M000316039

Jean Tirole

The Theory of Industrial Organization

The MIT Press
Cambridge, Massachusetts
London, England

Tenth printing, 1998

© 1988 Massachusetts Institute of Technology

All rights reserved. No part of this book may be reproduced in any form by any electronic or mechanical means (including photocopying, recording, or information storage and retrieval) without permission in writing from the publisher.

This book was set in Palatino by Asco Trade Typesetting Ltd. in Hong Kong, and printed and bound by Hamilton Printing in the United States of America.

Library of Congress Cataloging-in-Publication Data

Tirole, Jean.
  The theory of industrial organization.

  Includes bibliographies and indexes.
  1. Industrial organization (Economic theory)
I. Title
HD2326.T56   1988   302.3'5   88-2700
ISBN 0-262-20071-6

This book is based in part on a translation by John Bonin and Hélène Bonin of Jean Tirole's *Concurrence Imparfaite.*

The Theory of Industrial Organization

à Nathalie

Contents

Preface

Theoretical industrial organization has made substantial progress since the early 1970s, and has become a central element of the culture of microeconomics. This book is an attempt to give a straightforward account of the recent developments and to blend them into the tradition of industrial organization.

For advice, encouragement, and criticism I am particularly indebted to Philippe Aghion, Roland Bénabou, Patrick Bolton, Bernard Caillaud, Franklin Fisher, Paul Joskow, Bruno Jullien, Eric Maskin, Patrick Rey, Garth Saloner, Richard Schmalensee, and Michael Whinston. Dilip Abreu, Kyle Bagwell, John Bonin, Joel Demski, Peter Diamond, Drew Fudenberg, Robert Gertner, Robert Gibbons, Roger Guesnerie, Oliver Hart, Bengt Holmström, Jean-Jacques Laffont, Ariel Rubinstein, Stephen Salant, Steve Salop, Carl Shapiro, Andrea Shepard, Marius Schwartz, and Oliver Williamson offered very useful comments on specific chapters.

My debt to Paul Joskow and Richard Schmalensee—who encouraged me to undertake this endeavor, who read the entire manuscript, and who made pages and pages of critical comments—goes back to my days as a student at MIT. They are still teaching me about industrial organization. Former MIT students will recognize in the organization and in the choice of topics the influence of course 14.271, which Paul and Richard molded. My debt to Drew Fudenberg and Eric Maskin also goes back to my student days. While this debt extends well beyond the area of industrial organization, I must acknowledge that my vision of the game-theoretic aspects of industrial organization has been shaped by our ongoing collaboration. Eric taught me game theory and showed me how its tools could fruitfully be applied to various economic questions. Drew's input into this book is almost too obvious to be acknowledged. Part II and the Game Theory User's Manual borrow heavily from our joint research and surveys. David Kreps, Paul Milgrom, John Roberts, and Robert Wilson have also greatly influenced my views on strategic behaviors in markets. My intellectual debt extends to the many fine researchers who have built the modern theory of industrial organization and whose work I cite extensively.

The material in this book was taught in various forms at the undergraduate level at the Ecole Nationale de la Statistique et de l'Administration Economique and at the University of Lausanne, as part of a basic graduate sequence in industrial organization at MIT and at the Ecole des Hautes Etudes en Sciences Sociales, and at the advanced-topics level at MIT. The students at those institutions supplied useful comments and expositional suggestions.

I am very grateful to Benjamin Hermalin for his superb research assistance. Not only did he read the entire manuscript and check the exercises; he also offered many insightful comments. I could not have been more fortunate in finding a research assistant, with respect to both diligence and talent. I am also grateful to Bernice Soltysik for preparing the indexes and to Bruno Jullien for reading the proofs.

I began the writing of this book while I was at the Ecole Nationale des Ponts et Chaussées. My 1983 ENSAE lecture notes on industrial organization became *Concurrence Imparfaite*, published by Editions Economica in 1985. John and Hélène Bonin translated *Concurrence Imparfaite* with competence and alacrity, enabling me to start building *The Theory of Industrial Organization* on the basis of that French-language version shortly after its publication.

Although this book is very much the outcome of a group undertaking, none of those who contributed to it should be held responsible for any errors or omissions. I apologize to them for ignoring many of their good suggestions for completing and extending the exposition. My only excuse for not taking all their suggestions is that the book might have doubled in size had I included them all.

I was fortunate to have as my editor Paul Bethge, who handled the manuscript with much intelligence, experience, and humor. I am also grateful to the rest of the very able team at The MIT Press—particularly to economics editor Terry Vaughn, for his help and encouragement, and to designer Rebecca Daw, for a nice treatment of some naturally difficult material.

Very special thanks go to the skillful and multilingual Emily Gallagher, who suffered through the typing of many drafts, both in French and in English. With good cheer, she spent countless evenings and weekends so that the material could be ready for my students and then for publication. She did a beautiful job. The first French-language draft was typed by Patricia Maillebouis and Pierrette Vayssade.

I gratefully acknowledge generous research grants from the National Science Foundation, the Sloan Foundation, the Center for Energy Policy Research at MIT, the MIT Fund for the Arts, Humanities, and Social Sciences, and the Commissariat Général au Plan.

Jean Tirole
Cambridge, Massachusetts

The Theory of Industrial Organization

Introduction

Why Should One Be Interested in Industrial Organization?

This question sounds almost silly. To study industrial organization is to study the functioning of markets, a central concept in microeconomics. However, it took a long time and two waves of interest for industrial organization to become one of the main fields of economics.[1]

The first wave, associated with the names of Joe Bain and Edward Mason and sometimes called the "Harvard tradition," was empirical in nature. It developed the famous "structure-conduct-performance" paradigm, according to which market structure (the number of sellers in the market, their degree of product differentiation, the cost structure, the degree of vertical integration with suppliers, and so on) determines conduct (which consists of price, research and development, investment, advertising, and so forth), and conduct yields market performance (efficiency, ratio of price to marginal cost, product variety, innovation rate, profits, and distribution). This paradigm, although plausible, often rested on loose theories, and it emphasized empirical studies of industries. For instance, it was generally found that certain measures of conduct and performance were strongly linked with the market's structure—a typical regression had the form $\Pi_i = f(\text{CR}_i, \text{BE}_i, \ldots)$, where i denoted the industry, Π_i denoted some measure of firm or industry profitability, CR_i was a concentration ratio (a measure meant to summarize how noncompetitive the industry is), and BE_i (for barriers to entry) referred to variables that measured the difficulty of entering the industry (approximated by the minimum efficient scale of entry, the ratio of advertising to sales, and so on). Other variables could be introduced in the regression as well. The regression was run on cross-sectional data for a large sample of industries.[2]

---

1. This section draws on lectures given by Paul Joskow and Richard Schmalensee.

2. See Schmalensee 1986 for an excellent critical survey of this approach.

If one ignored the many issues having to do with measurement, such regressions produced a useful array of stylized facts. The links (or the absence of links) between variables must, however, be interpreted as correlations or "descriptive statistics," not as causal relationships. In the above example, the industry profit, the concentration ratio, and the ratio of advertising to sales are jointly endogenous. They are determined simultaneously by the market's "basic conditions" (exogenous variables) and the behavior of the firms.

The absence of a causal interpretation is troubling for an analyst. What is to be made of a regression showing that the rate of return in an industry grows with the concentration in that industry?[3] Well, it may suggest that there is market power in fairly concentrated industries and that the performance of such industries might not be optimal. However, it says little about the causes of concentration or market power, and it fails to guide our analyst as to whether, and in what form, government intervention can improve market performance.

The empirical tradition certainly tried to measure more basic (exogenous) conditions: technology (returns to scale, entry cost, proportion of capital sunk, existence of a learning curve, durable versus nondurable good, etc.), preferences and consumer behavior (structure of information about product quality, reputation and brand loyalty, etc.), "exogenous" technological change, and so on.[4] Although progress has been made in this direction, it is often difficult to gather data that are accurate measures of basic conditions and are comparable across industries.

The preceding comments are certainly too harsh a judgment on the empirical tradition, which, after all, set an agenda for industrial organization. I left unmentioned the fact that many informal stories were built around the regressions. (Actually, industry case studies preceded the wave of regressions and were made possible by antitrust cases. These case studies led to some informal stories. Regressions offered complementary material on industry behavior.) Those stories, together with antitrust analysis

and case studies, supported the subsequent theoretical wave. Nor is it fair to say that more formal theory was completely left aside. In particular, the "Chicago tradition," starting with Aaron Director and George Stigler, emphasized the need for rigorous theoretical analysis and empirical identification of competing theories. The Chicago tradition had an important methodological impact on the development of the field; it is also famous for its very permissive view of market behavior—for instance with respect to vertical restraints and predatory pricing (collusion is the main offense, on its view)—and for its relative distrust of government intervention in comparison with the Harvard tradition. Still, by the early 1970s it was felt that in many instances theory was more a way of explaining statistical results or of buttressing particular intellectual positions than a rigorous and systematic investigation. For instance, Paul Joskow offered the following observation:

In a sense, the ultimate test of the utility of the various models is whether they prove useful to people involved in analyzing problems involving actual markets or groups of markets. I suggest that not only aren't they particularly useful but also that they aren't really used. . . . Somehow one gets the distinct feeling that the important messages are being carried by the informal theories, stories, and behavioral observations, and that the formal models are trotted out ex-post to demonstrate that some kind of formal apparatus can explain or incorporate some of what is actually being observed. (Joskow 1975, p. 273)

The second wave of interest, which was mainly theoretical, started in the 1970s. It can be attributed to three factors. I have already mentioned, on the "demand side," the growing dissatisfaction with the limits of the cross-sectional empirical analysis that had come to dominate the field of industrial organization. There was a widespread feeling, exemplified by the above quote, that empirical work did not appeal to particular formal models of oligopoly markets. On the "supply side," two factors can be discerned. First, until the 1970s, economic theorists

---

3. Actually, this statistical relationship is weak. Introducing a market-share variable on the right-hand side of the regression tends to wipe out concentration-ratio effects. One explanation may be that industries with cost heterogeneity between firms tend to yield high concentration ratios (a few low-cost firms produce most of the output) as well as high profits (the low-cost firms are relatively free of competitive pressure from their rivals). The concentration-ratio variable might be picking up the effect of the missing-market-share variable. See chapter 5.

4. For instance, the returns to scale have been measured by various methods. The most common may be the estimation of a cost function (estimation of the parameters of a cost function of output level and input prices). Bain obtained "engineering production functions" from engineering data at the plant level; he also used "engineering managerial analysis"—asking managers what the optimal plant size is, for instance. Still another method is George Stigler's survivorship technique, which looks at the size of surviving firms.

(with a few exceptions) pretty much ignored industrial organization, which did not lend itself to elegant and general analysis the way the theory of competitive general equilibrium did. Since then, a fair number of top theorists have become interested in industrial organization.[5] Second, and crucial for the topics reviewed in part II of this book, noncooperative game theory imposed itself (not without some dissension) as the standard tool for the analysis of strategic conflict, thus bringing a unified methodology to the field. Furthermore, it made serious progress in two crucial areas: dynamics and asymmetric information. The stage was thus set for a reappraisal of the many informal stories that were floating around.

This book is mainly concerned with the accomplishments of the second wave, but I have tried not to forget that earlier contributions laid the foundations for this theoretical work. I think there is now sufficient agreement about the methodology to be employed in the theoretical study of industries to warrant such a text.

I have mentioned some historical developments without defining industrial organization (IO) or emphasizing its importance. I would actually like to avoid giving a precise definition of the field, as its frontiers are fuzzy. IO certainly begins with the structure and behavior of firms (market strategy and internal organization). This business-strategy aspect may explain why a few of the outstanding contributors in the area have appointments in business schools. But there is more to IO than business strategy. The other side of the coin is the outsider's (the academic economist's, the civil servant's, or the antitrust practitioner's) assessment of market efficiency. Imperfectly competitive markets (that is, most real markets) are unlikely to maximize social welfare. This does not necessarily mean that the government (the "social planner") can improve on the private outcome given its structure of information, nor does this observation indicate when and how the government should intervene. It does tell us that analyses that rely on models of perfect competition may be quite

unsatisfactory from a positive and from a normative perspective.

The scope of government intervention is itself ill defined. Roughly, the promotion of competition through antitrust action, as well as certain forms of "market regulation"[6] (taxes and subsidies, minimum quality standards, etc.), will be considered to lie within the scope of this book. Other instruments, such as price and entry or economic regulation at the firm level (including monopoly franchising, governmental procurement, and nationalization) will not. This division has some unfortunate effects. In particular, I will not be considering all modes of intervention in my models. My only excuse (and one that I will use for other purposes) is that the book is already very long. Considering selective regulation could well have doubled its length.

Theory versus Evidence

Industrial organization has become a fairly theoretical field in recent years. At first sight, even a theorist should regret the very high ratio of theory to evidence in a field in which theoretical models are often lacking in generality and in which practical implications are so crucial. While I feel there is an imbalance in the field, I also think the theoretical evolution has been very healthy.

The "new theoretical IO," having drawn from the old oral tradition of behavioral stories as well as from stylized facts,[7] can, I believe, help the people involved in analyzing actual markets. Not only has it formalized some of the old informal stories; it also has rejected others. I do not want to overemphasize the practical contributions of the theory. It may have put too much emphasis on positive (explanatory) analysis, to the detriment of normative (welfare) analysis, and it has done too little to help practitioners distinguish between competing theories. But it definitely has practical content.

Furthermore, the theoretical contributions should soon feed back to empirical analysis.[8] They suggest what evi-

---

5. This hardly explains the "performance" of recent theoretical research in IO. The "structure" of the market for theoretical research in the field (e.g., the number of top theorists with permanent or temporary interest in the area) is itself endogenous. One must look for more basic conditions that explain the inflow.

6. By "market regulation" I mean regulation that treats all firms in an industry (including potential ones) symmetrically.

7. Scherer 1980, a remarkable collection of facts about firm behavior, has been very instrumental in the development of the current theory.

8. The new intra-industry empirical studies are a good sign that such an evolution might take place. Some excellent contributions along these lines are Bresnahan 1987a, Joskow 1985, and Porter 1983. See Bresnahan 1987b for a useful survey.

dence to look for, separate the endogenous from the exogenous variables, and highlight the hypothesis to be tested.

Econometric analysis certainly isn't the only way of doing empirical research in IO. Because of unsatisfactory data, many applied researchers are paying more attention to the development of evidence on firm and industry behavior and performance through detailed case studies of firms or industries (to which one can add the evidence accumulated for antitrust purposes). Although these studies have their own drawbacks, they have yielded many interesting insights. Indeed, IO theorists have often felt more comfortable with case studies than with statistical analysis—perhaps because it may be easier to recover the industry's basic conditions and behavior from rich case studies than from selective statistics about profit, concentration, advertising, and so on drawn from a very large sample of disparate industries.

Still another method of collecting evidence that can benefit from the theoretical developments is the running of controlled experiments in laboratories.[9]

Thus, it is hoped that these three approaches to empirical work will be strengthened by the new theoretical developments. The book does not list the empirical implications of each model and does not explain how competing models might be distinguished. However, I hope that the presentation of the models is intuitive enough to highlight their testable features.

Scope of the Book

The book does not cover the empirical side of the field (including the antitrust experience). It also ignores some of the broad theoretical issues, such as economic regulation, international industrial organization,[10] imperfect competition in general equilibrium,[11] and the link between IO and macroeconomics.[12]

The methodology is also defined narrowly. Part I assumes optimizing behavior, and part II uses a generalization of optimization to multiperson decision making: the theory of noncooperative games. The book does little

justice to alternative approaches, such as satisficing (bounded rationality). The gain from this omission is a unified treatment.

To simplify things, I treat firms as single decision makers that maximize profits. In most of the book, problems of managerial control by shareholders, banks, or the capital market are assumed away. Delegation and control within a firm are also ignored. The preliminary chapter on the theory of the firm discusses these assumptions. Some allusions are made to agency problems in chapters 4 and 9. Because a fair treatment of agency theory would require a book in itself, I content myself with mentioning the issues. The topics will cry out loud for further development. And, indeed, I believe that the intersection between organization theory and IO is one of the most interesting areas for theoretical research in the years to come.

I clearly had to choose which topics to emphasize—a sometimes painful exercise. Although my choices reflect my own preferences, they should not necessarily be mistaken for value judgments. First, they are contingent on my current state of knowledge and reflection. I apologize to the authors whose contributions I underemphasized or left out because of ignorance, imperfect recall, or insufficient perspective. Second, the choices are sometimes guided by an expositional strategy. Some interesting contributions that would require long or technically difficult exposition are relegated to footnotes, remarks, or exercises.

How to Use the Book

General Organization

Part I (chapters 1 through 4) looks at those features of market behavior that are not related to (but are certainly not inconsistent with) strategic behavior. It considers a monopolist's choices of price and quality, the spectrum of goods, advertising, and the distribution structure. Most of the conclusions obtained there carry over to oligopolies. Part II analyzes the choice of price, capacity, product positioning, research and development, and other strate-

---

9. For a survey of this approach to IO, see Plott 1982.

10. See Helpman and Krugman 1985 for a recent contribution to IO in an open economy.

11. See Hart 1985 for a good survey of the corresponding literature.

12. See Carlton 1987.

gic variables in oligopoly. It makes heavy use of some elementary notions of game theory.

I have found this division into two parts useful for teaching purposes. Ignoring strategic considerations for a few weeks allows the student to become familiar with some key topics in IO without getting swamped by the simultaneous introduction of game theory. It also yields a clearer separation of those aspects that are specific to strategic behavior. I have included a "user's manual" on noncooperative game theory (chapter 11) to help the reader prepare for part II. It is not meant to be a substitute for a more formal course in game theory. Rather, it is designed to point out the relevant concepts and to familiarize the reader with their use. A separate course in game theory would be useful, but it is by no means a prerequisite for part II. I suggest that those unfamiliar with game theory read up to section 11.4 of the "user's manual" while progressing through part I of the book and read sections 11.4 and 11.5 before studying chapter 9.

As was mentioned above, part I is preceded by a discussion of the theory of the firm. The firm is the basic object of the book, and therefore we ought to inquire into its nature and objectives. The study of the firm is a preliminary to the analysis of markets. I fear (and, at the same time, hope) that the reader will find the discussion somewhat unsatisfactory. As it stands, it may seem intended to ease my conscience ("Now that we have talked about the firm, we can ignore it and treat it as a profit-maximizing black box") by allowing me to pay lip service to the relationship between internal organization and market structure. In fact, I include this discussion not because it enhances the book through its complementarity with subsequent chapters but because I believe that the theory of the firm is a crucial topic in economics as well as an integral part of industrial organization.

Relationships among Chapters

The chapters are relatively self-contained. Nonetheless, some connections are to be drawn. For instance, chapters 5 and 6 generalize parts of chapter 1 to strategic behavior, and chapter 7 does so with respect to chapter 2. The rent-dissipation hypothesis, mentioned in chapter 1, is carefully studied in part II. The appropriability of consumer surplus by a firm, introduced in chapter 2, is encountered again in chapters 7 and 10. Analogies will be stressed when it is appropriate.

Organization within Chapters

Each chapter is divided into a main text and a supplementary section. Undergraduates, first-year graduate students, and scholars unfamiliar with IO are advised to focus on the main text. Other graduate students and scholars familiar with IO will find some more advanced material in the supplementary section.

Exercises

Exercises have been included to help the reader become familiar with the concepts and to broaden his or her knowledge. Some exercises appear within a chapter; their solutions are sketched at the end of the chapter. In addition, review exercises (without answers) are offered at the back of the book. Readers who are not able to solve exercises in the text should not be discouraged; some of them are difficult. Those readers will find easier work in the review exercises. I have indexed the exercises by asterisks to reflect their difficulty:

*: simple application of concepts developed in the text
**: more difficult; requires more thought
***: advanced; the most challenging.

Prerequisites

Economics

An intermediate microeconomics course is desirable. Otherwise, the book is fairly self-contained. I have tried to give some motivation for the models when needed. Some familiarity with stylized facts, however, would give the reader a better perspective on these models. A preliminary or simultaneous reading of Scherer's classic text (1980) would be valuable. Books on business strategy (e.g. Porter 1980) and antitrust policy (e.g. Areeda 1974, Areeda and Turner 1976, Blair and Kaserman 1985, Posner and Easterbrook 1981) may also prove useful in this respect.

Mathematics

I try to present theories in a "reader-friendly" form. I often choose specific functional forms (such as linear demand) over general ones, two-period models over general dynamic ones, and duopoly situations over oligopolies. My hope is that the intuition behind the phenomena studied here will emerge strongly enough to convince the reader that the results have some robustness.

Very little mathematical knowledge is required. For the most part, elementary notions of calculus (e.g. unconstrained optimization) will suffice. The reader should know how to derive the first-order and second-order conditions associated with a maximization problem, be aware of the envelope theorem[13] and of the chain rule of differentiation, and have a few notions about concavity.[14] Some further notions will be used for specific, isolated points (integration by parts, Bayes' rule, dynamic programming). The required notions can generally be found in a simple form in the mathematical appendixes of Dixit and Norman 1980 or those of Varian 1978.[15]

Market Definition, Partial Equilibrium, and Welfare Criteria

The Competitive Paradigm

The best-developed and most aesthetically pleasing model in the field of economics is the competitive-equilibrium paradigm of Arrow and Debreu.[16] In brief, this model goes as follows: The model starts with a very fine description of available goods. An economic good is characterized by its physical properties, the date on which and the state of nature in which it is available, its location, and so forth. Consumers are perfectly informed about all goods' properties and have preferences over bundles of goods. Producers (firms), which are owned by consumers,

are endowed with production-possibility sets. A paradigm of market organization is then added. All agents are price takers. The consumers maximize their welfare given that their expenditures must not exceed their income (which stems from their endowment and their ownership of firms). This gives rise to demand functions ("correspondences," if there are several welfare-maximizing bundles). Producers maximize profits over their technological possibilities, giving rise to supply functions (or correspondences). A competitive equilibrium is a set of prices, with associated demands and supplies, such that all the markets (one for each good) clear (i.e., total demand does not exceed total supply).

Weak assumptions about preferences and technological possibilities yield general results on competitive equilibrium. The best-known of these may be the two fundamental welfare theorems. Roughly stated, the first says that a competitive equilibrium is Pareto optimal (that is, a benevolent and fully informed social planner could not replace the competitive allocation of goods with another feasible allocation that would increase all the consumers' welfare) and the second asserts that, under convexity assumptions (which rule out increasing returns to scale), any Pareto-optimal allocation can be decentralized (implemented by a market organization) by a choice of the right prices and an appropriate redistribution of income among consumers.

A key property of competitive equilibrium is that each good is sold at marginal cost. A producer would increase profit by expanding production of the good if its price

---

13. According to this theorem, the derivative of the value of an optimization problem (i.e., the maximum of the objective function) with respect to an exogenous parameter is equal to the partial derivative of the objective function with respect to the parameter. That is, only the direct effect of the change in the parameter should be taken into account (and not the indirect effect through the change in the endogenous (control) variables, which has only a second-order effect). Formally, let

$$V(a) = \max_x f(x, a).$$

Then

$$\frac{dV}{da} = \frac{\partial f}{\partial a}(x^*(a), a),$$

where $x^*(a)$ is the optimal control variable.

14. A function $f(x)$, where x is a vector of R^n, is concave if, for any λ in $[0, 1]$ and all x and x',

$$f(\lambda x + (1 - \lambda)x') \geqslant \lambda f(x) + (1 - \lambda)f(x').$$

For a differentiable function, an alternative characterization of concavity is the following: For all x and x',

$$f(x) \leqslant f(x') + \sum_{i=1}^{n} \frac{\partial f}{\partial x_i}(x')(x_i - x_i').$$

(For x in R, the reader can check this inequality by making a diagram.)

The function f is quasi-concave if the sets in R^n defined by $\{x | f(x) \geqslant y\}$ are convex for all y. For x in R, a slightly stronger and sufficient condition for quasi-concavity is that $f'' < 0$ whenever $f' = 0$. As a diagram will easily show, this stronger notion of quasi-concavity (which is weaker than concavity) is all that is needed for the second-order conditions in an optimization program to be satisfied. We will rarely need this notion, however.

15. More detailed treatments of optimization for economists include Dixit 1976 and Kamien and Schwartz 1981.

16. See the beautiful treatments by Debreu (1959), Arrow and Hahn (1970), and Mas-Colell (1985). The reader will find simpler versions in Varian 1978 (at the graduate level) and in various undergraduate microeconomics texts.

exceeded his marginal cost. Conversely, if he produced the good at all, he would contract production if the marginal cost were to exceed the price. This trivial result has important implications. When deciding whether to consume one more unit of the good, a consumer faces a price that is socially the "right one" and internalizes the cost of producing this extra unit. This is part of the intuition behind the Pareto optimality of competitive equilibrium.

The first fundamental welfare theorem strongly limits the scope of industrial organization. The organization of industries in such a world is necessarily efficient. The only potential concern for policy is income distribution among consumers, which the social planner may not judge optimal.[17]

The competitive-equilibrium paradigm makes relatively weak assumptions about preferences and production possibilities, but only within a given class. Among the conditions that are required are the absence of externalities between economic agents,[18] the private nature of goods,[19] and the perfect information of consumers about products. Although the treatment of externalities and public goods is traditionally part of the field of public finance, we will study a few situations involving externalities (e.g. network externalities) and public goods (e.g. the provision of information about new technologies). We will also relax the third condition when dealing with consumers' imperfect information about products (as in the case of product quality).

Perhaps the most conspicuous of all conditions is price-taking behavior. Though it is easy to exhibit markets that seem to be reasonably described by this assumption (e.g. some agricultural markets), most markets are served by a small number of firms with non-negligible market power.[20] The book is, to a large extent, concerned with the causes and consequences of this market power.

Partial Equilibrium, Downward-Sloping Demand Curves, and Consumer Surplus

Once some of the assumptions of competitive-equilibrium analysis are relaxed, very little can be said about economic allocations without more specific assumptions, as the "theory of the second best" has taught us. One of the costs of moving toward more realistic models of the organization of industries is the adoption of a partial-equilibrium setup. A good (or a group of related goods) is singled out, and the interaction with the rest of the economy is ignored.

We will come back to the notion of market shortly; for the moment, let us consider the validity of two assumptions that will be made throughout the book: that the demand for a good decreases with its price and that changes in consumer welfare can be measured by the so-called consumer surplus.

First, the notion of consumer surplus: Consider the market for a single good. The demand for this good is assumed to decrease with its own price and to be independent of the prices of other goods and of the consumers' income. To make this rigorous, consider "quasi-linear" utility functions:

$$U(q_0, q_1, \ldots, q_m) = q_0 + \sum_{h=1}^{m} V_h(q_h),$$

where good 0 is the numéraire and the functions V_h are increasing and concave. Maximizing U subject to the budget constraint

$$q_0 + \sum_{h=1}^{m} p_h q_h \leqslant I,$$

where I is the consumer's income, yields $V_h'(q_h) = p_h$ for all h. Thus, each consumer's demand function for good h, and therefore the aggregate demand function, satisfies the above conditions. (For the more general quasi-linear pref-

17. This is not to say that competitive equilibrium should be totally abandoned for IO purposes. Some positive implications can be derived from simple competitive models. For instance, there exists an interesting literature (not reviewed in this book) that uses the competitive paradigm to study, in a dynamic economy, the process of entry and exit in an industry and/or to find theoretical foundations for Gibrat's law (according to which the rate of growth of firms tends to be, on average, independent of firm size). See Lucas 1978, Jovanovic 1982, Lippman and Rummelt 1982, and Hopenhayn 1986.

18. An externality arises when the consumption of a good by a consumer directly affects the welfare of another consumer, or when a firm's production affects other economic agents. A consumer who increases the size of a telephone network by connecting to the network exerts a positive externality on other consumers. A firm that pollutes a river exerts a negative externality on consumers and other firms.

19. A public good is a good that can be consumed simultaneously by several consumers (e.g., national defense or a TV program).

20. For an ingenious estimation of the divergence between price and marginal cost in various industries, see Hall 1986.

erences $U(q_0, q_1, \ldots, q_m) = q_0 + W(q_1, \ldots, q_m)$, the demand functions exhibit cross-price effects but no income effect.)

Consider a homogeneous good. Dupuit (1844) introduced the first welfare measurement. (Dupuit's consumer surplus is also sometimes called the Marshallian consumer surplus—see Marshall 1920, p. 811. Henceforth, we will call it simply the *consumer surplus*.[21]) In figure 1, the consumer surplus is defined as the area between the demand curve and the horizontal line at the price level p^0. Dupuit contended that this area was a measure of what the consumers would be willing to pay in excess of what they already spend ($p^0 q^0$) for the right to consume q^0 units of the good. The reasoning is most simply explained when the demand curve is made up of a large number of "unit demands." That is, there are many consumers, who purchase either 0 or 1 unit of the goods. The consumers are heterogeneous, in that they have different valuations or willingnesses to pay (v_i) for the good, expressed in terms of money (that is, for the quasi-linear utility functions discussed above, $V_h(\cdot)$ is a step function for each consumer, equal to zero for a consumption of good h lower than 1 and equal to the consumer's willingness to pay for good h for a consumption equal to or greater than 1). Without loss of generality, let us rank these consumers by order of decreasing valuations: $v_1 \geqslant v_2 \geqslant \cdots$. A consumer with valuation v_i purchases if and only if $v_i \geqslant p^0$. The first consumer realizes a surplus $v_1 - p^0$, because he was willing to pay v_1. The second consumer realizes a surplus $v_2 - p^0$, and so forth until the marginal consumer (call him n), who realizes approximately no surplus. The total consumer surplus is then

$$(v_1 - p^0) + (v_2 - p^0) + \cdots + (v_{n-1} - p^0).$$

For n large, the stepped demand function can be approximated by the continuous aggregate demand function $q = D(p)$, and the consumer surplus takes the form

$$S^n = \int_{p^0}^{\bar{p}} D(p)dp. \tag{1}$$

S^n is the net consumer surplus. The gross consumer surplus, S^g, is equal to the net consumer surplus plus the

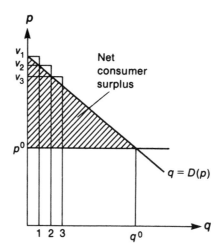

Figure 1
Consumer surplus.

consumer expenditure $p^0 D(p^0)$. $\bar{p}$ denotes the choke-off price (the lowest price at which there is no demand). It is equal to v_1 in the discretized version, but it could also be taken to be infinity without any change in the formula.

Let us now consider a single consumer with a downward-sloping demand $D(\cdot)$ for the good. Dupuit's reasoning is that this consumer can be thought of as composed of consumers with unit demands. That is, he is willing to pay v_1 for the first unit purchased, v_2 for the second, and so forth. Overall, his net surplus from consuming q^0 units of the good at price p^0 is given by equation 1. From now on, we will consider a single consumer. Only later will we come back to multiple consumers.

The changes in net and gross consumer surplus when the consumer price moves from p^0 to p^1 are defined by the following equations:

$$\Delta S^n = -\int_{p^0}^{p^1} D(p)dp,$$

$$\Delta S^g = -\int_{p^0}^{p^1} D(p)dp + [p^1 D(p^1) - p^0 D(p^0)]. \tag{2}$$

The producer surplus is defined as the profit of the firm in the industry. Figure 2 shows the marginal-cost curve (which coincides with the supply curve under perfect competition). Profit is equal to revenue ($p^0 D(p^0)$) minus

---

21. See Auerbach 1986 for an extensive review of various measures of surplus and excess burden. See also the classic discussions of consumer surplus by Hicks (1941) and Samuelson (1947).

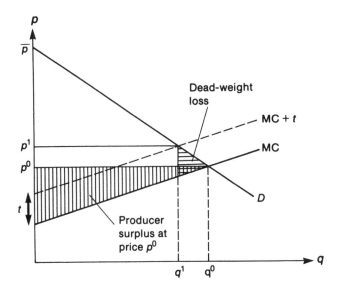

Figure 2
Dead-weight loss from commodity taxation.

cost. Cost is the integral of marginal cost.[22] Thus, the industry profit is equal to the area between the marginal-cost curve and the horizontal line at price p^0 (the vertical hatching in figure 2).

The aggregate welfare in the industry, or the total surplus, is equal to the consumer surplus plus the producer surplus. The total surplus is maximized when the consumer price is equal to the marginal cost (p^0 in figure 2).

A famous application of this is the derivation of a monetary measure of the welfare loss ("dead-weight loss") associated with commodity taxation. Suppose the industry is competitive, so that the initial price is the first best (p^0). Let us impose a unit tax t on each unit sold. The new equilibrium has price p^1 and consumption q^1. The welfare loss, equal to the difference in total surplus between the two situations, can be measured by the area of the horizontally hatched triangle in figure 2. (The total surplus involves the tax revenue for the government as well. The simplest way to compute the total surplus is to subtract

the total cost from the gross consumer surplus. Monetary transfers among consumers, producers, and government are irrelevant to the computation of the total surplus.) As Dupuit suggested, the dead-weight loss can thus be approximated by

$$\tfrac{1}{2}t|q^1 - q^0| = \tfrac{1}{2}t^2|D'(p^1)|$$

for a small tax and for a constant marginal cost.[23]

The rest of this section is more technical than most of the introduction and can be skipped in a first reading. It discusses the extension of consumer surplus to the multi-product case, and then goes on to find conditions under which the demand for each good is downward sloping and under which the consumer surplus is a good approximation of welfare.

There are two obvious questions about consumer surplus: Does it generalize to more than one good? Can it be expressed in terms of classical demand theory? To answer these questions, consider general demand functions $q_h = D_h(\mathbf{p}, I)$, where the demand for good h depends on the price vector $\mathbf{p}$ and the consumer's income I.

The generalization to a group of several goods seems straightforward; one can simply add up the consumer surpluses for the various goods. The variation in net consumer surplus from vector $\mathbf{p}^0$ to vector $\mathbf{p}^1$ is

$$\Delta S^n = \sum_h \Delta S_h = -\int_{p^0}^{p^1} \sum_h q_h dp_h. \qquad (3)$$

An unfortunate feature of this consumer surplus with many goods is that equation 3 does not always define a unique number. The integral in general depends on the path of integration from the initial price $\mathbf{p}^0$ to the final price $\mathbf{p}^1$, as is easily checked. It is path independent (and thus well defined) only if the demand functions exhibit no income effect (or, more generally, if the cross-partial derivatives of the demand functions are equal).[24]

This drawback is actually related to the link with foundations in demand theory. Hicks (1946) introduced two

---

22. If there exists a fixed cost of production, the latter must be subtracted from profit.

23. Hotelling (1938) and Harberger (1964) later proved the result more formally and generalized it to several goods. Boiteux (1951) and Debreu (1951) gave important measures of dead-weight loss in a general-equilibrium context.

24. To see this, consider two prices; change one first and then the other, and conversely. Taking the difference between the two measures and writing demand functions as the integral of their partial derivatives yields a term in $\partial D_2/\partial p_1 - \partial D_1/\partial p_2$. This term would be equal to zero if the demands were compensated ones (from the symmetry of the Slutsky matrix); however, these demands are ordinary ones. For a reminder of the notion of compensated demand, see Varian 1978. For a good presentation of the problems studied here, see Auerbach 1986.

further monetary measures for changes in consumer utility: the "compensating variation" of a price change (the amount of income that the consumer must receive to leave his utility unaffected by the price change) and the "equivalent variation" (the amount of income the consumer would be willing to forgo to avoid the price change).[25]

A crucial notion for what follows is the Hicksian or compensated-demand function, $\mathbf{D}^c(\mathbf{p}, u)$. This is the demand obtained when income is adjusted to keep the consumer's utility constant at level u. The compensated-demand function for each good is downward sloping. Furthermore, the ordinary-demand function and the compensated-demand function are known to be related by the Slutsky equation. Singling out a good h, we have

$$\frac{\partial D_h}{\partial p_h} = \frac{\partial D_h^c}{\partial p_h} - D_h \frac{\partial D_h}{\partial I}.$$

That is, the change in a good's demand brought about by a unit change in own price is the sum of two terms. The first is the derivative of the compensated demand with respect to price, and it is, as we just noted, negative. This term is called the *substitution effect*. The second term, called the *income effect*, is negative for a normal good and positive for an inferior good (and is equal to zero in the case of quasi-linear utility functions). It stems from the fact that a unit increase in p_h costs the consumer D_h units of income, which affects the demand for good h by $\partial D_h / \partial I$ each.

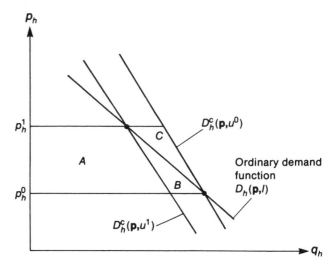

Figure 3
Compensating and equivalent variations and consumer surplus.

Consider a single price change (that of good h, say).

It is easily seen that the equivalent (respectively, compensating) variation from price $\mathbf{p}^0$ to price $\mathbf{p}^1$ is equal to the area under the compensated-demand curve at utility level u^1 (respectively, u^0).[26] Using the facts that $\mathbf{D}(\mathbf{p}^0, I) \equiv \mathbf{D}^c(\mathbf{p}^0, u^0)$ and $\mathbf{D}(\mathbf{p}^1, I) \equiv \mathbf{D}^c(\mathbf{p}^1, u^1)$, we can represent the consumer surplus and the equivalent and compensating variations as in figure 3 (which depicts the case of a normal good). The change in consumer surplus is equal to the area $A + B$, the equivalent variation is equal to the area A, and the compensating variation is equal to the area $A + B + C$.[27]

---

25. Let

$$E(\mathbf{p}, u) = \min_{\mathbf{q}} \{\mathbf{p} \cdot \mathbf{q}\},$$

subject to $U(\mathbf{q}) \geqslant u$, denote the consumer's expenditure function, where $U(\cdot)$ denotes the utility function. This is the amount of income required to reach utility level u at price vector $\mathbf{p}$. Let

$$V(\mathbf{p}, I) = \max_{\mathbf{q}} U(\mathbf{q}),$$

subject to $\mathbf{p} \cdot \mathbf{q} \leqslant I$, denote the indirect utility function. For a price change from $\mathbf{p}^0$ to $\mathbf{p}^1$, the compensating variation is

$$CV = E(\mathbf{p}^1, V(\mathbf{p}^0, I)) - I$$

and the equivalent variation is

$$EV = I - E(\mathbf{p}^0, V(\mathbf{p}^1, I)).$$

The equivalent variation is an acceptable measure of welfare in that comparing welfare at prices $\mathbf{p}^1$ and $\mathbf{p}^2$—i.e., $V(\mathbf{p}^1, I)$ and $V(\mathbf{p}^2, I)$—is equivalent to comparing the equivalent variations from $\mathbf{p}^0$ to $\mathbf{p}^1$ and from $\mathbf{p}^0$ to $\mathbf{p}^2$. This property, in general, does not hold for the compensating variation.

The two variations do not exhibit path dependence in the case of multiple price changes.

26. Formally, the equivalent variation is

$$E(\mathbf{p}^1, V(\mathbf{p}^1, I)) - E(\mathbf{p}^0, V(\mathbf{p}^1, I))$$

$$= \int_{p_h^0}^{p_h^1} D_h^c(\mathbf{p}, V(\mathbf{p}^1, I)) dp_h,$$

where $I = E(\mathbf{p}^1, V(\mathbf{p}^1, I)) = E(\mathbf{p}^0, V(\mathbf{p}^0, I))$ and where the envelope theorem and the definition of the expenditure function are used to obtain the derivative of the expenditure function with respect to price. Similarly for the compensating variation.

27. Here the two Hicksian variations bracket the consumer surplus. This may not hold when dead-weight losses, rather than surpluses or variations, are considered; see Hausman 1981.

For generalizations of the dead-weight loss to multiple price changes, see Mohring 1971 and Diamond and McFadden 1974. The equivalent and the compensating variation, respectively, are used in those papers.

How well does the consumer surplus approximate the Hicksian (equivalent or compensating) variations? Because the derivatives of these concepts with respect to price are the ordinary-demand function and the compensated-demand function, respectively, the Slutsky equation suggests that the discrepancy between consumer surplus and Hicksian variations is small when income effects are small. Willig (1976) provides bounds on the percentage error made by approximating the Hicksian variations by the consumer surplus, which depend on the income elasticity of demand and/or the expenditure share of the good.[28]

Along these lines, note that the income effect is likely to be small if the good in question represents only a small fraction of expenditure. If we let

$$\varepsilon_h \equiv -\frac{\partial D_h}{\partial p_h} \bigg/ \frac{D_h}{p_h}$$

and

$$\varepsilon_h^c \equiv -\frac{\partial D_h^c}{\partial p_h} \bigg/ \frac{D_h^c}{p_h}$$

denote the own-price elasticities of ordinary demand and compensated demand, and let

$$\varepsilon_h^I \equiv -\frac{\partial D_h}{\partial I} \bigg/ \frac{D_h}{I}$$

represent the income elasticity of ordinary demand, the Slutsky equation can be rewritten as

$$\varepsilon_h = \varepsilon_h^c + \left(\frac{p_h D_h}{I}\right) \varepsilon_h^I.$$

Thus, the intuition is that, if the consumer's expenditure $p_h D_h$ on good h is small relative to income, the income effect is negligible. Two very useful facts follow:

• The demand curve for good h is downward sloping, because the compensated-demand curve is downward sloping.

• The consumer surplus, and the dead-weight loss computed from it, are good welfare approximations.

This intuition goes back at least to Marshall (1920, p. 842), who argued that the above two statements should hold on the basis that the consumer's "expenditure on any one thing, as, for instance, tea, is only a small part of his whole income." Vives (1987) confirms Marshall's intuition. Under some assumptions,[29] he shows that when the consumer consumes a large number of goods n, the following statements hold:

• The income derivative of demand on one good is small (of order $1/\sqrt{n}$, and even $1/n$ if preferences are additively separable), and the demand curves are downward sloping.[30]

• For a single price change, the percentage error in approximating the Hicksian variations by the consumer surplus is small (of order $1/\sqrt{n}$ as well). Furthermore, the same thing holds for the approximation of the dead-weight loss.

• For a multiple price change, the Hicksian variations are also well approximated by the multigood consumer surplus, independent of the order of prices with respect to which integration takes place. (Recall that consumer surplus may not be defined uniquely when the prices of several goods change; it is path dependent.)

The goods and industries considered in this book generally represent only a small share of consumer expenditure. Price changes are therefore likely to generate small income effects, and it may be appropriate to assume that

---

28. Note, however, that a small percentage error in this approximation does not necessarily mean that the percentage error in the approximation of the dead-weight loss computed from the Hicksian variation by that computed from the consumer surplus is small. (To obtain the dead-weight loss, one must subtract the increase in income for the government or the firms.) See Hausman 1981.

29. In particular, Vives assumes that the preferences for different goods are symmetrical enough (so as to avoid the possibility that one good picks up most of the income effects), that no two goods are close to being perfect substitutes (to avoid the possibility that one good picks up most of the demand), and that the consumer's utility function satisfies a curvature condition. Then income effects vanish while the substitution effects remain large as the number of goods tends to infinity.

30. There exists a different literature on finding conditions under which the demand curve for a good is downward sloping. For instance, Hildenbrand (1983) shows that if all consumers have the same demand function and the distribution of income is given by a decreasing density, all demand functions are downward sloping. (See also Chiappori 1985.) This approach does not require a large number of goods (and the associated assumptions—see note 29). However, the assumptions of identical preferences and decreasing income density are quite strong.

The need for strong assumptions is not surprising in view of the earlier contributions of Sonnenschein (1973), Debreu (1974), and Mantel (1976) on the subject of excess-demand functions. Those authors showed that, as long as there are at least as many consumers as there are goods, absolutely no restriction (beyond homogeneity of degree 0 with respect to prices and Walras' law) could be put on aggregate demand functions.

demand is downward sloping and that the consumer surplus is a good approximation of welfare.

Extending the single-consumer case to multiple consumers creates new difficulties. One can, for instance, define the aggregate equivalent variation as the sum of individual equivalent variations without creating difficulty; however, the issue is that the aggregate equivalent variation is not, in general, insensitive to redistributions of income between the consumers. Only under strong conditions can one ignore the distribution of income.[31] (See Auerbach 1986 for more on this.)

In this book, I will treat income distribution as irrelevant. In other words, the redistribution of income from one consumer to another is assumed to have no welfare effect. (The marginal social utilities of income are equalized.) I certainly do not feel that actual income distributions are optimal, even with an optimal income-tax structure (because there are limits and costs to income taxation, as is emphasized by the optimal-taxation literature). Market intervention does have desirable or undesirable income-redistribution effects. But I will focus on the efficiency of markets, using Musgrave's (1959) framework in which the distribution branch of government worries about distribution and the allocation branch (the one considered in this book) deals with efficiency. The "compensation principle" of Hicks (1940) and Kaldor (1939) holds that we need only be concerned about efficiency; if total surplus increases, the winners can compensate the losers and everyone is made better off. The classic drawback of this approach is that the distribution branch may not function, and compensation need not occur (Samuelson 1947). This caveat should be borne in mind in all our welfare conclusions. For instance, the conclusion in chapter 3 that allowing a monopolist to price-discriminate perfectly improves welfare would be reversed if social planners were to put a much higher weight on the consumers' incomes than on the incomes of the firm's shareholders.

What Is a Market?

The notion of a market is by no means simple. Obviously we do not want to restrict ourselves to the homogeneous-good case. If we posit that two goods belong to the same market if and only if they are perfect substitutes, then virtually all markets would be served by a single firm—firms produce goods that are at least slightly differentiated (either physically or in terms of location, availability, consumer information, or some other factor). But most firms actually do not enjoy pure monopoly power. An increase in price leads consumers to substitute somewhat toward a small number of alternative goods. Therefore, the definition of a market should not be too narrow.[32]

The definition should not be too broad either. Any good is potentially a substitute for another, if only in an infinitesimal way. However, a market should not be the entire economy. In particular, it should allow partial-equilibrium analysis. It should also allow a single description of the main interactions among firms.

It is also important to realize that the "right" definition of a market depends on the use to which it will be put. For instance, consider the case of coal. If one is interested in broad issues of energy policy (such as the effect of subsidizing certain types of energy), the relevant market is the energy market, including coal, gas, oil, and nuclear power. The analysis of long-term contracting and vertical integration between U.S. coal producers and electric utilities is best conducted at the level of the region (e.g. the Northeast, the Midwest, and the West; see the chapter on the theory of the firm). To assess the competitive effects of a merger between two coal suppliers, one looks at a much narrower definition of a market, because of the high transportation costs.

There is no simple recipe for defining a market, as is demonstrated by the many debates among economists and antitrust practitioners about the degree of monopoly power in specific industries. Several useful (though imperfect) criteria have been offered, however. Robinson (1933)

---

31. More specifically, the demand function of consumer i must take the "Gorman polar form":

$$D^i(\mathbf{p}, I^i) = \Phi^i(\mathbf{p}) + \theta(\mathbf{p}) I^i,$$

where Φ^i is homogeneous of degree 0 in prices and θ is homogeneous of degree -1.

32. This subsection draws on lectures given by Paul Joskow and Richard Schmalensee.

suggested beginning with a given good and then looking at the good's substitutes, and the substitutes for these substitutes, and so on, until one finds a significant gap in the chain of substitutes. These gaps, she asserted, define the boundaries of the market around this good. This definition has several drawbacks. First, it may treat goods in a way that is too symmetric. Good 1 and good 3 may be strong competitors to good 2 but only weak competitors against each other. For instance, a Hyundai and a Rolls-Royce undoubtedly belong to the same chain of substitutes, but are they really in the same market? Second, the definition takes into account only existing competition and not potential competition. The third drawback is operational and relates to the exact definition of a gap.[33] Another criterion looks at the correlation between the prices of goods. The idea is that goods belonging to the same market tend to face similar cost and demand shocks, and that therefore their prices tend to be correlated. However, price correlation is at best a necessary condition for belonging to the same market. Boston Edison and Electricité de France, which both distribute electricity, are by no means competitors, although their prices are likely to be correlated because the prices of their fuels are. Concluding they belong to the same market just because their prices are highly correlated would be erroneous.

For the purpose of the present book, this empirical difficulty of defining a market will be ignored. It will be assumed that the market is well defined, and that it involves either a homogeneous good or a group of differentiated products that are fairly good substitutes (or complements) for at least one good in the group and have limited interaction with the rest of the economy.

References

Areeda, P. 1974. *Antitrust Analysis*, second edition. Boston: Little, Brown.

Areeda, P., and D. Turner. 1976. *Antitrust Law*. Boston: Little, Brown.

Arrow, K., and F. Hahn. 1970. *General Competitive Analysis*. San Francisco: Holden Day.

Auerbach, A. 1986. The Theory of Excess Burden and Optimal Taxation. In *Handbook of Public Economics*, volume 1, ed. A. Auerbach and M. Feldstein. New York: Elsevier.

Blair, R., and D. Kaserman. 1985. *Antitrust Economics*. Homewood, Ill.: Irwin.

Boiteux, M. 1951. Le "Revenu Distribuable" et les Pertes Economiques. *Econometrica* 19: 291–309.

Bresnahan, T. 1987a. Competition and Collusion in the American Automobile Industry: The 1955 Price War. *Journal of Industrial Economics* 35: 457–482.

Bresnahan, T. 1987b. Empirical Studies of Industries with Market Power. In *Handbook of Industrial Organization*, ed. R. Schmalensee and R. Willig. Amsterdam: North-Holland, forthcoming.

Carlton, D. 1987. The Theory and the Facts of How Markets Clear: Is Industrial Organization Valuable for Understanding Macroeconomics? In *Handbook of Industrial Organization*, ed. R. Schmalensee and R. Willig. Amsterdam: North-Holland, forthcoming.

Chiappori, P.-A. 1985. Distribution of Income and the "Law of Demand." *Econometrica* 53: 109–127.

Debreu, G. 1951. The Coefficient of Resource Allocation. *Econometrica* 19: 273–292.

Debreu, G. 1959. *The Theory of Value*. New York: Wiley.

Debreu, G. 1974. Excess Demand Functions. *Journal of Mathematical Economics* 1: 15–21.

Diamond, P., and D. McFadden. 1974. Some Uses of the Expenditure Function in Public Finance. *Journal of Public Economics* 3: 3–21.

Dixit, A. 1976. *Optimization in Economic Theory*. Oxford University Press.

Dixit, A., and V. Norman. 1980. *Theory of International Trade*. Welwyn: Nisbet.

33. The guidelines of the U.S. Department of Justice offer a somewhat related criterion: Starting with a given product and a given seller, keep adding close substitutes (not necessarily produced by the same seller) until the set of products as a whole has a sufficiently low own elasticity of demand that the sellers of these products would charge an average monopoly markup above some threshold level if they colluded. This group of products is called a market. Practitioners thus do not have to look for gaps, although they may do so in practice.

Dupuit, J. 1844. De la Mesure de l'Utilité des Travaux Publics. Translation in *AEA Readings in Welfare Economics*, ed. K. Arrow and T. Scitovsky.

Hall, R. 1986. The Relationship between Price and Marginal Cost in U.S. Industry. Working Paper E-86-24, Hoover Institution, Stanford University.

Harberger, A. 1964. Taxation, Resource Allocation and Welfare. In *The Role of Direct and Indirect Taxes in the Federal Reserve System*. Princeton University Press for NBER and Brookings Institution.

Hart, O. 1985. Imperfect Competition in General Equilibrium: An Overview of Recent Work. In *Frontiers of Economics*, ed. K. Arrow and S. Honkapohja. Oxford: Blackwell.

Hausman, J. 1981. Exact Consumer's Surplus and Deadweight-Loss. *American Economic Review* 71: 662–676.

Helpman, E., and P. Krugman. 1985. *Market Structure and Foreign Trade*. Cambridge, Mass.: MIT Press.

Hicks, J. 1940. The Valuation of Social Income. *Economica* NS 7: 105–129.

Hicks, J. 1941. The Rehabilitation of Consumer's Surplus. *Review of Economic Studies* 9: 108–116.

Hicks, J. 1946. *Value and Capital*, second edition. Oxford University Press.

Hildenbrand, W. 1983. On the Law of Demand. *Econometrica* 51: 997–1019.

Hopenhayn, H. 1986. A Competitive Stochastic Model of Entry and Exit to an Industry. Mimeo, University of Minnesota.

Hotelling, H. 1938. The General Welfare in Relation to Problems of Tarification and of Railway and Utility Raises. *Econometrica* 6: 242–269.

Joskow, P. 1975. Firm Decision-Making Process and Oligopoly Theory. *American Economic Review, Papers and Proceedings* 65: 270–279.

Joskow, P. 1985. Vertical Integration and Long Term Contracts: The Case of Coal-Burning Electric Generating Plants. *Journal of Law, Economics and Organization* 1: 33–80.

Jovanovic, B. 1982. Selection and the Evolution of Industry. *Econometrica* 50: 649–670.

Kaldor, N. 1939. Welfare Propositions in Economics. *Economic Journal* 49: 549–552.

Kamien, M., and N. Schwartz. 1981. *Dynamic Optimization*. Amsterdam: North-Holland.

Lippman, C., and R. Rummelt. 1982. Uncertain Imitability: An Analysis of Interfirm Differences in Efficiency under Competition. *Bell Journal of Economics* 13: 418–438.

Lucas, R. 1978. On the Size Distribution of Business Firms. *Bell Journal of Economics* 9: 508–523.

Mantel, R. 1976. Homothetic Preferences and Community Excess Demand Functions. *Journal of Economic Theory* 12: 197–201.

Marshall, A. 1920. *Principle of Economics*. London: Macmillan.

Mas-Colell, A. 1985. *The Theory of General Economic Equilibrium: A Differentiable Approach*. Cambridge University Press.

Mohring, H. 1971. Alternative Welfare Gain and Loss Measures. *Western Economic Journal* 9: 349–368.

Musgrave, R. 1959. *The Theory of Public Finance*. New York: McGraw-Hill.

Plott, C. 1982. Industrial Organization Theory and Experimental Economics. *Journal of Economic Literature* 20: 1485–1527.

Porter, M. 1980. *Competitive Strategy*. New York: Free Press.

Porter, R. 1983. A Study of Cartel Stability: The Joint Economic Committee: 1880–1886. *Bell Journal of Economics* 14: 301–314.

Posner, R., and F. Easterbrook. 1981. *Antitrust Cases, Economic Notes and Other Materials*, second edition. St. Paul: West.

Robinson, J. 1933. *The Economics of Imperfect Competition*. London: Macmillan.

Samuelson, P. 1947. *Foundation of Economic Analysis*. Cambridge, Mass.: Harvard University Press.

Scherer, F. 1980. *Industrial Market Structure and Economic Performance*, second edition. Chicago: Rand-McNally.

Schmalensee, R. 1986. Inter-Industry Studies of Structure and Performance. In *Handbook of Industrial Organization*, ed. R. Schmalensee and R. Willig. Amsterdam: North-Holland, forthcoming.

Sonnenschein, H. 1973. Do Walras' Identity and Homogeneity Characterize the Class of Community Excess Demand Functions? *Journal of Economic Theory* 6: 345–354.

Varian, H. 1978. *Microeconomic Analysis*. New York: Norton.

Vives, X. 1987. Small Income Effects: A Marshallian Theory of Consumer Surplus and Downward Sloping Demand. *Review of Economic Studies* 54: 87–103.

Willig, R. 1976. Consumer's Surplus without Apology. *American Economic Review* 66: 589–597.

The Theory of the Firm

The basic actors in this book are firms. But what is a firm, and how do firms behave? These two questions are the subjects of this preliminary chapter.

The notions of a "firm," of "vertical integration," and of "authority" are by no means simple, and consequently they have been given various meanings in the literature. The frequently used definitions that will be mentioned and classified here reflect different facets of the notions and can be thought of as complementary. They share the idea that a firm should be able to produce (or sell) more efficiently than would its constituent parts acting separately. These definitions thus entail very explicit optimizing approaches.

The behavior of firms is not a simple matter, either. There are many ways in which business decision makers may deviate from profit-maximizing behavior and many mechanisms that, in turn, limit managerial discretion. Furthermore, most of the recent developments in the study of firms' decision making and behavior are based on the theory of incentives, a full treatment of which is outside the scope of this book. Here, again, the main arguments will be introduced and classified.

This chapter is at worst a hodgepodge of received ideas; at best it is a road map of the relevant contributions. A large number of theories are reviewed at a fast pace. Numerous references are included for the interested reader, who may also find the surveys by Hart and Holmström (1987) and Holmström and Tirole (1987) useful.[1]

It is customary to distinguish—not always without ambiguity—the horizontal and vertical aspects of a firm's size. The horizontal dimension refers to the scale of production in a single-product firm or to its scope in a multiproduct one. The vertical dimension reflects the extent to which goods and services that can be purchased from

---

1. Hart and Holmström 1987 develops some of the themes of this chapter in more detail. Holmström and Tirole 1987 is less methodological and more issue-oriented, and covers a substantially broader selection of topics than the present chapter.

outsiders are produced in house. A wallpaper manufacturer merging with another wallpaper manufacturer or a tile producer engages in horizontal integration; a winemaker purchasing a bottle or cork factory engages in vertical integration.

This chapter is divided into two sections. Section 1 looks at various definitions of a firm. It does not focus on the advantages (limited liability, issuing of shares, etc.) brought about by the legal constitution of some form of firm (e.g., a limited partnership or a corporation).[2] Rather, it focuses on what determines the size of the firm. However, one legal aspect should be mentioned at the outset: Sometimes the internalization of transactions within a firm is a way of concealing practices deemed illegal under, say, antitrust laws. A couple of such examples are given, in which firms are integrated horizontally or vertically only in order to legally exercise monopoly power on the product market.

Section 1 is concerned mainly with the *efficiency (or "non-monopoly") reasons* for integration or disintegration. Efficiency motives are associated with the cost-minimizing organization of economic activity. They are not contingent on the existence of monopoly power on the product market. Indeed, if the product market is perfectly competitive, the private and social interests that are relative to the choice between alternative organizational forms generally coincide.[3]

First the firm will be regarded as a synergy between different units at a given point in time to exploit economies of scale or of scope.[4] This *technological* view will lead to discussions of the various forms of cost or demand complementarities and of the old "U-form" internal organization of a firm (in which units are gathered according to their functions).

The second view of the firm—the *contractual* view of a long-run arrangement of its units—brings us to the Williamsonian theory of the hazards of idiosyncratic exchange in a long-run relationship. Consider a buyer-supplier relationship in which the parties must sink trade-specific investments before trading. *Ex ante* (before agreement to trade) there may be many suppliers and buyers, but *ex post* (once investments have been made) the parties may be in a bilateral monopoly situation. The supplier may not find alternative outlets, and the buyer may not be able to contract with a new supplier on time. This absence of *ex post* competition raises the possibility of "hold-up" or "opportunism" (the confiscation of the gains associated with one party's investment by the other party). A long-term contract must *ex post* guarantee the parties a fair return in order to *ex ante* encourage specific investment. It must also *ex post* guarantee the efficient volume of trade by prohibiting monopoly pricing.

These first two views have relatively little to do with the legal definition of a firm (or with each other). Firms that agree to share some fixed costs (for instance, the study of export markets, the procurement of inputs, or some research and development), a manufacturer and a retailer who sign a contract specifying stringent vertical restraints, and a power plant and a coal mine located next to each other that sign a detailed thirty-year supply contract can all be considered at least partially integrated, although legally they remain separate entities. (Consider, in contrast, an employee hired for a particular task, or one who can quit or be fired without advance notice and without penalties for breach).

The third view of the firm—the *incomplete-contracting* view—comes somewhat closer to the legal definition(s). It emphasizes that firms and contracts are rather different "governance modes." It looks at the firm as a particular way of specifying what is to be done in the event of contingencies not foreseen in a contract. It starts from the idea that contracts are necessarily incomplete, because some contingencies are unforeseeable or because there are too many of them to specify in writing, so that cost minimization requires the original contract to define only the broad lines of the relationship. The ownership of machines and the employment relationship give the owner of the firm the power ("authority") to choose the way machines and personnel are to be employed, within certain limits. The degree of integration can then

---

2. See Alchian and Demsetz 1972 and Jensen and Meckling 1976 for economic analyses of the various ownership structures.

3. Unless there are production externalities between firms. Such externalities arise, for instance, when the input markets are noncompetitive. Or, as in the Hart model of managerial incentives mentioned below, the control of a firm's managers by its shareholders depends (for informational reasons) on the internal organization of other firms in the industry.

4. Very roughly, economies of scale exist when the production cost of a single product decreases with the number of units produced; economies of scope are cost-saving externalities between product lines (e.g., the production of good A reduces the production cost of good B).

be measured roughly by the extent to which authority is distributed between contracting parties.

Also discussed in section 1 are the factors limiting the firm's size according to the various definitions of a firm. Among these factors are exhaustion of returns to scale and scope, rare factors, the drawbacks of long-run relationships, and excessive concentration of power.

Section 2 takes firms as well-defined entities. Rather than analyze their size, it investigates how firms behave. Do firms actually maximize profits, as is presumed throughout this book? If they do not, is the profit-maximization hypothesis still a useful guide for predicting monopolistic behavior or strategic interaction? The various mechanisms that put a lid on managerial discretion (monitoring; the incentives of the product, labor, and capital markets) are reviewed, and the profit-maximization postulate is then discussed.

---

1 What Is a Firm?

In subsections 1.2–1.4 we shall examine three views of the firm as a cost-minimizing device. Before doing so, however, let us dispose of some motives for integration.

1.1 The Firm as a Loophole for the Exercise of Monopoly Power

Various trade practices are, rightly or wrongly, banned by antitrust regulations as evil manifestations of monopoly power. By internalizing these practices, firms can circumvent the legal framework to quietly exercise their monopoly power. (Because internal transactions are usually unobserved, they escape the law.[5])

Price Discrimination

As will be shown in chapter 3, a firm may want to sell a given product in different markets at different prices. This raises the possibility of arbitrage among the retailers serving these markets. To avoid arbitrage, the manufacturer may integrate into distribution and serve the low-price market himself. A similar phenomenon, but one induced by the law rather than by arbitrage, arises when the law forces a firm to treat two customers in "similar situations" symmetrically (as is the case in principle in the United States or in France) but the manufacturer desires to treat them differently or to foreclose one customer's access. By integrating with one customer, the manufacturer can treat the other differently or perhaps shut the intermediate-good market altogether.

Intermediate Price Controls

Suppose the price of an intermediate good traded between a large number of suppliers and a large number of buyers is set by regulatory agencies below the market equilibrium price determined by supply and demand. The good must then be distributed to the buyers by some rationing mechanism. This gives the suppliers an incentive to merge with some of their buyers. Why? The transaction (legal) price of the intermediate good is lower than the shadow price that the buyers are willing to pay. Therefore, there exist appropriable rents to be distributed between the suppliers and the rationed users. However, the suppliers, who could obtain their share of appropriable rents by increasing the price in an unconstrained market, cannot do so in the regulated case. Vertical integration allows suppliers to circumvent the law by generating internal—and consequently unobservable—transactions.

There are other legal reasons that may lead vertically related firms to integrate. One is the existence of a sales tax. The internalization of transactions avoids the payment of such a tax at the intermediate stage. (This phenomenon does not occur when the tax base is the value added rather than the accumulated value of the product up to the transaction. A value-added tax is neutral with respect to the integration decision.) Another reason is the existence of a rate-of-return regulation. A firm that is subject to such a regulation can earn more profits by integrating backwards into the equipment-supply industry if equipment-transfer prices are not regulated.[6]

Chapter 4 is dedicated to the study of the economic rather than the legal motives for vertical integration that are related to the exercise of monopoly power.

Remark Horizontal integration may also be motivated by the desire to exercise monopoly power. The obvious example is that of a merger of two firms that produce the

---

5. Furthermore, the law often distinguishes quite explicitly between internal and external transactions.

6. The regulated firm can inflate transfer prices so as to relax the rate-of-return regulation. See Dayan 1972.

same products. Such mergers, prominent during the great merger wave of 1887–1904 in the United States,[7] are often meant to eliminate the dissipation of monopoly profit through product competition (see chapter 5).[8]

1.2 The Firm as a Static Synergy

An old theme in industrial organization, following Viner's (1932) classic investigation of cost curves, is that the size and the number of the firms in an industry are related to the degree of returns of scale.

One of the main determinants of the size of a firm is the extent to which it can exploit economies of scale or of scope. As has been well documented by engineers,[9] higher levels of production permit the use of more efficient techniques. They vindicate the investment in cost-reducing technologies, and they allow workers to be more specialized. Unit costs decrease. Such economies of scale, related to the volume of a single product, are called *product-specific economies.* In this category we could include, although it is not customary to do so, the so-called *economies of massed reserves* (Robinson 1958). A plant with a larger number of machines can sustain a flow of output proportionally higher than one with a small number. This is because the random breakdown of a machine has less of an impact on output, as the flow of production through that machine can be reallocated to other machines. (In the limit, with many machines, the flow of output that can be sustained is perfectly deterministic, by the law of large numbers, when the machines' breakdowns are independent.) Similarly, a firm serving several markets with (imperfectly correlated) variable demands faces less uncertainty than a collection of separate firms serving these markets independently, and therefore can save on costly peak-load investment. Economies of massed reserves may also apply to multiproduct firms when the various products share production techniques.[10]

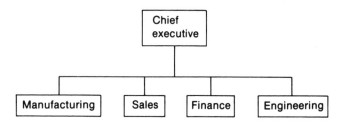

Figure 1

An example of unitary-form organization. Source: Williamson 1975, p. 134.

Alternatively, the gathering of activities, be they relative to the same product or to different products, may relate not to production in the narrow sense but to all the services that accompany production: auditing, marketing, personnel service, finance, distribution, materials procurement, research and development, and so forth. Such a gathering avoids duplication of fixed costs associated with these services, or at least it reduces these costs on the average. Demand complementarities may also be a motive for coordinating activities.[11]

The late nineteenth century witnessed the emergence of large, multifunctional firms, which were organized in a unitary (U) form,[12] with the units regrouped by their functions as shown in figure 1. This sort of organization can be seen as an attempt to exploit potential economies of scale. Within each unit, the large size reduces the unit cost of exercising the function (that is, producing the good or the service).

However pervasive they may be, returns to scale have their limits. Machines or functional divisions related to two production units can be advantageously pulled together only if they are not employed to their capacities. Similarly, the savings in peak-load capacity associated with the pooling of risk and the law of large numbers become smaller and smaller as the size of the firm grows. Furthermore, it is sometimes argued that there may exist

---

7. See, e.g., Scherer 1980, pp. 119–122. Mergers of this kind were later discouraged by the application of antitrust laws.

8. It is also often suggested that firms may gain by interacting in many (possibly unrelated) markets. This may be a cause of horizontal (here, conglomerate) merger. See chapter 6.

9. See Scherer 1980, pp. 81–84, for a few concrete examples.

10. A useful article along the lines of this paragraph is Arrow et al. 1972. The authors show the link between the repair of machines and increasing returns to scale. They derive an increasing-returns-to-scale production function, which

tends to a constant-returns-to-scale one when the number of machines tends to infinity.

11. One could think of firms specialized in making left shoes and others in making right shoes; however, the required coordination of designs creates a synergy.

12. For discussions of unitary and multidivisional forms, see Chandler 1966 and Williamson 1975. (The U-form—the logical one from a technological viewpoint—faces serious coordination and incentive problems and has often been replaced by the M-form. See page 47.)

rare factors, such as managerial talent, that cannot be duplicated as the firm expands.[13]

Let us now briefly consider the formalizations of returns to scale and to scope. (A much more complete treatment can be found in Baumol et al. 1982—see chapter 2 for the single-product case and chapters 3 and 4 for the multiproduct case.)

Let us begin with the single-product firm. Let $C(q)$ denote a firm's total cost of producing output q; that is, let $C(q)$ be the minimum cost of a bundle of inputs that allows the production of q units of output. For simplicity, assume that the cost function is twice differentiable, except possibly at zero output:

$$C(q) = \begin{cases} F + \int_0^q C'(x)dx & \text{for } q > 0 \\ \\ 0 & \text{otherwise} \end{cases}$$

where $F \geq 0$ denotes a fixed production cost.

Marginal costs are strictly decreasing if $C''(q) < 0$ for all possible q. Average costs are strictly decreasing if, for all q_1 and q_2 such that $0 < q_1 < q_2$,

$$\frac{C(q_2)}{q_2} < \frac{C(q_1)}{q_1}.$$

The cost function is said to be strictly subadditive if, for any n-tuple of outputs $q_1, \ldots, q_n$,

$$\sum_{i=1}^n C(q_i) > C\left(\sum_{i=1}^n q_i\right).$$

Subadditivity thus means that it costs less to produce the various outputs together than to produce them separately.

Figure 2 shows three shapes of average-cost (AC) and marginal-cost (MC) curves that are familiar from introductory and intermediate microeconomics textbooks. Figure 2a depicts the cost function $C(q) = F + cq$ for $q > 0$. The firm incurs a fixed cost F, and then has a constant

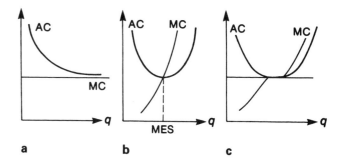

Figure 2

marginal cost. Average costs are everywhere declining (except at zero production), although at a vanishing rate. Figure 2b shows a U-shaped average-cost curve. The average cost declines until it reaches the "most efficient scale," MES, where it intersects the marginal-cost curve; then it increases. An example of such a cost curve is $C(q) = F + aq^2$ (where $a > 0$). The flat-bottomed average-cost curve depicted in figure 2c is intermediate between the first-two curves. Average cost stabilizes over a range of outputs before decreasing returns make it grow again.[14]

Everywhere-decreasing marginal costs imply everywhere-decreasing average costs,[15] and everywhere-decreasing average costs imply subadditivity.[16] The converses of these two propositions are, however, false. (See figure 2a for a counterexample to the first converse, and proposition 2A1 of Baumol et al. 1982 for a counterexample to the second.)

Remark Several meanings can be given of a natural monopoly, depending on the application that is being made. Suppose that there exists a commonly available technology $C(q)$ that produces some output q. Baumol et al. (1982) define an industry as a natural monopoly if, over the relevant range of outputs, the cost function is subadditive. This definition is the correct one for a well-informed planner (a planner who knows the cost function

---

13. Lucas (1967) and Prescott and Visscher (1980) build models in which adjustment costs slow the firm's expansion. Prescott and Visscher associate the adjustment cost with learning about the characteristics of the employees. The firm observes the employees' performance over time and slowly finds out which tasks suit each of them best. The trade-off is between growing quickly and making errors in job assignment, and growing more slowly and capturing the gains from more accurate information about the employees' comparative advantage. This theory reflects the common feeling among executives that human capital is a serious constraint in expansionary periods.

Lucas (1978) and Kihlstrom and Laffont (1979) consider economies with scarce managerial talents and identify firms with managers.

14. See Bain 1954 and chapter 4 of Scherer 1980 for discussions of the evidence on average-cost curves.

15. $\dfrac{d}{dq}\left(\dfrac{C(q)}{q}\right) = \dfrac{d}{dq}\left(\dfrac{F}{q}\right) + \dfrac{d}{dq}\left(\int_0^q C'(x)dx\Big/q\right) < 0,$

since $C'(q) < C'(x)$ for all $x \in (0, q)$ implies that $C'(q) - \int_0^q C'(x)dx/q < 0.$

16. Let $q \equiv \sum_i q_i$ (with $q_i > 0$). Then $C(q_i)/q_i > C(q)/q$, which implies

$\sum_i C(q_i) > \sum_i q_i C(q)/q = C(q).$

perfectly). The planner has no incentive to have several firms produce the output when the aggregate output could be produced more cheaply by a single firm.

In a more positive sense, one can look at behavior in an unregulated industry. Let $\Pi(n)$ denote the profit of a single firm when the number of firms in the industry is n. (For simplicity, assume that all the firms make the same profit.) This profit is the outcome of whatever type of competition the firms wage, and is net of all costs (including the fixed cost). It is natural to assume that $\Pi(n)$ decreases with n. An industry is a natural monopoly if $\Pi(1) > 0 > \Pi(2)$—that is, if one firm is viable, but not two or more.[17]

One can also consider the case of a regulator who has incomplete information about the cost function (or demand). Such a regulator may want to trade off returns to scale (which would favor a unique firm) and the extraction of the relevant information through competition among firms (on this see the discussion of tournaments in section 2 of the present chapter and the complementary section of chapter 4). A natural monopoly then arises when the regulator prefers production by a single firm.

For a multiproduct firm, subadditivity generalizes naturally. Suppose that $\mathbf{q}$ is now a production vector or plan: $\mathbf{q} = (q_1, \ldots, q_m)$ for the m outputs. Let $\mathbf{q}^1, \ldots, \mathbf{q}^n$ denote n such vectors. (Superscripts index production plans; subscripts here index goods.) The cost function C is strictly subadditive if

$$\sum_{i=1}^{n} C(\mathbf{q}^i) > C\left(\sum_{i=1}^{n} \mathbf{q}^i\right)$$

for all $\mathbf{q}$ such that $\sum_i \mathbf{q}^i \neq 0$. This definition applies to the single-product cost function as a special case. (Let the m goods be homogeneous, i.e., be the same good.) More interestingly, it gives one formulation of economies of scope. For example, let q_1 and q_2 denote two quantities of two different goods. Then, for a strictly subadditive cost function,

$$C(q_1, 0) + C(0, q_2) > C(q_1, q_2).$$

($C(q_1, 0)$ are $C(0, q_2)$ are called *stand-alone costs*.) For instance, a single railroad company producing both passenger travel and freight transport (two different economic goods) is technologically more efficient than two companies specialized in one of the two productions. Similarly, the production of peak-load and base-load demands is less costly when performed by a single electric-power company.[18]

Is the Technological View a "Theory of the Firm"?

The technological view aims at defining the size of a firm. Economies of scale encourage the gathering of activities. And the limit to the size stems from the fact that average-cost curves rise at high output, as in figures 2b and 2c. There are two related reasons why this view, as it stands, does not quite constitute a theory of firm size.

First, it is not clear why economies of scale should necessarily be exploited within the firm. They could, *a priori*, also be obtained through contracting between legally separate entities. For example, consider the above "economies of massed reserves" argument. As was noted, a firm serving several markets faces less uncertainty than a number of separate firms serving these markets independently. It can thus reduce costly investment in peak-load equipment. But a similar outcome could be obtained through an agreement to transfer the good at some (possibly contingent) prices. Indeed, electric utilities do engage in arrangements to pool electric power. Similarly, the "repairman problem" of Arrow et al. (1972), which involves an increasing-returns-to-scale production function, does not imply that all production should take place in a single firm. The various units could sign a contract in which they agree to share the services of repairmen, or an independent repair firm could be established that would supply the services to the units.

---

17. Similarly, one could define a natural duopoly as an industry such that $\Pi(2) > 0 > \Pi(3), \ldots$.

18. The returns-to-scale argument looks at cost or demand interdependencies. There can also be synergies between unrelated units. Two such synergies, based on uncertainty and the diversification of risks, have been put forward as attempts to explain conglomerate mergers (i.e., mergers not motivated by cost or demand interactions—waves of which occurred in the United States in the 1960s and the 1980s). First, it has been argued that a diversification into unrelated activities allows firms to reduce risk. (This argument does not explain why firms diversify their activities when their shareholders could duplicate this operation by diversifying their portfolios.) Second, when diversification still leaves the top managers in charge of all activities, the measurement of these managers' performance is less garbled by the randomness in each activity's profit (by the law of large numbers), so that managerial incentive schemes can relate more closely to actual performance (see Aron 1984).

Second, we should not take it for granted that average-cost curves rise at high output. For instance, if producing output $q_1 + q_2$ were to cost more than producing outputs q_1 and q_2 separately, a firm wanting to produce $q_1 + q_2$ could set up two independent divisions operated as quasi-firms. Its production technology would then exhibit no diseconomies of scale. A reformulation of this argument brings us to Williamson's "puzzle of selective intervention": Why can't one merge two firms into a single one and duplicate (and perhaps, through selective intervention, improve upon) the decentralized outcome? Why are there limits to firm size? (An element of the answer is given in subsection 1.4 below.)

1.3 The Firm as a Long-Run Relationship

In subsection 1.2 we investigated some reasons why, at a given point in time, some units might want to merge or coordinate their activities through a static contract. We now study the new problems associated with long-run relationships—in particular, why the rules that govern trade tomorrow ought to be determined today whenever this is feasible.[19] For simplicity, this discussion will be restricted to a vertical relationship between a supplier and a buyer. In the discussion of uncertainty, it will also be assumed that both parties are risk-neutral.

Idiosyncratic Investment and Asset Specificity

Long-run relationships are often associated with either switching costs or specific investments. Switching costs receive a detailed analysis in Williamson's (1976) enumeration of the hazards associated with a government's use of repeated bidding to allocate a natural monopoly.[20] Prominent among switching costs are the need of the new team to learn the ropes and the reluctance of the old team to transmit information to the new one. The same costs that may prevent a regulator from using repeated bidding to allocate the monopolistic supply of a good are likely also to prevent a buyer from repeatedly using the spot market to purchase certain goods or services from a supplier.

Switching costs, in a sense, are a case of idiosyncratic investment. Once the two parties have traded, staying together can yield a surplus relative to trading with other parties. More generally, idiosyncratic investment can be associated with the prospect of future trading rather than with current trading. This is the case, for instance, when a supplier must design equipment the characteristics of which are specific (dedicated) to a buyer's particular order (as is often the case with machine tools), or when a buyer spends money and effort to sell or promote a final product before an intermediate good used to produce this final product is delivered by the supplier (as when a concert organizer rents a concert hall before the singer performs), or when a user of raw materials buys machines that are adapted to the use of certain materials. Williamson (1975) distinguishes two further types of specificity: site specificity and specific investments in human capital. Site specificity is associated with the gain in trading with a nearby supplier or buyer. For instance, in the steel industry, the integration of smelting (upstream) and laminating (downstream) operations affords a reduction in transportation costs and avoids the need to reheat the steel. Similarly, the location of a power plant near a coal mine saves on transportation costs. Specific investments in human capital involve, for example, the learning of processes and team work.[21]

All these types of specificity have the same outcome: The parties that contract now know that later on there will be gains from trade between them to be exploited. It is important that these gains from trade be exploited correctly (i.e., that there be an efficient amount of trade *ex post*) and that they be divided properly in order to induce the efficient amount of specific investment *ex ante*.

A crucial aspect of specific investment is that even though the supplier and the buyer may select each other *ex ante* in a pool of competitive suppliers and buyers, they end up forming an *ex post* bilateral monopoly in that they have an incentive to trade between them rather than with outside parties. Under bilateral monopoly, each party wants to appropriate the common surplus *ex post*, thus jeopardizing the efficient realization of trade *ex post* and the efficient amounts of specific investments *ex ante*.[22]

---

19. For a discussion of incomplete contracts, see subsection 1.4.

20. Williamson responded to earlier contributions by Demsetz (1968), Stigler (1968), and Posner (1972), who suggested the use of repeated bidding as a means to prevent excessively deviant behavior by the regulated monopoly.

21. For an analysis of specific investments in a labor context, see Williamson et al. 1975.

22. The following discussion draws, in particular, from Farrell 1985, Grossman and Hart 1984, and Hall and Lazear 1984.

Bilateral Monopoly Pricing and the *Ex Post* Volume of Trade

To be concrete, let us assume that there are two periods: $t = 1$ (*ex ante*) and $t = 2$ (*ex post*). A supplier and a buyer may or may not contract in period 1. To focus on the *ex post* issue, we ignore for the moment first-period specific investments. At the beginning of period 2, the two parties learn how much they will gain from trading in period 2 (these variables can be seen at date 1 as being random). If they choose to do so, they trade one unit of an indivisible good (or the supplier realizes a "project"). Thus, the volume of trade is either 0 or 1 (in a more complicated model, it could be a continuous variable). The value of the good to the buyer is v, and its production cost to the supplier is c.[23] So, the gains from trade (if any) to be split between the two parties are equal to $v - c$. If p is the trading price, the buyer's surplus from the relationship is $v - p$ and the seller's surplus is $p - c$. In the absence of trade, the surplus is nil for the two parties.

Bargaining

Let us assume that no contract is signed in period 1. Then some bargaining occurs in period 2 to determine whether to trade and at what price.

If v and c are common knowledge (i.e., if both parties learn v and c before bargaining), we should expect the efficient amount of trade (i.e., that trade occurs if and only if $v \geq c$). To see why, suppose that $v > c$ and that no trade will take place, so that the two parties expect no surplus. Then one of the parties could suggest trading at a price p in the interval (c, v) that leaves a net surplus to both. Such a solution would be preferred by both parties to no trade at all. If $v < c$, and both parties trade, one of the parties must realize a negative surplus and would be better off refusing to trade. More generally, bargaining under symmetric information is efficient, so the issue of an inefficient *ex post* volume of trade in a bargaining situation does not arise. (This is a version of the Coase

[1960] theorem.) As we now see, asymmetric information may yield bargaining inefficiencies.

Often the buyer's value v and the supplier's cost c are "private information." The value is observed only by the buyer, the cost only by the seller.[24] The efficient volume of trade may then not be reached because of the (bilateral) monopoly pricing problem. The inefficiency stems from the fact that both parties would like to appropriate the gains from trade but, because of asymmetric information, run the risk of forgoing trade in order to get a larger share of the pie in case of trade. They may be too demanding.

A simple example helps to illustrate how the "wrong distribution of bargaining power" creates trade inefficiencies: Suppose that the cost c is known to both parties, that the value v is known to the buyer only, and that the supplier's beliefs about v are represented by a cumulative probability distribution $F(v)$ with density $f(v) > 0$ on an interval $[\underline{v}, \overline{v}]$ (with $F(\underline{v}) = 0$ and $F(\overline{v}) = 1$). Assume that gains from trade exist with positive probability (i.e., $\overline{v} > c$) and, for simplicity, that this probability is less than 1 (i.e., $\underline{v} < c$). Suppose further that the supplier has all the bargaining power in period 2—that is, the supplier can make a "take it or leave it" price offer p to the buyer. (Of course, in a bilateral monopoly situation one would expect bargaining power to be more evenly distributed; but this extreme case offers simple and illustrative conclusions.) If the supplier offers p, the buyer accepts only if $v \geq p$. Thus, the probability of trading is $1 - F(p)$ and the supplier's expected profit is

$$(p - c)[1 - F(p)].$$

Maximizing with respect to p yields the first-order condition[25]

$$[1 - F(p)] - (p - c)f(p) = 0. \tag{1}$$

Equation 1 says that an increase in price from p to $p + dp$ yields extra profits dp with probability $1 - F(p)$ and leads to a loss of trade, and hence to a loss of net profit $p - c$ with probability $f(p)dp$. At the optimum, these two effects

---

23. The value and the cost may reflect outside opportunities as well. For instance, v may be the difference between the value to the buyer in this relationship and that in an alternative relationship.

24. In some instances, these values could be inferred *ex post* from accounting data in the case of trade. However, such accounting data may be garbled. For instance, the supplier's cost may be hard to distinguish from costs associated with other projects; also, it may be garbled by "moral hazard" (the unobserv-

able level of cost-reducing effort exerted *ex post* by the supplier). Similarly, how much the trade in this intermediate good contributes to the buyer's overall profit may be hard to discern.

25. The local second-order condition is $-2f(p) - (p - c)f'(p) \leq 0$. Using the first-order condition, the reader will check that the local second-order condition is satisfied if and only if the "hazard rate" of the distribution $f/(1 - F)$ is increasing.

cancel. Notice that the volume of trade is suboptimal.[26] The efficient volume of trade would arise if and only if $p = c$ (the buyer pays exactly the supplier's cost and thus makes the "right decision" of whether or not to trade). But equation 1 yields $p > c$ instead. The reason for this inefficiency is as follows: Charging a price equal to cost yields no profit to the supplier; raising the price above cost yields a profit with some probability; the forgone volume of trade associated with this increase is costless because the initial price-cost margin is zero.

Equation 1 is nothing but the familiar monopoly pricing formula (see chapter 1) for demand curve $q = D(p) = 1 - F(p)$. For a risk-neutral seller, a continuum of buyers with unit demands and valuations distributed according to some cumulative distribution $F(\cdot)$ is equivalent to a single buyer with unit demand and a random valuation determined by $F(\cdot)$.[27]

Remark More generally, it can be shown that as long as both value and cost are private information, as long as gains from trade do not arise with certainty (i.e., there is some probability that $v < c$), and as long as the parties are free not to trade (i.e., can guarantee themselves a zero surplus by quitting the bargaining process), there exists no efficient bargaining process (see Myerson and Satterthwaite 1983).[28] Bargaining creates some inefficiency (in general, in the direction of too little trade). The intuition is that the previous monopoly-pricing in-

efficiency is bound to arise because each bargainer has incomplete information about the other party.

Contracting

Ex post trade inefficiency gives the parties incentives to contract *ex ante* to avoid or limit this inefficiency. In the preceding case, in which only the buyer's value is private information, there is a simple way to do so. It suffices to give the "informed party"—the buyer—the right to choose the price (i.e., to reverse the bargaining power). Since c is known, no inefficiency will arise. The buyer's monopoly price is equal to the price that leaves the seller indifferent about either accepting or refusing to trade: $p = c$. The buyer *ex post* appropriates all the gains from trade. An unconditional *ex ante* payment from the buyer to the supplier can be negotiated to create any division of this optimal joint surplus. (More generally, the contract aims to create the largest possible "pie." The division of this pie depends on *ex ante* relative bargaining powers.)

Similarly, if the buyer's value is common knowledge and the supplier's cost is private information, giving the supplier the right to fix the price is efficient. Such rights are somewhat similar to a sequential authority relationship (see subsection 1.4) in which one party has the authority to choose the price and the other party has only the authority over the trade decision.

In the case in which one of the parties' value or cost is already common knowledge at the contract date, this

---

26. If it is common knowledge that there are gains from trade (i.e., $\underline{v} > c$), the volume of trade may or may not be efficient.

27. Similarly, dynamic bargaining between a buyer and a seller in which the seller makes offers sequentially can be reinterpreted as an intertemporal monopoly price discrimination problem (see the supplementary section at the end of chapter 1). Indeed, the monopoly pricing problem examined here is the one-period version (or the multiperiod version with commitment) of the intertemporal price discrimination problem.

28. The advanced reader may check this in the following way. Let the supplier's cost c be distributed on $[\underline{c}, \bar{c}]$ according to the c.d.f. $G(\cdot)$ with density $g(\cdot)$, and let the buyer's valuation v be distributed according to the c.d.f. $F(\cdot)$, with density $f(\cdot)$. For exchange to be efficient, the parties must trade if and only if $v \geqslant c$. Thus, the total *ex ante* expected surplus is

$$W = \int_{\underline{c}}^{\bar{c}} \left(\int_{c}^{\bar{v}} (v - c) f(v) dv \right) g(c) dc.$$

Next, let $V(v)$ denote the buyer's expected profit in the bargaining process (the expectation being taken over the seller's cost). One has $\dot{V}(v) = G(v)$; i.e., the expected profit grows at a rate equal to the probability that a buyer with valuation v trades. (To see this, note that a buyer with valuation v can always behave like a buyer with valuation $v + dv$, so $V(v + dv) - V(v)$

$\leqslant G(v + dv) dv$. And conversely.) Similarly, if $C(c)$ denotes the supplier's expected profit when his cost is c, then $\dot{C}(c) = -[1 - F(c)]$. Last, free participation implies that $V(\underline{v}) \geqslant 0$ and $C(\bar{c}) \geqslant 0$. Hence,

$$V(v) \geqslant \int_{\underline{v}}^{v} G(x) dx$$

and

$$C(c) \geqslant \int_{c}^{\bar{c}} [1 - F(x)] dx.$$

A simple integration by parts then shows that

$$\int_{\underline{v}}^{\bar{v}} V(v) f(v) dv + \int_{\underline{c}}^{\bar{c}} C(c) g(c) dc$$

strictly exceeds W if $\bar{c} > \underline{v}$ (overlapping supports)—a contradiction.

Myerson and Satterthwaite (1983) characterize the optimal bargaining mechanisms (of course, the actual bargaining process need not be one of these). Cramton et al. (1987) show that inefficiency need not result if ownership of the good is initially distributed in a more symmetric way (as in a partnership), and generalize the Myerson-Satterthwaite characterization of optimal mechanisms.

efficient arrangement takes the even simpler form of a *fixed-price contract*. For instance, if c is common knowledge at the contracting date, the contract can be written in the following manner: "The buyer determines the quantity to be delivered (here, 0 or 1). The delivery price is c."

With bilateral asymmetric information, assigning one party the right to choose the price, or to choose the quantity at a previously agreed-upon price, in general is no longer efficient. The parties will want to consider alternative arrangements. A particularly simple rule, the "rigid norm," fixes the amount of trade and the price in advance. It specifies that the parties will trade, whatever the realizations of v and c. Such a rule, of course, is efficient if and only if the parties are *ex ante* certain that there will be gains from trade. (In this case, the rigid norm is generally strictly superior to giving either party the right to choose the price.[29])

In summary: *Ex post* bargaining may not lead to the efficient volume of trade. Some constraints (if possible, simple ones) on the second-period decision process must be contracted for. When one party's information is (respectively, becomes after contracting) common knowledge, the other party should be given the right to choose whether to trade at a given price (respectively, to choose the price). *The power should go to the informed party.*

To apply this to an example, consider a publisher–printer relationship where the publisher is the buyer, the printer is the supplier, and trading means running an additional printing. If the costs of an additional printing run are known and equal c, the publisher should have the authority to order a new printing, for which he should pay c. If, by contrast, c is private information (because of outside opportunities for the printer, say) while v can be measured precisely (it could, for instance, result from

a fixed order for the book at an observable price), the printer should be given the authority to pick the price.

Specific Investment and the Hold-up Problem

Suppose that at date 1 a supplier invests in cost reduction (his investment reduces c) and a buyer invests in value enhancement (his investment increases v). These investments are specific in that they would not reduce cost or increase value if the parties were to trade with other parties.

Bargaining

Let us, as above, start by assuming that no contract is signed in period 1. Thus, the two parties bargain in period 2 over whether to trade and at what price.

Obviously, if the *ex post* volume of trade is not efficient, investments will be affected accordingly. If there is too little trade, the supplier and the buyer have an incentive to invest less than under efficient trade, because the probability that their investments are "used" is smaller than the optimal one.[30] To separate the issues of efficient trade and efficient investment, we will assume that, *ex post*, v and c are common knowledge. Thus, the parties trade if and only if $v \geq c$. We can thus focus on the dependence of *ex ante* specific investments on the *ex post* split of gains from trade. What fraction of his own value-enhancing (cost-reducing) investment can the buyer (supplier) recoup?

Assume that the buyer's value is known at the contract date to be $v = 3$. The supplier can "invest" (spend $I = 2$) or "not invest" (spend $I = 0$). If he invests, his *ex post* marginal cost is $c = 0$. If he does not invest, his marginal cost is "high" (> 3). Suppose that *ex post* the parties'

---

29. Inefficiency does not arise if the parties sign an optimal contract before learning their private information as was shown by Arrow (1979) and d'Aspremont and Gerard-Varet (1979). The advanced reader may check this as follows: Suppose that v is, *a priori*, distributed on $[\underline{v}, \overline{v}]$ according to the c.d.f. F with density f and c on $[\underline{c}, \overline{c}]$ according to the c.d.f. G with density g, and that the two distributions are independent. Suppose further that the two parties agree *ex ante* to simultaneously announce their private information to a third party (referee) after learning it in the second period. Let $\tilde{v}$ and $\tilde{c}$ denote the announcements (which need not be truthful). The rule specifies that trade occurs if and only if $\tilde{v} \geq \tilde{c}$. Thus, it is efficient if the parties tell the truth. The payment from the buyer to the seller is $p(\tilde{v}, \tilde{c})$ and is unconditional on trade (is made even if $\tilde{v} < \tilde{c}$). It is given by

$$p(\tilde{v}, \tilde{c}) = \int_{\underline{c}}^{\tilde{v}} w\, g(w)\, dw - \int_{\underline{v}}^{\tilde{c}} b\, f(b)\, db + \text{constant}.$$

This payment induces the parties to announce the truth. It is called an *expected externality payment* because, for instance, the buyer, by increasing the announcement from $\tilde{v}$ to $\tilde{v} + dv$, increases the payment by $\tilde{v} g(\tilde{v}) dv$, which is nothing but the expectation of the cost of the extra volume of trade created. (The new trade occurs when $c = \tilde{c}$ belongs to $[\tilde{v}, \tilde{v} + dv]$, which occurs with probability $g(\tilde{v}) dv$.) For extensions of this mechanism (which violates the *ex post* nonnegative surplus condition for some values) see Maskin 1985, Pratt and Zeckhauser 1985, and Johnson et al. 1986.

The expected-payment mechanism described here is always efficient, but is more complex to set up than the ones envisioned in the text. (Subjective distributions must be described, and the private information must be conveyed to a third party—or a recording machine—*ex post*. The good to be traded must also be precisely described at date 1.)

30. The effect of this reduction in the volume of trade is emphasized in Tirole 1986a.

bargaining leads to the Nash solution[31]: They split evenly any gain from trade. Thus, if $c = 0$, the gains from trade are 3 and the price at which they trade is 1.5 (so that each party's surplus is 1.5). If c is high, there are no gains from trade; hence, there is no trade and the parties' surplus is 0. Let us next consider specific investment. The supplier makes profit 0 if he does not invest. He makes profit $-2 + 1.5 < 0$ (assuming no discounting) if he invests. So no investment takes place. Investment, however, would be socially desirable. It would yield net gains of $3 - 2 > 0$.

This example can easily be generalized to a continuous choice of investment. Suppose that the production cost is a deterministic function of the supplier's investment: $c(I)$, with $c'(I) < 0$ and $c''(I) > 0$ (investment lowers cost, but at a decreasing rate). Let v denote the (deterministic) value. To simplify, assume that $v \geqslant c(0)$. Let the price be *ex post* determined by the Nash bargaining solution: $p(I) = [c(I) + v]/2$ (so that $v - p(I) = p(I) - c(I)$), once I has been invested (using $v \geqslant c(I)$). The supplier's profit is

$$\max_I [p(I) - c(I) - I] = \max_I [v/2 - c(I)/2 - I].$$

In other words, \$1 of cost reduction yields only 50 cents to the supplier. The other 50 cents are held up by the buyer. The privately optimal investment is $-c'(I) = 2$. In contrast, the socially optimal investment solves

$$\max_I [v - c(I) - I],$$

so $-c'(I) = 1$. Because c is convex ($-c'$ is decreasing), *the actual (privately optimal) investment is suboptimal.*[32]

The problem is, of course, that the party investing does not capture all the cost savings (increments in value) generated by his investment. The other party can use the threat of not trading to appropriate some of these savings. Williamson (1975) calls this *opportunism.* As he emphasizes, *ex post* bilateral monopoly plus bargaining yields underinvestment in specific assets. A power company will not invest heavily when locating near a coal mine if it knows that it will not appropriate the benefits

of the investment once it is sunk, an employee will not invest in learning firm-specific skills if he has no guarantee that the firm will not exploit his captive position later on, and so forth.

This simple model also allows us to see the effect of the degree of *asset specificity* and the existence of *outside opportunities.* Introduce (*ex ante* and *ex post*) a large number of buyers who all are willing to pay v for the good. But there is still asset specificity in that the investment, I, is geared to a particular buyer ("the specific buyer"). If the supplier trades with any other buyer, his production cost corresponds to a fictitious investment of λI, where λ belongs to [0, 1]. ($\lambda = 0$ is the most extreme form of asset specificity, and $\lambda = 1$ corresponds to the absence of specificity.) Suppose that the supplier has invested I. By not trading with the specific buyer, he obtains price v (because of the competitive behavior of other buyers) and gets surplus $v - c(\lambda I)$. Hence, still under the assumption that bargaining with the specific buyer leads to an equal division of the gains from trade, trade takes place with this specific buyer at price p such that

$$v - p = [p - c(I)] - [v - c(\lambda I)].$$

One immediately sees that the supplier has a higher incentive to invest than in the absence of outside opportunities. Outside opportunities for the supplier raise his status quo (disagreement) payoff and put him in a better bargaining position. The supplier's intertemporal payoff is now

$$v - \tfrac{1}{2}[c(I) + c(\lambda I)] - I.$$

The *ex ante* choice of investment yields

$$-[c'(I) + \lambda c'(\lambda I)] = 2.$$

When $\lambda = 1$ (no asset specificity), $p = v$ and the investment is socially optimal. When $\lambda = 0$ (full asset specificity), the investment level is the same as in the absence of outside opportunities. For λ in (0, 1), as long as the curvature of the cost function is not too high, the investment increases with λ.

---

31. See Nash 1953. Nash used an axiomatic approach to derive his bargaining solution; he also justified it as the outcome of a simultaneous-move "demand game." One justification of the Nash solution in terms of sequential, non-cooperative bargaining is that given by Rubinstein (1982) and Binmore (1982) for the case where the parties have no outside opportunity. (See the section on

dynamic games of complete information in the Game Theory User's Manual at the end of the present book.)

32. For an application of this type of reasoning to labor markets, see Grout 1984.

Contracting

Let us now assume that the two parties can write *ex ante* contracts specifying the process through which the amount of trade and the transfer are determined *ex post*. We will suppose that specific investments are observable by the two parties, but not verifiable. By this is usually meant that, although each party can observe the other party's amount of specific investment before trading, this investment is not measureable by a court, so that the contract cannot be contingent on its realized level. (If investments were verifiable, they could be specified *ex ante* and enforced *ex post*, so that the issue of asset specificity would not arise. In this respect, it is interesting to note that General Motors and other manufacturers sometimes pay for their suppliers' tools.) We will also assume that valuation and cost are commonly observable, but not verifiable. That is, they are known by the involved parties, but they cannot be assessed by a court.

As the threat of termination (no trade) is often the vehicle that allows parties to appropriate a share of common gains from trade in bargaining situations, it may be desirable to contract *ex ante* to impose penalties for breach. These penalties bind the parties to each other and prevent opportunism. The extreme case of penalties for breach is when the parties agree in advance to trade at a given price "no matter what" (this corresponds to infinite penalties). Because the price is given, specific investments cannot be expropriated (mathematically, the dependence of p on I is eliminated).

High penalties for breach are in a sense a measure of a long-run relationship. They automatically keep the relationship going. One of their drawbacks is, for course, that they force parties to trade even when there are no gains from trade (i.e., if it turns out that the value is low or the cost is high, or, equivalently, that the parties have better outside opportunities). More flexible and sensitive mechanisms must be contracted for when there is a non-negligible probability of no gains from trade. There are some simple cases, however. For instance, suppose that v

and c are random from a first-period viewpoint (with the possibility that $v < c$) but become common knowledge between the two parties at the beginning of the second period. Suppose further that only one party—the supplier, say—invests (so that c depends stochastically on investment I). In this case, the sequential authority mechanism by which the supplier chooses the price and the buyer accepts or refuses to trade at this price is efficient (i.e., yields the optimal levels of investment and trade). Because of *ex post* symmetric information, the volume of trade is optimal. The supplier offers price v if $v \geq c$ and any price strictly greater than v if $v < c$. Trade takes place if and only if $v \geq c$ and all the *ex post* gains from trade go to the supplier. Because the volume of trade is optimal *and* the price does not depend on investment, the supplier chooses the socially optimal investment.[33] If v is already known at date 1, this mechanism amounts to fixing the price at v at that date and letting the supplier choose whether to trade in period 2. Thus, the rough rule is that *the party investing should have the authority* over the price, or over the trading decision if the other party's information is known in advance.[34] (Gains from trade can be divided *ex ante* through a lump-sum transfer.)

Exercise 1** In the text, it is assumed that the supplier's investment reduces his production cost. Assume instead that the *ex ante* investment affects the quality of the product and thus the value to the buyer. The buyer's *ex post* value is $v(I) = 3I - \frac{1}{2}I^2$. Hence, the buyer's surplus in case of trade is $v(I) - p$. The supplier's surplus is then $p - c - I$ (where $c < \frac{1}{2}$ is now a constant production cost). Suppose that I (and, hence, v) is observable by the buyer; however, it is not verifiable by a court, so that it cannot be specified by a contract.

(i) Determine the efficient amount of investment.

(ii) Suppose that there is no contract and the two parties bargain *ex post* according to the Nash bargaining solution. Is the investment optimal? Point out the externality.

(iii) Suppose that the parties sign a contract specifying that the buyer has the right to buy the good at a given

---

33. Let $F(v)$, $f(v)$, $G(c|I)$, and $g(c|I)$ denote the cumulative distributions and densities of v and c (with $\partial G/\partial I > 0$). The supplier solves

$$\max_I \left(\int_{\{v \geq c\}} [p(v,c) - c]f(v)g(c|I)dvdc - I \right),$$

which is also the socially optimal program, because $p(v,c) = v$ whenever $v \geq c$.

34. Bilateral investment or supplier's investment and asymmetric information about v calls for even more sophisticated mechanisms. The expected-externality-payment mechanism described in footnote 29 yields the efficient volume of investment (as well as trade) even when both parties invest and there is *ex post* bilateral asymmetric information.

price p. Is this contract efficient? What if the supplier has the right to sell at a given price?

(iv) What happens if the supplier is given the right to choose the price *ex post*?

Remark The preceding discussion suggests that v and c be audited when that is feasible. In bargaining, perfect auditing makes the value and the cost common knowledge and thus prevents inefficiencies associated with incomplete information. In a contracting framework, it allows the disconnection of the trading decision and the transfers so that the trading decision can be based entirely on auditing. More information gives rise to gains in efficiency wherever the contract is inefficient in the absence of auditing.[35] Williamson (1975, p. 29) has argued that integrated firms may be more susceptible to auditing than nonintegrated ones.[36] In particular, he suggests that it is easier to audit an internal division than an outside contractor offering the same services, because external auditors are regarded suspiciously and face collusive behavior on the part of employees, who may impede the release of information.[37] Another argument may be that a firm has the legal right to audit its divisions but no such right to audit outside contractors (except in extreme circumstances). Grossman and Hart (1986) argue that integration *per se* is unlikely to change the structure of information, on the grounds that nonintegrated parties can sign a contract that mimics the auditing possibilities of the integrated firm. In particular, each party can waive his right not to be audited by the other party.[38]

The Limitations of Long-Run Relationships

The most obvious and important limitation of a long-run relationship is the presence of outside opportunities. As was noted above, forcing the parties to stick to each other through high penalties for breach may hurt them if there are no gains from trade or, equivalently, if better outside opportunities are available to one or both of the parties. As breach may be desirable, the contract must find the optimal trade-off between flexibility and the prevention of opportunism.[39]

The loss of advantageous outside opportunities is not the only hazard of long-run contracts. Long-run relationships tend to promote collusion between the units' personnel (Tirole 1986b). A long time horizon gives them time to reciprocate favors and to become confident that collusion is sustainable. For instance, Pettigrew (1972) notes how managers of a business firm may, in the long run, identify with particular suppliers.[40] The possibility that such collusion will create inefficiencies calls for the rotation of personnel within each unit, or, when that is costly (because of job-related human capital, say), the occasional switching of suppliers or buyers.

Another limitation of long-run relationships may be due to the fact that a short-term relationship is generally more advantageous to a party who knows he will have good outside opportunities in the future. Because good outside opportunities tomorrow are related to his general ability to perform well and thus improve his bargaining position today, this party has an incentive to signal them through the signature of a short-term contract (possibly disguised as a long-term contract).[41]

---

35. Often, of course, v and c can be audited only *ex post* (i.e., after trade is realized). Indeed, before trading they are often subjective estimates. *Ex post* auditing may not be an issue even if the trading decision must be based on its outcome. The parties can commit to revealing their estimates before trading and can be punished *ex post* if their announcements were erroneous. (In order for such a mechanism to work when the original estimate is not a perfect predictor of realized cost or value, the parties must not be too risk-averse.)

36. For a model of vertical integration that presumes that integration yields a superior auditing technology, see Arrow 1975.

37. This is not to say that collusive behaviors do not impair accounting within a firm. See, e.g., Dalton 1959, p. 206.

38. This argument relies on the possibility of writing a contract that specifies the right to audit specific items related to the parties' trade in case a party does not want to grant the other party the right to audit his whole firm. If delineating specific auditing rights is costly or hard to perform *ex ante*, internal organization may be superior in auditing respects. Williamson (1975, p. 146) applies a similar argument to argue that a firm's general office has superior auditing

possibilities with regard to its divisions relative to the capital market. See subsection 1.4 on incomplete contracts and authority. For a discussion of why, in an incomplete-contract framework, the structure of authority may affect the structure of information, see Holmström and Tirole 1987.

39. For a model of search over the possibility of superior outside opportunities, see Harris and Holmström 1983.

40. In a similar spirit, some Department of Defense officials become friendly with the firms they have repeatedly dealt with, and some consultants lose their objectivity when they stay with a firm for a long time. For analogous reasons, auditing firms rotate their personnel.

41. This point is most strikingly made by Hermalin (1986) in the context of labor markets. Hermalin examines the implications of this signaling behavior for training. See also, in Aghion and Bolton's (1987) reconsideration of the market-foreclosure doctrine, the case of a current monopoly supplier of a good who tries to signal that the technology makes entry unlikely in his market by lowering penalties for breach for the buyer. A short-term contract is a long-term contract that does not specify penalties for breach.

An Application: Repeated Franchise Bidding

We can now come back to Williamson's warning against the hazards of franchise bidding.[42] First, he argues that the incumbent's specific investments, in order to be transferred to an alternative supplier at a fair rate (so as to induce the incumbent to make them), must be observable and verifiable. But equipment is often hard to evaluate. Good records must have been kept, physical depreciation must be measured adequately, and no kickbacks may have been received by the incumbent in exchange for an inflated price for equipment. Even harder to measure are specific investments in the human capital of the incumbent's personnel. So a fair reimbursement of investment cannot come from simple accounting data. Rather, it must be ensured by bidding over the equipment.[43] After all, the market assigns higher values to firms that have committed more investment. But this also creates problems. On the one hand, the incumbent's transferable investments may not be observable by the other bidders. On the other hand, some of these investments (such as human capital) may not be recoverable by them.[44] The use of franchise bidding is thus likely to be costly in industries with high specific investments (such as the electric power, gas, telephone, and cable television industries) and more advantageous in industries in which only a small fraction of investments is sunk (as—perhaps—in the case of the allocation of airline routes, or as in Demsetz's hypothetical example of the production of automobile license plates under increasing returns with general-purpose equipment).[45]

Empirical Investigations

The Williamsonian theory of long-run relationships suggests that firms should write long and detailed contracts where that is feasible and not too costly, and that the incentive to do so increases with the lack of *ex post* outside opportunities and the specificity of investments. Joskow (1985, 1987) has made a detailed study of contracts between coal mines and electric utilities in the United States. (Most such relationships are run by contracts; vertical integration is rare.) The specific investments that run the risk of being expropriated here are, for the coal mines (suppliers), investments in mining capacity; for the electric utilities (buyers), they are investments in generating units and in boilers adapted to a particular type of coal.[46]

One can distinguish between two polar geographical cases (of course, in practice things are not that clear cut). In one case, there are a large number of electric utilities and coal mines in the region, and transportation facilities for coal (railroads, barges) are numerous and competitive so that parties have a large choice of their partners (even *ex post*). Furthermore, the coal produced by the various mines is quite homogeneous, so boiler design is fairly irrelevant. In such a region, the hazard of expropriation of specific assets is small, so spot markets (short-run contracts) are relatively efficient. In the other case, there are few coal mines, transportation facilities are limited, and the quality of coal is very variable. One would then expect complex long-term contracts (or vertical integration) to support exchange.

As Joskow shows, the regional differences in the United States offer a dramatic illustration of Williamsonian predictions. In the East, underground mining (60 percent of production) offers few returns to scale; as a consequence there are many small mines. Transportation facilities are numerous, and the quality of coal is relatively homogeneous. In the West, where surface mining is prevalent, there are large returns to scale, so there are only few large mines. There is also less competition for transportation than in the East, and the quality of coal is very variable. Joskow's study shows that contracts are of a much longer duration in the West than in the East (and that the spot market for coal is very important in the East and virtually

---

42. See Joskow and Schmalensee 1983 for a specific analysis in the case of electric power generation.

43. Here we must distinguish between bidding for the equipment (the proceeds of which go to the incumbent) and bidding for the monopoly position (the proceeds of which go to the regulator).

44. To these inconveniences can be added the pre-bidding costs associated with the "ratchet effect." The incumbent firm has little incentive to be efficient before the new award of the monopoly situation, because this would convey favorable information about its technology, inducing competitors to bid higher

and possibly inducing the regulator to fix a higher minimum price in the auction. For related analyses of the ratchet effect, see Freixas et al. 1985 and Laffont and Tirole 1988; and for an application to the labor market, see Gibbons 1987.

45. See Laffont and Tirole 1987 for an analysis of franchise bidding with unobservable transferable and nontransferable investments.

46. Coal-specific boilers are more efficient than boilers designed to allow flexibility in the use of coal.

nonexistent in the West). Note here that the lack of outside opportunities is related to asset specificities.

Another check of the theory involves "mine-mouth plants"—electricity-generating plants located near coal mines. Lack of competition and high transportation costs may induce an electric utility to locate near a coal mine, which creates site specificities. Joskow found that mine-mouth plants tend to rely on long-term contracts (or even vertical integration); typically, they sign twenty- to fifty-year contracts that prohibit price renegotiation for twenty years, give a detailed description of quantities to be supplied over the period, specify the quality of coal, and index costs and the prices of substitutes. (They also usually contain provisions for arbitration in case of disputes.) This *ex ante* specification of the terms of the contract may well prevent specific investments from being expropriated.

1.4 The Firm as an Incomplete Contract[47]

In subsections 1.2 and 1.3 we looked at organizations in terms of efficient short-term and long-term contracts. In practice, however, contracts are fairly incomplete, owing to "transaction costs."[48] Coase (1937) and Williamson (1975) have distinguished four types of transaction costs, two of which occur at the contracting date and two of which occur later. First, some contingencies which the parties will face may not be foreseeable at the contracting date. Second, even if they could be foreseen, there may be too many contingencies to write into the contract.[49] Third, monitoring the contract (i.e., checking that the other party abides by its terms) may be costly. Fourth, enforcing contracts may involve considerable legal costs. Coase and Williamson assert that the minimization of transaction costs is a major concern of organization design.

The *ex ante* causes of incompleteness are hard to formalize. We have no well-established theories of complexity or of individual decision-making under unforeseeable

contingencies—two economically important phenomena. Most existing contracts do not specify many relevant contingencies. When these unspecified contingencies occur, the actions of the concerned parties are likely to lead to conflicts. We can distinguish two polar cases of decision processes that, *ex post*, handle the unforeseen contingencies.

The simplest decision process, bargaining, was considered in subsection 1.3. There, we first assumed that no contract at all was signed *ex ante*, and that the parties bargained over the trading and transfer decisions after investing and learning their valuations and costs. The bargaining process was unconstrained by previous contracting; there was only the legal constraint that *ex post* trading be voluntary. We contrasted the solution with the one obtained under a complete contract.

Intermediate forms of contracting which exist between no contract (and unconstrained *ex post* bargaining) and a complete contract are also available. These intermediate forms can save on transaction costs relative to complete contracts, but without the perverse effects of unconstrained bargaining. We distinguish two possibilities. The first is that the two concerned parties resort to a third party. This third party is supposed to make the efficient decisions that most closely resemble those that a complete contract would have specified. His *ex post* trading and transfer decisions must, therefore, yield *ex post* the efficient volume of trade and encourage *ex ante* the right amounts of specific investments. The second possibility gives one of the two concerned parties, rather than a third party, the right to determine what happens in an unspecified contingency.

Arbitration

The first type of resort to a third (unconcerned) party is *external arbitration*. For instance, a union and a firm may agree to go to binding arbitration if negotiations on a labor contract become stalled. Similarly, a supplier

---

47. A broader perspective on incomplete contracts can be found in Holmström and Tirole 1987.

48. A "complete contract" is a contract that has the relevant decisions (transfer, trade, etc.) depend on all verifiable variables, including possibly announcements by the parties (concerning their valuation, cost, etc.). By abuse of the terminology, one can also call a contract that is *a priori* incomplete a "complete contract" if it yields the parties the same payoffs as the optimal complete contract.

49. Empirically it may be difficult to distinguish between the two. For instance, the adaptation of secretarial tasks to the introduction of word processors may well not have been included in labor contracts before their introduction, not because nobody had thought about the possibility of their advent but because thinking about all the potential forms of word processing and including them into the contract would have been prohibitively time consuming and costly.

and a buyer may agree to accept arbitration by outside experts.[50]

External arbitration is likely to be costly. Outsiders may not possess the relevant information with which to formulate an efficient decision. They may have to hire experts or spend time learning about the specificities of the situation. In this respect, *internal arbitration*, if feasible, is likely to be more efficient. One of the main advantages of internal arbitration is that it gives the organization's chief executives the authority to resolve conflicts among its divisions or its employees. Day-to-day contact with the operations and personal experience with the employees are likely to make internal arbitrators more knowledgeable about a situation than external ones could be.[51] Williamson (1975, p. 29) insists on the superiority of internal arbitration in the settling of disputes.

An arbitrator must be able to learn about and understand the situation at relatively low cost, and must be independent. The first condition may, as we have seen, restrict the use of external arbitrators. It may also create difficulties with internal arbitration. In large firms, chief executives may be too overloaded with decisions to arbitrate between their subordinates. The efficacy of authority is jeopardized when executives are poorly informed.[52] The second condition, independence, requires that the arbitrator not be both judge and party. He must make decisions that conform to the aggregate interests of the two parties, and not favor one to the detriment of the other. Independence may fail, for instance, when a chief executive officer has kept close ties with a particular division. More generally, the internal arbitrator, like the external one, must be trusted, or else must develop a reputation for settling disputes "fairly" (that is, the arbitrator must confirm the parties' expectation that he will make the efficient decisions—the ones that would have been specified in a complete contract).[53]

Authority

The power to fill unspecified contingencies—*authority*—may be given to one of the concerned parties rather than to an arbitrator. As Grossman and Hart (1986) and Hart and Moore (1985) note, authority does not mean that the concerned parties do not negotiate *ex post*. The preferred decision of the party who has authority may be very costly to the other party. Some alternative decision may be mutually advantageous, and the party with authority may coerce some benefits by not exercising this authority. An important insight of the Grossman-Hart-Moore analysis is that *authority changes the status-quo point in the bargaining process*—it puts the party that has it in a better bargaining situation. In turn, the *ex post* division of the gains from trade will affect *ex ante* investments.

To see how authority redistributes the gains from trade, suppose with Grossman and Hart that, *ex post*, the parties (the buyer and the supplier) must make some decision d in a set D. They have *ex post* monetary payoffs $B_i(d)$ where $i = 1, 2$.[54] Giving authority to party 1 (the buyer or the supplier) means that he is allowed to choose *ex post* the d that he prefers. Thus, if the two parties cannot agree on an alternative decision, party 1 chooses d_1^* so as to maximize $B_1(d)$. But if d_1^* does not maximize party 2's payoff, the two parties will, in general, have an incentive to renegotiate to implement d^* (the decision that maximizes their joint payoff $B_1(d) + B_2(d)$). Assuming that the transfer t from party 2 to party 1 is such that gains from renegotiation are evenly distributed (i.e., assuming the Nash bargaining solution), we have

$$[B_1(d^*) + t] - B_1(d_1^*) = [B_2(d^*) - t] - B_2(d_1^*).$$

Letting B_1 and B_2 denote the final benefits (given the transfer and decision d^*), we have

$$B_1 = B_1(d_1^*) + \tfrac{1}{2}[B_1(d^*) + B_2(d^*) - B_1(d_1^*) - B_2(d_1^*)]$$

---

50. To this can be added the potential resort to court action. The difference is that this resort need not be contracted for in advance. However, courts—beyond enforcing "reasonable contracts"—only rule on "unfair practices" (i.e., rule out some types of behavior in the absence of agreement). Arbitrators can be given more extensive powers (e.g., to choose the outcome in the absence of agreement).

51. Courts and arbitrators are aware of this informational superiority, and try to mimic internal arbitration. For instance, in the French *tribunaux de commerce*, a number of the judges in charge of a commercial case have business or engineering backgrounds rather than legal ones. Similarly, the arbitrators listed by the International Chamber of Commerce are often experts rather than lawyers.

Conversely, internal arbitration may adopt procedures similar to those of external arbitration. In particular, some firms have internal grievance procedures.

52. Authority may then have to be delegated to lower levels, e.g. the divisions.

53. Managers' reputations for setting disputes fairly (i.e., efficiently) make up part of what is meant by "corporate culture."

54. The decision d may be a trading decision, and B_i may be a value or a cost. But the issue is much more general. For instance, d could denote a quality or a design decision, or B_i could denote the effort exerted by party i. Note that d can be multidimensional.

and

$$B_2 = B_2(d_1^*) + \tfrac{1}{2}[B_1(d^*) + B_2(d^*) - B_1(d_1^*) - B_2(d_1^*)].$$

It is clear that party 1 benefits from having authority because, by definition,

$$B_1(d_1^*) \geqslant B_1(d_2^*),$$

$$B_2(d_1^*) \leqslant B_2(d_2^*),$$

so that

$$B_1(d_1^*) - B_2(d_1^*) \geqslant B_1(d_2^*) - B_2(d_2^*).$$

More important, if *ex post* benefits depend on *ex ante* investment (as in subsection 1.3) as well as on the *ex post* decision, then the distribution of authority affects the parties' incentives to invest in specific assets. Intuitively, at the status-quo point, party 1's investments cannot be expropriated, because he is the decision maker. (Party 2's may well be expropriated.) Thus, in the absence of renegotiation, party 1's authority affects both parties' incentives to invest. Under renegotiation, the status quo, even if it is not observed, influences final payoffs; thus, the distribution of authority still affects the incentives for investment. To be more specific, one must describe how specific investments and the decisions affect payoffs (see the example below).

Grossman and Hart (1986) call *supplier control* (respectively, *buyer control*) the situation in which the supplier (the buyer) has the authority over the decision. *Integration* is defined as the allocation of residual rights of control to one of the parties. *Nonintegration* refers to the case in which the decision space has at least two dimensions and each party has authority on at least one of its dimensions (as opposed to integration, in which a party has authority over all dimensions).[55] The optimal arrangement is the one that best protects the specific investments (or, in a situation of inefficient bargaining, the one that yields the highest gains from trade). In the absence of complete contracts, ownership is a second-best solution to protect one's investment. Thus, in professions such as hairdressing and law, where a firm often assigns previously accumulated customers to new employees, the customers belong to the firm rather than to the employee; this distribution of ownership is enforced by a noncompetition clause. (Sometimes an implicit distinction is made between old clients and those brought in by the employee, as the theory would predict.) An engineer cannot easily quit his firm and patent an invention made possible by his firm's research effort. Grossman and Hart also cite the fact that insurance companies tend to use direct writers (i.e., employees who do not own their lists of clients) when the agent's specific investment in keeping customers is weak (as in life insurance) and independent agents (who do own their lists) when it is substantial.

Example

In the spirit of the Grossman-Hart analysis, this example shows how the distribution of authority affects the division of the gains from trade and the incentive to invest.

A buyer and a supplier contract to trade tomorrow. Trading is not an issue, and the parties agree that the good is to be exchanged in any case. The only uncertainty concerns the final specification of the good. A basic design is contracted for at date 1, but an opportunity to improve its quality may arise at date 2 that cannot be described at date 1 (one can imagine that there is an "infinity" of such potential improvements, of which only one will prove relevant). Whether the quality improvement will be made cannot be directly determined at date 1. The relevant quality improvement is learned by both parties at date 2. The second-period cost to the supplier, c, is greater than zero. For simplicity, we suppose that c is known at date 1 and is independent of the particular improvement. The buyer picks an investment in period 1. His second-period value for the improvement is $v > c$ with probability x and 0 with probability $1 - x$; the cost of investment, I, is equal to $x^2/2$. It is not clear to outsiders which level of investment has been chosen, so that the parties cannot contract on it. Note that v and c are *extra* valuation and cost (beyond the values corresponding to the basic design).

---

55. For instance, a supplier and a buyer may have freedom over their personnel management, while the buyer may have authority over whether the quality of the delivered product is acceptable. Similarly, a foreman and a worker may decide what clothes they will wear in the shop, but the foreman may have authority on shop management matters. These examples show that because the dimensionality of decision making is high, nonintegration with respect to the all decisions is prevalent. To make the distinction more relevant, it is natural to focus on a small dimension of the authority structure, such as those decisions that result from the ownership of a few physical assets; this is what Grossman and Hart do.

The interpretation of the investment technology is as follows: The buyer invests in flexibility. A higher investment increases the probability that the improvement that comes about can be used. For instance, an employer (a buyer) can train his workers to adjust to changing technologies, as in Piore and Sabel's (1984) theory of flexibility, or a power company (a buyer) can choose a more costly and flexible boiler designed to adapt to some variations in the coal from a mine (the supplier).

Let us first look at the social optimum in this model. Obviously the quality improvement should be made if and only if the buyer has value v. The optimal investment is then given by

$$\max_{x} [x(v - c) - x^2/2].$$

Thus, $x^* = v - c$. The joint surplus is $W^* = (v - c)^2/2$. (Here and in the following it is assumed that the values of the parameters are such that the constraint $x \leqslant 1$ is never binding.)

Now assume that the parties are self-interested. The quality improvement, although not specifiable at date 1, can be contracted for at date 2. We will consider three institutions: unconstrained bargaining (the parties bargain in the second period over whether to make the improvement; if they cannot agree, the improvement is not made, because it was not specified in the contract), "buyer control" (the buyer has the right to decide whether the improvement is to be made), and "supplier control" (the supplier has the right to decide whether to make the improvement). We assume that in the last two cases, the party who has the authority can bargain and offer to give this authority away (so, for instance, the buyer can offer not to impose the improvement on the supplier if the latter gives him a transfer in exchange). We will also assume that in any bargaining situation, any gains from trade are shared. Last, we assume that the parties choose the institution that maximizes expected joint surplus, on the grounds that gains from changing the institution to a more efficient one can always be redistributed through a transfer at date 1.

Under *unconstrained bargaining*, the parties trade if and only if $v > c$. Each gets $(v - c)/2$. So the buyer's investment solves

$$\max_{x} \left(\frac{x(v - c)}{2} - \frac{x^2}{2} \right).$$

Hence,

$$x^{B} = (v - c)/2 = x^*/2.$$

This result is nothing but our previous underinvestment result under unconstrained bargaining. Joint surplus is equal to

$$W^{B} = x(v - c) - x^2/2 = 3(v - c)^2/8 = 3W^*/4.$$

Supplier control in this simple model is equivalent to unconstrained bargaining, because the status-quo point is the same: If the parties disagree, the supplier chooses not to make the improvement (the less costly action for him). His right allows him to use strict compliance with the original contract as a threat to get a good bargaining position. This situation describes roughly what happens in negotiations between the Department of Defense and defense contractors over design changes. The contractors are, in general, able to use their right not to make the changes to derive large profits from such changes. Because of the equivalence, $x^{SC} = x^{B}$ and $W^{SC} = W^{B}$ (where SC stands for supplier control). Again the buyer's investment is "half-expropriated," and the buyer consequently underinvests.

Under *buyer control*, the improvement would always be made if the status quo were not renegotiated. (Actually, when the value to the buyer is zero, the buyer is indifferent between imposing the improvement and not doing so; we assume he does. On the one hand, he would do so if the value were only slightly positive; on the other hand, our conclusions would be even stronger if he did not impose the improvement.) If the value is v, the status quo is efficient and no bargaining occurs. The buyer gets v by imposing the improvement. If the value is 0, the status quo is inefficient and bargaining divides evenly the gain (c) of not making the improvement. In particular, the buyer gets $c/2$. Thus, the optimal choice of investment for the buyer is given by

$$\max_{x} \left(xv + (1 - x)\frac{c}{2} - \frac{x^2}{2} \right),$$

which yields

$$x^{BC} = v - c/2 > x^*$$

and

$$W^{BC} = \tfrac{1}{2}(v - c/2)(v - 3c/2).$$

The striking result here is that the buyer now overinvests. This is due to the fact that his authority will allow him not to pay the production c if his value is v. Because he does not internalize this production cost, he overinvests in the activity that makes production more likely.

It is easy to see that it may be optimal to give the authority to the buyer or to the supplier. When $c = 0$, buyer control is socially efficient (there is no noninternalized production cost); supplier control is not. If $v = c > 0$, then no investment is optimal, and supplier control (or unconstrained bargaining) is optimal; buyer control encourages investment and yields a negative joint surplus.

The Scope of Authority

We have assumed that the decision set D from which the party with the authority can choose is well delineated *ex ante*. This may be inconsistent with the transaction-cost hypothesis. If contingencies are unforeseeable or are too numerous to be included in the original contract, the decision set that includes these contingencies is also likely to be unforeseeable or too complex to be described in that contract (indeed, the contingencies may be the feasible actions themselves). But how is D defined if it is not precisely specified in the original contract? Grossman and Hart trace authority to the ownership of some physical asset; the idea is that the owner of a machine has the right to use the machine as he wishes. Kreps (1984) notes that ownership may also pertain to intangible assets, such as reputation. It can also be identified with a function within a firm, through delegation of authority. The foreman may have some authority over shop management.

Although ownership (possibly in a delegated form) helps define the set D, it cannot fully determine it. Even if the owner of a machine is free to allocate it between different uses, his elimination of its noise dampener may not be considered by the workers or the courts to be within the scope of his authority. A division manager may have a recognized authority to choose whether secretaries use typewriters or word processors, but not to require secretaries to use word processors with sight-damaging screens. The Department of Defense may have the authority to impose some uncontracted but standard safety devices on defense contractors, but not to require major design changes. As Kreps rightly notes, there must be some common understanding as to the scope of authority, even when this scope is not specified in advance; and such an understanding (an aspect of corporate culture) is facilitated when unforeseen contingencies follow patterns.

The *ex post* definition of the scope of authority creates a role for arbitration similar to that created by the definition of the decision d itself: An internal or external arbitrator may not be competent to fine-tune the decision but may have enough information to delineate the set of acceptable decisions. Indeed, in a typical firm the exercise of delegated authority (foreman over worker, say) is made possible by the presence of a superior authority (a manager, say) with powers of arbitration.

Another possible safety valve against the abuse of authority is to allow the party without authority to terminate the relationship, so that, *ex post*, he has the authority to reject the other party's authoritarian decision.

Empirical Investigations

Vertical integration, like long-term contracts, is more likely the more specific the investments are. This may make it difficult to distinguish between the two empirically. The main conclusion of the Coase-Williamson analysis in this respect is that vertical integration is more likely (relative to a long-term contract) when "transaction costs" are high. One can, of course, conjecture that transaction costs are high in situations with considerable technological uncertainty. (This may explain why coal mines and power plants are rarely integrated, although another explanation for the low level of vertical integration in this industry is the regulator's resistance to it.) Unfortunately, degrees of "unforeseeability" and complexity are hard to measure empirically; good proxies must be found.

Most case studies and regression analyses have focused on the effect of the specificity of investment on the likelihood of vertical integration. Klein, Crawford, and Alchian (1978) offer a particularly interesting analysis of how asset specificities led to vertical integration between General Motors and Fisher Body and between pipeline firms and oil explorers or refineries. Monteverde and Teece (1982) look at the procurement of automotive components by U.S. automakers. To explain why some are purchased whereas others are manufactured internally, they use (in particular) the following variables: the specificity of a component to the automaker (Is the component designed specifically for that automaker? Can it be bought from other suppliers on short notice?) and the complexity of the system in which the component must be inserted (engine, chassis, etc.).[56] They show that, in particular, the specificity variable is a significant determinant of the integration decision. Masten (1984) finds analogous results for aerospace manufacturers. In a similar spirit, Anderson and Schmittlein (1984) study the integration of the sales force (manufacturer's representative versus employee salesperson) and show that the degree of human-specific capital (measured by the manager's assessment of the difficulty in learning the ins and outs of the company, the nature of the product, the nature of the consumers, and so forth) is negatively related to the probability of using independent representatives.[57]

Reputation as a Substitute for Contracts or Integration

The concept behind this and previous subsections is that, in order to avoid future hazards, parties should sign complete contracts, or, if contracts are too costly or impossible to write, should at least make a correct use of the authority structure (restricted contract). In practice, however, MaCaulay (1963) found that relations between firms tended to be more informal than was predicted by the theory. This is often true even when firms engage in long-run relationships. Efficiency is then sustained by the firms' reputation. A firm that cheats at some date (i.e., makes decisions that are not jointly efficient) runs the risk of losing future profitable deals with its partner (see Williamson 1975, chapter 6, Kreps 1984, subsection 2.2 of this chapter, and chapters 2 and 6 below). Reputation allows a firm to save on the costs of writing complete contracts or even on the costs of distributing authority. On the other hand, informality exposes the firms to the threat of opportunism. Thus, one would expect infor-mality to be most prevalent when specific investments are limited and when trade is sufficiently frequent that the incentive to cheat is low.

Dual Sourcing as a Substitute for Contracts

An alternative way of avoiding the *ex post* hold-up problem is to introduce *ex post* competition whenever that is feasible. Farrell and Gallini (1986) and Shepard (1986) have analyzed Williamsonian models in which the buyer invests in specific assets and the seller chooses, *ex post*, some *ex ante* noncontractible variable (call it "quality").[58] *Ex post*, the seller has an incentive to choose low quality[59]; therefore, *ex ante*, the buyer invests little in the relationship. Dual sourcing consists in having two or more suppliers, who compete *ex post* on quality. This raises the equilibrium level of quality and the *ex ante* investment. Competition can thus alleviate the *ex post* bilateral monopoly problem and raise efficiency. Farrell and Gallini and Shepard argue that this is a persuasive explanation of why Intel licenses its microprocessor technologies and why IBM adopts an "open architecture" policy in regard to its personal computers.

2 The Profit-Maximization Hypothesis

It is a postulate of this book, and of most economic theory, that firms maximize expected profits. There is, however, a widespread feeling that in practice their managers have other objectives (e.g., maximizing the firm's size and growth and the perquisites of the managerial position).[60] This section presents arguments for and against the profit-maximization hypothesis. It also discusses the power of the current theory of industrial organization in the presence of non-profit-maximizing firms.

The shareholders of a firm are claimants for its revenue, net of various input costs. Thus, if they were able to run the firm, they would choose decisions that would

---

56. The idea behind the introduction of this variable is as follows. Both Williamson (1975) and Scherer (1980, p. 90) have argued that vertical integration permits executive fiat to obtain better coordination (because the exact timing of the production process is generally left indeterminate in the incomplete contract). A complex system may require more coordination of inputs.

57. See Williamson 1985 for other interesting examples.

58. This variable is a price in Farrell and Gallini 1986 and a delivery lag in Shepard 1986.

59. In these models, a high price or a long delivery lag.

60. See the models of firm behavior of the 1950s and the 1960s (e.g., Baumol 1962, Marris 1964).

minimize cost and maximize profit.[61] Thus, non-profit-maximization is mainly associated with the separation of ownership and control.[62] Adherents of the principal–agent theory and its emanations have, since the early 1970s, taken the approach that firms' deviations from profit-maximizing behavior should be explained rather than postulated and that deviations should be traced to the inability of shareholders to adequately monitor the managers and discover the firm's cost-and-demand situation. For instance, managerial discretion (e.g. the granting of perquisites) is permitted by the managers' informational superiority relative to the shareholders. The firm's concern for size or growth may not be attributable directly to its shareholders' or its managers' intrinsic preference for such attributes; rather, it may be due to conflicts between shareholders and managers. For instance, the shareholders' incomplete information about the firm's technology may allow the managers to inflate the need for personnel, lowering pressure on the job (or, equivalently, increasing on-the-job leisure). Similarly, the firm's growth may be desired by the managers not for its own sake but because it allows them and their subordinates to enjoy greater opportunities for promotion.

Reviewing the principal–agent literature and alternative approaches is beyond the scope of this chapter.[63] This treatment will be restricted to the main issues. First we will consider the basic moral-hazard problem and how direct monetary incentives, yardstick competition, takeover bids, product-market competition, and supervision can reduce managerial slack or discretion. The limits of these control mechanisms will be pointed out. It will then be argued that even if managerial slack invalidates the profit-maximization hypothesis, the implications of this hypothesis for industrial organization need not be erroneous.

The managerial rewards that will be discussed below should be taken in a broad sense. Such rewards can be monetary (as in the models below), but could also consist of promotions, tolerance of perquisites, prestige, assignment of cash flow to one's division, and so on. Furthermore, it should be noted that the principal–agent relationship will be discussed mainly in the context of the separation of ownership and control between shareholders and managers. Clearly, many of the incentive devices described below apply to other tiers of the firm's hierarchy; indeed, some of them apply more to lower tiers than to executive officers.

2.1 The Basic Incentive Problem

The agency problem in its moral-hazard form (the focus of this subsection) stems from a basic conflict between insurance and incentives. On the one hand, the theory of optimal insurance demonstrates that the optimal division of a pie of a random size (the profit) between a risk-neutral party (the shareholders) and a risk-averse one (the manager)[64] has the risk-neutral party bear all the risk, if incentive issues are left aside. (See, e.g., Arrow 1970 and Borch 1963.) Suppose there is a pie of random size Π to be divided between the two parties, and that this random variable is not affected by the parties' actions. Let Π take values in a discrete set $\Pi_1 < \cdots < \Pi_i < \cdots < \Pi_n$,

---

61. There are two reasons why shareholders might not want to maximize expected profit (or market value). First, they may be risk-averse; they may then want the firm to make decisions that lead the firm's profit to be negatively correlated with the economy's fluctuations (so as to get a less risky portfolio) even if these decisions do not quite maximize expected profit. Second, and also in a general-equilibrium context, a firm's price for one of its products, say, influences the shareholders' welfare not only through the firm's profit but also through their consumption of the firm's good as long as the firm is not perfectly competitive. (Actually, shareholders may not even agree on the firm's best decision in such cases.) These two general-equilibrium effects are important theoretically, but they do not look very strong empirically. The shareholders' portfolio is relatively well diversified, and it is not clear how most decisions of the firm relates to aggregate shocks in the economy. Furthermore, the shareholders' (at least the influential ones') consumption of their firms' products is usually very small, so that price effects are small relative to the income effect generated by the firm's profit levels.

62. For a review of some evidence on the separation of ownership and control, see Scherer 1980, pp. 32–33.

63. See Arrow 1985 for an informal introduction to the subject. One generally distinguishes between "hidden-action" (or "moral-hazard") models and "hidden-knowledge" models. In a hidden-action model, the agent takes some action that is unobservable to the principal. In a hidden-knowledge model, he has superior information about some exogenous environmental variable. Hidden-knowledge models are subdivided into two groups, depending on whether the agent obtains his information after or before signing the contract (the latter case refers to an "adverse selection" situation). Hart and Holmström (1986) offer a useful discussion of non-adverse-selection models (as well as of incomplete contract theory). For recent surveys of the adverse-selection literature in a context of procurement or regulation, see Baron 1986, Caillaud et al. 1988, and Sappington and Stiglitz 1987. Most of this section is concerned with moral-hazard issues.

64. With respective objective functions Ex and $Eu(x)$, where x is the income, u is an increasing and strictly concave utility function, and $E(\cdot)$ denotes the expectation over x (the random variable.)

with probabilities $p_1, \ldots, p_i, \ldots, p_n$ (where $p_i > 0$ and $\sum_{i=1}^{n} p_i = 1$). Let $\Pi - w(\Pi)$ and $w(\Pi)$ denote the allocations to the risk-neutral party and the risk-averse party when the realization is Π. The parties' expected utilities are

$$\mathop{E}_{\Pi} [\Pi - w(\Pi)] = \sum_i p_i(\Pi_i - w_i)$$

and

$$\mathop{E}_{\Pi} u(w(\Pi)) = \sum_i p_i u(w_i),$$

respectively, where $w_i \equiv w(\Pi_i)$. An efficient (or Pareto-optimal) contract maximizes the utility of one party given the level of utility of the other party. It satisfies

$$\max_{\{w_i\}} \sum_i p_i(\Pi_i - w_i) \text{ s.t. } \sum_i p_i u(w_i) \geqslant U_0,$$

where U_0 is a constant. The Lagrangian for this program is

$$L = \sum_i p_i(\Pi_i - w_i) + \lambda \left(\sum_i p_i u(w_i) - U_0 \right).$$

Taking the derivatives with respect to the w_i, one gets for all i

$$u'(w_i) = 1/\lambda.$$

So w_i is independent of i if the manager is strictly risk-averse ($u'' < 0$). The same result holds for a continuous distribution for Π.

Thus, the risk-averse party should get full insurance (i.e., should have a constant income over all states of nature). This is where the issue of incentives arises. Suppose the risk-averse party takes some unobservable action that affects the size of the pie to be divided (in a stochastic sense) and that this action is costly to him. Think of this action as a level of effort (it could be a more general discretionary choice). Suppose, further, that the risk-neutral party observes only the realization of the pie (the level of profit). The risk-averse party, if given an income that does not depend on this realization, has no incentive to exert effort, because his effort does not affect his income. So full insurance conflicts with incentives. Indeed, the trade-off between insurance and incentive objectives generally leaves the parties with both suboptimal insurance and suboptimal profits.

There is one case in which this trade-off does not arise. Assume that both parties are risk-neutral (in particular, u'

is constant), so that the party who takes the unobservable action (the agent) does not need to be insured. The other party (the principal) can ensure that the agent takes the jointly optimal action by "selling" the pie to him—that is, the principal receives a transfer price independent of the size of the pie, and the agent becomes the *residual claimant* for the remainder of the pie. Because the agent's expected income is equal (up to the fixed transfer price) to the expected size of the pie, the agent has all the incentive to pick the optimal action, i.e., the action that maximizes the expected size of the pie net of the action's cost (see section 3). The agent bears all the risk under this arrangement, but this does not matter because he is risk-neutral. Residual claimancy for the party that takes the unobservable action offers a very general solution to the incentive problem, and it will be encountered again in chapter 3 and especially in chapter 4. However, it is clear that for a risk-averse agent the residual claimancy conflicts with the insurance objective.

Finding the optimal incentive scheme when the agent is risk-averse is a complex task. (The supplementary section contains a few results.) The following simple examples illustrate the issues.

Example 1

A firm's profit may take one of two values: Π_1 and Π_2 (with $\Pi_1 < \Pi_2$). The firm is run by a manager, who chooses between two levels of effort: high ("work") and low ("shirk"). The manager has utility $U = u(w - \Phi)$ when he works and $U = u(w)$ when he shirks, where w is the manager's wage, u is an increasing, concave function (with $\lim_{w \to -\infty} u'(w) = +\infty$), and Φ (the monetary disutility of high effort) is strictly positive. The manager's objective function is the expectation of u. Working outside the firm, he would get $U_0 \equiv u(w_0)$. So, to ensure his participation, the shareholders must give him an expected utility of at least U_0. (w_0 is called the *reservation (net) wage*). The shareholders' objective function is the expectation of the net profit $\Pi - w$.

The technology is as follows: If the manager works, the profit is Π_2 with probability x and equal to Π_1 with probability $1 - x$. If he does not work, the profit is Π_2 with probability y and Π_1 with probability $1 - y$. One has $0 < y < x < 1$.

Assume that the manager's contract is chosen by the shareholders.

First, suppose that the manager's effort is observed by the shareholders, who can then choose any level of effort they want and impose it on the manager (with the threat of a large punishment if he disobeys). Because effort is observable, there is no incentive issue; hence, the optimal contract calls for full insurance. Suppose first that they demand a low level of effort. Optimal insurance implies that $w_1 = w_2 = w_0$, where the second equality is due to the fact that the shareholders neither want nor need to give the manager more than his reservation wage. The shareholders' profits are

$$y\Pi_2 + (1 - y)\Pi_1 - w_0.$$

Now, suppose the shareholders demand a high level of effort. Optimal insurance again calls for a constant *net* wage for the manager, so

$$w_1 - \Phi = w_2 - \Phi = w_0.$$

The shareholders' expected profits are then

$$x\Pi_2 + (1 - x)\Pi_1 - (w_0 + \Phi).$$

To make things interesting, assume that it is optimal for the shareholders to demand the high effort:

$$x\Pi_2 + (1 - x)\Pi_1 - (w_0 + \Phi)$$
$$> y\Pi_2 + (1 - y)\Pi_1 - w_0,$$

or

$$(x - y)(\Pi_2 - \Pi_1) > \Phi. \qquad (2)$$

In words, the increase in expected profits exceeds the disutility of effort.

Now consider the more interesting case in which the manager's effort is not observable by the shareholders. As has been noted, a high effort cannot be induced by a constant wage structure. Instead, the shareholders must reward the manager when profits are high. Suppose that the shareholders still want to induce the high effort. They must design a wage structure that satisfies the "incentive-compatibility" constraint:

$$x u(w_2 - \Phi) + (1 - x)u(w_1 - \Phi)$$
$$\geqslant y u(w_2) + (1 - y)u(w_1), \qquad (3)$$

where w_i is the wage paid when realized profits are Π_i. (Equation 3 implies that $w_2 > w_1$.[65])

To the incentive-compatibility constraint we must add the "individual-rationality" or "participation" constraint:

$$x u(w_2 - \Phi) + (1 - x)u(w_1 - \Phi) \geqslant u(w_0). \qquad (4)$$

The shareholders' expected profit is then

$$x(\Pi_2 - w_2) + (1 - x)(\Pi_1 - w_1).$$

It is easily seen that, in the maximization of the shareholders' profits with respect to equations 3 and 4, both constraints are binding. (Suppose the incentive-compatibility constraint is not binding. Maximization of expected shareholders' profit subject to the participation constraint yields full insurance ($w_1 = w_2$), as has been shown, but this wage structure does not satisfy the incentive-compatibility constraint. Conversely, suppose that only the incentive-compatibility constraint is binding. Then the shareholders can reduce w_1, say, and keep this constraint satisfied; if the decrease in w_1 is not too large, the participation constraint is still satisfied.) Thus, in this simple case, the optimal wage structure, given that the high effort is to be induced, is obtained from equations 3 and 4 satisfied with equality:

$$x u(w_2 - \Phi) + (1 - x)u(w_1 - \Phi)$$
$$= y u(w_2) + (1 - y)u(w_1), \qquad (3')$$

$$x u(w_2 - \Phi) + (1 - x)u(w_1 - \Phi) = u(w_0). \qquad (4')$$

The shareholders' profit is lower under unobservability—equation 4' and the concavity of u imply that the expected wage bill, $x w_2 + (1 - x)w_1$, strictly exceeds $w_0 + \Phi$, as figure 3 shows.[66] Hence, to induce the high effort and obtain the high profit with probability x, the wage bill must be higher than under effort observability.

On the other hand, if the shareholders wanted to induce the low effort under effort observability, they would not suffer from effort unobservability. The full-information wage is constant ($w_1 = w_2 = w_0$), and it also induces the low effort under unobservability. Thus, the relative desirability of inducing the high effort is lower under unobservability; that is, the shareholders may be happier

---

65. The left-hand side of equation 3 is strictly lower than $x u(w_2) + (1 - x)u(w_1)$, which is lower than the right-hand side if $w_2 \leqslant w_1$ (recall that $x > y$).

66. Figure 3 is an illustration of Jensen's inequality, according to which the expectation of a concave function of a random variable is lower than the value of this function evaluated at the expectation of the random variable.

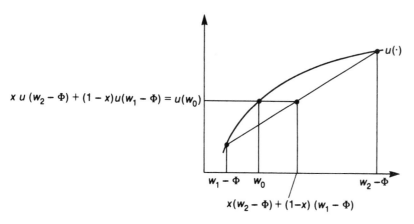

$x\,u(w_2 - \Phi) + (1 - x)u(w_1 - \Phi) = u(w_0)$

$w_1 - \Phi$ w_0 $w_2 - \Phi$

$x(w_2 - \Phi) + (1-x)(w_1 - \Phi)$

Figure 3

with the low effort under unobservability even if equation 2 is satisfied.

In summary: This simple model highlights the following points: Effort, if it is not observed, must be induced through incentives. The manager's wage must grow with the realized profit. Because such incentive structures destroy insurance, the expected wage bill required to obtain effort is higher under nonobservability. This, in turn, may make the shareholders not wish to induce effort; that is, they may tolerate slacking.

Two further important points can be derived from straightforward variants of this model.

Observability, Verifiability, and Authority

The difference between "observability" and "verifiability" (which has not been explored up to this point) relates to the possibility that the principal can observe the agent's performance but cannot verify his observations (i.e., cannot supply sufficient evidence) to a court. Because performance cannot be verified by a court, contracts that are contingent on performance (e.g., contracts that read "If the agent's performance meets such and such standard, we will pay him so much") cannot be made, as the courts will be unable to enforce them.[67] For example, when the agent is part of a productive team, reliable accounting procedures may measure only the team's performance, not individual contributions. However, an insider (the chief executive officer or a supervisor, say) may be able to disentangle these contributions, whereas an outsider (a judge) cannot. This applies equally well to the performance of complementary divisions (manufacturing and marketing, for instance) or to that of team workers.

Now, suppose that in an agency problem Π is observable by the principal but is not verifiable, so the contract cannot depend directly on the agent's performance. Can the principal be trusted to announce truthfully what he observes? *A priori*, no: Suppose that in the previous model the optimal contract induces effort when profit is verifiable. When profit is only observable, the principal has an incentive to claim that it is low (Π_1) even when it is high (Π_2), since $w_1 < w_2$. There is a simple conflict of interest for the principal.

The picture changes dramatically when the principal oversees many agents (division managers, workers, etc.). To simplify, consider a large number N of agents, each of whom produces an observable but unverifiable profit. As in the previous model, the probability that the individual performance is Π_2 rather than Π_1 is x or y, depending on whether or not the agent exerts effort. The probabilities are independent.[68] Consider the following commitment by the principal: "I will pay a wage w_2 to x percent of my agents (the ones I announce to be the most productive ones), and a wage w_1 to the rest," where w_1 and w_2 solve equations 3' and 4' (i.e., are the optimal wages under verifiability). Clearly, the total wage bill,

$$N[xw_2 + (1 - x)w_1],$$

---

67. In the model discussed above, Π need not represent the firm's profit; it could also represent an employee's performance.

68. Correlation between the production processes is not required here, as it is in the case of the tournament mechanism given below.

is fixed, and the principal does not have an incentive to misrepresent the individual performances.[69] Conversely, if the agents all exert effort, they know that x percent of them will yield profit Π_2 (by the law of large numbers) and will receive wage w_2. Those yielding profit Π_1 will receive wage w_1. Hence, the incentive-compatibility constraint and the individual-rationality constraint are satisfied. With many agents, the principal can be given the authority to choose rewards, because he can commit himself to an overall reward policy. Thus, verifiability is obtained indirectly.[70]

Remark The rewarding of observable but unverifiable performance through authority is a more general phenomenon. Here, the fixed size of the aggregate reward prevents authority from becoming arbitrary by removing the principal's incentive to misrepresent the agents' performances. An alternative but similar mechanism, which works even with a single agent, exists if the principal has a reputation to defend. For instance, an employer who has a reputation for treating his employees fairly (rewarding them according to their performance)—that is, an employer who does not abuse authority—is able to offer his employees better incentives, and therefore may be reluctant to milk his reputation by not rewarding them fairly simply to increase short-run profit.

Limited Punishment and Managerial Rents

In the previous model, it was shown that the manager's individual-rationality constraint is binding. The argument was that if it were not binding, the shareholders could reduce the wage w_1 a bit; this would not impair incentives and would still induce the manager to participate. In some circumstances, however, reducing the wage may not be possible. Suppose that, because of limited liability and laws against slavery, the harshest punishment that can be imposed on the manager is for him to receive w_0 (so $w_i \geqslant w_0$ for all i is a new constraint in the design of the wage structure). One can interpret w_0 as the equivalent in terms of utility of the wage that the manager can get elsewhere net of the search costs.[71] Alternatively, one might imagine that the manager becomes infinitely risk-averse under w_0; w_0 could be like a subsistence level, a fall slightly below which would yield utility $-\infty$ ("death") to the manager.

Because w_2 and w_1 necessarily exceed w_0 (weakly), and because the manager can always choose not to work, the participation constraint is automatically satisfied. Suppose the shareholders still want to induce effort (which will be the case if $\Pi_2 - \Pi_1$ is large enough). To do so they need to impose a wage differential between the two levels of profit: $w_2 > w_1 \geqslant w_0$. Again, because the manager can always choose not to work, his expected utility is no less than

$$y\,u(w_2) + (1 - y)u(w_1) > u(w_0).$$

The participation constraint is not binding, which means that the manager enjoys a rent within the firm.[72] (Here w_1 is equal to w_0, and w_2 is then given by equation 3'.)

The possibility of rents (Calvo 1977; Calvo and Wellisz 1978, 1979) underlies much of the efficiency-wage hypothesis for involuntary unemployment, according to which workers inside a firm are given a rent relative to unemployed ones as a way of giving them work incentives in the face of limited punishments (see, e.g., Shapiro and Stiglitz 1984).[73]

Example 2

The purpose of this example is to confirm our earlier intuitions on a simple example with a continuous choice of effort.[74] The manager chooses a level of effort e on the real line. His utility is equal to $u(w - Re^2/2)$, where R is a parameter of disutility of labor and u satisfies the assumptions of example 1. His net reservation wage is w_0, so the participation constraint is

---

69. As long as he does not collude with some of the agents.

70. A similar argument is made in Bhattacharya 1983, Carmichael 1983, and Malcomson 1984. It still holds with a finite number of agents (i.e., not a large one), though not in such a stark way.

71. There are some subtle issues of timing of production and profit accounting here, but a dynamic model would complicate the argument. Note also that the harshest punishment can be slightly below w_0 without any change in the reasoning.

72. Technically, the existence of a rent is associated with the impossibility of imposing punishments beyond a given level. For a sufficient condition to rule out rents, see the earlier reasoning and (more generally) proposition 2 in Grossman and Hart 1983.

73. See Milgrom 1986 for a further discussion of rents attached to jobs.

74. This example is taken from Parsons 1984, where it is attributed to Berhold (1971) and Stiglitz (1975).

$$\mathrm{E}\, u(w - Re^2/2) \geqslant u(w_0), \tag{5}$$

where the expectation is with respect to ε. The gross profit for the shareholders is $\Pi = e + \varepsilon$, where ε is a random variable such that $\mathrm{E}\varepsilon = 0$. (We will continue assuming that randomness occurs after the choice of effort, although in the current model it could occur and be observed by the agent between the signature of the contract and the choice of effort without any change in the argument.)

If the shareholders can observe effort, the optimal contract involves a fixed wage $w = \bar{w}$. For a given effort level e, this wage is given by the participation constraint:

$$\bar{w} = w_0 + Re^2/2.$$

Maximization of the shareholders' expected profit

$$\mathrm{E}(e + \varepsilon - w_0 - Re^2/2) = e - w_0 - Re^2/2$$

yields $e^* = 1/R$ (assuming $w_0 \leqslant 1/2R$). Suppose that effort is not observable, but profit is.

We will restrict ourselves to *linear* incentive schemes,[75] so let $w(\Pi) = a + b\Pi$. Now determine the optimal scheme in this class. The manager's expected utility is

$$\mathrm{E}\, u(a + be + b\varepsilon - Re^2/2).$$

Maximization with respect to e yields $e = b/R$. Effort grows with the slope of the incentive scheme, and for $b = 1$ the manager is residual claimant and $e = e^*$. The manager's expected utility is, thus,

$$\mathrm{E}\, u(a + b^2/2R + b\varepsilon).$$

The shareholders' expected net profit is

$$\Pi^e \equiv \mathrm{E}(e + \varepsilon - a - be - b\varepsilon) = \frac{b}{R}(1 - b) - a.$$

To find the optimal linear incentive scheme, solve

$$\max_{\{a,b\}} \Pi^e = \frac{b}{R}(1 - b) - a$$

subject to

$$\mathrm{E}\, u\left(a + \frac{b^2}{2R} + b\varepsilon\right) \geqslant u(w_0).$$

Substituting a into the participation constraint (which is binding here) yields

$$\mathrm{E}\, u\left(-\Pi^e + \frac{b}{R} - \frac{b^2}{2R} + b\varepsilon\right) = u(w_0). \tag{6}$$

It is clear that if Π^e is to be maximized, the shareholders must choose b so as to maximize the left-hand side of equation 6. Hence, we have

$$(\mathrm{E}\, u')\frac{1 - b}{R} + \mathrm{E}(u'\varepsilon) = 0. \tag{7}$$

If the manager is risk-neutral, u' is a constant independent of ε, and equation 7 yields $b = 1$. This confirms the principle of residual claimancy for risk-neutral agents. If u' is strictly concave, we claim that b lies between 0 and 1. Suppose that $b \leqslant 0$. Then the first term on the left-hand side of equation 7 is strictly positive. The second term, which is equal to the covariance of u' and ε (recall that $\mathrm{E}\varepsilon = 0$), is non-negative, so equation 7 cannot hold. The reason the covariance is non-negative is that for $b \leqslant 0$ the manager's income is nonincreasing in ε, so that his marginal utility, which is a decreasing function of income, is nondecreasing in ε. The reasoning for $b \geqslant 1$ is similar, but here the first term is negative, and the covariance is also negative.

We thus infer that the optimal linear wage structure is a profit-sharing scheme—a compromise between a fixed wage ($b = 0$), which yields optimal insurance, and residual claimancy ($b = 1$), which yields optimal incentives.

Remark In the above example, the manager was assumed to be rewarded on the basis of profit. In practice, managerial compensation is contingent on the value of the firm as well as on its current profits. Lewellen (1971) documents that a firm's stock options are often a large portion of its managerial portfolios. The general idea behind rewarding managers on the basis of stock value rather than profits is that profits are a very garbled measure of managerial performance (Lewellen 1968, chapter 4; Grossman and Hart 1980, p. 48). For instance, a profitable investment reduces current profits without reflecting managerial slack or ineptitude. But such factors, which are unverifiable because of accounting manipulations, may be observable

---

75. This is a strong restriction. The supplementary section at the end of this chapter looks at optimal nonlinear schemes. Holmström and Milgrom (1987) and Laffont and Tirole (1986) offer two different special contexts in which the optimal incentive scheme indeed turns out to be linear.

by the market and thus may be reflected in the firm's valuation. Stock options in particular are seen as an incentive for an otherwise transient manager to care about the firm's future profits as well as its current profits.[76]

2.2 Limits to Discretion

In the preceding subsection we considered the use of performance measures to limit managerial discretion. In practice, the shareholders may want to use other pieces of information as well. We will look at other factors that restrict managerial discretion even further.

Yardstick Competition

An agent's individual performance, even if it is verifiable, is only a garbled measure of the agent's effort (see examples 1 and 2 above). For instance, a firm's low profit may be due to a decrease in demand or an increase in costs rather than to managerial slack. Such effects can be detected, to some extent, by comparing the agent's performance with that of other agents placed in similar conditions.[77]

To see how yardstick competition works, consider example 1 above. Suppose that the shareholders oversee two managers in charge of two similar divisions. The shareholders' profits are equal to the sum of the profits generated by each manager, net of the expected wage bill. As before, the probability of generating profit Π_2 rather than Π_1 is x or y depending on whether the manager works or not. Furthermore, the uncertainties facing the managers are perfectly correlated, in that the same level of effort yields the same profit. Thus, if both managers choose to work, the realized profit is either Π_2 for both (with probability x) or Π_1 for both (with probability $1 - x$), and similarly when they both choose not to work. One may have in mind, for instance, the case of two divisions serving two distinct geographical markets whose demands are perfectly correlated.

In these circumstances, the shareholders can use the following contract: "If both managers reach the same level of profit (be it Π_1 or Π_2), both receive the full-information wage $w_1 = w_2 = w_0 + \Phi$; if profits differ, the high-profit manager gets $w_2 = w_0 + \Phi$ and the low-profit manager gets heavily punished." Each manager's wage thus depends on the other manager's performance as well as on his own. Clearly, both managers exerting effort is an equilibrium of the subsequent game between the managers. If a manager is expected to work, and yields the high profit, the other manager automatically reveals that he did not work by obtaining the low profit. He cannot attribute his poor performance to "adverse circumstances," and he is heavily fined.[78]

Exercise 2*** In this exercise, which concerns sole sourcing versus dual sourcing, we build a simple model in which the managers' objective function is such that monetary incentives are rather ineffective. A firm has a project of a given size. The cost of the project is $C = \beta - e$. The variable β is random on $[\underline{\beta}, \bar{\beta}]$ with expectation $E\beta$. The variable e denotes the effort exerted by the manager assigned to the project. A manager has utility function $U(w, e) = u(w) - \Phi(e)$, where $\Phi' > 0$, $\Phi'' > 0$, $\Phi'(0) > 0$, and

$$u(w) = \begin{cases} -\infty & \text{if } w < \bar{w} \\ \bar{u} + \lambda(w - \bar{w}) & \text{if } w \geq \bar{w}. \end{cases}$$

Thus, $\bar{w}$ can be interpreted as a subsistence wage. λ is a "small," positive parameter; mathematically, $\lambda \leq \Phi'(e)$ for all e. The manager is infinitely risk-averse over the states of nature β, so he is only interested in his utility in the worst state of nature: $\min_\beta U(w, e)$. The manager learns β after signing the contract and before choosing e. The principal observes C, but not β or e. So the wage structure is a function of C, $w(C)$, and the manager's objective can be written

$$\min_\beta \left(\max_e (u(w(\beta - e)) - \Phi(e)) \right).$$

Let U_0 denote the manager's reservation utility, and let

---

76. Of course, to preserve incentives it is important to prevent the manager from diversifying away the risks associated with the firm's performance. Stock options that cannot be sold serve this purpose.

77. The theory of yardstick competition and tournaments was developed by Lazear and Rosen (1981), Green and Stokey (1983), Nalebuff and Stiglitz (1983), and Shleifer (1985).

78. This suggests the possibility of multiple equilibria. Indeed, with our formulation, both not working is also an equilibrium. On the issue of multiplicity and incentive design to prevent it, see Mookherjee 1984.

$e^* > 0$ be defined by $u(\bar{w}) - \Phi(e^*) = U_0$. The principal wants to minimize the expected cost of the project.

(i) Show that if β and/or e were observable by the principal, the optimal contract would yield $w = \bar{w}$ and $e = e^*$ for all β, and that the expected cost of the project is $\bar{w} + E\beta - e^*$.

(ii) Under asymmetric information, show that the optimal contract is

$$w \begin{cases} = \bar{w} & \text{if } C \leqslant \bar{\beta} - e^* \\ < \bar{w} & \text{otherwise} \end{cases}$$

and that the expected cost of the project is $\bar{w} + \bar{\beta} - e^*$.

(iii) Suppose that the project can be given to two managers. The cost to the principal (net of the wage bill) is $\min(C_1, C_2)$, where $C_i = \beta - e_i$ and e_i is manager i's effort $(i = 1, 2)$. That is, β is the same for both managers. Show that an optimal contract is

$$w_i(C_i, C_j) \begin{cases} = \bar{w} & \text{if } C_i = C_j \\ < \bar{w} & \text{if } C_i > C_j \\ = \bar{w} + \Phi'(e^*)(C_j - C_i)/\lambda & \text{if } C_i < C_j. \end{cases}$$

It is concluded that the principal prefers dual sourcing to sole sourcing if and only if $\bar{w} \leqslant \bar{\beta} - E\beta$. Interpret.

Remark The preceding example and the exercise assumed perfect correlation between the agents' technologies. But the idea of yardstick competition carries over to environments with imperfect correlation (a more reasonable assumption). Indeed, Baiman and Demski (1980) and Holmström (1982) have used the Holmström-Shavell sufficient-statistics result (see section 3) to show that an agent's optimal wage structure depends only on his performance if and only if performances are independent.

Remark Yardstick competition is somewhat analogous to the use of authority to reward agents when their performance is observable but not verifiable, in that both rest on a comparison of the agents' performances. However, the two arguments differ in spirit. Yardstick competition relies on the correlation of the agents' technologies, but not on the nonverifiability of performances; furthermore, comparison can be made with outside parties, such

as competing firms. With authority the result stems from nonverifiability, and does not rely on the correlation of the technologies, and the comparison is made within a group of agents overseen by a principal.

The potential applications of yardstick competition are numerous. The performances of managers of divisions facing similar cost or demand conditions may be compared by chief executive officers. Similarly, the rewards of one company's managers can be made contingent on the performance of a competitor's managers. More generally, managerial rewards can be based on average industry profit. The Department of Defense and many private firms sometimes use dual sourcing to procure their supplies, even in spite of the possible loss in returns to scale. Medicare pays hospitals a fixed fee for treating all patients within a diagnostically related group. The size of this fee is based on the average cost of treating patients in this group at comparable hospitals (Shleifer 1985).

Yardstick competition also has its limits. The units that are to be compared may face different conditions (e.g., the correlation between the situations may be fairly imperfect). Furthermore, their performance may be garbled by accounting idiosyncrasies or measurement errors. Last, the managers' performance depends on the assets they have inherited. (Although it may not be a problem in theory, this effect requires yardstick competition to be more sophisticated and, therefore, makes it more unlikely.) This may explain why there is little yardstick competition in the electricity-generation industry (see Joskow and Schmalensee 1986).[79]

Takeovers

Manne (1965) and Marris (1964) have argued that failure to maximize profits lowers the stock value of a firm, and that it induces outside entrepreneurs (raiders) to buy the firm, replace its management, and direct the firm toward profit maximization. The threat of such takeovers serves to discipline managers.

But why should managers be concerned with the threat of a takeover? For the argument to hold, managers must suffer greatly from the takeover. This could be true either because managers are immediately punished when their

---

79. See Antle and Smith 1986 for an empirical assessment of the use of yardstick competition in executive compensation.

firm is taken over (since a takeover is an indicator of poor management) or because, by being removed, they lose the rents they had enjoyed within the firm. The first reason does not seem convincing; because of limited liability and a prohibition on slavery, direct punishments are hard to impose. Actually, far from being punished, managers usually receive princely amounts of money ("golden parachutes") when they are fired after a raid.[80] The threat of losing rents attached to managerial jobs is a more credible explanation. One such rent is prestige or reputation. Another may be on-the-job leisure (slack) due to the asymmetry of information between shareholders and managers. To the extent that mismanagement increases the likelihood of a takeover, the fear of losing their rents may make managers less prone to slack. Formulations of this idea have been put forth by Scharfstein (1985a) and by Demski, Sappington, and Spiller (1987).[81]

Takeovers, however, have their limits. Costly information must be collected about the firm's inefficiencies and areas for improvement. Outsiders have an incentive to collect information and spend the takeover costs only if they can derive substantial profits from the takeover. Grossman and Hart (1980) point out a potential free-rider problem that may impair this incentive: In the event of a takeover, a shareholder may not want to tender his shares, because if he keeps them he can enjoy the increase in the stock price brought about by the raid. On the other hand, the raider can make a profit only if the tender price of shares is lower than their post-raid price. Hence, he cannot both buy the shares and make a profit on them.

There are ways out of the free-rider problem. Dilution—a provision in the firm's constitution allowing a successful raider to sell part of the firm's assets to another company owned by the raider at disadvantageous terms for minority shareholders or to issue himself new shares— is tantamount to a reward to the raider, and encourages takeovers (Grossman and Hart 1980). Another possibility is that the raid may be undertaken by a large shareholder of the firm. Even if the other shareholders free-ride on him

(by not tendering their shares), a large shareholder at least enjoys the increase in the value of his own shares (Shleifer and Vishny 1986).

These anti-free-rider factors are themselves limited. On the one hand, because dilution is basically a gift to the raider, incumbent shareholders may be reluctant to allow it on a large scale. Furthermore, the U.S. courts have restrained its use. On the other hand, the large shareholders internalize only the increase in the value of their shares. They do not take the positive externality on the other incumbent shareholders into account, so their incentive to monitor the firm and to undertake a takeover may be too small.

Potential resistance by the current management to a raid imposes a second limit on the efficacy of takeovers. Managers can make the firm unattractive to the raider through antitrust litigation or "poison pills."[82] If this does not work, they can collude with the raider and buy his shares of the firm (if any) at a substantial premium over the market price in exchange for his signing a standstill agreement, which prohibits him from owning shares of the firm for a certain period of time. The other shareholders may well be losers in such a "greenmail" maneuver, because the takeover does not take place (management is not removed) and the firm purchases the raider's shares at a high price (however, see Shleifer and Vishny 1984). Finally, managerial resistance can be reduced (for instance, by offering "golden parachutes" to removed managers), but only at a substantial cost.

These effects may, to some extent, explain Scherer's (1980, p. 38) observation (made before the recent wave of takeovers) that "the available evidence provides at best only weak support for the hypothesis that takeovers generate an effective disciplinary mechanism against departures from profit maximization."

A takeover threat may have perverse incentive effects. First, it lowers the managers' incentive to make long-run investments, as they may not be around to reap the benefits. That is, managers are led to behave myopically

---

80. In some instances the takeover may hurt the managers' future careers by conveying bad news about their abilities. The sanction is then imposed by the market for managerial talent and is delayed. (For models of managerial careers, see the next subsection.)

81. Demski et al. present their formulation in the related context of second sourcing (i.e., the replacement of a supplier by another). See also Anton and Yao 1987 and Caillaud 1985.

82. For instance, they may purchase one of the raider's competitors, making the raider's takeover subject to antitrust laws. Or, by purchasing another firm (even one not related to the raider's activity), they may increase their own firm's debt enough to scare off a cash-constrained raider. "Poison pills" are preferred stock rights that are inactive unless they are triggered by a tender offer for a large fraction of the firm. They are somewhat similar to an entry fee to be paid by the raider.

(Laffont and Tirole 1987). Second, it destroys the managers' job stability and exacerbates their career concerns, which may lead to managerial decisions that are contrary to the firm's interest (Hermalin 1987). Third, it shortens the term of the relationship between managers and workers, and may prevent the development of trust between them (Shleifer and Summers 1987).

Managerial Incentives: The Dynamic Perspective

Another bound on the managers' discretion is the concern for their own careers, both within the firm and outside the firm. The arguments presented here relate mainly to the interaction between adverse selection (How efficient or trustworthy is the manager?) and moral hazard (How hard does he work?).

Within a firm, a manager who has performed poorly may not be trusted to do well in the future. His prospects for internal promotion may be weak. To formalize this, some authors have focused on the repeated aspects of the relationship between a firm and its employees. Suppose that in each period the employee's performance is of a high or a low quality. Quality is observable by the employer, but it is not verifiable. The firm offers a rent to its employees in each period (where a rent means that the employee strictly prefers to stay with the firm rather than quit—it may, for instance, represent a wage above the market wage), as long as the employee has performed with high quality before. If the employee "cheats" and turns in a low-quality performance, the firm stops offering him the rent (for instance, does not promote him or does not increase his salary). The threat of losing this rent puts some discipline on the employee. Mathematically, the formalization of this idea involves either the theory of supergames or the theory of reputation under asymmetric information (see chapters 2, 6, and 9). The idea is similar to the one in chapter 2 where consumers stop patronizing a firm that starts producing low-quality products.[83]

Let us now turn to the possibility that the manager will leave the firm. The threat of outside offers may discipline the firm and force it to treat its managers fairly when the quality of their work is observable but not verifiable. Suppose that a manager turns in a high-quality job, which is a signal of the manager's ability as well as of his effort, but is not rewarded by a wage increase. If his performance is observed by other firms, the latter may be able to bid him away. Because of this threat, the firm must reward the manager fairly. Consider a professor at a university. Let the quality of his work be the quality of his research and the richness of his interactions with colleagues and students. Now, this quality may be observable by the profession but hard for a court to assess.[84] His threat to move to another university tends to equalize his position within and outside his university. This idea, pioneered by Fama (1980), was studied further by Holmström (1982a), who combined the distinction between observability and verifiability and the outside pressure mechanism.

The possibility of getting good opportunities outside his present firm, like that of being rewarded within the firm, certainly gives a manager incentives to perform satisfactorily. When the manager's internal or external supervisors observe only his performance, any amount of shirking on his part may be mistaken for a lack of trustworthiness or ability, and thus may hurt his career. Holmström shows that, in such circumstances, a manager at the beginning of his career may work even harder than is socially optimal.[85]

Remark Two other mechanisms that enable a firm to reward its employees' observable-but-unverifiable performance by fiat, but fairly, have already been described. One was based on the firm's commitment to reward a given percentage of its employees; the other was based on the firm's reputation. The outside pressure mechanism may work better for top managers than for other employees, because the former have more outside visibility than the latter.

---

83. For elaborations of this idea in the context of internal organization or business relations, see Telser 1980, Kreps 1984, Bull 1985, Hart and Holmström 1987, and MacLeod and Malcomson 1986. In the context of business relations, Kreps posed the further question of why transient managers of a firm would want to sustain the firm's reputation. Cheating on an implicit agreement yields a current benefit, whereas some of the future losses associated with the loss of reputation will be incurred after the managers have left the firm. Kreps notes that if the managers own the firm, they internalize the full effects of their decisions, because the value of the firm reflects future as well as current profits.

84. Of course, the courts might hire experts in the profession to assess the quality (which they sometimes do). But the legal costs would generally be incommensurate with the issue at stake.

85. Gibbons (1985) shows that it may be optimal to reduce the manager's outside visibility at the beginning of his career in order to reduce this effect. He argues that the junior members of a law firm often have such a reduced visibility. Wolfson (1985) demonstrates that a reputation effect alleviates the moral-hazard problem somewhat in oil drilling ventures.

Supervision

Except in the discussion of takeovers, we have mainly taken the principal's information as given and studied the optimal use of this information to control the agent. We now turn to the internal incentive to monitor.

Alchian and Demsetz (1972) argue that nonseparabilities or increasing returns to scale are essential to the understanding of organization design. The product of a team exceeds the sum of the products of its members in isolation; however, Alchian and Demsetz note, team production may hinder the metering of productivity and rewards. For instance, unless each worker is accountable for a particular part of production (as is the case with piecework), accounting data measure only the output of the shop. In one of their examples, Alchian and Demsetz show that it may be hard to disentangle the relative performances of two workers who jointly lift heavy cargo into trucks. At a more aggregate level, a high level of sales of a product may be due to a good design, to the high quality of the product, or to an appropriate marketing campaign, and there may be no clean measure of each functional division's contribution.

Nonseparabilities create a free-rider problem among the members of a team. Suppose, for instance, that two employees in a team share equally every extra dollar the team creates. Then each employee, when generating $1 for the team, receives only 50¢. This means that each employee has too small an incentive to contribute to the team's production. One solution is to increase the monetary incentives further (see the remark below). The other solution is the introduction of a third party (a monitor or a supervisor) to measure the individual performance of each employee. How is the monitor monitored? What are his incentives to supervise the employees? Alchian and Demsetz suggest that the monitor be given a title to the net earnings of the team (net of payments to other inputs). In the jargon of incentives theory, the supervisor is made the *residual claimant* or *sink*. At the margin, he captures any extra profit of the team. He thus has a strong incentive to exert effort to measure the employees' individual performances.

In summary: Alchian and Demsetz's organization (or "firm") is a particular policing device utilized in the presence of team production. Indeed, among the bundle of rights associated with ownership of a firm, Alchian and Demsetz list the right to be residual claimant and to observe the behavior of employees.[86]

Remark Holmström (1982b) offers an alternative theory of the firm based on team production and the impossibility of measuring individual performance. He argues that one of a *corporation's* roles is to break the rule that the benefits of an organization must be split among employees (the way it is done in a partnership). The idea is as follows: To face the right incentives in his production decisions, an employee must be the "residual claimant" for these decisions; if a decision yields one extra dollar to the firm or unit, the employee must receive that extra dollar. Consider a two-employee unit, and suppose that only the unit's performance (equal to the sum of the two employees' performances) is observable. Then, each time the unit's profit grows by $1, each employee must be given $1. The *marginal* distribution of profits must be $2 for each extra dollar earned by the unit. This is possible only if there exists a "source" (shareholders? other units?) that "breaks the budget constraint" at the margin.[87] The Holmström and Alchian-Demsetz theories differ except for the starting point (the impossibility of disentangling individual contributions at an accounting level) and for the conclusion that the budget constraint of a team must be broken. Alchian and Demsetz rely on supervision by a third party who is made a sink in order to give him the incentive to monitor (at the margin, the employees receive $0 for every $1 they create; i.e., they have a fixed wage). In contrast, Holmström disciplines team members through monetary incentives provided by a marginal source.

Williamson (1975, p. 49) argues that the importance of nonseparabilities in production should not be overstressed. Because a monitor can supervise only a limited number of employees, the theory can at best explain the organiza-

---

86. Other listed rights are those to be the central party common to all contracts with inputs, to alter the membership of the team, and to sell these rights.

87. For an argument that follows Holmström's see exercise 4.4. Note that the use of a source requires that the employees be unable to collude against this

source. Because every time an employee increases output by $1 the other employee also receives $1, the employees have an incentive to get together to expand production beyond its noncooperative level.

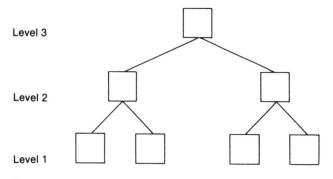

Level 3

Level 2

Level 1

Figure 4

tion of small groups. In large firms, supervision must be delegated.[88]

This brings us to an interesting class of hierarchical models which were pioneered by Williamson (1967) and by Calvo and Wellisz (1978, 1979) and developed further by Rosen (1982) and by Keren and Levhari (1983). Suppose that the firm is organized according to a pyramidal structure, as shown in figure 4. Level 1 is the productive tier of the firm (the workers). Level-1 employees are supervised by level-2 employees, presumably because of nonseparabilities in production. A level-2 employee does not supervise all level-1 employees, because the quality of supervision decreases with the span of supervision. In turn, level-2 employees' incentives to supervise are provided by level-3 supervision. Level 3 is assumed to be composed by a single agent (or unit), who is the residual claimant for the firm's profit net of wage and input payments. For instance, level 3 can be the shareholders (respectively, the executive officers) and level 2 the executive officers (respectively, the division officers). An attractive property of these models is that the horizontal and vertical sizes of the firm are not fixed. The span of control of each employee and the number of tiers are supposed to be chosen by the top tier to maximize profits. What may then put a lid on the firm's size is the deterioration of supervision as the firm grows. More workers require more level-2 supervisors, and the supervision of level-2 employees by the top tier worsens. (Alternatively, an extra layer can be created between the top tier and level 2; but this addition is costly.) Calvo and

Wellisz also derive some interesting implications for the wage structure within the firm from this type of model.

In Tirole 1986b it is argued that the exercise of supervision and authority in an organization is limited by the possibility of collusion between groups of its members. An employee obtains power over another when given the right to evaluate the other's performance (supervision) or to make decisions in unforeseen contingencies that affect him (authority). This power gives rise to the possibility of collusion between the two parties, which is enforced by side-transfers (promise of a similar counter favor, money, evolution of their personal relationship, etc.). Organizational design is then partly geared toward preventing collusion by recognizing a supervisor's incentive to act as an advocate for rather than as a prosecutor of the supervisee, and by limiting authority through the imposition of bureaucratic rules.

Product-Market Competition

As Scherer (1980, p. 38) notes,

When forced into the trenches on the question of whether firms maximize profits, economists resort to the ultimate weapon in their arsenal: a variant of Darwin's natural selection theory. Over the long pull, there is one simple criterion for the survival of a business enterprise: Profits must be nonnegative. No matter how strongly managers prefer to pursue other objectives, and no matter how difficult it is to find profit-maximizing strategies in a world of uncertainty and high information costs, failure to satisfy this criterion means ultimately that a firm will disappear from the economic scene.

For instance, Winter (1971) suggests that a competitive firm that makes inefficient decisions (about techniques, for instance) incurs losses because it cannot simply transmit its extra costs to the consumers (the market price is taken as given). The firm is thus led to search for new and better decisions in order to survive. Hence, firms in a competitive environment are more hard-pressed to reduce costs, and end up being more efficient. This is clearly a rather realistic story; however, as Hart (1983) notes, "a question which Winter does not analyze, at least formally, is why firms choose inefficient techniques in the first place." The

---

88. Indeed, most of the supervisors in organizations have only limited stakes in them. In particular, they are usually far from being the residual claimants for the teams they supervise.

answer to this question may lie in the problems of delegation and monitoring mentioned above.[89]

The effects of the threat of bankruptcy and of competitive pressure on managerial incentives have not yet been formulated in a satisfactory way. However, some of the effects of competitive pressure on incentives (not those related to the survival issue) have been studied.

One obvious effect stems from the possibility of yardstick competition. The shareholders of a competitive firm can base managerial rewards on the competitors' profits or on the market price, which would not be possible were the firm a monopoly.

The effect of product-market competition on internal incentives becomes more subtle when outside data, such as competitors' profits and the market price, are not available to the firm. Hart (1983) has shown that the form of competition in the product market still has an influence on internal control when the owners of the firm observe only that firm's performance.[90]

In Hart's model, competition operates through the variability of the market price, which, together with a cost shock, determines the variability of the firm's profit and therefore determines the extent to which the firm's managers can manipulate the owners' uncertainty in order to engage in slack. Roughly, a profit that is exogenously more variable leaves more leeway for misrepresentation by the managers and less opportunity for control by the shareholders. Hart considers a competitive industry with two types of firms: managerial firms (in which the shareholders delegate the decision power to managers and are therefore exposed to the above-mentioned control hazards) and entrepreneurial firms (which are run by the entrepreneurs themselves).[91]

Intuitively, when the marginal cost of production (which is perfectly correlated across the firms) is low, entrepreneurial firms expand their output. The managers of the managerial firms, if they do not respond much to monetary incentives, take advantage of the good times to slack. If the proportion of entrepreneurial firms increases, the output is thus more sensitive to a cost decrease. This reduces the market price in good times, thus mitigating the influence of the low cost on profit. In particular, the managerial firms' profits become less sensitive to outside uncertainty when the proportion of entrepreneurs grows. This makes their control by shareholders easier, which results in less slack. To the extent that entrepreneurs are a symbol of competition,[92] more competition in the output market leads to less slack in managerial firms. Unfortunately, this result is sensitive to the description of the managers' utility function, as Scharfstein (1985b) shows. If managers do react to monetary incentives sufficiently, a larger proportion of entrepreneurs increases slack in managerial firms.[93]

An Application: The M-Form Firm

The analysis of managerial incentives may shed some light on the emergence of the so-called multidivisional-form (M-form) firm.[94]

Recall from section 1 that the technologically rational organization of a firm is the unitary form, with its specialization by function. However, this type of organization collapsed with the horizontal expansion of firms. According to Chandler (1966), this collapse is mainly due to the loss of control by the top management. This might be explained as follows. To control the functional divisions,

---

89. Another possibility, unrelated to the issue of incentives, is that firms must try techniques before learning their efficiency. Hence, a firm may enter a market, discover it has inherited an inefficient technique, suffer losses, and exit the market. In the long run, only firms that have developed efficient techniques survive. Jovanovic (1982), Lippman and Rumelt (1982), and Hopenhayn (1986) derive some interesting conclusions from such dynamic competitive selection models.

90. This material is more advanced than the rest of this chapter. The reader may wish to omit it on the first reading.

91. The division between the two types of firms is explained by a fixed cost of becoming an entrepreneur.

92. Note, however, that no firm has market power.

93. Readers familiar with the principal–agent literature will understand the following explanation: Obtaining separation between the different states of nature (i.e., obtaining variations of one's firm's profits when the cost parameter varies) is very costly to the shareholders if the managers respond little to monetary incentives (because much money must then be spent to achieve separation). In particular, as in Hart's model, when the managers are infinitely income-risk-averse, they are best required to reach a profit target—i.e., to bunch (reach the same level of profit in all states of nature). Bunching means that in good states of nature the managers slack more. In contrast, when managers do react to monetary incentives to a decent extent, the optimal incentive scheme leads to separation. In that case, as is well known, there is no distortion of effort in the best state of nature (at least if the disutility of effort has a monetary representation; that is, $u = u(w - Re)$), and there is slack in worse states of nature. This reverses the result.

94. The following is but a naive attempt to promote incentive theory as a partial explanation of the M form. For a richer approach see Chandler 1966 and Williamson 1975.

the top management can basically use one of two methods: rewarding each functional division for good performance (i.e., basing incentive schemes on output) and supervising the divisions directly in order to assess individual contributions (i.e., to measure inputs). The first method clearly faces the accounting problem of separating the contributions of the various divisions. The sales of a product or the profits of the firm depend on the quality of each division's performance, which may be hard to measure. This gives rise to an Alchian-Demsetz-type team problem. The second method can be employed only if the firm is small. A loss in the supervisory possibilities of top management may have accounted for the difficulties of the unitary-form firm in an expansionary phase.

The multidivisional form emerged in the 1920s and became prevalent after World War II. It consists of organizing the firm into quasi-firms resembling "scaled down, specialized U-form structures" (Williamson 1975, p. 136). These divisions are defined by product, brand, or geographic lines, and are fairly autonomous. See, for example, figure 5.

In the M-form firm, a relatively precise measure of divisional performance is available. And, indeed, the role of the general office (top management) is to audit and allocate resources among the competing divisions.[95] Within a division, by contrast, the supervisory mode is more prevalent, and that allows some assessment of the relative contributions of functional subdivisions.

This rough analysis leaves an important question unanswered: If divisions are quasi-firms, why should they be organized within a single structure? Why aren't they separate legal entities? Indeed, Williamson views the M-form firm as a "miniature capital market"; however, he argues further that the general office has better auditing capabilities, as well as better takeover capabilities, than the capital market (1975, pp. 146–148). His argument is related to incomplete contracts.

2.3 Doubts about the Neoclassical Methodology

Progress made since the early 1970s has shown that the neoclassical firm is not the unrealistic, profit-maximizing

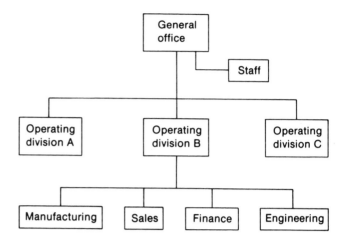

Figure 5
An example of the multidivisional form. Source: Williamson 1975, p. 138.

entity that organization theorists ridiculed in the 1950s and the 1960s. Still, the neoclassical theory leaves many questions unanswered, and this raises some doubts about its ability to cope with certain complex organizational phenomena. Simon 1976 and chapters 3 and 5 of Nelson and Winter 1982 are particularly instructive in this respect. Among the neglected topics are the following.

Optimizing Behavior

The neoclassical theory presumes that members of an organization act so as to maximize an objective function of a few standard variables (such as income and effort). This raises two questions: Does their objective include other variables (prestige, ego, power, number of subordinates, size of the budget, conviviality, friendship, etc.)? Do they even have a well-defined objective function, or do they use rules of thumb or "satisfice"?

Concerning the first issue (arguments of the objective function), we must recognize that a number of goals other than income and effort seem to mobilize the members' energy. Of course, it is interesting to wonder whether these enter directly into the member's utility function or whether they are intermediate objectives that help achieve the primitive goals. As was mentioned earlier, it might be the case that a manager enjoys a large number

---

95. Other roles include advisory services and strategic planning. The important thing to note is that the top management is removed from the routine operational activities—including, to some extent, the direct supervision of divisions.

of subordinates not *per se* but rather because this acts as a signal to the labor market (a manager in charge of an important division is likely to be an able manager) or because it allows for smoother operation and thus reduces on-the-job pressure (effort). The economist faces a familiar dilemma here. An increase in the number of explanatory variables (arguments of the objective function) makes it easier to explain real-world phenomena. At the same time, the theory loses predictive power: By adding enough arguments, one can always "explain" any kind of behavior. By contrast, the restriction to a small number of predetermined primitive variables restores some discipline. How "inspired" the neoclassical economists have been in their choices of primitive variables is not yet known.

The second issue—the possibility that economic agents do not optimize—is, of course, a matter of concern. Indeed, members of an organization often use rules of thumb instead of performing complex computations. However, many behaviors that *look* nonoptimizing may actually be the outcomes of optimization under constraints, and therefore may be not at all irrational. For instance, a member generally does not have time to sample all the information that is relevant to decision making; he may thus make decisions that, viewed with better information, look irrational. However, the decisions may be rational, given the shadow price of the time necessary to gather the information. Similarly, the time and effort required to compute optimal decisions in complex problems are traded off against inefficiencies in decision making. It remains to be seen how successful such "rational explanations" of bounded rationality will be.[96]

Communication and Knowledge

Neoclassical theory pays only lip service to the issue of communication. Information flows between members of an organization are limited only because of incentive compatibility. A member keeps his information private when he would suffer from its becoming public. Private incentives certainly limit information flows considerably. However, even well-intentioned members of an organiza-tion (i.e., members who do not manipulate information to their advantage) may have trouble communicating all the information they possess to their relevant co-members, because it is too time consuming or because the information is hard to "codify" (see Arrow 1974) to make it understandable to its receivers. Thus, decisions that would be profit maximizing under full communication will not be made under imperfect communication.[97]

This brings us to the notion of knowledge. Several contributions (among the most recent Nelson and Winter 1982, Kreps 1984, and Cremer 1986) have endowed a firm with a stock of knowledge that guides the organization's members in their decisions and coordination in a world of imperfect communication:

The context of the information possessed by an individual member is established by the information possessed by all other members.... To view organization memory as reducible to individual member memories is to overlook, or undervalue, the linking of those individual memories by shared experiences in the past, experiences that have established the extremely detailed and specific communication system that underlies routine performance. (Nelson and Winter 1982, p. 105)

Organizational culture is the pattern of basic assumptions that a given group has invented, discovered or developed in learning how to cope with its problems of external adaptation and internal integration, and that have worked well enough to be considered valid, and, therefore, to be taught to new members as the correct way to perceive, think, and feel in relation to these problems. (Schein 1984, p. 3)

Organizational memory helps the members to find relatively satisfactory decisions in the presence of complex decision making ("satisficing" or individual bounded rationality) and to coordinate their respective actions in the absence of perfect communication (collective bounded rationality).

Dynamics of Organizations

Neoclassical theory has focused on the optimal design of an organization at a given point of time. Little has been said about reorganizations. Because most reorganizations

---

96. An important area where this reformulation has been fairly successful is search theory, which explicitly formalizes the trade-off between costly acquisition of information and (*ex post*) inefficient decision making.

97. Neoclassical theory has recently made some progress in the formalization of these issues (Geanakoplos and Milgrom 1984) and their consequences (Sah and Stiglitz 1985), but much work remains to be done.

Marshak and Radner (1972) analyze optimal decision rules that coordinate members of an organization under imperfect communication.

are, in general, not specified in the initial organizational design, they are much influenced by the authority and bargaining relationships at the time of the reorganization. As the formalization of these relationships is still in its infancy, even in the static neoclassical theory of the firm, it is not surprising that neoclassical theory has had little to say about reorganizations.

Group Behavior

Sociologists (e.g. Dalton [1959] and Crozier [1967]) and organization theorists (e.g. Cyert and March [1963]) have emphasized that organizational behavior is often best predicted by the analysis of group incentives as well as individual incentives. In contrast, neoclassical theory has tended to focus only on individual incentives.[98]

The reader will have perceived in this discussion of the current lacunae of the neoclassical approach much intellectual imperialism. Most of it conveys the following message: "Sociologists and organization theorists are right to claim that neoclassical theory has not tackled some important aspects of organizations. But give the theory enough time to develop and resolve adequate models." Of course, this is a pure act of faith, and much of the controversy may revolve around whether the neoclassical approach is indeed able to cope with these aspects.

2.4 The Profit-Maximization Hypothesis and Industrial Organization

As has been noted, there are many ways in which discretion can be curbed. However, none of them is perfect, and we should expect some possibly important deviations from profit-maximizing behavior.[99] Does this mean that the profit-maximizing models of this book are fundamentally flawed? Not necessarily. Consider the familiar problem of monopoly pricing (see chapter 1). Let a monopoly have the profit function

$$\Pi = P(q)q - c(e, \varepsilon)q - w,$$

where q is the firm's output, $P(\cdot)$ is the inverse demand function, w is the manager's wage, and c is the unit cost (a function of the manager's effort e and some random variable ε). Suppose that the shareholders observe every variable except e and ε. In particular, they observe the realization of the unit cost c. This unit cost plays the same role that the profit variable plays in examples 1 and 2 of subsection 2.1. It can easily be shown that the optimal wage structure, $w(c)$, is based solely on the realization of c, because c conveys all the relevant information about effort (mathematically, it is a sufficient statistic for effort). Now, we know from subsection 2.1 that if the manager is risk-averse, the effort e induced by the optimal wage structure differs from e^*, the optimal level that would be obtained if effort were observable by the shareholders. The firm is profit-maximizing only in a constrained sense, and the manager engages in X-inefficiency ($e \neq e^*$) in the sense of Leibenstein 1966.

However, given the effort e induced by the optimal wage structure, $w(\cdot)$, let $\tilde{c} \equiv c(e, \varepsilon)$ denote the resulting random cost. The shareholders' expected profit is

$$E\Pi = P(q)q - (E\tilde{c})q - E w(\tilde{c}).$$

Because the choice of q does not change the managerial-control problem (recall that $\tilde{c}$ is a sufficient statistic), the shareholders (or the manager) might as well pick q so as to maximize $P(q)q - (E\tilde{c})q$. Hence, for an outside observer, the firm's behavior is *observationally equivalent* to that of a firm that does not engage in X-inefficiency, but has a cost distribution $\tilde{c}$ for the efficient (full-information) level of effort. So never mind that the distribution of the unit cost is biased toward high levels because of informational asymmetries; the monopoly-pricing model developed in chapter 1 is still valid.

This is only an example; it is not meant to convey the impression that this "separability" between internal organization and product-market or input-market decisions is the rule.[100] Indeed, one of the most exciting research agendas in industrial organization for years to

---

98. According to Nelson and Winter (1982, p. 56): "Although the business press frequently reports the internal policy struggles of large firms in a manner that clearly involves informal use of a coalition model, there is little scholarly literature in economics that takes this perspective. The proposals of March [1962] and Cyert and March [1963] have been largely ignored."

99. Scherer (1980, p. 41) concludes: "... assuming profit maximization provides

a good first approximation in describing business behavior. Deviations, both intended and inadvertent, undoubtedly exist in abundance, but they are kept within more or less narrow bounds by competitive forces, the self-interest of stock-owning management, and the threat of managerial displacement by important outside stockholders and takeover raiders."

100. For a counterexample, see the long-purse story in chapter 9.

come is the determination of the scope and importance of such interactions. However, this author feels and hopes that many of the conclusions of the theory of industrial organization will remain valid (at least at a descriptive level) when the profit-maximization postulate is abandoned for a full-fledged model of internal organization.

3 Supplementary Section: The Principal–Agent Relationship[101]

The purpose of this section is to introduce the moral-hazard issue in a more general framework than the one in the text.

Suppose that shareholders are risk-neutral. Their objective function is equal to the expected gross profit of the firm minus the expected wage payment. For ease of exposition, assume that there is a unique manager. This manager makes an unobservable decision e in an interval $[\underline{e}, \overline{e}]$. This decision will be interpreted as an effort level, but more generally it could be any discretionary or moral-hazard variable (perquisites, care, etc.); it is not observable by the shareholders. Given e, the realization of the profit depends on the realization of a random variable ε: $\Pi(e, \varepsilon)$. Presumably, Π increases with e. The shareholders observe only the profit level and reward the manager according to a wage function of the only observable variable: $w(\Pi)$. Thus, the shareholders' objective function is

$$\mathop{\mathrm{E}}_{\varepsilon}\big[\Pi(e, \varepsilon) - w(\Pi(e, \varepsilon))\big].$$

The manager's objective function is the expectation of his utility. The latter depends on the monetary reward and on the level of effort exerted: $U(w, e)$. Presumably, U increases with w and decreases with e. Assume also that U is concave in w (income risk aversion). Thus, the manager's objective function is

$$\mathop{\mathrm{E}}_{\varepsilon} U(w(\Pi(e, \varepsilon)), e).$$

(Hereafter, all expectations are taken with respect to ε.)

In the traditional principal–agent framework, the shareholders design a wage contract $w(\cdot)$. There exists *ex ante* a competitive supply of identical managers, with some reservation utility U_0 (the expected utility that they would obtain by working somewhere else). The shareholders are able to fill the managerial position only if the highest possible expected utility for a manager over all potential levels of effort exceeds U_0. In the jargon of incentive theory, the manager's "individual rationality" or "participation" constraint,

---

101. This supplementary section is partly inspired by part 1 of Hart and Holmström 1987.

$$\max_e \mathrm{E}\, U(w(\Pi(e,\varepsilon)),e) \geqslant U_0, \qquad (8)$$

must be satisfied. Next, if the shareholders want to induce a given level of effort e^* from the manager, they must design a wage structure that is "incentive compatible":

e^* maximizes $\mathrm{E}\, U(w(\Pi(e,\varepsilon)),e))$ over all e. $\qquad (9)$

Now consider the *shareholders' problem*: Choose a wage structure $w^*(\cdot)$ and induce a level of effort e^* for the manager that maximizes

$$\mathrm{E}[\Pi(e,\varepsilon) - w(\Pi(e,\varepsilon))]$$

subject to constraints 8 and 9.

Solving this problem is, in general, a complex task.[102] There are two polar cases, however, in which the solution is straightforward.

Before exposing those cases, it is useful to derive the solution in the case in which e and ε would be observable (*full information*). Because the shareholders observe e, they can impose any level they want consistent with the manager's participation (by threatening a large penalty if the manager does not conform). Thus, the only relevant constraint is 8. Now, from the theory of optimal insurance, for a given e, the risk-neutral shareholders should give a constant wage w to the manager, i.e., should give him *full insurance*.[103] The choice of the level of effort is, in general, slightly more complex. Let us simply assume that the optimal effort under full information is not $\underline{e}$ (the lowest possible effort for the manager).

Let us now return to our asymmetric-information framework, in which the shareholders observe only the profit. Obviously, because the contract is contingent on fewer variables, the shareholders have less control and therefore can expect, at most, their expected full-information profit. (The allocation they induce by using a small number of observables can always be duplicated with a larger one by dropping the extra observables.)

The first polar case is that of an income-risk-neutral manager. In this case,

$$U(w,e) = w - \Phi(e).$$

The term $\Phi(e)$ represents the disutility of effort expressed in terms of money. The shareholders' objective function can then be written as

$$\mathrm{E}(\Pi - w) = \mathrm{E}\Pi - \mathrm{E}\, U(w,e) - \Phi(e)$$
$$= [\mathrm{E}\,\Pi(e,\varepsilon) - \Phi(e)] - U_0,$$

where use is made of the manager's risk neutrality and of the individual rationality constraint (which can easily be shown to be binding in this case). Let e^* optimize $\mathrm{E}\,\Pi(e,\varepsilon) - \Phi(e)$ (the expected profit net of the disutility of effort). By definition, e^* is the optimal effort under full information (because under full information only the individual rationality constraint matters). Thus, under full information the shareholders' net profit is

$$\mathrm{E}\,\Pi(e^*,\varepsilon) - \Phi(e^*) - U_0.$$

Under asymmetric information, suppose the shareholders offer to sell the firm to the manager at price $p = \mathrm{E}\,\Pi(e^*,\varepsilon) - \Phi(e^*) - U_0$. If the manager accepts, he becomes the *residual claimant* for the firm's profit. The sale of the firm to the manager is formally equivalent to an incentive scheme in which the shareholders would remain the claimants for the firm's profit but would pay a wage $w(\Pi) = \Pi - p$. To see whether the manager accepts, look at his objective function:

$$\max_e[\mathrm{E}\,\Pi(e,\varepsilon) - \Phi(e) - p] = U_0.$$

So the manager accepts, and the shareholders make exactly the same expected profit as under full information. As is explained above, the intuition for this result is that the manager faces an incentive scheme that exactly reflects the vertical structure's objective. Thus, he chooses the full-information level of effort. The potential drawback is that the manager may bear all the risk. That would not matter, however, because the manager is risk-neutral.

The other polar case is that of an infinitely income-risk-

---

102. The pioneers in this area were Wilson (1968, 1969), Ross (1973), Mirrlees (1974, 1975), Harris and Raviv (1978), Holmström (1979), Shavell (1979), and Grossman and Hart (1983). Very few general results can be obtained in the absence of more specific assumptions (see Grossman and Hart 1983).

103. To prove this, fix e and let $\tilde{\Pi} \equiv \Pi(e,\varepsilon)$ denote the random profit. Let $\tilde{U}(w) \equiv U(w,e)$. The shareholders maximize over $w(\tilde{\Pi})$ their objective function

$$\max_{\tilde{\Pi}} \mathrm{E}\,[\tilde{\Pi} - w(\tilde{\Pi})]$$

subject to the constraint $\mathrm{E}\,\tilde{U}(w(\tilde{\Pi})) \geqslant U_0$. Forming the Lagrangian for this problem and taking the first derivative yields $\tilde{U}'(w(\tilde{\Pi})) = $ constant, so the wage is independent of profit.

averse manager. Such a manager prefers a random wage $\tilde{w}_1$ and effort e_1 to a random wage $\tilde{w}_2$ and effort e_2 if and only if $\min \tilde{w}_1 > \min \tilde{w}_2$, or $\min \tilde{w}_1 = \min \tilde{w}_2$ and $e_1 < e_2$. That is, the manager is concerned primarily with his minimum wage, but in case of a tie he prefers the allocation with the lowest level of effort. Suppose further that the distribution of Π given e has support equal to an interval $[\underline{\Pi}, \bar{\Pi}]$ whatever e, so that the distribution of e but not its support moves with e.[104] Then, whatever his effort, the manager's lowest possible wage is effort-independent, so he chooses $e = \underline{e}$. In this case, no incentive can be given to the manager. He is given a constant wage, the value of which is chosen to make the individual rationality constraint binding given effort $\underline{e}$.

The case of a general managerial utility function $U(w, e)$ is more complex. Let us simplify the model by assuming that the utility function is separable in income and effort: $U(w, e) = u(w) - \Phi(e)$. Assume that $u' > 0$, $u'' < 0$, $\Phi' \geqslant 0$, $\Phi'' > 0$, $\Phi'(0) = 0$, and $\Phi'(\infty) = \infty$. We will also use the "parametrized distribution formulation of uncertainty" (pioneered by Mirrlees [1974] and Holmström [1979]), according to which the cumulative distribution of Π given e is described by a cumulative distribution function $F(\Pi; e)$ on $[\underline{\Pi}, \bar{\Pi}]$, with density $f(\Pi; e) > 0$. These functions are assumed to be differentiable in effort. That effort increases profit (stochastically) is formalized by the first-order stochastic dominance relation on $(\underline{\Pi}, \bar{\Pi})$:

$$e_1 > e_2 \Rightarrow F(\Pi; e_1) < F(\Pi; e_2);$$

that is, the distribution for e_1 puts more weight on the upper tail. For a differentiable cumulative distribution function, this means that $F_e(\Pi; e) < 0$.

The manager's optimization problem for a given incentive scheme $w(\cdot)$,

$$\max_{e} \left(\int_{\underline{\Pi}}^{\bar{\Pi}} u(w(\Pi)) f(\Pi; e) d\Pi - \Phi(e) \right),$$

yields the first-order condition

$$\int_{\underline{\Pi}}^{\bar{\Pi}} u(w(\Pi)) f_e(\Pi; e) d\Pi - \Phi'(e) = 0. \tag{10}$$

Of course, this condition is not sufficient for optimality of effort; the second-order condition must also be satisfied if a maximum is to be obtained. For the moment, ignore the second-order condition. If the optimal solution for the *shareholders* found by ignoring the second-order condition for the manager can later be shown to satisfy the second-order condition, then it is truly optimal.

The manager must also be willing to participate:

$$\int_{\underline{\Pi}}^{\bar{\Pi}} u(w(\Pi)) f(\Pi; e) d\Pi - \Phi(e) \geqslant U_0. \tag{11}$$

The "first-order approach" for the shareholders consists of finding a wage structure $w(\cdot)$ and an effort level e that maximizes

$$L = \int_{\underline{\Pi}}^{\bar{\Pi}} [(\Pi - w(\Pi)) f(\Pi; e) \\ + \lambda(u(w(\Pi)) - \Phi(e) - U_0) f(\Pi; e) \\ + \eta(u(w(\Pi)) f_e(\Pi; e) - \Phi'(e) f(\Pi; e))] d\Pi,$$

where λ and η are positive (they are actually strictly positive, as can easily be shown). The derivative of L is taken with respect to e, and that of the integrand with respect to w for all Π. We will be concerned only with the second differentiation, which yields

$$-f(\Pi; e) + \lambda f(\Pi; e) u'(w(\Pi)) + \eta f_e(\Pi; e) u'(w(\Pi)) = 0,$$

or

$$\frac{1}{u'(w(\Pi))} = \lambda + \eta \frac{f_e(\Pi; e)}{f(\Pi; e)}. \tag{12}$$

(Equation 12 need only be true for almost every Π, i.e., everywhere except possibly on a set of Π with measure zero.) It is left to the reader to compute the derivative of L with respect to e and to check that the second-order conditions for the choice of $w(\Pi)$ and e are satisfied (conditional on the manager's second-order condition being satisfied).

The interpretation of the result is particularly simple when there are only two possible levels of effort—low and high (e_L and e_H)—rather than a continuum. On the

---

104. The case of a moving support is uninteresting, at least if the wage function $w(\cdot)$ is unconstrained. Suppose, for instance, that $\underline{\Pi}$ is a strictly increasing function of e. Suppose further that the shareholders want to induce an arbitrary level of effort, e_0. Then it suffices to impose a very large penalty on the manager if the realized profit Π turns out to be lower than the presumed lower bound $\underline{\Pi}(e_0)$. This deters the manager from choosing any level of effort $e < e_0$. (Such extreme punishments are not feasible if $w(\cdot)$ is constrained, say, by limited liability.) Thus, a moving support is basically equivalent to full information. The same phenomenon can also occur with nonmoving, infinite support, as was shown by Mirrlees (1974).

assumption that the shareholders want to induce the high level of effort, the incentive-compatibility constraint becomes

$$\int_{\underline{\Pi}}^{\overline{\Pi}} u(w(\Pi))f_H(\Pi)d\Pi - \Phi(e_H)$$

$$\geq \int_{\underline{\Pi}}^{\overline{\Pi}} u(w(\Pi))f_L(\Pi)d\Pi - \Phi(e_L) \qquad (3')$$

where $f_H(\cdot)$ and $f_L(\cdot)$ denote the densities for effort levels e_H and e_L. Equation 12 then becomes

$$\frac{1}{u'(w(\Pi))} = \lambda + \eta\left(1 - \frac{f_L(\Pi)}{f_H(\Pi)}\right), \quad \lambda, \eta > 0. \qquad (12')$$

Because u' is decreasing, $1/u'$ is increasing. Thus, the higher the relative probability that effort was high when profit Π was observed, the higher the manager's wage will be. The term $f_L(\Pi)/f_H(\Pi)$ is called the *likelihood ratio*. The optimal wage function is increasing with the realized profit if the likelihood ratio is decreasing. (See Milgrom 1981 for a useful discussion of likelihood ratios.) This property is a natural one to assume (although it is trivial to construct conditional distributions that do not satisfy it). *If higher profits are indeed a correct signal of higher effort, managerial compensation increases with observed profits.*

When is the first-order approach valid? In other words, when does the optimal solution satisfy the manager's second-order condition? As was shown with increasing generality by Mirrlees (1975), Grossman and Hart (1983), and Rogerson (1985), the following conditions are sufficient for the first-order approach to be valid (and, in particular, for equation 12 or 12' to describe the optimal compensation scheme):

Monotonic-likelihood-ratio property: f_e/f increases with Π (or in the two-level-of-effort case, f_H/f_L increases with Π).

Convexity of the distribution function: $F_{ee} \geq 0$, or (more generally) for all e_1, e_2, Π, and any α in $[0, 1]$,

$$F(\Pi; \alpha e_1 + (1 - \alpha)e_2) \leq \alpha F(\Pi; e_1) + (1 - \alpha)F(\Pi; e_2).$$

That is, the deterministic effort $\alpha e_1 + (1 - \alpha)e_2$ is stochastically superior to effort e_1 with probability α and to effort e_2 with probability $1 - \alpha$. This convexity assumption has the flavor of decreasing returns to scale.[105]

Equation 12 also teaches us something interesting about the value of a signal. Suppose that the shareholders observe not only profit Π but also some other signal, s. This signal could be the price of inputs, the performances of other firms, or sunspots. If $G(\Pi, s; e)$ denotes the joint distribution of Π and s for an effort e, with density $g(\Pi, s; e)$, then equation 12 becomes

$$\frac{1}{u'(w(\Pi, s))} = \lambda + \eta\frac{g_e(\Pi, s; e)}{g(\Pi, s; e)}. \qquad (12'')$$

Equation 12'' gives the same wage structure as equation 12 (i.e., w depends only on Π) if

$$\frac{g_e(\Pi, s; e)}{g(\Pi, s; e)} = \frac{f_e(\Pi; e)}{f(\Pi; e)}. \qquad (13)$$

However, equation 13, if integrated with respect to e, is equivalent to the existence of two functions m and n such that

$$g(\Pi, s; e) = m(\Pi, e)n(\Pi, s). \qquad (14)$$

Equation 14 says that Π is a sufficient statistic for (Π, s) with respect to e. Thus, the optimal incentive scheme uses the extra information s if and only if s is informative about e given that Π is already available. This theorem is proved more formally in Holmström 1979 and in Shavell 1979.

General results for the moral-hazard problem are rare. For instance, a reasonable prediction would be that a $1 increase in profit results in an increase in the manager's wage of between $0 (full insurance) and $1 (residual claimancy). However, this need not hold. Even for a separable utility function for the manager ($U = \phi(e)u(w) - \Phi(e)$—a special case of which, $\phi \equiv 1$, was used above), one can prove only that the reward function must be increasing at *some* level of profit and has slope < 1 at *some*

---

105. To see why these conditions yield a concave objective function for the manager, integrate the latter's objective by parts to obtain

$$\int_{\underline{\Pi}}^{\overline{\Pi}} u(w(\Pi))f(\Pi; e)d\Pi - \Phi(e) = -\int_{\underline{\Pi}}^{\overline{\Pi}} u'(w(\Pi))w'(\Pi)F(\Pi; e)d\Pi - \Phi(e)$$

$$+ \text{constant},$$

where the constant is independent of e (because $F(\underline{\Pi}; e) = 0$ and $F(\overline{\Pi}; e) = 1$ for all e). Because $w'(\Pi) \geq 0$ (from equation 12), $F_{ee} \geq 0$, and $\Phi'' \geq 0$, this objective function is concave in e.

(possibly different) level of profit (Grossman and Hart 1983). Only when there are two possible profit levels, Π_1 and Π_2, does one necessarily have

$$0 < \frac{w_2 - w_1}{\Pi_2 - \Pi_1} < 1$$

(where w_i corresponds to Π_i). Alternatively, one can suppose that the likelihood ratio is monotonic and that the distribution function is convex in the effort to apply the first-order approach and its conclusions (such as the monotonicity of the reward function). Getting more specific results requires stronger assumptions on the distribution and the utility functions.

Answers and Hints

Exercise 1

(i) The efficient amount of investment is given by

$$\max_{I}[v(I) - I].$$

This yields $I^* = 2$.

(ii) *Ex post* bargaining leads to $v(I) - p = p - c$, so $p = [v(I) + c]/2$. *Ex ante*, the supplier maximizes

$$\frac{v(I) + c}{2} - c - I = \frac{I}{2} - \frac{c}{2} - \frac{I^2}{4}.$$

This yields $I = 1$ (suboptimal investment). Not investing at all is not profitable, because $c < \frac{1}{2}$.

(iii) If the buyer has the right to buy at price p, the supplier either will not invest or will invest the minimum amount so that the buyer buys: $v(I) = p$. The second strategy yields profit $p - c - v^{-1}(p)$. If $p = v(2) = 4$, the investment is 2 and the profit is $2 - c > 0$. If $p < 4$, investment is suboptimal or nonexistent. If the supplier has the right to sell at a given price, investment is nil.

(iv) Efficient investment.

Exercise 2

(i) $U(w, e)$ should be constant for insurance purposes. Thus, $u(w) - \Phi(e) = U_0$ for all β. But the minimization of $w + \beta - e$ subject to the previous constraint yields $w = \bar{w}$ and $e = e^*$ for all β if λ is small (i.e., if $\lambda \leqslant \Phi'(e^*)$).

(ii) Let $w(\beta)$ and $e(\beta)$ denote the wage and the effort in state β. Incentive compatibility requires that

$$\bar{u} + \lambda(w(\beta) - \bar{w}) - \Phi(e(\beta))$$
$$\geqslant \bar{u} + \lambda(w(\bar{\beta}) - \bar{w}) - \Phi(e(\bar{\beta}) - (\bar{\beta} - \beta))$$

or

$$\lambda(w(\beta) - w(\bar{\beta})) \geqslant \Phi(e(\beta)) - \Phi(e(\bar{\beta}) - (\bar{\beta} - \beta)).$$

Using the convexity of Φ and the condition $\lambda \leqslant \Phi'(e)$ for all e, we get

$$w(\beta) + \beta - e(\beta) \geqslant w(\bar{\beta}) + \bar{\beta} - e(\bar{\beta}).$$

Thus, the cost for the principal cannot be lower in state β than in state $\bar{\beta}$. For any wage structure, the manager's utility is

$$\max_e [u(w(\bar{\beta} - e)) - \Phi(e)].$$

(Because of the previous incentive-compatibility constraint, the worst state of nature for the manager is $\bar{\beta}$.) These two properties imply that the contract in the text is optimal. Because monetary incentives are too costly, the principal contents himself with a given cost target.

(iii) The cost of having two managers under *full* information is $2\bar{w} + E\beta - e^*$. But this cost is reached under the yardstick-competition scheme in the text: In state β, manager i maximizes

$$\max_{e \geq e^*} [\bar{u} + \Phi'(e^*)(e - e^*) - \Phi(e)].$$

Hence, $e = e^*$ for all β.

References

Aghion, P., and P. Bolton. 1987. Entry Prevention through Contracts with Customers. *American Economic Review* 77: 388–401.

Alchian, A., and H. Demsetz. 1972. Production, Information Costs, and Economic Organization. *American Economic Review* 62: 777–795.

Anderson, E., and D. Schmittlein. 1984. Integration of the Sales Force: An Empirical Investigation. *Rand Journal of Economics* 15: 385–395.

Antle, R., and A. Smith. 1986. An Empirical Investigation of the Relative Performance Evaluation of Corporate Executives. *Journal of Accounting Research* 24: 1–39.

Anton, J., and D. Yao. 1987. Second Sourcing and the Experience Curve: Price Competition in Defense Procurement. *Rand Journal of Economics* 18: 57–76.

Aron, D. 1984. Ability, Moral Hazard, and Firm Diversification, Part I. Mimeo, Department of Economics, University of Chicago.

Arrow, K. 1970. *Essays in the Theory of Risk Bearing*. Amsterdam: North-Holland.

Arrow, K. 1974. *The Limits of Organization*. New York: Norton.

Arrow, K. 1975. Vertical Integration and Communication. *Bell Journal of Economics* 6: 173–183.

Arrow, K. 1979. The Property Rights Doctrine and Demand Revelation under Incomplete Information. In *Economics and Human Welfare*. New York: Academic.

Arrow, K. 1985. The Economics of Agency. In *Principals and Agents: The Structure of Business*, ed. J. Pratt and R. Zeckhauser. Cambridge, Mass.: Harvard Business School Press.

Arrow, K., D. Levhari, and E. Sheshinski. 1972. A Production Function for the Repairmen Problem. *Review of Economic Studies* 39: 241–250.

Baiman, S., and J. Demski. 1980. Economically Optimal Performance Evaluation and Control Systems. *Journal of Accounting Research*, supplement, 18: 184–234.

Bain, J. 1954. Economies of Scale, Concentration and Entry. *American Economic Review* 44: 15–39.

Baron, D. 1986. Design of Regulatory Mechanisms and Institutions. In *Handbook of Industrial Organization*, ed. R. Schmalensee and R. Willig (Amsterdam: North-Holland, forthcoming).

Baumol, W. 1962. On the Theory of Expansion of the Firm. *American Economic Review* 52: 1078–1087.

Baumol, W., J. Panzar, and R. Willig. 1982. *Contestable Markets and the Theory of Industry Structure*. New York: Harcourt Brace Jovanovich.

Berhold, M. 1971. A Theory of Linear Profit-Sharing Incentives. *Quarterly Journal of Economics* 85: 460–482.

Bhattacharya, S. 1983. Tournaments, Termination Schemes and Forcing Contracts. Mimeo.

Binmore, K. 1982. Perfect Equilibria in Bargaining Models. Discussion Paper 82-58, ICERD, London School of Economics.

Borch, K. 1963. *The Economics of Uncertainty.* Princeton University Press.

Bull, C. 1985. The Existence of Self-Enforcing Implicit Contracts. Mimeo, New York University.

Caillaud, B. 1985. Regulation, Competition, and Asymmetric Information. *Journal of Economic Theory,* forthcoming.

Caillaud, B., R. Guesnerie, P. Rey, and J. Tirole. 1988. Government Intervention in Production: A Review of Recent Contributions. *Rand Journal of Economics,* spring.

Calvo, G. 1977. Supervision and Utility and Wage Differentials across Firms. Mimeo, Columbia University.

Calvo, G., and S. Wellisz. 1978. Supervision, Loss of Control, and the Optimal Size of the Firm. *Journal of Political Economy* 86: 943–952.

Calvo, G., and S. Wellisz. 1979. Hierarchy, Ability, and Income Distribution. *Journal of Political Economy* 87: 991–1010.

Carmichael, L., 1983. Firm-Specific Human Capital and Promotion Ladders. *Bell Journal of Economics* 14: 251–258.

Chandler, A. 1966. *Strategy and Structure.* New York: Doubleday (Anchor Book edition).

Coase, R. 1937. The Nature of the Firm. *Economica* n.s. 4: 386–405. Reprinted in *Readings in Price Theory,* ed. G. Stigler and K. Boulding (Homewood, Ill.: Irwin, 1952).

Coase, R. 1960. The Problem of Social Cost. *Journal of Law and Economics* 3: 1–44.

Cramton, P., R. Gibbons, and P. Klemperer. 1987. Dissolving a Partnership Efficiently. *Econometrica* 55: 615–632.

Cremer, J. 1986. Corporate Culture: Cognitive Aspects. Mimeo, Virginia Polytechnic Institute and State University.

Crozier, M. 1967. *The Bureaucratic Phenomenon.* University of Chicago Press.

Cyert, R., and J. March. 1963. *A Behavioral Theory of the Firm.* Englewood Cliffs, N.J.: Prentice-Hall.

Dalton, M. 1959. *Men Who Manage.* New York: Wiley.

D'Aspremont, C., and L. A. Gerard-Varet. 1979. Incentives and Incomplete Information. *Journal of Public Economics* 11: 25–45.

Dayan, D. 1972. Vertical Integration and Monopoly Regulation. Ph.D. dissertation, Princeton University.

Demsetz, H. 1968. Why Regulate Utilities? *Journal of Law and Economics* 11: 55–66.

Demski, J., D. Sappington, and P. Spiller. 1987. Managing Supplier Switching. *Rand Journal of Economics* 18: 77–97.

Fama, E. 1980. Agency Problems and the Theory of the Firm. *Journal of Political Economy* 88: 288–307.

Farrell, J. 1985. Allocating and Abrogating Rights: How Should Conflicts Be Resolved under Incomplete Information? Mimeo, GTE Labs, Waltham, Mass.

Farrell, J., and N. Gallini. 1986. Second-Sourcing as a Commitment: Monopoly Incentives to Attract Competition. Working Paper 8618, University of California, Berkeley.

Fershtman, C., and K. Judd. 1986. Strategic Incentive Manipulation in Rivalrous Agency. Technical Report 496, IMSSS, Stanford University.

Freixas, X., R. Guesnerie, and J. Tirole. 1985. Planning Under Incomplete Information and the Ratchet Effect. *Review of Economic Studies* 52: 173–191.

Geanakoplos, J., and P. Milgrom. 1984. A Theory of Hierarchies Based on Limited Managerial Attention. Mimeo.

Gibbons, R. 1985. Optimal Incentive Schemes in the Presence of Career Concerns. Mimeo, Massachusetts Institute of Technology.

Gibbons, R. 1987. Piece-Rate Incentive Schemes. *Journal of Labor Economics* 5: 413–429.

Green, J., and N. Stokey. 1983. A Comparison of Tournaments and Contests. *Journal of Political Economy* 91: 349–364.

Grossman, S., and O. Hart. 1980. Takeover Bids, the Free Rider Problem and the Theory of the Corporation. *Bell Journal of Economics* 11: 42–64.

Grossman, S., and O. Hart. 1983. An Analysis of the Principal–Agent Problem. *Econometrica* 51: 7–45.

Grossman, S., and O. Hart, 1984. Vertical Integration and the Distribution of Property Rights. Mimeo, University of Chicago.

Grossman, S., and O. Hart. 1986. The Costs and Benefits of Ownership: A Theory of Lateral and Vertical Integration. *Journal of Political Economy* 94: 691–719.

Grout, P. 1984. Investment and Wages in the Absence of Binding Contracts: A Nash Bargaining Approach. *Econometrica* 52: 449–460.

Hall, R., and E. Lazear. 1984. The Excess Sensitivity of Layoffs and Quits to Demand. *Journal of Labor Economics* 2: 233–258.

Harris, M., and B. Holmström. 1983. On the Duration of Agreements. Technical Report 424, IMSSS, Stanford University.

Harris, M., and A. Raviv. 1978. Some Results on Incentive Contracts with Applications to Education and Unemployment, Health Insurance, and Law Enforcement. *American Economic Review* 68: 20–30.

Hart, O. 1983. The Market Mechanism as an Incentive Scheme. *Bell Journal of Economics* 74: 366–382.

Hart, O., and B. Holmström. 1987. The Theory of Contracts. In *Advances in Economic Theory, Fifth World Congress,* ed. T. Bewley. Cambridge University Press.

Hart, O., and J. Moore. 1985. Incomplete Contracts and Renegotiation. Mimeo, London School of Economics.

Hermalin, B. 1986. Adverse Selection and Contract Length. Mimeo, Massachusetts Institute of Technology.

Hermalin, B. 1987. Adverse Effects of the Threat of Takeovers. Mimeo, Massachusetts Institute of Technology.

Holmström, B. 1979. Moral Hazard and Observability. *Bell Journal of Economics* 10: 74–91.

Holmström, B. 1982a. Managerial Incentive Problems: A Dynamic Perspective. In *Essays in Economics and Management in Honor of Lars Wahlbeck*. Helsinki: Swedish School of Economics.

Holmström, B. 1982b. Moral Hazard in Teams. *Bell Journal of Economics* 13: 324–340.

Holmström, B., and P. Milgrom. 1987. Aggregation and Linearity in the Provision of Intertemporal Incentives. *Econometrica* 55: 303–328.

Holmström, B., and J. Tirole. 1987. The Theory of the Firm. In *Handbook of Industrial Organization*, ed. R. Schmalensee and R. Willig (Amsterdam: North-Holland, forthcoming).

Hopenhayn, H. 1986. A Competitive Model of Entry and Exit to an Industry. Mimeo, University of Minnesota Department of Economics.

Jensen, M., and W. Meckling. 1976. Theory of the Firm: Managerial Behavior, Agency Costs and Ownership Structure. *Journal of Financial Economics* 3: 305–360.

Johnson, S., J. Pratt, and R. Zeckhauser. 1986. Efficiency Despite Mutually Payoff-Relevant Private Information. Mimeo, John F. Kennedy School of Government, Harvard University.

Joskow, P. 1985. Vertical Integration and Long Term Contracts: The Case of Coal-Burning Electric Generating Plants. *Journal of Law, Economics and Organization* 1: 33–79.

Joskow, P. 1987. Contract Duration and Relationship-Specific Investments: The Case of Coal. *American Economic Review* 77: 168–185.

Joskow, P., and R. Schmalensee. 1983. *Markets for Power*. Cambridge, Mass.: MIT Press.

Joskow, P., and R. Schmalensee. 1986. Incentive Regulation for Electric Utilities. *Yale Journal on Regulation* 4: 1–49.

Jovanovic B. 1982. Selection and the Evolution of Industry. *Econometrica* 50: 649–670.

Katz, M. 1987. Game-Playing Agents: Contracts as Precommitments. Mimeo, Princeton University.

Keren, M., and D. Levhari. 1983. The Internal Organization of the Firm and the Shape of Average Costs. *Bell Journal of Economics* 14: 474–486.

Kihlstrom, R., and J.-J. Laffont. 1979. A General Equilibrium Entrepreneurial Theory of the Firm Based on Risk Aversion. *Journal of Political Economy* 87: 719–748.

Klein, B., R. Crawford, and A. Alchian. 1978. Vertical Integration Appropriable Rents and the Competitive Contracting Process. *Journal of Law and Economics* 21: 297–326.

Kreps, D. 1984. Corporate Culture and Economic Theory. Mimeo, Graduate School of Business, Stanford University.

Laffont, J.-J., and J. Tirole. 1988. The Dynamics of Incentive Contracts. *Econometrica* 56.

Laffont, J.-J., and J. Tirole. 1986. Using Cost Observation to Regulate Firms. *Journal of Political Economy* 94: 614–641.

Laffont, J.-J., and J. Tirole. 1987. Repeated Auctions of Incentive Contracts, Investment and Bidding Parity, with an Application to Takeovers. Mimeo, University of Toulouse.

Lazear, E., and S. Rosen. 1981. Rank-Order Tournaments as Optimal Labor Contracts. *Journal of Political Economy* 89: 841–864.

Leibenstein, H. 1966. Allocative Efficiency as "X-Inefficiency." *American Economic Review* 56: 392–415.

Lewellen, W. 1968. *Executive Compensation in Large Industrial Corporations*. New York: Columbia University Press.

Lewellen, W. 1971. *The Ownership Income of Management*. New York: Columbia University Press.

Lippman, S., and R. Rumelt. 1982. Uncertain Imitability: An Analysis of Interfirm Differences in Efficiency Under Competition. *Bell Journal of Economics* 13: 418–438.

Lucas, R. 1967. Adjustment Costs and the Theory of Supply. *Journal of Political Economy* 75: 321–339.

Lucas, R. 1978. On the Size Distribution of Business Firms. *Bell Journal of Economics* 9: 508–523.

MaCaulay, S. 1963. Non-Contractual Relations in Business. *American Sociological Review* 28: 55–70.

MacLeod, B., and J. Malcomson. 1986. Implicit Contracts, Incentive Compatibility and Involuntary Unemployment. Mimeo, Queen's University.

Malcomson, J. 1984. Work Incentives, Hierarchy, and Internal Labor Markets. *Journal of Political Economy* 92: 486–507.

Manne, H. 1965. Mergers and the Market for Corporate Control. *Journal of Political Economy* 73: 110–120.

March, J. 1962. The Business Firm as a Political Coalition. *Journal of Politics* 24: 662–678.

Marris, R. 1964. *The Economic Theory of "Managerial" Capitalism*. London: Macmillan.

Marshak, J., and R. Radner. 1972. *Economic Theory of Teams*. New Haven: Yale University Press.

Maskin, E. 1985. Unpublished Notes on Public Goods with Correlated Values. Harvard University.

Masten, S. 1984. The Organization of Production: Evidence From the Aerospace Industry. *Journal of Law and Economics* 27: 403–418.

Milgrom, P. 1981. Good News and Bad News: Representation Theorems and Applications. *Bell Journal of Economics* 12: 380–391.

Milgrom, P. 1986. Quasi-Rents, Influence, and Organization Form. Mimeo, Yale University.

Mirrlees, J. 1974. Notes on Welfare Economics, Information and Uncertainty. In *Essays in Economic Behavior in Uncertainty*, ed. M. Balch, D. McFadden, and S. Wu. Amsterdam: North-Holland.

Mirrlees, J. 1975. The Theory of Moral Hazard and Unobservable Behavior, Part I. Mimeo, Nuffield College, Oxford.

Monteverde, K., and D. Teece. 1982. Supplier Switching Costs and Vertical Integration in the Automobile Industry. *Bell Journal of Economics* 13: 206–213.

Mookherjee, D. 1984. Optimal Incentive Schemes with Many Agents. *Review of Economic Studies* 51: 433–446.

Myerson, R., and M. Satterthwaite. 1983. Efficient Mechanisms for Bilateral Trading. *Journal of Economic Theory* 28: 265–281.

Nalebuff, B., and J. Stiglitz. 1983. Prices and Incentives: Towards a General Theory of Compensation and Competition. *Bell Journal of Economics* 14: 21–43.

Nash, J. 1950. The Bargaining Problem. *Econometrica* 18: 155–162.

Nash, J. 1953. Two-Person Cooperative Games. *Econometrica* 21: 128–140.

Nelson, R., and S. Winter. 1982. *An Evolutionary Theory of Economic Change*. Cambridge, Mass.: Harvard University Press.

Parsons, D. 1984. The Employment Relationship: Job Attachment, Work Effort, and the Nature of Contracts. In *Handbook of Labor Economics*, ed. O. Ashenfelter and E. Lazear. Amsterdam: North-Holland.

Pettigrew, A. 1972. Information Control as a Power Resource. *Sociology* 6: 187–204.

Piore, M., and C. Sabel, 1984. *The Second Industrial Divide*. New York: Basic Books.

Posner, R. 1972. The Appropriate Scope of Regulation in the Cable Television Industry. *Bell Journal of Economics* 3: 98–129.

Pratt, J., and R. Zeckhauser. 1985. Incentive-Based Decentralization: Expected Externality Payments Induce Efficient Behavior in Groups. In *K. Arrow and Economic Theory*, ed. G. Feiwel. London: Macmillan.

Prescott, E., and M. Visscher. 1980. Organization Capital. *Journal of Political Economy* 88: 446–461.

Robinson, E. 1958. *The Structure of Competitive Industry*, revised edition. University of Chicago Press.

Rogerson, W. 1985. The First-Order Approach to Principal–Agent Problems. *Econometrica* 53: 1357–1368.

Rosen, S. 1982. Authority, Control, and the Distribution of Earnings. *Bell Journal of Economics* 13: 311–323.

Ross, S. 1973. The Economic Theory of Agency: The Principal's Problem. *American Economic Review* 63: 134–139.

Rubinstein, A. 1982. Perfect Equilibrium in a Bargaining Model. *Econometrica* 50: 97–109.

Sah, R., and J. Stiglitz. 1985. Human Fallibility and Economic Organization. *American Economic Review* 75: 292–297.

Sappington, D., and J. Stiglitz. 1987. Information and Regulation. In *Public Regulation: New Perspectives on Institutions and Policies*, ed. E. Bailey. Cambridge, Mass.: MIT Press.

Scharfstein, D. 1985a. The Disciplinary Role of Takeovers. Mimeo, Massachusetts Institute of Technology.

Scharfstein, D. 1985b. Product Market Competition and Managerial Slack. Mimeo, Massachusetts Institute of Technology.

Schein, E. 1984. Coming to a New Awareness of Organizational Culture. *Sloan Management Review* 25: 3–16.

Scherer, F. 1980. *Industrial Market Structure and Economic Performance*, second edition. Chicago: Rand-McNally.

Shapiro, C., and J. Stiglitz. 1984. Equilibrium Unemployment as a Worker Discipline Device. *American Economic Review* 74: 433–444.

Shavell, S. 1979. Risk Sharing and Incentives in the Principal and Agent Relationship. *Bell Journal of Economics* 10: 55–73.

Shepard, A. 1986. Licensing to Enhance Demand for New Technologies. Mimeo, Yale University.

Shleifer, A. 1985. A Theory of Yardstick Competition. *Rand Journal of Economics* 16: 319–327.

Shleifer, A., and L. Summers. 1987. Hostile Takeovers and Breaches of Trust. Mimeo, Harvard University.

Shleifer, A., and R. Vishny. 1984. Greenmail, White Knights, and Shareholders' Interest. Mimeo, Massachusetts Institute of Technology.

Shleifer, A., and R. Vishny. 1986. Large Shareholders and Corporate Control. *Journal of Political Economy* 94: 461–488.

Simon, H. 1957. *Models of Man*. New York: Wiley.

Simon, H. 1976. *Administrative Behavior*, third edition. London: Macmillan.

Stigler, G. 1968. *The Organization of Industry*. Homewood, Ill.: Irwin.

Stiglitz, J. 1975. Incentives, Risk and Information: Notes Towards a Theory of Hierarchy. *Bell Journal of Economics* 6: 552–579.

Telser, L. 1980. A Theory of Self-Enforcing Agreements. *Journal of Business* 53: 27–44.

Tirole, J. 1986a. Procurement and Renegotiation. *Journal of Political Economy* 94: 235–259.

Tirole, J. 1986b. Hierarchies and Bureaucracies. *Journal of Law, Economics and Organization* 2: 181–214.

Viner, J. 1932. Cost Curves and Supply Curves. *Zeitschrift für Nationalökonomie* 3: 23–46. Reprinted in *Readings in Price Theory*, ed. G. Stigler and K. Boulding (Homewood, Ill.: Irwin, 1952).

Williamson, O. 1967. The Economics of Defense Contracting: Incentives and Performance. In *Issues in Defense Economics*, ed. R. McKean. New York: Columbia University Press.

Williamson, O. 1975. *Markets and Hierarchies: Analysis and Antitrust Implications*. New York: Free Press.

Williamson, O. 1976. Franchise Bidding for Natural Monopoly—In General and With Respect to CATV. *Bell Journal of Economics* 7: 73–107. Elaborated version: O. Williamson, *The Economic Institutions of Capitalism* (New York: Free Press, 1985), chapter 13.

Williamson, O. 1985. *The Economic Institutions of Capitalism*. New York: Free Press.

Williamson, O., M. Wachter, and J. Harris. 1975. Understanding the Employment Relation: The Analysis of Idiosyncratic Exchange. *Bell Journal of Economics* 6: 250–280.

Wilson, R. 1968. The Structure of Incentives for Decentralization under Uncertainty. In *La Decision*, ed. M. Guilbaud. Paris: CNRS.

Winter, S. 1971. Satisficing, Selection, and the Innovating Remnant. *Quarterly Journal of Economics* 85: 237–261.

Wolfson, M. 1985. Empirical Evidence of Incentive Problems and their Mitigation in Oil and Tax Shelter Programs. In *Principals and Agents: The Structure of Business*, ed. J. Pratt and R. Zeckhauser. Boston: Harvard Business School Press.

Part I

The Exercise of Monopoly Power

Part I concerns the behavior of a monopoly—in particular, single-product and multiple-product pricing (chapter 1), the choice of quality, spectrum of goods, and advertising (chapter 2), price discrimination (chapter 3), and vertical control (chapter 4).

A more general concern of these chapters is the exercise of monopoly power. That is, most of the phenomena considered here could be derived even in the presence of competitors as long as the firm retained some market power.

The study of monopoly is justified by expositional convenience. Trying to address strategic competition at the same time would complicate the derivations and would sometimes obscure the main points. The focus on monopoly also delays the introduction of game theory.

Monopoly

This chapter discusses various arguments made in favor of and in opposition to monopoly power. We will assume here that the goods produced by the monopolist are given, and that their qualities are known by the consumers. We will also assume that the monopolist charges the same price per unit of good for each good produced. (More specifically, there is no price discrimination at a given point of time. We will, however, consider intertemporal price discrimination.)

The best-known monopoly distortion, that related to pricing strategy, will be tackled in section 1.1. In contrast with the behavior of a competitive firm whose product demand is infinitely elastic by definition (and which takes the price as given), a firm exercising monopoly power over a given market can raise its price above marginal cost without losing all its clients. Such behavior leads to a price that is too high and to a "dead-weight" welfare loss for society (unless the firm is able to "price-discriminate" perfectly, as we shall see in chapter 3).

We shall recall the main aspects of the pricing behavior of a single-product monopolist. We shall then consider a multiproduct monopolist with interrelated production costs of or interrelated demands for his various products. Last, we shall study the intertemporal pricing behavior of a durable-good monopolist.

Other distortions may also exist. On the one hand, both theory and practice suggest that it is more difficult for the owners of a firm to keep control over its costs when the firm has monopoly power on the product market. Thus, a monopolist may produce given outputs at a higher cost than a competitive firm (section 1.2). On the other hand, the monopoly rent may give rise to a contest among several firms to obtain or secure it. This contest may involve socially wasteful expenditures, which partly dissipate the monopoly rent. Therefore, monopoly profit should not always be taken into account in the expression of welfare (section 1.3).

Naturally, the conclusions would hold as well for monopsony power (i.e., monopoly power in the input markets).

1.1 Pricing Behavior

The best-known monopoly distortion results from the monopolist's pricing behavior. To focus on this distortion, we assume that the monopolist's products are given and that their existence and quality are known to consumers. We start by reviewing the distortionary markup by a monopoly producer of a single good. We then study the multiproduct monopolist. Last, we consider the issue of intertemporal pricing by a durable-good monopoly.

1.1.1 A Single-Product Monopolist

1.1.1.1 The Inverse Elasticity Rule

Let $q = D(p)$ be the demand for the good produced by the monopoly, with inverse demand function $p = P(q)$. Let $C(q)$ be the cost of producing q units of this good. Assume that demand is differentiable and decreasing with the price (i.e., $D'(p) < 0$),[1] and that cost is differentiable and increasing with the output. A profit-maximizing monopolist chooses the monopoly price p^m so as to

$$\max_{p} \left[p D(p) - C(D(p)) \right].$$

The first-order condition for this problem is

$$p^m - C'(D(p^m)) = -\frac{D(p^m)}{D'(p^m)},$$

or

$$\frac{p^m - C'}{p^m} = \frac{1}{\varepsilon}, \tag{1.1}$$

where $\varepsilon = -D'p^m/D$ denotes the demand elasticity at the monopoly price p^m. Letting $q^m \equiv D(p^m)$ denote the monopoly output, one can rewrite the first-order condition as the equality between marginal revenue and marginal cost:

$$\mathrm{MR}(q^m) \equiv P(q^m) + P'(q^m)q^m = C'(q^m).$$

For now, we ignore the second-order condition of the maximization problem. Equation 1.1 indicates that the relative "markup"—the ratio between the profit margin (price minus marginal cost) and the price; also called the

Lerner index—is inversely proportional to the demand elasticity. The monopoly sells at a price greater than the socially optimal price, which is its marginal cost.[2] The price distortion is larger when consumers, facing a price increase, reduce their demand only slightly. The intuition, of course, is that the monopolist is more wary of the perverse effect of a high price on consumption when consumers react to a price increase by greatly reducing their demand.

If the elasticity of demand is independent of price (the demand function is $q = kp^{-\varepsilon}$, where k is a positive constant), the Lerner index is constant. The monopolist adjusts his price to shocks on the marginal cost by using a constant (relative) markup rule. For instance, if his technology exhibits constant returns to scale so that the marginal cost is equal to the average cost or unit cost and if the elasticity of demand is 2, the monopolist systematically charges twice the unit cost. Thus, if we observe a monopolist using such a "rule of thumb," we should not necessarily conclude that this monopolist's pricing behavior is not (privately) optimal.

More generally, observe that a monopoly always operates in a price region such that the elasticity of demand (from equation 1.1) exceeds 1. Where the elasticity is lower than 1, the monopolist's revenue—and, *a fortiori*, his profit—are decreasing in quantity (i.e., increasing in price).

It is a simple yet a very general property of monopoly pricing that the monopoly price is a nondecreasing function of marginal cost. To see this, consider two alternative cost functions for the monopolist: $C_1(\cdot)$ and $C_2(\cdot)$. Assume that these cost functions are differentiable, and that $C_2'(q) > C_1'(q)$ for all $q > 0$. No other assumption on these cost functions is required. Let p_1^m and q_1^m denote the monopoly price and quantity when the cost function is $C_1(\cdot)$; p_2^m and q_2^m are defined similarly. When the cost function is $C_1(\cdot)$, the monopolist prefers charging p_1^m rather than any other price. In particular, he could charge price p_2^m and sell quantity q_2^m. Thus,

$$p_1^m q_1^m - C_1(q_1^m) \geqslant p_2^m q_2^m - C_1(q_2^m). \tag{1.2}$$

Similarly, the monopolist prefers to charge p_2^m rather than p_1^m when his cost function is $C_2(\cdot)$:

---

1. See the introduction.

2. See the introduction.

$$p_2^m q_2^m - C_2(q_2^m) \geqslant p_1^m q_1^m - C_2(q_1^m). \qquad (1.3)$$

Adding equations 1.2 and 1.3 yields

$$[C_2(q_1^m) - C_2(q_2^m)] - [C_1(q_1^m) - C_1(q_2^m)] \geqslant 0, \qquad (1.4)$$

or

$$\int_{q_2^m}^{q_1^m} [C_2'(x) - C_1'(x)]dx \geqslant 0. \qquad (1.5)$$

Because $C_2'(x) > C_1'(x)$ for all x, equation 1.5 implies that $q_1^m \geqslant q_2^m$. In other words, the monopoly price is a non-decreasing function of marginal cost.[3]

1.1.1.2   The Dead-Weight Loss

Equation 1.1 provides a quantification of price distortion, but from a normative viewpoint the appropriate measure of distortion is the loss of social welfare. To measure the latter, we compare the total surplus at the monopoly price with that at the competitive (marginal-cost) price. The total surplus is equal to the sum of the consumer surplus and the producer surplus (or profit), or to the difference between total consumer utility and production costs.[4] In figure 1.1 this surplus is represented by the area $DGAD$ under marginal-cost pricing and by the area $DEFAD$ under monopoly pricing.

The net consumer surplus under monopoly is the area of the "triangle" CDE in figure 1.1. The monopolist's profit is equal to the total revenue, $p^m q^m$, minus the integral of the marginal cost—i.e., equal to the area of the "trapezoid" $ACEF$. Thus, the "dead-weight" welfare loss is equal to the area of the "triangle" EFG. (These are a proper triangle and trapezoid only if the demand and marginal-cost curves are linear.)

The welfare loss does not necessarily decrease with the elasticity of demand, even though the relative markup does (from equation 1.1). The monopoly situations for which we observe strong price distortions correspond to those in which demand elasticity is low, so that consumers decrease their quantity demanded only slightly in response to a unit price increase. Consequently, in precisely these situations, price changes do not affect quantity consumed very much; rather, they elicit a large

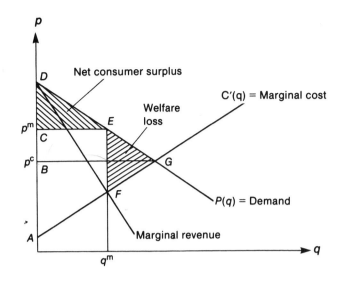

Figure 1.1

monetary transfer from consumers to the firm. Hence, we cannot conclude that the welfare loss is monotonic in the elasticity of demand.

Exercise 1.1**   In a monopolized industry, the demand function has a constant elasticity: $q = D(p) = p^{-\varepsilon}$ where $\varepsilon > 1$ is the elasticity of demand. Marginal cost is constant and equal to c.

(i) Show that a social planner (or a competitive industry) would yield a total welfare of

$$W^c = c^{1-\varepsilon}/(\varepsilon - 1).$$

(ii) Compute the welfare loss, WL, under monopoly.

(iii) Show that the ratio WL/W^c (relative dead-weight loss) increases with ε, that WL is nonmonotonic in ε, and that the fraction Π^m/W^c of potential consumer surplus that can be captured by the monopolist increases with ε. Discuss the result. (Note that the "size" of the market changes with ε.)

Exercise 1.2*   Suppose that all consumers have unit demand. They buy 0 or 1 unit of the good produced by the monopolist. They are identical, and they have willingness to pay (valuation) $\bar{s}$ for the good. Show that monopoly pricing does not create a welfare loss.

---

3. This style of proof is familiar from the literature on incentives. Though less familiar in industrial organization, it will be used occasionally in this book.

The monopoly price may be nonunique owing to nonconcavities in the profit function. It is then a correspondence rather than a function. The result

then says that *any* optimal price for cost function $C_2(\cdot)$ (weakly) exceeds *any* optimal price for cost function $C_1(\cdot)$.

4. This criterion ignores problems of income distribution; see the introduction.

Of course, the dead-weight welfare loss represents only what can be gained from moving from a monopoly situation to an ideal situation. It thus yields an upper bound on the efficiency gain to be realized by correcting monopoly pricing. The actual efficiency gain must be computed for any policy intervention that does not yield marginal-cost pricing. To put it another way, a high total distortion associated with the monopolization of an industry is a signal that some public intervention might be desirable, but it does not suggest a course of action. An analyst or a government should begin analyzing the causes of monopolization (see chapter 8), as well as the set of potential interventions. The latter will depend crucially on the information available to the social planner concerning industry conditions (cost structure, demand).

Remark The welfare loss can be measured empirically by estimating the demand curve and the marginal-cost curve. For a discussion of methodology and results see Scherer 1980, p. 461. Harberger's (1954) estimate of a total welfare loss not exceeding 0.1 percent of the gross national product implied that economists were wasting their time focusing on the monopoly-pricing problem and gave rise to much controversy about both the data and the methodology.[5] Industrial-organization economists are, in general, mainly interested in industries which are monopolized to at least some extent. An economy-average number understates the typical distortion in those industries because it includes many fairly competitive industries in the sample. The dead-weight loss is only one of the harmful effects of monopoly, as we shall see below. (Including some of the other distortions, such as those associated with rent seeking, some researchers found welfare losses of up to 7 percent of GNP. See Cowling and Mueller 1978 and Jenny and Weber 1983; see Scherer 1980 for a skeptical view of these high estimates.)

1.1.1.3 The Effect of Commodity Taxation

Consider one possible policy prescription for restoring the social optimum in the presence of monopoly. Suppose that the government taxes monopoly output at the rate t.

Then the monopolist chooses p to

$$\max_{p}[p\,D(p+t) - C(D(p+t))],$$

from which it follows that

$$D(p+t) + D'(p+t)(p - C') = 0$$

or

$$[D(p+t) - t\,D'(p+t)] + D'(p+t)(p+t-C') = 0.$$

To restore the social optimum, marginal cost C' must coincide with the price faced by the consumers ($p + t$) and thus with the marginal utility in terms of money to the consumers. Therefore, we must set

$$t = D(p^c)/D'(p^c) < 0$$

(i.e., $t/p^c = -1/\varepsilon$), where p^c is the competitive price (determined by the intersection of the demand and marginal-cost curves in figure 1.1). Since $t < 0$, we must subsidize the output of the monopolist. We can explain this rather paradoxical result as follows: The problem with monopoly pricing is that it induces consumers to consume too little of the good. In order to achieve an efficient allocation of resources, we induce them to consume more by subsidizing the good.

Exercise 1.3* A monopolist's marginal cost of supplying a good to consumers is $\tilde{c} = c + t$ (where t is a unit commodity tax). Let $p^m(\tilde{c})$ denote the corresponding monopoly price.

(i) Compute $dp^m/d\tilde{c}$ for the following demand functions: $p = q^{-1/\varepsilon}$, $p = \alpha - \beta q^\delta$, $p = a - b\ln q$.

(ii) Sumner (1981) uses an ingenious approach to estimate the elasticity of demand—and thus the degree of monopoly power—in the American cigarette industry. He notes that in the United States, commodity taxes—and therefore the generalized cost $\tilde{c}$—vary across states. Although data on c are hard to obtain, data on t are readily available. Sumner uses varying levels of taxation across states to estimate the elasticity of demand. Bulow and Pfleiderer (1983) argue that the method has limited applicability. What do you think?

---

5. In particular, Harberger assumed unit demand elasticities, which creates a downward bias in the estimation of welfare losses. Furthermore, Bergson (1973) showed that Harberger's partial-equilibrium approach can be a major source of bias on either side. Another drawback of Harberger's approach is the identification of the competitive profit rate with the *mean* (cross-sectional) profit rate, which incorporates monopoly profits.

Despite the simplicity of the result, the subsidy solution has only a few advocates. Its critics point out that the concept of total surplus accords equal weight to consumer surplus and to the monopoly profit of the firm's shareholders, so that a pure transfer from consumers to shareholders has no reported social cost. The implementation of such a policy raises further problems. It is difficult for the government to estimate demand elasticity and to determine the marginal cost of the monopolist. Of course, it is in the firm's self-interest for the state to err in granting too large a subsidy.[6] Faced with this situation, the firm will seek to "inflate" the subsidy by its actions and in its dealings with the government. To use such a subsidy policy in a discriminating way, the government will most likely need to obtain some information about demand and cost directly, and not through the monopolist. Demand information can be obtained through sampling, although this technique is potentially expensive and may be hard to implement if the monopolist supplies only a few large customers. Cost information is even harder to extract, because the monopolist is, for obvious reasons, reluctant to release accurate estimates of its cost structure.[7] Alternatively, the government can offer the monopolist incentives to reveal its cost structure. For instance, it can reward (in a lump-sum way) the monopolist when the latter charges low prices. The government may thus induce the monopolist to charge a low price when he has a low marginal cost. This type of policy tends to reduce the dead-weight loss.

By considering "sophisticated" incentive schemes, we are moving away from industrial organization proper into regulation—a realm in which a subsidy policy is not optimal any longer, as there exist alternative regulatory schemes that yield lower welfare losses.[8] Why stay away from regulation? First, it is a large field that can hardly be treated in a concise manner; second, its theoretical foundations require some familiarity with the theory of incentives, which would require further developments. The point here is simply that the government's incomplete information about market conditions creates difficulties for intervention. For a correct treatment of the matter, informational asymmetries should be explicitly introduced into the model; then the efficiency of various types of intervention (including commodity taxation) should be analyzed.

1.1.1.4 Second-Order Conditions

Let us return briefly to second-order conditions, which require concavity or quasi-concavity of the objective function. It happens that the profit function of the monopolist is not always concave even if his cost function is convex. The problem is that the revenue function may not be concave—that is, marginal revenue may not be decreasing everywhere. The second derivative of the revenue function $R(p) = p D(p)$ is

$$R''(p) = 2 D'(p) + p D''(p).$$

Our assumption that demand is downward sloping ensures that the first term in $R''(p)$ is negative. The second term is nonpositive if demand is linear or, more generally, concave. If demand is convex, the revenue function—and thus the profit function—may not be concave.[9]

Exercise 1.4* Assume that demand has constant elasticity ε:

$$q = D(p) = p^{-\varepsilon}.$$

Suppose that the cost function is convex. Show that the monopolist's profit function is quasi-concave if $\varepsilon > 1$.

1.1.2 Multiproduct Monopoly

Consider now the case of a multiproduct firm which has monopoly power over all the goods it manufactures. It

---

6. The "envelope theorem" supports this. Where Π denotes the monopolist's profit, $d\Pi/dt = (p - C')D' = -D$ using the first-order condition.

7. The monopolist may not know the exact cost structure himself, of course. What matters for the argument, however, is simply that the monopolist has private information about the technology.

8. For an analysis of optimal price regulation under asymmetric information about the technology, see the pioneering papers by Baron and Myerson (1982) and Sappington (1982) on the single-product monopolist and that by Sappington (1983) on the multiproduct monopolist. For an analysis of optimal price and

cost regulation under asymmetric information about the technology and under moral hazard, see Laffont and Tirole 1986. For surveys of this line of research and further topics (*ex ante* and *ex post* competition, dynamics, etc.), see Baron 1986, Besanko and Sappington 1987, Caillaud et al. 1988, and Sappington and Stiglitz 1987.

9. If the objective function is not concave, the achievement of the social optimum by a subsidy policy becomes still more difficult. (The monopolist's reaction function—the determination of the price, p, depending on the tax, t, imposed—is discontinuous. See Guesnerie and Laffont 1978 for a discussion of this point.)

produces goods $i = 1, \ldots, n$, charges prices $p = (p_1, \ldots, p_n)$, and sells quantities $q = (q_1, \ldots, q_n)$, where $q_i = D_i(p)$ is the demand for good i. The cost of producing the output vector is $C(q_1, \ldots, q_n)$.

In subsection 1.1.1 we analyzed the case of a single-product monopoly or, equivalently, that of a multi-product monopoly for which demands are independent: $q_i = D_i(p_i)$ (the demand for good i depends only on the price of good i) *and* total cost can be decomposed in n subcosts:

$$C(q_1, \ldots, q_n) = \sum_{i=1}^{n} C_i(q_i)$$

(cost separability). The pricing problem can then be decomposed into n subsidiary pricing problems. Equation 1.1 tells us that the monopolist imposes a higher markup on those goods with a lower elasticity of demand. We will derive a straightforward implication of this result in chapter 3, where we will reinterpret a manufacturer selling the same good in several distinct markets as a multi-product monopolist. This result represents the simplest form of "Ramsey pricing," which depicts how markups should vary with the elasticities of demand.[10]

More generally, the multiproduct monopolist maximizes

$$\sum_{i=1}^{n} p_i D_i(p) - C(D_1(p), \ldots, D_n(p)).$$

This results in the following formula, which generalizes the equality between marginal revenue and marginal cost:

$$\left(D_i + p_i \frac{\partial D_i}{\partial p_i} \right) + \sum_{j \neq i} p_j \frac{\partial D_j}{\partial p_i} = \sum_{j} \frac{\partial C}{\partial q_j} \frac{\partial D_j}{\partial p_i} \quad \text{for all } i. \quad (1.6)$$

To analyze this formula, we will consider the two polar cases. (The second-order conditions for equation 1.6 will not be discussed here.) We will phrase the results in terms of the biases that would result if the firm were operated by n independent divisions, each producing one good and maximizing profit on that good.

1.1.2.1   Dependent Demands, Separable Costs

Let us assume that the total cost can be split into n costs:

$$C(q_1, \ldots, q_n) = \sum_{i=1}^{n} C_i(q_i).$$

Then, after some algebraic manipulation, equation 1.6 becomes

$$\frac{p_i - C_i'}{p_i} = \frac{1}{\varepsilon_{ii}} - \sum_{j \neq i} \frac{(p_j - C_j') D_j \varepsilon_{ij}}{R_i \varepsilon_{ii}},$$

where $\varepsilon_{ii} \equiv -(\partial D_i / \partial p_i)(p_i / D_i)$ is the own elasticity of demand (which we will assume to be positive), $\varepsilon_{ij} \equiv -(\partial D_j / \partial p_i)(p_i / D_j)$ is the cross-elasticity of demand for good j with respect to the price of good i, and $R_i \equiv p_i D_i$ is the revenue associated with good i.

First, consider the case of goods that are *substitutes*, i.e., for all j different from i, $\partial D_j / \partial p_i > 0$ or $\varepsilon_{ij} < 0$. In this case, the Lerner index for each good i exceeds the inverse of the own elasticity of demand. This can be explained simply: An increase in the price of good i raises the demand for good j. So, if the firm is decomposed into n divisions, each producing and marketing its own good and maximizing its own revenue ($R_i - C_i$), each division charges too low a price from the point of view of the aggregate firm. The divisions are *de facto* competitors because of the substitutability between their goods. Hence, they must be given incentives to raise their own price (eliminate the externalities between them).

Second, for *complements* ($\partial D_j / \partial p_i < 0$ for all j different from i), the inverse of the own elasticity of demand exceeds the Lerner index for each good. This can easily be understood: A decrease in the price of good i raises the demand for good j. An interesting phenomenon that may arise with complements is that one or several of the goods may be sold below marginal cost (so their Lerner index may be negative), so as to raise the demand for other goods sufficiently. This possibility will be demonstrated in chapter 3.

---

10. See Ramsey 1927 and Robinson 1933. The result is due to Robinson; the link with Ramsey's contribution was made later. The traditional Ramsey context is that of a multiproduct firm whose objective is the maximization of social welfare rather than profit. Boiteux (1956) constructed a general-equilibrium model in which the social planner, having authority over some public firms, maximizes a social-welfare function subject to the constraint that these firms make non-negative profits. The general Ramsey formula naturally depends on the cross-elasticities of demand and on the elasticities of supply. On this topic see also Baumol and Bradford 1970, Sheshinski 1986, and Brown and Sibley 1986.

These models contain no endogenous explanation of the budget constraint for the public sector.

Exercise 1.5* A firm has monopoly power on the production of nuts (good 1) and bolts (good 2). Nuts and bolts are perfect complements. Thus, demand depends only on the total price: $D_i(p_1, p_2) = D(p_1 + p_2)$ for all i. Show that equation 1.6 boils down to the monopoly-pricing formula in a single composite market.

An Application: Intertemporal Pricing and Goodwill

Consider a monopoly producer of a single good. This good is sold in two consecutive periods: $t = 1, 2$. At date 1 the demand is $q_1 = D_1(p_1)$ and the production cost is $C_1(q_1)$; at date 2 the demand is $q_2 = D_2(p_2, p_1)$ and the production cost is $C_2(q_2)$. There is a goodwill effect, in that a lower first-period price raises first-period demand and raises second-period demand as well: $\partial D_2 / \partial p_1 < 0$.[11] The monopolist's profit is thus

$$p_1 D_1(p_1) - C_1(D_1(p_1))$$
$$+ \delta(p_2 D_2(p_2, p_1) - C_2(D_2(p_2, p_1))),$$

where δ is the discount factor. Letting $\tilde{D}_2 \equiv \delta D_2$ and $\tilde{C}_2 \equiv \delta C_2$, we can rewrite this profit as that of a multiproduct monopoly with interdependent demands. The two economic goods are the single good at the two different dates. From our previous analysis, we can conclude the following: As $\partial D_1 / \partial p_2 = 0$, the monopolist charges the monopoly price in the second period conditional on the goodwill accumulated in the first (in other words, the second-period Lerner index is equal to the inverse of the second-period elasticity of demand). In the first period, however, the monopolist charges a price under the static monopoly price, i.e., under the price that maximizes $p_1 D_1(p_1) - C_1(D_1(p_1))$. This is very natural, because the monopolist realizes that a lower price today raises demand tomorrow. He then takes a dynamic perspective by sacrificing some short-run profits to raise future profits.

1.1.2.2 Independent Demands, Dependent Costs

Let us now assume that the demand for good i depends on its price only: $q_i = D_i(p_i)$. Designing a taxomony for dependent costs is a bit more complex than designing one for dependent demands. Indeed, although in the dependent-demand case one can easily envision a set of divisions, each in charge of one product, it may be rather unnatural to separate total cost into several components. Yet there are some cases in which such a decomposition may be reasonable. The application below, also drawn from an intertemporal problem, illustrates this. Before turning to the application, however, the reader would do well to tackle the following exercise.

Exercise 1.6** A power plant (or a hotel, or an airline) faces two types of demand: off-peak ($q_1 = D_1(p_1)$) and peak ($q_2 = D_2(p_2)$), where $D_1(p) = \lambda D_2(p)$ with $\lambda < 1$. (For simplicity, the demands are independent.) The marginal cost of production is c (as long as capacity is not satiated). The marginal cost of investing one unit of capacity is γ. The same capacity serves peak and off-peak demands.[12]

(i) Show that if off-peak demand is small relative to peak demand (where "small" is to be defined), the monopolist equates marginal revenues to c and $(c + \gamma)$ respectively.

(ii) Treat the case in which off-peak demand is not small. Solve the case in which demands have constant elasticity.

Application: Learning by Doing

In some industries, cost reductions are achieved over time simply because of learning. Through repetition of its activity, the firm gains proficiency. Learning by doing is especially apparent in industrial activity. For example, in the 1920s the commander of Wright-Patterson Air Force Base noted that the number of direct labor hours required to assemble a plane decreased as the total number of

---

11. The "reduced-form" demand function is not quite satisfactory. The rational foundations of goodwill must be based on the analysis of consumer behavior; see chapter 2.

The astute reader may have noticed that the formalization of the demand curve in period 1 implicitly assumes that the monopolist chooses the two prices sequentially, i.e., does not commit himself about p_2 in period 1. Otherwise, with rational consumers living for two periods, the announcement of a low p_2 in period 1 encourages the consumers to try the good, because they will enjoy a high surplus if they like the good. In this case, D_1 decreases with p_2.

The reader may also feel that calling $D_1(p_1)$ a "first-period demand function"

is a bit misleading, because rational consumers consider the possibility of repeat purchase when deciding whether to buy in the first period. Maybe the best way of thinking about this model at the current stage is as follows: One can envision two different groups of consumers at the two dates. The goodwill effect stems from word of mouth between the two generations. The more consumers there are at date 1, the more the generation-2 consumers learn about the characteristics or the existence of the product.

12. Optimal pricing by a firm producing several goods from the same capacity was first studied by Boiteux (1949).

aircraft assembled increased. More recently, learning by doing has been observed in the manufacture of semiconductors and computers.[13]

Consider a single-good monopolist producing at dates $t = 1, 2$. At date t, the demand is $q_t = D_t(p_t)$ (demand can be time dependent). The total cost is $C_1(q_1)$ at date 1 and $C_2(q_2, q_1)$ at date 2, where $\partial C_2 / \partial q_1 < 0$. We are thus assuming that a higher production at the beginning lowers the production cost later—i.e., that "practice makes perfect." The monopolist's profit is then

$$p_1 D_1(p_1) - C_1(D_1(p_1))$$
$$+ \delta(p_2 D_2(p_2) - C_2(D_2(p_2), D_1(p_1))).$$

The maximization of this profit with respect to p_1 and p_2 (i.e., equation 1.6) leads to equality between the marginal revenue and the marginal cost (with respect to current output) in the second period. However, in the first period the marginal revenue is lower than the marginal cost. Thus, the monopolist charges less than the one-period (myopic) monopoly price (the price that maximizes $p_1 D_1(p_1)$ $- C_1(D_1(p_1))$) in the first period; this policy enables him to sell more, which increases production and learning.[14] Put differently, the firm would underproduce in the first period if it were run by two consecutive managers maximizing short-term profit. Exercise 1.7 shows in a slightly more general model that one can obtain a further result if the demand is stationary and costs decrease with experience: that the firm's output grows over time. This result would be very natural if the firms behaved myopically. The decrease in marginal cost due to learning by doing leads to an output expansion. However, a nonmyopic firm also desires to produce much in the first period in order to learn. The result shows that the second effect is dominated by the first.

Exercise 1.7***[15] The monopoly producer of a single good has a constant unit cost $c(\omega(t))$ at time t, where $\omega(t)$ is the firm's "experience" at that date. (Assume $c > 0$, $c' < 0$, and $\lim_{t \to \infty} c(t) > 0$.) Time is continuous and runs from zero to infinity. Experience accumulates with

production: $d\omega(t)/dt = q(t)$, where $q(t)$ is production at date t. (Those who have done the empirical work have assumed, as we do, that production exhibits constant instantaneous returns to scale and that the appropriate measure of experience is cumulative output.) Let $R(q)$ denote the revenue function as a function of quantity (supposing demand is invariant). Assume $R' > 0$ and $R'' < 0$. Let r denote the interest rate. The monopolist's objective function is

$$\int_0^\infty [R(q(t)) - c(\omega(t))q(t)]e^{-rt}dt.$$

(i) Show that at each instant the monopolist sets marginal revenue equal to the average (discounted) unit cost in the future:

$$A(t) = \int_t^\infty c(\omega(s)) r e^{-r(s-t)} ds.$$

Hint: Consider the current cost and the future savings from changing $q(t)$ slightly.

(ii) Show that output increases over time.

1.1.3 A Durable-Good Monopolist

As was noted above, in the case of a product that gives rise to goodwill the firm ought to take a dynamic perspective and sacrifice some current profits to enhance future profits. Repeat purchases (which will be studied more generally in chapter 2) are an instance of a dynamic link between the periods: Customers are more likely to buy tomorrow if they do so today. Here we investigate another kind of intertemporal link on the demand side—one that is associated with the durability of goods. We now assume that the lifetime of the good exceeds the basic "period" (i.e. length of time between price revisions). In contrast with the goodwill paradigm for nondurable goods, a customer who buys a durable good today is unlikely to buy the same good tomorrow. Thus, the goods offered by the monopolist at two different dates are substitutes rather than complements. (Intertem-

---

13. One of the very first theoretical analyses of this phenomenon is Arrow 1961.

14. Learning by doing can also be viewed, to some extent, as a form of dynamic increasing returns to scale (see Scherer 1980, chapter 4). In particular, it is easily seen that a competitive equilibrium cannot exist under learning by

doing if instantaneous costs exhibit constant returns to scale (see Fudenberg and Tirole 1983). For an existence theorem with convex instantaneous production costs, see Rasmussen 1986.

15. This exercise is drawn from Fudenberg and Tirole 1983.

poral pricing by a durable-good monopolist is studied in much detail in the supplementary section; only the broad issues will be mentioned here.)

As we have seen, a durable-good monopolist creates his own competition. By selling today, he reduces demand tomorrow. As we will see, to sell to the residual demand, the monopolist lowers the price tomorrow. But consumers ought to expect a price decrease and hold back on their purchases today. These rational expectations hurt the monopolist.

Suppose that there are seven consumers. These consumers have "willingnesses to pay" or "valuations" $v = 1, 2, \ldots, 7$, respectively; v represents the present discounted value of the flow of services from the date of purchase on. Each consumer can derive utility from only one unit of the durable good. Assume further that there is no cost to produce the good and that the good is infinitely durable. Time is discrete: $t = 1, 2, \ldots$. The discount factor between periods is δ.

Assume first that the monopolist makes a once-and-for-all offer in the first period. (This thought experiment is meant to describe what happens in the absence of intertemporal effects.) The monopolist then charges the monopoly price, $p^m = 4$, and sells to consumers with valuation 4 to 7. (The monopoly profit is equal to 16.) Now consider the multiperiod model. Suppose that the monopolist charges 4 in period 1, and that consumers with valuations exceeding 4 accept. At the beginning of period 2, the monopolist is left with a residual demand, composed of the consumers with valuations 1 through 3. The monopolist is then tempted to charge a lower second-period price. For instance, if the second period is the last period at which the monopolist sells,[16] he charges the monopoly price corresponding to the residual demand, i.e., 2. Now, consider what happens when the consumers realize in period 1 that the monopolist will have, *ex post*, an incentive to lower the price in period 2. Consumers with high valuations may still accept paying 4 because they are eager to get the good.[17] However, the consumer with valuation 4, for instance, does not buy, because he would get a zero surplus whereas by waiting he could get

a positive surplus. Thus, the expectation of future price cuts reduces the demand in period 1.

To solve for the equilibrium, one must find a sequence of prices and consumers' expectations such that the expectations are rational given the firm's behavior and such that the firm's behavior is optimal given the consumers' expectations. The supplementary section explains how to do this. The equilibrium takes the form of a decreasing price sequence. Thus, the monopolist price-discriminates over time: He first charges a high price and sells only to the consumers who are most eager to buy the good. He then cuts his price to reach a slightly less eager clientele, and so on. This type of intertemporal discrimination behavior is often encountered in practice. For instance, books are often introduced in hardcover and then published in paperback form a few months or years later. It is well known that the production-cost difference between a hardcover and a paperback is fairly small. Thus, most of the price differential can be explained by the intertemporal-discrimination model. Another example is the first-run movie feature that is shown later on television, as a home video, on airlines, or at second-run moviehouses.

The flexibility that the monopolist has to adjust his price over time actually hurts him. Indeed, it can be shown that he would be better off if he could *ex ante commit* himself not to haggle, i.e., not to lower the price once high-valuation consumers have bought. ("No haggling" is actually optimal for the monopolist when he can commit. The fixed price is then, of course, the monopoly price.) This is explained by the fact that consumers wait for the day when the monopolist will cut his price. Here, price discrimination is *involuntary*—the firm would, *ex ante*, prefer not to be able to discriminate. Further, it can be shown that the profit loss for the monopolist under non-commitment becomes very high when his price adjustments are frequent; in fact, a conjecture due to Coase (and proved by other researchers; see supplementary section) states that when price adjustments become more and more frequent the monopolist's profit converges to zero. All trade takes place almost instantaneously, at prices

16. This may occur if the monopolist has "outside opportunities" or a fixed cost of production and/or marketing, which induce him to leave the market.

17. In order for the consumer to accept, v must satisfy $v - 4 \geq \delta(v - 2)$ or $v \geq (4 - 2\delta)/(1 - \delta)$. Such v's exist if the discount factor is not too close to unity—i.e., if consumers are impatient.

close to marginal cost. This result may be extreme, but it illustrates the issue well.

The supplementary section describes these points in a more formal way. It also discusses credibility of commitment and how, in practice, the monopolist can escape the Coase problem to some extent. That section is preceded by an example in which the monopolist produces a good that is recycled. The example is constructed in such a way that the modeling of the buyers' expectations is irrelevant. Thus, it forms a simple introduction to the durable-good problem. It also serves as a background for a brief discussion of monopoly power in the aluminum market.

1.1.4 Learning the Demand Curve

Throughout this chapter—and most of the book—we assume that the monopolist knows his demand curve perfectly. One way of justifying this is to assume that the monopolist conducts market surveys. But such surveys are costly and imperfect, and they always leave some residue of uncertainty about the demand curve. A complementary way of learning demand is to experiment by changing prices over time, which usually allows a better estimation of the demand curve than keeping one's price constant.

There is a small literature on optimal intertemporal pricing by a monopolist in a Bayesian setting.[18] There are few general conclusions about the price path to be followed by the monopolist, which obviously need not be monotonically increasing or decreasing over time. One thing is certain: When setting his price at a given date, the monopolist should not maximize expected current profit given his current (posterior) beliefs about the demand curve. Rather, he should also take into account the value of information thus obtained for future pricing. Aghion, Bolton, and Jullien (1988) and Lazear (1986) have studied models of a stable (nonstochastic) demand curve. Aghion et al. ask whether the monopolist eventually learns his demand curve and therefore charges the full-information monopoly price in the long run. The answer is intuitive. Suppose that it is initially known that the profit function is concave and continuous, but that its exact shape is unknown. Then the monopolist will not stop experimenting before reaching the monopoly price. For assume that he keeps his price constant from some period on. By charging a price slightly different from this price, he learns the slope of the profit function at this price, and he does not affect his expected current profit much. But learning the slope is very valuable for the future, and is therefore desirable. The trick is that, by altering his price by an arbitrarily small amount, the monopolist can make his experimentation costs arbitrarily small and still learn very useful information about the gradient of his objective function. Aghion et al. show that nonconcavities or discontinuities in the profit function may prevent the monopolist from learning his true monopoly price even if the demand curve is deterministic. (See Rothschild 1974 and McLennan 1984 for further results of finite experimentation in models that allow stochastic demands.) For instance, in the case of a nonconcave profit function the previous local-experimentation reasoning shows that the monopolist will eventually reach a local maximum of the profit function. To reach a global maximum, however, would require nonlocal experimentation (large changes in price), which may prove too costly if the discount factor is not sufficiently high. Thus, the monopolist may well settle for incomplete learning, even in the long run. Lazear (1986) looks at a simple case of learning and obtains a few interesting comparative-statics results. For instance, he shows how thin markets (such as that for a mansion) are likely to exhibit a fairly rigid intertemporal pricing pattern, whereas thicker markets (such as that for a very ordinary condominium) will yield larger price changes, the idea being that in a thick market the seller learns more about the demand curve from observing current demand. Similarly, markets with a very diffuse prior probability distribution on the demand curve will also exhibit large price changes.

1.1.5 Inventories

It is assumed throughout most of the book that, in each period, sales originate from current production. In practice, inventories may allow firms to separate production from sales. A sizable and interesting literature treats the

---

18. The papers usually abstract from other intertemporal pricing considerations mentioned in this chapter (intertemporal substitution by consumers for durable goods, inventories, goodwill, learning by doing) to focus on the learning aspect.

dynamics of quantity and price adjustments, when a firm faces shocks and can smooth its price path and its production path through inventory holdings. For instance, Blinder (1982) analyzes how a monopolist's production, inventories, and price adjust to demand shocks depending on whether these shocks are transitory or permanent. He assumes that in each period the marginal cost of production is increasing with output. Because of the cost convexity, the monopolist prefers a deterministic production to a random one with the same mean. In an intertemporal context, this means that he prefers a stable production to a fluctuating one. Thus, he would like to smooth demand shocks over time; this is exactly what inventories allow him to do. Consider first a transitory (single-period) upward shock in demand. In Blinder's model, in the absence of inventories, the price and the output adjust upward. They still do so in the presence of inventories, but to a lesser extent. The firm can reduce its inventory temporarily and replenish it later. The effect of a single-period increase in demand can thus be spread at the production stage over several periods. A permanent shock in demand cannot be smoothed as much. A high demand today implies a high demand in the future. That is, the marginal cost of production will be high tomorrow as well. Thus, production (as well as price) reacts more to a permanent shock than to a transitory shock.[19]

Another common theme in the literature on inventory behavior is the asymmetric price response to upward and downward shocks. In particular, Reagan (1982; see also Reagan and Weitzman 1982 for the competitive case) assumes that the monopolist can sell only from existing inventories. That is, there is a lag between the use of inputs and the availability of outputs. Current inventories act as a capacity constraint on sales in each period. When demand is high, output is determined entirely by inventories and the firm's price adjusts so as to clear the market (i.e., to satisfy demand). In contrast, when demand is low, the inventory constraint is not binding (sales are lower than inventories). The firm reacts both by choosing a low price and by reducing production. Because of this possibility of quantity adjustment for low demand, but not for high demand, the monopolist's price tends to react

more to upward shocks in demand than to downward shocks, as Reagan showed.[20]

1.2 Cost Distortions

In section 1.1 the emphasis was on the distortion on the demand side associated with a monopolist's pricing behavior. Monopoly power can also have perverse effects on the supply side. In particular, for given goods produced by the monopolist and given quantities of those goods to be supplied to the consumers, a monopolist may produce at a higher cost than would a competitive firm. In particular, it has often been suggested that firms in a monopoly situation tend to pay little attention to cost-cutting strategies, engage in slack, and so forth. Hicks (1935), for instance, noted that "the best of all monopoly profits is a quiet life." Machlup (1967) suggested that managerial slack can exist only if product markets are not perfectly competitive. These ideas may seem paradoxical; after all, the monopoly power is on the output side, and it is not easy to figure out why output distortions should have any effect on the cost of producing a given amount of a good.

To investigate this question, we must go back to the concept of cost function—more precisely, to the delegation problem. As was discussed in the chapter on the theory of the firm, a firm's shareholders, who wish to maximize profits, may have a hard time monitoring and controlling the activities of the firm's employees (executives, workers). The latter naturally seek objectives other than profit maximization, and unless the shareholders perfectly observe the technological environment and the employees' behavior (which is highly unrealistic) the firm is likely to engage in "X-inefficiency" (Leibenstein 1966). Indeed, we know from the chapter on the theory of the firm that, whatever the market structure, the firm will generally be able to engage in such inefficiency (i.e., that Machlup's suggestion holds only in very special cases). The question here is how this inefficiency is affected by market power on the product market.

As we saw in that preliminary chapter, shareholders

---

19. See also the discussion of Blinder in Schutte 1983.

20. For other references on this topic, see Phlips 1980, 1983 and Amihud and Mendelson 1983.

can use the performances of firms with related technologies (or demands) as a yardstick to control the performance of their firm. For instance, the shareholders may be suspicious of their firm's claim that it is facing adverse exogenous conditions when other firms known to face similar supply or demand conditions are doing well. In such a case, the managers' use of the excuse that "times are hard" to conceal slack and justify low profits is not as credible as when there is no other firm with which to compare their firm. This "tournament" idea—basing the incentive structure of one's firm on a comparison with the performance of related firms—does not rely on the existence of competition in the product market; one could, *a priori*, compare the performances of two power plants generating power in two independent regions. But the same type of argument can be made when firms compete on the product market. Thus, it seems natural to base the rewards of Ford managers on the performance of General Motors. It can even be argued that, because the exogenous conditions facing two firms are more likely to be correlated when these two firms are in the same product market, yardstick competition will *in practice* be more useful in industries with several competitors than in product-market monopolies.

This yardstick competition, when it is applicable, may explain why a competitive firm's managers are better controlled by the shareholders than a monopoly's managers.[21] However, Hicks' statement is only half-true: Although a monopoly's managers may engage in more slack (the "quiet life"), they may not benefit from it, because the slack is anticipated. In other words, their "participation" constraint may nevertheless be binding. A lower effort, say, is then offset by lower rewards.

1.3 Rent-Seeking Behavior

Section 1.1 described how monopoly pricing lowers consumer surplus and raises a firm's profit relative to a competitive behavior. The decrease in surplus exceeds the increase in profit by an amount equal to the dead-weight loss. Section 1.2 discussed how, for a given output, a monopoly position may inflate costs. These extra costs add to the dead-weight loss. This section discusses a third distortion associated with monopoly: the wasteful expenses incurred to secure or maintain a monopoly position.

Consider the rent associated with monopoly pricing. Abstracting from the control problem discussed in section 1.2 (so that the cost function can be defined independent of the monitoring technology), one can see that this rent is equal to the monopoly profit represented by the trapezoid *CEFAC* in figure 1.1. It is clear that the existence of this potential rent may lead to rent-seeking behavior. Firms will tend to spend money and exert effort to acquire the monopoly position; once installed in that position, they will tend to keep on spending money and exerting effort to maintain it.

A firm may incur both strategic and administrative expenses to obtain or keep a monopoly position. An example of a strategic expense is the research-and-development cost of obtaining a patent, which secures a monopoly position for the patented product (see chapter 10). Other examples are the accumulating of various forms of capital and the erecting of barriers to entry (chapter 8). Among the administrative expenses are the costs of lobbying and advertising campaigns aimed at influencing the public and its elected representatives ("Our firm is at the service of the consumer") and of legal defense against charges of antitrust violations.

Posner (1975) analyzes an extreme case of rent-seeking behavior in a contest between firms to become a monopolist and concludes that all monopoly rents should be counted in the costs of monopoly. In other words, the actual dead-weight loss is represented in figure 1.1 by the area *CEGFAC*. The two main axioms leading to this conclusion are the following.

(1) *rent dissipation:* The total expenditure by firms to obtain the rent is equal to the amount of the rent.

---

21. These reflections also imply that the public sector may be more inefficient than the private sector and, at the same time, not introduce any unnecessary inefficiency. The reason is that in many countries the public sector encompasses many industries that are "natural monopolies." Because of the existence of large fixed costs, say, an industry cannot be competitive and is nationalized or regulated (e.g., railroads, the postal service, electricity companies, the telecommunications industry). Hence, the public sector forms a biased sample in terms of product-market power, which naturally leads to more slack. However, the public sector may not be more inefficient *per se*, because many of its firms would have engaged in X-inefficiency anyway had they remained private.

(2) *socially wasteful dissipation:* This expenditure has no socially valuable by-products.[22]

Axiom 1 is the zero-profit free-entry condition. The idea is that entry (or increases in rent-seeking expenses) occurs until the expected rent—i.e., the probability of obtaining the rent times the amount of the rent—equals the rent-seeking cost for each firm. In equilibrium, for instance, ten firms may spend $1 each to have a 10 percent chance of obtaining $10 in rent, in which case the total cost is equal to the rent.

The plausibility of axiom 1 depends on the way the contest is organized. One cannot *a priori* measure rent dissipation without going into the microfoundations of the particular situation.[23] Axiom 1 may not be satisfied for many reasons (see Fisher 1985). First, monopolies can be obtained through luck rather than through foresight. An extreme and somewhat contrived case is that of the patenting of a fortuitous invention. Second, and more important, the contenders may not begin on equal footing; one firm may already have patents, access to particular mineral resources, private information about technology or demand, or incumbency advantages,[24] which will make it the most powerful candidate for the monopoly position. Because a firm's competitors may be less willing to spend money to obtain the monopoly position, it may be able to keep some of the rent. Consider the case in which firms must bid for the privilege of becoming a franchise monopoly. If all the firms are symmetric, the highest bid equals the (common) monopoly rent. With asymmetric bidders, however, the firm with the highest potential rent is able to keep some of the surplus. Third, even with symmetric or almost-symmetric firms, the rent need not be dissipated.[25]

Axiom 2 says that the expenses are socially wasteful. This may be the case when a regulated monopoly position (e.g., the allocation of import franchises) is allocated on the basis of lobbying influence.[26] However, if the same monopoly allocation is allocated through an auction, the expenses are received by the government and thus are not wasteful (in the symmetric case, axiom 1 is satisfied but axiom 2 is violated). There are also intermediate cases in which the expenses are somewhat wasteful. For instance, when air-travel prices and entry on routes were regulated in the United States, airlines competed for customers (the "rent") by offering lavish services. This type of rent-seeking behavior was not entirely wasteful, because customers enjoyed the services. However, the same consumers would have happily traded some of these services for price reductions corresponding to the cuts in services.

An interesting case is that of monopoly rents that are partially transferred to input suppliers. For example, a monopoly rent of 10 may be split into 5 for the owners of the firm and 5 for the workers if the union's bargaining power enables it to appropriate half of the pie. If this represents a simple transfer from the owners to the workers (the labor supply is not altered by the redistribution), the "dissipation" of monopoly profit involves no social loss; the recorded profit (equal to 5) simply underestimates the monopoly rent (equal to 10). However, if the labor supply is affected by the redistribution (for instance, if the existing workers respond to a higher wage by increasing the labor supply), some distortion in allocation is introduced as well.

The bottom line is that rent-seeking behaviors certainly waste some of the monopoly profit. That the monopoly profit may be part of the welfare loss associated with monopoly is a well-taken point. However, we should refrain from drawing any general conclusion about which fraction of the monopoly profit should be counted as a welfare loss. Only a careful description of the rent-seeking game can allow us to give an order of magnitude for this

---

22. A further assumption is that the inputs used to obtain the rent cannot be bid up (their supply is perfectly elastic). An example where they might be bid up is the case considered below of firms vying for favors from civil servants to obtain a regulated monopoly position. The rent, instead of being dissipated, may then be transferred to the civil servants (through bribes in extreme cases). But, as Krueger (1974) notes, becoming a civil servant in charge of the attribution of these rents may lead to rent-seeking behavior at that stage. A seminal paper on rent-seeking activities is Tullock 1967. A useful discussion can be found in Varian 1987.

23. See the discussion of patent races in chapter 10 of this book.

24. On incumbency advantages and Posner's approach, see Rogerson 1982.

25. See the discussion of preemption games in chapter 8.

26. The analysis here is very vague. What is needed is an equilibrium model in which lobbying activities have influence. Incomplete information ought to be the key to building such a model that would explain why lobbying occurs (information, collusion with decision makers, and so on) and whether lobbying expenses are socially wasteful.

fraction. As the rent-seeking games vary considerably in practice, we are obliged to analyze the issue case by case.

1.4 Concluding Remarks

Monopoly power results in high prices and a dead-weight welfare loss. There may also exist other, more subtle distortions, such as X-inefficiency and dissipation of the monopoly profit. (The next chapter considers a further distortion associated with product selection.)

Although pricing distortions are relatively well understood, cost distortions and rent-seeking behaviors have not yet been mastered by economists. To extend sections 1.2 and 1.3 at a theoretical level and to develop empirical methodologies to measure such distortions are two challenges posed by this chapter.

Some mitigating factors balance these perverse effects of monopoly power to an extent.

First, under increasing returns to scale, production by a single firm is technologically more efficient. Indeed, one of the most often-heard arguments in defense of the monopolization of an industry is that it prevents a wasteful duplication of fixed costs. Williamson (1968) questions the refusal of the U.S. courts to recognize a defense of economies of scale in horizontal-merger cases under the Clayton Act.[27] He argues that, under reasonable assumptions about the elasticity of demand, only a small reduction in fixed costs is necessary to offset the dead-weight loss created by the price increase in the case of a merger.

Second, as Joseph Schumpeter suggested, monopoly may be a necessary condition for a decent amount of research and development. In particular, innovation may require the assignment of monopoly property rights (patents).[28]

One cannot express a view on the merits of monopoly without considering its alternatives (e.g., competition, regulated monopoly) and the ways in which these alternatives may be fostered or obstructed (e.g., subsidies, antitrust proceedings, regulation). The relevance of the various arguments for and against monopoly eventually depends on the relative efficiency of all arrangements[29]

and on the information possessed by antitrust, regulatory, and other governmental authorities who promote them. This chapter, like most of this book, is more satisfactory at the positive level (How do firms behave on the product market?) than at the normative one (How should the government correct distortions?). Another challenge offered by this chapter is to develop the normative side.

---

27. Note, however, that economies of scale are considered in merger cases under the present Department of Justice guidelines.

28. We shall return to this argument in chapter 10.

29. For instance, chapter 6 is mainly concerned with the question of whether the pricing distortion is eliminated by competition.

1.5 Supplementary Section: Durable Goods and Limits on Monopoly Power

In this section, we examine how a durable-good monopolist creates his own future competition. The central theme is that his monopoly power can be eroded by the existence of this nurtured competition. We start with a case of a good that has a short lifetime, after which it can be recycled by a competitive industry. The purchasers of the good dispose of it at the end of the lifetime, and this allows us to ignore the purchasers' expectations about future prices. Although extreme, this case offers a simple and instructive introduction to the subject. In the second example (an "intertemporal price-discrimination problem"), we consider a good that does not depreciate, and we focus on the role of consumers' expectations. This example shows how consumers who anticipate a price decrease restrict their purchases.

1.5.1 Recycling

Consider the case of a monopolist producing a good that is recycled by a competitive industry. As a motivation for this case, recall the famous 1945 U.S. Supreme Court case concerning the Aluminum Company of America (Alcoa). Alcoa had about 90 percent of the primary aluminum market. It was considered a monopoly, and was prohibited from expanding (in that the court ordered that the aluminum plants built by the government during the war not be sold to Alcoa), which led rapidly to a more competitive market in primary aluminum.[30] Some economists opposed the court's decision on the grounds that there already existed an approximately competitive industry, independent from Alcoa, that recycled the aluminum Alcoa produced. If this secondary market for aluminum was taken into account, Alcoa's market share was only 64 percent. In fact, the price charged by Alcoa seemed moderate for a monopolist. Some even suggested that Alcoa's price was close to its marginal cost. Let us examine this argument using a simple model.[31]

Consider discrete time periods labeled $1, 2, \ldots, t$. Suppose that there is a demand function in each period: $q_t = D(p_t)$. This demand corresponds to the consumption demand for aluminum (primary or secondary). Let $p_t = P(q_t)$ be the inverse demand function. The aluminum consumed in period t is either lost or recycled by a competitive industry. Let $x_{t+1} \in [0, 1]$ be the fraction of the aluminum that is recycled. The recycling cost is $C(x_{t+1})$, where C is a convex, increasing function (i.e., the recycling technology exhibits decreasing returns). Moreover, assume that $C(0) = 0$, that $C'(0) = 0$, and that $C(1) = +\infty$ (it is impossible to recoup the entire input). If p_{t+1} is the price of aluminum (primary and secondary) in period $t + 1$, the recycled fraction x_{t+1} is

$$p_{t+1} = C'(x_{t+1})$$

(the competitive recycling industry recycles until its marginal cost equals the price of aluminum). We can then write x_{t+1} as an increasing function of p_{t+1}:

$$x_{t+1} = x(p_{t+1}).$$

Remark We are implicitly assuming that the profits from recycling (which are positive because the recycling cost function is convex) accrue to the recycling industry. In other words, the buyers of aluminum at date t dispose of their used aluminum at date $t + 1$. This assumption allows us to write a per-period demand function $p_t = P(q_t)$. As will be seen below, if the consumers are able to reuse the good or resell it, their demand at date t depends on the price they expect at date $t + 1$, say. The anticipations about future prices must then be modeled. One way of justifying this assumption is to envision a recycling industry composed of a large number of recycling firms so that none of them has any power on the (primary plus secondary) aluminum market (i.e., they are price takers). Each of these firms, however, has a local monopoly power in its geographically delineated input market. Thus, they can charge the monopoly price to obtain the scrapped aluminum; i.e., if the aluminum cannot be used without being recycled, it is obtained for free by the recycling

30. The Supreme Court did not actually hear the Alcoa case. Too many of the justices had conflicts—because the case had taken so long to get through the court system, a majority of the justices had served in the Justice Department while the case was in progress. A special three-judge Appeals Court panel was established to make the final resolution of the case.

31. The following discussion is based on Martin 1982. See also Gaskins 1974 and Swan 1980.

firms. Thus, the recycling firms are competitive only at the output level.

Suppose that primary aluminum is produced by a monopolist at a constant unit cost c. The monopoly profit in period t is

$$\pi_t = [P(q_t) - c](q_t - x_t q_{t-1}).$$

(Note that $q_0 = 0$.) q_t is the total production of aluminum (new plus recycled), and $q_t - x_t q_{t-1}$ is the new aluminum provided by the monopolist.

Assume that the monopolist maximizes the present discounted value of his profits:

$$\Pi = \sum_{t=1}^{\infty} \delta^t \pi_t, \quad \text{where } \delta = \frac{1}{1+r} < 1.$$

It is left as an exercise for the reader to show that, in a stationary state (in which, by definition, quantities and prices are constant over time),

$$(p - c)(1 - \delta x - x'P'q) = -P'(1 - x)q. \tag{1.7}$$

Furthermore, it is assumed that the second-order conditions are satisfied.

Since $x' > 0$ and $P' < 0$, equation 1.7 indicates that $p > c$. In fact, *the long-run price for aluminum can be close to the competitive price only if the fraction recycled is close to* 1. This does not seem to have been the situation in the Alcoa case (in addition, one must take into account the fact that during the period under consideration the demand was increasing greatly, so that even if x had been high Alcoa's market share would have been maintained).

Let

$$\varepsilon = -\frac{D'p}{D} = -\frac{P}{P'q}$$

be the elasticity of demand. Equation 1.7 can be rewritten as

$$\frac{p - c}{p} = \frac{1}{\varepsilon}\left(\frac{1 - x}{1 - \delta x - x'P'q}\right).$$

Since $\delta < 1$, $x < 1$, $x' > 0$, $P' < 0$, and $(p - c) > 0$,

$$\frac{p - c}{p} < \frac{1}{\varepsilon}.$$

Therefore, in this situation, *the relative profit margin (Lerner index) is lower than the one chosen by a monopolist in an industry without recycling* ($1/\varepsilon$). In fact, in the long run, consumers benefit from the existence of recycling. The following can also be shown:

• An improvement in the recycling technology diminishes the monopoly rent.[32] Indeed, when the recycling technology is very inefficient, almost none of the aluminum is recycled, and the monopoly realizes its static monopoly profit in every period.

• If consumers benefit from the existence of recycling in the long run, they take a loss when it is first introduced. Suppose that until period 2 there is no recycling. Compare market prices in period 1 depending on whether or not there will be a recycling industry starting in period 2. If the monopolist anticipates the future existence of recycling, he reduces his output relative to that of the static optimum (given by $(p - c)/p = 1/\varepsilon$) so that he will not "nurture" future competition. Therefore, prices are higher during period 1 for consumers. In the longer run, recycling increases the supply of the product, and—in spite of the initial reduction in monopoly output—the price decreases.

• Growth in the aluminum market increases the monopolist's profit margin. (Here, we assumed that the market was stationary.) The basic idea is that during a period of market growth, recycled aluminum—which depends on the lower past demand but not on the higher present demand—obtains a lower market share.

For an analysis of the decomposition of the technology of recycling of raw materials and a study of recycling proper and of the effects of vertical integration, see Martin 1982.

1.5.2 Durable Goods and Intertemporal Price Discrimination

Assume now that the consumers can enjoy a certain durable good during several periods. The price at which

---

32. The monopolist may benefit from an improvement in the recycling technology if its production cost c is high and the consumers are able to obtain a substantial part of the rent associated with recycling (in contrast with the assumption made above). Recycling then makes the good more desirable to the consumers. See, however, the discussion of intertemporal price discrimination below.

consumers are willing to buy the good today then depends on their expectation of the price at which they will be able to buy it tomorrow, because today's purchases are an (imperfect) substitute for tomorrow's. We first set up a simple two-period model, which illustrates the main ideas. We show that, whenever feasible, the manufacturer of the durable good prefers to lease it rather than to sell it. We then consider the general issue of intertemporal price discrimination and its most extreme form, the so-called Coase conjecture. This conjecture (now a result) asserts that the producer of an infinitely durable good loses all his monopoly power when the period between his price adjustments converges to zero. This result must be qualified by the fact that, in many situations, the monopolist may be able to recoup some of his monopoly power, as we will see. We then consider the implications of intertemporal price discrimination for the monopolist's choice of the durability of the good.

1.5.2.1 Leasing versus selling

When a good (e.g., a computer or a photocopying machine) is durable, its producer has the option to lease or to sell.[33] We will consider here the idea that a monopolistic producer of a durable good prefers leasing to avoid the problems of intertemporal credibility associated with selling. This idea can be illustrated with the help of a very simple model. There are two periods: $t = 1, 2$. The good produced and used during period 1 may be used again in period 2, with no depreciation. For simplicity, assume that after period 2 the good becomes obsolete (is replaced by a new product), and hence there is no demand for it. The model and the ideas can easily be generalized to the case in which the good does not become obsolete. To simplify the calculation, assume that the cost of producing this good is zero, so that the monopolist can produce as much as he wishes in each period without incurring any cost. The monopolist and the consumers have discount factor $\delta = 1/(1 + r)$, where r is the interest rate. The consumption (utilization) demand for this good in each period is $D(p) = 1 - p$.

The monopolist has two options: (1) to lease the good in each period and (2) to sell in each period. In the latter case, a resale market exists in which the good bought during the first period may change hands in the second period. In each period, the owners of the good may lease it to other consumers if they wish.

Compare the two options:

(1) Suppose that the monopolist decides to lease. His price in each period t maximizes $p_t D(p_t)$. The monopolist charges $p_1 = p_2 = \frac{1}{2}$. Then he produces $q_1 = \frac{1}{2}$ during period 1 and $q_2 = 0$ during period 2 (since there is no depreciation). The present discounted value of his intertemporal profit is

$$\Pi^\ell = \tfrac{1}{4} + \tfrac{1}{4}\delta = \tfrac{1}{4}(1 + \delta).$$

(2) Suppose that the monopolist decides to sell. The quantity sold during period 1 is "re-offered"[34] on the market during period 2. Having sold quantity q_1 in period 1, the monopolist chooses to sell quantity q_2 (which maximizes his profit) during period 2. The accompanying price, p_2, is that for which the total quantity offered $(q_1 + q_2)$ is equal to the quantity demanded; that is, $p_2 = 1 - q_1 - q_2$. Therefore, to maximize his profit, the monopolist chooses q_2 in order to solve

$$\max_{q_2} q_2(1 - q_1 - q_2).$$

From this, we determine $q_2 = (1 - q_1)/2$. The profit in period 2 is then $(1 - q_1)^2/4$.

Now let us examine the first period. The price that the buyers of the durable good are willing to pay (whether they will use it themselves or lease it) depends on their expectation of the market price during period 2. Let p_2^a be this expected price. The consumers are willing to pay $(1 - q_1) + \delta p_2^a$, since the current rental price is $1 - q_1$. Therefore, we have

$$p_1 = (1 - q_1) + \delta p_2^a.$$

To complete the model, we assume that the consumers anticipate correctly the price charged in period 2: $p_2^a = p_2$. From this, knowing q_1, they expect the producer to sup-

---

33. In certain cases, the leasing option is less attractive or not relevant at all. For example, the leasing market for cars is rather small relative to the sales market because of both moral hazard (consumers take little care of the car) and potential adverse selection problems (the market would tend to attract the less careful drivers).

34. To say that the good is reoffered does not imply that it will necessarily change hands. A consumer and owner of the good during period 1 is prepared to lease it to another consumer during period 2 when the market price exceeds the value he himself attaches to the good.

ply $q_2 = (1 - q_1)/2$ during period 2 with a corresponding price:

$$p_2 = 1 - q_1 - \left(\frac{1 - q_1}{2}\right) = \frac{1 - q_1}{2}.$$

Therefore, we derive

$$p_1 = (1 - q_1) + \delta\left(\frac{1 - q_1}{2}\right) = (1 - q_1)\left(1 + \frac{\delta}{2}\right).$$

Note, in particular, that the quantity demanded at price p_1 is lower than in the case where the monopolist would commit himself not to produce during period 2 (in this case, $p_1 = (1 - q_1)(1 + \delta)$). Note also that the first-period price necessarily exceeds the second-period one. Then the monopolist chooses q_1 to maximize

$$\Pi^s = \max_{q_1}\left[q_1(1 - q_1)\left(1 + \frac{\delta}{2}\right) + \delta\frac{(1 - q_1)^2}{4}\right].$$

It is left to the reader to check that

$$q_1 = 2/(4 + \delta),$$

that

$$p_1 = \frac{(2 + \delta)^2}{2(4 + \delta)} < \frac{1 + \delta}{2},$$

and, more important, that $\Pi^s < \Pi^\ell$. Because of this last inequality, the monopolist prefers leasing.[35]

1.5.2.2 The Coase Problem

Why does selling create a problem for the monopolist? The reason is that the consumers (or investors) are unready to pay a high price for the good during period 1, knowing that the monopolist can "flood the market" in period 2—which, in effect, he does. (Equivalently, the monopolist could make the good bought in period 1 obsolete by introducing a new model.) To simplify, consider the case in which the linear demand curve stems from a continuum of consumers with unit demands and per-period willingness to pay in $[0, 1]$. Suppose that the monopolist charges the monopoly price $(1 + \delta)/2$ in the first period and that, naively, those consumers

whose per-period willingness to pay exceeds $\frac{1}{2}$ buy. In the second period, the monopolist faces a residual demand $D(p) = \frac{1}{2} - p$ from those consumers whose per-period willingness to pay is lower than $\frac{1}{2}$. This tempts the monopolist to lower his price (to $\frac{1}{4}$ in this case). Thus, in retrospect, some consumers with willingness to pay near $\frac{1}{2}$ would have wanted to refrain from buying in the first period. For instance, a consumer with willingness to pay equal to $\frac{1}{2} + \varepsilon$, where ε is small and positive, enjoys a surplus of $\varepsilon(1 + \delta)$ if he buys naively and a surplus of $\delta(\frac{1}{4} + \varepsilon) > \varepsilon(1 + \delta)$ if he waits. Therefore, the prospect of a price adjustment tomorrow changes the monopolist's demand curve today. Facing a lower demand under perfect foresight than under naive expectations, the monopolist is forced to charge a lower first-period price. Here we have the phenomenon of *intertemporal price discrimination*. In equilibrium, only the high-valuation consumers buy in the first period at the high price; their high surplus for the good leads them to purchase then rather than to wait for a low price. Consumers with an intermediate valuation buy at the low price in the second period. Those with a low valuation do not buy at all.

The monopolist suffers from the consumers' rational belief that he will flood the market. This problem takes an extreme form in the following setting: Suppose that both the monopolist and the consumers are infinitely lived and that the good is infinitely durable. The consumers have unit demands. Each consumer's valuation now represents the present discounted value of the services brought by the good from the date of purchase on. Assume that the consumers' valuations are distributed on $[c, +\infty)$ according to some smooth density function, where c is the unit production cost of the good. (Consumers with valuations under c are irrelevant because the monopolist will never charge a price under c, as can easily be shown.) Let $\delta = e^{-r\Delta}$, where r is the rate of interest and Δ is the length of time between the price adjustments. The *Coase conjecture* (Coase 1972), proved formally by Bulow (1982) and Stokey (1981) for particular demand functions and equilibria and by Gul, Sonnenschein, and Wilson (1986) for

---

35. This result is contingent on the absence of threat of entry. Bucovetsky and Chilton (1986) and Bulow (1986) show that a monopolist would sell some if he tried to deter a rival's entry. A sale lowers the potential demand for the entrant, whereas leasing does not commit customers to stay with the incumbent firm in case of entry. This idea is somewhat related to the market-foreclosure issue discussed in the supplementary section of chapter 4.

more general demand structures,[36] states that when Δ tends to zero the intertemporal profit tends to zero. In other words, a monopolist who can change his price very quickly (as would be expected) loses his monopoly power completely. In equilibrium, consumers expect him to charge prices close to the competitive price c at any future instant and, as they can wait for the next offer without much delay cost, they cannot be induced to accept higher prices. Thus, the monopolist ends up charging prices close to the competitive price, vindicating the consumers' belief.

The appendix to this chapter gives a heuristic proof of the Coase conjecture; exercise 1.8 explores the mechanics of the reasoning in a simple case.

Exercise 1.8***[37] Both the monopolist and the consumers are infinite-lived. The unit production cost is 0. The consumers' valuations, v, are uniformly distributed on $[0, 1/(1 - \delta)]$ (which amounts to saying that the per-period valuation is uniformly distributed on $[0, 1]$). A consumer with valuation v has utility $\delta^t(v - p_t)$ if he buys at date t at price p_t, where δ is the discount factor. The monopolist's intertemporal profit is

$$\sum_{t=1}^{\infty} \delta^t p_t q_t,$$

where q_t is the quantity sold (the number of consumers who buy) at time t. Look for a linear and stationary equilibrium: When facing at some date a price p, any consumers with valuations exceeding $w(p) = \lambda p$ buy and consumers with lower valuations do not buy, where $\lambda > 1$. Conversely, if at some date consumers with valuations exceeding v have bought and the others have not, the monopolist charges $p(v) = \mu v$, where $\mu < 1$.

(i) Compute the monopolist's intertemporal payoff from date t on when only consumers with valuations below v remain and the monopolist charges $p_t, p_{t+1}, \ldots$ and the consumers follow their linear rule.

(ii) Show that the monopolist's optimization over p_t leads to a linear rule, where λ is given (implicitly) as a function of μ by

$$1 - 2\lambda\mu + \delta\lambda^2\mu^2 = 0.$$

(iii) Write consumer $w(p)$'s indifference equation to obtain

$$(\lambda - 1) = \delta\lambda(1 - \mu).$$

(iv) Conclude that when δ tends to 1, the monopolist's profit tends to zero.

1.5.2.3 Evading the Coase Problem

The credibility issue drives the durable-good monopolist's profit to zero in the Coase conjecture. Although this problem is a serious one (for the monopolist, not the consumer), there exist many reasons why a durable-good monopolist can in practice make a profit. We now investigate these reasons.

• As we have seen, leasing (or renting) allows the monopolist to keep clear of the Coase problem. The intuition is that the good is implicitly returned to the manufacturer. When flooding the market, the manufacturer puts pressure on the price of his own good but not on the quantity owned by the consumers (as in the selling case). The monopolist thus realizes the static monopoly profit in each period. It is interesting in this respect that the U.S. government has required the dominant firm(s) in some industries (computers, copiers, and shoe machinery) to sell rather than rent.

Leasing, however, may create some serious hazards that were not formalized in the model. If the consumers' consumption mode (maintenance, care, etc.) matters, the monopolist must be able to monitor at the end of each period the exact condition of the good. Such a monitoring technology, however, may be extremely costly, and leasing may lose its virtues. This is one reason why automobiles are more commonly sold than rented.

---

36. See also exercise 1.8 (which is inspired by Sobel and Takahashi's [1983] treatment of exponential demand curves). See Fudenberg et al. 1985 for the derivation of the Coase conjecture when the buyers' valuations are bounded away from the monopolist's production cost (in this case, the Coase conjecture says that the monopolist sells at a price close to the buyers' lowest valuation). Gul et al. (1986) consider the (often more realistic) case in which the buyers' lowest possible valuation is lower than the production cost. Their derivation of the Coase conjecture assumes that the buyers' decision on whether to accept a

price depends only on this price and not on the history of the market. Ausubel and Deneckere (1986) challenge this assumption and show that many outcomes (including, possibly, outcomes near the monopoly one) may be obtained once it is dropped. See Ausubel and Deneckere 1987 and Gul 1987 for discussions of the durable-good problem in the context of oligopolies.

37. This exercise follows Sobel and Takahashi 1983.

Leasing may face other hazards when the customers are not anonymous (and anonymity cannot be restored through the transfer of the good between customers). Then, within a given period, the monopolist can discriminate between customers on the basis of their past consumption. Customers who have leased in the past have signaled a high willingness to pay for the good, and therefore should be charged high rental rates. This reduces the demand for the good considerably in the early periods of the relationship between a customer and the seller. Indeed, it can be shown that in the absence of buyer anonymity the monopolist does even worse when leasing than when selling: $\tilde{\Pi}^\ell < \Pi^s$ (where the sale profit Π^s is not affected by whether the customer is anonymous, because once the good is sold no discrimination is feasible any more).[38] In such a situation, it seems that the seller would have an incentive to at least mimic a sale contract by offering a long-term lease at guaranteed prices. This would protect the customer against future price discrimination based on his current consumption, and would raise current demand. In this respect, Hart and Tirole (1987) prove that if the two parties can sign a long-term contract (which is enforced if either of the parties wants it to be enforced, but can be renegotiated if both parties find it advantageous to do so),[39] the market organization with long-term leasing contracts is the same as that for the sale of a durable good without commitment. That is, everything is as if the good were sold to the customer. The price and consumption dynamics are as described in the subsections on "leasing versus selling" and "the Coase problem," and the monopolist's profit is equal to Π^s.

Now assume that leasing is impossible (say, because of moral hazard on the consumer side). We will see that in a number of circumstances the monopolist can evade the Coase problem, at least partially.

• Notice first that the monopolist can achieve the same (optimal) profit as under leasing if, at date 1, he can *commit* himself credibly to a sequence of prices. Assume in our two-period example that he announces $p_1 = (1 + \delta)/2$ and $p_2 \geq \frac{1}{2}$—that is, he quotes the intertemporal monopoly price in the first period and commits himself not to lower the price in the second. The quantities bought are $q_1 = \frac{1}{2}$ and $q_2 = 0$, and consumers are indeed willing to pay $(1 + \delta)/2$ in the first period. Hence, the monopolist's profit is

$$p_1 q_1 = (1 + \delta)/4 = \Pi^\ell.$$

An important lesson of the previous analysis is that commitment must be credible. In the second period the residual demand facing the monopolist is $q_2 = \frac{1}{2} - p_2$. Thus, as before, the monopolist would *ex post* wish to reduce the price under $\frac{1}{2}$. But, if this were possible, the consumers would then refrain from buying in the first period. Thus, *ex ante* the monopolist would actually be hurt by his *ex post* flexibility. This result is actually much more general: *An economic agent can always do as well when he can commit himself as when he cannot.* This is because, under commitment, he can always duplicate what he does under no commitment. For instance, in this case he could announce at date 1 the two prices that would prevail under noncommitment. The consumers' behavior would be unaffected, because we assumed that under noncommitment they have rational expectations. This simple paradox—that one generally gains by imposing self-constraints—is an important phenomenon in industrial economics. We will encounter it again—for instance, in chapter 8.

Remark The fact that in the optimal commitment price pattern the price decreases over time is an artifact of our assumption that the good becomes obsolete after two periods. Actually, one can see that the price *per period of utilization* (where the second period is discounted) is constant and equal to the static (per period) monopoly price. This result is very general. Exercise 1.9 demonstrates the result for a good that never becomes obsolete.

*Exercise 1.9**** Consider the framework of exercise 1.8 (infinite-lived consumers and monopolist and an infinitely durable good). In contrast with exercise 1.8, assume that the monopolist commits himself to a sequence of prices $(p_1, p_2, p_3, \ldots)$.

---

38. See Hart and Tirole 1987. Another result is that when the relationship is sufficiently long and the discount factor "not too small" (but not necessarily close to unity) the monopolist loses all power to discriminate; with two potential per-period valuations for the customer, the monopolist keeps charging the lower of the valuations until close to the end of the horizon.

39. The concept of mutually advantageous renegotiation was introduced by Dewatripont (1985).

(i) Show that, when searching for the optimal price policy, the monopolist restricts himself to sequences satisfying $p_1 \geqslant p_2 \geqslant p_3 \geqslant \cdots$.

(ii) Set up the monopolist's optimization problem and derive the first-order conditions.

(iii) Show that an optimal sequence is $p_1 = p_2 = p_3 = \cdots = p^m = 1/2(1 - \delta)$.

In practice, there are several ways for the monopolist to commit himself:

• A possibility rarely practiced is for the monopolist to put into escrow with a *third party* (an "arbitrator") a sufficient amount of money, with the clause that, if in the future he produces more than the specified quantity or charges less than the specified price, he will lose this money to the third party.[40]

• The monopolist's *reputation* can enter into consideration when the relationship between the producer and the consumers is long-lived. For example, DeBeers, the diamond monopoly, has the reputation of refusing to allow prices to fall.

• To commit himself not to add to the existing stock of the good tomorrow, the monopolist may *destroy his factory* after today's production (if he is incapable of rebuilding another one at little expense). For instance, an artist can destroy the limestone used to create a lithograph. (Another strategy would be to number the lithographs and indicate the total number produced.)

• In a less extreme way, the existence of increasing marginal production costs (*decreasing returns to scale*) prevents the monopolist from flooding the market too fast (Kahn 1986); thus, increasing costs allow the monopolist to commit himself not to cut prices in a Coasian fashion.[41]

• The monopolist can offer a *money-back guarantee* (sometimes called the "most-favored-nation" clause) if he lets the price of the good fall. In the above model, he can charge $p_1 = (1 + \delta)p^m$ in the first period (where $p^m = \frac{1}{2}$)

and commit himself to reimburse $p^m - p_2$ to his first-period customers if the second-period price p_2 falls under p^m. Formally, everything is as if consumers paid

$$(1 + \delta)p^m - \delta(p^m - p_2) = p^m + \delta p_2$$

—that is, as if they were charged the one-period monopoly price in the first period and p_2 in the second period. Hence, the monopolist has an incentive to charge $p_2 = p^m$ in the second period—that is, not to produce in the second period if the good is perfectly durable. Thus, the monopolist is, *de facto*, able to commit himself not to lower the market price, and is thus able to realize the monopoly profit. The intuition for this result is that the monopolist reimburses the consumers for any capital loss his opportunistic second-period behavior would inflict relative to the promised (commitment) behavior. Thus he totally internalizes the consumers' concern about price reductions.

Such price protection clauses may be hard or costly to enforce. The seller must be unable to give secret price discounts to new customers. (In May 1963, when General Electric announced that if it were to lower the prices of its turbine generators it would grant retroactively reductions to customers who had purchased them in the preceding six months, it also hired a public accounting firm to audit its compliance with the price-protection policy upon the request of any customer.) Furthermore, the seller must be unable to affect quality. Thus, price-protection policies are difficult to enforce in industries where goods are tailored to the customer. In such an industry, a price cut can be dissimulated in a quality improvement. That is, the good must be a well-specified and standard one to allow price protection.[42]

• The durable-good monopolist may have an *opportunity cost* of staying in this market. Suppose that, for some reason,[43] the monopolist produces the good at the date of supply (i.e., cannot produce everything at date 0), and that production at each date involves a fixed cost inde-

---

40. This scheme would not necessarily "work," because *ex post* (in the second period, say) the third party and the monopolist would have an incentive to renegotiate their contract. The third party, knowing that he would not receive the money in escrow if he did not renegotiate, would be willing to accept a small bribe to renegotiate and let the monopolist lower his market price.

41. See Moorthy 1980 for a model in which the monopolist's capacity constraint is unknown to consumers.

42. This is hardly the case for turbine generators. However, General Electric also published a price book containing fixed and simplified pricing formulas. The price of a turbine generator was to be computed according to the book (depending on the specifications of the various parts) and then multiplied by a uniform multiplier. The price protection then applied to a single price: the multiplier. For more on pricing in the electrical industry see Sultan 1975.

43. For instance, the monopolist could be capacity constrained, or storage might be expensive.

pendent of the scale of production. (Alternatively, one could think of a fixed marketing cost, or of the opportunity cost of the managers' time—i.e., the profit that could be realized if the firm were to make another product instead.) The monopolist keeps on producing the good as long as the current profit associated with it exceeds the fixed cost. This implies that the Coase reasoning breaks down: If either the price or the quantity bought were to tend to zero at some point in time, the monopolist would exit the market. This, in turn, puts pressure on the buyers to buy before the good disappears from the market.[44]

• The buyers may not be informed about the exact marginal production cost of the durable-good monopolist. Even under the conditions of the Coase conjecture, this allows the monopolist to realize some profits when he has a low production cost—he can always duplicate the pricing strategy that he would use if he were to have a high production cost, and earn at least the corresponding cost savings on the units sold.

An interesting possibility in this respect, analyzed by Vincent (1986) and Evans (1987), is that the producer may signal quality through delays. To be more precise, suppose that the producer is either a high-quality producer or a low-quality one. Buyers value quality, but they do not know it before purchasing. A high-quality seller faces a higher marginal cost of production than a low-quality one, which implies that a low-quality seller is more impatient to sell (his margin is higher at any given price). This suggests that in equilibrium the seller of a high-quality good delays trade in order to "demonstrate" that he is a high-quality seller. Vincent and Evans confirm this intuition and show that a non-negligible delay arises even for rapid price offers. (The reader will find it easier

to understand this result after studying Akerlof's lemons model in chapter 2.[45])

• Last, there may be a constant inflow of new customers. The inflow of new customers at each instant raises the demand curve (normalized by the number of customers) because the consumers who wait longer to buy are those with the lowest valuations. Thus, "on average," the old customers in the market (those who were around, but have not bought yet) have lower valuations than the new customers. In a sense, the existence of new customers reduces the monopolist's propensity to cut his price. Conlisk, Gerstner, and Sobel (1984) show that the constant inflow of new customers leads to "price cycles": The monopolist, from time to time, offers a sale to cater to the existing stock of low-valuation buyers. For a few periods, he charges high prices so as to extract the surplus of high-valuation buyers, until the proportion of low-valuation buyers in the sample of unserved customers becomes so high that he cannot resist selling to these customers at a lower price. This sale temporarily reduces the proportion of low-valuation buyers among potential customers, and the monopolist starts charging high prices again.[46]

Which of these many factors mitigating the Coase result play a role in practice depends on the industry under consideration. However, in general, the above analysis suggests that, although the intertemporal credibility of the pricing behavior is a serious problem facing durable-good monopolists, one should not expect that it forces them to charge the competitive price and make no profit.

1.5.2.4 Monopoly and Planned Obsolescence

From the preceding discussion, we can easily derive a theory of planned obsolescence. Suppose that the dura-

---

44. Fudenberg et al. (1987), who argue that the existence of the fixed cost commits the monopolist not to charge low prices, show how a finite-horizon timing can be endogenized from the existence of outside opportunities. (There are some differences, however, with the case of an exogenously fixed horizon.)

45. To get a very rough idea of this now, suppose that a high-quality good is valued 5 by the buyer and costs 4 to the seller and that a low-quality good is valued 1 by the buyer and costs nothing to produce. The two qualities are equally likely *a priori*. Suppose that, as in the Coase conjecture, all socially desirable trade takes place almost instantaneously. Here this means that the two parties trade immediately with probability 1. Because trade occurs almost instantaneously, it must take place at a single price (more precisely, at prices very close to each other). Furthermore, this price must exceed 4 in order for a high-quality seller to be willing to trade. The buyer's expected surplus is then at most

$\frac{1}{2}(5) + \frac{1}{2}(1) - 4 = -1 < 0$

—which is impossible, as he can refuse to trade. Hence, non-negligible delay (inefficiency in the trading process) must occur. In chapter 2 we will see that asymmetries of information in static markets (no sequence of trading prices) generally imply that gains from trade are not realized (which can be viewed as an infinite delay in trading).

46. Another way of introducing a steady-state demand for the durable good is to assume that the good depreciates over time. (In the extreme case of full depreciation, the good is nondurable and the firm enjoys full monopoly power over the demand curve, i.e., is not handicapped by price commitment). Bond and Samuelson (1984) and Suslow (1986) analyze the problem of a durable-good monopoly in conjunction with depreciation.

bility of a good now becomes a decision variable for the monopolist and that the consumers are informed of the product's durability.

First, assume that the monopolist can commit himself to a sequence of prices, or that (equivalently) he can lease the good. The leasing interpretation actually leads to a straightforward derivation of the optimal durability for the monopolist. On this interpretation, the monopolist is the owner of the stock of the durable good at each instant. For any plan he formulates as to the intertemporal evolution of the stock of the durable good, he has an incentive to choose durability so as to minimize the intertemporal production cost. Thus, conditional on this plan, the monopolist chooses the socially optimal (cost-minimizing) durability. In this sense, there is no "planned obsolescence"; the monopolist does not produce a good with an uneconomically short life so that customers have to make repeat purchases. Thus, we obtain Swan's optimal-durability result in our context (see Swan 1972 and the discussion of durability in chapter 2 below).

The picture changes dramatically in the sale (non-commitment) case. Then, by decreasing durability, the monopolist reduces the quantity of the good carried over to the next period, increases the next period's residual demand, and therefore increases the next period's price. Thus, reducing durability is a way of committing oneself not to lower the price tomorrow, which induces consumers to buy today. (When the monopolist can commit himself directly, this effect is irrelevant. Hence, there is no point to distorting the durability decision.) We see that the monopolist has an incentive to choose a durability below that which minimizes his intertemporal cost of production—i.e., to plan obsolescence. A typical example of an "obsolescence-planning monopolist" is the textbook publisher who frequently introduces revised editions. Doing so kills off the secondary (used-book) market and is thus tantamount to producing a low-durability good. (A slight difference with our model is that the durability of the good is anticipated rather than observed at the date of purchase.)

The following exercise (based on Bulow 1986) makes these ideas slightly more formal.[47]

Exercise 1.10** Consider the previous two-period model (in which the good becomes obsolete after two periods). Introduce a constant unit-production cost of $c_1(x)$ in the first period and c_2 in the second period. x is the probability that the first-period good is still usable in the second period. Thus, if q_1 is the first-period production, xq_1 is the number of units of the durable good still around at date 2 before further production by the monopolist. (Assume $c_1' > 0$, $c_1'' > 0$; and $c_1'(0)$ "small" and $c_1'(1)$ "large," so as to obtain an interior solution.)

(i) Show that if the monopolist can commit, he chooses the cost-minimizing durability: $c_1'(x) = \delta c_2$.

(ii) Show that if the monopolist cannot commit, durability is suboptimal:

$$c_1'(x) = \delta \left(c_2 + \frac{\partial p_2(xq_1)}{\partial (xq_1)} xq_1 \right) < \delta c_2,$$

where $p_2(xq_1)$ is the second-period price chosen by the monopolist given that the residual demand is equal to demand minus existing stock (xq_1). Interpret.

Thus, the choice of durability is biased by the absence of commitment. Another bias in technological choices, also noted by Bulow, concerns investments. Suppose, for instance, that the durable-good monopolist chooses between not investing today and facing a high marginal cost in all future periods, and investing so as to face a lower marginal cost. The monopolist may choose not to invest in the absence of commitment, whereas he would invest if he could commit. Choosing a high-marginal-cost technology makes possible a certain commitment not to flood the market in the future and may thus be profitable.

---

47. See Bulow 1986 for somewhat more general conditions under which planned obsolescence can be obtained and for an analysis of the oligopoly context. For further developments on the issue of durability, see Schmalensee 1974, 1979 and Liebowitz 1982.

Answers and Hints

Exercise 1.1

(i) W^c is equal to consumer surplus plus profit:

$$W^c = \max_p \left(\int_p^\infty x^{-\varepsilon} dx + (p - c)p^{-\varepsilon} \right).$$

The maximum is, of course, obtained through marginal-cost pricing: $p = c$. This yields

$$W^c = \int_c^\infty x^{-\varepsilon} dx = c^{1-\varepsilon}/(\varepsilon - 1) \quad \text{for } \varepsilon > 1.$$

(ii) Welfare under monopoly, W^m, corresponds to price $p^m = c/(1 - 1/\varepsilon)$. Some computations yield

$$\text{WL} \equiv W^c - W^m$$

$$= \left(\frac{c^{1-\varepsilon}}{\varepsilon - 1} \right) \left[1 - \left(\frac{2\varepsilon - 1}{\varepsilon - 1} \right) \left(\frac{\varepsilon}{\varepsilon - 1} \right)^{-\varepsilon} \right] > 0.$$

(iii) Tedious computations show that WL is nonmonotonic in ε. Such a result is not very instructive, as the size of the market decreases with ε. Next, note that

$$\frac{\text{WL}}{W^c} = 1 - K(\varepsilon),$$

where $\ln K(\varepsilon) = \ln(2\varepsilon - 1) - \ln(\varepsilon - 1) - \varepsilon \ln \varepsilon + \varepsilon \ln(\varepsilon - 1)$. Therefore,

$$\frac{K'(\varepsilon)}{K(\varepsilon)} = \frac{2}{2\varepsilon - 1} - \frac{1}{\varepsilon - 1} - 1 - \ln \varepsilon + \frac{\varepsilon}{\varepsilon - 1}$$

$$+ \ln(\varepsilon - 1),$$

or

$$\frac{K'(\varepsilon)}{K(\varepsilon)} = \frac{2}{2\varepsilon - 1} + \ln \left(\frac{\varepsilon - 1}{\varepsilon} \right).$$

It is easy to show that the right-hand side of this last equation is increasing in ε, and therefore that it reaches its maximum, equal to zero, at $\varepsilon = +\infty$. Thus, $K'(\varepsilon) < 0$, and WL/W^c is an increasing function of ε.

Finally,

$$\Pi^m = \frac{c^{1-\varepsilon}}{(\varepsilon - 1)^{1-\varepsilon}} \varepsilon^{-\varepsilon},$$

so that

$$\frac{\Pi^m}{W^c} = \frac{\varepsilon^{-\varepsilon}}{(\varepsilon - 1)^{-\varepsilon}}.$$

The right-hand side of this last equation is increasing in ε.

Exercise 1.2

The monopolist charges $p^m = \bar{s}$. The quantity consumed is equal to the number of consumers, and is the same as under marginal-cost pricing. Monopoly pricing simply transfers the surplus $(\bar{s} - c)$ per consumer from the consumers to the firm.

Exercise 1.3

(i) For $p = q^{-1/\varepsilon}$,

$$\frac{dp^m}{d\tilde{c}} = \frac{1}{1 - 1/\varepsilon}.$$

For $p = \alpha - \beta q^\delta$,

$$\frac{dp^m}{d\tilde{c}} = \frac{1}{1 + \delta}.$$

For $p = a - b \ln q$,

$$\frac{dp^m}{d\tilde{c}} = 1.$$

(The sensitivity of price to marginal cost is the same as in a competitive market here, in spite of the fact that the elasticity of demand is not equal to infinity.)

(ii) Only when the elasticity of demand is constant is the sensitivity of price to marginal cost unambiguously related to the elasticity of demand. This can be seen from the monopoly-pricing equation:

$$p = P(q) = \frac{c + t}{1 - 1/\varepsilon(q)}.$$

For general demand functions, the elasticity of demand varies with the "size" of the market (which depends not only on market conditions but also on the level of the tax). Thus, even with a constant marginal cost, the supply equation (i.e., the above first-order condition) cannot be estimated separately from the demand equation (the identification problem) unless one is confident that the demand function belongs to the constant-elasticity-of-substitution class.

Exercise 1.4

Let $R(p) \equiv p D(p) = p^{1-\varepsilon}$. The first-order condition is

$$R'(p) - C'(D(p))D'(p) = 0.$$

The second-order condition is

$$R''(p) - C''(D(p))[D'(p)]^2 - C'(D(p))D''(p) < 0.$$

Quasi-concavity is obtained if the second-order condition holds for any p satisfying the first-order condition. That is, substituting the first-order condition into the second-order condition,

$$R''(p) - C''(D(p))[D'(p)]^2 - \frac{R'(p)D''(p)}{D'(p)} < 0.$$

The second term of this last inequality is negative. Hence (using the fact that $R'(p) < 0$ from the first-order condition), it suffices that

$$\frac{R''(p)}{R'(p)} > \frac{D''(p)}{D'(p)}.$$

This is easily checked using logarithmic derivatives.

If $\varepsilon < 1$, then $R'(p) > 0$. Thus, the first-order condition has no solution (the optimal price and the monopoly profit are infinite).

Exercise 1.5

$q_1 = q_2 = D(p_1 + p_2)$. Equation 1.6 can be written, for all i, as

$$D + p\frac{\partial D}{\partial p} = \left(\sum_i \frac{\partial C_i}{\partial q_i}\right)\frac{\partial D}{\partial p}, \quad \text{where } p \equiv p_1 + p_2.$$

Letting $\tilde{C} = C_1 + C_2$ and adding the two equations yields

$$\tilde{D} + p\frac{\partial \tilde{D}}{\partial p} = \frac{\partial \tilde{C}}{\partial \tilde{q}}\frac{\partial \tilde{D}}{\partial p}.$$

Exercise 1.6

(i) The capacity constraint is not binding for small off-peak demand. Hence, the marginal cost of production is c, which leads to $\text{MR}_1(p_1^\star) = c$. For peak demand, the marginal cost is $c + \gamma$. Hence, $\text{MR}_2(p_2^\star) = c + \gamma$. This holds as long as the constraint $D_1(p_1^\star) \leq D_2(p_2^\star)$ is not binding —i.e., as long as off-peak demand (i.e., λ) is small.

(ii) For large off-peak demand, the constraint $D_1(p_1) \leq D_2(p_2)$ is binding. The distinction between off-peak

and peak is somewhat blurred, because both types of demand are capacity constrained. At the optimum, a small increase in capacity is matched by a decrease in both p_1 and p_2 so that the new capacity can be used in both states of demand. The monopolist maximizes

$$R_1(p_1) + R_2(p_2) - (c + \gamma/2)[D_1(p_1) + D_2(p_2)]$$

subject to the constraint $D_1(p_1) = D_2(p_2)$. Using the Kuhn-Tucker conditions (or, simpler, maximizing with respect to output instead of prices), one obtains

$$p_1\left(1 - \frac{1}{\varepsilon_1}\right) + p_2\left(1 - \frac{1}{\varepsilon_2}\right) = 2c + \gamma,$$

where ε_1 and ε_2 are the elasticities of demand. This equation together with $D_1(p_1) = D_2(p_2)$ gives p_1 and p_2 (note that $p_1 < p_2$). For instance, for $D_1(p_1) = \alpha_1 p_1^{-\varepsilon}$ and $D_2(p_2) = \alpha_2 p_2^{-\varepsilon}$ (where $\lambda = \alpha_1/\alpha_2 < 1$),

$$p_2 = \frac{2c + \gamma}{(1 - 1/\varepsilon)[1 + (\alpha_1/\alpha_2)^{1/\varepsilon}]}.$$

Exercise 1.7

(i) For a formal proof, use the Pontryagin theory of optimal control (see, e.g., Arrow and Kurz 1970; Dixit 1976; Intriligator 1971; Kamien and Schwartz 1981). The intuition behind the optimality condition is as follows: Raising $q(t)$ by dq at time t yields $\text{MR}(q(t))dq$ in terms of revenue. It raises current cost by $c(\omega(t))dq$. It also raises experience at all times $s \geq t$ by dq, which reduces unit cost by $-c'(\omega(s))dq$. The number of units affected is $q(s)$ (one can ignore the change in $q(s)$ when using the equivalent of the envelope theorem). Marginal revenue must equal current cost minus future cost savings:

$$\text{MR}(q(t)) = c(\omega(t)) + \int_t^\infty c'(\omega(s))q(s)e^{-r(s-t)}ds$$
$$= A(t).$$

(Integrate by parts, remembering that $d\omega(s)/ds = q(s)$.)

(ii) $dA(t)/dt = r[-c(\omega(t)) + A(t)] < 0$, because current cost is higher than average future cost. Thus, $d(\text{MR})/dt < 0$, or $dq/dt > 0$.

Exercise 1.8

(i) Because the buyers' decision function, summarized by $w(p) = \lambda p$, is stationary, the monopolist cannot gain by charging a price that is accepted by no buyer (he will face the same decision problem in the next period and will have lost one period). From the buyers' decision function, we know that at any given point of time t there exists a valuation v such that buyers with a valuation above v have already bought and other buyers have not. (This property is actually very general; see Fudenberg et al. 1985 and Gul et al. 1986. It is just an "incentive compatibility constraint" for this Bayesian game.) The monopolist's intertemporal profit from date t on is

$$V(v) = \frac{1}{v}[(v - \lambda p_1)p_1 + \delta(\lambda p_1 - \lambda p_2)p_2 + \cdots],$$

where $v > \lambda p_1 > \lambda p_2 > \cdots$.

(ii) Differentiating with respect to p_1 gives

$$v - 2\lambda p_1 + \delta \lambda p_2 = 0.$$

But $p_1 = \mu v$ and $p_2 = \mu(\lambda p_1) = \lambda \mu^2 v$. We thus obtain

$$1 - 2\lambda\mu + \delta\lambda^2\mu^2 = 0.$$

(Check the second-order conditions!)

(iii) A buyer with valuation λp is indifferent between buying now and waiting one more period, so

$$(\lambda p - p) = \delta(\lambda p - \mu(\lambda p)).$$

(iv) Solving for λ and μ gives

$$\lambda\mu = (1 - \sqrt{1 - \delta})/\delta,$$

$$\lambda = (\sqrt{1 - \delta})^{-1},$$

$$\mu = (\sqrt{1 - \delta} - (1 - \delta))/\delta.$$

Notice that $\lim_{\delta \to 1} \mu = 0$.

Exercise 1.9

(i) A price $p_t \geq p_{t-k}$ for some positive k will be accepted by no consumer, because a consumer could buy at the lower price p_{t-k} and enjoy the good earlier. Thus, choosing $p_t = \min_{k>0}(p_{t-k})$ leads to the same outcome.

(ii) A consumer with valuation v is indifferent between accepting p_t and waiting for p_{t+1} if and only if

$$(v - p_t) = \delta(v - p_{t+1}).$$

Thus, the monopolist's optimization problem can be written as

$$\max\left[V\left(\frac{1}{1 - \delta}\right)\right] = p_1\left(\frac{1}{1 - \delta} - \frac{p_1 - \delta p_2}{1 - \delta}\right)$$
$$+ \delta p_2\left(\frac{p_1 - \delta p_2}{1 - \delta} - \frac{p_2 - \delta p_3}{1 - \delta}\right) + \cdots.$$

The first-order conditions are

$$p_1 = \tfrac{1}{2} + \delta p_2,$$

$$t \geq 2,$$

$$p_t = \frac{p_{t-1} + \delta p_{t+1}}{1 + \delta}.$$

(iii) The sequence with constant price $1/2(1 - \delta)$ is obviously a solution to the first-order conditions (check the concavity of the objective function). This is actually the unique solution, as the sequence $p_t - p_{t+1} = (p_{t-1} - p_t)/\delta$ leads to negative prices if $p_{t-1} - p_t > 0$ for some time t.

The no-haggling result is actually more general and holds for any distribution of valuations, not only for the uniform one.

There is a more elegant way to prove the no-haggling result using the theory of mechanism design. Since this theory is beyond the scope of this book, we preferred to use a more "mechanical" approach.

For a more general model of monopoly pricing of a durable good under commitment, see Stokey 1979.

Exercise 1.10

(i) Write the firm's intertemporal profit and maximize with respect to p_1, p_2, and x.

(ii) The second-period profit is

$$\pi_2(q_1 x) = \max_{p_2}\{(p_2 - c_2)[D(p_2) - xq_1]\}.$$

The envelope theorem implies that

$$\frac{\partial \pi_2}{\partial(xq_1)} = -[p_2(xq_1) - c_2].$$

The equation in the statement of the exercise is obtained by maximizing

$$q_1[P(q_1) + \delta p_2(xq_1)x - c_1(x)] + \delta\pi_2(xq_1)$$

with respect to x (to obtain the complete solution, maximize this expression with respect to q_1 as well).

Appendix: A Heuristic Proof of the Coase Conjecture

The following heuristic proof of the Coase conjecture, which is for the advanced reader, is inspired by Wilson 1985.

Consider an infinite horizon, $t = 1, 2, \ldots$. It can easily be shown that for any sequence of past prices charged by the monopolist, $\{p_1, \ldots, p_{t-1}\}$, the seller's posterior beliefs at the beginning of period t are that the buyers with valuations b in $[0, b_t]$ have not yet purchased the good whereas the buyers with valuations b in $(b_t, +\infty)$ have already purchased it for some b_t. That is, the monopolist's posterior beliefs necessarily coincide with a truncation of his prior beliefs (this results from the fact that a high-valuation buyer is more impatient to buy). Following Gul et al. 1986, assume that the buyers follow a simple, "stationary" strategy. When charged price p_t at date t, buyers with valuations exceeding $\beta(p_t)$ buy (if they have not yet done so) whereas those with valuation under $\beta(p_t)$ do not, where $\beta(\cdot)$ is an increasing function and $\beta(p_t) > p_t$ for all $p_t > 0$. (The importance of this stationarity assumption was proved by Ausubel and Deneckere [1986].) For notational simplicity, let $c = 0$ denote the monopolist's marginal cost and let $F(b)$ denote the cumulative distribution of the buyers' valuations on $[0, +\infty)$ (with $F(0) = 0$, $F(b) > 0$ for $b > 0$, and $F(+\infty) = 1$). Last, $\delta = \exp(-r\Delta)$ denotes the discount factor, where Δ is the length of real time between the periods. We will be interested by what happens when Δ tends to 0.

Because of the stationarity of the buyers' strategy, the monopolist's present discounted value of profits from a given date t on depends only on the distribution of remaining buyers, which is summarized by the "cut-off valuation" b_t. Let $V(b_t)$ denote this present discounted profit. Note that $V(\cdot)$ is a nondecreasing function, and let $F_t \equiv F(b_t)$ denote the proportion of buyers who have not purchased before date t.

Fix a real time $\varepsilon > 0$, and let Δ converge to 0. For any $\eta > 0$, there exists a Δ sufficiently small and a t (such that $(t + 2)\Delta < \varepsilon$) satisfying

$$F_t - F_{t+2} \equiv F(b_t) - F(b_{t+2}) < \eta. \tag{A1}$$

That is, as the number of periods between 0 and ε tends to infinity, one can always find two consecutive periods such that the total quantity sold during these two periods is bounded by a given number.

Coase's intuition was that if the profit $V(b_{\varepsilon/\Delta})$ from real time ε on were not negligible, the monopolist would have an incentive to speed up the process by cutting price faster. For instance, between dates t and $t + 2$ he does not sell very much, and he does not gain much from discrimination either, because the real time between these two periods is short (so the price cannot decrease much between these periods; otherwise the buyers would wait and no one would buy between these two periods). Thus, in a sense, the gain from discrimination is of the second order, whereas by making at date t the offer he plans to make at date $t + 1$ the monopolist would speed the process by one period and obtain a first-order gain (in Δ) if $V(b_{\varepsilon/\Delta})$ were not small. To formalize this intuition, let us write the condition under which the monopolist prefers to charge p_t at date t and p_{t+1} at date $t + 1$ rather than p_{t+1} at date t directly:

$$p_t(F_t - F_{t+1}) + \delta p_{t+1}(F_{t+1} - F_{t+2}) + \delta^2 V(b_{t+2})$$
$$\geq p_{t+1}(F_t - F_{t+2}) + \delta V(b_{t+2}). \tag{A2}$$

This is equivalent to

$$(p_t - p_{t+1})F_t - (p_t - \delta p_{t+1})F_{t+1} + (1 - \delta)p_{t+1}F_{t+2}$$
$$\geq \delta(1 - \delta)V(b_{t+2}). \tag{A3}$$

By definition of b_{t+1}, the buyer with valuation b_{t+1} is indifferent between accepting p_t and accepting p_{t+1}; thus,

$$b_{t+1} - p_t = \delta(b_{t+1} - p_{t+1}), \tag{A4}$$

which implies that

$$p_t - \delta p_{t+1} = (1 - \delta)b_{t+1} \tag{A5}$$

and

$$p_t - p_{t+1} = (1 - \delta)(b_{t+1} - p_{t+1}). \tag{A6}$$

Substituting equations A5 and A6 into equation A2 and dividing by $(1 - \delta)$, we obtain

$$(b_{t+1} - p_{t+1})F_t - b_{t+1}F_{t+1} + p_{t+1}F_{t+2} \geq \delta V(b_{t+2}); \tag{A7}$$

that is,

$$b_{t+1}(F_t - F_{t+1}) - p_{t+1}(F_t - F_{t+2}) \geq \delta V(b_{t+2}). \tag{A8}$$

But $t + 2 \leq \varepsilon/\Delta$ implies that $b_{t+2} \geq b_{\varepsilon/\Delta}$ and thus that $V(b_{t+2}) \geq V(b_{\varepsilon/\Delta})$. Also, $F_{t+1} \geq F_{t+2}$. Hence, equation A8 becomes

$$(b_{t+1} - p_{t+1})(F_t - F_{t+2}) \geqslant \delta V(b_{\varepsilon/\Delta}), \qquad \text{(A9)}$$

which implies that by choosing η sufficiently small we can make the seller's present discounted value of profits from real time ε on arbitrarily small. We thus conclude that we can make the present discounted value of profits from any time on (including times close to zero) arbitrarily small by choosing Δ sufficiently small. The end of the "proof" of the Coase conjecture is then routine. The profit can go to zero only if prices tend to zero (more generally, to marginal cost). All trade takes place in "the twinkling of an eye."[48]

References

Aghion, P., P. Bolton, and B. Jullien. 1988. Learning through Price Experimentation by a Monopolist Facing Unknown Demand. Mimeo, Harvard University.

Amihud, Y., and H. Mendelson. 1983. Price Smoothing and Inventory. *Review of Economic Studies* 50: 87–98.

Arrow, K. 1961. Economic Welfare and the Allocation of Research for Invention. In *The Rate and Direction of Inventive Activity: Economic and Social Factors*, ed. R. Nelson. Princeton University Press.

Arrow, K., and M. Kurz. 1970. *Public Investment, The Rate of Return, and Optimal Fiscal Policy*. Baltimore: Johns Hopkins University Press.

Ausubel, L., and R. Deneckere. 1986. Reputation in Bargaining and Durable Goods Monopoly. Mimeo, Northwestern University.

Ausubel, L., and R. Deneckere. 1987. One is Almost Enough for Monopoly. *Rand Journal of Economics* 18: 255–274.

Baron, D. 1986. Design of Regulatory Mechanisms and Institutions. In *Handbook of Industrial Organization*, ed. R. Willig and R. Schmalensee (Amsterdam: North-Holland, forthcoming).

Baron, D., and R. Myerson. 1982. Regulating a Monopolist with Unknown Costs. *Econometrica* 50: 911–30.

Baumol, W. J., and D. Bradford. 1970. Optimal Departures from Marginal Cost Pricing. *American Economic Review* 60: 265–283.

Bergson, A. 1973. On Monopoly Welfare Losses. *American Economic Review* 63: 853–870.

Besanko, D., and D. Sappington. 1987. Designing Regulatory Policy with Limited Information. In *Fundamentals of Pure and Applied Economics*, ed. J. Lesourne and H. Sonnenschein. London: Harwood.

Blinder, A. 1982. Inventories and Sticky Prices: More on the Microfoundations of Macroeconomics. *American Economic Review* 72: 334–348.

Boiteux, M. 1949. La Tarification des Demandes en Pointe. *Revue Générale de l'Electricité* 58: 321–340.

Boiteux, M. 1956. Sur la Gestion des Monopoles Publics Astreints à l'Equilibre Budgétaire. *Econometrica* 24: 22–40. Published in English as On the Management of Public Monopolies Subject to Budgetary Constraints, *Journal of Economic Theory* 3: 219–240.

Bond, E., and L. Samuelson. 1984. Durable Good Monopolies with Rational Expectations and Replacement Sales. *Rand Journal of Economics* 15: 336–345.

Brown, S., and D. Sibley. 1986. *The Theory of Public Utility Pricing*. Cambridge University Press.

48. A number of details have been swept under the rug here. In particular, we implicitly assumed that the seller uses a pure strategy, which is not required for the result. The real proof is more complicated and can be found in Gul et al. 1986.

Bucovetsky, S., and J. Chilton. 1986. Concurrent Renting and Selling in a Durable Goods Monopoly under Threat of Entry. *Rand Journal of Economics* 17: 261–278.

Bulow, J. 1982. Durable Goods Monopolists. *Journal of Political Economy* 90: 314–332.

Bulow, J. 1986. An Economic Theory of Planned Obsolescence. *Quarterly Journal of Economics* 51: 729–750.

Bulow, J., and P. Pfleiderer. 1983. A Note on the Effect of Cost Changes on Prices. *Journal of Political Economy* 91: 182–185.

Caillaud, B., R. Guesnerie, P. Rey, and J. Tirole. 1988. The Normative Economics of Government Intervention in Production. *Rand Journal of Economics*, forthcoming.

Coase, R. 1972. Durability and Monopoly. *Journal of Law and Economics* 15: 143–149.

Conlisk, J., E. Gerstner, and J. Sobel. 1984. Cyclic Pricing by a Durable Goods Monopolist. *Quarterly Journal of Economics* 99: 489–505.

Cowling, K., and D. Mueller. 1978. The Social Costs of Monopoly Power. *Economic Journal* 88: 724–748.

Dewatripont, M. 1985. Renegotiation and Information Revelation over Time in Optimal Labor Contracts. Mimeo, Harvard University.

Dixit, A. 1976. *Optimization in Economic Theory*. Oxford University Press.

Evans, R. 1987. Sequential Bargaining with Correlated Values. Mimeo, Cambridge University.

Fisher, F. 1985. The Social Costs of Monopoly and Regulation: Posner Reconsidered. *Journal of Political Economy* 93: 410–416.

Fudenberg, D., and J. Tirole. 1983. Learning-by-Doing and Market Performance. *Bell Journal of Economics* 14: 522–530.

Fudenberg, D., D. Levine, and J. Tirole. 1985. Infinite-Horizon Models of Bargaining with One-Sided Incomplete Information. In *Game-Theoretic Models of Bargaining*, ed. A. Roth. Cambridge University Press.

Fudenberg, D., D. Levine, and J. Tirole. 1987. Incomplete Information Bargaining with Outside Opportunities. *Quarterly Journal of Economics* 102: 37–50.

Gaskins, D. 1974. Alcoa Revisited: The Welfare Implications of a Second-Hand Market. *Journal of Economic Theory* 7: 254–271.

Guesnerie, R., and J.-J. Laffont. 1978. Taxing Price Makers. *Journal of Economic Theory* 19: 423–455.

Gul, F. 1987. Foundations of Dynamic Oligopoly. *Rand Journal of Economics* 18: 248–254.

Gul, F., H. Sonnenschein, and R. Wilson. 1986. Foundations of Dynamic Monopoly and the Coase Conjecture. *Journal of Economic Theory* 39: 155–190.

Harberger, H. 1954. Monopoly and Resource Allocation. *American Economic Review* 44: 77–87.

Hart, O., and J. Tirole. 1987. Contract Renegotiation and Coasian Dynamics. *Review of Economic Studies*, forthcoming.

Hicks, J. 1935. Annual Survey of Economic Theory: The Theory of Monopoly. *Econometrica* 3: 1–20.

Intriligator, M. 1971. *Mathematical Optimization and Economic Theory*. Englewood Cliffs, N.J.: Prentice-Hall.

Jenny, F., and A. Weber. 1983. Aggregate Welfare Loss due to Monopoly Power in the French Economy: Some Tentative Estimates. *Journal of Industrial Economics* 32: 113–130.

Kahn, C. 1986. The Durable Goods Monopolist and Consistency with Increasing Costs. *Econometrica* 54: 275–294.

Kamien, M., and N. Schwartz. 1981. *Dynamic Optimization*. Amsterdam: North-Holland.

Krueger, A. 1974. The Political Economy of the Rent-Seeking Society. *American Economic Review* 64: 291–303.

Laffont, J.-J., and J. Tirole. 1986. Using Cost Observation to Regulate Firms. *Journal of Political Economy* 94: 614–641.

Lazear, E. P. 1986. Retail Pricing and Clearance Sales. *American Economic Review* 76: 14–32.

Lazear, E. P. and S. Rosen. 1981. Rank-Order Tournaments as Optimal Labor Contracts. *Journal of Political Economy* 89: 841–64.

Leibenstein, H. 1966. Allocative Efficiency vs. 'X-Efficiency.' *American Economic Review* 56: 392–415.

Liebowitz, S. 1982. Durability, Market Structure and New-Used Goods Models. *American Economic Review* 72: 816–824.

Machlup, F. 1967. Theories of the Firm: Marginalist, Behavioral, Managerial. *American Economic Review* 57: 1–33.

Martin, R. 1982. Monopoly Power and the Recycling of Raw Materials. *Journal of Industrial Economics* 30: 405–419.

McLennan, A. 1984. Price Dispersion and Incomplete Learning in the Long Run. *Journal of Economic Dynamics and Control* 7: 331–347.

Moorthy, S. 1980. Notes on Durable Goods Monopolists and Rational Expectations Equilibria. Mimeo, Graduate School of Business, Stanford University.

Phlips, L. 1980. Intertemporal Price Discrimination and Sticky Prices. *Quarterly Journal of Economics* 94: 525–542.

Phlips, L. 1983. *The Economics of Price Discrimination*. Cambridge University Press.

Posner, R. 1975. The Social Costs of Monopoly and Regulation. *Journal of Political Economy* 83: 807–827.

Ramsey, F. 1927. A Contribution to the Theory of Taxation. *Economic Journal* 37: 47–61.

Rasmussen, E. 1986. The Learning Curve in a Competitive Industry. Mimeo, Graduate School of Management, University of California, Los Angeles.

Reagan, P. 1982. Inventory and Price Behavior. *Review of Economic Studies* 49: 137–142.

Reagan, P., and M. Weitzman. 1982. Asymmetries in Price and Quantity Adjustments by the Competitive Firm. *Journal of Economic Theory* 27: 410–420.

Robinson, J. 1933. *The Economics of Imperfect Competition.* London: Macmillan.

Rogerson, W. 1982. The Social Costs of Monopoly and Regulation: A Game-Theoretic Approach. *Bell Journal of Economics* 13: 391–401.

Rothschild, M. 1974. A Two-Armed Bandit Theory of Market Pricing. *Journal of Economic Theory* 9: 185–202.

Sappington, D. 1982. Optimal Regulation of Research Development under Imperfect Information. *Bell Journal of Economics* 13: 354–368.

Sappington, D. 1983. Optimal Regulation of a Multi-Product Monopoly with Unknown Technological Capabilities. *Bell Journal of Economics* 14: 453–463.

Sappington, D., and J. Stiglitz. 1987. Information and Regulation. In *Public Regulation: New Perspectives on Institutions and Policies,* ed. E. Bailey. Cambridge, Mass.: MIT Press.

Scherer, F. 1980. *Industrial Market Structure and Economic Performance,* second edition. Chicago: Rand-McNally.

Schmalensee, R. 1974. Market Structure, Durability, and Maintenance Effort. *Review of Economic Studies* 41: 277–287.

Schmalensee, R. 1979. Market Structure, Durability and Quality: A Selective Survey. *Economic Inquiry* 17: 177–196.

Schutte, D. 1983. Inventories and Sticky Prices: Note. *American Economic Review* 73: 815–816.

Sheshinski, E. 1986. Positive Second-Best Theory: A Brief Survey of the Theory of Ramsey Pricing. In *Handbook of Mathematical Economics,* volume 3, ed. K. Arrow and M. Intriligator, Amsterdam: Elsevier.

Sobel, J., and I. Takahashi. 1983. A Multi-Stage Model of Bargaining. *Review of Economic Studies* 50: 411–426.

Stokey, N. 1979. Intertemporal Price Discrimination. *Quarterly Journal of Economics* 93: 355–371.

Stokey, N. 1981. Rational Expectations and Durable Goods Pricing. *Bell Journal of Economics* 12: 112–128.

Sultan, R. 1975. Pricing in the Electrical Oligopoly, volumes 1 and 2. Division of Research, Harvard Graduate School of Business Administration.

Sumner, D. 1981. Measurement of Monopoly Behavior: An Application to the Cigarette Industry. *Journal of Political Economy* 89: 1010–1019.

Suslow, V. 1986. Commitment and Monopoly Pricing in Durable Goods Models. *International Journal of Industrial Organization* 4: 451–460.

Swan, P. 1972. Optimum Durability, Second-Hand Markets, and Planned Obsolescence. *Journal of Political Economy* 80: 575–585.

Swan, P. 1980. Alcoa: The Influence of Recycling on Monopoly Power. *Journal of Political Economy* 88: 76–99.

Tullock, G. 1967. The Welfare Costs of Tariffs, Monopolies and Theft. *Western Economic Journal* 5: 224–232. Reprinted in *Toward a Theory of the Rent Seeking Society,* ed. J. Buchanan et al. (Texas A&M University Press, 1980).

Varian, H. 1987. Measuring the Deadweight Costs of DVP and Rent Seeking Activities. Mimeo, University of Michigan.

Vincent, D. 1986. Bargaining with Common Values. Mimeo, Princeton University.

Williamson, O. 1968. Economies as an Antitrust Defense: The Welfare Tradeoffs. *American Economic Review* 58: 18–36.

Wilson, R. 1985. Economic Theories of Price Discrimination and Product Differentiation: A Survey. Mimeo, Graduate School of Business, Stanford University.

Product Selection, Quality, and Advertising

One of the functions of the production system is to select the commodities that are produced and sold. This selection involves real economic choices; owing in particular to increasing returns to scale, only some of the potentially producible goods are actually manufactured. In the preceding chapter we assumed that the set of goods produced by the monopolist was given. In this chapter we relax that assumption by letting the monopolist choose a position in a "product space." This is not to say that other monopoly decisions are entirely put aside. For instance, the monopolist's choice between different qualities depends on how these qualities can be marketed, so pricing behavior cannot be ignored.

This chapter starts with a brief description of the product space. It then discusses the choice of product by a monopolist, assuming that the characteristics of the product become known to the consumers before they purchase. Depending on the application, the monopolist may offer too high or too low a quality and too much or too little product variety relative to the social optimum. The monopolist has no reason to choose the optimal products; however, in contrast with the case of pricing behavior, one cannot sign the bias without further analysis of the consumers' preferences and the production technology (section 2.2).

Sections 2.3 and 2.4 consider goods whose characteristics are learned by the consumers only after purchase ("experience goods"). The main issues in regard to such goods are whether there are incentives for firms to supply quality and whether variables such as price and advertising provide any (indirect) information about it. The main incentive to provide quality is the possibility of repeat purchases by consumers, which induces firms to sustain quality so as not to hurt their reputation and lose future sales. The key ideas behind signaling and reputation are mentioned in the body of the chapter and developed in the supplementary section.

2.1 The Notion of Product Space

As is well known, it is hard to come up with a satisfactory definition of the notion of an industry or a market. On the one hand, two goods are almost never perfect substitutes (in the sense that all consumers are indifferent between the goods when they have the same price). Goods are almost always differentiated by some characteristic. On the other hand, a group of products (an "industry") always interacts to some extent with other goods in the economy; the pricing of goods outside the industry enters into the demand for the goods in the industry not only through income effects but also through substitution effects. The notion of an industry is an idealization or a limit case.

There remains the question of how to describe the differentiation between the goods within an industry. This question has been addressed by, among others, Hotelling (1929), Chamberlin (1951, 1962), and Lancaster (1966). A good can be described as a bundle of characteristics: quality, location, time, availability, consumers' information about its existence and quality, and so on. Each consumer has a ranking over the mix of variables.

Introducing all potential characteristics provides a rich description of a good, but is likely to be of little help in studying issues of industrial organization. Both in empirical work and in theoretical work, researchers focus their attention on a small subset of characteristics and on a special (but, if possible, reasonable) description of preferences. There are three types of cases that are commonly used.

2.1.1 Vertical Differentiation

In a vertically differentiated product space, all consumers agree over the most preferred mix of characteristics and, more generally, over the preference ordering. A typical example is quality. Most agree that higher quality is preferable—for instance, that a Volvo is preferable to a Hyundai. (However, more consumers may still purchase the latter. The consumers' income and the prices of the cars, and of servicing them, determine the consumers' ultimate choice. See below.) Similarly, a smaller and more powerful computer is preferable to a larger, less powerful one. At equal prices there is a natural ordering over the characteristic space.

Example

A simple example of a vertical-differentiation model is the following. Each consumer consumes one or zero units of a "good." The good is characterized by a quality index s (we will use s, for "services," so as not to confuse quality with quantity, which is denoted by q). When the monopolist produces several qualities, we will often talk about these different qualities as being "different goods." For the moment, we shall confine ourselves to the single-quality/good monopolist. A consumer has the following preferences:

$$U = \begin{cases} \theta s - p & \text{if he buys a good with quality } s \\ & \text{at price } p, \\ 0 & \text{if he does not buy.} \end{cases}$$

U should be thought of as the surplus derived from the consumption of the good. s is a positive real number that describes the quality of the good. The utility is separable in quality and price. θ, a positive real number, is a taste parameter. All consumers prefer high quality, for a given price; however, a consumer with a high θ is more willing to pay to obtain high quality. Modeling a distribution of tastes consists of assuming that θ is distributed in the economy according to some density $f(\theta)$ with cumulative distribution function $F(\theta)$ on $[0, +\infty)$, where $F(0) = 0$ and $F(+\infty) = 1$. Thus, $F(\theta)$ is the fraction of consumers with a taste parameter of less than θ.

An interesting reinterpretation of these preferences views θ as the inverse of the marginal rate of substitution between income and quality rather than as a taste parameter. As far as the choice between buying and not buying is concerned, the consumer's preferences could be read as

$$U = \begin{cases} s - (1/\theta)p & \text{if he buys a good with quality } s \\ & \text{at price } p, \\ 0 & \text{if he does not buy.} \end{cases}$$

On this interpretation, all consumers derive the same surplus from the good, but they have different incomes and, therefore, different marginal rates of substitution between income and quality $(1/\theta)$. Wealthier consumers have a lower "marginal utility of income" or, equivalently, a higher θ.[1]

Let us derive the demand function(s) for this particular utility function. If only one quality, s, is offered at price p, the demand for the good is equal to the number of consumers with taste parameter θ such that $\theta s \geqslant p$. In other words, the demand for the good is

$$D(p) = N[1 - F(p/s)],$$

where N is the total number of consumers.

If there are several qualities offered in the market, the consumers choose among these qualities as well as choosing whether to buy at all (assuming they have unit demands—i.e., they consume at most one unit of the good —whatever the quality). Suppose, for instance, that goods of two qualities, $s_1 < s_2$, are sold at prices $p_1 < p_2$. (The price inequality makes the problem nontrivial, as a low-quality good that is more expensive than a high-quality one will never be purchased.) First, assume that the "quality per dollar" is higher for quality 2: $s_2/p_2 \geqslant s_1/p_1$. Then, all consumers always prefer quality 2 to quality 1 if they purchase at all:

$$(\theta s_2 - p_2) - (\theta s_1 - p_1)$$
$$= p_2(\theta s_2/p_2 - 1) - p_1(\theta s_1/p_1 - 1)$$
$$\geqslant (p_2 - p_1)(\theta s_1/p_1 - 1)$$
$$\geqslant 0$$
$$\text{if } \theta s_1 \geqslant p_1.$$

The demand for the high-quality good is then

$$D_2(p_1, p_2) = N[1 - F(p_2/s_2)],$$

and the demand for the low-quality good is zero. The more interesting case occurs when the low-quality good is not "dominated." Then, the consumers with a taste parameter exceeding $\tilde{\theta} \equiv (p_2 - p_1)/(s_2 - s_1)$ buy the high-quality good, since $\theta s_2 - p_2 \geqslant \theta s_1 - p_1 \Leftrightarrow \theta \geqslant \tilde{\theta}$, those with a taste parameter lower than $\tilde{\theta}$ but exceeding p_1/s_1 buy the low-quality good, and the others do not

buy. Thus, the demands are

$$D_2(p_1, p_2) = N[1 - F((p_2 - p_1)/(s_2 - s_1))]$$

and

$$D_1(p_1, p_2) = N[F((p_2 - p_1)/(s_2 - s_1)) - F(p_1/s_1)].$$

2.1.2 Horizontal Differentiation

For some characteristics, the optimal choice (at equal prices) depends on the particular consumer. Tastes vary in the population. An obvious example is the case of colors. Another example is location. Bostonians are likely to prefer goods that are available in Boston to goods that are physically the same but are available only in Paris. Similarly, consumers will prefer to go to a shop or a supermarket that is nearby. In such cases of horizontal or "spatial" differentiation, there are no "goods" or "bads."

Example

A simple model of horizontal differentiation is given in Hotelling 1929. Consider a "linear city" of length 1. Consumers are distributed uniformly along the city. As the analysis greatly resembles the vertical-differentiation example, let us start directly with a "two-good" example, which is used in exercise 2.3 below. Two shops, located at the two ends of the city, both sell the same physical good. The location of shop 1 is $x = 0$, and that of shop 2 is $x = 1$. (See figure 2.1.) Consumers have transportation cost t per unit of length (this cost can include the consumers' value of time). They have unit demands; they consume zero or one unit of the good. Let p_1 and p_2 denote the prices charged by the two shops. The "gen-

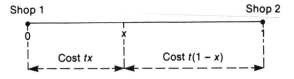

Figure 2.1
The linear city.

---

1. Suppose that consumers have identical ordinal preferences and differ only in their incomes. Consider the following separable representation of a consumer's utility function: $U = u(I - p) + s$, where I is the consumer's income. (Taking a slightly more general function $U = u(I - p) + \Phi(s)$ with Φ increasing would not change anything; it would amount to a redefinition of "quality.") Let p

be much smaller than I; i.e., the expenditure on this particular good is small relative to income. A first-order Taylor expansion yields $U \simeq -u'(I)p + s$. Let $\theta \equiv 1/u'(I)$. If u is concave, wealthier consumers have a low $u'(I)$ and therefore a high θ.

Product Selection, Quality, and Advertising

eralized price" of going to shop 1 (respectively, shop 2) for a consumer with coordinate x is $p_1 + tx$ (respectively, $p_2 + t(1 - x)$). If $\bar{s}$ denotes the surplus enjoyed by each consumer when he is consuming the good, the utility of a consumer located at x is

$$\bar{s} - p_1 - tx$$

if he buys from shop 1,

$$\bar{s} - p_2 - t(1 - x)$$

if he buys from shop 2, and zero otherwise. Let us derive the demand functions for three cases.

If the price difference between the two shops does not exceed the transportation cost t along the whole city, and if prices are "not too high" (see below), there exists a consumer with location $\tilde{x}$ who is indifferent between buying from shop 1 and buying from shop 2:

$$p_1 + t\tilde{x} = p_2 + t(1 - \tilde{x}) \Leftrightarrow \tilde{x}(p_1, p_2) = (p_2 - p_1 + t)/2t.$$

Then the demands are

$$D_1(p_1, p_2) = N\tilde{x}(p_1, p_2)$$

and

$$D_2(p_1, p_2) = N[1 - \tilde{x}(p_1, p_2)],$$

where N is the total number of consumers.

If the price difference between the two shops exceeds t (say, $p_2 - p_1 \geqslant t$), shop 2 has no demand. Shop 1 has demand $D_1(p_1, p_2) = N$ if $p_1 \leqslant \bar{s} - t$ (i.e., if all consumers are willing to buy at shop 1) and demand $D_1(p_1, p_2) = N(\bar{s} - p_1)/t$ if $p_1 > \bar{s} - t$. In the latter case, the market is "not covered," in that some consumers do not buy at all.

The third case is that in which each shop has a local monopoly power (and the market is not covered). This occurs when both p_1 and p_2 belong to $[\bar{s} - t, \bar{s}]$ and the consumer located at $\tilde{x}(p_1, p_2)$ who would be indifferent between the two shops does not buy. (This is equivalent to the condition $p_1 + p_2 + t > 2\bar{s}$.) The three cases are illustrated in figure 2.2.

Figures 2.2a–2.2c represent the generalized costs for the consumers as a function of their locations, as well as the market shares of the two products. In figure 2.2a, the two products compete for consumers. A reduction in one product's price reduces the demand for the other product. In figures 2.2b and 2.2c, the pricing policy of one product

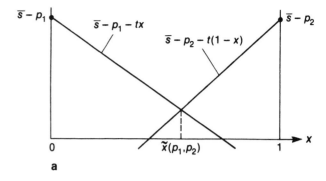

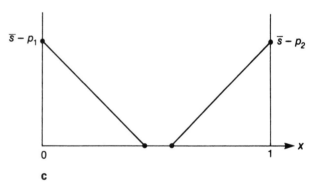

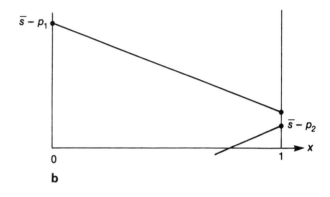

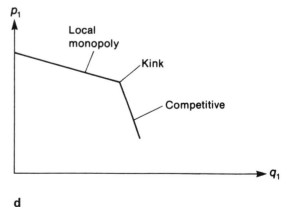

Figure 2.2

does not affect (locally, at least) the demand for the other product. Figure 2.2d depicts the residual demand for good 1, taking the price of good 2 as given. This demand curve exhibits a kink at the price at which the local monopoly and the competitive regimes meet (a borderline case in figures 2.2a and 2.2c). At this point, a unit increase in p_1 lowers the demand for good 1 by $1/t$ whereas a unit decrease in p_1 raises the demand for good 1 by only $1/2t$.[2]

2.1.3 "Goods–Characteristics" Approach

Goods are defined as bundles of characteristics, and the consumers have preferences over characteristics. The consumers may have heterogeneous preferences over characteristics. In the vertical- and horizontal-differentiation approaches, it was assumed that consumers purchase only one good—in other words, that they do not get extra utility from consuming a variety of goods. In contrast, one could assume that consumers can consume several goods and, furthermore, that all they care about in a good is its characteristics. For example, assume that what the consumer cares about in foods is protein and vitamins. If one unit of food 1 supplies two units of protein and one unit of vitamins, one unit of food 2 one unit of protein and two units of vitamins, and one unit of food 3 one unit of each, the consumer is indifferent between one unit of foods 1 and 2 and three units of food 3. In other words, the consumer ultimately cares only about the characteristics of the bundles of goods, i.e., the sum of the characteristics of the goods in the bundle. This is the approach pioneered by Lancaster (1966).

The goods–characteristics approach makes sense in a number of cases. For instance, when buying light bulbs, the consumer certainly cares mainly about the total number of hours of lighting provided by the bundle of bulbs. The key to the approach is to be able to sum up the characteristics. In some cases this approach is less handy —in particular, where there are indivisibilities of consumption, as in the vertical- and horizontal-differentiation

examples above. The Lancaster framework must then be amended.[3]

2.1.4 Traditional Consumer-Theory Approach

In its extreme form, the Lancasterian approach ignores the notion of good to focus on that of characteristic; goods are here only to provide characteristics. Conversely, one can ignore the notion of characteristic and focus on that of good. This is indeed the approach taken by classical general-equilibrium theory: Both production functions and utility functions are defined as functions of the quantities of the various goods. One cannot be more general than by writing a utility function $U(q_0, q_1, q_2, \ldots, q_n)$ with components the consumptions of goods $0, 1, 2, \ldots, n$. The questions are these: How can we impose more structure and get results? What does this added structure imply about products?

The following utility function is commonly used to study product selection (see chapter 7). There are two sectors in the economy. The "representative consumer" (all consumers are identical) consumes a quantity q_0 of the unique good produced by the first sector and quantities $\{q_i\}_{i=1}^n$ of the n goods produced by the second sector, which is called "the sector of differentiated products." His utility function is

$$U = U\left(q_0, \left(\sum_{i=1}^n q_i^\rho\right)^{1/\rho}\right).$$

For U to be quasi-concave, ρ must be $\leqslant 1$. If p_i is the price of the differentiated product i, and if the good in the first sector is the numéraire and I is the consumer's income, the representative consumer maximizes U subject to the budget constraint

$$q_0 + \sum_{i=1}^n p_i q_i \leqslant I.$$

The "sub utility function" for the differentiated goods is a constant-elasticity-of-substitution (CES) utility function.

---

2. There is also a large literature in marketing that deals with the notion of product space. Schmalensee and Thisse (1987) draw the link between the "perceptual mapping" techniques used in that literature and the location techniques considered here.

3. As Rosen (1974) notes, "two six-foot cars are not equivalent to one twelve [feet] in length, because they cannot be driven simultaneously" (or, "two fiddles don't make a Stradivarius"). Rosen departs from the Lancasterian framework on

the assumption of divisibility. As a consequence, the "hedonic prices," which give the total cost of a bundle of characteristics, may not be linear in the amounts of the characteristics even under perfect competition. That is, one cannot compute the price of a good by simply adding the amounts of its characteristics weighted by prices affected to unit amounts of these characteristics. See also Lancaster 1975, 1979.

As was noted above, the approach in terms of goods rather than characteristics is very general (for instance, the basic Lancasterian form simply presumes linear functional forms). However, for applications to industrial organization, it may have some drawbacks. As it does not make explicit the characteristics over which firms are competing, it sometimes gives limited intuition concerning the plausibility of preferences. Or else, it may be very specific, as in the case of the CES utility function given above. The latter utility function treats all the differentiated products in a symmetric way. When a firm introduces a product, it does not choose its degree of differentiation relative to other products. This contrasts with the horizontal- and vertical-differentiation approaches as well as with the goods–characteristics approach, in that there is no notion of "remoteness" or "neighborhood" relative to the other products. In particular, this approach is poorly adapted to describe a confined space.[4] Industrial-organization economists generally feel that a new product does not compete as closely with each and every other product.

2.2 Product Selection

Let us now investigate what kind of bias a monopolist introduces in his choice of product(s). Throughout this section we will follow fairly closely the work of Spence (1975, 1976).[5] We start with the choice of quality (a vertical characteristic) by a single-product monopolist. We then look at the closely related question of whether a monopolist supplies too few or too many products (from a social standpoint).

2.2.1 Product Quality

Assume that a monopolist produces a single good, for which he chooses two real numbers: a price p and a quality s. Let $p = P(q, s)$ denote the inverse-demand curve, i.e., the price that creates a demand for q units of the good at quality s. Quality is desirable, in that P increases with s. Let $C(q, s)$ denote the total cost of producing q units of

a good with quality s. It is natural to assume that C increases with s.

Let us first consider the choice of quality by a social planner, who would choose price and quality (or, equivalently, quantity and quality) so as to maximize the difference between gross consumer surplus and production cost. Taking quality and quantity as the decision variables, the social planner maximizes

$$W(q, s) = \int_0^q P(x, s)dx - C(q, s).$$

We approximate gross consumer surplus by the integral under the demand curve given the specification of quality. The first-order conditions are

$$P(q, s) = C_q(q, s) \tag{2.1}$$

and

$$\int_0^q P_s(x, s)dx = C_s(q, s), \tag{2.2}$$

where subscripts denote partial derivatives. Equation 2.1 is the now-familiar equality between price and marginal cost. Equation 2.2 stems from the choice of quality. It states that the partial derivative of gross surplus with respect to quality is equal to the marginal cost of producing this quality. To understand this formula, it may be helpful to think of the demand curve as stemming from a large number of consumers with unit demands, ranking them in decreasing order of willingness to pay. $P(x, s)$ is then the price that makes the xth consumer indifferent between buying one unit of the good of quality s and not buying. Thus, $P_s(x, s)$ is equal to the willingness to pay (in terms of money) by consumer x for one more unit of quality. Alternatively, $P_s(x, s)$ is the marginal valuation for quality for the marginal consumer when the price is $P(x, s)$. Hence, the marginal gross surplus is equal to output q times the average marginal valuation of quality over the market, which is

$$\left(\int_0^q P_s(x, s)dx \right) \Big/ q.$$

---

4. As we will see, in the case of such a utility function for large n, a change in the price of good $i \geqslant 1$ does not trigger a change in the price of good $j \geqslant 1$. This abstract utility function is, however, very convenient to use when studying the number of products, because it allows one to concentrate on the entry

decision ("zero or one") without complicating it with choices of location, quality, etc. See chapter 7.

5. See also Sheshinski 1976.

The monopolist is concerned not with social surplus but with profits. Thus, he maximizes

$$\Pi^m(q, s) = q P(q, s) - C(q, s).$$

This leads to the first-order conditions

$$P(q, s) + q P_q(q, s) = C_q(q, s) \tag{2.3}$$

and

$$q P_s(q, s) = C_s(q, s). \tag{2.4}$$

Equation 2.3 is the familiar equality between marginal revenue and marginal cost, which is the expression of optimal pricing by the monopolist. Equation 2.4 determines the optimal quality for a given output q. It states that the marginal revenue associated with a unit increase in quality is equal to the marginal cost of producing this quality.

The difference between equations 2.1 and 2.3 is familiar; the monopolist is concerned with the effect of output on price, whereas the social planner (or a competitive firm) is not. More interesting here is the comparison between equations 2.2 and 2.4. The social planner's concern about the average marginal valuation for quality is replaced by the monopolist's concern about the "marginal marginal" valuation $P_s(q, s)$, where the first marginal refers to the consumer and the second to quality. (For ease of notation, we will often delete the "marginal" corresponding to quality.) This is easily understood. The social planner looks at the effect of an increase in quality on *all* consumers; the monopolist considers the effect of an increase in quality on the *marginal* consumer. When raising the quality by Δs, the monopolist can raise the price by $P_s(q, s)\Delta s$ while keeping the same demand (i.e., keeping the marginal consumer at the same utility level). This price increase, however, can be passed on to all inframarginal consumers, which generates an extra revenue $q P_s(q, s)\Delta s$.

In summary: *The incentive to provide quality is related to the marginal willingness to pay for quality, for the marginal consumer in the case of a monopolist and for the average consumer in the case of a social planner.*

Hence, it is natural to compare $P_s(q, s)$ and $(\int_0^q P_s(x, s)\, dx)/q$. A caveat: This comparison tells us which way the monopolist biases his choice of quality only if the output is the same in both arrangements. This property generally does not hold, because, as we have seen, the monopolist

tends to restrict output for a given quality. Hence the qualifier in the following proposition: *For a given output q, the monopolist undersupplies quality relative to the optimum when*

$$\left(\int_0^q P_s(x, s)\,dx \right) \Big/ q > P_s(q, s),$$

and conversely. Because there is no *a priori* reason why the marginal consumer is representative of the population (i.e., has the same marginal valuation for quality as the inframarginal consumers), the monopolist, in general, introduces a bias in product selection at a given output level.

In both the case of choice of quality and that of monopoly pricing, the monopolist is concerned with the effect of his decision on the marginal consumer's demand; the social planner cares about the effect of the decision variable on the inframarginal consumers' welfare as well. The analogy becomes trivial in the extreme case in which services are a perfect substitute for price reductions (this may be the case, for instance, when the "service" is the price of delivery of the good). Suppose that the consumers care only about the "real price" $p - s$, where s denotes the monetary value of services; their demand function is $q = D(p - s)$, so their inverse demand function is linear in services:

$$p = D^{-1}(q) + s \equiv P(q, s).$$

Suppose further that the cost of supplying the service is $C(q, s) = sq$. Then s is the equivalent of a price reduction from the point of view of consumers and seller. It is left to the reader to check that equation 2.4 is satisfied. From here on, we will be interested in those quality variables that are imperfect substitutes for price reductions. It is useful for some intuitions to think of this trivial case of perfect substitutes.

The previous proposition gives a simple condition to determine whether the monopolist oversupplies or undersupplies quality. This may seem a weak proposition, in that it relies on an assumption—same output in the two arrangements—that is very unlikely to be satisfied. We should pause for a moment here and ask how important it is to compare the monopolist's and the social planner's choices of qualities once the difference in pricing behaviors (in outputs) is taken into account. Such a comparison makes sense if we are interested in moving from a monopoly to a perfect socially oriented organization. When making a choice between a monopoly and a socially oriented organization, one may want to focus on the total dead-weight loss associated with monopoly, and not only on the quality distortion. If, in contrast, the private monopoly arrangement is not at stake, and one simply wants to affect the monopolist's choice of product quality through subsidies, minimum quality standards, and so forth, then the previous proposition, which takes output as given, becomes more relevant. For instance, an increase in quality is socially desirable if the average valuation for quality exceeds the marginal valuation for quality *and* if the policy that brings forth this increase in quality does not induce the monopolist to contract output (remember that an increase in output at the monopoly solution is socially desirable). The bottom line is, as usual, that the relevant issue depends on the policy move being considered.

2.2.1.1 Applications

Swan's (1970) Optimal-Durability Theorem

Suppose that the quality variable is the durability of the good. For instance, let s denote the number of lighting hours of a light bulb. A consumer who buys q bulbs obtains qs hours. Assume that the consumers care only about the total number of hours, and not about the way these hours are obtained. In this Lancasterian world, the price per unit of durability that induces consumers to buy q units of a good of quality s depends only on the product of these two variables; $P(q, s)/s \equiv \tilde{P}(qs)$.[6] Let $\tilde{q} \equiv qs$ denote total consumption (and, similarly, let $\tilde{x} = xs$, where x denotes an arbitrary consumption level). Further, assume that the production cost is linear in output: $C(q, s) = c(s)q$. (Unit production cost naturally rises with quality $c'(s) > 0$.)

The social planner (or a competitive industry) maximizes total welfare:

$$W(q, s) = \int_0^q P(x, s)dx - c(s)q$$

$$= \int_0^q s\,\tilde{P}(xs)dx - c(s)q$$

$$= \int_0^{\tilde{q}} \tilde{P}(\tilde{x})d\tilde{x} - \left(\frac{c(s)}{s}\right)\tilde{q}.$$

The maximization with respect to q and s is equivalent to that with respect to $\tilde{q}$ and s. In particular, we see that the social planner minimizes the unit cost of durability $c(s)/s$.

The monopolist maximizes profit:

$$\Pi^m(q, s) = q\,P(q, s) - c(s)q$$

$$= qs\left(\tilde{P}(qs) - \frac{c(s)}{s}\right)$$

$$= \tilde{q}\left(\tilde{P}(\tilde{q}) - \frac{c(s)}{s}\right).$$

The first-order condition with respect to s shows that the monopolist also minimizes the unit cost of durability. Hence, monopoly power does not introduce a distortion in the choice of durability. This result is part of the Swan invariance theorem, which states that, if consumers care only about total services $\tilde{q} = qs$ and if the production function exhibits constant returns to scale in output, the choice of durability is independent of the market structure.

This invariance is quite natural. The consumers actually care about the *composite* good $\tilde{q}$. The firm, in all arrangements, wants to minimize the cost of producing this composite commodity. Under constant returns to scale, its unit production cost $c(s)/s$ is independent of output. Thus, durability and price decisions are disjoint. (The invariance result does not hold if the cost function $C(q, s)$ cannot be written as a product. And, of course, the assumption that consumers consider two one-year bulbs to be perfect substitutes for one two-year bulb is also crucial to the result.[7])

The Dorfman-Steiner (1954) Condition

In their seminal paper on advertising, Dorfman and Steiner assumed that the demand facing the firm is a function of price and advertising, so that $P(q, s)$ denotes the inverse demand function, where s denotes the total expenses of advertising. This formulation is not appropriate for welfare analysis; rational consumers, in general, may not en-

---

6. More formally, consider for simplicity a representative consumer, and let $U(qs)$ denote the gross surplus for this consumer consuming q units of the good with durability s. The net surplus is $U(qs) - pq$. The consumer's optimal consumption is given by $s\,U'(qs) = p$. The expression $\tilde{P}(qs)$ in the text is nothing but $U'(qs)$. This analysis is easily generalized to the case of heterogeneous consumers.

7. For more on the durability and invariance issues, see Hirshleifer 1971, Kihlstrom and Levhari 1977, and Liebowitz 1982.

joy advertising *per se.* The reasons why advertising affects demand are not made explicit here and are subsumed in the "reduced-form" demand function $P(q,s)$.[8] Thus, we study only the monopolist's program, and not the planner's. The monopolist's profit is

$$\Pi^m(q,s) = q\,P(q,s) - C(q) - s.$$

The cost function is assumed to be additive in output and advertising. Conditions 2.3 and 2.4 can be written as

$$P(q,s) + q\,P_q(q,s) = C_q$$

and

$$q\,P_s(q,s) = 1.$$

To obtain the Dorfman-Steiner condition, it turns out to be convenient to maximize over price and advertising rather than over quantity and advertising. Let $q = D(p,s)$ denote the demand at price p and advertising level s. The monopolist's profit can be rewritten as

$$\Pi^m(p,s) = p\,D(p,s) - C(D(p,s)) - s.$$

The first-order conditions for the maximization with respect to p and s are

$$D(p,s) + p\,D_p(p,s) = C'(D(p,s))D_p(p,s)$$

and

$$p\,D_s(p,s) - C'(D(p,s))D_s(p,s) = 1.$$

Let

$$\varepsilon_p \equiv -\frac{\partial D}{\partial p}\frac{p}{q}$$

and

$$\varepsilon_s \equiv \frac{\partial D}{\partial s}\frac{s}{q}$$

denote the elasticities of demand with respect to price and

advertising, respectively. Then, rearranging the two first-order conditions yields the desired formula:

$$\frac{s}{pq} = \frac{\varepsilon_s}{\varepsilon_p}.$$

The monopolist's optimal advertising/sales ratio is equal to the ratio of the elasticities of demand with respect to advertising and to price.[9] (Because sales and advertising are selected simultaneously, one should not conclude that sales determine advertising in a causal sense.)

Exercise 2.1* Show that if demand is of the Cobb-Douglas type—$q = p^{-\alpha}s^{\beta}$, where α and β are positive—the advertising/sales ratio is a constant. (In particular, show that it is independent of the cost structure.)

An Example of "Underprovision" of Quality

Consider the example of vertical differentiation given above. Consumers have utility (net surplus) $U = \theta s - p$ if they purchase and 0 otherwise. θ is distributed over the population with cumulative distribution F. If we normalize $N = 1$ (there is no loss of generality in doing so), the demand function is $q = 1 - F(p/s)$, or $p = P(q,s) = s\,F^{-1}(1 - q)$, where F^{-1} (the inverse of F) is an increasing function. The average marginal valuation for quality, which guides the social planner's quality decision, is

$$\frac{1}{q}\int_0^q P_s(x,s)dx = \frac{1}{q}\int_0^q F^{-1}(1 - x)dx.$$

The marginal valuation for quality of the marginal consumer, which guides the monopolist's decision, is

$$P_s(q,s) = F^{-1}(1 - q).$$

Because for $x \leqslant q$

$$F^{-1}(1 - x) \geqslant F^{-1}(1 - q),$$

the average valuation for quality exceeds the marginal

---

8. An example of such a specification (from Butters 1977) is the following: Suppose that the role of advertising is to inform consumers about the existence of the product and its price. Let N, the number of consumers, be large. Assume that the monopolist sends a total number s of messages (ads) randomly to consumers (thus, some consumers get no ads, while others get several). A consumer's probability of not getting an ad is

$$(1 - 1/N)^s \simeq e^{-s/N}$$

for N large. Letting $d(p)$ denote the representative consumer's demand function

(or the average demand over different types of consumers), we have

$$D(p,s) = N(1 - e^{-s/N})d(p).$$

Note that D has a multiplicative form in s and p. We will use this specification in chapter 7.

9. See Nerlove and Arrow 1962 and Schmalensee 1972 for dynamic versions of this formula.

---

valuation, and, for a given q, the monopolist under-supplies quality. This is easily understood: The marginal willingness to pay for quality of the marginal buyer is lower than that of other buyers, who have higher θ. An exogenous and small increase in quality starting from the monopoly quality would thus benefit society.

As was mentioned above, it is not clear, however, that the quality in the monopoly case is lower than that in the social-planning case. The social planner charges a low price and thus reaches a lower θ than the monopolist. Hence, the average valuation for quality given the social planner's pricing policy may end up being lower than the marginal valuation for the monopolist. Indeed, in the exercise below the quality is the same in both arrangements.

Exercise 2.2* In the above vertical-differentiation model, let θ be uniformly distributed on $[0, 1]$. The cost function is

$$C(q, s) = \left(\frac{cs^2}{2}\right)q.$$

(i) Check that, at q given,

$$\frac{1}{q}\int_0^q P_s(x, s)dx > P_s(q, s).$$

(ii) Show that, when the difference in output is taken account of, the monopoly and the social planner choose the same quality.

An Example of "Overprovision" of Quality

A consumer with "type" θ has utility $\theta + (\alpha - \theta)s - p$ if he purchases the good and utility 0 otherwise. The parameter θ is distributed on $[0, \alpha]$. Consider the situation where consumers enjoy the good *per se* (i.e., get utility θ from it) and also enjoy some extra services $s < 1$ that are attached to the good. But they enjoy these services more when their "intrinsic" willingness to pay for the good θ is lower. For instance, a monopoly concert hall may offer concerts and also distribute booklets explaining the music and introducing the conductor. The benefit from these side services may be higher for low-θ consumers. (High-θ consumers may be wealthy people who can afford to buy music books, have more education, etc.) It is easy to check that for this specification of preferences there is over-provision of services at a given output. The marginal

consumer values services more than the average consumer who purchases the good. Again, this result is contingent on the output being fixed. A social planner would want to reach lower θ and, therefore, might want to provide more services than the monopolist.

2.2.2 Too Many or Two Few Products?

In the preceding subsection we considered the case of a monopolist choosing the quality of the single good he produces. In general, he may produce several goods. How does the monopolist's choice of diversity compare with the socially optimal product diversity? The preceding example (which focused on the choice of a continuous variable rather than on the number of products) strongly suggests that the monopolist may choose either too many or too few products. As previously, "too many" or "too few" depends on the type of intervention one has in mind. In this subsection, we consider simple examples of the comparison between the monopoly solution and the social-planning solution (we do not study, for instance, the comparative statics of the monopoly situation). In chapter 7 we will return to the issue of product diversity in a framework of monopolistic competition.

2.2.2.1 Nonappropriability of the Social Surplus and Underprovision of Diversity

A firm that creates a new product generally cannot capture all the gross surplus generated by the product. Consider the case with only one potential design. The monopolist produces either one product or none. Assume that there exists a fixed cost f of introducing or producing the good (on top of the variable production cost). The monopolist introduces the product only if the monopoly profit Π^m (measured in figure 1.1 by the area of the trapezoid $CEFAC$) exceeds f. The social planner introduces the good if and only if the social welfare W (measured in figure 1.1 by the area of the triangle ADG) exceeds f. Note that $W > \Pi^m$. Hence, if the fixed cost satisfies $W > f > \Pi^m$, the monopolist does not introduce the good; the social planner does. Thus, with only one potential product, monopoly may imply "too few products" and never entails "too many products." This can be explained by the fact that the monopolist, in general, cannot appropriate the social surplus. $W - \Pi^m$ represents the sum of the dead-weight loss (measured by the triangle FEG) and the consumer net surplus (measured by the triangle *CDE*). An attempt to capture the consumer surplus by raising the price raises the dead-weight loss. What matters for the efficiency of product selection is what fraction of net potential surplus is capturable by the monopolist.

Remark 1 Even if the firm charges the monopoly price (thus introducing a dead-weight loss), there is still a tendency to have too few products under monopoly because the monopoly cannot capture the net consumer surplus.

Remark 2 There is a case in which the monopolist can capture the whole potential surplus from the introduction of the good. This case arises when the monopolist can price discriminate perfectly (i.e., can capture the whole consumer surplus without introducing a dead-weight loss). As we will see in chapter 3, perfect discrimination requires a perfect knowledge of individual demand functions (and not only of the aggregate demand function), a nonlinear pricing schedule if consumers' demands are not unit demands, and the absence of arbitrage between consumers.

Remark 3 We will see in chapter 10 that an analogous problem of appropriability is the basis for Schumpeter's reflections on the incentives for research and development (where the "good" is an invention).

Remark 4 A first intuition would be that the tendency to lose products is higher for higher elasticities of demand, because the monopolist is then induced to charge a lower price. However, for a constant-elasticity demand the fraction of potential surplus which the monopolist can appropriate increases with the elasticity (see exercise 1.1). Thus, underprovision of a product occurs more frequently for low-elasticity products.

2.2.2.2 Multiproduct Monopoly and Overprovision of Diversity

When a monopolist can manufacture several goods, a new effect appears which tends to create too much diversity. Suppose that a monopolist can produce two goods which are substitutes ($\partial D_j / \partial p_i > 0$, $i \neq j$, $i = 1, 2$). The price he charges for good 1 exceeds the marginal cost of producing that good. Thus, the demand function for good 2 is shifted up by the use of monopoly power for the first good. This may make it profitable to produce good 2, which it would not be profitable to do if the monopolist were to charge the competitive (socially optimal) price in the first market. The monopolist may produce good 2 when this is not socially optimal. The exercise below gives an instance in which this is indeed the case.

Exercise 2.3** Consider the horizontal-differentiation example in subsection 2.1.2. Consumers are uniformly distributed along a linear city of length 1, have transportation costs t per unit of distance, and have unit demands. Except for their location, they are all identical and have gross surplus $\bar{s}$ for the good sold by the monopolist. The monopolist can sell the good at different sites, and product diversity is then measured by the number of sites. For simplicity, a law requires that the shops be at the borders of the city (at abscissa 0 and 1). The fixed set-up cost of establishing a site is f. The marginal cost of producing the good is zero. Assume that $t/2 > f > t/4$, and that $\bar{s}$ is "sufficiently large" (so that the market is covered even if there is only one site). Show that the monopolist sets up two shops whereas the social planner sets up only one. Explain.

The conclusion of this subsection is that a monopolist can provide too many or too few products. Besides the two effects identified here, we will identify a third effect which affects product diversity when we introduce monopolistic competition. This third effect is linked to the externality between firms.

2.2.3 Product Selection and Discrimination

A monopolist who faces consumers with differing tastes is eager to learn which taste each particular consumer has. If he can do so, he may be able to charge a high price to a consumer with a high willingness to pay for his good and a low price to a consumer with a lower willingness to pay ("have the rich pay and still sell to the poor"), assuming that the consumers cannot resell the good (arbitrage). However, asking a consumer for his taste parameter is not "incentive compatible"; the consumer has a strong incentive to claim that he has a low willingness to pay so that he will be charged a low price. As we will see in chapter 3, the monopolist can nevertheless try to discriminate between consumers by using variables that are related to the willingness to pay. One such variable is the quantity purchased by the consumer if the latter has a downward-sloping demand: Higher purchases are usually a signal of higher willingness to pay. This will lead to a justification of "nonlinear tariffs." Another such variable is the quality of the product purchased; for instance, in the unit-demand vertical-differentiation model of subsection 2.1.1, a consumer with a high θ is more eager to consume high-quality goods than a consumer with a low θ. The monopolist can then use his product line or spectrum of goods (priced at different rates) to discriminate between consumers (to tell them apart). This is described in the supplementary section of chapter 3. We will see that under reasonable assumptions the quality sold to a particular consumer is suboptimal, and that the monopolist tends to offer "too many products."

2.3 Quality and Information

The quality of some goods (e.g. dresses) can be ascertained by consumers before a purchase. In other cases the quality is learned after the good is bought; this is the case, for instance, with the taste of canned food or the quality of a restaurant. For still other goods, aspects of the quality (e.g. the amount of fluoride in a toothpaste, the timeliness of a doctor's intervention) is rarely learned, even after consumption. These three types of goods have been christened "search goods," "experience goods" (Nelson 1970), and "credence goods" (Darby and Karni 1973). To be sure, most goods cannot be classified in this simple manner because they possess attributes that are learned before purchase, after purchase, or never. But this classification is quite useful for analysis.

The previous section focused on search goods. The main issue for such goods is product selection (quality, product diversity). For experience goods, the main issue is information: How do consumers learn the quality? What incentives do firms have to supply it? We will see that repeat purchases offer some consumer control over quality for such goods. Credence goods face the informational issue with a vengeance. For obvious reasons, they often require government intervention.

In a broad sense, search goods include "warranty goods." It is not always necessary to observe quality before purchasing a good. If the producer offers to compensate the buyer in full should the quality of the good end up differing from the announced characteristics, quality is no longer an issue; the buyer does not worry whether the producer's announcement of quality is accurate. It remains to be seen whether the producer has an incentive to give full warranty. It can be shown that, if it

is possible *ex post* to evaluate the quality (performance) of the good, and if variations in the good's performance can be attributed entirely to the producer, the producer indeed wants to give full warranty (see the Game Theory User's Manual, example 3 of section 5). The intuition is this: Were the producer to give less than full warranty, the buyers would become suspicious; they would correctly infer that the reason the producer is afraid to give a full warranty is that the product is very likely defective and thus very likely to lead the producer to pay the compensation. Thus, a low warranty would be a signal of low quality. In contrast, a full-warranty system makes the producer internalize any consumer misperceptions and suppresses informational problems. Thus, the quality problem could be eliminated by a perfect warranty system.

In many interesting real-world situations, however, the warranty system is nonexistent or imperfect. When quality means durability, the good must be consumed in order for the buyer to know its exact quality; if, as is usual, the eventual performance of the good depends on the way the buyer consumes it as well as on its intrinsic quality, there is a moral-hazard problem on the consumer side: The buyer has no incentive to take care of the good if he is to be fully reimbursed in case of a breakdown (i.e., breakdown imposes no cost on him). The natural way to proceed is to make the consumer internalize some of the costs associated with his behavior by giving a less than full warranty. Limited warranties can also be motivated by adverse selection considerations; for obvious reasons, goods carrying full warranties tend to attract heavy users or "high-risk" consumers, while (cheaper) goods associated with lower coverage are purchased by consumers who are less likely to benefit from a warranty.

Moral hazard and adverse selection certainly explain many of the restrictions on the warranty system. For instance, those parts of a car that are considerably affected by the owner's driving style or maintenance behavior (e.g. the tires) are unlikely to be guaranteed by the manufacturer. But there are other causes of imperfect warranties for experience goods. The quality may be impossible or very costly to measure for a court, while still being observed by the consumer. On the one hand, it may be subjective (do the colors of a color TV after one year of use "conform to expectations"?). On the other hand, the enforcement costs may be incommensurate with the issue (the buyer does not sue the manufacturer when a very inexpensive item breaks down). When a manufacturer's description of quality involves many attributes and/or much uncertainty about the final performance pattern over the sample of produced items, the warranty not only may require high enforcement costs but may also become very complex to evaluate for the consumer.

In this section we consider experience goods. To obtain clear conclusions, we assume away warranties. We first describe the informational issue when the consumers buy a good only once. We then suggest how repeat purchases and reputation can give a producer incentives to supply an adequate level of quality. Repeat purchases are studied in much greater detail in the supplementary section.

2.3.1 One-Shot Relationships: Moral Hazard and "Lemons"

2.3.1.1 Moral Hazard

A manufacturer who sells an experience good to one-time consumers and who can neither offer a warranty nor be sued for faulty quality has strong incentives to cut quality (as long as quality is costly) to the lowest possible level, because the market price cannot respond to the unobservable quality. The minimum level may be a legal standard or the level at which consumers can supply convincing evidence of underprovision of quality. Thus, there is "moral hazard" on the producer side.

The moral-hazard problem explains, for instance, why the food in restaurants in some tourist areas of Paris is not what it could be: The transient nature of consumption there does not allow reputation to play an important role. More generally, for one-shot purchases, the quality *chosen* by a manufacturer is likely to be poor.

Consider the following simple model (the repeated version of which will be studied in the supplementary section). Consumers are all identical. They have preferences $U = \theta s - p$ if they buy the monopolist's product at price p and the product has quality s, and $U = 0$ otherwise. The monopolist chooses a price p and a quality s. The unit cost of production is c_s for quality s. The quality can be "high" ($s = 1$; cost $c_1 > 0$) or "low" ($s = 0$; cost c_0 in $[0, c_1]$). Assume that $\theta > c_1$, so that producing the high

quality is socially efficient. The monopolist's profit is $(p - c_s)$ if he sells quality s at price p and 0 if he does not sell. (Without loss of generality, we normalize the number of consumers to one.) Assume further that the consumers do not observe quality before purchasing. It is clear that an equilibrium in which the monopolist sells and provides high quality cannot exist. The monopolist would save $c_1 - c_0$ by cutting quality, and this would not reduce demand. If $c_0 = 0$, equilibrium in this model consists of $s = 0$ and, hence, $p = 0$. If $c_0 > 0$, the market disappears, since consumers are unwilling to pay for goods of quality 0, and so the monopolist cannot recover costs.

In the simple example above, we assumed that consumers could not learn the quality of the product before buying. In a number of interesting cases, however, *some* consumers do learn information related to a product's quality before the purchase. For instance, they perform technical tests, or they develop skills that aid them in judging quality by simply looking at the product, or they read *Consumer Reports*. Another possibility (considered in Bagwell and Riordan 1986) is that consumers enter the market sequentially, so that at a given point in time some consumers know the quality and some do not.

The informed consumers exert a positive externality on the uninformed ones. By being more demanding, they drive up the quality of the monopolist's product.[10] To see this, suppose that in the previous model an exogenously given fraction α of consumers are perfectly informed (i.e., observe the quality before buying). These consumers are willing to pay θ if quality is high and 0 otherwise. The remaining $1 - \alpha$ consumers observe product quality only after they purchase. Suppose that the monopolist charges a price p in $[0, \theta]$. The informed consumers buy if quality is high, yielding a profit $\alpha(p - c_1)$, and do not buy if quality is low. Consider the uninformed consumers' behavior. Suppose first that they do not buy. Then the only demand comes from informed consumers, and the monopolist's optimal choice is the high quality (as long as $p \geqslant c_1$). Hence, the uninformed consumers should expect quality to be high, and should thus purchase (as we assumed that $p \leqslant \theta$)—a contradiction. Suppose next that the uninformed consumers buy. The monopolist's profit is

10. The following argument borrows elements from Wolinski's (1983) work on prices as signals of quality and from Salop's (1977) and Salop and Stiglitz's (1977) work on price search. See also Farrell 1980, Chan and Leland 1982, and Cooper and Ross 1984, 1985.

$$p - c_1$$

if he provides the high quality and

$$(1 - \alpha)(p - c_0)$$

if he provides the low quality. He thus provides the high quality if and only if

$$p - c_1 \geq (1 - \alpha)(p - c_0);$$

i.e.,

$$\alpha p \geq c_1 - (1 - \alpha)c_0.$$

From this inequality, we can infer two interesting economic phenomena.

First, the monopolist will supply the high quality only if the price is sufficiently high. When the price is high, the monopolist is afraid of losing his high profit margin on informed customers; this makes the low quality less attractive. In this sense, *high prices can signal high qualities* to uninformed consumers when there also exist informed customers (and the monopolist cannot offer different qualities to the different types of customers). Indeed, if

$$\theta \alpha \geq c_1 - (1 - \alpha)c_0,$$

the monopolist in equilibrium charges $p = \theta$ and provides the high quality.[11]

Second, our condition is more likely to be satisfied the higher the fraction α of informed customers.[12] This is natural, because the informed consumers are those who prevent the monopolist from cutting quality. We thus infer that increasing the number of informed customers favors efficiency.[13]

The latter conclusion offers an argument for government intervention. Whether consumers become informed or not depends on their relative costs of becoming informed (how bored they get reading *Consumer Reports*, how receptive they are to learning about new products,

etc.). But when deciding whether to become informed, a consumer takes only the private cost and the private benefit into account. He does not take into account the fact that, by being better informed, he induces (or allows) the monopolist to credibly offer the high quality. Thus, consumers' information should be encouraged beyond its privately optimal level. One such encouragement may be the subsidization of magazines like *Consumer Reports*.[14]

Exercise 2.4** In the previous example, show that if

$$\alpha p < c_1 - (1 - \alpha)c_0,$$

in equilibrium only a fraction of uninformed customers purchase and the monopolist randomizes between high and low quality.

2.3.1.2 The Lemons Problem

Akerlof (1970) showed that the same issues arise when the quality of goods is not a choice variable but putting the good on the market is. The basic idea, as before, is that if the buyers do not know the quality of the good when purchasing, the purchase price must be independent of the actual quality. This implies that sellers put their goods on the market only if the goods are of low quality; otherwise, they are better off "consuming" the goods themselves.

Robinson Crusoe (agent 1) is the monopoly owner of a goat. Friday (agent 2) is the potential purchaser of the animal. The goat is characterized by s, the amount of milk it produces daily (a quality parameter). Robinson has a surplus of $\theta_1 s$ if he keeps the goat and p if he sells it at price p. Friday has a surplus of $\theta_2 s - p$ if he buys at price p and zero otherwise. Assume that, for technical reasons, milk cannot be traded; only the animal can. Friday's marginal valuation for quality exceeds Robinson's: $\theta_2 > \theta_1$ (these parameters are known to both parties). Thus, trad-

---

11. Note that $\theta - c_1 \geq (1 - \alpha)(\theta - c_0)$ and that $p = \theta$ is an upper bound on what the monopolist can charge informed consumers when quality is high.

12. The condition requires that $p > c_1$, which implies that $p > c_0$.

13. In this simple model, the producer realizes all the efficiency gains by charging θ for the high quality. More generally, the consumers will obtain some extra surplus as well if they have different tastes or if they have downward-

sloping demands (and the monopolist cannot price discriminate perfectly—see chapter 3).

14. The monopolist could duplicate the government intervention by contracting with a third party (a laboratory, for instance) to supply estimates of the product's quality. However, the independence of this third party from the monopolist is likely to be dubious. Underwriters' Laboratories and Good Housekeeping try to provide such a service nevertheless.

ing is Pareto optimal regardless of s. However, trading must be voluntary. Robinson has experience with the goat and knows s perfectly. Friday knows only that s is, a priori, uniformly distributed on the interval $[0, s_{max}]$ (this is the usual distribution for goats, from which Robinson's goat has been drawn). Assume further that Friday is risk-neutral (his objective function is $\theta_2 s^a - p$, where s^a is the expected quality of the goat, conditional on its being offered for sale). Is there a price p ($\leqslant \theta_1 s_{max}$) at which Robinson and Friday can agree to trade? Suppose there is. Friday should then infer the following: If Robinson is willing to sell his goat at price p, the quality s must satisfy $p \geqslant \theta_1 s$. This means that Robinson sells if and only if s belongs to the interval $[0, p/\theta_1]$. Given that s is, a priori, uniformly distributed, the average (expected) quality of the goat *given that it is offered for sale* is

$$s^a(p) = \frac{1}{2} \frac{p}{\theta_1}.$$

The average quality is biased downward by the decision to put the goat on the market ($s^a(p) \leqslant \frac{1}{2} s_{max}$ for $p \leqslant \theta_1 s_{max}$). This is the so-called *adverse-selection or lemons problem*.[15]

Friday agrees to buy the goat if and only if his expected surplus from the transaction is positive, i.e., iff $\theta_2 s^a(p) \geqslant p$ or $\theta_2 \geqslant 2\theta_1$. If tastes do not differ too much in the sense that $\theta_2 < 2\theta_1$, there exists no price at which Robinson is willing to sell *and* Friday is willing to buy.[16] In this case the market breaks down completely. Whatever s, a socially desirable transaction does not occur. The exercise below develops this example in a bit more detail.

The reason why the market disappears in this example is clear. Suppose that the price is high and the seller is willing to sell, but the buyer does not want to buy. The traditional way to balance the market is to lower the price to reduce excess supply.[17] However, this mechanism may not work here. A decrease in price reduces the average quality on the market. (The fact that the good is still offered becomes, in a sense, "bad news." The actual quality is endogenously given.) This may turn out to reduce demand instead of increasing it.

In general, the market may not disappear; it may only shrink because of adverse selection. This situation arises in the used-car market, where the frequency of transactions is certainly smaller than it would be were the information structure about qualities perfect (leaving aside other transaction costs). It also arises in the insurance market—high-risk consumers are more likely to wish to purchase health or life insurance.

Are there counteracting forces that attenuate this problem? We have already mentioned the possibility of repeat purchases (which is studied in the next subsection) and that of warranties. Another way around adverse selection involves multidimensional contracts that specify several attributes in addition to the price. The buyer can then use the variation in the mixes of these different attributes to obtain a relatively satisfactory selection of goods and sellers; alternatively, the seller can use the mix he offers to signal the unknown characteristics of his good. For instance, a consumer with a high probability of accident is more eager to be fully insured against an accident than a consumer with a low probability. An insurance company can introduce two-dimensional contracts—{price, amount of reimbursement in case of an accident}—and can select low-probability consumers by charging them a lower price but reimbursing them only partially in case of an accident. (Deductibles are a form of partial insurance.) The organization of markets in such circumstances is a fascinating topic, but lies outside the scope of this book.[18] We simply note that this discrimination on the basis of the level of reimbursement, if privately optimal, is not socially optimal, even conditional on the imperfect information structure.

Government regulation or intervention is quite powerful in some markets; it can take the form of quality controls, minimum quality standards, occupational licensing and

15. Akerlof used as an example the market for used cars. Bad cars are called "lemons."

16. To be complete, note that a price $p \geqslant \theta_1 s_{max}$ always induces the seller to sell. The average quality is then $s_{max}/2$. Again, if $\theta_2 < 2\theta_1$, the market cannot be in equilibrium.

17. There is no income effect here. Thus, under perfect information, the "demand curve" is downward sloping, and the Walrasian tâtonnement process is stable.

18. See, e.g., Rothschild and Stiglitz 1976, Wilson 1977, Stiglitz and Weiss 1981, Bester 1985, and Hellwig 1986a. On the organization of markets with moral hazard with or without adverse selection, see, e.g., Arnott and Stiglitz 1982 and Hellwig 1986b.

certification (as for doctors, accountants, and lawyers), or safety regulations.[19,20]

*Exercise 2.5**[21]* Potential sellers and buyers of used cars are in equal number, N (where N is "large"). The distribution of qualities in the population of potential sellers is given by the c.d.f. $F(s)$ with density $f(s)$ on $[s_{min}, s_{max}]$. All sellers have surplus $\{\theta_0 s\}$ when keeping a car with quality s, and p when selling it (so all sellers are identical but for the quality of their car). A buyer has surplus $\{\theta s - p\}$ when buying a car of quality s and 0 when not buying. Buyers are heterogeneous: θ is distributed on $[\theta_{min}, \theta_{max}]$ according to the c.d.f. $G(\theta)$ and the density $g(\theta)$. Assume that $\theta_{min} < \theta_0 < \theta_{max}$. Sellers know the quality of their cars, but buyers do not (asymmetric information).

(i) Determine the efficient volume of trade (i.e., the volume of trade under symmetric information) and the efficient mix.

(ii) Compute the demand and supply curves under asymmetric information. Explain why the demand curve is not necessarily downward sloping (in spite of the absence of income effects).

(iii) Solve for a competitive equilibrium for f and g uniform on $[0, 1]$. Check that trade is suboptimal.

(iv) Argue that, in general, there can exist multiple equilibria. Then assume that this is the case. Show that a higher-price equilibrium Pareto dominates a lower-price one. Compare with the first fundamental theorem of welfare economics.

(v) Show that a minimum quality standard $s_0 > 0$, if enforceable, may improve welfare.

2.3.2 Repeat Purchases

In the absence of warranties, repeat purchases offer consumers some means of monitoring quality. By experimenting, consumers learn about the attributes of a product. As long as their current experience is somehow related to the future quality, they obtain valuable information as to whether they should repeat their purchases. There are two ways in which this mechanism can operate. First, the quality of the good may remain the same over time. For instance, a consumer may try a wine of a given vintage and vineyard. If he likes it, he is likely to like other bottles of the same vintage and vineyard. Past consumption then brings *direct* information on quality (or match). Often, however, the quality may change over time. A good meal at a restaurant may not imply that the next meal at the same restaurant will also be good. The chef may use lower-quality ingredients, spend less time preparing the food, and so on. If the producer can change quality over time, current quality is not necessarily informative about future quality. In such cases, the repeat-purchases mechanism must operate in an *indirect* way.

Repeat purchases are studied in detail in the supplementary section; here, a few important ideas are sketched.

Consider first the polar case in which quality is unalterable, so that consumption brings direct information. For the moment, take the quality as given in order to abstract from the moral-hazard problem. The only issue for the producer of a high-quality item is how to induce consumers to try his product. Consumers are not reluctant to try new products if the psychological cost of trying is low and the prospect of many future purchases high. For many products, however, the cost of experimenting may be perceived as high, even if the trial reveals the true quality. Can the producer then use a pricing strategy or some alternative instrument to induce the consumers to try?

An apparently natural way to do this is to charge a low price in the introductory period. But the consumers may still be reluctant to buy if a low price somehow means bad news about quality. Hence, we must study whether the manufacturer of a high-quality item has more incentive to offer a low price to encourage consumers to experiment

---

19. Of course, the seller and the buyer could duplicate the terms specified by the regulatory agency or the law in their contract. However, in many cases, they would not do so because of transaction and enforcement costs. On the one hand, it is costly to foresee and write everything in a contract; on the other hand, government control of quality may be more efficient if the seller sells several units—there are increasing returns to scale in enforcement. (The seller could set up a control agency exploiting these returns to scale, but the independence of the agency with respect to the seller would be somewhat problematic.)

20. Leland (1979) examines the effect of a minimum quality standard in an Akerlof-type model. Shaked and Sutton (1981) extend Leland's examination in

the context of occupational licensing to allow for the possibility that those excluded from a profession by licensing enter a para-profession. Shapiro (1986) distinguishes between occupational licensing (an input regulation, which requires a minimum level of human-capital investment by the professional) and certification (in which consumers are provided with information about the professional's training level, possibly above the licensing level). He shows that both government interventions benefit consumers who value quality of service highly at the expense of those who do not. He also notes that certification may lead to excessive signaling by the professional.

21. This exercise is inspired by Wilson 1980.

than he would have if his product were of low quality. For simplicity, assume that quality can be "high" or "low," [22] and that the low quality is so low that it does not generate repeat purchases.

The answer to our question lies in the comparison between two effects. On the one hand, a high-quality product generates more repeat purchases (Nelson 1974). Thus, attracting a customer yields more future revenues to the high-quality producer than to the low-quality one. Hence, a high-quality producer is more willing to sacrifice current profits (charge a low price) to attract customers. On the other hand, a low-quality product, for a given price, generally yields high profits because of a lower production cost (Schmalensee 1978). Thus, from a static point of view, a low-quality producer has more incentive to attract customers. Because a low-quality producer can always duplicate the introductory pricing strategy of a high-quality one, the difference in gain due to repeat purchases must exceed the cost advantage enjoyed by the low-quality producer in order for the price to convey any information about product quality. If this condition is met, the high-quality producer can sacrifice current profit by charging a low price to signal the quality. The low-quality producer is not willing to duplicate this sacrifice, because customers are not worth as much to him. Hence, under some circumstances *a low price may signal a high quality*. In essence, the high-quality producer says: "I will be in the market for a while because my quality is high. To prove this to you, I am willing to lose money now. You know that it would not be in my interest to do so, were my quality low. Try me."

The signal of quality need not actually be an introductory price. Any conspicuous initial expenditure that the monopolist can make to "prove" he will be in the market for a long time will do. Indeed, Nelson originally argued that apparently uninformative advertising can be a signal of quality. For instance, a wasteful advertising campaign that brings no direct information to consumers may sometimes be interpreted as a statement of persistence in the market. This, of course, raises the question whether a wasteful expenditure or an introductory offer is the cheapest method to signal quality—a question discussed in the supplementary section.

If persistence in the market is not an issue—i.e., if the low-quality producer keeps his goodwill (and is simply forced to charge a low price once consumers are informed)—the high-quality producer may want to signal through a *high* price. This is due to the fact that, even under full information about quality, a low quality may generate a higher profit margin than a high quality because of the cost differential. So it may turn out that purchases are more valuable to the low-quality producer. In this case, the way to signal high quality is a high price to "prove" that the firm is not afraid of contracting demand.[23] Furthermore, advertising by the high-quality producer may then be a necessary ingredient of the optimal signaling package (Milgrom and Roberts 1986).

The reader may be puzzled by the conclusion that low prices can signal high quality. In the discussion of moral hazard, emphasis was placed on the idea that, in the presence of a fraction of directly informed consumers, the producer is more afraid of losing consumers as the price becomes higher, and that the producer therefore has a higher incentive to provide high quality. The circumstances under which a low or a high price signals high quality differ. Low prices correspond to the existence of repeat purchases, high prices to that of informed consumers. A manager planning a strategy to introduce new items or an outsider observing the launching of new products should keep these two models in mind and try to

---

22. In the following, "the high-quality producer" will be used as shorthand for "the producer when the quality is high."

A reader who is not familiar with signaling theory may want to glance through the review of the Spence signaling model in the Game Theory User's Manual. Here, a low price may signal high quality if it attracts more consumers than a high price, and the marginal revenue of an additional consumer is higher for a high-quality monopolist than for a low-quality one.

23. In the Bagwell-Riordan (1986) model of intertemporal pricing, the high-quality firm signals its quality through high prices for precisely this reason. Because in the Bagwell-Riordan model a high-quality product is more costly to produce than a low-quality one, a high-quality monopolist has incentive to signal with a high price instead of a low one. (A low-quality monopolist has more to lose from a demand contraction.) An interesting innovation of their

model is that there is a continual mix of "new" and "old" consumers. Over time, the proportion of old consumers grows as some consumers who had not yet experimented with the product try it. The growing fraction of old consumers ("informed consumers," in the jargon of subsection 2.3.1.1) reduces the incentive to signal, and the high-quality monopolist eventually lowers his price to the full-information (high-quality) monopoly price. Bagwell and Riordan thus obtain a declining price path (in contrast with the increasing price path obtained when signaling is performed through an introductory offer).

See Crémer 1984 and Riordan 1986 for somewhat different models, in which the seller can commit to prices over a period of repurchases and in which a declining price path is obtained when the consumers are uncertain of their taste for the product (Crémer) or of the quality of the product *per se* (Riordan).

accurately determine the nature of demand. Naturally, a mixing of the two ingredients—informed customers and repeat purchases—is likely to blur the informational content of prices. For instance, introducing some initially informed customers into the repeat-purchase model ought to make the high-quality producer more reluctant to offer low introductory prices (because he can charge a high price to informed consumers); it also makes wasteful and conspicuous expenditures such as advertising a more likely signal of quality.

Let us next consider the other polar case, in which the monopolist chooses a new quality every "period" (where a period means the length of time it takes consumers to learn the quality). Repeat purchases can play a role in avoiding the moral-hazard problem described in subsection 2.3.1.1 only if a high quality yesterday somehow signals that the monopolist is likely to choose a high quality again today, i.e., if the monopolist has developed a *reputation* for high quality. The supplementary section describes two models that explain how "reputation" can form: the Klein-Leffler/Shapiro model of quality premia and the Kreps-Wilson/Milgrom-Roberts model of asymmetric information.

Roughly, the model of quality premia is based on the idea that in a repeated game the consumers can react to the monopolist's choice of low quality by not repeating their purchase. This reaction constitutes a punishment for the monopolist only if high quality commands a profit margin. Such a margin is called a "quality premium." One can thus construct equilibria in which the monopolist sustains a high quality through fear of retaliation by consumers. The consumers purchase as long as quality remains high. The quality premium must be such that the cost associated with the future loss of sales exceeds the current cost savings of cutting quality. (This story requires an infinite horizon. With a finite horizon T, the monopolist has incentive to cut quality in the last period, and therefore in the next to last period, and so on. The market equilibrium then unravels to become the bad equilibrium described in subsection 2.3.1.1 repeated T times. The asymmetric-information story does not require an unbounded horizon.)

The Kreps-Milgrom-Roberts-Wilson theory of reputation is based on the consumers' incomplete information about the monopolist. More precisely, it starts from the premise that the consumers are not quite sure that the monopolist has an incentive to provide a low-quality product even in a one-shot relationship (i.e., that he supplies high quality "naturally"). For instance, there can be at least a small probability that high quality is actually not more costly than the low one; or else profit maximization may not be the monopolist's only objective, and "honesty"—the reluctance to provide a low quality when one announces the high one—may lead the monopolist to provide high quality even when his reputation is not at stake. This literature shows that, even if the monopolist's static profit-maximizing choice is a low quality, he may want to sustain high quality (a reputation) for a while. Doing so, he entertains the possibility that he might supply quality naturally (and therefore keep providing the high quality in the future); and, because of their confusion about the real "identity" of the monopolist, consumers are willing to repeat their purchase. If the horizon is bounded, the profit-maximizing type milks his reputation at the end by cutting quality, which prompts consumers to stop purchasing after observing the low quality. The main insight of this literature is that even a small probability that the monopolist is not profit-maximizing induces the profit-maximizing type to develop a reputation as long as consumers repeat their purchases sufficiently often (the horizon is long enough). The supplementary section discusses and compares the two approaches to reputation.

When are repeat purchases likely to induce a firm to provide quality?[24] Clearly, two necessary conditions are that the consumers learn the quality of a purchased item sufficiently quickly and that they renew their purchase sufficiently often. Only under those conditions does the manufacturer have an incentive to provide quality. These conditions, it can be argued, can be met by a restaurant that caters to a stable population (or, in the case of a chain of franchised restaurants, if the franchiser can monitor the franchisees' quality).

It is convenient to distinguish between two polar types of qualities. The first type, which is the one considered

---

24. Repeat purchases need not be made by the same consumer at the same outlet or of the same good in order to have an effect. First, word of mouth between consumers may do the job; one may deal with a real-estate agent or a contractor infrequently, but learn about the quality of their recent services through family or friends. Second, brand names and chains can support the development of reputation when the repeat purchases concern similar but different goods.

in the supplementary section, has been described as the "vertical-product-space model": The product has some characteristic which the consumers enjoy. The consumers' gross surplus associated with the consumption of the product at a given instant is an increasing function of the amount of this attribute. The second type is durability. The consumers' gross surplus is fixed as long as the product "works." Quality is then measured by the amount of time between purchase and breakdown of the product. The reputation mechanism, although certainly possible, may be less efficient in this second type of quality. The issue is that a high-quality item—i.e., a durable one—generates fewer repeat sales than a low-quality one. In the extreme case, a product that never breaks down does not generate repeat sales; hence, the producer does not want to produce such a product, because it is more expensive than a low-durability one (this contrasts with Swan's optimal-durability proposition, which assumes that the durability is observable *before* purchase).[25]

2.3.3 Quality, Information, and Public Policy

The mere fact that some products may have low quality or fail is not by itself an argument for government intervention, because the government may be facing the same informational difficulties as the consumers. On the other hand, there is no reason why the market allocation should be efficient even when informational asymmetries are taken account of. The purpose of this subsection is to give some hints as to when government intervention is likely to be desirable.[26]

2.3.3.1 Failure of the Coase Theorem and Product Liability

To assess potential policy interventions, we first assume that the government *a priori* has the same information about product quality that a consumer has before making a purchase.

Such an assumption raises the question of what a government can do that cannot be mimicked by the producer through contract with consumers. Any efficiency gain stemming from government intervention, so runs the argument, could also be obtained by the monopolist through detailed contract provisions; furthermore, the monopolist could appropriate these efficiency gains by raising the price. Thus, any desirable government intervention would already be realized by private means, implying that there is no scope for such interventions. This loose reasoning, it seems, might be supported by an extension of the Coase theorem.[27] But, as we shall now see, the Coase theorem is not likely to be applicable here.

The efficiency of private contracts generally requires perfect information, the absence of transaction costs, and the absence of externalities toward third parties.

Imperfect Information

Imperfect information is the basis for the quality issue. However, one might think that, even though the equilibrium may not be fully Pareto efficient, it might be (constrained) Pareto efficient relative to the structure of information. (Because the government is assumed to have the same information as the consumers, it cannot enlarge the scope of private contracts.) This conjecture turns out to be false. In a second-best situation, there are generally externalities between economic agents that must be corrected. In a one-shot relationship, informed customers exert a positive externality on uninformed ones. The government may then improve welfare by subsidizing the acquisition of information.

Transaction Costs

Transaction costs may lead to incomplete contracts. This is particularly true for contracts between a firm and its customers. Often, the contract does not exist (is implicit) or is of a standard form. To illustrate the problem, let us modify our framework slightly and assume that *ex post* some dimensions of quality are publicly observable. For instance, consider the case of a soda-pop bottle which has a small probability of exploding. A consumer who buys a

---

25. For an evolutionary model of product durability, see Smallwood and Conlisk 1979.

26. A complete study of public policy with regard to product quality lies outside the scope of this book.
   There exists a large and interesting literature in law and economics that covers the topics of this subsection (and more). See, e.g., Shavell 1980, 1984 and Polinsky 1983, and the legal references therein.

27. The Coase theorem (1960) asserts that an optimal allocation of resources can always be achieved through market forces, irrespective of the legal liability assignment, if information is perfect and transactions are costless. (This theorem should not be mistaken for the Coase *conjecture* studied in chapter 1.)

soda pop will not bother to require that the manufacturer sign a detailed contract; doing so would involve costs incommensurate with the surplus associated with the consumption of this particular good. However, efficiency calls for the producer to be liable in case the bottle explodes and hurts the consumer. This is required to give the firm incentives to produce safe bottles. The law may thus be a substitute for incomplete contracts. This is actually a major argument in favor of product liability (*caveat venditor*).[28]

Opponents of product-liability legislation might object to the previous argument by arguing that the producer would be better off supplying a standard-form contract that promises to compensate consumers in case of an accident. However, the consumers usually do not have time to read the contract, or do not understand its subtleties. Furthermore, there may exist contingencies that are not foreseen by consumers; if these contingencies are detrimental to the consumers, the producer will not draw attention to them.[29] For instance, a consumer may foresee that the paint he uses for his house may not last, but not be aware that this paint may contain lead and poison his children.

We conclude that the Coase theorem is unlikely to apply here and that selective government intervention may be desirable.

2.3.3.2 Creation of Information

We assumed that the government does not acquire superior information relative to the consumers. Sometimes quality tests may speed up consumer learning.[30] This applies to experience goods. It applies with a vengeance to credence goods, for which information is never obtained or is obtained slowly and too late; take the example of a chemical substance that causes cancer or affects genes. This example illustrates a limit of product liability. First, consumers can hardly be compensated for the damage. Second, a firm that faces the threat of a series of very costly lawsuits usually goes bankrupt. This means that the punishment is mild relative to the damage.[31] In such a case, product liability is a very incomplete inducement to supply the right quality (in the above case, to make sure that the chemical substance is not highly toxic). Direct quality controls may then complement, or even supplement, product-liability laws.

2.3.3.3 Consumers' Misperceptions

Product liability has also been supported on the basis of consumers' misperceptions. In this chapter (as in almost all of the book), we assume that consumers form their expectations rationally. Even though they may not be fully informed about product quality, they exhibit no systematic bias in their predictions. Spence (1977) assumes that consumers systematically overestimate the probability that the product will not fail. The producer, who has rational expectations, then gains from offering a low warranty in exchange for a low price.[32] The consumers are willing to accept this arrangement, because they wrongly perceive the probability of failure as low. In turn, this low warranty induces the producer to undersupply reliability. Such misperceptions naturally call for the government to increase liability beyond the private-contract level.[33,34]

---

28. Of course, assigning the liability to the consumer (*caveat emptor*) may still make sense when the main moral hazard lies on the consumer side.

29. This argument was suggested by D. Scharfstein.

30. Testing could also be performed by consumer associations or the like. Of course, information is a public good. It is collectively valuable. However, each consumer would prefer other consumers to generate this information, because this saves the costs of testing. The usual resolution of a public-good issue is through collective action.

31. The punishment should actually be higher than the damage, to correct for the probability that the damage is not discovered.

32. Spence assumes that consumers are risk-averse. (If they were risk-neutral the solution would be unbounded, as is well known from the theory of bets with divergent prior views of the world.) See Spence's article for an example in which a two-part liability—to the customer and to the government (or a third party)—is optimal.

33. Of course, the issue is whether consumers do underestimate risks. There is some evidence in this direction (see Calabresi 1970). The remark that "such things always happen to the other guy" is common. In particular instances, such proclaimed misperceptions may be due to cognitive dissonance; i.e., they may be *ex post* attempts to justify the agent's behavior (carelessness, signature of incomplete contracts, etc.); this should be investigated.

34. An alternative model of consumer misperceptions is that of Shapiro (1982). Shapiro's consumers have, at each instant of time, t, utility $U(q(t), s)$, which depends on the flow quantity purchased and the true quality of the good. (s is a general quality parameter and should not necessarily be interpreted as reliability.) Instead of knowing or inferring s, the consumers have a (mis)-perception of quality $R(t)$, where R stands for reputation. R need not coincide with s. Consumers start with some perception $R(0)$. Shapiro, however, allows for long-term learning. The reputation grows (or decreases) over time with the difference $s - R(t)$. Shapiro shows that, under very general conditions, *any* self-fulfilling quality levels (i.e., satisfying $R(0) = R(t) = s$ for all t and being part of the solution of the monopolist's intertemporal profit-maximization problem given $R(0)$) lie below the quality level that would be chosen by the monopolist under full information about product quality. A similar result is obtained when the monopolist can affect his quality over time.

2.4 Advertising

Advertising has long been perceived as wasteful and manipulative. One reason for this may be that advertising is one of the topics in the study of industrial organization for which the traditional assumptions (especially those with regard to consumer behavior) are strained most. The advertising of a product has strong psychological and sociological aspects that go beyond optimal inferences about objective quality. For instance, ad agencies constantly try to appeal to the consumers' conscious or unconscious desire for social recognition, a trendy lifestyle, and the like. Advertising also has important economic aspects (Dorfman and Steiner 1954; Kaldor 1940–41; Nelson 1970, 1974; Schmalensee 1972). Naturally, we shall focus on the economic side.[35]

We can distinguish between advertising that conveys "hard" (direct) information and advertising at conveys "soft" (indirect) information or none at all. Hard information includes the existence of the product, its price, the retail outlets in which it is distributed, its physical appearance, and so on. Most TV commercials provide no information beyond existence. As Nelson (1974) notes, if advertising were solely concerned with distributing hard information there should be much more advertising for search goods (goods whose quality can be assessed before a purchase). The data contradict this prediction: Experience goods are advertised heavily.

The Dorfman-Steiner model, reinterpreted (as in footnote 8) to describe advertising as a bunch of messages about product existence, offers a simple paradigm of hard advertising. The signaling model suggested in section 2.3 and taken up in the supplementary section concerns soft information. Because we have already developed these models, and because some interesting features of advertising are related to product competition, we will leave the analysis of advertising under monopoly at this point.[36]

2.5 Concluding Remarks

Even when product characteristics are observable before a purchase (as in the case of a search good), a monopolist generally chooses these characteristics in a socially sub-optimal way because of his concern for the marginal consumer rather than the average consumer. Although the existence of a bias in product selection is fairly clear, its sign is model dependent. For instance, product quality can be oversupplied or undersupplied by the monopolist. A closely related issue is that of product diversity. If only one product is at stake, the monopolist tends to under-supply the product (i.e., not to introduce it when it would be optimal to do so), because he does not internalize the associated net consumer surplus. A multiproduct monopolist, however, can introduce too many goods, because pricing one product above the marginal cost may create an artificial demand for another of his products.

A further issue arises in the case of experience goods. Then, for moral-hazard and adverse-selection reasons, quality tends to be undersupplied. Consumer information, repeat purchases, warranties, and signaling by the monopolist (price, advertising) may alleviate this informational problem.

Although the bias in product selection is now relatively well understood at a theoretical level, work remains to be done to see how these models apply to specific industries. Also, this chapter puts too much emphasis on the positive side. A more careful welfare analysis, based on a study of the structure of information (including the government's information) and of the alternative policy instruments (fiscal, legal, and regulatory) would be desirable.

---

35. For a challenging analysis of welfare when advertising affects tastes, see Dixit and Norman 1978. See also the comments of Fisher and McGowan (1979) and Shapiro (1980).

36. This section does even less justice to its field than other sections. The interested reader will consult, beyond the works already mentioned, the references in Schmalensee 1986.

2.6 Supplementary Section: Repeat Purchases

As was suggested above, the possibility of repeat purchases can operate in two different ways. If quality is unalterable, current observation of quality brings direct information about future quality. If quality can be manipulated over time, current quality may still act as a signal.

We begin our analysis of repeat purchases by assuming that the quality of a good is exogenously given and unalterable. In this simple framework, there are two main questions: (1) What is the value of goodwill to the producer, and should the producer make "introductory offers" to broaden his goodwill? (2) If the producer knows the quality of the good, can he signal this quality through a judicious choice of price, advertising, etc.?

To distinguish the first question from the second, we develop a model in which the producer and the consumers have the same imperfect information. The informational problem arises only from the fact that a given consumer does not know in advance whether he will like a product. Liking a product is a matter of "match" between the consumer and the product rather than a matter of quality, in that the probability of liking the product (a measure of quality) is known. The issues associated with the producer's superior knowledge of quality (question 2) are then taken up. That discussion is followed by an analysis of reputation in models with sequential moral hazard.

2.6.1 Repeat Purchases in the Absence of Moral Hazard

2.6.1.1 Goodwill and Introductory Offers[37]

Consider the following matching model. There are a large number of consumers. A consumer with taste θ has the following per-period preferences for the good produced by the monopolist:

$$U = \begin{cases} \theta s - p & \text{if he buys at price } p \\ 0 & \text{otherwise,} \end{cases}$$

where s denotes the quality to the consumer (see section 2.1). Quality here is purely "idiosyncratic" or "subjective" —in other words, it is not correlated between consumers. There are two potential levels of idiosyncratic quality: $s = 0$ ("no match") and $s = 1$ ("match"). The probability of a match between the consumer and the product is x, belonging to $(0, 1)$. As was mentioned earlier, x is common knowledge. The taste parameter θ is distributed over the population of consumers with the cumulative distribution $F(\theta)$. We normalize the population to be equal to 1 (without loss of generality). The unit cost of producing the good is c.

There are two periods: $t = 1, 2$. The monopolist charges p_1 and p_2. For simplicity, we assume that he cannot commit himself to a second-period price at date 1.[38] Consumers who have purchased the good in period 1 know whether they like it or not; they purchase in period 2 if and only if they liked the product in period 1 and $\theta \geq p_2$. By the law of large numbers, the proportion of consumers who like the product is x.

First, consider the case in which the consumers and the producer are myopic. Their common discount factor δ is then equal to 0. In the first period, a consumer with parameter θ buys at price p_1 if and only if his expected surplus from buying is positive: $E(\theta s) - p_1 \geq 0$, or $\theta \geq p_1/x$. Thus, the demand at price p_1 is $1 - F(p_1/x)$. The monopolist's first-period profit is

$$(p_1 - c)[1 - F(p_1/x)].$$

For the consumers, a price p_1 associated with a probability x of liking the product is equivalent to a price p_1/x to be paid only if they are satisfied (if such a contract can be enforced):

$$\theta x - p_1 = x(\theta - p_1/x).$$

Let us thus introduce $\tilde{p}_1 \equiv p_1/x$, and let $\tilde{c} \equiv c/x$. The monopolist's first-period profit can be written as

$$x(\tilde{p}_1 - \tilde{c})[1 - F(\tilde{p}_1)].$$

This profit is nothing but the profit that the monopolist would realize if the fraction x of consumers who are going to like the product knew it *in advance*, except that the unit production cost is the production cost "per satisfied cus-

---

37. This section is based on Farrell 1984, 1986 and Milgrom and Roberts 1986.

38. As in Farrell 1986, little would be affected by the possibility of commitment.

---

tomer," $\tilde{c}$, instead of c. The real cost is higher than c because the monopolist cannot predict matches. Let $p^m(\gamma)$ denote the monopoly price under full information when the unit cost is γ; i.e., $p^m(\gamma)$ maximizes $x(p - \gamma)[1 - F(p)]$.

In the first period, the monopolist chooses $\tilde{p}_1 = p^m(\tilde{c})$. Because $\tilde{c} \geqslant c$, $\tilde{p}_1 \geqslant p^m(c)$ (see chapter 1). Or, $p_1 \geqslant x p^m(c)$. We conclude that the price exceeds the full-information monopoly price adjusted by the probability of the consumers' not liking the product. This is due to the fact that the unit cost per customer satisfied exceeds the unit cost of production (unless the latter is 0).

Consider now the second-period price in this myopic setting. The second-period demand curve is shown in figure 2.3. The monopolist has two strategies: to cater only to his goodwill (first-period) customers and to try to reach new customers. Let us start with the first strategy. The marginal consumer in period 1 has parameter $\tilde{p}_1 = p^m(\tilde{c}) \geqslant p^m(c)$. Since the first-period customers are perfectly informed and the marginal cost of production is c, the monopolist charges $p_2 = \tilde{p}_1$.[39] The monopolist's second period profits is then

$$x(\tilde{p}_1 - c)[1 - F(\tilde{p}_1)].$$

The second strategy, charging $p_2 \leqslant x\tilde{p}_1$, attracts new customers. The monopolist's second-period profit is then

$$(p_2 - c)\{x[1 - F(\tilde{p}_1)] + F(\tilde{p}_1) - F(p_2/x)\}.$$

Such a strategy is dominated—notice that the profit can be written as

$$x(\hat{p}_2 - \tilde{c})\{x[1 - F(\tilde{p}_1)] + F(\tilde{p}_1) - F(\hat{p}_2)\}$$

$$< x(\hat{p}_2 - \tilde{c})[1 - F(\hat{p}_2)],$$

where $\hat{p}_2 \equiv p_2/x$.

Thus, with myopic consumers and a myopic monopolist, the monopolist charges $p_2 = p_1/x$ and caters exactly to his first-period customers (those with whom he has established goodwill). The second-period price is higher than the first-period one; this is natural, as the customers know that they like the product.

Does this mean that the monopolist makes an "intro-

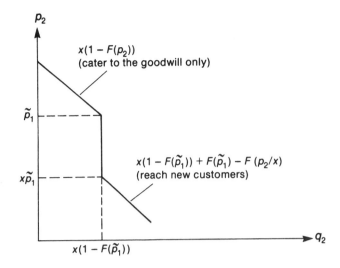

Figure 2.3
Demand curve with goodwill.

ductory offer"? Notice that the consumers would, in the first period, be indifferent between paying p_1 for sure and paying p_2 conditional on their liking the product. Let us, with Farrell (1984), define an introductory offer as a first-period price that is strictly lower than the second-period (full-information) price times the first-period probability of the customers' liking the good.[40] In this sense, the monopolist makes no introductory offer.

Let us more generally consider nonmyopic parties. The monopolist and the consumers have a common discount factor, δ. A first intuition would suggest that, when taking a dynamic perspective, the monopolist should try to accumulate a large clientele in the first period so as to take advantage of it in the second period. This intuition, however, is flawed (Farrell 1986; Milgrom and Roberts 1986).

As in the myopic case, it is easy to show that the monopolist does not try to reach a new clientele in the second period. Contrary to the case of a durable-good monopolist discussed in chapter 1, a period-2 decrease in price to reach new customers also benefits period-1 customers. Overall, the monopolist is better off resting on his laurels and milking his goodwill.

The interesting question is whether the monopolist

---

39. The reader may wonder whether a concavity assumption on the profit function is not required for this argument. A more careful argument runs as follows: The monopolist's profit function for prices exceeding $\tilde{p}_1$ is the same in the second period as in the first, except that the unit cost has become c instead of $\tilde{c}$. Thus, the second-period price cannot exceed the first-period price. On the

other hand, prices under $\tilde{p}_1$ either do not attract new customers (and then are dominated by $\tilde{p}_1$) or attract new customers (a case studied below).

40. More generally, one could adjust each period's price by the expected quality of the good at the beginning of the period.

would like to cater only to part of his goodwill clientele. To show that such a strategy is not profitable requires two steps. First notice that, if this were the case, the marginal consumer in period 1 would make a myopic decision in that period, because he knows that he will not buy in period 2. Hence, the demand at price $p_1 = x\tilde{p}_1$ is

$$1 - F(\tilde{p}_1),$$

and the firm's first-period profit is the same as in the myopic case:

$$x(\tilde{p}_1 - \tilde{c})[1 - F(\tilde{p}_1)].$$

Second, suppose that the firm charges $p_2 \geqslant \tilde{p}_1$ in period 2. Only consumers with parameters $\theta \geqslant p_2$ will purchase, conditional on their having liked the good in period 1. Hence, the second-period profit is

$$x(p_2 - c)[1 - F(p_2)].$$

Because $c \leqslant \tilde{c}$, p_2 cannot exceed $\tilde{p}_1$. Hence, even with a dynamic perspective, the monopolist makes no introductory offer.

Exercise 2.6* A dynamic perspective, however, leads to a greater goodwill. Show that the first-period and second-period prices decrease with the discount factor δ. Give the intuition for this result.

The no-introductory-offer result can be interpreted as meaning that there is no point in "bending over backwards" to attract customers to whom one does not intend to cater later.

2.6.1.2 Signaling an Existing Quality

Let us now turn to the possibility that a producer who knows the quality of his good signals it through his choice of price, advertising, and so on. Modify the previous model in two respects. First, assume that s is perfectly correlated between consumers instead of being uncorrelated—in other words, that all or none of the consumers like the product. Then s is an objective measure of quality (vertical product space); $s = 0$ denotes a low quality and $s = 1$ a high quality. Second, suppose that the

monopolist knows the quality of his product, whereas the consumers learn it only if they try the product. Assume further that only consumers who try the product learn the quality.[41] Let c_0 (c_1) denote the unit cost of producing a low-quality (a high-quality) item.

The monopolist would always want the consumers to believe that the quality is high, regardless of the true quality. The consumers ought to understand this, and the question arises whether the monopolist can credibly signal a high quality.

In this model, the monopolist has two potential instruments for signaling: the price of the product, and conspicuous (and wasteful) expenditures. An example of the latter is an advertising campaign that conveys no direct information about the quality of the product. There is some similarity between the two instruments (for instance, from the monopolist's viewpoint, an introductory offer is a bit like throwing money away). They differ in that introductory prices entail a cost proportional to demand, whereas wasteful expenditures are a fixed cost. Also, consumers enjoy introductory offers, whereas wasteful expenditures bring them no direct benefit.

Nelson (1974) suggested that wasteful expenditures (or introductory prices) may signal quality. His idea is that a high-quality product generates repeat purchases. Therefore, the future returns from the formation of goodwill are higher for a high-quality product than for a low-quality one. Suppose that consumers associate high quality with some minimum amount of wasteful expenditures. Then the monopolist may want to waste this amount if the quality of his product is high in order to create goodwill and reap future benefits. A monopolist producing a low-quality product may not want to do so. In this case, the consumers' expectations are fulfilled, even though wasteful expenditures convey no *direct* information about quality.

Schmalensee (1978) pointed out that it is not clear that a high-quality monopolist has a higher incentive to attract customers than a low-quality one. Although the high-quality monopolist's future gains from doing so are likely to be higher (per Nelson's argument), his current gains may well be lower. This is due to the fact that a high-

---

41. If we assumed that consumers can learn by word of mouth or by reading *Consumer Reports*, all consumers would know the quality in period 2 regardless of what happened in period 1 (if aggregate consumption were not zero). Thus,

the dynamics of learning would be uninteresting. Neither the firm nor the consumers would take a dynamic perspective. Intermediate assumptions are also possible.

quality monopolist is likely to have higher production costs than a low-quality monopolist ($c_1 > c_0$). Thus, for a given first-period price p_1, the profit margin per customer is higher for a low-quality monopolist: $p_1 - c_0 > p_1 - c_1$. This effect may render wasteful expenditures ineffective as a signal of quality. Klein and Leffler (1981), and especially Kihlstrom and Riordan (1984) and Milgrom and Roberts (1986), have treated the issue in more detail.

The formal signaling model was developed by Spence (1973) to describe how efficient workers can signal their ability to employers by engaging in (possibly wasteful) education expenditures. Transposed to our quality problem, the moral of Spence's analysis is that a high-quality producer is able to use an instrument—e.g. price or wasteful expenditures—to signal his quality if his cost (his return from) using this instrument is lower (respectively, higher) than that of a low-quality producer.

We now consider an example in which an introductory price and wasteful expenditures are essentially equivalent, so that the monopolist has only one way of signaling quality. (Multidimensional signaling, a more complex issue which will be considered briefly later, requires the investigation of which instrument is the less costly signal.)

Suppose that all consumers are identical (i.e., have the same taste parameter θ). Their gross surplus is θ if the good is of high quality and 0 if it is of low quality. For simplicity, assume that only consumers who have consumed at date 1 can consume at date 2. (As the preceding subsection suggests, this assumption could be relaxed without a change in the results.) We will assume that $x\theta < c_0$, where x is the *a priori* probability that quality is high. As we will see, this condition implies that the high-quality producer is driven out of the market by the possibility of low quality if he cannot signal his product's quality. (In the absence of new information, consumers are willing to pay $x\theta$.) Let A denote the level of wasteful expenditures in the first period. (As is easily seen, there is no need to engage in wasteful expenditures in the second period.) These expenditures are ostentatious, in that they

are observed by consumers. If all consumers buy the good, the monopolist's first-period profit is $p_1 - c - A$. Thus, an increase in A is equivalent to an equivalent decrease in p_1. In the following we will focus on price signaling, assuming that $A = 0$. When signaling by price and wasteful expenditures are indeed equivalent, it will be noted.

Suppose that consumers buy in the first period. In the second period, they do not repeat their purchase if the quality is low; they do repeat it if the quality is high and the second-period price p_2 does not exceed θ. Thus, the high-quality monopolist charges $p_2 = \theta$ in the second period.

Can the first-period price signal (reveal) the quality? Suppose it does. A low-quality monopolist is then unable to sell and makes zero profit. The high-quality monopolist charges a price p_1 and makes a profit of

$$\Pi_1 = (p_1 - c_1) + \delta(\theta - c_1).$$

For this to be an equilibrium, the monopolist must not be willing to duplicate this strategy when his good has low quality (otherwise, he would do so and p_1 would not be informative). His profit from doing so would be $p_1 - c_0$, since he does not generate repeat purchases. Thus, we require $p_1 \leqslant c_0$. This implies that

$$\Pi_1 \leqslant \delta(\theta - c_1) - (c_1 - c_0).$$

Hence, there are two cases:

• $\delta(\theta - c_1) < c_1 - c_0$. In this case, necessarily, $\Pi_1 < 0$. There exists no revealing (or separating) equilibrium. In equilibrium, the monopolist charges the same price, regardless of the quality of the good. The price is thus uninformative. If x denotes the *a priori* probability that the good has high quality, the highest price that can be charged in the first period is $p_1 = x\theta$. The high-quality monopolist produces only if $(x\theta - c_1) + \delta(\theta - c_1) \geqslant 0$. If this condition is not satisfied, the high-quality monopolist does not produce. Neither does the low-quality monopolist, in this model.[42] Thus, the possibility of a low

---

42. To be more formal: If the high-quality producer sells, the low-quality one makes a strictly positive profit, as he always has the option of duplicating the high-quality strategy. However, from Bayes' law we know that there must exist some equilibrium price p_1 such that the consumers' posterior beliefs following p_1, $x'(p_1)$, satisfy $[x'(p_1)\theta - c_1] + \delta(\theta - c_1) < 0$ (because $x = \sum_{p_1} x'(p_1)\mathrm{Prob}(p_1)$, where $\mathrm{Prob}(p_1)$ is the probability that p_1 is charged in

equilibrium and where $(x\theta - c_1) + \delta(\theta - c_1) < 0$ by assumption). As consumers are not willing to pay more than $x'(p_1)\theta$, the high-quality monopolist does not charge p_1; hence, $x'(p_1) = 0$. This means that the low-quality monopolist does not charge p_1 either, which contradicts our assumption that p_1 is an equilibrium price. If the high-quality monopolist is out of the market, so is the low-quality one, because consumers are not willing to pay for a low-quality item.

quality may drive a high-quality producer out of the market, as in the lemons problem.[43]

• $\delta(\theta - c_1) \geqslant c_1 - c_0$. In this case, there exists a revealing equilibrium in which the monopolist charges $p_1 = c_0$ if his good has high quality. He actually does not need to charge under c_0 to signal high quality, because a low-quality monopolist would never charge below c_0, regardless of how such an action would be interpreted.[44] The low-quality monopolist does not sell.

Thus, a revealing equilibrium may or may not exist. The cost of signaling is independent of quality (a reduction in price reduces the monopolist's profit uniformly over qualities), but the return to signaling depends on quality. The existence of a revealing equilibrium hinges on the comparison of two effects. The first is the *Nelson effect*: A high-quality producer generates repeat purchases, with value $\delta(\theta - c_1)$. The second is the *Schmalensee effect*: A given demand generates a cost differential $(c_1 - c_0)$ in favor of the low-quality producer (assuming that $c_1 \geqslant c_0$—if $c_1 < c_0$, the revealing equilibrium always exists). The price can be revealing only if the Nelson effect dominates the Schmalensee effect.

The high-quality monopolist in a revealing equilibrium charges below marginal cost in the first period (if $c_0 < c_1$) and makes an introductory offer (in the sense given above).

Remark Let us briefly consider wasteful expenditures as a substitute signaling device. Letting p_1 denote the high-quality monopolist's price, we have $p_1 - A = c_0$ in a revealing equilibrium. The consumers' utility is $\theta - p_1 = \theta - c_0 - A$. In order for the consumer to purchase, θ must be $\geqslant c_0 + A$. Thus, only pairs $\{p_1, A\}$ such that $p_1 - A = c_0$ and $A \leqslant \theta - c_0$ can form a revealing equilibrium. Thus, as long as A does not exceed $\theta - c_0$, wasteful expenditures and introductory prices are perfect substitutes. Needless to say, consumers prefer introductory prices to wasteful expenditures. Hence, if an equilibrium that Pareto dominates all other equilibria is postulated

to be the "right" or "focal" one, there are no wasteful expenditures in equilibrium.

The conclusion of this study is that low prices (or wasteful expenditures) can signal high quality only if the cost differential between qualities is small relative to the repeat-purchase premium of high-quality products.

The result that high quality must be signaled through a low price depends crucially on our assumption that low quality would not be profitable under full information (the unit production cost c_0 exceeds θs_0, which here is zero). Under this assumption, the low-quality monopolist sells for one period at most, i.e., is constrained to use a "fly-by-night" strategy. Because at any given first-period price a low-quality monopolist earns larger short-term profits than a high-quality one, the high-quality monopolist can reveal his type only by charging a price that makes it unprofitable in the short term for the low-quality monopolist to pretend to be a high-quality one.

The picture changes dramatically if the low-quality monopolist can earn profits under full information, i.e., if $\theta s_0 > c_0$. Under the assumptions that either all consumers buy or no consumers buy (remember, consumers are identical) and that $(\theta s_0 - c_1) + \delta(\theta s_1 - c_1) > 0$ (high quality is profitable even if it is initially thought to be low quality), the first-period price is not at all informative. Hence, the price charged by the firm is independent of the quality of its product. To see why, first note that both types will sell in equilibrium. In particular, they can always generate sales by charging $p_1 = \theta_0 s_0$ and, thus, make positive profits. Second, as all equilibrium prices are, by assumption, accepted by all consumers, both types ought to charge the highest equilibrium price, which means that the price is uninformative.

If the low-quality monopolist can earn profits under full information, and if consumers differ (in contrast with the previous model), then the high-quality monopolist may signal the quality of his product through a high or a low price, depending on the values of the parameters[45]

---

43. The analogy with the lemons problem is twofold. First, because of the impossibility of signaling, the producer must charge the same price regardless of quality. Second, the high-quality producer has a higher cost of producing than the low-quality one; this is similar to Crusoe's being more willing to keep his goat when the goat is more productive.

44. Dominated strategies (charging under c_0 for a low-quality monopolist) are

implicitly eliminated here. This suffices to obtain a unique *revealing* equilibrium. To obtain a unique equilibrium, one could apply the intuitive criterion (Cho and Kreps 1987), which refines the notion of equilibrium in dynamic games of incomplete information. For a more formal treatment, see the Game Theory User's Manual.

45. The following discussion is inspired by Milgrom and Roberts 1986.

—a result opposite to the one obtained in industries where the producer tries to convince the consumer that he will still be around after consumer learning. The point is that under consumer heterogeneity a high price generates lower sales than a low price.[46] The value of goodwill may be higher or lower to a high-quality producer than to a low-quality one. It may be higher because the high quality allows the manufacturer to extract more consumer surplus in the second period; it may be lower because high quality costs more, so that the high-quality manufacturer may want to supply fewer customers. If prices signal quality at all (which requires some restrictive conditions), high quality is signaled through a low (high) price if the first (second) effect dominates. The following exercise illustrates these two possibilities.[47]

Exercise 2.7*** Suppose that in the previous model there are two types of consumers, with taste parameters θ_1 and θ_0 ($\theta_1 > \theta_0$), in proportions q_1 and $1 - q_1$. The high quality is s_1 and costs c_1 per unit. The low quality is s_0 and costs c_0 per unit ($c_1 \geq c_0$). Consider two sets of parameters:

$$S_1 = \{c_1 = \tfrac{1}{2}; c_0 = 0; \theta_1 = 2; \theta_0 = 1; s_1 = 1;$$
$$s_0 = \tfrac{1}{2}; \delta = 1; \tfrac{1}{3} \leq q_1 \leq \tfrac{1}{2}\}$$

and

$$S_2 = \{c_1 = c_0 = 1; \theta_1 = 2; \theta_0 = 1; s_1 = 2;$$
$$s_0 = 1; \delta = 1; q_1 \leq \tfrac{1}{3}\}.$$

(i) Assume first that consumers know product quality. Show that under S_1 the high-quality monopolist sells only to θ_1 consumers and the low-quality monopolist sells to all consumers. Show that this conclusion is reversed under S_2.

(ii) Suppose that consumers learn the quality in the first period, and that only consumers who have purchased in that period can purchase in the second period. Show that under S_1 there exists a revealing equilibrium in which the high-quality monopolist charges a higher price than the low-quality monopolist. Show that under S_2 there exists a revealing equilibrium in which the high-quality monopolist charges a lower price than the low-quality one.

Remark Bagwell (1985) provides an alternative signaling explanation of introductory offers, according to which the monopolist signals not the quality of his good (which is known to the consumers) but his production cost. In a world where consumers must decide each period whether to obtain at a cost a price quotation from the monopolist (i.e., to engage in search), a low first-period price may encourage consumers to come back and get a second-period price quotation. A low-cost producer benefits more than a high-cost producer from repeat purchases, which makes the firm willing to sacrifice some profit in the first period. Hence, consumers are vindicated in their beliefs that a low first-period price signals a low second-period price. This leads to a theory of shops with a reputation for low prices. The idea is similar to the reputation story developed below in subsection 2.6.2.2.

2.6.2 Adjustable Quality and Reputation

In the previous subsection we focused on how consumers can learn an unalterable quality. As mentioned earlier, there are many instances in which a producer can affect quality over time. In this subsection we study the other polar case, in which the monopolist makes a new quality decision each period. The question then arises as to how repeat purchases can discipline the producer. Is there any mechanism that prevents him from choosing the cheapest quality each period? Obviously, if such a mechanism exists, it must be the case that the observation of a low quality today generates pessimistic consumer expectations for the future. We now consider two models in which such expectations are rational. In both models, we assume that the monopolist's choice of quality is learned by *all* consumers one period after the purchase.

---

46. At least it must be so in an equilibrium; otherwise, the low price would never be charged.

47. Milgrom and Roberts (1986) offer examples in which the high-quality monopolist uses both advertising and prices to signal. See their paper for more details.

2.6.2.1 Quality Premia and Bootstrap Equilibria

We first consider a simplified version of the Klein-Leffler (1981)–Shapiro (1983) model of quality premia.[48] Consider the model of subsection 2.6.1.2. There are two potential qualities: low ($s = 0$) and high ($s = 1$). The unit cost of producing the low (high) quality is c_0 (respectively, $c_1 > c_0$). Consumers are all identical and have per-period surplus $\theta s - p$ if they buy at price p a good with quality s, and 0 if they do not buy. In this subsection we modify the model in three respects. First, the monopolist chooses quality in each period (in 2.6.1.2 we assumed that quality was exogenous). Second, there are an infinite number of periods: $t = 1, 2, \ldots$. As we shall see, the results cannot be derived in a two-period or, more generally, in a finite-horizon model. Let $\delta = 1/(1 + r)$ denote the discount factor. Third, all the consumers learn at the beginning of period $t + 1$ the quality chosen by the monopolist at date t. This may result, for instance, from an article in *Consumer Reports* or from efficient word-of-mouth communication between consumers. We make this assumption to abstract from the considerations concerning the number of informed consumers, which were central to the previous subsection.

If there were only one period, the producer would have an incentive to choose quality $s = 0$ regardless of the price he charged, and the consumers would not purchase the good. Thus, in the one-period model there is an extreme lemons problem[49] (see section 2.3).

Let us look for an equilibrium of the following type:

• Consumers base their expectations of quality on the firm's "reputation." This reputation at t is measured by the quality chosen by the monopolist at $t - 1$: $R_t = s_{t-1}$. So, they expect $s_t = R_t$. Assume $R_1 = 1$ (the consumers have a favorable prior).

• The monopolist starts with a price p_1 and keeps on charging the same price. He also always provides the high quality. If he were to deviate and provide the low quality in some period, then he would keep providing a low quality from then on and charge $p_0 = 0$; the consumers would then stop buying.

These strategies depict a special form of reputation: The consumer believes that the monopolist will keep producing the same quality whatever this quality is. And, the monopolist indeed maintains the same quality.

We will now see that, for a judicious choice of p_1, these strategies form an equilibrium. We must demonstrate that the consumers' apparently naive expectations are indeed rational (they do not fool themselves), and that, given the consumers' expectations and for any initial reputation, the monopolist maximizes his present discounted value of profits.

The consumers' expectations are trivially rational, because the monopolist's strategy dictates that in each period he chooses the quality chosen a period earlier.

If the monopolist follows his prescribed strategy, he obtains an intertemporal profit of

$$(p_1 - c_1)(1 + \delta + \delta^2 + \cdots) = \frac{p_1 - c_1}{1 - \delta}$$

$$= \left(\frac{1 + r}{r}\right)(p_1 - c_1).$$

If instead he were to deviate and sell a low quality at price p_1 (he might as well charge p_1 if he produces the low quality), he would obtain $p_1 - c_0$ in the deviation period and 0 thereafter. Hence, a necessary condition for equilibrium is that the "fly by night" strategy be unprofitable:

$$\left(\frac{1 + r}{r}\right)(p_1 - c_1) \geqslant p_1 - c_0$$

or

$$p_1 - c_1 \geqslant r(c_1 - c_0).$$

Thus, in order for the monopolist not to cut quality, the high-quality price must command a *premium*: It exceeds marginal cost by at least $r(c_1 - c_0)$. This is easily understood. By cutting quality now, the monopolist saves on production cost $(c_1 - c_0)$. However, he loses his reputation rent:

$$(p_1 - c_1)(\delta + \delta^2 + \cdots) = (p_1 - c_1)/r.$$

---

48. See also Allen 1984. Rogerson (1987) allows producers to differ in their cost structures and provides further support for the equilibria selected by Shapiro (see below).

49. In the lemons problem, the seller does not choose the quality; rather, he chooses whether to sell the product. However, the situation is somewhat similar to the one considered here, in that the seller offers his product only if it is of low quality.

Next, p_1 must be such that the monopolist would not want to rebuild his reputation if he lost it. To do so, he could sell for one period at zero (or slightly negative) price and high quality. This would cost him c_1 in the short run and would bring back the reputation rent $(p_1 - c_1)/r$. Thus, we need

$$-c_1 + (p_1 - c_1)/r \leqslant 0$$

or

$$p_1 - c_1 \leqslant rc_1.$$

(We must also have $p_1 \leqslant \theta$ in order for the consumers to purchase the good.)

The moral of this model is straightforward: The producer has an incentive to produce a high-quality item only if high quality implies a rent that the producer is afraid of losing if he cuts quality.[50] The minimum quality premium $r(c_1 - c_0)$ increases with the rate of interest. Suppose, for instance, that the time lag between periods increases. This means that the consumers take longer to observe past quality. For a given interest rate per unit of time, the interest rate per period grows with the information lag. The monopolist is more tempted to cut quality, because such a cut takes longer to be detected. The quality premium must increase to keep the monopolist from cutting quality (milking his reputation).

Finally, consider the bootstrap aspect of this equilibrium. Reputation matters only because consumers believe it matters. If they did not, and if they believed instead that, whatever the past qualities, the monopolist would supply the low quality in the future, the monopolist would have no incentive to sustain quality, and the consumers' expectations would again be fulfilled. Thus, we have another equilibrium with an extreme lemons effect: Whatever the history, the monopolist always produces products of the lowest quality, and the consumers expect him to do so. In this equilibrium, repeat purchases have no effect. Thus, the analysis suggests only that repetition *may* offer incentives to supply quality, not that it necessarily will.

This second equilibrium is actually the one that would be obtained if the horizon were finite. Let T denote the horizon. At date T, the monopolist has a dominant strategy: to produce the lowest quality (for any price that he charges). This is because there is no future, and the problem is identical to a one-period problem. Thus, consumers should expect $s_T = 0$, whatever the past. As quality at date T is independent of what happens at date $T - 1$, the quality decision at $T - 1$ is made without regard to the future, and so it is again the same as in the one-period model. The monopolist produces the lowest quality regardless of history. By backward induction (see chapter 11), the lemons problem folds back and the monopolist produces the lowest quality in each period.

The infinite-horizon model can also be interpreted as a model in which, at each period, there is a fixed probability y in $(0, 1)$ that the market "disappears" (because of the introduction of a superior product or a change in taste, for instance). The discount factor to be used in computing the equilibria is a modified one:

$$\delta = \left(\frac{1}{1 + r}\right)(1 - y),$$

where r is the rate of interest per period.

The monopoly version of the model can be recast in a competitive mold by allowing free entry by firms, where free entry implies that each producer's intertemporal profit must be 0 (otherwise, other firms would come in). A zero profit requires that the firm loses some money when entering because the flow of subsequent profits $(p_1 - c_1)$ is positive. For instance, the firm may make an introductory offer below marginal cost c_1 (with the specification that if it does not make this introductory offer or if it does not supply the high quality, it will not be trusted by the consumers in the future). Alternatively, the firm could sink some money into uninformative but conspicuous advertising. See Shapiro 1983 for more on this issue.

2.6.2.2 Asymmetric Information and Reputation

The Klein-Leffler/Shapiro theory of quality premia is economically appealing. It relies strongly on the unbounded-

---

50. This idea is not new. Klein and Leffler offer the following quote from Adam Smith: "... the wages of labour vary according to the small or great trust which must be reposed in the workman. The wages of goldsmiths and jewellers are everywhere superior to those of many other workmen, not only of equal, but of much superior ingenuity, on account of the precious metals with which they are intrusted. We trust our health to the physician; our fortune and sometimes our life and reputation to the lawyer and attorney. Such confidence could not safely be reposed in people of a very mean or low condition." (Smith 1776, p. 105)

ness of the horizon, however; furthermore, even for an infinite horizon, the positive effect of repeat purchases on product quality is a possibility, not a certainty (there are many equilibria, including the one in which no reputation forms). Kreps and Wilson (1982) and Milgrom and Roberts (1982) showed that reputation effects can be obtained even with a finite horizon, as long as the consumers are not informed about the firm's technology or its objective function.[51] The idea is the following: Suppose that in the one-period problem there is a positive probability, from the consumers' point of view, that the monopolist does not want to provide the lowest quality. For instance, the monopolist might be "honest," i.e., be reluctant to supply a low quality when he has announced a high quality, even though that strategy would yield a higher monetary payoff. Alternatively, there could be a positive probability that the monopolist's cost of producing the high quality does not exceed that of producing the low quality. Thus, consider two potential types[52] for the monopolist. The "dishonest" type is as described in subsection 2.6.2.1; in the one-period and T-period games, he would provide the low quality if the consumers were aware of his type. The "honest" type always provides the high quality.

Suppose that only the monopolist knows his type, and consider a two-period horizon. The dishonest type may behave as if the consumers knew his type from the start and provide a low quality in the first period. The consumers would then infer that he is of a dishonest type and would expect a low quality in the second period. But another strategy may prove superior: The dishonest type can provide a high quality in the first period in an attempt to *convince* the consumers that he is honest. The consumers then expect a high quality in the second period and are willing to pay for it. The dishonest type can then milk his reputation by providing the low quality at a high price.[53] This strategy entails a first-period loss (due to investment in reputation), which is offset by a second-period gain from reputation. The story might, for instance, apply to a restaurant that offers high-quality food

for a year or two, then reduces quality, and finally shuts down.

Consider a more formal version of this argument in which a monopolist chooses between two qualities, $s = 0$ and $s = 1$, in each of two periods ($t = 1, 2$). The high quality costs c_1, the low quality c_0 ($c_1 > c_0 \geqslant 0$). The consumers are all identical and have a per-period utility of ($\theta s_t - p_t$) if they purchase and 0 otherwise. The monopolist can be of two potential types: "honest" (with probability x_1) and "dishonest" (with probability $1 - x_1$). The monopolist knows his type, but the consumers do not. An honest monopolist always supplies the high quality. A dishonest monopolist maximizes intertemporal profits. In particular, he always provides the low quality in the second period (because it is cheaper, and there is no point keeping a reputation).

For each period, the monopolist quotes a price and then picks a quality. The consumers observe only the price immediately; they observe the quality a period later. We assume for simplicity that in a given period all consumers behave identically—they all accept or reject the price offered by the monopolist. Furthermore, we look for equilibrium behaviors that are independent of the price quoted in the first period. Indeed, we will see that there exists an equilibrium in which any p_1 is totally uninformative. Let us fix an arbitrary first-period price and consider the quality choice of the dishonest monopolist. We will then determine which price can be charged in the first period. If the consumers do not purchase the product in that period, the quality choice is irrelevant.

Assume that the product is bought. The dishonest monopolist can save $c_1 - c_0$ by providing the low quality. He then makes a profit of 0 in the second period, because the consumers learn that he is dishonest and that he will therefore provide low quality in the second period (the moral hazard problem under complete information— see subsection 2.6.2.1 or section 2.3). By providing a high quality in the first period, he gains, at most, $\delta(\theta - c_0)$ in the second period. This is because, at best, the consumers believe that he is honest and are willing to pay θ; milking

51. Kreps, Milgrom, Roberts, and Wilson actually developed their reputation story in the context of predation by a chain store (see chapter 9). However, the ideas are similar enough to be straightforwardly applied to the quality problem.

52. For the notion of type in games of incomplete information, see the Game Theory User's Manual.

53. Of course, consumers should realize that such a strategy may be optimal for the monopolist. See below.

the reputation in the second period then yields $\theta - c_0$. Now, if $c_1 - c_0 > \delta(\theta - c_0)$, the dishonest monopolist has a dominant strategy: to provide the low quality in the first period. The maximum price at which the good can be sold at date 1 is then $p_1 = \theta x_1$.

More interesting is the case where $c_1 - c_0 < \delta(\theta - c_0)$.[54] The cost savings due to low quality are dominated by the value of the reputation of being honest. This suggests that the dishonest monopolist may want to mimic ("pool with") the honest monopolist and provide the high quality in the first period. Can this be an equilibrium? If both types of monopolists provide the same high quality, observing a high quality does not bring any information. Thus, the consumers' posterior (date 2) probability that the monopolist is honest is still x_1. Hence, the consumers are willing to pay $E(\theta s_2) = \theta x_1$. In turn the dishonest monopolist is willing to provide the high quality only if $c_1 - c_0 < \delta(\theta x_1 - c_0)$. If this condition is satisfied, the monopolist does provide the high quality for one period before milking his reputation. Of course, he does not succeed in fully convincing the consumers that he is honest; however, he lets the doubt persist, which allows him to sell in the second period at price θx_1. Thus we have obtained an elementary example of *investment in reputation*.

When $\delta(\theta - c_0) > c_1 - c_0 > \delta(\theta x_1 - c_0)$, the unique equilibrium has the dishonest monopolist randomize (be indifferent) between the high and the low quality in the first period.

*Exercise 2.8*** Show that, if $\delta(\theta - c_0) > c_1 - c_0 > \delta(\theta x_1 - c_0)$, the dishonest monopolist establishes a reputation for the second period with probability

$$\alpha = \frac{x_1[\delta(\theta - c_0) - (c_1 - c_0)]}{(1 - x_1)(c_1 - c_0 + \delta c_0)}.$$

Note that $\lim_{x_1 \to 0} \alpha = 0$. Interpret.

Notice that the choice of quality and the second-period price are independent of p_1. To complete the description of equilibrium, let us specify the following consumer behavior:

If $c_1 - c_0 > \delta(\theta - c_0)$, the first period reveals the monopolist's type. Hence, $E(\theta s_1) = \theta x_1$. Both types charge θx_1.

If $c_1 - c_0 < \delta(\theta x_1 - c_0)$, both types of monopolist provide the high quality. Hence, $E(\theta s_1) = \theta$. The consumers are willing to pay up to $p_1 = \theta$. Both types charge θ.

If $\delta(\theta x_1 - c_0) < c_1 - c_0 < \delta(\theta - c_0)$, the dishonest monopolist randomizes:

$$E(\theta s_1) = \theta[x_1 + (1 - x_1)\alpha],$$

where α is given by exercise 2.8. The consumers are willing to pay up to $p_1 = \theta[x_1 + (1 - x_1)\alpha]$. Both types charge this price.

Note that the higher the incentive to keep a reputation (for instance, the lower $(c_1 - c_0)$), the higher the first-period price will be.

Thus, we have considered an equilibrium in which the dishonest monopolist reveals his type immediately, or tries to keep his reputation (where reputation means the consumers' perception of the possibility of honesty), depending on the values of the parameters.

Let us compare this equilibrium with the reputation equilibrium of the quality-premium story. In both cases, the high price associated with a reputation may induce a dishonest monopolist not to cut quality (at least in the short run in the quality-premium story). There are, however, important differences. First, the new equilibrium is based on an asymmetry of information rather than on bootstrapping. Second, low cost savings $(c_1 - c_0)$ lower the incentive to cut quality in both models; however, in the quality-premium story, it implies that a lower price premium is required to keep incentives. Thus, the market price can be lower. In the asymmetric-information story, lower cost savings make the dishonest monopolist more likely to produce the high quality. This raises the market price on average (both in the first and in the second period).

The asymmetric-information theory of reputation can be studied more generally in a T-period model. The generalization of the earlier equilibrium can be derived using the same techniques used before. In general, it takes the following form: In the early periods, the dishonest monopolist always provides the high quality. Later on, he

---

54. For the sake of brevity, we do not consider the borderline case $c_1 - c_0 = \delta(\theta - c_0)$. Similarly, we will ignore another borderline case below.

randomizes between the high and the low quality (and once he has provided the low quality, he keeps doing so until the end). At the end of the horizon, he always provides the low quality (see exercise 2.9).

One of the main points of the Kreps-Milgrom-Roberts-Wilson contribution is that if the horizon is sufficiently long and the discount factor δ sufficiently close to 1 (so that the monopolist does not discount the future too much), even small initial probabilities x_1 that the monopolist is honest lead to non-negligible investments in reputation (which is not the case in the two-period model; see exercise 2.8).

*Exercise 2.9**** In the T-period version of the previous model, derive the equilibrium in which (as previously) each period's price does not act as a signal. Let $K \equiv \theta\delta/(c_1 - c_0 + \delta c_0)$. Show that if $K \leqslant 1$ the equilibrium behavior reveals the monopolist's type in the first period. Show that if $K > 1$ the monopolist pools at period t with probability 1 if the current posterior beliefs that the monopolist is honest satisfy $x_t \geqslant 1/K^{T-t}$. Interpret.

In our equilibrium, the market price does not act as a signal of the monopolist's price. One may wonder whether, in the cases in which the dishonest monopolist duplicates the honest monopolist's quality choice in the first period, the honest monopolist would not want to signal through an introductory price, as in subsection 2.6.1.2. For this question to be well posed, the objective function of the honest monopolist must be specified more thoroughly. If the honest monopolist simply enjoys providing quality, it is not clear why he would try to raise his intertemporal profit by making an introductory offer. On the other hand, he may also enjoy profits. (Quality comes first, however, either because of lexicographic preferences or because, for this type, the cost of providing the higher quality is lower than that of providing the lower one.)

Answers and Hints

Exercise 2.1

$$\varepsilon_s = \frac{p^{-\alpha}\beta s^{\beta-1}s}{p^{-\alpha}s^{\beta}} = \beta \quad \text{and} \quad \varepsilon_p = \frac{\alpha p^{-\alpha-1}s^{\beta}}{p^{-\alpha}s^{\beta}}p = \alpha.$$

A Cobb-Douglas function implies constant elasticities.

Exercise 2.2

The demand function is given by $1 - p/s = q$ or $p = s(1 - q)$.

(i) $\dfrac{1}{q}\displaystyle\int_0^q P_s(x, s)\,dx = 1 - \dfrac{q}{2} > P_s(q, s) = 1 - q.$

(ii) The monopoly solution is given by equations [2.3] and [2.4].[55] Here

$$s(1 - q) - qs = \frac{cs^2}{2} \qquad [2.3]$$

and

$$(1 - q)q = (cs)q, \qquad [2.4]$$

which yields $q = \frac{1}{3}$ and $s = 2/3c$.

Note that output is independent of c.

The social planner's optimum is given by equations [2.1] and [2.2]. Here

$$s(1 - q) = \frac{cs^2}{2} \qquad [2.1]$$

and

$$(1 - q/2)q = (cs)q, \qquad [2.2]$$

which yields $q = \frac{2}{3}$ and $s = 2/3c$.

Exercise 2.3

(i) Monopoly: With only one site, the monopolist charges $\overline{s} - t$. (If $\overline{s}$ is big, he prefers to cover the market, i.e., to reduce price sufficiently so that everybody buys.) With two sites, he can increase the price to $\overline{s} - t/2$ and

---

55. Equations [2.3] and [2.4] specialize the general formulas 2.3 and 2.4 (given in the text above) to this particular demand function. Equations [2.1] and [2.2] do much the same.

still cover the market. The increase in profit from adding the second site is $\Delta\Pi^m = t/2 - f > 0$.

(ii) *Social planner*: The consumer surplus is given (inelastic consumption). The only thing that the number of sites affects is the total transportation cost. Thus, the increase in welfare from adding a second site is

$$\Delta W = \int_0^1 txdx - 2\int_0^{1/2} txdx - f = t/4 - f < 0.$$

Exercise 2.4

It was shown in the text that if $\alpha p < c_1 - (1 - \alpha)c_0$ not all uninformed consumers can buy, because otherwise the monopolist would cut quality. It was also shown that some uninformed consumers must buy, because otherwise the monopolist would offer the high quality. Let γ in $(0, 1)$ denote the fraction of uninformed consumers who buy. The monopolist must randomize between the two qualities (otherwise, γ would be 0 or 1). Thus he must be indifferent between the two:

$$[\alpha + \gamma(1 - \alpha)](p - c_1) = \gamma(1 - \alpha)(p - c_0),$$

or

$$\alpha p = c_1 - (1 - \alpha)[(1 - \gamma)c_1 + \gamma c_0].$$

This equation defines γ. Note that γ grows with α. Next, the uninformed consumers must be indifferent between buying and not buying. Let β denote the probability that the monopolist provides the high quality:

$$\theta\beta - p = 0, \text{ or } \beta = p/\theta.$$

Exercise 2.5

(i) The efficient volume of trade is $N[1 - G(\theta_0)]$. High θ's should get high s's.

(ii) Much as in the Robinson Crusoe example, the supply of cars, $O(p)$, at price p is $O(p) = NF(p/\theta_0)$. The average quality in the market is

$$s^a(p) = \left(\int_{s_{\min}}^{p/\theta_0} xf(x)dx\right) \Big/ F(p/\theta_0).$$

A crucial check is that $ds^a(p)/dp > 0$.

A buyer with parameter θ buys iff $\theta s^a(p) \geqslant p$. Hence,

$$D(p) = N\left(1 - G\left(\frac{p}{s^a(p)}\right)\right).$$

(iii) A competitive equilibrium satisfies $O(p) = D(p)$. For the specification of the model,

$$O(p) = \frac{Np}{\theta_0}, \; s^a(p) = \frac{p}{2\theta_0}, \; D(p) = N(1 - 2\theta_0).$$

Thus, if $\theta_0 \geqslant \frac{1}{2}$, there cannot be any trade (as in the Robinson Crusoe example). If $\theta_0 \leqslant \frac{1}{2}$, there exists a unique competitive equilibrium at $p = \theta_0 - 2\theta_0^2$. The volume of trade is $N(1 - 2\theta_0) < N(1 - \theta_0)$.

(iv) By varying F and G, one can easily obtain multiple intersections between O and D. Let p_1 and p_2 denote two equilibrium prices, with $p_1 < p_2$. Suppliers clearly prefer the equilibrium at p_2. Buyers also do; a higher supply at p_2 means that the demand is higher as well. Hence,

$$\frac{p_2}{s^a(p_2)} < \frac{p_1}{s^a(p_1)}$$

$$\to \text{ for all } \theta, \; \theta - \frac{p_2}{s^a(p_2)} > \theta - \frac{p_1}{s^a(p_1)}$$

$$\to \text{ for all } \theta, \; \theta s^a(p_2) - p_2 > \theta s^a(p_1) - p_1.$$

It turns out that the highest-price Walrasian equilibrium need not be optimal, even when account is taken of informational constraints (i.e., a central planner can do better even if he does not know the private characteristics). For instance, some rationing may be desirable. See Wilson 1980.

(v) Consider the specification of question iii. Under a minimum quality standard s_0, the average quality at price p becomes

$$s^a(p) = (p/\theta_0 + s_0)/2.$$

Take $\theta_0 = \frac{1}{2}$, for example. If $s_0 = 0$, no trade occurs. For $s_0 > 0$, trade occurs at $p = \frac{1}{2}\sqrt{s_0 + s_0^2}$.

Exercise 2.6

The intertemporal profit can be written as

$$x(\tilde{p}_1 - \tilde{c})[1 - F(\tilde{p}_1)] + \delta x(\tilde{p}_1 - c)[1 - F(\tilde{p}_1)]$$

$$= (1 + \delta)x[\tilde{p}_1 - c(\delta)][1 - F(\tilde{p}_1)],$$

where $c(\delta) = (\tilde{c} + \delta c)/(1 + \delta)$ is the average discounted cost (remember that the cost of producing a clientele of N consumers is $Nc/x = N\tilde{c}$). Note that $c(\delta)$ decreases with δ. The maximization of this profit is equivalent to that of a monopolist with unit cost $c(\delta)$. Hence, the market price is a decreasing function of δ. The intuition is that the cost of building goodwill is offset more and more by the second-period benefit from goodwill when the discount factor increases.

When δ goes to infinity (which corresponds to the case in which the consumers learn very quickly and the monopolist can milk his informed clientele for a long time), the demand (size of goodwill) converges to the monopoly demand under full information.

Exercise 2.7

(i) For the low-quality type, the monopoly price is determined by the comparison of $\theta_0 s_0 - c_0$ (sell to all consumers) and $q_1(\theta_1 s_0 - c_0)$ (sell only to high-valuation consumers). For the high-quality type, replace s_0 with s_1 and c_0 with c_1.

(ii) Assume the set of parameters S_1. The low-quality monopolist, who in a separating equilibrium reveals that quality is low, does best by choosing his monopoly solution. From (i), he sells to all consumers and makes profit $(\theta_0 s_0 - c_0)(1 + \delta)$. He should not want to duplicate the high-quality type's strategy. Assume that the latter sells at p_1 to θ_1 consumers only. (This requires that $p_1 \geqslant \theta_0 s_1$.) Then we have

$$(\theta_0 s_0 - c_0)(1 + \delta) \geqslant q_1(p_1 - c_0 + \delta(\theta_1 s_0 - c_0)).$$

Next, the high-quality type does not want to duplicate the low-quality type's strategy:

$$q_1(p_1 - c_1 + \delta(\theta_1 s_1 - c_1))$$
$$\geqslant \theta_0 s_0 - c_1 + \delta q_1(\theta_1 s_1 - c_1),$$

where use is made of the optimal monopoly strategy in the second period. These two equations, the condition $p_1 \geqslant \theta_0 s_1$, and the non-negativity of profits are satisfied for parameters S_1 and $p_1 = \theta_0 s_1$, say. To complete the proof, suppose that consumers believe that quality is s_0 when the first-period price differs from $\theta_0 s_0$ and $\theta_0 s_1$. Similar computations yield the result under S_2.

Exercise 2.8

In the text, it is shown that the dishonest monopolist chooses the low quality with probability 1 only if $c_1 - c_0 > \delta(\theta - c_0)$ and chooses the high quality with probability 1 only if $c_1 - c_0 < \delta(\theta x_1 - c_0)$. Hence, in equilibrium the dishonest monopolist must randomize. Let α

denote the probability that he chooses the high quality. From Bayes' rule, the consumers' posterior probability that the monopolist is honest, given that he has provided the high quality in the first period, is

$$x_2 = x_1/[x_1 + (1 - x_1)\alpha].$$

The dishonest monopolist's indifference between the two choices requires that $c_1 - c_0 = \delta(\theta x_2 - c_0)$. Hence the formula in the text.

When x_1 is small, the dishonest type cannot choose the high quality with non-negligible probability. Otherwise, the consumers put most of the weight on him, which lowers the benefits from reputation.

Exercise 2.9

(The following proof is a mere adaptation of the Kreps-Milgrom-Roberts-Wilson proof in their predatory-pricing model).

Work by backward induction from the last period. x_t denotes the period-t (posterior) probability that the monopolist is honest.

At T, the dishonest monopolist provides the low quality whatever x_T.

At $(T - 1)$, the game is identical with the two-period case analyzed in the text for initial beliefs x_{T-1}. We know that if $K \leqslant 1$ the equilibrium involves full revelation for any x_{T-1}. If $K > 1$, the equilibrium is either a "pooling equilibrium" (the dishonest type provides the high quality with probability 1) or a "semi-revealing equilibrium" (the dishonest type provides the high quality with probability α_{T-1} in [0, 1]). The dishonest type has intertemporal payoff from $T - 1$ on: $\theta K x_{T-1} - c_0$ in the semi-revealing region and $\theta - c_1 + \delta(\theta x_{T-1} - c_0)$ in the pooling region. The semi-revealing region is defined by $0 \leqslant x_{T-1} \leqslant \overline{x}_{T-1}$ and the pooling region by $\overline{x}_{T-1} \leqslant x_{T-1} \leqslant 1$, where the cutoff probability $\overline{x}_{T-1}$ is defined by

$$\theta K \overline{x}_{T-1} - c_0 = \theta - c_1 + \delta(\theta x_{T-1} - c_0) \Leftrightarrow \overline{x}_{T-1} = 1/K.$$

First, get rid of the uninteresting case $K \leqslant 1$. At $T - 2$, the consumers and the monopolist know that the dishonest type will provide the low quality at date $T - 1$ anyway. Thus, everything is as if $T - 1$ were the end of the horizon (i.e., as if we were in a two-period model). Hence, the dishonest type provides the low quality for any beliefs x_{T-2}. By backward induction, this property holds for all t.

Next, assume that $K > 1$ and consider period $T - 2$. Can the dishonest monopolist reveal his type with probability 1? If this were so, he would save $c_1 - c_0$ relative to waiting until $T - 1$ and milking the reputation then. (Such a strategy at $T - 1$ is actually dominated.) But he would lose $\delta(\theta - c_0) > c_1 - c_0$. Thus, the equilibrium cannot be revealing. Again, there are two regions. The semi-revealing region $(x_{T-2} \leqslant \bar{x}_{T-2})$ is such that the monopolist ends up in the $T - 1$ semi-revealing region if he provides the high quality at $T - 2$. Hence, the cutoff point between the two regions at date $T - 2$ is determined by

$$c_1 - c_0 = \delta(\theta K \bar{x}_{T-2} - c_0).$$

(At the cutoff point, the monopolist produces the high quality with probability 1, which implies $x_{T-1} = \bar{x}_{T-2}$). Hence, $\bar{x}_{T-2} = 1/K^2$.

In the semi-revealing region, the dishonest type has intertemporal payoff $\theta K^2 x_{T-2} - c_0$, and, by induction, $\bar{x}_t = 1/K^{T-t}$.

For any fixed t, $\bar{x}_t$ tends to zero when T goes to infinity. Hence, for any x_1 and any t, the dishonest monopolist produces the high quality with probability 1 at least until t as long as T is sufficiently large.

References

Akerlof, G. 1970. The Market for "Lemons": Qualitative Uncertainty and the Market Mechanism. *Quarterly Journal of Economics* 84: 488–500.

Allen, F. 1984. Reputation and Product Quality. *Rand Journal of Economics* 15: 311–327.

Arnott, R., and J. Stiglitz. 1982. Equilibrium in Competitive Insurance Markets and The Welfare Economics of Moral Hazard. Reports DP 465 and 483, Queen's University.

Bagwell, K. 1985. Introductory Price as Signal of Cost in a Model of Repeat Business. Discussion Paper 130, Studies in Industrial Economics, Stanford University.

Bagwell, K., and M. Riordan. 1986. Equilibrium Price Dynamics for an Experience Good, Discussion Paper 705, CMSEMS, Northwestern University.

Bester, H. 1985. Screening vs. Rationing in Credit Markets with Imperfect Information. *American Economic Review* 75: 850–855.

Butters, G. 1977. Equilibrium Distributions of Sales and Advertising Prices. *Review of Economic Studies* 44: 465–491.

Calabresi, G. 1970. *The Costs of Accidents: A Legal and Economic Analysis.* New Haven: Yale University Press.

Chamberlin, E. 1951. Monopolistic Competition Revisited. *Economica* 18: 343–362.

Chamberlin, E. 1962. *The Theory of Monopolistic Competition,* eigth edition. Cambridge, Mass.: Harvard University Press.

Chan, Y., and H. Leland. 1982. Prices and Qualities in Markets with Costly Information. *Review of Economic Studies* 49: 499–516.

Cho, I. K., and D. Kreps. 1987. Signaling Games and Stable Equilibria. *Quarterly Journal of Economics* 102: 179–221.

Coase, R. 1960. The Problem of Social Cost. *Journal of Law and Economics* 1: 1–44.

Cooper, R., and T. Ross. 1984. Prices, Product Qualities and Asymmetric Information: The Competitive Case. *Review of Economic Studies* 51: 197–208.

Cooper, R., and T. Ross. 1985. Monopoly Provision of Product Quality with Uninformed Buyers. *International Journal of Industrial Organization* 3: 439–449.

Crémer, J. 1984. On the Economics of Repeat Buying. *Rand Journal of Economics* 15: 396–403.

Darby, M., and E. Karni. 1973. Free Competition and the Optimal Amount of Fraud. *Journal of Law and Economics* 16: 67–88.

Dixit, A., and V. Norman. 1978. Advertising and Welfare. *Bell Journal of Economics* 9: 1–17.

Dorfman, R., and P. Steiner. 1954. Optimal Advertising and Optimal Quality. *American Economic Review* 44: 826–836.

Farrell, J. 1980. Prices as Signals of Quality. Ph.D. dissertation, Brasenose College, Oxford.

Farrell, J. 1984. Moral Hazard in Quality, Entry Barriers and Introductory Offers. Discussion Paper 344, Department of Economics, Massachusetts Institute of Technology.

Farrell, J. 1986. Moral Hazard as an Entry Barrier. *Rand Journal of Economics* 17: 440–449.

Fisher, F., and J. McGowan. 1979. Advertising and Welfare: Comment. *Bell Journal of Economics* 10: 726–727.

Hellwig, M. 1986a. A Sequential Approach to Modelling Competition in Markets with Adverse Selection. Mimeo, Universität Bonn.

Hellwig, M. 1986b. Moral Hazard, Adverse Selection and Competition in Insurance Markets. Mimeo, Universität Bonn.

Hirshleifer, J. 1971. Suppression of Inventions. *Journal of Political Economy* 79: 382–383.

Hotelling, H. 1929. Stability in Competition. *Economic Journal* 39: 41–57.

Kaldor, N. 1940–41. Economic Aspects of Advertising. *Review of Economic Studies* 18: 1–27.

Kihlstrom, R., and D. Levhari, 1977. Quality, Regulation, Efficiency. *Kyklos* 30: 214–234.

Kihlstrom, R., and M. Riordan. 1984. Advertising as a Signal. *Journal of Political Economy* 92: 427–450.

Klein, B., and K. Leffler. 1981. The Role of Market Forces in Assuring Contractual Performance. *Journal of Political Economy* 81: 615–641.

Kreps, D., and R. Wilson. 1982. Reputation and Imperfect Information. *Journal of Economic Theory* 27: 253–279.

Lancaster, K. 1966. A New Approach to Consumer Theory. *Journal of Political Economy* 74: 132–157.

Lancaster, K. 1975. Socially Optimal Product Differentiation. *American Economic Review* 65: 567–585.

Lancaster, K. 1979. *Variety, Equity and Efficiency*. New York: Columbia University Press.

Leland, H. 1979. Quacks, Lemons and Licensing: A Theory of Minimum Quality Standards. *Journal of Political Economy* 87: 1328–1346.

Liebowitz, S. 1982. Durability, Market Structure, and New-Used Goods Models. *American Economic Review* 72: 816–824.

Milgrom, P., and J. Roberts. 1982. Predation, Reputation, and Entry Deterrence. *Journal of Economic Theory* 27: 280–312.

Milgrom, P., and J. Roberts. 1986. Prices and Advertising Signals of Product Quality. *Journal of Political Economy* 94: 796–821.

Nelson, P. 1970. Information and Consumer Behaviour. *Journal of Political Economy* 78: 311–329.

Nelson, P. 1974. Advertising as Information. *Journal of Political Economy* 81: 729–754.

Nerlove, M., and K. Arrow. 1962. Optimal Advertising Policy Under Dynamic Conditions. *Economica* 29: 524–548.

Polinsky, M. 1983. *An Introduction to Law and Economics*. Boston: Little, Brown.

Riordan, M. 1986. Monopolistic Competition with Experience Goods. *Quarterly Journal of Economics* 101: 265–280.

Rogerson, W. 1987. Advertising as a Signal when Prices Guarantee Quality. Discussion Paper 704, CMSEMS, Northwestern University.

Rosen, S. 1974. Hedonic Prices and Implicit Markets: Product Differentiation in Pure Competition. *Journal of Political Economy* 82: 34–56.

Rothschild, M., and J. Stiglitz. 1976. Equilibrium in Competitive Insurance Markets: An Essay in the Economics of Imperfect Information. *Quarterly Journal of Economics* 90: 629–650.

Salop, S. 1977. The Noisy Monopolist. *Review of Economic Studies* 44: 393–406.

Salop, S., and J. Stiglitz. 1977. Bargains and Ripoffs: A Model of Monopolistically Competitive Price Dispersion. *Review of Economic Studies* 44: 493–510.

Schmalensee, R. 1972. *The Economics of Advertising*. Amsterdam: North-Holland.

Schmalensee, R. 1978. A Model of Advertising and Product Quality. *Journal of Political Economy* 86: 485–503.

Schmalensee, R. 1986. Advertising and Market Structure. In *New Developments in the Analysis of Market Structure*, ed. J. Stiglitz and F. Matthewson. Cambridge, Mass.: MIT Press.

Schmalensee, R., and J. Thisse. 1987. Perceptual Maps and the Optimal Location of New Products. *International Journal of Research in Marketing* 4.

Shaked, A., and J. Sutton. 1981. The Self-Regulating Profession. *Review of Economic Studies* 48: 217–234.

Shapiro, C. 1980. Advertising and Welfare: Comment. *Bell Journal of Economics* 11: 749–752.

Shapiro, C. 1982. Consumer Information, Product Quality, and Seller Reputation. *Bell Journal of Economics* 13: 20–35.

Shapiro, C. 1983. Premiums for High Quality Products as Rents to Reputation. *Quarterly Journal of Economics* 98: 659–680.

Shapiro, C. 1986. Investment, Moral Hazard, and Occupational Licensing. *Review of Economic Studies* 53: 843–862.

Shavell, S. 1980. Damage Measures for Breach of Contract. *Bell Journal of Economics* 11: 466–490.

Shavell, S. 1984. On the Design of Contracts and Remedies for Breach. *Quarterly Journal of Economics* 99: 121–148.

Sheshinski, E. 1976. Price, Quality and Quantity Regulation in Monopoly. *Econometrica* 43: 127–137.

Smallwood, D., and J. Conlisk. 1979. Product Quality in Markets where Consumers are Imperfectly Informed. *Quarterly Journal of Economics* 93: 1–23.

Smith, A. 1776. *An Inquiry into the Nature and Causes of the Wealth of Nations.* New York: Modern Library, 1937.

Spence, M. 1977. Consumer Misperceptions, Product Failure, and Producer Liability. *Review of Economic Studies* 44: 561–572.

Spence, M. 1973. Job Market Signaling. *Quarterly Journal of Economics* 87: 355–374.

Spence, M. 1975. Monopoly, Quality and Regulation. *Bell Journal of Economics,* 6: 417–429.

Spence, M. 1976. Product Differentiation and Welfare. *American Economic Review* 66: 407–414.

Stiglitz, J., and A. Weiss. 1981. Credit Rationing in Markets with Imperfect Information. *American Economic Review* 71: 393–410.

Swan, P. 1970. Market Structure and Technological Progress: The Influence of Monopoly on Product Innovation. *Quarterly Journal of Economics* 84: 627–638.

Wilson, C. 1977. A Model of Insurance Markets with Incomplete Information. *Journal of Economic Theory* 16: 167–207.

Wilson, C. 1980. The Nature of Equilibrium in Markets with Adverse Selection. *Bell Journal of Economics* 11: 108–130.

Wolinsky, A. 1983. Prices as Signals of Product Quality. *Review of Economic Studies* 50: 647–658.

Price Discrimination

For most of chapters 1 and 2 we assumed that a monopolist produces a single good and sells it at a uniform price (per unit). In general, uniform pricing leaves some surplus to the consumers. (Indeed, we saw in chapter 2 that this nonappropriability of the consumer surplus is a force pushing toward the introduction of too few products by a monopolist.)

Uniform pricing may be a good generalization for most retail markets. However, examples abound in which the same economic good is sold at different prices to different consumers. A doctor may charge a rich patient more than a poor one, or may charge an insured patient more than an uninsured one. The price of a consumer good may vary across areas of a city or a country, even in the absence of any significant cost differential. The same economic good may also be sold at two different prices to the same consumer. This occurs, for instance, when the producer practices quantity discounts, in which the marginal unit can be purchased at a lower price than the inframarginal ones. Such examples may be viewed as attempts by the producer to capture a higher fraction of consumer surplus than he would if he charged a uniform price.

It is hard to come up with a satisfactory definition of price discrimination. Roughly, it can be said that the producer price-discriminates when two units of the same physical good are sold at different prices, either to the same consumer or to different consumers.

This definition is unsatisfactory, and sometimes it must be amended or extended. First, consider the case of a cement producer serving a geographic area. To the producer's costs must be added the freight costs. Suppose that the cement producer is vertically integrated and thus provides his own transportation. In such a case, a uniform delivered price is discriminatory, whereas delivered prices that respond fully to transportation-cost differentials among consumers located at different distances from the factory are not. Hence, we will say that there is no price discrimination if differences in prices between consumers exactly reflect differences in the costs of serving these consumers (this amounts to considering the *net* cost of serving a consumer). Second, it should not be inferred that price discrimination does not occur when differentiated products are sold to different consumers.[1] The use of different qualities of services (e.g., classes in trains and airplanes) is also partly an attempt to capture consumer surplus by separating consumers into different groups, as we shall see. Thus, it is difficult to offer an all-encompassing definition. A general-equilibrium theorist might rightly point out that goods delivered at different dates, at different locations, in different states of nature, or of different quality are distinct economic goods and thus that the scope of "pure" discrimination is very limited.[2]

The possibility of price discrimination is linked to the possibility of arbitrage. It is conventional to distinguish between two types of arbitrage.

The first type of arbitrage is associated with the *transferability of the commodity*. It is clear that if the transaction (arbitrage) costs between two consumers are low, any attempt to sell a given good to two consumers at different prices runs into the problem that the low-price consumer buys the good to resell it to the high-price one. For instance, the introduction of quantity discounts (which, as we will see below, is often optimal) implies that, in the absence of transaction costs between consumers, only one consumer buys the product and resells it to other consumers. For example, if each consumer buys according to the "two-part tariff" $T(q) = A + pq$ (where $A > 0$ is a fixed fee and p is the marginal price), only one consumer will pay the fixed fee. Hence, if there are many consumers, everything is almost as if the manufacturer sold at the linear (or uniform) price. If consumers can arbitrage perfectly, the producer is generally forced to charge a uniform or fully linear price: $T(q) = pq$.

Transaction costs offer a clue as to when price discrimination is feasible. Services such as medical treatment and travel are much less transferable than most retail commodities. Similarly, the consumer can hardly engage in arbitrage for electricity or telephone calls.

Of course, perfect (costless) arbitrage and no arbitrage

are two extreme cases. In general, some limited arbitrage may occur, depending on the relative cost and benefit: Consider the use of a false student ID card in order to enjoy a student discount. An interesting case of partial arbitrage, and therefore partial discrimination, is that of a manufacturer who sells his product to several retailers. The retailers may arbitrage if the manufacturer tries to charge different marginal prices to different retailers. This prevents the manufacturer from imposing general non-linear tariffs $T(q)$ to his retailers. However, even though he may not be able to observe the exact quantity sold by each retailer, he may observe that a retailer carries his product. Then (ignoring legal constraints) he can charge a two-part tariff $T(q) = A + pq$, where A is a fixed premium (a "franchise fee," in this case).

Two-part tariffs will also be applicable whenever the (variable) consumption of the arbitraged good is linked with the (fixed) consumption of a complementary product, as in the case of razor blades and razors or that of Polaroid film and Polaroid cameras. If pictures (rather than film and camera) are thought of as the final consumption good, the producer can manipulate the relative prices of the two inputs that produce pictures to discriminate (i.e., can charge two different prices for different units of the good "picture"). The analogy with the franchising example is that the fixed fee must in practice be paid by every consumer, while the good which is consumed in variable proportions may be subject to arbitrage.

The second type of arbitrage is associated with the *transferability of demand* between different packages or bundles offered to the consumers. Here there is no physical transfer of good between consumers. The consumer simply chooses between the different options offered. For instance, a consumer may have a choice between buying two units of the good at total price $T(2)$ and buying one unit at price $T(1)$ (this is known as a price-quantity package) or between first-class and second-class accommodations on a train (a price-quality package). As we will see, if consumers' tastes differ, the producer generally wants to target a specific package for each consumer. However, in the absence of information about the identity of each

---

1. In the example of the cement producer, consumers indeed buy spatially differentiated goods. However, each consumer can consume only a well-defined commodity ("cement delivered at the consumer's location"). We want to extend the notion of discrimination to cases in which the consumer is given a choice among several differentiated goods.

2. See Phlips 1983 for an extensive discussion of the notion of discrimination. This introduction to chapter 3 is influenced by his introduction to the topic. Varian 1987 and Wilson 1985 are two other useful treatments of price discrimination.

consumer (the producer only knows the aggregate distribution of tastes), the producer must make sure that each consumer indeed chooses the package designed for him and not the package designed for another consumer. For instance, the traveler to whom first class is targeted should not want to travel second class because the price savings more than offset the reduction in quality. This, as we will see, puts "incentive compatibility" constraints on the set of packages offered by the producer. The producer must use "self-selection devices."

In terms of the consequences of discrimination, the two types of arbitrage are naturally very different. The transferability of the product tends to prevent discrimination, whereas the transferability of demand may induce the producer to increase discrimination. In the supplementary section we will see that, under reasonable assumptions, the producer enlarges the quantity spectrum or the quality spectrum when he has information about aggregate demand rather than about individual demands.

Following Pigou (1920), it is customary to distinguish three types of price discrimination. *First-degree* price discrimination is perfect price discrimination—the producer succeeds in capturing the entire consumer surplus. This occurs, for instance, when consumers have unit demands and the producer knows exactly each consumer's reservation price and (if these reservation prices differ) can prevent arbitrage between consumers. It then suffices for the producer to charge an individualized price equal to the consumer's reservation price. Perfect price discrimination is unlikely in practice, either because of arbitrage or because of incomplete information about individual preferences. In the case of incomplete information about individual preferences, the producer may still be able to extract consumer surplus imperfectly by using the self-selecting devices mentioned earlier. This is called *second-degree* price discrimination.[3] Also, the producer may observe some signal that is related to the consumer's preferences (e.g. age, occupation, location) and use this signal to price-discriminate; this is termed *third-degree* price discrimination. The important difference between second-degree and third-degree price discrimination is that

third-degree discrimination uses a direct signal about demand, whereas second-degree discrimination selects indirectly between consumers through their choice between different packages.

We will not quite follow the traditional ordering. After considering when perfect price discrimination is feasible (section 3.1), we will study third-degree price discrimination (section 3.2). The ideas contained in section 3.2 are direct applications of previous material on multi-product monopoly and the inverse elasticity rule (see section 1.1). To clearly differentiate this type of imperfect discrimination from second-degree price discrimination, we will assume that the monopolist is able to divide the market into n segments of customers on the basis of direct signals, but that he is unable to discriminate between consumers within a group (either because of unit demands or because of commodity arbitrage). We will then tackle the newer concept of second-degree price discrimination by assuming that the monopolist knows how consumers' preferences are distributed within a group but does not know each consumer's preferences. This will lead to a consideration of screening or self-selection devices, which is developed in more detail in the supplementary section. Our study of second-degree price discrimination will also be extended to exhibit the analogy between discrimination over quality spectra and nonlinear tariffs.

3.1 Perfect Price Discrimination

The simplest kind of perfect price discrimination occurs when a single consumer (or, equivalently, a number of identical consumers) has unit demand. Suppose that each consumer has v as his willingness to pay (valuation) for a good. The monopolist, by charging price $p = v$, extracts the whole consumer surplus.

Next, consider the case of identical downward-sloping demands. Suppose that the n consumers in the market all have the same demand, $q = D(p)/n$, for the monopolist's product, and that this demand function (and, therefore, the aggregate function $q = D(p)$) is known by the mo-

---

3. We encountered an instance of second-degree price discrimination in the supplementary section of chapter 1, where we saw how time could screen consumers with different valuations for a durable good. High-valuation consumers are more eager to buy early. They pay a higher price than low-valuation buyers, who wait to purchase the good. A difference with the examples below

is that in the earlier example the monopolist actually loses from price discrimination. As we saw, he would prefer to commit to a fixed (uniform) price path (also, the model was constructed so that in a one-period framework the monopolist would be unable to discriminate). In section 3.3, we will assume the credibility issue away.

nopolist. By using an appropriate pricing schedule, the monopolist can increase his profits over those achieved with a linear pricing schedule (which yields $p^m D(p^m) - C(D(p^m))$); he can even extract all of the potential social surplus. By *pricing schedule*, or *tariff*, we mean the total amount of money T to be paid by the consumer as a function of consumption q. A linear pricing schedule corresponds to a single price: $T(q) = pq$. An affine pricing schedule corresponds to a two-part tariff: $T(q) = A + pq$.

Imagine first that the monopolist adopts the competitive pricing schedule, i.e., $T(q) = p^c q$, where p^c is the competitive price (see figure 3.1). Let S^c be the corresponding net consumer surplus:

$$S^c = \int_0^{q^c} [P(q) - p^c] dq,$$

where $P(q) \equiv D^{-1}(q)$ is the inverse demand function. Now suppose that, in order to have the right to buy at p^c, the consumer must pay a fixed premium. This fixed premium, A, may go as high as S^c/n without inducing the consumers to refrain from buying anything. By offering the "affine" (but nonlinear) pricing schedule or "two-part tariff,"

$$T(q) = \begin{cases} p^c q + \dfrac{S^c}{n} & \text{if } q > 0 \\ 0 & \text{if } q = 0, \end{cases}$$

the monopolist realizes a profit equal to

$$\Pi = S^c + p^c q^c - C(q^c),$$

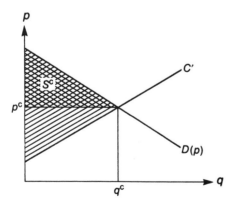

Figure 3.1
(Π is the area of the shaded section.)

which is simply the social surplus at the optimum. This is to be expected, since the marginal price charged by the monopolist is equal to his marginal cost, and consumers have zero surplus after the fixed premium S^c/n is subtracted. It is easy to see that this strategy affords the monopolist his maximum profit. (In particular, he makes more profit than with the optimal linear schedule, which yields a profit equal to $p^m q^m - C(q^m)$.) Unless the monopolist uses coercive means, the consumers can always guarantee themselves a zero surplus by not buying at all. Since the sum of the consumer surplus and the monopoly profit is equal to the total surplus, the maximal profit of the monopolist is equal to the maximal total surplus.

Exercise 3.1*

(i) Show that an alternative way to realize the optimal profit under discrimination is to charge each consumer a tariff equal to his *gross* surplus:

$$T(q) = \int_0^q P(x) dx / n.$$

(ii) Generalize to the case of a monopolist facing a competitive fringe at $p_0 > p^c$. (By definition, a competitive fringe is willing to supply any demand at price p_0 but supplies nothing for a lower price.) What is the optimal two-part tariff? To implement an alternative way of appropriating consumer surplus, how can one redefine "gross surplus"?

So far, we have assumed that consumers are identical. Now suppose that the consumers have different demand curves and assume that the monopolist knows each individual demand curve. For the monopolist, the optimal pricing scheme consists of charging for the marginal unit a price (p^c) equal to the marginal cost and demanding a personalized fixed premium equal to the net surplus S_i^c from consumer i at the price p^c. A special application of this result is the case where the aggregate demand function is derived from unit demand functions (each consumer consumes one or zero unit of the good) of consumers each of whom has a different willingness to pay. Then, the two-part tariff is equivalent to a simple system of personalized prices, with each consumer paying a sum equal to his willingness to pay.

Of course, there are considerable disclosure problems. Certainly a consumer is not likely to reveal that he is among those willing to pay a higher price for the good. This may destroy the possibility of discrimination. For instance, when consumers have unit demands and the producer knows only the distribution of valuations over the population but not the individual valuations, a single price is charged—i.e., discrimination does not occur. (The optimal price is then equal to the monopoly price for the downward-sloping demand curve formed by the addition of unit demands.)[4]

We now turn to imperfect price discrimination.

3.2 Multimarket (Third-Degree) Price Discrimination

3.2.1 The Inverse-Elasticity Rule Again

Suppose that a monopolist produces a single product at a total cost of $C(q)$, and that he is able to divide the aggregate demand into m "groups" or "markets" on the basis of some "exogenous" information (e.g. age, sex, occupation, location, or first-time vs. second-time buyer). These m groups have m distinct downward-sloping demand curves for the product. The demand curves are known to the monopolist. We will assume that arbitrage cannot occur *between* groups but that, at the same time, the monopolist cannot discriminate (even in a second-degree sense) *within* a group. (These conditions will have to be checked in each application.) Hence, the monopolist charges a linear tariff for each group. Let

$$\{p_1, \ldots, p_i, \ldots, p_m\}$$

denote the prices in the different markets, and let

$$\{q_1 = D_1(p_1), \ldots, q_i = D_i(p_i), \ldots, q_m = D_m(p_m)\}$$

denote the quantities demanded. Let

$$q = \sum_{i=1}^{m} D_i(p_i)$$

denote the aggregate demand. The monopolist chooses prices to maximize his profit:

$$\sum_{i=1}^{m} p_i D_i(p_i) - C\left(\sum_{i=1}^{m} D_i(p_i)\right).$$

Formally, this price-discrimination program is a special case of the multiproduct monopolist's pricing problem described in chapter 1, where demands are independent and costs are (possibly) dependent. We know from this analysis that relative price margins are given by the inverse-elasticity rule: For all i,

$$\frac{p_i - C'(q)}{p_i} = \frac{1}{\varepsilon_i},$$

where $\varepsilon_i = -D_i'(p_i)p_i/D_i(p_i)$ is the elasticity of demand in market i. *Optimal pricing implies that the monopolist should charge more in markets with the lower elasticity of demand.*

This rule explains why students and senior citizens are given discounts by private firms with no redistribution intention, why legal and medical services are priced according to the customer's income or amount of insurance coverage, why the prices of goods in different countries sometimes do not reflect transportation costs and import taxes, and why first-time subscribers to a magazine are given discounts.[5]

3.2.2 Welfare Aspects

When a monopolist's various products are actually the same physical good sold to different markets, an interesting question is: What would happen if the monopolist were forced to charge the same (uniform) price in all markets? Comparing the two situations gives a measure of the effect of third-degree price discrimination. The monopolist is better off under price discrimination, because "at worst" he can always charge the uniform price in each market. *Consumers in low-elasticity markets are adversely*

---

4. Discrimination could operate if the monopolist could charge a tariff function of the *probability* for the consumer to get the good (i.e., whether the consumer gets the good or not is not determined in advance, but depends on the "toss of a coin"). However, it can be shown that if both the monopolist and the consumers are "risk-neutral," such complicated mechanisms are not optimal for the monopolist.

5. In this last example, price discrimination could also be explained by matching issues—see the supplementary section of chapter 2. The idea here is more similar to that developed in the supplementary section of chapter 1; the consumers who have not yet subscribed are perceived by the monopolist as less eager to buy the magazine than those who have already subscribed.

affected by the discrimination and would prefer a uniform price; consumers in high-elasticity markets prefer discrimination.[6]

To compute the associated change in welfare, assume constant returns to scale: $C(\sum_i q_i) = c(\sum_i q_i)$.[7]

Under discrimination, the monopolist charges p_i in market i. The demand is $q_i = D_i(p_i)$. The aggregate net consumer surplus is $\sum_i S_i(p_i)$, and the firm's profit is $\sum_i (p_i - c)q_i$. Suppose next that discrimination is prohibited. The monopolist charges a uniform price $\bar{p}$ and sells $\bar{q}_i = D_i(\bar{p})$ in market i. The profit is $\sum_i (\bar{p} - c)\bar{q}_i$, and the consumer surplus is $\sum_i S_i(\bar{p})$. Let $\Delta q_i \equiv q_i - \bar{q}_i$.

The difference in total welfare between discrimination and no discrimination is equal to the change in surplus plus the change in profits:

$$\Delta W = \left(\sum_i [S_i(p_i) - S_i(\bar{p})] \right)$$
$$+ \left(\sum_i (p_i - c)q_i - \sum_i (\bar{p} - c)\bar{q}_i \right).$$

We now derive an upper and a lower bound for ΔW. To do so, we make use of the fact that the net surplus function is convex in the market price. (Recall that the derivative of the net surplus with respect to price is equal to minus the demand, and that the demand curve is downward sloping: $S'(p) = -D(p)$ implies $S''(p) = -D'(p) > 0$.)

A well-known property of a convex function is that it is everywhere above its tangents, as figure 3.2 shows. Hence,

$$S_i(p_i) - S_i(\bar{p}) \geqslant S_i'(\bar{p})(p_i - \bar{p}).$$

Using this inequality and the fact that $S_i'(\bar{p}) = -D_i(\bar{p})$, we obtain

$$\Delta W \geqslant \sum_i (p_i - c)\Delta q_i. \qquad (3.1)$$

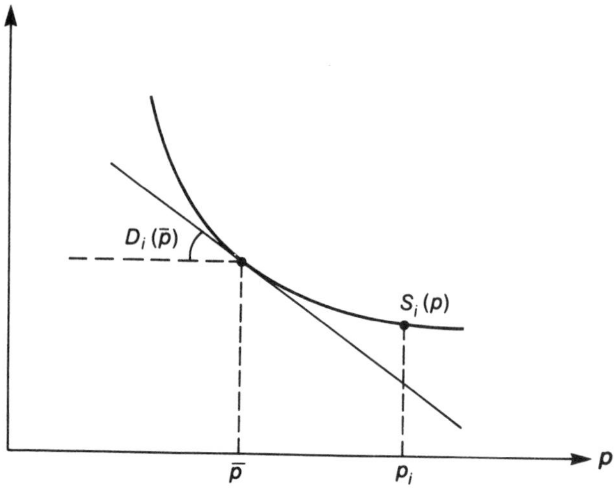

Figure 3.2

Similarly, we have

$$S_i(\bar{p}) - S_i(p_i) \geqslant S_i'(p_i)(\bar{p} - p_i),$$

which yields

$$\Delta W \leqslant (\bar{p} - c)\left(\sum_i \Delta q_i \right). \qquad (3.2)$$

That price discrimination reduces welfare if it does not increase total output (a fact implied by equation 3.2) is intuitive. Price discrimination causes marginal rates of substitution to differ among consumers, and is thus socially inferior to uniform pricing if the goal is to distribute a given amount of good between them. Thus, a necessary condition for price discrimination to be preferred socially is that it raise total output (i.e., that it reduce the traditional monopoly pricing distortion). (To obtain the bounds 3.1 and 3.2, we make no assumptions about the firm's behavior. However, to obtain specific results we will need to use the fact that the producer maximizes monopoly profits.)

---

6. Under a uniform price $\bar{p}$ and a constant marginal cost c, the monopolist maximizes

$$(\bar{p} - c)\left(\sum_i D_i(\bar{p}) \right),$$

which yields a price-cost margin of

$$(\bar{p} - c)/\bar{p} = -\left(\sum_i D_i(\bar{p}) \right) \Big/ \bar{p}\left(\sum_i D_i'(\bar{p}) \right)$$
$$= \left(\sum_i D_i(\bar{p}) \right) \Big/ \left(\sum_i D_i(\bar{p})\varepsilon_i \right).$$

Thus, the inverse of the price-cost margin is a weighted average of the elasticities of demand, where the weights are the quantities demanded. (As an exercise, write the price-cost margin as a weighted average of the inverse elasticities.) Hence,

$$\min_i (1/\varepsilon_i) \leqslant (\bar{p} - c)/\bar{p} \leqslant \max_i (1/\varepsilon_i).$$

7. This discussion is inspired by Varian 1985. Hausman and Mackie-Mason (1986) give general conditions under which price discrimination is welfare improving when the production technology exhibits increasing returns to scale.

3.2.2.1 An Application to Linear Demand Curves

Assume that the demand curve in market i is $q_i = a_i - b_i p$. Assume further that, for all i, $a_i > c b_i$. This condition ensures that under discrimination all markets are served.

The monopolist, if he can discriminate, chooses a price p_i in market i so as to maximize $(p_i - c)(a_i - b_i p_i)$. Straightforward computations show that

$$p_i = (a_i + cb_i)/2b_i$$

and

$$q_i \equiv (a_i - cb_i)/2.$$

Suppose next that the monopolist is forced to charge a uniform price $\bar{p}$ across markets. Assume that all markets are served at the optimum (see the caveat below). The monopolist chooses $\bar{p}$ so as to maximize

$$(\bar{p} - c)\left[\sum_i a_i - \left(\sum_i b_i\right)\bar{p}\right].$$

This leads to

$$\bar{p} = \left[\sum_i a_i + c\left(\sum_i b_i\right)\right]\Big/ 2\left(\sum_i b_i\right)$$

and

$$\sum_i \bar{q}_i = \left[\sum_i a_i - c\left(\sum_i b_i\right)\right]\Big/ 2.^8$$

Total output is the same in the two arrangements: $\sum_i q_i = \sum_i \bar{q}_i$, or $\sum_i \Delta q_i = 0$—a result obtained by Robinson (1933). From equation 3.2, welfare is lower under price discrimination (Schmalensee 1981).

3.2.2.2 Caveat

The conclusion that price discrimination lowers welfare when the demand curve is linear is contingent on the assumption that all markets are served under a uniform price. This assumption is actually quite strong. When

forced to charge a uniform price, the monopolist *de facto* "robs Peter to pay Paul"—he raises the price in high-elasticity markets and lowers that in low-elasticity markets (see footnote 6). The increase in price in the high-elasticity markets may induce consumers in those markets to stop purchasing.

To see that the welfare conclusion can be reversed, suppose that there are two markets ($m = 2$) and that, under a uniform price, the second market is not served. The uniform price is then equal to the monopoly price for the first market: $\bar{p} = p_1^m$ and $\bar{q}_1 = q_1^m$. On the other hand, $\bar{q}_2 = 0 \leqslant q_2$. From equation 3.1, welfare is higher under price discrimination. Indeed, price discrimination leads to a Pareto improvement. The monopolist makes more profit, and the surplus of the consumers in market 2 becomes positive while that of the consumers in market 1 is unchanged.

3.2.2.3 Summary

To summarize our welfare analysis: The welfare effects of third-degree price discrimination are ambiguous. One has to weigh the losses of consumers in low-elasticity markets against the gains of those in high-elasticity markets and of the producer. The elimination of price discrimination may be particularly dangerous if it leads to the closure of markets.[9]

The previous discussion assumes that welfare is equal to the sum of all consumer surpluses and profits, i.e., that the government has efficiency concerns but no redistribution concerns. Of course, one of the main policy issues in regard to price discrimination is its effect on income distribution. As we saw, price discrimination redistributes income away from the low-elasticity groups toward consumers in the high-elasticity groups and the monopolist. Of course, raising monopoly profits at the expense of consumers may not be very desirable. On the other hand, the low-elasticity groups are often (but not always) the richer consumers.[10] Thus, it is clear that one cannot *a*

---

8. All markets are served if, for all i, $a_i - b_i \bar{p} \geqslant 0$.

9. The higher profit associated with discrimination may also increase wasteful competition to obtain the monopoly rent. This led Posner (1976) to notice that if the monopoly rent is completely dissipated (see section 1.3), price discrimination is more likely to be harmful. It now suffices that consumer surplus is lower under discrimination for uniform pricing to be preferable. Indeed, under perfect price discrimination there is no surplus left and price discrimination is clearly detrimental—a reversal of our previous conclusion. (However, even with

wasteful rent dissipation, price discrimination is not always harmful. See the previous two-class example, in which uniform pricing leads to the closure of one market.) This remark is, of course, also valid for second-degree price discrimination. As usual, the validity of the wasteful rent dissipation argument requires further analysis.

10. In the examples given at the end of subsection 3.2.1, the high-elasticity groups are students, the elderly, indigent patients and legal assistees, or poor countries.

priori make a case against price discrimination on the basis of income distribution.

3.2.3 Applications

A few examples of discrimination based on observable characteristics follow.

3.2.3.1 Application 1: Spatial Discrimination

Consider the location model described in section 2.1. Suppose that a monopolist produces a good at a single plant. To simplify, assume that the transportation cost per unit of good is proportional to the distance to the plant; i.e., it is tx for a customer located at a distance x. Suppose that the producer transports the good himself. He charges this customer a delivered price $p(x)$; equivalently, he could charge a free-on-board (f.o.b.) or mill price of $p(x) - tx$ and let the customer take care of the transportation (of course, this second policy would tend to lend itself to arbitrage). The production cost is c per unit.

Suppose that the firm's customers are located at various distances from the plant. To focus on the spatial issue, assume that all customers have the same demand at a given delivered price; let $q = D(p)$ denote this demand. Assume that the firm charges the same price to all customers located at the same location. (One could, for instance, imagine that customers located at the same site engage in arbitrage. For a discussion of the possibility of arbitrage between sites, see below.) The monopolist maximizes monopoly profit in the market formed by customers located at x; in other words, he maximizes $(p - tx - c)D(p)$.

The transportation cost (tx) is analogous to an excise tax. In the terminology of chapter 1, p is equivalent to the "consumer price" and $p - tx$ to the "producer price." We know from chapter 1 that, in general, excise taxes are not fully passed on to the consumer. For instance, for a linear demand, the producer bears half of an increase in the excise tax. For an exponential demand function, the consumer bears the entirety of any tax increase. For a constant-elasticity demand function, the consumer bears more than the entirety of a tax increase (see exercise 1.3).

Reinterpreted in our location model, an increase of dx in the distance to the plant implies an increase in the (delivered) monopoly price of $dp = t\,dx$ in the exponential case, $dp = t\,dx/2$ in the linear case, and $dp = t\,dx/(1 - 1/\varepsilon)$ in the constant-elasticity case. An exponential demand leads to the absence of price discrimination: Any difference in cost is fully reflected in the delivered price. In other words, the f.o.b. price is the same for all customers. In the linear-demand case, the consumer does not pay the full transportation cost. The monopolist practices "freight absorption" and discriminates against his nearest customers. In the constant-elasticity-of-demand case, discrimination plays against the farthest consumers.

The possibility of arbitrage between consumers at different locations invalidates the type of discrimination that would otherwise occur under constant elasticity of demand. If the transport technology used by the monopolist is commonly available, the customers located near the factory will buy and resell to the consumers located farther away. In such contexts the producer must content himself with nondiscriminatory prices. The policy of freight absorption is immune to the possibility of arbitrage between the consumers. Thus, although the way discrimination operates is theoretically very sensitive to the demand function, the possibility of arbitrage suggests that only freight absorption will be observed.

Freight absorption is commonly observed in practice.[11] The possibility of arbitrage may not be the only explanation for this. In some circumstances, our assumption that the demand function is the same at each location is likely to be violated. Consumers located farther away from the factory are more likely to be able to buy from an alternative source than consumers nearby; a cement consumer located 50 miles from each of two competing cement producers that are 100 miles apart has more substitution possibilities than a consumer located 10 miles from one producer and 90 miles from the other. Price discrimination is, then, a useful way for each producer to compete for the marginal consumers without granting price concessions to the inframarginal (captive) ones. At the current stage, it suffices to think of the elasticity of demand as increasing

---

11. See pp. 24–25 of Phlips 1983 for examples of uniform delivered prices in the cement, plasterboard, and clay brick industries, and for an analysis of the use for discriminatory purposes of the basing-point system. The basing-point system expresses the delivered price as a base price plus the transport cost from a basing point (which need not be the factory's location). Basing-point pricing is often used as a collusive device that allows competitors to coordinate their pricing policies and to easily detect defections from collusive behavior.

with the distance to the factory. Strategic interactions between spatial oligopolists will be considered in chapter 7.

Exercise 3.2* Suppose that consumers have a linear demand function and are located uniformly from distance $x = 0$ to distance $x = 1$. The transportation cost to distance x is tx.

(i) Compute the optimal f.o.b. prices when discrimination is allowed.

(ii) Suppose that transportation is operated through a competitive sector at the same unit cost, t. Compute the optimal uniform (i.e. nondiscriminatory) f.o.b. price, assuming that the whole market is served. Can one say that in the no-discrimination case some consumers "cross-subsidize" others?

(iii) Which arrangement serves the largest market in general?

3.2.3.2 Application 2: Vertical Controls as an Instrument of Discrimination

Suppose that a monopolist produces a good which is used as an input by two competitive industries producing different final goods (or, alternatively, that the monopolist's good is sold by competitive retailers to two classes of consumers). The final goods ($i = 1, 2$) face two independent demands, which have elasticities such that $\varepsilon_2 > \varepsilon_1$ (for the following, it may be convenient to think of constant-elasticity demands). Also assume, for simplicity, that each industry converts one unit of input into one unit of output.

Because of the technology and the fact that downstream industries are competitive, each final good's price is equal to the intermediate price charged to the industry manufacturing it. Hence, everything is as if the monopolist sold his good directly to the consumers in the two industries. The downstream industries are but a "veil." Hence, the intermediate good's optimal prices are

$$p_2^* = \frac{c}{1 - 1/\varepsilon_2} < p_1^* = \frac{c}{1 - 1/\varepsilon_1}.$$

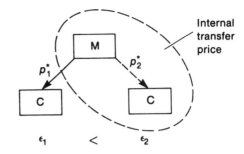

Figure 3.3

The solution in which the monopolist operates the two downstream technologies himself (and sells to consumers) is called the "vertically integrated solution."[12]

There is a caveat, however. To realize the vertically integrated profit, the monopolist must be able to prevent arbitrage between the two industries. Industry 2 might buy the intermediate good at the low price, p_2^*, and resell it to industry 1. If the monopolist cannot prevent arbitrage directly by precluding industry 2 from reselling some of the input to industry 1 and thereby undoing the policy of discrimination, his optimal solution involves selling nothing to industry 2. To accomplish this, the monopolist can buy a firm in industry 2, then set this firm's final price at p_2^*, and sell the intermediate good at price p_1^* to other firms (see figure 3.3). Only the firms in industry 1 will buy the good, since the firms in industry 2 will not be able to compete effectively with the monopolist's subsidiary in the sale of consumption good 2. For instance, in the United States, Alcoa had monopoly power in the production of virgin-aluminum ingots, an intermediate good. It integrated into markets with high elasticities of demand (rolled sheet) and, through its pricing policy for the intermediate good, squeezed its downstream competitors in these markets.[13]

Therefore, vertical integration can be used as a substitute for price discrimination when an upstream firm cannot control directly the resale of its product among its buyers, and legal rules against price discrimination may lead to vertical integration.

---

12. For more on vertical control and third-degree price discrimination, see Perry 1978.

13. For a general discussion of price squeezes in nonregulated and regulated environments, see Joskow 1985. Judge Learned Hand, who wrote the opinion in the Alcoa case, proposed the "transfer price test" to assess whether a firm is engaged in a price squeeze. This test considers whether the integrated firm can

sell the final output profitably at prevailing prices, assuming it has to pay the same price for the input it produces internally as it charges its downstream competitors. If the answer is No, then the firm is said to practice a price squeeze. In the Alcoa case, the Court found that Alcoa's downstream profits would have been negligible or negative if the downstream unit had paid the market price rather than the internal price to the upstream unit.

A monopolist who adopts the "reverse policy" and serves the low-elasticity market himself may have to impose some further control over the industry serving the other market. For example, in an antitrust case in the United States concerning the White Motor Company, the industry with low demand elasticity was made up of various public agencies (local and federal) and was served by the manufacturer himself. The one with high demand elasticity was a private market serviced by retailers. The manufacturer had forbidden these retailers to sell to public agencies.

3.2.4 Third-Degree Price Discrimination in Intermediate-Goods Markets

The previous analysis assumed that the buyers of the monopolist's good are consumers—i.e., that the good is a final one. However, U.S. laws restricting third-degree price discrimination are particularly concerned with intermediate-goods markets. The aim of the Robinson-Patman act (which has not been very strictly enforced lately) was to protect small businesses from "unfair" advantages possessed by large buyers in such markets. A typical situation that act was concerned with is that of a chain store that is able to obtain discounts below the prices charged to local stores from suppliers. Katz (1987) notes two reasons why the previous analysis cannot straightforwardly be applied to intermediate-goods markets. First, the demand of the "consumers" is interdependent. For instance, the chain store and the local store compete on the product market; thus, how much one of the competitors purchases from the monopolist depends not only on the price charged to him but also on the price charged to the other competitor. Solving for product-market competition, one obtains a case of interdependent demands (see chapter 1). Second, distributors are much more likely than consumers to integrate backward into production. In particular, the chainstore, if it does not obtain advantageous conditions from the monopolist, may decide to supply the good itself. (The local store is less likely to do so, because of the existence of increasing returns to scale at the production stage—for example, the fixed cost of production may be too high for a low-volume producer.)

In Katz's analysis of such a chain store–local store model, the chain store competes in each of several geographic markets with a single local store (so there are as many local stores as there are markets). Integrating backward costs $F + vq$, where F is a fixed cost and where v is the marginal cost of production (which is assumed to be not lower than the marginal cost c for the monopolist). The monopolist chooses two prices, one for the chain store and one for the local stores. Katz shows that integration does not occur. (If the chain store integrated, the monopolist could charge price v to the chain store instead, which would not affect downstream competition and would prevent integration while not lowering the monopolist's profit.)

Katz then considers an alternative regime, in which price discrimination is prohibited. Under uniform pricing, integration by the chain store may or may not occur (the local stores never integrate backward). An interesting result is that if there is no integration under either regime, both prices may be higher under price discrimination than under uniform pricing—a phenomenon that could never happen if the buyers were ordinary consumers (see above). To get a rough intuition about why this may be so, suppose that under uniform pricing the "integration constraint" (the condition that the chain store does not want to integrate) is binding. That is, the monopolist would increase his profit by raising the uniform price if there were no integration possibilities, but he cannot do so and keeps the price low so as to prevent integration. When discrimination is allowed, he can raise the price for the local store. Under some conditions, this may reduce the chain store's incentive to integrate, which allows the monopolist to increase the price for the chain store as well.[14] In such a case, price discrimination is clearly detrimental to welfare, as it raises all prices.

3.3 Personal Arbitrage and Screening (Second-Degree Price Discrimination)

Suppose that a monopolist faces a demand composed of heterogeneous consumers. If the monopolist knows each consumer's taste, he can, in general, offer personalized

---

14. That raising the price for the local store reduces the chain store's incentive to integrate is by no means trivial. If the conditions alluded to are not satisfied,

other patterns may emerge. For instance, the price charged to the local store may go down while that to the chain store goes up.

packages or bundles (price and quantity, price and quality, etc.) to consumers. He then achieves perfect discrimination. Suppose, however, that the monopolist cannot tell the consumers apart. In particular, assume (in contrast with the preceding section) that there is no exogenous signal of each consumer's demand function (such as age or occupation).[15] This does not mean that the monopolist will not try to discriminate between consumers and will content himself with a unique bundle for all consumers. He can offer a menu of bundles to choose from. In doing so he must, however, take into account the possibility of personal arbitrage, i.e., the possibility that a consumer to whom a given bundle is directed may want to choose a bundle directed to another consumer. This introduces "self-selection" or "incentive-compatibility" constraints, which, in general, make perfect price discrimination impossible (see the example in section 3.1 involving consumers with unit demands).

This section starts with a simple example of two-part pricing. Because a two-part tariff is generally not optimal, it then proceeds to a consideration of more general nonlinear pricing schemes. It goes on to demonstrate the strong analogy between discrimination through price-quantity bundles and discrimination through price-quality bundles. Optimal pricing is considered in more detail in the supplementary section, along with discrimination in the insurance market.

3.3.1 Two-Part Tariffs[16]

A two-part tariff ($T(q) = A + pq$) offers a menu of bundles $\{T, q\}$ (a continuum of them, actually) located on a straight line. Unlike the line representing a pure linear tariff, this straight line need not pass through the origin.

Two-part tariffs are commonly used in practice. Table 3.1 gives a few examples.

The main appeal of two-part tariffs is their simplicity. For instance, what the consumer pays to enter an amusement park could be (and sometimes is) a more complicated function of the number of rides than it is under a two-part tariff; however, it is costly to keep track of the number of rides each person has taken. Sometimes two-part tariffs may also be justified by the possibility of

Table 3.1

	Fixed premium (A)	Charge varying according to
Telephone, gas, electricity	Rental	Number of units
Polaroid camera	Camera purchase	Amount of film
Amusement park	Entrance fee	Number of rides
Taxi	Initial meter reading	Distance

limited arbitrage, as was noted above. But arbitrage cannot be complete; it must not be the case that only one consumer can pay the fixed fee A and resell the good to other consumers. This assumption is met by the examples given in table 3.1. Note that two-part tariffs correspond, *de facto*, to a quantity discount scheme: The average price of the good decreases with the number of units bought.

We now investigate the consequences of this tariff in terms of profit and welfare. To do so, we will use a simple example. Suppose that consumers have the following preferences:

$$U = \begin{cases} \theta V(q) - T & \text{if they pay } T \text{ and consume } q \\ & \text{units of the good} \\ 0 & \text{if they do not buy,} \end{cases}$$

where $V(0) = 0$, $V'(q) > 0$, and $V''(q) < 0$ (i.e., there is a decreasing marginal utility of consumption in this representation of the utility function). θ is a taste parameter that varies across consumers; $V(\cdot)$ is the same for all consumers.

As in chapter 2, these preferences could be justified by identical preferences over the good, combined with differences in incomes. Suppose that all consumers have preferences $U(I - T) + V(q)$—i.e., preferences that are separable in net income $(I - T)$ and quantity, where $U' > 0$, $U'' < 0$, $V(0) = 0$, $V' > 0$, and $V'' < 0$. Then, if the amount of money spent on the good is small relative to initial income $(T \ll I)$, preferences can be approximated by $U(I) - T U'(I) + V(q)$. All that is relevant to a consumer's choice concerning this good is summarized by $\theta V(q) - T$, where $\theta \equiv 1/U'(I)$ is the inverse of the

15. Alternatively, one could look at price discrimination within a class identified by a signal.

16. For more on two-part tariffs, see Oi 1971 and Schmalensee 1982a.

"marginal utility of income." Hence, we can generate apparent differences in tastes simply from differences in income.[17]

Assume that there are two groups of consumers. Consumers with taste parameter θ_1 are in proportion λ; those with taste parameter θ_2 are in proportion $1 - \lambda$. (The absolute number of consumers does not matter with constant marginal cost, and can be normalized to 1.) Assume that $\theta_2 > \theta_1$ and that the monopolist produces at constant marginal cost $c < \theta_1 < \theta_2$.

To simplify the computations, assume that

$$V(q) = \frac{1 - (1 - q)^2}{2}$$

(so that $V'(q) = 1 - q$ is linear in quantity).

We shall consider, in sequence, the case of perfect discrimination, the case of uniform, nondiscriminatory monopoly pricing, and the case of a two-part tariff. (We are interested in the first two cases only for comparison with the third.)

As a preliminary, let us compute the demand function for consumer θ_i facing marginal price p. (With this demand function, the fixed premium affects only the decision whether to buy the good. If he has decided to buy, the consumer does not take it into account when choosing how much of the good to buy.) The consumer maximizes

$$\{\theta_i V(q) - pq\},$$

which yields

$$\theta_i V'(q) = p.$$

For our specification of preferences, $\theta_i(1 - q) = p$. The demand function is thus

$$q = D_i(p) = 1 - p/\theta_i.$$

The net consumer surplus is

$$S_i(p) = \theta_i V(D_i(p)) - p D_i(p)$$

(leaving out the fixed fee, if any). In this special case,

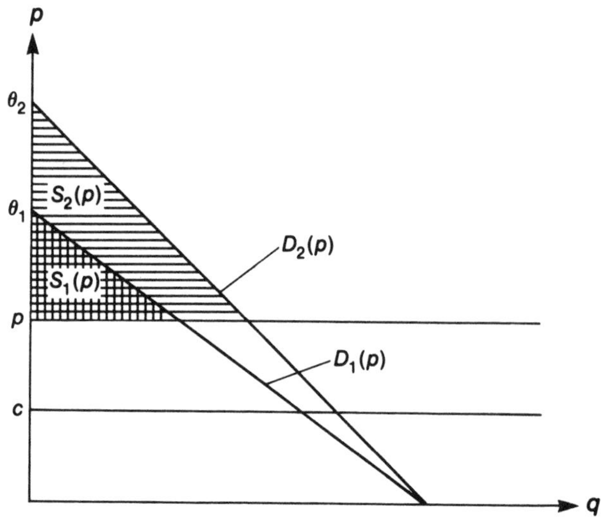

Figure 3.4

$$S_i(p) = \theta_i \left(\frac{1 - [1 - D_i(p)]^2}{2} \right) - p D_i(p)$$

$$= \frac{(\theta_i - p)^2}{2\theta_i}.$$

(Note that $S_i(\theta_i) = 0$, and that the surplus is always higher for θ_2 types.) The demand curves and the net surpluses are depicted in figure 3.4.

Let θ denote the "harmonic mean" of θ_1 and θ_2:

$$\frac{1}{\theta} \equiv \frac{\lambda}{\theta_1} + \frac{1 - \lambda}{\theta_2}.$$

Then the aggregate demand at price p can be written as

$$D(p) = \lambda D_1(p) + (1 - \lambda)D_2(p) = 1 - p/\theta.$$

3.3.1.1 Perfect Discrimination

Suppose that the monopolist can differentiate among consumers, i.e., can observe θ_i directly. As we saw in section 3.1, he can charge a marginal price $p_1 = c$ and demand a personalized fixed premium equal to each consumer's net surplus at price c. For consumer i ($i = 1, 2$), the fixed premium is

---

17. The analysis in this subsection, as well as that for the fully nonlinear case, could easily be extended to preferences $V(q, \theta) - T$ as long as $\partial V/\partial \theta > 0$ and $\partial^2 V/\partial q \partial \theta > 0$.

$$A_i = S_i(c) = \frac{(\theta_i - c)^2}{2\theta_i}.$$

The fixed premium is naturally higher for the high-demand consumer. The monopolist's profit is

$$\Pi_1 = \lambda \frac{(\theta_1 - c)^2}{2\theta_1} + (1 - \lambda) \frac{(\theta_2 - c)^2}{2\theta_2}.$$

As we saw in section 3.1, welfare is optimal (as long as there is no redistributive concern).

If the monopolist did not observe the consumers' types, the perfect-discrimination allocation could not be implemented. The high-demand consumers, whose surplus is fully extracted, would have an incentive to claim that they are low-demand consumers. Doing so would give them a strictly positive utility, because for the low-demand bundle the low-demand consumers have zero utility.[18] Hence, the high-demand consumers would exercise personal arbitrage. (The low-demand consumers would not.) In subsection 3.3.2 it will be shown that preventing the high-demand consumers from buying the bundle directed to the low-demand ones is costly to the monopolist.

3.3.1.2 Monopoly Price

Suppose that there is full arbitrage between consumers, so that the monopolist is forced to charge a fully linear tariff: $T(q) = pq$. The monopoly price, p_2 (or p^m), maximizes $(p - c)D(p)$, where $D(p)$ is the aggregate demand: $D(p) = 1 - p/\theta$. Thus, the monopoly price is

$$p_2 = \frac{c + \theta}{2}$$

and the monopoly profits are

$$\Pi_2 = \frac{(\theta - c)^2}{4\theta}.$$

A caveat: These computations assume that the monopolist decides to serve the two types of consumers. Another strategy might be to serve only type-θ_2 consumers. Such a strategy will be optimal if the monopoly price relative to this category (which is $(c + \theta_2)/2$) exceeds θ_1 and

the fraction of type-θ_1 consumers is sufficiently small. To reduce the number of cases to be considered, we will assume either that

$$(c + \theta_2)/2 \leqslant \theta_1$$

or that λ is not too small, so that both types are served under a linear tariff.

Exercise 3.3* Show that a monopolist practicing uniform pricing serves both classes of consumers if either θ_1 or λ is "large enough."

3.3.1.3 Two-Part Tariff

Let us now look for the optimal two-part tariff. Again, we will assume that the monopoly serves the two types of consumers.

Suppose the marginal price is p. The highest fixed fee that is consistent with type-θ_1 consumers buying the good is $A = S_1(p)$. Type-θ_2 consumers then buy, because

$$S_2(p) > S_1(p) = A.$$

Hence, the monopolist maximizes

$$S_1(p) + (p - c)D(p).$$

The monopolist always does at least as well under the optimal two-part tariff as under a fully linear tariff. To the variable profit $(p - c)D(p)$ he adds the fixed fee $S_1(p)$ received from all types of consumers. (Another way to see this is to think of a linear tariff as a special case of a two-part tariff, with $A = 0$.) Straightforward computations yield

$$p_3 = \frac{c}{2 - \theta/\theta_1}.$$

3.3.1.4 Comparison

To see that $\Pi_1 \geqslant \Pi_3 \geqslant \Pi_2$ requires no computation. The monopolist gets the maximum profit under perfect price discrimination. And he can always duplicate a linear tariff with a two-part tariff, so that $\Pi_3 \geqslant \Pi_2$. More interesting is the comparison of the marginal prices and welfare. As can easily be checked (under our assumption that

---

18. More formally, they would get a utility

$(\theta_2 - \theta_1)V(D_1(c)) > 0$.

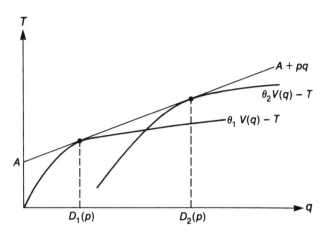

Figure 3.5
A two-part tariff.

all types are served),

$$p_1 = c < p_3 < p_2 = p^m.$$

Thus, the marginal price is intermediate between the competitive price (which would be paid by the marginal consumer under perfect discrimination) and the monopoly price. The intuition is as follows: Starting from the monopoly price p^m, consider a small reduction of price ($\delta p < 0$). By the definition of the monopoly price, the change in price has only a second-order effect on the variable profit $(p - c)D(p)$. However, the consumers' surplus increases by an amount proportional to the reduction in price, a first-order effect. In particular, the monopolist can increase the fixed premium by an amount proportional to the reduction,

$$\delta A = \delta S_1(p) = -D_1(p)\delta p > 0,$$

and can therefore gain. Next, start from the competitive price. Raising the price by $\delta p > 0$ and lowering the fixed premium correspondingly to keep the type-θ_1 consumers indifferent between buying and not buying leads to the same profit from these consumers, because perfect price discrimination is realized for these consumers. Thus, a small change in price has only a second-order effect on

the profit coming from low-demand consumers, but it has a first-order effect on the profit coming from high-demand consumers. The latter save on the fixed fee, which is reduced by $D_1(c)\delta p$. On the other hand, they pay $D_2(c)\delta p$ more for what they demand. (There is a third effect: the reduction in demand. However, as the profit margin $(p - c)$ is zero, the monopolist's variable profit is not affected by the change in demand.) Hence, the net effect on profit is

$$(1 - \lambda)[D_2(p) - D_1(p)]\delta p > 0.$$

This analysis strongly suggests that the optimal marginal price should be somewhere between c and p^m (as it actually is).

Note also that welfare is higher under a two-part tariff than under a linear tariff; because the marginal price is lower, both types of consumers consume more, which reduces the distortion.[19] As we have seen, under a two-part tariff the monopolist can reduce the marginal price below the monopoly price and recoup lost profits through the fixed fee. The fixed fee thus induces the monopolist to lower prices, which is good for welfare.

*Exercise 3.4**[20]* Consider the previous model with two types of consumers. Show that for any linear tariff $T(q) = pq$ with $p > c$ there exists a two-part tariff $\tilde{T}(q) = \tilde{A} + \tilde{p}q$ such that, if consumers are offered the choice between T and $\tilde{T}$, both types of consumers and the firm are made better off. Hint: Offer a two-part tariff that includes the high-demand consumers' bundle under the linear tariff (i.e., going through $(D_2(p), p\,D_2(p))$).[21]

3.3.1.5   A Variant: Tie-in Sales as a Price-Discrimination Tool

Sometimes a manufacturer produces a "basic" good that is consumed in a fixed quantity (typically one unit), while a complementary good—which may be supplied by a competitive industry—is consumed in variable amounts. For instance, consider the punch cards once used with

---

19. Remember that aggregate welfare is

$$\lambda S_1^g(p) + (1 - \lambda)S_2^g(p) - c[\lambda D_1(p) + (1 - \lambda)D_2(p)];$$

it decreases with p when $p \geqslant c$ (S_i^g is consumer θ_i's gross surplus.)

20. This exercise demonstrates a special case of a general result due to Willig (1978).

21. This exercise shows that everybody can be made better off relative to a linear tariff, even under the informational constraint on the consumers' types. This does not mean that the *optimal* nonlinear tariff for the monopolist Pareto dominates (or even is welfare-superior to) this optimal linear tariff.

computers. The manufacturer of the computer (the good consumed in fixed quantity) would generally gain by requiring that the customers purchase the complementary good (the punch cards) from him as well, if he could avoid arbitrage (i.e., if he could check that the customers did not purchase the complementary good on the competitive market). Such a practice is called a *tie-in sale*. Higher consumption of the complementary good signals higher valuations for the good (higher θ, in our model); the sale of the complementary product serves as a counting (metering) device.[22] Hence, the manufacturer can use tie-in sales to practice second-degree price discrimination. This may explain why IBM required its customers to purchase only IBM punch cards. Xerox practiced a similar policy by charging a per copy fee on its copying machines (another alternative is to require the tied purchase of Xerox paper, if arbitrage can be prevented).[23]

To illustrate this within our model, suppose that a consumer, if he purchases at all, buys one unit of a good produced by a manufacturer and q units of a complementary good. As before, his utility is $\theta V(q) - T(q)$ if he purchases and 0 otherwise. $T(q)$ is the two-part tariff charged by the manufacturer through a tie-in sale. The producer produces the basic good at cost c_0 and the complementary good at c per unit. c is also the competitive price for the complementary good, as there are many firms willing to produce the complementary good at price c. The manufacturer has a monopoly on the market for the basic good.

This set-up is similar to that in the above analysis of two-part pricing, except that the manufacturer must pay a fixed cost c_0 per customer served. Thus, if we make the assumption that both types of consumers are served,

the magnitude of c_0 is irrelevant and the previous solution is obtained. In contrast with that analysis, suppose that the manufacturer is prohibited from using tie-in sales. A consumer with taste θ buys the complementary good on the competitive market at price c, so as to maximize $\{\theta V(q) - cq\}$. A type-θ_i consumer's net surplus is $S_i(c)$. Assuming again that the manufacturer serves both types of customers, he charges a price for the basic good equal to the lower willingness to pay: $S_1(c)$.[24]

The above analysis of two-part tariffs enables us to assess the effect of a tie-in sale without further computations. *The price of the complementary (tied) good is higher under a tie-in sale*: $p > c$ (where p was computed previously), whereas *the price of the basic (tying) good is lower*: $S_1(p) < S_1(c)$.[25]

A curiosum here is that the derivation of the optimal price structure for the monopolist is independent of the cost c_0 of producing the basic good (Oi 1971). By choosing c_0 sufficiently high (but not so high as to induce the monopolist to serve only the high-demand consumers), one can generate examples in which the price of the basic good is below its marginal cost.

There is, however, one important difference between the case of a tie-in and the more classical analysis of two-part pricing: *The tie-in sale reduces welfare as long as the manufacturer serves both types of customers.* To see this, notice that when tie-in sales are prohibited, customers purchase the variable good at marginal cost. Hence, the full potential social surplus is realized.[26] In contrast, the two-part tariff associated with a tied sale introduces a marginal price distortion ($p > c$), which leads to a consumption distortion. Hence, a tie-in sale is detrimental to welfare if the manufacturer always serves both types of

---

22. See Bowman 1957 and Burstein 1960a,b. The tied good need not be complementary with the tying good. One can also think of situations in which the consumption of the tied good brings the monopolist information about the consumer's willingness to pay for the tying good. On this, see Burstein 1960a, Adams and Yellen 1976, and the discussion on commodity bundling in the supplementary section.

23. See also Blackstone's (1975) study of the copying-machine industry. SCM, a copying-machine firm, used a process (electrofax) that required special coated paper. As long as it had a monopoly position in the manufacture of this paper, SCM charged high markups on paper (about 200 percent) and low ones on machines (around 25 percent). Entry into the electrofax-paper industry, however, led this firm to struggle to keep its discriminatory policy. In particular, SCM used its monopoly power in the replenisher and service industries (where entry was slower) to force the customers to use its paper. Replenishers and service requirements were subsidized contingent on buying the paper. Similarly, SCM tried to tie the rental of its machines to the use of its paper.

24. When λ is small, the manufacturer wants to serve only type-θ_2 consumers. He then charges $S_2(c)$. One can also easily see that, for an "intermediate λ," the manufacturer serves both types under a tie-in sale and only the high-demand type when tie-in sales are prohibited.

25. This explains why SCM charged relatively low prices for machines and much higher prices for supplies (Blackstone 1975). In the same way, automobile manufacturers sell repair parts at prices well above marginal cost (Crandall 1968). (Auto parts are not tied; however, part specificity and increasing returns to scale in the production of repair parts tend to lock customers in with the automobile manufacturer, even for repair parts.)

26. The manufacturer's profit is $S_1(c) - c_0$, the type-θ_1 consumers' net surplus is 0, and the type-θ_2 consumers' net surplus is $S_2(c) - S_1(c)$. Total welfare is

$$S_1(c) - c_0 + (1 - \lambda)[S_2(c) - S_1(c)]$$

$$= \lambda S_1(c) + (1 - \lambda)S_2(c) - c_0.$$

consumers. The important caveat here is, of course, that the prohibition of a tie-in sale makes it more likely that the manufacturer serves only the high-demand consumers. The result that tie-in sales are detrimental may then be reversed, as the following exercise will show.

Exercise 3.5** Assume $c_0 = 0$.

(i) Show that the aggregate social surplus when tie-in sales are prohibited is

$$(1 - \lambda)S_2(c)$$

if $(1 - \lambda)S_2(c) \geqslant S_1(c)$.

(ii) Let $c = 1$, $\theta_1 = 2$, $\theta_2 = 3$, $\lambda = \frac{5}{8}$, and $D_i(p) = 1 - p/\theta_i$. Show that prohibiting tie-in sales decreases aggregate welfare.

Exercise 3.6** In the United States, the fast-food chain Chicken Delight used to tie paper packaging items—"buckets" for large orders and "kits" for individual dinners —to the use of the franchise name. Can you think of a potential explanation for this practice? (Hint: The franchisees were serving differentiated, exclusive territories.)

3.3.2 Fully Nonlinear Tariffs and Quantity Discrimination[27]

Two-part tariffs are simple and common. However, a manufacturer who can fully prevent commodity arbitrage (but not personal arbitrage) can increase his profit beyond that obtained with the optimal two-part tariff by adopting a more complex scheme.

Figure 3.6, which depicts the (q, T) space, explains why. The straight line represents the optimal two-part tariff $T(q) = A + pq$. The two types of consumers' indifference curves are concave, because $V(q)$ is. Because $\theta_2 > \theta_1$, the type-θ_2 consumers' indifference curve is steeper than the type-θ_1 consumers' when the curves cross.[28] Under the optimal two-part tariff, the type-θ_1 consumers pick the bundle B_1 and the type-θ_2 consumers pick B_2. By construction, the low-demand consumers have no net sur-

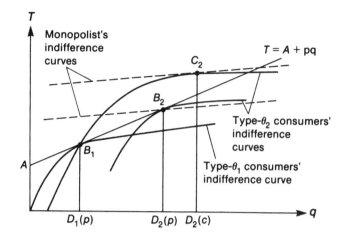

Figure 3.6

plus (their indifference curve through B_1 goes through the origin), whereas the high-demand consumers have a positive net surplus. Figure 3.6 also shows the indifference curves for the monopolist ($T - cq = $ constant). Because $c < p$, these indifference curves are flatter than the optimal two-part tariff.

An important feature of a two-part tariff is that none of the personal-arbitrage constraints are binding. In particular, high-demand consumers strictly prefer B_2 to B_1. Indeed, when the indifference curve for these consumers is drawn through B_1, any point on or below this curve is accepted by them. It is then immediately apparent that the monopolist can increase his profit by still offering type-θ_2 consumers a bundle under type-θ_2's indifference curve through B_1 and above the monopolist's indifference curve through B_2. Actually, the optimal such point is C_2, where the monopolist's indifference curve is tangent to the type-θ_2 consumers' indifference curve through B_1. Since the curve for type θ_2 is steeper, it cannot contain the origin, because type θ_1's curve does. Thus, type θ_2 makes a rent.[29] The profit from low-demand consumers is unchanged, and that from high-demand consumers is increased. Hence, the two-part tariff is not optimal.

An interesting feature of the construction of C_2 is that the monopolist's and the high-demand consumers' indif-

27. This subsection is more abstract than the rest of the chapter. The reader may nevertheless want to invest in the techniques developed here and in the supplementary section, because virtually the same techniques are used in the theories of optimal taxation, regulation under asymmetric information, labor contracts, auctions, etc.

28. This condition—familiar in the literature on incentives—is called the "sorting condition," or the "single crossing condition," or the "Spence-Mirrlees condition." In the present context it makes it possible to separate the two types of consumers by offering a higher consumption to the type-θ_2 consumers.

29. The type-θ_1 consumers do not want to exercise personal arbitrage by choosing C_2.

ference curves are tangent. Hence, at C_2, type θ_2's consumption is socially optimal: $q_2 = D_2(c)$.

To derive the optimal nonlinear tariff, one must find two bundles (q_1, T_1) and (q_2, T_2) that maximize the monopolist's profit under the constraints that personal arbitrage does not occur and consumers are willing to buy. This is done in the supplementary section, which basically shows that the optimal nonlinear tariff resembles the couple (B_1, C_2).

Conclusion 1   Low-demand consumers derive no net surplus, while high-demand consumers derive a positive net surplus.

Conclusion 2   The binding (or relevant) personal-arbitrage constraint is to prevent high-demand consumers from buying the low-demand consumers' bundle.

Conclusion 3   The high-demand consumers purchase the socially optimal quantity, $q_2 = D_2(c)$,[30] while the low-demand consumers purchase a suboptimal quantity, $q_1 < D_1(c)$.

Conclusion 3 is the economically most significant one. Relative to the social optimum, the monopolist *enlarges the spectrum of consumption patterns*: $(D_1(c), D_2(c))$ becomes $(q_1 < D_1(c), D_2(c))$. The intuition is as follows. The monopolist would like to extract the type-θ_2 consumers' large surplus, but this policy faces the threat of personal arbitrage: A high-demand consumer can consume the low-demand consumers' bundle if his own bundle does not generate enough surplus. To relax this personal-arbitrage constraint, the monopolist offers a relatively low consumption to the low-demand consumers. Because high-demand consumers suffer more from a reduction in consumption than low-demand ones,[31] this relaxes the personal-arbitrage constraint. Hence, the monopolist reduces the quantity consumed by the low-demand consumers so that the high-demand consumers will be less tempted to consume the low-demand consumers' bundle. Conversely, low-demand consumers are not tempted to exercise personal arbitrage, and there is no point to introducing a distortion in the high-demand consumers' con-

sumption (any welfare gains stemming from a move of the marginal price toward the marginal cost can be captured by the monopolist through an increase in T_2).

The supplementary section develops these ideas in more detail and shows how the analysis can be pursued for more than two types of consumers. It also draws the link between the optimal nonlinear prices employed for second-degree price discrimination and the Ramsey prices considered in the study of third-degree price discrimination.

3.3.2.1   Welfare

The welfare analysis of nonlinear tariffs is ambiguous. There is no doubt that the nonlinear tariff chosen by a monopolist is socially suboptimal. However, we must compare this tariff not with the socially optimal one but with that which would arise from a given government intervention. A much-studied policy intervention consists in forcing a monopolist to charge a linear price. (Such a limited policy is so eagerly considered because it does not require the government to have any information whatsoever concerning the distribution of tastes among consumers, the firm's cost structure, etc.) The monopolist is made worse off by such an intervention because he loses flexibility in his pricing policy. The consumers, however, do not necessarily gain. Under nonlinear pricing, the monopolist could extract some of the high-demand consumers' net surplus while still selling to low-demand consumers. Under linear pricing, the monopolist may stop serving the low-demand consumers in order to extract the high-demand consumers' surplus; hence, his output may well decrease.

For more on the welfare analysis of nonlinear tariffs, see Spence 1977, Roberts 1979, and Katz 1983.

3.3.3   Quality Discrimination

In subsections 3.3.1 and 3.3.2, the monopolist discriminated among consumers by offering different quantities of the same good at different prices to consumers with different tastes for the good. A monopolist can also discriminate among consumers with different tastes for qual-

---

30. This conclusion is known in the literature of optimal taxation (Mirrlees 1971; Seade 1977) as "absence of distortion at the top."

31. This is nothing but the sorting condition alluded to in footnote 28. Consider a small decrease in consumption $\delta q_1 < 0$ for type-θ_1 consumers compen-

sated by a reduction in price: $\delta T_1 \simeq \theta_1 V'(q_1)\delta q_1 < 0$. By construction, this change leaves type-θ_1 consumers indifferent. However, it hurts type-θ_2 consumers if they consume q_1; their utility changes by

$$\theta_2 V'(q_1)\delta q_1 - \delta T_1 = (\theta_2 - \theta_1)V'(q_1)\delta q_1 < 0.$$

ity (or service) by offering an array of qualities. For instance, railroads and airlines offer several classes. Airline tickets also differ in ease of cancellation, in existence of a waiting list, and in other respects.

It turns out that quality discrimination is very similar to quantity discrimination.[32] To see the analogy, consider the vertical differentiation space studied in chapter 2. Consumers have unit demands for a good. The good comes in various qualities, indexed by s. Consumers have preferences $U = \theta s - p$ (if they purchase), where s is the quality of the good purchased, p is the price paid, and θ is the taste parameter. In general, the price depends on the quality: $p(s)$. Suppose that producing one unit of the good with quality s costs the monopolist $c(s)$, where c is increasing and convex.

By a simple relabeling of variables, this quality model can be transformed into the previous quantity model. To this purpose, let $q \equiv c(s)$ denote the cost of quality s. Let $s = V(q) \equiv c^{-1}(q)$ denote the inverse function, i.e., the quality obtained for cost q (note that c increasing and convex implies V is increasing and concave). The consumers have preferences

$$U = \theta V(q) - p(V(q)) = \theta V(q) - \tilde{p}(q)$$

(where $\tilde{p}(q) \equiv p(V(q))$) if they purchase. And, by construction, the monopolist's cost function is linear in q (with the coefficient of proportionality equal to 1). Hence, *at a formal level the two models are identical*, and we can transpose the conclusions of the quantity model to the quality model. In particular, we have (in the case of two types of consumers) the following conclusion:

Conclusion 3′ The consumers with a high valuation for quality (type-θ_2 consumers) purchase the socially optimal quality; the consumers with a low valuation for quality (type-θ_1 consumers) purchase a suboptimal quality.[33]

In other words, *the monopolist enlarges the quality spectrum*, as was shown by Mussa and Rosen (1978). (See also O'Keefe 1981.) The monopolist uses lower-quality goods as a market-segmentation technique.

For a real-world example of such a behavior, consider

Dupuit's (1849) discussion of railroad tariffs for passenger traffic:

It is not because of the few thousand francs which would have to be spent to put a roof over the third-class carriages or to upholster the third-class seats that some company or other has open carriages with wooden benches. . . . What the company is trying to do is prevent the passengers who can pay the second-class fare from traveling third-class; it hits the poor, not because it wants to hurt them, but to frighten the rich. . . . And it is again for the same reason that the companies, having proved almost cruel to third-class passengers and mean to second-class ones, become lavish in dealing with first-class passengers. Having refused the poor what is necessary, they give the rich what is superfluous.[34]

(Note, however, that the optimal policy is to give the rich not what is superfluous but the socially optimal quality. The high quality may, however, seem exaggerated in comparison with the other, suboptimal qualities.)

3.3.3.1 Application 1: Discrimination in Insurance Policies

In the insurance market, the type of a consumer refers to the probability that the consumer has an "accident" (is robbed, etc.). The quality of service corresponds to the amount of reimbursement in case of accident. If consumers are divided into two classes (high and low probability of accident), it can be shown that the high-risk consumers value the reimbursement more than the low-risk consumers (in the same sense that type-θ_2 consumers value quantity or quality more than type-θ_1 consumers in the previous interpretations). The analogue of conclusion 3 for the insurance market is the following: A risk-neutral monopoly insurance company optimally discriminates between the consumers by giving full insurance (the socially optimal policy) to high-risk consumers and suboptimal insurance (i.e., reimbursing less than the damage) to low-risk consumers. Again, introducing a distortion for type-θ_1 (low-risk) consumers is meant to make type-θ_2 (high-risk) consumers less tempted to choose the "wrong" insurance policy (Rothschild and Stiglitz 1976; Stiglitz 1977; Wilson 1977).

---

32. This subsection is inspired by part of Maskin and Riley's (1984) analysis.

33. The socially optimal qualities s_1 and s_2 are given by $c'(s_1) = \theta_1$ and $c'(s_2) = \theta_2$.

34. Quoted by Ekelund (1970, p. 275) and Phlips (1983, p. 216).

Optimal discrimination in the insurance market is studied in the supplementary section.

3.3.3.2 Application 2: Discrimination through Waiting Time or Price Dispersion

Sometimes the variable s refers to some disamenity associated with the purchase of the good. For instance, consumers usually do not like to travel to faraway stores, to bargain at length, or to buy from stores with few services. Or, they incur a cost searching for the lowest price for a given good. In more general terms, the purchased good is tied to another good (a "bad," rather), which represents the time spent (or, more generally, the disamenities incurred) in obtaining the good.

At first, it may seem that a firm ought to reduce the costs incurred in purchasing its goods as much as is possible in the context of its own cost structure. This is because cost savings for the consumer can be appropriated by the firm through a higher price for the good. For instance, if the firm incurs no cost in charging a uniform price in different locations, it might as well do so in order to lower consumers' search cost. This makes consumers more willing to purchase the product. Similarly, consumers are willing to pay more for the convenience of nearby outlets and quick service.

The previous reasoning, however, implicitly assumes that consumers are homogeneous. Under consumer heterogeneity, the monopolist may use the consumption of the bad as a signal of the consumer's willingness to pay for the good (valuation, demand).[35] For this to work, the consumers with the highest willingness to pay for the good (which the firm tries to determine) must also be the ones with the highest distaste for the bad.[36] If this is the case, the firm may offer several bundles. A high (low) price for the good is associated with a low (high) consumption of the bad. The high consumption of the bad for a low price for the good is meant to prevent the high-demand consumers from exercising personal arbitrage, in the same way that Dupuit's railroad monopolist refused to put a roof over the third-class carriages in order to frighten the rich.

Salop (1977) presents a model in which consumers differ in search cost[37] as well as in demand for the good and shows that discrimination through price dispersion may be a profitable strategy for a monopolist.[38] Similar in spirit is the model of Chiang and Spatt (1982), whose monopolist discriminates through waiting times.

On the welfare side, the policy of tying more of the bad to the good than is socially optimal need not be detrimental to welfare if the alternative is to force the monopolist to treat all consumers uniformly. As in the quantity and quality models, discrimination allows the monopolist to appropriate some of the surplus of high-demand consumers while still serving low-demand consumers. Preventing discrimination may eliminate some excessive consumption of the bad (i.e., may lead the monopolist to put a roof on the third-class carriages), but may also lead the monopolist to stop serving low-demand consumers (discontinue third-class services). Hence, the welfare effects of the prohibition of discrimination are ambiguous. Indeed, Chiang and Spatt (1982) show that waiting-time discrimination by a monopolist can be Pareto superior (preferred by all consumers and the firm) to the situation in which the monopolist is forced to charge a uniform price to consumers and, therefore, offers the same waiting time to all consumers.

The above analysis is a little inexact in that it ignores the issue of the individual rationality constraint—i.e., the fact that the monopolist cannot coerce the consumers to buy if they will receive a negative net surplus from his

---

35. The monopolist would generally prefer to bundle a positive amenity that is related to the consumer's willingness to pay, but such an amenity may not exist.

36. For instance, Chiang and Spatt (1982) suppose that the consumer, who has unit demands, has utility $v(\theta) - \theta t - p$, where v is the valuation for the good, t is the waiting time ($s = -t$ in our previous notation), and p is the price of the good. The assumption is that $v'(\theta) > 0$.

37. Here the search cost represents the cost of sampling store prices and, more broadly, the costs of consulting with friends and sales personnel and reading *Consumer Reports* and newspaper advertisements.

38. Since Diamond's (1971) pathbreaking work on the integration of individual search with market equilibrium, a sizeable literature has formalized the link between price dispersion and consumer or producer heterogeneity. Reinganum (1979) generates price dispersion from differences in production costs among firms. Price dispersion can also be obtained when consumers have different search costs (Salop 1977; Salop and Stiglitz 1982; Axel 1977; von zur Muehlen 1980; Rob 1985; Stiglitz 1985), receive a different number of price offers (Butters 1977; Burdett and Judd 1983), or have different valuations for the good (Diamond 1987). Rosenthal (1980), Shilony (1977), and Varian (1980) look at price dispersion in oligopoly with heterogeneous consumers; Png and Hirschleifer (1987) also allow price matching. In Bénabou 1986, the price dispersion results from the inflationary environment and from costly price adjustments (under consumer homogeneity or heterogeneity).

product. This may create problems. In the quantity and quality models, it suffices to impose this condition for the lowest-demand consumers. It is then automatically satisfied for consumers with a higher demand, because they derive a higher net surplus than the low-demand consumers from a given consumption bundle and they can exercise personal arbitrage. However, in the case of waiting-time discrimination or search discrimination a consumer with a higher willingness to pay also has a higher distaste for the bad. Hence, it is not clear that the high-demand consumer derives more net surplus from a given bundle than a low-demand consumer. This makes the analysis more complex.

3.4 Concluding Remarks

Both second-degree and third-degree price discriminations are widespread. Their importance has triggered a vast and useful literature in economics. Much work remains to be done, however.

Although we have assumed a single firm, most price discrimination takes place in oligopolistic markets. As long as the competitors are differentiated along some dimension (brand loyalty, location, consumer information, etc.), each competitor is tempted to price-discriminate on his residual-demand curve. It is then interesting to study the competitive aspects of price-discrimination instruments, such as sales, coupons, frequent-flyer programs, bundling, and offers to match one's rival's price. The extension of the theory toward oligopolistic markets is thus an important area of research.[39]

Furthermore, in our study of second-degree price discrimination we have assumed that the monopolist discriminates along a single dimension (either quantity or quality). In many interesting situations (e.g. computer systems, WATS lines, industrial equipment), the consumer chooses both a quantity variable and a quality variable (for instance, the time pattern of usage of the units purchased). Panzar and Sibley (1978) and Oren, Smith, and Wilson (1985) have studied the issue of pricing for capacity and usage.[40]

Another important assumption of our study of second-degree price discrimination is the independence of consumers' demands from those of other consumers. The quality offered to a consumer may, however, depend on the choices of other consumers. This is the case when service is ranked by priorities of access because of limited capacity (as in the telephone, electric power, and air travel industries). Suppose that an electric utility, with a fixed capacity for a given period of time, faces uncertain demand or supply. During peak load, electricity must be rationed to some consumers. Random rationing generally is not efficient, as some consumers suffer more than others from the interruption of service. A spot market, on the other end, would allocate the limited capacity efficiently among consumers in each state of nature, as those who would pay the spot price are those who suffer most from an interruption. Such a spot market, however, is generally infeasible because of the high transaction costs of setting it up. As an imperfect substitute for spot markets, the firm may offer priority of service, i.e., probability of being interrupted. In practice, this takes the form of a few priority ranks. Here the interdependence of demands is apparent: if all consumers choose the top priority, no one has any priority. Thus, the firm must adequately compute the tariff for each priority class to match capacity and demand. Wilson (1986) makes important progress in this direction in his study of priority servicing by a monopolist, an oligopolist, and a social planner.[41]

---

39. For pioneering work in this area, see Borenstein 1985; Champsaur and Rochet 1986; Katz 1984a,b; Oren, Smith, and Wilson 1983; Thisse and Vives 1986.

40. Panzar and Sibley assume that the tariff is linear in both capacity and usage (a generalization of the two-part tariff studied in subsection 3.3.1); Oren et al. consider general nonlinear tariffs.

41. For instance, Wilson concludes that, in many cases, priority servicing allows a social planner to realize most of the efficiency gains attributed to spot markets. See also Reitman 1986 and the references in these two papers.

3.5 Supplementary Section: Nonlinear Pricing

This supplementary section develops the study of non-linear tariffs begun in subsections 3.3.2 and 3.3.3. We derive explicitly the optimal tariff and study whether this tariff exhibits quantity (or quality) discounts. The first part of this supplementary section emphasizes techniques that can be applied to a variety of problems in economics, including topics relevant to industrial organization, such as the theories of optimal regulation[42] and optimal auctions.[43]

3.5.1 Nonlinear Prices[44]

Let us take up the model of subsection 3.3.1. A firm produces a single good.[45] Consumers receive utility $\theta V(q) - T(q)$ if they purchase a quantity q and utility 0 otherwise. The unit cost of producing the good is constant and equal to c. We consider first the case in which θ takes two values and second the case in which θ takes a continuum of values in an interval.

3.5.1.1 The Two-Type Case

This is the case considered in the text above. A monopolist offers two bundles: (q_1, T_1), which is directed at type-θ_1 consumers (in proportion λ), and (q_2, T_2), which is directed at type-θ_2 consumers (in proportion $1 - \lambda$). It is assumed that the monopolist serves both types of consumers (which will occur if λ is "sufficiently large").

The monopolist's profit is

$$\Pi^m = \lambda(T_1 - cq_1) + (1 - \lambda)(T_2 - cq_2).$$

The monopolist faces two kinds of constraints. The constraints of the first kind require that consumers be willing to purchase. (These are "individual rationality constraints," in the jargon of the incentives literature.) In particular,

the net surplus of the low-demand consumers must be positive:

$$\theta_1 V(q_1) - T_1 \geqslant 0. \tag{3.3}$$

If this condition is satisfied, the high-demand consumers are automatically willing to purchase (because they can choose to buy q_1 at price T_1 and get net surplus $\theta_2 V(q_1) - T_1 > 0$). The constraints of the second kind require that the consumers not exercise personal arbitrage. (These are known as "incentive-compatibility constraints.") In particular, the high-demand consumers should not want to consume the low-demand consumers' bundle:

$$\theta_2 V(q_2) - T_2 \geqslant \theta_2 V(q_1) - T_1. \tag{3.4}$$

Our previous analysis strongly suggests that the other incentive-compatibility constraint is not relevant—the idea is to induce high-demand consumers to "reveal" that they have a high demand, not the reverse. Thus, we will ignore the second incentive-compatibility constraint and later check that it is indeed satisfied in the solution of the "subconstrained problem." (See figure 3.6 for the intuition.)

Thus, the monopolist maximizes Π^m subject to the constraints 3.3 and 3.4. Because the monopolist benefits from high prices, constraint 3.3 implies that $T_1 = \theta_1 V(q_1)$. Constraint 3.4 then implies that

$$T_2 = \theta_2 V(q_2) - \theta_2 V(q_1) + T_1$$
$$= \theta_2 V(q_2) - (\theta_2 - \theta_1) V(q_1).$$

Notice the economic content of these equations. The transfer T_1 can be chosen so as to appropriate the type-θ_1 consumers' surplus entirely. T_2 must leave some net surplus to the type-θ_2 consumers, because they can always buy the bundle (q_1, T_1) and have net surplus

$$\theta_2 V(q_1) - T_1 = (\theta_2 - \theta_1) V(q_1).$$

42. See, e.g., Baron and Myerson 1982, Sappington 1982, and Laffont and Tirole 1986.

43. See, e.g., Maskin and Riley 1980, Milgrom and Weber 1982, Myerson 1979, and Riley and Samuelson 1981.

44. For expositions of optimal nonlinear pricing see Goldman, Leland, and Sibley 1984; Maskin and Riley 1984; Oren, Smith, and Wilson 1984.

45. Nonlinear pricing for a multiproduct firm (but still assuming a one-dimen-
sional parameter for the consumers' type) is considered in Mirman and Sibley 1980 and in Oren et al. 1982. For an exposition of techniques involved in the study of discrimination with several goods, see Guesnerie and Laffont 1984. For an examination of the quality-discrimination problem when the monopoly can also offer warranties, see Matthews and Moore 1987.

The study of multidimensional type spaces is somewhat complex. For a start on this in related models, see Laffont et al. 1982, Kohllepel 1983, Quinzii and Rochet 1985, and Engers 1987.

Substituting into the objective function, the monopolist solves the following unconstrained problem:

$$\max_{\{q_1, q_2\}} \{\lambda[\theta_1 V(q_1) - cq_1]$$
$$+ (1 - \lambda)[\theta_2 V(q_2) - cq_2 - (\theta_2 - \theta_1) V(q_1)]\}.$$

The first-order conditions are

$$\theta_1 V'(q_1) = c \bigg/ \left(1 - \frac{1 - \lambda}{\lambda} \frac{\theta_2 - \theta_1}{\theta_1}\right) \qquad (3.5)$$

and

$$\theta_2 V'(q_2) = c. \qquad (3.6)$$

From equation 3.6, the quantity purchased by the high-demand consumers is socially optimal (the marginal utility of consumption of the good is equal to the marginal cost). From equation 3.5 and the assumption that the monopolist serves both types of consumers, the quantity purchased by the low-demand consumers is suboptimal ($\theta_1 V'(q_1) > c$). (These two properties also imply that $q_2 > q_1$.) This proves conclusion 3 in the text.

Last, let us check that the low-demand consumers do not want to choose the high-demand consumers' bundle. Because they do not realize a net surplus, we require that

$$0 \geqslant \theta_1 V(q_2) - T_2.$$

But this condition is equivalent to

$$0 \geqslant -(\theta_2 - \theta_1)[V(q_2) - V(q_1)],$$

which is satisfied.

Upward-Binding Individual Rationality Constraints

A monopolist faces two types of constraints: The consumer can exert personal arbitrage among various bundles offered by the firm (incentive compatibility), and he can refuse to buy from the firm (individual rationality). We assumed that if the consumer does not buy from the firm, he does not buy at all. This type of individual rationality is downward binding, in that consumers with a low valuation for the good (low θ) are more tempted not to buy. A similar situation would generally occur if there existed an inferior substitute. Sometimes the substitute may be superior. For instance, it could, in the context of the previous model, yield utility $k\theta V(\tilde{q})$, where $\tilde{q}$ is the consumption of this substitute (mutually incompatible with the consumption of the monopolist's good) and $k \geqslant 1$. Assume further that this substitute is sold competitively at marginal cost $\tilde{c}$ (where $\tilde{c} \geqslant kc$). In this situation, the individual rationality constraint facing the monopolist may be "upward binding." The problem may be to prevent the high-valuation consumers from buying the "superior" good.[46] If this is the case, the spectrum of quantities may again be enlarged relative to the first-best (perfect-discrimination) case, but in the opposite way: The consumption of the high-valuation consumers may exceed the socially optimal one. For more on this, see Champsaur and Rochet 1986.[47]

3.5.1.2 The Continuum-of-Types Case

To further develop the techniques of nonlinear pricing and obtain a few additional results, let us assume that the taste parameter θ is distributed across the population of consumers according to the density $f(\theta)$ (with cumulative distribution function $F(\theta)$) on an interval $[\underline{\theta}, \overline{\theta}]$ (where $0 \leqslant \underline{\theta} < \overline{\theta}$).

The monopolist offers a nonlinear tariff, $T(q)$. A consumer with taste parameter θ purchases $q(\theta)$ units and pays $T(q(\theta))$. The monopolist's profit is then

$$\Pi^m = \int_{\underline{\theta}}^{\overline{\theta}} [T(q(\theta)) - c q(\theta)] f(\theta) d\theta.$$

The monopolist maximizes this profit subject to two constraints.

First, all consumers must be willing to purchase: For all θ,

$$\theta V(q(\theta)) - T(q(\theta)) \geqslant 0. \qquad (3.7)$$

(The monopolist may want to exclude some consumers

---

46. The constraint can then be written

$$\theta_2 V(q_2) - T_2 \geqslant \tilde{U}(\theta_2) = \max_{\tilde{q}_2} [k\theta_2 V(\tilde{q}_2) - \tilde{c}\tilde{q}_2].$$

47. An alternative application of this idea would pertain to vertical integration. If the customer were a downstream firm, he would have the choice between buying one of the upstream monopolist's bundles and producing the inter-

mediate good himself (i.e., vertically integrating). In the latter case, he would pay a fixed investment cost K to have access to the technology of production at marginal cost $\tilde{c}$ (and k might be equal to 1 in this context). The high-demand customers would have a higher incentive to vertically integrate (as in Katz's model of *third*-degree price discrimination mentioned in the text), so the individual-rationality constraint might be upward binding.

from consumption; at a formal level, this can be represented by $q(\theta) = T(q(\theta)) = 0$ for these consumers.) As in the two-type case, it actually suffices to require that the individual-rationality constraint 3.7 hold for the lowest-demand consumer:

$$\underline{\theta} \, V(q(\underline{\theta})) - T(q(\underline{\theta})) \geqslant 0. \qquad (3.8)$$

If constraint 3.8 is satisfied, a type-θ consumer also realizes a non-negative net surplus, because he can always choose to consume the type-$\underline{\theta}$ consumer's bundle and obtain utility

$$\theta \, V(q(\underline{\theta})) - T(q(\underline{\theta})) \geqslant (\theta - \underline{\theta}) V(q(\underline{\theta})) \geqslant 0.$$

Second, a type-θ consumer must not choose the bundle chosen by type-$\tilde{\theta}$ consumers (where $\tilde{\theta} \neq \theta$). The incentive-compatibility constraints are, for all θ and $\tilde{\theta}$,

$$U(\theta) = \theta \, V(q(\theta)) - T(q(\theta)) \geqslant \theta \, V(q(\tilde{\theta})) - T(q(\tilde{\theta})). \quad (3.9)$$

The constraints represented by 3.9 are not very tractable. Fortunately, in this problem it will suffice to require that the incentive constraints are satisfied "locally"—i.e., that for $\tilde{\theta} = \theta - d\theta$ close to θ (see footnote 52)

$$\theta \, V(q(\theta)) - T(q(\theta)) \geqslant \theta \, V(q(\theta - d\theta)) - T(q(\theta - d\theta)).$$

Assuming that $q(\cdot)$ and $T(\cdot)$ are strictly increasing and differentiable,[48] we obtain for all θ

$$\theta \, V'(q(\theta)) - T'(q(\theta)) = 0, \qquad (3.10)$$

which expresses the fact that a small increase in the quantity consumed by the type-θ consumer generates a marginal surplus $\theta \, V'(q(\theta))$ equal to the marginal payment $T'(q(\theta))$. Hence, the consumer does not want to modify the quantity at the margin. Equation 3.10 can be used to obtain the payment function once the quantity function $q(\theta)$ is known: Assuming that the optimal $q(\theta)$ is strictly monotonic in θ (which will be derived shortly), one has

$$T'(q) = \alpha(q) V'(q), \qquad (3.11)$$

where $\alpha(\cdot)$ is the inverse of the quantity function—i.e., $\alpha(q)$ is the type that consumes quantity q ($\alpha(q(\theta)) \equiv \theta$).

To derive the optimal quantity function, it is actually convenient to use a perhaps less natural representation of the incentive constraint.[49] Let $U(\theta)$ denote (as before) the utility, or net surplus, of the type-θ consumer. From the incentive-compatibility constraint,

$$U(\theta) \equiv \theta \, V(q(\theta)) - T(q(\theta)) = \max_{\tilde{\theta}} \, [\theta \, V(q(\tilde{\theta})) - T(q(\tilde{\theta}))].$$

From the envelope theorem, the derivative of U with respect to θ takes into account only the direct effect of θ, and not the indirect effect stemming from the adjustment in quantity:

$$\frac{dU}{d\theta} \equiv U'(\theta) = V(q(\theta)). \qquad (3.12)$$

Integrating equation 3.12, we can express the utility of the type-θ consumer as[50]

$$U(\theta) = \int_{\underline{\theta}}^{\theta} V(q(u)) du + U(\underline{\theta}) = \int_{\underline{\theta}}^{\theta} V(q(u)) du, \qquad (3.13)$$

where use is made of the individual rationality constraint ($U(\underline{\theta}) = 0$).

The fact that the consumer's utility as a function of θ grows at a rate that increases with $q(\theta)$ will turn out to be crucial. Higher quantities "differentiate" different types more, in that the utility differentials are higher. Because leaving a surplus to the consumer is costly to the monopolist (recall that the transfer $T(q(\theta))$ is equal to $\theta \, V(q(\theta)) - U(\theta)$), the monopolist will tend to reduce U and, to do so, to induce the consumer to consume a suboptimal quantity. Equation 3.13 suggests that it is more desirable to reduce the quantity (relative to the socially optimal quantity defined by $\theta \, V'(q(\theta)) = c$) more for low-$\theta$ consumers—an increase of $\delta q > 0$ in the quantity purchased by a type-θ consumer raises the utility of all types $\theta' > \theta$ by $V'(q(\theta)) \delta q > 0$ but does not affect the utility of types $\theta' < \theta$). Hence, we expect the low-demand consumers to consume much less than their socially optimal quantity and the highest-demand consumer ($\theta = \bar{\theta}$) to consume exactly his socially optimal quantity—a conclusion

---

48. It can indeed be shown that these two functions necessarily are differentiable almost everywhere: From equation 3.9, q must be nondecreasing in θ, using the same proof as the one in chapter 1 showing that the monopoly price increases with marginal cost (T must obviously be nondecreasing in q; otherwise some bundles would not be chosen); and a monotonic function is almost everywhere differentiable.

49. This trick was first used by Mirrlees (1971).

50. Equation 3.13 is the analogue of the equation

$$U(\theta_2) = (\theta_2 - \theta_1) V(q(\theta_1))$$

in the two-type case.

analogous to conclusion 3 in the text. If this is indeed so, the monopolist enlarges the quantity spectrum toward low quantities (i.e., low qualities in the quality interpretation). Let us now prove these results formally.

Since $T(q(\theta)) = \theta V(q(\theta)) - U(\theta)$, the monopolist's profit can be written as

$$\Pi^m = \int_{\underline{\theta}}^{\overline{\theta}} \left(\theta V(q(\theta)) - \int_{\underline{\theta}}^{\theta} V(q(u))du - c q(\theta) \right) f(\theta)d\theta.$$

Integrating by parts[51] yields

$$\Pi^m = \int_{\underline{\theta}}^{\overline{\theta}} \{ [\theta V(q(\theta)) - c q(\theta)]f(\theta)$$
$$- V(q(\theta))[1 - F(\theta)] \} d\theta.$$

The maximization of Π^m with respect to the schedule $q(\cdot)$ requires that the term under the integral be maximized with respect to $q(\theta)$ for all θ:

$$\theta V'(q(\theta)) = c + \frac{1 - F(\theta)}{f(\theta)} V'(q(\theta)). \qquad (3.14)$$

We thus obtain the conclusion that the marginal willingness to pay for the good exceeds the marginal cost, except for the highest-demand consumer ($\theta = \overline{\theta}$). Hence, the monopolist induces consumers to purchase a suboptimal quantity.[52]

Next, for this type of consumer preference, one can get a simple expression for the "price-cost margin." Let $T'(q)$ $\equiv p(q)$ denote the price of an extra unit when the consumer already consumes q units. We know from consumer optimization that

$$T'(q(\theta)) = \theta V'(q(\theta)).$$

Substituting into equation 3.14, we get

$$\frac{p - c}{p} = \frac{1 - F(\theta)}{\theta f(\theta)}, \qquad (3.15)$$

where $p = p(q(\theta))$.

An assumption commonly made in the literature is that the "hazard rate" of the distribution of types

$$\frac{f(\theta)}{1 - F(\theta)}$$

increases with θ.[53] This property is satisfied by many distributions, including the uniform, the normal, the Pareto, the logistic, the exponential, and any distribution with nondecreasing density. On the assumption that the hazard rate is increasing,

$$\theta - \frac{1 - F(\theta)}{f(\theta)}$$

increases with θ. From equation 3.14 and the fact that V is concave, $q(\theta)$ increases with θ. Furthermore,

$$\frac{1 - F(\theta)}{\theta f(\theta)}$$

---

51. In this integration by parts, it is convenient to take $-[1 - F(\theta)]$ as the integral of $f(\theta)d\theta$.

52. We represented the incentive-compatibility constraints by the first-order condition 3.10. To be certain that $q(\theta)$ is indeed the optimal choice of a type-θ consumer, we must check the second-order condition associated with the consumer's optimization over quantities, both locally and globally. Let $U(\theta, \tilde{\theta})$ denote the utility of a consumer with taste θ when he consumes the quantity of a consumer with taste $\tilde{\theta}$:

$$U(\theta, \tilde{\theta}) \equiv \theta V(q(\tilde{\theta})) - T(q(\tilde{\theta})).$$

The first-order condition is, for all θ,

$$U_{\tilde{\theta}}(\theta, \theta) = 0,$$

where subscripts denote partial derivatives. In other words, choosing $q(\theta)$ is optimal for a type-θ consumer. Differentiating the first-order condition with respect to θ gives

$$U_{\tilde{\theta}\tilde{\theta}}(\theta, \theta) = -U_{\theta\tilde{\theta}}(\theta, \theta).$$

The local second-order condition is thus equivalent to

$$U_{\theta\tilde{\theta}}(\theta, \theta) \geqslant 0.$$

But

$$U_{\theta\tilde{\theta}}(\theta, \theta) = V'(q(\theta))\frac{dq(\theta)}{d\theta} \geqslant 0, \text{ as } \frac{dq(\theta)}{d\theta} \geqslant 0.$$

To check the global second-order condition, suppose that

$$U(\theta_1, \theta_2) > U(\theta_1, \theta_1)$$

for some θ_1 and θ_2. This implies

$$\int_{\theta_1}^{\theta_2} U_{\tilde{\theta}}(\theta_1, x)dx > 0.$$

Suppose, for instance, $\theta_2 > \theta_1$. Because $U_{\theta\tilde{\theta}}(\theta, \tilde{\theta}) \geqslant 0$, we have

$$U_{\tilde{\theta}}(\theta_1, x) \leqslant U_{\tilde{\theta}}(x, x) = 0$$

for $x \geqslant \theta_1$ (where use is made of the first-order condition). We thus obtain a contradiction. And similarly for $\theta_2 < \theta_1$.

53. To understand why this is called the hazard rate, suppose that one moves along the θ axis from $\underline{\theta}$ toward $\overline{\theta}$ and eliminates types that are "passed by." Arriving at θ and moving by $d\theta$ to the right, one finds that the conditional probability that the consumer's type belongs to $[\theta, \theta + d\theta]$ and is thus eliminated is $f(\theta)d\theta/[1 - F(\theta)]$.

decreases with θ, so that *the price-cost margin decreases with the consumer's type and, therefore, decreases with output.*

Let us derive some further properties of the optimal payment function $T(\cdot)$. Recall that $T'(q) = p(q)$. Hence,

$$T''(q) = \frac{dp}{dq} = \frac{dp}{d\theta} \Big/ \frac{dq}{d\theta}.$$

But $dq/d\theta > 0$, and, from equation 3.15, $dp/d\theta < 0$. Hence, the payment function is concave. It is represented in figure 3.7.

Two properties result from figure 3.7:

• The average price per unit, $T(q)/q$, decreases with q.[54] (This is the Maskin-Riley quantity-discount result.)

• Because a concave function is the lower envelope of its tangents, the optimal nonlinear payment schedule can also be implemented by offering a menu of two-part tariffs (where the monopolist lets the consumer choose

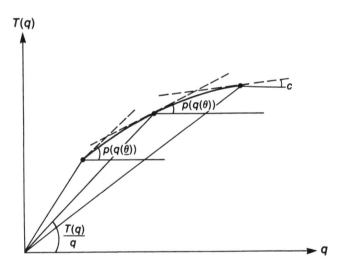

Figure 3.7

among the continuum of two-part tariffs). This can be seen in the figure, where a consumer of type θ indeed chooses the two-part tariff with slope $p(q(\theta))$.[55,56]

More General Demand Functions

As we earlier noted, the above theory holds for more general gross surplus functions $V(q, \theta)$ as long as $\partial V/\partial \theta > 0$ (which is just a normalization) and $\partial^2 V/\partial q \partial \theta > 0$ (the single-crossing or sorting condition). Equation 3.14 then becomes

$$\frac{\partial V}{\partial q}(q(\theta), \theta) = c + \frac{1 - F(\theta)}{f(\theta)} \frac{\partial^2 V}{\partial q \partial \theta}(q(\theta), \theta). \qquad (3.14')$$

The following exercise, inspired by Spulber (1981) and Wilson (1985), makes use of equation 3.14'.

*Exercise 3.7*** A monopolist with marginal cost c sells to heterogeneous consumers. The latter differ in their transportation cost tq for purchasing quantity q. The parameter t is distributed according to a c.d.f. $G(t)$ on $[0, +\infty)$, with density $g(t)$. The monopolist does not supply transportation. (Assume, further, that the consumers cannot arbitrage among themselves.) The consumer's utility function is

$$[1 - (1 - q)^2]/2 - tq - T(q)$$

when purchasing q units.

(i) How would you define θ, $V(q, \theta)$, $F(\theta)$, and $f(\theta)$ so as to be able to apply the general theory?

(ii) Let $p(q) \equiv T'(q)$. Use equation 3.14' to compute the optimal $p(q)$.

(iii) Assume that $G(t) = t^\alpha$ on $[0, 1]$ (where $\alpha > 0$). Compute the optimal nonlinear tariff and show that it exhibits quantity discounts.

---

54. The slope of T at $q(\underline{\theta})$ is indeed smaller than that of the ray through the origin and the point $(q(\underline{\theta}), T(q(\underline{\theta})))$:

$$\underline{\theta} \, V'(q(\underline{\theta})) < \underline{\theta} \, \frac{V(q(\underline{\theta}))}{q(\underline{\theta})},$$

because V is concave.

55. This point is made in a different context in Laffont and Tirole 1986. There, a government offers a menu of contracts to a regulated firm having private information about its technology. The optimal contracts can actually be chosen linear in cost overruns. That is, the government discriminates on the basis of the

fraction of cost overruns reimbursed to the firm. The use of linear (i.e., two-part) tariffs is more interesting in this incentive context because of the presence of uncertainty. Under risk neutrality, the linear contracts are still robust (optimal) under any kind of cost uncertainty or measurement error.

56. With two types of consumers, it turns out that two two-part tariffs do not allow for the implementation of the optimal nonlinear tariff. This looks bizarre, as it would seem that it would be more difficult to use two-part tariffs with more types. However, think of a two-point distribution as a continuous distribution with two atoms. This distribution is not well behaved, in that its hazard rate is not monotonic (which was a sufficient condition for the implementation with two-part tariffs).

Quantity Discounts and Quantity Premia

Maskin and Riley's result on quantity discounts relies on their plausible assumptions about the shape and distribution of consumers' preferences. In general, however, the optimal nonlinear tariff may involve quantity premia instead of quantity discounts. Suppose that a good can be consumed only in integer numbers and that there are two types of consumers. A low-demand consumer wants to consume exactly one unit of the good. His gross surplus is 1 if he consumes one unit or more and 0 otherwise. A high-demand consumer wants to consume exactly two units of the good. His gross surplus is 4 if he consumes two units or more and 0 otherwise. The optimal tariff for the monopolist is clearly $T(q) = 1$ for $q = 1$ and $T(q) = 4$ for $q = 2$. In this special case, the monopolist can discriminate perfectly; and more important, the average price is 1 for a purchase of one unit and 2 for a purchase of two units.

Under the quality interpretation of the model, a good example of a premium involves automobile manufacturers, who typically try to extract surplus from high-valuation consumers (i.e., consumers who highly value luxury and prestige). The profit margins on top-of-the-line cars and optional equipment are generally higher than those on basic cars and equipment,[57] and this suggests the existence of quality premia.

Thus, we cannot determine on *a priori* grounds whether quantity (or quality) discounts or premia are optimal. Only a careful consideration of the likely shape and distribution of consumer preferences can determine the optimal business strategy.

Welfare Aspects

Katz (1983) shows that nonlinear pricing may yield too little or too much output in comparison with the social optimum. (Furthermore, the distribution of this given output between consumers is not welfare maximizing, because the efficient means of rationing a fixed output is uniform pricing.) However, if the single-crossing condition holds (as is assumed here), the monopolist generally produces too little output.

3.5.1.3   Optimal Nonlinear Tariffs as Ramsey Prices[58]

Let us draw the analogy between the optimal nonlinear tariff (given by equation 3.15, say) and the inverse-elasticity rule, in order to unify the theories of second-degree and third-degree price discrimination.

To this purpose, let us decompose the aggregate-demand function into independent demands for marginal units of consumption. Fix a quantity q and consider the demand for the qth unit of consumption. This unit has, by definition, price p. The proportion of consumers willing to buy this unit is

$$D_q(p) \equiv 1 - F(\theta_q^*(p)),$$

where $\theta_q^*(p)$ denotes the type of consumer who is indifferent between buying and not buying the qth unit at price p:

$$\theta_q^*(p)V'(q) = p.$$

The demand for the qth unit is independent of the demand for the $\bar{q}$th unit for $\bar{q} \neq q$.[59] We can thus apply the inverse-elasticity rule. The optimal price for the qth unit is given by

$$\frac{p - c}{p} = -\frac{dp}{dD_q}\frac{D_q}{p}.$$

However,

$$\frac{dD_q}{dp} = -f(\theta_q^*(p))\frac{d\theta_q^*}{dp} \quad \text{and} \quad \frac{d\theta_q^*}{\theta_q^*} = \frac{dp}{p}.$$

We thus obtain

$$\frac{p - c}{p} = \frac{1 - F(\theta_q^*(p))}{\theta_q^*(p)f(\theta_q^*(p))},$$

which is nothing but equation 3.15.

---

57. Scherer (1980, p. 394) quotes a memorandum on the 1966 Ford Galaxie four-door sedan revealing that, whereas the wholesale price of the basic car with standard equipment exceeded standard accounting costs by 17 percent, the markups on optional equipment were characteristically much higher—"e.g., 293 percent for a more powerful V-8 engine, 123 percent for power steering, and 58 percent for air conditioning."

58. This subsection is inspired by Brown and Sibley 1986 and by Goldman et al. 1984.

59. This independence is due to the absence of income effects. The price charged for the inframarginal units has no influence on the demand for the marginal unit.

3.5.2 Commodity Bundling

3.5.2.1 Homogeneous Good

We saw that a discriminating monopolist may want to practice quantity discounts. The price of two units of a good is then lower than twice the price of one unit. In a sense, the two units purchased by a consumer are bundled (cannot be bought separately at no extra cost). However, we cannot conclude that the monopolist induces consumers to consume more by offering quantity discounts. We must give a precise definition of "consuming more." If we take the efficient solution as a reference, we actually see that discrimination by the monopolist may lead to suboptimal consumption.

The monopolist's offering the choice between one and two units of the good is an instance of what Adams and Yellen (1976) call "mixed commodity bundling" (for instance, airline companies offer one-way as well as round-trip tickets). Pure commodity bundling occurs when the monopolist offers only the two-unit bundle. Although such an all-or-nothing policy is not, in general, optimal,[60] it is easily justified in circumstances in which there are economies of scale in production or in distribution. It may be cheaper to manufacture or sell two units together rather than twice one unit.

To understand when pure bundling may occur in the absence of economies of scale, recall the price-discrimination model. Suppose that there are two types of consumers, with low and high demands. Suppose further that the efficient allocation is for the low-demand consumers to consume one unit of a good and for the high-demand consumers to consume two units (to simplify, the good must be consumed in integer numbers). As we saw in section 3.3, if the proportion of high-demand consumers is high, the monopolist does not want to serve the low-demand consumers in order to extract the high-demand consumers' surplus; thus, he induces them to consume

zero units rather than one. The optimal policy is then to offer the two-unit package only (for a payment equal to the high-demand consumers' gross surplus for two units). We thus have an instance of pure commodity bundling.

Pure commodity bundling becomes even more likely when, for technological or marketing reasons, a good must be sold in either one-unit or two-unit packages, but not both. (Think of a firm having to choose one size—either size 1 or size 2—for its product.[61]) In the previous example, the same profit was obtained by selling two units to the high-demand consumers and zero to the low-demand consumers, and the monopolist chose the size-2 technology.[62] In this example, however, the profitability of serving the two types of consumers is reduced, because the single-size constraint prevents price discrimination. This makes the policy of serving high-demand consumers only (and, hence, offering a two-unit consumption deal only) more appealing. The following exercise illustrates this reasoning.

Exercise 3.8** Consumers have preferences $U = \theta V(q) - T$. The consumption q can take a value of 0, 1, or 2. $V(0) = 0$, $V(1) = 1$, and $V(2) = \frac{7}{4}$. The unit production cost is $c = \frac{3}{4}$ whatever the size of the bundle. There are two types of consumers: $\theta_1 = 1$ (in proportion λ) and $\theta_2 = 2$ (in proportion $1 - \lambda$). The consumers can engage in personal arbitrage.

(i) Show that, in the absence of a technological constraint (i.e., in a case where the monopolist can product both sizes), the monopolist uses pure commodity bundling if and only if $\lambda < \frac{4}{5}$.

(ii) Suppose that, for technological reasons, the monopolist must choose to produce the good in either size 1 or size 2. Show that the monopolist chooses the size-2 technology if and only if $\lambda < \frac{6}{7}$.

Exercise 3.9* Buying a season ticket is sometimes the only means of attending a certain sports or cultural event.

---

60. As Adams and Yellen show, mixed bundling always dominates pure bundling. Intuitively, the monopolist has more "instruments." Suppose that the pure-bundling price is p_B. The monopolist can still sell the bundle at price p_B and sell each unit at price $p_B - c$ (where c is the unit cost). This policy cannot generate a lower profit than the pure-bundling one. The reasoning easily extends to the bundling of heterogeneous goods.

61. We still rule out economies of scale. The cost of producing two units is the same whether the monopolist has chosen the one-unit or the two-unit package size. We only assume that the two sizes are mutually incompatible.

62. This allocation cannot be reached using the size-1 package. To extract the high-demand consumers' gross surplus for two units, the monopolist would have to charge half this gross surplus. But because the gross-surplus function is strictly concave, the high-demand consumers would only consume one unit—mathematically,

$$\theta_2 V(1) - \frac{\theta_2 V(2)}{2} > \theta_2 V(2) - 2\left(\frac{\theta_2 V(2)}{2}\right) = 0.$$

Often, however, tickets can also be bought for specific events as well. Discuss this in light of the above arguments (and, possibly, others that you may want to bring in).

Heterogeneous Goods

The previous discussion focused on bundling of several units of a single commodity. Commodity bundling can also affect several commodities. For instance, a restaurant ties the consumption of several dishes into a menu, a bank offers an indivisible array of services (e.g., checking, safe deposit, and travelers' checks), and a tour operator sells comprehensive vacation plans.

Formally, the tying of units of several goods is similar to that of several units of the same good. However, while one can make reasonable assumptions about the cross-distribution of marginal utilities for the good in the single-commodity framework,[63] it is harder to formulate *a priori* restrictions on the cross-distribution of the utilities for the various goods. It is, therefore, not surprising that the theory of multi-commodity bundling has focused on examples. The exercise below gives one example; other examples and theoretical developments can be found in Adams and Yellen 1976, Telser 1979, Schmalensee 1984, and Lewbel 1985.

Exercise 3.10* A common practice in the U.S. film industry (before it was outlawed) was the bundling of several films at the distribution level. Stigler (1963) offered the following simple model to formalize this practice, which was also called "block booking": There are two downstream units (theaters), two films, and one monopoly film producer. The first downstream unit values film 1 at 4 and film 2 at 1. The second values film 1 at 3 and film 2 at 2. The value of a bundle to each downstream unit is equal to the sum of its valuations for the two films (there is no interdependence effect). Show that the film producer wants to bundle the two films.

It was mentioned above that mixed bundling dominates pure bundling (weakly, at least). It also dominates unbundled sales (for the same reason: the monopolist has more instruments). But, as Schmalensee (1982b) shows, it need not *strictly* dominate unbundled sales; a monopolist does not gain from bundling his product to another product that is produced competitively if the consumers' reservation values (valuations) for the two products are independent.[64] McAfee, McMillan, and Whinston (1987) provide very general conditions under which, even for independent reservation prices, the monopolist strictly prefers mixed bundling over unbundled sales.[65]

3.5.3 The Insurance Market

Finally, consider the analogy between an insurance market, in which consumers differ in their risk, and the quality-differentiation model. A consumer with initial income I can face either of two states of nature. In state of nature 2 ("accident"), which occurs with probability θ, he incurs a loss with monetary equivalent L. In state of nature 1 ("no accident"), which occurs with probability $(1 - \theta)$, he incurs no loss. The probability θ is exogenous (there is no "moral hazard"). The consumer has a von Neumann–Morgenstern utility function U.

A risk-neutral firm, which (to simplify) has monopoly power, can supply insurance to the consumer. For a fixed premium p, to be paid in all states of nature, the firm reimburses an amount s in case of an accident. s can be seen as an insurance service. The consumer's expected utility for the insurance policy (p, s) is

$$\theta\, U(I - p - L + s) + (1 - \theta) U(I - p),$$

and the firm's expected profit is $p - \theta s$.

Assume first that everything (except the realization of the state of nature) is known to both parties. The firm offers an insurance contract to the consumer before the realization of the state of nature. The contract is accepted by the consumer only if it gives him an expected utility exceeding that in the absence of insurance contract. The

---

63. For example, one can make the Spence-Mirrlees assumption that the marginal utility of the good at any quantity increases with the consumer's "type."

64. Let c' denote the unit cost and price of the other product. If the monopolist charges p_B for the bundle, he can do the same by selling his good separately at price $p_B - c'$. This result does not extend to correlated valuations. Schmalensee

shows that if the consumers' reservation prices for the two goods are negatively correlated (the above exercise yields an example of negative correlation), the monopolist may strictly gain by pursuing mixed bundling.

65. See also Chae 1987 for an analysis of bundling for a specific (independent) distribution of reservation prices.

individual rationality constraint can be written as

$$\theta U(I - p - L + s) + (1 - \theta)U(I - p)$$

$$\geqslant \theta U(I - L) + (1 - \theta)U(I). \tag{3.16}$$

The maximization of the expected profit $(p - \theta s)$ over the contract (p, s) subject to constraint 3.16 implies that $s = L$. The firm fully reimburses the consumer in case of accident (full insurance). This is a classic result in the theory of insurance. Just as efficiency requires that marginal rates of substitutions be equated across goods and consumers, Borch's (1968) rule says that the consumer's rates of substitution between income in the two states of nature,

$$\frac{U'(I - p - L + s)}{U'(I - p)},$$

must equal the firm's $(1/1)$, or

$$I - p - L + s = I - p;$$

that is, $s = L$.[66]

Second, assume that the consumer knows his risk parameter θ, but that the firm does not. This is the Rothschild-Stiglitz (1976)–Wilson (1977) model of discrimination in the insurance market.[67] Assume for simplicity that there are only two potential probabilities of accident: $\theta_1 < \theta_2$. (The case with a continuum of types can be treated as in subsection 3.5.1.2.) The insurance company then offers two contracts: $\{p_1, s_1\}$ and $\{p_2, s_2\}$.

Let $u(p, s, \theta)$ denote the utility of a consumer with probability of accident θ for the contract (p, s). This consumer's marginal rate of substitution between insurance services and income is, by definition, equal to

$$\frac{\partial u}{\partial s} \bigg/ \left(-\frac{\partial u}{\partial p}\right).$$

A straightforward computation shows that

$$\frac{\partial}{\partial \theta}\left[\frac{\partial u}{\partial s}\bigg/\left(-\frac{\partial u}{\partial p}\right)\right] > 0. \tag{3.17}$$

This inequality means that when the probability of accident increases, the consumer is more eager to buy insurance services. In other words, he is willing to pay a higher marginal premium for a given marginal increase in services. Hence, in our discrimination problem, type-θ_2 ("high-risk") consumers are more eager to buy insurance than type-θ_1 ("low-risk") consumers.

Inequality 3.17 is the sorting (or Spence-Mirrlees) condition for the insurance market. It implies that the only way to discriminate between the two types of buyers is to induce high-risk consumers to get more insurance: $s_2 \geqslant s_1$. There is a strong analogy between this model and the quality-discrimination model.

Although the model does not quite fit the consumers' objective function of subsection 3.5.1, the previous techniques and conclusions can be extended.[68] In particular, conclusion 3 becomes as follows: The high-risk consumers get full insurance ($s_2 = L$), while the low-risk consumers get suboptimal insurance ($s_1 < L$). As before, the intuition is that the firm wants to prevent the high-risk consumers from consuming the low-risk consumers' bundle.[69] It reduces the services offered to the low-risk consumers to discourage the high-risk consumers from exercising personal arbitrage. This policy is indeed profitable, because a reduction in services is relatively less costly to the low-risk than to the high-risk consumers. Figure 3.8 illustrates this result.

The derivation of the optimal insurance contracts follows a few simple geometrical considerations (see Stiglitz 1977 for a formal argument). The figures are drawn in the consumption space rather than in the (p, s) space.

In figure 3.8a, E depicts the bundle of consumptions in the two states of nature in the absence of insurance ($p = s = 0$). This bundle is the same for both types of consumers. The consumers' indifference curves through

---

66. The different states of nature can be thought of as different goods. The theory of uncertainty considers the same physical good available in two different states of nature as two different economic goods. See Debreu 1959, chapter 7.

67. The monopoly case is actually considered in Stiglitz 1977. Rothschild and Stiglitz (1976) and Wilson (1977) couch the problem in a competitive insurance market.

68. The Maskin-Riley framework includes the insurance market as a special

case. One similarity with the quality-discrimination model is that the type who is most eager to buy the services benefits from the asymmetry of information if and only if the other type is served by the monopolist. See below.

69. In the quality or the quantity model, the low type would pay less than the high types for the right to buy at marginal cost if the firm could tell different types apart (i.e., if the firm had full information). Here, under full information, the firm would offer the low type a lower premium for the service $s = L$ because the low type does better without insurance than the high type.

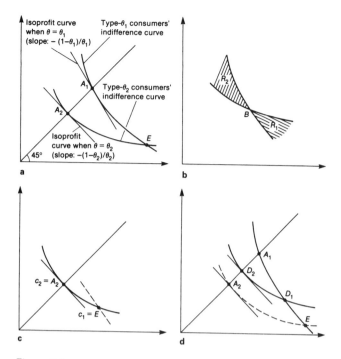

Figure 3.8
(a) Complete information. Vertical axis represents income (accident) $(= I - p - L + s)$; horizontal axis represents income (no accident) $(= I - p)$. (b) Incomplete information: screening possibilities. (c) Incomplete information: λ small. Low-risk consumers do not buy insurance. (d) Incomplete information: λ large. Low-risk consumers buy a suboptimal amount of insurance.

net surplus from the insurance policy (point c_2); their utility, as in the full-information case, is the same as the one they would obtain in the absence of insurance. Low-risk consumers do not buy insurance (point c_1). To understand why this allocation is not easily upset by offering some insurance to low-risk customers, one can draw the latter's indifference curve through E. Any contract that is accepted by them lies to the northeast of this indifference curve. Furthermore, to generate gains from trade between the risk-neutral insurance company and the risk-averse low-risk customers, this point must represent a move from E toward the diagonal (i.e., must involve positive insurance). However, the monopolist must then leave a positive net surplus to the high-risk consumers in order for them not to buy the low-risk consumers' bundle. This is too costly to the monopolist if the proportion of high-risk consumers is large. The new trade generated by the new contract is not worth its cost in terms of incentives.

When the proportion of low-risk consumers is smaller, the trade-off operates the opposite way (figure 3.8d). The monopolist prefers to sell to both types of consumers. The low-risk consumers, who choose D_1, do not derive a net surplus from the possibility of insurance; the high-risk ones do by choosing D_2. The high-risk consumers' net surplus is the minimum one consistent with their not choosing D_1.

In both cases, the high-risk consumers are efficiently (i.e., fully) insured and the low-risk consumers are suboptimally insured.

E are represented. The low-risk consumers' indifference curve is always steeper than the high-risk consumers'. Under complete information about θ, the monopolist offers full insurance at the minimal level at which consumers buy (point A_i for type θ_i). Thus, the individual-rationality constraint is binding. Note also that the high-risk consumers would like to be able to purchase the low-risk consumers' full insurance policy.

Figure 3.8b depicts how the two types of consumers can be separated when the monopolist does not observe θ. For instance, if B is the bundle directed at low-risk consumers, any allocation for the high-risk consumers must lie in region R_2 (it must be preferred to B by type-θ_2 consumers, but it must not induce type-θ_1 consumers to abandon B). Conversely, if B is the allocation targeted for type-θ_2 consumers, that for type-θ_1 consumers must belong to region R_1.

Figure 3.8c depicts the optimal allocation when the market is composed mainly of high-risk consumers. High-risk consumers obtain full insurance but do not derive any

Answers and Hints

Exercise 3.1

(i) The consumer maximizes gross surplus minus the tariff. But this objective function is equal to zero for any level of consumption. Thus, the consumer is willing to consume the competitive level $q = q^c/n$. Because the consumers' surplus is completely captured, the monopolist's profit is equal to the maximum social surplus. The reader who worries about the consumer's indifference among all levels of consumption can imagine that the tariff is equal to the gross consumer surplus for $q \neq q^c/n$ and equal to the gross consumer surplus minus ε for $q = q^c/n$. The consumer then strictly prefers the competitive quantity.

(ii) The new (residual) inverse-demand curve for the monopolist is

$$\tilde{P}(q) = \begin{cases} p_0 & \text{for } q \leqslant D(p_0) \\ P(q) & \text{for } q \geqslant D(p_0). \end{cases}$$

Assuming for simplicity a constant marginal cost c and a single consumer, the optimal two-part tariff is $p = c$ and $A = \int_0^{q^c} [\tilde{P}(q) - c]dq$. Alternatively, the monopolist can charge the fully nonlinear tariff: $T(q) = \int_0^q \tilde{P}(x)dx$. These results are depicted in figure 3.9.

Exercise 3.2

Let $q = a - b(p + tx)$ denote the demand function, where p is now the f.o.b. price for a consumer located at x.

(i) Under nonuniform f.o.b. prices, the producer maximizes

$$(p - c)(a - bp - btx).$$

for all x. This yields a delivered price of

$$p(x) + tx = \frac{a}{2b} + \frac{c}{2} + \frac{tx}{2}.$$

Note that there is a 50 percent freight absorption.

(ii) Under a uniform f.o.b. price $\bar{p}$, the producer maximizes

$$\int_0^1 (\bar{p} - c)(a - b\bar{p} - btx)dx.$$

This yields

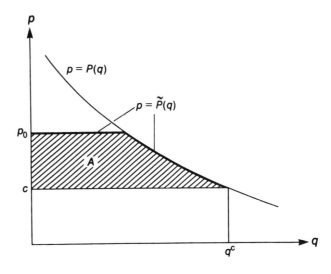

Figure 3.9

$$\bar{p} + tx = \frac{a}{2b} + \frac{c}{2} + tx - \frac{t}{4}.$$

Under discrimination, the delivered price is higher for $x < \frac{1}{2}$ and lower for $x > \frac{1}{2}$. Hence, uniform pricing involves a cross-subsidization from distant customers to local ones.

(iii) A uniform f.o.b. price tends to reduce the market, since the delivered price for the consumer located at $x = 1$ is higher.

Exercise 3.3

Serving both types yields

$$\Pi_2 = (\theta - c)^2/4\theta,$$

as is seen in the text. Serving only the high type (at monopoly price $(c + \theta_2)/2)$) yields

$$\Pi_2' = (1 - \lambda)(\theta_2 - c)^2/4\theta_2.$$

$\Pi_2 - \Pi_2'$ grows with λ. (Warning: θ depends on λ.) For $\lambda = 1$,

$$\Pi_2 - \Pi_2' = \Pi_2 > 0,$$

and for $\lambda = 0$,

$$\Pi_2 - \Pi_2' < 0.$$

Hence, $\Pi_2 > \Pi_2'$ only if λ is "large enough." Alternatively, if $\theta_1 > (c + \theta_2)/2$, monopoly pricing for the type-θ_2 consumers yields consumption by the type-θ_1 consumers.

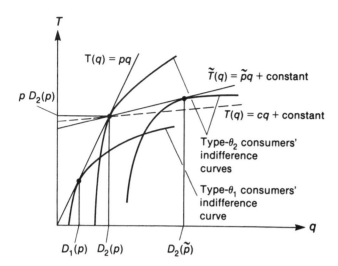

Figure 3.10

Exercise 3.4

Figure 3.10 depicts the issue.

Suppose that the monopolist offers, along with the linear tariff $T(q) = pq$, the two-part tariff $\tilde{T}(q) = \tilde{A} + \tilde{p}q$, where

$$c < \tilde{p} < p$$

and

$$p D_2(p) = \tilde{A} + \tilde{p} D_2(p).$$

The second condition says that the type-θ_2 consumers can also afford their initial bundle with the two-part tariff.

It is clear from figure 3.10 that the type-θ_1 consumers stick to their old consumption pattern (i.e., they use the linear tariff). The type-θ_2 consumers are made better off because their opportunity set (the lower envelope of the linear and two-part tariffs) is improved. They increase their consumption by

$$D_2(\tilde{p}) - D_2(p).$$

The monopolist enjoys this increase in consumption, because his profit margin on these extra units is $(\tilde{p} - c) > 0$.

More formally, the increase in the monopolist's profit from type-θ_2 consumers is

$$(1 - \lambda)[\tilde{A} + (\tilde{p} - c)D_2(\tilde{p}) - (p - c)D_2(p)]$$

$$= (1 - \lambda)(\tilde{p} - c)[D_2(\tilde{p}) - D_2(p)] > 0.$$

The picture changes dramatically when the consumers' demands are interrelated (as is the case when consumers are firms competing on the same product market). Purchases by low-demand consumers may be reduced by the discount offered to high-demand consumers, and there may exist no nonlinear tariff that is Pareto superior to a uniform price (as has been shown by Ordover and Panzar [1980]).

Exercise 3.5

(i) In the absence of tie-ins, the monopolist can either sell to both types and capture only the low-demand type's surplus (profit $S_1(c)$) or sell to high-demand consumers only (profit $(1 - \lambda)S_2(c)$).

(ii) For these numerical values: Under prohibition,

$$S_1(c) \leqslant (1 - \lambda)S_2(c).$$

Aggregate welfare is equal to

$$(1 - \lambda)S_2(c).$$

With tie-ins, the manufacturer prefers to sell to both types, as

$$S_1(p) + (p - c)D(p) > (1 - \lambda)S_2(c),$$

where p is the optimal price computed in the text ($p = \frac{7}{6}$); welfare is equal to

$$\lambda S_1(p) + (1 - \lambda)S_2(p) + (p - c)D(p) > (1 - \lambda)S_2(c),$$

as $S_2(p) > S_1(p)$.

Exercise 3.6[70]

Chicken Delight claimed that the tie was motivated by quality-control considerations. However, it was not tying the purchase of chicken, a more likely target of quality control; furthermore, repeat sales mattered a lot to franchisees, so their incentive to buy leaky buckets was weak.

Suppose that a franchisee can serve either of two types of geographical area. The first type is composed of consumers of single dinners with a fairly high reservation price; the second type is composed of families purchasing bulk orders and having a lower reservation price (because home meal preparation is more common). Chicken Delight may have wanted to extract the extra profit

---

70. Here we follow the analysis of Klein and Saft (1984).

from franchisees serving the first type of area. (It could, alternatively, have imposed franchise fees tailored to the geographical site, but such "discrimination" between retailers is often considered illegal.) Chicken Delight could have used the relative price of buckets and kits to price-discriminate.

In favor of the price-discrimination hypothesis, note that "single dinners were, on a per piece of chicken basis, priced higher than bucket sales" and that "the implied royalty payment of a typical Chicken Delight store selling mostly chicken dinners was significantly higher than a typical store selling mostly bulk orders" (Klein and Saft 1984, p. 11).

Exercise 3.7

(i) Define

$\theta \equiv -t$,

$V(q, \theta) \equiv [1 - (1 - q)^2]/2 + \theta q$,

$\frac{\partial V}{\partial \theta} = q > 0$,

$\frac{\partial^2 V}{\partial \theta \partial q} = 1 > 0$,

and

$\frac{\partial V}{\partial q} = 1 - q + \theta$.

Also define $F(\theta) \equiv 1 - G(-\theta)$ and $f(\theta) = g(-\theta)$ for θ in $(-\infty, 0]$.

(ii) $p(q) = 1 - q + \theta$ results from consumer optimization. Furthermore, equation 3.14' yields

$$p(q) = c + \frac{1 - F(\theta)}{f(\theta)}.$$

(iii) Using the previous two equations and the specific functional form, we obtain

$p(q) = 1 - q - t$,

$p(q) = c + t/\alpha$.

Eliminating t yields

$$p(q) = \left(\frac{\alpha}{1 + \alpha}\right) c + \left(\frac{1}{1 + \alpha}\right)(1 - q).$$

Thus, $p(q)$ is decreasing in q.

Exercise 3.8

(i) The efficient quantity for high-demand consumers is $q = 2$, because the marginal utility of the second unit is

$\theta_2(V(2) - V(1)) = \frac{3}{2} > c = \frac{3}{4}$.

That for low-demand consumers is $q = 1$ (the second unit actually yields a zero social surplus). Pure commodity bundling involves offering only the two-unit package at price $\theta_2 V(2) = \frac{7}{2}$. This yields a profit equal to

$(1 - \lambda)(\frac{7}{2} - \frac{3}{2}) = 2(1 - \lambda)$.

To serve both consumers, the monopolist charges $T(1) = \theta_1 V(1) = 1$ and $T(2)$ so as to satisfy

$\theta_2 V(2) - T(2) = \theta_2 V(1) - T(1)$.

Thus, $T(2) = \frac{5}{2}$. Total profit is

$\lambda(1 - \frac{3}{4}) + (1 - \lambda)(\frac{5}{2} - \frac{3}{2}) = \lambda/4 + (1 - \lambda)$.

Hence, pure commodity bundling is preferred to mixed commodity bundling if and only if

$2(1 - \lambda) \geqslant \lambda/4 + (1 - \lambda)$,

or $\frac{4}{5} > \lambda$.

(ii) If the monopolist chooses the size-2 technology, he obtains $2(1 - \lambda)$ (unless he charges a low price so as to serve the low-demand consumers, but this policy, which yields $\frac{1}{4}$, is easily seen not to affect our result). If the monopolist chooses the size-1 technology, he has the choice between four prices p per unit, which are the four marginal utilities of units (two per type of buyer). If $p = 1$, the profit is

$\lambda(1 - \frac{3}{4}) + (1 - \lambda)(2 - \frac{3}{2}) = \lambda/4 + (1 - \lambda)/2$.

If $p = \frac{3}{4}$, the low-demand buyers buy two units, but, as $p = c$, the monopolist makes no profit. If $p = 2$, only the high-valuation buyer buys, and still just one unit. The profit is

$(1 - \lambda)(2 - \frac{3}{4}) = 5(1 - \lambda)/4$,

which is clearly dominated by the profit for a size-2 package. If $p = \frac{3}{2}$, only the high-valuation consumers buy, and they buy two units. The profit is

$(1 - \lambda)(3 - \frac{3}{2}) = 3(1 - \lambda)/2$,

which is also dominated. Hence, the size-2 technology is chosen if and only if

$2(1 - \lambda) > \lambda/4 + (1 - \lambda)/2,$

or $\frac{6}{7} > \lambda$.

Exercise 3.10

By selling film 1 separately, the monopolist gets $\max(4, 2 \times 3) = 6$. By selling film 2 separately, he gets $\max(2, 2 \times 1) = 4$. Thus, the total profit is 8. By bundling the two, he gets $2 \times 5 = 10$, because the total willingness to pay for each unit is equal to 5.

References

Adams, W., and J. Yellen. 1976. Commodity Bundling and the Burden of Monopoly. *Quarterly Journal of Economics* 90: 475–498.

Axell, B. 1977. Search Market Equilibrium. *Scandinavian Journal of Economics* 79: 20–40.

Baron, D., and R. Myerson. 1982. Regulating a Monopolist with Unknown Costs. *Econometrica* 50: 911–930.

Bénabou, R. 1986. Optimal Price Dynamics: Speculation and Search under Inflation. Ph.D. thesis, Massachusetts Institute of Technology.

Blackstone, E. 1975. Restrictive Practices in the Marketing of Electrofax Copying Machines and Supplies: The SCM Corporation Case. *Journal of Industrial Economics* 23: 189–202.

Borch, K. 1968. *The Economics of Uncertainty*. Princeton University Press.

Borenstein, S. 1985. Price Discrimination in Free-Entry Markets. *Rand Journal of Economics* 16: 380–397.

Bowman, W. 1957. Tying Arrangements and the Leverage Problem. *Yale Law Journal* 67: 19–36.

Brown, S., and D. Sibley. 1986. *The Theory of Public Utility Pricing*. Cambridge University Press.

Burdett, K., and K. Judd. 1983. Equilibrium Price Dispersion. *Econometrica* 51: 955–990.

Burstein, M. 1960a. The Economics of Tie-in Sales. *Review of Economics and Statistics* 42: 68–73.

Burstein, M. 1960b. A Theory of Full-Line Forcing. *Northwestern University Law Review* 55: 62–95.

Butters, G. 1977. Equilibrium Distributions of Sales and Advertising Prices. *Review of Economic Studies* 44: 465–491.

Chae, S. 1987. Subscription Television. Mimeo, Rice University.

Champsaur, P., and J.-C. Rochet. 1986. Multiproduct Duopolists. Mimeo, ENSAE.

Chiang, R., and C. Spatt. 1982. Imperfect Price Discrimination and Welfare. *Review of Economic Studies* 49: 155–181.

Crandall, R. 1968. The Decline of the Franchised Dealer in the Automobile Repair Market. *Journal of Business* 43: 19–30.

Debreu, G. 1959. *The Theory of Value*. New York: Wiley.

Diamond, P. 1971. A Model of Price Adjustment. *Journal of Economic Theory* 3: 156–168.

Diamond, P. 1987. Consumer Differences and Prices in a Search Model. *Quarterly Journal of Economics* 102: 429–436.

Dupuit, J. 1849. On Tolls and Transport Charges. Translated in *International Economic Papers* (London: Macmillan, 1952); original version in *Annales des Ponts et Chaussées* 17.

Ekelund, R. 1970. Price Discrimination and Product Differentiation in Economic Theory: An Early Analysis. *Quarterly Journal of Economics* 84: 268–278.

Engers, M. 1987. Signalling with Many Signals. *Econometrica* 55: 663–674.

Goldman, M., H. Leland, and D. Sibley. 1984. Optimal Nonuniform Pricing. *Review of Economic Studies* 51: 305–320.

Guesnerie, R., and J.-J. Laffont. 1984. A Complete Solution to a Class of Principal-Agent Problems with an Application to the Control of a Self-Managed Firm. *Journal of Public Economics* 25: 329–369.

Hausman, J., and J. Mackie-Mason. 1986. Price Discrimination and Patent Policy. Working paper, University of Michigan.

Joskow, P. 1985. Mixing Regulatory and Antitrust Policies in the Electric Power Industry: The Price Squeeze and Retail Market Competition. In *Antitrust and Regulation: Essays in Memory of John J. McGowan*, ed. F. Fisher. Cambridge, Mass.: MIT Press.

Katz, M. 1983. Nonuniform Pricing, Output and Welfare under Monopoly. *Review of Economic Studies* 50: 37–56.

Katz, M. 1984a. Firm-Specific Differentiation and Competition among Multiproduct Firms. *Journal of Business* 57: 149.

Katz, M. 1984b. Price Discrimination and Monopolistic Competition. *Econometrica* 52: 1453–1471.

Katz, M. 1987. The Welfare Effects of Third Degree Price Discrimination in Intermediate Goods Markets. *American Economic Review* 77: 154–167.

Kohllepel, L. 1983. Multidimensional "Market Signalling." Mimeo, Universität Bonn.

Klein, B., and L. Saft. 1984. Tie-in Contracts as Franchising Quality Control Mechanisms. Mimeo, University of California, Los Angeles.

Laffont, J., and J. Tirole. 1986. Using Cost Observation to Regulate Firms. *Journal of Political Economy* 94: 614–641.

Laffont, J.-J., E. Maskin, and J.-C. Rochet. 1982. Optimal Nonlinear Pricing with Two-Dimensional Characteristics. Mimeo.

Lewbel, A. 1985. Bundling of Substitutes or Complements. *International Journal of Industrial Organization* 3: 101–108.

McAffee, P., J. McMillan, and M. Whinston. 1987. Multiproduct Monopoly, Commodity Bundling and Correlation of Values. Discussion Paper 1296, HIER, Harvard University.

Maskin, E., and J. Riley. 1980. Auctioning an Indivisible Object. Working Paper 87D, Kennedy School of Government, Harvard University.

Maskin, E., and J. Riley. 1984. Monopoly with Incomplete Information. *Rand Journal of Economics* 15: 171–196.

Matthews, S., and J. Moore. 1987. Monopoly Provision of Quality and Warranties: An Exploration in the Theory of Multidimensional Screening. *Econometrica* 55: 441–468.

Milgrom, P., and R. Weber. 1982. A Theory of Auctions and Competitive Bidding. *Econometrica* 50: 1089–1122.

Mirman, L., and D. Sibley. 1980. Optimal Nonlinear Prices for Multiproduct Monopolies. *Bell Journal of Economics* 11: 659–670.

Mirrlees, J. 1971. An Exploration in the Theory of Optimum Income Taxation. *Review of Economic Studies* 38: 175–208.

Mussa, M., and S. Rosen. 1978. Monopoly and Product Quality. *Journal of Economic Theory* 18: 301–317.

Myerson, R. 1979. Optimal Auction Design. *Mathematics of Operations Research* 6: 58–73.

Oi, W. Y. 1971. A Disneyland Dilemma: Two-Part Tariffs for a Mickey Mouse Monopoly. *Quarterly Journal of Economics* 85: 77–90.

O'Keefe, M. 1981. Quality and Price Discrimination. Ph.D. thesis, Harvard University.

Ordover, J., and J. Panzar. 1980. On the Nonexistence of Pareto Superior Outlay Schedules. *Bell Journal of Economics* 11: 351–354.

Oren, S., S. Smith, and R. Wilson. 1982. Linear Tariffs with Quality Discrimination. *Bell Journal of Economics* 13: 455–471.

Oren, S., S. Smith, and R. Wilson. 1983. Competitive Nonlinear Tariffs. *Journal of Economic Theory* 29: 49–71.

Oren, S., S. Smith, and R. Wilson. 1984. Pricing a Product Line. *Journal of Business* 57, no. 1: S73–S100.

Oren, S., S. Smith, and R. Wilson. 1985. Capacity Pricing. *Econometrica* 53: 545–566.

Panzar, J., and D. Sibley. 1978. Public Utility Pricing under Risk: The Case of Self Rationing. *American Economic Review* 68: 888–895.

Perry, M. 1978. Price Discrimination and Forward Integration. *Bell Journal of Economics* 9: 209–217.

Phlips, L. 1983. *The Economics of Price Discrimination.* Cambridge University Press.

Pigou, A. C. 1920. *The Economics of Welfare*, fourth edition. London: Macmillan.

Png, I., and J. Hirshleifer. 1987. Price Discrimination through Offers to Match Price. *Journal of Business* 60: 365–384.

Posner, R. 1976. *The Robinson-Patman Act: Federal Regulation of Price Differences.* City: American Enterprice Institute.

Quinzii, M., and J.-C. Rochet. 1985. Multidimensional Signalling. *Journal of Mathematical Economics* 14: 261–284.

Reinganum, J. 1979. A Simple Model of Equilibrium Price. *Journal of Political Economy* 87: 851–858.

Reitman, D. 1986. Competition in Congested Markets. Ph.D. dissertation, Graduate School of Business, Stanford University.

Riley, J., and W. Samuelson. 1981. Optimal Auctions. *American Economic Review* 71: 381–392.

Rob, R. 1985. Equilibrium Price Distributions. *Review of Economic Studies* 52: 487–504.

Roberts, K. 1979. Welfare Implications of Nonlinear Prices. *Economic Journal* 89: 66–83.

Robinson, J. 1933. *Economics of Imperfect Competition*. London: Macmillan.

Rosenthal, R. 1980. A Model in which Increase in the Number of Sellers Leads to a Higher Price. *Econometrica* 40: 1575–1579.

Rothschild, M., and J. Stiglitz. 1976. Equilibrium in Competitive Insurance Markets: An Essay on the Economics of Imperfect Information. *Quarterly Journal of Economics* 90: 629–650.

Salop, S. 1977. The Noisy Monopolist: Imperfect Information, Price Dispersion, and Price Discrimination. *Review of Economic Studies* 44: 393–406.

Salop, S., and J. Stiglitz. 1982. A Theory of Sales: A Simple Model of Equilibrium Price Dispersion with Identical Agents. *American Economic Review* 72: 1121–1130.

Sappington, D. 1982. Optimal Regulation of Research and Development under Imperfect Information. *Bell Journal of Economics* 13: 354–368.

Schmalensee, R. 1981. Output and Welfare Implications of Monopolistic Third-Degree Price Discrimination. *American Economic Review* 71: 242–247.

Schmalensee, R. 1982a. Monopolistic Two-Part Pricing Arrangements. *Bell Journal of Economics* 12: 445–466.

Schmalensee, R. 1982b. Commodity Bundling by a Single Product Monopolist. *Journal of Law and Economics* 25: 67–71.

Schmalensee, R. 1984. Gaussian Demand and Commodity Bundling. *Journal of Business* 57: S211–S230.

Seade, J. 1977. On the Shape of Optimal Tax Schedules. *Journal of Public Economics* 7: 203–235.

Shilony, Y. 1977. Mixed Pricing in Oligopoly. *Journal of Economic Theory* 14: 373–388.

Spence, A. 1977. Nonlinear Prices and Welfare. *Journal of Public Economics* 8: 1–18.

Spulber, D. 1981. Spatial Nonlinear Pricing. *American Economic Review* 71: 923–933.

Stigler, G. 1963. A Note on Block Booking. *Supreme Court Review*. Reprinted in *The Organization of Industry* (University of Chicago Press, 1983).

Stiglitz, J. 1977. Monopoly, Nonlinear Pricing, and Imperfect Information: The Insurance Market. *Review of Economic Studies* 44: 407–430.

Stiglitz, J. 1985. Competitivity and the Number of Firms in a Market: Are Duopolies More Competitive than Atomistic Markets? Technical Report 478, IMSSS, Stanford University.

Telser, L. 1979. A Theory of Monopoly of Complementary Goods. *Journal of Business* 52: 211–230.

Thisse, J.-F., and X. Vives. 1986. On the Strategic Choice of Spatial Price Policy. Mimeo, University of Pennsylvania.

Varian, H. 1980. A Model of Sales. *American Economic Review* 70, 651–659.

Varian, H. 1985. Price Discrimination and Social Welfare. *American Economic Review* 75: 870–875.

Varian, H. 1987. Price Discrimination. In *Handbook of Industrial Organization*, ed. R. Schmalensee and R. Willig (Amsterdam: North-Holland, forthcoming).

von zur Muehlen, P. 1980. Monopolistic Competition and Sequential Search. *Journal of Economic Dynamics and Control* 2: 257–281.

Willig, R. 1978. Pareto-Superior Nonlinear Outlay Schedule. *Bell Journal of Economics* 9: 56–69.

Wilson, C. 1977. A Model of Insurance Markets with Incomplete Information. *Journal of Economic Theory* 16: 167–207.

Wilson, R. 1985. Economic Theories of Price Discrimination and Product Differentiation: A Survey. Parts I, II, III. Mimeo, Graduate School of Business, Stanford University.

Wilson, R. 1986. Efficient and Competitive Rationing via Priority Service. Mimeo, Graduate School of Business, Stanford University.

Vertical Control

In chapters 1 through 3 we assumed that the firm under discussion supplied final consumers directly, and we focused on monopoly pricing and product selection. We will now study the relationships between an "upstream firm" possessing monopoly power in an intermediate-good market and the users of that good: the "downstream firms." In these situations, the monopolist does not supply the final users himself. Examples of downstream firms include manufacturing or service companies using an intermediate input, wholesalers, and retailers (in the latter two cases, the final good is often close or identical to the intermediate one). Because downstream firms are customers of the upstream firms, many of the features studied previously are also relevant to the study of vertical relationships. For instance, the upstream firm may want to discriminate among the downstream firms, either with regard to the sectors or areas they serve or with regard to their cost structures.

However, vertical relationships among firms are often much richer and more complex than those between a firm and its consumers. Ordinary consumers often just consume the good, but industrial consumers (downstream firms) transform the good and/or market it. In other words, some further decisions (technological use, determination of final price, promotional effort, and so forth) are made after the intermediate good is sold by the upstream firm. Because these decisions affect its profit, the upstream firm has an incentive to control them. Beyond the pricing policy and the product specification for its good, it will exert further vertical control on downstream operations to the extent that such control is feasible. For instance, it may fix the final (retail) price for the good, delineate the area of distribution of each retailer, or impose tie-in purchases of other goods.

Vertical control was touched on in the chapter on the theory of the firm. In this chapter, we abstract from the issues of transaction costs, incomplete contracts, and ownership, and other issues that are crucial even in a world of perfect product-market competition. We focus on the monopoly reasons for vertical control; that is, on the factors that create an incentive for vertical control only when the market for the intermediate good is noncompetitive.

A school of thought sometimes associated with the University of Chicago holds that there is no monopoly reason for vertical control, and that observed vertical controls are meant only to improve the efficiency of real-world vertical relationships and not to exercise monopoly power on the intermediate-good market. A firm that has monopoly power in its market, so runs the argument in its simplest form, can always exhaust this monopoly power by raising the linear price it charges its customers. Hence, vertical control is purely an internal, welfare-enhancing matter within the vertical structure (i.e., it does not hurt third parties, such as consumers). We will consider the validity of this argument below.

To conform to the industrial-organization tradition, we will say that the upstream firm is vertically integrated if it controls (directly or indirectly) all the decisions made by the vertical structure. The "vertically integrated profit" is the maximum aggregate (manufacturer's plus retailers') profit that the vertical structure can obtain—that is, the aggregate profit that the structure would get if all the decision variables were costless to observe, verify, and specify in the contract. The vertically integrated solution is a particularly useful benchmark because it demonstrates which decisions the monopolist would like the downstream firm to make concerning matters he cannot directly control. Readers who have skipped the chapter on the theory of the firm are warned that the term *vertical integration* as used in this chapter may be misleading. On the one hand, a monopolist who absorbs the downstream firms (the usual meaning of vertical integration) may not be able to exert total control over these firms (because decisions must be delegated within a vertical structure, be it integrated or not). On the other hand, full vertical control may sometimes be achieved in the absence of vertical integration through adequate contracts specifying "vertical restraints," as we will see below.

The chapter proceeds as follows. Section 4.1 defines a basic vertical framework, which is used to introduce the most commonly observed vertical restraints. Section 4.2

then presents the control problem. The need for control is traced to the existence of externalities between downstream firms and the upstream firms, or among downstream firms themselves. (The use of vertical control to implement price discrimination has been studied in chapter 3, and will not be developed here.) The emphasis here is on the way vertical restraints are used to cope with these externalities.[1] Sections 4.3 and 4.4 deal with intra-brand and inter-brand competition. The supplementary section treats the effect of uncertainty on vertical relationships and the virtues of downstream competition in promoting economic efficiency and offers a more general analysis of market foreclosure.

4.1 Linear Prices versus Vertical Restraints

Much of economic theory is concerned with the case of linear prices, in which the buyer pays the seller an amount proportional to the quantity bought. Vertical relationships, however, often involve more complex contracting arrangements, broadly named *vertical restraints*. They range from simple nonlinear prices (for example, the imposition of franchise fees, as considered in chapter 3) to instruments that restrict intra-brand or inter-brand competition (such as exclusive territories and exclusive dealing). To introduce some common vertical restraints in a natural way, we start with a basic model, which we enrich progressively.

4.1.1 Basic Framework

A single supplier, called the *monopolist* or the *manufacturer*, produces an intermediate good at a constant unit cost, c. He is the only producer of this good, and he sells it to a single downstream firm, called the *retailer*. (The downstream firm could equally well be a wholesaler or an industrial user of the intermediate good.) The retailer resells the product; for simplicity, he has no retailing cost. Formally, after signing the contract, the retailer has a monopoly on a technology that transforms one unit of the intermediate good into one unit of the final good. p_w denotes the wholesale (intermediate) price and p the consumer (or retail or final) price. q denotes the quan-

---

1. Sections 4.1 and 4.2 draw from Rey and Tirole 1986a. Blair and Kaserman (1983) and Caves (1984) survey a different selection of topics.

tity bought by the retailer; it also denotes the final consumption if the retailer does not throw away any of the intermediate good. The consumers' downward-sloping demand function is denoted $q = D(p)$. (We will later assume that demand also depends on a promotional service s exerted by the retailer: $q = D(p, s)$.)

Some of the most common forms of contracting between manufacturers and retailers are defined as follows:

A *linear price* is a contract specifying only a payment, $T(q) = p_w q$, from the retailer to the manufacturer. q is the retailer's choice (see figure 4.1).

A *franchise fee*, A, gives rise to the simplest example of a nonlinear price (or payment function). The retailer then pays $T(q) = A + p_w q$. As in chapter 3, the manufacturer may more generally be able to charge a more complicated (fully nonlinear, i.e. non-affine) payment.

Resale-price maintenance (RPM) is a provision in the contract dictating the choice of the final price, p, to the retailer. Variants of this restraint are a price ceiling ($p \leqslant \overline{p}$) and a price floor ($p \geqslant \underline{p}$). (RPM is thus a price ceiling plus a price floor, such that $\underline{p} = \overline{p}$.)

Quantity fixing specifies the amount, q, to be bought by the retailer. Variants of this restraint are quantity forcing ($q \geqslant \underline{q}$) and quantity rationing ($q \leqslant \overline{q}$). If demand is known and depends on the final price only, and if the retailer cannot throw the good away, quantity forcing is equivalent to a price ceiling and quantity rationing to a price floor (and quantity fixing to RPM).

Why have industrial-organization theorists focused on such primitive restraints, and when can these restraints be imposed? The most obvious cause of the focus is that these restraints are simple and commonly used. But also, they may not be as primitive as they look in the environments in which they have been studied.

Consider first a deterministic environment (see section 4.2 for more details). The manufacturer's concern is to ensure that the retailer picks the "right actions" (for instance, final price or promotional effort)—which, because of the absence of uncertainty, are known. The retailer's decision is, as we will see, generally dictated by the marginal price he pays for the intermediate good. In a deterministic environment, however, the amount of

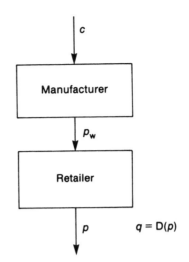

Figure 4.1

the intermediate good consumed—and, thus, its marginal price—can be foreseen perfectly. Thus, there is no loss in adopting a two-part tariff (i.e., a franchise fee plus a fixed marginal price)—at least, there is no loss if the retailer's objective function is concave—so there is no point in considering more complex nonlinear prices. This vindicates the focus on franchise fees.

The above justification of two-part tariffs does not hold in a stochastic, asymmetric information environment. As is well known in regard to adverse selection[2] and moral hazard,[3] a constant marginal price is not generally desirable. Thus, the manufacturer may wish to use more complex nonlinear prices. However, arbitrage may prevent him from doing so (see chapter 3). Although it is easy to control the quantity bought directly by the retailer, it is much harder to observe the quantity he actually sells. Consequently, if there are several retailers (e.g., in different geographical markets), some retailers may engage in "bootlegging" to other retailers, thereby preventing total price discrimination by the monopolist. The conventional result is that, with many arbitraging buyers, the upstream unit can only charge linear prices. In the present context, however, the manufacturer is generally assumed to observe whether the retailer carries his product; thus, he can demand the payment of a franchise fee (as long as the courts confirm this right). Thus, two-part tariffs may be used despite arbitrage.

2. See chapter 3 of the present book. See Baron and Myerson 1982, Sappington 1982, and Laffont and Tirole 1986 for examples in a regulatory context.

3. See, e.g., Holmström 1979, Shavell 1979, and Grossman and Hart 1983.

This brings us to a seemingly trivial but actually important point: The set of vertical restraints that can be used in practice depends on the informational environment—i.e., on what can be observed and enforced by the manufacturer. (If the enforcement mechanism is associated with the legal system, the courts must also be able to verify the manufacturer's information.) Thus, for example, RPM is not possible if the retailer can give hidden discounts to his customers.[4] Similarly, quantity fixing is essentially meaningless in an environment in which the retailers engage in arbitrage.

4.1.2 Intrabrand Competition

Let us now introduce the possibility of competition among several retailers on the same market. The new type of restraint that can be used by the manufacturer is that of *exclusive territories*, which divides the final market among the retailers (figure 4.2). (A similar restraint is a limit on the density of retailers.)

Territories can be understood in a spatial sense, but also (more broadly) in a market-segmentation sense (for instance, public versus private markets). The informational requirements for such a restraint to be feasible are strong. For example, in the spatial interpretation of the model, the manufacturer must be able to trace customers[5] and to prove (in case of cheating) that the retailer was aware of their place of origin (or, if he was not cheating, that he was negligent in not obtaining that information). Thus, exclusive territories are more commonly used when the downstream units are wholesalers. However, note that the allocation of a retail monopoly situation (in an isolated territory) serves the purpose of exclusive territories. A similar remark can be made about refusals to deal.

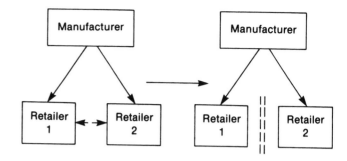

Figure 4.2
Exclusive territories.

4.1.3 Several Inputs

Let us assume that the downstream unit uses several inputs to produce the final good. Here, the downstream unit can be a producer. It can also be a retailer who sells complementary products to the customer. A new restraint specific to this feature is a *tie-in*, in which one of the input suppliers forces the downstream unit to purchase the other inputs from him. (To be precise, we should distinguish between "bundling," which fixes the quantities of other inputs per unit of manufacturer input, and "requirements contracting," in which the manufacturer simply requires that the retailer buy the other inputs from him. The distinction matters under uncertainty.) And intermediate products are thus tied. In particular, he can charge prices for the other inputs that differ from their market prices.[6]

The manufacturer can use another instrument if the retailer's level of sales is observable and verifiable: He can impose a payment, called a *royalty*, proportional to the number of units sold downstream.[7]

---

4. Discounts may affect nonmonetary (less observable) dimensions of exchange between retailers and customers, as well. For instance, they can take the form of extra services or free delivery. Also, even if discounts can be observed by the manufacturer, such price controls may be prohibitively costly. Suppose that one of the roles of the retailers is to analyze customers so as to price-discriminate among them. (The manufacturer knows only the distribution of tastes in the population of customers.) A full control of the retailer's pricing policy then requires knowing *ex post* the *whole* distribution of prices that he charged, which is very costly for the manufacturer or a court to assess. (In other words, monitoring costs cannot be saved by inspecting randomly.)

5. Methods that can be employed to do so include the use of private investigators and the existence of warranty cards or discount coupons that must be sent

back to the manufacturer with the customer's address written in. The same methods may be used to enforce RPM.

6. Making a product incompatible with complementary products manufactured by other firms (but not with one's own complementary products, of course) is similar to a tie-in.

7. A royalty could be imposed in the single-input case. However, this instrument is redundant with the wholesale price if, as we have assumed here, one unit of input is transformed into one unit of output. If p_w and r denote the wholesale price and the royalty rate, the effective marginal cost for the retailer is $p_w + r$. Hence, anything that can be done with a royalty rate can also be done without a royalty but with a higher wholesale price. In general, nonlinear royalty payments are superior to linear ones, as was suggested in chapter 3.

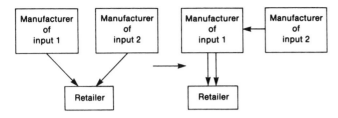

Figure 4.3
Example of a tie-in.

4.1.4 Interbrand Competition

The retailer may sell goods that are close substitutes for the good supplied by the manufacturer. The manufacturer may then impose *exclusive dealing* on the retailer, which prevents him from selling goods that compete directly with the manufacturer's product.[8]

This does not exhaust the list of possible contractual provisions between manufacturer and retailer, which are often dependent on the environment. For instance, if the manufacturer is in charge of national advertising for the product, the contract may include a provision concerning the expenses of the advertising.

4.1.5 Legal Status of Restraints

A few words about the always-changing legal status of these restraints in the United States are necessary. Roughly, franchise fees are legal; indeed, their legality might lead one to reserve the term *vertical restraint* for other restraints. RPM is currently illegal *per se*. Exclusive territories, after having been forbidden *per se*, are now judged according to a rule of reason. Tie-ins are, in principle, illegal *per se*, but their actual status is closer to being determined by a rule of reason.

4.2 Externalities and Vertical Control

4.2.1 Methodology

The vertical structure, as a whole, determines a number of (possibly dependent) decision variables: wholesale price, franchise fee, quantity purchased by the retailer, consumer price, promotional effort, retail location, and so forth. In practice, only a few of these variables are observable and verifiable (in the sense of section 4.1); these variables are called *instruments*. They can serve as the basis for the monetary transfers in the contract between the manufacturer and the retailer(s). Next we define targets. To this purpose, let us call the sum of the manufacturer's and the retailers' profits the *aggregate profit*. The *targets* form another subset of decision variables, which are those directly affecting the aggregate profit. The promotional effort and the retail price are targets. The franchise fee and the wholesale price are not targets, because they do not *directly* affect the aggregate profit.[9] The control problem consists in knowing how to use the instruments to reach, or come close to, the desired values of the targets —that is, the values that maximize the vertical structure's aggregate (vertically integrated) profit. The literature actually often looks at situations where there are "enough" instruments to obtain the vertically integrated profit; Mathewson and Winter (1984, 1986) say that the set of instruments is then *sufficient*.

In what follows we will, for simplicity, assume that the manufacturer chooses the contract. The retailers accept the contract only if it guarantees them at least what they would get by refusing it. We normalize this "outside opportunity" to be zero; thus the retailers accept the contract only if it gives them a non-negative profit. The assumption that the manufacturer chooses the contract makes sense when there exists a competitive supply of potential retailers.[10]

---

8. Another (and a very different) degree of freedom concerning interbrand competition is the length of contracts, or the level of penalties for breach of contract. See the supplementary section.

9. They directly affect only "internal" transfers. They may indirectly affect targets through incentives, but this is irrelevant to the present classification.

10. Furthermore, this assumption is innocuous as long as the contract can specify a franchise fee and there is no uncertainty. To see this, define a "constrained efficient contract" as a contract that maximizes the aggregate profit subject to the incentive constraints (decentralization of those decision variables that are targets, but not of instruments). In other words, a "constrained efficient contract" yields the maximum feasible aggregate profit (which, if the set of

instruments is sufficient, coincides with the vertically integrated profit). The bargaining between the manufacturer and the retailers over the contract can then be decomposed into two steps: the design of a constrained efficient contract (which yields the greatest possible "pie") and the division of the pie through the franchise fee. Because the franchise fee is a lump-sum transfer, it does not interact with the determination of the targets. Thus, even if we have little information about the parties' relative bargaining power (which determines the franchise fee), we can characterize the optimal contract (up to the franchise component). In the absence of franchise fees, the maximum feasible aggregate profit may not be reached, and the complete outcome (and not only the division of profits) is, in general, sensitive to the parties' bargaining power.

4.2.2   The Basic Vertical Externality

In chapter 1 we saw that under linear pricing a monopolist charges a price above marginal cost. Doing so allows him to realize a positive profit margin (at the expense of a contraction in demand). Similarly, in the context of a vertical structure, the monopoly producer of an intermediate good who uses linear pricing charges $p_w > c$. The retailers then face a marginal cost for their input (the intermediate good) equal to p_w, and they make their pricing, promotional, and technological decisions on this basis. The vertical externality is that any decision made by a retailer that increases his demand for the intermediate good by one unit generates an incremental profit of $p_w - c$ for the manufacturer. However, the retailer, who maximizes his own profit, does not take the manufacturer's incremental profit into account, and therefore tends to make decisions that lead to too low a consumption of intermediate good. The problem is that the retailer's cost (p_w) for the good differs from the vertical structure's (c). The aggregate profit is then lower than the vertically integrated one, which gives the manufacturer an incentive to impose vertical restraints that eliminate this externality.

Three famous illustrations of this basic externality in the simple manufacturer-and-retailer context deal with the downstream unit's choice of price, promotional effort, and production technology respectively.

Example 1:   Double Marginalization (Spengler 1950)

Suppose that the retailer's only decision (and, therefore, the vertical structure's only target) is the retail price. The vertically integrated quantity q^m and retail price p^m are determined by

$$q^m = D(p^m),$$

and p^m maximizes $(p - c)D(p)$, where $D(\cdot)$ is the demand curve.

Consider the decentralized structure and the retailer's choice of the consumer price p under a linear wholesale tariff $T(q) = p_w q$. Assume that the manufacturer chooses the linear tariff first and the retailer chooses the consumer price second, and that the retailer is himself a monopolist in his retail market.

The retailer maximizes his own profit, $(p - p_w)D(p)$. In chapter 1 we saw that the monopoly price is an increasing

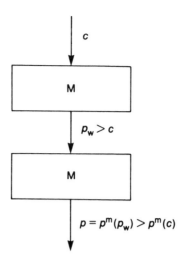

Figure 4.4
Double marginalization.

function of marginal cost. Because the retailer is a monopolist and because his marginal cost is equal to p_w, we have $p > p^m$ as long as the manufacturer charges above the marginal cost ($p_w > c$). The retail price is higher in the decentralized structure than in the integrated one, because of two successive mark-ups (marginalizations). As mentioned earlier, the externality arises because the retailer does not take the manufacturer's marginal profit, $(p_w - c)D'(p)$, into account when choosing a retail price.

To see this, assume that the final-demand function is $D(p) = 1 - p$ and that $c < 1$. Let Π_m and Π_r denote the manufacturer's and the retailer's profits. First determine the equilibrium for the nonintegrated industry. The retailer solves

$$\max_p [(p - p_w)(1 - p)],$$

from which it follows that

$$p = \frac{1 + p_w}{2}.$$

Then, the demand for the final good (and, therefore, that for the intermediate good) is

$$q = \frac{1 - p_w}{2},$$

and the retailer's profit is

$$\Pi_r = \left(\frac{1 - p_w}{2}\right)^2.$$

The manufacturer solves

$$\max_{p_w} \left[(p_w - c)\left(\frac{1 - p_w}{2}\right) \right],$$

from which it follows that

$$p_w = \frac{1 + c}{2}.$$

Notice that

$$\Pi^{ni} = \Pi_m + \Pi_r = \frac{(1 - c)^2}{8} + \frac{(1 - c)^2}{16} = \tfrac{3}{16}(1 - c)^2$$

and that

$$p = \frac{3 + c}{4}.$$

Now consider the integrated industry, which pays c per unit for its input. It maximizes

$$\max_p [(p - c)(1 - p)],$$

from which it follows that

$$p = \frac{1 + c}{2}.$$

Then the total profit is

$$\Pi^i = \frac{(1 - c)^2}{4} > \Pi^{ni}.$$

Therefore, the integrated industry makes more profit than the nonintegrated industry, and the consumer price is lower in the case of the integrated industry. These two properties are very general, as we have seen. The objective of vertical integration is to avoid the double price distortion that occurs when each firm adds its own price-cost margin at each stage of production. ("What is worse than a monopoly? A chain of monopolies.")

Exercise 4.1** Show that in the double-marginalization set-up the ratio of the retailer's margin over the manufacturer's margin,

$$\frac{p - p_w}{p_w - c},$$

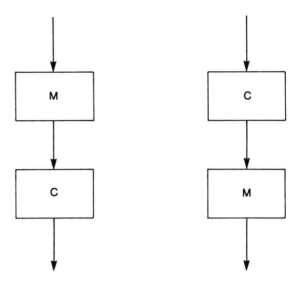

Figure 4.5

is equal to (greater than, lower than) $\frac{1}{2}$ if the demand function is linear (convex, concave).[11] (Hint: Look at the retailer's and the manufacturer's first-order conditions. To obtain the sensitivity of the retail price to the wholesale price, differentiate the retailer's first-order condition; use this first-order condition again to reach the conclusion.)

If (as in figure 4.5) one of the two firms is competitive in the sense that it sells at marginal cost, then vertical integration does not increase the profit of the monopoly firm. The intuition behind this result is that the competitive sector does not introduce a price distortion. Thus, the monopoly sector does not exercise an externality on the competitive sector, whose price-cost margin is zero. (As we will see in example 3, the result does not hold if, for instance, the downstream competitive sector uses several inputs.)

The double-marginalization (or chain-of-monopolies) problem is very similar to that of two monopoly producers of perfectly complementary goods. After all, production and retailing are complements, and consumers often consume both of them in fixed proportions. The following exercise shows, similarly, that the monopoly producers of complementary goods have an incentive to integrate (horizontally) in order to avoid double marginalization and an excessive demand contraction.

11. This exercise follows Bresnahan and Reiss 1985. See that article for a test of the relationship in the case of automobile dealerships.

*Exercise 4.2*** Two firms ($i = 1, 2$) produce one good each, at marginal cost c_i ($i = 1, 2$). Each firm has a monopoly power in the production of its good. The goods are perfect complements. The demand curve is $q = D(p)$, where $p \equiv p_1 + p_2$ is the price of the composite good and p_i is the price of good i ($i = 1, 2$). Let $c \equiv c_1 + c_2$.

(i) Reinterpret the variables to show that the case of a single good produced by a manufacturer and distributed by a retailer fits into this model.

Assume that the elasticity of demand, $\varepsilon = -D'p/D$, is constant in order to simplify computations.

(ii) What is the optimal p for the horizontally integrated structure?

(iii) Consider the nonintegrated structure. Suppose that firm 1 chooses its price first and takes into account the effect of its choice on firm 2's price. Show that the Lerner index is higher than under integration. More precisely, show that

$$p = c/(1 - 1/\varepsilon)^2.$$

(iv) Suppose now that the two firms choose their prices simultaneously. Assume that each firm maximizes its profit given the other firm's price—that is, the choices are simultaneous; a firm does not try to influence the other firm's price (see chapter 5). Show that the Lerner index is even higher than in the case of sequential choice of prices. More precisely, show that

$$p = c/(1 - 2/\varepsilon).$$

Interpret this result. (Hint: Start from the simultaneous-choice equilibrium and change firm 1's price slightly.)

Sufficient Vertical Restraints

Franchise fee The benefit of vertical integration is related to the extreme simplicity of the linear-price contract. Indeed, the manufacturer can realize the integrated profit without integration by using a two-part tariff: $T(q) = A + p_w q$. With a little thought it will be evident which marginal price p_w he ought to choose. Recall that the issue with the linear price is that the downstream unit's marginal cost is not equal to the vertical structure's mar-

ginal cost. To eliminate this distortion, take $p_w = c$. The downstream unit does not affect the upstream unit by its choice of final price, so there is no externality. The retailer maximizes

$$(p - c)D(p) - A$$

and thus chooses

$$p = p^m.$$

His profit is equal to

$$\Pi^m - A,$$

where $\Pi^m = (p^m - c)D(p^m)$. The manufacturer can then appropriate the retailer's profit by imposing a franchise fee equal to the vertical structure's profit ($A = \Pi^m$).

The idea of charging a marginal price equal to the upstream marginal cost in order to avoid downstream distortion—an idea already encountered in chapter 3—is very general. This policy amounts to "selling the vertical structure" (at price A) to the downstream monopolist, who is made the "residual claimant" (the receiver of any marginal profit). The downstream monopolist therefore has all the incentive to make the "right decisions" (here, to choose the monopoly price). The two-part tariff also solves the externalities in promotional effort and input choices considered below.

Drawbacks of franchise fees A franchise fee is a simple and powerful instrument in this environment. However, in more complex environments a franchise fee can also have drawbacks. First, when the retailer is risk-averse and the retail cost or the final demand is random, the retailer—because he claims all the residual profits—bears too much risk. A reduction in the franchise fee, together with an increase in the wholesale price above marginal cost, gives the retailer some insurance and is called for.[12] (See section 4.6 for an analysis of risk sharing.) Second, suppose that at the contracting date the retailer possesses private information about the retail cost or the (local) final demand that the manufacturer does not have. Because the retailer's profit is not known to the manufacturer, it is difficult for him to tailor the franchise fee so as to appropriate the

---

12. If the uncertainty is about final demand, the retailer clearly faces less risk when the wholesale price increases, because his margin per unit sold at a given price decreases with p_w. The reason this is true for retail-cost uncertainty is slightly more subtle. An increase in the wholesale price leads to an increase in

the final price—that is, to a contraction in demand. As total retail cost is equal to unit retail cost times demand, the variability of total retail cost is reduced for a given variability in unit retail cost.

retailer's profit. The manufacturer must then use screening devices similar to those analyzed in chapter 3. By analogy, we can derive the optimal discriminatory policy for the manufacturer: A low-retail-cost or a high-final-demand retailer here corresponds to a high-demand consumer in the theory of price discrimination; hence, the optimal two-part tariff has a wholesale price higher than the marginal cost ($p_w > c$) and a franchise fee equal to the retailer's profit when the demand is low or the retail cost is high.[13] Third, when there are several retailers, a retailer is not in general made the residual claimant for the vertical structure by buying the input at marginal cost. Franchise fees, in general, will not suffice to realize the vertically integrated profit, as we will see later.

Resale-price maintenance Rather than using a franchise fee, the manufacturer can sell the intermediate good at price $p_w = p^m$ and then impose resale-price maintenance at $p = p^m$. The retailer then makes a zero profit, and the vertical structure's aggregate profit (which is equal to the manufacturer's profit) equals Π^m. Hence, RPM is a sufficient instrument here. Actually, a price ceiling ($p \leqslant p^m$) —or, equivalently, quantity forcing ($q \geqslant q^m$)—would also allow the manufacturer to realize the integrated profit. The more commonly encountered version of price maintenance—a price floor—would not allow this (which suggests that there are other explanations for price maintenance than the double-marginalization problem).

Like the franchise system, RPM is not sufficient once one introduces uncertainty. For one thing, its insurance properties are poor when the retailer is risk-averse and faces retail-cost uncertainty; he is not able to pass retail-cost variations into the final price, so he (and not the manufacturer) bears all the risk of such variations.

Welfare The welfare analysis of vertical integration (or, equivalently, of sufficient vertical restraints) is simple. The vertical structure (manufacturer plus retailer) makes more money under vertical integration than under a linear price because it realizes the vertical structure's monopoly profit. Consumers are better off under vertical integration because they face a lower price. Thus, welfare is unambiguously increased by the elimination of the double marginalization. The same conclusion holds for the two additional illustrations of the basic vertical externality considered in examples 2 and 3 below.

Example 2:   Downstream Moral Hazard

Retailers often provide services that make the manufacturer's good more attractive to consumers: trading stamps, free alterations, free delivery, credit, pre-sale information, elaborate premises, excess sales help to keep waiting lines short, and so on. We can gather all these under the heading "promotional effort" or "services." To the extent that promotional effort affects the demand for the good, the manufacturer wants to encourage the retailer to supply it. The simplest way to do so would be to specify the level of promotional services in the contract. But such a contract would generally not be enforceable, as courts (and even the parties) cannot measure such services precisely. Thus, incentives must be given to the retailer to overcome the associated moral-hazard problem.[14]

Promotional services can be formalized as a real number, s. As in chapter 2, s is a parameter measuring the good's position in a vertical product space. The consumers' demand is $q = D(p, s)$ (see section 2.1 for an example of the derivation of such a demand function). D decreases with p and increases with s. Assume that supplying a level s of services costs the retailer $\Phi(s)$ per unit of output, and that this cost can be observed only by the retailer. Φ increases with s. The total service cost is thus $q\,\Phi(s)$.

The vertically integrated consumer price (p^m) and services (s^m) maximize

$$[p - c - \Phi(s)]D(p, s).$$

13. Conversely, if, at the contract date, the manufacturer has private information about the aggregate demand for his product, he charges $p_w = c$ when the demand is "low" and $p_w > c$ when the demand is "high." The intuition is that, to "prove" that demand is high, the manufacturer accepts a cut in the franchise fee in exchange for a higher wholesale price. (The Spence-Mirrlees condition alluded to in chapter 2 says that, because a manufacturer with a high demand is more interested in the variable profit than one facing a low demand, higher demand can be signaled only through a higher wholesale price.) See the "fran-chising game" in the supplementary section of the Game Theory User's Manual (a similar point is made by Gallini and Wright 1987.)

14. Formally, the double-marginalization and input-substitution problems also relate to moral hazard. For an example in which a promotional effort is equivalent to (the opposite of) a second marginalization, see below. Here, we limit the extent of moral hazard to the provision of effort and services.

Let

$$\Pi^{m} = [p^{m} - c - \Phi(s^{m})]D(p^{m}, s^{m}).$$

In the decentralized structure, and for a linear price p_{w}, the profits are

$$(p_{w} - c)D(p, s)$$

for the manufacturer and

$$[p - p_{w} - \Phi(s)]D(p, s)$$

for the retailer. The manufacturer charges price $p_{w} > c$ in order to maximize his profit. The retailer then maximizes his own profit with respect to p and s. The distortion in retail price—the second marginalization—is familiar from example 1. The distortion in services resembles the distortion in retail price: The retailer does not take into account the extra profit for the manufacturer associated with an increase in services,

$$(p_{w} - c)\frac{\partial D}{\partial s}.$$

Again, this is because the manufacturer's mark-up makes the retailer's profit margin smaller than that of the vertical structure. Thus, for any retail price, the retailer provides too few services and so causes the demand to be too small.

The analogy between services and retail prices is not fortuitous. As in chapter 2, it is useful to consider the extreme case in which services are perfect substitutes for price discounts—i.e., $q = D(p - s)$ and $\Phi(s) = s$—and high prices thus correspond to low services. Of course, the interesting and general case arises when services and price discounts are imperfect substitutes.

To encourage more promotional effort and obtain the vertically integrated profit, the manufacturer can (as above) make the retailer a residual claimant by choosing $p_{w} = c$, and can appropriate the retailer's residual profit through a franchise fee of $A = \Pi^{m}$.

RPM alone is no longer sufficient. To realize the vertically integrated profit, the manufacturer should set the retail price at $p = p^{m}$. However, the service externality remains.[15]

*Exercise 4.3*** Show that quantity forcing is a sufficient instrument (i.e., that, together with quantity forcing, a linear price yields the vertically integrated profit).

Bilateral moral hazard arises when the manufacturer provides services that are hard to measure precisely (brand advertising, product quality, and so forth). In such cases the manufacturer generally exerts an externality on the retailer, because his services affect the retailer's demand and profit. This externality would not matter if the retailer's profit margin were zero; however, as we saw, the manufacturer may want to leave the retailer a positive profit margin in order to encourage him to supply promotional services. The vertical structure must then design an incentive scheme that alleviates the moral-hazard problem on both sides. For this purpose, a simple two-part tariff is no longer sufficient. As we saw, to induce the retailer to provide the correct amount of promotional effort, one must make him the residual claimant. The manufacturer's profit margin, $p_{w} - c$, is then zero, which means that the manufacturer has no incentive to expand demand (and, thus, no incentive to supply services). Conversely, if the manufacturer is made a residual claimant, the retailer has no incentive to supply promotional effort; more sophisticated schemes must then be designed. The following exercise shows that both parties can simultaneously be made residual claimants through the use of a third party (Holmström 1982). However, the corresponding scheme is not immune to collusion between the retailer and the manufacturer.

*Exercise 4.4*** Let the demand function be $q = D(p, s, S)$, where S denotes the services offered by the manufacturer. (D increases with S.) To simplify, assume that, to supply S, the manufacturer incurs a cost $\phi(S)$ that is independent of the quantity sold ($\phi' > 0$). Let (p^{m}, s^{m}, S^{m}) maximize the vertically integrated profit,

$$[p - c - \Phi(s)]D(p, s, S) - \phi(S).$$

---

15. In the same way that the manufacturer may try to control the retail price in order to eliminate the price externality, he may try to control services to eliminate the service externality. Direct supervision of the provision of services is often used as a complement of monetary incentives to induce a retailer to provide these services. The manufacturer can then use termination of the contract as a threat against cuts in services. (In order for termination to impose a cost on the retailer, it must be the case that the retailer enjoys a rent from his relationship with the manufacturer, i.e., that he obtains more than his reservation profit. On this, see the chapter on the theory of the firm.)

In the decentralized structure, p and s are chosen by the retailer, and S by the manufacturer. The manufacturer and the retailer can contract jointly with a third party. This third party, called a *marginal source*, is willing to sign any contract that gives him a non-negative profit.

(i) Show that the vertically integrated profit can be realized in the following way: The intermediate good is transferred through the third party. The third party pays the manufacturer according to a linear tariff $T_1(q) = p_w q$, with $p_w \equiv p^m - \Phi(s^m)$, and is paid by the retailer according to a two-part tariff $T_2(q) \equiv A + cq$. How would you choose A?

(ii) Explain the term "marginal source." Is the three-way contract immune to a manufacturer-retailer coalition?

Example 3:   Input Substitution

Now suppose that the downstream unit is an industry that produces the final good from several inputs. To simplify, assume that the downstream unit uses two inputs: the manufacturer's good and a second intermediate good produced competitively at cost (and sold at price) c'. Aside from the final price, the downstream unit must choose inputs x and x' to produce output $q = f(x, x')$. The two inputs are substitutes in the production function. Assume, further, that the technology exhibits constant returns to scale (f is homogeneous of degree 1). The demand function is $q = D(p)$ (we abstract from promotional effort, for simplicity). The vertically integrated profit is

$$\Pi^m = \max_{x, x'} [P(f(x, x'))f(x, x') - cx - c'x'],$$

where $P(\cdot) \equiv D^{-1}(\cdot)$ is the inverse demand function. Let x^m and x'^m denote the optimal inputs.

Consider the decentralized structure in which the manufacturer of the first input x and (for the moment) the downstream industry have monopoly power. See figure 4.6. (Obtaining the basic externality does not require the monopolization of the downstream industry when there are several inputs. The differences introduced by downstream competition will be discussed below.)

Under linear pricing, the monopoly manufacturer charges a wholesale price $p_w > c$, while the competitive manufacturers charge $p'_w = c'$ for the second input. Hence, the relative price of inputs for the downstream unit, $p_w/p'_w = p_w/c'$, exceeds their true relative price, c/c', for the vertical structure. The downstream unit thus substitutes

toward the second input and consumes too little of the manufacturer's intermediate good (Vernon and Graham 1971; Schmalensee 1973; Warren-Boulton 1974). The downstream unit, when substituting toward the second input, does not take the upstream monopolist's marginal profit ($p_w - c$) into account (whereas it does not exert any externality on the second input industry, whose margin is zero).

Of course, the input-substitution problem arises only when substitution is possible. It cannot occur in a fixed-proportion situation, consumption of left and right shoes or of bolts and nuts. (As Bowman [1957] notes, "a monopoly of bolts if nuts are competitive is as good as a monopoly of bolts and nuts.")

To realize the vertically integrated profit, the upstream monopolist need not integrate toward the second input industry, because the latter exerts no externality (it contents itself with selling at marginal cost). Thus, it suffices to integrate vertically, as shown in figure 4.7. Alterna-

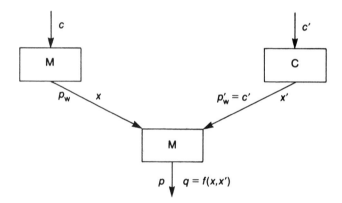

Figure 4.6

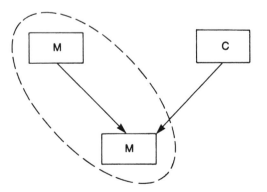

Figure 4.7
Vertical integration with several inputs.

tively, several vertical restraints can be substituted for vertical integration:

Franchise fee   The monopolist can make the downstream unit the residual claimant:

$$p_w = c,$$

$$A = P(f(x^m, x'^m))f(x^m, x'^m) - cx^m - c'x'^m.$$

As in examples 1 and 2, vertical control increases welfare. The downstream monopolist pays a lower marginal price for the first input and therefore charges a lower price to consumers. Furthermore, the input mix is now efficient.

Tie-in together with RPM   As was shown by Blair and Kaserman (1978), tie-ins have a very desirable property in the presence of input substitution: They allow the relative price of inputs to be the "correct" one. To see this, let the upstream monopolist force the downstream unit to buy the second intermediate good from him at price p'_w (figure 4.8). Suppose that the upstream monopolist chooses prices for the intermediate goods proportional to their marginal cost:

$$p_w/p'_w = c/c'. \tag{4.1}$$

The downstream unit minimizes cost over the two inputs. A well-known condition for cost minimization is that the marginal rate of substitution between inputs be equal to the ratio of their prices. Hence,

$$\frac{\partial f}{\partial x}(x, x') \bigg/ \frac{\partial f}{\partial x'}(x, x') = \frac{p_w}{p'_w}$$

$$= \frac{c}{c'}$$

$$= \frac{\partial f}{\partial x}(x^m, x'^m) \bigg/ \frac{\partial f}{\partial x'}(x^m, x'^m). \tag{4.2}$$

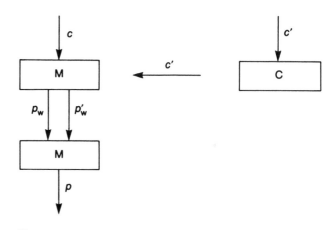

Figure 4.8
Tie-in.

Equation 4.2 ensures that the downstream unit uses the inputs in the right proportions.[16] Furthermore, it takes us back to the one-input case. Equation 4.2 determines x' as a function of x, say. Hence, the upstream monopolist needs only one more instrument to take care of the retail-price externality. Resale-price maintenance is such an instrument. To realize the vertically integrated profit Π^m, the upstream monopolist must obviously impose $p = p^m$. Last, to appropriate the downstream unit's profit, the upstream monopolist chooses a p_w and a p'_w satisfying equation 4.1 and

$$p_w x^m + p'_w x'^m = p^m f(x^m, x'^m). \tag{4.3}$$

Because f is homogeneous of degree 1, the downstream unit cannot improve on the monopoly allocation[17] and makes zero profit.

A limit to the use of tie-ins is that, in general, there are many inputs (including labor), and the monopoly producer of an input must tie all other inputs (or at least all those that are good substitutes with his product). Such broad ties are infrequent. The case of a durable-

---

16. For instance, for a Cobb-Douglas production function

$$f(x, x') = k x^\alpha (x')^{1-\alpha},$$

one has

$$x/x' = [\alpha/(1 - \alpha)](c'/c) = x^m/x'^m.$$

More generally, the partial derivatives of a function that is homogeneous of degree 1 are homogeneous of degree 0. Hence,

$$\frac{\partial f(\lambda x^m, \lambda x'^m)}{\partial x} = \frac{\partial f(x^m, x'^m)}{\partial x},$$

and similarly for the derivative with respect to x'. The solutions to equation 4.2 have the form

$$\{x = \lambda x^m, x' = \lambda x'^m\}.$$

17. To minimize cost, the downstream unit would choose $x = \lambda x^m$ and $x' = \lambda x'^m$ for some $\lambda \geqslant 0$. However, from equation 4.3 and the homogeneity of f,

$$p_w x + p'_w x' = \lambda(p_w x^m + p'_w x'^m)$$

$$= p^m(\lambda f(x^m, x'^m))$$

$$= p^m f(x, x').$$

good monopolist, in which the substitute "input" is maintenance, is a good application of the previous analysis (see exercise 4.5).

Let us briefly consider the new features associated with a competitive downstream industry. Assume that the downstream industry sells at its marginal cost (the minimal cost given intermediate prices p_w and p_w').[18] A franchise fee with $p_w = c$ is no longer sufficient; the downstream industry then sells at a price equal to the marginal cost for intermediate prices c and c'. Thus, the consumer pays the vertical structure's marginal cost (too low a price, from the viewpoint of the vertical structure), and no profit is realized. Hence, no franchise fee can be imposed on the downstream firms.

In contrast, a tie-in (with prices determined by equations 4.1 and 4.3) is a sufficient instrument. RPM is not needed, because downstream competition eliminates the second marginalization.

A royalty on the final output is also sufficient; the upstream monopolist charges $p_w = c$ in order not to induce input distortion, and then realizes the integrated profit by taxing final output.[19]

*Exercise 4.5*** Some durable-good producers tie the purchase of spare parts and maintenance to the purchase of the good. (For instance, Boeing used to tie spare parts to the sale of commercial jets through requirements provisions, and required subcontractors to destroy any production overruns of spare parts.) The purpose of this exercise is to show that the input-substitution model offers a possible explanation of this practice. (Can you think of alternative explanations?)

A monopolist produces a durable good at unit cost c. A competitive industry offers maintenance at unit cost $p_w' = c'$. Another competitive downstream industry uses the durable good to produce the final output. One unit of the durable good in working condition produces one unit of the final output per unit of time. Time is continuous,

and the rate of interest is r. The firms in the downstream industry consume x' units of maintenance per unit of durable good and per unit of time. The conditional probability of breakdown of the durable good is $\alpha(x')dt$ between t and $t + dt$, where $\alpha' < 0$ and $\alpha'' > 0$. (Breakdown means that the durable good must be replaced.) Let p_w denote the price of the durable good (assume that this price is constant over time, to avoid the commitment issues discussed in the supplementary section of chapter 1).

(i) Show that the price of the final good is

$$p = c'x' + p_w[r + \alpha(x')],$$

where x' minimizes the right-hand side.

(ii) Show that the downstream industry "consumes" too much maintenance from the vertical structure's point of view. How can the durable-good monopolist solve this problem?

(iii) Draw the analogy with the input-substitution model.

These three famous examples—double marginalization, downstream moral hazard, and input substitution—show that vertical integration or vertical restraints need not be detrimental to welfare, even when they are meant to increase monopoly profit.[20] In such circumstances, the issue is the existence of a monopoly power *per se*, not its by-products (vertical integration or vertical restraints). We will see in the supplementary section that vertical restraints may be privately desirable and at the same time socially undesirable. One should be cautious when assessing the effects of such restraints, but unqualified hostility toward vertical restraints is inappropriate.

4.3 Intrabrand Competition

In most of section 4.2 we assumed that the retailer had monopoly power. In this section we examine the polar case in which the downstream sector is competitive. We focus on the provision of promotional services.[21]

---

18. Because f exhibits constant returns to scale, the marginal cost is independent of the scale of operations.

19. The adequate royalty per unit of output is

$(p^m q^m - c x^m - c' x'^m)/q^m$.

20. The above models do not "explain" the existence of vertical restraints (such as resale-price maintenance and tie-ins). In all these models, a franchise fee suffices to obtain the vertically integrated profit. And it is difficult to argue that

franchise fees are more costly to administer (involve higher transaction costs) than RPM or tie-ins.

21. The issue of double marginalization disappears because downstream competition brings the second price-cost margin to zero. (The case of "differentiated retailers" [see chapter 7 for the definition of differentiated products] is intermediate between the monopoly case and the competitive case. Differentiation allows retailers to introduce a second marginalization.) The effect of competition on the input-substitution problem was analyzed in example 3.

4.3.1 Intrabrand Competition and Retail Services[22]

Here we use the model of example 2 of section 4.2. The demand function for the final good is $q = D(p, s)$ for a package of p (final price) and s (services). To abstract from the discrimination issues of chapter 3, we assume that all consumers are identical. Their net consumer surplus is $S(p, s)$, with $\partial S/\partial p = -D(p, s)$. The retailers, who are all identical, incur cost $\Phi(s)$ per unit of output for service s.

The vertically integrated profit is obtained by choosing p^m and s^m so as to maximize

$$[p - c - \Phi(s)]D(p, s).$$

The first-order condition for services is

$$[p^m - c - \Phi(s^m)]\frac{\partial D}{\partial s} = \Phi'(s^m)D. \tag{4.4}$$

Consider now the decentralized structure.

Consumers will buy from the retailer who offers them the best package of price and services. We can then formalize perfect competition in this model as retailers offering consumers their most preferred price and services package subject to the condition that the retailers not lose money. In other words, the competitive price and level of services maximize $S(p, s)$ subject to $p = p_w + \Phi(s)$, where p_w is the intermediate price charged by the monopolist. Substituting p, the competitive sector maximizes $S(p_w + \Phi(s), s)$. The first-order condition for services is (remember, the derivative of consumer surplus with respect to price equals $-D$)

$$\frac{\partial S}{\partial s} = \Phi'(s)D. \tag{4.5}$$

Comparing equations 4.4 and 4.5, we see that competition introduces a bias in the choice of services. The right-hand side is the same for the decentralized and the integrated structures: The cost of a unit increase in services equals the marginal cost of services times demand. The left-hand side differs between the two arrangements. The integrated structure considers the marginal revenue accruing from the increase in demand. Competition con-

siders the marginal surplus, which embodies the increase in demand for all inframarginal units

$$\left(\frac{\partial S}{\partial s} = \int_p^\infty \frac{\partial D}{\partial s}(u, s)du\right).$$

The comparison is thus analogous to that in chapter 2 between the qualities chosen by a monopolist (who considers only the effect of an increase in quality on the *marginal* consumer) and a social planner (who considers the effect of an increase in quality on the *average* consumer). This analogy is not coincidental; the vertically integrated solution is nothing but the monopoly solution, and competition maximizes social welfare subject to the fact that input is bought at price p_w rather than c.

From the analysis in chapter 2, we conclude that the competitive retailers may provide too few or too many services (from the vertical structure's point of view), depending on whether services are more valued by marginal or inframarginal consumers. The welfare analysis of vertical integration can be shown to be ambiguous. The provision of services under retail competition is socially optimal given the wholesale price. However, the wholesale price is the monopolist's choice and may exceed the fictitious wholesale price under vertical integration.[23]

*Exercise 4.6*** In the previous model, which of the following instruments is sufficient?

(i) a franchise fee

(ii) resale-price maintenance

4.3.2 The Horizontal Externality

In the previous model, the retailers exerted an externality on the manufacturer through their competition (they did not offer the level of services he preferred). In this subsection, we tackle the issue of externalities among retailers. We shall consider the provision of pre-sale information (or advertising) by one retailer to consumers who ultimately buy from other retailers. Pre-sale information (e.g., literature, test drives, demonstrations by salespeople) matters for complex durable goods, such as automobiles, cameras, and stereo equipment. Telser (1960) argues that

---

22. The exposition here follows Caillaud and Rey 1986.

23. This fictitious wholesale price is equal to $p^m - \Phi(s^m)$. From example 2 in section 4.2, the manufacturer can realize the vertically integrated profit by granting one retailer a monopoly position on retail (or, equivalently in this

model, granting exclusive territories on portions of the total demand to several retailers) and using an instrument that is sufficient in the one-retailer case (a franchise fee, for instance). Hence, we have an example in which eliminating retail competition increases the manufacturer's profit.

retail competition may prevent the provision of such information. A retailer who incurs the cost of providing the information must charge a higher price than a retailer who does not provide the information. Consumers then have an incentive to visit the first retailer to obtain information and then buy from the second.

This phenomenon is starkly illustrated by considering the polar case in which services cannot be appropriated by the retailer who provides them. Suppose that the demand is $q = D(p, \bar{s})$, where $\bar{s}$ is the maximum of services offered by any retailer and p is the lowest price charged by any retailer.[24] $\Phi(s)$ is now the unit cost of services to a consumer who visits the store and does not buy. Assume that $\Phi(0) = 0$. A retailer who offers services $\bar{s}$ must make enough in sales to cover his additional costs. At the same time, his retail price must not exceed the wholesale price, because another retailer could lower his price slightly, provide no services, and take all the demand. In other words, the competitive price for a given $\bar{s}$ is $p = p_w$. However,

$$p - [p_w + \Phi(\bar{s})] \leqslant 0.$$

Hence, $\bar{s} = 0$. No services are provided.

More generally, the horizontal externality gives rise to a public-good problem. Retailers free-ride on one another. The public good—the information provided to the consumers—is therefore undersupplied. (It is not supplied at all in our extreme example.) To encourage an adequate provision of services by retailers, competition must be reduced or eliminated. The manufacturer must give the retailers a property right on their services by protecting them against unfair competition. Competition-reducing restraints, such as RPM and exclusive territories, are adequate to serve that purpose. RPM prevents the emergence of discount stores and encourages consumers to buy where the services are provided (because they will not find a better price elsewhere). Exclusive territories will also suffice. For instance, the manufacturer can grant a monopoly position to a retailer. The absence of competition precludes any horizontal externality. Such restraints are generally welfare-enhancing, because they allow the retailers to supply valuable information to the consumers (although one must, as usual, be cautious and consider the change in final price associated with the change in services when moving from the downstream competitive solution to the downstream monopoly solution).[25]

Mathewson and Winter (1984) build a model in which retailers are differentiated by their locations (see the model of spatial differentiation in section 2.1). They advertise the product locally (i.e., to their own customers), but some spillovers (due to word-of-mouth communication among consumers, say) create a positive externality on other retailers in other geographical areas.[26] As above, this externality must be encouraged. For instance, if exclusive territories are granted, the optimal two-part tariff makes each retailer a "more than residual claimant": $p_w < c$. The intermediate good is subsidized, giving each retailer an extra margin that encourages him to advertise more, which benefits the manufacturer through the positive externality on other retailers.

The horizontal-externality argument is often invoked to explain the existence of RPM. Often, however, RPM is imposed on goods that involve relatively few inappropriable pre-sale services.[27] Lately the externality argument has been extended to goods for which the distributor offers quality certification. The idea is that pre-sale services need not take the form of time spent with the customer, free brochures, and the like. Rather, the simple fact that a certain retailer carries the product may signal that the product is of high quality. Prestigious stores such as Bloomingdale's have built reputations for picking quality items. Such a store is willing to engage its reputation by carrying a given product only if the product is sufficiently profitable—in particular, if it is not carried by discount stores. Resale-price maintenance is one way of keeping consumers from buying from a discount store

---

24. A finer description of the effect of pre-sale information on demand would be desirable here. One can imagine that consumers go first to the retailer with the highest level of pre-sale information and then choose from among retailers on the basis of price only.

25. See Perry and Porter 1986 for an analysis of retail-service externalities in a different product-differentiation space.

26. A similar externality arises among a group of franchisees using a common name. A McDonald's franchisee who cuts quality hurts the other McDonald's franchisees. Indeed, McDonald's goes to great lengths to measure quality at each location using a "quality-service-cleanliness index."

27. See Overstreet 1983 and Steiner 1985 for critiques of the too-frequent application of this theory.

after getting the message about the high quality of the good from a prestigious store.[28]

4.3.3 Differentiated Retailers

In the previous two examples, retail competition hurts the manufacturer, who might as well grant a retail monopoly. In general, however, a manufacturer may want to keep several retailers. First, competition may discipline the retailers, as we shall see in the next subsection. Second, consumers may be heterogeneous, and having retailers located at different points in geographical or quality space (see section 2.1) enables a manufacturer to better appropriate their surplus.[29] The manufacturer can choose the number of retailers either directly, or indirectly through the level of the franchise fee (the retailers then enter until they make zero profit). Of course, the manufacturer cares not only about the number of retailers but also about their locations. It turns out that for homogeneous geographical spaces (such as a uniform distribution of consumers along a circle—see chapter 7) there is no conflict between the manufacturer and a given number of retailers as to their locations. This is because the retailers try to differentiate themselves as much (i.e., locate as far apart) as they can in order to avoid intense intrabrand competition (see chapter 7). The vertically integrated structure would also differentiate retailers as much as possible in order to capture consumer surplus. In contrast, a conflict as to location arises in more general product spaces (see Bolton and Bonanno 1985 for a model of quality differentiation with such a conflict; see also subsection 4.3.1 above).

4.3.4 Retail Competition as an Incentive Device

Since a retailer is an agent for the manufacturer (in an economic sense, not necessarily in a legal sense), he must be given incentives to choose the adequate level of promotional services, retail price, etc. The deterministic environment of section 4.2 allowed the manufacturer to perfectly control each retailer's actions and to realize the "vertically integrated" (symmetric-information) profit—for instance, by using the two-part tariff. However, as was emphasized in the chapter on the theory of the firm,

uncertainty and asymmetric information generally create a real control problem by introducing a basic trade-off between insurance and incentives. The risk-averse agent (retailer), who is provided with some insurance, tends to have too little incentive to take actions that are costly to him (high promotional effort, low retail price, etc.) but profitable to the principal (manufacturer).

Competition on the retail market may alleviate the agency problem, because (as bizarre as this may seem) it provides some insurance to the retailers. Suppose, for instance, that a retailer is hurt by an increase in retail cost (a direct effect). If he competes on the retail market and his rivals are also hurt by the increase in retail cost (such a correlation is not unreasonable, given that they are in the same market), these rivals raise their prices or lower their services, which raises the demand for the first retailer and reduces his loss in profit. This indirect effect does not exist for a monopoly retailer. Thus, competition smoothes the retailer's profit stream over states of nature (potential retail costs). The same argument applies to shocks in demand in this retail market. Because competition has desirable insurance properties, and thus alleviates the trade-off between insurance and incentives, the manufacturer can give more incentives to his retailers when the latter compete in the product market. Thus, competition can also be seen as an incentive device.

On the other hand, competition is destructive of profit, as will be emphasized throughout part II. Yet a monopoly retailer is not constrained by competitive pressure, and can fully extract the monopoly profit from his retail market. We thus conclude that the manufacturer faces a trade-off between high incentives (provided by retail competition) and the optimal exploitation of monopoly power (obtained by allowing a single retailer, or else by imposing exclusive territories). For a formal model, and for a discussion of the welfare implications of this, see the supplementary section.

4.3.5 Dealer Cartels

Competing retailers may pressure a manufacturer to impose competition-reducing vertical restraints. As an extreme example, consider the case of a group of retailers

---

28. See Oster's analysis of Levi Strauss and Greening's of Florsheim Shoes in Lafferty et al. 1984. For a formal analysis of quality certification, see Marvel-McCafferty 1984.

29. See Dixit 1983 and Mathewson and Winter 1984, 1986 for spatial models.

who purchase an intermediate good at its competitive price, $p_w = c$. That is, assume away upstream monopoly power. These retailers compete on the final price. Thus, the final price is equal to their marginal cost (that is, if they do not have other retail costs, $p = c$), and they do not make a profit. (See chapter 5 for a discussion of this conclusion.) Suppose now that they have the clever idea of creating a "trademark." They create an institution that "certifies" the product. (Recall, however, that there is no quality problem here.) In turn, this upstream institution "imposes" resale-price maintenance or exclusive territories on them. RPM specifies a minimum retail price (for instance, the monopoly price) that exceeds the marginal cost c; exclusive territories divide the market into submarkets in which a retailer has monopoly power. In both cases, the creation of a phony upstream institution allows the retailers to make profits by reducing competition.

Of course, this simple story begs some questions: What happens if a retailer does not comply with the trademark agreement? Can the retailers impose vertical restraints on noncompetitive upstream manufacturers? However, it starkly illustrates the issue. In this framework, the vertical restraints are not meant to enhance the efficiency of the vertical structure. They are introduced only to allow the retailers to raise the consumer prices above marginal cost. Such vertical agreements are just a veil for horizontal collusion. They lower welfare in the same way that monopoly pricing lowered welfare in chapter 1.

At the current level of comprehension of the issue, it is generally admitted that restraints imposed by a retailers' cartel are harmful. Even economists associated with the Chicago school, who usually see vertical integration and vertical restraints as increasing the efficiency of vertical structures and welfare,[30] have argued against the legality of retailer-imposed restraints.[31]

4.4 Interbrand Competition

Here the link between vertical control and the consumers' choice between products will be discussed briefly. Two cases will be distinguished. In the first, the vertical restraint is imposed as a way to enhance efficiency by encouraging the manufacturer to provide services. In the second, the manufacturer imposes a vertical restraint to affect the behavior of its upstream rivals.[32]

4.4.1 Exclusive Dealing and Efficiency

Exclusive dealing—the stipulation that a retailer may not sell a brand that competes with the manufacturer's product—may result in a loss of returns to scale. For instance, the retailer's employment is increased and consumers' search costs are reduced when the retailer carries several products. However, exclusive dealing may also bring a gain in efficiency. The argument here is the mirror image of that advanced in subsection 4.3.2, which was that a retailer may have to be granted an exclusive territory (or, more generally, a downstream-competition-reducing restraint) to give him incentives to provide presale information. Similarly, exclusive dealing (a priori, an upstream-competition-reducing restraint) may induce the manufacturer to supply promotional services. The point is that the manufacturer may promote the product, give the retailer a certain location, and so forth, but the retailer may induce the consumers who visit him to buy the competing brand (which, presumably, carries a higher profit margin for the retailer if the competing manufacturer does not incur the same promotional expenses). Exclusive dealing is then seen as a way of giving the manufacturer a property right on his promotional expenses (Marvel 1982).

4.4.2 Vertical Restraints and Upstream Strategic Behavior

It has been argued that some vertical restraints are used by manufacturers to restrict upstream competition.

The first and best-known argument is that exclusivity contracts (exclusive dealing, long-term contracts with retailers) form a barrier to entry. Such contracts force new manufacturers to set up their own distribution networks

---

30. See, e.g., Posner 1981.

31. See, e.g., Posner 1976. In 1981, the new assistant attorney general in charge of the antitrust division of the U.S. Department of Justice, William Baxter, testifying before a congressional committee, stated: "In my view, there is no such thing as a vertical 'problem'.... The only possible adverse competitive consequences of vertical arrangements inhere in their horizontal effects. Only

where vertical arrangements facilitate restricted output and raised prices—horizontal impacts—should they be inhibited." (quoted in Howard 1983 on pp. 150–151)

32. This case relates to strategic competition, which is the subject of part II of the book. Thus, only the main arguments will be mentioned here.

(which is costly, whether or not the new distributors can quickly offset their disadvantages in terms of goodwill and experience). Thus, new manufacturers are less inclined to enter. (A variant of this important argument is studied in the supplementary section, where it is shown that private contracting tends to excessively foreclose the access to markets for new entrants.)

The second argument is one of market discipline. Telser (1960) and Posner (1977) have argued that RPM can help competing manufacturers sustain collusion by reducing the efficacy of secret wholesale-price cuts (see chapter 6 on the factors that facilitate or hinder collusion). In a somewhat different vein, Bonanno and Vickers (1986), Gal-Or (1987), and Rey and Stiglitz (1986) have shown that restraints that reduce downstream competition (such as exclusive territories) may also soften upstream competition. Thus, the manufacturers may also adopt vertical restraints for strategic purposes.[33]

4.5 Concluding Remarks

In a single-manufacturer, single-retailer, deterministic environment, the basic vertical externality associated with linear pricing creates an excessive demand contraction, even from the viewpoint of the vertical structure. Restraints that correct this externality tend to be welfare improving. Thus, vertical restraints that reduce competition (either downstream or upstream) seem better candidates for the economist's attention. Although the horizontal-externality argument associated with pre-sale services rightly calls for the suppression of downstream competition, the two models of competition analyzed in the supplementary section (of retail competition as an incentive device, and of long-term contracts as a barrier to entry) both yield the conclusion that private contracting yields too much market foreclosure (too little competition) from a social point of view. Competition-reducing restraints should be a focus of research, as much work remains to be done in this crucial area of vertical control.

Theoretically, the only defensible position on vertical restraints seems to be the rule of reason. Most vertical restraints can increase or decrease welfare, depending on the environment. Legality or illegality *per se* thus seems unwarranted. At the same time, this conclusion puts far too heavy a burden on the antitrust authorities. It seems important for economic theorists to develop a careful classification and operative criteria to determine in which environments certain vertical restraints are likely to lower social welfare.

---

33. The treatment of these contributions, which requires a good comprehension of parts of chapters 5 and 8, is beyond the scope of this overview of vertical restraints. See review exercise 19.

4.6 Supplementary Section: Competition-Reducing Restraints

In this section we shall analyze two models of market foreclosure. In the first, the manufacturer decides whether to let simultaneous (product-market) competition operate between his retailers (or licensees, or downstream firms). The second model considers sequential competition in a model of supplier switching, and analyzes whether equilibrium long-term contracts between a buyer and a supplier forms a barrier to entry for other suppliers. In both models, it is found that private contracting yields too much foreclosure—i.e., too little competition—from a social viewpoint.

4.6.1 The Role of Retail Competition in Promoting Efficiency[34]

We saw in section 4.3 how retail competition may hurt the manufacturer. Competition puts constraints on retailers and prevents them from extracting the monopoly profit. To realize the (higher) vertically integrated profit, the manufacturer prevented competition through, for instance, exclusive territories. A retailer who is given a monopoly situation on part of the demand and who purchases the intermediate good at marginal cost internalizes the vertical structure's objectives. He thus makes the decisions that yield the vertically integrated profit, which can then be captured by the manufacturer through a franchise fee. In such a world, the imposition of exclusive territories cannot hurt the manufacturer. Nor can the imposition of the other main intrabrand-competition-reducing restraint, resale-price maintenance. If retailers face no uncertainty, the manufacturer can perfectly foresee the final price they will charge, so he could always duplicate the situation without restraints by imposing the retail price that would then prevail.

This supplementary section begins with a demonstration that in the presence of uncertainty and asymmetric information, competition-reducing restraints have some drawbacks. First, they may not allow the efficient use of the information held by retailers. Second, they may give

the retailers an inadequate amount of insurance. Competition among retailers may become a profitable option for the manufacturer[35] (although competition creates its own vertical inefficiencies, particularly by constraining the retailers' choices).

After discussing these issues in broad terms, we consider a more formal model of retail competition. In this model, retail competition either is or is not optimal for the manufacturer; however, it is always socially superior to no retail competition. We explain why the consumers, whose interests are not accounted for in the arrangement between manufacturer and retailers, prefer retail competition.

4.6.1.1 Uncertainty, Delegation, and Insurance

Uncertainty

Two types of uncertainty faced by retailers in a given market can be distinguished (think of retailers within the same geographic area): demand uncertainty and retail-cost uncertainty. Demand varies with the consumers' tastes or with the degree of interbrand competition; retail cost is affected by technological progress, wages, input prices, and so forth. Assume that the uncertainty affects all retailers in a given market in the same manner. At the point in time when retailers and manufacturers make contracts, everyone has the same beliefs about the potential realizations of demand and retail-cost uncertainty. After the contracts are signed, the uncertainty is resolved and learned by the retailers, who then take some actions (for instance, the choice of the retail price or promotional effort) that affect the vertical structure's targets. The right to make decisions in response to changes in the economic environment is delegated to the retailers.

To illustrate the issues, it suffices to consider the following simple framework (the formal development of this framework is given below): There are n retailers in a given market ($n > 1$). The manufacturer charges two-part tariffs to his retailers. As before, the form of the tariffs is

$$T(q) = A + p_w q,$$

where q is the quantity of the intermediate good bought

---

34. These comments are derived from Rey and Tirole 1986b.

35. In the chapter on the theory of the firm, it was noted that product competition may help to discipline the firm's managers (see, e.g., the Hart argument). A somewhat similar phenomenon occurs here with the retailers—with the important difference that the existence of product competition is a choice variable for the manufacturer.

by the retailers. Under retail competition, the retailers choose retail prices. Consumers, who consider the retailers to be identical, go to the retailer with the lowest price. Their demand is $q = D(p, d)$, where p is the lowest retail price and d is the parameter of demand uncertainty (D decreases with p and increases with d). The retailers have a retail cost γ per unit of sales, where γ, like d, is uncertain at the contract date but is revealed to the retailers before the final price is chosen. The manufacturer may impose exclusive territories or RPM, depending on whether such restraints are enforceable. Exclusive territories divide consumers into n groups. Each retailer then has monopoly power and faces demand $q = D(p, d)/n$. For RPM, the manufacturer fixes p in the contract. Assume that the retailers then share the demand equally: Each sells $q = D(p, d)/n$.[36]

Delegation

The manufacturer would like the vertical structure to yield the vertically integrated profit (even if this profit is realized by retailers, because a franchise fee can be used to appropriate the retailers' profits). The *ex post* vertically integrated profit is

$$\max_{p} \left[(p - c - \gamma) D(p, d) \right].$$

The retail price that maximizes this profit is contingent on the realizations of the demand and retail-cost parameters; assume that $p^m(d, \gamma)$ grows with d and γ (see chapter 1 for a proof that p^m grows with γ; reasonable conditions can be found so that p^m grows with d as well). For instance, if

$$D(p, d) = d - p$$

(linear demand), then

$$p^m(d, \gamma) = (d + c + \gamma)/2.$$

The delegation problem consists of inducing the retailers to choose actions that come as close as possible to optimal actions—here, $p^m(d, \gamma)$—for all realizations

of demand and retail-cost uncertainty. Let us examine the properties of competition and those of competition-reducing restraints in this respect.

Under competition, the retail price is driven down to the retailers' total marginal cost, which is equal to the wholesale price plus the retail cost: $p = p_w + \gamma$.[37] The retail price is then entirely determined by cost. The price is not responsive to the demand parameter, and fully embodies the retail cost. In contrast, the vertically integrated price is responsive to the demand parameter and may embody only part of the retail cost (in the case of linear demand, it embodies only 50 percent of the cost). As in section 4.3, competition constrains retailers in the search for the monopoly profit.

Like competition RPM uses decentralized information nonoptimally. Indeed, the retail price is fixed before the uncertainty is resolved, so it is not responsive to demand and retail-cost conditions at all.

In contrast, exclusive territories create local monopolies which can adjust to the realization of uncertainty without being constrained by the manufacturer (as with RPM) or by other retailers (as in the case of competition). Indeed, if the manufacturer does not distort the intermediate price ($p_w = c$), each retailer maximizes

$$(p - c - \gamma) D(p, d)/n - A$$

and thus chooses the right retail price, $p^m(d, \gamma)$. Thus, exclusive territories make excellent use of decentralized information.

Insurance

If retailers are risk-averse,[38] the manufacturer is concerned with the amount of risk the retailers bear. Any increase in risk for the retailers reduces the franchise fee the manufacturer can extract from them. Thus, the monopolist wants to keep the retailers from bearing risk. Let us assume that the manufacturer is risk-neutral.[39]

Competing retailers are perfectly insured. Their margin

---

36. Here, imposing exclusive territories on top of RPM would be redundant.

37. See chapter 5. We take a sharp view here of competition by assuming that the retailers cannot use tacit collusion. Also, the assumption that retailers are not differentiated (either naturally, or through cost and demand shocks) is meant to formalize the notion of pure competition.

38. Their objective function is

$$\mathrm{E}\, U((p - p_w - \gamma)q - A),$$

where q is the quantity they sell, U is a concave von Neumann–Morgenstern utility function, and E denotes the expectation over d and γ.

39. This assumption is justified, for instance, when the manufacturer serves a large number of independent markets.

$(p - p_w - \gamma)$ is equal to zero for any realization of the cost uncertainty. Thus, their profit is deterministic. The intuition is as follows: When, for instance, a retailer's retail cost increases, his competitors' retail costs also increase. The competitive pressure is lowered, in the sense that the competitors' prices increase. Thus, competition has very desirable insurance properties.

RPM makes the retailers bear all the fluctuations in the retail cost that cannot be passed on to the consumers. Whether the retailers bear fluctuations in demand depends upon whether the contract leaves them a positive profit margin $(p - p_w - \gamma)$.

Last, exclusive territories let the retailers bear the fluctuations of the vertical structure—at least, they do so if the retailers are made the residual claimants $(p_w = c)$, in which case the manufacturer bears no risk. Hence, exclusive territories give mediocre insurance to the retailers.

Thus, competition is superior to competition-reducing restraints in that it gives more insurance to retailers. (This is from the vertical structure's point of view; as we will see below, competition offers other advantages to the consumers.)

Let us now develop the vertical structure's trade-off between competition and a competition-reducing restraint by completing and justifying the previous model, and let us introduce the welfare analysis into the model.

4.6.1.2   A Model of Retail Competition

Consider the model exposited in subsection 4.6.1.1: Consumer demand is equal to $q = D(p, d)$, where p is the retail price and d is the uncertain demand parameter. The common and uncertain retail cost per unit of sales is equal to γ. Retailers are *ex ante* and *ex post* identical. First, they sign a contract with the manufacturer; second, they learn the realizations of the demand and retail-cost parameters; third they choose a retail price.

To define the set of feasible contracts, let us now make assumptions about what the manufacturer observes (i.e., on what the contract can be contingent). As we will see, these assumptions imply that the only feasible contracts are competition and exclusive territories, both combined

with a two-part tariff (in particular, RPM is not enforceable under these assumptions).

Assumption 1   The manufacturer observes how much of the intermediate good a retailer buys directly from him, and whether the retailer carries the product.

Assumption 2   The manufacturer does not observe the realization of the uncertainty (d and γ), the quantity sold by a retailer, and the retailers' prices and profits.

Assumption 3   The manufacturer serves many independent markets,[40] and retailers engage in arbitrage (they "bootleg").

Assumptions 1 and 3, and the nonobservability of the quantity sold by the retailer, mean that the manufacturer cannot charge different marginal prices because of arbitrage (as discussed above), but he can still impose a two-part tariff as he observes whether the retailer carries his product.

The assumption that a retailer's consumer price is not observed by the manufacturer can be justified in two ways: First, the retailer may give secret price discounts to his customers. Second, the retailer can include in the sales package services that are not observable by the manufacturer (or, at least, not verifiable by a court). For instance, suppose that the retailer offers services that have a monetary equivalent s for the consumers. The "real retail price" for the consumer is then $p - s$, where p is the nominal price charged by the retailer. The demand function is then $q = D(p - s, d)$. Suppose further that the cost of providing services s per unit of sales is $\Phi(s) = s$. Then the retailers' margin is $p - s - p_w - \gamma$. It is clear that even if p were observable, the unobservable choice of services means that the retailer chooses a "generalized retail price" $\tilde{p} = p - s$ which is not observable by the manufacturer. The model can also be interpreted as a model of *retailers' incentives to supply services*. Anticipating what follows, we will obtain the conclusion that product-market competition acts as an incentive device. We saw in the chapter on the theory of the firm that there is a basic conflict between insurance and incentives in agency. As competition is a good insurance device, the manufacturer can thus

---

40. Here "independent" means that the realizations of the uncertainty in different markets are statistically independent, as (for instance) in the case of geographic markets (cities, regions, etc.) with local demand and cost conditions.

induce the retailers to supply more services (promotional effort) by forcing them to sell in the same market.

Hence, only two-part tariffs are enforceable. To introduce a choice between competition and a competition-reducing restraint, let us make another assumption:

Assumption 4 The manufacturer can divide the market into n submarkets over which a retailer has monopoly power (exclusive territories) if he so chooses.

The optimal contract between the manufacturer and retailers is thus a two-part tariff, accompanied either by price competition among retailers or by exclusive territories.[41]

The manufacturer is risk-neutral. His profit for a total quantity $Q = nq$ sold is

$n(A + p_w q)$.

A retailer makes a profit of

$(p - p_w - \gamma)q - A$

when he sells an amount q. He is risk-averse, and he has a von Neumann–Morgenstern utility function U ($U' > 0$, $U'' \leqslant 0$). His reservation profit is zero. The expected utility derived from the retailing contract must exceed the retailer's utility when he does not sign this contract:

$$E\, U((p - p_w - \gamma)q - A) \geqslant U(0), \qquad (4.6)$$

where the expectation is taken over d and γ. It is clear that, in equilibrium, equation 4.6 is satisfied with equality because the manufacturer can always raise the franchise fee if the retailer's expected utility strictly exceeds his reservation utility. We will consider a family of utility functions indexed by their Arrow-Pratt index of absolute risk aversion,[42]

$$-\frac{U''(\cdot)}{U'(\cdot)}.$$

This family includes the polar cases of risk neutrality (i.e., $E\, U(x) = Ex$—the retailer cares only about his expected profit) and infinite risk aversion (i.e., $E\, U(x) = \min x$—the retailer cares only about his worst possible income). An increasing index means that the retailer is more risk-averse. Last, all retailers have identical preferences.

We can now prove the following proposition:

Proposition 1 The difference between the manufacturer's profits under competition and under exclusive territories grows with the retailers' risk aversion. The manufacturer imposes exclusive territories for low risk aversion. Sufficient conditions for the manufacturer to let competition play for high risk aversion are that, under monopoly, demand and the monopoly price are nondecreasing in the demand parameter, and that the monopoly price does not respond more than fully to changes in marginal cost ($\partial D(p, d)/\partial d \geqslant 0$, $\partial p^m(c, d)/\partial d \geqslant 0$, and $\partial p^m(c, d)/\partial c \leqslant 1$ for all p, c, and d). (These sufficient conditions are in particular satisfied for linear demand $D(p, d) = d - p$, for which the first derivative is equal to 1 and the last two derivatives are equal to $\frac{1}{2}$.)

The proof of this proposition is simple. First, note that under competition the manufacturer's profit does not depend on the retailers' degree of risk aversion. This is because retailers are perfectly insured (see subsection

---

41. Could the manufacturer not do better by using the perfect correlation between the retailers' realizations of uncertainty, as is done in the "yardstick competition" literature (see the chapter on the theory of the firm)? Here, final sales are not observed. Hence, any information that the manufacturer obtains about the realization of uncertainty must come from "costless" announcements by the retailers. It is easily seen that the set of equilibria and payoffs of such an announcement game is independent of the realization of uncertainty— at least when preferences are exponential (including risk-neutral and infinitely risk-averse preferences). Thus, under the reasonable assumption that the retailers coordinate on the same announcement equilibrium (whatever the realization), the manufacturer cannot gain by designing such an announcement game.

We also ruled out the possibility of auctioning off the market to one retailer *after* the realization of uncertainty (this assumption can be justified by the need for several retailers, either because of prior capacity investments or increasing marginal cost of distribution or, in a slight departure from the model, by the existence of retailers' goodwill or differentiation).

42. See Arrow 1970 and Pratt 1964. A utility function U_1 is said to exhibit more risk aversion than a utility function U_2 if, for all realizations of x,

$$-U_1''(x)/U_1'(x) \geqslant -U_2''(x)/U_2'(x).$$

The Arrow-Pratt theorem asserts that, for a given distribution of the random variable x, the certainty equivalent $\bar{x}_1$ for utility U_1, defined by

$$U_1(\bar{x}_1) \equiv E\, U_1(x),$$

is lower than the certainty equivalent $\bar{x}_2$ for utility U_2, defined by

$$U_2(\bar{x}_2) \equiv E\, U_2(x).$$

An example of such a family is given by $U(x) = -e^{-\xi x}$, where ξ is the index of absolute risk aversion.

4.6.1.1), and thus risk aversion plays no role. (Note in passing that, because the retailers make no marginal profit, the franchise fee is zero.) In contrast, the profit under exclusive territories decreases with risk aversion, since retailers bear risk under exclusive territories. From the Arrow-Pratt theorem (see footnote 42), the less risk-averse the retailers are, the greater is the certainty equivalent of their random profit

$$\max_{p} [(p - p_w - \gamma)D(p, d)/n - A],$$

where the certainty equivalent is the value z such that

$$U(z) = E\, U\left[\left(\max_{p}(p - p_w - \gamma)D(p, d)/n\right) - A\right].$$

So, for a given wholesale price (which entirely determines the distribution of the random profits), the less risk-averse the retailers, the greater the franchise fee can be while still keeping equation 4.6 satisfied. Hence, the manufacturer benefits from a decrease in risk aversion.

Under risk neutrality, we know from subsection 4.6.1.1 that the monopolist makes more profits by imposing exclusive territories than under competition. This is because there is no insurance problem, and exclusive territories make perfect use of decentralized information (exclusive territories yield the vertically integrated profit) whereas competition does not.

Last, under infinite risk aversion (the other polar case), its insurance properties make the competitive arrangement more profitable for the manufacturer than exclusive territories. See the following exercise.

Exercise 4.7** Assume that the conditions in the last part of proposition 1 are satisfied. Show that under retailers' infinite risk aversion, an exclusive territories arrangement yields less profit than a competitive arrangement in which no franchise is imposed and in which the wholesale price is equal to the exclusive-territories retail price in the worst state of nature minus the highest possible retail cost. (The worst state of nature occurs for the lowest possible demand parameter $\underline{d}$ and the highest possible retail cost $\overline{\gamma}$.)

The conclusion of this study is that competition—although it limits the retailers' reactions to their environment—may be desirable from the manufacturer's point of view. When the retailers are risk-averse, if the manufacturer grants exclusive territories, he must distort the intermediate price ($p_w > c$) in order to bear some of the retailers' risk. The retailers exert a vertical externality on the manufacturer through his profit margin when choosing the retail price (or services, in the other interpretation). Thus, the manufacturer would like to control the retailers' behavior. However, he cannot do so, because he lacks information about the retailers' environment. And, further, the only kind of franchise fee he can impose is one that is not contingent on their environment. In contrast, competition, by preventing the retailers from making profits, does not expose them to risk. Consequently, the manufacturer does not distort the intermediate price to account for risk, nor does he worry about being unable to tailor the franchise fee to each realization of the uncertainty.

4.6.1.3 Welfare Analysis

The main issue with vertical contracts is that, although they are usually efficient from the viewpoint of the parties who sign them,[43] they do not take into account the interests of consumers (or, more generally, third parties). Hence, there may be externalities, which may have to be corrected through public intervention. We saw in the text that vertical integration and vertical restraints often exert positive externalities on consumers. It was pointed out in subsection 4.2.2 that contracts help avoid an excessive contraction of output, thus benefitting consumers. The picture is quite different in the model of retailer competition developed here, however. To see this, let us simplify the model by making demand a linear function of price:

$$q = D(p, d) = d - p.$$

The consumer net surplus is then

$$S = S(p, d) = \int_{p}^{\infty} (d - u)du = (d - p)^2/2.$$

Because of the uncertainty on d and γ, we must take the

---

43. At least this is the case if, on the date when the contracts are signed, all the involved parties are symmetrically informed. They clearly should not settle for an inefficient contract when they can all be given a higher utility.

expectation of consumer surplus over d and γ:

$$E\,S = \mathrm{E}[(d-p)^2/2] = [(d^e - p^e)^2 + \mathrm{var}(d-p)]/2,$$

where the superscript e denotes an expected (or average) value of a variable and var denotes its variance. The expectation of d, d^e, is given. *The expected net consumer surplus decreases with the average retail price and increases with the variance of consumption.*

The aggregate welfare is defined as the sum of the expected net consumer surplus and the manufacturer's profit. The retailers are always put at their reservation utility, so that their utility does not depend on the arrangement that is chosen.

Proposition 1 compared the two arrangements from the manufacturer's point of view. Proposition 2 deals with consumers and aggregate welfare.

Proposition 2 Suppose that demand is linear: $D(p,d) = d - p$. For any concave utility function U for the retailers, both the expected net consumer surplus and the aggregate welfare are higher under competition than under exclusive territories.

This result shows that consumers do prefer competition. Furthermore, it shows that when the retailers' risk aversion is low, the manufacturer imposes a socially undesirable restraint on intrabrand competition (aggregate welfare is higher under competition). The intuition for this result[44] is that, under competition, the expected retail price is lower and the variance of consumption is higher. Why is this so?

First, uncertainty creates a difference in expected retail prices between the two arrangements. In a deterministic

environment, the two-part tariff accompanied by either competition or exclusive territories is a sufficient restraint, as was shown in sections 4.2 and 4.3. Thus, in the absence of uncertainty, the retail price is equal to the vertically integrated retail price in both cases.[45] Introducing uncertainty around the mean of d and γ affects neither the wholesale price nor the expected retail price under retailer competition, because retailers are perfectly insured.[46] Under exclusive territories, however, the retailers bear some risk, and the manufacturer decides to share some of this risk by setting $p_w > c$ (whereas in the deterministic case the retailer was made the residual claimant, as p_w was set equal to c; see section 4.2). This rise in the wholesale price is partially passed into the retail price (see chapter 1). Hence, under uncertainty the average retail price is higher with exclusive territories.

Second, consumption has a higher variance under competition. To see this, recall that the competitive retail price reacts fully to cost disturbances and not at all to demand disturbances ($p = p_w + \gamma$). Hence, consumption ($q = d - p = d - p_w - \gamma$) reacts fully to both types of uncertainty. In contrast, under exclusive territories, monopoly pricing implies a partial adjustment of the retail price and, thus, only a partial adjustment of consumption to both types of uncertainty.[47]

We thus conclude that consumers prefer retailer competition on this count as well.[48] Indeed, their preference for competition is so strong that even when the manufacturer prefers exclusive territories, a social planner will want to prohibit this restraint on intrabrand competition.

A very interesting analogy (suggested by Michael Whinston) can be drawn with third-degree price discrimi-

---

44. For a proof, see Rey and Tirole 1986b.

45. Hence, the argument that consumers prefer competition because it reduces the retailers' margin is fallacious. It does not take account of the adjustment in wholesale price between the two arrangements.

46. The retail price is $p_w + \gamma$, and the franchise fee must equal zero. Hence, the manufacturer maximizes

$$\mathrm{E}(p_w - c)[d - (p_w + \gamma)] = (p_w - c)(d^e - p_w - \gamma^e).$$

Therefore, p_w and the average retail price ($p_w + \gamma^e$) are not affected by the introduction of uncertainty around the means γ^e and d^e.

47. The retailer *ex post* maximizes

$$(p - p_w - \gamma)(d - p)/n - A,$$

which yields

$$p = \frac{d + p_w + \gamma}{2}.$$

Hence,

$$\frac{\partial p}{\partial d} = \frac{\partial p}{\partial \gamma} = \tfrac{1}{2},$$

and thus

$$\frac{\partial}{\partial d}(d - p) = \left|\frac{\partial}{\partial \gamma}(d - p)\right| = \tfrac{1}{2}.$$

48. When the retail price is observable, RPM becomes enforceable (although not necessarily optimal for the manufacturer). It can similarly be shown that, for linear demand, the expected net consumer surplus and aggregate welfare are higher under competition than under RPM.

nation in the case of retailer risk neutrality and demand shocks. First, because of risk neutrality, the manufacturer captures the retailers' expected profit, even under exclusive territories (in which case the monopoly retailers face a wholesale price equal to the marginal cost c). Second, the difference between exclusive territories and competition is exactly that between third-degree price discrimination and uniform pricing. Exclusive territories yield the monopoly price for each specification of the demand parameter d. (Think of demand d as a group of consumers with proportion equal to the probability of parameter d.) The outcome is thus the third-degree-price-discrimination outcome. In contrast, under competition the manufacturer "fixes" a retail price (equal to the wholesale price plus the retail cost) that is independent of d. He thus obtains the monopoly profit under uniform pricing. Thus, for retailer risk neutrality and demand shocks, proposition 2 is nothing but Robinson's theorem that uniform pricing socially dominates third-degree price discrimination for linear demands (see subsection 3.2.2.1). This analogy also highlights the role of the linearity of demand in proposition 2.

This model exhibits one destructive aspect of competition. That competition reduces industry profit is more general, as will be emphasized throughout part II. Another destructive effect of competition was actually developed in subsection 4.3.2, where competition reduced the supply of pre-sale services; however, there rent dissipation was socially wasteful (hurt the consumers)—it is not here, as the consumers enjoy increased retailer incentives.

4.6.2 Market Foreclosure

Few topics in industrial organization are as controversial as market foreclosure. Very loosely, market foreclosure are commercial practices (including mergers) that reduce the buyers' access to a supplier (which we will call *upstream foreclosure*) and/or limit the suppliers' access to a buyer (*downstream foreclosure*). There are many tools used to achieve market foreclosure. A buyer may purchase a supplier or set up his own production unit so as to manufacture the intermediate good internally; or he can fill at least some of his requirements internally (*tapered integra-*

tion). The upstream division may then refuse to deal with external buyers or, equivalently, may engage in a "price squeeze" (i.e., charge them an exhorbitant price). A supplier may sign exclusive-dealing or exclusive-territory contracts with his buyers. A manufacturer of two complementary products may impose a tie-in or make his basic good incompatible with the complementary goods sold by other manufacturers.

Though market foreclosure is a "hot" issue among those concerned with antitrust proceedings and with regulation, economists still have a very incomplete understanding of its motivations and effects. Nor can they always successfully explain why a particular tool is employed to achieve foreclosure. A general survey of the theory of market foreclosure would be very premature. The following subsections are meant only to introduce some of the issues at hand.

4.6.2.1 Generalities on Market Foreclosure

For convenience, let us distinguish two kinds of market foreclosure. In the first, one of the sectors (upstream or downstream) is already monopolized. The goal is then for the monopoly supplier or buyer to exploit its monopoly power efficiently. The exclusion of trading partners, or the reduction of competition among these partners, may serve this purpose. In the second kind of market foreclosure, neither sector is monopolized, and foreclosure increases the monopolization of one of the two sectors.

Foreclosure as the Efficient Exploitation of Existing Monopoly Power

We already discussed reasons why a monopoly supplier may want to deal with a single buyer.[49] In the model of Rey and Tirole (see subsection 4.6.1) the manufacturer may impose exclusive territories on his retailers (or wholesalers). The explanation was that retail competition destroys profit and therefore does not allow the manufacturer to enjoy full monopoly power. (The counterpart of this is that retail monopoly power destroys downstream incentives.) Such behavior is an instance of upstream fore-

---

49. The issue of foreclosure may also arise in the case of a monopoly buyer. We saw in the chapter on the theory of the firm that a buyer may want to keep several suppliers or sources for incentive purposes. On the other hand, effi-

ciency may require that fixed costs not be duplicated, so that the buyer creates a monopoly supplier (i.e., engenders downstream foreclosure).

closure. The manufacturer *de facto* denies the competing retailers fair access to his good.

Another motive for upstream foreclosure is price discrimination. We saw in chapter 3 that a monopoly manufacturer whose intermediate good is used in two downstream markets has an incentive to integrate into the high-elasticity market and to charge a high intermediate price to the firms supplying the low-elasticity market. Joskow (1985) notes that discrimination often motivates a "price squeeze." Considering a situation in which a monopoly supplier is integrated downstream, he defines the occurrence of a price squeeze as the situation in which "the monopoly input supplier charges a price for the input to its downstream competitors that is so high they cannot profitably sell the downstream product in competition with the integrated firm" (p. 186). That is, the manufacturer charges a lower (internal) price to his downstream division than to the downstream competitors. In the above price-discrimination example, the manufacturer need only drive his downstream competitors out of the high-elasticity market. The notion of a price squeeze was introduced by Judge Learned Hand in a price-discrimination context (in the Alcoa case—see chapter 3).[50]

The same motives may apply in the case of complementary products. As was shown earlier in this chapter, producing complementary products is very similar to operating a vertically integrated firm. A typical example is the problem of competitive access in the rail industry, where not infrequently the route from location A to location B (called the *bottleneck*) is owned by a railroad monopolist while the route from location B to location C is served by the same monopolist as well as by a rival firm. Assume that there are customers who desire to ship from A to C, and that using the monopolist from A to B and his competitor from B to C is ruled out by costly handling of the merchandise. To serve such customers, the competitor's trains must use the monopolist's tracks from A to B. One way of regarding this situation is to think of the bottleneck transportation as the upstream good—produced monopolistically—and the competitive transportation as the downstream good. We can then use the previous framework. The issue is whether the monopolist and its competitor should freely negotiate the transfer price to be paid by the competitor for the trackage rights from A to B. Should the Interstate Commerce Commission prevent foreclosure, if any, of the access to the bottleneck route, or should it (more generally) regulate a "fair transfer price"? Does the monopolist value competition sufficiently (see Baumol 1983, Grimm and Harris 1983, and Tye 1986a, b)? A similar situation arose prior to 1984 in the telephone industry. AT&T, an integrated firm, had a monopoly on the local calls but was in competition with other firms (e.g., MCI and Sprint) on the long-distance market. Its long-distance competitors had to be connected to AT&T's local network, however. One important regulatory issue was to determine the transfer price charged to AT&T's competitors for access to this network.[51]

Beyond foreclosing the market through refusal to deal or engaging in a price squeeze, the manufacturer of two complementary products who has monopoly power on one of them can use two other tools: tie-in and incompatibility. For instance, International Salt, which had substantial monopoly power on machines that inject salt into canned products, was challenged by antitrust authorities for tying the complementary product (salt), which was produced more competitively, and IBM was accused of making some of its products incompatible to gain a competitive edge. (See Ordover and Willig 1981 for an analysis of predatory product incompatibility. See also example 8 of chapter 8.)

Monopolization

Suppose now that both the upstream and the downstream industries are oligopolistic. It is often alleged that in such a situation market foreclosure tends to create monopoly power, either upstream or downstream. For instance, in the *Interstate Circuit* case (mentioned in Krattenmaker and Salop 1986), a Texas movie-theater company obtained promises from film distributors that the distributors would

---

50. For other examples of such price discrimination, see Joskow (1985) on discrimination by privately owned electric utilities and Scherer (1980, p. 325) on discrimination by IBM. Howard (1983, pp. 151–54) also discusses price squeezes. Ordover et al. (1985) shed further theoretical light on price discrimination and squeezes.

51. This issue did not disappear with the 1984 divestiture. Although the operating companies in charge of the local networks are now independent of AT&T, regulatory constraints (such as equal access for long-distance companies) must ensure that the operating companies do not duplicate through contracting the market foreclosure that might arise under integration. For more on the telephone industry, see Brock 1981, Evans 1983, and Temin 1987.

raise their prices to competing exhibitors. An extreme case of such behavior is Alcoa's reported purchase of exclusionary convenants from power companies not to sell to other aluminum producers (while they did not even sell to Alcoa). Such moves are part of a general strategy to monopolize the downstream market by raising rivals' costs (Krattenmaker and Salop 1986; Salop and Sheffman 1983).[52]

The threat of monopolization through mergers or exclusionary vertical restraints has always been of concern to antitrust authorities. For instance, the merger between Brown Shoe (which accounted for 5 percent of U.S. shoe production) and Kinney Shoe Stores (which represented 1.6 percent of U.S. shoe distribution) was considered illegal. Similarly, exclusive dealing arrangements have been frowned upon. The *Standard Fashion* case of 1922 involved the exclusion of 40 percent of all dress-pattern outlets from dealing with a dress manufacturer's rivals. (The critical market share covered by an exclusive dealing agreement with a manufacturer has been narrowed over time.[53]) More recently, there has been concern over computer reservation systems, which are rented by airlines to travel agents (in particular, the systems promoted by American Airlines and United Airlines cover 70 percent of the travel-agent system).[54]

Progress has recently been made toward formalizing the effects of a particular type of market foreclosure—vertical integration—on the competitive structure of the downstream and upstream industries and on welfare (see Greenhut and Ohta 1979; Groff and Perry 1985; McAfee and McMillan 1986; Salinger 1984, 1986; Krattenmaker and Salop 1986; Ordover et al. 1987; Vassiliakis 1985; Ordover and Saloner 1987). For instance, in Vassiliakis 1985 the upstream firms face a fixed cost of production; entry is otherwise free (see chapter 7). Integrated production by a downstream firm is costly because the fixed cost of production is amortized on too small a number of units (it is assumed that an integrated firm does not sell or buy on the intermediate-goods market). But integration prevents the double marginalization considered in the text; the independent suppliers play a Cournot game (see chapter 5) and therefore price above marginal cost, which introduces a distortion in the downstream choice. From this trade-off, Vassiliakis obtains an equilibrium fraction of integrated firms and goes on to derive interesting comparative-statics results.[55]

Because these issues refer to strategic considerations studied in part II of this book, no attempt will be made here to summarize this interesting and growing literature. Also, much work remains to be done. First, in the set-up where there are integrated and nonintegrated firms, it remains to be explained why integrated firms do not sell or buy on the intermediate-goods market.[56] If they indeed participate in this market, the foreclosure argument may have to be reconsidered. Similarly, the set of feasible contracts for nonintegrated firms (linear pricing, two-part pricing, etc.) ought to be spelled out, if possible, from primitive economic assumptions such as arbitrage, information problems, or transaction costs. Second, as is usually the case with vertical restraints, careful consideration must be given to alternative instruments. For instance, if vertical mergers for foreclosure are to be prohibited, can't the concerned firms duplicate the merger allocation through a contract?[57] Third, it may be useful to study the dynamics of market foreclosure. For example, in the cement industry, acquisition of a producer of

---

52. The Krattenmaker-Salop paper contains a fascinating discussion of various ways of foreclosing access to suppliers or buyers, as well as examples of such behavior (some of which are quoted below).

53. See, e.g., the *Standard Stations* case, 337 U.S. 293 (1949). For more on exclusive dealing, see Marvel 1982 and Mathewson and Winter 1985.

54. The display bias becomes particularly important when airlines compete on the same routes. It is also asserted that independent vendors of computer reservation systems are at a disadvantage (they cannot bias displays in their favor, because they are not integrated), and, similarly, that small carriers are at a disadvantage (American may not bias too much against United because of the threat of retaliation). Little theoretical work has been done on these issues. First, entry into the computer-reservation-system industry is made excessively difficult by exclusionary contracts. Not only are natural switching costs (learning, new printers, etc.) for the travel agent non-negligible; in addition, the airlines impose important liquidated damages or buy-out penalties for switching, and the contracts are exclusive and run for four to five years (on this, see subsection 4.6.2.2). Second, each computer reservation system has a display bias that favors the airline selling it, and offers instantaneous confirmation of reservations and boarding passes for that airline.

55. For instance, as the demand side of the economy is replicated so that the number of firms goes to infinity, the fraction of integrated firms goes to zero; but welfare does not converge to the social optimum.

56. Exceptions include Salinger 1984 and Ordover et al. 1987.

57. If not, the distinction is likely to stem from incomplete contracting and the allocation of residual rights of control, as is explained in the chapter on the theory of the firm.

ready-mixed concrete by a cement company may trigger similar behavior by other cement companies (the *bandwagon effect*).[58] These puzzles are challenging. Their solution will require a solid understanding of both contract theory and strategic competition; their importance makes one hope that much progress will be made.

Certain cases of horizontal foreclosure have a similar flavor. For instance, in the *Aspen Ski* case, the firm that controlled three of the four major downhill skiing facilities in Aspen, Colorado, refused to market access to all facilities jointly with the owner of the fourth facility. This is a case of refusal to deal when *network externalities* create gains from trade. (Recall IBM's attempts to make its products incompatible with those of other manufacturers.) We will return to the formalization of this issue in chapter 10.[59] Similarly, refusing to engage in joint ventures may, to some extent, foreclose the access of some firms to a new technology.

4.6.2.2 Contracts as Barriers to Entry

It is often alleged that long-term leasing contracts or contracts that impose substantial penalties for breach foreclose access to the downstream market for entering suppliers. Such reasoning underlies the decision of Judge Wyzanski that the United Shoe Machinery Corporation (which controlled 85 percent of the shoe-machinery market) had attempted to prevent entry into the market by offering binding leasing contracts to shoe manufacturers. This decision was criticized by the prominent Chicago School proponents Posner (1976) and Bork (1978), who made the point that customers of United Shoe Machinery Corporation might not have signed contracts that would have strengthened this supplier's monopoly position. (In the Chicago tradition, Posner and Bork attribute such contracts to efficiency reasons.)

Aghion and Bolton (1987) reconsider the entry-deterrence doctrine of market foreclosure and show that, despite the buyers' concern for monopolization, long-term contracts may be signed that inefficiently deter entry.

The Aghion-Bolton model is simple. Initially, a seller (the "incumbent") and a buyer contract for the delivery of one unit of an intermediate good. The buyer has a unit demand for the intermediate good and has valuation 1 (alternatively, he could buy a backstop substitute at price 1). The seller's cost of producing this unit is $\frac{1}{2}$. After the contract is signed, a competing supplier (the "entrant," unidentified at the date of the contract) will come up with a cost c of producing the good. Assume that c is *a priori* uniformly distributed between 0 and 1. (There is no loss of generality in assuming that an entrant appears; a high c corresponds, *de facto*, to no entry.) Assume, further, that c is known only to the entrant.

Consider first the optimal allocation for the integrated structure imposed by the incumbent and the buyer. Because the incumbent's cost ($\frac{1}{2}$) is lower than the buyer's valuation (1), the buyer always consumes one unit of the intermediate good. The issue is only to minimize the vertical structure's expected production cost. The trade-off is between producing internally at cost $\frac{1}{2}$ and procuring from the entrant at price p. This is a simple monopoly pricing problem. The vertical structure minimizes

$$p\,\mathrm{Prob}(c \leqslant p) + \tfrac{1}{2}\,\mathrm{Prob}(c > p) = p^2 + \tfrac{1}{2}(1 - p),$$

because the price offer from the incumbent, p, is accepted if and only if it exceeds c, and the distribution of c is uniform. This yields $p = \frac{1}{4}$. In the same way that monopoly pricing leads to a welfare loss (consumers with valuations above the marginal cost do not buy—see chapter 1), the vertical structure's price offer to the entrant yields an inefficient production structure: When the entrant's cost lies between $\frac{1}{4}$ and $\frac{1}{2}$, the incumbent supplies the intermediate good.

The next question is whether the nonintegrated structure can realize the same outcome through a contract. To see that this is the case, suppose that the incumbent makes a take-it-or-leave-it offer of the following contract to the buyer: The buyer can buy from the incumbent at price $\frac{3}{4}$. The penalty for breach (liquidated damages) is $\frac{1}{2}$. Suppose that the entrant makes the buyer a take-it-

58. According to Scherer (1980, p. 90): "When vertical integration induced by fewness of supply sources thins the market further, other buyers may be stampeded into integrating as well despite appreciable scale economy sacrifices. Dynamics of this sort can be observed in the histories of the U.S. and European refrigerator-freezer industries, the U.S. automobile industry, and the movement by American steel makers into iron ore mining."

59. Other cases include the expulsion from a wholesale purchasing cooperative in *Northwest Stationers* and the exclusion of nonmembers in *Associated Press* (see Krattenmaker and Salop 1986).

or-leave-it offer (for simplicity, we put the bargaining power on the entrant's side in its negotiation with the buyer). The buyer will accept such an offer only if it does not exceed $\frac{3}{4} - \frac{1}{2} = \frac{1}{4}$. Thus, a profit-maximizing entrant makes an offer if and only if his cost is lower than $\frac{1}{4}$, and the offer made is exactly equal to $\frac{1}{4}$. Hence, the allocation and the vertical structure's expected profit are the same as in the integrated case. But we still have to answer Posner's and Bork's concern that the buyer may not want to accept a contract that helps the incumbent monopolize the intermediate-good market. For this, we must specify what happens if the buyer rejects the incumbent's contract. There are several ways of specifying this outcome. Fortunately, the precise specification chosen affects only the price to be paid to the incumbent and the penalty for breach, but not the difference between the two. That is, it affects the way the profits are divided between the incumbent and the buyer, but not the real allocation. Let us assume that if $c < \frac{1}{2}$, the entrant enters and Bertrand competition between the two suppliers drives the price to a Bertrand price of $\frac{1}{2}$ (see chapter 5). If $c \geqslant \frac{1}{2}$, the entrant is the high-cost supplier and does not enter; the incumbent then charges the monopoly price, 1, to the buyer. Thus, the expected price paid by the buyer, if he does not sign the contract, is

$$\text{Prob}(c < \tfrac{1}{2}) \times \tfrac{1}{2} + \text{Prob}(c \geqslant \tfrac{1}{2}) \times 1$$

$$= (\tfrac{1}{2} \times \tfrac{1}{2}) + (\tfrac{1}{2} \times 1) = \tfrac{3}{4}.$$

But accepting the contract has the buyer pay $\frac{3}{4}$ whatever c (once the penalty for breach is included), so the buyer accepts the exclusionary contract.[60,61]

We thus conclude that the buyer and the incumbent can realize the vertically integrated outcome through a long-term contract that specifies a penalty for breach in case the buyer switches to another supplier. As we have seen, this contract creates an inefficiently low probability of entry from a social point of view. There is too much market foreclosure (too little competition).[62]

Aghion and Bolton then analyze the externalities among several buyers. (To abstract from downstream competition, let us assume that the buyers are in different industries.) If the entrant produces under constant returns to scale (in particular, if he does not face a fixed cost of entry or production, i.e., a cost that is independent of the scale of operation), the buyers are "unrelated" and the contract signed between the incumbent and one buyer exerts no externality on the other buyers. The contract is then the same as in the one-buyer case. When the entrant faces a fixed cost, however, a buyer who signs a contract with the incumbent that reduces the entrant's profitability of dealing with the buyer (because of penalties for breach) reduces the size of the entrant's market and thus reduces the probability of entry. Because the fixed cost can be recovered only through mass production, a buyer's exclusivity or long-term contract exerts negative externalities on the other buyers.

An obvious observation is that the incumbent may be able to extract large surpluses from the individual buyers, which he could not do if the buyers colluded. To see why, suppose that there are many small buyers, and suppose that the entrant's fixed cost is sufficiently large that entry to supply a single buyer is never profitable. Then if all the other buyers accept a contract tying them to the incumbent, an individual buyer has no threat to turn to the entrant. The incumbent can then obtain the natural-monopoly price (equal to 1). In general, however, the incumbent may offer a contract that allows the entrant to enter with some probability (as in the one-buyer case), and can do even better than a natural monopoly by extracting some of the efficiency gains from letting the entrant produce (as long as the buyers do not organize to synchronize their decisions).

An issue not analyzed in Aghion and Bolton 1987 but

---

60. Even if the incumbent has all the bargaining power in his negotiation with the buyer (i.e., makes a take-it-or-leave-it offer), he cannot realize the whole integrated structure's profit, which is $\frac{9}{16}$. His profit is only $\frac{5}{16}$, because the buyer can threaten to get $\frac{1}{4}$ by rejecting the contract.

61. As was noted above, the exact division of surplus and the final allocation of production depend on the relative bargaining powers, and on the assumption about price competition in case of rejection. But the incentive for the incumbent and the buyer to exploit their monopoly power with respect to the entrant remains.

62. There are reasons why it may be socially efficient to bias the recontracting process in favor of the incumbent. In particular, it can be shown that, both socially and privately, the initial contract should favor the incumbent at the contract-renewal stage (relative to a bidding procedure) if the incumbent invests in *transferable* assets (e.g., machines or know-how that can be used by the entrant in case of entry); see Laffont and Tirole 1987. This result does not contradict the conclusion of Aghion and Bolton (1987) that there is too little switching in equilibrium, but it may make its application more difficult in cases involving non-negligible transferable investments (how distant is the private bias from the socially optimal one?).

which could in principle be analyzed in an extended version of their model is that of the optimal timing of contracts for the incumbent. This might shed some light on the validity of the common allegation that established suppliers optimally deter entry through staggered contracts with their downstream customers (as is done with computer reservation systems).

Last, Aghion and Bolton show that an incumbent who has private information about the probability of entry (presumably because of superior knowledge of the technology) tends to lower the penalties for breach (i.e., to offer "shorter-run" contracts) relative to the case in which the buyer is as well informed as the incumbent. The idea is that the incumbent tries to push the buyer to accept his terms by signaling that the probability of entry is small (i.e., that the distribution of c is biased toward high costs). The way to signal a low probability of entry is to impose a low penalty for breach in order to "prove" that one is not concerned about the possibility of entry.

Answers and Hints

Exercise 4.1

Start with the retailer:

$$\max_{p}(p - p_w)D(p)$$

implies that

$$D(p) + (p - p_w)D'(p) = 0, \tag{1}$$

which defines a function $p^*(p_w)$ (assuming that the objective function is concave). We have

$$[2 D'(p) + (p - p_w)D''(p)]dp^* - D'(p)dp_w = 0.$$

Hence, using equation 1, we obtain

$$\frac{dp^*}{dp_w} = \frac{1}{2 - D(p)D''(p)/D'^2(p)}. \tag{2}$$

Hence, dp^*/dp_w is greater or less than $\frac{1}{2}$ if the demand function is convex or concave.

The manufacturer maximizes $(p_w - c)D(p^*(p_w))$:

$$D(p) + (p_w - c)D'(p)\frac{dp^*}{dp_w} = 0. \tag{3}$$

Equations 1–3 yield the desired result.

Exercise 4.2

(i) To obtain the equivalence, let firm 1 be the manufacturer and let firm 2 be the retailer. p_1 stands for the wholesale price p_w; $p_2 \equiv p - p_w$; p is the price of the final good; c_1 is the unit manufacturing cost; c_2 is the unit retail cost (zero in the text).

(ii) The vertically integrated price is

$$p = \frac{c}{1 - 1/\varepsilon}$$

(see chapter 1).

(iii) Firm 2, knowing p_1, chooses p_2 (or, equivalently, $p = p_1 + p_2$) so as to maximize

$$(p_2 - c_2)D(p) = [p - (p_1 + c_2)]D(p).$$

Thus, everything is as if firm 2 faced marginal cost $p_1 + c_2$ (recall the analogy with the vertical structure here). From chapter 1, we know that firm 2 chooses

$$p = \frac{p_1 + c_2}{1 - 1/\varepsilon}.$$

Let $p(p_1)$ denote this final price. (c_2 and ε are constant, so we do not include them in this function.) We have

$$p' \equiv \frac{dp}{dp_1} = \frac{1}{1 - 1/\varepsilon};$$

any increase in the first price is *magnified* by the second distortion. Firm 1 maximizes

$$(p_1 - c_1)D(p(p_1)).$$

Hence, by the chain rule of differentiation,

$$(p_1 - c_1)D'p' + D = 0.$$

Straightforward computations lead to

$$p = \frac{c}{(1 - 1/\varepsilon)^2}.$$

(iv) In the simultaneous-choice case, firm i chooses p_i so as to maximize

$$(p_i - c_i)D(p_i + p_j),$$

where p_j is considered as given ($j \neq i$). Thus,

$$(p_i - c_i)D' + D = 0.$$

Adding these equations for the two firms gives

$$(p - c)D' + 2D = 0,$$

or

$$p = \frac{c}{1 - 2/\varepsilon}.$$

Note that $p > c/(1 - 1/\varepsilon)^2$.

Explanation

Consider the price charged by firm 1 in the simultaneous mode. If in the sequential mode firm 1 charges the same price, then firm 2 will also choose the same price as in the simultaneous mode (since its price is optimal given firm 1's). Now consider a slight decrease in firm 1's price. If firm 2 did not change its price, firm 1's profit would be affected only to the second order (because firm 1's price is optimal given firm 2's). But this also has an effect on firm 2's price, which is reduced (see iii). This effect increases demand, and thus increases firm 1's profit, as $p_1 - c_1 > 0$.

Hence, a small price decrease is profitable for firm 1. This type of reasoning will be developed more systematically in chapters 5 and 8.

Exercise 4.3

Clearly, the manufacturer must impose a minimum quantity: $\underline{q} = q^m$. The retailer maximizes

$$[p - p_w - \Phi(s)]D(p, s)$$

subject to the constraint $D(p, s) \geqslant q^m$. In order for the manufacturer to realize the vertically integrated profit, the solution to this program must be $p = p^m$ and $s = s^m$ (so that the vertical structure's profit is maximized), and p_w must be equal to $p - \Phi(s) = p^m - \Phi(s^m)$ (so that the retailer's profit is appropriated by the manufacturer). Conversely, suppose that the retailer maximizes

$$[p - p^m + \Phi(s^m) - \Phi(s)]D(p, s)$$

subject to the constraint $D(p, s) \geqslant q^m$. If we forget about the constraint, the retailer will choose p and s such that $D(p, s) < q^m$, because he faces a cost $p^m - \Phi(s^m)$ for the intermediate good that exceeds the vertical structure's marginal cost c. Hence, in the absence of the constraint, the retailer would induce a lower demand than q^m. (The proof of this is almost identical to that for the result in chapter 1 that the monopoly price increases with the marginal cost.) Thus, the constraint is binding: $D(p, s) = q^m$. The maximization program is now equivalent to $\max[p - \Phi(s)]$ subject to $D(p, s) \equiv q^m$. However, from the maximization program for the vertically integrated structure, the solution to this program is $p = p^m$ and $s = s^m$.

Exercise 4.4**

On multilateral moral hazard and the role of third parties, see Holmström 1982.

(i) The marginal revenue for the manufacturer is $p^m - \Phi(s^m)$, who chooses the right amount of services, S^m, if the retailer chooses p^m and s^m. The retailer buys the intermediate good at marginal cost. Hence, he ought to choose p^m and s^m. The presence of the third party allows both the retailer and the manufacturer to be residual claimants. (The role of a third party in breaking the budget balance between two parties was particularly emphasized by Groves [1973] and Holmström [1982].) To appropriate the retailer's profit, the manufacturer should set

$A = [p^m - c - \Phi(s^m)]D(p^m, s^m, S^m).$

The third party makes a zero profit:

$-[p^m - \Phi(s^m)]q^m + cq^m + [p^m - c - \Phi(s^m)]q^m = 0.$

(ii) The third party is a marginal source, in that a unit increase in output yields him

$c + \Phi(s^m) - p^m < 0.$

(The third party's margin is equal to minus the vertically integrated margin, which is not surprising.) The manufacturer and the retailer, if they collude, have a joint profit margin of

$[p - c - \Phi(s)] + [p^m - c - \Phi(s^m)],$

which exceeds the joint profit margin in the absence of a source:

$p - c - \Phi(s).$

Hence, collusion between these two parties leads to an output above q^m, and—because marginal units are costly to the source—to a negative profit for the source.

Exercise 4.5

Another explanation was given in chapter 3: The tie-in of spare parts or maintenance can be used as a counting device to discriminate between high-use and low-use consumers. For a more general discussion of tie-ins and their link with the input substitution model, see Shughart 1985.

(i) Informally: The rental cost of the capital (the jet) equals the interest on the durable good, rp_w, plus the product of the probability that the good breaks down, $\alpha(x')$, and the replacement cost, p_w. To this must be added the maintenance cost, $c'x'$. Thus, the marginal cost of one unit of output is

$\min_{x'}\{c'x' + p_w[r + \alpha(x')]\}.$

More formally: If the downstream industry buys the durable good, the expected total cost (gross of maintenance costs) of owning one unit of the durable good permanently is

$C = p_w + \int_0^\infty \alpha e^{-\alpha t} e^{-rt} C \, dt.$

The owner must pay p_w now. The probability at date 0 of

the durable good's breaking down between t and $t + dt$ is $\alpha e^{-\alpha t}$. The owner then faces an expected total cost of C anew. Integrating, we obtain

$rC = p_w(r + \alpha).$

Thus, again, the cost per unit of time is $p_w(r + \alpha) + c'x'$.

(ii) The monopolist sells at $p_w > c$. The first-order condition for the downstream industry is

$c' + p_w\alpha'(x') = 0,$

and that for the vertically integrated structure is

$c' + c\alpha'(x') = 0.$

Because $\alpha'' > 0$, x' is smaller under vertical integration. (The result that cost minimization is destroyed by excessive maintenance downstream was obtained by Schmalensee [1974]. In contrast with a sale policy, the rental policy yields cost minimization and is preferred by the monopolist.) Sufficient restraints include a tie-in and a royalty.

(iii) Introduce a fictitious variable,

$x \equiv r + \alpha(x').$

(Note that $dx/dx' < 0$ and $d^2x/dx'^2 > 0$.) Thus, the downstream industry minimizes

$c'x' + p_w x(x').$

In the input-substitution problem in the text, the downstream industry minimizes $c'x' + p_w x$ subject to $f(x, x')$ = constant (a cost-minimization program). The constraint can be written as $x = x(x')$ with $dx/dx' < 0$ (inputs are substitutes) and $d^2x/dx'^2 > 0$ (the production function is concave).

Exercise 4.6

(i) A franchise fee is not sufficient. Whatever the marginal wholesale price p_w, competition generally does not lead to the vertically integrated level of services. (Actually, $A = 0$ because competition drives retailers' profits down to zero.)

(ii) RPM is sufficient. The choice of p and p_w fixes the competitive level of services: $\Phi(s) = p - p_w$. Hence, it suffices to impose $p = p^m$ and charge the wholesale price $p_w = p^m - \Phi(s^m)$. Quantity fixing is also a sufficient instrument.

Exercise 4.7

Let $p^m(p_w + \gamma, d)$ denote the monopoly price in state of demand d with total input price $p_w + \gamma$, where p_w denotes the wholesale price under exclusive territories. The manufacturer's profit under exclusive territories is

$$E[(p_w - c)D(p^m(p_w + \gamma, d), d)]$$
$$+ [p^m(p_w + \overline{\gamma}, \underline{d}) - p_w - \overline{\gamma}]D(p^m(p_w + \overline{\gamma}, \underline{d}), \underline{d}).$$

The second term in this profit represents the sum of the franchise fees over all retailers. (Because the retailers are infinitely risk-averse, their utility is equal to their profit in the worst state of nature minus the franchise fee; and this utility must be non-negative.)

Because we assumed that the monopoly price responds less than fully to variations in cost,

$$p^m(p_w + \overline{\gamma}, \underline{d}) - p^m(p_w + \gamma, \underline{d}) \leqslant \overline{\gamma} - \gamma,$$

and that the monopoly price is nondecreasing in the demand parameter,

$$p^m(p_w + \gamma, \underline{d}) \leqslant p^m(p_w + \gamma, d),$$

we have

$$D(p^m(p_w + \gamma, d), d) \leqslant D(p^m(p_w + \overline{\gamma}, \underline{d}) - \overline{\gamma} + \gamma, d).$$

The manufacturer's profit under exclusive territories is clearly bounded above by that under the alternative competitive arrangement, which is equal to

$$E[D(p^m(p_w + \overline{\gamma}, \underline{d}) - \overline{\gamma} + \gamma, d)(p^m(p_w + \overline{\gamma}, \underline{d}) - \overline{\gamma} - c)].$$

References

Aghion, P., and P. Bolton. 1987. Contracts as a Barrier to Entry. *American Economic Review* 77: 388–401.

Arrow, K. 1970. *Essays in the Theory of Risk Bearing.* Amsterdam: North-Holland.

Baron, D., and R. Myerson. 1982. Regulating a Monopolist with Unknown Costs. *Econometrica* 50: 911–930.

Baumol, W. 1983. Some Subtle Issues in Railroad Rate Regulation. *International Journal of Transport Economics* 10: 341–355.

Blair, R., and D. Kaserman. 1978. Vertical Integration, Tying and Antitrust Policy. *American Economic Review* 68: 397–402.

Blair, R., and D. Kaserman. 1983. *Law and Economics of Vertical Integration and Control.* New York: Academic.

Bolton, P., and G. Bonanno. 1985. Resale Price Maintenance and Competition in Post-Sales Services. Mimeo; *Quarterly Journal of Economics,* forthcoming.

Bonanno, G., and J. Vickers. 1986. Vertical Separation. Mimeo, Nuffield College, Oxford.

Bork, R. 1978. *The Antitrust Paradox.* New York: Basic Books.

Bowman, W. 1957. Tying Arrangements and the Leverage Problem. *Yale Law Journal* 67: 19–36.

Bresnahan, T., and P. Reiss. 1985. Dealer and Manufacturer Margins. *Rand Journal of Economics* 16: 253–268.

Brock, G. 1981. *The Telecommunications Industry.* Cambridge, Mass.: Harvard University Press.

Caillaud, B., and P. Rey. 1986. A Note on Vertical Restraints with the Provision of Distribution Services. Mimeo, INSEE and Massachusetts Institute of Technology.

Caves, R. 1984. Vertical Restraints in Manufacturer-Distributor Relations: Incidence and Economic Effects. Mimeo.

Dixit, A. 1983. Vertical Integration in a Monopolistically Competitive Industry. *International Journal of Industrial Organization* 1: 63–78.

Evans, D., ed. 1983. *Breaking Up Bell.* Amsterdam: North-Holland.

Gallini, N., and R. Winter. 1985. Licensing in the Theory of Innovation. *Rand Journal of Economics* 16: 237–252.

Gallini, N., and B. Wright. 1987. Technology Licensing under Asymmetric Information. Mimeo, University of Toronto.

Gal-Or, E. 1987. Duopolistic Vertical Restraints. Working Paper 650, Graduate School of Business, University of Pittsburgh.

Greenhut, M., and H. Ohta. 1979. Vertical Integration of Successive Oligopolists. *American Economic Review* 69: 137–147.

Grimm, C., and R. Harris. 1983. Vertical Foreclosure in the Rail Freight Industry: Economic Analysis and Policy Prescriptions. *ICC Practitioners Journal* 50: 508–531.

Groff, R., and M. Perry. 1985. Resale-Price Maintenance and Forward Integration into a Monopolistically Competitive Industry. *Quarterly Journal of Economics* 100: 1293–1312.

Grossman, S., and O. Hart. 1983. An Analysis of the Principal-Agent Problem. *Econometrica* 51: 7–46.

Groves, T. 1973. Incentives in Teams. *Econometrica* 41: 617–631.

Holmström, B. 1979. Moral Hazard and Observability. *Bell Journal of Economics* 10: 74–91.

Holmström, B. 1982. Moral Hazard in Teams. *Bell Journal of Economics* 13: 324–340.

Howard, M. 1983. *Antitrust and Trade Regulation: Selected Issues and Case Studies*. Englewood Cliffs, N.J.: Prentice-Hall.

Joskow, P. 1985. Mixing Regulatory and Antitrust Policies in the Electric Power Industry: The Price Squeeze and Retail Market Competition. In *Antitrust and Regulation: Essays in Memory of John J. McGowan*, ed. F. Fisher. City: Publisher.

Kamien, M., and Y. Tauman. 1983. The Private Value of a Patent: A Game Theoretic Analysis. Discussion Paper 576, Northwestern University.

Katz, M., and C. Shapiro. 1984. On the Licensing of Innovations. Discussion Paper 82, Woodrow Wilson School, Princeton University.

Krattenmaker, T., and S. Salop. 1986. Anticompetitive Exclusion: Raising Rivals' Costs to Achieve Power over Price. *Yale Law Journal* 96: 209–295.

Lafferty, R., R. Lande, and J. Kirkwood, eds. 1984. *Impact Evaluation of Federal Trade Commission Vertical Restraints Cases*. U.S. Federal Trade Commission.

Laffont, J.-J., and J. Tirole. 1986. Using Cost Observation to Regulate Firms. *Journal of Political Economy* 94: 614–641.

Laffont, J.-J., and J. Tirole. 1987. Repeated Auctions of Incentive Contracts, Investment and Bidding Parity. Mimeo, Massachusetts Institute of Technology.

McAfee, P., and J. McMillan. 1986. Strategic Vertical Integration. Mimeo, University of Western Ontario.

Marvel, H. 1982. Exclusive Dealing. *Journal of Law and Economics* 25: 1–26.

Marvel, H., and S. McCafferty. 1984. Resale Price Maintenance and Quality Certification. *Rand Journal of Economics* 15: 346–359.

Mathewson, F. 1983. The Incentives for Resale Price Maintenance under Imperfect Information. *Economic Enquiry* 21: 337–348.

Mathewson, F. and R. Winter. 1984. An Economic Theory of Vertical Restraints. *Rand Journal of Economics* 15: 27–38.

Mathewson, F., and R. Winter. 1985. Is Exclusive Dealing Anticompetitive? Working Paper 85/7, University of Toronto.

Mathewson, F., and R. Winter. 1986. The Economics of Vertical Restraints in Distribution. In *New Developments in the Analysis of Market Structures*, ed. F. Mathewson and J. Stiglitz. Cambridge, Mass.: MIT Press.

Ordover, J., and G. Saloner. 1987. Predation, Monopolization, and Antitrust. In *Handbook of Industrial Organization*, ed. R. Schmalensee and R. Willig (Amsterdam: North-Holland, forthcoming).

Ordover, J., and R. Willig. 1981. An Economic Definition of Predation: Pricing and Product Innovation. *Yale Law Journal* 91: 8–53.

Ordover, J., G. Saloner, and S. Salop. 1987. Equilibrium Vertical Foreclosure. Mimeo, Massachusetts Institute of Technology.

Ordover, J., A. Sykes, and R. Willig. 1985. Noncompetitive Behavior by Dominant Firms toward the Producers of Complementary Products. In *Antitrust and Regulation: Essays in Memory of John J. McGowan*, ed. F. Fisher. Cambridge, Mass.: MIT Press.

Overstreet, T. 1983. *Resale Price Maintenance: Economic Theories and Empirical Evidence*. U.S. Federal Trade Commission.

Perry, M., and R. Porter. 1986. Resale Price Maintenance and Exclusive Territories in the Presence of Retail Service Externalities. Mimeo, SUNY Stony Brook.

Posner, R. 1976. *Antitrust Law: An Economic Perspective*. University of Chicago Press.

Posner, R. 1977. The Rule of Reason and the Economic Approach: Reflections on the *Sylvania* Decision. *University of Chicago Law Review* 45: 1–20.

Posner, R. 1981. The Next Step in the Antitrust Treatment of Restricted Distribution: *Per se* Legality. *University of Chicago Law Review* 48: 6–26.

Pratt, J. 1964. Risk Aversion in the Small and in the Large. *Econometrica* 32: 122–136.

Rey, P., and J. Stiglitz. 1986. The Role of Exclusive Territories. Mimeo.

Rey, P., and J. Tirole. 1986a. Vertical Restraints from a Principal-Agent Viewpoint. In *Marketing Channels: Relationships and Performance*, ed. L. Pellegrini and S. Reddy. Lexington, Mass.: Lexington Books.

Rey, P., and J. Tirole. 1986b. The Logic of Vertical Restraints. *American Economic Review* 76: 921–939.

Salinger, M. 1984. Vertical Mergers and Market Foreclosure. Working Paper FB-84-17, Graduate School of Business, Columbia University.

Salinger, M. 1986. Vertical Mergers and Market Foreclosures with Differentiated Products. Mimeo, Columbia University.

Salop, S., and D. Sheffman. 1983. Raising Rivals' Costs. *American Economic Review* 73: 267–271.

Sappington, D. 1982. Optimal Regulation of Research and Development under Imperfect Information. *Bell Journal of Economics* 13: 354–368.

Scherer, F. 1980. *Industrial Market Structure and Economic Performance*, second edition. Boston: Houghton Mifflin.

Schmalensee, R. 1973. A Note on the Theory of Vertical Integration. *Journal of Political Economy* 81: 442–449.

Schmalensee, R. 1974. Market Structure, Durability and Maintenance Effort. *Review of Economic Studies* 41: 277–287.

Shavell, S. 1979. Risk Sharing Incentives in the Principal and Agent Relationship. *Bell Journal of Economics* 10: 55–73.

Shughart, W. 1985. Durable Goods, Tying Arrangements, and Anti-trust. Mimeo, George Mason University.

Spengler, J. 1950. Vertical Integration and Anti-trust Policy. *Journal of Political Economy* 58: 347–352.

Steiner, R. 1985. The Nature of Vertical Restraints. *Antitrust Bulletin* 30: 143–197.

Telser, L. 1960. Why Should Manufacturers Want Fair Trade?" *Journal of Law and Economics* 3: 86–105.

Temin, P. 1987. *The Fall of the Bell System*. Cambridge University Press.

Tye, W. 1986a. Post-Merger Denials of Competitive Access and Trackage Rights in the Rail Industry. *Transportation Practitioners Journal* 53: 413–427.

Tye, W. 1986b. Sunk Cost, Transaction Costs, and Vertical Foreclosure in the Rail Industry. Mimeo, Putnam, Hayes and Bartlett, Cambridge, Mass.

Vassiliakis, S. 1985. On the Division of Labor. Mimeo, Johns Hopkins University.

Vernon, J., and D. Graham. 1971. Profitability of Monopolization by Vertical Integration. *Journal of Political Economy* 79: 924–925.

Warren-Boulton, F. 1974. Vertical Control with Variable Proportions. *Journal of Political Economy* 82: 783–802.

Winter, R. 1985. Contracts in Intermediate Markets with Variable Proportions. Mimeo, University of Toronto.

Part II

Strategic Interaction

Introduction

Price and Nonprice Competition

In an oligopolistic market structure, a firm no longer encounters a passive environment. Therefore, we need to incorporate the strategic interactions of various decision makers in our models. To do this, we will make extensive use of the theory of noncooperative games.

Firms can use many instruments to compete in a market. Grossly simplifying, we can classify these instruments according to the speed at which they can be altered. In the short run, price is often the main instrument that a firm can change easily (other instruments include advertising and sales-force effort). Therefore, we begin our analysis with price competition in the context of rigid cost structures and product characteristics. In the somewhat longer run, cost structures and product characteristics can be altered, either together or separately. Production techniques can be rearranged and improved upon; capacity can be increased. Product characteristics (quality, product design, delivery delay, location of outlets, and so forth) can be changed. The consumers' perception of the product, which influences the demand function, can be modified by advertising. Ultimately, there is the decision of whether or not to enter or stay in the market (a "0-1" choice). Finally, in the long run, the product characteristics and the cost structures may be changed, not only by simple adjustments within the existing set of products and feasible costs, but also by a modification of this set. Research and development allows firms to expand their choice sets. "Process innovation" alters the technological production possibilities, and "product innovation" affords the creation of new products.

We can very crudely schematize the different stages of competition as in figure 1.

Chapter 5 deals with short-run price competition, examines the Bertrand paradox (in which two or more identical firms producing a homogeneous good with a

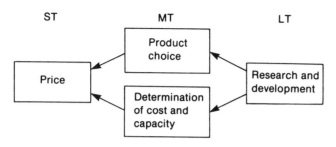

ST   MT   LT

Figure 1

constant-returns-to-scale technology in equilibrium sell at marginal cost and make no profit), discusses why the Bertrand conclusion is disturbing, and suggests three factors that, in practice, smooth price competition. The effect of capacity constraints is studied later in the chapter. Chapter 6 looks at repeated price competition, and chapter 7 introduces product differentiation. The last three chapters deal with barriers to entry, accommodation, predation, and exit (chapters 8 and 9) and with competition in research and development and the adoption of new technologies (chapter 10).

Noncooperative Games and Strategic Behavior

We shall model oligopolistic behavior as noncooperative games in which each firm behaves in its own self-interest. We are especially interested in the equilibria of these games. Nash equilibrium is the basic solution concept in game theory. A set of actions[1] is in Nash equilibrium if, given the actions of its rivals, a firm cannot increase its own profit by choosing an action other than its equilibrium action. For example, take two firms (the analysis generalizes trivially to n firms). Firm i ($i = 1, 2$) earns profit $\Pi^i(a_i, a_j)$, where a_i is the action of firm i and a_j is the action of its rival. We say that a pair of feasible actions is in Nash equilibrium if, for all i and any feasible action a_i,

$$\Pi^i(a_i^*, a_j^*) \geqslant \Pi^i(a_i, a_j^*). \tag{1}$$

The strategies we study here are pure strategies; each firm chooses a simple action. We could also consider mixed strategies where each firm chooses randomly from a set of actions. Of course, in order for firm i to be willing

to choose randomly from this set of different actions, all actions in it must yield the same profit (or expected profit, if firm j also plays a mixed strategy), and this profit must be optimal relative to the set of feasible actions a_i.

Nash equilibrium generalizes naturally to dynamic situations and to problems of incomplete information. We shall consider first the dynamic concept of Nash equilibrium (designated "perfect" in the jargon of game theory). This idea becomes particularly important as soon as there are many time periods and any intertemporal dependency of profits or feasible action sets; that is, when the actors make choices in period t that affect their objective functions or their set of feasible choices in a future time period $t + t'$, where $t' > 0$. To determine the consequences of actions taken in t, the players must forecast what will happen in $t + t'$ given the state of the game at the beginning of that period (which is influenced by their actions in t). To calculate these expectations, each player assumes that all other players will play an optimal strategy in $t + t'$. Therefore, the solution of a dynamic game is "backward looking." For example, in a two-period game, we start by solving the second-period Nash equilibrium as a function of the state of the game at the beginning of the second period (that is, on the basis of what happened during the first period). This means that the players can determine the future consequences of their first-period actions, because their first-period actions determine which second-period equilibrium will ensue; in a sense, given their first-period actions, the remainder of the game is a foregone conclusion. Therefore, the players choose their first-period actions with an eye toward their consequences in *both* periods. Thus, it suffices to determine the Nash equilibrium of the corresponding game in which players take only first-period actions but with the same set of consequences as in the original two-period game. All this may appear rather abstract, but it will become much clearer with some examples.

The Nash concept also generalizes to situations of asymmetric information. For instance, a firm may *ex ante* have one of two cost structures and be the only party to know which of these two is realized. The other parties must then figure out how this firm plays optimally for each possible realization of the cost structure. The no-

---

1. For expositional simplicity, we blur the distinction between action and strategy here. See the Game Theory User's Manual for more details.

tion of Bayesian equilibrium shows precisely how Nash equilibrium may be extended to this type of situation. Finally, in dynamic games with asymmetric information, the notions of perfect equilibrium and Bayesian equilibrium can be combined to further extend the relevance of Nash equilibrium.

Because most problems of industrial organization can be solved with a handful of basic game-theoretic concepts, it is recommended that the reader develop at least a casual familiarity with game theory. Although most of the arguments in part II can be understood at an intuitive level, the reader will benefit from a formal acquaintance with the concept of Nash equilibrium and its extensions, in the same way that optimization techniques clarify the study of the exercise of monopoly power. The reader may find the Game Theory User's Manual (chapter 11) useful in this respect.

Does noncooperative game theory remain relevant in situations in which firms appear to collude? In industrial organization, as in other fields, collusion and noncooperative behavior are not inconsistent. First, an altruistic party's objective function may embody the objectives of another party. In such a case, the first party's own interest is to make decisions that help the other party. (Here, altruism means cooperative actions taken purely for reason of self-interest.) Second, in the absence of altruism, parties facing conflicts may wish to change the rules of the game they are playing if this game has disastrous consequences for them. Signing a contract is a way of doing so. For instance, duopolists may agree to share the market in order to avoid cutthroat competition. However, signing a contract is formally only a part of a bigger noncooperative game. These two reasons why collusion can emerge from self-interested behavior may have limited relevance in IO. First, firms are rarely thought of as altruistic. Second, signing collusive contracts to prevent competition is often illegal. A third and more important reason is that, in a dynamic context, a firm may want to "pull its punches" because an aggressive action would trigger a rational reaction or retaliation from its opponents. (This will be emphasized in chapter 6 and, to a lesser extent, in chapter 8.) Again, the collusion is only apparent; it re-

sults from optimal noncooperative behavior. (This type of collusion is sometimes called *tacit* collusion.)

Reaction Functions: Strategic Complements and Substitutes

Consider a simultaneous-move game between (for simplicity) two firms. Assume that each action belongs to the real line and that the profit functions $\Pi^i(a_i, a_j)$ are twice continuously differentiable in the actions. The (necessary) first-order condition for a Nash equilibrium is that for each firm i

$$\Pi^i_i(a^*_i, a^*_j) = 0, \tag{2}$$

where a subscript denotes a partial derivative (e.g., $\Pi^i_i \equiv \partial \Pi^i / \partial a_i$). The second-order condition is that $a_i = a^*_i$ yields a local maximum:

$$\Pi^i_{ii}(a^*_i, a^*_j) \leqslant 0. \tag{3}$$

Assume that each firm's profit function is strictly concave in its own action everywhere: $\Pi^i_{ii}(a_i, a_j) < 0$ for all (a_i, a_j). Then the second-order condition is satisfied and, furthermore, the first-order condition given in equation 2 is sufficient for a Nash equilibrium. A Nash equilibrium is then given by a system of two equations with two unknowns (equation 2).

Let us define $R_i(a_j)$ as the best action for firm i given that firm j chooses a_j:

$$\Pi^i_i(R_i(a_j), a_j) = 0. \tag{4}$$

$a_i = R_i(a_j)$ is unique from our strict-concavity assumption,[2] and is called firm i's reaction to a_j. A Nash equilibrium is a pair of actions (a^*_1, a^*_2) such that $a^*_1 = R_1(a^*_2)$ and $a^*_2 = R_2(a^*_1)$. In such an equilibrium, each firm reacts optimally to the other firm's anticipated action.

A crucial element of part II is the sign of the slope of reaction functions for the various strategic variables we consider. This slope is obtained by differentiating equation 4:

$$R'_i(a_j) = \frac{\Pi^i_{ij}(R_i(a_j), a_j)}{-\Pi^i_{ii}(R_i(a_j), a_j)}. \tag{5}$$

---

2. We will assume that it exists and is an interior solution. In other words, going to the boundary of the feasible set of actions (e.g., $-\infty$ or $+\infty$) is not optimal for firm i.

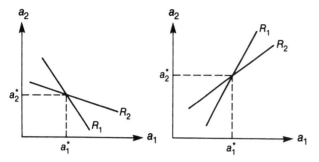

Strategic substitutes ($\Pi^i_{ij} < 0$) Strategic complements ($\Pi^i_{ij} > 0$)

Figure 2

We thus have sign(R'_i) = sign(Π^i_{ij}). Π^i_{ij} is the cross-partial derivative of firm i's profit function, i.e., the derivative of its marginal profit with respect to its opponent's action. The reaction curve is upward sloping if $\Pi^i_{ij} > 0$ and downward sloping if $\Pi^i_{ij} < 0$. Following Bulow, Geanakoplos, and Klemperer,[3] we will also consider the actions of the two firms to be strategic complements if $\Pi^i_{ij} > 0$ and strategic substitutes if $\Pi^i_{ij} < 0$.[4] As we shall see further on, prices are often strategic complements, and capacities are often strategic substitutes.

The construction of the reaction functions in a simultaneous-move game, performed in figure 2, is no more than a technical and illustrative device. By definition of simultaneous choices, a firm chooses its action before observing that of its opponent. Hence, it has no possibility of reacting. Reaction functions depict what a firm would do if it were to learn of a change in its opponent's action (which it does not). Points other than the Nash point on the reaction curves are never observed.

In contrast, reaction functions have real economic content in dynamic (sequential) games. For instance, if firm i chooses a_i first and firm j observes this choice before choosing a_j, firm i can use the function R_j to compute how a change in its behavior affects its opponent's behavior.

3. J. Bulow, J. Geanakoplos, and P. Klemperer, "Multimarket Oligopoly: Strategic Substitutes and Complements," *Journal of Political Economy* 93 (1985): 488–511.

4. This terminology is inspired by demand theory. Two goods are complements for a consumer if a decrease in the price of one good makes the other good more attractive to the consumer. Here, a decrease in a_j induces a decrease in a_i if $\Pi^i_{ij} > 0$, and conversely for substitutes.

Short-Run Price Competition

The study of price competition—a fundamental part of oligopoly theory—is one of its weakest links. It so happens that the most obvious natural formalization yields a result that is sometimes unconvincing. Deeper reflection shows that this formalization is economically naive, and alternative approaches come to mind.

In this chapter we assume that firms "meet only once" in the market. They simultaneously and noncooperatively charge a price. The Bertrand paradox, discussed in section 5.1, states that under these circumstances even oligopolists behave like competitive firms—that is, the number of firms in the industry is irrelevant to the study of price behavior. Section 5.2 offers an overview of the three alternative approaches that will be developed below and in the next two chapters. Section 5.3 introduces one such approach which is associated with decreasing returns to scale or capacity constraints; it studies foundations for the rival model to the Bertrand paradigm, the Cournot model of competition in quantities. The Cournot model assumes that firms pick quantities rather than prices, and that an auctioneer chooses the price to equate supply and demand. This model has been justly criticized on the grounds that no such auctioneer exists and that firms ultimately choose prices. The point of section 5.3 is that Cournot competition may be thought of as a two-stage game in which firms first choose capacities (or, more generally, scale variables) and then compete through prices. Section 5.4 reviews the main properties of the Cournot paradigm. Section 5.5 discusses concentration indices. The supplementary section completes sections 5.3 and 5.4 with a discussion of capacity-constrained price competition and other aspects of the Cournot model.

5.1 The Bertrand Paradox

To simplify, let us take the case of a duopoly. The analysis generalizes straightforwardly to the case of n firms.

Assume that two firms produce identical goods which are "nondifferentiated" in that they are perfect substitutes in the consumers' utility functions. Consequently, consumers buy from the producer who charges the lowest price. If the firms charge the same price, we must make an assumption about the distribution of consumers between them. We assume that each firm faces a demand schedule equal to half of the market demand at the common price (the half is not a crucial assumption). Further, we assume that the firm always supplies the demand it faces (this assumption is not crucial here). The market demand function is $q = D(p)$. Each firm incurs a cost c per unit of production. Therefore, the profit of firm i is

$$\Pi^i(p_i, p_j) = (p_i - c)D_i(p_i, p_j), \qquad (5.1)$$

where the demand for the output of firm i, denoted D_i, is given by

$$D_i(p_i, p_j) = \begin{cases} D(p_i) & \text{if } p_i < p_j \\ \frac{1}{2}D(p_i) & \text{if } p_i = p_j \\ 0 & \text{if } p_i > p_j. \end{cases}$$

The aggregate profit,

$$\min_{p_i}(p_i - c)D(p_i),$$

cannot exceed the monopoly profit,

$$\Pi^m = \max_p (p - c)D(p).$$

Each firm can guarantee itself a non-negative profit by charging a price above the marginal cost. Hence, any reasonable prediction must yield

$$0 \leqslant \Pi^1 + \Pi^2 \leqslant \Pi^m.$$

The firms choose their prices both simultaneously and noncooperatively. Simultaneity means that each firm has not yet observed the other firm's price when choosing its own. Rather, a firm anticipates it. We assume that it does so correctly. A Nash equilibrium in prices—sometimes referred to as a Bertrand equilibrium—is a pair of prices (p_1^*, p_2^*) such that each firm's price maximizes that firm's profit given the other firm's price. Formally, for all $i = 1$, 2 and for all p_i,

$$\Pi^i(p_i^*, p_j^*) \geqslant \Pi^i(p_i, p_j^*).$$

The Bertrand (1883) paradox states that the unique equilibrium has the two firms charge the competitive price: $p_1^* = p_2^* = c$. The proof is as follows: Consider, for example,

$$p_1^* > p_2^* > c.$$

Then firm 1 has no demand, and its profit is zero. On the other hand, if firm 1 charges

$$p_1 = p_2^* - \varepsilon$$

(where ε is positive and "small"), it obtains the entire market demand, $D(p_2^* - \varepsilon)$, and has a positive profit margin of

$$p_2^* - \varepsilon - c.$$

Therefore, firm 1 cannot be acting in its own best interest if it charges p_1^*. Now suppose that

$$p_1^* = p_2^* > c.$$

The profit of firm 1 is

$$D(p_1^*)(p_1^* - c)/2.$$

If firm 1 reduces its price slightly to $p_1^* - \varepsilon$, its profit becomes

$$D(p_1^* - \varepsilon)(p_1^* - \varepsilon - c),$$

which is greater for small ε. In this situation, the market share of the firm increases in a discontinuous manner. Because no firm will charge less than the unit cost c (the lowest-price firm would make a negative profit), we are left with one or two firms charging exactly c. To show that both firms do charge c, suppose that

$$p_1^* > p_2^* = c.$$

Then firm 2, which makes no profit, could raise its price slightly, still supply all the demand, and make a positive profit—a contradiction.

The conclusions of this simple model are the following:

(i) that firms price at marginal cost, and

(ii) that firms do not make profits.

These conclusions suggest that the monopoly results of chapter 1 are very special. Even a duopoly would suffice to restore competition. We call this the Bertrand *paradox* because it is hard to believe that firms in industries with few firms never succeed in manipulating the market price to make profits.[1]

In the asymmetric case (say, where firm i has constant unit cost c_i, where $c_1 < c_2$), conclusions i and ii do not hold. Indeed, the following can be shown (up to some technical considerations, see exercise 5.1):

(iii) that both firms charge price $p = c_2$ (actually, firm 1 charges an ε below c_2 to make sure it has the whole market), and

(iv) that firm 1 makes a profit of $(c_2 - c_1)D(c_2)$, and firm 2 makes no profit (as long as $c_2 \leqslant p^m(c_1)$, where $p^m(c_1)$ maximizes $(p - c_1)D(p)$; otherwise, firm 1 charges $p^m(c_1)$).

Thus, firm 1 charges above marginal cost and makes a positive profit, and the Bertrand equilibrium is no longer welfare-optimal. But, again, the conclusion is a bit strained. Firm 1 makes very little profit if c_2 is close to c_1, and firm 2 makes no profit at all.

*Exercise 5.1** Prove conclusions iii and iv.

5.2 Solutions to the Bertrand Paradox: An Introduction

We can resolve the Bertrand paradox by relaxing any one of the three crucial assumptions of the model. Each of these generalizations brings more realism to the problem of price determination. The first is studied in section 5.3; the other two are taken up in chapters 6 and 7. In the present section we will sketch these possible solutions.

5.2.1 The Edgeworth Solution

Edgeworth (1897) solved the Bertrand paradox by introducing capacity constraints, by which firms cannot sell more than they are capable of producing. To understand this idea, suppose that firm 1 has a production capacity smaller than $D(c)$. Is $(p_1^*, p_2^*) = (c, c)$ still an equilibrium price system? At this price, both firms make zero profit. Suppose that firm 2 increases its price slightly. Firm 1 then faces demand $D(c)$, which it cannot satisfy. Then,

rationing dictates that some consumers must resort to firm 2. Firm 2 has a (residual) nonzero demand at a price greater than its marginal cost and, therefore, makes positive profit. Consequently, the Bertrand solution is no longer an equilibrium.

To solve explicitly for the equilibrium, we must introduce a more specific assumption concerning the manner in which consumers are rationed. As a general rule, in models with capacity constraints, firms make positive profit and the market price is greater than the marginal cost. The crucial question now is whether or not this property is relevant: Won't firms accumulate capital *ex ante* until they are capable of satisfying the entire market demand at marginal cost? The answer is No. To accumulate capital is expensive, and it is not in the self-interest of the firms to do so if such behavior yields zero gross profit (without netting out capital costs).[2]

Using capacity constraints to justify noncompetitive prices is quite reasonable in some applications. For example, imagine the case of two hotels in a small town. In the short run, these hotels cannot adjust the number of beds (capacity). It is useless for them to get involved in cutthroat price competition if they are incapable of satisfying market demand individually. In the longer run they do not increase their capacity very much, because they expect keen competition in a situation of collective overcapacity. One can also consider the case where the production of a good requires a certain delay. Then, the available quantities for sale in the very short run cannot be adjusted at all, and therefore they act as capacity constraints at the time of price competition.

The existence of a rigid capacity constraint is a special case of a decreasing-returns-to-scale technology. In our previous example, a firm has marginal cost that is equal to c up to the capacity constraint and is then equal to infinity. More generally, the marginal cost may increase with the output. Except in special cases (such as the hotel example), a firm usually has some leeway to increase its production beyond its "efficient level"—extra machines can be rented, existing ones can be utilized beyond their efficient intensity of use, inputs can be provided on short

---

1. Another paradox of the model is that one wonders why firms bother to enter at all if they do not make any profit. Along the same lines, suppose that the firms face a fixed cost of entering the market. Then, if one firm enters, the other firm will not follow suit, however small the fixed cost. Thus, if one

believes in the existence of at least a small fixed cost of production or of entry, the market is likely to yield a monopoly.

2. See sections 5.3 and 5.7.

notice, and workers can work overtime. The cost of producing these extra units exceeds that for the inframarginal ones, but is, in general, not infinite.

5.2.2 The Temporal Dimension

The second crucial assumption underlying the Bertrand paradox is the "timing" of the game, which does not always seem to reflect economic reality as it stands. To see this, consider a crucial condition for the Bertrand solution. In particular, why is $p_1 = p_2 > c$ not an equilibrium? The answer is that firm 1, for example, would benefit from a slight decrease in its price (i.e., to $p_2 - \varepsilon$) and from its resulting takeover of the entire market. What would happen then? Nothing, given Bertrand's crucial condition that players are assumed to play only once. Firm 2 would lose all its customers, and would make zero profit because it would not react. In reality, firm 2 would probably decrease its price in order to regain its share of the market. If we introduce this temporal dimension and the possibility of reaction, it is no longer clear that firm 1 would benefit from decreasing its price below p_2. Firm 1 would have to compare the short-run gain (the increase of its market share) to the longer-run loss in a price war. Chapter 6 shows that more collusive behavior than in the Bertrand equilibrium can be sustained by the threat of future losses in a price war.

5.2.3 Product Differentiation

An important assumption in the Bertrand analysis is the perfect substitutability of the firms' products. Consumers are indifferent between the goods at equal price and, thus, buy from the lowest-priced producer. This creates a pressure on price, which is somewhat relaxed when the firms' products are not quite identical (see chapter 2 for a description of a few differentiation spaces). Then, in general, the firms do.not charge their marginal cost. For instance, think of two firms selling the same good but located at different places. Suppose that firm 1 charges $p_1 = c$. Firm 2, by charging $p_2 = c + \varepsilon$ (for ε small), keeps at least some consumers who are located near it. For these consumers, the price differential is more than offset by the difference in transportation cost. Hence, the zero-profit price system ($p_1 = c$, $p_2 = c$) is no longer an equilibrium. (An extreme case of product differentiation occurs when the demands for the firms' products are unrelated. Each

firm then charges its monopoly price.) Price competition with differentiated products is analyzed in chapter 7.

5.2.4 What to Make of the Bertrand Analysis

Bertrand competition is interesting because it depicts a polar case. It represents what we have in mind when we think of sharp small-number competition. In general, of course, oligopoly pricing will lead to an outcome intermediate between the Bertrand one and the outcome of the other polar case (the monopoly situation). Most of our analysis of price rivalry will concern the determination of the factors that induce tough or soft competition.

5.3 Decreasing Returns to Scale and Capacity Constraints

5.3.1 Rationing Rules

Assume now that both firms' cost functions exhibit decreasing returns to scale. $C_i(q_i)$ is increasing and convex: $C_i'(q_i) > 0$ and $C_i''(q_i) \geqslant 0$ for $q_i > 0$.

As figure 5.1 shows, an extreme case of decreasing returns to scale is that of a capacity constraint: The marginal cost of production becomes infinite at some output $\bar{q}_i$ (called the *capacity level*).

At a given price p, a firm is not willing to supply more than its competitive supply $S_i(p)$, which is defined by the equality of price and marginal cost:

$$p \equiv C_i'(S_i(p)).$$

Now, suppose that firm i charges the lowest price, p, and that $S_i(p) < D(p)$. Not all consumers who want to buy from firm i are able to do so. Because of rationing, the other firm faces some *residual demand*. The exact form

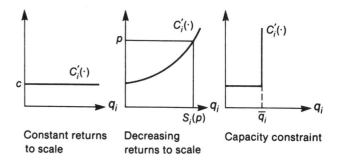

Figure 5.1

of the residual-demand function depends on which consumers are served by the low-price firm—i.e., on the rationing rule.

Two rationing rules have often been considered in the literature. The following subsections give their interpretation for the case of a demand function stemming from unit demands. The interpretation for individual downward-sloping demands is left to the reader.

Let $p_1 < p_2$ denote the two prices charged by the two firms. By abusing notation, we can allow $\bar{q}_1 \equiv S_1(p_1)$ to denote firm 1's supply. ($S_1(p_1)$ is a self-imposed capacity constraint.)

5.3.1.1 The Efficient-Rationing Rule

Suppose that $\bar{q}_1 < D(p_1)$. Firm 1 cannot satisfy all of its demand. The efficient-rationing rule presupposes a residual-demand function for firm 2:

$$\tilde{D}_2(p_2) = \begin{cases} D(p_2) - \bar{q}_1 & \text{if } D(p_2) > \bar{q}_1 \\ 0 & \text{otherwise.} \end{cases}$$

Thus, everything is as if the most eager consumers bought from firm 1. Firm 2 then faces the translated demand curve shown in figure 5.2.

This rationing is called efficient because it maximizes consumer surplus. In particular, when $D(p_2) > \bar{q}_1$, the marginal consumer who consumes the good has valuation p_2 for the good, which is the marginal cost of obtaining the good for consumers. The residual-demand function defined by the efficient-rationing rule is the one that would be obtained if the consumers were able to costlessly resell the good to each other (i.e., to engage in arbitrage).[3]

Efficient rationing is also called *parallel rationing*, for obvious geometrical reasons. It also arises when the demand curve stems from identical individual downward-sloping demand curves and consumers are all rationed fairly (i.e., each of n consumers gets $\bar{q}_1/n$ at price p_1).

5.3.1.2 The Proportional-Rationing Rule

By this rationing rule (also called the *randomized-rationing rule*), all consumers have the same probability of being

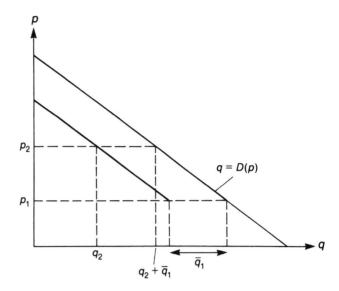

Figure 5.2
The efficient-rationing rule.

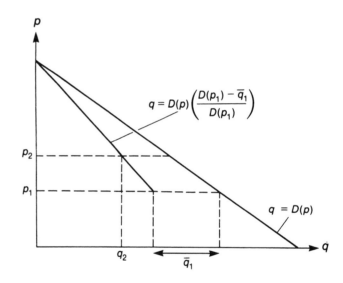

Figure 5.3
The proportional-rationing rule.

---

3. This is because we know that the competitive exchange market between consumers is efficient. Note that the existence of a frictionless arbitrage between consumers is a strong assumption. (Recall that on the other side of the market, firms are assumed not to be able to change prices; thus, we may be putting too much friction on the supply side and too little on the demand side.)

rationed. The probability of not being able to buy from firm 1 is

$$\frac{D(p_1) - \bar{q}_1}{D(p_1)}.$$

Hence, the residual demand facing firm 2 is

$$\tilde{D}_2(p_2) = D(p_2)\left(\frac{D(p_1) - \bar{q}_1}{D(p_1)}\right).$$

This rule is not efficient for consumers—some consumers with valuation below p_2 (the marginal cost of the good for the population of buyers) buy the good because they obtain the bargain price p_1. However, firm 2 prefers this rule to the efficient-rationing rule, because its residual demand is higher at each price.

Of course, there are many other possible rationing rules. The most realistic one cannot be found in the abstract. For example, if rationing is achieved by queueing and waiting, we need to know the degree of correlation between the value of the good and the value of the time for each consumer. If the consumers who are the most eager to buy the good are also those with the highest value of time, and if rationing is accomplished through waiting time, one may want to consider rationing rules in which the least eager consumers tend to buy the good at the lowest price. One must also wonder whether consumers can engage in arbitrage after buying the good and whether one firm can buy from the other.[4] In the following, we will use rationing rules as a substitute for a complete analysis of consumer behavior.

5.3.2 Price Competition

Price competition under constant returns to scale yields a price equal to the constant marginal cost. The natural generalization for decreasing returns to scale would be the "competitive outcome":

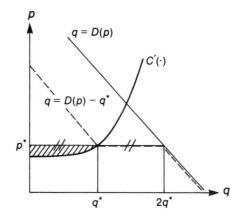

Figure 5.4

$$p^* = C_1'(q_1) = C_2'(q_2),$$

or

$S_1(p^*) + S_2(p^*) = D(p^*)$. Unfortunately, both firms charging the competitive price, p^*, is generally not an equilibrium. Consider, for example, the symmetric marginal-cost curves depicted in figure 5.4. The competitive-equilibrium price is p^*, and the competitive supply per firm is q^*. The rationing rule here is the efficient-rationing one, and each firm's residual-demand curve when the other firm charges p^* is represented by the dashed line.

Suppose that $p_1 = p_2 = p^*$ is a Nash equilibrium. Then each firm's profit is equal to the area of the shaded region in figure 5.4 (possibly minus a fixed cost of production). Now, it is clear from the figure that there exist prices $p > p^*$ that yield a higher profit for a firm given that the other firm charges p^*.[5] Thus, the competitive equilibrium is not a Nash equilibrium. The economic intuition behind this result is simple. At the competitive equilibrium, each firm is on its supply curve, so one will not supply more if the other raises its price. The firm that raises its price slightly above the competitive price loses some demand; however, this is only a second-order effect, as the last

---

4. For instance, if consumers are rationed according to the efficient-rationing rule, firm 2 would want to buy firm 1's whole capacity if it could do so. The residual demand would then be equal to the demand, and firm 2's profit would be

$$p_2 D(p_2) - p_1\bar{q}_1 - c[D(p_2) - \bar{q}_1] > (p_2 - c)[D(p_2) - \bar{q}_1]$$

for linear costs, say.

5. Mathematically, a firm's profit for price $p \geqslant p^*$ when the other firm charges p^* is

$$p[D(p) - q^*] - C[D(p) - q^*].$$

The derivative of this profit with respect to p at $p = p^*$ is

$$D(p^*) - q^* + \{p - C'[D(p) - q^*]\}D'(p^*) = q^* > 0,$$

using $D(p^*) = 2q^*$. So the profit is locally increasing in one's own price at the competitive price. The reader should check this property for a more general rationing rule yielding a residual demand curve $\tilde{D}(p, p^*)$ that is right-differentiable at $p = p^*$ (for instance, the proportional-rationing rule).

units were sold at marginal cost. At the same time, that firm raises the price on inframarginal units and realizes a first-order increase in profit.

Deriving the (or an) equilibrium under increasing marginal costs is often a complex matter. In particular, it generally involves mixed strategies.[6] But one property of equilibrium is that *both firms' prices exceed the competitive price*.[7] This property formalizes the notion that decreasing returns to scale soften price competition. In the following example (which differs from the previous analysis in that the marginal-cost functions are not differentiable), the equilibrium is nicely characterized (the firms charge a market-clearing price).

5.3.2.1 A Capacity-Constrained Example

Let the demand curve be

$$D(p) = 1 - p,$$

or

$$p = P(q_1 + q_2) = 1 - q_1 - q_2.$$

The two firms have capacity constraints, so firm i's output must satisfy $q_i \leq \overline{q}_i$. The capacity $\overline{q}_i$ has been acquired previous to the price game at a unit cost c_0 belonging to the interval $[\frac{3}{4}, 1]$. The marginal cost of production c (once the capacity is installed) is, without loss of generality, 0 up to $\overline{q}_i$, and ∞ after $\overline{q}_i$ (for instance, the capacity could correspond to an *ex ante* production). The efficient-rationing rule is in effect.

We can restrict ourselves to capacities of less than $\frac{1}{3}$, because a firm's profit (gross of investment costs) in the price game cannot exceed the monopoly profit

$$\max_p p(1 - p) = \frac{1}{4}.$$

Thus, firm i's total profit (net of investment costs) is at most $\frac{1}{4} - c_0 \overline{q}_i$, and is negative for $\overline{q}_i \geq \frac{1}{3}$—whatever their expectations about the market outcome, firms would not rationally invest more than $\frac{1}{3}$. (From now on, profits

will be computed gross of the investment cost except where another method is mentioned.)

Assume that $\overline{q}_1$ and $\overline{q}_2$ belong to $[0, \frac{1}{3}]$. Let us show that both firms charging

$$p^* = 1 - (\overline{q}_1 + \overline{q}_2)$$

is an equilibrium. (This equilibrium is unique.) At this price, both firms "dump" their capacities on the market, and the consumers are not rationed. There is no point to charging a lower price; firm i cannot supply more than $\overline{q}_i$ and thus would simply supply an output equal to capacity at a lower price.

Is it worth raising one's price above p^*? Firm i's profit from price $p \geq p^*$ is

$$p(1 - p - \overline{q}_j) = (1 - q - \overline{q}_j)q,$$

where q is the quantity sold by firm i at price p. (Note that $q \leq \overline{q}_i$, because $p \geq p^*$.) But this later profit is the same as the one realized by a firm that gives output q to an auctioneer who then equates supply and demand, given that the other firm supplies $\overline{q}_j$. We will later call this profit a *Cournot profit*. The profit function

$$(1 - q - \overline{q}_j)q$$

is concave in q. Its derivative at $q = \overline{q}_i$ is

$$1 - 2\overline{q}_i - \overline{q}_j > 0,$$

because $\overline{q}_i$ and $\overline{q}_j$ are lower than $\frac{1}{3}$. Hence, lowering the output below $\overline{q}_i$ (or, equivalently, raising the price above p^*) is not optimal.

The conclusion of this study is that everything is as if the two firms put outputs equal to their capacities on the market and an auctioneer equaled supply and demand. The difference is that the firms choose the market-clearing price themselves. For capacities $\overline{q}_1$ and $\overline{q}_2$ in $[0, \frac{1}{3}]$, the firms' *reduced-form profit functions* after solving for price competition are

$$\Pi^{ig}(\overline{q}_i, \overline{q}_j) = [1 - (\overline{q}_i + \overline{q}_j)]\overline{q}_i \qquad (5.2)$$

(gross of investment cost)

---

6. This feature makes the static model of price choices particularly suspect. Suppose that each firm randomizes between different prices. A firm's price may be optimal *ex ante* (before the firm knows the realization of the other firm's price). But *ex post* (after learning this realization) the firm may want to change its price. This suggests that we look at the price dynamics.

7. The advanced reader may check this on mixed strategies. The intuition can be derived from pure strategies: If $p_2 > p_1$ and $p_1 < p^*$, then firm 1 is a local monopolist (i.e., its profit is the monopoly profit for prices around p_1). We know that a monopolist does not sell at a price below marginal cost. If $p_2 = p_1 < p^*$, the same reasoning as in footnote 5 shows that each firm wants to raise its price.

and

$$\Pi^{in}(\overline{q}_i, \overline{q}_j) = \{[1 - (\overline{q}_i + \overline{q}_j)] - c_0\}\overline{q}_i \qquad (5.3)$$

(net of investment cost).

We later will say that such profit functions have the *exact Cournot reduced form*. As was explained above, these are the profit functions that would obtain if the firms produced quantities $\overline{q}_i$ and an auctioneer picked the price so as to clear the market.

Exercise 5.2* Let the demand function be

$$q = D(p) = 1 - p.$$

Suppose that both firms' marginal cost (once the capacities are installed) is zero. Suppose further that $\overline{q}_1$ and $\overline{q}_2$ are lower than $\frac{1}{4}$. Show that under *proportional rationing* both firms charge

$$p^* = 1 - (\overline{q}_1 + \overline{q}_2),$$

and that

$$\Pi^{ig}(\overline{q}_i, \overline{q}_j) = \overline{q}_i(1 - \overline{q}_i - \overline{q}_j).$$

Our assumption of large investment costs was meant to guarantee small capacities. The result that for small capacities the reduced-form profit functions have the exact Cournot form was obtained by Beckman (1967) in the case of proportional rationing and by Levitan and Shubik (1972) in the case of efficient rationing. For larger capacities, no pure-strategy equilibrium exists (unless capacities allow each firm to supply the whole demand at the competitive price). The equilibrium is thus in mixed strategies, and it was computed in closed form by Beckman (1967) for proportional rationing and by Levitan and Shubik (1972) for efficient rationing in the special case of symmetric capacities. Kreps and Sheinkman (1983) characterized the mixed-strategy equilibrium for efficient rationing for asymmetric capacities as well—see section 5.7.[8] (The characterization of the asymmetric case is important for the study of the two-stage game, in which firms are allowed to choose different capacities.)

5.3.3 *Ex Ante* Investment and *Ex Post* Price Competition

In the above example, price competition was subsumed in a very simple manner. Each firm knew that both firms chose exactly the price that allowed them to dump their capacities on the market. As Kreps and Scheinkman (1983) noted,[9] this suggests that we look at a two-stage game in which both firms simultaneously choose capacities $\overline{q}_i$ and then, knowing each other's capacity, they simultaneously choose prices p_i.

From our characterization of the second-stage price game, it follows that this two-stage game is equivalent to the one-stage game in which firms choose *quantities* $\overline{q}_i$ and an auctioneer determines the market price that clears the market: $p = P(\overline{q}_1 + \overline{q}_2)$. This one-stage game is indeed the quantity competition game envisioned by Cournot (1838).[10] Cournot has often (rightly) been criticized on the ground that prices are ultimately chosen by firms, not by an auctioneer. This type of two-stage-game construction shows that it may be possible to vindicate Cournot by introducing capacity constraints and considering the Cournot profit function (equation 5.3) as a reduced-form profit function in which later price competition has been subsumed.

Kreps and Scheinkman (1983) have shown that if the demand function is concave and if the rationing rule is the efficient one (but the investment cost c_0 is arbitrary), the outcome (capacity choices, market price) of the two-stage game is the same as that of the one-stage Cournot game—as the title of their paper proclaims, "quantity precommitment and Bertrand competition yield Cournot outcomes."[11] (See section 5.7.)

The idea of looking at a two-stage game in which firms choose an investment decision and then a price is not restricted to capacity choices. Indeed, in chapters 7 and 8 we will study two-stage games in which the investment decision refers to a choice in a product space (e.g. location). These games will have similar features. For instance, we will see that when choosing a location, firms try to differentiate themselves from other firms so as to avoid

---

8. See also further closed-form computations or characterizations of equilibrium in various contexts by Benoit and Krishna (1987), Davidson and Deneckere (1986), Ghemawat (1986), and Osborne and Pitchik (1986). For early work on the topic, see Shubik 1959.

9. Davidson and Deneckere (1986) trace the idea back to Sherman (1972).

10. The idea of Nash equilibrium can be found in Cournot. A Nash equilibrium for the quantity game is often called a Cournot-Nash or Cournot equilibrium.

11. However, the reduced-form profit functions do not have the exact Cournot form for "large capacities"(see section 5.7).

the intense Bertrand competition associated with perfectly substitutable products (in the same way that firms here avoid accumulating "too much capacity" in order to soften price competition). Such two-stage games are attractive because they formalize the idea that investment decisions are generally made before price decisions (or that they are long-run or medium-run choices while prices are fairly flexible.)

5.3.4 Discussion

As was noted above, the two-stage game is meant to convey the idea that price competition is the final stage of competition *and* the idea that scale decisions must be made before firms arrive on the market. Of course, in situations where firms can produce while or after demand is formulated, the second condition is not met. However, the existence of *ex ante* choice of scale may be reasonable in a number of situations. For instance, our hotel example is based on the fact that a hotel cannot adjust its capacity very quickly as a function of demand. Similarly, the street vendor of a perishable food first goes and buys a certain amount of the food (capacity), and in a second stage sells part or all of this amount.

There are two potential results of interest for the foundations of Cournot competition:

Exact Cournot reduced form The capacity-constrained price game yields reduced-form profit functions that are identical to Cournot profit functions, in which quantities are to be interpreted as capacities.

Cournot outcome in the two-stage game The equilibrium of the two-stage (capacity and then price) game coincides with the Cournot equilibrium, in which quantities are to be interpreted as capacities.

The first result implies the second. And, unlike the second, it allows the analysis of variants of Cournot competition, such as sequential timing for the choice of capacities. It is important to realize that these results rest on very strong assumptions. For instance, Davidson and Deneckere (1986) show that rationing rules even slightly different from the efficient-rationing rule do not yield the Cournot outcome if the cost of investment c_0 is small. The re-

sults also rest on the absence of intertemporal price competition (see chapter 6) and product differentiation (see chapter 7).[12]

Furthermore, even when such results hold in this simple setting, one must exercise caution when justifying Cournot competition using a reduced-form argument in more general settings. This point can be seen in a simple model where a firm's actions signal information to its rivals. As we shall see in chapter 9, firms may attempt to infer from their opponents' behavior information about the cost structures or the level of demand. Now, a one-stage quantity game and a two-stage quantity (capacity) and price game may be different, because the ability to make inferences may vary across different types of actions (in a one-stage game, a firm's actions do not convey the same information as the actions in the two-stage game it is meant to summarize). At the present point in the book, this may be obscure, and the reader may wish to return to this issue after having read the next chapters. But the moral is that the assumptions underlying the two-stage "vindication" of the Cournot model may not be consistent with the application of this theory to any given situation. In particular, caution must be exercised so that folding a two-stage game back into a reduced-form one-stage game does not eliminate important features of the two-stage game (e.g., the type of inferences firms may draw from their opponents' behavior).

Another caveat: In most cases, firms do not face rigid capacity constraints, as we noted earlier. The cost function induced by the investment choice does not have the (inverted) L shape. That is, there is generally no "capacity level" that gives a meaning to the quantity variable in the Cournot profit functions.

So, what is left of the analysis in this section? Three points:

First, the predictions and welfare results of the traditional Cournot model (see sections 5.4 and 5.7) can be provided with foundations in some extreme cases. Overall, the exact-Cournot-reduced-form and the Cournot-outcome results are more likely to hold when the investment cost c_0 is high. A high c_0 creates a large discrepancy between the first-period (*ex ante*) costs and the second-period (*ex post*) costs, and therefore creates a higher

---

12. They also require capacities to be observable before prices are chosen. If a firm's capacity is not observable by its rival(s), scale and price choices must be represented as simultaneous rather than sequential. The results are then modified (see section 5.7).

willingness to dump existing capacity (i.e., adopt market-clearing behavior) *ex post*.

Second, the two-stage game illustrates the idea that firms may want to choose non-price actions that soften price competition (here, each firm restricts its capacity as a commitment not to choose a low price later).[13] This idea is much more general than this particular situation and will be developed in much detail in chapter 8.

Third, in many (descriptive) applications of Cournot competition, the ability to write the profit functions in the exact Cournot reduced form is not crucial. The main property of Cournot competition is often that the cross-partial derivative of firm i's profit with respect to the actions of that firm and its rival is negative (strategic substitutes). This property holds, for instance, under the Kreps-Scheinkman assumptions (in the pure strategy region,

$$\frac{\partial^2 \Pi^i}{\partial \overline{q}_i \partial \overline{q}_j} = \frac{\partial^2 ([P(\overline{q}_i + \overline{q}_j) - c]\overline{q}_i)}{\partial \overline{q}_i \partial \overline{q}_j} = P' + P''\overline{q}_i < 0$$

for a concave demand function), but it may also hold for models in which the exact Cournot form is invalid—although the exact assumptions under which capacities are indeed strategic substitutes remain to be determined.

More generally, what we mean by quantity competition is really a *choice of scale that determines the firm's cost functions and thus determines the conditions of price competition*. This choice of scale can be a capacity choice, but more general investment decisions are also allowable.

To give an example of this reasoning, let us jump ahead. In chapter 7, we will consider price competition between two firms located at the two extremes of a spatial-differentiation model on a line (see chapter 2 for the set-up). Assuming that the segment has length 1, that the parameter of differentiation is t, and that the firms face constant marginal costs of production c_1 and c_2, we will show that, solving for price competition, the reduced-form profit functions are

$$\Pi^i(c_i, c_j) = \left(t + \frac{c_j - c_i}{3}\right)^2 \bigg/ 2t.$$

Now consider a first stage, in which the firms "choose their unit costs"—that is, they choose a level of monetary investment I_i that determines the *ex post* unit cost $c_i(I_i)$ (with $c_i'(\cdot) < 0$). These investments (or the resulting unit costs) can be considered scale variables by abuse of terminology, and they satisfy the strategic-substitutes condition:

$$\partial^2 \Pi^i / \partial I_i \partial I_j < 0 \quad (\text{and } \partial^2 \Pi^i / \partial c_i \partial c_j < 0).$$

5.4 Traditional Cournot Analysis

We now analyze the one-stage game in which firms choose their quantities (understand their capacities) simultaneously. We will use either the general reduced form for the profit function, $\Pi^i(q_i, q_j)$, or the more specific exact Cournot form:

$$\Pi^i(q_i, q_j) = q_i P(q_i + q_j) - C_i(q_i)$$

(see the caveats on this exact form in section 5.3).

Each firm maximizes its profit given the quantity chosen by the other firm. Assuming that the profit function Π^i is strictly concave in q_i and twice differentiable, we get

$$q_i = R_i(q_j), \tag{5.4}$$

where R_i is firm i's reaction curve:

$$\Pi^i_i(R_i(q_j), q_j) = 0.$$

Recall from the introduction to part II that if we assume that firm i's marginal profit is decreasing with the other firm's quantity, then the reaction functions are downward sloping. The equilibrium quantities are depicted in figure 5.5 by the intersection of the two reaction curves. Of course, such an intersection need not be unique; in that case we would have multiple equilibria.

To be a bit more specific, let us consider the first-order condition for profit maximization for the exact Cournot form:

$$\Pi^i_i = P(q_i + q_j) - C_i'(q_i) + q_i P'(q_i + q_j) = 0. \tag{5.5}$$

This has a simple interpretation. The first two terms yield

---

13. Along these lines, Ghemawat (1986) finds that in an example of an asymmetric-capacity price game, the firm with a low capacity prices more aggressively than the one with a high capacity, because it is more at risk to be undersold. This confirms the idea that a high capacity threatens one's rivals and forces them to price aggressively.

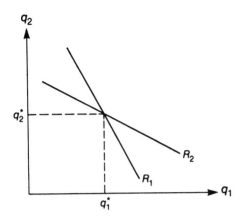

Figure 5.5

the profitability of an extra unit of output, which is equal to the difference between price and marginal cost. The third term represents the effect of this extra unit on the profitability of inframarginal ones. The extra units create a decrease in price P', which affects the q_i units already produced. Equation 5.5 is similar to the formulas obtained for a competitive firm and a monopoly. For a competitive firm there is no third term, because the firm is too small to affect the market price; for a monopoly, q_i is equal to the output of the industry.

The preceding comparison actually illustrates the negative *externality* between the firms: When choosing its output, firm i takes into account the adverse effect of the market-price change on its own output, rather than the effect on aggregate output. Hence, each firm will tend to choose an output that exceeds the optimal output from the industry's point of view[14] (but, of course, not from a welfare point of view). Thus, *the market price will be lower than the monopoly price, and the aggregate profit will be lower than the monopoly profit*. Another interesting consequence of equation 5.5 is that Cournot equilibrium does not equalize marginal costs except in the symmetric case. Not only is too little produced, but *the industry's cost of production is not minimized*.

Equation 5.5 can be rewritten as

$$L_i = \frac{\alpha_i}{\varepsilon}, \tag{5.6}$$

where

$$L_i \equiv \frac{P - C_i'}{P}$$

is the Lerner index (price-cost margin) for firm i;

$$\alpha_i \equiv \frac{q_i}{Q}$$

is firm i's market share ($Q \equiv q_i + q_j$), and

$$\varepsilon \equiv -\frac{P'}{P}Q$$

is the elasticity of demand. Thus, the Lerner index is proportional to the firm's market share and inversely proportional to the elasticity of demand. This index is positive—that is, firms sell at a price exceeding marginal cost. Thus, the Cournot equilibrium is not socially efficient.

A technical note about the concavity of the firm's objective function and the sign of the cross-partial derivative: From equation 5.5, we obtain

$$\Pi_{ii}^i = 2P' + q_i P'' - C_i'' \tag{5.7}$$

and

$$\Pi_{ij}^i = P' + q_i P''. \tag{5.8}$$

Recall that $P' < 0$. For the objective function to be concave ($\Pi_{ii}^i < 0$), it suffices that the firm's cost be convex ($C_i'' \geq 0$) and that the inverse-demand function be concave ($P'' \leq 0$). The latter assumption suffices for quantities to be strategic substitutes ($\Pi_{ij}^i < 0$). These two assumptions are met, for instance, for linear demand ($P'' = 0$) and constant returns to scale ($C_i'' = 0$). For more on the concavity of the objective function and the existence of a Cournot equilibrium see section 5.7.

The Cournot equilibrium is easily derived in the case of linear demand and cost. Suppose that $D(p) = 1 - p$ (or $P(Q) = 1 - Q$) and $C_i(q_i) = c_i q_i$. Then the reaction functions are

$$q_i = R_i(q_j) = \frac{1 - q_j - c_i}{2}.$$

Hence, the Cournot equilibrium is given by

$$q_i = \frac{1 - 2c_i + c_j}{3},$$

---

14. This is obtained by replacing $q_i P'$ in equation 5.5 with $(q_i + q_j)P'$.

and the profit is

$$\Pi^i = \frac{(1 - 2c_i + c_j)^2}{9}.$$

A firm's output decreases with its marginal cost. More interestingly, it increases with its competitor's marginal cost; this is because a higher c_j leads firm j to produce less, which raises the residual demand faced by firm i, encouraging firm i to produce more.

That a firm's output decreases with its marginal cost and increases with its competitor's marginal cost can be obtained for more general demand and cost functions as long as the following two conditions are satisfied: (a) the reaction curves are downward sloping (quantities are strategic substitutes) and (b) the reaction curves cross only once (there exists a unique Cournot equilibrium) and the slope of R_2 in the (q_1, q_2) space is smaller in absolute value than the slope of R_1.[15]

It is easily shown that an increase in a firm's marginal cost shifts the firm's reaction curve down. To prove this, recall from chapter 1 that a monopolist's price (respectively, quantity) increases (respectively, decreases) with the firm's marginal cost. But in duopoly, for a given output q_j, firm i is a monopolist on the residual-demand curve $P(\cdot + q_j)$. Hence, the proof of chapter 1 applies, and firm i's optimal output given q_j is a decreasing (more precisely, a nonincreasing) function of firm i's marginal cost. This result is completely general; conditions such as (a) or (b) are not required. (The reader is advised to go through the argument again as an exercise.)

Figure 5.6 depicts reaction curves satisfying (a) and (b), and shows the effect of an increase in firm 1's marginal cost. Firm 1's equilibrium output is reduced, while firm 2's increases.

The results generalize straightforwardly to the case of n firms. Let

$$Q \equiv \sum_{i=1}^{n} q_i.$$

Equation 5.5 then becomes

$$P(Q) - C_i'(q_i) + q_i P'(Q) = 0. \tag{5.9}$$

Firm i's Lerner index is still equal to the ratio of its market

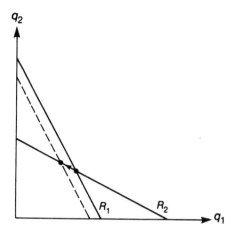

Figure 5.6
Effect of an increase in firm 1's marginal cost.

share to the elasticity of demand. For instance, for the symmetric case with linear cost and demand,

$$P(Q) = 1 - Q$$

and $C_i(q_i) = cq_i$

for all i (with $c < 1$), equation 5.9 becomes

$$1 - Q - c - q_i = 0. \tag{5.10}$$

The equilibrium is symmetric for this symmetric model: $Q = nq$, where q is the output per firm. Hence, we obtain

$$q = \frac{1 - c}{n + 1}. \tag{5.11}$$

The market price is

$$p = 1 - nq = c + \frac{1 - c}{n + 1}, \tag{5.12}$$

and each firm's profit is

$$\Pi = \frac{(1 - c)^2}{(n + 1)^2}. \tag{5.13}$$

The market price and each firm's profit decrease with the number of firms. Furthermore, because the market price decreases with n, so does the aggregate profit $n\Pi$. Indeed, *when the number of firms becomes very large* ($n \to \infty$), *the market price tends to the competitive price c.* Thus, a Cournot

---

15. This "stability condition" is treated in chapter 8. A sufficient condition is that, for $i = 1, 2$, $|R_i'| < 1$—that is, a decrease in one firm's production yields

a decrease in aggregate output even if its rival reacts (optimally) to the decrease in production. For instance, for a linear demand, $|R_i'| = \frac{1}{2}$.

equilibrium with a large number of firms is approximately competitive. This is natural, because each firm has only a small influence on the price and thus acts almost like a price taker.

See section 5.7 for more on the convergence to the competitive equilibrium, and for a discussion of the existence and uniqueness of a Cournot equilibrium.

Exercise 5.3* There are three identical firms in the industry. The demand is $1 - Q$, where $Q = q_1 + q_2 + q_3$. The marginal cost is zero.

(i) Compute the Cournot equilibrium.

(ii) Show that if two of the three firms merge (transforming the industry into a duopoly), the profit of these firms decreases. Explain.

(iii) What happens if all three firms merge?

(iv)** If the firms were competing in prices and sold differentiated products, would a merger between two of them be profitable? (Work at an intuitive level, and assume that prices are strategic complements.)

Exercise 5.4* Consider a duopoly producing a homogeneous product. Firm 1 produces one unit of output with one unit of labor and one unit of raw material. Firm 2 produces one unit of output with two units of labor and one unit of raw material. The unit costs of labor and raw material are w and r. The demand is $p = 1 - q_1 - q_2$, and the firms compete in quantities.

(i) Compute the Cournot equilibrium.

(ii) Show that firm 1's profit is not affected by the price of labor (over some range). To prove this elegantly, use the envelope theorem. Explain.

Exercise 5.5* This exercise illustrates the strategic considerations faced by a multimarket firm. It is inspired by the more general theory of Bulow et al. (1985).

There are two firms in a market. They produce perfect substitutes at cost $C(q) = q^2/2$. The demand is $p = 1 - (q_1 + q_2)$.

(i) Compute the Cournot equilibrium.

(ii) Suppose now that firm 1 has the opportunity to sell the same output on another market as well. The quantity sold on this market is x_1, so firm 1's cost is $(q_1 + x_1)^2/2$. The demand on the second market is $p = a - x_1$. Con-

sider the Cournot game in which firm 1 chooses q_1 and x_1 and firm 2 chooses q_2 simultaneously. Show that $q_1 = (2 - a)/7$ and $q_2 = (5 + a)/21$ over the relevant range of a. Show that for $a = \frac{1}{4}$ a small increase in a hurts firm 1. (Use the envelope theorem.) Interpret.

5.5 Concentration Indices and Industry Profitability

The Bertrand model and the Cournot model are the basic models for nonrepeated interaction among oligopolists producing the same good. Like the models that will be developed in the next chapters, they give prices, quantities, profits, and consumer surplus as functions of the cost structures, the demand function, and the number of firms (unless the latter variable is endogenized through choice of entry, as in chapter 7). In practice, the observation of a market price (if such a thing exists) tells us little about the competitiveness of the corresponding industry unless we observe prices in industries with similar cost structures (for instance, different geographical markets), or we observe the temporal pattern of the industry price (see chapter 6), or we are able to measure accurately the firms' marginal cost. More readily informative variables are the rates of profit and the firms' market shares.

Industrial-organization economists have long tried to summarize the distribution of market shares among firms in a single index to be used in econometric and antitrust analysis. Such an aggregate index is called a *concentration index*. With $\alpha_i \equiv q_i/Q$ denoting firm i's market share (where $i = 1, \ldots, n$ and $\Sigma_{i=1}^n \alpha_i = 1$), the following are examples of concentration indices.

• the *m-firm concentration ratio* (for $m < n$), which adds up the m highest shares in the industry:

$$R_m \equiv \sum_{i=1}^m \alpha_i$$

(ordering the firms so that $\alpha_1 \geqslant \cdots \geqslant \alpha_m \geqslant \cdots \geqslant \alpha_n$),

• the *Herfindahl index*, which is equal to the sum of the squares of the market shares[16]:

$$R_H \equiv \sum_{i=1}^n \alpha_i^2,$$

---

16. In the literature, R_H is usually denoted by H.

- the *entropy index*, which is equal to the sum of the shares times their logarithm:

$$R_e \equiv \sum_{i=1}^{n} \alpha_i \ln \alpha_i.$$

Of course, such indices should be related to our idea of concentration. Encaoua and Jacquemin (1980) give an axiomatic derivation of "allowable" concentration indices. They require a concentration index $R(\alpha_1, \ldots, \alpha_n)$ to satisfy the following properties: It must be symmetric between firms (invariant to permutations of market shares between firms); it must satisfy the Lorenz condition that a mean-preserving spread[17] (i.e., a further spread of the distribution of market shares toward its tails) increases R; and the concentration for symmetric firms must decrease when the number of firms grows from n to $n + 1$,

$$\left(R\left(\frac{1}{n}, \ldots, \frac{1}{n}\right) \geqslant R\left(\frac{1}{n+1}, \ldots, \frac{1}{n+1}\right) \right).$$

They show that a family of concentration indices satisfying these properties takes the form

$$R(\alpha_1, \ldots, \alpha_n) = \sum_{i=1}^{n} \alpha_i h(\alpha_i),$$

where h is an arbitrary nondecreasing function such that $\alpha h(\alpha)$ is convex. The Herfindahl index and the entropy index are two such concentration indices (with $h(\alpha) = \alpha$ and $h(\alpha) = \ln \alpha$, respectively). The m-firm concentration ratio satisfies these properties, although it does not belong to the family.

Although the previous requirements seem reasonable, they do not tell us what use to make of concentration indices. Do they reflect a useful economic variable for measurement or policy evaluation? One possibility is that they are related to the profitability of the industry. In-

deed, Bain (1951, 1956) hypothesized that concentration facilitates collusion between firms and increases industry-wide profits. At this point we cannot assess the (mainly dynamic) collusion part of the statement, but we can already look at the link between concentration and industry profits in light of the static Bertrand and Cournot models. Most of the cross-section analysis has actually focused on the relationship between concentration indices and profitability.[18]

Let us first consider *symmetric* firms with equal market shares. The only reasonable measures of concentration are then equivalent to the number of firms in the industry (i.e., the concentration indices are decreasing with the number of firms in the industry—e.g., $R_m = m/n$, $R_H = 1/n$, $R_e = \ln(1/n)$). The Bertrand model tells us that market price and industry profits are independent of the number of firms in the industry. Thus, profitability and concentration are unrelated. The Cournot model, however, exhibits a negative correlation between number of firms and profitability (see section 5.4).[19]

When firms have *asymmetric* market shares (because of cost differences, say), there is no longer an unambiguous measure of concentration. In some simple cases it can be shown that industry profitability is related to a simple index of concentration. For instance, following Cowling and Waterson (1976), suppose that firms have constant marginal costs $C_i(q_i) = c_i q_i$, and that they compete in quantities. Industry-wide profits are

$$\Pi = \sum_{i=1}^{n} \Pi^i = \sum_{i=1}^{n} (p - c_i) q_i = \sum_{i=1}^{n} \frac{p \alpha_i q_i}{\varepsilon} = \frac{pQ}{\varepsilon} \left(\sum_{i=1}^{n} \alpha_i^2 \right),$$

(5.14)

where use is made of expression 5.6 for the Lerner index. Assume further that consumers spend a fixed amount of income on the good—i.e., the elasticity ε of their demand

---

17. See Rothschild and Stiglitz 1970, Atkinson 1970, Kolm 1966, and Kolm 1969. Consider two industries of equal size with market shares $\{\alpha_i\}_{i=1}^{n}$ and $\{\tilde{\alpha}_i\}_{i=1}^{n}$. Let R_m and $\tilde{R}_m$ denote the m-firm ratios. Suppose that for all m between 1 and n, $R_m \geqslant \tilde{R}_m$: The aggregate share of the m biggest firms in the first industry is greater than or equal to the share of the m biggest firms in the second industry, for all m. Then, the concentration index R must be higher for the first industry (the Lorenz criterion). This condition can be shown to be equivalent to the transfer principle, according to which the transfer of a part of a firm's share to a bigger firm must not decrease the concentration index. For a given number of firms in the industry, this condition implies that the concentration index R takes on its minimum value when the firms have equal shares, and its maximum value when a single firm captures the whole market.

18. See chapters 3 and 9 of Scherer 1980 and, especially, Schmalensee 1986 for detailed discussions of the empirical literature and references. Most cross-sectional analyses find a weak but statistically significant link between concentration and profitability. Beyond the issue of measurement of profitability, the interpretation of this link is complicated by the fact that the relationship is a reduced form between two endogenous variables, which, furthermore, can be obtained from fairly different models of competition. Other good discussions of concentration measurement are Hannah and Kay 1977 (especially chapter 4) and Curry and George 1983.

19. One must be careful here. The number of firms is assumed to be exogenous. If the number of firms depends on the cost of entry, then a higher cost of entry yields a higher concentration but may offset the resulting increase in gross profits (see chapter 7).

is equal to 1: $Q = k/p$, where k is a positive constant. We then obtain

$$\Pi = k\left(\sum_{i=1}^{n} \alpha_i{}^2\right) = kR_H. \tag{5.15}$$

The Herfindahl index then yields an exact measure (up to the proportional constant) of industry profitability.

Exercise 5.6*

(i) Show that under constant returns to scale and Cournot competition the ratio of total industry profit to total industry revenue is equal to the Herfindahl index divided by the elasticity of demand.

(ii) Show that under Cournot competition the "average Lerner index" ($\Sigma_i \alpha_i L_i$) is equal to the Herfindahl index divided by the elasticity of demand.

This chapter suggests that intrinsic asymmetries among firms are likely to yield both high concentration indices and high industry profitability. Indeed, Demsetz (1973) offered this argument as an alternative, noncollusive reason for Bain's hypothesis about the positive correlation between the two variables. For instance, in Bertrand competition with constant marginal cost, the lowest-cost firm charges a price equal to the second-lowest cost, takes all of the market (yielding the highest possible concentration index, whatever index satisfying the Encaoua-Jacquemin axioms is chosen), and makes a positive profit. With symmetric firms, concentration is generally not so high and the firms make no profit. The following exercise also gives a (Cournot) example in which exogenous increases in cost asymmetries create a positive relationship between concentration indices and industry profit.

Exercise 5.7* Suppose that demand is linear ($Q = 1 - p$) and that there are two firms with constant marginal costs c_1 and c_2 such that $c_1 + c_2 = 2c$ (where c is a constant). Show that when the firms become more asymmetric (c_i moves away from c) Cournot competition yields a higher concentration index and a higher industry profit.

We will not investigate the generality of Demsetz's conclusion. (For more on the Demsetz argument and for some tests, see Schmalensee 1987.) The intuition behind the positive correlation in the above examples is clear: Cost asymmetries yield output asymmetries, increasing the concentration index. At the same time, they allow

low-cost firms to enjoy a rent, thus increasing industry profit.

One would also want to relate concentration and welfare. In the symmetric case, the number of firms is unrelated to welfare for Bertrand competition and positively related to welfare for Cournot competition. With asymmetric firms, a given concentration index need not be related in a systematic manner to welfare for either type of competition (in the same way that it need not be related in a systematic manner to profitability).

Exercise 5.8** Dansby and Willig (1979) have proposed a look at the effect of small changes in a firm's output on aggregate surplus (consumer surplus plus industry profit). Assume that, for some unspecified reason, firm i's output moves from q_i to $q_i + \delta q_i$ (for all i).

(i) Argue that the change in total surplus, δW, is equal to

$$\sum_{i=1}^{n} (p - C_i')\delta q_i.$$

(ii) Suppose that a change $\delta q = (\delta q_1, \ldots, \delta q_n)$ must be constrained to be smaller than a given number in Euclidean norm:

$$\sum_{i=1}^{n} (\delta q_i)^2 \leqslant k.$$

Show that for Cournot competition the upper bound on δW associated with this change is proportional to the square root of the Herfindahl index. Discuss.

Concentration indices are useful in that they give an easily computable and interpretable indication of how competitive the industry is. However, they have no systematic relationship with economic variables of interest for assessing changes in cost, demand, or policy. Furthermore, they are endogenous, so they do not allow simple observations of correlation to be interpreted in a causal way.

5.6 Concluding Remarks

Price competition among even a few firms yields, according to Bertrand, competitive (socially optimal) outcomes. However, price competition is softened when the firms face sharply rising marginal costs (capacity constraints, in an extreme case), when they compete repeatedly, or when their products are differentiated. This chapter has treated the first softening factor.

If firms choose their capacities before competing in price, under strong assumptions, they *ex post* choose the price that an auctioneer would pick so as to clear the market (i.e., to adjust demand to existing capacity). This result provides some foundations for the Cournot model, in which firms choose quantities and an auctioneer then chooses the price so as to clear the market, as long as quantities are reinterpreted as capacities. Thus, the Bertrand and Cournot models should not be seen as two rival models giving contradictory predictions of the outcome of competition in a given market. (After all, firms almost always compete in prices.) Rather, they are meant to depict markets with different cost structures. The Bertrand model may be a better approximation for industries with fairly flat marginal costs; the Cournot model may be better for those with sharply rising marginal costs.

One should be cautious when justifying the Cournot model by the existence of capacity constraints. The validity of the justification must be checked in each model.

Last, quantity competition can more generally be seen as competition in choices of scale, where a firm's choice of scale determines its cost function and thus the conditions of price competition.

5.7 Supplementary Section: Quantity Competition

5.7.1 Traditional Cournot Analysis: Existence, Uniqueness, and Limit Behavior

This subsection presents an incomplete account of the technical analysis and research that has been conducted on the one-stage Cournot model (no price competition) considered in chapter 5.

5.7.1.1 Existence of a Pure-Strategy Equilibrium

Pure-strategy equilibria have attractive properties. First, they are simple. Second, no firm has *ex post* regret after observing the choice of the other firm. So, no further adjustment is desired even if firms can change their capacities. A mixed-strategy equilibrium requires firms to be unable to adjust their capacities (even upward), because one firm's realization of capacity may not be optimal against the other firm's. They are thus more sensitive to the possibility of adjustment. The existence of a pure-strategy equilibrium has attracted much attention among researchers. Two sets of assumptions have historically been considered for this purpose. We will consider existence in the two-firm case; it is straightforward to extend the reasoning to more firms. For simplicity, we will also assume that profit functions are twice continuously differentiable.

The first approach assumes that each firm's profit function is concave in its own output (see, e.g., Szidarovsky and Yakowitz 1977). From the analysis in the text, we know that a sufficient condition for this is that the cost functions be convex ($C_i''(q_i) \geqslant 0$) and the demand function concave ($P'' \leqslant 0$). With concave profit functions, one can define continuous reaction functions $R_i(q_j)$.[20] To make sure that these reaction functions intersect, one can impose the following technical conditions:

$$P(0) > C_i'(0)$$

for all i (each firm would like to produce at least a small quantity if it were a monopoly) and

$$R_j^{-1}(0) > R_i(0) = q_i^m$$

---

20. We will assume that $\Pi_{ii}^i < 0$, for simplicity. In this case, reaction functions are single-valued.

(firm i's output that induces firm j to produce nothing exceeds firm i's monopoly output). These conditions, as well as the strict concavity of the profit functions with respect to own output, are satisfied for linear demand and constant marginal costs as long as the latter are "not too high." The existence can be obtained from figure 5.7.[21]

Remark The existence of a pure-strategy Cournot equilibrium is not an issue for an industry with a large number of firms. To see this intuitively, recall that the second derivative of Π^i is

$$q_i P''(Q) + 2 P'(Q) - C_i''(q_i).$$

Suppose that $C_i'' \geqslant 0$, and suppose that (as in the example in the text) one increases the number of firms keeping demand constant, and that the aggregate output converges to the competitive one. $P'(Q)$ then converges to a strictly negative constant. If q_i converges to zero (as in the example in the text), Π^i is clearly strictly concave and the previous existence result can be applied. If q_i does not converge to zero, and competitive equilibrium is obtained through the replication of the consumption side or else through a reduction of the most efficient scale (see subsection 5.7.1.3), more work is required to obtain this type of result. Novshek and Sonnenschein (1978) show that for their model there exists a Cournot equilibrium in which the proportion of firms using a mixed strategy converges to zero when the economy is replicated.[22]

Unfortunately, the profit function is not necessarily concave. It may not be, in particular, if the demand function is "sufficiently convex." (See Friedman 1983 and Roberts and Sonnenschein 1977 for robust counterexamples to concavity of the profit functions and existence of pure-

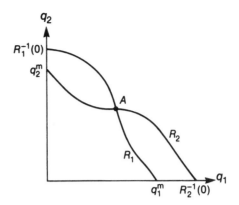

Figure 5.7

strategy equilibria even with convex costs.) The reaction functions need not be continuous (may involve jumps) if the profit functions are nonconcave. A second approach (McManus 1962, 1964; Roberts and Sonnenschein 1976; Vives 1985) proves existence for *symmetric* firms with a convex cost function. The key to the proof is to show that the convex-cost assumption implies that jumps in the reaction function (which is the same for all firms) are jumps up.[23] As figure 5.8 indicates, only jumps down are a problem when one is proving the existence of a firm's output q such that q is an optimal reaction to itself (symmetric pure-strategy equilibrium).

A more recent approach (Novshek 1985; for a related result see Bamon and Fraysse 1985) shows that if a firm's marginal revenue increases with the other firm's output, a pure-strategy equilibrium exists.

5.7.1.2 Uniqueness

Even if it exists, a pure-strategy Cournot equilibrium need not be unique (see figure 5.9). One can, nevertheless, find

---

21. The more general proof for $P'' < 0$ and $C_i'' > 0$ is as follows: Define the (single-valued) function $q_i(Q)$ by the first-order condition

$$P(Q) - C_i'(q_i) + q_i P'(Q) = 0,$$

or by 0 if this equation has no solution. Note that $q_i(Q)$ is continuous and nonincreasing; so is $\sum_i q_i(Q)$. A pure-strategy Cournot equilibrium is obtained by finding an aggregate output such that $Q = \sum_i q_i(Q)$, i.e., by finding a fixed point of the function $Q \to \sum_i q_i(Q)$. The Brouwer theorem asserts that a continuous function from a compact set into itself admits at least one fixed point, which proves the result. (Compactness is easily obtained by assuming that $\sum_i q_i(0) \geqslant 0$ and $\sum_i q_i(Q) < Q$ for any Q such that $P(Q) = 0$.) The equilibrium is then unique, because all the functions $q_i(Q)$ are decreasing when strictly positive. (To see this, it may be convenient to draw a diagram.)

22. They also show in a general-equilibrium model that the demand curve,

which we naturally assume to be downward sloping in our partial-equilibrium context, must indeed be downward sloping in equilibrium for a large economy.

23. Assume that $P'' \geqslant 0$ (case that creates problems with the first proof of uniqueness). Assume for simplicity that costs are nil. Suppose that for $q_1 - \varepsilon$ the optimal reaction is q_2, and that for $q_1 + \varepsilon$ it is $q_2' < q_2$, where ε is positive and arbitrarily small. Profit maximization requires that

$$q_2 P(q_1 - \varepsilon + q_2) \geqslant q_2' P(q_1 - \varepsilon + q_2')$$

and

$$q_2' P(q_1 + \varepsilon + q_2') \geqslant q_2 P(q_1 + \varepsilon + q_2).$$

Adding these two inequalities and using a first-order Taylor expansion in ε yields a contradiction for $P'' \geqslant 0$. Thus, there cannot be any jump down. The reader may check the property for general convex cost functions.

sufficient conditions for uniqueness. For instance, consider the two-firm case. Assume that profit functions are strictly concave in own output. The differentiation of the first-order condition

$$\Pi_i^i(R_i(q_j), q_j) = 0$$

with respect to q_j gives the slope of the reaction curve:

$$|R_i'(q_j)| = \left| \frac{\Pi_{ij}^i(R_i(q_j), q_j)}{\Pi_{ii}^i(R_i(q_j), q_j)} \right|.$$

A sufficient condition for reaction curves to intersect only once is that whenever they intercept, R_1 is steeper than R_2 (see points A and C in figure 5.9). In turn, a sufficient condition for this to hold is that the derivatives of the reaction functions be less than 1 in absolute value over the relevant range ($|R_i'| < 1$). Thus, $|\Pi_{ii}^i| > |\Pi_{ij}^i|$ is sufficient for uniqueness.[24] This condition is satisfied for linear demand and constant returns to scale, for which the slope of the reaction functions is $\frac{1}{2}$.

5.7.1.3 Convergence to the Competitive Equilibrium

In the text, we saw in a simple example that when the number of firms goes to infinity, the Cournot equilibrium converges toward the competitive equilibrium. The reason is that a small firm is more willing to expand output than a big one, because the effect of such an expansion on the market price is small for a small firm. (Although the global effect of a unit increase in q_i on p is the same as in the monopoly or the duopoly case, most of it is a negative externality on the other firms if firm i is small.[25])

There are several ways of increasing the number of firms. The one used in the text is a simple replication of the number of firms. When the technology exhibits nonconstant returns to scale, one may want to replicate the consumption side along with the production side to avoid noncompetitive outcomes of the type discussed in chapter 7 below. (For example, replicating the number of firms does not make the industry more competitive if high fixed costs and a limited consumer market restrict the

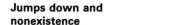

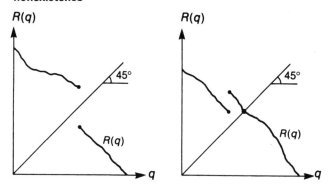

Figure 5.8

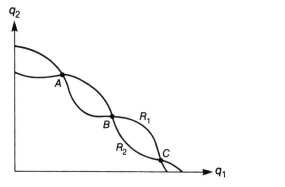

Figure 5.9
Multiple Cournot equilibrium.

number of viable firms.) This is done in Gabszewicz and Vial 1972, for instance. One may also allow "free entry" from the start (the number of potential firms is infinite, and the number of operating firms is limited by the existence of a fixed cost or increasing returns to scale over some range and by the extent of the market) and either replicate the consumption side or lower the minimum efficient scale to induce more entry. Though the extensive literature on this subject (see Novshek and Sonnenschein 1978, Hart 1980, Roberts 1980, Mas-Colell 1982, and the symposium in the April 1980 *Journal of Economic Theory*) will not be reviewed here, it should be mentioned that

---

24. With n firms, the condition

$$p_i \geqslant C_i' \rightarrow |\Pi_{ii}^i| > \left| \sum_{j \neq i} \Pi_{ij}^i \right|$$

is sufficient. This condition actually does not require goods to be perfect substitutes; see Friedman 1983.

25. This type of result fits with the Roberts-Postlewaite (1976) result for more abstract contexts, which demonstrates the impossibility of economic agents' manipulating the competitive process in a large economy.

much of this literature is concerned with a larger framework. In particular, starting with Gabszewicz and Vial 1972, the results are often obtained in general equilibrium.[26] Here, we shall content ourselves with a simple partial-equilibrium example due to Novshek and Sonnenschein (1978).

Suppose that in the original economy each firm has a U-shaped average-cost curve $C(q)/q$, as in figure 5.10. Producing 0 costs 0. The most efficient scale (MES)—i.e., the output that minimizes average cost—can be set equal to 1 without loss of generality. Let c denote the minimum average cost. Let us keep the consumption side constant (the demand is $p = P(Q)$) and reduce the MES. To this purpose, we introduce the family of cost functions $C_\alpha(q) = \alpha C(q/\alpha)$. The MES of C_α is α, and the minimum average cost is still c.[27]

For any α, we allow free entry. There are an infinite number of potential firms. They all choose an output simultaneously. Of course, for a given α, only a finite number of firms will enter (operate) because of initial increasing returns to scale. A Cournot equilibrium implies, in particular, that all operating firms (i.e., firms that choose $q_i > 0$) make a non-negative profit and that any non-operating firm would make a nonpositive profit were it to enter.

When α tends to zero, firms can enter on a small scale—that is, it is possible to produce a small output at unit cost c. This induces more competitive behavior. Indeed, if an equilibrium exists (as it does—see Novshek and Sonnenschein 1978 or the remark in subsection 5.7.1.1), the equilibrium total output Q must belong to the interval $[Q^* - \alpha, Q^*]$, where Q^* is the Walrasian output of the limit economy: $Q^* = D(c)$. To show this, suppose first that $Q > Q^*$. Then,

$$P(Q) < c \leqslant \frac{C_\alpha(q_i)}{q_i} \quad \text{for all } q_i > 0.$$

Thus, operating firms make a negative profit. They would be better off choosing $q_i = 0$ and making zero profit. Now suppose that $Q < Q^* - \alpha$. Consider a nonoperating firm i; it makes a zero profit. By entering at scale $q_i = \alpha$,

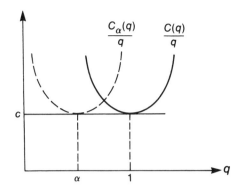

Figure 5.10

it would drive the total output to $Q + \alpha < Q^*$. Its profit would then be

$$\alpha P(Q + \alpha) - C_\alpha(\alpha) > \alpha c - C_\alpha(\alpha) = \alpha\left(c - \frac{C_\alpha(\alpha)}{\alpha}\right) = 0$$

—a contradiction. Thus, one indeed gets a competitive equilibrium in the limit when α converges to zero.

Hart (1979) pointed out that having a large number of competitors is not always necessary to obtain a competitive outcome. What matters is that a firm be small relative to the market for its good so that it is little affected by the effect of its decisions on the market price. This point is best exemplified in the case of a monopoly producer. Suppose that the producer has exactly ten units of such a producer's good for potential sale (i.e., he has a capacity constraint of 10, and a marginal cost of 0 before an output of 10 and infinity thereafter). If there are ten consumers, with unit demands and valuations 10, 9, 8, ..., the monopolist will sell only the monopoly quantity 5. If the consumption side is replicated at least ten times (say there are at least ten identical islands on which the monopolist can sell), the monopolist can sell his ten units at price 10. He then introduces no distortion in the economy. Figure 5.11 gives the intuition for the result in the case of a continuously increasing marginal cost. That figure replicates the consumption side; for an economy of $K \geqslant 1$ islands, the quantity demanded is $q = KD(p)$. (K plays the role of $1/\alpha$, in the previous reasoning.) Thus, for production q, the market price is

26. See Hart 1985 for a very useful survey of the general-equilibrium results and methodology.

27.
$$\underset{q}{\text{Min}} \, \frac{C_\alpha(q)}{q} = \underset{q}{\text{min}} \, \frac{C(q/\alpha)}{(q/\alpha)}$$

is reached for $q/\alpha = 1$ and is equal to c.

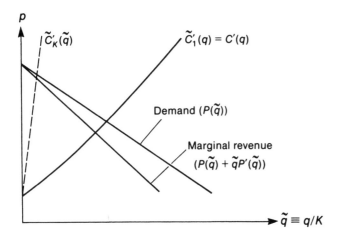

Figure 5.11

$P(q/K) = P(\tilde{q})$,

where $\tilde{q} \equiv q/K$ is the "output per island." The cost function per island as a function of $\tilde{q}$ can then be written

$\tilde{C}_K(\tilde{q}) = C(q)/K = C(K\tilde{q})/K$.

Thus, the marginal cost $\tilde{C}'_K(\tilde{q}) = C'(K\tilde{q})$ shifts to the northwest. The monopolist chooses the output per island to equalize marginal revenue and marginal cost. When K is large, the firm basically operates in the upper part of the demand curve, and thus takes the price (approximately equal to the highest valuation) almost as given.

Allen and Hellwig (1986) have studied the capacity-constrained price game when the number of firms tends to infinity. They assume that each firm capacity is an exogenous constant (there is no first stage determining capacities) and show that the equilibrium price distribution converges (in distribution) toward the perfectly competitive outcome.[28]

5.7.2 Capacity-Constrained Price Games

Here we informally consider part of Kreps and Scheinkman's (1983) ingenious construction, which shows that under some circumstances the Cournot outcome holds for capacity-constrained price games. Specifically, we first set up the price game with (rigid) capacity constraints and efficient rationing. We show that firms sell up to capacity within a region where capacities are not too large, and that in the two-stage game the first-period choice of capacities ends up in this region and the outcome is equivalent to the Cournot outcome. We will then discuss the timing of the game.

5.7.2.1 The Price Game

Suppose there are two firms ($i = 1, 2$). Firm i has a rigid capacity constraint $\overline{q}_i$; it can produce any quantity $q_i \leqslant \overline{q}_i$ at unit cost c. It cannot produce more than $\overline{q}_i$. Assume that $c = 0$ for simplicity. The marginal production cost is represented in figure 5.1. The firm sells up to capacity if $q_i = \overline{q}_i$. Assume efficient rationing.[29] The demand function P is concave ($P'' \leqslant 0$), and the firms choose their prices simultaneously.

The analysis proceeds as follows: We first consider the existence of a pure-strategy equilibrium (i.e., the firms do not randomize in their choice of price). We show that such an equilibrium exists if and only if the capacities are "not too high" (i.e., belong to some region just above the origin in the capacity space). The equilibrium in this region is such that both firms charge the price at which demand equals aggregate capacity. Thus, both firms basically dump their quantities in the market, in a manner analogous to Cournot behavior (the only difference is that firms, rather than the auctioneer, quote the market price). The next step in the analysis is to characterize the (necessarily mixed-strategy) equilibrium when capacities are "high." This is complex, but a lemma shows that the profit of the highest-capacity firm is equal to the Stackelberg follower profit (i.e., the profit that this firm makes when it reacts optimally to the other firm's output, which is assumed to be equal to its capacity). The analysis of the prior choice of capacities is then simple. It is easily seen that the Cournot capacities or quantities lead to a price equilibrium in the pure-strategy region, and that if a firm

---

28. They assume proportional rationing. They find that although there is convergence in distribution, there is no convergence in support. That is, monopoly prices persist for any number of firms (but their probability tends to zero).

Vives (1986) shows that for the efficient rationing rule, the support of the equilibrium price distribution converges to the competitive price as well.

29. See section 5.3.

chooses its Cournot capacity the other firm also is best off choosing its Cournot capacity.

LEMMA 1 In a pure-strategy equilibrium, $p_1 = p_2 = P(\bar{q}_1 + \bar{q}_2)$. Firms sell up to capacity.

Proof Suppose first that $p_1 = p_2 = p > P(\bar{q}_1 + \bar{q}_2)$. Then the price is too high, in that at least some firm i cannot sell to capacity: $q_i < \bar{q}_i$. Now, by charging $p - \varepsilon$, firm i gets all of the market and can sell $\bar{q}_i$. Thus, for ε small, firm i would gain from undercutting (i.e., $q_i p < \bar{q}_i(p - \varepsilon)$). If $p_1 = p_2 = p < P(\bar{q}_1 + \bar{q}_2)$, both firms strictly ration their customers. By raising its price a bit, each firm would still be able to sell its capacity and would make more profit. Last, $p_i < p_j$ is not feasible: The low-price firm always wants to raise its price as long as it is capacity constrained; or else p_i is firm i's monopoly price at cost $c = 0$, and firm i supplies the entire demand at this price. Thus, firm j makes no profit, whereas it could make a strictly positive profit by undercutting to $p_i - \varepsilon$. Q.E.D.

The following simple lemma conveys most of the intuition about the relationship with Cournot competition. Let $R_i(q_j)$ denote firm i's optimal reaction to output q_j in the one-stage simultaneous-choice-of-quantity game in the absence of cost of accumulating capacity: $R_i(q_j)$ maximizes $q_i P(q_i + q_j)$. Because the demand is concave, R_i is single-valued and decreasing (see section 5.4).

LEMMA 2 In a pure-strategy equilibrium, firm i never charges less than $P(\bar{q}_j + R_i(\bar{q}_j))$ in the capacity-constrained price game.

That is, there is no point charging a (low) price that leads the firm to produce beyond the optimal reaction to the other firm's capacity (if it can do so).

Proof Let p_i denote the price charged by firm i. If firm j charges a price $p_j > p_i$, firm i must charge its monopoly price, and firm j makes no profit (whereas it could make a profit by charging $p_i - \varepsilon$). If

$$p_i = p_j < P(\bar{q}_j + R_i(\bar{q}_j)),$$

firm i can raise its price slightly and make profit

$$(p_i + \varepsilon)\bar{q}_i > p_i \bar{q}_i$$

if it is capacity constrained. If firm i is not capacity constrained, firm j must be; at least one firm must be con-

strained, because otherwise they would undercut. So firm i's profit is

$$p_i(D(p_i) - \bar{q}_j) = q_i P(q_i + \bar{q}_j) \leq R_i(\bar{q}_j)P(R_i(\bar{q}_j) + \bar{q}_j),$$

where the inequality comes from the definition of the reaction function. If firm j charges a price $p_j < p_i$, firm i's profit is

$$p_i(D(p_i) - \bar{q}_j)$$

(or $p_i \bar{q}_i$ if $\bar{q}_i < D(p_i) - \bar{q}_j$; but, as noted above, a strictly capacity-constrained firm is better off raising its price slightly, so we need not consider this case). Since firm i is not capacity constrained, we can rewrite its profit as

$$q_i P(q_i + \bar{q}_j).$$

But this is the Cournot profit for output $\bar{q}_j$, so

$$q_i = R_i(\bar{q}_j)$$

by definition of the reaction function. Therefore,

$$p_i = P(\bar{q}_j + R_i(\bar{q}_j)), \text{ as was stated. Q.E.D.}$$

Lemmas 1 and 2 imply that a pure-strategy equilibrium exists only if, for all i,

$$\bar{q}_i \leq R_i(\bar{q}_j).$$

To see this, let $\bar{q}_i > R_i(\bar{q}_j)$, but suppose that a pure-strategy equilibrium exists. By lemma 1,

$$p_i = P(\bar{q}_1 + \bar{q}_2).$$

Then

$$p_i < P(\bar{q}_j + R_i(\bar{q}_j)),$$

which contradicts lemma 2; hence, by contradiction, a pure-strategy equilibrium cannot exist. Above either reaction curve, the only possible equilibrium is a "mixed-strategy" one (see figure 5.12). Conversely, if the capacities lie under both reaction curves, $p = p_1 = p_2 = P(\bar{q}_1 + \bar{q}_2)$ is an equilibrium. Lowering the price is senseless, because firms cannot sell more. Raising the price implies that the quantity sold is smaller than the optimal reaction:

$$p(D(p) - \bar{q}_j) = q_i P(q_i + \bar{q}_j)$$

and

$$q_i \leq \bar{q}_i \leq R_i(\bar{q}_j).$$

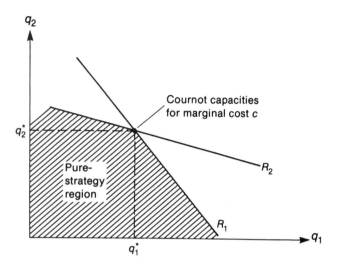

Figure 5.12

In particular, if the capacities are the Cournot capacities (q_1^*, q_2^*), (corresponding to marginal cost c), the equilibrium price is $P(q_1^* + q_2^*)$. More generally, in the pure-strategy region, the reduced-form profits have the exact Cournot reduced form.

The latter property does not hold for proportional rationing. Suppose that the capacities are the Cournot capacities (q_1^*, q_2^*) and that both firms charge $p^* \equiv P(q_1^* + q_2^*)$. Firm 1's profit for $p > p^*$ is

$$p\left[D(p)\left(\frac{D(p^*) - q_2^*}{D(p^*)}\right)\right] = [p\,D(p)]\left(\frac{q_1^*}{q_1^* + q_2^*}\right).$$

Hence, firm 1 is best off charging the monopoly price (maximizing $p\,D(p)$), which, from section 5.4, exceeds the Cournot price p^*. This suggests that this analysis cannot be extended to proportional rationing (and, indeed, it cannot). See subsection 5.7.2.3.

Outside the pure-strategy region, one must look for mixed-strategy equilibria. (See Dasgupta and Maskin 1986 for general results on the existence of mixed-strategy equilibria with discontinuous payoffs.) We will not reproduce Kreps and Scheinkman's equilibrium construction; we will but simply characterize equilibrium behavior in order to show that investing in capacity beyond the pure-

strategy region in the first stage is not in either firm's interest.

A mixed strategy for firm i is a cumulative distribution of prices $F_i(p_i)$ on some interval $[\underline{p}_i, \overline{p}_i]$.[30] In order for such a strategy to be optimal for firm i, it must be the case that only prices that maximize firm i's expected profit are chosen by firm i (that is, all prices that are chosen yield the same—optimal—payoff). See the Game Theory User's Manual for a discussion of mixed strategies.

LEMMA 3   In the mixed-strategy region ($\overline{q}_i > R_i(\overline{q}_j)$ for at least some firm i), the highest-capacity firm (i, say) makes a profit equal to its "Stackelberg follower profit":

$$\Pi^i = \Pi^F(\overline{q}_j) = R_i(\overline{q}_j)P(\overline{q}_j + R_i(\overline{q}_j)).$$

The proof of lemma 3 (a sketch of which is given below) is long and involved; it should be skipped in a first reading.

Proof (Sketch)   Let $\underline{p}_i$ and $\overline{p}_i$ denote the lower and upper bounds of the support of firm i's optimal strategy. First, let us show that $\underline{p}_1 = \underline{p}_2 \equiv \underline{p}$, and that at $\underline{p}$ each firm sells up to capacity or its opponent charges $\underline{p}$ with probability 0. If $\underline{p}_i < \underline{p}_j$, we know by previous arguments that $\underline{p}_i$ must be firm i's monopoly price. As the monopoly profit is the most firm i can get, it will charge $\underline{p}_i$ with probability 1 and firm j will never make a profit; however, firm j could make a strictly positive profit by undercutting to $\underline{p}_i - \varepsilon$, which contradicts the supposition that $\underline{p}_j$ is the lower bound of the support of firm j's optimal strategy. Second, if firm j charges $\underline{p}$ with positive probability ("plays an atom"), firm i will be better off charging $\underline{p} - \varepsilon$ if at $\underline{p}$ it cannot sell to capacity. Thus, by charging $\underline{p}$, each firm i can sell $\overline{q}_i$ with probability 1. Because $\underline{p}$ is an optimal price,[31] firm i's profit is $\underline{p}\overline{q}_i$. Note that $\underline{p} > P(\overline{q}_1 + \overline{q}_2)$.

Now consider the highest prices, $\overline{p}_1$ and $\overline{p}_2$. Suppose that $\overline{p}_i > \overline{p}_j$, or that $\overline{p}_i = \overline{p}_j$ and that firm j charges $\overline{p}_j$ with probability 0. Firm i's profit is

$$\overline{p}_i(D(\overline{p}_i) - \overline{q}_j) = q_i P(q_i + \overline{q}_j),$$

---

30. Note that F_i is increasing. Technically, $F_i(\cdot)$ is required to be right continuous—i.e., for all p_i,

$$F_i(p_i) = \lim_{p \to p_i^+} F_i(p).$$

An atom at p_i is defined by

$$F_i(p_i) > \lim_{p \to p_i^-} F_i(p).$$

The equilibrium distributions actually have densities, with possibly an atom at the upper bound of the support.

31. By continuity, if $\underline{p}$ is an infimum rather than a minimum.

where q_i is the quantity sold at $\bar{p}_i$. Hence, $q_i = R_i(\bar{q}_j)$,[32] and firm i's profit is

$$\Pi^F(\bar{q}_j) \equiv R_i(\bar{q}_j)P(\bar{q}_j + R_i(\bar{q}_j)).$$

(The superscript F refers to the fact that firm i is the "Stackelberg follower," i.e., that it reacts to firm j's choice of $\bar{q}_j$. See chapter 8.) But, in a mixed-strategy equilibrium, all optimal strategies for a firm must yield the same profit—in particular,

$$\Pi^F(\bar{q}_j) = \underline{p}\bar{q}_i. \tag{5.16}$$

On the other hand, suppose that $\bar{q}_j > \bar{q}_i$. Then, by charging $P(\bar{q}_i + R_j(\bar{q}_i))$, firm j can guarantee itself $\Pi^F(\bar{q}_i)$, because we are in the mixed-strategy region, so that $\bar{q}_j > R_j(\bar{q}_i)$, and because $\bar{q}_i < \bar{q}_j$ implies that[33]

$$P[\bar{q}_i + R_j(\bar{q}_i)] > P[\bar{q}_j + R_i(\bar{q}_j)].$$

So we have

$$\underline{p}\bar{q}_j \geqslant \Pi^F(\bar{q}_i). \tag{5.17}$$

Eliminating $\underline{p}$, we obtain $\Pi^F(\bar{q}_j)\bar{q}_j \geqslant \Pi^F(\bar{q}_i)\bar{q}_i$. Simple algebraic manipulations[34] then show that $\bar{q}_i \geqslant \bar{q}_j$—a contradiction.

Or, each firm plays an atom at $\bar{p} = \bar{p}_i = \bar{p}_j$. However, in a mixed-strategy equilibrium, $\bar{p} > \underline{p}$; and, from our earlier analysis, $\bar{p} > P(\bar{q}_i + \bar{q}_j)$. Thus, at $\bar{p}$ each firm is unable to sell to capacity with strictly positive probability. Hence, each firm would be better off charging slightly less than $\bar{p}$ than charging $\bar{p}$.

We thus conclude that *the firm with the highest capacity —say, i ($\bar{q}_i \geqslant \bar{q}_j$)—earns profit $\Pi^F(\bar{q}_j)$*.

To construct a mixed-strategy equilibrium, one can look for increasing probability distributions for each firm over some (coincident) interval $[\underline{p}, \bar{p}]$ so that each firm is indifferent between playing any price in this interval (see Kreps and Scheinkman 1983). We will not need to do so. Given the above characterization, we need only to know that an equilibrium exists; we need not worry about its particular shape.

5.7.2.2 Choice of Capacities

Let us now add a prior and simultaneous choice of capacities; let $c_0 > 0$ denote the unit cost of installing capacity. Let us show that the Cournot outcome

$$(\bar{q}_1 = q^{**}, \bar{q}_2 = q^{**}),$$

where q^{**} maximizes

$$q[P(q + q^{**}) - c_0 - c]$$

is an equilibrium ($c = 0$ here).

Figure 5.13 illustrates the reaction curves when the capacity cost is sunk and when it is not. In the second-period price game, the capacity cost is alreay sunk and therefore it is irrelevant (bygones are bygones). Each firm would like to put more output on the market than it would if capacity were yet to be paid for. Hence, the reaction curves move upward from the first to the second period. In particular, $R(q^{**}) > q^{**}$, where R denotes the second-period reaction function.

Suppose that firm i plays q^{**}. Firm j, if it plays $q \leqslant R(q^{**})$, gets

---

32. If $q_i > R_i(\bar{q}_j)$, firm i could raise its price toward

$$P(\bar{q}_j + R_i(\bar{q}_j))$$

and make a higher profit. If $q_i < R_i(\bar{q}_j)$, $q_i = \bar{q}_i$ and $\bar{p}_i = P(\bar{q}_1 + \bar{q}_2) = \underline{p}$, so the equilibrium is in pure strategies, a contradiction.

33. The following inequality is due to the fact that reaction curves are identical and have slope < 1, as can easily be shown by differentiating the first-order conditions for Cournot equilibrium.

34. Suppose that $\bar{q}_i < \bar{q}_j$, which implies $\bar{q}_j > R_j(\bar{q}_i)$, and consider

$$\Delta \equiv \Pi^F(\bar{q}_j)\bar{q}_j - \Pi^F(\bar{q}_i)\bar{q}_i$$

$$= \int_{\bar{q}_i}^{\bar{q}_j} \frac{d}{dq}[q R(q)P(q + R(q))]dq$$

$$= \int_{\bar{q}_i}^{\bar{q}_j} [R(q)P(q + R(q)) + q R(q)P'(q + R(q))]dq,$$

where R denotes the reaction function and use is made of the envelope theorem

($R(q)$ maximizes the profit of the firm that reacts to q). Using the first-order condition for Cournot competition, we have

$$\Delta = -\int_{\bar{q}_i}^{\bar{q}_j} R P'(R - q)dq.$$

If $\bar{q}_i \geqslant R(\bar{q}_i)$, then for all $q > \bar{q}_i$ we have $R(q) < R(\bar{q}_i) \leqslant \bar{q}_i < q$ and thus $\Delta < 0$. Suppose next that $\bar{q}_i < R(\bar{q}_i)$. From footnote 32, $\bar{q}_j \geqslant R^{-1}(\bar{q}_i)$. For q in $[R^{-1}(\bar{q}_i), \bar{q}_j]$,

$$R(q) \leqslant \bar{q}_i \leqslant R^{-1}(\bar{q}_i) \leqslant q.$$

Hence,

$$\Delta \leqslant \int_{\bar{q}_i}^{R^{-1}(\bar{q}_i)} - R P'(R - q)dq$$

$$\leqslant R^{-1}(\bar{q}_i)\bar{q}_i P(\bar{q}_i + R^{-1}(\bar{q}_i)) - R(\bar{q}_i)\bar{q}_i P(\bar{q}_i + R(\bar{q}_i))$$

$$< 0,$$

as $R(\bar{q}_i)$ is a better reaction to $\bar{q}_i$ than $R^{-1}(\bar{q}_i)$.

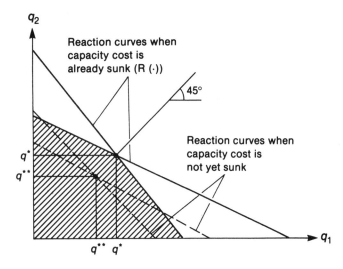

Figure 5.13

$$q[P(q + q^{**}) - c_0] \leqslant q^{**}[P(2q^{**}) - c_0],$$

where R still denotes the second-stage reaction function. If $q > R(q^{**})$, firm j gets exactly

$$\Pi^F(q^{**}) = R(q^{**})\{P[R(q^{**}) + q^{**}] - c_0\}.$$

But, by definition of q^{**}, $q^{**}(< R(q^{**}))$ is the best first-period reaction to q^{**}. So,

$$\Pi^F(q^{**}) \leqslant q^{**}[P(2q^{**}) - c_0].$$

We conclude that the Cournot equilibrium with cost c_0 is the equilibrium in the first-stage capacity game. And, from the analysis of the price game, the second-stage price is equal to $P(2q^{**})$.

To prove uniqueness in the choice of capacities requires more work, but not much; see Kreps and Scheinkman 1983.

5.7.2.3 Discussion of the Rationing Rule

Davidson and Deneckere (1986) argue that for virtually any rationing rule other than the efficient one, the Cournot outcome cannot emerge as an equilibrium of the two-stage game. Their reasoning can be sketched as follows: If we let c and c_0 denote the production cost and the capacity-installation cost, the first-order condition for firm

2's profit maximization in the Cournot game is

$$P'(q_1 + q_2)q_2 + P(q_1 + q_2) - c - c_0 = 0$$

at $q_1 = q_2 = q^{**}$. Let $p^{**} \equiv P(2q^{**})$ denote the Cournot price, and let $D(p_2|p_1)$ denote firm 2's residual demand when it charges price $p_2 \geqslant p_1$. Note that $D(p^{**}|p^{**}) = q^{**}$ if both firms have accumulated the Cournot capacity in the first stage (a necessary condition for the Cournot outcome to occur). Assuming that $D(p_2|p_1)$ is differentiable with respect to p_2 to the right of p_1, and assuming that the two firms have accumulated the Cournot capacities and charge the Cournot price p^{**}, firm 2's increase in profit associated with a slight increase in price above p^{**} is proportional to

$$A = D(p^{**}|p^{**}) + (p^{**} - c)D'(p^{**}|p^{**}).$$

(Recall that the investment cost is sunk in the second period.)

Following Davidson and Deneckere, assume further that, for p_2 just above p^{**},

$$D(p_2|p^{**}) > D(p_2) - q^{**}.$$

That is, the residual demand exceeds the one obtained with the efficient-rationing rule. The idea here is that if rationing is instantaneous and costless, q^{**} consumers are served by firm 1 and the rest turn to firm 2. The worst that can happen to firm 2 is that firm one serves the q^{**} consumers with the highest valuations. This is precisely what occurs under efficient rationing. That is, efficient rationing yields the lowest residual-demand curve.[35]

Let us actually make the slightly stronger assumption that

$$D'(p^{**}|p^{**}) > D'(p^{**}) = \frac{1}{P'(2q^{**})},$$

where the left-hand side refers to the residual-demand curve and the right-hand side to the ordinary-demand curve. Using the first-order condition for a Cournot equilibrium, we obtain

$$A > \frac{c_0}{P'(2q^{**})}.$$

---

35. There is, of course, a need to return to the microfoundations of rationing here. If rationing is not instantaneous and costless, one can think of residual demands that are even worse for firm 2 than the one associated with efficient rationing—for instance, consumers may maintain their order with firm 1 in the hope of buying at the low price if rationing is not instantaneous.

Now, suppose that $c_0 = 0$. Then, $A > 0$. Thus, firm 2, say, has an incentive to raise its price above the market-clearing price at the Cournot capacities. The Cournot outcome cannot be an equilibrium of the two-stage game. More generally, the same holds if c_0 is small, and the residual-demand curve is sufficiently above the one obtained for the efficient rationing rule.

5.7.2.4 Discussion of the Timing

A model of price competition occurring after capacity competition reflects the idea that prices adjust more quickly than capacities. Thus, it may make sense to consider capacities as given when prices are chosen. An important assumption of the previous analysis, though, is that a firm's capacity is observed by its competitor(s) before the price stage. It then acts as an indicator of the price the firm is about to charge. If capacities are imperfectly observable, this feature disappears and, formally, everything is as if capacities and prices were chosen simultaneously (although they need not be).

Gertner (1985) analyzes simultaneous quantity-price games. Each firm i chooses a quantity q_i and a price p_i without first observing the choices made by its competitors. Although Gertner allows decreasing and increasing returns to scale, let us focus on the simpler case of constant returns to scale, in which producing q_i costs cq_i to firm i. And, for simplicity, assume that there are two firms.

It is clear that no pure-strategy equilibrium exists. The logic closely follows the Bertrand-Edgeworth spirit. If a pure-strategy equilibrium existed, the two firms would have to sell at the same price. Otherwise, the low-price firm (say, firm i) would have the whole market; knowing that the other firm charges a higher price, it would confidently be able to produce the whole demand at its lower price. However, either $p_i = c$ and firm i would be better off raising its price by at least a small amount or $p_i > c$ and firm j could make a strictly positive profit by undercutting firm i. Next, in a pure-strategy equilibrium one would need $p_1^* = p_2^* = c$; if the market price exceeded c, each firm could increase its profit by undercutting slightly and supplying the whole market. But the competitive price cannot be an equilibrium either. At least one firm

would supply strictly less than $D(c)$ (otherwise, the firms would lose money); so the other firm could raise its price a bit, still get customers, and make a positive profit.

Gertner shows that a (unique) mixed-strategy equilibrium exists. It is similar to Bertrand's equilibrium in that firms make a zero expected profit.[36] It resembles Cournot's equilibrium in that the expected price exceeds the competitive price c. (This second result stems from the fact that firms never charge less than c, and (c, c) is not an equilibrium.) The qualitative difference with the case in which quantities (capacities) are observed is that a firm cannot commit itself not to "flood the market" by choosing a limited capacity. This raises competitive pressure and drives profits down, as in the Bertrand equilibrium. The firm that ends up charging the lower price supplies the whole market and makes a positive profit, and the firm with the higher price makes a negative profit (it produces and does not sell). The following exercise demonstrates the logic of the argument.

Exercise 5.9** Consider a two-firm simultaneous quantity-price game. Let $\bar{p}$ denote the supremum of prices at which there is a demand: $D(\bar{p}) = 0$. Look for a mixed-strategy equilibrium.

(i) Show that both firms make a zero profit. (Hint: Consider the lowest and the highest price charged by each firm.)

(ii) Suppose that each firm i plays according to some continuous distribution $F_i(p)$ on $[\underline{p}_i, \bar{p}_i]$ (which can be demonstrated). Show that each firm produces $D(p)$ when it charges p, if the other firm also produces to satisfy the demand at the price it charges.

(iii) Show that $F(p) = 1 - c/p$ for $p < \bar{p}$ and $F(\bar{p}) = 1$ is a symmetric equilibrium price distribution. Do these results depend on the rationing rule?

Both the sequential and the simultaneous quantity-price games involve mixed-strategy equilibria. This feature is a bit unsatisfactory if one indeed believes that prices can be changed much more quickly than capacities. Under mixed strategies, one firm generally ends up with a higher price than its competitor and faces little or no residual demand. Clearly, this firm would like to react and revise its price downward to increase its market share.

---

36. With decreasing returns (increasing marginal costs), firms make a profit.

Thus, mixed strategies call for price dynamics. Indeed, when Edgeworth introduced capacity constraints to escape the Bertrand paradox, he suggested the possibility of price cycles rather than the use of mixed strategies. Another feature worth studying when capacity precommitments take the form of production prior to sales and when the game in which both capacity and price decisions are made is repeated is the possibility of inventories.

5.7.2.5 Competition for Inputs

We assumed earlier that the firms on the output market have unrelated cost functions. In some circumstances, they may compete for the same input(s) for which they have monopsony power. A firm's cost of obtaining the input then depends on the other firm's purchasing strategy An important feature is that each firm can overbid its competitor on the input market and foreclose access to the input supply (or at least make this access more expensive). If the inputs can be identified with capacity (think of wholesalers buying crops from farmers, or of final-good producers buying machines from suppliers), each firm can restrict its competitor's capacity by bidding input supplies up. Stahl (1985) assumes that the input-supply industry is competitive and posits some other conditions; he shows that the outcome of the two stage game in which in the first stage firms bid for inputs (capacities) and in the second stage they choose prices, is competitive. As in Bertrand equilibrium, even two firms producing the final good cannot prevent the price from falling to the level at which the consumers' marginal willingness to pay is equal to the marginal cost of supplying the final good.

Answers and Hints

Exercise 5.1

First, there cannot be an equilibrium in which both p_1 and p_2 are strictly above c_2 (by the same reasoning as for the symmetric case). Second, firm 2 does not charge less than c_2 (it would make a negative profit if it sold).[37] Third, firm 1 can guarantee itself a profit as close as possible to $(c_2 - c_1)D(c_2)$ by charging $c_2 - \varepsilon$ (with ε small and positive). But since the market price (the minimum of the two prices) does not exceed c_2, this profit is also the highest that firm 1 can obtain. There is an "openness problem": Unless one assumes that at common price c_2 firm 1 gets all the demand, there is no equilibrium *stricto sensu*—firm 1 will want to choose ε as close as possible to, but different from, 0. Such an ε does not exist. But this is a technical detail. One can define the equilibrium as the limit, so $p_1 = c_2$ and firm 1's profit is $(c_2 - c_1)D(c_2)$.[38]

When $p^m(c_1) < c_2$, firm 1 can charge its monopoly price without worrying about firm 2's threat.

Exercise 5.2

Suppose that firm 1 charges

$$p^* = 1 - (\overline{q}_1 + \overline{q}_2) \geqslant \tfrac{1}{2}.$$

Clearly, firm 2 has no incentive to charge less than p^*. Suppose that it charges $p > p^*$. The residual demand is

$$(1 - p)\left(\frac{1 - p^* - \overline{q}_1}{1 - p^*}\right).$$

Thus, firm 2's profit is

$$p(1 - p)\left(\frac{1 - p^* - \overline{q}_1}{1 - p^*}\right).$$

This implies that firm 2 must choose $p = \tfrac{1}{2}$ (which is the monopoly price in the absence of capacity constraint). However, $p^* > \tfrac{1}{2}$. From the concavity of its objective function above p^*, firm 2 can do no better than to charge p^*.

---

37. Here we are making the reasonable assumption that firm 2 does not play a "dominated strategy." We thus put some constraint on the Nash concept (see the Game Theory User's Manual).

38. Show that the same result is obtained (still under the assumption that firm 2 does not play a dominated strategy) when the firms are free to supply whatever demand they face.

Exercise 5.3

(i) $q = \frac{1}{4} \Rightarrow \Pi^i = \frac{1}{16}$.

(ii) In duopoly, $q = \frac{1}{3} \Rightarrow \Pi^i = \frac{1}{9} < 2 \times \frac{1}{16}$.

(iii) A monopoly would clearly do better: It would make an aggregate profit of $\frac{1}{4}$.

(iv) In price competition, a firm that carries two substitute products charges higher prices for these products than two separate firms would. This is because, when pricing a product, the firm internalizes the reduction of demand on the other product associated with a price decrease. Now, if there is a third firm producing a third, differentiated product, this firm charges a higher price for its own product if the other two products are sold by a single firm. Here, merging is here a "puppy-dog strategy," in the language of chapter 8. Merging firms become less aggressive and, therefore, trigger a less aggressive response from the third firm.

For more details on mergers and Cournot competition, see Davidson and Deneckere 1984, Salant et al. 1983, and Szidarowsky and Yakowitz 1982; on mergers and Bertrand competition, see Deneckere and Davidson 1985.

Exercise 5.4

(i) Let $c_1 = w + r$ and $c_2 = 2w + r$ denote the unit costs. In Cournot equilibrium,

$$q_1 = (1 - 2c_1 + c_2)/3 \text{ and } q_2 = (1 - 2c_2 + c_1)/3$$

or

$$q_1 = (1 - r)/3 \text{ and } q_2 = (1 - r - 3w)/3.$$

(ii) $\Pi^1 = \max_{q_1}\{q_1[1 - q_1 - q_2 - (r + w)]\}$.

From the envelope theorem,

$$\frac{\partial \Pi^1}{\partial w} = q_1\left(-\frac{\partial q_2}{\partial w} - 1\right) = q_1(1 - 1) = 0.$$

A change in w has two effects: It raises firm 1's cost and it weakens firm 2's strategic position. Because firm 2 is highly labor intensive, it must reduce its output considerably. In general, either effect may dominate.

Exercise 5.5

(i) $\max_{q_1}[(1 - q_1 - q_2)q_1 - q_1{}^2/2] \Rightarrow 1 - 3q_1 - q_2 = 0$.

By symmetry, $q_1 = q_2 = \frac{1}{4}$, and $\Pi^1 = \Pi^2 = \frac{3}{32}$. Note that the marginal cost is $\frac{1}{4}$.

(ii) The two firms' outputs are obtained by solving

$$\Pi^1 = \max_{\{q_1, x_1\}} [q_1(1 - q_1 - q_2) + x_1(a - x_1) - (q_1 + x_1)^2/2]$$

and

$$\Pi^2 = \max_{\{q_2\}}[q_2(1 - q_1 - q_2) - q_2{}^2/2].$$

The first-order conditions yield the solution.

From the envelope theorem,

$$\frac{d\Pi^1}{da} = -q_1\frac{\partial q_2}{\partial a} + x_1 = -\frac{q_1}{21} + x_1.$$

However, for $a = \frac{1}{4}$, $x_1 = 0$; so $d\Pi^1/da < 0$.

Interpretation: When $a = \frac{1}{4}$, firm 1 is indifferent between selling one unit in market 2 and not doing so (because $P(0) = a = \frac{1}{4} = $ MC). But the "strategic effect" plays against firm 1: Firm 2 knows that for $a = \frac{1}{4} + \varepsilon$ firm 1 sells a bit in the second market and therefore has a higher marginal cost. So firm 2 increases its output. If firm 1 could commit to staying out of market 2, it would do so (for $a = \frac{1}{4} + \varepsilon$. This abstention is an example of the "lean-and-hungry-look strategy" ("stay thin to remain aggressive") developed in chapter 8.

Exercise 5.6

(i) $\frac{\Sigma_i \Pi^i}{R} = \frac{\Sigma_i(p - c_i)q_i}{pQ} = \frac{\Sigma_i \alpha_i^2}{\varepsilon} = \frac{R_H}{\varepsilon}$.

(ii) $L_i = \frac{p - C_i'}{p} = -q_i\frac{P'}{P}$

implies

$$L = \sum_i \alpha_i L_i = \frac{\Sigma_i \alpha_i^2}{\varepsilon}.$$

Exercise 5.7

Outputs and profits are derived in section 5.4. Note that

$$Q = q_1 + q_2 = \frac{1}{3}(2 - c_1 - c_2) = \frac{2}{3}(1 - c).$$

Thus, total output does not depend on the degree of cost asymmetry. Let firm 1 be the low-cost firm: $c_1 \leqslant c \leqslant c_2$. When c_1 decreases (and $c_2 = 2c - c_1$ increases), q_1 increases and q_2 decreases. Hence, α_1 increases and α_2

decreases. Thus, any concentration index satisfying the Lorenz criterion (like the three mentioned in the text) increases.

Total profit is

$$\Pi = \tfrac{1}{9}[18c_1(c_1 - 2c) + (2 - 4c + 20c^2)].$$

Π is a convex function of c_1 with a minimum at $c_1 = c$.

Exercise 5.8

(i) W is equal to net consumer surplus plus industry profit, or to gross consumer surplus minus total cost. The change in gross consumer surplus is equal to $p\delta Q$, where $\delta Q \equiv \Sigma_{i=1}^{n} \delta q_i$; the change in cost is equal to $\Sigma_{i=1}^{n} C_i' \delta q_i$.

(ii) Maximize δW subject to the constraint

$$\sum_{i=1}^{n} (\delta q_i)^2 \leqslant k.$$

δW is then called the *industry performance gradient index*. The Lagrangian is equal to

$$\sum_{i=1}^{n} [(p - C_i')\delta q_i - \lambda \delta q_i^2] + \lambda k.$$

We get

$$\delta q_i = (p - C_i')/2\lambda.$$

Thus,

$$\delta W = \left(\sum_{i=1}^{n} (p - C_i')^2 \right) \Big/ 2\lambda.$$

Using the aforementioned constraint, we get

$$\sum_{i=1}^{n} (p - C_i')^2/4\lambda^2 = k.$$

Substituting λ gives

$$\delta W = p\sqrt{k} \sqrt{\sum_{i=1}^{n} \left(\frac{(p - C_i')^2}{p^2} \right)} = \frac{p\sqrt{k}}{\varepsilon} \sqrt{R_{\mathrm{H}}} \,,$$

where ε is the elasticity of demand.

Looking at small changes is usually (informally) justified by the possibilities that the exogenous variables (e.g. cost) underlying Cournot competition do move slowly, and that those of these variables that are controlled by the government ought to be changed slowly (for informational reasons, in particular—the tax-reform literature emphasizes that the elasticities of demand and supply

functions are known only locally, which makes radical moves hazardous).

The manner in which changes in exogenous variables and changes in output are linked is an open question. In particular, one must look at how close the actual change in δq induced by (say) a policy change comes to the change that maximizes δW subject to the norm constraint. Only this exercise will allow us to assess whether bigger potential welfare improvements are indeed associated with higher concentration indices.

For more examples of types of competition and indices, see Dansby and Willig.

Exercise 5.9

Take an "arbitrary" rationing rule.

(i) Let $\underline{p}_i$ and $\bar{p}_i$ denote the lower and upper bounds of the support of firm i's mixed strategy. Suppose first that $\bar{p}_i > \bar{p}_j$ or $\bar{p}_i = \bar{p}_j$ and firm j charges $\bar{p}_j$ with zero probability. Then firm i makes zero profit, because when charging $\bar{p}_i$ it sells with zero probability. Next, firm j also makes zero profit; either $\underline{p}_j = c$, or $\underline{p}_j > c$ (in the latter case, firm i could secure a positive profit by charging $\underline{p}_j - \varepsilon$ and producing $D(\underline{p}_j - \varepsilon)$—a contradiction). So we are left with $\bar{p}_i = \bar{p}_j$ and both firms playing an atom at this price (i.e., playing this price with positive probability). If $D(\bar{p}_i) > 0$, each firm can reduce its price slightly, still produce $D(\bar{p}_i)$, and be able to sell the whole of $D(\bar{p}_i)$ if the other firm charges $\bar{p}_i$ (which it does with positive probability). So $\bar{p}_i = \bar{p}_j = \bar{p}$, where $D(\bar{p}) = 0$. And, again, neither firm makes a profit.

(ii) If firm j produces $D(p_j)$ when it charges p_j, consumers are never rationed by firm j and firm i's profit from charging p_i is

$$\{[1 - F_j(p_i)]p_i - c\}q_i, \quad \text{for } 0 \leqslant q_i \leqslant D(p_i)$$

and

$$[1 - F_j(p_i)]p_i D(p_i) - cq_i, \quad \text{for } q_i > D(p_i).$$

Clearly, the optimal quantity for price p_i is $q_i = D(p_i)$ (or zero).

(iii) If $F(p) = 1 - c/p$, for all p in $[c, \bar{p}]$,

$$\{[1 - F(p)]p - c\}D(p) = 0.$$

Each firm plays an atom at $\bar{p}$.

References

Atkinson, A. B. 1970. On the Measurement of Inequality. *Journal of Economic Theory* 2: 244–263.

Allen, B., and M. Hellwig. 1986. Bertrand-Edgeworth Oligopoly in Large Markets. *Review of Economic Studies* 53: 175–204.

Bain, J. 1951. Relation of Profit Rate to Industry Concentration: American Manufacturing, 1936–1940. *Quarterly Journal of Economics* 65: 293–324.

Bain, J. 1956. *Industrial Organization*. New York: Wiley.

Bamon, R., and J. Fraysse. 1985. Existence of Cournot Equilibrium in Large Markets. *Econometrica* 53: 587–597.

Beckman, M. 1967. Edgeworth-Bertrand Duopoly Revisited. In *Operations Research-Verfahren, III*, ed. R. Henn. Meisenheim: Verlag Anton Hein.

Benoit, J.-P., and V. Krishna. 1987. Dynamic Duopoly: Prices and Quantities. *Review of Economic Studies* 54: 23–36.

Bertrand, J. 1883. Théorie Mathématique de la Richesse Sociale. *Journal des Savants*, pp. 499–508.

Bulow, J., J. Geanakoplos, and P. Klemperer. 1985. Multimarket Oligopoly: Strategic Substitutes and Complements. *Journal of Political Economy* 93: 488–511.

Cournot, A. 1838. *Recherches sur les Principes Mathématiques de la Théorie des Richesses*. English edition (ed. N. Bacon): *Researches into the Mathematical Principles of the Theory of Wealth* (New York: Macmillan, 1897).

Cowling, K., and M. Waterson. 1976. Price-Cost Margins and Market Structure. *Economic Journal* 43: 267–274.

Curry, B., and K. George. 1983. Industrial Concentration: A Survey. *Journal of Industrial Economics* 31: 203–255.

Dansby, R., and R. Willig. 1979. Industry Performance Gradient Indexes. *American Economic Review* 69: 249–260.

Dasgupta, P., and E. Maskin. 1986a. The Existence of Equilibrium in Discontinuous Economic Games, I: Theory. *Review of Economic Studies* 53: 1–26.

Dasgupta, P., and E. Maskin. 1986b. The Existence of Equilibrium in Discontinuous Games, II: Applications. *Review of Economic Studies* 53: 27–41.

Davidson, C., and R. Deneckere. 1984. Horizontal Mergers and Collusive Behavior. *International Journal of Industrial Organization* 2: 117–132.

Davidson, C., and R. Deneckere. 1986. Long-Term Competition in Capacity, Short-Run Competition in Price, and the Cournot Model. *Rand Journal of Economics* 17: 404–415.

Demsetz, H. 1973. Industry Structure, Market Rivalry and Public Policy. *Journal of Law and Economics* 16: 1–10.

Deneckere, R., and C. Davidson. 1985. Incentives to Form Coalitions with Bertrand Competition. *Rand Journal of Economics* 16: 473–486.

Edgeworth, F. 1897. La Teoria Pura del Monopolio. *Giornale degli Economisti* 40: 13–31. In English: The Pure Theory of Monopoly, in *Papers Relating to Political Economy*, volume 1, ed. F. Edgeworth (London: Macmillan, 1925).

Encaoua, D., and A. Jacquemin. 1980. Degree of Monopoly, Indices of Concentration and Threat of Entry. *International Economic Review* 21: 87–105.

Friedman, J. 1977. *Oligopoly and the Theory of Games*. Amsterdam: North-Holland.

Friedman, J. 1983. *Oligopoly Theory*. Cambridge University Press.

Friedman, J. 1986. On the Strategic Importance of Prices vs. Quantities. Mimeo, University of North Carolina.

Gabszewicz, J., and J. P. Vial. 1972. Oligopoly "à la Cournot" in General Equilibrium Analysis. *Journal of Economic Theory* 4: 381–400.

Gertner, R. 1985. Simultaneous Move Price-Quantity Games and Non-Market Clearing Equilibrium. Mimeo, Massachusetts Institute of Technology.

Ghemawat, P. 1986. Capacities and Prices: A Model with Applications. Mimeo, Harvard Business School.

Hannah, L., and J. Kay. 1977. *Concentration in Modern Industry: Theory, Measurement and the U.K. Experience*. London: Macmillan.

Hart, O. 1979. Monopolistic Competition in a Large Economy with Differentiated Commodities. *Review of Economic Studies* 46: 1–30.

Hart, O. 1980. Perfect Competition and Optimal Product Differentiation. *Journal of Economic Theory* 22: 279–312.

Hart, O. 1985. Imperfect Competition in General Equilibrium: An Overview of Recent Work. In Frontiers of Economics, ed. K. Arrow and S. Honkapohja. Oxford: Blackwell.

Kay, J. 1977. *Concentration in Modern Industry*. London: Macmillan.

Kolm, S.-C. 1966. Les Choix Financiers et Monétaires: Théorie et Techniques Modernes. Editions Dunod.

Kolm, S.-C. 1969. The Optimal Production of Social Justice. In *Public Economics*, ed. J. Margolis and H. Guitton. London: Macmillan.

Kreps, D., and J. Scheinkman. 1983. Quantity Precommitment and Bertrand Competition Yield Cournot Outcomes. *Bell Journal of Economics* 14: 326–337.

Levitan, R., and M. Shubik. 1972. Price Duopoly and Capacity Constraints. *International Economic Review* 13: 111–122.

Levitan, R., and M. Shubik 1980. Duopoly with Price and Quantity as Strategic Variables. *International Journal of Game Theory* 7: 1–11.

McManus, M. 1962. Numbers and Size in Cournot Oligopoly. *Yorkshire Bulletin of Social and Economic Research* 14.

McManus, M. 1964. Equilibrium, Number and Size in Cournot Oligopoly. *Yorkshire Bulletin of Social and Economic Research* 16: 68–75.

Mas-Colell, A. 1982. The Cournotian Foundations of Walrasian Equilibrium Theory: An Exposition of Recent Theory. In Advances in Economic Theory, ed W. Hildenbrand. Cambridge University Press.

Nash, J. 1950. Equilibrium Points in *n*-Person Games. *Proceedings of the National Academy of Sciences* 36: 48–49.

Novshek, W. 1985. On the Existence of Cournot Equilibrium. *Review of Economic Studies* 52: 85–98.

Novshek, W., and H. Sonnenschein. 1978. Cournot and Walras Equilibrium. *Journal of Economic Theory* 19: 223–266.

Osborne, M., and C. Pitchik. 1986. Price Competition in a Capacity Constrained Duopoly. *Journal of Economic Theory* 38: 238–260.

Roberts, K. 1980. The Limit Points of Monopolistic Competition. *Journal of Economic Theory* 22: 256–279.

Roberts, J., and A. Postlewaite. 1976. The Incentives for Price-Taking Behavior in Large Exchange Economies. *Econometrica* 44: 115–128.

Roberts, J., and H. Sonnenschein. 1976. On the Existence of Cournot Equilibrium without Concave Profit Functions. *Journal of Economic Theory* 13: 112–117.

Roberts, J., and H. Sonnenschein. 1977. On the Foundations of the Theory of Monopolistic Competition. *Econometrica* 45: 101–113.

Rothschild, M., and J. Stiglitz. 1970. Increasing Risk: I. A Definition. *Journal of Economic Theory* 2: 225–243.

Salant, S., S. Switzer, and R. Reynolds. 1983. Losses Due to Merger: The Effects of an Exogenous Change in Industry Structure on Cournot-Nash Equilibrium. *Quarterly Journal of Economics* 48: 185–200.

Scherer, F. 1980. *Industrial Market Structure and Economic Performance*, second edition. Chicago: Rand-McNally.

Schmalensee, R. 1986. Inter-Industry Studies of Structure and Performance. In *Handbook of Industrial Organization*, ed. R. Schmalensee and R. Willig (Amsterdam: North-Holland, forthcoming).

Schmalensee, R. 1987. Collusion versus Differential Efficiency: Testing Alternative Hypotheses. *Journal of Industrial Economics* 35: 399–425.

Sherman, R. 1972. *Oligopoly: An Experimental Approach*. Cambridge, Mass.: Ballinger.

Shubik, M. 1959. *Strategy and Market Structure*. New York: Wiley.

Stahl, D. 1985. Bertrand Competition for Inputs, Forward Contracts and Walrasian Outcomes. Duke University.

Szidarowsky, F., and S. Yakowitz. 1977. A New Proof of the Existence and Uniqueness of the Cournot Equilibrium. *International Economic Review* 18: 787–789.

Szidarowsky, F., and S. Yakowitz. 1982. Contribution to Cournot Oligopoly Theory. *Journal of Economic Theory* 28: 51–70.

Vives, X. 1985. Nash Equilibrium in Oligopoly Games with Monotone Best Responses. CARESS W. P. 85–10, University of Pennsylvania.

Vives, X. 1986. Rationing and Bertrand-Edgeworth Equilibria in Large Markets. *Economic Letters* 27: 113–116.

Dynamic Price Competition and Tacit Collusion

The analysis in chapter 5 assumed one-shot competition; firms simultaneously quoted their prices, then "disappeared." In practice, though, firms are likely to interact repeatedly. Durable investments, technological know-how, and barriers to entry promote long-run interactions among a relatively stable set of firms (this is especially true of industries with only a few firms). As was mentioned in chapter 5, repeated interaction may upset the Bertrand outcome. With repeated interaction, a firm must take into account not only the possible increase in current profits but also the possibility of a price war and long-run losses when deciding whether to undercut a given price.

Chamberlin (1929) suggested that in an oligopoly producing a homogeneous product, firms would recognize their interdependence and, therefore, might be able to sustain the monopoly price without explicit collusion. The threat of a vigorous price war would be sufficient to deter the temptation to cut prices. Hence, the oligopolists might be able to collude in a purely noncooperative manner. This possibility of *tacit collusion* was a challenging one at a time when economists were primarily concerned with overt collusion. Chamberlin even suggested that in the absence of hindering factors (to be discussed below), the monopoly price was the most likely outcome.

The purpose of this chapter is to offer an introduction to the theory of repeated interaction. Section 6.1 briefly reviews the conventional wisdom on collusion and the factors that are supposed to hinder or facilitate collusion. (The reader may want to complement this section with the much richer description of the conventional wisdom in chapters 5 through 7 of Scherer 1980.) Because the dynamics of price behavior are hard to analyze, and the tool to do so (the theory of dynamic games) has been developed only recently, there is a considerable literature that attempts to formalize the dynamic aspects in a static context. This literature, which generally presumes some anticipation of one's opponent's reaction to the choice of one's price, is reviewed in section 6.2. Sections 6.3 through 6.5 use different approaches to develop full-fledged models of dynamic price competition.[1] In all those approaches, price cutting yields short-run profits to the undercutting firm but triggers a price war, and prices above marginal cost (for instance, the monopoly price) may be sustained in equilibrium. The motives for "retaliation" differ in the three approaches, however. In the first approach (that of the well-established supergame literature), the price war is a purely self-fulfilling phenomenon. A firm charges a low price because it expects the other firms to do so ("bootstrap" behavior). The signal that triggers such a noncooperative phase is previous undercutting by one of the firms. The second approach presumes short-run price rigidities; the reaction by one firm to a price cut by another firm is motivated by its desire to regain a market share that has been and continues to be eroded by its rival's aggressive pricing strategy. The third approach (reputation) focuses on (nonphysical) intertemporal links that arise from the firms' learning about each other. A firm reacts to a price cut by charging a low price itself because the previous price cut has conveyed the information that its opponent either has a low cost or cannot be trusted to sustain collusion and is therefore likely to charge relatively low prices in the future.

Thus, we will consider a variety of theories that can explain tacit collusion. These should be thought of as describing complementary aspects of repeated price interaction. To paraphrase Scherer (1980, p. 151), the proliferation of theories is mirrored by an equally rich array of behavioral patterns actually observed under oligopoly.

Section 6.5 briefly reviews an alternative to optimizing approaches—the evolutionary theory of price behavior—and the supplementary section provides a further and more advanced treatment of the dynamic-game approaches to tacit collusion.

6.1 Conventional Wisdom (Factors Facilitating and Hindering Collusion)

Starting with Chamberlin, several authors felt that repeated interaction between oligopolists should facilitate collusion. They also identified some factors that may hinder it.

6.1.1 Collusion

Consider a small number of identical firms producing a homogeneous product. Chamberlin conjectured that in such a situation the firms in the industry would charge the monopoly price, i.e., the price that maximizes industry profit:

If each seeks his maximum profit rationally and intelligently, he will realize that when there are only two or a few sellers his own move has a considerable effect upon his competitors, and that this makes it idle to suppose that they will accept without retaliation the losses he forces upon them. Since the result of a cut by any one is inevitably to decrease his own profits, no one will cut, and although the sellers are entirely independent, the equilibrium result is the same as though there were a monopolistic agreement between them. (1933, p. 48)

Several contributions published before World War II tried to formalize the discipline imposed by the possibility of reactions; some of them will be reviewed in section 6.2. By far the best-known is the story of the *kinked demand curve* (Hall and Hitch 1939; Sweezy 1939): Consider two firms with marginal cost c. Let $q = D(p)$ denote the demand function and let $\Pi(p) = (p - c)D(p)$ denote the industry profit when the lowest price charged is p. Start from a situation in which firms charge the monopoly price p^m and each makes profit $\Pi^m/2$, where $\Pi^m \equiv \Pi(p^m)$. Suppose that a firm contemplates deviating from the monopoly price and has the following conjecture about its rival's reaction: Its rival will stay put at p^m if it raises its price above p^m, and will follow suit (match the price) if it cuts its price. It is clear that, under such a conjecture, deviating from the monopoly price is not profitable. An increase in price leads to a complete loss in market share and a zero profit. A reduction in price to $p < p^m$ yields a profit of $\Pi(p)/2 \leqslant \Pi^m/2$. (The term "kinked demand curve" will be explained in section 6.2.)

As Chamberlin recognized, there are factors that may hinder collusion. We distinguish two such factors: detection lags and asymmetries between firms. The consequences of the first factor can be obtained easily from any of the dynamic-game approaches mentioned above. Unfortunately, efforts to formulate the second factor have not been as successful.

---

1. Shapiro 1986 contains an excellent critical discussion of models of dynamic price competition.

6.1.2 Detection Lags

Chamberlinian tacit collusion is enforced by the threat of retaliation. But retaliation can occur only when it is learned that some member of the industry has deviated. In many industries, the prices charged by a manufacturer can be observed fairly quickly by its competitors. In others, however, prices may remain somewhat hidden. This may be the case, for instance, when the manufacturers sell to a small number of big buyers. Rather than quoting a price, they make deals that are particular to each buyer and that the other competitors may observe only with a lag. (They may observe only the effects of these deals on their market shares.) Because retaliation is delayed, it is less costly to a price-cutting firm; therefore, tacit collusion is harder to sustain. (In the extreme, suppose that a price cut is never observed. Then everything is as if firms chose prices simultaneously—there are never prices around that competitors can react to. We know from chapter 5 that in such a situation, absent capacity constraints, firms charge their marginal cost and make no profit.)

Information lags make the future more distant and thus make dynamic interaction less relevant. A similar point can be made about the existence of some large sales situation, such as the arrival of a big order from a large buyer. In such a situation, one would predict that collusion will tend to break down because the short-run private gain from undercutting is large relative to the long-term losses associated with a subsequent price war.[2]

Oligopolists are likely to recognize the threat to collusion posed by secrecy, and consequently may take steps to eliminate it.

First, they may create an industry trade association that (among other functions) collects detailed information on the transactions executed by the association's members or allows its members to cross-check price quotations. The members of the industry can also give advance notice of their price changes.

Second, the oligopolists may impose resale-price maintenance on their wholesalers or their retailers (Telser 1960). The idea here is that any deviation from collusive behavior is easily detected because a manufacturer's good is sold at a single price ungarbled by distribution idiosyncrasies and price discrimination. (The "most favored nation" clause, requiring that the seller charge a buyer a price no higher than what it charges any other buyer, serves a similar purpose and is a significant deterrent to price cutting; see Scherer 1980, p. 225.)

Third, when firms sell hundreds or thousands of different products (as do department stores and manufacturers of products with a large number of attributes), rule-of-thumb pricing—such as a uniform margin over all products or the use of representative prices—helps firms to quickly analyze one another's pricing behavior in the presence of complexity. (Consider, for example, an auto-repair shop that sets standard job-completion times and then sets an hourly rate.) Similarly, trade associations may impose standardization agreements to discourage price cutting in a multiple-attribute world, and industries producing products whose transportation costs are high relative to their value (e.g. cement, steel, wood, sugar) are often alleged to use basing-point pricing to collude.[3] An example of basing-point pricing consists in charging a unique mill price; prices to various destinations are then equal to the announced mill price plus freight to those destinations.[4,5,6]

---

2. See Scherer 1980, pp. 220–225, for some interesting examples of difficulties of substaining collusion under lumpiness or secrecy, and Stigler 1964 and Orr and MacAvoy 1965 for early analyses of the topic.

3. See chapter 3 for a study of third-degree price discrimination in spatial markets.

4. Some types of rule-of-thumb pricing require a good deal of common information. In the case of uniform margins, for example, it would be necessary for firms to know each other's costs to verify that the rule of thumb was being obeyed. Basing-point pricing and pricing according to standard job-completion times require less common information.

5. The practices reviewed in this paragraph allow a firm's rivals to infer a change in its pricing strategy from a single price observation. They reduce informational delays and thus hasten retaliation. It is also often alleged that these practices (in particular, basing-point pricing) are used to aid coordination (rather than information collection) by restricting attention to a single price. According to this theory, the firms would have trouble focusing on a "focal equilibrium" in a complex environment (perhaps because of bounded rationality).

Neither the information-collection theory nor the coordination theory explains how the rule-of-thumb or representative price is chosen (for instance, why a particular basing-point pricing system is used rather than f.o.b. pricing, or how an auto-repair shop sets standard job-completion times).

6. A good example of an industry in which such practices are used is the turbine generator industry, which is dominated by General Electric and Westinghouse. The buying process for turbine generators by electric utilities is highly secret. In 1963, General Electric, quickly followed by its rival, announced a new pricing policy. First it published a new price book, which contained simplified and exhaustive pricing formulas for computing the price of a turbine generator as a function of its specifications. (The old price book left a lot of leeway for interpretation, in particular for some technical trade-offs and for the price of spare parts.) The resulting price was then multiplied by a uniform

6.1.3 Asymmetries

Chamberlin's suggestion that the likely market outcome is *the* monopoly price raises the question of what happens if the oligopolists have divergent preferences about prices and, in particular, different monopoly prices. For instance, their marginal costs may differ, so the lower-cost firms would like to coordinate on a lower price than the higher-cost firms (see chapter 1 for a proof that a low marginal cost implies a low monopoly price). The firms may also offer differentiated products (differentiated according to quality, location, distribution channels, etc.). It is often felt that heterogeneity in both costs and products may make coordination on a given price difficult (see Scherer's chapter 7).[7]

Under symmetric conditions, the price to coordinate on seems to be naturally the monopoly price. This price maximizes profit and involves a symmetric repartition of profits.[8] Under asymmetric costs, there is no "focal" price on which to coordinate.[9]

The following exercise describes the trade-off between maximization of industry profits and a "fair" distribution of these profits when firms face different marginal costs.

Exercise 6.1*** Suppose there are two firms, with unit costs $c_1 < c_2$. Let $p^m(c)$ denote the monopoly price for unit cost c; it maximizes $(p - c)D(p)$. If the two firms could get together and sign a contract, they would let firm 1 produce everything and charge $p^m(c_1)$. This would maximize industry profit. The "pie" could then be divided between the two firms through an arbitrary lump-sum transfer from firm 1 to firm 2. But suppose that it is illegal for the firms to overtly agree and use side payments. We can determine the set of industry allocations that are efficient for the two firms, *constrained* by the fact that side payments are prohibited. (Exercise 6.5 involves the question whether such "constrained efficient allocations" can be sustained by equilibrium behavior in repeated interaction.) To this purpose, we fix a profit target $\bar{\Pi}^2$

for firm 2 in the interval $[0, \Pi^m(c_2)]$ and look for profit-sharing agreements (without transfers) in which both firms charge the same price p. They choose market shares s_1 and s_2 such that $s_1 + s_2 = 1$. The interpretation of these market shares is that firm i produces exactly $q_i = s_i D(p)$; if $s_i < \frac{1}{2}$, the consumers who go to firm i and are rationed buy from firm j. Given a profit target of $\bar{\Pi}^2$ for firm 2, the efficient allocation is a choice of price p and market shares s_1 and s_2 so as to maximize Π^1:

$$\max_{\{p, s_1, s_2\}} \Pi^1 = (p - c_1)s_1 D(p) \tag{6.1}$$
$$\text{s.t. } \Pi^2 = (p - c_2)s_2 D(p) \geqslant \bar{\Pi}^2 \text{ and } s_1 + s_2 = 1.$$

Suppose that the profit function $(p - c)D(p)$ is concave for all p and c.

(i) After substituting s_1, obtain the first-order condition. Show that

$$p^m(c_1) \leqslant p \leqslant p^m(c_2).$$

Show that the objective function is quasi-concave.

(ii) Show that

$$[(p - c_1)D'(p) + D(p)] + \frac{(c_2 - c_1)\bar{\Pi}^2}{(p - c_2)^2} = 0.$$

(iii) Conclude that as $\bar{\Pi}^2$ grows, both p and s_2 grow.

(iv) Show that the Pareto frontier is convex.

(v) What do you conclude from (iv)?

(vi) Show that if one now allows the firms' prices to differ, for the *efficient*-rationing rule (see chapter 5), deterministic efficient market-sharing allocations indeed imply identical prices for both firms.

6.1.4 Other Factors

Factors that weaken price competition in a static context might also facilitate collusion in a repeated-price-interaction situation. In particular, *decreasing returns to scale* (or capacity constraints) make undercutting less profitable today. However, they also weaken the strength of future

---

multiplier, just as in the case of an auto-repair shop that sets a uniform hourly rate. (The two rivals used the same book prices, and even ended up using the same multipliers.) Second, GE announced that it would not price-discriminate between different buyers (including intertemporally—its contracts included a six-month price-protection clause, which was enforced by a public accounting firm hired by GE). For more on this, see Sultan 1975 and Porter 1983.

7. Of course, if the firms' products are very differentiated, there is no real

competition anyway, and the problem of collusive coordination does not arise. The informal literature is a bit confused concerning these differentiation effects.

8. The reasoning here is very loose; there is no formal argument justifying it.

9. For a discussion of Schelling's (1960) theory of focal points, see Scherer 1980, pp. 190–193. For a discussion of why collusion might be more complex with asymmetric firms, see Scherer 1980, pp. 156–160.

retaliations, as they limit the output that firms can supply in the market. Thus, the effect of decreasing returns to scale is *a priori* ambiguous.[10]

Multimarket contact is generally thought to blunt the incentives for rivalry. Corwin Edwards puts it in the following way:

[Firms that compete against each other in many markets] may hesitate to fight vigorously because the prospects of local gain are not worth the risk of general warfare.... A prospect of advantage from vigorous competition in one market may be weighted against the danger of retaliatory forays by the competitor in other markets. (quoted in Bernheim and Whinston 1986)

However, as Bernheim and Whinston note, a firm might also fight vigorously and simultaneously in all markets, so that its short-term gains would be not local but general. In section 6.3 we will review the multimarket contact argument.

The number of firms in the industry is, of course, thought of as affecting the possibility of collusion. Indeed, Bain's (1956) original concern with *market concentration* was based on an intuitive view that high concentration is necessary (if not sufficient) for collusive outcomes.

6.2 Static Approaches to Dynamic Price Competition

6.2.1 Kinked Demand Curve

As was mentioned in section 6.1, the story of the kinked demand curve was designed to explain why oligopolists shy away from frequent price cutting. Suppose that there are two firms, $i = 1, 2$, with unit cost c. The demand function is $q = D(p)$.

The simplest version of the kinked-demand-curve story assigns a special role to a given price; we will call this the "focal price," p^f. We can think of p^f as the current market price or as what firms believe is the steady-state (long-run) price. Each firm has the following conjecture: If it charges $p > p^f$, its rival will not follow suit (i.e., will keep

charging p^f). If, instead, a firm cuts its price to $p \leqslant p^f$, its rival will exactly match the price cut. The residual demand for a firm that increases its price is zero; the residual demand for a firm that charges $p \leqslant p^f$ is $D(p)/2$. In summary, each firm envisions for its rival the "reaction curve" shown in figure 6.1. The perceived-demand curve for firm i is shown in figure 6.2.

With such beliefs about its rival's reaction, firm i maximizes $(p_i - c)D(p_i)/2$ subject to $p_i \leqslant p^f$. If we assume that the profit function $(p - c)D(p)$ is increasing to the

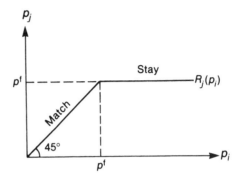

Figure 6.1
Reaction function for kinked demand curve.

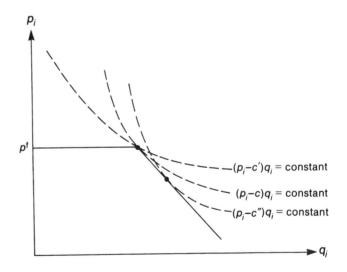

Figure 6.2
Kinked demand curve.

---

10. Brock and Scheinkman (1985) consider a dynamic price model in which firms are constrained by the same exogenously given capacity. The price game at each period is similar to the capacity-constrained price games considered in

chapter 5. They justify the previous intuition and show that, for the equilibrium they select, the collusive price is not necessarily a monotonic function of industry capacity.

left of p^m and decreasing to its right (i.e., that it is quasi-concave), the optimal price for firm i is thus equal to p^f if $p^f \leqslant p^m$ and to p^m if $p^f > p^m$. We conclude that both firms charging any p^f is an "equilibrium" as long as p^f lies between c and p^m *and* each firm expects its rival to react as described above.

The kinked-demand-curve story can be criticized on many grounds. First, beyond the general issue of modeling dynamic situations in a static framework (an issue taken up below), one may worry about the embarrassment of riches associated with the large number of equilibria. Like the supergame theory described in section 6.3, the kinked-demand-curve story is, in a sense, too successful in explaining tacit collusion. Indeed, any price between marginal cost and the monopoly price can be the outcome of price competition. We have no indication of how firms end up at a given focal price. Nevertheless, it can be argued that $p^f = p^m$ is the logical outcome, because it is the best focal price for both firms and thus the firms have an incentive to coordinate on it. Second, does the focal price change when costs change? Again, this question is left unanswered. Some have assumed that, when feasible, the focal price is invariant to small changes in cost. This assumption has important consequences for economy-wide price rigidities. Suppose that for initial unit cost c the focal price is $p^m(c)$. Assume that, at some point of time, the cost is permanently increased to $c' > c$ (see figure 6.2). The price remains at $p^m(c)$. However, if the unit cost becomes $c'' < c$, then $p^m(c)$ cannot be a focal price any longer, since $p^m(c'') < p^m(c)$, and we can assume that the price goes down to the new focal price, $p^m(c'')$. Thus, the assumption of an invariant focal price yields upward rigidity but not downward rigidity. Yet, according to Scherer (1980, p. 168), prices tend to be at least as rigid downward as they are upward in well-disciplined oligopolies. However, one could make the equally likely assumption that the focal price automatically adjusts to the new monopoly price when the costs change. The asymmetry between upward and downward price adjustment would then disappear. The conclusion is that, because we have little insight into how the focal price is selected, the kinked-demand-curve story has little predictive power. (For more criticism of the story, see Stigler 1947.) The most sensible aspects of the story may well be the suggestions it makes about reactions and rivalry.

6.2.2 Conjectural Variations

Like the story of the kinked demand curve, the story of conjectural variations (Bowley 1924) assumes that each firm believes that its choice of price will affect the price selected by its rival. The difference is that this story generally anticipates a smoother, less asymmetric reaction. The analogy is that, for instance, firm 1 believes that firm 2 will react according to $R_2(p_1)$ and maximizes $\Pi^1(p_1, R_2(p_1))$ over p_1.[11] As with the choice of a focal price in the kinked-demand-curve story, we have little insight into the choice of the conjectural variation R_2.

6.2.3 Discussion

The modelling of dynamic features in a static framework is, *a priori*, very appealing. As we will see, dynamic price competition is complex, and for many applications one would like it to be subsumed in some kind of "reduced-form" static competition. This is precisely what the kinked-demand-curve and conjectural-variations approaches attempt to do. However, this methodology suffers one major drawback: A static game is, by definition, a game in which each firm's choice is independent of its rivals' choices. By the very timing and information structure of the game, firms cannot react to one another. Thus, any conjecture about one's opponents' reaction that differs from no reaction is irrational. We conclude that this methodology is not theoretically satisfactory, as it

---

11. The profit function is nondifferentiable (when prices are equal) for perfect substitutes. If Π^1 were differentiable (see the case of differentiated commodities in chapter 7), as well as R_2, one could write the first-order condition

$$\Pi_1^1(p_1, R_2(p_1)) + \Pi_2^1(p_1, R_2(p_1))R_2'(p_1) = 0,$$

where Π_j^i denotes the partial derivative of Π^i with respect to price p_j.

For a homogeneous product, use is generally made of "Cournot competition." For instance, with two firms, firm 1 perceives that firm 2 reacts to output q_1 by producing $q_2 = R_2(q_1)$ (and conversely). On the assumption that R_2 is differentiable, the maximization of

$$P(q_1 + R_2(q_1))q_1 - C_1(q_1)$$

yields

$$P - C_1' + q_1 P'(1 + R_2') = 0.$$

Cournot competition corresponds to "zero conjectural variations": $R_2' = 0$. The competitive solution is obtained for a negative conjectural variation: $R_2' = -1$—that is, each firm perceives that any increase in its output is exactly offset by a decrease in the rival's output, so total output (and, therefore, price) is perceived as exogenous. The reader may check that the collusive (industry-profit-maximizing) outcome is obtained for positive conjectural variations.

does not subject itself to the discipline imposed by game theory.[12]

Now, it may be that some conjectured reactions in the static model yield the same outcome(s) as a full-fledged dynamic price game. However, to know this, one must have studied the dynamic game. One must also have checked that the two approaches yield the same response to exogenous demand and cost shocks (which is unlikely, because the static approach cannot describe the adjustment path following a shock). Absent such verifications, it is not clear what is achieved by the static approaches.

6.3 Supergames

6.3.1 The Theory

We now take up the two-firm model introduced in section 5.1. The two firms produce perfect substitutes with the same marginal cost, c. The lower-price firm gets the whole market, and the firms share the market when they charge the same price. The only difference here is that we replicate the basic Bertrand game $T + 1$ times, where T can be finite or infinite. The game is then called a *repeated game*, or a *supergame*. Let $\Pi^i(p_{it}, p_{jt})$ be firm i's profit at date t ($t = 0, \ldots, T$) when it charges p_{it} and its rival charges p_{jt}. Each firm seeks to maximize the present discounted value of its profits; that is,

$$\sum_{t=0}^{T} \delta^t \Pi^i(p_{it}, p_{jt}),$$

where δ is the discount factor ($\delta = e^{-r\tau}$, where r is the instantaneous rate of interest and τ is the real time between "periods"). δ close to 1 represents low impatience, or rapid price changes.

At each date t, the firms choose their prices (p_{1t}, p_{2t}) simultaneously. There is no physical link between the periods; the previous choice of price by one's rival is already obsolete when one chooses a price. Nevertheless, we will allow price choices at date t to depend on the history of previous prices. Thus, the price strategy p_{it} depends on the history

$$H_t \equiv (p_{10}, p_{20}; \ldots; p_{1,t-1}, p_{2,t-1}).$$

We require strategies to form a "perfect equilibrium" (see the Game Theory User's Manual). That is, for any history H_t at date t, firm i's strategy from date t on maximizes the present discounted value of profits given firm j's strategy from that date on.

First we assume that the horizon is finite: $T < +\infty$. What is the equilibrium of the dynamic price game? As is explained in the Game Theory User's Manual, we need to proceed by "backward induction" to obtain the perfect equilibrium. First, let us ask how, given the history H_T of the game, the firms choose prices in the last period T. Because the past prices do not affect the profits in period T, each firm ought to maximize its "static profit" $\Pi^i(p_{iT}, p_{jT})$, given its rival's price. Hence, the equilibrium is, for any history, the Bertrand one:

$$p_{1T} = p_{2T} = c.$$

What will the equilibrium prices in period $T - 1$ be? Since price choices at T do not depend on what happens at $T - 1$, everything occurs as if $T - 1$ was the last period. Therefore, the firms also choose the competitive price at $T - 1$, regardless of the history up to this period: For any H_{T-1},

$$p_{1,T-1} = p_{2,T-1} = c.$$

And so forth by backward induction. The outcome of the $(T + 1)$-period price game is the Bertrand solution repeated $T + 1$ times. Therefore, the dynamic element contributes nothing to the model.

The picture changes dramatically when the horizon is infinite ($T = +\infty$). On the one hand, it is easy to verify that the Bertrand equilibrium repeated infinitely is an equilibrium of this game. To see this, consider the following strategy: Each firm chooses a price equal to the marginal cost in each period t, regardless of the history of the game up to t. Given that the rival firm charges a price equal to c in this manner, each firm can do no better than to charge c itself. On the other hand, the interesting feature of this game is that the repeated Bertrand equilibrium is no longer the only equilibrium. Let p^m denote the

---

12. However, the conjectural-variations approach may have been a useful way of empirically estimating the degree of noncompetitiveness in an industry— see, e.g., Appelbaum 1982; Bresnahan 1981, 1987a, Iwata 1974; Sumner 1981. (The empirical definition of conjectural variations does not completely coincide

with the theoretical one. See Bresnahan 1987b.) Although it is hoped that the testing of full-fledged dynamic models will develop, it must be acknowledged that such models are complex, and that little attention has been paid to their testable implications.

monopoly price (it maximizes $(p - c)D(p)$) and consider the following (symmetric) strategies: Each firm charges p^m in period 0. It furthermore charges p^m in period t if in every period preceding t both firms have charged p^m; otherwise it sets its price at marginal cost c forever.[13] These strategies are called *trigger strategies*, because a single deviation triggers a halt in the cooperation. They constitute an equilibrium if the discount factor is sufficiently high: In charging p^m, a firm earns half the monopoly profit in each period. By deviating from this price, a firm can earn maximum profit, Π^m, during the period of deviation (indeed it can earn approximately Π^m by slightly undercutting price p^m), but then it receives zero forever more. Therefore, if

$$\frac{\Pi^m}{2}(1 + \delta + \delta^2 + \cdots) \geqslant \Pi^m,$$

which follows if $\delta \geqslant \frac{1}{2}$, then these trigger strategies are equilibrium ones.

This result is a formalization of tacit collusion. If a firm undercuts the monopoly price, it gains during the period of deviation but it destroys collusion in the later periods —the firms revert to the "grim strategy" (i.e., they play purely competitively forever, which we know is an equilibrium). Note that collusion is enforced through a purely noncooperative mechanism.

There are many other equilibria in this game. The previous reasoning actually implies that any price between the competitive price and the monopoly price can be sustained as a (time-invariant) equilibrium price as long as the discount factor is greater than $\frac{1}{2}$ (which implies that any symmetric per-period profit between 0 and Π^m can be an equilibrium profit). Let p belong to $[c, p^m]$, and let each firm charge price p as long as neither has yet deviated from that price. If either firm has deviated in the past, both charge the competitive price forever. Again, these strategies are equilibrium strategies. By conforming to p, each firm gets

$$\frac{\Pi(p)}{2}(1 + \delta + \delta^2 + \cdots).$$

If a firm deviates, it gets at most $\Pi(p)$ during the deviation period (because its rival charges p). Thus, it gains at most $\Pi(p)/2$ during that period, and it loses half of the profit at price p forever after:

$$\frac{\Pi(p)}{2}(\delta + \delta^2 + \cdots) = \Pi(p)\frac{\delta}{2(1 - \delta)}.$$

So if $\delta \geqslant (1 - \delta)$—that is, $\delta \geqslant \frac{1}{2}$—deviating from price p is not privately optimal.

The preceding result is one facet of a general result, known as the *Folk theorem*. For the repeated price game under consideration, the Folk theorem asserts that any pair of profits (Π^1, Π^2) such that

$$\Pi^1 > 0, \Pi^2 > 0, \text{ and } \Pi^1 + \Pi^2 \leqslant \Pi^m$$

is a *per-period equilibrium payoff* for δ sufficiently close to 1. That is, there exist perfect equilibrium strategies

$$\{p_{1t}(H_t), p_{2t}(H_t)\}$$

that form a perfect equilibrium such that, for all i, firm i's associated per-period payoff,

$$(1 - \delta) \sum_{t=0}^{\infty} \delta^t \Pi^i(p_{it}, p_{jt}),$$

is equal to Π^i.[14] This is depicted in figure 6.3.

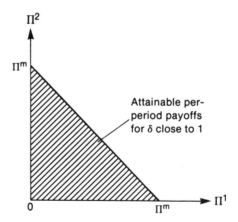

Figure 6.3
The Folk theorem for the repeated price game.

---

13. Formally: $p_{it}(H_t) = p^m$ if $H_t = (p^m, p^m; \ldots; p^m, p^m)$, and $p_{it}(H_t) = c$ otherwise.

14. Multiplying the intertemporal payoff by $1 - \delta$ amounts to normalizing it to a per-period equivalent. Notice in particular that if $\Pi^i(p_{it}, p_{jt})$ is independent of time and equal to Π^i, then

$$(1 - \delta) \sum_{t=0}^{\infty} \delta^t \Pi^i(p_{it}, p_{jt}) = (1 - \delta)(1 + \delta + \delta^2 + \cdots)\Pi^i = \Pi^i.$$

Exercise 6.2*** Show that any payoff (Π^1, Π^2) such that $\Pi^1 > 0$, $\Pi^2 > 0$, and $\Pi^1 + \Pi^2 \leqslant \Pi^m$ is an equilibrium payoff for δ close to 1.

Exercise 6.3*** Show that for $\delta < \frac{1}{2}$ the only equilibrium profit is the competitive (zero) profit. Restrict yourself to pure strategies. Hint: Consider the highest (supremum) per-period profit that is attainable by a firm in a perfect equilibrium.

Thus, when δ is close to 1, everything is an equilibrium ("everything" because aggregate profit cannot exceed Π^m, and because equilibrium profits cannot be negative—a firm can always guarantee itself non-negative profits by charging prices above marginal cost or by exiting the market).

The Folk theorem demonstrated here was proved by Friedman (1971, 1977). More general versions of this theorem have been provided by Aumann and Shapley (1976), Rubinstein (1979), and Fudenberg and Maskin (1986). See also subsection 6.7.3 below.

Remark The easiest way to enforce a given price (and, possibly, given market shares) is to punish deviations as harshly as possible. In the context of a price game with perfect substitutes, maximal punishments take a simple form: They correspond to the competitive Bertrand (static and dynamic) equilibrium, in which all firms make no profit. (There do not exist harsher punishments, because a firm can always exit the market—or, equivalent, charge a very high price—and guarantee itself a zero profit after it has deviated.) Of course, such a punishment is also harsh to its enforcers, but along the equilibrium path it has no cost because it is not observed (deviations do not occur). Thus, to see whether a given behavior is indeed sustainable in equilibrium it suffices to assume that any deviation leads to an eternal reversion to Bertrand behavior. This reasoning is part of a more general principle (see Abreu 1983, 1986)[15]; as we will see in subsection 6.3.3,

it depends crucially on all price choices being perfectly observable.

The supergame theory is, in a sense, too successful in explaining tacit collusion. The large set of equilibria is an embarrassment of riches. Somehow the firms must coordinate on a "focal equilibrium" in order for the equilibrium concept to remain attractive. How is this equilibrium chosen? A selection process often used in the literature makes the assumption that in a symmetric game the focal equilibrium is symmetric and the assumption that the focal equilibrium must be Pareto optimal from the viewpoint of the two firms (i.e., must yield a payoff on the frontier of the attainable set of per-period profits). In the previous example, these assumptions clearly select equilibrium strategies that yield per-period profits $\Pi^1 = \Pi^2 = \Pi^m/2$ when $\delta \geqslant \frac{1}{2}$ (enforced, e.g., by the strategy of charging p^m as long as every firm has charged p^m earlier, and charging c in case of a deviation).

6.3.2 Applications

Let us now apply the theory to obtain a formalization of some aspects of the conventional wisdom reviewed in section 6.1. (Because the supergame framework is technically the easiest to work with, we discuss the conventional wisdom here.) We will content ourselves with illustrative examples; the theories have generally been developed in a more general context than is presumed here.[16]

6.3.2.1 Application 1: Market Concentration

As was mentioned earlier, Bain's (1956) original concern with market concentration was based on an intuitive relationship between high concentration and collusion. There is a sense in which tacit collusion is easier to sustain with a smaller number of firms: Consider a homogeneous-good industry with n firms facing the same constant marginal cost, and look at the fully collusive outcome, in which all firms charge the monopoly price and share the market

---

15. A maximal punishment is clearly optimal when deviations are perfectly detected. Abreu shows that maximal punishments exist in games with a continuum of actions (1983, 1987). He also looks at optimal *symmetric* punishments in dynamic oligopoly supergames (1986), and unveils a simple stick-and-carrot two-dimensional nature of these punishments (ibid.).

16. The reader who has little familiarity with supergame theory may want to skip these applications in a first reading. The advanced reader may study further

applications of the supergame methodology: e.g., Mookherjee and Ray 1986 (on repeated games under learning by doing or increasing returns to scale), Rotemberg and Saloner 1985a (on strategic inventories), Rotemberg and Saloner 1985b (on price leadership), and Slade 1985 (on price wars as an information-gathering device when industry demand is subject to periodic and unobserved random shocks).

equally. The per-period and per-firm profit is Π^m/n, a decreasing function of n. A large number of firms reduces the profit per firm and thus the cost of being punished for undercutting. In contrast, the short-run gain from undercutting the monopoly price slightly is

$$\Pi^m(1 - 1/n) - \varepsilon,$$

and thus increases with n. The discount factor must exceed $1 - 1/n$ for collusion to be sustainable; in this sense, market concentration facilitates tacit collusion.

6.3.2.2 Application 2: Long Information Lags and Infrequent Interaction

The threat of a punishment operates only if the punishment comes fairly soon after a price cut. Punishment might be delayed for two related reasons. First, a firm's price cut may be learned of by its rival only with a lag. This may happen when manufacturers contract with a few big buyers (wholesalers or downstream manufacturers). The secrecy of contracts may then be an obstacle to collusion. Indeed, if price cuts were never detected, collusion could not be sustained. Second, infrequent interaction (due to a lumpiness in orders, for instance) delays the punishment and makes current price cutting more attractive.

The second reason is straightforwardly formalized in the supergame framework. A more infrequent interaction corresponds to a decrease in δ. But we know that if δ lies between 0 and $\frac{1}{2}$ no collusion is sustainable, and that if δ exceeds $\frac{1}{2}$ any outcome is possible, including collusive ones (this supergame vindication of infrequent interaction as a cause of breakdown of collusion is weak because the theory only predicts that collusion *can* occur in equilibrium).

The first reason is harder to formalize, unless one is willing to make the strong assumption that profits and demands are observed with a lag as well. For instance, consider the duopoly model, and assume that prices are observed two periods (instead of one) after they are chosen. Assume further that a firm's profit and demand in a given period are observed by this firm at least two periods later, so that a firm cannot infer from the observation of its past profits and demands anything it does not know about its rival's pricing behavior. In such a situation, a firm can deviate and cut its price for two periods before being detected. The monopoly price (or any other

price) is sustainable in equilibrium if and only if

$$\frac{\Pi^m}{2}(1 + \delta + \delta^2 + \cdots) \geqslant \Pi^m(1 + \delta)$$

or

$$\delta \geqslant \frac{1}{\sqrt{2}}.$$

Thus, the condition is more stringent than the previous one ($\delta \geqslant \frac{1}{2}$), as $1/\sqrt{2} > \frac{1}{2}$. In this sense, information lags are also a cause of breakdown of collusion. However, the assumption that profit and (especially) demand are observed with a lag is strong. In subsections 6.3.3 and 6.7.1 we make the polar assumption that prices are completely secret (never revealed to a firm's rival), but that a firm learns its demand and its profit immediately (i.e., one period after the price choices).

6.3.2.3 Application 3: Fluctuating Demand

Let us now consider Rotemberg and Saloner's (1986) theory of price wars during booms. Suppose that demand is stochastic. At each period t, it can be low ($q = D_1(p)$) with probability $\frac{1}{2}$, or high ($q = D_2(p)$) with probability $\frac{1}{2}$. Assume that $D_2(p) > D_1(p)$ for all p. To simplify, assume that the demand shock is identically and independently distributed over time. At each period the two firms learn the current state of demand *before* choosing their prices simultaneously.

We look for a pair of prices $\{p_1, p_2\}$ such that (a) both firms charge price p_s when the state of demand is s, (b) the price configuration $\{p_1, p_2\}$ is sustainable in equilibrium (i.e., there exists an equilibrium in which deviating from p_s in state s is not privately optimal), and (c) the expected present discounted profit of each firm along the equilibrium path

$$V = \sum_{t=0}^{\infty} \delta^t \left(\frac{1}{2} \frac{D_1(p_1)}{2}(p_1 - c) + \frac{1}{2} \frac{D_2(p_2)}{2}(p_2 - c) \right)$$

$$= \left(\frac{1}{2} \frac{D_1(p_1)}{2}(p_1 - c) + \frac{1}{2} \frac{D_2(p_2)}{2}(p_2 - c) \right) \bigg/ (1 - \delta)$$

is not Pareto dominated by other equilibrium payoffs (i.e., one cannot find an equilibrium that both firms would prefer).

We know from the maximal-punishment principle (see the remark in subsection 6.3.1) that in order to enforce the pair of prices $\{p_1, p_2\}$ one can assume that after a deviation the two firms charge their competitive price c forever (and thus make no profit).

We first examine whether the "fully collusive outcome" is sustainable in equilibrium. By "fully collusive outcome" we mean that the two firms charge the monopoly price p_s^m in each state of demand s (where p_s^m maximizes $\Pi_s(p) = (p - c)D_s(p)$). We let

$$\Pi_s^m \equiv (p_s^m - c)D_s(p_s^m)$$

denote the monopoly profit in state s. If the monopoly profit can always be sustained, then

$$V = \frac{(\Pi_1^m + \Pi_2^m)/4}{1 - \delta}.$$

From the maximal-punishment principle, the future loss from deviating at some date, discounted at that date, is δV. Undercutting p_s^m slightly in state of demand s yields an extra gain of almost

$$\Pi_s^m - \frac{\Pi_s^m}{2} = \frac{\Pi_s^m}{2}$$

to the firm that deviates. Thus, for p_s^m to be sustainable for all s, one must have

$$\frac{\Pi_s^m}{2} \leqslant \delta V \tag{6.2}$$

for all s. However, because $\Pi_1^m < \Pi_2^m$, this condition is satisfied if and only if

$$\frac{\Pi_2^m}{2} \leqslant \delta V, \tag{6.3}$$

or substituting for V,

$$\delta \geqslant \delta_0 \equiv \frac{2\Pi_2^m}{3\Pi_2^m + \Pi_1^m}. \tag{6.4}$$

Because $\Pi_2^m > \Pi_1^m$, δ_0 lies strictly between $\frac{1}{2}$ and $\frac{2}{3}$.

This result already offers some insight. When demand is high, the temptation to undercut is important. The

punishment entails the loss of an average of high and low profit and is therefore less severe than it would be if the high demand were to persist with certainty in the future. Thus, when δ lies between $\frac{1}{2}$ and δ_0, full collusion cannot be sustained in the high-demand state, contrary to the case of a deterministic demand.

The interesting case is that of a discount factor in the interval $[\frac{1}{2}, \delta_0]$. We must choose p_1 and p_2 so as to maximize the firms' expected payoff subject to the incentive (no undercutting) constraints:

$$\max \left(\frac{1}{2}\frac{\Pi_1(p_1)}{2} + \frac{1}{2}\frac{\Pi_2(p_2)}{2} \right) \bigg/ (1 - \delta) \tag{6.5}$$

subject to

$$\frac{\Pi_1(p_1)}{2} \leqslant \delta \left(\frac{1}{2}\frac{\Pi_1(p_1)}{2} + \frac{1}{2}\frac{\Pi_2(p_2)}{2} \right) \bigg/ (1 - \delta) \tag{6.6}$$

$$\frac{\Pi_2(p_2)}{2} \leqslant \delta \left(\frac{1}{2}\frac{\Pi_1(p_1)}{2} + \frac{1}{2}\frac{\Pi_2(p_2)}{2} \right) \bigg/ (1 - \delta). \tag{6.7}$$

Intuitively, the binding constraint should be 6.7, because the temptation to undercut is higher when demand is high. Indeed, it can easily be shown that this is the case: Note that the program is equivalent to

$$\max\{\Pi_1(p_1) + \Pi_2(p_2)\} \tag{6.5'}$$

subject to

$$\Pi_1(p_1) \leqslant K\Pi_2(p_2) \tag{6.6'}$$

and to

$$\Pi_2(p_2) \leqslant K\Pi_1(p_1), \tag{6.7'}$$

where

$$K \equiv \delta/(2 - 3\delta) \geqslant 1.$$

Ignore 6.6' and maximize 6.5' subject to 6.7'. Clearly, choosing $p_1 = p_1^m$ increases the objective function and relaxes constraint 6.7' as much as possible. And, p_2 is then chosen under p_2^m so that $\Pi_2(p_2) = K\Pi_1(p_1^m) = K\Pi_1^m$.[17,18]

---

17. Such a p_2 exists because, by the definition of δ_0,

$$K\Pi_1^m = \delta\Pi_1^m/(2 - 3\delta) \leqslant \Pi_2^m$$

for $\delta \leqslant \delta_0$. One must choose $p_2 < p_2^m$ rather than the other root of the equation $\Pi_2(p_2) = K\Pi_1(p_1^m)$ because otherwise a firm could undercut to p_2^m in the high

state of demand. Note also that the ignored constraint 6.6' is satisfied as $K\Pi_2(p_2) = K^2\Pi_1^m \geqslant \Pi_1^m$ from $K \geqslant 1$.

18. Maximizing 6.5' with respect to 6.6', ignoring 6.7', would similarly yield $p_2 = p_2^m$ and $\Pi_1(p_1) = K\Pi_2^m$. However, because $K \geqslant 1$ and $\Pi_1^m < \Pi_2^m$, no such p_1 exists, so this cannot be the solution.

We thus conclude the following: For δ in $[\frac{1}{2}, \delta_0]$, some collusion is sustainable. In the low state of demand, firms charge the monopoly price in that state: $p_1 = p_1^m$. In the high state of demand, firms charge below the monopoly price in that state: $p_2 < p_2^m$. (p_2 can be higher or lower than p_1, depending on the demand function.) Rotemberg and Saloner interpret this as demonstrating the existence of a price war during booms—i.e., as representing a situation in which firms are forced to lower the amount of their collusion in good times.[19] This is not a price war in the usual sense, because the price may actually be higher during booms than during busts; thus, that oligopoly prices move countercyclically is not an implication of (but is consistent with) the Rotemberg-Saloner model.

The Rotemberg-Saloner analysis seems plausible. At the micro (industry) level, cartels tend to break down when a big order arrives. For instance, Scherer (1980, p. 222), in reviewing the market for the antibiotic tetracycline, observes that pure discipline broke down when the Armed Services Medical Procurement Agency placed a large order in October 1956. Industry demand or cost conditions can also fluctuate with factors that may be relatively exogenous to the industry: input prices or aggregate demand. A second contribution of Rotemberg and Saloner's 1986 paper is an empirical analysis of some links between industry behavior and economy-wide performance. In particular, they show that the price of cement—a good produced by an oligopolistic industry—tends to move countercyclically, which is consistent with (but, as we observed, not necessarily predicted by) their theory. See also their discussion of R. Porter's (1983a) study of the railroad cartel on the Chicago–New York route in the 1880s and Bresnahan's (1981) analysis of the American automobile industry in the mid-1950s.

Exercise 6.4* Consider an n-firm supergame framework. The firms have constant marginal cost c. The demand function at date t is $q_t = \mu^t D(p_t)$, where $\mu\delta < 1$ (δ is the discount factor).[20] Derive the set of discount factors such that full collusion (i.e., the monopoly solution) is sustain-

able as an equilibrium of the supergame. What would this model predict about the relative ease of sustaining collusion in expanding and declining industries?

6.3.2.4   Application 4: Cost Asymmetries

In section 6.1 we saw that two firms with unit costs $c_1 < c_2$ have conflicting preferences on the price to be charged. Efficient market-sharing arrangements may, for instance, call for firm 2 to supply less than the demand it faces in exchange for firm 1's charging above its monopoly price, or they may even involve the two firms taking turns supplying the market. The following exercise illustrates that a variety of market-sharing patterns can be sustained in a supergame when the firms are not too impatient.

Exercise 6.5** Consider the deterministic efficient market-sharing allocations derived in exercise 6.1. Let $\{p^*, s_1^*\}$ denote an efficient market-sharing allocation, and let

$$\Pi^{1*} \equiv s_1^* D(p^*)(p^* - c_1)$$

and

$$\Pi^{2*} \equiv (1 - s_1^*) D(p^*)(p^* - c_2)$$

denote the corresponding per-period profits. Consider the following strategies: Each firm i charges p^* and produces $s_i^* D(p^*)$ as long as both have complied with this rule earlier. If anyone has deviated in the past, both firms revert to Bertrand behavior forever.[21] Determine the set of efficient market-sharing allocations that can be enforced in this manner.

One issue that was alluded to earlier is the choice of an equilibrium allocation. Even if one accepts the idea of selecting a Pareto-optimal allocation, one has little clue as to how to choose p^* (or s_1^*) in the feasible range. In the symmetric case, one could invoke the idea that a symmetric equilibrium is focal; but whatever worth this argument may have, it is not applicable to rivalry under asymmetric costs. The difficulty of picking a focal equilib-

---

19. We will later identify another factor leading to price wars between booms stemming from price rigidities. On the other hand, price wars during recessions are likely to occur if the capital market is imperfect (see the long-purse story in chapter 9).

20. This is the same as the situation discussed by Rotemberg and Saloner,

except for two things: Shocks are perfectly anticipated, and there is a trend (the market grows if $\mu > 1$ and shrinks if $\mu < 1$).

21. Under asymmetric payoffs, the reversion to Bertrand behavior is *not* the maximal punishment for the low-cost firm. The worst equilibrium outcome is a zero profit. See section 6.7. The qualitative analysis would not be affected by this consideration.

rium has been perceived by some as hindering tacit collusion.

6.3.2.5 Application 5: Multimarket Contact

To understand why multimarket contact may help, recall the incentive constraint for a constant price (e.g., the monopoly price) to be sustained in a single market:

$$\frac{\Pi^m}{2} \leqslant \delta \frac{\Pi^m}{2}(1 + \delta + \cdots),$$

or

$$1 \leqslant \frac{\delta}{1 - \delta}.$$

As has been noted, $\delta = \frac{1}{2}$ is sufficient for full collusion to be sustainable. A higher δ is "overkill"; the punishment is then more than sufficient to keep market discipline.

Now suppose that there are two *identical* and *independent* markets, and that both firms participate in both markets. Assume further that market 1 "meets more frequently" than market 2—i.e., either orders arrive more rapidly or the information lag is shorter. To be concise, let us assume that market 1 meets every period and market 2 meets every even period. If the discount factor between periods is δ, the implicit discount factor for market 2 is equal to δ^2. Suppose that $\delta^2 < \frac{1}{2} < \delta$. Then we know from subsection 6.3.1 that, in the absence of multimarket contact, collusion is sustainable in market 1 but not in market 2. On the other hand, with multimarket contact, full collusion on both markets is sustainable if

$$2 \times \frac{\Pi^m}{2} \leqslant \frac{\Pi^m}{2}(\delta + \delta^2 + \delta^3 + \cdots)$$

$$+ \frac{\Pi^m}{2}(\delta^2 + \delta^4 + \delta^6 + \cdots) \qquad (6.8)$$

or

$$0 \leqslant 4\delta^2 + \delta - 2 \quad (\text{or } \delta \geqslant 0.593). \qquad (6.9)$$

Let us derive 6.8. The highest temptation to undercut occurs every even period, when both markets are open.

A firm that undercuts might as well undercut on both markets simultaneously, given that it will be punished in both markets for its deviation anyway. The gain from undercutting the monopoly price is $\Pi^m/2$ per market and, hence, Π^m overall. The right-hand side of 6.8 represents the future loss of collusive profits on both markets associated to the reversion to Bertrand behavior (the maximal punishment).

So, for instance, for $\delta = 0.6$, full collusion on both markets can be sustained under multimarket contact, whereas no amount of collusion is sustainable in market 2 under single-market contact.

The intuition for this result is that the loss of collusion on market 1 may be so large as to deter deviations not only on market 1 but also on market 2. (Technically, the incentive (no-undercutting) constraints on the two markets are pooled into a single constraint—i.e., 6.8. If they are both satisfied, then 6.8 is also satisfied. However, the converse does not hold, as has just been shown. The set of sustainable allocations cannot be smaller under multimarket contact than under single-market contact.)

Bernheim and Whinston (1986) offer a much more complete treatment of multimarket contact and tacit collusion.[22]

*Exercise 6.6** Consider two firms interacting in two identical and independent markets. The markets differ in that in market 1 a firm's price at time t is observed at $t + 1$, whereas in market 2 it is learned only at $t + 2$. Thus, although each of the markets meets every period, market 2 has longer information lags.

(i) Argue that in the absence of multimarket contact, collusion in market 2 would be sustainable if and only if $\delta \geqslant 1/\sqrt{2} \simeq 0.71$.

(ii) Show that under multimarket contact, collusion in both markets is sustainable if (and only if) $\delta \geqslant \underline{\delta}$, where $\underline{\delta} \simeq 0.64$.

6.3.3 Secret Price Cuts

In subsections 6.3.1 and 6.3.2 it was assumed that after some information lag, a firm's past price choice is perfectly observed by its rival. However, one can think of

---

22. Multimarket contact may raise the firms' profits, but need not raise the price in both markets. As Bernheim and Whinston show, the price may be higher in one market and smaller in the other.

instances in which prices are not observable. As was mentioned in the supplementary section of chapter 4, a firm may offer a price discount to a customer, or may increase the quality of its services without raising the price. If its rival's price is unobservable, a firm must rely on the observation of its own realized market share or demand to detect any price undercutting by the rival. However, if the demand function is random and shocks are unobservable, this inference process is garbled. A low market share may be due to the aggressive behavior of one's rival or to a slack in demand. Hence, when demand is very random, price cuts are hard to detect. As Stigler (1964) noted, this tends to hinder collusion.

E. Green and R. Porter (1984; see also Porter 1983b) have developed a supergame model that formalizes the issue of secret price cutting.[23] As was mentioned above, the maximal-punishment principle need not apply to such a situation. When price choices are perfectly observable, it makes sense to resort to extreme punishments because such punishments are never observed on the equilibrium path and therefore are costless to the firms (they are just threats). Under uncertainty, mistakes are unavoidable and maximal punishments (eternal reversion to Bertrand behavior) need not be optimal.

As the analysis of collusion under price secrecy is more complicated than that under perfectly observable prices (because optimal punishments must be determined), it is postponed until the supplementary section. There we will content ourselves with a simple example: Firms charge the monopoly price as long as their profit has been high in the past. If a firm observes a low profit, which a priori could be due to a price cut by its rival or to a low demand, or if it itself has undercut the monopoly price in the last period, it charges a low price for some period of time T, and so does its rival (this is a punishment phase). The firms revert to the collusive phase (i.e., charge the monopoly price) after the punishment phase is completed, until the next deviation or slump in demand. The increase in the probability of reversion to a punishment phase makes price cutting unprofitable for the firms. The model then predicts periodic price wars, contrary to the perfect-observation models of subsections 6.3.1 and 6.3.2. Price wars are *involuntary*, in that they are triggered not by a price cut but by an unobservable slump in demand. (Indeed, in the collusive phase both firms charge the monopoly price until their profit is adversely affected by a demand shock.) Note also that price wars are triggered by a recession, contrary to the Rotemberg-Saloner model.

Under imperfect information, the fully collusive outcome cannot be sustained. It could be sustained only if the firms kept on colluding (charging the monopoly price) even when making small profits, because even under collusion small profits can occur as a result of low demand. However, a firm that is confident that its rival will continue cooperating even if its profit is low has every incentive to (secretly) undercut—price undercutting yields a short-term gain and creates no long-run loss. Thus, full collusion is inconsistent with the deterrence of price cuts.[24]

Exercise 6.7* A procurement agency repeatedly purchasing supplies for a federal, state, or local government uses sealed competitive auctions. Price quotations are opened publicly at a predetermined date. What are the potential adverse effects of this procedure?

6.3.4 Discussion

As we have seen, the supergame framework is simple and lends itself to many applications. This subsection identifies the main features of the supergame model and discusses its methodology.

6.3.4.1 Synchronic Timing

We assume that firms always choose their prices simultaneously. That is, a firm's current profit is no longer affected by its rival's previous price choices when it chooses its own price. As is easily seen, the synchronicity assumption is not crucial to the main supergame result (the Folk theorem for low impatience). However, it implies specific conduct. The firms' strategies are *bootstrap* strategies in the following sense: At any point in time, past prices do not affect current (or future) profits. Hence, the only reason a firm conditions its pricing behavior (in

---

23. See Porter 1983a for a test of the existence of price wars (an implication of the Green-Porter model) using data from the U.S. railroad industry in the 1880s.

24. For an example of a supergame showing that full collusion between two parties may be impossible even for δ close to 1 if these parties' actions are observable only with noise (i.e., under "bilateral moral hazard"), see Maskin et al. 1986. Fudenberg, Levine, and Maskin (1988) provide general conditions for full collusion to be sustainable.

collusive equilibria) on previous price choices is that the other firms do so. The achievement of collusion stems from a subtle self-fulfilling expectation. Firms do not follow simple business strategies, such as regaining one's market share when the latter has been (and still is) eroded by one's rival's aggressive price behavior. In a supergame, the market share is no longer eroded by the time the firm reacts. If we eliminate the bootstrap equilibria, we are left with noncollusiveness (repeated Bertrand behavior).

6.3.4.2 Infinite Horizon

As we saw, collusion cannot be sustained in the supergame framework, even for a long but finite horizon. Thus, an unbounded horizon is crucial to the results. This raises the possibility that the results are not robust to finite-length price interaction—a reasonable assumption. The infinite-horizon assumption need not be taken too seriously. Suppose that at each period there is a probability x in $(0, 1)$ that the market "survives," i.e., that the firms keep competing on this market (one can think of $1 - x$ as the probability that the good becomes obsolete or intense competition emerges). The game then ends in finite (but stochastic) time with probability 1. However, everything is as if the horizon were infinite and the firms' discount factor were equal to $\tilde{\delta} = \delta x$, as is easily checked on the payoff function (explanation: The future is discounted with discount factor δ, but exists only with probability x). Thus, if both δ and x are sufficiently high, supergame collusion can be enforced. Note, however, that this result relies on probability x being constant over time. Unfortunately, little is known about the set of equilibria when, for instance, a time-varying x_t declines sharply at some point in time (although one would suspect that supergame collusion would be hard to sustain in such an environment).

6.3.4.3 Multiplicity of Equilibria

As was noted earlier, the supergame story is too successful in explaining tacit collusion. The multiplicity of equilibria is an embarrassment of riches. We must have a reasonable and systematic theory of how firms coordinate on a particular equilibrium if we want the theory to be predictive and allow for comparative statics. One natural method is to assume that the firms coordinate on an equilibrium that yields a Pareto-optimal point in the set of the firms' equilibrium profits. One can further cut the set of remaining equilibria by choosing a symmetric equilibrium if the game is symmetric. This is a useful methodology, but it raises two problems. First, the game may be asymmetric (e.g. because of intrinsic cost differences), or it may become asymmetric when a richer context is studied (e.g. when firms make investment decisions).[25] Second, the choice of an efficient equilibrium raises the issue of "renegotiation." Suppose that the firms initially coordinate on the monopoly-price equilibrium, and that some firm deviates by undercutting in the first period. The equilibrium strategies specify some punishment from period 2 on. For instance, we considered the maximal punishment in which firms charge the competitive price forever after a deviation. But the firms, who expect no profit from period 2 on, have an incentive to renegotiate to avoid the punishment phase and reach an efficient equilibrium anew. And, indeed, there is no reason why the firms could not coordinate on an efficient equilibrium at date 2 if they were able to do so at date 1.[26]

The possibility of renegotiating undermines the strength of punishments and, therefore, the incentive not to undercut. (To impose discipline, firms would prefer to commit to not renegotiate; but such a commitment is not credible.) Farrell and Maskin (1986), Pearce (1987), and van Damme (1986) offer analyses of supergames that account for the possibility of renegotiation.

6.4 Price Rigidities

As was discussed in subsection 6.3.1, the above supergame description of repeated price interaction is very special in that firms never react to variables that currently affect their profits. In reality, prices cannot be adjusted continuously. Firms incur costs in deciding price changes,

---

25. Even when the firms are symmetric and make symmetric investment decisions in equilibrium, they must contemplate the outcome of the repeated price game under asymmetric investments when they make their investment decisions.

26. Of course, the managers of a firm that has been undercut often comment that "the managers of the other firm cannot be trusted to cooperate anymore." But such a comment refers to the firm's managers learning information about the other firm or its managers. Hence, it relates more to the situation described in section 6.5.

sending new price lists and catalogs to retailers, changing price tags, advertising price cuts to consumers, and so on. These "menu costs" are generally small, so firms are able to change their prices frequently if they elect to do so. However, changing one's price every day or every minute would often be prohibitively expensive, so prices are likely to exhibit short-run rigidities. Beyond price rigidity, there are other channels through which past price choices affect current profits. On the demand side, past prices may affect the firms' current goodwill through consumers' learning about the good or switching costs. On the supply side, past prices affect current inventories (or current workload, if orders take time to be filled).

The presence of price rigidities raises the possibility that price reactions are not bootstrap reactions but are simply attempts to regain or consolidate market share. The simplest way to (roughly) formalize short-run rigidities and reactions to payoff-relevant prices is to assume that firms choose their prices *asynchronously*.[27] For simplicity, let us consider two firms producing perfect substitutes. At odd (respectively, even) periods, firm 1 (respectively, firm 2) chooses its price. A price p_{it} chosen by firm i at date t is fixed for two periods: $p_{i,t+1} = p_{i,t}$. In period $t + 2$, firm i may choose a new price, which again will be locked in for two periods. (Our exogenous asynchronicity assumption will be motivated later on.)

Firm i's objective is to maximize the present discounted value of its profit:

$$\sum_{t=0}^{\infty} \delta^t \Pi^i(p_{i,t}, p_{j,t}).$$

Now the model is identical to the supergame model, except that asynchronicity replaces synchronicity.

We look for a perfect equilibrium in which the firms' price choices are simple in that they depend only on the "payoff-relevant information." More precisely, at date $2k + 1$, firm 2 is still committed to the price $(p_{2,2k})$ it chose a period earlier. This price affects firm 1's profit at date $2k + 1$ and, therefore, will be termed payoff-relevant. We assume that $p_{1,2k+1} = R_1(p_{2,2k})$—that is, firm 1's strategy is conditioned on as little information as is consistent with rationality (no bootstrapping). And similarly for firm 2: $p_{2,2k+2} = R_2(p_{1,2k+1})$. $R_1(\cdot)$ and $R_2(\cdot)$ are

called *Markov reaction functions*. A Markov perfect equilibrium is a perfect equilibrium in which the firms use Markov strategies. For any current price $p_{2,2k}$ at time $2k + 1$, firm 1's reaction must maximize its objective function given that the firms will react according to $R_1(\cdot)$ and $R_2(\cdot)$ in the future. Mathematically, firm 1's intertemporal profit from date $2k + 1$ on when it reacts to $p_{2,2k} = p_2$ by choosing $p_{1,2k+1} = p_1$ is

$$V^1(p_2) = \max_{p_1} [\Pi^1(p_1, p_2) + \delta \Pi^1(p_1, R_2(p_1))$$

$$+ \delta^2 \Pi^1(R_1(R_2(p_1)), R_2(p_1)) + \cdots],$$

since firm 2 will react with $R_2(p_1)$ in the next period, and then firm 1 will react in two periods to $R_2(p_1)$ with $R_1(R_2(p_1))$, and so on. (Here we are appealing to the "one-period-deviation criterion." It is clearly necessary for an equilibrium that no firm wants to deviate from the reaction rule for one period and then conform to this rule. Conversely, this one-period-deviation criterion is sufficient for equilibrium, as an intertemporal deviation from the rule can be decomposed into sequential one-period deviations. See section 6.7.) In equilibrium, $p_1 = R_1(p_2)$ must maximize the expression in brackets for all p_2. Firm 2 behaves similarly.

In subsection 6.7.2 we will derive the conditions to be satisfied by an equilibrium pair of reaction functions; here, we content ourselves here with a simple example and consider some implications of the model.

6.4.1 A Kinked-Demand-Curve Example

Let $D(p) = 1 - p$, and let $c = 0$ for the two firms. The price grid is discrete: $p_h = h/6$, where $h = 0, 1, \ldots, 6$. Now, $p_0 = 0$ is the competitive price, and $p_3 = \frac{1}{2}$ is the monopoly price. Consider the symmetric reaction function $R_1(\cdot) = R_2(\cdot) = R(\cdot)$ in table 6.1. (The right-most column indicates the industry profit when the lowest price charged is p.) These strategies can be shown to form an equilibrium for any discount factor sufficiently close to 1 (rapid price adjustments). See section 6.7.

This equilibrium is highly reminiscent of the kinked-demand-curve story. The focal price (the steady state) is the monopoly price p_3 here. Starting from this price, if a

---

27. The following exposition follows Maskin and Tirole 1988. Eaton and Engers 1987 study this model with differentiated products.

Table 6.1

p	$R(p)$	$(36)\Pi(p)$
p_6	p_3	0
p_5	p_3	5
p_4	p_3	8
p_3	p_3	9
p_2	p_1	8
p_1	$\begin{cases} p_3 \text{ with probability } \alpha \\ p_1 \text{ with probability } 1 - \alpha \end{cases}$	5
p_0	p_3	0

Note: α depends on δ.

firm raises its price, its rival does not follow suit; it stays at the focal price. If the firm undercuts to p_2, its rival reacts with a price war. In this particular equilibrium, the price war has two stages: In turn, the rival undercuts to p_1. At that low price, the firms then engage in a "war of attrition." Both firms want the price to go back up to the focal price. However, each firm would like the other firm to move first, because the relenting firm loses market share in the short run. The outcome is a mixed-strategy behavior, in which each firm either continues the price war or cracks and raises its price. The difference with the kinked-demand-curve (KDC) story is that the reactions are real and fully rational. (A small difference lies in the fact that the price-war phase here differs from the matching behavior of the KDC story.)

Let us, for instance, check that at the focal price no firm wants to undercut. Given the equilibrium strategies, firm 1, say, gets an intertemporal profit (all profits are multiplied by 36) of

$$V(p_3) = (1 + \delta + \delta^2 + \delta^3 + \cdots)4.5 = 4.5/(1 - \delta).$$

By undercutting to p_2, it gets a profit of 8 today. In the next period it is undercut to p_1 by firm 2 and, therefore, gets 0. Two periods from now, it is firm 1's turn to choose a price. According to the equilibrium strategy, one optimal action is to revert to the focal price. (To compute a firm's payoff, one can take any equilibrium action when the firm plays a mixed strategy, because the equilibrium condition is that all actions played with positive probability yield the same payoff.) Firm 1 makes no profit in that

period, and brings the industry back to the focal price from the following period on. Thus, undercutting to p_2 yields

$$8 + \delta \cdot 0 + \delta^2 \cdot 0 + (\delta^3 + \delta^4 + \cdots)4.5 < V(p_3)$$

for δ close to 1. This computation illustrates the trade-off between the short-run gain from undercutting and the longer-run loss due to the price war. Firm 1's profit is increased by $(8 - 4.5) = 3.5$ today, but is reduced by 4.5 in the following two periods (if we suppose that firm 1 elects to relent at price p_1).

Remark 1 The above equilibrium suggests a "strategic" theory of excess capacity. We have assumed to this point that the firms can satisfy their demand. Now, let us assume that they must first install their capacities before competing over prices (as in chapter 5, but with dynamic price competition as the "second stage"). In the stationary state, the firms need capacity equal to half the total market demand at p_3—that is, $\frac{1}{4}$. However, a firm's threat to charge p_1 if the other firm charges p_2 is no longer credible if the capacity of the former firm is $\frac{1}{4}$. At price p_1, the former firm is far from able to satisfy demand ($\frac{5}{6}$). Equilibrium at p_3 is no longer an equilibrium when this level of capacity is chosen. In fact, it can be shown that the firms benefit from installing capacities which they will not use, but which they would use if the other firm became more "aggressive."[28]

Remark 2 There also exist equilibria in which the price never settles. For instance, in the previous example, the symmetric strategies $\{R(p_6) = R(p_5) = p_4; R(p_4) = p_3; R(p_3) = p_2; R(p_2) = p_1; R(p_1) = p_0;$ and $R(p_0) = p_0$ with probability β and p_5 with probability $1 - \beta\}$ (where β depends on δ) form another equilibrium for δ close to 1. At this equilibrium, market dynamics consist of a price war followed by a rapid relenting phase followed by a new price war, and so on. A market onlooker thus observes a cyclical path of market prices. Each firm undercuts because, with good reason, it anticipates that maintaining its price will not prevent the other firm from

---

28. See Maskin and Tirole 1985 for an example of strategic excess capacity; see Benoit and Krishna 1987 and Davidson and Deneckere 1985 for examples of similar behavior in a supergame context. Rotemberg and Saloner (1985a) make a similar point with respect to inventories. A nonstrategic reason for maintaining excess capacity is the fluctuation in demand over time (either in a seasonal

manner or over the business cycle). See Arrow, Beckmann, and Karlin 1958 and (for a related idea in an inventory context) the contributions in Arrow, Karlin, and Scarf 1958, Mills 1962, and Zabel 1972. See also the discussion of inventories in chapter 1 of the present volume.

being aggressive. In that sense, mistrust is a self-justifying attitude.[29]

6.4.2 Discussion

Remark 2 above shows that, despite the restriction to simple (Markov) strategies, multiple equilibria exist (indeed, there also exist several kinked-demand-curve equilibria). However, it can be shown that in any Markov perfect equilibrium, profits are always bounded away from the competitive profit (which is 0). For instance, the average industry profit in a symmetric equilibrium is equal to at least half of the monopoly profit for δ close to 1. The intuition here is that if firms were stuck in the competitive price region, with the prospects of small profits in the future, a firm could raise its price dramatically and lure its rival to charge a high price for at least some time (the rival would not hurry back to nearly competitive prices). Thus, tacit collusion is not only possible (as in the supergame approach) but necessary. Furthermore, it can be shown that there exists only one pair of equilibrium strategies that sustain industry profits close to the monopoly profit. These strategies (which are described in subsection 6.7.2) form a symmetric kinked-demand-curve equilibrium at the monopoly price, and they are the only symmetric "renegotiation-proof" equilibrium strategies (whatever the current price, the firms cannot find an alternative Markov perfect equilibrium that they both prefer).

Price rigidities suggest the possibility that price adjustments are more sluggish during booms than during busts. The point is that during a bust in demand, price adjustments operate downward and thus result in a temporary increase in the market share of the firm initiating the adjustment. During a boom, each firm is reluctant to adjust (upward) because this results in a temporary loss of market share.[30]

Asynchronicity was exogenously imposed in order to allow the formulation of the notion of reaction to payoff-relevant variables. But it can be shown that if firms can choose their prices whenever they want, subject to the constraint that their price is locked in for two periods once it is chosen (short-run commitment), the firms effectively end up moving asynchronously. This vindicates the use of alternating timing. Of course, the two-period commitment is a conceit. Optimally, one would wish to describe the price frictions evoked at the beginning of this section in more detail. Gertner (1986) takes this route, and assumes that there exists a fixed menu cost of changing prices.[31] His results reaffirm the previous ones (in particular, that the monopoly price is sustainable by some Markov-perfect-equilibrium strategies, and that equilibrium profits are bounded away from the competitive profit).

Price rigidities cannot formalize tacit collusion in situations of repeated auctions (see page 222 of Scherer 1980 for a description of collusion and breakdown of collusion in the antibiotic industry, where the federal government was the major buyer). Then new prices are quoted in each auction, and the timing is constrained to be synchronous. (Ortega-Reichert [1967] has developed a theory of tacit collusion for first-bid auctions, which is similar to the theory of tacit collusion developed in section 6.5 below. The idea is that by charging a high price in the current auction, each firm tries to *signal* to the other firms that it is less cost effective than it really is, and thereby to indicate that it will not price aggressively in the next auction. It thus induces its rival to price less aggressively in the future. The consistency of this strategy with rational behavior will be examined in section 6.5 and in chapter 9 in related contexts.)

6.5 Reputation for Friendly Behavior

Section 6.4 shows how short-run price rigidities can sustain price collusion. More generally, this approach presumes that firms react to payoff-relevant variables that are determined by past price choices (the payoff-relevant variables can be the prices themselves, but they can also

---

29. Such an equilibrium price cycle arises in the absence of capacity constraint. (Edgeworth suggested the possibility of price cycles as a consequence of the potential nonexistence of a pure-strategy equilibrium in the static price game with capacity constraints—see chapter 5 above.)

30. See Maskin and Tirole 1988 for a preliminary example of such behavior based on unforeseen demand shocks and using the renegotiation-proof equilibrium behaviors.

31. The literature on menu costs stems from Barro 1972, Sheshinski and Weiss 1977, and Sheshinski and Weiss 1983. Important recent research in this area (in monopoly or competitive frameworks) has been done by Caplin and Spulber (1987) and Bénabou (1985). In macroeconomics there exists a large literature on costly price adjustments. Of particular relevance to the dynamic study of effects of menu costs is Blanchard's (1983) analysis of asynchronic price movements.

stem (less directly) from consumer inertia or from technological intertemporal links). It thus emphasizes the role of tangible variables. In reality, history matters not only through its effect on tangible variables but also through the information it conveys about competitors. Oligopolists are concerned with many variables that they cannot estimate precisely. Among these are the cost structure (or, more generally, the objective function) of their rivals, the state of demand, and the potential of the market. Beyond individual or industry surveys, firms rely on market information (such as past price choices and observed demand) to estimate these variables. Thus, history also matters through intangible variables (beliefs). This raises the possibility that the firms may want to manipulate their rivals' information in order to derive benefits later on.

Chapter 9 is devoted to the general study of strategic interaction under incomplete information. The purpose of the present section is to suggest why asymmetries in information are likely to induce firms to raise their prices in a situation of repeated price interaction.

The basic intuition (which will be systematically developed in chapters 8 and 9) is the following: In a one-shot interaction, a firm is more likely to charge a high price if it knows that its rival is likely to charge a high price (this step must be taken for granted for the time being, but it is quite intuitive). Hence, because a firm likes its rival to charge high prices, it would like to convince its rival that it is likely to charge high prices itself. In a one-shot situation, there is little that a firm can do to convince its rival of this. Talk is cheap and cannot be trusted to supply useful information. In a dynamic framework, however, a firm can send costly signals. For instance, in a two-period price game, a firm can in the first period charge a price that exceeds its first-period expected-profit-maximizing price in order to signal that it is likely to charge a high price in the second period. (This signal may be credible precisely because it is costly—it implies a first-period sacrifice of profit.) Why should a high first-period price convey the information that the firm is likely to charge a high second-period price? Suppose that the firm has private information about its production cost (or about the demand curve).[32] In a one-shot relationship, the firm tends to charge a high price if its marginal cost is high (or if it has information that demand is high) and a low price otherwise. Thus, *absent strategic manipulation of information*, a high first-period price reveals that the firm has a high cost (or that the demand is high). If costs (or demand) are positively correlated over time (in particular, if they are time invariant), the firm will also charge a high price in the second period. Hence, a rival ought to use the information conveyed by the firm's first-period price to predict its second-period behavior. Of course, a rational firm realizes this and generally wants to manipulate its rival's information. To do so, it charges a price above the first-period expected profit-maximizing price given its marginal cost (or its information about demand). In turn, the rival ought to anticipate the firm's incentive to charge high prices, and modify its inference process accordingly. The proper extension of the Nash perfect-equilibrium concept to this type of situation is described in section 11.5 below. The study of equilibrium indeed confirms the intuition just developed. *In a repeated price game with asymmetric information about marginal cost or demand, each firm sacrifices short-run profit by raising its price in order to build a reputation for charging high prices.* (Of course, in a two-period game this effect operates only in the first period. In the second period, each firm maximizes its expected second-period profit given its second-period information, because there is no future to carry reputation over to.)

As was mentioned in the previous section, this reasoning may be applicable to repeated auctions. Suppose that the government procures its supplies (concrete, weapons, antibiotics, etc.) through first-bid auctions.[33] In a single auction, a firm generally does not charge a price equal to its marginal cost. By charging above its marginal cost, it makes a positive profit in case the other firms bid even higher. (This departure from the Bertrand outcome can be attributed to the possibility of a cost differential between the firms. See the Game Theory User's Manual

---

32. A firm need not have private information for the phenomenon described to operate. It can also jam its rivals' information through the choice of unobservable actions (here, secret price adjustments), as in Riordan's (1985) model. See chapter 9 below.

33. A first-bid auction has all the bidders announce a price at which they are willing to supply the good; the lowest-price firm is picked and receives its bid to supply the good. A first-bid auction is thus equivalent to Bertrand competition with perfect substitutes (a minor difference is that the quantity bought by the buyer—e.g., the government—is often fixed, i.e. inelastic, rather than due to a downward-sloping demand).

for an example of an equilibrium of a first-bid auction.) In a repeated auction, each firm bids even higher than this in order to try to convince its rival that it is inefficient and, therefore, likely to bid high in the future (Ortega-Reichert 1967, chapter 8).

6.5.1 A Metaphor: The Repeated "Prisoner's Dilemma" Game

Because dynamic games of incomplete information are technically hard to solve, we will put off studying them until chapter 9. Here, we will consider a simple example that looks somewhat like a price game. Figure 6.4 depicts the so-called "prisoner's dilemma" game (see the Game Theory User's Manual for its motivation). There are two players. Both can choose between cooperating (C) and finking (F). If they both cooperate, they both obtain 3. If they both fink, they both obtain 0. If one cooperates and the other finks, they get −1 and 4, respectively. In the one-shot version of this game, finking is a dominant strategy for both players. That is, each player gains from finking, regardless of the other player's choice. Hence, the only Nash equilibrium is (F, F). Although the prisoners' dilemma is not a faithful representation of a price game, it contains some elements that illustrate price competition and the Bertrand paradox. In particular, both players would be better off cooperating (charging a high price) rather than finking (undercutting), but each player is individually better off finking. It also shares with the Bertrand price game the property that repeating the game T times does not help sustain collusion: In the last period, both players will fink; so they will in the penultimate period, and so on. Thus, unless the game is repeated an infinite number of times (in which case, if the discount factor is sufficiently large, collusion—i.e. (C, C)—can easily be sustained by means of threats to revert to (F, F) in the future if one of the players does not cooperate today), the (F, F) equilibrium is still the only noncooperative equilibrium in each period.

The basic insight of Kreps et al. 1982 is that a small uncertainty about the preferences of the players (technically, about the above payoff matrix) can have a significant amount of influence on the players' behavior if

Player 1 \ Player 2	C	F
C	3,3	−1,4
F	4,−1	0,0

Figure 6.4

the game is repeated long enough (but not necessarily repeated an infinite number of times). To see this, suppose that with probability $1 - \alpha$ each player is "sane," meaning that his payoff is then given by the payoff matrix in figure 6.4 (so that, for instance, the payoff corresponding to (F, C) is 4 for player 1). With probability α, each player is "crazy." His preferences are not given by the previous payoff matrix; rather, he behaves in the following way: He starts cooperating at date 1. He continues cooperating at date t as long as his opponent has cooperated up to that date; otherwise he finks. (One can think of this crazy type as representing a preference for cooperation—or a distaste for finking—coupled with a strong desire to punish a noncooperative opponent.) "Craziness" does not reflect a value judgment, but refers to behavior (or preferences) that deviates from the norm (which is associated with preferences defined by the payoff matrix). One can think of α as small if one feels that craziness is relatively unlikely.

Let us briefly return to our metaphor, in which a firm can charge one of two prices (cooperating corresponds to charging the high price, and finking to charging the low price). There, one might think of the "sane type" as facing a low production cost (and therefore benefiting from an unanswered price cut), and the "crazy type" as facing a high enough cost (say, above the low price) that it never pays to undercut the rival's high price.[34,35]

Let us assume that the game is repeated from $t = 0$ to $t = T$, and, to simplify computations, that the discount factor δ is 1. Each player knows his preferences ("sane" or "crazy"), but does not know his opponent's. Because the

---

34. On this interpretation, α need not be small

35. The metaphor is imperfect as it stands, in that it is not clear why a

high-cost firm should charge a low price after a deviation. The reason why this prisoner's dilemma is useful in building some intuition about the price game will be given in chapter 9.

behavior of a crazy type is determined, we will derive player i's strategy assuming that he is sane.

Suppose that at date 0 player 1 finks. Because a crazy player never takes the initiative to fink first, player 1 must be sane. Both players finking from date 1 on (up to the end of the game) is an equilibrium: By the very definition of craziness, player 2, if he is crazy, retaliates for the date-0 deviation from cooperation. If he is sane he might as well fink, given that player 1 will fink no matter what. Similarly, player 1, who is sane, cannot do better than to fink. This actually is the only equilibrium from date 1 on[36] after a deviation from cooperation at date 0. This means that if player 1 is sane and finks at date 0, his payoff is at most 4 (he gets at most 4 at date 0, and gets 0 at dates $1, \ldots, T$). Now, consider the strategy that consists for player 1 in cooperating up to T unless player 2 deviates at some date t, in which case player 1 finks from $t + 1$ to T. This strategy need not (and actually is not) optimal for player 1 if he is sane; however, as will now be shown, it dominates finking at date 0 for T sufficiently large, and therefore finking at date 0 cannot be optimal even for a sane player. If player 2 is crazy, player 1 gets $3(T + 1)$ from this strategy. If player 2 is sane, player 1 gets at worst -1, because he gets caught cooperating while his opponent finks for at most one period, after which he plays noncooperatively. Hence, player 1's payoff from this strategy is at least

$$\alpha[3(T + 1)] + (1 - \alpha)(-1) > 4$$

for T sufficiently large. However small α may be, there exists T_0 such that for $T \geq T_0$ finking at date 0 cannot be optimal for player 1 even if he is sane. And similarly for player 2. This means that, *for a sufficiently large horizon, each player cooperates at the beginning of the horizon,* even when from a myopic (static) perspective finking is a dominant strategy for a sane player. More generally, cooperation by both players is observed as long as $t \leq T - T_0$.[37]

The intuition for this result is straightforward. Each player, by cooperating, exposes himself to the risk that the other player finks, and that he obtains a low profit during one period (after which, having learned his lesson, he will no longer try to cooperate). However, by finking, he reveals that he is not of a cooperative (crazy) type and, therefore, loses future gains from cooperation if the other player is of a cooperative type. If the horizon is long enough, the loss of future cooperation exceeds that for being cheated on. In a sense, at the beginning of their relationship, the players want to keep their reputation for possibly be willing to cooperate; that is, they do not want to reveal that they are noncooperative.

Because we have obtained our main result (that cooperation can be sustained for sufficiently large horizons even for small probabilities of craziness), we do not give a complete description of the equilibrium of this game. A sane player cooperates for some period of time. Then, near the end of the horizon, he starts milking his reputation; the loss of future cooperation becomes comparable to that of being cheated upon. Hence, collusion breaks down at the end of the relationship (if at least one of the players is not cooperative).[38]

6.5.2 Discussion

A striking feature of the model in subsection 6.5.1 is the powerful effect of small uncertainties about each other's objective function on equilibrium behavior if the horizon is sufficiently long and the players are not very impatient. As Kreps et al. (1982) show, cooperation is sustainable for a small probability α of being crazy, whereas it is not for $\alpha = 0$.

Of course, the possibility of sustaining collusion or another outcome depends on the type of craziness one is willing to assume. For instance, if we assumed that a crazy player likes to cooperate no matter what (that is, is not "revenge hungry" after his opponent cheats), collusion would not be sustainable for any α.[39] Finking would imply no future loss of cooperation with a crazy player,

---

36. At date T, everybody finks (the sane players do so because finking is a dominant strategy in the last period; a crazy player 2 does so because he still retaliates for the period-0 deviation). The same is true at date $T - 1$, and at any date $t \geq 1$, by backward induction.

37. If both types of players' best strategy is to cooperate at date $0, \ldots, t - 1$, each player still has posterior beliefs given by $(1 - \alpha, \alpha)$ at date t when both have cooperated until then.

38. The equilibrium and its derivation are formally similar to the model of a monopolist's reputation for quality. See the supplementary section of chapter 2.

39. By backward induction, finking is a "dominant" strategy for the sane type at each date. Thus, the sane players play F in each period, and not only at the end of the horizon.

and therefore nothing would deter a sane player from finking.

On the other hand, Kreps et al. show that the (cooperative) conclusion of subsection 6.5.1 still holds if craziness means playing "tit for tat." (The tit-for-tat strategy is to cooperate at date 0 and then do whatever the other player did on the previous move.)

The high sensitivity of equilibrium behavior to beliefs about one's opponent's objective for a long horizon and a high discount factor raises the question of the size of the set of equilibria spanned by small amounts, but *arbitrary* descriptions, of "craziness." Fudenberg and Maskin (1986a) show that a kind of Folk theorem holds, i.e., "any outcome" can be sustained as an equilibrium of a sufficiently long and little discounted game with incomplete information, as long as one is willing to assign a probability $\alpha > 0$ that each player is crazy in a particular way (see subsection 6.7.3 for more details). The set of equilibria is then the same as the set of equilibria for the infinitely repeated game (supergame) between the sane types only. Thus, we again face an embarrassment of riches. While the supergame approach forces us to choose between a large multiplicity of equilibria of a single model, the reputation approach with long horizon (which, because of the finite horizon, reduces the set of equilibria dramatically for a given model) offers a large multiplicity of models (descriptions of uncertainty) and associated outcomes to choose from.

The Fudenberg-Maskin criticism suggests two routes that can yield predictive power to the reputation model. The first consists of being reasonably confident about the sort of craziness that is likely to arise in practice.[40] The second is more consistent with the general neoclassical approach of presuming full rationality (in the sense of profit-maximizing behavior) to obtain predictive power. According to this approach, each player views his opponent as rational and is rational himself; however, he does not know some parameters, such as the opponent's marginal cost or estimate of demand (see the above metaphor).

Besides sticking to the rationality axiom, this approach has the advantage of looking at a type of asymmetric information which is more likely to be "large" (as opposed to the probability of craziness, which we would presume to be "small"). (The equilibria of dynamic games of incomplete information tend to be less sensitive to the exact specification of uncertainty when the magnitude of the uncertainty is non-negligible.) In chapter 9, we will generally take this second approach.

It should, however, be pointed out that the approach outlined in subsection 6.5.1 was motivated by the many experiments that show that collusion is likely to be sustained in long but finite games. For instance, Axelrod (1980) proposed a prisoner's dilemma (such as the one illustrated by figure 6.4) to game theorists in economics, psychology, sociology, political science, and mathematics. The game was supposed to be repeated $T = 200$ times. Axelrod ran the strategies submitted by the game theorists against one another in a round-robin tournament. The highest average score was realized by the tit-for-tat strategy rather than the "rational" strategy of finking at each period.

Such experiments point at the following ideas: Under such circumstances, collusion does not seem to be explained by the second approach—in contrast with industrial-organization environments, there is no asymmetric information about cost, demand, etc.: If one assumes that each participant's preferences are increasing with his final wealth, there is no real asymmetry of information about payoffs between the participants. Thus, the failure to get defection (F) in each period seems to be traceable to the rationality axiom. And, indeed, it is reasonable to presume that at least a small fraction of the participants (the "crazy" players) have not performed the backward-induction reasoning that yields defection in each period, or are unable to do it, or believe that with some probability some other participants have not performed this computation. The important contribution of the approach of Kreps et al. is to show that if the game is repeated long

---

40. An interesting result due to Fudenberg and Levine (1987) states that under some conditions an informed player will, in the long run, succeed in convincing his rivals that he is "crazy" and that his form of craziness is the (sane) informed player's "preferred" craziness. Informally, this preferred type of craziness is the one that, in a one-shot game, would induce the rival to take an action that is most favorable to the sane type of the informed player. The conditions are that the informed player is a long-run player who faces a (long) sequence of short-run players (e.g., players who play for a single period each), that the short-term players have observed the long-term player's past behavior, and that they put a positive prior probability on the preferred type of craziness. The intuition behind the result is that, if the informed player is very patient and the horizon is very long, it is worth taking the time and incurring the losses associated with building the best possible reputation. The time frame to build such a reputation is, however, longer than the one in the approach of Kreps et al., in which craziness can take only one form, and the opponents do not have to distinguish among various types of craziness.

enough, even a sane player who has performed all the required computations may want to behave like a crazy player, and do better than he would do by finking.

6.5.3 The Evolutionary Approach

The reputation approach described in subsection 6.5.1 relies on a small probability of craziness. But it does not disassociate itself totally from the rational approach, in that a large fraction of the population attempts to maximize total payoff. The evolutionary approach goes all the way by not requiring maximizing behavior at all. However, it recognizes that, first, economic agents cannot, in the long run, use totally suboptimal rules (because they will notice it or else disappear[41]) and, second, allowing all kinds of irrationality implies a complete loss of predictive power. This approach—which was pioneered, in the tradition of Darwin, by (among others) Alchian (1950), Hirshleifer (1977), and especially Nelson and Winter (1982) in economics and Maynard Smith (1974, 1978) in biology—looks at strategies, or (better terminology) rules, that are "robust" in the sense that they do relatively well against a variety of other rules.[42] For instance, Axelrod (1981) points out that in the repeated prisoner's dilemma, tit for tat tends to be a robust rule because it cooperates, is provoked into retaliation by the defection of the opponent, and yet is forgiving after it takes its one retaliation. (In contrast, the "always fink" rule forbids gains from cooperation with cooperative types, as was seen in subsection 6.5.2, while the "always fink after a deviation" rule is not forgiving enough in case of a "mistake."[43])

The evolutionary approach assumes that, in the long run, only actors who use robust rules will stay around. The actors who use fragile rules will die (in a biological context) or go bankrupt (in an economic one), or will experiment with new rules; the more successful actors will see their rules imitated by new generations:

The biological motivation for this approach is based on the interpretation of the payoffs in terms of fitness (survival and fecundity). All mutations are possible, and if any could invade *a given population it would have had the chance to do so. Thus only a collectively stable strategy is expected to be able to maintain itself in the long-run equilibrium as the strategy used by all. Collectively stable strategies are important because they are the only ones which an entire population can maintain in the long run if mutations are introduced one at a time. (Axelrod 1981, p. 310)*

The predictive power of the evolutionary theory remains to be determined. What is meant by "robust rule" is *a priori* contingent on the set and the probability distribution of mutations, and on the set of strategies the robust rule is allowed to be compared to.

6.6 Concluding Remarks

The full-fledged dynamic models of repeated price interaction are complex; however, they provide the best approach for formalizing tacit collusion. Game theory imposes discipline by forcing the economist to think about and give a precise description of the strategic environment (including, here, the frequency and timing of price changes and the information structure). In principle, this discipline allows for a better assessment of the relevance of the models; few would believe in a model simply because it formalizes some of the conventional wisdom (tacit collusion for high market concentration, kinked demand curve, price secrecy as a hindering factor, and so on). In the absence of conclusive econometric evidence of the predictive power of various models, precious information can be gained from looking at whether the very mode of competition presumed by the model (the "extensive form" of the game), and not only its outcome (the equilibrium prices or profits, say) fits the informal descriptions of the business press or those of the industry case studies.

Why should we be interested in three (or more) approaches to price collusion? The cynical view is that the absence of rigorous tests makes it difficult to reject an approach as irrelevant. But it may be the case that "theoretical heterogeneity" is needed here. As was men-

---

41. E.g., by going bankrupt if there is sufficient experimentation or mutation.

42. The recent literature on repeated games played by automata (e.g., Abreu and Rubinstein 1986, Aumann and Sorin 1986, Kalai and Stanford 1986, and Rubinstein 1986) should also be mentioned.

43. Another advantage of tit for tat in an evolutionary context (in which successful strategies survive and grow) is that it allows the survival of other cooperative strategies (such as "always cooperate"). For a general overview of Axelrod's approach to cooperation, see his book *The Evolution of Cooperation* (1984) and Milgrom's 1984 review thereof.

tioned in the introduction, the rich array of behavioral patterns across industries may justify a proliferation of theories. Thus, the approaches developed in this chapter, and other approaches, may be complements rather than competitors.

This brings us to three important questions about "comparative modeling" that have been only partially addressed in this chapter and in the literature: How would one go about testing the various approaches? Which one is most relevant in a particular industry? Do they generate different policy conclusions? These difficult questions should be given high priority on the research agenda.

6.7 Supplementary Section: Dynamic Games and Tacit Collusion

6.7.1 Secret Price Cuts

6.7.1.1 Price Competition

To formalize the intuition of section 6.3.3, we will now develop a straightforward model of collusion under imperfect observability of prices. Because the Green-Porter model is slightly *ad hoc* in that it considers quantity competition and therefore assumes the presence of an auctioneer (if we are to take the informational assumption seriously), we shall depart from it by presuming direct price competition.[44] Thus, we shall make Stigler's (1964) assumption that firms do not observe their rivals' prices but rather infer them (imperfectly) from their own demand. The analysis, however, follows in the spirit of the Green-Porter model.

The framework is that of the basic supergame. Two firms choose prices every period. The goods are perfect substitutes and are produced at constant marginal cost c, so the consumers all buy from the low-price firm. The demand is split in halves if both firms charge the same price. In each period, there are two possible states of nature. With probability α, there is no demand for the product sold by the duopolists (the "low-demand state"). With probability $1 - \alpha$, there is a positive demand, $D(p)$ (the "high-demand state"). The monopoly price and the monopoly profits in the high-demand state are denoted by p^m and Π^m. We assume that the realizations of demand are independently and identically distributed (i.i.d.) over time.

A firm that does not sell at some date is unable to observe whether the absence of demand is due to the realization of the low-demand state or to its rival's lower price. It is always common knowledge that at least one firm makes no profit. If this occurs because of the absence

---

44. The fact that different modes of competition have different informational contents is more general. For instance, Milgrom (1985) makes the point that collusion may be easier to sustain for infinitely repeated "descending" auctions than for infinitely repeated sealed-bid auctions. Suppose, e.g., that two firms facing the same cost c to supply a buyer quote prices. In a sealed-bid auction they quote prices simultaneously. In a descending auction the price goes down by itself until one of the firms gives up, in which case the other firm supplies at the current price. In a single auction or a finite number of auctions, the equilibrium in both types of auctions is the competitive price (the buyer pays c). A repeated sealed-bid auction is similar to the repeated price game studied in section 6.3. Collusion can be sustained only if the horizon is infinite and the discount factor is sufficiently high. In a repeated descending auction, a deviation is discovered immediately (instead of one period later) and thus can be made unprofitable, even from a static point of view (the deviator's rival can refuse to give up before the price equals c in the current auction). Collusion is feasible for any discount factor. The market organization thus affects detection lags and the amount of feasible collusion.

of demand, neither firm makes a profit. If this occurs because one firm undercuts the monopoly price, this firm knows that the other firm makes no profit.

The all-or-nothing demand function is clearly contrived. However, it allows the firms to face a nontrivial signal-extraction problem: A firm cannot say for sure whether a low demand stems from its rival's price cut. The model thus follows Stigler's approach. (With general demand functions for differentiated products, a firm could not perfectly infer a price cut.)

In a nonrepeated game or a finitely repeated game, both firms charge the competitive price c (the Bertrand outcome). In the infinitely repeated version of the game, we look at an equilibrium with the following strategies: There is a collusive phase and a punishment phase. The game begins in the collusive phase. Both firms charge p^m until one firm makes a zero profit (as was noted above, such an event is observed by both firms, even though a firm does not observe its rival's profit).[45] The occurrence of a zero profit triggers a punishment phase. Both firms charge c for exactly T periods, where T can *a priori* be finite or infinite. At the end (if any) of the punishment phase, the firms revert to the collusive phase and charge p^m as long as they both make positive profits.

Let us look for a length of the punishment phase such that the expected present discounted value of profits of each firm is maximal subject to the constraint that the associated strategies form an equilibrium.

The strategies are always optimal in the punishment phase. Given that its rival charges the competitive price no matter what during T periods, each firm cannot improve on the competitive price itself.

Let V^+ (respectively, V^-) denote the present discounted value of a firm's profit from date t on, assuming that at date t the game is in the collusive phase (respectively, starts the punishment phase). By stationarity, V^+ and V^- do not depend on time. By definition, we have

$$V^+ = (1 - \alpha)(\Pi^m/2 + \delta V^+) + \alpha(\delta V^-) \qquad (6.10)$$

and

$$V^- = \delta^T V^+. \qquad (6.11)$$

Equation 6.10 says that in the collusive phase, both firms charge p^m. With probability $1 - \alpha$, demand is high, firms make current profit $\Pi^m/2$ each, and the game remains in the collusive phase, so that both firms have valuation V^+ again next period. With probability α, there is no demand today, and the game will be in the punishment phase tomorrow. Equation 6.11 yields the present discounted value of profits at the beginning of the punishment phase. During T periods, both firms make zero profit, after which they revert to the collusive phase.

Last, we must add the "incentive constraint," which states that no firm would wish to undercut in the collusive phase:

$$V^+ \geqslant (1 - \alpha)(\Pi^m + \delta V^-) + \alpha(\delta V^-). \qquad (6.12)$$

This equation expresses the trade-off for each firm. If a firm undercuts, it gets $\Pi^m > \Pi^m/2$. However, undercutting automatically triggers the punishment phase, which yields valuation V^- instead of V^+ (these effects exist only if demand is high; for a low demand, nothing changes). Thus, to deter undercutting, V^- must be sufficiently lower than V^+. This means that the punishment must last long enough. But because punishments are costly and occur with positive probability, T should be chosen as small as possible given that equation 6.12 must be satisfied. Mathematically, equation 6.12 is equivalent to (using equation 6.10)

$$\delta(V^+ - V^-) \geqslant \Pi^m/2. \qquad (6.13)$$

On the other hand, equations 6.10 and 6.11 yield

$$V^+ = \frac{(1 - \alpha)\Pi^m/2}{1 - (1 - \alpha)\delta - \alpha\delta^{T+1}} \qquad (6.14)$$

and

$$V^- = \frac{(1 - \alpha)\delta^T\Pi^m/2}{1 - (1 - \alpha)\delta - \alpha\delta^{T+1}}. \qquad (6.15)$$

Substituting equations 6.14 and 6.15 into equation 6.13 yields, after some computations,

$$1 \leqslant 2(1 - \alpha)\delta + (2\alpha - 1)\delta^{T+1}. \qquad (6.16)$$

Because the game starts in the collusive phase, the highest profit for the firms is obtained by solving the following program:

---

45. This model possesses the same "bang-bang" property as its complete-information counterpart; i.e., there is no reason for the firms to try to implement any price less than p^m (in contrast with the Green-Porter quantity model—see exercise 6.9).

max V^+

subject to equation 6.16.

As is easily verified from equation 6.14, V^+ is a decreasing function of T; that is, longer punishments reduce the expected profits. So we must choose the lowest possible T consistent with equation 6.16. (The fact that equation 6.16 is not satisfied for $T = 0$ confirms our remark that non-negligible punishments are required.) The right-hand side of equation 6.16 increases with T if and only if $\alpha < \frac{1}{2}$. Thus, if $\alpha \geqslant \frac{1}{2}$, there exists no T satisfying equation 6.16. The intuition for this is that the temptation to undercut increases when the expected gains from future collusion decrease. If $\alpha < \frac{1}{2}$, then the right-hand side of equation 6.16 is maximal for $T = +\infty$.

Assuming that $(1 - \alpha)\delta \geqslant \frac{1}{2}$ guarantees that the high price is sustainable using maximal punishments ($T = +\infty$). It generalizes the condition for deterministic demand, which corresponds to $\alpha = 0$ (see section 6.3).

To maximize V^+ subject to the incentive constraint 6.16, it thus suffices to choose the smallest T that satisfies the incentive constraint. We thus obtain a (finite) optimal length of punishment.[46]

*Exercise 6.8*** Work your way through the Green-Porter model with price competition and two i.i.d. states of demand (no demand or positive demand). Rederive the optimal length of punishment. Show that for a probability $\alpha = \frac{1}{4}$ of no demand, δ must exceed $\frac{2}{3}$ in order for collusion to be sustainable; show also that at least two periods of punishment are required.

6.7.1.2 Quantity Competition

*Exercise 6.9*** Consider the Green-Porter model with *quantity* as a choice variable. Assume that the market price at time t is

$$p_t = \theta_t P(q_{1t} + q_{2t}),$$

where θ_t is an i.i.d. multiplicative demand shock at date t, distributed according to the c.d.f. F. Firm i observes only p_t, not θ_t or q_{jt}. Let

$$\Pi(q) \equiv \underset{\theta}{E}[(\theta P(2q) - c)q]$$

denote the expected per-period profit when both firms produce q, and let q^c denote the symmetric Cournot output (which we assume is unique). Thus, q^c maximizes

$$\Pi^i(q_i, q^c) = \underset{\theta}{E}[(\theta P(q_i + q^c) - c)q_i].$$

Suppose that a price war is triggered when p_t falls under some threshold level p^+. Thus, when the firms' outputs are q_i and q_j, the probability of a price war is

$$\alpha(q_i, q_j) = F\left(\frac{p^+}{P(q_i + q_j)}\right).$$

Let q^+ and q^c denote the per-firm outputs in the collusive and punishment phases ($q^+ < q^c$). Note the constraint that punishments must be Cournot.

(i) Using the same notation as in the text, show that

$$V^+ = \frac{\Pi(q^c)}{1 - \delta} + \frac{\Pi(q^+) - \Pi(q^c)}{1 - \alpha^+ \delta^{T+1} - (1 - \alpha^+)\delta},$$

where $\alpha^+ = \alpha(q^+, q^+)$.

(ii) Again using the same notation, show that the optimal output q^+, trigger price p^+, and length of punishment T are given by

$$\max_{\{q^+, p^+, T\}} \quad V^+$$

$$\text{s.t.} \quad \frac{\partial \Pi^i}{\partial q_i}(q^+, q^+)$$

$$= \delta \frac{\partial \alpha}{\partial q_i}(q^+, q^+)\left(\frac{\Pi(q^+) - \Pi(q^c)}{1 - \alpha^+ \delta^{T+1} - (1 - \alpha^+)\delta}\right)(1 - \delta^T).$$

(The optimal T can be finite or infinite.)

(iii) Use intuitive reasoning to argue that $q^+ > q^m$, where q^m maximizes the expected value of $(\theta P(2q) - c)q$. (Hint: Explain in terms of first- and second-order effects starting at $q^+ = q^m$.) Show that q^+ converges to q^m when the amount of noise tends to zero (the distribution of θ becomes degenerate).

The Green-Porter equilibrium (described in exercise 6.9) is optimal in a limited class of strategies. First, punishments are restricted to Cournot punishments, while worse punishments exist (some intuition about this may be

---

46. A residual issue is that the root of equation 6.16 may not be an integer. One may then either take the smallest integer above this root or (better) use a randomizing device to determine whether the length of punishment is this integer or the highest integer under the root (where the probabilities are chosen so that the constraint 6.16 is exactly binding).

gained from section 6.7.3). Second, the price war is based on a "tail test." It is triggered by a price p_t lower than some threshold level p^+, so no use is made of the actual level of p_t beyond its comparison with p^+. Thus, the model presumes special forms for the collusive and punishment phases. Abreu, Pierce, and Stacchetti (1985, 1986) look at optimal collusive strategies without restrictions on the class of strategies. Two assumptions that allow these authors to obtain very crisp results are that the firms' objective functions are concave and that the conditional distribution of the market price p_t, given aggregate output Q_t, satisfies the "monotone likelihood ratio property" (MLRP). Informally, the latter condition means that a low p_t is more likely to result from a high Q_t than from a low one.[47]

Abreu et al. show that one can indeed restrict attention to a collusive phase and a punishment phase, characterized by payoffs V^+ and V^-, where V^+ and V^- are now the best and worst elements in the set of symmetric perfect-equilibrium payoffs. Furthermore, the collusive phase and the punishment phase take simple forms. In the collusive phase, the firms produce output q^+. The punishment phase is triggered by a tail test, i.e., it starts if the market price falls under some threshold level p^+. Thus, the collusive phase is qualitatively similar to that presumed in Porter 1983b and in Green and Porter 1984. The punishment phase, however, does not have a fixed length; rather, it resembles the collusive phase. The two firms produce (presumably high) output q^- each. If the market price exceeds a threshold price p^-, the game remains in the punishment phase; if it lies below p^-, the game goes back to the collusive phase. Thus, the evolution between the two phases follows a Markovian process. The reader may be surprised by the "inverse tail test" in the punishment phase. The idea is that a harsh punishment requires a high output (higher than is even privately desirable); to ensure that the firms produce a high output, it is specified that in the case of a high price (which signals a low output) the game remains in the punishment phase.[48]

6.7.2 Price Rigidities and the Kinked Demand Curve

The following is a technical analysis of the alternating-move price game of section 6.4.

6.7.2.1 The One-Period-Deviation Criterion

The reader may be puzzled by the statement in the text that no single-period deviation from equilibrium behavior being profitable is sufficient to ensure that strategies (R_1, R_2) are optimal; indeed, when computing $V^1(p_2)$ at date t, we assumed that firm 1 would react at dates $t + 2$, $t + 4, \ldots$ according to the prescribed reaction function, $R_1(\cdot)$. Could it be possible that a single deviation from $R_1(\cdot)$ at date t is not profitable but that a sequence of deviations from $R_1(\cdot)$ at dates $t, t + 2, \ldots$ is? The answer is No. (The following reasoning applies to much more general games and, in particular, to the supergames considered in section 6.3.) First, a finite sequence of deviations during n periods cannot be profitable for the deviating firm if a single-period deviation is not, for the nth deviation is unprofitable because it amounts to a single-period deviation. Thus, if the firm benefits from the n deviations, it a fortiori benefits from the $n - 1$ first deviations. If we eliminate the last deviation, the $(n - 1)$th deviation becomes a single-period deviation and therefore is not optimal, and so forth. Next, consider a profitable infinite sequence of deviations from $R_1(\cdot)$. If it yields an extra payoff of $\varepsilon > 0$ relative to following $R_1(\cdot)$ all the time, then (because $\delta < 1$ makes the distant future almost insignificant in terms of payoffs) the first n deviations alone yield an extra payoff of $\varepsilon' > 0$ for n sufficiently large. However, we know that finite deviations will not do.

6.7.2.2 The Dynamic Programming Equations

To simplify the notation, we look for the necessary and sufficient conditions that correspond to a symmetric equilibrium—that is, to conditions for which $R_1 = R_2 = R$.

---

47. See the supplementary section of the chapter on the theory of the firm for a similar use of this condition. Formally, let $F(p_t|Q_t)$ denote the cumulative distribution of the price conditional on the aggregate output, with density $f(p_t|Q_t)$. It satisfies the MLRP if

$$\frac{\partial}{\partial p_t}\left(\frac{\partial f/\partial Q_t}{f}\right) < 0.$$

48. If one restricted punishments to be of the Cournot type, the optimal length of punishment would be $T = +\infty$, from the Abreu-Pearce-Stacchetti result on the harshest possible punishment V^-. This is to be contrasted with Porter's (1983b) demonstration that if the previous assumptions do not hold, the optimal length of Cournot punishments can be finite. This also differs from the above price game, where (Bertrand) punishments are finite. The price game and the quantity game are technically different; the quantity game exhibits a commonly observed variable (the market price) whereas the price game does not.

Consequently, we no longer index the variables by the name of the firm. We assume that there is a finite number of possible prices p_h. R will be interpreted as a Markov chain. That is, there is a finite number of possible states, where the state refers to the price to which one of the firms is currently committed. The reaction function defines a transition from the current state to a new state, which is the price chosen by the other firm in reaction to the current state. Let $\alpha_{hk} \geq 0$ be the transitional probability that the firm (1 or 2) reacts to price p_h by charging price p_k:

$$\sum_k \alpha_{hk} = 1.$$

Finally, let $\Pi(p_k, p_h)$ be the instantaneous profit of the firm (1 or 2) when its price is p_k and the price of its competitor is p_h.

We introduce the valuation functions from dynamic programming. V_h is the discounted value of the profit of a firm that chooses its price when the other firm has chosen p_h in the preceding period. The discounted value of the profit of the second firm is denoted W_h. Using our notation, we have

$$V_h = \max_{p_k} [\Pi(p_k, p_h) + \delta W_k].$$

This yields the following set of equations:

$$V_h = \sum_k \alpha_{hk} [\Pi(p_k, p_h) + \delta W_k],$$

$$W_k = \sum_\ell \alpha_{k\ell} [\Pi(p_k, p_\ell) + \delta V_\ell],$$

$$[V_h - \Pi(p_k, p_h) - \delta W_k] \alpha_{hk} = 0,$$

$$V_h \geq \Pi(p_k, p_h) + \delta W_k,$$ $$(6.17)$$

$$\sum_k \alpha_{hk} \geq 1,$$

$$\alpha_{hk} \geq 0.$$

The first two of these equations simply use the definitions of functions V and W. The third is a relation of complementary slackness. In order for price p_k to be an optimal reaction to price p_h in the maximization exercise associated with the first equation ($\alpha_{hk} > 0$), the discounted

value corresponding to p_k, $\Pi(p_k, p_h) + \delta W_k$, must achieve a maximum of V_h with respect to p_k.

The set of equations 6.17 has as unknowns $\{V_h, W_k, \alpha_{hk}\}$. We are interested only in α_{hk}, which determines the reaction functions. (The system is known mathematically as a complementary bilinear program.)

To check that the kinked-demand-curve strategies of subsection 6.4.1 form an equilibrium, it suffices to compute V_h and W_h for all h from the presumed strategies and check that equations 6.17 are satisfied.

Exercise 6.10** Compute the valuation functions for the strategies described in subsection 6.4.1, compute α, and check that the strategies are in equilibrium for δ close to 1.

6.7.2.3 Profits Are Bounded away from Zero

In the text, it was stated that profits cannot be close to the competitive profit in a Markov perfect equilibrium. Let us show that in a symmetric equilibrium the average industry profit per period must exceed $\Pi(p^m)/2$ (where $\Pi(p) \equiv (p - c)D(p)$) for δ close to 1. (A basically similar proof shows that, even in an asymmetric equilibrium, at least one firm must earn an average profit of no less than $\Pi(p^m)/4$.)

Let $V(p)$ and $W(p)$ denote the present discounted value of profits of the firm whose turn it is to choose a price and of its rival. The price grid is assumed discrete[49] with size k, where k is "small" (e.g., prices are denominated in cents). Let p^m denote the monopoly price, and consider price $p^m + k$. Let p^* be the smallest price that solves

$$\max \left(\max_{p < p^m + k} [\Pi(p) + \delta W(p)], \right.$$

$$\frac{\Pi(p^m + k)}{2} + \delta W(p^m + k), \max_{p > p^m + k} \delta W(p) \left. \right).$$

Then a firm's reaction to $p^m + k$ is not lower than p^*.

Case a: $p^* \geq p^m$

In this case, starting from any price, each firm's payoff

---

49. The reason for taking a discrete-price grid is technical. Even in a static framework, a firm's best reaction to its rival's price is not well defined for perfect substitutes and a continuous price grid (because this firm generally

would like to come as close as possible to its rival's price while strictly undercutting it).

when it plays is at least

$$\delta^2[\Pi(p^m - k) + \delta W(p^m - k)],$$

since it could raise its price to $p^m + k$ and then, after its rival's reaction (which exceeds p^m), undercut to $p^m - k$. For the same reason, we have

$$W(p^m - k) \geqslant \delta^3[\Pi(p^m - k) + \delta W(p^m - k)].$$

Thus,

$$W(p^m - k) \geqslant \frac{\delta^3 \Pi(p^m - k)}{1 - \delta^4},$$

and, hence,

$$\delta^2[\Pi(p^m - k) + \delta W(p^m - k)] \geqslant \frac{\delta^2 \Pi(p^m - k)}{1 - \delta^4}.$$

Thus, each firm's intertemporal profit is at least

$$\left(\frac{\delta^2}{1 + \delta + \delta^2 + \delta^3}\right) \frac{\Pi(p^m - k)}{1 - \delta}$$

when it charges a price, and at least δ times this when it has chosen its price last period. For δ close to 1, this profit is at least

$$\frac{1}{4}\left(\frac{\Pi(p^m - k)}{1 - \delta}\right),$$

which amounts to a per-period profit

$$\frac{\Pi(p^m - k)}{4}$$

close to

$$\frac{\Pi(p^m)}{4}$$

for a fine price grid.

Case b: $p^* < p^m$

In this case we have

$$\Pi(p^*) + \delta W(p^*) \geqslant \Pi(p^m) + \delta W(p^m).$$

On the other hand,

$$W(p^m) \geqslant \delta \frac{\Pi(p^*)}{2} + \delta^2 W(p^*).$$

The latter inequality holds because a firm that is committed to p^m is at worst undercut to p^* and can react to p^* by charging p^* itself. (If its rival charges $p > p^*$, the firm makes at least

$$\delta \Pi(p^*) + \delta^2 W(p^*)$$

by undercutting to p^*.) Multiplying the first inequality by δ and adding the two inequalities yields

$$(1 - \delta)W(p^m) \geqslant \frac{\delta}{1 + \delta}\left(\Pi(p^m) - \frac{\Pi(p^*)}{2}\right).$$

From the definition of the monopoly price, we have

$$\Pi(p^m) - \frac{\Pi(p^*)}{2} \geqslant \frac{\Pi(p^m)}{2},$$

and

$$\frac{\delta}{1 + \delta} \simeq \frac{1}{2}$$

for δ close to 1. Thus, again, the average profit per period and per firm exceeds one-fourth of the monopoly profit.

It can further be shown that in a kinked-demand-curve equilibrium, each firm's per-period profit exceeds $\frac{4}{7}\Pi(p^m)$ for δ close to 1. Conversely, the set of focal prices (steady states for some kinked-demand-curve equilibrium) is exactly the set of prices p under p^m such that $\Pi(p) \geqslant \frac{4}{7}\Pi(p^m)$ and above p^m such that $\Pi(p) \geqslant \frac{2}{3}\Pi(p^m)$. Thus, even though there is no approximately competitive equilibrium, there is a large number of equilibria.

6.7.2.4 The Renegotiation-Proof Equilibrium

Let $\underline{p}$ denote the price under p^m such that

$$(1 + \delta)\Pi(\underline{p}) \geqslant \frac{\delta \Pi(p^m)}{2} > (1 + \delta)\Pi(\underline{p} - k)$$

(where k is, as before, the size of the price grid). Note that for δ close to 1

$$\Pi(\underline{p}) \simeq \Pi(p^m)/4,$$

and consider the following symmetric reaction function:

$$R^*(p) = \begin{cases} \underline{p} & \text{if } \underline{p} < p < p^m \\ p^m & \text{otherwise.} \end{cases}$$

Exercise 6.11** Show that (R^*, R^*) forms a Markov perfect equilibrium for δ close to 1.

(R^*, R^*) turns out to be the unique pair of equilibrium reaction functions that yield average industry profit close to $\Pi(p^m)$ for δ close to 1 (see Maskin and Tirole 1988). This property trivially implies that this is the unique symmetric renegotiation-proof equilibrium for δ close to 1. (It is renegotiation-proof because any other equilibrium yields less aggregate profit, and therefore a lower profit for at least one firm; furthermore, starting from any price, any other symmetric Markov perfect equilibrium yields less profit than this one to both firms, who therefore would have an incentive to "renegotiate" to move to this equilibrium.)

6.7.3 Folk Theorems

In this subsection we recall the existing versions of the Folk theorem.

6.7.3.1 Infinitely Repeated Games of Complete Information

Consider an n-person "static" game defined by action spaces A_i for each player $i = 1, \ldots, n$, and payoff functions $\Pi^i(a_1, \ldots, a_i, \ldots, a_n)$ for each player i, where a_j belongs to A_j. Suppose for simplicity that the set of pure strategies is finite (for instance, in a price game, prices have to be denoted in cents, are non-negative, and are bounded above by a large number). We do not distinguish between pure and mixed strategies, so that we can think of A_i as the set of probability distributions (mixed strategies) over the pure strategies available to player i. (It is also technically convenient to assume that the players can play correlated strategies, i.e., that they can make their actions contingent on the outcome of a public randomizing device; but we will ignore this here.) The static game is often called the "constituent game." We will use the notation

$$a_{-i} = (a_1, \ldots, a_{i-1}, a_{i+1}, \ldots, a_n),$$

and $\Pi^i(a_i, a_{-i})$ for player i's profit.

We define player i's *reservation utility* as the worst outcome player i can be forced to take in this game:

$$\Pi^{i*} = \min_{a_{-i}} \max_{a_i} \Pi^i(a_i, a_{-i}).$$

Anticipating actions a_{-i} by its rivals, player i maximizes $\Pi^i(a_i, a_{-i})$ in a static framework. Clearly, player i cannot get less than Π^{i*} in the constituent game (or less than Π^{i*} "on average" if the constituent game is repeated over time).

A payoff vector $\Pi = (\Pi^1, \ldots, \Pi^i, \ldots, \Pi^n)$ is *individually* rational if, for all i, $\Pi^i > \Pi^{i*}$. It is *feasible* if there exist feasible strategies $a = (a_1, \ldots, a_i, \ldots, a_n)$ such that, for all i, $\Pi^i = \Pi^i(a)$.

For instance, in the Bertrand price game or the Cournot quantity game, the individually rational profits are equal to zero. (Firms cannot be forced to make negative profits; on the other hand, one's opponents' charging a zero price or producing quantities that make the price fall below one's marginal cost prevents the realization of profit.) It is easy to check that any set of profits whose sum does not exceed the monopoly profit is feasible.

Consider the infinitely repeated version of the constituent game. Let δ denote the discount factor. Player i then has payoff

$$V^i = \sum_{t=0}^{\infty} \delta^t \Pi^i(a_1(t), \ldots, a_n(t))$$

and average payoff

$$v^i = (1 - \delta) V^i,$$

where $a_i(t)$ denotes the action chosen by i at t (which is a function of past history).

Our first Folk theorem is due to Friedman (1971). It states that any average payoff vector that is better for all players than a Nash-equilibrium payoff vector of the constituent game can be sustained as the outcome of a perfect equilibrium of the infinitely repeated game if the players are sufficiently patient. More precisely, let

$$\Pi^{iN} = \Pi^i(a_1^N, \ldots, a_n^N),{}^{50}$$

and let $v = (v^1, \ldots, v^n)$ such that v is feasible and $v^i > \Pi^{iN}$ for all i. Then there exists $\delta_0 < 1$ such that, for all $\delta \geq \delta_0$, v is an equilibrium payoff vector.

The proof of this Folk theorem is basically the same as that in the text. For expositional simplicity, suppose that there exist pure strategies $a = (a_1, \ldots, a_n)$ such that $v^i = \Pi^i(a_1, \ldots, a_n)$ for all i. Specify the following behaviors:

---

50. That is, $\Pi^i(a_i^N, a_{-i}^N) \geq \Pi^i(a_i, a_{-i}^N)$ for all i and a_i in A_i.

Each player plays a_i as long as all players have stuck to strategies a before. If someone has deviated in the past, the player plays a_i^N. Thus, collusion on a is enforced through Nash threats—i.e., threats to revert to Nash behavior forever. By deviating today, a player gains at most a bounded amount; on the other hand, he loses the gain from future cooperation:

$$(v^i - \Pi^{iN})(\delta + \delta^2 + \cdots),$$

which tends to infinity as δ tends to 1.

For the Bertrand game (which is potentially one of the most interesting applications of the theory of long repeated interaction, because prices are locked in for short periods of time), this theorem gives a full description of the set of equilibria for δ close to 1. This is because if firms have identical marginal costs, the Nash equilibrium of the constituent game yields zero profits and thus yields the reservation payoffs. The previous theorem then shows that all individually rational and feasible payoffs are equilibrium payoffs for δ close to 1. For other constituent games (e.g., Cournot competition), the Nash points do not yield reservation values (see figure 6.5).

In games in which Nash equilibria lie above the reservation values, the question arises whether other equilibrium payoff vectors beyond those given by the previous theorem can be enforced. The answer is that every individually rational and feasible payoff vector can be enforced in perfect equilibrium. Aumann and Shapley (1976) and Rubinstein (1979) show this in the case $\delta = 1$.[51] The intuition as to why any payoffs above reservation values can be sustained is as follows:

... as long as everyone has previously conformed, players continue to play their a_i's, leading to payoff v_i. If some player j deviates, he is, as before, minimaxed but, rather than forever, only long enough to wipe out any possible gain that he obtained from this deviation. After this punishment, the players go back to their a_i's. To induce the punishers to go through with their minimaxing, they are threatened with the prospect that, if any one of them deviates from his punishment strategy, he in turn will be minimaxed by the others long enough to

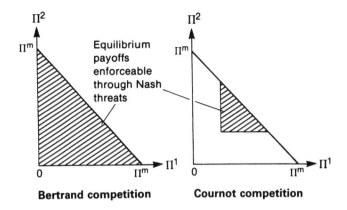

Figure 6.5
Nash threats.

make such a deviation not worthwhile. Moreover, his punishers will be punished if any one of them deviates, etc. Thus, there is a potential sequence of successively higher-order punishments where the punishment at each level is carried out for fear the punishment at the next level will be invoked. (Fudenberg and Maskin 1986a, p. 538)

Fudenberg and Maskin (1986) show that, under a mild regularity condition, lower-hemi continuity holds at $\delta = 1$: All individually rational and feasible payoffs can be sustained in perfect equilibrium for δ sufficiently close to 1.

6.7.3.2 Finitely Repeated Games of Complete Information with Multiple Equilibria in the Constituent Game

We saw in the text that even with a long horizon, collusion cannot be sustained in the finitely repeated Bertrand price game (or prisoner's dilemma). However, when the constituent game has several Nash equilibria, it is possible to play with the various Nash equilibria and obtain equilibria other than the Nash equilibria in the repeated version of the game. This is illustrated for the constituent game (game of coordination) in figure 6.6.

This game has two pure-strategy Nash equilibria: (U, L) and (D, R). Suppose that this game is repeated three times

---

51. In the absence of discounting, the sum of a player's payoffs over time may not be defined (may be infinite). One can then use either the limit (infimum) of the average payoff

$$\frac{1}{T} \sum_{t=0}^{T} \Pi^i(a(t))$$

when T tends to infinity, or the so-called "overtaking criterion" (see Rubinstein 1979).

Player 2 / Player 1	L	R
U	5,5	0,0
D	0,0	1,1

Figure 6.6

and that there is no discounting. Then (D, L), yielding zero payoff to both players in the first period, can be sustained in that period by the promise of coordinating on (U, L) in the two subsequent periods if both players comply, and by the threat of coordinating on (D, R) in the two subsequent periods if anyone deviates in the first period. Because

$$5 + 1 + 1 < 0 + 5 + 5,$$

(D, L) can thus be sustained in the first period.

Benoit and Krishna (1985) show that, under some conditions, the set of equilibria of a repeated game with multiple equilibria in the constituent game converges to the set of individually rational and feasible outcomes.

6.7.3.3 Finitely Repeated Games of Incomplete Information

Here we consider the generalization of the model in subsection 6.5.1. Consider a finitely repeated game in which, with probability $1 - \alpha$, player i is "sane" and is described by the action space A_i and the payoff $\Pi^i(a_1, \ldots, a_n)$ in each period, and in which player i is "crazy" with probability α. (This player's preferences or strategy are then at the disposal of the modeler. See below.)

Fudenberg and Maskin (1986) show that, under a mild condition, the Folk theorem applies, in the sense that any individually rational and feasible payoff vector of the constituent game (for sane players) can be sustained as a perfect Bayesian equilibrium of the finitely repeated game for arbitrary small probability α, as long as the horizon is sufficiently large and the discount factor is sufficiently close to 1.

The proof that any payoff that exceeds a Nash payoff is sustainable is, as usual, simple (see also section 6.5.1). Let us sketch it. Let $a^N = (a_1^N, \ldots, a_n^N)$ denote a Nash equilibrium of the constituent game when players are sane with probability 1. Let Π^{iN} denote the corresponding payoffs, let

$$v^i = \Pi^i(a_1, \ldots, a_n) > \Pi^{iN},$$

and let the crazy player i play a_i as long as all players have done so in the past and a_i^N if anyone has deviated in the past. The one-period payoff from deviating for a sane player is bounded above. At the same time, the loss of future cooperation with the crazy players is $\alpha^{n-1}(v^i - \Pi^{iN})T$ if T is the horizon and if, for simplicity, there is no discounting ($\delta = 1$). This loss goes to infinity as T tends to infinity. Hence, for $T \geq T_0$ it cannot be optimal for player i to deviate from a_i even if he is sane. More generally, collusion on a is sustained during at least $T - T_0$ periods, which means that the average payoff for a sane player i tends to v^i when T tends to infinity.

As usual, this proof yields the full Folk theorem for the Bertrand game. For more general games, the proof of the Folk theorem is more involved; see Fudenberg and Maskin 1986a.

Answers and Hints

Exercise 6.1[52]

(i) Let $\Phi_i(p) \equiv (p - c_i)D(p)$. Note that Φ_i is (by assumption) concave, increases up to the monopoly price p_i^m, and decreases thereafter. After substituting s_1, one gets

$$\Pi^1 = \max_p \Phi_1(p)\left(1 - \frac{\bar{\Pi}^2}{\Phi_2(p)}\right).$$

The first-order condition is

$$\Phi_1'(p)\left(1 - \frac{\bar{\Pi}^2}{\Phi_2(p)}\right) + \Phi_1(p)\frac{\bar{\Pi}^2\Phi_2'(p)}{\Phi_2^2(p)} = 0.$$

This implies that Φ_1' and Φ_2' have opposite signs. Because $p_1^m < p_2^m$, we have $\Phi_1' \leqslant 0 \leqslant \Phi_2'$ and $p_1^m \leqslant p \leqslant p_2^m$. The second-order derivative of the objective function is

$$\Phi_1''(p)\left(1 - \frac{\bar{\Pi}^2}{\Phi_2(p)}\right) + \frac{\Phi_1(p)\bar{\Pi}^2\Phi_2''(p)}{\Phi_2^2(p)}$$
$$- \frac{2\Phi_1(p)\bar{\Pi}^2(\Phi_2'(p))^2}{\Phi_2^3(p)} + \frac{2\Phi_1'(p)\bar{\Pi}^2\Phi_2'(p)}{\Phi_2^2(p)}.$$

The first three terms in this expression are negative. The fourth term is negative when the first-order condition is satisfied. Hence, the objective function is quasi-concave, and we do have an optimum.

(ii) This is straightforward.

(iii) Take the derivative of the first-order condition with respect to p and $\bar{\Pi}^2$. Writing

$$s_2 = -(p - c_2)\Phi_1'(p)/(c_2 - c_1)D(p)$$

and taking the derivative shows that s_2 is an increasing function of p and therefore of $\bar{\Pi}^2$. When the profit target for firm 2 is zero, the highest profit for firm 1 is its monopoly profit and is obtained for $p = p^m(c_1)$ and $s_2 = 0$. Conversely, in order for $\bar{\Pi}^2 = \Pi^m(c_2)$ to be obtained, the price must be $p = p^m(c_2)$, and firm 2 must serve the whole market. More generally, there is a trade-off between aggregate efficiency (which requires $p = p^m(c_1)$ and $s_2 = 0$) and sharing of profits. The higher the profit target for firm 2, the higher the market price and the higher firm 2's market share. See figure 6.7.

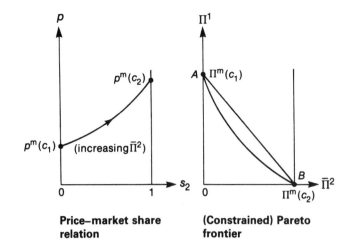

Figure 6.7
Efficient market-sharing allocations.

(iv) From the envelope theorem,

$$\frac{d\Pi^1}{d\bar{\Pi}^2} = -\frac{\Phi_1(p)}{\Phi_2(p)}.$$

Using the chain rule,

$$\frac{d^2\Pi^1}{d\bar{\Pi}^2} = \left(\frac{-\Phi_2(p)\Phi_1'(p) + \Phi_1(p)\Phi_2'(p)}{\Phi_2^2(p)}\right)\frac{dp}{d\bar{\Pi}^2} > 0,$$

because

$$\Phi_1'(p) \leqslant 0 \leqslant \Phi_2'(p),$$

and from question iii,

$$\frac{dp}{d\bar{\Pi}^2} > 0.$$

Schmalensee (1987) uses axiomatic bargaining theory to select a point on this convex Pareto frontier. He observes that, if the leading firm's cost advantage is substantial, its likely gains from collusion are relatively small. (In the extreme case, if the low-cost firm's monopoly price is lower than its rival's marginal cost, the low-cost firm cannot gain from colluding.)

(v) Question iv implies that our "efficient market-sharing allocation" is optimal only in the class of *deterministic* allocations. The firms could obtain higher expected payoffs by "tossing a coin" to decide who will be the monopolist. More formally, the firms could achieve any point on

---

52. This exercise is derived from Bishop 1960 and Schmalensee 1987.

the straight line between A and B in figure 6.7 by letting one of them be a monopolist depending on the realization of a random variable. Alternatively, in a repeated-game context with little impatience (so that the firms' objective is approximately the average of their profits—see section 6.3), the firms could take turns being the monopolist.

(vi) Suppose that firm 1 sells q_1 at price $p_1 < p_2$. Firm 2's residual demand is $D(p_2) - q_1$ under efficient rationing. This demand would be left unaffected if firm 1 raised its price. Hence, firm 1 could continue selling q_1 at a price higher than p_1 without hurting firm 2.

Exercise 6.2

We content ourselves with showing that any payoff (Π^1, Π^2) can be approximated as closely as desired for δ close to 1. Choose a price p in $[c, p^m]$ such that $\Pi(p) = \Pi^1 + \Pi^2$, and let $\Pi^1 \equiv \alpha \Pi(p)$ and $\Pi^2 = (1 - \alpha)\Pi(p)$. Consider the ratio $\alpha/(1 - \alpha)$. We know that any real number can be approximated as closely as is wished by a rational number. Let m/n denote a rational approximation of $\alpha/(1 - \alpha)$. Consider the following strategies: "During the first m periods, firm 1 charges p and firm 2 charges a price strictly exceeding p; for the n subsequent periods, firm 2 charges p and firm 1 charges a price strictly exceeding p; during the m subsequent periods, it is firm 1's turn to have the market at price p; and so forth. If anyone deviates, the firms charge the marginal cost forever." These strategies clearly form an equilibrium for δ close to 1. Furthermore, the per-period payoff for firm 1 is

$$(1-\delta)\Pi(p)[(1 + \delta + \cdots + \delta^{m-1}) + (\delta^{m+n} + \cdots + \delta^{2m+n-1}) + \cdots]$$

$$= \frac{1 + \delta + \cdots + \delta^{m-1}}{1 + \delta + \cdots + \delta^{n+m-1}} \Pi(p) \simeq \frac{m}{m+n}\Pi(p) \simeq \alpha\Pi(p)$$

for δ close to 1.

Exercise 6.3 [53]

The highest possible per-period profit, $\bar{\Pi}$, is the same for both firms (because the game is symmetric, the set of attainable per-period profits is also symmetric). Consider an equilibrium in which firm 1, say, gets a per-period profit $\bar{\Pi} - \varepsilon$ (where ε is positive and small), and consider

a price p such that $\Pi(p) \geqslant \bar{\Pi} - \varepsilon$, price p is the lowest price charged for some period t, and firm 1 makes profits $s_1\Pi(p) \geqslant \bar{\Pi} - \varepsilon$ in that period. (Such a price and period must exist; otherwise firm 1 could not make $\bar{\Pi} - \varepsilon$ "on average.") At t firm 2 ought to deviate and charge slightly less than p. By doing so, it would gain $s_1\Pi(p)/2$ at date t (because it would capture the whole market). But the loss of future collusion costs at most

$$\bar{\Pi}(\delta + \delta^2 + \cdots) = \bar{\Pi}\frac{\delta}{1 - \delta} < \bar{\Pi} - \varepsilon.$$

It suffices to choose ε such that

$$\frac{\bar{\Pi} - \varepsilon}{\bar{\Pi}} > \frac{\delta}{1 - \delta}$$

to obtain the contradiction.

Exercise 6.4

The monopoly price is sustainable if

$$\left(\frac{n-1}{n}\right)\Pi^m \leqslant \frac{\Pi^m}{n}(\delta\mu + \delta^2\mu^2 + \cdots).$$

(The LHS is the gain from deviating; the RHS is the long-term loss.) That is,

$$\delta\mu \geqslant 1 - \frac{1}{n}.$$

For a given δ, this condition is more easily satisfied if the market is expanding. (The intuition is that the future weighs more heavily in such circumstances.)

Exercise 6.5

Let $\{p^*, s_1^*\}$ denote an efficient market-sharing allocation, and let

$$\Pi^{1*} \equiv s_1^* D(p^*)(p^* - c_1)$$

and

$$\Pi^{2*} \equiv (1 - s_1^*)D(p^*)(p^* - c_2)$$

denote the corresponding per-period profits. Consider the following strategies: "Each firm i charges p^* and produces

53. The following proof is from Bernheim and Whinston 1986.

$s_i^* D(p^*)$ as long as both have complied with this rule earlier. If anyone has deviated in the past, both firms revert to Bertrand behavior forever."

Look at the most profitable deviation from equilibrium. For firm 1 it consists of undercutting to its monopoly price. Thus, firm 1 makes a short-term gain equal to $\Pi^{1m} - \Pi^{1*}$, where $\Pi^{1m} \equiv \max[D(p)(p - c_1)]$. The long-term loss is

$$\delta(\Pi^{1*} - (c_2 - c_1)D(c_2))/(1 - \delta),$$

where $(c_2 - c_1)D(c_2)$ is firm 1's profit in the Bertrand equilibrium. Thus, the market-sharing allocation must satisfy

$$\Pi^{1m} - \Pi^{1*} \leqslant \delta(\Pi^{1*} - (c_2 - c_1)D(c_2))/(1 - \delta). \quad (1)$$

Note that, for a given δ, this is satisfied if and only if Π^{1*} exceeds some given level, or $s_1^* \geqslant \underline{s}_1(\delta) > 0$, where $\underline{s}_1(\delta)$ is defined by (1) (recall that Π^{1*} is a linear function of s_1^*).

Firm 2's optimal deviation from p^* is to undercut slightly and capture the whole market (because $p^* \leqslant p^m(c_2)$). It then realizes a short-term gain of almost $s_1^* D(p^*)(p^* - c_2)$. The long-term loss is $\Pi^{2*}/(1 - \delta)$, because the firm makes no profit in the Bertrand equilibrium. Thus, we must have

$$s_1^* D(p^*)(p^* - c_2) \leqslant \delta(1 - s_1^*)D(p^*)(p^* - c_2)/(1 - \delta);$$

that is,

$$s_1^*/(1 - s_1^*) \leqslant \delta/(1 - \delta),$$

or

$$s_1^* \leqslant \delta.$$

Hence, the efficient market-sharing allocation is sustainable in equilibrium if $\underline{s}_1(\delta) \leqslant s_1^* \leqslant \delta$.[54] This naturally means that *an efficient market-sharing arrangement can be sustained only if it is "not too unfair" to one of the firms.*

As was noted in section 6.2, the firms could do even better by taking turns being monopolists, because the Pareto frontier in the payoff space is convex. For instance, firm 1 could supply the whole demand at p_1^m in odd periods and firm 2 the whole demand at price p_2^m in even periods. (In case of deviation, the firms would revert to competitive behavior.) The per-period profits would then be approximately $\Pi_1^m/2$ and $\Pi_2^m/2$, respectively, for δ close to 1.

Exercise 6.6

(i) The implicit discount factor in market 2 is δ^2—a firm can deviate during two consecutive periods without being detected.

(ii) The optimal deviation is to start with market 2 and then deviate on both markets in the following period (a deviation in market 1 triggers punishment in the following period). Thus, the maximal gain from deviating is

$$\frac{\Pi^m}{2}(1 + 2\delta).$$

The loss is

$$\delta^2 \Pi^m/(1 - \delta),$$

because the deviation is detected with a two-period lag, and collusive profits are $\Pi^m/2$ per market.

Exercise 6.7

Making price quotations public reduces the scope for bribery and favoritism. However, it may help the participating firms to tacitly collude by giving the industry information about price cuts. At least, so runs the conventional wisdom: "It would ... be hard to find a device less calculated to foster open and aggressive competition among [oligopolistic] sellers." (Cook 1963) (See also Scherer 1980, p. 224.)

Things are more complicated in fact. The theory developed in this section and in subsection 6.7.1 assumes a random and unobservable demand, whereas in the case of public bids the demand is generally known to all parties (so firms may learn that undercutting took place by observing who wins, even if bids are kept secret). More work seems warranted to assess this facet of the conventional wisdom.

---

54. Such s_1^* may not exist. But, as can be checked, it does exist as long as

$\Pi^{1*} > (c_2 - c_1)D(c_2)$

and δ is sufficiently close to 1.

Exercise 6.8

See section 6.7. For $\alpha = \frac{1}{4}$, T is the lowest time such that $3\delta - \delta^{T+1} \geqslant 2$. Hence, $\delta \geqslant \frac{2}{3}$ if this condition is to be satisfied for some T. For $T = 1$, it is not satisfied unless $\delta = 1$.

Exercise 6.9

See Green and Porter 1984.

Exercise 6.10

(All payoffs are multiplied by 36.)

$$V_6 = V_5 = V_4 = 9 + \delta[4.5/(1-\delta)] = 4.5\left(\frac{2-\delta}{1-\delta}\right),$$

$$V_3 = 4.5/(1-\delta) = W_3,$$

$$V_2 = 5 + \delta W_1,$$

$$V_1 = V_0 = \frac{\delta}{1-\delta}4.5 = W_6 = W_5 = W_4 = W_0,$$

$$W_2 = \frac{\delta^2}{1-\delta}4.5,$$

$$W_1 = \alpha\left(5 + \frac{\delta}{1-\delta}4.5\right) + (1-\alpha)\left(2.5 + \frac{\delta^2}{1-\delta}4.5\right).$$

The probability α is such that $V_1 = 2.5 + \delta W_1$ (each firm is indifferent between staying at p_1 and relenting to the monopoly price). Thus,

$$\alpha = (4\delta + 9\delta^2 - 5)/(5\delta + 9\delta^2)$$

(that is, α is approximately equal to $\frac{4}{7}$ for δ close to 1).

Checking that the strategies form an equilibrium is a bit tedious. We saw in the text that undercutting from p_3 to p_2 is not profitable. Let us simply show that at p_2 a firm prefers to undercut to p_1 rather than to revert to the monopoly price. By undercutting, it gets

$$5 + \delta W_1 = 5 + (V_1 - 2.5)$$

$$= 2.5 + V_1 = 2.5 + \frac{\delta}{1-\delta}4.5 > \frac{\delta}{1-\delta}4.5,$$

which is what it would get by relenting.

Exercise 6.11

See Maskin and Tirole 1988.

References

Abreu, D. 1983. Repeated Games with Discounting: A General Theory and an Application to Oligopoly. Ph.D. thesis, Department of Economics, Princeton University.

Abreu, D. 1986. Extremal Equilibria of Oligopolistic Supergames. *Journal of Economic Theory* 39: 191–225.

Abreu, D. 1987. On the Theory of Infinitely Repeated Games with Discounting. *Econometrica*, forthcoming.

Abreu, D., and A. Rubinstein. 1986. The Structure of Nash Equilibria in Repeated Games with Finite Automatas. Mimeo, Harvard University.

Abreu, D., D. Pearce, and E. Stachetti. 1985. Optimal Cartel Equilibria with Imperfect Monitoring. *Journal of Economic Theory* 39: 251–269.

Abreu, D., D. Pearce, and E. Stachetti. 1986. Toward A Theory of Discounted Repeated Games with Imperfect Monitoring. Mimeo.

Alchian, A. 1950. Uncertainty, Evolution and Economic Theory. *Journal of Political Economy* 58: 211–222.

Appelbaum, E. 1982. The Estimation of the Degree of Oligopoly Power. *Journal of Econometrics* 19: 287–299.

Arrow, K., M. Beckmann, and S. Karlin. 1958. The Optimal Expansion of the Capacity of a Firm. In Arrow, Karlin, and Scarf 1958.

Arrow, K., S. Karlin, and H. Scarf. 1958. *Studies of Mathematical Theory of Inventory and Production.* Stanford University Press.

Aumann, R., and L. Shapley. 1976. Long Term Competition: A Game Theoretic Analysis. Mimeo.

Aumann, R., and S. Sorin. 1986. Bounded Rationality and Cooperation. Mimeo, Hebrew University, Jerusalem.

Axelrod, R. 1980. Effective Choice in the Prisoner's Dilemma. *Journal of Conflict Resolution* 24: 3–25.

Axelrod, R. 1981. The Emergence of Cooperation among Egoists. *American Political Science Review* 28: 1–12.

Axelrod, R. 1984. *The Evolution of Cooperation.* New York: Basic Books.

Axelrod, R., and W. Hamilton. 1981. The Evolution of Cooperation. *Science* 211: 1390–1396.

Bain, J. 1956. *Barriers to New Competition.* Cambridge, Mass.: Harvard University Press.

Barro, R. 1972. A Theory of Monopolistic Price Adjustment. *Review of Economic Studies* 39: 17–26.

Bénabou, R. 1985. Optimal Price Dynamics and Speculation with a Storable Good. Ph.D. thesis, Department of Economics, Massachusetts Institute of Technology.

Benoit, J.-P., and V. Krishna. 1985. Finitely Repeated Games. *Econometrica* 53: 890–904.

Benoit, J.-P., and V. Krishna. 1987. Dynamic Duopoly: Prices and Quantities. *Review of Economic Studies* 54: 23−36.

Bernheim, D., and M. Whinston. 1986. Multimarket Contact and Collusive Behavior. Mimeo, Department of Economics, Harvard University.

Bishop, R. 1960. Duopoly: Collusion or Warfare? *American Economic Review* 50: 933−961.

Blanchard, O. 1983. Price Asynchronization and Price Level Inertia. In *Inflation, Debt and Indexation*, ed. R. Dornbusch and M. Simonsen. Cambridge, Mass.: MIT Press.

Bowley, A. 1924. *The Mathematical Groundwork of Economics.* Oxford University Press.

Bresnahan, T. 1981. The Relationship between Price and Marginal Cost in the U.S. Automobile Industry. *Journal of Econometrics* 17: 201−227.

Bresnahan, T. 1987a. Competition and Collusion in the American Automobile Industry: The 1955 Price War. *Journal of Industrial Economics* 35: 457−482.

Bresnahan, T. 1987b. Empirical Studies of Industries with Market Power. In *Handbook of Industrial Organization*, ed. R. Schmalensee and R. Willig (Amsterdam: North-Holland, forthcoming).

Brock, W., and J. Scheinkman. 1985. Price Setting Supergames with Capacity Constraints. *Review of Economic Studies* 52: 371−382.

Caplin, A., and D. Spulber. 1987. Inflation, Menu Costs, and Endogenous Price Variability. *Quarterly Journal of Economics* 102: 703−726.

Chamberlin, E. 1929. Duopoly: Value Where Sellers Are Few. *Quarterly Journal of Economics* 43: 63−100.

Chamberlin, E. 1933. *The Theory of Monopolistic Competition.* Cambridge, Mass.: Harvard University Press.

Cook, P. 1963. Facts and Fancy on Identical Bids. *Harvard Business Review* 41: 67−72.

Davidson, C., and R. Deneckere. 1985. Excess Capacity and Collusion. Discussion Paper 675, DMSEMS, Northwestern University.

Eaton, J., and M. Engers. 1987. International Price Competition. Mimeo, University of Virginia.

Farrell, J., and E. Maskin. 1986. Renegotiation in Repeated Games. Mimeo, Harvard University.

Friedman, J. 1971. A Noncooperative Equilibrium for Supergames. *Review of Economic Studies* 28: 1−12.

Friedman, J. 1977. *Oligopoly and the Theory of Games.* Amsterdam: North-Holland.

Fudenberg, D., and D. Levine. 1987. Reputation and Equilibrium Selection in Games with a Patient Player. Mimeo, Massachusetts Institute of Technology.

Fudenberg, D., and E. Maskin. 1986. The Folk Theorem in Repeated Games with Discounting and with Incomplete Information. *Econometrica* 54: 533−54.

Fudenberg, D., Levine, D., and Maskin, E. 1988. The Folk Theorem in Discounted Repeated Games with Imperfect Public Information. Mimeo, MIT.

Gertner, R. 1986. Dynamic Duopoly with Price Inertia. Ph.D. thesis, Department of Economics, Massachusetts Institute of Technology.

Green, E., and R. Porter. 1984. Non-cooperative Collusion Under Imperfect Price Information. *Econometrica* 52: 87−100.

Hall, R., and C. Hitch. 1939. Price Theory and Business Behavior. *Oxford Economic Papers* 2: 12−45.

Hirshleifer, J. 1977. Economics from a Biological Viewpoint. *Journal of Law and Economics* 20: 1−52.

Iwata, G. 1974. Measurement of Conjectural Variations in Oligopoly. *Econometrica* 42: 947−966.

Kalai, E., and W. Stanford. 1986. Finite Rationality and Interpersonal Complexity in Repeated Games. Mimeo, Northwestern University.

Kreps. D., P. Milgrom, J. Roberts, and R. Wilson. 1982. Rational Cooperation in the Finitely Repeated Prisoner's Dilemma. *Journal of Economic Theory* 27: 245−252.

Maskin, E., and J. Tirole. 1985. A Theory of Dynamic Oligopoly: II: Price Competition. MIT Working Paper 373.

Maskin, E., and J. Tirole. 1988. A Theory of Dynamic Oligopoly: II: Price Competition, Kinked Demand Curves and Edgeworth Cycles. *Econometrica*, forthcoming.

Maskin, E., R. Myerson, and R. Radner. 1986. An Example of a Repeated Partnership Game with Discounting and with Uniformly Inefficient Equilibria. *Review of Economic Studies* 53: 59−70.

Maynard Smith, J. 1974. The Theory of Games and the Evolution of Animal Conflict. *Journal of Theoretical Biology* 47: 209−221.

Maynard Smith, J. 1978. The Evolution of Behavior. *Scientific American* 239, no. 3: 176−192.

Milgrom, P. 1984. Axelrod's *The Evolution of Cooperation. Rand Journal of Economics* 15: 305−309.

Milgrom, P. 1985. Auction Theory. In *Advances in Economic Theory*, ed. T. Bewley (Cambridge University Press, forthcoming).

Mills, E. 1962. *Price, Output and Inventories.* New York: Wiley.

Mookherjee, D., and D. Ray. 1986. Collusive Market Structure under Learning by Doing and Increasing Returns. Report RP 884-R, Stanford University Graduate School of Business.

Nelson, R., and S. Winter. 1982. *An Evolutionary Theory of Economic Change.* Cambridge, Mass.: Harvard University Press.

Orr, D., and P. MacAvoy. 1965. Price Strategies to Promote Cartel Stability. *Econometrica* 32: 186−197.

Ortega-Reichert, A. 1967. Models for Competitive Bidding under Uncertainty. Ph.D. thesis, Stanford University.

Pearce, D. 1987. Renegotiation-Proof Equilibria: Collective Rationality and Intertemporal Cooperation. Mimeo, Yale University.

Porter, M. 1983. *Cases in Competitive Strategy*. New York: Free Press.

Porter, R. 1983a. A Study of Cartel Stability: The Joint Economic Committee, 1880–1886. *Bell Journal of Economics* 14: 301–314.

Porter, R. 1983b. Optimal Cartel Trigger Price Strategies. *Journal of Economic Theory* 29: 313–338.

Riordan, M. 1985. Imperfect Information and Dynamic Conjectural Variations. *Rand Journal of Economics* 16: 41–50.

Rotemberg, J., and G. Saloner. 1985a. Strategic Inventories and the Excess Volatility of Production. Mimeo, Massachusetts Institute of Technology.

Rotemberg, J., and G. Saloner. 1985b. Price Leadership. Mimeo, Massachusetts Institute of Technology.

Rotemberg, J., and G. Saloner. 1986. A Supergame-Theoretic Model of Business Cycles and Price Wars during Booms. *American Economic Review* 76: 390–407.

Rubinstein, A. 1979. Equilibrium in Supergames with the Overtaking Criterion. *Journal of Economic Theory* 21: 1–9.

Rubinstein, A. 1986. Finite Automata Play the Repeated Prisoner's Dilemma. *Journal of Economic Theory* 39: 83–96.

Schelling, T. 1960. *The Strategy of Conflict*. Cambridge, Mass.: Harvard University Press.

Scherer, F. 1980. *Industrial Market Structure and Economic Performance*, second edition. Chicago: Rand-McNally.

Schmalensee, R. 1987. Competitive Advantage and Collusive Optima. *International Journal of Industrial Organization* 5: 351–368.

Shapiro, C. 1986. Theories of Oligopolistic Behavior. In *The Handbook of Industrial Organization*, ed. R. Schmalensee and R. Willig (Amsterdam: North-Holland, forthcoming).

Sheshinski, E., and Y. Weiss. 1977. Inflation and Costs of Price Adjustment. *Review of Economic Studies* 44: 287–304.

Sheshinski, E., and Y. Weiss. 1983. Optimum Pricing Policy under Stochastic Inflation. *Review of Economic Studies* 50: 513–529.

Slade, M. 1985. Price Wars in Price Setting Supergames. Mimeo, University of British Columbia.

Stigler, G. 1947. The Kinky Oligopoly Demand Curve and Rigid Prices. *Journal of Political Economy* 55: 442–444.

Stigler, G. 1964. A Theory of Oligopoly. *Journal of Political Economy* 72: 44–61.

Sultan, R. 1975. Pricing in the Electrical Oligopoly. Division of Research, Harvard Graduate School of Business Administration.

Sumner, D. 1981. Measurement of Monopoly Behavior: An Application to the Cigarette Industry. *Journal of Political Economy* 89: 1010–1019.

Sweezy, P. 1939. Demand under Conditions of Oligopoly. *Journal of Political Economy* 47: 568–573.

Telser, L. 1960. Why Should Manufacturers Want Fair Trade? *Journal of Law and Economics* 3: 86–105.

van Damme, E. 1986. Renegotiation-Proof Equilibria in Repeated Prisoner's Dilemma. Mimeo, Universität Bonn.

Zabel, E. 1972. Multiperiod Monopoly under Uncertainty. *Journal of Economic Theory* 5: 524–536.

Product Differentiation: Price Competition and Non-Price Competition

One of the crucial assumptions behind the Bertrand paradox (chapter 5) is that firms produce a homogeneous product. Hence, price is the only variable of interest to consumers, and no firm can raise its price above marginal cost without losing its entire market share. In practice, such an assumption is unlikely to be satisfied. Some consumers will prefer buying the firm's brand even at a small premium because it is available at a closer store, can be delivered sooner, or comes with superior post-sale services; some other consumers will remain faithful to the high-price firm because they are unaware of the existence of other brands; still other consumers will be concerned that alternative brands do not have the same quality or will not satisfy their preferences as well. In short, the products are differentiated; the cross-elasticity of demand is not infinite at equal prices. As was noted in chapter 5, it is clear that a price above marginal cost can (and therefore will) be sustained under product differentiation. Diversity prevents unbridled competition for customers, even in a nonrepeated relationship. This chapter addresses two main issues: the determination of prices under differentiated products (assuming a nonrepeated interaction) and the choice of products in oligopoly. This chapter thus extends the analysis of chapter 2 by including the effects of strategic interaction.

Prices can often be adjusted faster than product characteristics can. To formalize this we will assume that firms competing in prices take these characteristics as given. Consequently, firms will choose their products anticipating that their location in product space will affect the intensity of price competition. In making these assumptions, we conform to the literature, which envisions a world where products are chosen first and prices second (similar to the way capacities were chosen before prices in chapter 5).

The main points will be illustrated by means of two classic models. The first is the so-called *location* or *spatial-*

differentiation model,[1] in which different consumers are located at different places (see Hotelling 1929). Another interpretation of this model is that consumers have heterogeneous tastes which lie on a continuum; for instance, a consumer's "location" may represent the degree of sweetness he prefers most. Firms are not located at each potential location, possibly as the result of fixed costs. Thus, consumers pay transportation costs when going to purchase the good. (In the taste interpretation, they incur a utility loss from not consuming their preferred commodity.)

We begin solving this model by finding the Bertrand-Nash equilibrium of the (static) price competition game, taking the firms' locations as given. Calculating the equilibrium prices, we obtain the firms' reduced-form profit functions conditional on their locations. The next stage looks at the firms' entry and location decisions (non-price competition). At this stage, it suffices to work with the reduced-form profit functions and consider only the entry and location decision of each firm.

We then develop the *principle of differentiation*, according to which firms generally do not want to locate at the same place in the product space. The reason is simply the Bertrand paradox: Two firms producing perfect substitutes face unbridled price competition (at least in a static framework). In contrast, product differentiation establishes clienteles ("market niches," in the business terminology) and allows firms to enjoy some market power over these clienteles. Thus, firms usually wish to differentiate themselves from other firms. However, market conditions place certain restrictions on this differentiation. For example, supermarkets cannot be located just anywhere, and little diversity is possible among laundry detergents, food flavorings, or even cameras. (Firms may nonetheless seek to differentiate themselves through gadgetry or advertising.)

As was just mentioned, not all technically feasible goods will be produced. Often two or three models are selected even though thousands are possible *a priori*. This incomplete spectrum of goods is closely related to the existence of fixed costs (capital, personnel, research and development, etc.). To produce all imaginable goods would imply a huge expense in fixed costs, and the demand for most of these products would never be sufficient to make them profitable. Therefore, fixed costs limit the spectrum.

Next, we make the assumption that there are many potential firms (more than the number of firms that will eventually be operative, and perhaps an infinite number). Since in later chapters we will consider technological differences, we also assume here that all potential firms have the same technology. These two properties combine to yield an assumption of "free entry." What is the effect of this assumption on equilibrium profit? We already know that an entering firm must make a non-negative profit. Under the assumption of free entry, the profit of existing firms (assuming that the profit is the same for all firms) cannot be too large; otherwise, entry would occur until profit had decreased sufficiently to make further entry unprofitable. Therefore, the assumption of free entry naturally leads to that of approximately zero profit (actually, this intuition is valid only if the market is sufficiently large). To simplify our calculations, we will often assume that profits are zero. This assumption may lead to the number of firms being calculated as a noninteger. In such a case the actual solution, which must be an integer, is the integer closest to but not exceeding the real number calculated.

In section 7.1 we develop two standard models of spatial differentiation: "on the line" and "on the circle." We use these examples to demonstrate the nature of Bertrand competition with differentiated products, to enunciate the principle of differentiation, and to study free-entry equilibria. We also discuss product diversity and the number of goods in both a market economy and a social optimum. We conclude that section by discussing some factors that reduce the incentive to differentiate from other firms. In the supplementary section we consider another important model of product differentiation—one that uses the vertical-differentiation model introduced in chapter 2—to formalize quality competition. Because the analysis here closely parallels that of horizontal differentiation, the points of divergence between the quality model and the location model will be indicated.[2]

In section 7.2 we consider the concept of "monopolistic competition," introduced by Chamberlin (1933).

---

1. See chapter 2 for a description of horizontal differentiation.

2. For interesting applications of these models to the beer industry and the automobile industry, see Baker and Bresnahan 1985 and Bresnahan 1987.

Monopolistic competition refers to an "industry" with a large number of firms, each facing a downward-sloping demand (for differentiated products) but making no profit because of fixed costs, and such that strategic interaction is absent (i.e., each firm can ignore its impact on other firms). As we will see, this latter property distinguishes the monopolistically competitive situations from the zero-profit equilibrium studied in the spatial-differentiation model. The supplementary section applies the familiar model of Dixit and Stiglitz (1977) and Spence (1976) to an analysis of product diversity in a monopolistically competitive economy.

In section 7.3, ideas developed in sections 7.1 and 7.2 are used to study informational differentiation, another type of product differentiation that results from consumers' uneven information about the characteristics (existence, price, quality, etc.) of various products. We focus on the link between advertising and differentiation. After reviewing the conventional wisdom on advertising, we will see how informative advertising can increase the elasticity of demand for a product and foster competition. We will also see that competition may yield (from a social standpoint) too much or too little informative advertising.

7.1 Spatial Competition

7.1.1 The Linear City

We first consider a model (originally due to Hotelling [1929]) in which a "linear city" of length 1 lies on the abscissa of a line and consumers are uniformly distributed with density 1 along this interval. There are two firms or stores, which sell the same physical good. For simplicity, and as a first step, these two stores are located at the extremes of the city; store 1 is at $x = 0$ and store 2 at $x = 1$. The unit cost of the good for each store is c. Consumers incur a transportation cost t per unit of length (this cost may include the value of time spent in travel). Thus, a consumer living at x incurs a cost of tx to go to store 1 and a cost of $t(1 - x)$ to go to store 2. The consumers have unit demands; i.e., each consumes one or zero unit of the good. Each consumer derives a surplus

from consumption (gross of price and transportation costs) equal to $\bar{s}$.

We will also consider a variant of this model in which the transportation costs are quadratic instead of linear. In this case, a consumer at x incurs a cost of tx^2 to go to store 1 and a cost of $t(1 - x)^2$ to go to store 2. In this version, the marginal transportation cost increases with the distance to the store. As we will see, the quadratic model is sometimes more tractable than the linear one.

7.1.1.1 Price Competition

In this subsection we take the firms' locations as given and look for the Nash equilibrium in prices. Assuming that firms choose their prices p_1 and p_2 simultaneously,[3] we derive the demand function for *quadratic* transportation costs. Let us assume that the prices of the two firms do not differ so much that one firm faces no demand, and that the prices are not too high relative to $\bar{s}$ (so that all consumers buy—i.e., the market is covered). The first condition must clearly be satisfied in equilibrium, because a firm with no demand makes no profit and therefore has an incentive to lower its price to gain market share. The second condition is satisfied in equilibrium if the consumers' surplus from the good $\bar{s}$ is sufficiently large.

A consumer who is indifferent between the two firms is located at $x = D_1(p_1, p_2)$, where x is given by equating generalized costs; i.e.,

$$p_1 + tx^2 = p_2 + t(1 - x)^2.$$

The firms' respective demands are

$$D_1(p_1, p_2) = x = \frac{p_2 - p_1 + t}{2t}$$

and

$$D_2(p_1, p_2) = 1 - x = \frac{p_1 - p_2 + t}{2t}.$$

When the firms are located at the two extremes of the city, the demand functions are the same for linear cost as for quadratic cost. (This is not robust. It does not hold if the market is not covered, and, as we will see shortly, it is contingent on the locations' being the two

3. For the derivation of the demand functions for linear transportation costs, see section 2.1.

extremities of the city.) In both cases, firm i's profit is

$$\Pi^i(p_i, p_j) = (p_i - c)(p_j - p_i + t)/2t.$$

The goods produced by the two firms are strategic complements in prices ($\Pi^i_{ij} > 0$). This important property will hold for all the models in this chapter except that of monopolistic competition, in which interaction is absent. Its role will be clarified in the next chapter.

For either linear or quadratic transportation costs, firm i chooses p_i so as to maximize its profit given the price p_j charged by its rival; i.e.,

$$\Pi^i = \max_{p_i} [\Pi^i(p_i, p_j)].$$

The first-order condition for firm i is

$$p_j + c + t - 2p_i = 0,$$

and the second-order condition is satisfied. Using the symmetry of the problem, we obtain the competitive prices and profits under product differentiation:

$$p_1^c = p_2^c = c + t \qquad (7.1)$$

and

$$\Pi^1 = \Pi^2 = t/2. \qquad (7.2)$$

We speak of differentiated products even though they are physically identical. The products are differentiated more for the consumer when the transportation cost is higher. When t increases, both stores compete less strenuously for "the same consumers"; indeed, the neighboring clientele of a store becomes more captive, giving the store "monopoly power" (which, in turn, allows it to increase its price). On the other hand, when $t = 0$ all the consumers can go to either store for the same cost (0). The absence of product differentiation leads to the Bertrand result.

Because we are also interested in the firms' choice of product differentiation, we would like to know how the equilibrium prices vary with the firms' locations. We have

looked at one polar case—the one in which firms are located as far as possible from each other (maximal differentiation). The other polar case is that in which they produce the same product—i.e., they are located at the same point (say x_0) and their goods are perfect substitutes. Comparing the generalized costs $p_i + t|x - x_0|$ (or, in the quadratic case, $p_i + t(x - x_0)^2$) for a consumer located at any point x amounts to just comparing prices p_1 and p_2. Hence, the Bertrand result holds for identical locations:

$$p_1^c = p_2^c = 0 \qquad (7.3)$$

and

$$\Pi^1 = \Pi^2 = 0. \qquad (7.4)$$

More generally, let us assume that firm 1 is located at point $a \geq 0$ and firm 2 at point $1 - b$, where $b \geq 0$ and, without loss of generality, $1 - a - b \geq 0$ (firm 1 is to the "left" of firm 2; $a = b = 0$ corresponds to maximal differentiation and $a + b = 1$ corresponds to minimal differentiation, i.e., perfect substitutes). The linear-cost model is not very tractable if firms are located inside the interval, because when a firm lowers its price to the point that it just attracts the consumers located between the two firms it also attracts all consumers located on the other side of the rival.[4] The firms' demand functions are discontinuous. Their profit functions are discontinuous and nonconcave. Consequently, the price-competition problem is not well behaved. Indeed, d'Aspremont, Gabszewicz, and Thisse (1979) show that if the firms are located close to the center of the segment (but not at the same location), no pure-strategy price equilibrium exists.[5]

The quadratic-cost model allows us to sidestep these technical issues. The demand and profit functions are well behaved (continuous and concave). We obtain

$$D_1(p_1, p_2) = x = a + \frac{1 - a - b}{2} + \frac{p_2 - p_1}{2t(1 - a - b)} \qquad (7.5)$$

---

4. Suppose that a consumer is located at $x \geq 1 - b > a$. This consumer belongs to firm 2's "turf" or "back yard." His choice between the two firms is determined by the comparison between

$$p_1 + t(x - a)$$

and

$$p_2 + t[x - (1 - b)],$$

i.e., between p_1 and $p_2 - t(1 - a - b)$. Thus, all consumers located to the right of firm 2 always make the same brand choice as the consumer located at firm 2's location. This means that at $p_1 = p_2 - t(1 - a - b)$ the demand functions are discontinuous; all consumers on firm 2's turf switch to firm 1 for a small reduction in p_1.

5. A mixed-strategy price equilibrium does exist. See Dasgupta and Maskin 1986.

and

$$D_2(p_1, p_2) = 1 - x = b + \frac{1 - a - b}{2} + \frac{p_1 - p_2}{2t(1 - a - b)}$$
(7.6)

(as long as these are non-negative and do not exceed 1 and as long as $\bar{s}$ is sufficiently large that the market is covered).

To interpret equation 7.5, notice that for equal prices firm 1 controls its own turf (of size a) and receives the half of the consumers located between the two firms who are closer to firm 1 (numerically, $(1 - b - a)/2$). The third term of equation 7.5 expresses the sensitivity of demand to the price differential.

The Nash equilibrium in prices, which always exists, is

$$p_1^c(a, b) = c + t(1 - a - b)\left(1 + \frac{a - b}{3}\right),$$
(7.7)

$$p_2^c(a, b) = c + t(1 - a - b)\left(1 + \frac{b - a}{3}\right).$$
(7.8)

Exercise 7.1* Check equations 7.5 through 7.8.

7.1.1.2 Product Choice

Suppose now that there are two firms and that each firm is allowed to choose only one product (that is, only one location). This defines a two-stage game in which (1) the firms choose their locations simultaneously and (2) given the locations, they choose prices simultaneously. As was mentioned earlier, each firm must anticipate how its choice of location affects not only its demand function but also the intensity of price competition. Therefore, to study location (product) competition, we use the reduced-form profit functions, e.g.,

$$\Pi^1(a, b) = [p_1^c(a, b) - c]D_1[a, b, p_1^c(a, b), p_2^c(a, b)],$$
(7.9)

where D_1 is given by equation 7.5. An equilibrium in location is such that firm 1 maximizes $\Pi^1(a, b)$ with respect to a, taking b as given, and similarly for firm 2. (This procedure is similar to the two-stage, capacity-and-then-price competition studied in chapter 5.)

D'Aspremont et al. (1979) show that for quadratic transportation costs, the equilibrium has the two firms locating at the two extremes of the city (*maximal differentiation*). Each firm locates far from its rival in order not

to trigger a low price from the rival, and thus price competition is softened. To show this, we could compute the reduced-form profit functions $\Pi^i(a, b)$ explicitly using equations 7.5 through 7.8 and solve for a Nash equilibrium; however, it is more elegant and instructive to proceed otherwise. Suppose, without loss of generality, that in equilibrium

$$0 \leq a \leq 1 - b \leq 1.$$

We know that to maximize $\Pi^1(a, b)$ (given by equation 7.9) with respect to a we need not take the derivative

$$\frac{\partial \Pi^1}{\partial p_1} \frac{\partial p_1^c}{\partial a}.$$

This is due to the envelope theorem: Firm 1 maximizes with respect to price in the second period, so $\partial \Pi^1 / \partial p_1 = 0$. Thus, we need only look at the direct effect of a on Π^1 (the *demand effect*) and the indirect effect through the change in firm 2's price (the *strategic effect*). That is,

$$\frac{d\Pi^1}{da} = (p_1^c - c)\left(\frac{\partial D_1}{\partial a} + \frac{\partial D_1}{\partial p_2} \frac{dp_2^c}{da}\right).$$

Using equations 7.5, 7.7, and 7.8 we get

$$\frac{\partial D_1}{\partial a} = \frac{1}{2} + \frac{p_2^c - p_1^c}{2t(1 - a - b)^2} = \frac{3 - 5a - b}{6(1 - a - b)},$$
(7.10)

and using equations 7.5 and 7.8 we get

$$\frac{\partial D_1}{\partial p_2} \frac{dp_2^c}{da} = \left(\frac{1}{2t(1 - a - b)}\right)\left[t\left(-\frac{4}{3} + \frac{2a}{3}\right)\right]$$

$$= \frac{-2 + a}{3(1 - a - b)}.$$
(7.11)

Adding equations 7.10 and 7.11 and using the fact that the mark-up ($p_1^c - c$) is positive, we can easily show that $d\Pi^1/da < 0$. Hence, firm 1 always wants to move leftward if it is to the left of firm 2, and similarly for firm 2. Therefore, the equilibrium in locations exhibits maximal differentiation.

Use of the envelope theorem (which will be reiterated in the next chapter) is also instructive. It exhibits the conflict between two effects. First, equation 7.10 shows that if a is not too big (in particular, if it does not exceed $\frac{1}{2}$, using $1 - b \geq a$), firm 1 will want to move toward the center to increase its market share given the price structure. This is part of a more general result that, for given prices, the two firms want to locate at or near the center (see subsection 7.1.3). However, firm 1 also acknowledges that the associated decrease in product differentiation forces firm 2 to lower its price. The computations show that this strategic effect dominates the market-share effect.

It is interesting to compare the market-determined locations to the socially optimal ones. Suppose that the social planner chooses locations for the two firms. Because consumption is fixed, the social planner minimizes the consumers' average transportation cost (this holds whether the firms exercise their market power as above or are forced to price at marginal cost; for given locations, and as long as the market is covered, the pricing structure does not affect the sum of consumer surplus and profits in this inelastic-demand model). By symmetry of the problem, the social planner chooses to locate the two firms equidistantly on either side of the middle of the segment, so that for equal prices a firm serves the left or the right half of the market. Hence, the location that minimizes the average transportation cost on a market segment is the middle of this market segment when the density of consumers is uniform. Thus, the socially optimal locations are $\frac{1}{4}$ and $\frac{3}{4}$. In this example, the market outcome yields socially too much product differentiation.

*Exercise 7.2*** Consider the model of differentiation on the line. The two firms' locations are fixed, and they are the two extremities of the segment. Transportation costs are linear in distance, and the distribution of consumers is uniform along the segment. The firms have constant marginal costs, c_1 and c_2, which are not necessarily equal (but, for simplicity, assume that they do not differ too much, so that each firm has a positive market share in equilibrium).

(i) Compute the reaction functions $p_i = R_i(p_j)$. Infer the Nash-equilibrium prices $p_i(c_i, c_j)$ and the reduced-form profits $\Pi^i(c_i, c_j)$ as functions of the two marginal costs.

(ii) Show that $\partial^2 \Pi^i / \partial c_i \partial c_j < 0$.

(iii) Suppose that, before competing in price, the firms play a first-period game in which they simultaneously choose their marginal cost. (Think of an investment cost $\phi(c)$ of choosing marginal cost c, with $\phi' < 0$ and $\phi'' > 0$.) Show that, as in the previous choice-of-location game, this investment game gives rise to a direct effect and a strategic effect.

7.1.2 The Circular City

7.1.2.1 The Model

The above consideration of a linear city allowed us to examine price competition with differentiated products, as well as the choice of product in duopoly. Now let us study entry and location when there are no "barriers to entry" other than fixed costs or entry costs. Assuming that there exist a large number of identical potential firms, we will look at the number of firms entering the market. To do so, it is actually more convenient to consider a circular city with a uniform distribution of consumers. In this case, the product space is completely homogeneous (no location is *a priori* better than another), which makes the study of the issue at hand more tractable.

The following model is due to Salop (1979). Consumers are located uniformly on a circle with a perimeter equal to 1. Density is unitary around this circle. Firms are also located around the circle, and all travel occurs along the circle (like the linear city, this is a bit contrived in order to simplify the analysis, but one may think of a city around a lake, with boats being an inefficient transportation technology; or of supermarkets in a circular suburbia with a costly-to-cross city at its center; or else of aircraft departure times).

As before, consumers wish to buy one unit of the good, have a unit transport cost t (for simplicity, we will consider only linear transportation costs), and are willing to buy at the smallest generalized cost so long as the latter does not exceed the gross surplus they obtain from the good ($\bar{s}$). Each firm is allowed to locate in only one location (we will discuss this assumption below, and especially in the next chapter, where we will examine the possibility of entry deterrence through brand proliferation). In order to address the issue of the number of firms, we introduce a fixed cost of entry, f. Once a firm is in and is located at a point on the product space, it faces a marginal cost c (smaller than $\bar{s}$). Thus, firm i's profit is $(p_i - c)D_i - f$ if it enters (where D_i is the demand it faces), and 0 otherwise.

Salop considers the following two-stage game: In the first stage, potential entrants simultaneously choose whether or not to enter. Let n denote the number of entering firms. Those firms do not choose their location, but rather are automatically located equidistant from one another on the circle (figure 7.1). Thus, maximal differentiation is exogenously imposed. In the second stage, firms compete in prices given these locations.

For realism, one would want firms to choose their locations either at the same time or after their entry decision, rather than having an auctioneer pick the particular location pattern. However, the point of Salop's model is not to look at the particular product choice but rather to study the extent of entry (in this respect, this approach is similar to that outlined in sections 7.2 and 7.5.2). Omitting the choice of location allows us to study the entry issue in a simple and tractable way. We will come back to the issue of location choice later.

We have assumed free entry (a large number of identical firms). Consequently, the equilibrium profit of entering firms is zero (up to the integer problem) As has already been indicated, we must (1) determine the Nash equilibrium in prices for any number of firms and calculate the reduced-form profit functions and (2) determine the Nash equilibrium in the entry game.

Assume that n firms have entered the market. Because they are located symmetrically, it makes sense to look for an equilibrium in which they all charge the same price p (see figure 7.1). For the moment, we will consider only the case in which there are enough firms in the market (which will correspond to f not too high) so that the firms are indeed competing among themselves. In practice, firm i has only two real competitors, namely the two surrounding it.[6] Suppose that it chooses price p_i (see figure 7.2). A consumer located at the distance $x \in (0, 1/n)$ from firm i is indifferent between purchasing from firm i and purchasing from i's closest neighbor if

$$p_i + tx = p + t(1/n - x).$$

Then firm i faces a demand of

$$D_i(p_i, p) = 2x = \frac{p + t/n - p_i}{t}.$$

Therefore, firm i seeks to maximize

$$\max_{p_i} \left[(p_i - c)\left(\frac{p + t/n - p_i}{t}\right) - f \right].$$

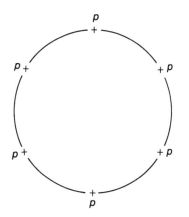

Figure 7.1

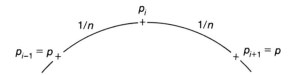

Figure 7.2

Differentiating with respect to p_i and then setting $p_i = p$ yields

$$p = c + \frac{t}{n}.$$

This result is analogous to the one found for the linear city. The profit margin $(p - c)$ decreases with n. However, the number of firms is endogenous; it is determined from the zero-profit condition for the existing firms:

$$(p - c)\frac{1}{n} - f = \frac{t}{n^2} - f = 0.$$

Therefore, the number of firms and the market price in a situation of imperfect competition with free entry are, respectively,

$$n^c = \sqrt{t/f}$$

and

$$p^c = c + \sqrt{tf}.$$

---

6. This feature is due to the particularities of this location model. For instance, Archibald and Rosenbluth (1975) show that in a Lancasterian world (see chapter 2) with four characteristics, an average brand may have $n/2$ direct competitors, where n is the number of products.

A trivial but important point of models of this type is that firms price above marginal cost and yet do not make profits. Thus, an empirical finding that firms do not make supranormal profits in an industry should not lead one to conclude that firms do not have market power, where "market power" is defined as pricing above marginal cost. (An economist's definition of market power differs from a policy-maker's definition. Policy-makers generally mean pricing above *average* cost. For this second meaning, the firms in our free-entry model have no market power.)

The above equations show that an increase in *fixed* costs causes a decrease in the number of firms and an increase in the profit margin ($p^c - c$). An increase in the transportation cost increases the profit margin and therefore increases the number of firms—firms see that there is an increased possibility of differentiation. Finally, we note that the consumer's average transportation cost is

$$\frac{t}{4n^c} = \frac{\sqrt{tf}}{4}$$

and that this does not increase as rapidly as t.

When the entry cost or fixed production cost f converges to zero, the number of entering firms tends to infinity and the market price tends toward marginal cost. (Similarly, an increase in consumer density, with the fixed cost kept constant, would increase the number of entering firms and push prices toward marginal cost.) Thus, with very low entry costs, each consumer purchases a product very close to his preferred product, and the market is approximately competitive. (As we will see in the supplementary section, this property may not hold in vertical-differentiation models.)

We continue with our previous locational-choice model by considering the equilibrium from a normative viewpoint. To this end, we compare the free-entry equilibrium with the allocation selected by a social planner. We already know that the price charged by the firms is greater than the marginal cost. However, in this case, where consumers all receive the same utility from the good and each consumes only one unit, this price introduces no distortion. The quantity consumed—one unit—is not affected by the mark-ups. Thus, the profit margin is only a monetary transfer from the consumers to the firms. The question is whether there are too many or too few firms in relation to the social optimum. In deriving the social optimum, we will not be concerned with gross consumer surplus ($\bar{s}$), since it is the same as in the case of imperfect competition. An omniscient planner would choose $n = n^*$ in order to minimize the sum of the fixed costs and the consumers' transportation costs:

$$\min_n \left[nf + t \left(2n \int_0^{1/2n} x\, dx \right) \right],$$

or, equivalently,

$$\min_n (nf + t/4n).$$

Therefore, we have

$$n^* = \tfrac{1}{2}\sqrt{t/f} = \tfrac{1}{2} n^c.$$

From this, we conclude that the market generates too many firms. (Because there is no distortion of consumption through pricing, whether or not the social planner is able to force firms to price at marginal cost in the regulated-entry context does not affect this conclusion.) The following exercise shows that similar results hold for quadratic transportation costs.

Exercise 7.3* Show that if transportation costs are td^2, where d is the consumer's distance to his selected shop, Salop's model yields

$$p = c + t/n^2,$$

and that, with free entry,

$$n^c = (t/f)^{1/3} > n^* = (t/6f)^{1/3}.$$

Thus, under linear or quadratic costs, we obtain too many products.[7] Firms have too much of an incentive to enter. Clearly, the private and the social incentive to enter have no reason to coincide. Entry is socially justified here by the savings in transportation costs (or, more generally, by the greater product diversity offered to the consumers). In contrast, the private incentive to enter is linked with "stealing the business" of other firms while still being able to impose a mark-up. We will come back

---

7. More generally, the market offers too many products for transportation costs tx^α for any $\alpha > 0$ (R. Costrell, private communication).

later to this effect, which is sometimes called the *trade-diversion effect*.

Remark   In the preceding model, we assumed implicitly that the market equilibrium was such that

$$p^c + \frac{t}{2n^c} < \bar{s} \left(\text{i.e., } \tfrac{3}{2}\sqrt{tf} < \bar{s} - c, \text{ or } f < \bar{f} = \frac{4}{9t}(\bar{s} - c)^2 \right).$$

In other words, the consumer furthest from a store (having to travel a distance of $1/2n^c$) receives a strictly positive net surplus. This assumption does not create any problems for small fixed costs. When fixed costs increase, however, the number of firms decreases and both the distance between the firms and the prices increase. When f exceeds $\bar{f}$, the equilibrium can no longer be described as above, since consumers located halfway between two firms will no longer purchase anything. See Salop 1979 for a study of this case (see also the following exercise).

Exercise 7.4**   Show that if $f \geq \bar{f}$ but f is small enough so that the market remains "covered," there exists an equilibrium in which the firms charge $p = \bar{s} - t/2n$. To do this, construct the "residual demand curve"—that is, the demand curve $D_i(p_i|p_{-i})$ for firm i when the other firms charge a price equal to $\bar{s} - t/2n$. Demonstrate that this demand curve has a kink at $\bar{s} - t/2n$, and draw the iso-profit curve in the same space (D_i, p_i). Derive n^c and p^c as functions of f and t. Argue that the results obtained are *a priori* "counterintuitive," and explain them.

7.1.2.2   Discussion

The above model was built to address the question of the number of firms. There are three natural extensions that would make it more realistic: the introduction of a location choice, the possibility that firms do not enter simultaneously, and the possibility that a firm locates at several points in the product space.

Location Choice

The model assumes that firms locate equidistantly. This assumption is appealing given the maximal-differentiation result of d'Aspremont et al. for quadratic transportation

costs in a linear city. It has been justified in the context of the circular city only in the case of quadratic transportation costs. Economides (1984) considers a three-stage game in which firms choose whether to enter, then choose locations on the circle, and then compete in prices. He vindicates the equal-spacing assumption by showing that for quadratic costs there exists a free-entry symmetric equilibrium (in locations and prices).

Sequential Entry

The assumption that all firms enter simultaneously is convenient because it eliminates the strategic aspects of product positioning (a product choice may deter entry or affect one's rival subsequent choice of product). However, one generally thinks of the firms *possibly* (but not necessarily) entering in sequence.[8] There are two issues here. First, positing that firms move sequentially, what is the *equilibrium pattern of location*, given that firms take into account the fact that their location decision in the product space affects future locations? (Prescott and Visscher [1977] did some pioneering work in this area, studying sequential location decisions by firms in a linear city.) Second, what is the optimal *timing* of entry?[9] Giving a satisfactory answer to this second question requires the introduction of further elements into the model (for instance, in a spatial model, the rate of growth of demand or population, or the rate at which the production cost decreases).

Brand Proliferation

A crucial assumption in the previous analysis is that each firm is allowed only one brand. But a firm may produce several brands and crowd the product space, leaving no room for entry by another firm (this possibility is all the more likely if preemption is feasible). Indeed, it will be argued in subsequent chapters that because a monopoly makes more profit than an oligopoly carrying the same brands and facing the same technology (because competition lowers profits), an incumbent firm has a greater incentive to introduce new products than a entrant has. As we will see, this *efficiency effect* tends to bias the market structure toward multibrand monopoly.[10]

---

8. The real world is often better approximated by a continuous-time entry model than by a one-period entry model. The one-period set-up can be obtained only in special cases, such as the case where long information lags about one's rivals' entry decisions cause firms to (*de facto*) move simultaneously.

9. This question raises the important issue of preemption, which will be examined in various models in chapters 8 and 10.

10. See chapters 8 and 10 for more detail, and for a description of offsetting effects that encourage an oligopoly structure.

7.1.3 Maximal or Minimal Differentiation?

Clearly, the spatial models, and others like them (e.g., the vertical-differentiation (quality) model in the supplementary section), are only abstractions. Nevertheless, they are quite useful, for they shed light on the nature of price rivalry. Furthermore, they make important predictions about business strategies. One such prediction is the principle of differentiation: Firms want to differentiate to soften price competition. This corresponds to the recommendation found in most marketing texts concerning market segmentation, and to the observation that firms do successfully differentiate in the real world.[11] In some cases, firms look for maximal product differentiation. While these recommendations are economically very appealing, there exist forces that oppose maximal product differentiation, and even forces that oppose any product differentiation. These can be put into three categories:

Be where the demand is It is clear that, although firms like to differentiate for strategic purposes, they also all want to locate where the demand is (e.g., near the center of the linear city). In the example of d'Aspremont et al., these two forces conflict, and we did not derive any intuition as to why the strategic effect dominates. Thus, it is not surprising that one can construct examples in which firms differentiate, but not fully.[12] This is even clearer in markets where demand is concentrated around a few poles,[13] which may explain the abundance of ice cream parlors and bookstores near universities. (In other product spaces, differentiation in laundry detergents or gasoline is not of much interest to most consumers.) Of course, if firms are to locate at the same place, they must be able to relax price competition somehow. From chapters 5 and 6, we know that this may be implemented either by restraining capacity or by tacitly colluding. Another possibility is that firms may be differentiated by attributes other than location. For instance, not all consumers may have the same taste for various brands of ice cream independent of their generalized costs,[14] or they may not all have the same information about products (see section 7.3).

Positive externalities between firms There may be externalities that induce firms to locate near one another. On the cost side, one can think of common installations and trade centers; for instance, fishermen may converge to the same harbor to sell their fish, even if this means more intense competition. Another possibility is that many firms may locate near a source of raw materials. On the demand side, search by consumers may encourage firms to gather. Doing so lowers search costs and increases aggregate demand for these firms. If the increase in demand is not offset by a considerable increase in price competition, such a strategy may be worthwhile. This may explain the scores of furniture stores along the Faubourg Saint Antoine in Paris[15]; the point here is that in a world with at least some amount of product differentiation other than location (e.g., different furniture designs), consumers find it convenient to search next door if they do not find their preferred item in a given shop.[16]

Absence of price competition Product differentiation is meant to relax price competition. In some instances, there

---

11. For instance, in the personal computer industry, Apple's products are easy to use and are directed toward home use whereas IBM's are intended mainly for office or professional use. (Apple is, however, trying to crack the office market. This relates to the need—discussed below—to be where the demand is.) A vertical-differentiation example is that of Mercedes and Rolls-Royce, which have found profitable niches in the automobile product space. See also the discussion on advertising and information in section 7.3.

12. A trivial example is obtained by fictitiously extending the city in the example of d'Aspremont et al. (e.g., to cover the segment located between $x = -1$ and $x = 2$). However, the subsegments between $x = -1$ and $x = 0$ and between $x = 1$ and $x = 2$ are uninhabited; the consumers are uniformly distributed between 0 and 1. Clearly, the analysis of d'Aspremont et al. is not affected; however, the equilibrium locations ($x = 0$ and $x = 1$) are no longer extreme in the city's territory.

In a more interesting example, Economides (1986) takes up the linear-city model with transportation cost td^α, where d is the distance to the shop and α belongs to $[1, 2]$. He shows that a pure-strategy price equilibrium exists for $\alpha > 1.26$, and that differentiation is not maximal for α in $[1.26, 1.67]$, whereas it is for α in $[1.67, 2]$.

13. Here we take poles as exogenous. They may in fact result not only from the consumers' location pattern but also from the decisions by firms selling goods that are complements (or even imperfect substitutes) to locate near one another—think of shopping malls. See Stahl 1982a and Eaton 1982.

14. De Palma et al. (1985) introduce this possibility in the linear-city model with linear transportation costs. Instead of assuming that the consumers all derive the same surplus $\bar{s}$ from any product, they consider a product-specific surplus: $\bar{s}_i = \bar{s} + \mu\varepsilon_i$, where μ is a parameter and ε_i is a consumer-and-firm-specific random variable. They find that if μ becomes large enough, there exists an equilibrium in which both firms locate at the center. When μ is large, products are very differentiated even if they have the same spatial location, so the strategic effect is weak. The direct, demand effect then commands firms to locate where the demand is.

15. Other Parisian examples include the Au Printemps and the Galeries LaFayette department stores and the seafood restaurants on Place Clichy. It would be interesting to study whether the disappearance of some districts in New York is due to a decrease in search costs and information costs.

16. The literature on the interaction between consumer search and firm location is scant. Stahl (1982b) has made a start.

may exist legal or technical reasons why the scope of price competition is limited. For instance, the prices of airline tickets in the United States (before deregulation) were determined exogenously, as the prices of gas and books in France once were.[17] (Similarly, consumer prices may be determined by resale-price-maintenance agreements imposed by manufacturers.) It is, thus, clear that the incentive to differentiate products decreases when firms do not compete in prices. Indeed, Hotelling (1929) enunciated the principle of *minimal differentiation* in such circumstances. To see why minimal differentiation may arise in some location models, consider his model of a linear city with two firms. Suppose that the price ($p > c$) is exogenously fixed, and that each firm chooses a location on a segment of length 1 with a uniform distribution of consumers. Suppose further that the firms share demand equally if they are located identically. Because the prices and the profit margins are fixed, the firms choose their locations so as to maximize demand. Let firm 1 locate at point a and firm 2 at point $1 - b$, where, without loss of generality, $0 \leqslant a \leqslant 1 - b \leqslant 1$. Suppose that these locations differ: $a < 1 - b$. Let us show that firm 1, for instance, would like to move toward b. Its demand is

$$a + \frac{1 - b - a}{2};$$

it therefore increases with a. This is natural, as the firms are competing for the consumers located between them. Thus, an equilibrium must involve identical locations: $a = 1 - b$. Suppose now that $a = 1 - b < \frac{1}{2}$. Each firm's demand is $\frac{1}{2}$. But by moving to the right by $\varepsilon > 0$, firm 2, for instance, would have demand

$$(b - \varepsilon) + \frac{1 - b + \varepsilon - a}{2} \simeq b > \frac{1}{2}.$$

Thus, the firms would want to move toward the center. By the same reasoning, for $a = 1 - b = \frac{1}{2}$ neither firm would want to move. Thus, the only equilibrium has both firms located at the center of the city.[18] In this example, the products are socially too close to each other. Transportation costs could be reduced by having the firms move away from the center. (As was noted in subsection 7.1.1, the locations midway between the center and the extremities minimize transportation costs.) Such a location model without price competition may explain why political platforms tend to cluster around the center, and why similar TV shows (news, movies, etc.) compete in the same time slots of the major networks in many countries.

7.2 Monopolistic Competition

Monopolistic competition was introduced by Chamberlin (1933) to formalize the following industry configuration (here we continue to assume that each firm produces at most one product, in order to abstract from the issue of brand proliferation by a given firm):

(i) Each firm faces a downward-sloping demand.

(ii) Each firm makes no profit.

(iii) A price change by one firm has only a negligible effect on the demand of any other firm.[19]

Properties i and ii are satisfied by the zero-profit equilibrium of the Salop model of section 7.1. Property iii distinguishes monopolistic competition from the previous oligopolistic competition with free entry. It says that each firm or product has no direct neighbor in the product space. This absence of cross-effects has been widely criticized. Except in a few cases (see the monopolistic competition model of informational product differentiation in

---

17. To be sure, some forms of "non-price decisions" are meant to substitute for price cuts. For instance, some big book retailers in France have offered to buy used books back at advantageous prices and have introduced benefits for faithful consumers, and airlines once supplied lavish on-board services. Firms will always find ingenious loopholes in the regulatory system; however, such non-price competition is not necessarily a perfect substitute for price competition, and therefore it may yield some undesirable welfare losses besides the benefits intended by the regulators. Consumers may prefer a direct price reduction.

18. It can be shown, for instance, that with three firms no pure-strategy location equilibrium with exogenously fixed price exists. (For some nonexistence results, see Eaton and Lipsey 1975. For more references and for mixed-strategy equilibrium, see Dasgupta and Maskin 1986.) However, an equilibrium does exist if firms enter sequentially rather than simultaneously (Prescott and Visscher 1977). The first and second firms locate at $\frac{1}{4}$ and $\frac{3}{4}$, and the third firm locates between them.

19. Other (nonequivalent) properties sometimes replace property iii to yield alternative definitions of monopolistic competition. One such property (weaker than iii) is the *perfect-symmetry axiom* (also called the *absence-of-localization axiom*): A change in the demand for good i (due to a change in its price, advertising level, etc.) does not affect the ratio of good j's sales to good k's sales for all j, $k \neq i$. Schmalensee (1985) has developed an econometric test for the presence of localized competition. The application of this test to data on the U.S. ready-to-eat-breakfast-cereal industry signals a misspecification of the perfect-symmetry model.

section 7.3), existing products compete directly with a few products (or when they do not, as in the monopoly case, property ii is likely to be violated). The point of monopolistic competition is thus not to study strategic aspects between products (such as product positioning and price competition), but rather to abstract from them to simplify the analysis and study other issues, such as the number of products offered by a market economy.

There has long been a "conventional wisdom" that monopolistic competition yields too many firms from a social viewpoint, or that the existing firms produce too little to exhaust returns to scale ("excess capacity"). The reasoning runs as follows: Suppose that firms have U-shaped average-cost curves. Let $D_i(p_i, p_{-i})$ be the residual demand curve of firm i; that is, its demand curve given the vector of prices p_{-i} charged by the other firms. A free-entry equilibrium requires that each firm make zero profit or, simply, that firm i produce at a point (p_i^c, q_i^c) such that the residual demand curve is tangent to the average-cost curve at this point (see figure 7.3, where $AC(q_i)$ is the average cost at q_i). The quantity produced is less than the quantity (q_i^*) that minimizes average cost. Therefore, the fixed cost is spread over too few units, and waste occurs.

Actually, this reasoning is flawed. If no other firm produces the same good (the other goods are different from that of firm i), the introduction of this good can be justified even if its production does not exhaust economies of scale. (This is even more obvious in the preceding location example, where the average cost is $c + f/q_i$ and the quantity that minimizes average cost—the most efficient scale—is therefore $q_i^* = +\infty$.) Therefore, the reasoning must require firm i to produce a good that is already being produced by another firm. But then its demand curve is horizontal at the price (p_j) charged by the other firm (or at the minimum of such prices if there are many other firms that produce this good), and decreasing thereafter; see figure 7.4.

Geometrically, it is easy to see that the only output for firm i that can satisfy both the condition that firm i makes zero profit and the condition that firm j sells a positive quantity (otherwise, its own profit must be negative because of the fixed cost) is q_i^* (with $p_i = p_i^*$). Therefore, we cannot conclude that there is "excess capacity" or that there are too many firms.

More recent research (Dixit and Stiglitz 1977, Spence 1976) has shown that this argument cannot be patched

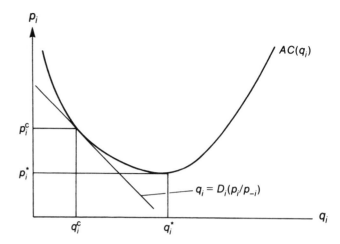

Figure 7.3

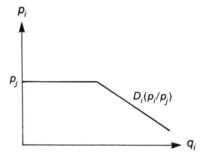

Figure 7.4
Demand curve for perfectly substitutable goods.

up. In general, there are two effects operating in opposite directions:

Nonappropriability of social surplus This effect, discussed in the monopoly case in chapter 2, says that a firm cannot generally capture the whole consumer surplus associated with the introduction of a good. The positive externality on consumers implies that firms tend to introduce socially too few products.

Business stealing (trade diversion) By introducing a product, a firm steals consumers from other firms. The rivals, who have a positive profit margin, lose income from these diverted consumers. This negative externality on other firms implies that firms tend to introduce too many products.

In general, the free-entry outcome (like the monopoly outcome; see chapter 2) can involve socially too few or too many products. More definite conclusions can be obtained only for specific models.

For more on the Dixit-Stiglitz-Spence model, see subsection 7.5.2.

7.3 Advertising and Informational Product Differentiation

Let us now apply some of the above ideas to informational differentiation. We will focus on the effect of advertising on consumer demand and product differentiation.

Advertising has many media, including television, radio, newspapers, magazines, and direct mail.[20] It constitutes a non-negligible industry in itself (2 to 3 percent of the GNP in the United States in 1984, somewhat less in other developed countries).[21]

Competition in advertising is one of the main dimensions of non-price competition. As was mentioned in chapter 2, the study of advertising strains the rational-consumer model perhaps more than other topics. Though it will be argued that advertising may foster competition by increasing the elasticity of demand (reducing "differentiation"), it is easy to find cases in which the reverse is true. For instance, ads seem to succeed in differentiating products that are physically almost identical (laundry detergents, beers, etc.). Subsection 7.3.1 reviews the conventional wisdom about advertising.

Subsection 7.3.2 presents the best case for advertising. We adopt the view that advertising brings useful information to the consumer (this view stems from Telser's (1964) response to economists' traditional distaste for advertising—see, e.g., Kaldor 1950). We formalize advertising as yielding information about the very existence of the product and its price (information about location or product characteristics would follow a somewhat similar pattern). The assumption in this subsection is that informational issues can be solved—at a cost—through advertising (in the terminology of chapter 2, the good is a *search good*). We investigate whether advertising reduces product differentiation, and whether the market supplies too much or too little advertising.

Subsection 7.3.3 briefly mentions another link between consumer information and product differentiation. There we consider *experience goods* rather than search goods. We assume that manufacturers cannot directly inform consumers about product quality through advertising, and that consumer learning occurs through consumption. Different consumers at a given point in time have different information about the various products' qualities, which stems from their earlier patterns of consumption. Thus, a consumer may fail to perceive two goods that are equal in quality (and not differentiated on other characteristics) as perfect substitutes because he has tried and knows the quality of only one of the goods.

7.3.1 Views on Advertising[22]

We can distinguish two polar views on advertising.

The *partial view* sees advertising as providing information to the consumers and thus enabling them to make rational choices. Advertising announces the existence of a product, quotes its price, informs consumers about retail locations, and describes the product's quality. It reduces the consumers' search costs and helps them choose between brands. Thus, advertising reduces product differentiation associated with a lack of information about some products and fosters competition. Similarly, it facilitates the entry of new firms, who can capture the demand of established firms. It also encourages the production of high-quality goods. High-quality firms have an incentive to reveal their quality through advertising, which puts low-quality firms at a disadvantage.

Newspapers are the favorite medium of the proponents of this view. Newspaper advertising in the United States is, for the most part, local. It often contains information about price, attributes, and retail location. The favorite products of these proponents are eyeglasses, prescription drugs, and food. Benham (1972) argues that the average price of eyeglasses is significantly higher in states where advertising is prohibited. The explanation seems to be that advertising informs consumers and fosters price com-

---

20. To give orders of magnitude: The shares of total advertising expenditures in 1984 in the United States were 23% for television (network, spot, local, and cable), 7% for radio, 27% for newspapers, 6% for magazines, and 16% for direct mail. There are also non-advertising promotional expenses, e.g. salespersons, lobbyists, and public-relations staffs.

21. Advertising expenditures vary greatly according to the product. For instance, according to 1975 data from the Federal Trade Commission, drugs,

perfumes, and breakfast cereals had media-advertising expense-to-sales ratios between 10% and 20% (between 20% and 35% if one includes all selling expenses). Of course, beet sugar, railroad equipment, and guided missiles are hardly advertised.

22. This section was inspired by lectures given by Paul Joskow and Richard Schmalensee.

petition[23] (see also Cady [1976] on prescription drugs and Steiner [1973] on how the availability of network television advertising changed the nature of competition in the toy industry). These proponents also point to efforts of some professionals (e.g. pharmacists, medical professionals, and lawyers) to impose legal restrictions on advertising.

The *adverse view* claims that advertising is meant to persuade and fool consumers. It creates differentiation that is not real, rather than reducing real informational differentiation (see, e.g., Galbraith 1967 and Solow 1967 on the view that consumers are manipulated by Madison Avenue). Thus it reduces product competition; it also increases barriers to entry.

The favorite medium of the proponents of this view is network television. Network TV advertising is mainly national. It is very image-oriented, and it conveys little information beyond the existence of the product. Their favorite products are cigarettes, Clorox (which commands a high price premium although it is basically identical to rival products), and beer. They point to Nichols' (1951) famous study of the cigarette industry, which shows that, from the 1920s on, cigarette manufacturers competed through advertising and brand proliferation rather than through price cuts (prices seem to have been fairly collusive) or improvements in quality. Hence, competition in this industry seems to have been socially wasteful.

Certainly, each of these views has some merit. The relevance of each seems to depend on the product, the nature of consumer demand, and the advertising medium. In the rest of this section, we will investigate the role of advertising assuming full consumer rationality.

7.3.2 Search Goods and Informative Advertising

In this subsection, we assume that advertising conveys information on existence and price.[24] We consider two such models. The first, due to Butters (1977), is one of monopolistic competition (each of a large number of firms faces a downward-sloping demand, but their effects on the rivals are negligible). Differentiation between products stems entirely from consumers' knowing about only a restricted number of brands (possibly one or none). The second model, due to Grossman and Shapiro (1984), looks at oligopolistic interaction in a Butters-type model; it also allows product differentiation along another dimension (location). Our main focus is on whether monopolistic or oligopolistic interaction yields socially too much or too little advertising. As will become clear, our discussion rejoins the previous study of product diversity.

7.3.2.1 Monopolistic Competition

In Butters' model, all firms offer the same product (there is no horizontal or vertical differentiation). Production of the good exhibits constant returns to scale, at unit cost c. Each consumer has unit demand for this product. A consumer's utility is $U = \bar{s} - p$ if he buys one unit at price p and 0 if he does not buy. If the consumers were perfectly informed about all firms, Bertrand competition would drive the price to the marginal cost, and each consumer would buy one unit and enjoy utility $\bar{s} - c$. However, we assume that informing the consumers about the existence and the price of a brand is costly. More specifically, let us assume that the only way to reach consumers is to send advertisements at random. An advertisement also quotes the price charged by the firm that sends it. (Because the consumers cannot search in this model, the term *search good* is unfortunate here.) If there are N consumers, each consumer has a probability $1/N$ of receiving a given ad. A consumer thus can receive 0, 1, 2, ... ads. If he receives none, he buys nothing; if he receives one, he buys from the corresponding firm as long as the price does not exceed $\bar{s}$; if he receives several, he chooses the lowest price if it does not exceed $\bar{s}$. In the case of a tie, he chooses randomly between low-price brands.

As in section 2.2, let s denote the total number of ads sent to consumers by all firms. A consumer's probability of not getting an ad at all is

---

23. There might be a change in the quality of services. Benham mentions that in 1963, 83.4% of consumers were served by physicians and optometrists in states where advertising was prohibited, versus 53.2% in states where it was permitted. However, Kwoka (1984) presents empirical evidence that advertising leads to no erosion of quality in this industry.

24. The field owes much to the early analyses of Dehez and Jacquemin (1975), Dorfman and Steiner (1954), Friedman (1983), Nerlove and Arrow (1962),

Schmalensee (1972, 1976, 1978), and Spence (1980), all of whom assumed that the demand for a product depends on its price and on the amount of advertising. Their approach is useful for positive analysis (prediction of price and advertising expenditures). It is less amenable to normative analysis, because it does not detail the channel through which advertising enters the consumers' preferences. To perform welfare analysis, we choose to be more explicit (and also less general) about the effect of advertising on demand. For a more general overview of advertising and market structure, see Schmalensee 1986a.

$$1 - \Phi \equiv \left(1 - \frac{1}{N}\right)^s \simeq e^{-s/N}$$

for N large. Conversely, where c' denotes the unit cost of sending an ad (again, we assume constant returns), the social cost of making sure that the fraction Φ in $(0, 1)$ of consumers receives at least one ad is

$$A(\Phi) = c's = c'N \ln\left(\frac{1}{1 - \Phi}\right).$$

The advertising cost per consumer is thus

$$c'\ln\left(\frac{1}{1 - \Phi}\right).$$

Assume that $\bar{s} > c + c'$ (otherwise, no advertising and production would ever take place).

Let us first consider a *free-entry equilibrium*. Firms here do not face entry costs or fixed costs. Each firm is negligible with respect to the market. Clearly, ads specifying prices below $c + c'$ or above $\bar{s}$ will not be sent (pricing below $c + c'$ yields negative profit; pricing above $\bar{s}$ automatically induces no demand). Butters shows that any price between $c + c'$ and $\bar{s}$ is advertised in equilibrium by some firm. The trade-off between two prices is the following: A higher price yields a higher profit margin, but has a lower probability of being accepted, as the probability increases that the consumer receives another ad with a lower price. More formally, let $x(p)$ denote the probability that an ad at price p is accepted by the consumer who receives it, i.e., the probability that this consumer does not receive another ad specifying a lower price. $x(p)$ can be thought of as a (downward-sloping) demand function. In equilibrium, an ad must make a zero expected profit whatever its price (if it made a positive profit, new firms would enter the market and send ads at the same price until the probability of acceptance fell enough to reestablish the zero-profit condition). That is, for all p in $[c + c', \bar{s}]$,

$$(p - c)x(p) - c' = 0. \tag{7.12}$$

Note that $x(c + c') = 1$; otherwise, an ad at $c + c'$ would

lose money. Conversely, one can recover the distribution of ads from the probability $x(p)$.

As we will see shortly, the important datum for assessing welfare in this model is the level of advertising. This level is obtained from equation 7.12. The probability $1 - \Phi^c$ that a consumer does not receive an ad is equal to the probability $x(\bar{s})$ that an ad at the highest possible price of the good triggers a sale (the only chance that such an ad will trigger a sale is if it is the only ad received by the consumer). From equation 7.12,

$$1 - \Phi^c = \frac{c'}{\bar{s} - c}.$$

Let us now consider social welfare. Because of the unit-demand assumption and the homogeneity of consumers, the market does not introduce any consumption distortion. A consumer who receives at least one ad consumes one unit of the good, which is socially optimal. The only potential distortion in this economy is related to the number of ads, or equivalently, to the fraction $(1 - \Phi)$ of consumers who are not reached by any ad. Because consumption by a consumer yields social surplus $\bar{s} - c$, a social planner would choose a fraction Φ^* so as to maximize as follows:

$$\max_{\Phi} \left[\Phi(\bar{s} - c) - c'\ln\left(\frac{1}{1 - \Phi}\right) \right].$$

The first-order condition is

$$\bar{s} - c - \frac{c'}{1 - \Phi^*} = 0 \text{ or } \Phi^* = \Phi^c.$$

Thus, *the monopolistically competitive level of advertising is socially optimal.* To understand this result, note that, from the zero-profit condition, the firm's incentive to send an ad, $(p - c)x(p)$, is independent of price p (in other words, all ads at prices between $c + c'$ and $\bar{s}$ yield the same profit). This incentive is equal to the gain from sending an ad at price $\bar{s}$. Such an ad yields $\bar{s} - c$ with a probability equal to the probability that the consumer receives no ad. But this is exactly the social planner's incentive. An ad increases the social surplus (by $\bar{s} - c$) only if the consumer receives no other ad.[25]

---

25. For prices $p < \bar{s}$, the private incentive can be decomposed into two effects. The firm's profit margin, $p - c$, is lower than the social surplus, $\bar{s} - c$; the firm does not appropriate the whole surplus. However, the ad generates demand with probability $x(p)$, which exceeds the socially relevant probability that the consumer receives no other ad $(1 - \Phi)$. The difference between the two prob-

abilities corresponds to the probability that the firm diverts the consumer from another firm (a business-stealing effect). We will come back to these two effects when we discuss oligopoly. Note that the optimality result means that the two effects offset each other exactly here.

This optimality result is quite striking. Even though it does not hold for more general models (see below), it shows that informative advertising need not be distorted in market equilibrium. It relies on specific assumptions (unit demands, consumer homogeneity, etc.). An interesting variant of the model, considered by Butters, allows consumer search. Thus, consumers can be informed through two channels: advertising and (if they receive no ad) personal search. Butters shows that the monopolistically competitive equilibrium involves too much advertising and not enough search.

Another striking result reported by Butters is the equilibrium price dispersion. There is a vast literature on price dispersion when consumers get informed through search rather than advertising. See Bénabou 1986a,b for a general model of search and for references to earlier work.[26]

7.3.2.2 Oligopoly

Grossman and Shapiro (1984) build on Butters to analyze informative advertising in oligopolistic interaction. They combine the preceding model with the circular-city one. Thus, firms are differentiated along two dimensions: information and location. We shall employ a model slightly simpler than theirs and shall abstract from the entry question they consider to focus on the effect of advertising on the elasticity of individual demands and on the appropriability and business-stealing effects.

Let us use the linear-city model of section 7.1. (There are two firms located at the two extremes of a segment of length 1. Consumers are distributed uniformly along the segment with density 1; they derive gross surplus $\bar{s}$ from consuming the good, and they incur transportation cost t per unit of distance.) As in Butters' case, a consumer can consume a product if and only if he receives an ad from the corresponding firm. Let Φ_i ($i = 1, 2$) denote the fraction of consumers who receive an ad from firm i. Like Grossman and Shapiro, we assume that advertising is not localized. Thus, consumers located along the segment have equal chances of receiving a given ad. (Extending the model to allow the targeting of ads would be worthwhile.) The cost of reaching fraction Φ_i of consumers is $A(\Phi_i)$, where $A' > 0$ and $A'' > 0$. (With the Butters technology,

$$A(\Phi_i) = c' \ln\left(\frac{1}{1 - \Phi_i}\right).$$

However, the technology can be more general. To simplify the computations, we will assume that $A(\Phi_i) = a\Phi_i^2/2$, with a maximum advertising expenditure of $a/2$.)

The potential demand for firm 1, say, has size Φ_1. It can be decomposed into two parts. A fraction $1 - \Phi_2$ of this potential demand does not receive an ad from firm 2. It can thus be considered firm 1's turf. Each consumer in this market segment is willing to pay a price up to $\bar{s}$ minus the transportation cost to firm 1. A fraction Φ_2 also receives at least one ad from firm 2, and therefore constitutes a more elastic or competitive fragment of demand. We assume that firms cannot price-discriminate. They choose prices p_1 and p_2. In the sequel, we consider only the case in which the two firms compete for this "common demand." In particular, we look at equilibria with overlapping market areas for firms among the fully informed consumers. Thus, we focus on the competitive case, which will allow useful comparisons with the no-advertising model of section 7.1.[27] Recall from section 7.1 that the demand for firm 1 under full information is

---

26. Bénabou (1986b) obtains price dispersion in a monopolistic competition model in which nominal prices are costly to adjust (because of "menu costs") and inflation creates a need for nominal price adjustments. He shows that inflation generates price dispersion, which makes search potentially more profitable and thereby increases price competition. Inflation thus yields lower real prices and fewer firms in equilibrium.

Gertner (1987) considers an oligopoly model in which a higher variance of inflation increases the firms' market power for high search costs. The idea is that for a deterministic inflation rate, the consumers interpret a firm's high price as stemming from a high idiosyncratic cost and may keep on searching for a lower-cost firm (depending on their search cost). Under a random inflation rate, the high price is due either to a high idiosyncratic cost or to a high inflation, which then affects the firm's rivals as well. The consumers' incentive to keep searching is thus reduced, and the firms' market power is increased. It is interesting to note that Bénabou finds a negative correlation between the *level*

of inflation and market power, whereas Gertner finds a positive correlation between the *variance* of inflation and market power. (Of course, the two effects may offset each other somewhat, as the inflation rate and its variance are generally positively correlated.)

Bénabou (1986a) also looks at price reputation and repeat purchases with search.

27. Roughly, the competitive case arises if the advertising costs are not too high, so that a large fraction of the market is covered by both firms. In this case, charging a high price and focusing on one's own turf does not yield enough demand, and firms indeed try to compete for the common demand. In the quadratic-cost-of-advertising example, this is guaranteed if a does not exceed $t/2$ too much. (Values $a \leq t/2$ are not considered here, because they yield $\Phi_1 = \Phi_2 = 1$ in equilibrium, which is the full-information case considered in section 7.1.)

$(p_2 - p_1 + t)/2t$.

Thus,

$$D_1 = \Phi_1\left[(1 - \Phi_2) + \Phi_2\left(\frac{p_2 - p_1 + t}{2t}\right)\right].$$

Note that the elasticity of demand at $p_1 = p_2 = p$ and $\Phi_1 = \Phi_2 = \Phi$ is

$$\varepsilon_1 = -\left.\frac{\partial D_1}{\partial p_1}\right/\frac{D_1}{p_1} = \frac{\Phi p}{(2 - \Phi)t}.$$

The elasticity of demand is an increasing function of Φ, and thus is increasing with advertising.

Consider the game in which the two firms simultaneously choose prices and advertising levels. For instance, firm 1's behavior is described by

$$\max_{\{p_1, \Phi_1\}}\left\{\Phi_1\left[(1 - \Phi_2) + \Phi_2\left(\frac{p_2 - p_1 + t}{2t}\right)\right](p_1 - c) - A(\Phi_1)\right\},$$

and firm 2's behavior similarly. Now specialize the model to quadratic advertising costs $A(\Phi_i) = a\Phi_i^2/2$. The two first-order conditions are (note that a firm's pricing policy is independent of its advertising level)

$$p_1 = \frac{p_2 + t + c}{2} + \frac{1 - \Phi_2}{\Phi_2}t \qquad (7.13)$$

and

$$\Phi_1 = \frac{1}{a}(p_1 - c)\left[1 - \Phi_2 + \Phi_2\left(\frac{p_2 - p_1 + t}{2t}\right)\right]. \qquad (7.14)$$

These equations have straightforward interpretations. The first term on the right-hand side of 7.13 is the reaction function under full consumer information. The second term is an extra mark-up associated with the existence of a turf; it reflects the fact that the elasticity of demand is lower than under full information. Equation 7.14 states the equality between the marginal cost of advertising $a\Phi_1$ and the marginal benefit, which is equal to the profit margin times the probability of sale. Be-

cause the game is symmetric, let us look for a symmetric equilibrium ($p_1^c = p_2^c = p^c$, and $\Phi_1^c = \Phi_2^c = \Phi^c$). Solving equations 7.13 and 7.14, assuming $a \geqslant t/2$, yields

$$p^c = c + t\frac{2 - \Phi^c}{\Phi^c} = c + \sqrt{2at}, \qquad (7.15)$$

$$\Phi^c = \frac{2}{1 + \sqrt{2a/t}}, \qquad (7.16)$$

and

$$\Pi^1 = \Pi^2 = \frac{2a}{(1 + \sqrt{2a/t})^2}. \qquad (7.17)$$

Several interesting conclusions can be derived from this simple model (these conclusions are, of course, valid only in the competitive range):

• The price, p^c, exceeds that under full information ($c + t$). This is due to the lower elasticity of demand associated with informational differentiation. As in section 7.1, the price increases with the parameter of horizontal differentiation, t (but not as rapidly, because more horizontal differentiation yields a higher margin and therefore encourages more advertising and creates a bigger common market). The price also increases with the cost of advertising, a.

• The lower the advertising cost and the higher the horizontal differentiation, the more the firms advertise.

• Profits increase with the transportation cost, as in section 7.1. What is more remarkable, they increase with the cost of advertising. The direct effect of an increase in a (for p and Φ given) is to reduce the firms' profits. However, there is a strategic effect: An increase in advertising costs reduces advertising and thus increases informational product differentiation. This allows firms to raise the price. In this example, they gain more from costlier advertising than they lose. This result is not general, but it strongly exemplifies the role of advertising in reducing product differentiation. It may also shed some light on why some professions do not resist—and sometimes encourage—legal restrictions on advertising.[28]

---

28. In this model, a small limitation on advertising (such as a small tax on it) helps the firms. An outright prohibition would hurt them, because they would then be unable to reach consumers at all. Of course, in reality, in the absence of advertising, consumers would substitute for advertising by searching (including using word of mouth). Thus, a reasonable description of such a prohibition would require enriching the model.

Peters 1984 constructs a model of a homogeneous-good industry in which price advertising is costless. In an advertising equilibrium, all consumers are

Compare the market level of advertising to the socially optimal level of advertising, Φ^*.[29] It is easy to see that Φ^c can be either greater or less than Φ^*—there can be either excessive or suboptimal advertising in equilibrium. This result should not surprise us very much. Advertising, as described in this model, is very much like creating a good, in that it offers a new good to the consumer who receives the ad. The following effects can now be distinguished:

Nonappropriability of social surplus Because of the competitive pressure, the firms' profit margin is lower than the social surplus associated with the consumption of the good. Thus, each firm has too low an incentive to create the good (i.e., to advertise).

Business stealing Here a firm creates little social surplus if its ad is received by a consumer who also receives an ad from its rival; it saves at most some transportation t, and usually less (because it captures the segment located next to it, it saves an average of $3t/4 - t/4 = t/2$ on such a consumer). But the markup exceeds t. The loser is not the consumer, who saves on transportation costs, but the rival, who loses the profit margin $p^c - c$ on the diverted consumer. Thus, there may be excessive advertising.

This type of model is too crude to allow definite conclusions (beyond that there may be overadvertising or underadvertising). However, it constitutes the first step toward a richer analysis, and it also supplies a framework with which empirical findings can be confronted. For instance, consider the following stylized fact: "In broad samples of manufacturing industries, especially those producing consumer goods, advertising intensity is positively related to industry-average profitability." (Schma-

lensee 1986b, stylized fact 3-10).[30] As Schmalensee warns us, such correlations should not be interpreted as causal relationships. Advertising does not increase profits, and profits do not generate advertising. Both variables are jointly determined (i.e., endogenous), as is shown, for example, by the reduced-form equations 7.16 and 7.17. In the previous model, the exogenous variables are t and a. If horizontal differentiation increases, both advertising and profit increase, which is consistent with the stylized fact. However, if the cost of advertising increases, advertising goes down and profits go up, implying a negative relationship between the two. Thus, it all depends on which exogenous variable varies significantly in the sample distribution. If we take this crude model as a paradigm, we attribute the positive correlation to the possibility that product differentiation varies more than advertising costs across manufacturing industries.[31]

7.3.3 Experience Goods: Informational Differentiation and Goodwill

The previous analysis dealt with search goods. Advertising could bring the consumers information about the good's existence, retail location, price, characteristics, and so forth. Goods were differentiated, because costly (and therefore incomplete) advertising campaigns did not inform all consumers about all goods. For experience goods, informational differentiation may also arise from the consumers' imperfect knowledge of the products' quality or fit with their preferences (see chapter 2 for quality and matching models in monopoly). Consumers, who learn their utility of consuming a good from experience, generally know about only one brand or only a few,

---

informed about all prices. When price advertising is prohibited, consumers must search. There are two classes of consumers: zero-search-cost consumers' who get costlessly informed about all prices, and high search-cost buyers, who visit only one seller. Peters shows that high-production-cost producers are made better off by advertising restrictions and that those with low production costs are made worse off. (His other conclusions, such as that advertising restrictions may cause average prices in an industry to fall, are more ambiguous.)

29. The latter is obtained by maximizing

$$\Phi^2(\bar{s} - c - t/4) + 2\Phi(1 - \Phi)(\bar{s} - c - t/2) - 2(a\Phi^2/2).$$

(An average consumer has transportation cost $t/4$ when receiving two ads, which occurs with probability Φ^2, and transportation cost $t/2$ when receiving one ad, which occurs with probability $2\Phi(1 - \Phi)$.) This maximization yields

$$\Phi^* = \frac{2(\bar{s} - c) - t}{2(\bar{s} - c) - 3t/2 + 2a}.$$

Because $a \geq t/2$, $\Phi^* < 1$. The market-determined advertising level exceeds the socially optimal level for a close to $t/2$. In contrast, there is socially too little advertising when a and t are small. (To see this, fix a and t such that $a > t/2$, and consider the parameters $\{\lambda a, \lambda t\}$. Φ^c is independent of λ, whereas Φ^* tends to 1 when λ tends to 0.)

30. For more on empirical analyses of advertising, see Telser 1964, Schmalensee 1972, Comanor and Wilson 1974, Comanor 1979, Lambin 1976, and Porter 1976.

31. Schmalensee also states two stylized facts related to entry and concentration: "Among consumer goods industries, advertising intensity increases with concentration at low levels of concentration; the relation may vanish or change sign at high levels of concentration" (stylized fact 5.7), and "Advertising intensity is negatively related to entry in manufacturing industries" (stylized fact 5.9). Grossman and Shapiro (1984) look at free-entry equilibria in their circularity model.

because experimenting is costly. Thus, consumers do not treat products they have experienced and products they have not experienced as identical even if the products are in fact the same. Consumers who have experienced a good match with a product or observed its high quality will not try a rival product unless it is considerably cheaper. Thus, again, the demand curve of a given brand is downward sloping rather than perfectly elastic.

Some of the interesting questions here are related to market dynamics: How do consumers come to try brands? Is there consumer inertia? Do pioneering brands have an advantage over entering brands? Bain (1956) argued that informational differentiation can be a barrier to entry, because consumers tend to be loyal to the pioneering brands. Schmalensee (1982) confirmed Bain's intuition in a formal model, showing how a high-quality incumbent can earn supranormal profit without encouraging the entry of even a high-quality entrant. Bagwell (1985), who considered the possibility of signaling product quality through pricing,[32] showed that even a low-quality incumbent may deter entry of a high-quality entrant thanks to informational differentiation.[33]

7.4 Concluding Remarks

The idea that product differentiation softens price competition fits well with the observation that firms often search for market niches when positioning their products. However, as we have seen, there are limits to differentiation. Fixed prices, discrete concentration of demand in the product space, and cost and demand gains from the agglomeration of firms all may foster product homogeneity.

Another lesson of this chapter is that free-entry equilibria yield too many or too few firms. Although economists generally feel that entry is socially desirable, this opinion may be based on considerations other than those discussed in this chapter, such as the existence of barriers to entry (see chapters 8 and 9).

Through most of this chapter we have assumed that firms are differentiated along a single dimension (horizontal, vertical, or informational). Actual differentiation is multidimensional. An interesting and largely unexplored issue is that of the demand complementarity and substitutability of various product characteristics (e.g., quality and advertising) and of the optimal strategic mix of these characteristics.

Two other limitations of the models considered in this chapter are the firms' simultaneous entry decision and their choice of a single product. Market preemption and firm-level brand proliferation are two important real-world phenomena that will be explored in the next chapters.

---

32. See also Farrell 1984. On price and advertising signaling in a monopoly situation, see chapter 2 above.

33. The formalization of these important issues is complex. See the original papers (cited in the text) for more detail.

7.5 Supplementary Section:
Vertical Differentiation and Monopolistic Competition

7.5.1 Vertical Differentiation

Vertical (quality) differentiation was introduced in chapter 2. Chapter 3 described how a monopolist manipulates the spectrum of products he puts on the market to better price-discriminate. Here we shall consider oligopolistic competition under quality differentiation. As with horizontal differentiation, we will first analyze price competition with given qualities (one per firm) and then look at the *ex ante* choice of qualities. The analysis presented here was developed by Gabszewicz and Thisse (1979, 1980) and Shaked and Sutton (1982, 1983).[34] Because the study of vertical differentiation so closely resembles that of horizontal differentiation, we will concentrate more on the points of divergence.

Let the consumers' preferences be described by $U = \theta s - p$ if the consumer consumes one unit (of quality s) and pays price p, and by 0 otherwise. The parameter θ of taste for quality is uniformly distributed across the population of consumers between $\underline{\theta} \geqslant 0$ and $\overline{\theta} = \underline{\theta} + 1$. The density is 1.

There are two firms. Firm i produces a good of quality s_i, where $s_2 > s_1$. The unit cost of production is c. The cost is the same for both qualities (we will return to this assumption later). We make the following assumption for the moment:

Assumption 1 $\overline{\theta} \geqslant 2\underline{\theta}$.

This assumption says, roughly, that the amount of consumer heterogeneity is sufficient for what follows. We also make a second assumption,

Assumption 2 $c + \dfrac{\overline{\theta} - 2\underline{\theta}}{3}(s_2 - s_1) \leqslant \underline{\theta}s_1$,

which ensures that in the price equilibrium the market is "covered" (that is, each consumer buys one of the two brands).

Let $\Delta s \equiv s_2 - s_1$ denote the quality differential, and let $\overline{\Delta} \equiv \overline{\theta}\Delta s$ and $\underline{\Delta} \equiv \underline{\theta}\Delta s$ be the monetary values of this quality differential for the highest- and the lowest-demand-for-quality consumers.

We first consider price competition. We look for an equilibrium in which the market is covered and both firms compete for consumers. High-θ consumers buy the high-quality good; low-θ consumers buy the low-quality good (which must be priced lower to attract any consumer). A consumer with parameter θ is indifferent between the two brands if and only if $\theta s_1 - p_1 = \theta s_2 - p_2$. This yields the following demand functions (see chapter 2):

$$D_1(p_1, p_2) = \frac{p_2 - p_1}{\Delta s} - \underline{\theta},$$

$$D_2(p_1, p_2) = \overline{\theta} - \frac{p_2 - p_1}{\Delta s}.$$

In Nash equilibrium, each firm i maximizes

$$(p_i - c)D_i(p_i, p_j)$$

with respect to p_i.

The reaction functions are

$$p_2 = R_2(p_1) = (p_1 + c + \overline{\Delta})/2$$

and

$$p_1 = R_1(p_2) = (p_2 + c - \underline{\Delta})/2.$$

The Nash equilibrium satisfies $p_i^c = R_i(p_j^c)$, which implies

$$p_1^c = c + \frac{\overline{\Delta} - 2\underline{\Delta}}{3} = c + \frac{\overline{\theta} - 2\underline{\theta}}{3}\Delta s$$

and

$$p_2^c = c + \frac{2\overline{\Delta} - \underline{\Delta}}{3} = c + \frac{2\overline{\theta} - \underline{\theta}}{3}\Delta s > p_1^c.$$

These yield demands

$$D_1^c = (\overline{\theta} - 2\underline{\theta})/3$$

and

---

34. See also Gabszewicz, Shaked, Sutton, and Thisse 1981. This section follows Shaked and Sutton 1982 particularly closely. We will use a different representation of consumer preferences. For consistency, we will stick to the preferences used in chapters 2 and 3. Bonanno (1986) and Gal-Or (1983) consider vertical product differentiation under quantity competition rather than price competition and report that, in general, Cournot competition does not lead to less product differentiation than price competition.

$$D_2^c = (2\bar{\theta} - \underline{\theta})/3$$

and profits

$$\Pi^1(s_1, s_2) = (\bar{\theta} - 2\underline{\theta})^2 \Delta s/9$$

and

$$\Pi^2(s_1, s_2) = (2\bar{\theta} - \underline{\theta})^2 \Delta s/9.$$

Thus, the high-quality firm charges a higher price than the low-quality producer. It also makes a higher profit.

As with the horizontal model, undifferentiated firms ($\Delta s = 0$) charge their marginal cost and make no profit. When we look at the choice of quality, we will thus obtain the principle of differentiation.

Consider now a two-stage game in which firms first compete in quality (one per firm) and then compete in price. Assume for the moment that the choice of quality is costless. Suppose further that s_i must belong to $[\underline{s}, \bar{s}]$, where $\underline{s}$ and $\bar{s}$ satisfy assumption 2.[35] In the first stage, firm 1 maximizes $\Pi^1(s_1, s_2)$ over s_1, and similarly for firm 2. Let us look for pure strategies. Because undifferentiated firms make no profit, s_1 and s_2 will differ in equilibrium. Suppose, e.g., that $s_1 < s_2$. Because both firms make more profit when they are more differentiated, firm 1 gains from reducing its quality toward $\underline{s}$ and firm 2 from increasing its quality toward $\bar{s}$. Hence, there are two pure Nash equilibria in location: $\{s_1^c = \underline{s}, s_2^c = \bar{s}\}$ and the one obtained by reversing the firms' indices. Both equilibria exhibit maximal differentiation. The intuition is the same as for the spatial model: Firms try to relax price competition through product differentiation. Of course, if one of the firms entered first (sequential choice of quality), that firm would choose the high quality $\bar{s}$ and the other the low quality $\underline{s}$, so the equilibrium would be unique. This suggests the possibility, in real time, of both firms trying to be first. To describe such a preemption game, one would introduce a (possibly time-decreasing) cost of introducing each quality, and possibly a rate of growth of demand (formalized, for instance, by the rate of growth of the density of consumers). The firms then would face a trade-off between obtaining a leadership position (i.e.,

occupying the most profitable niche) and introducing the good too early (see chapters 8 and 10 for such preemption games).

The maximal-differentiation result is interesting because it formalizes the effect of strategic behavior in an extreme way. Even though quality is costless to produce, the low-quality firm gains from reducing its quality to the minimum because this softens price competition (lower quality otherwise reduces demand). This result is, however, not very robust. In particular, if the lowest quality is fairly low (i.e., if assumption 2 is invalid) the low-quality firm ends up facing no demand; this effect prevents maximal differentiation (it is reinforced if marginal production costs differ, so that price competition is less intense). But the principle of differentiation is more robust.

An interesting phenomenon arises when assumption 1 is violated. Suppose that $\bar{\theta} < 2\underline{\theta}$ (low consumer heterogeneity). Then, in the price equilibrium, firm 1 faces no demand. It charges c, and firm 2 charges $c + (\bar{\Delta}/2)$. Firm 1 makes no profit, and firm 2 makes profit $\bar{\Delta}/2$. Thus, even though we assumed costless entry and constant returns to scale, there is only one firm making positive profits in the markets, and the other firm does not gain any share of the market. This property contrasts with the location model. In that model, under costless entry, a firm always enters and has a positive market share. By charging just above the marginal cost, it always makes a positive profit from consumers located nearby (given that its rivals never charge under the marginal cost). With low consumer heterogeneity, intense price competition drives the low-quality firm out. The intuition is that if the lower quality is "low" it cannot compete with the higher quality, whereas if it is "high" (close to the higher quality) it triggers rough price competition, which swamps the increase in demand associated with the increase in quality.

More generally, Shaked and Sutton (1983) show the following "finiteness result"[36]: Suppose that quality s costs $c(s)$ per unit (c was constant in our example). Suppose further that, if all qualities were produced and sold at marginal cost $p(s) = c(s)$, all consumers would buy the highest quality.[37] Then there can be at most a *finite* num-

---

35. That is, $c + [(\bar{\theta} - 2\underline{\theta})/3](\bar{s} - \underline{s}) \leq \underline{\theta}\underline{s}$. This implies that assumption 2 is satisfied for any quality choices.

36. The Shaked-Sutton model actually differs from this one in two respects. First, they use a different family of consumer preferences; second, they study a three-stage game, with sequential entry, quality, and price decisions.

37. Consumer θ would maximize $\theta s - c(s)$. Assuming $c' \geq 0$ and $c'' \geq 0$, the condition is equivalent to $\underline{\theta} \geq c'(\bar{s})$; that is, the lowest-valuation-for-quality consumer would choose the highest quality $\bar{s}$. This is satisfied in particular in our model, in which $c' \equiv 0$. More generally, the assumption is that potential qualities are ranked in the same way by all consumers if sold at marginal cost.

ber of firms with positive market share in the industry (regardless of the relative sizes of demand and entry costs). Again, price competition among the high-quality firms drives prices down to a level at which there is no room for low-quality products. This result must be contrasted with that obtained in the location model of section 7.1, in which, when the entry cost tends to zero or when the density of consumers tends to infinity, the equilibrium number of firms tends to infinity (and the prices converge to marginal cost).

In a sense, the finiteness property requires that the marginal cost of quality not increase too quickly with quality. Shaked and Sutton thus conclude that this finiteness property is more likely to hold if the main burden of quality improvements falls on research-and-development costs or fixed costs rather than on more variable costs, such as those of labor and raw materials.

7.5.2 A Symmetric Model of Monopolistic Competition

In the horizontal- and the vertical-differentiation model, a product competes more with some products (its close neighbors in the product space) than with others. The purpose of this subsection is to introduce a model (due to Dixit and Stiglitz [1977] and Spence [1976]) in which there is no such asymmetry in the substitutability of various products in the industry. Other differences with the horizontal- and the vertical-differentiation model are that there exists a single, representative consumer (i.e., there is no heterogeneity in taste) and that this consumer consumes a little bit of every available good instead of consuming only his most preferred product.

The model has two sectors. The utility function of the "representative" consumer has as its two arguments q_0 (the quantity consumed of the unique good produced by the first sector[38]) and a "subutility function" that depends on the consumptions q_i of all goods i in the second sector (which is called "the sector of differentiated products"). More precisely,

$$U = U\left(q_0, \left(\sum_{i=1}^{n} q_i^\rho\right)^{1/\rho}\right).$$

Thus, the subutility function for the differentiated goods has the constant-elasticity-of-substitution (CES) form. We assume U to be concave, which, in particular, requires that $\rho \leqslant 1$. If p_i is the price of the differentiated product i, the representative consumer maximizes U subject to the budget constraint

$$q_0 + \sum_{i=1}^{n} p_i q_i \leqslant I,$$

where I is the (exogenous) income of the representative consumer.[39]

The number of potential producers in the differentiated sector is infinite. Each producer i is identified by a good i. The production of the differentiated good i involves a fixed cost f and a marginal cost c, both denominated in terms of the numéraire.

Because of the fixed cost, only a finite number n of differentiated goods will be produced (of course, $nf < I$). To simplify calculations, we will assume that n is large. Finally, we will make the free-entry assumption, so that the profit of entering firms is zero. For this reason, profit is not relevant to the income of the representative consumer.

As was mentioned earlier, the utility function chosen is very specific, as it treats all the differentiated products in a symmetric way. When a firm introduces a product, it does not choose its degree of differentiation relative to other products. The utility function used here is thus somewhat abstract, but it allows us to concentrate on the entry decision ("0 or 1") without complicating this by a simultaneous choice of "location."

Maximization of consumer utility with respect to q_i yields (after substitution of the budget constraint into U)

$$U_1 p_i = U_2 \left(\sum_{j=1}^{n} q_j^\rho\right)^{1/\rho - 1} q_i^{\rho - 1}, \tag{7.18}$$

where U_h is the partial derivative of U with respect to its hth argument. Since n is large, a change of q_i has little effect on

$$\sum_{j=1}^{n} q_j^\rho$$

---

38. This unique good is taken as the numéraire.

39. For example, we may assume that the consumer generates I units of the nondifferentiated good by his labor.

and, therefore, little effect on U_1 and U_2. The resulting demand function for product i can be approximated as

$$q_i = kp_i^{-1/(1-\rho)} \ (k > 0).$$

Therefore, the demand elasticity for product i is approximately

$$\varepsilon_i = -\frac{\partial q_i}{\partial p_i} \bigg/ \frac{q_i}{p_i} = \frac{1}{1-\rho}.$$

The limiting case where $\rho = 1$ corresponds to the situation where products are perfect substitutes for one another.

The producer of good i, if he decides to enter, chooses p_i in order to maximize his profit:

$$\max_{p_i} \ [(p_i - c)q_i - f].$$

It follows that

$$p_i(1 - 1/\varepsilon_i) = c$$

(see chapter 1), or

$$p_i = c/\rho. \tag{7.19}$$

The less substitutable are the differentiated products, the higher the price. Now, we determine the number of firms n by imposing the zero-profit condition. Given the symmetry of the problem, all the firms of the differentiated sector produce the same quantity: $q_i = q$. Hence, the zero-profit condition can be written as

$$(c/\rho - c)q = f. \tag{7.20}$$

Using equation 7.18, we derive

$$U_1 \frac{c}{\rho} = U_2 q^{\rho-1}(nq^\rho)^{1/\rho-1},$$

or

$$c\,U_1\left(I - \frac{ncq}{\rho}, n^{1/\rho}q\right) = n^{1/\rho-1}\rho\,U_2\left(I - \frac{ncq}{\rho}, n^{1/\rho}q\right). \tag{7.21}$$

The problem is now solved: q is given by equation 7.20; and after the substitution of q, equation 7.21 determines the number of firms, n. Let (q^c, n^c) be these two numbers.

We now compare this free-market outcome with that chosen by a social planner. There are several assumptions that can be made concerning what the social planner can do. One possibility (considered in different models by von Weizsäcker [1980] and Mankiw and Whinston [1986]) is that he can control only entry (i.e., n). Another is that he can also regulate prices (i.e., n and q). One cannot, in the abstract, determine the relevant benchmark, which depends on the social planner's feasible set of interventions. We here consider the "first-best" benchmark, in which the social planner chooses both the level of entry (n^*) and the output of entering firms (q^*). To be sure, the planner would price at marginal cost c. He would finance the fixed costs $\{n^*f\}$ by a lump-sum tax on the consumer's income. Then the consumer would choose the quantity q of each differentiated product (identical, from the fact of the symmetry of the problem) in order to maximize as follows:

$$\max_q \ U(I - nf - ncq, qn^{1/\rho}).$$

Consequently, the planner would choose n in order to maximize the corresponding indirect utility function. Therefore, it suffices to maximize U with respect to q and n (for which we can use the "envelope theorem"). Then we would obtain two equations in two unknowns, from which we would solve for q^* and n^*.

After these calculations, it is possible to compare q^c with q^*, and n^c with n^*. For practical purposes, taking a simple functional form, as Dixit and Stiglitz have done, facilitates these calculations. Those authors show that the comparison between q^c and q^* depends crucially on the derivative of the "rate of appropriability of the surplus by the firm" in their example. This rate, $\mu(q)$, is defined as the ratio of the firm's total revenue to the *gross* consumer surplus generated by the introduction of the differentiated product:

$$\mu(q) \equiv \frac{pq}{S(q)} = \frac{S'(q)q}{S(q)}.$$

In their example, q^c is larger or smaller than q^* depending on whether μ increases or decreases with q.[40] Quite

---

40. Dixit and Stiglitz's example is slightly more general with regard to the second argument of U. They use $\sum_{i=1}^{n} v(q_i)$ for this argument. For the utility function used above, we can show that $\mu(q) = \rho$. In this case $\mu'(q) = 0$ and $q^c = q^*$.

naturally, when the rate of appropriability increases with the quantity produced, the firm (whose objective is to maximize profit) has more incentive to increase output than does the planner (whose objective is to maximize surplus). It can also be shown that n^c may be larger or smaller than n^*.

As for monopoly or oligopoly, the conclusion of this study of monopolistic competition is that only the detailed examination of each situation allows us to say whether or not there is "excess capacity" ($q^c < q^*$) or "excess diversity" ($n^c > n^*$).

Monopolistic competition has, even more recently, received very rigorous foundations in papers by Deneckere and Rothschild (1986), Hart (1985a,b), Perloff and Salop (1985), Sattinger (1984), and Wolinsky (1986), in comparison with which the previous arguments were only approximate. (With a large but finite number of brands, there is a little bit of strategic interaction, profits are not exactly zero, and so on.) These authors look for foundations for demand functions, such as the Spence-Dixit-Stiglitz one, that give rise to monopolistic competition. Instead of positing a representative consumer, they build probability models in which tastes differ and are random. With some variants, these models resemble the horizontal- and vertical-differentiation models of this chapter, in that each consumer consumes only one brand in the differentiated-goods sector. An important distinction with these models, however, is that the valuations for the various brands are drawn independently from some probability distribution,[41] whereas in the horizontal-differentiation model the "net valuation" (valuation minus transportation cost) for the various brands follows a pattern that varies in a well-defined and nonrandom way among consumers.[42]

Answers and Hints

Exercise 7.1

The consumer at abscissa x in figure 7.5 is indifferent between the two brands if

$$p_1 + t(x - a)^2 = p_2 + t(1 - b - x)^2.$$

This yields the demand functions

$$D_1(p_1, p_2) = x$$

and

$$D_2(p_1, p_2) = 1 - x.$$

To obtain the Nash equilibrium, maximize

$$(p_i - c)D_i(p_i, p_j)$$

with respect to p_i.

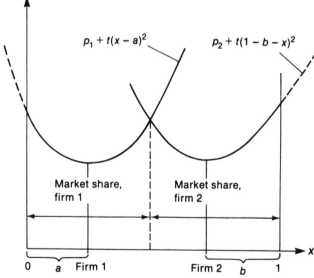

Figure 7.5
Generalized costs under quadratic transportation costs.

---

41. For instance, Sattinger shows that if a consumer's valuation for a brand is drawn from the Pareto distribution, one obtains aggregate demand functions resembling those derived from the CES form used by Spence and by Dixit and Stiglitz.

42. See Deneckere and Rothschild 1986 for a more precise definition of this. They also argue that, "other things being equal," monopolistic competition is much more competitive than competition on the circle, owing to the fact that every firm is competing with every other firm rather than with two neighbors.

Exercise 7.2

(i) The demand functions are given by

$$D_i(p_i, p_j) = (p_j - p_i + t)/2t.$$

(See chapter 2.) Firm i maximizes

$$(p_i - c_i)D_i(p_i, p_j),$$

which yields

$$p_i = R_i(p_j) = (p_j + t + c_i)/2.$$

The Bertrand-Nash equilibrium satisfies

$$p_i = R_i[R_j(p_i)],$$

or

$$p_i(c_i, c_j) = t + \frac{2c_i + c_j}{3}.$$

The reduced-form profits are

$$\Pi^i(c_i, c_j) = \left(t + \frac{c_j - c_i}{3}\right)^2 \bigg/ 2t.$$

(ii) This is straightforward.

(iii) In the first stage, firm i maximizes

$$[p_i(c_i, c_j) - c_i][p_j(c_i, c_j) - p_i(c_i, c_j) + t]/2t - \phi(c_i).$$

Using the envelope theorem, we can ignore the derivative with respect to p_i. We are thus left with two terms (besides the marginal cost of investment, $\phi'(c_i)$): $-D_i$ (the direct effect: a unit cost reduction operates on D_i units of demand) and

$$(p_i - c_i)\frac{\partial p_j}{\partial c_i}\bigg/ 2t > 0$$

(the strategic effect: firm i's cost reductions imply a decrease in p_i, and therefore a decrease in p_j because the reaction curves are upward sloping).

Exercise 7.3

Assume that there are n firms. Consider firm i's choice of p_i, given that the other firms charge p. A consumer located at a distance of $x < 1/n$ from firm i is indifferent between firm i and the nearest competitor if

$$p_i + tx^2 = p + t(1/n - x)^2.$$

This yields the following demand function:

$$D_i(p_i, p) = 2x = \frac{1}{n} - \frac{n(p_i - p)}{t}.$$

Maximizing $(p_i - c)D_i$ and using symmetry yields

$$p = c + t/n^2.$$

Profits per firm are

$$\Pi = \left(\frac{t}{n^2}\right)\frac{1}{n} - f = \frac{t}{n^3} - f.$$

The zero-profit condition implies $n^c = (t/f)^{1/3}$ and $p^c = c + f^{2/3}t^{1/3}$. To get the social optimum, minimize total costs (because of unit demands and covered market, there is no distortion of consumption due to market power):

$$\min_n \left(nf + 2nt\int_0^{1/2n} x^2 dx\right) = \min_n \left(nf + \frac{t}{12n^2}\right).$$

This yields $n^* = [t/6f]^{1/3}$.

Exercise 7.4

See Salop 1979.

References

Archibald, G., and G. Rosenbluth. 1975. The "New" Theory of Consumer Demand and Monopolistic Competition. *Quarterly Journal of Economics* 89: 569–590.

Bagwell, K. 1985. Informational Product Differentiation as a Barrier to Entry. Discussion Paper 129, Studies in Industry Economics, Stanford University.

Bain, J. 1956. *Barriers to New Competition*. Cambridge, Mass: Harvard University Press.

Baker, J., and T. Bresnahan. 1985. The Gains from Merger or Collusion in Product Differentiated Industries. *Journal of Industrial Economics* 35: 427–444.

Bénabou, R. 1986a. Search Market Equilibrium, Heterogeneity and Repeat Purchases. Mimeo, CEPREMAP.

Bénabou, R. 1986b. Search, Price-Setting and Inflation. CEPREMAP Working Paper 8622 (*Review of Economic Studies*, forthcoming).

Benham, L. 1972. The Effects of Advertising on the Price of Eyeglasses. *Journal of Law and Economics* 15: 337–352.

Bonanno, G. 1986. Vertical Differentiation with Cournot Competition. *Economic Notes* 15: 68–91.

Bresnahan, T. F. 1987. Competition and Collusion in the American Automobile Industry: The 1955 Price War. *Journal of Industrial Economics* 35: 457–482.

Butters, G. 1977. Equilibrium Distribution of Prices and Advertising. *Review of Economic Studies* 44: 465–492.

Cady, J. 1976. An Estimate of the Price Effects of Restrictions on Drug Price Advertising. *Economic Inquiry* 14: 493–510.

Chamberlin, E. 1933. *The Theory of Monopolistic Competition*. Cambridge, Mass.: Harvard University Press.

Comanor, W. S. 1979. The Effect of Advertising on Competition: A Survey. *Journal of Economic Literature* 17: 453–476.

Comanor, W. S., and T. A. Wilson. 1974. *Advertising and Market Power*. Cambridge, Mass.: Harvard University Press.

Dasgupta, P., and E. Maskin. 1986. The Existence of Equilibrium in Discontinuous Economic Games, II: Applications." *Review of Economic Studies* 53: 27–42.

d'Aspremont, C., J. Gabszewicz, and J.-F. Thisse. 1979. On Hotelling's Stability in Competition. *Econometrica* 17: 1145–1151.

Dehez, P., and A. Jacquemin. 1975. A Note on Advertising Policy under Uncertainty and Dynamic Conditions. *Journal of Industrial Economics* 24: 73–78.

Deneckere, R., and M. Rothschild. 1986. Monopolistic Competition and Preference Diversity. Discussion Paper 684, CMSEMS, Northwestern University.

de Palma, A., V. Ginsburgh, Y. Papageorgiou, and J.-F. Thisse. 1985. The Principle of Minimum Differentiation Holds Under Sufficient Heterogeneity. *Econometrica* 53: 767–782.

Dixit, A., and J. Stiglitz. 1977. Monopolistic Competition and Optimum Product Diversity. *American Economic Review* 67: 297–308.

Dorfman, R., and P. O. Steiner. 1954 Optimal Advertising and Optimal Quality. *American Economic Review* 44: 826–836.

Eaton, B. C. 1982. An Economic Theory of Central Places. *Economic Journal* 92: 56–72.

Eaton, B. C., and R. Lipsey. 1975. The Principle of Minimum Differentiation Reconsidered: Some New Developments in the Theory of Spatial Competition. *Review of Economic Studies* 42: 27–49.

Economides, N. 1986. Minimal and Maximal Product Differentiation in Hotelling's Duopoly. *Economic Letters* 21: 67–71.

Economides, N. 1984. Symmetric Equilibrium Existence and Optimality in Differentiated Product Markets. Mimeo, Columbia University.

Farrell, J. 1984. Moral Hazard in Quality, Entry Barriers, and Introductory Offers. Working Paper 344, Department of Economics, Massachusetts Institute of Technology.

Friedman, J. 1983. Advertising and Oligopolistic Equilibrium. *Bell Journal of Economics* 14: 464–473.

Gabszewicz, J., and J.-F. Thisse. 1979. Price Competition, Quality and Income Disparities. *Journal of Economic Theory* 20: 340–359.

Gabszewicz, J., and J.-F. Thisse. 1980. Entry (and Exit) in a Differentiated Industry. *Journal of Economic Theory* 22: 327–338.

Gabszewicz, J., A. Shaked, J. Sutton, and J.-F. Thisse. 1981. Price Competition Among Differentiated Products: A Detailed Study of Nash Equilibrium. Discussion Paper 81/37, ICERD, London School of Economics.

Galbraith, K. 1967. *The New Industrial State*. Boston: Houghton Mifflin.

Gal-Or, E. 1983. Quality and Quantity Competition. *Bell Journal of Economics* 14: 590–600.

Gertner, R. 1987. Inflation and Monopoly Power in a Duopoly Model with Search. Mimeo, University of Chicago Graduate School of Business.

Grossman, G., and C. Shapiro. 1984. Informative Advertising with Differentiated Products. *Review of Economic Studies* 51: 63–82.

Hart, O. 1985a. Monopolistic Competition in the Spirit of Chamberlin: A General Model. *Review of Economic Studies* 52: 529–546.

Hart, O. 1985b. Monopolistic Competition in the Spirit of Chamberlin: Special Results. *Economic Journal* 95: 889–908.

Hotelling, H. 1929. Stability in Competition. *Economic Journal* 39: 41–57.

Kaldor, N. 1950. The Economic Aspects of Advertising. *Review of Economic Studies* 18: 1–27.

Kwoka, J. 1984. Advertising and the Price and Quality of Optometric Services. *American Economic Review* 74: 211–216.

Lambin, J. J. 1976. *Advertising, Competition, and Market Conduct in Oligopoly Over Time.* Amsterdam: North-Holland.

Lane, W. 1980. Product Differentiation in a Market with Endogenous Sequential Entry. *Bell Journal of Economics* 11: 237–260.

Mankiw, G., and M. Whinston. 1986. Free Entry and Social Inefficiency. *Rand Journal of Economics* 17: 48–58.

Nerlove, M., and K. J. Arrow. 1962. Optimal Advertising Policy Under Dynamic Conditions. *Economica* 29: 524–548.

Nichols, W. 1951. *Price Policies in the Cigarette Industry.* Nashville: Vanderbilt University Press.

Perloff, J., and S. Salop. 1985. Equilibrium with Product Differentiation. *Review of Economic Studies* 52: 107–120.

Peters, M. 1984. Restrictions on Advertising. *Journal of Political Economy* 92: 472–485.

Porter, M. E. 1976. *Interbrand Choice, Strategy, and Bilateral Market Power.* Cambridge, Mass.: Harvard University Press.

Prescott, E., and M. Visscher. 1977. Sequential Location Among Firms with Foresight. *Bell Journal of Economics* 8: 378–393.

Riordan, M. 1986. Monopolistic Competition with Experience Goods. *Quarterly Journal of Economics* 101: 265–279.

Salop, S. 1979. Monopolistic Competition with Outside Goods. *Bell Journal of Economics* 10: 141–156.

Sattinger, M. 1984. Value of an Additional Firm in Monopolistic Competition. *Review of Economic Studies* 43: 217–235.

Schmalensee, R. 1972. *The Economics of Advertising.* Amsterdam: North-Holland.

Schmalensee, R. 1974. Brand Loyalty and Barriers to Entry. *Southern Economic Journal* 40: 579–588.

Schmalensee, R. 1976. A Model of Promotional Competition in Oligopoly. *Review of Economic Studies* 43: 493–507.

Schmalensee, R. 1978. A Model of Advertising and Product Quality. *Journal of Political Economy* 86: 485–503.

Schmalensee, R. 1982. Product Differentiation Advantages of Pioneering Brands. *American Economic Review* 72: 349–365.

Schmalensee, R. 1985. Econometric Diagnosis of Competitive Localization. *International Journal of Industrial Organization* 3: 57–70.

Schmalensee, R. 1986a. Advertising and Market Structure. In *New Developments in the Analysis of Market Structure,* ed. J. Stiglitz and F. Mathewson. Cambridge, Mass.: MIT Press.

Schmalensee, R. 1986b. Inter-Industry Studies of Structure and Performance. In *Handbook of Industrial Organization,* ed. R. Schmalensee and R. Willig (Amsterdam: North-Holland, forthcoming).

Shaked, A., and J. Sutton. 1982. Relaxing Price Competition through Product Differentiation. *Review of Economic Studies* 49: 3–13.

Shaked, A., and J. Sutton. 1983. Natural Oligopolies. *Econometrica* 51: 1469–1484.

Solow, R. 1967. The New Industrial State or Son of Affluence. *Public Interest* 9: 100–108.

Spence, M. 1976. Product Selection, Fixed Costs and Monopolistic Competition. *Review of Economic Studies* 43: 217–235.

Spence, M. 1977. Non-Price Competition. *American Economic Review* 67: 225–259.

Spence, M. 1980. Notes on Advertising, Economies of Scale, and Entry Barriers. *Quarterly Journal of Economics* 95: 493–508.

Stahl, K. 1982a. Location and Spatial Pricing Theory with Nonconvex Transportation Cost Schedules. *Bell Journal of Economics* 13: 575–582.

Stahl, K. 1982b. Consumer Search and the Spatial Distribution of Retailing. *Journal of Industrial Economics* 31: 97–114.

Steiner, R. 1973. Does Advertising Lower Consumer Prices? *Journal of Marketing* 37: 19–26.

Telser, L. G. 1964. Advertising and Competition. *Journal of Political Economy* 72: 537–562.

von Ungern-Sternberg, T. 1986. Monopolistic Competition and General Purpose Products. Mimeo, Université de Lausanne.

von Weizsäcker, C. 1980. A Welfare Analysis of Barriers to Entry. *Bell Journal of Economics* 11: 399–420.

Wolinsky, A. 1986. True Monopolistic Competition as a Result of Imperfect Information. *Quarterly Journal of Economics* 101: 493–511.

Entry, Accommodation, and Exit

In the preceding chapter we saw how fixed costs (or, more generally, increasing returns) generate an imperfectly competitive market structure by limiting entry. However, even when fixed costs do restrict entry, positive (supranormal) profits are not ensured. Indeed, in the free-entry equilibrium, the firms make zero profit (up to the integer problem). In order to explain why the profit rate is systematically greater in certain industries than in others, some type of restriction to entry must exist in these industries to prevent other firms from taking advantage of the profitable market situations. Along these lines, Bain (1956) defined as a barrier to entry anything that allows incumbent firms to earn supranormal profits without threat of entry.[1]

Occasionally government restricts entry—for example, by introducing permits, licenses, patents, and taxi medallions. These restrictions may generate above-normal profits.[2] Other examples include the use of certain government purchasing policies or the granting of import licences (in situations that are not already domestically competitive, perhaps because of significant fixed costs) to form domestic monopolies.[3] In this chapter we consider barriers to entry not created by government.

Bain (1956) informally identified four elements of market structure that affect the ability of established firms to prevent supranormal profits (rents) from being eroded by entry:

---

1. Stigler (1968) offered an alternative definition based on cost asymmetries between incumbents and entrants. Von Weizsäcker's definition (1980a, p. 400) that "a barrier to entry is a cost of producing that must be borne by a firm which seeks to enter an industry but is not borne by firms already in the industry and that implies a distortion in the allocation of resources from the social point of view" is related to Stigler's. For comprehensive treatments of barriers to entry, see Encaoua et al. 1986 and von Weizsäcker 1980b.

2. In New York, a taxi medallion sells for $100,000. That can be interpreted as the present discounted value of the positive profits to be earned in the market, entry into which is legally restricted.

3. Another institutional barrier to entry may well be the lags and costs imposed by regulatory processes. For instance, MCI spent $10 million in regulatory and legal costs and waited seven years to gain permission to construct a microwave system, which cost $2 million and took seven months to complete. The established regulated firm, AT&T, which had a staff of lawyers and economists expert in regulatory matters, skillfully argued there was no need for the new service and that MCI only intended to enter the profitable part of the market, which, AT&T claimed, was used to subsidize some less profitable services ("cream skimming"). For criticisms of the Noerr-Pennington doctrine, which (particularly in the AT&T case) shields businesses from liability for their participation in governmental proceedings, see Brock and Evans 1983 and Brock 1983b. Those authors argue that business' interference in the regulatory process may be pure waste and that, because abuses are unlikely to be caught, this interference (called "regulatory-process predation") should be dealt with severely.

Economies of scale (e.g., fixed costs) Bain argued that if the minimum efficient scale is a significant proportion of the industry demand, the market can sustain only a small number of firms that make supranormal profits without inviting entry. This argument is examined in section 8.1, where we examine natural monopoly or oligopoly situations and the theory of contestability. See also section 8.6.1.

Absolute cost advantages The established firms may own superior production techniques, learned through experience (learning by doing) or through research and development (patented or secret innovations). They may have accumulated capital that reduces their cost of production. They may also have foreclosed the entrants' access to crucial inputs through contracts with suppliers. In sections 8.2 and 8.6.1 we consider the accumulation of capital by incumbents. Section 4.6.2 examined the market-foreclosure doctrine. R&D activity is studied in chapter 10.

Product-differentiation advantages Incumbents may have patented product innovations (which, of course, can be seen as a cost advantage relative to the product), or they may have cornered the right niches in the product space, or they may enjoy consumer loyalty. (The niche argument is examined in section 8.6.2.)

Capital requirements According to this controversial element of entry barriers, entrants may have trouble finding financing for their investments because of the risk to the creditors. One argument is that banks are less eager to lend to entrants because they are less well known than incumbents; another (which will be examined in section 9.7) is that entrants may be prevented from growing as incumbents inflict losses on them in the product market in order to reduce their ability to find financing for new investments.

Bain also suggested three kinds of behavior by incumbents in the face of an entry threat:

Blockaded entry The incumbents compete as if there were no threat of entry. Even so, the market is not attractive enough to entrants.

Deterred entry Entry cannot be blockaded, but the incumbents modify their behavior to successfully thwart entry.

Accommodated entry The incumbents find it (individually) more profitable to let the entrant(s) enter than to erect costly barriers to entry.

Bain's suggestions obviously begged for further analysis. The most famous model of barriers to entry is the "limit pricing model" (Bain 1956; Sylos-Labini 1962; Modigliani 1958), the basic idea of which is that, under some circumstances, incumbent firms may sustain a price so low that it discourages entry. This story remained controversial until Spence (1977), Dixit (1979, 1980), and Milgrom and Roberts (1982) clarified its underlying aspects.[4] Very roughly, the Spence-Dixit reconsideration (section 8.2 below) offers to regard the Stackelberg model of sequential quantity competition as one of sequential capacity choices. That is, although product-market competition (if any) determines the market price in the short run, in the longer run firms compete through the accumulation of capacity. (See chapter 5 for the reinterpretation of quantities as capacities.) An incumbency advantage (the possibility of early capital accumulation) leads the incumbent firm to accumulate a large capacity (and therefore to charge a low price) in order to deter or limit entry. The Milgrom-Roberts reconsideration of the limit-pricing story (studied in chapter 9) is based on the asymmetry of information between the incumbent and the entrant. In their model, the incumbent charges a low price not because he has a large productive capacity (capacity constraints play no role there) but because he tries to convey the information that either the demand or his own marginal cost is low, thus signaling a low profitability of entry to the potential entrant(s). These two models have fairly distinct positive and normative implications.

Erecting barriers to entry is only one aspect of strategic competition. Inducing exit of rivals is another. And even if neither entry nor exit is at stake (the "accommodation" case), firms battle for market shares. Chapter 6 examined examples of such battles, in which firms repeatedly compete in price. Firms also compete in non-price aspects

---

4. Part of the controversy is due to the fact that the timing of the underlying game and the strategic instruments were not completely described (for instance, the "Sylos-Labini postulate" holds that potential entrants expect established firms to maintain the same output if entry occurs, yet the story is named "limit-pricing"), nor was the commitment value of either quantity or price carefully examined.

(capacities, technology, R&D, advertising, product differentiation, etc.). Chapters 5 and 7 offered examples of non-price competition, but there we focused on once-and-for-all (static) situations in which firms choose their non-price variables simultaneously; the important possibility of influencing rivals' subsequent non-price behavior was ignored. This chapter examines strategic interaction in a dynamic context.

There are a variety of business strategies available to a firm, depending on whether it wants to deter entry, to induce exit, or (if those goals are too costly) to do battle with its rivals. As we will see, optimal strategies also depend on whether reaction curves are sloping upward (strategic complements) or downward (strategic substitutes). Section 8.3 offers a taxomony of relevant business strategies, all of them meant to soften the rivals' behavior. Section 8.4 applies these strategies to a number of strategic situations.

The excellent surveys of Gilbert (1986, 1987), Kreps and Spence (1984), Shapiro (1986), and Wilson (1984) address some of the points raised in this chapter. Much of the material of this chapter and the following one is derived from Fudenberg and Tirole 1986 (see also Fudenberg and Tirole 1984). Section 8.1 draws from Fudenberg and Tirole 1987.

8.1 Fixed Costs: Natural Monopoly and Contestability

This section addresses the role of fixed costs as a barrier to entry. Recall Bain's argument that under increasing returns to scale, only a finite number of firms are viable, and these firms make positive (supranormal) profits without triggering entry—for instance, if potential entrants know that a duopoly yields negative profits, an established firm can quietly enjoy a monopoly profit without worrying about the threat of entry. This conclusion was challenged by Baumol, Panzar, and Willig (1982), who argued that having one or a limited number of firms does not mean there is no competition and that potential competition (the threat of entry) may serve to discipline established firms.[5]

8.1.1 Fixed Costs versus Sunk Costs

In a one-period (i.e., timeless) view of the world, a fixed cost is easily defined as a cost that a firm must incur in order to produce and that is independent of the number of units of output. For instance, a firm may incur cost $C(q) = f + cq$ for $q > 0$ and cost $C(q) = 0$ for $q = 0$. (Fixed costs are instances of increasing returns to scale. See the chapter on the theory of the firm for the notions of subadditivity and natural monopoly.) The timeless model of production is, of course, an abstraction. Once time is introduced, one must carefully define the notion of production period. To see this, suppose (with Weitzman [1983]) that a firm produces output $q > 0$ per period in two consecutive periods at cost $2(f + cq)$, where f is the per-period fixed cost. Absent entry and exit costs, it would be cheaper to produce output $2q$ in the first period and 0 in the second. This would cost $f + 2q$ and save f. (We ignore interest and storage costs, assuming that the lag between the periods is short; we also ignore uncertainty about future demand, which may lead firms to wait to produce future supply.) More generally, dividing the production period by 2 and doubling the production intensity saves on fixed costs, so that all production should take place over a very short interval of time and fixed costs should be negligible relative to variable costs. To avoid this extreme conclusion, it is important to realize that fixed costs are always sunk to some extent. The presence of market imperfections prevents instantaneous rental of capital or hiring of labor. Or the firm may need to buy up front specific investment that has no intrinsic value to other firms (and therefore has no value on a second-hand market) and cannot be allocated to another use within the firm.

We will define fixed costs as costs that are independent of the scale of production and are locked in (committed, sunk) for some short length of time, which defines the "period." For example, suppose that deciding to produce a positive quantity requires a firm to immobilize machines, capital, land, legal, public relations, and advertising services, and general staff for one month. The firm cannot get away with incurring half of the relevant fixed costs and doubling its production rate during fifteen days, stop

5. See Baumol et al. 1982 for further references. See also Brock 1983a, Spence 1983, Baumol et al. 1986, and Schwartz 1986.

production, and save the remaining half during the second fortnight (and possibly resume production thereafter). Thus, one can envision a discrete-time model in which a firm incurs a cost of $f + cq$ in each period if it produces at that date and zero otherwise. The real time length of each period indicates the length of time over which the cost is incurred.[6]

The distinction between "fixed costs" and "sunk costs" is one of degree, not one of nature. Fixed costs are sunk only in the short run. (Of course, there is the question of how short the short run is, and how the length of commitment to investments compares with the time scale of product competition, e.g., of price changes. We will come back to this issue when discussing the contestability theory.) Sunk costs are those investment costs that produce a stream of benefits over a long horizon but can never be recouped. A machine will be labeled a fixed cost if the firm rents it for a month (or can sell it without capital loss a month after its purchase) and a sunk cost if the firm is stuck with it.

The notions of fixed and sunk costs are idealizations for several reasons. First, there is clearly a continuum of degrees of commitment between these two polar cases of short and eternal commitment. Second, both notions assume that the investment cost cannot be recouped at all during the commitment period (whatever it is). In practice, a machine would have some value lower than its original value on the second-hand market. Also, leasing and labor contracts can be breached at some penalty cost. Thus, commitment is not quite an all-or-nothing notion. What we really mean by period of commitment is a period of time over which the cost of being freed from the commitment within the period is sufficiently high that it does not pay to be freed. For simplicity, we will content ourselves with assuming that investment costs are completely sunk for the whole period. Third, and a related point, our notion of commitment is largely a purely technological one (though filtered through the existing set of input-market institutions). In practice, the date at which a firm resells its assets or modifies its rental or labor contracts may also depend on how well the firm is doing in the product market and on strategic considerations in this market.

8.1.2 Contestability

Following Baumol et al. 1982, let us consider a homogeneous-good industry with n firms. All firms have the same technology, and producing output q costs $C(q)$ with $C(0) = 0$. We split the set of firms into two groups: m "incumbents" (without loss of generality, we can assume that the incumbents are firms $i = 1, \ldots, m$) and $n - m \geq 0$ "potential entrants."

An industry configuration is a set of outputs $\{q_1, \ldots, q_m\}$ for the incumbents and a price p charged by all incumbents (the potential entrants stay out of the market).

The industry configuration is *feasible* if the market clears (i.e., if total output is equal to total demand at price p: $\sum_{i=1}^{m} q_i = D(p)$) and if firms make non-negative profits (for any incumbent firm, $pq_i \geq C(q_i)$). It is *sustainable* if no entrant can make a profit taking the incumbents' price as given (there do not exist a price $p^e \leq p$ and an output $q^e \leq D(p^e)$ such that $p^e q^e > C(q^e)$).

A *perfectly contestable market* is one in which any equilibrium industry configuration must be sustainable.

These definitions extend straightforwardly to multi-product technologies; it suffices to allow outputs and prices to be multidimensional vectors. Indeed, the theory of contestability has been partly motivated by multiproduct technologies, and some of its interesting developments are related to the issue of "cross-subsidization." (See footnote 7 below.)

Here we will content ourselves with an exposition of the single-product case.

To illustrate the concept of sustainability, let us consider our standard example of increasing-returns technology:

$$C(q) = f + cq.$$

Let

$$\tilde{\Pi}^m \equiv \max_q \{[P(q) - c]q\}$$

denote the monopoly profit gross of the fixed cost. Assume that a monopoly is viable: $\tilde{\Pi}^m > f$. Figure 8.1 depicts the unique sustainable configuration in this industry. There exists only one incumbent in the industry, charging price p^c and supplying output q^c. The other firms stay out. The contestable price-output pair $\{p^c, q^c\}$ is obtained

---

6. See page 363 of Baumol et al. 1986 for a more complete discussion of this point.

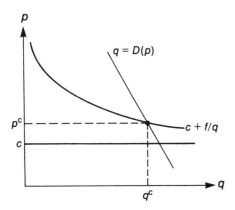

Figure 8.1

from the intersection of the average-cost curve and the demand curve:

$$(p^c - c)D(p^c) = f.$$

A firm that charges $p < p^c$ and produces a positive quantity loses money, because its price is below the average cost. (This also shows that the contestable price is smaller than the monopoly price p^m.) Conversely, a price above p^c is not sustainable, because an entrant can undercut this price and still make a strictly positive profit.

In this example, the theory of contestability predicts the following conclusions:

(1) There is a unique operating firm in the industry (technological efficiency).

(2) This firm makes zero profit.

(3) Average-cost pricing prevails. Furthermore, the allocation is constrained efficient, in the sense that it is socially efficient, given the constraint that a social planner does not use subsidies.[7]

Thus, the mere "threat of entry" has an effect on the market behavior of the incumbent firm (conclusion 2 and first part of conclusion 3). The second part of conclusion 3 is not surprising. The fixed cost is not duplicated in the sustainable outcome. Thus, only the market price matters in the assessment of efficiency. Clearly, the first-best outcome is obtained when the incumbent charges the marginal cost; however, in the absence of a subsidy, the firm would lose f and would not be willing to operate. Short of the first-best outcome, a social planner prefers the lowest price that allows the firm to make a non-negative profit, i.e., p^c.[8]

This set of conclusions is striking. It has long been argued that an industry subject to non-negligible increasing returns could not behave competitively and therefore should be nationalized, or at least carefully regulated. If, however, such an industry behaves like a perfectly contestable market, it comes as close to marginal-cost pricing as is consistent with viable firms (if subsidies are prohibited). In the absence of actual competition, potential competition is very effective in disciplining the incumbent firms. Hence, the unregulated organization of industries with increasing returns to scale should be less of a problem than would appear at first glance. Clearly,

---

7. In the multiproduct case, Baumol et al. (1982) show that a sustainable allocation, if it exists, satisfies the following conditions: (a) Industry cost minimization holds (a generalization of conclusion 1). (b) Firms make no profit (conclusion 2). (c) The revenue made by a firm on a subset of products is at least as big as the cost savings that would result from not producing these products (keeping the outputs of the other products as given). (d) The price of a product exceeds its marginal production cost for any firm that produces it. They are equal if more than one firm supplies the good. (e) Under some assumptions (see Baumol et al. 1977), Ramsey prices and outputs—i.e., those that are welfare optimal subject to the constraint that the firm earns a profit equal to the maximum profit permitted by barriers to entry—are sustainable.

The intuition for condition c (the no-cross-subsidization result) is that if a set of products were not viable, an entrant could come in with the same production as an incumbent except that it would drop these products and thus make money. Condition d is a generalization of Bertrand competition.

8. To be rigorous, we must check that the social planner could not do better by forcing the firm to randomize between different prices. To see that price randomization lowers welfare, it suffices to show that the aggregate welfare $W(p)$ is concave in p. If this is the case, then from Jensen's inequality $E\,W(p) \leqslant W(Ep)$, and welfare is higher under the deterministic price Ep than under the random price p (where E denotes expectation over the price). If,

furthermore, the profit function $\Pi(p)$ is concave in p, the firm makes non-negative profits under the deterministic price Ep if it makes non-negative profit under the random price p (since $\Pi(Ep) \geqslant E\,\Pi(p) \geqslant 0$), so the firm's non-negative profit constraint is harder to satisfy with a random price than with a deterministic one. For our purpose, let us assume that

$$D'(p) + (p - c)D''(p) \leqslant 0.$$

Then

$$\Pi''(p) \equiv 2\,D'(p) + (p - c)D''(p) < 0.$$

Also,

$$
\begin{aligned}
W''(p) &\equiv [S(p) + \Pi(p)]'' \\
&= [-D(p) + D(p) + (p - c)D'(p)]' \\
&= D'(p) + (p - c)D''(p) \leqslant 0
\end{aligned}
$$

(where S denotes the net consumer surplus). Thus, both Π and W are concave. For a much more general result on the undesirability of random prices, see Samuelson 1972.

such a theory, if applicable, has strong implications for the deregulation of the airlines and similar industries.

Baumol et al. (1982) show that, for different demand and cost functions, natural monopolies may not be sustainable. That is, there may not exist a price-output pair $\{p^c, q^c\}$ such that firms make non-negative profits, the market clears, and the allocation cannot be upset by profitable entry at price-output pair $\{p^e, q^e\}$ such that $p^e \leq p^c$ and $q^e \leq D(p^e)$. That is, constrained efficient market structures may not be sustainable against entry.

*Exercise 8.1*** In a one-good industry, consider a U-shaped average-cost curve. Suppose that the demand curve intersects the average-cost curve slightly to the right of the most efficient scale (i.e., the average-cost-minimizing output). Using a diagram, show that there exists no sustainable allocation.

The natural question is this: Which situation is depicted by the contestability axioms—in particular, the sustainability axiom? One would want to describe (at least in a stylized way) competition in a natural-monopoly industry, and to compare its outcome with the contestable one.

One game that yields the contestable outcome is the following: Suppose that firms first choose prices simultaneously and then choose outputs. (Picking an output involves deciding whether to enter—i.e., whether to choose a strictly positive output.) This two-stage game is the reverse of the two-stage game described in chapter 5, in which firms chose quantities before prices. Suppose that all potential firms choose price p^c. Then one of them chooses output q^c and the others stay out (produce nothing). This is clearly an equilibrium. All firms make zero profit. If a firm were to undercut p^c, it could not supply the market profitably.[9] As Baumol et al. rightly note, the theory of perfectly contestable markets can thus be seen as a generalization of Bertrand competition to markets with increasing returns to scale.[10]

The preceding game portrays the vision of an industry in which prices adjust more slowly than decisions about quantities or entry. Prices are considered rigid at the time firms choose their quantities. As prices are generally thought of as amenable to relatively quick adjustment, the technology thus involves a fixed cost in the sense of subsection 8.1.1. This vision is implicit in the slightly more sophisticated "hit-and-run entry" story offered by the proponents of contestability. Suppose that the incumbent's price is rigid for a length of time τ, and that entry and exit are costless. If the incumbent's price exceeds p^c, an entrant can enter, undercut p^c slightly (thereby conquering the incumbent's entire market share), and exit the industry before τ units of time having elapsed—i.e., before the incumbent can respond by lowering his price. The entrant (who, by assumption, incurs no entry or exit cost) thus makes a positive profit. Thus, only price p^c is "sustainable."

This interpretation of contestability has come under attack on the grounds that prices seem to adjust more rapidly than decisions about quantities or entry. Price adjustment does seem faster in the railroad industry, where entry and expansion entail a long-process of buying up parcels of land (generally requiring powers of eminent domain), engineering and building the railroad, and so on. It may be even faster in the airline industry, where opening a new route is a relatively fast process.[11,12]

---

9. To prove that this is the unique equilibrium, consider the highest price $\bar{p} > p^c$ charged in equilibrium by any firm. Show that this price has probability 1 of being *strictly* higher than the lowest price charged by the other firms. Conclude that this firm makes zero profit, which in turn implies that the lowest price charged by the other firms is p^c with probability 1.

10. See Grossman 1981 for an alternative approach to contestability in a one-good industry. Grossman assumes that firms announce supply curves rather than prices.

11. However, Bailey and Panzar (1981) argue that the theory of contestable markets is relevant to city-pair airline markets. There are returns to scale in this industry, but fixed costs are not sunk. (The aircraft can be recovered at little cost. Sunk costs, such as those for runways, towers, and ground facilities, are incurred by municipalities.) Bailey and Panzar offer some evidence that monopolists (almost 70% of routes are served by a single carrier) behave more or less competitively on their long-haul routes immediately after deregulation. In contrast, Bailey et al. (1985) and other find that fares are higher when concentration is higher when all else is equal (but the relation, although statistically strong, is not economically large).

12. Brock and Scheinkman (1983) study "quantity sustainability." They say that a price-quantity allocation $(\bar{p}, \bar{q})$ is quantity sustainable if any production plan by an entrant q^e makes negative profit at the market-clearing price for quantity $\bar{q} + q^e$. That is, the entrant assumes that the established firm's output remains fixed after entry. Brock and Scheinkman show that under some assumptions price sustainability implies quantity sustainability, and that in the single-product case the allocation (p^c, q^c) at which the demand curve intersects the average-cost curve is quantity sustainable (it is not necessarily price sustainable—see exercise 8.1).

Perry (1984) considers price strategies but departs from the uniform-pricing assumption made by Baumol et al. (1982). The incumbent announces a price-quantity schedule: He stands ready to supply q_1 units of the good at price p_1, then q_2 more units at price $p_2 > p_1$ (so that his total supply at price p_2 is $q_1 + q_2$), and so on. The entrant reacts by announcing a price-quantity schedule himself. Sustainability is easier to obtain than under uniform pricing, because

---

If one takes the view that prices generally adjust more rapidly than capacities, the incumbent's price is unlikely to be locked in when the entrant finishes assembling his production facilities. That is, entry ought to induce the incumbent to reduce his price fairly quickly to adjust to competitive pressure. If the incumbent's price reacts quickly to entry (where "quickly" is relative to the time scale of the entrant's investment), hit-and-run entry is not profitable, as there is no scope for two price-competing firms in a natural monopoly.

An alternative way of thinking about contestability is to envision short-run capacity commitments rather than price rigidities. In this view, prices adjust "instantaneously." (This, of course, is not realistic; it is a metaphor for the idea that prices adjust quickly relative to the time scale of the capacity game.) That is, at any point in time, each firm chooses its price so as to maximize its profit, given the current vector of capacities.

An old intuition in industrial organization states that if the incumbent is committed to his capacity only in the short run, he and the potential entrant are almost on equal footing, so that barriers to entry (and the incumbent's profit) are low. Indeed, in a model where firms are stuck with their capacity choices for a short period of time, it can be shown that there exists an equilibrium in which only the incumbent produces; this apparent monopolist accumulates and constantly renews (approximately) capacity q^c and makes (almost) no profit. If the incumbent's equilibrium capacity were lower (allowing positive profits), an entrant could come in and, because the incumbent's capacity commitment is short, would incur duopoly losses for a short time before the incumbent would exit. The entrant would then take over the market and enjoy incumbency. Thus, the prospect of high steady-state profits together with the brevity of the fight to kick out the incumbent would encourage entry. This approach to contestability is developed in more detail in the supplementary section.

8.1.3 War of Attrition

Another popular approach to natural monopoly is the war of attrition. Like the short-run capacity-commitment approach sketched in the preceding paragraph, it assumes that price adjustments take place more quickly than quantity adjustments.

The war of attrition was introduced in theoretical biology, by Maynard Smith (1974), to explain animals' fights for prey. Two animals fighting for prey may resemble two firms fighting for control of an increasing-returns industry. Fighting is costly to the animals; at the very least, they forgo the opportunity of other activities and become exhausted. Similarly, duopoly competition may be costly because it generates negative profits. In both cases, the object of the fight is to induce the rival to give up. The winning animal keeps the prey; the winning firm obtains monopoly power. The loser is left wishing it had never entered the fight. (For such a fight to take place, its outcome cannot be deterministic. Each player must have at least some chance of winning in order to be willing to participate.) In a war of attrition, each player waits and suffers for a while. If at some point in time his rival has not yet quit, a player gives up.

The simplest example of a war of attrition is the following: Suppose time is continuous from 0 to $+\infty$. The rate of interest is r. There are two firms, with identical cost functions $C(q) = f + cq$ if $q > 0$ and $C(0) = 0$, per unit of time. Price adjustments are instantaneous. If the two firms are in the market at time t, price equals marginal cost c (Bertrand competition) and each firm loses f per unit of time. If only one firm is in the market, the price is equal to the monopoly price, p^m, and the firm makes instantaneous profit $\tilde{\Pi}^m - f > 0$; the other firm makes zero profit. Both firms are in the market at date 0. At each instant, each firm decides whether to exit (conditional on the other firm's still being in the market at that date). Exit is costless. For simplicity, assume that a firm that drops out never returns (however, the equilibrium we describe below

---

profitably undercutting an incumbent is more difficult. The incumbent can sell just enough units at low prices so that the entrant's residual demand curve is moved to the left of his average-cost curve; in a sense, the incumbent is able to commit to a certain output through low prices on these units but can still make money through high prices on the marginal units. Perry shows that the

incumbent generally makes a strictly positive profit, and that the existence of a sustainable price-quantity strategy may not even require the natural-monopoly assumption (which assumption is necessary but not sufficient for the existence of a sustainable allocation under uniform pricing).

is still an equilibrium if costless reentry is allowed). Because the market is profitable for a monopoly, the remaining firm stays in forever after its rival has dropped out.

We now construct a symmetric equilibrium in which, at any instant, each firm is indifferent between dropping out and staying. For a firm to be indifferent, the expected profits from the two actions must be the same. Because dropping out at t means zero profits *from that date on*, each firm's expected present discounted value of profits from any date on must equal zero. If both firms are still in the market at date t, each firm drops out with probability $x\,dt$ between t and $t + dt$, where $x \equiv rf/(\tilde{\Pi}^m - f)$. To see that these strategies form an equilibrium, suppose that at date t both firms are still in the market. If firm 1 drops out, it obtains 0 from t on. If firm 1 stays in until time $t + dt$, it incurs duopoly loss $f\,dt$. However, with probability $x\,dt$, firm 2 drops out during this short interval of time. Firm 1 then becomes a monopoly and, from then on, earns total (discounted) profits $(\tilde{\Pi}^m - f)/r$. If firm 2 is still in at date $t + dt$, firm 1 is willing to drop out and thus make 0 from that date on. Firm 1 is indifferent between dropping out at date t and staying until $t + dt$ if

$$0 = -f\,dt + (x\,dt)[(\tilde{\Pi}^m - f)/r] + 0.$$

The industry outcome is stochastic. Each firm drops out according to a Poisson process with parameter x.[13]

This equilibrium is consistent with free reentry because the value of being in is 0, so there is no reason to reenter once one has left. The equilibrium is not unique,[14]; however, if we depart from our perfect-information assumption and allow uncertainty about rival's fixed (opportunity) costs (see chapter 9), and if the support of this uncertainty is sufficiently large, then the symmetric equilibrium is also the unique equilibrium.

The war of attrition yields the following conclusions:

(1') There are two firms in the industry for a (random) length of time (technological inefficiency); then one exits.

(2') Firms earn no *ex ante* rents, but may have *ex post* profits.

(3') The price is first competitive and then equal to the monopoly price. The allocation is not constrained efficient, and welfare is lower than under contestability.

The second part of conclusion 3' results from the fact that the contestable allocation is optimal, subject to the no-subsidy constraint. The following exercise checks this result for a simple specification of demand.

Exercise 8.2** All the firms in an industry have the same production cost: $C(q) = f = \frac{3}{16}$. (The marginal cost is 0.) The demand is $D(p) = 1 - p$.

(i) Is this a "natural monopoly"?

(ii) Compute the contestable allocation. Calculate the welfare level.

(iii) Derive the symmetric equilibrium of the infinite-horizon, continuous-time war of attrition between two firms. Calculate the expected intertemporal welfare, and compare it with the welfare level from question ii. (Hint: For a Poisson process with parameter y, the probability that no arrival has occurred by time t is e^{-yt}.)

Figure 8.2 illustrates the difference in price dynamics in the contestability and war-of-attrition theories.

It may be instructive to look at the natural monopoly issue from the viewpoint of the literature on rent seeking. As was noted in chapter 1, Posner argued that the prospect of monopoly profits creates a contest to appropriate those profits. All monopoly profits must be added to the usual dead-weight-loss triangle if two postulates

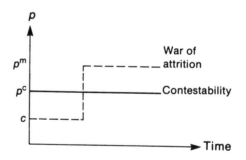

Figure 8.2
Price dynamics in natural monopoly.

---

13. That is, the cumulative probability that a firm drops out before date t, conditional on the other firm's not dropping out, is $1 - e^{-xt}$ (an exponential distribution).

14. There also exist asymmetric equilibria: For example, at each date firm 1 stays in and firm 2 exits (another equilibrium is obtained by switching the names of the firms).

hold: the rent-dissipation (or zero-profit) postulate, which asserts that the firms' total expenditure on obtaining the monopoly profit is equal to the monopoly profit, and the wastefulness postulate, which asserts that this expenditure has no socially valuable by-products.

Both the contestable allocation and the war-of-attrition equilibrium satisfy the rent-dissipation postulate. Competition for the monopoly position drives industry profits down to zero.[15] The contestable allocation yields an interesting reversal of the wastefulness postulate. Because rent dissipation occurs through low prices, it benefits the consumer and is socially useful. The war-of-attrition equilibrium comes closer to satisfying the wastefulness postulate than the contestable allocation. Some of the profits are dissipated wastefully (for a while, the fixed production cost is duplicated). But the consumers also enjoy marginal-cost pricing for some time before facing the monopoly price (Posner's allocation would correspond to monopoly pricing at each instant). Thus, welfare is higher than that predicted by the rent-seeking literature and lower than that associated with the contestable allocation.

Another interesting analogy relates to the free-entry biases discussed in chapter 7. As Whinston (1986) notes, one can view the exit decision as a reverse entry decision. Therefore, this decision is subject to the same biases—imperfect appropriability of the consumer surplus and business-stealing effect—as the entry decision. Let $w(p)$ denote the social welfare per unit of time, gross of fixed cost. To illustrate the two biases, assume that there are two consumers, with unit demands, and that $c = 0$. First, to focus on the business-stealing effect, suppose that the two consumers have the same valuation v for the good. The flow monopoly profit is then $\tilde{\Pi}^m = v$. A monopolist captures the full consumer surplus and introduces no distortion in consumption. Thus,

$$w(c) - w(p^m) = v - v = 0 < f.$$

The social gain from competition per unit of time is lower than the flow fixed cost of production. It is socially optimal to have a single firm at any point of time even if its pricing behavior cannot be regulated. Thus, there is too little exit. Second, suppose that the two consumers have different valuations $v_1 < v_2$ and that $v_2 > 2v_1$, so that a monopolist charges price v_2. By charging v_1 (which would induce a socially optimal consumption), it would capture only part of the total consumer surplus. Now, if f is lower than

$$w(c) - w(p^m) = (v_1 + v_2) - v_2 = v_1,$$

competition is valuable.[16] That is, when a firm chooses to exit (because its private incentive to stay is zero), a social planner would like it to stay—there is socially too much exit, because the firms do not appropriate the gain in consumer surplus due to competition. Thus, in a second-best world in which pricing cannot be regulated, a social planner would want to prevent any exit.

The preceding analysis relies on strong price competition between the two firms. Suppose they succeed in tacitly colluding in prices while both are still in the market (see chapter 6 for a discussion of tacit collusion). The market price is then equal to p^m, independent of the number of remaining firms. Thus, a social planner would want one of the firms to exit at date 0 in order to avoid wasteful duplication of the fixed cost. However, suppose that the firms wage a war of attrition, and they lose $(f - \tilde{\Pi}^m/2) > 0$ per unit of time while competing. In the symmetric equilibrium, each firm exits with probability $x'dt$ between t and $t + dt$, where x' is given by

$$(f - \tilde{\Pi}^m/2)dt = [x'(\tilde{\Pi}^m - f)/r]dt,$$

which yields $x' < x$. Because fighting for a monopoly position is less costly under tacit collusion, firms exit at a slower rate precisely when a social planner would prefer a single firm. Here we have an example of the business-stealing effect. Staying in has no social value; all profits are derived from diverting half the monopoly profit from one's rival (and the full monopoly profit if this rival exits). Under tacit collusion, there is socially too little exit.[17]

The war-of-attrition paradigm has been used to try to predict whether big firms or small firms are more likely to

---

15. One way of looking at this is as follows. The monopoly profit in a contestable market turns out to be zero. No expenditure is made to obtain it. In contrast, in the war of attrition, the monopoly profit is the regular one. The expenditure corresponds to the duopoly losses incurred prior to giving up or getting the monopoly situation.

16. In this example, $\tilde{\Pi}^m = v_2 > 2v_1 > 2f$. As long as firms wage Bertrand competition, $f > 0$ is sufficient for the market to be a natural monopoly.

17. See Mankiw and Whinston 1986 and review exercise 24 for analyses of the free-entry biases in a homogeneous-good industry in a static context.

exit first in a declining industry with increasing returns to scale. Ghemawat and Nalebuff (1985) argue that big firms will exit earlier, leaving the industry to the small firms. The intuition is that if demand declines, a big firm loses viability more quickly (it is too big relative to the market). Thus, in a monopoly situation, a big firm would exit earlier than a small firm. In a competitive duopoly, the small firm's anticipation that the big firm will eventually leave is an incentive for the small firm to stay in the market. As Ghemawat and Nalebuff show, this forces the big firm to exit as soon as its instantaneous duopoly profit becomes negative (i.e. no real war of attrition takes place on the equilibrium path).[18] Londregan (1986) extends this model to allow a complete product life cycle, in which the market grows and then declines.[19]

Whinston (1986) shows that the Ghemawat-Nalebuff result depends crucially on the big firms' inability to "go on a diet." He argues that, in practice, a big firm may be able to reduce the number of plants and become a small firm when demand declines. He then solves for equilibrium when firms can scrap plants (exit then occurs when the last plant is closed) and shows that a variety of potential outcomes are feasible. Indeed, Whinston notes that in the declining industry producing the antiknock additive for leaded gasoline, the smallest producer was the first to leave. Ghemawat and Nalebuff (1985) give a few exam-

ples, including the synthetic-soda-ash industry and the British steel-castings industry, in which the largest firms exited first.

There is a simple case for which the outcome can be predicted without intimate knowledge of the industry. Ghemawat and Nalebuff (1987) and Whinston (1986) show that if firms can decrease their capacities after a downward shock in demand that calls for exit, the bigger firm reduces its capacity until it is equal in size to its rival, and thereafter the two firms reduce their capacities symmetrically (so they remain of equal size).[20]

In chapter 9 we will consider another aspect of the war of attrition: the possibility that each firm has incomplete information about its rivals' production or opportunity costs. The length of time already spent in a ruinous oligopoly contest is then a signal that a firm is efficient (or has low outside opportunities, or that the market exerts beneficial spillovers on its other product lines). The link between the war of attrition, Bayesian updating, and Darwinian selection in an industry will be discussed.

8.2 Sunk Costs and Barriers to Entry: The Stackelberg-Spence-Dixit Model

A fascinating aspect of sunk costs is their commitment value. A firm that buys equipment today signals that it

---

18. The Ghemawat-Nalebuff model assumes that each firm faces a flow cost of maintaining capacity, which is proportional to the firm's capacity (there is no fixed cost independent of productive scale). With $P(K, t)$ denoting the inverse demand function at time t, where $K = K_1 + K_2$ is industry capacity, and c denoting the maintenance-cum-production cost, firm i's instantaneous profit (assuming that both firms are still in at t) is

$$[P(K_1 + K_2, t) - c]K_i.$$

Assume that $\partial P/\partial K < 0$, and $\partial P/\partial t < 0$ (i.e., the industry is declining). Assume further that the firm's exit decision is lumpy (so a firm's capacity jumps directly from K_i to 0). Let t_i^* be defined by

$$P(K_i, t_i^*) \equiv c.$$

If $K_1 > K_2$, then $t_1^* < t_2^*$. That is, firm 1 would exit earlier than firm 2 in a monopoly situation. Backward induction shows that firm 1 exits first at time $t < t_1^*$ such that $P(K_1 + K_2, t) = c$, and firm two stays until t_2^*. (Hint: At date t_1^*, it is a dominant strategy for firm 1 to exit. At date $t_1^* - \varepsilon$, for ε small, firm 2 would be foolish to exit: At worst, it loses some profit during ε, and then becomes a profitable monopolist from t_1^* to t_2^*; so, assuming costly reentry, firm 2 stays and firm 1 exits.)

19. See Huang and Li 1986 and Fine and Li 1986 for analyses of the war of attrition when the profits follow a stochastic process.

20. The model of Ghemawat and Nalebuff is a continuous-time, continuous-capacity-adjustment one. That of Whinston assumes discrete periods and indivisible plants of equal sizes; it does not require almost continuous reduction, but uses a Markov-like assumption.

The following is a heuristic description of equilibrium. Consider the continuous-time model in note 18. Let $R(K_j, t)$ denote firm i's static reaction function at t; it maximizes

$$[P(K_i + K_j, t) - c]K_i$$

over K_i. Let $(K^*(t), K^*(t))$ denote the static Nash equilibrium, defined by $K^*(t) \equiv R(K^*(t), t)$. Under mild assumptions, $\partial R/\partial t < 0$, which implies that $dK^*/dt < 0$. Consider now the dynamic model and assume for simplicity that firms can only reduce capacity. The equilibrium strategies are: If

$$K_i(t) < R(K_j(t), t) \text{ for } i = 1, 2,$$

no firm reduces its capacity at date t. If

$$K_i(t) < R(K_j(t), t) \text{ and } K_j(t) \geqslant R(K_i(t), t),$$

firm i does not reduce its capacity; firm j stays on or moves to its reaction curve (that is, it reduces its capacity continuously if it is on its reaction curve and discontinuously if it is above its reaction curve). If $K_i(t) \geqslant R(K_j(t), t)$ for $i = 1, 2$, both firms move to the static Nash equilibrium $(K^*(t), K^*(t))$. They then reduce their capacities so as to remain on their reaction curve. The equilibrium is nothing but a sequence of myopic (static) Cournot outcomes.

will be around tomorrow if it cannot resell the equipment. Thus, we may conjecture that the buying of equipment—if it is observed by one's rivals—may have strategic effects, and therefore is not a purely internal cost-minimization issue. Rivals may interpret the purchase of equipment as bad news about the profitability of the market and may reduce their scale of entry or not enter at all. The purpose of this section is to verify this conjecture.

For the modeling, we will need an explicitly dynamic model. Sunk costs are, by definition, a multiperiod phenomenon, as is entry deterrence. We will also introduce temporal asymmetries. Some firms will enter the market early, possibly because of a technological lead. We will see that these established firms (also called incumbents) accumulate a quantity of "capital" sufficient to limit the entry of other firms or even to make their entry unprofitable. First-mover advantages thus allow the established firms to restrict or prevent competition. We will think of "capital" as equipment or machines; however, as will be discussed later, the concept of capital can be interpreted more broadly.

8.2.1 Accommodated, Deterred, and Blockaded Entry

We start with a prototypical model whose extremely simplistic structure allows us to highlight the concept of a barrier to entry. This model is due to Heinrich von Stackelberg (1934).

Consider a two-firm industry. Firm 1 (the existing firm) chooses a level of capital K_1, which is then fixed. (We shall return to this assumption later.) Firm 2 (the potential "entrant") observes K_1 and then chooses its level of capital K_2, which is also fixed.

Assume that the profits of the two firms are specified by

$$\Pi^1(K_1, K_2) = K_1(1 - K_1 - K_2)$$

and

$$\Pi^2(K_1, K_2) = K_2(1 - K_1 - K_2).$$

These functions will be interpreted later. (Recall from chapter 5 that they are the reduced-form profit functions that come from short-run product-market competition with given capacities.) For the moment, note that these functions have two properties that are necessary for the generalization of the results to more general profit func-

tions: First, each firm dislikes capital accumulation by the other firm ($\Pi_j^i < 0$). Second, each firm's marginal value of capital decreases with the other firm's capital level ($\Pi_{ij}^i < 0$). That is, the capital levels are strategic substitutes (see the introduction to part II).

For now, assume that there is no fixed cost of entry. The game between the two firms is a two-period one. Firm 1 must anticipate the reaction of firm 2 to capital level K_1. Profit maximization by firm 2 requires that

$$K_2 = R_2(K_1) = \frac{1 - K_1}{2},$$

where R_2 is the reaction function of firm 2 (that is, $R_2(K_1)$ maximizes $K_2(1 - K_1 - K_2)$ with respect to K_2). Therefore, firm 1 maximizes

$$\Pi^1 = K_1\left(1 - K_1 - \frac{1 - K_1}{2}\right),$$

from which we can determine the "perfect" Nash equilibrium:

$$K_1 = \tfrac{1}{2}, K_2 = \tfrac{1}{4}, \Pi^1 = \tfrac{1}{8}, \Pi^2 = \tfrac{1}{16}.$$

Despite identical profit functions, firm 1 is in a position to obtain more profit than firm 2 by limiting the size of firm 2's entry. This illustrates the first mover's advantage. We know that if the two firms were to choose their levels of capital simultaneously, each would react to the other optimally, so that $K_2 = R_2(K_1)$ and $K_1 = R_1(K_2)$. Using the symmetry, the simultaneous-move solution yields

$$K_1 = K_2 = \tfrac{1}{3}$$

and

$$\Pi^1 = \Pi^2 = \tfrac{1}{9}.$$

The simultaneous-move and sequential-move outcomes are illustrated in figure 8.3. The broken lines represent the isoprofit curves. By definition of the reaction curves, firm 1's isoprofit curve is horizontal when it crosses R_1 and firm 2's isoprofit curve is vertical when it crosses R_2. To conform with common usage, S and N are used to denote the equilibrium outcomes in the sequential and the simultaneous game, respectively. They are usually called Stackelberg and Nash equilibria, but that terminology is actually misleading. The equilibrium concept is the same in both cases: (perfect) Nash equilibrium. The games simply differ in their timing. In the Stackelberg game, firm 1 has a chance to choose its level of capital before firm 2 and, therefore, to influence firm 2.

We conclude that temporal asymmetry allows firm 1 to limit firm 2's capital level. To do this, it accumulates more capital than it would have done in a simultaneous equilibrium. Consequently, the profitability of a marginal investment for firm 2 is diminished, providing an incentive for this firm not to accumulate too much capital. The intuition is the same for more general profit functions; by raising K_1, firm 1 reduces the marginal profit from investing (Π_2^2) for firm 2 (as long as $\Pi_{12}^2 < 0$). Thus, firm 2 invests less, which benefits its rival ($\Pi_2^1 < 0$).

The role of the irreversibility of capital levels (i.e., the fact that they may not be reduced in the future) should be stressed. Firm 1 is not on its reaction curve *ex post*; its best response to $K_2 = \frac{1}{4}$ is $K_1 = \frac{3}{8} < \frac{1}{2}$. If, after the choice of K_2, firm 1 could reduce K_1, it would do so. However, firm 2 would then choose $K_2 > \frac{1}{4}$ in anticipation of this response. In this sense, firm 1 loses by being flexible. The fact that the investment cost is sunk is a barrier to exit and allows the incumbent to commit to a high capital level.

Therefore, it is important that the capital investment be somewhat difficult to reverse if it is to have a commitment value. In particular, if the machines operated by the established firm may easily be resold on a second-hand market, then it will not satisfy this condition. The commitment effect is stronger the more slowly capital depreciates and the more specific it is to the firm (that is, when its resale involves large losses).

The value of commitment and the corresponding notion of "burning one's bridges" have widespread applicability beyond economics. An oft-quoted example is that of two armies wishing to occupy an island located between their countries and connected by a bridge to both (figure 8.4). Each army prefers letting its opponent have the island to fighting. Army 1, which is somewhat knowledgeable in game theory, occupies the island and burns the bridge behind it. Army 2 then has no option other than to let army 1 have the island, because it knows that army 1 has no choice other than to fight back if army 2 attacks. This is the paradox of commitment: Army 1 does better by reducing its set of choices.

The above equilibrium demonstrates how the incumbent (firm 1) can reduce firm 2's scale of entry. Following Caves and Porter (1977), we denote this as a *barrier to mobility*. We will also say that firm 1 *accommodates* entry, in that it takes entry for granted and simply tries to affect

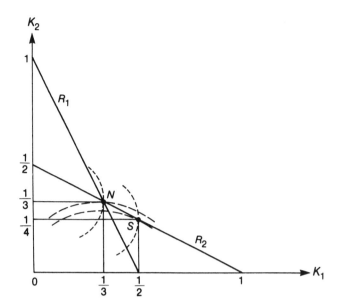

Figure 8.3
Stackelberg outcome.

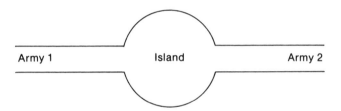

Figure 8.4

firm 2's subsequent behavior. Firm 1 cannot deter entry in this model. Firm 2 declines to enter ($K_2 = R_2(K_1) = 0$) only if $K_1 \geq 1$, which would yield negative profits to firm 1. In economic terms, this means that it is always worthwhile for firm 2 to enter, even on a small scale. If firm 1 makes positive profits, firm 2 can choose a small level of capital, hardly affect the market price, and make a profit itself.

Such small-scale entry becomes unprofitable under increasing returns to scale. To illustrate the possibility of *entry deterrence*, let us introduce a fixed cost of entry, f, into our model. Assume that firm 2 has the following profit function:

$$\Pi^2(K_1, K_2) = \begin{cases} K_2(1 - K_1 - K_2) - f & \text{if } K_2 > 0 \\ 0 & \text{if } K_2 = 0. \end{cases}$$

Suppose that $f < \frac{1}{16}$. If firm 1 chooses $K_1 = \frac{1}{2}$ as before, firm 2 chooses $K_2 = \frac{1}{4}$ and makes a profit of $(\frac{1}{16} - f) > 0$.

However, this choice of K_1 may not be optimal for firm 1, which may be able to increase its profit by completely preventing the entry of firm 2. K_1^b, the capital level that discourages entry, is given by[21]

$$\max_{K_2}[K_2(1 - K_2 - K_1^b) - f] = 0,$$

or

$$K_1^b = 1 - 2\sqrt{f} > \tfrac{1}{2}.$$

Firm 2's reaction curve, depicted in figure 8.5, coincides with that in figure 8.3 up to K_1^b, and then coincides with the horizontal axis. When entry is deterred, the profit of firm 1 is

$$\Pi^1 = (1 - 2\sqrt{f})[1 - (1 - 2\sqrt{f})] = 2\sqrt{f}(1 - 2\sqrt{f}).$$

If f is close to $\tfrac{1}{16}$, this profit is greater than $\tfrac{1}{8}$. Therefore, firm 1 is interested in completely discouraging, not simply restricting, the entry of firm 2. Firm 1 accomplishes this by choosing $K_1 = K_1^b$, because accumulating beyond K_1^b would reduce profit (K_1^b is greater than the monopoly capital level of $\tfrac{1}{2}$).[22]

In Bain's terminology, the equilibrium for f a bit below $\tfrac{1}{16}$ is one of deterred entry, whereas the one for $f = 0$ (or, more generally, f small) is one of accommodated entry. With $f > \tfrac{1}{16}$, firm 1 blockades entry simply by choosing its monopoly capital level, $K_1^m = \tfrac{1}{2}$.[23]

*Exercise 8.3** Indivisibilities may, like a fixed cost, lead to a monopolistic structure if combined with a first-mover advantage. Suppose that firms must build an integer number of plants: 0, 1, 2, ... Building n plants costs $(3.5)n$. Each plant produces one unit of output, there is no variable cost, and the market price is $p = 6 - K$, where K is the industry's total capacity (number of plants).

(i) Show that a monopolist installs one plant.

(ii) Consider duopolists simultaneously choosing their numbers of plants, K_1 and K_2. Let $p = 6 - K_1 - K_2$. Show that in the Cournot equilibrium each firm builds one plant.

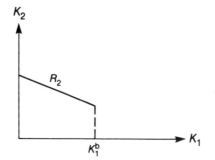

Figure 8.5
A fixed cost of entry implies a minimum capital level.

(iii) Suppose that firm 1 builds before firm 2. Show that firm 1 builds two plants and firm 2 stays out. Comment on the similarities and differences with the continuous-investment-*cum*-fixed-cost case.

8.2.2 Discussion and Extensions

8.2.2.1 Reduced-Form Profit Functions

We now return to the interpretation of the profit functions. Stackelberg actually wrote his two-stage game in terms of quantities. This left (at least) three questions unanswered: What does quantity competition mean? Why does one of the firms enjoy a first-mover advantage (i.e., choose its quantity first)? Why does quantity have a commitment value? Spence (1977, 1979) and Dixit (1979, 1980) made the Stackelberg story consistent, basically by interpreting Stackelberg's quantity variable as a capacity (as we did notationally). Doing so provides answers to the three questions: First, the profit functions represent reduced-form profit functions after one has solved for short-run product-market competition given the capacity levels. Second, the first-mover advantage may come from the fact that one of the firms obtains the technology earlier or is quicker to act than the other firm. Third, capacities have a commitment value to the extent that they are sunk.

Remark 1 In chapter 5, we derive the reduced-form profit functions by solving capacity-constrained price competi-

---

21. The superscript b stands for *barrier*.

22. Technically, $K_1 = \tfrac{1}{2}$ satisfies the first-order condition and the second-order condition locally for firm 1. However, since the reaction function of firm 2 is discontinuous at K_1^b, firm 1's objective function is not globally concave. Thus, $K_1 = \tfrac{1}{2}$ is not necessarily the maximum.

23. That the monopoly level coincides with the incumbent's capital level under accommodated entry is an artifact of the quadratic profit functions we have chosen.

tion. Spence and Dixit depart from this in two respects. First, they take short-run competition to be quantity competition rather than price competition. Second, they allow firms to accumulate more capacity during product-market competition. Consider Dixit's (1980) model. In the first period, firm 1 chooses capacity K_1 at cost $c_0 K_1$. This capacity may subsequently be increased, but cannot be reduced. Firm 2 observes K_1. Then, in the second period, the two firms choose their outputs (q_1 and q_2) and their capacities ($\tilde{K}_1$ and K_2) simultaneously, with $\tilde{K}_1 \geqslant K_1$. Production involves cost c per unit of output. Output cannot exceed capacity: $q_i \leqslant K_i$ for all i. The price is equal to the market-clearing price, given the outputs.

Firm 2 faces short-run and long-run marginal costs equal to $c_0 + c$ and clearly chooses identical capacity and outputs ($K_2 = q_2$). For $q_1 \leqslant K_1$, firm 1 incurs the short-run marginal cost c; any unit of output beyond K_1 costs the long-run marginal cost, $c_0 + c$. The short-run marginal-cost curve is represented in figure 8.6, which suggests why capacity has a commitment value: It lowers the *ex post* marginal cost of producing up to K_1 and hence makes the production of the first K_1 units attractive in the second period. To make this precise, we can consider two reaction functions. Were firms to choose their levels of capital and output simultaneously (that is, were there no first-mover advantage), they would face cost $c_0 + c$ for each unit of output at the date of the production decision. With the demand curve assumed linear ($p = a - bq$), firm i would maximize

$$q_i(a - b(q_i + q_j) - c_0 - c).$$

(There is obviously no point in accumulating capacity that is not used for production here.) Thus, the reaction function is

$$R_i(q_j) = (a - bq_j - c_0 - c)/2b.$$

Next consider the Dixit two-stage game in which firm 1 chooses its capacity in the first period and its production in the second period, whereas firm 2 chooses both capacity and production in period 2. Firm 2's reaction function at date 2 is

$$R_2(q_1) = (a - bq_1 - c_0 - c)/2b.$$

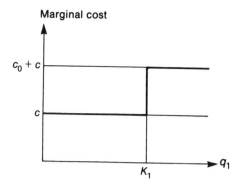

Marginal cost

Figure 8.6
Short-run marginal cost.

However, firm 1 at date 2 has a different reaction function, called a *short-run* reaction function. Up to K_1, it incurs marginal cost c only, and therefore it has reaction function

$$\tilde{R}_1(q_2) = (a - bq_2 - c)/2b > R_1(q_2).$$

Beyond K_1, the short-run and long-run reaction functions coincide:

$$\tilde{R}_1(q_2) = R_1(q_2).$$

The second-period equilibrium as a function of K_1 can thus be obtained from the intersection of $\tilde{R}_1$ and R_2 in figure 8.7.

As can been seen from figure 8.7, firm 1 has no incentive to invest in the first period in capacity that it does not use *ex post*.[24] Furthermore, firm 1 gains by investing beyond the Nash capacity K_1^N, because this moves the equilibrium to the right of N along R_2, which increases firm 1's profit.

This does not explain how prices are determined. It is assumed that the market price "clears the market." For instance, the market price for linear demand $p = a - bq$ is

$$p = a - b(q_1 + q_2).$$

Assuming that the firms in the second stage produce to capacity, $q_i = K_i$ (this actually is part of the derivation), we can write the reduced-form profit functions

$$\Pi^i(K_i, K_j) = K_i(a - c_0 - c - b(K_i + K_j)),$$

---

24. There would be idle capacity if firm 1's short-run reaction curve intersected firm 2's reaction curve at some $q_1 < K_1$. Firm 1 could obtain the same product-market outcome by accumulating only q_1, thus saving $c_0(K_1 - q_1)$.

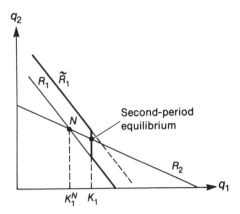

Figure 8.7
Short-run and long-run reaction functions.

which have the previous form for $a - c_0 - c \equiv 1$ and $b \equiv 1$.

As usual, the presence of an auctioneer is not completely satisfactory. A more realistic description of the Spence-Dixit game might involve a "double-capacity-constrained game." The first capacity constraint refers to the *production* capacity, which limits the level of output; the marginal cost is c as long as $q_i \leqslant K_i$. The second capacity constraint refers to the *selling* capacity, which limits the level of sales—firm i cannot sell more than it has produced: $x_i \leqslant q_i$, where x_i is the level of sales. This interpretation simply adds a third stage, in which firms choose prices constrained by their outputs.

A question studied by the literature is whether the incumbent firm uses its capacity after deterring entry. That is, does firm 1 hold idle capacity to deter firm 2's entry? Using quantity competition as the paradigm of short-run product-market competition, Spence answered in the affirmative. But Dixit showed that Spence's result was due to the fact that his equilibrium was not a perfect equilibrium.[25] Indeed, with a concave demand function, any capacity held to deter entry is used by the monopolist. Bulow et al. (1985a) show that Spence's excess capacity may reappear when the demand function is so convex that the reaction curves are upward sloping.

Schmalensee (1981) uses the Spence-Dixit model; however, instead of introducing a fixed cost of entry, he assumes that a firm cannot produce below some minimum level of output K_0 if it produces at all (so $q_i \geqslant K_0$). He

interprets K_0 as a minimum efficient scale. Using empirical evidence that the minimum efficient scale is often low relative to industry demand (generally under 10 percent), he argues that such barriers to entry cannot account for established firms' high profits.

*Exercise 8.4*** The first part of this exercise recalls how reduced-form profit functions can be deduced from short-run price competition. The second part (inspired by Matsuyama and Itoh [1985]) shows how the model of barriers to entry can be used to analyze the desirability of protecting an infant industry.

(i) Two firms produce perfect substitutes at zero marginal cost (up to a capacity constraint). The demand function is $p = 4 - (q_1 + q_2)$. Firms are capacity constrained: $q_i \leqslant K_i$. Capacity costs 3 per unit. Use the monopoly solution to show that K_i cannot exceed 1. Use this upper bound to conclude that when firms are capacity constrained and choose their prices simultaneously (with the capacities fixed and common knowledge), both firms quote price $p = 4 - K_1 - K_2$; to show this, posit either the efficient-rationing rule or the proportional-rationing rule.

(ii) Firm 1 is a foreign firm, firm 2 a domestic one. Consider the following "no-protection" 3-stage game:

1. Firm 1 chooses capacity K_1.

2. Firm 2 chooses capacity K_2, knowing K_1.

3. Firms choose prices simultaneously, knowing K_1 and K_2.

(That is, the foreign firm has a first-mover advantage.) The domestic firm faces an entry cost $f = \frac{1}{16}$. Compute the equilibrium and the welfare (where welfare = consumer surplus + profit of domestic firm). Show that a policy of "limited protection," which forces the foreign firm to wait until period 2 to invest domestically (so that both firms choose K_1 and K_2 simultaneously) increases welfare.

Remark 2 Interpreting profit functions as reduced-form functions for price competition under capacity constraints allows us to perform some welfare analysis. In the Stackelberg example (see subsection 8.2.1), let $p = 1 - K$ denote the demand function, where $K = K_1 + K_2$ denotes industry capacity and output. (The intercept of the demand

---

25. See the Game Theory User's Manual on the notion of perfect equilibrium.

function is net of investment and production costs—see remark 1). The social optimum in this industry is to produce industry output $K = 1$. In duopoly, the welfare loss is measured by the area of the triangle between the demand curve and the marginal-cost curve (which, here, is the horizontal axis, as the marginal cost is normalized to zero); see chapter 1. If p is the market price, the welfare loss from monopoly or duopoly pricing is equal to $p^2/2$. If the entrant enters, the fixed cost f of entry must be added to the welfare loss, because the socially optimal production involves only one firm (the entrant does not bring any cost savings).

First, assume away the entry cost. The market price is higher when the two firms invest simultaneously ($p = \frac{1}{3}$) than when firm 1 invests before firm 2 ($p = \frac{1}{4}$). Thus, a social planner would not mind sequential entry.

The picture may be altered dramatically by the presence of an entry cost. The welfare loss is equal to $f + \frac{1}{18}$ if the two firms invest simultaneously.[26] When firm 1 invests first, the welfare loss is equal to $(2\sqrt{f})^2/2 = 2f$ if the fixed cost is sufficiently large that firm 1 deters entry.[27] Thus, the welfare loss is higher under sequential entry than under simultaneous entry if $f > \frac{1}{18}$ (and the reverse is the case if $f < \frac{1}{18}$ as long as entry is deterred). That the welfare analysis of entry deterrence is ambiguous should not be a surprise, because we know from chapter 7 that entry can result in biases in either direction. While the entrant takes the incumbent's capacity as fixed, the entrant's addition to the capacity of the industry is socially beneficial if it is privately beneficial from the nonappropriability-of-consumer-surplus effect (as long as the capacity is used). The incumbent's increase in capacity to deter entry also yields some increase in the industry's capacity without wasting the entry cost.

8.2.2.2 Multiple Incumbents

Several authors have studied either entry deterrence with several incumbents or models of sequential entry—Bernheim (1984), Gilbert and Vives (1986), McLean and Riordan (1985), Vives (1985), and Waldman (1987), among others.

One of the issues[28] addressed in this literature is whether entry deterrence is a public good. The one incumbent–one entrant model considered above suggests the following conjecture: To deter entry, the incumbent incurs a cost. With several incumbents, entry deterrence becomes a public good; if the first incumbent deters entry by accumulating a large amount of capital, the other incumbents also benefit. Every incumbent would like entry to be deterred but would prefer not to incur the associated cost.

To understand why underinvestment by the incumbents to deter entry might occur, it is useful to come back to the classic noncooperative subscription problem. Consider a community with two individuals. This community can implement a project that costs $1. Each member of the community has value $2/3 for the project. Thus, no one is willing to bear the whole cost; however, cooperative action is desirable, because the social value of the project, $4/3, exceeds its cost, $1. Suppose that the members choose simultaneously how much to invest in the project. If $1 or more is collected, the project is implemented; otherwise it is not. (Any remaining money is redistributed according to some rule.) There are two kinds of pure-strategy Nash equilibria in this game. In the first, no one contributes and the project is not implemented. In the second, each member i contributes by subscribing an amount a_i such that $a_1 + a_2 = 1$ and the project is implemented. (There is a continuum of such equilibria, indexed by, say, a_1 in $[\frac{1}{3}, \frac{2}{3}]$, if the money is given back to the contributors because the project is not realized.)[29]

Now consider a situation in which two incumbents (firms 1 and 2) choose their capacities simultaneously. The entrant (firm 3) stays out if and only if $K_1 + K_2 \geqslant K^b$, where K^b is the entry-deterring industry capacity. The capacities K_1 and K_2 are analogous to the subscriptions in the preceding paragraph. It would seem that we face a public-good problem, with the possibility of too little

---

26. This assumes that both firms choose their Cournot outputs equal to $\frac{1}{3}$. Note that the entrant in this equilibrium makes profit $\frac{1}{9} - f > 0$. This is the only pure-strategy equilibrium under our assumption that $f < \frac{1}{16}$. (For $f \geqslant \frac{1}{16}$, there exists another equilibrium, with firm 1 producing its monopoly output, $\frac{1}{2}$, and firm 2 not entering.)

27. That is, $2\sqrt{f} - 4f > \frac{1}{8}$ or $f \geqslant 0.0054$. We assume as before that the incumbent uses its entry-deterring capacity, $2\sqrt{f}$. See remark 1 above.

28. Some policy interventions against entry deterrence are ambiguous. For instance, as Bernheim notes, making entry deterrence harder for the second firm entering a market reduces this firm's prospects and makes entry deterrence easier for the first firm in the market.

29. See exercise 11.6 in the Game Theory User's Manual for an underinvestment result with a continuous-size project choice.

aggregate investment from the point of view of the incumbents. Gilbert and Vives (1986) show that this intuition may be misleading. The reason is that, contrary to the usual public-good problem, supplying the public good (and thus contributing to entry deterrence) is not necessarily costly. Suppose that entry is deterred and $K_1 + K_2 = K^b$. Let incumbent i's profit be

$$K_i(P(K^b) - c_0 - c),$$

where $P(\cdot)$ is the inverse demand function and where c_0 and c are the investment and *ex post* variable costs per unit. Because the price must exceed the total unit cost, each firm would like to have the highest possible capital level for this given price. Thus, conditional on the actual deterrence of entry, each firm would like to contribute to entry deterrence as much as it can (in contrast with the public-good situation). Gilbert and Vives actually find that only overinvestment can occur. The exercise below suggests in more detail why this is so. For more general models, the conclusions are more ambiguous; see Waldman 1987 and McLean and Riordan 1985.

Exercise 8.5*** Consider the two incumbents–one entrant game above. Let

$$\Pi^i = K_i(P(K_1 + K_2 + K_3) - c_0 - c)$$

denote firm i's profit for $i = 1, 2$, where

$$K_3 = \begin{cases} R_3(K_1 + K_2) & \text{for } K_1 + K_2 < K^b \\ 0 & \text{for } K_1 + K_2 \geqslant K^b \end{cases}$$

(firm 3 faces a fixed cost of entry). Let

$$\Pi^b \equiv K^b(P(K^b) - c_0 - c)$$

denote the industry profit when firms 1 and 2 just deter firm 3's entry. Show that if the noncooperative equilibrium between the incumbents allows entry, then $\Pi^1 + \Pi^2 \geqslant \Pi^b$ (so there is no underinvestment in entry deterrence by the incumbents).

8.2.2.3   Entry for Buyout

We assumed that the post-entry market organization takes the form of competition between the incumbent and the entrant (if the entrant enters). However, suppose that

there are no impediments to mergers—i.e., there is no legal prohibition, there is no asymmetry of information about the value of assets, there are no direct costs of transferring assets, and it is possible for the asset seller to commit not to come back and reinvest in this market. The market structure may then be a monopoly if the incumbent buys the entrant or vice versa. Indeed, if mergers are costless, firms have an incentive to merge after the entrant enters, because a monopoly can do at least as well as duopolists as long as it owns the two firms' assets. Of course, the distribution of the gains from monopolization is determined in the bargaining process for buyout and depends on the "threat point," i.e., on the profits the two firms would make if they were to reach no agreement and compete in the product market. As long as the entrant has some bargaining power, he can extract part of the increase in industry profits associated with the merger. This means that, for a given investment (here, capacity), the possibility of a merger increases the entrant's post-entry profit. The bottom line is that the prospect of buyouts encourages entry. But we should note that the merger *ex post* increases market concentration. One example of a socially perverse effect is that the incumbent may buy the entrant's capacity and scrap part of it (that is, the incumbent may hold excess capacity after the merger). For more on these ideas, see Rasmusen 1987.

8.2.2.4   Uncertainty

Maskin (1986) extends Schmalensee's version of the Spence-Dixit model to allow for uncertainty about demand or short-run marginal cost. He argues that uncertainty forces the incumbent to choose a higher capacity to deter entry than he would under certainty. This increases the cost of entry deterrence, making it less likely.

8.2.2.5   Capital Accumulation

The basic model is very simplistic in that it assumes that firms can accumulate their capacities all at once. Furthermore, these capacities cannot be reduced and do not depreciate. In practice, capacities are accumulated and adjusted over time (possibly in a lumpy way, owing to technological indivisibilities). Capacity expansion imposes adjustment costs.[30] Furthermore, demand grows at the

---

30. See Prescott and Visscher 1980 for a model of internal organization that explains adjustment costs.

beginning of the product's life cycle, making early complete capacity accumulation a costly strategy. Thus, it is worthwhile to study capital-accumulation games, in which firms vie for a Stackelberg leadership position; see section 8.6.1.

8.2.3 Other Forms of Capital

We saw how physical capital may facilitate the erection of barriers to entry. Other kinds of capital may have the same effect if they have commitment value (that is, they are irreversible, at least in the short run). Consider the following three examples.[31]

• *Learning by doing* In certain industries, the experience acquired by the established firms during previous production periods reduces their current production costs and thus may be considered to be a form of capital. This experience gives the existing firms a competitive advantage, and therefore it can discourage others from entering. Indeed, certain consulting firms (the Boston Consulting Group, for example) have suggested that intense early production promotes learning by doing and thus can be used strategically for this purpose. The argument is, however, a bit less clear-cut than it seems, as will be shown in section 8.4.

*Exercise 8.6*** (i) A monopolist faces demand curve $q = 1 - p$ in each of two periods (A and B). Its unit cost is c in period A and $c - \lambda q^A$ in period B, where q^A is the first-period output (the firm learns by doing). The discount factor between the periods is $\delta = 1$. Show that the first-period output is $d/(2 - \lambda)$, where $d \equiv 1 - c$.

(ii) Suppose now that the monopolist (firm 1) faces an entrant (firm 2, with unit cost c) in the second period. They play Cournot (quantity) competition, which yields profits

$$\Pi_i^B = (1 + c_j^B - 2c_i^B)^2/9$$

and outputs

$$q_i^B = (1 + c_j^B - 2c_i^B)/3.$$

Write the first-order conditions determining q_1^A when (a) q_1^A is not observed by the entrant before second-period competition and (b) q_1^A is observed by the entrant. In which case is the monopolist's first-period output higher? (You need not compute q_1^A; just give the intuition and the interpretation in terms of business strategy.) What could change if the entrant were to face a fixed cost of entry?

• *Developing a clientele* The decision to develop a clientele is a capital decision that increases the demand for the product of the established firm. Clearly, if the clientele attached to the existing firm is considerable, the potential demand for the entrant is weak. This is well understood by firms that launch advertising and promotional campaigns not only to make their product known but also to "preempt" demand. The more imperfect the consumers' information and the more important the costs of switching suppliers, the greater the clientele effect.[32]

• *Setting up a network of exclusive franchises* This is a capital decision that increases the entrant's distribution costs.[33] The established supplier can assure himself of the services of the more capable franchisees by selecting them initially and imposing exclusivity on them.[34] Such an explanation is offered by some economists for the initial difficulty encountered by foreign producers attempting to enter the American automobile market (however, this argument is debatable because exclusive contracts are often of short duration).

The last two barriers—developing a clientele and franchising in the distribution network—are preemptive strategies. Two other important examples of such strategies are the following:

• Choosing a "strategic place" in a geographical or product space is often important because of its commitment

---

31. These are enunciations of the conventional wisdom, which may oversimplify reality. Two of the examples will be discussed in more detail below.

32. Considering a clientele as a form of capital suggests that the existing firm should overinvest to block the entry of other firms. Even though such a strategy may be possible, it is not necessarily optimal, for the following reason. If entry does occur, the established firm has two types of customers after entry: its own clients (over whom it still has monopoly power) and the other consumers (for whom it is competing with the entrants). Of course, the firm wants to set a high price for the captive clientele and a lower price for the other consumers. If it cannot price-discriminate, the firm must charge an intermediate price; this intermediate price is higher the more important is the captive clientele. Consequently, the existing firm is less aggressive after entry, when it has a large clientele; it has become a "fat cat," which may make entry profitable. Therefore, overinvesting in clientele may not necessarily be the best way to prevent entry. See Schmalensee 1983. (See also Baldini 1983, Fudenberg and Tirole 1984, and note 43 below.)

33. Salop and Scheffman (1983) include this type of strategic behavior in their category of behaviors that "raise the rival's costs."

34. See subsection 4.6.2.

effect (the fixed cost of establishing oneself cannot be easily recouped; "the firm is here to stay"). See subsection 8.6.2 for further discussion.

• A new product can preempt rival firms, especially when it is patented.

Preemption and the "race" to be first which it engenders are important concepts in the theory of imperfect competition.

• *The problem of "apparently innocent" behavior* From a theoretical viewpoint, it is possible to prescribe policies for government intervention in each situation of noncompetitive behavior by existing firms. Those responsible for fostering competition (antitrust authorities) are well aware that things are not so simple. They have a very difficult time proving that a certain type of behavior is detrimental to competition. In fact, they have less information than the firms about demand functions, cost structures, the quantities of accumulated capital, and so on. Government decision-makers face a dilemma. Certainly they cannot prosecute an existing firm for increasing the demand for its product by providing information to consumers, for decreasing its own costs by investing in R&D and in physical capital, or for accumulating experience. But how can we know if a firm has accumulated its "capital" in a totally innocent fashion? The problem is that most of the decisions that make a firm healthy also elevate it to a power position with respect to potential entrants.[35]

8.3 A Taxonomy of Business Strategies

The point of the Stackelberg model is that commitments matter because of their influence on the rivals' actions. In the capacity-accumulation game, the incumbent overinvests to force the entrant to restrict his own capacity. The goals of this section are to define the notions of "overinvestment" and "underinvestment" and, more generally, to supply a two-period framework within which to think of business strategies, including a taxonomy of possible strategies. The ideas that underlie this section have been known informally for a long time.

Recently Fudenberg and Tirole (1984) and Bulow, Geanakoplos, and Klemperer (1985b) have independently offered a framework that systematizes these ideas.[36] The outcomes of many strategic interactions in industrial organization can be predicted using the basic framework of strategic effects in the simple two-period model.

Consider the following two-period, two-firm model. In period 1, firm 1 (the incumbent) chooses some variable K_1 (for example, capacity). We will call K_1 an investment, although, as we will see, that word must be taken in a very large sense. Firm 2 observes K_1 and decides whether to enter. If it does not enter, it makes zero profit. The incumbent then enjoys a monopoly position in the second period and makes profit

$$\Pi^{1m}(K_1, x_1^m(K_1)),$$

where $x_1^m(K_1)$ is the monopoly choice in the second period as a function of K_1 (for instance, x_1 is firm 1's output). If firm 2 enters, the firms make simultaneous second-period choices x_1 and x_2. Their profits are then

$$\Pi^1(K_1, x_1, x_2)$$

and

$$\Pi^2(K_1, x_1, x_2).$$

By convention, firm 2's entry cost is part of Π^2. These functions are assumed to be differentiable.

Suppose that firm 1 chooses some level K_1 (take it as given in this paragraph) and that firm 2 enters. The postentry choices x_1 and x_2 are determined by a Nash equilibrium. The subsequent analysis of the effect of changes in K_1 on the Nash equilibrium assumes that this Nash equilibrium,

$$\{x_1^*(K_1), x_2^*(K_1)\},$$

is unique and stable. "Stability" has to do with the following thought experiment: Suppose that firm 1 picks an arbitrary x_1. Let firm 2 react by choosing an action $R_2(x_1)$ that maximizes $\Pi^2(K_1, x_1, x_2)$ over x_2. Then let firm 1 react to $R_2(x_1)$ by choosing an action $R_1(R_2(x_1))$ that maximizes $\Pi^1(K_1, \tilde{x}_1, R_2(x_1))$ over $\tilde{x}_1$. And so forth. This yields a sequential adjustment process in which both firms

---

35. In the next section we will see how actions by established firms have direct ("innocent") effects on their profits as well as strategic effects.

36. The terms *strategic complements* and *strategic substitutes* were coined by Bulow et al. The "animal" terminology is taken from Fudenberg and Tirole.

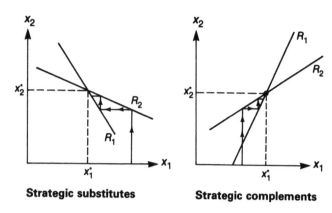

Strategic substitutes **Strategic complements**

Figure 8.8
Stable second-period equilibrium.

are myopic (i.e., they ignore the effect that their adjustment has on their rival; alternatively, they are rational but have discount factor $\delta = 0$). The Nash equilibrium,

$$\{x_1^*(K_1), x_2^*(K_1)\},$$

is stable if such an adjustment process converges to the equilibrium allocation from any initial position.[37] Stability is illustrated in figure 8.8.

Let us now consider the incumbent's first-period choice of K_1. We will say that entry is deterred if K_1 is chosen such that

$$\Pi^2(K_1, x_1^*(K_1), x_2^*(K_1)) \leqslant 0.$$

(This includes the case where entry is blockaded, that is, where the monopoly choice of K_1 deters entry.) Entry is accommodated if

$$\Pi^2(K_1, x_1^*(K_1), x_2^*(K_1)) > 0.$$

Which of the two cases must be examined depends on whether the incumbent finds it advantageous to deter or to accommodate entry. For simplicity, we will also assume that

$\Pi^1(K_1, x_1^*(K_1), x_2^*(K_1))$ and $\Pi^{1m}(K_1, x_1^m(K_1))$

are strictly concave in K_1 and that the functions $x_i^*(\cdot)$ are differentiable.

8.3.1 Deterrence of Entry

We ignore the uninteresting case in which entry is blockaded (that case is void of strategic interactions). Thus, the incumbent chooses a level of K_1 so as to just deter entry[38]:

$$\Pi^2(K_1, x_1^*(K_1), x_2^*(K_1)) = 0.$$

Let us consider which strategy firm 1 can use to make firm 2's entry unprofitable. For this, let us take the total derivative of Π^2 with respect to K_1. From the second-period optimization,

$$\frac{\partial \Pi^2}{\partial x_2}(K_1, x_1^*(K_1), x_2^*(K_1)) = 0.$$

Thus, the effect of K_1 on Π^2 through firm 2's second-period choice should be ignored (this is the envelope theorem). Only two terms remain:

$$\frac{d\Pi^2}{dK_1} = \underbrace{\frac{\partial \Pi^2}{\partial K_1}}_{\text{Direct effect}} + \underbrace{\frac{\partial \Pi^2}{\partial x_1}\frac{dx_1^*}{dK_1}}_{\text{Strategic effect}}.$$

By changing K_1, firm 1 may have a *direct effect* on firm 2's profit ($\partial \Pi^2/\partial K_1$). For instance, if K_1 is the clientele accumulated by firm 1 before the entry of firm 2, a greater clientele reduces the size of the market and thus lowers firm 2's profit independent of any strategic effect. Often, however, $\partial \Pi^2/\partial K_1 = 0$. This is the case when K_1 is an investment that affects only firm 1's technology, such as the choice of a capacity or a technique.[39] Any effect on

---

37. For more on stability in oligopoly models, see Cournot 1838, Fisher 1961, Hahn 1962, Seade 1980, and Dixit 1986. The condition for local stability is $\Pi_{11}^1 \Pi_{22}^2 > \Pi_{12}^1 \Pi_{12}^2$. (Hint: Compare the slopes at the Nash equilibrium.) For a version in which firms behave rationally (that is, anticipate subsequent reactions and discount the future), see subsection 8.6.1.1.

38. From the continuity of Π^1 and Π^2 and the uniqueness of x_1^* and x_2^*, $x_1^*(K_1)$ and $x_2^*(K_1)$ are continuous in K_1 (from the "theorem of the maximum"). Hence, Π^2 is continuous in K_1. Suppose that

$$\Pi^2(K_1, x_1^*(K_1), x_2^*(K_1)) < 0.$$

Then firm 1 can increase or decrease K_1 a bit while still deterring entry (from the continuity of Π^2). This means that the constraint that firm 1 deters entry is not locally binding at the optimal K_1. From the concavity of Π^1 and that of Π^{1m}, the entry-deterrence constraint is not binding globally, which means that entry is blockaded (the case we ruled out).

39. Unless firm 1's investment bids up the price of investment goods for firm 2, or firm 1's investment has spillover or learning effects on firm 2.

firm 2's profit is then channeled through firm 1's post-entry choice. The *strategic effect* comes from the fact that K_1 changes firm 1's *ex post* behavior (by dx_1^*/dK_1), thus affecting firm 2's profits (in proportion to $\partial\Pi^2/\partial x_1$). The total effect of K_1 on Π^2 is the sum of the direct and strategic effects.

We will say that investment makes firm 1 *tough* if $d\Pi^2/dK_1 < 0$ and *soft* if $d\Pi^2/dK_1 > 0$.

Obviously, to deter entry, firm 1 wants to look tough. Now consider the following taxonomy of business strategies:

top dog: Be big or strong to look tough or aggressive.

puppy dog: Be small or weak to look soft or inoffensive.

lean and hungry look: Be small or weak to look tough or aggressive.

fat cat: Be big or strong to look soft or inoffensive.

If investment makes firm 1 tough, then firm 1 should "overinvest" to deter entry; that is, it should use the "top dog" strategy. If investment makes firm 1 soft, that firm should "underinvest" (i.e., stay lean and hungry) to deter entry.[40]

Example For simplicity, consider a slightly modified version of the Spence-Dixit model of section 8.2 (the same kind of reasoning holds for the original game). In this version, firm 1 chooses an investment K_1. This investment determines firm 1's second-period marginal cost $c_1(K_1)$, with $c_1' < 0$.[41] In the second period, firms 1 and 2 compete in quantities: $x_1 = q_1$, $x_2 = q_2$ (for the sake of exposition, we ignore firm 2's choice of investment). In the second period, firm 1 maximizes

$$q_1(P(q_1 + q_2^*) - c_1),$$

where P is the inverse demand function and c_1 is firm 1's marginal cost. A higher K_1 shifts firm 1's reaction curve to the right.[42] Assuming that quantities are strategic sub-

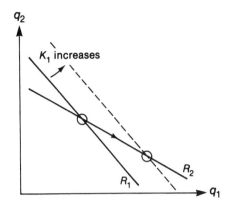

Figure 8.9
A firm's reaction curve moves outward with a decrease in marginal cost.

stitutes, the effect of an increase in K_1 can be represented as in figure 8.9. When firm 1's cost decreases, that firm has an incentive to produce more, which lowers the marginal value of output for firm 2. The new equilibrium involves a higher output for firm 1 and a lower output for firm 2. The main point, though, is that investment makes firm 1 tough (it raises q_1^*, which hurts firm 2). Hence, the "top dog" strategy is appropriate to deter firm 2's entry.

Exercise 8.7* Suppose that, in the modified version of the Spence-Dixit game discussed above (where firm 1's investment reduces its marginal cost), the second-period competition is in prices. The two products are differentiated and are substitutes (see, e.g., the location model of chapter 7). Prices are strategic complements. Using a diagram, argue that firm 1 must overinvest to deter entry (assuming that entry is not blockaded).

Example A case was mentioned earlier in which K_1 was firm 1's pre-entry clientele. (One may, for instance, think of K_1 as firm 1's expenditures that makes switching costly

---

40. The concepts of over- and underinvestment can be characterized in an alternative way. Consider the hypothetical situation in which K_1 is not observed by firm 2 before the entry and second-period decisions. The corresponding equilibrium is usually called an *open-loop* equilibrium, because firm 2's strategy cannot be contingent on the actual choice of K_1, which is not observed at the date of decision. (A closed-loop strategy would depend on the actual level of K_1.) The open-loop case is an interesting benchmark against which to compare the effect of an observable change in K_1. If investment makes firm 1 tough,

the equilibrium, entry-deterring level of K_1 exceeds the open-loop level (overinvestment); and conversely if investment makes firm 1 soft.

41. In section 8.2, the investment was a capacity level, and c_1 was not constant with output. But the important feature is that the investment reduces the marginal cost.

42. The proof of this is the same as the proof that a monopoly's optimal price increases with its marginal cost (see chapter 1).

to at least some of its customers.[43]) The direct effect of K_1 is to reduce firm 2's potential market ($\partial\Pi^2/\partial K_1 < 0$). However, the strategic effect has the opposite impact on firm 2's profit if firm 1 is not able to price-discriminate between its consumers; ideally, firm 1 would like to charge a high price to its captive clients and a low price to the noncaptive segment of the market, for which it is competing with firm 2. In the absence of price discrimination, however, an intermediate price is quoted, which intuitively increases with the size of the captive clientele. That is, a sizable clientele may make one a pacifistic fat cat, which is bad for entry deterrence. The overall effect $d\Pi^2/dK_1$ is thus ambiguous, and, depending on the parameters, either the "top dog" strategy or the "lean and hungry look" strategy may be appropriate to deter entry.

8.3.2 Accommodation of Entry

Suppose now that firm 1 finds deterring entry too costly. Whereas firm 1's first-period behavior in the entry-deterrence case was dictated by firm 2's profit, which had to be driven down to zero, it is dictated by firm 1's profit in the entry-accommodation case. The incentive to invest is given by the total derivative of

$$\Pi^1(K_1, x_1^*(K_1), x_2^*(K_1))$$

with respect to K_1.

From the envelope theorem, the effect on Π^1 of the change in firm 1's second-period action is of the second order. Thus, our basic equation in the entry-accommodation case is

$$\frac{d\Pi^1}{dK_1} = \underbrace{\frac{\partial\Pi^1}{\partial K_1}}_{\substack{\text{Direct}\\\text{effect}}} + \underbrace{\frac{\partial\Pi^1}{\partial x_2}\frac{dx_2^*}{dK_1}}_{\substack{\text{Strategic}\\\text{effect}}}.$$

Again, we can decompose this derivative into two effects. The *direct* or *"cost minimizing"* effect is $\partial\Pi^1/\partial K_1$. This effect would exist even if firm 1's investment were not observed by firm 2 before the choice of x_2, and therefore could not affect x_2. Thus, we will ignore this effect for the purpose of our classification. The *strategic* effect results from the influence of the investment on firm 2's second-period action. In the case of entry accommodation, we will say that firm 1 should overinvest (underinvest) if the strategic effect is positive (negative).[44]

The sign of the strategic effect can be related to the investment making firm 1 tough or soft and to the slope of the second-period reaction curve. To do this, assume that the second-period actions of both firms have the same nature, in the sense that $\partial\Pi^1/\partial x_2$ and $\partial\Pi^2/\partial x_1$ have the same sign. For instance, if the second-period competition is in quantities (prices), $\partial\Pi^i/\partial x_j < 0$ (> 0). Using the fact that

$$\frac{dx_2^*}{dK_1} = \left(\frac{dx_2^*}{dx_1}\right)\left(\frac{dx_1^*}{dK_1}\right) = [R_2'(x_1^*)]\left(\frac{dx_1^*}{dK_1}\right)$$

by the chain rule, and arranging, we obtain

$$\text{sign}\left(\frac{\partial\Pi^1}{\partial x_2}\frac{dx_2^*}{dK_1}\right) = \text{sign}\left(\frac{\partial\Pi^2}{\partial x_1}\frac{dx_1^*}{dK_1}\right) \times \text{sign}(R_2').$$

---

43. For other examples of clienteles, see Schmalensee 1983, Baldini 1983, and Fudenberg and Tirole 1984. Of particular interest here are the switching-cost models of Klemperer and that of Farrell and Shapiro. Klemperer (1984, 1985a, b) analyzes the effect of switching costs in a two-period duopoly model in which there is competition in the first period and *ex post* monopoly (due to lock-in) in the second period. He shows how frequent-flyer discounts given by airlines to consumers in the first period to be used in the second period lead to weak price competition in the second period and may not benefit the consumers. (Frequent-flyer discounts differ from the most-favored-nation clause, discussed in section 8.4 below, in that the second-period discounts are not attached to the first-period price. They otherwise have similar collusive second-period effects.) More generally, the second-period rents stemming from switching costs induce intense first-period competition. Farrell and Shapiro (1987) introduce successive cohorts of consumers (via a model in which generations overlap) and show how a larger firm with a clientele may "milk" that clientele by charging a high price whereas a smaller firm charges a low price to attract young customers and build a clientele. For background on switching costs, see von Weizsäcker 1984 and the discussion of clienteles in chapter 2 of the present volume.

44. Again the concepts of over- and underinvestment can be characterized by comparing the optimal K_1 to the open-loop solution (i.e., the solution of the same game except that K_1 is not observable by firm 2 prior to its decision). See footnote 40. Given the concavity of Π^1, the optimal K_1 exceeds the open-loop solution if and only if the strategic effect is positive. Hint: In the open-loop solution, $\hat{K}_1$ is given by

$$\frac{\partial\Pi^1}{\partial K_1}(\hat{K}_1, x_1^*(\hat{K}_1), x_2^*(\hat{K}_1)) = 0.$$

This implies that for a positive strategic effect

$$\frac{d\Pi^1}{dK_1}(\hat{K}_1, x_1^*(\hat{K}_1), x_2^*(\hat{K}_1)) > 0.$$

This characterization does not generalize to the case in which both firms make decisions K_1 and K_2 in the first period. Even if both firms' strategic effect is positive, firm 2 (say) may invest less because firm 1 invests more and reduces the marginal value of firm 2's investment (this may occur, e.g., when the strategic effect is much stronger for firm 1).

The sign of the strategic effect, and therefore the over- or underinvestment prescription, is contingent on the sign of the strategic effect in the entry-deterrence case (which is equivalent to whether investment makes firm 1 tough or soft, when there is no direct effect in the entry-deterrence case) and on the slope of firm 2's reaction curve. We are thus led to distinguish four cases, depending on whether investment makes firm 1 tough or soft[45] and on whether second-period actions are strategic substitutes or complements (i.e., whether reaction curves are downward or upward sloping—see the introduction to part II). In all these cases, firm 1 tries to induce a softer behavior by firm 2 through its investment strategy.

• If investment makes firm 1 tough and the reaction curves are downward sloping, investment by firm 1 induces a softer action by firm 2; therefore, firm 1 should overinvest for strategic purposes (i.e., should follow the "top dog" strategy).

• If investment makes firm 1 tough and the reaction curves are upward sloping, firm 1 should underinvest (the "puppy dog" strategy) so as not to trigger an aggressive response from firm 2.

• If investment makes firm 1 soft and the reaction curves are downward sloping, firm 1 should stay lean and hungry.

• If investment makes firm 1 soft and the reaction curves are upward sloping, firm 1 should overinvest to become a fat cat.

These results, and those for the entry-deterrence case, are summarized in figure 8.10.

Example

Consider the modified Spence-Dixit game. Firm 1's investment reduces its marginal cost. Second-period competition is either in prices or in quantities. As before, assume that prices are strategic complements and quantities are strategic substitutes. A reduction in marginal cost increases firm 1's output in the quantity game and reduces firm 1's price in the price game (see subsection 8.3.1).

In the quantity game, a higher output for firm 1 yields a lower output for firm 2. Firm 1 thus wants to overinvest

	Investment makes firm 1	
	Tough	Soft
Strategic complements ($R' > 0$)	**A** Puppy dog / **D** Top dog	**A** Fat cat / **D** Lean and hungry
Strategic substitutes ($R' < 0$)	**A and D** Top dog	**A and D** Lean and hungry

Figure 8.10
Optimal business strategies. (A stands for accommodation of entry, D for deterrence.)

—i.e., be a top dog. Thus, firm 1's strategy is the same whether it wants to deter or to accommodate entry, because being tough both hurts and softens firm 2 in the quantity game.

The picture is different in the price game. A lower price for firm 1 forces firm 2 to charge a lower price, which hurts firm 1. Thus, firm 1 should underinvest (i.e., keep a puppy-dog profile) so as not to look aggressive and trigger an aggressive reaction by firm 2. Firm 1's strategy is then very different depending on whether it wants to deter or to accommodate entry (deterrence calls for the "top dog" strategy), because being tough both hurts and toughens firm 2 in the price game.

At this point, one is likely to think: "I have a clear picture of the entry-deterrence case, in which firm 1 ought to overinvest. In the entry-accommodation case, however, the optimal strategy relies too much on the type of *ex post* competition (price or quantity); how can I make up my mind whether firm 1 should be a top dog or a puppy dog?" An element of the answer to this query can be found in chapter 5, where we interpreted quantity competition as capacity competition. To find the optimal strategy, we must wonder whether the investment K_1 reduces the marginal cost of accumulating capacity or that of producing. In the context of this model, we would thus predict strong strategic investment to accommodate entry when this investment reduces the costs of accumulating capacity. In contrast, a firm may be less eager to reduce

---

45. We assume that $\partial \Pi^2/\partial K_1 = 0$, so that we can identify "toughness" or "softness" with the sign of the strategic effect in the entry-deterrence case. If $\partial \Pi^2/\partial K_1 \neq 0$, the taxonomy under accommodation is relative to the sign of this effect rather than to "toughness" and "softness."

production costs and trigger tough price competition under entry accommodation.

8.3.3 Inducement of Exit

The above model treats only entry deterrence and accommodation. What about firm 1's incentive to invest in period 1, supposing that firm 2 is in the market at that date and must decide whether to stay or to exit in period 2? Inducing exit is very similar to deterring entry. In both cases, firm 1 wants to make firm 2 unprofitable in the second period. That is,

$$\Pi^2(K_1, x_1^\star(K_1), x_2^\star(K_1)) \leqslant 0$$

is the relevant objective for firm 1, where Π^2 includes entry or exit costs. Thus, firm 1's behavior is driven by firm 2's profit, and the strategic taxonomy is identical in both cases. In particular, D can be replaced by "D or E" in figure 8.10, where E stands for exit inducement.

8.4 Applications of the Taxonomy

We now turn to some applications of section 8.3. Other applications will be given in chapters 9 and 10.[46] We start with two examples of entry accommodation encountered in chapters 5 and 7. We then consider some new ones. We treat these examples mostly in an informal manner; the emphasis is on explaining how often optimal business strategies and market performance can be predicted from educated guesses. (References are given for more formal analyses.)

In section 8.3, K_1 was interpreted as an investment. More generally, it could be any action taken prior to date-2 competition; for instance, in example 4 below, K_1 refers to whether the firm offers a most-favored-customer clause and at what price. What matters is whether this action is observed by firm 2 and whether it makes firm 1 tough or soft in the second-period competition. Actually,

K_1 need not even be an action taken by firm 1; it can be any variable that influences date-2 competition. In example 5 below, K_1 refers to firm 1's presence in another market. In example 6, K_1 denotes some variable outside the control of firm 1 (a quota, a tariff, or a subsidy). Again, the taxonomy can be applied as long as we can determine whether K_1 makes firm 1 tough or soft. The only modification is verbal: When K_1 is not controlled by firm 1, the "over- or underinvestment" prescription is replaced by the prescription that a higher K_1 benefits or hurts firm 1. We can also enlarge the set of applications to cases in which all firms play strategically in period 1, or to multiperiod games. The simple model of section 8.3 is again the key to understanding these slightly more complicated models.

In the following applications, we will assume that prices are strategic complements and that quantities (i.e., capacities) are strategic substitutes. This crucial assumption will be discussed in section 8.5.

Example 1: Voluntary Limitation of Capacity

In chapter 5 we analyzed a two-stage (accommodation) game in which firms accumulated capacities and then charged prices. We observed that firms accumulate noncompetitive amounts of capacity (under some circumstances, the Cournot levels). Prior capacity accumulation was seen as one way out of the Bertrand paradox. What prevents a firm from accumulating a large amount (a competitive level) of capacity is that by accumulating a small capacity, each firm signals that it will not play an aggressive price strategy, and there is no point to cutting the price if one cannot satisfy demand. This signal softens the pricing behavior of the firm's rivals. Such a voluntary limitation of capacity is an instance of "puppy dog" behavior. Gelman and Salop (1983) make this point nicely. They consider a model in which an entrant enters on a very small scale so as not to trigger an aggressive response by a large-capacity incumbent.[47] (The entrant is the strategic player in this example.) As Wilson notes,

---

46. See Shapiro 1986 for a useful and more extensive list of applications.

47. This is similar to the Stackelberg follower behavior in section 8.2. The game considered by Gelman and Salop is, however, different. The entrant, firm 2, chooses both a capacity (K_2) and a price (p_2). The incumbent, firm 1, has no capacity constraint, and chooses price p_1 after observing K_2 and p_2. Clearly, firm 2 does not pick p_2 above the monopoly price p^m, because firm 1 would then undercut to this monopoly price. Hence, when faced with $\{p_2 < p^m, K_2\}$, the incumbent's optimal strategy is either to undercut p_2 by ε (which firm 2 wants to avoid) or to charge $p_1 > p_2$ so as to maximize its profit given the

residual demand. For instance, for the efficient-rationing rule (see chapter 5), the residual demand is $D(p_1) - K_2$. Firm 2 thus chooses $p_2 < p^m$ and K_2 so as to maximize $(p_2 - c)K_2$ subject to the no-undercutting constraint:

$$\max_{p_1} \{(p_1 - c)[D(p_1) - K_2]\} \geqslant (p_2 - c)D(p_2).$$

To make undercutting unattractive to firm 1, firm 2 chooses a low enough price and restricts its capacity. Gelman and Salop call this strategy "judo economics." Their paper also includes an interesting theoretical account of the 1979 coupon war among the major airlines in the United States.

A useful example is an incumbent hotel in a resort location: an entrant that builds a comparable but small hotel with lower rates (a pension) can expect accommodation from a large hotel, since it is in the larger one's interest to serve the overflow from the smaller one rather than to cut its price to compete directly.... There are various ways to accomplish a commitment to capacity limitation. Besides a direct restriction on available supplies, the entrant can also tailor its product to a limited market segment. In the hotel example a menu of health foods might suffice. (1984, p. 41)

Example 2: The Principle of Differentiation

In chapter 7 we considered two-stage (accommodation) games of entry and location followed by price competition. We enunciated the principle of differentiation, according to which firms may not want to locate next to one another in the product space in order to avoid vigorous price competition. Here the first-period variable is location.

It is particularly instructive to recall the location game studied in section 7.1, in which two firms choose locations along a segment. When analyzing a firm's optimal decision, we saw that there are two effects: Moving toward the center of the segment increases the firm's market share and profit at given prices. This corresponds to the direct or cost-minimizing (here, profit-maximizing) effect of section 8.3. Moving toward the other firm increases the intensity of price competition. This strategic effect dictates that a firm locate as far as possible from the other firm. We saw that firms differentiate their products. (In our example, the strategic effect is so strong that maximal differentiation occurs.) Product differentiation is another instance of "puppy dog" behavior.[48] Identifying a firm's capital as the closeness of its location to the center of the segment, each firm is willing to accumulate less capital (i.e., locate away from the center) than it would do if its rival's action (price) were fixed.

Example 3: Learning by Doing[49]

It is often argued that experience effects can be used for strategic purposes. Indeed, in the 1970s some consulting firms recommended to their clients that they sacrifice short-run profits early in the product life cycle in order to gain strategic position, on the ground that by producing a lot early (i.e., by cutting its price) a firm can quickly slide down the learning curve and deter the entry (or at least restrict the expansion) of other firms—see, e.g., Boston Consulting Group 1972.

Learning by doing is similar to investing in technology or in capacity in that both reduce the firm's future cost. (Here we assume specific learning. Learning externalities are analyzed later.) There is an important difference, however, between learning by doing and other investments: The cost of learning by doing is not exogenous to the market, but rather follows from the firm's production experience.

For ease of exposition, let us consider a two-firm rivalry. Let each firm's second-period marginal cost decrease with its first-period output. Suppose first that competition takes place in quantities in both periods. By increasing its output in period 1, a firm signals that it will produce a higher output in period 2 because of the learning effect. With strategic substitutes, this reduces the other firm's output at date 2. Thus, the "top dog" strategy of accumulating experience early is optimal under accommodation and quantity competition. It is also optimal to deter entry, because the incumbent firm's lower second-period cost hurts the entrant.

Determining the optimal strategy under price competition is slightly more complex. The "top dog" strategy is still optimal for entry deterrence: By charging a low price today, the incumbent accumulates experience, which induces it to charge a low price tomorrow. Entry accommodation when there is only one firm in the market at date 1 (as in section 8.3) yields the opposite result: Experience induces a low price, which triggers a low price from the rival. The "puppy dog" strategy of underinvestment in experience (i.e., high first-period price) is then called

---

48. This is a bit loose, because the case of entry deterrence or exit inducement involves a direct effect: If $K_1 = a$ (in the notation of chapter 7), then $\partial \Pi^2 / \partial K_1 < 0$. But $(\partial \Pi^2 / \partial p_1) \cdot (\partial p_1^* / \partial K_1)$ is also negative, so we can identify "toughness" and the strategic effect.

49. The strategic aspects of learning by doing with and without spillovers have been analyzed by Spence (1981, 1984), Fudenberg and Tirole (1983a), Stokey (1986), and Mookherjee and Ray (1986), among others. The present discussion follows Fudenberg and Tirole 1986. This field owes much to the early analysis of Arrow (1962).

for. In contrast, accommodation when both firms are in the market at date 1 yields ambiguous results. On the one hand, a low price today increases the firm's output and hence its experience, making the firm aggressive tomorrow and triggering a low price from its rival (this is the previous strategic effect); however, a low price also reduces the rival's market share and, therefore, reduces its experience. The rival faces a higher second-period cost and, therefore, is less aggressive in that period. This second effect, which does not exist for quantity competition because a firm cannot affect its rival's current output, calls for the "top dog" strategy. It is not clear *a priori* which effect dominates.

To summarize: With specific learning by doing, the "top dog" strategy of accumulating lots of experience is optimal to deter entry or induce exit. It is also optimal for entry accommodation under quantity competition, but it may or may not be optimal under price competition. Thus, for entry accommodation it matters whether the learning by doing refers to a reduction in investment costs (quantity competition) or to a reduction in production costs (price competition).

Let us now consider the possibilities of diffusion of learning across firms (spillovers).[50] Such externalities can take place through interfirm mobility of employees, through spying, or through reverse engineering (i.e., taking a product apart to learn how it was built). Learning by doing then somewhat resembles a public good and is therefore likely to be undersupplied. The new strategic effect arising from the diffusion of learning runs counter to the "top dog" tendency associated with specific learning: No firm is willing to accumulate experience that helps its rival to reduce its cost and thus to be more aggressive.[51]

Example 4: Most-Favored-Customer Clause

A firm competing in price in an accommodation framework ought to look inoffensive so as not to force its rivals to cut price. It would thus like to take actions that commit it to charge a high price. As we saw earlier, this can be achieved by restraining investments that reduce production costs. There are, of course, other ways to commit to a high price. One way is to grant current customers a most-favored-customer status or price protection. (See Hay 1982 and Salop 1986. The analysis here relies more particularly on Cooper's [1986] formal treatment of such policies.)

The most-favored-customer policy guarantees a firm's current customers that they will be reimbursed the difference between the current price and the lowest price offered in the future (up to some specified date). For instance, in the 1960s and the early 1970s the two manufacturers of turbine generators, General Electric and Westinghouse, offered a price-protection policy effective during the six months following a sale.[52]

Before we consider why such a policy may help firms collude, it may be useful to recall the Stackelberg *price-leadership* story. Consider a duopoly producing differentiated products. Figure 8.11 depicts the reaction curves and the Nash (simultaneous-move) equilibrium (p_1^*, p_2^*). Suppose now that firm 1 chooses its price before firm 2. If it raises its price slightly above p_1^* to $\mathring{p}_1$, its profits are affected only to the second order by the fact that p_1^* is

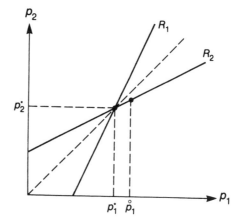

Figure 8.11
Stackelberg price leadership.

---

50. See Lieberman 1984 for evidence of the diffusion of experience in the chemical industry.

51. For instance, with linear demand and quantity competition, the firms' first-period output can be shown to decrease with the degree of diffusion by learning (in spite of the fact that diffusion increases total experience and

therefore increases second-period output, making first-period learning more desirable). See, e.g., Fudenberg and Tirole 1983a.

52. These firms ended the practice as part of a settlement to avoid antitrust action.

an optimal response to p_2^* (according to the envelope theorem). To this direct effect can be added the indirect effect that firm 2 reacts by raising its price. This indirect effect raises firm 1's profit to the first order. Firm 1, the Stackelberg leader, thus chooses a price exceeding p_1^*.[53]

The Stackelberg story gives the intuition of why even unilateral commitments to a price-protection policy may be desirable. Consider a two-period duopoly price game. The firms choose their prices simultaneously in each period. The demand functions $D_i(p_i, p_j)$ and the cost functions (which we take as linear for notational simplicity) are independent of time. To simplify, there is no discounting between the two periods. In the absence of price-protection policies, the price equilibrium is the Nash equilibrium (p_1^*, p_2^*) in each period.

With price protection, the previous Nash equilibrium (without price protection) is no longer an equilibrium. That is, it would pay a firm to *unilaterally* impose price protection. To see this, suppose that firm 1 charges a price $\mathring{p}_1$ a bit above p_1^* in the first period *and* offers to reimburse the difference between $\mathring{p}_1$ and the price it will charge in the second period if the former exceeds the latter. Assume that the buyers behave myopically; that is, it is not because they expect firm 1 to lower its price and pay some cash back that they buy from that firm. (We will see later that these myopic consumers are actually rational, as firm 1 will not lower its price.) Thus, firm 1's first-period demand is

$$\mathring{q}_1 \equiv D_1(\mathring{p}_1, p_2^*).$$

Firm 1's second-period profit is thus

$$\dot{\Pi}^1(p_1, p_2) = \begin{cases} \Pi^1(p_1, p_2) & \text{if } p_1 \geqslant \mathring{p}_1 \\ \Pi^1(p_1, p_2) - (\mathring{p}_1 - p_1)\mathring{q}_1 & \text{if } p_1 < \mathring{p}_1 \end{cases}$$

where $\Pi^1(p_1, p_2) \equiv (p_1 - c)D_1(p_1, p_2)$.

Thus, firm 1's marginal profit in the second period exhibits a discontinuity at $p_1 = \mathring{p}_1$. To see that

$$\{p_1 = \mathring{p}_1, p_2 = R_2(\mathring{p}_1)\}$$

is the second-period price equilibrium, draw firm 1's second-period reaction curve $\mathring{R}_1$. (Firm 2, which by assumption has not imposed price protection, has its usual reaction curve, R_2.) Whenever the optimal reaction to p_2 calls for $p_1 \geqslant \mathring{p}_1$ in the usual (no price protection) case, $\mathring{R}_1$ and R_1 clearly coincide. Let $\mathring{p}_2$ be such that $R_1(\mathring{p}_2) = \mathring{p}_1$. By definition of $R_1(\cdot)$,

$$\Pi_1^1(\mathring{p}_1, \mathring{p}_2) = 0.$$

This implies that

$$\Pi_1^1(\mathring{p}_1, \mathring{p}_2) + \mathring{q}_1 > 0.$$

It is thus easy to see that for $\mathring{p}_2 - \varepsilon$, firm 1 wants to react by $\mathring{p}_1$ rather than $R_1(\mathring{p}_2 - \varepsilon)$. This is also true for a range of prices for firm 2. Only when firm 2's price becomes very low will firm 1 cut below its first-period price and (with regret) bring the price-protection policy into play.[54] Firm 1's second-period discontinuous reaction curve is depicted in figure 8.12. A useful way to under-

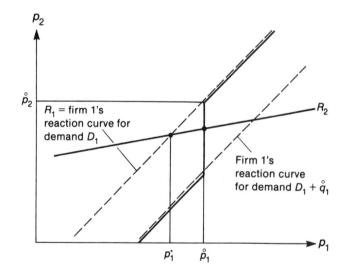

Figure 8.12
Second-period reaction curves when firm 1 offers price protection at p_1.

---

53. However, in contrast with quantity competition, being the leader may not be desirable. For instance, with symmetric profit functions, one has $R(p) < p$ for $p > p^*$. That the follower benefits more than the leader from the sequential timing follows from

$$\Pi(R(\mathring{p}), \mathring{p}) > \Pi(\mathring{p}, \mathring{p}) > \Pi(\mathring{p}, R(\mathring{p})),$$

where the first inequality comes from the optimality of the firm's reaction to $\mathring{p}$

and the second inequality from the fact that each firm's profit increases with its rival's price.

54. This very low price, p_2', is given by

$$\Pi^1(\mathring{p}_1, p_2') = \max_{p_1 < \mathring{p}_1} [\Pi^1(p_1, p_2') - (\mathring{p}_1 - p_1)\mathring{q}_1].$$

stand this reaction curve is to notice that for $p_1 < \mathring{p}_1$

$$\dot{\Pi}^1 = (p_1 - c)[D_1(p_1, p_2) + \mathring{q}_1] - (\mathring{p}_1 - c)\mathring{q}_1 .$$

The second term in this expression is irrelevant as far as marginal choices are concerned, so everything is as if firm 1 faced demand $D_1(p_1, p_2) + \mathring{q}_1$ for $p_1 < \mathring{p}_1$. Thus, the reaction is that for demand $D_1(p_1, p_2) + \mathring{q}_1$ whenever the reaction falls strictly below $\mathring{p}_1$, and that for demand $D_1(p_1, p_2)$ whenever the reaction exceeds $\mathring{p}_1$.

Now recall that we choose $\mathring{p}_1$ just greater than p_1^*. From figure 8.12, the second-period price equilibrium is given by $p_1 = \mathring{p}_1$ and $p_2 = R_2(\mathring{p}_1)$.[55] In words: Firm 1 has succeeded in becoming the Stackelberg leader, thus driving firm 2's price up. Firm 1 increases its profit to the first order, which more than offsets the second-order loss in the first period. Thus, it pays for a firm to impose a price-protection policy, even if the other firm does not impose such a policy. By making future price cuts costly, a firm uses a profitable "puppy dog" strategy. It shifts down its second-period profit function (i.e., it becomes weak) in order to commit to a high second-period price (so as to look inoffensive). But, as in the Stackelberg price game, the firm that offers price protection gains less from this policy than its rival. See Cooper 1986 for the complete solution to the game (in equilibrium, either one or both firms will offer price protection).

Remark 1 Despite its strategic attractiveness, the most-favored-customer clause is not widespread. Several reasons can be found for this: (1) Rebates to other customers must be made observable to each buyer, because unrecorded rebates would benefit (*ex post* but not *ex ante*) a manufacturer who had offered price protection in the past. That is, discount secrecy removes the credibility of the price-protection policy. Other transaction costs include the cost of indexing the price to inflation and input costs. (2) The design of the good may be altered over time, so that again the price-protection policy has little applicability.[56] (3) The practice may face antitrust prosecution. (4) Price-protection policies are not very profitable when other firms threaten to enter the market. Indeed, a "puppy dog" strategy (here, the established firms' commitment to a high price) encourages entry. (5) Even in the accommodation case, the application of price-protection policies may be delayed by the fact that each firm wants to be the follower rather than the leader (as is the case when only one firm elects to offer the policy in the simultaneous-move game). This may give rise to situations similar to the war of attrition.[57]

Remark 2 Price protection is one method of softening future price competition. Another method (as in example 2) is to increase product differentiation. Klemperer (1984) has argued that discounts for repeated purchases increase the cost of customers' interbrand switching and thus differentiate the products in the future. This raises prices in the future. However, price competition is more intense at the beginning, because the value of a customer to a firm is raised.[58]

Example 5: Multimarket Oligopoly

The presence of a firm in one market may affect its strategic position in another market if the two markets are somehow related. This is the case when producing for two markets involves economies (or diseconomies) of scale or scope. Alternatively, the demands on the two markets may be interdependent.[59]

Bulow et al. (1985b) consider a duopoly model in which firms 1 and 2 are rivals in market 1 and firm 1 is a monopoly in market 2. (For concreteness, the two markets can be thought of as two different regions.) Here K_1, rather than a choice variable for firm 1, is a parameter related to profitability in market 2 (it can be thought of as a demand parameter). Bulow et al. show that an increase in firm 1's profitability in market 2 may actually reduce its total profit. This is because of the strategic effect in

---

55. The reaction curves for demands D_1 and $D_1 + \mathring{q}_1$ do not converge to each other (i.e., stay far apart) when $\mathring{p}_1$ converges to p_1^*.

56. As Cooper (1986) observes, General Electric and Westinghouse published books that contained relative prices for each component in order to face the issue that turbine generators are custom-made. They changed the prices by adjusting the multiplier.

57. Still another possibility is that firms compete in capacities. We know that results under accommodation are usually reversed with quantity competition. In this case, a firm wants to look tough (which a price-protection policy does not help it achieve). Checking this intuition would require solving the game in which firms choose capacities, prices, and protection policy.

58. See note 43 above.

59. For an example of multimarket rivalry with interdependent demands, see subsection 8.6.2 below.

market 1. Suppose that the firms compete in quantities, that firm 1's production cost depends on the sum of its outputs in the two markets, and that this technology exhibits decreasing returns to scale. All quantities (the two outputs for firm 1 and the output for firm 2) are chosen simultaneously and noncooperatively. Suppose that demand increases in market 2. This induces firm 1 to sell more in that market, which raises firm 1's marginal cost of production and lowers its output in market 1. Firm 2, observing the increase in demand in market 2, will infer that firm 1 will decrease its output in market 1, and so firm 2 will raise its output in market 1. In other words, the increased profitability of market 2 raises firm 1's marginal cost in market 1, which puts it at a strategic disadvantage (a "puppy dog" look is detrimental under strategic substitutes).[60] Similarly, if firms compete in prices and firm 1's technology exhibits increasing returns to scale, an increase in firm 1's profitability in market 2 lowers its marginal cost in market 1 and therefore makes it aggressive in this market, which triggers a low price by firm 2. Again, this strategic effect may offset the profitability increase for firm 1. Either with quantity competition and economies of scale or with price competition and decreasing returns to scale, an increase in the profitability of market 2 unambiguously increases firm 1's profit.

Example 6: Quotas and Tariffs

Strategic interaction in an international context is affected by countries' trade policies. Exercise 8.4 showed how a protection policy can help a domestic firm to gain an edge in a domestic capacity-accumulation contest with a foreign firm (when goods are costly to trade between countries). More generally, subsidies, tariffs, and quotas (which can be interpreted as the variable K_1 of the general model) may have a non-negligible impact on the strategic positions of foreign and domestic firms (Brander and Spencer 1984; Dixit 1984; Dixit and Grossman 1986; Eaton and Grossman 1983; Eichberger and Harper 1986; Krishna 1983; Krugman 1984).[61]

For instance, if a domestic and a foreign firm compete in quantities in the foreign market, an export subsidy

induces the domestic firm to expand its output, which induces the foreign firm to contract its own. That is, the export subsidy makes the domestic firm a top dog (to its advantage). The following exercises develop other examples.

Exercise 8.8* "A foreign firm that competes in prices with a domestic firm in the domestic market suffers from facing a quota." True or false?

Exercise 8.9* Suppose that two firms, producing substitute but differentiated products, compete in prices. (The equilibrium is unique and "stable," and the profit functions are concave.) Show that a government-imposed floor on firm 1's price may increase that firm's profit. Explain.

Example 7: Vertical Control

The contracts signed between owners and managers or between manufacturers and their retailers influence competition between downstream units (managers or retailers) if these contracts are observable. For instance, Rey and Stiglitz (1986) show how exclusive territories may soften not only intrabrand competition but also interbrand competition. Exclusive territories may allow firms to behave like puppy dogs in a price game.[62] Bonanno and Vickers (1986) show that in duopoly a manufacturer may prefer to sell his product through an independent retailer rather than directly to consumers, in order to induce more friendly behavior from the rival manufacturer (see also McGuire and Staelin 1983 and Moorthy 1987). For some general results on the link between observable agency contracts and interbrand competition, see Fershtman and Judd 1986 and Katz 1987.

Example 8: Tying

Whinston (1987) reconsiders the old leverage theory, according to which tying may allow a firm with monopoly power in one market to monopolize a second market. His simplest model is as follows: Suppose there are two firms and two completely unrelated markets (the reasoning can be extended to the case in which the goods are comple-

---

60. See exercise 5.5.

61. See Itoh and Kiyono 1987 for other reasons why export subsidies may be desirable.

62. See review exercise 19. In a financial context, Brander and Lewis (1986) show that the contract between a bank and a firm affects market competition. In their model, a high level of debt makes a firm a top dog in a quantity competition. See also Mathewson and Winter 1985 for a strategic analysis of exclusive dealing.

ments). Market A is monopolized by firm 1. Consumers all have willingness to pay v for good A. Normalize the demand in this market to be 1 (as long as the price does not exceed v). Market B is a differentiated market and is served by firms 1 and 2. Let $q_i = D_i(p_i, p_j)$ denote firm i's demand in this market. For simplicity, assume that the consumers are the same and have unit demands in the two markets, so that $D_i(\cdot, \cdot) \leqslant 1$. Let c and c_1 denote firm 1's unit production costs in markets A and B. Does firm 1 have an incentive to tie its products? For simplicity, assume that firm 1 offers the two products either separately or together (i.e., that there is no mixed bundling, in the language of chapter 4).

Suppose first that firm 1 takes price p_2 as given. This situation arises when firms 1 and 2 choose their prices, and firm 1 chooses whether to tie its two products simultaneously. It is easily seen that firm 1 does not gain from tying the two goods—under tying, firm 1 offers the bundle at price P_1 so as to maximize

$$(P_1 - c_1 - c)D_1(P_1 - v, p_2),$$

as the fictitious price for its good in market B is $P_1 - v$. Where P_1^* denotes the optimal price, firm 1 can realize at least the tying profit by selling the two goods separately at prices v and $P_1^* - v$, respectively:

$$(v - c) + [(P_1^* - v) - c_1]D_1(P_1^* - v, p_2)$$

$$\geqslant (P_1^* - c - c_1)D_1(P_1^* - v, p_2),$$

where $D_1 \leqslant 1$. Absent strategic considerations (as is the case here, where firm 1 takes p_2 as given and acts as a monopolist on its residual-demand curve), tying generally hurts firm 1 by reducing the number of degrees of freedom in its pricing strategy. (We know from chapter 4 that this conclusion is not general, as a monopolist may gain from tying. On this, see also review exercise 27. But this modeling choice will make the conclusions more striking and help us to identify the strategic effect.)

An important property is that under pure bundling, the fictitious price $\tilde{p}_1 \equiv P_1^* - v$ is lower than the price p_1 in market B, under no bundling, for any p_2. That is, *bundling shifts firm 1's reaction curve westward in market B*. To see this, note that under bundling P_1 maximizes

$$(P_1 - c_1 - c)D_1(P_1 - v, p_2),$$

which means that $\tilde{p}_1$ maximizes

$$\{\tilde{p}_1 - [c_1 - (v - c)]\}D_1(\tilde{p}_1, p_2).$$

In the absence of bundling, however, p_1 maximizes

$$(p_1 - c_1)D_1(p_1, p_2).$$

(The constant term $(v - c)$ in firm 1's profit function can be ignored.) Thus, everything is as if bundling reduced firm 1's cost of producing in market B by $v - c$ as far as pricing in market B is concerned. This is very natural, as a unit loss of sales in market B costs $v - c$ to firm 1 in market A under bundling, so that the "real" marginal cost of selling in market B is reduced by $v - c$. Now, we know from chapter 1 that a monopoly price increases with marginal cost. The consequence of this is that a firm's reaction curve in oligopoly shifts outward when the marginal cost increases (because this firm is a monopoly on its residual-demand curve). For any p_2, therefore, $\tilde{p}_1 < p_1$. Furthermore, in this model bundling is formally identical to an investment in cost reduction. Firm 1 pays a fixed investment cost $v - c$ (which corresponds to the loss in revenue from selling in market A separately) for a fictitious technology that reduces its marginal cost in market B from c_1 to

$$c_1 - (v - c).$$

As the number of units sold in market B is generally lower than the number sold in market A ($D_1 < 1$), such an investment cannot be profitable in the absence of strategic considerations.

Suppose now that firm 1 decides whether to bundle before the two firms compete in prices. Thus, firm 1 first chooses to market the two goods separately (no bundling) or together (pure bundling); then the two firms choose their prices simultaneously. Think of a technological decision concerning the packaging of the product or (more likely in the case of complements) the decision whether to make the product intended for market A incompatible with firm 2's product.[63] Here bundling hurts not only firm 1 but also firm 2, as it commits firm 1 to charge a low fictitious price in market B. Thus, bundling is not a good strategy if firm 2's entry or exit decision is not at stake. It hurts firm 1 both directly and indirectly,

---

63. See example 9 for related arguments.

as it forces firm 2 to reduce its price. However, if firm 1 wants to deter the entry or induce the exit of firm 2, bundling may be profitable. In terms of our cost-reduction analogy, firm 1 may overinvest in cost reduction (i.e., bundle) to foreclose market B. Again, the "top dog" strategy is optimal under entry deterrence and the "puppy dog" strategy is optimal under accommodation. (The "puppy dog" strategy is actually the no-bundling strategy; firm 1 cannot underinvest in bundling here.)

We conclude, with Whinston, that technological pre-commitment to bundling has important strategic effects and may allow a firm to use the leverage provided by its power in one market to foreclose another market.

Example 9: Systems and Product Compatibility

This example, which is related to example 8, involves systems of complementary products (for example, computer hardware and software; cameras, lenses, and film processing; tape decks, amplifiers, and speakers). The products in these lines cannot be consumed separately, but they can be purchased individually—consumers can "mix and match" products as long as they are compatible. In contrast, a manufacturer that makes its system incompatible with other systems imposes a *de facto* tie-in (see chapter 4) of its various components.

Matutes and Regibeau (1986) analyze the compatibility decisions of two producers of competing lines. They consider a duopoly in which each firm produces two complementary products, X and Y, which constitute a system. Their model extends the differentiation on the line model of chapter 7 to a two-dimensional case. The consumers are uniformly located on a square of dimension 1, and the firms' products are at diametrically opposed locations. Firm 1 is located at the origin and firm 2 at the point (1, 1). (See figure 8.13.) A consumer located at the coordinates (x_1, y_1) is $tx_1 + ty_1$ away from his preferred system when buying firm 1's system, where t is a taste parameter (the analog of a "transportation cost"). Thus, if p_1 is the price of the system (i.e., the two bundled components) sold by firm 1, the generalized price paid by the consumer for this system is

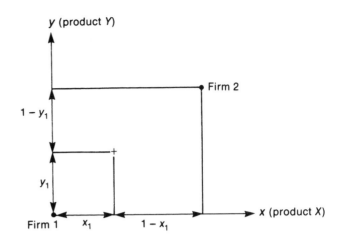

Figure 8.13

$$\tilde{p}_1 = p_1 + t(x_1 + y_1).$$

Similarly, the generalized price for the system sold by firm 2 is

$$\tilde{p}_2 = p_2 + t[(1 - x_1) + (1 - y_1)].$$

Under incompatibility, the consumer chooses the system with the lower generalized price, $\tilde{p} = \min\{\tilde{p}_1, \tilde{p}_2\}$. His demand is then downward sloping: $q = a - b\tilde{p}$.[64] If the systems are compatible and the products are sold separately, the consumer can mix and match. For example, the generalized cost of buying product X from firm 1 and product Y from firm 2 is

$$p_1^X + p_2^Y + t[x_1 + (1 - y_1)],$$

where p_1^X and p_2^Y are respectively the price charged by firm 1 for product X and the price charged by firm 2 for product Y. By mixing, the consumer can choose among four systems—*product variety is increased*. Again, the consumer chooses the system with the lowest generalized price.

Thus, as in chapter 7, the demand function for each firm's system (under incompatibility) or each firm's product (under compatibility) can be determined as a function of the prices. One can then solve for the Nash equilibrium in prices. Suppose, for simplicity, that the unit production cost is the same for both firms and both products. The

---

64. In chapter 7 we assumed that demand was equal to 1 (although we could just as well have considered the case of a downward-sloping demand at each location). For audio systems, the demand function is mainly a unit demand per consumer. The way to justify a downward-sloping demand *at a given location* is to envision a large number of consumers with different tastes for the system at this location.

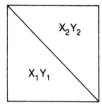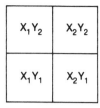

Incompatibility   Compatibility

Figure 8.14

equilibrium demands for each product are symmetric and are as represented in figure 8.14 (assuming that the whole market is covered in equilibrium). In the figure, $\{X_i, Y_j\}$ means that the consumer consumes good X from firm i and good Y from firm j. Under compatibility, the consumers located in the northwest and in the southeast corner of the square buy a system that is better suited to their preferences than the system they would buy under incompatibility.

What are the incentives to achieve compatibility? First, compatibility raises demand, because it makes products better adapted to the consumers' tastes. Second, compatibility softens price competition, as Matutes and Regibeau show. To see the latter, note that when firm 1 decreases its price for good X_1 it increases the demand for systems that include X_1 (because the generalized prices for those systems decrease). Under incompatibility, the only system that includes X_1 is $X_1 Y_1$. (Properly speaking, a decrease in the price of X_1 is then equivalent to the same decrease in the system's price.) Thus, firm 1 enjoys the full benefit associated with the increase in demand. Under compatibility, there are two systems that include X_1 ($X_1 Y_1$ and $X_1 Y_2$), so some of the benefit from increased demand accrues to firm 2. This noninternalization of part of the increase in demand reduces firm 1's incentive to cut its price.[65] Thus, the firms price their components less aggres-

sively than they would do if the components were bundled in an incompatible system. These two effects imply that *firms have a common interest in achieving compatibility.*[66]

Remark The desire for compatibility stems from the assumption that the firms accommodate each other (i.e., do not try to force each other out of the market). In contrast, we know from Whinston's version of the leverage theory (see example 8) that tie-ins may serve as a barrier to entry. Similarly, a dominant firm that wants to induce its rival's exit might well want to make its products incompatible with those of the rival.[67] Incompatibility hurts the rival in two ways: It reduces demand and it leads to more aggressive price competition. It is therefore apt to induce exit. Thus, a firm's optimal strategy (here, concerning the compatibility decision) again hinges on whether it wants to accommodate its rivals or to deter entry or induce exit.[68]

8.5 Epilogue: Prices versus Quantities

A crucial assumption in the interpretation of examples 1 through 9 is that prices are strategic complements and quantities are strategic substitutes. This characterization is particularly crucial in accommodation games, where firms wanting not to look aggressive when they compete in prices may take actions that will later turn them into puppy dogs and where firms competing in quantities may try to become top dogs in the future. It is therefore not surprising that two-period price games (respectively, quantity games) are often more collusive (respectively, more competitive) than their static (one-period) counterparts.[69] The strategies in an entry-deterrence or an exit-inducement situation usually differ less between price and quantity games than in an entry-accommodation situation. As we saw in section 8.3, the important thing is then

---

65. This effect is reminiscent of the observation in chapter 4 that producers of complementary products tend to charge prices that are too high from an industry viewpoint. The incompatible case makes systems fairly good substitutes, whereas compatibility introduces some complementarity.

66. The welfare analysis is less clear cut. In particular, the social welfare relative to consumers purchasing $X_1 Y_1$ and $X_2 Y_2$ under compatibility has gone down, as they face a higher price for their systems and their product selection is the same as under incompatibility. The consumers purchasing $X_1 Y_2$ and $X_2 Y_1$ under compatibility buy a more suitable system than under incompatibility but also pay a higher price, so the welfare analysis is ambiguous without further assumptions.

67. It has been alledged that IBM makes its products incompatible with those of its rivals in order to maintain dominance.

68. See Ordover and Willig 1981 for a discussion of predatory incompatibility decisions.

69. The infinite-horizon Markov analysis of Maskin and Tirole (1987, 1988b) also emphasizes the role of the cross-partial Π_{ij}', and suggests that these results are somewhat robust. There, repetition yields a collusive outcome in the price game and a more competitive outcome than the Cournot one in the quantity game.

to look tough. For instance, by reducing costs, one hurts one's rival, whether competition is in price or in quantity. The bottom line is that, before applying the above taxonomy, one should look at the microstructure of the industry and determine the type of competition that is being waged.

The characterization of prices and quantities as strategic complements and substitutes is a presumption, not a general law, as the following will show.

Quantities Assume that profits have the exact Cournot form (see chapter 5)

$$\Pi^i(q_i, q_j) = q_i P(q_i + q_j) - C_i(q_i),$$

where C_i is firm i's cost function. A simple computation yields the cross-partial derivative:

$$\Pi^i_{ij} = P' + q_i P''.$$

We already know that $P' < 0$. To obtain the strategic-substitute property, it suffices that the price function be linear ($P'' = 0$) or concave ($P'' < 0$). The property may fail for sufficiently convex price functions.[70]

Prices Let $q_i = D_i(p_i, p_j)$ denote the demand curves. The profit functions are

$$\Pi^i(p_i, p_j) = p_i D_i(p_i, p_j) - C_i(D_i(p_i, p_j)).$$

This yields the cross-partial derivative:

$$\Pi^i_{ij} = \frac{\partial D_i}{\partial p_j} + (p_i - C_i') \frac{\partial^2 D_i}{\partial p_i \partial p_j} - C_i'' \frac{\partial D_i}{\partial p_i} \frac{\partial D_i}{\partial p_j}.$$

As in the case of quantities, this cross-partial derivative depends on the details of the demand function. Assume that the demand is linear (over the relevant range),

$$D_i(p_i, p_j) = a - b p_i + d p_j,$$

and that the marginal cost is constant. If the goods are demand substitutes ($d > 0$), then $\Pi^i_{ij} > 0$, so the goods are strategic complements. If they are demand complements ($d < 0$), then they are strategic substitutes. More generally, if we assume that the goods are demand substitutes, and we note that $p_i - C_i' > 0$ in equilibrium (from firm i's first-order condition), it suffices that $\partial^2 D_i / \partial p_i \partial p_j$ be non-negative in order for the goods to be strategic complements in the neighborhood of a price equilibrium.[71]

---

70. For instance, Bulow et al. (1985b) note that for $P(q_1 + q_2) = (q_1 + q_2)^{-\alpha}$ where $0 < \alpha < 1$, Π^i_{ij} is proportional to $\alpha - q_j/q_i$. Thus, if because of cost differences the equilibrium involves a big firm and a small firm (q_1/q_2 very large, say), quantities are strategic complements for one firm and strategic substitutes for the other near the equilibrium point. In particular, an increase in the small firm's output raises the big firm's optimal reaction to this output.

71. It is easy to construct examples in which this property is not satisfied. What is more, the goods generally are not strategic complements in prices over the whole range of potential prices, as Maskin and Tirole (1988b) note. To see why, suppose that the goods are fairly good demand substitutes. Fix p_j and let p_i vary. When $p_i \gg p_j$, firm j obtains the whole demand, and firm i's demand and profit are not affected much by a unit change in firm j's price. (In the limit, with perfect substitutes, demand remains 0 and thus is not affected at all.) So Π^i_j is very small. Similarly, when $p_i \ll p_j$, a unit change in p_j has little effect on firm i's demand and profit; again, Π^i_j is very small. When p_i is close to p_j, a unit change in p_j has a big effect on firm i's demand and profit (think of perfect substitutes); hence, Π^i_j is big. Thus, Π^i_j cannot be monotonic in p_i. Now, this did not matter in our applications, because the second-period simultaneous-move price equilibrium occurred in the region where $\partial D_i / \partial p_j$ is large and Π^i_{ij} is positive. In more dynamic games, this may have some relevance. For instance, in Maskin and Tirole 1988a,b the reaction curves are monotonic (downward sloping) in the quantity game and nonmonotonic in the price game.

8.6   Supplementary Section:
Strategic Behavior and Barriers to Entry or Mobility

This section, which covers some of the recent research on barriers to entry, serves two purposes. First, on a technical level, it goes beyond the somewhat contrived two-period model of sections 8.2–8.4 to analyze the full-fledged dynamic interaction between firms. Second, and perhaps more important, it studies in detail two distinct barriers to entry. Section 8.6.1 compares short-term and long-term capital accumulation. (The analysis follows Fudenberg and Tirole 1986 and 1987.) Section 8.6.2 deals with differentiated markets; it shows how a firm may want to preempt its rivals to occupy the profitable market niches and how a firm can use product proliferation to restrict entry.[72]

8.6.1   Capital Accumulation

The commitment value of capital is higher the longer its lifetime and the more costly its disposal or resale. Thus, the extent to which capital is sunk determines the monopoly power and profit enjoyed by established firms. We will examine two polar cases here: one in which investments are sunk only in the very short run and one in which capital cannot be resold and does not depreciate (i.e., is completely sunk).

8.6.1.1   Short-Term Capital Accumulation and Contestability

This subsection explores two related investment-based dynamic models of a natural monopoly. In these models there is room for only one firm in the market, and there is actually a single firm in equilibrium. This firm makes a profit and deters entry through capital accumulation. Capital is sunk only in the short run and must be "renewed" periodically. The length of time over which capital is sunk determines the period of commitment. When commitment is short, the established firm enjoys only small incumbency advantages over potential entrants (because an entrant can kick the incumbent out of the market quickly). Thus, it must accumulate capital to deter entry. In the limit for very short commitments, the incumbent firm makes almost no profit, so Posner's rent-dissipation

postulate (which says that monopoly profit is dissipated through competition—here, potential competition) is satisfied for very-short-run commitments. Posner's wastefulness postulate (according to which profits are dissipated in a socially wasteful way) may or may not hold, depending on whether the incumbent's capital is excess capital or contributes to production.

Wasteful Rent Dissipation

The first theory of short-run commitments, developed by Eaton and Lipsey (1980), considers an industry with two firms. Time is continuous, and the horizon is infinite. One unit of capital (e.g., a plant) is necessary for production and gives access to constant marginal cost, c. A second unit of capital is useless in the sense that it does not reduce the marginal cost of production. One unit of capital costs f per unit of time and has deterministic durability H (after the unit of capital is installed, it undergoes no physical depreciation for H units of time and full depreciation thereafter[73]). The fixed cost of production (equal to $\int_0^H fe^{-rt}dt$, where r is the rate of interest) is paid when the unit is installed, so the firm cannot avoid paying the fixed cost by leaving the market before H units of time have elapsed. Therefore, with equipment of age $\tau < H$, the firm never has an incentive to leave the market, even if another firm enters. Thus, H is a measure of commitment.

If at date t only one firm is active (i.e., has at least one unit of capital), that firm's flow profit, gross of capital cost, is

$$\tilde{\Pi}^m = \max_q[P(q)q - cq].$$

Suppose that $f < \tilde{\Pi}^m < 2f$. A monopoly is feasible, because $\tilde{\Pi}^m > f$. If two firms operate (i.e., have at least one unit of capital each), they wage Bertrand competition with marginal cost c and make zero gross profit; thus, each loses f per unit of time. The Bertrand assumption is meant to simplify computations. More generally, the firms could make a positive gross duopoly profit; the assumption $\tilde{\Pi}^m < 2f$ would still guarantee a negative net profit for at least one of them, since the gross monopoly

---

72. Readers not familiar with dynamic games may want to skip subsection 8.6.1 in a first reading; it is technically more difficult than the rest of the section.

73. This is the "one-horse shay" manner of depreciation.

profit is an upper bound on gross industry profits under duopoly.

The firms' sole decision is when to build units of capital. One firm invests at time 0. (Think, for instance, of a technological edge that allows this firm to enter first.) The strategies constructed by Eaton and Lipsey are otherwise symmetric. They also are Markovian, in that they depend only on the current payoff-relevant state (here, the two firms' capital structures, i.e., the number and the age of their productive plants). The incumbent firm (the one with capital) always purchases a second unit of capital Δ ($< H/2$) years before its current unit depreciates. The other firm invests in a unit of capital if the incumbent has only one unit and this unit is more than $H - \Delta$ years old. In equilibrium, the length Δ is chosen such that when the incumbent's unit of capital is $H - \Delta$ old, the potential entrant is indifferent between entering and not entering. If he does not enter, the incumbent remains a monopoly forever, and the entrant makes no profit. If he enters, he makes a profit of $-f$ for Δ years (because the incumbent is still committed: The fixed cost on his current unit is sunk) and enjoys monopoly profit forever after. The incumbent's investment path is represented in figure 8.15. Along the equilibrium path, the incumbent always renews his capital before it depreciates. The potential entrant never enters; he is kept out of the market by the incumbent's commitment to stay in for at least Δ years after entry (which inflicts short-term losses on the entrant).

Let us now compute Δ. In equilibrium, the incumbent's present discounted profit from date 0 on (or from any date at which he buys one new unit of capital) is

$$V = \int_0^\infty \tilde{\Pi}^m e^{-rt} dt$$

$$- \left(\int_0^H f e^{-rt} dt \right) \left(1 + e^{-r(H-\Delta)} + e^{-r2(H-\Delta)} + \cdots \right).$$

The first term represents the flow monopoly profit forever. The second is the cost of one unit of capital, repeated at dates 0, $H - \Delta$, $2(H - \Delta)$, ..., $n(H - \Delta)$, ... Some simple mathematics yields

$$V = \frac{\tilde{\Pi}^m}{r} - \frac{f}{r} \left(\frac{1 - e^{-rH}}{1 - e^{-r(H-\Delta)}} \right). \tag{8.1}$$

Now suppose the potential entrant wants to enter. Obviously, there is no point in entering strictly before the

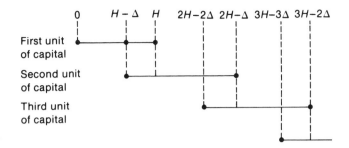

Figure 8.15
Incumbent's equilibrium investment strategy.

incumbent buys a second unit of capital (because the net duopoly profit flow is negative), so the entrant will wait and preempt the incumbent just before the latter buys its second unit (i.e., when the incumbent's current unit is $H - \Delta$ old). If the entrant does so, the incumbent does not buy a second unit, but he sticks around with his old unit for Δ units of time before exiting the market. The entrant's profit from the entry date on is thus equal to V minus the monopoly profit forgone during the entrant's first Δ years of existence (that is, the only difference between the incumbent at date 0 and an entrant who takes over is that the entrant is in a duopoly situation for Δ units of time):

$$V - \int_0^\Delta \tilde{\Pi}^m e^{-rt} dt = V - \tilde{\Pi}^m \frac{1 - e^{-r\Delta}}{r}.$$

Because the second unit of capital is costly and is useless for productive purposes, the incumbent chooses Δ as small as is consistent with deterring entry:

$$V - \tilde{\Pi}^m \frac{1 - e^{-r\Delta}}{r} = 0, \tag{8.2}$$

or, substituting V,

$$\frac{\tilde{\Pi}^m}{f} = \frac{1 - e^{-rH}}{e^{-r\Delta} - e^{-rH}}. \tag{8.3}$$

Under our assumptions, equation 8.3 implies that $\Delta < H/2$.

We are particularly interested in what happens in cases of very short commitments. Let H (and thus Δ) tend to zero. Performing first-order Taylor approximations on equation 8.3, we get

$$\frac{\tilde{\Pi}^m}{f} \simeq \frac{rH}{rH - r\Delta} = \frac{H}{H - \Delta}.$$

Thus,

$$\frac{\Delta}{H} \simeq 1 - \frac{f}{\tilde{\Pi}^m}. \tag{8.4}$$

This means that the incumbent has two units of capital $\Delta/(H - \Delta) \simeq (\tilde{\Pi}^m - f)/f$ percent of the time. More interesting, perhaps, equation 8.2 yields

$$V \simeq 0. \tag{8.5}$$

Thus, even though there is only one firm in the industry in equilibrium, this firm does not make profits. The monopoly rent is entirely dissipated by the accumulation of the second unit of capital. This is natural. If the value V of being a monopolist were large, the entrant would come in, lose money for a very short period of time (because H is small and therefore Δ is small), and capture V. Thus, for short-run commitments, *potential* competition drives the monopolist's profit down to zero.

Even for short-run commitments, we do not obtain the contestability outcome. Actually, we obtain Posner's wasteful-rent-dissipation postulate exactly: The monopolist charges the monopoly price and yet makes no profit. The total welfare loss per unit of time is equal to the loss in consumer surplus (see the triangle in figure 1.2) plus the net monopoly profit ($\tilde{\Pi}^m - f$) (see chapter 1). This should not be surprising; the only possible avenue for rent dissipation in this model is excess capital, which by definition has no social value. This brings us to our second model, in which rent dissipation is socially useful.

Contestability

Our second model is due to Maskin and Tirole (1988a). Though it is similar in spirit to the first model, the formulation differs in some respects. Time is discrete, and the horizon is infinite. There are two firms, which compete in capacities. A capacity is locked in for two periods once chosen. Let $\tilde{\Pi}(K_i, K_j)$ denote the per-period profit of a firm with capacity K_i when its rival has capacity K_j (gross of the per-period fixed cost f). As usual, Π decreases with K_j, and the cross-partial derivative $\partial^2 \tilde{\Pi}/\partial K_1 \partial K_2$ is negative (capacities are strategic substitutes). The period length is T, and the discount factor between periods is $\delta = e^{-rT}$.

The firms choose their capacities sequentially. (The model actually is equivalent to a continuous-time model in which firms choose capacities K, which, as in Eaton and Lipsey 1980, depreciate in a "one-horse shay" manner, but according to a Poisson process—i.e., H is stochastic.[74]) Firm 1 picks capacities in odd periods and firm 2 in even periods.[75] A firm picks a capacity for two periods of production and sinks in the first of these two periods a fixed cost: $f(1 + \delta)$ for capacity $K > 0$, zero for $K = 0$. Let

$$\tilde{\Pi}^m \equiv \max_K [P(K)K - (c + c_0)K],$$

where c is the marginal cost of production and c_0 is the marginal cost of installing capacity. As before, assume that $f < \tilde{\Pi}^m < 2f$. Thus, one firm is viable, but not two. Strategies are required to be "Markov" (i.e., payoff relevant)—that is, firm i reacts to the capacity K_j chosen by

---

74. Consider a continuous-time model with rate of interest r. Let $\Pi^i(K_1, K_2)$ denote firm i's gross profit flow per unit of time. When a firm chooses a capacity, its period of commitment to that capital is stochastic. The probability that the commitments will lapse between date t and date $t + \Delta t$ is independent of time and is equal to $\lambda \Delta t$. One can think of this technology as an uncertain working lifetime (the time independence of depreciation is clearly an extreme assumption). Letting $V^i(K_j)$ (respectively, $W^i(K_i)$) denote the present discounted value of firm i's profit when firm i renews its capital and reacts to firm j's current capital K_j (respectively, when firm j renews its capital and reacts to firm i's current level K_i). From dynamic programming, we have

$$V^1(K_2) = \max_{K_1} \{[\Pi^1(K_1, K_2) - f]\Delta t$$
$$+ \lambda \Delta t\, W^1(K_1)e^{-r\Delta t}$$
$$+ (1 - \lambda \Delta t)V^1(K_2)e^{-r\Delta t}\},$$

which yields

$$V^1(K_2) = \max_{K_1} \left(\frac{\Pi^1(K_1, K_2) - f}{\lambda + r} + \frac{\lambda}{\lambda + r} W^1(K_1) \right).$$

Thus, the continuous-time model is equivalent to the discrete-time, sequential-move model with gross profit function

$$\tilde{\Pi}^1(K_1, K_2) \equiv \frac{\Pi^1(K_1, K_2)}{\lambda + r}$$

and discount factor

$$\delta = \frac{\lambda}{\lambda + r}.$$

For the dynamic programming equations in the discrete time framework, see the next subsection.

75. When we "endogenize" timing by letting firms choose their capacities whenever they want, subject to the constraint that a capacity is locked in for two periods once chosen, the symmetric equilibrium is the same as described below. (Another way of endogenizing the timing is given in note 74.)

its rival in the last period and still in place for the current period by choosing a capacity $K_i = R_i(K_j)$.[76]

As in Eaton and Lipsey 1980, there exists a unique symmetric equilibrium. For δ sufficiently large, it takes the following form (illustrated in figure 8.16): In equilibrium only one firm operates, at capacity level K^*. A firm chooses to enter if and only if its rival's capacity is less than the entry-deterring capacity K^*; if it enters, it accumulates capacity K^* itself. In equilibrium, K^* is such that the entrant is indifferent between entering and not entering:

$$[\tilde{\Pi}(K^*, K^*) - f] + \frac{\delta}{1 - \delta}[\tilde{\Pi}(K^*, 0) - f] = 0. \qquad (8.6)$$

This equation reflects the fact that the entrant gets $\tilde{\Pi}(K^*, K^*) - f < 0$ when entering (recall that $2\tilde{\Pi}(K, K) \leqslant \tilde{\Pi}^m < 2f$ for all K). The incumbent exits in the following period, and the entrant becomes a monopolist who keeps deterring entry by choosing K^* forever. Then the entrant's future profits are given by

$$\delta[\tilde{\Pi}(K^*, 0) - f] + \delta^2[\tilde{\Pi}(K^*, 0) - f] + \cdots$$
$$= \frac{\delta[\tilde{\Pi}(K^*, 0) - f]}{1 - \delta}.$$

The incumbent chooses its own capacity so as to just deter entry; accumulating beyond K^* is costly because, as we will see shortly, K^* already exceeds the monopoly capacity K^m.

In summary: The equilibrium involves a single firm, operating at a capacity level K^*.[77] This firm engages in some form of limit pricing. It accumulates more capacity than a monopolist facing no threat of entry would. It therefore charges a price that is less than the monopoly price (see below).

We will now investigate the case of *short-run commitments* (where T tends to 0—i.e., δ tends to 1). From equation 8.6 we see that when δ converges to 1, $\tilde{\Pi}(K^*, 0) - f$ converges to 0. That is, the monopolist's profit converges to 0. (Note in particular that K^* exceeds K^m.) The intuition for this rent-dissipation result is the same as

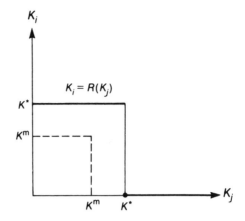

Figure 8.16

before. The established firm enjoys an important incumbency advantage only if it can inflict a duopoly loss on the entrant for a sufficient amount of time. The entrant is lured by the prospect of becoming a monopolist after only a brief fight, so the incumbent must raise its capacity to deter entry.

An important difference from the previous model is that the rent dissipation need not be wasteful. Indeed, if the established firm's capacity K^* is used (so output q is equal to K^*), the dissipation is socially useful. Rent dissipation occurs through price reduction rather than through excess capacity. The outcome in the limit is the one predicted by the contestability school (see section 8.1). Whether the monopolist uses all of his capacity K^* is an empirical question. As in chapter 5, K^* installed is used if the marginal cost of investment c_0 is sufficiently large relative to the marginal cost of production c.

For smaller discount factors, entry is blockaded. That is, by accumulating the monopoly capacity, the established firm deters entry.

No Fixed Cost: The Dynamics of Cournot Competition

In the two preceding subsections we assumed the existence of large fixed costs, which made the industry a natural monopoly. The incumbent firm overinvested to deter entry. In the absence of fixed costs (or in the presence of low fixed costs), there is room for two firms.

---

76. In other words, the strategies do not depend on the payoff-irrelevant history of the game.

77. In both the Eaton-Lipsey model and the Maskin-Tirole model, there are two asymmetric Markov-perfect equilibria for sufficiently short commitments.

In these equilibria, one of the firms enjoys unconstrained monopoly power in a steady state (that is, it does not renew its capital early in the first model, and it accumulates K^m in the second). This firm never quits the market, and it reacts to entry by assuming that the entrant will exit once its commitment has elapsed. This aggressive behavior is self-fulfilling and ends up deterring entry.

Entry, Accommodation, and Exit

Rather than deter entry, the firms accommodate each other. This subsection analyzes accommodation in an industry with short-run commitments and presents the argument that some of the principles governing accommodation under quantity competition in two-period models (see sections 8.3 and 8.4) carry over to full-fledged dynamic games.

Consider the sequential-move capacity competition model of the preceding subsection, but assume that the firms incur no fixed cost ($f = 0$). (The analysis here follows one presented by Maskin and Tirole [1987] and is based on the earlier model of Cyert and DeGroot [1970].) Firm 1 chooses capacities in odd periods (which are locked in for two periods and can be freely changed after two periods), and firm 2 chooses capacities in even periods. Firm i's intertemporal profit at time t is

$$\sum_{s=0}^{\infty} \delta^s \Pi^i(K_{1,t+s}, K_{2,t+s}).$$

As before, we make the usual assumptions on the profit function: $\Pi_{ii}^i < 0$, $\Pi_j^i < 0$, $\Pi_{ij}^i < 0$. We look for a pair of dynamic reaction functions, $R_1(\cdot)$ and $R_2(\cdot)$, that form a Markov perfect equilibrium. Thus, if firm 2's current (locked-in) capacity is K_2, firm 1 reacts by choosing capacity $K_1 = R_1(K_2)$ to maximize its present discounted profit given that both firms will then move according to R_1 and R_2. As in section 6.7, let $V^i(K_j)$ denote the present discounted profit of firm i when it reacts to its rival's capacity K_j, and let $W^i(K_i)$ be firm i's present discounted profit when it is locked into K_i and its rival reacts. The equilibrium conditions are the following:

$$V^1(K_2) = \max_K [\Pi^1(K, K_2) + \delta W^1(K)\}, \qquad (8.7)$$

$R_1(K_2)$ maximizes $[\Pi^1(K, K_2) + \delta W^1(K)]$, $\qquad (8.8)$

$$W^1(K_1) = \Pi^1(K_1, R_2(K_1)) + \delta V^1(R_2(K_1)), \qquad (8.9)$$

and similarly for firm 2.

The first common feature with traditional analysis is that, because capacities are strategic substitutes ($\Pi_{ij}^i < 0$), the reaction curves are downward sloping. To show this, it suffices to write the optimality of reaction functions (an identical technique is used to prove the monotonicity of incentive-compatible allocations in incentive problems). Consider two capacity levels, K_2 and $\tilde{K}_2$. Let $R_1(K_2)$ and $R_1(\tilde{K}_2)$ denote the optimal reactions to K_2 and $\tilde{K}_2$. By definition, $R_1(K_2)$ is a better response to K_2 than $R_1(\tilde{K}_2)$:

$$\Pi^1(R_1(K_2), K_2) + \delta W^1(R_1(K_2))$$
$$\geq \Pi^1(R_1(\tilde{K}_2), K_2) + \delta W^1(R_1(\tilde{K}_2)). \qquad (8.10)$$

Similarly, $R_1(\tilde{K}_2)$ is a best response to $\tilde{K}_2$:

$$\Pi^1(R_1(\tilde{K}_2), \tilde{K}_2) + \delta W^1(R_1(\tilde{K}_2))$$
$$\geq \Pi^1(R_1(K_2), \tilde{K}_2) + \delta W^1(R_1(K_2)). \qquad (8.11)$$

Adding equations 8.10 and 8.11, we obtain

$$\Pi^1(R_1(K_2), K_2) - \Pi^1(R_1(\tilde{K}_2), K_2)$$
$$+ \Pi^1(R_1(\tilde{K}_2), \tilde{K}_2) - \Pi^1(R_1(K_2), \tilde{K}_2) \geq 0, \qquad (8.12)$$

which is equivalent to

$$\int_{\tilde{K}_2}^{K_2} \int_{R_1(\tilde{K}_2)}^{R_1(K_2)} \Pi_{12}^1(x, y) dx dy \geq 0. \qquad (8.13)$$

But, by assumption, $\Pi_{12}^1 < 0$. Thus, equation 8.13 implies that $R_1(K_2) \leq R_1(\tilde{K}_2)$ if $K_2 > \tilde{K}_2$. The reaction curves are necessarily downward sloping.

To find equilibrium reaction functions, we must solve the system of equations 8.7–8.9.[78] For quadratic profit functions, such as

$$\Pi^i = K_i(d - K_i - K_j),$$

there exists a particularly simple solution. Each firm's reaction function is linear in its rival's capacity: $R_1 = R_2 = R$, where $R(K) = a - bK$. This solution also has the remarkable property that it is the limit of each firm's reaction function at any date when the horizon is finite but tends to infinity.[79]

---

78. To find a differentiable solution (if such a solution exists), we can differentiate equation 8.9 and take the first-order condition in 8.7. After some substitutions, we obtain a system of difference-differential equations in the two reaction functions. This system is generally hard to solve, but is easy in the case of quadratic profit functions.

79. The finite-horizon solution is too complex to be derived in closed form. Indeed, Cyert and DeGroot (1970) computed it numerically. To show conver-

gence toward the infinite-horizon, linear, Markov-perfect equilibrium, one shows that the finite-horizon solution belongs to the class of linear reaction functions with slopes between $-\frac{1}{2}$ and 0 and intercepts between 0 and d, that it is obtained by backward induction through a contraction mapping in the space of such functions, and that the fixed point of the contraction mapping (which is the limit of the reaction function for large horizons) satisfies the difference-differential equations for (R_1, R_2) derived from equations 8.7 through 8.9.

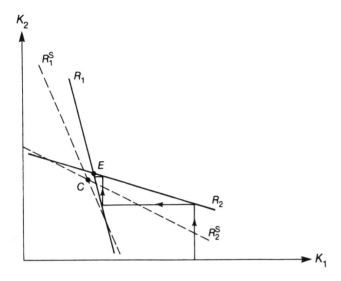

Figure 8.17

The dynamics of the game are illustrated in figure 8.17. The solid lines depict the dynamic reaction functions for δ in $(0, 1)$, the broken lines represent the static Cournot reaction functions R_1^s and R_2^s, E denotes the steady-state allocation, and C denotes the Cournot outcome.

For $\delta = 0$, the firms are myopic. They react according to the static reaction function

$$R(K) = \frac{d}{2} - \frac{K}{2},$$

which maximizes $\tilde{K}(d - K - \tilde{K})$. Thus, $a = d/2$ and $b = \frac{1}{2}$. The industry dynamics are then called the *tâtonnement process*. The steady state is the Cournot allocation C. For $\delta > 0$, each firm takes into account not only its current profit but also its rival's future reaction. Because reaction curves are downward sloping, the intuition is that a firm should invest beyond its short-run interest so as to induce its rival to curtail capacity (as in the Stackelberg game of section 8.2). Indeed, it can be shown that when δ increases, the steady-state symmetric level of capacity, given by $K = a - bK$ or $K = a/(1 + b)$, increases and thus moves away from the Cournot level. The process is dynamically stable—for any initial level of capacity, the capacities of the two firms converge to the steady-state capacities. This generalizes the Cournot tâtonnement process in that each firm rationally anticipates the influence of its capacity choices on its rival's behavior.

The moral of such a simple infinite-horizon model is that the intuitions derived in two-period models carry over: Strategic substitutes yield downward-sloping reac-

tion curves, so each firm overinvests for strategic reasons. The outcome can be thought of as symmetric Stackelberg leadership.

8.6.1.2 Long-Term Capital-Accumulation Games

In the other polar case, investment creates a long-term commitment to be in the market. Specifically, we assume that investment, once in place, does not depreciate and cannot be resold. That is, investment is irreversible. The following model is due to Spence (1979); the version presented here is from Fudenberg and Tirole 1983b.

Consider a duopoly, with firms indexed by $i = 1, 2$. Time is continuous, and the horizon is infinite. Firm i's flow profit at any time t, gross of investment expenditures, is given by

$$\Pi^i(K_1(t), K_2(t)),$$

where $K_i(t)$ is firm i's capital stock at date t (as usual, $\Pi_{ii}^i < 0$, $\Pi_j^i < 0$, and $\Pi_{ij}^i < 0$).

Capital at date t is equal to cumulative investment to date:

$$\dot{K}_i(t) \equiv \frac{dK_i(t)}{dt} = I_i(t),$$

where $I_i(t)$ is the rate of investment. It is assumed that the cost of investment is linear. One unit of investment costs \$1. To avoid instantaneous investment at date 0, we bound each firm's investment above by $\bar{I}_i$. This technology is an example of convex investment cost. Investment must be non-negative, and there is no depreciation. Thus, the capital stocks are nondecreasing. Firm i's net profit at time t is

$$\Pi^i(K_1(t), K_2(t)) - I_i(t).$$

Firm i's strategy is a path of investment $\{I_i(t)\}$ satisfying $0 \leq I_i(t) \leq \bar{I}_i$. Each firm's investment at date t depends on the current capital stocks $(K_1(t), K_2(t))$ (again, we assume that the strategies are of the Markov type, in that they depend only on the payoff-relevant state of the game and not on the whole history). Both firms enter the market at time $t = 0$ without any capital.

Firm i's objective function is equal to its present discounted profit:

$$\int_0^\infty [\Pi^i(K_1(t), K_2(t)) - I_i(t)]e^{-rt}dt.$$

In this subsection we will only consider the limit game in which both firms become infinitely patient (that is, r tends to 0). In this case, the firms maximize their time-average payoffs, so that only the eventual steady-state capital levels matter (no firm will choose to invest forever). Thus, firm i's objective function is $\Pi^i(K_1^{ss}, K_2^{ss})$, where ss stands for steady state. This simplification allows us to ignore the private cost of investment and focus on its strategic aspect, and to use a simple diagrammatic approach.[80]

Let us first examine the "precommitment" or "open-loop" equilibria.[81] In a precommitment equilibrium, the firms simultaneously commit themselves to entire time paths of investment. Thus, the precommitment equilibria are really static, in that there is only one decision point for each firm. The precommitment equilibria are just like Cournot-Nash equilibria, but with a larger strategy space. In the capacity game, the precommitment equilibrium is exactly the same as if both firms built their entire capital stocks at the start (because there is no discounting). In the resulting "Cournot" equilibrium, each firm invests to the point at which the marginal productivity of capital equals zero, given the steady-state capital level of its opponent. All of the many different paths that lead to this steady state are precommitment equilibria. For example, each firm's strategy could be to invest as quickly as possible to its Cournot level. We can highlight the similarity of this solution to a Cournot equilibrium by defining the "steady-state reaction curves" that give each firm's desired steady-state capital level as a function of its rival's steady-state capital level. Under our assumptions, these reaction curves look the same as usual "nice" Cournot reaction curves. The reaction curves R_1 and R_2 are displayed in figure 8.18, where IGP is the investment-growth path (the path along which both firms are investing as rapidly as they can). The precommitment (open-loop) equilibrium is at $C = (C_1, C_2)$, the intersection of the two curves. We have seen that the use of the concept of precommitment transforms an apparently dynamic game into a static one. As a modeling strategy, this transformation is ill advised: "... one should not allow precommitment to enter by the back door.... If it is possible, it should be explicitly modeled ... as a formal choice in the game." (Kreps and Spence 1984)

Now allow firm i's investment at time t to depend on the capital stocks at that time (the firms employ closed-loop strategies). The capital stocks are the "state variables" (i.e., the capital stocks at any date and the investment programs from that date on are all the information one needs to compute the payoffs). A Markov perfect equilibrium is a pair of Markov strategies

$$\{I_i(K_1(t), K_2(t))\}_{i=1,2}$$

that form a "closed-loop" Nash equilibrium from any possible initial state (K_1^0, K_2^0) and not only from the initial state $(0, 0)$.

Consider figure 8.19, which depicts a Markov perfect equilibrium. The arrows indicate the direction of motion. The motion is vertical if only firm 2 is investing, horizon-

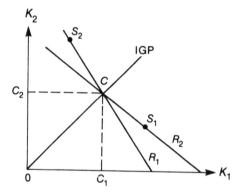

Figure 8.18

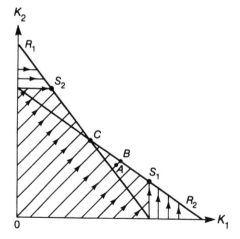

Figure 8.19

---

80. For analyses of the discounting case, see Fudenberg and Tirole 1983b and Nguyen 1986.

81. The analysis here follows Fudenberg and Tirole 1986, pp. 8–13.

tal if only firm 1 is investing, diagonal if each is investing as quickly as possible, and nonexistent if neither firm invests (because of the linearities, the optimal strategies are, in the jargon of optimal-control theory, "bang-bang"). Note that we have defined choices at every state, and not just those along the equilibrium path—we must do this in order to test for perfectness. Looking at figure 8.19, we see that unless firm 1 has a head start it cannot enforce its Stackelberg outcome S_1, because it cannot accumulate enough capital before firm 2 reaches its reaction curve. If firm 1 can invest to its Stackelberg level before firm 2 reaches its reaction curve, it does so and then stops; firm 2 then continues investing up to R_2. If for some reason firm 1's capital stock already exceeds its Stackelberg level, it stops investing immediately. The situation is symmetric on the other half of the diagram, which corresponds to states in which firm 2 has a head start. Thus, this equilibrium demonstrates how an advantage in investment speed or initial conditions can be exploited. The conditions of the growth phase (which firm got there first, the costs of adjustment, and so on) have a permanent impact on the structure of the industry.

It turns out that the equilibrium depicted in figure 8.19 is not unique. There are many others. To understand why, consider point A in the figure. This point is close to firm 2's reaction curve and past firm 1's reaction curve. The strategies specify that from point A on both firms invest until R_2 is reached. However, both firms would prefer the status quo at A. Firm 1 in particular would not want to invest even if firm 2 stopped investing; it just invests in self-defense to reduce firm 2's eventual capital level. Both firms' stopping at A is an equilibrium in the subgame starting at A, enforced by the credible threat of going to B (or close to B) if anyone continues investing past A. Thus, the Markov restriction does not greatly restrict the set of equilibria in the investment game.[82]

In this study we presume that capital does not depreciate. An open issue, analyzed by Hanig (1985) and Reynolds (1987), is the behavior of investment in the

industry when capital depreciates. Intuition suggests that capital ought to lose some of its commitment value and that the steady-state levels of capital should be less sensitive to the initial head start of one of the firms. Hanig and Reynolds consider quadratic payoff functions,

$$\Pi^i = K_i(1 - K_i - K_j),$$

and quadratic investment costs,

$$C^i(I_i) = cI_i^2/2.$$

They allow depreciation ($\dot{K}_i = I_i - \mu K_i$) and discounting, and they look for Markov-perfect-equilibrium investment strategies that are linear in the capital levels ($I_i(t) = -\alpha K_i(t) - \beta K_j(t) + \gamma$, where $\alpha, \beta, \gamma > 0$). They use differential-games techniques[83] to obtain such a solution. The main result is that the steady-state level of capital for both firms strictly exceeds the Cournot level; thus, both firms are beyond their reaction curves in the long run. The intuition is the same as for the model of short-run commitments (and no fixed cost) described above. Each firm at each instant keeps more capacity than it would if it could not influence its rival's accumulation. It thus forces its rival to reduce its capacity. Because both firms behave in this Stackelberg fashion, their capital levels exceed the Cournot ones. The commitment value of capital is inversely related to its rate of depreciation. In particular, capital that depreciates rapidly involves only a short-term commitment.

If we ignore fixed costs and barriers to entry, these models point at the following conclusion for dynamic competition under Markov strategies: Relative to static competition (see chapter 5), repeated interaction promotes collusion under price competition (see chapter 6) and fosters competition under capacity competition in the Hanig (1985), Maskin-Tirole (1987), and Reynolds (1987) models.[84] This conclusion makes economic sense. By raising its price, a firm creates incentives for its rival to do the same; by increasing its capital level, it induces its rival to reduce its own. Thus, the distinction between strategic

---

82. Fudenberg and Tirole (1983b) single out a reasonable "early-stopping" equilibrium (i.e., an equilibrium with steady state under the upper envelope of the reaction curves) through arguably intuitive arguments, including the elimination of Pareto-dominated equilibria. In the symmetric case, this equilibrium coincides with the joint profit-maximizing outcome. MacLeod (1985) offers a more formal argument that lends some support to this selection.

83. See Starr and Ho 1969 and Fudenberg and Tirole 1986. The differenti-

ability of the investment strategies in the capital levels required by the theory of differential games is not an innocuous assumption. Its rules out the above early-stopping equilibria, in which a firm invests to some level, stops, and threatens to resume investment if its rival does so.

84. We must be careful here because of the potential multiplicity of equilibria. The previous no-depreciation capital-accumulation game admitted nondifferentiable equilibria, which are quite collusive. See note 82.

substitutes and complements has some relevance for the study of long-run competition.

The Stackelberg-Spence-Dixit model (see section 8.2) illustrates the fact that with low fixed costs and in the absence of substantial indivisibilities in production, established firms do not deter entry but only try to limit the expansion of entrants. The dynamic rivalry models discussed above make this point even more forcefully. The Stackelberg-Spence-Dixit model also shows that under large fixed costs and/or indivisibilities, entry deterrence becomes optimal for the incumbents. This point too was confirmed by the dynamic rivalry models discussed above.

8.6.2 Product Proliferation, Preemption, and the Persistence of Monopoly

In many industries, firms do not choose a continuous scale variable (like capacity in the previous investment game). Rather, because of indivisibilities or fixed costs, they face a discrete choice: They invest in plants that are most efficient in terms of scale (as in the case of a U-shaped cost curve); they choose among a limited set of products; they locate at a restricted set of geographical places; and so on. The advantage of being the first mover then takes an extreme form: that of preemption. Certainly, preemption occurs in the above long-term capital-accumulation game. Each firm would like to enter first so as to reach its Stackelberg capacity before its rival has accumulated enough capital to dissuade it from doing so. The effect of indivisibilities is that firms wish to preempt with a vengeance. In the investment game, a firm that delays its investment a bit loses a bit of its first-mover advantage (in the absence of depreciation, the steady state will involve a bit less capital for this firm and a bit more for its rival). In contrast, a firm that fails to install a plant or to occupy the right market niche on time may not be able to prevent an entrant from installing a plant or occupying the niche. A little delay may allow entry and thus have large consequences for the firms' profits.[85]

In this subsection we will study discrete choice and preemption. The discussion will be limited to situations in which the preempting firm does not physically deter

entry but, rather, makes it unprofitable. (Exclusionary investments will be studied in chapter 10 in the context of patentable innovations.)

A natural focus of preemption games is the timing of the introduction of plants or products. As in the model of Eaton and Lipsey (1980), the established firms will tend to invest early. Another focus is the persistence of monopoly. Will the established firm always be able to deter its rivals from entering by investing early? Should we expect a monopolistic or an oligopolistic structure in the long-run?

8.6.2.1 Product Proliferation

As we saw in chapter 7, firms want to differentiate their products so as to avoid intense price competition (with some exceptions). Therefore, potential entrants look for unfilled market niches. To deter entry, the established firms may try to pack the product space and leave no profitable market niche unfilled. For instance, Scherer (1980, pp. 258–259) describes General Motors' 1921 decision to offer a complete spectrum of automobiles, and GM chairman Alfred P. Sloan's strategic approach to the decision. He also notes how the Swedish Tobacco Company, upon losing its legal monopoly position in 1961, reacted by offering twice as many brands (and by increasing its advertising twelvefold in the following years). Schmalensee (1978) observes that the six leading manufacturers of ready-to-eat breakfast cereals introduced eighty brands between 1950 and 1972 (the year in which the Federal Trade Commission issued a complaint against the four largest manufacturers, who had cornered 85 percent of the market and who enjoyed large profits).

Schmalensee (1978) shows formally how a cartel (a group of firms that act as a single monopolist) crowds a product space. In the context of a circular location model, he asks how many products a cartel should introduce to make further entry unprofitable; and he shows that it is indeed in a cartel's interest to deter entry in this way. Schmalensee's model is static and therefore is silent on the optimal timing of preemption. Subsequent research has developed models in which, over time, demand grows or the cost of introducing new products decreases, and the date of introduction of a new product is a choice variable.

---

85. A similar phenomenon would occur in an investment game with a fixed cost of entry.

Further persistence-of-monopoly results were discovered by Eaton and Lipsey (1979), who described preemption in a location model[86]; Gilbert and Newberry (1982), who demonstrated a similar result and clearly identified the reason for persistence in the context of a patent race; and Gilbert and Harris (1984), who determined the "threat dates" at which an established firm can build indivisible plants so as to deter entry.[87] We now look at the results for a simple product-differentiation model.[88]

Let us return to the simple model developed in chapter 7 and consider a linear city of length 1. We will assume that there are only two possible store locations: one at each of the extremities of the city. This assumption, although not crucial, simplifies the presentation. The consumers, who are distributed evenly along the segment, have a transportation cost t per unit of distance. Time is continuous and belongs to the interval $[0, +\infty)$. At date 0, the consumer density is unitary. It remains unitary until date T, when it doubles instantly; then it remains 2 forever. (The discontinuous growth of the population, which is somewhat contrived, gives us a simple way of modeling locational choice in an expanding city.)

There are two firms. At date 0, firm 1 (the existing firm) serves the entire market from its single store at the left end of the city. At any future moment, each of the two firms can build a shop at the right end of the city with an accompanying fixed investment cost f. For the time being, we assume that a firm does not exit after sinking the investment cost.

We could assume that each firm can build a store at a location where its rival already has a store. However, because Bertrand competition with undifferentiated products yields zero profit, it is easy to see that such a policy is not profitable in our model; therefore, we will not consider it (but see below). The problem is to determine which firm will invest in building at the second location and at what moment this will occur.

Before date T, firm 1 earns a profit per unit of time of Π_0^m if neither of the two firms has built at the right end of the city, Π_1^m (without subtracting the fixed building cost) if it has built, and Π^d if firm 2 (the entrant) was the first to build. In the last case, firm 2 also earns Π^d per unit of time. If the unit production cost (net of the fixed building cost of the store) is constant, these flow profits are doubled after date T because of the population growth. We assume that $\Pi_1^m > \Pi_0^m$ and $\Pi_1^m > 2\Pi^d$. The first of these inequalities simply says that, if we ignore the cost of building the store, the existing firm prefers to have two stores rather than one; the second inequality says that for a given number of stores (here, two), the total profit of the industry is smaller for a duopoly because of competition. These conditions are quite general. That they hold in the case where the consumers have unitary demands, where $\bar{s} > 2t$ ($\bar{s}$ is the consumers' valuation for the good sold by both stores), and where the production cost c is zero is due to $\Pi_0^m = \bar{s} - t$, $\Pi_1^m = \bar{s} - t/2$, and $\Pi^d = t/2$.

Let $t_1 > 0$ denote the preemption date, that is, the date at which one of the firms invests (first) and builds at the right end of the city. Let $L_i(t_1)$ (respectively, $F_i(t_1)$) be the present discounted value of profit, at date 0, for firm i when it is first to invest and does so at date t_1 (respectively, is preempted). L and F stand for *leader* and *follower*. (The leadership is endogenous.) For $t_1 < T$, these functions are given by

$$L_1(t_1) = \int_0^{t_1} \Pi_0^m e^{-rt} dt + \int_{t_1}^T \Pi_1^m e^{-rt}$$
$$+ \int_T^\infty 2\Pi_1^m e^{-rt} dt - fe^{-rt_1},$$

$$F_2(t_1) = 0,$$

$$L_2(t_1) = \int_{t_1}^T \Pi^d e^{-rt} dt + \int_T^\infty 2\Pi^d e^{-rt} - fe^{-rt_1},$$

$$F_1(t_1) = \int_0^{t_1} \Pi_0^m e^{-rt} dt + \int_{t_1}^T \Pi^d e^{-rt} dt + \int_T^\infty 2\Pi^d e^{-rt} dt,$$

---

86. Precursors include Hay 1976, Prescott and Visscher 1977, and Rothschild 1976. For an account of these contributions, see Gabszewicz and Thisse 1986. Bonanno (1987) analyzes a Prescott-Visscher-type model of sequential entry in a spatial market. He allows firms to open several stores, whereas Prescott and Visscher restrict the analysis to one store or none per firm. At date i ($i = 1, \ldots, n$), firm i decides whether to enter and (if it chooses to enter) how many stores to open and where to locate them. At date $n + 1$, after the n firms have made their investment decisions, price competition takes place. The main result is that monopoly persists: Firm 1 deters entry. In fact, for some values of the parameters, entry deterrence is not achieved through product proliferation; rather, firm 1 opens the same number of stores as a protected monopolist, but rearranges the locations of these stores to deter entry. If this strategic location choice is not sufficient or not the most profitable way to deter entry, product proliferation occurs.

87. See Rao and Rutenberg 1979 for the optimal timing of plant installation when entry cannot be deterred.

88. The following analysis follows Fudenberg and Tirole 1986, pp. 41–45, which builds on Eaton and Lipsey 1979.

where r is the interest rate and f is the investment cost. For $t_1 > T$, we can define L_i and F_i in a similar way.

Now suppose that

$$\frac{2\Pi^d}{r} > f > \frac{\Pi^d}{r}.$$

The first inequality tells us that after the doubling of the population, the present discounted value of duopoly profit is greater than the investment cost. This condition guarantees that firm 2's entry into the industry is profitable. The second inequality says that at any moment before T, the duopoly profit (Π^d) does not cover the interest (rf) on the investment cost. These two inequalities imply that in the absence of a preemptive threat by firm 1, firm 2 wishes to invest exactly at date T (that is, L_2 reaches its maximum at date T). The functions L_i and F_i are depicted in figure 8.20.

We define $T_2 < T$ such that, at date T_2, firm 2 is indifferent between preempting and being preempted; i.e.,

$$L_2(T_2) = F_2(T_2) = 0.$$

We can verify that $L_2(t_1) > F_2(t_1)$ if and only if $t_1 > T_2$, and we can verify that $L_1(t_1) > F_1(t_1)$ for any $t_1 \geqslant T_2$ (using $\Pi_1^m - \Pi^d > \Pi^d$).

Suppose that $(\Pi_1^m - \Pi_0^m) < rf$. In other words, in the absence of a threat of entry, the established firm does not choose to invest before T.[89] That is, L_1 is increasing before T. Figure 8.20 fully summarizes the preemption game between the two firms.

We can now solve the preemption game. To do this, we consider the problem by looking back in time from date T. At that moment, the established firm (firm 1) wishes to invest (if no one has done so before) regardless of firm 2's subsequent strategy. Knowing this, firm 2 will not allow investment by firm 1; it will preempt at some earlier moment $T - \varepsilon$, because $L_2(T - \varepsilon) > F_2(T)$. Firm 1, knowing the entrant's preemptive choice at $T - \varepsilon$, will wish to preempt by investing just before that moment, and so forth. This preemptive spiral stops at moment T_2, when firm 2 finds further preemption too costly. Therefore, in order to preempt firm 2, it is sufficient for firm 1

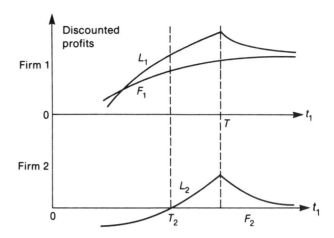

Figure 8.20

to invest just before T_2. Since L_1 is increasing before T_2, firm 1 waits until that date (or just slightly before it) to preempt. Therefore, equilibrium is characterized by the following two properties:

• The established firm preempts the entrant and retains its monopoly.

• Preemption occurs before the increase in the population, at the first date when the entrant would have been willing to enter in the absence of preemption.

A correct formalization of the equilibrium strategies can be found for a similar game in Fudenberg and Tirole 1985.[90]

The basic result of the above example is the persistence of monopoly. The intuitive reasoning behind the more general property goes as follows: Competition is destructive of profits; a monopolist with the same production technology as a duopoly industry earns more profit than the two rival firms together (at worst, the monopolist can always make its stores choose the strategies followed by the competing firms). This property, called the *efficiency effect* and reflected here by the inequality $\Pi_1^m \geqslant 2\Pi^d$, is very general and forms the basis for the phenomenon of monopoly persistence. At the time of entry, the potential entrant bases his decisions on duopoly profit per unit of time Π^d. Now consider the choices available

89. This inequality was satisfied above: $\Pi_1^m - \Pi_0^m = t/2 = \Pi^d < rf$.

90. The above reasoning is very loose. Familiar strategies for continuous-time games—called "distributional strategies," and specifying a (right continuous) cumulative probability distribution that a firm has moved by any date t—are not "rich" enough to describe such preemption games. Richer and more satisfactory strategies are obtained by taking the limit of the discrete-time model while allowing reasonable behavior. See Simon and Stichcombe 1986 and Simon 1987 for useful elaborations on this theme.

to the existing firm, i.e., either to allow or to preempt entry. Allowing entry implies a loss of $\Pi_1^m - \Pi^d$ per unit of time. Since $\Pi_1^m - \Pi^d > \Pi^d$, *the existing firm has more of an incentive to preempt than the entrant has to enter.*

The monopolist's rent is dissipated, although not fully, by the necessity to invest earlier than it desires (in order to preempt the entrant). In the above example with identical unit demands and linear transportation cost, this rent dissipation turns out to be socially wasteful, as in Eaton and Lipsey 1980. Thus, a social planner would wish to eliminate the threat of entry.[91]

It is worthwhile to compare preemption games such as the one just solved with war-of-attrition games such as the one considered in section 8.1. Both are "games of timing." In such games, each firm makes a single decision (when to enter in the preemption game; when to exit in the war of attrition). In the preemption game, each firm prefers to be first (at least over a period of time preceding the optimal date for moving), but would like to move "late" if it could be sure that its rival would not preempt. In the war of attrition, each firm prefers to "move" second (e.g., not to exit) but would like to move "early" if it could be sure that it would be outlasted by its rival. These two standard games are only polar examples of games of timing, and more general industrial-organization situations may involve different patterns; however, the techniques and intuitions derived for these games help us to apprehend the more complex situations (see Katz and Shapiro 1984).

8.6.2.2 Is Spatial Preemption Credible?

The general line of reasoning based on the efficiency effect suggests that monopoly situations remain monopoly situations, which of course is not always the case. We will consider what may be wrong with this reasoning. For the moment, let us observe that the incumbent's investment has a preemptive value only if the incumbent is somehow committed to this investment (see Judd 1985). A multiproduct incumbent who can withdraw some of his products at low cost may not be able to use crowding as a barrier to entry. This seems logical; we have been insisting all along that investment deters entry more easily when committed. Judd's interesting insight is that if a multiproduct firm competes with a single-product rival on some market, *the multiproduct firm has more incentive to quit the market than its rival as long as a low price in this market depresses the demand for its other goods.* Thus, existing products may have little commitment value.

To see how the multiproduct firm may be forced to exit a market, consider the previous model of a linear city. Suppose that the incumbent has preempted the entrant and has two stores, located at the two extremities. Suppose further that the entrant follows suit and enters the right-end location itself. If no firm exits, Bertrand competition drives the price of the two right-end stores down to marginal cost c. Hence, each firm makes a zero profit at its right-end store. Firm 1 makes a positive profit at its left-end store. Because of the transportation cost, the goods sold by the left- and right-end stores are differentiated, and firm 1 can keep its price a bit above c without losing all its customers (see chapter 7). However, its profit is meager, because the good sold at the right-end location is sold at the low price c. Now compare the two firms' incentives to quit the right-end location, assuming that the firms do not recoup their building cost f when exiting and do not incur any extra exit cost. Firm 2 has little incentive to exit, because it makes a zero profit whether it exits or stays when firm 1 stays. Firm 1, however, makes more money by exiting than by staying, if firm 2 stays. By exiting the right-end location, it raises the price at this location and therefore increases the residual demand for the good sold at the left-end location. For instance, for linear transportation costs, uniform density of consumers, and a city of length 1, the duopoly price is $c + t > c$ (see chapter 7). Because firm 1 was not making any money from the consumers purchasing at its right-end branch, it cares only about the residual demand faced by its left-end branch; thus, it increases its profit by exiting. To summarize loosely: Exiting the right-end location, a weakly dominated strategy for firm 2, raises firm 1's profit. Thus,

---

91. Because of the inelastic demand structure, the flow increase in welfare (before T) associated with the introduction of the right-end store is equal to the savings in average transportation costs: $t/2 - t/4 = t/4$ (assuming that the monopoly always covers the market). The flow cost of the store is equal to rf. But, by assumption, $rf > \Pi^d = t/2 > t/4$.

in equilibrium, *firm 1 exits immediately and firm 2 stays; the result is a duopoly.*[92]

Solving for the overall game, notice that firm 2 kicks firm 1 out of its right-end location immediately if both firms are located there, and recall that no firm wanted to enter the right-end location before date T except for preemptive purposes. Thus, the equilibrium is such that *firm 1 never enters the right-end location; firm two enters this location at date T.* No preemption occurs. We conclude that small exit costs together with product substitution may place the incumbent firm at a disadvantage and prevent it from credibly preempting the entrant through product proliferation.

Exercise 8.10* Two differentiated goods, apples and oranges, are located at the two extremes of a linear product space (a segment of length 1). The utility of a consumer located at x is

$$\bar{s} - tx^2 - p_1$$

if he consumes one apple,

$$\bar{s} - t(1 - x)^2 - p_2$$

if he consumes one orange, and 0 otherwise (consuming both yields indigestion). The price of an apple is p_1; the price of an orange is p_2. Consumers are located uniformly along the segment. (This is exactly like the transportation model, where spatial preferences are reinterpreted as tastes, except that transportation costs are quadratic instead of linear.) The marginal cost of each good is c. Firm 1 is an apple monopoly, firm 2 an orange monopoly.

(i) Show that the demand functions are

$$D_1 = (p_2 - p_1 + t)/2t$$

and

$$D_2 = (p_1 - p_2 + t)/2t$$

in the relevant range ($|p_2 - p_1| \leqslant t$ and prices not too high).

(ii) Solve for the Bertrand equilibrium. Compute the profits.

(iii) Suppose that firm 1 is an apple monopoly, but that both firms produce oranges. Compute the Bertrand equilibrium. Show that Π^1 is smaller (by a factor of 4) than in question ii. Explain.

(iv) Suppose that there are no exit costs, that entry costs are sunk, that firm 1 is in both markets, and that firm 2 is in the orange market (as in question iii). Which firm has an incentive to exit the orange market? What do you conclude about the role of sunk costs or exit costs with regard to the possibility of entry deterrence through product proliferation (e.g., firm 1 entering first in orange markets)?

8.6.2.3 Do Monopolies Persist?

Subsection 8.6.2.1 unveiled an important factor favoring the persistence of monopolies: the efficiency effect. *Because competition destroys industry profits, an incumbent has more incentive to deter entry than an entrant has to enter.*[93] In general, however, this efficiency effect is not sufficient for the persistence-of-monopoly result. (This is fortunate for the theory: In the United States there are

---

92. This is a very informal description of the game. Exiting is a weakly dominated strategy for firm 2, because by always charging c it can guarantee itself a zero intertemporal profit. Furthermore, staying is profitable if firm 1 exits. (This weak-domination argument actually assumes that reentry is impossible, but a more sophisticated argument can be used to derive the same outcome when reentry is allowed.) Suppose now that we rule out weakly dominated strategies as eligible for equilibrium behavior (as is done, for instance, in Selten's notion of trembling-hand perfect equilibrium in discrete games—see the Game Theory User's Manual). Firm 2 stays, and firm 1 has no other choice than to exit.

If firms could recoup part of their fixed cost f when exiting, exiting would no longer be a weakly dominated strategy for firm 2, but firm 1 would still gain more by exiting than firm 2. The exit game would then resemble a war of attrition. (In the mixed-strategy equilibrium of this war of attrition, firm 2's probability of exit exceeds firm 1's.)

93. This efficiency effect rests on the comparison between a monopoly and a duopoly. One might conjecture that, more generally, a big firm has more

incentive to preempt than a small firm. This, however, is not correct. Suppose, for instance, that the initial market structure is a duopoly. Firm 1 (the big firm) has unit cost 1 and firm 2 (the small firm) has unit cost 3. There is no fixed cost, and the firms wage Cournot competition. Suppose that an innovation comes along that makes a technology with unit cost 2 accessible at low adoption cost. Even in the case where a firm can buy an exclusive right to this technology (thus excluding its rival), it is not clear that firm 1 will preempt its rival and purchase the new technology (which it would do only for competitive purposes, and not for productive purposes). It may be the case that the cost reduction for firm 2 offsets the loss in industry revenues stemming from more intense competition. Thus, firm 2 may have more incentive to buy the technology than firm 1 (see Leung 1984 and Kamien and Tauman 1983 for related ideas). This comes from the fact that we are comparing an initial duopoly situation with a subsequent duopoly situation. If the initial industry configuration were an unconstrained monopoly (firm 2 starting with a large unit cost), then the efficiency effect would prevail.

very few pure monopolies. In the absence of regulatory restrictions, multifirm markets are the norm.)

First, preemption must be *effective*. Either it allows the preemptor to establish a property right on the technology (e.g. through a patent or exclusive licensing) or it commits the firm to intense price competition if the rival follows suit. An example in which preemption is not fully effective (in the sense that it allows entry) is the Stackelberg game without fixed costs (see section 8.2). In this example, the Stackelberg leader does not own property rights on capital; furthermore, capacity constraints prevent fierce price competition, so that the only way the leader can deter entry is to accumulate enough capacity to serve the whole market at a price equal to the marginal cost of investment plus production (and thus make no profit itself). By simply accumulating the Stackelberg follower's capacity on top of the leader's, the leader does not deter entry. Another example in which preemption is not effective is when the incumbent's investment has no commitment value, as in the example of product dropping considered in the preceding subsection.

Second, the technology of preemption must be *deterministic*. That is, firms must have a means of preempting their rivals. With a nondeterministic technology (as in the patent contests considered in chapter 10), there may be no way for the incumbent to guarantee that it will obtain the technology first.[94]

Third, even in a situation in which preemption is both effective and deterministic, it is hard to believe that a monopolist always keeps his privileged situation. Indeed, several variations of the preemption model give rise to a positive probability that an oligopolistic structure emerges:

(1) The incumbent does not possess the entrant's technology. In this obvious case, the incumbent cannot duplicate the entrant's strategy a bit earlier, which may leave scope for entry. In the product-differentiation model, for instance, the incumbent might not be able to build at the right-end location.

(2) The incumbent may not have time to preempt the entrant. This is the case when an innovation appears that both the incumbent and entrant would like to adopt immediately. Preemption would then require the incumbent to adopt the innovation before its appearance, which is impossible. This lack of time is also present (in a disguised way) in the simultaneous models of entry, in which there is only one period to invest. The models of competition in location and of monopolistic competition analyzed in chapter 7 belong to this category. In the case of the linear city with two locations, it is easy to see that there exist two equilibria in pure strategies if entry decisions are made simultaneously. In one equilibrium, the existing firm is the only one to invest and build at the right end of the city (monopoly persistence); in the other, the entrant is the only one to invest and build at this location (entry).[95]

The lack of time is also implicit in the investment models in which firms are not allowed to build more than one plant or introduce more than one product. The implicit assumption there is that rapid investment (in a second or third plant or product) is very costly, and that single-plant or single-product firms can enter before the established firms can pursue their expansion.

In a sense, the simultaneous-entry models of chapter 7 correspond to very long information lags: There is no way a firm can observe its rivals' choices before making its own. This is clearly an extreme assumption, even in situations where the firms' investment decisions take a while to be observed.[96] More generally, one may consider dynamic rivalry under non-negligible information lags (imperfect information). Fudenberg et al. (1983) consider a game in which, under perfect information (no information lags), only the incumbent conducts research and development, whereas with information lags competition may arise. If the entrant did not try to enter, the incumbent would delay its investment decision (as in the preemption game, the incumbent would like to move "slowly") and it would pay the entrant to enter. But the entrant will try to enter only if it has a chance of being first. Thus,

---

94. Furthermore, we will see in chapter 10 that, because the date of preemption is random, the incumbent may not want to hasten its own replacement and may therefore have less incentive than the entrant to invest in R&D.

95. As is usual in the simultaneous-entry models of a natural monopoly (where "natural monopoly" refers to the right-end location and not to the whole market), there exists a third, mixed-strategy equilibrium, in which both firms are indifferent between entering and not entering.

96. And where firms cannot communicate their investment decisions in a credible way. Indeed, it may be in the interest of a firm to release investment decisions so as to deter entry. (Firms actually do announce construction of plants or, like IBM, preannounce their products.) Conversely, the absence of announcement signals the absence of investment (unless announcements reveal precious technological information).

there is a positive probability that the monopoly will not persist.

(3) The existing firm may not have complete information about the entrant's characteristics. Without complete information, it cannot calculate exactly the optimal preemption date T_2. (In the case of an information lag, the existing firm does not observe its rival's action; in the case of incomplete information, it may not observe its rival's cost structure.) Since the existing firm wants to invest as late as possible (L_1 is increasing) and to preempt entry, it may bide its time even when this entails the risk of entry. The firm must evaluate the gain related to waiting and estimate the probability of not preempting entry. Therefore, incomplete information introduces a nonzero probability that the potential entrant will actually enter. To see this in the context of the model of subsection 8.6.2.1, suppose that the entrant's entry cost is either "high" or "low," and that it is known only to the entrant. The optimal date of preemption, T_2, is much later for a high-cost entrant than for a low-cost entrant. Intuitively, if the probability that the entrant has a high entry cost is sufficiently high, it does not pay for the incumbent to make sure he preempts the low-cost entrant. The benefits of obtaining a higher L_1 offset the loss associated with the probability of being preempted.

Answers and Hints

Exercise 8.1

The situation is depicted in figure 8.21. Let $C = \{p^c, q^c\}$ denote the point at which the average-cost curve intersects the demand curve, let q^* denote the most efficient scale, and let p^* denote the minimum average cost. A market-clearing, profit-making allocation must lie on the demand curve to the northwest of C. In particular, the market price must (weakly) exceed p^c. Now suppose that an entrant comes in at a lower price p^e between p^* and p^c, and produces $q^e = q^*$. That is, the entrant rations the consumers at price p^e. Because the price charged by the entrant strictly exceeds its average cost (which is p^*), the entrant makes a strictly positive profit and the initial allocation is not sustainable. Thus, there exists no sustainable allocation.

Exercise 8.2

(i) There are several meanings to "natural monopoly" (the notion depends on the application to be made). One meaning refers to the socially efficient production pattern. Because of increasing returns to scale, one firm is the optimal arrangement (if its price can be controlled). Another meaning looks at the maximum (upper bound on the) number of firms in the industry. Here, even if firms can somehow collude, they make at most $\Pi^m = \max[p(1-p)] = \frac{1}{4}$. Since $f = \frac{3}{16}$, if there are two firms at least one of them loses money.

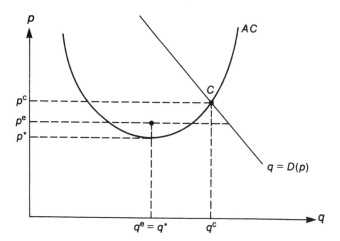

Figure 8.21

(ii) The contestable price satisfies $p(1 - p) = f$, or $p = \frac{1}{4}$ $= p^m/2$. Welfare is equal to net consumer surplus plus profit (i.e., here, net consumer surplus). Here,

$$w^c = (1 - p)^2/2 = (\tfrac{3}{4})^2/2 = \tfrac{9}{32}.$$

(The social optimum is reached for $p = c = 0$, which yields $w^* = \frac{1}{2} - \frac{3}{16} = \frac{5}{16}$.) In continuous time, welfare is equal to $W^c = w^c/r$.

(iii) In the symmetric equilibrium of a war of attrition, each firm exits with probability $x\,dt$ between t and $t + dt$ if both firms are still in. Indifference requires

$$x\left(\frac{\frac{1}{4} - \frac{3}{16}}{r}\right) = \frac{3}{16}, \text{ or } x = 3r.$$

To compute the expected intertemporal welfare, first notice that instantaneous welfare is equal to

$$w_2 = \tfrac{1}{2} - 2(\tfrac{3}{16}) = \tfrac{1}{8}$$

when there are two firms (because they charge the competitive price) and

$$w_1 = \tfrac{1}{8} + (\tfrac{1}{4} - \tfrac{3}{16}) = \tfrac{3}{16}$$

when only one firm is left. The arrival of a monopoly situation is a Poisson process with parameter $2x$. Hence, intertemporal welfare is equal to

$$W = \int_0^\infty [e^{-2xt}w_2 + (1 - e^{-2xt})w_1]e^{-rt}dt.$$

(The probability that there are still two firms at t is e^{-2xt}.) Hence,

$$W = \left(\frac{2x}{2x + r}\right)\frac{w_1}{r} + \left(\frac{r}{2x + r}\right)\frac{w_2}{r}.$$

(W is a weighted average of w_1/r and w_2/r.) That is,

$$W = \frac{5/28}{r} < W^c.$$

Here we know, trivially, that $W < W^c$, because both w_1 and w_2 are lower than w^c. But these inequalities hold more generally.

Exercise 8.3

(i) Profit is 1.5 for one plant and 1 for two plants. Accumulating three or more plants is irrational: Profit is negative if all plants are used, and the corresponding

output is sold on the market; and there is no point in building capacity that is not used.

(ii) Each firm makes equilibrium profit 0.5. Building a second plant drives the market price down to 3, which is below the unit cost of constructing a plant.

(iii) By building two plants, the Stackelberg leader appropriates the Cournot industry profit $2 \times \frac{1}{2} = 1$. Building one plant allows entry of firm 2 with one plant and yields the same outcome as in (ii).

The first-mover advantage results in the monopolization of the industry. However, in contrast with the fixed-cost case discussed in the text, the monopoly structure yields the same social welfare as the duopoly structure corresponding to simultaneous entry.

See Gilbert and Harris 1984 for a description of competition with lumpy investments with a more sensible time structure and time-dependent demand; see also the discussion of the persistence of monopoly in section 8.6.

Exercise 8.4

(i) See chapter 5.

(ii) Because any capacity is used *ex post*, everything is as if the consumers' demand were

$$\tilde{p} = 1 - K_1 - K_2$$

(subtracting the capacity cost 3 from the intercept). The consumer surplus is

$$(K_1 + K_2)^2/2,$$

and the domestic firm's profit is

$$K_2(1 - K_1 - K_2) - f$$

if it enters, 0 otherwise. Welfare is the sum of the two.

No protection From our derivations in the text, entry is blockaded by the foreign firm. The latter invests the monopoly capacity $K_1 = \frac{1}{2}$, and the domestic firm stays out:

$$\max_{K_2}[K_2(1 - K_1 - K_2) - f] = 0.$$

Welfare is equal to consumer surplus: $W_1 = \frac{1}{8} = 0.125$.

Limited protection In this case, K_1 and K_2 are chosen simultaneously. In equilibrium, $K_1 = K_2 = \frac{1}{3}$. The consumer surplus is $\frac{2}{9}$, and the domestic firm's profit is $\frac{1}{9} - \frac{1}{16}$. Thus, the welfare is given by $W_2 \simeq 0.271 > W_1$, because by preventing entry from being blockaded the government increases competition and consumer surplus (it also raises the domestic firm's profit at the expense of the foreign firm). Actually, in this example, full protection would be optimal; a domestic monopoly would accumulate $K_2 = \frac{1}{2}$. Consumer surplus would be lower than under limited protection, but the domestic firm's profit would increase; overall, the aggregate welfare would jump to $W_3 = 0.3125$.

Matsuyama and Itoh (1985) offer a continuous-investment model similar to that of subsection 8.6.1.2; they show that temporary protection can help domestic firms compete with foreign firms. However, in their model permanent protection is detrimental, as it leads to high domestic prices. They argue that the model fits well with the Japanese experience in the 1960s. (See Matsuyama 1987 for an analysis of the case in which the government can commit to a protection policy in the short run but not in the long run.)

Exercise 8.5

Let K_1 and K_2 denote an entry-accommodating equilibrium. They satisfy

$$\Pi^1 + \Pi^2 = (K_1 + K_2)[P(K_1 + K_2 + R_3(K_1 + K_2)) - c_0 - c].$$

Suppose that

$$\Pi^b > \Pi^1 + \Pi^2,$$

and let

$$\Delta \equiv K^b - (K_1 + K_2).$$

We claim that firm 1 would be better off investing $K_1 + \Delta$ instead of K_1. By definition of Δ, this would deter entry. Firm 1's profit would be

$$\tilde{\Pi}^1 = (K_1 + \Delta)[P(K^b) - c_0 - c]$$

$$= \Pi^b - K_2(P(K^b) - c_0 - c)$$

$$> \Pi^1 + K_2[P(K_1 + K_2 + R_3(K_1 + K_2)) - P(K^b)].$$

Because P is decreasing, it suffices to prove that

$$K_1 + K_2 + R_3(K_1 + K_2) \leqslant K^b$$

to obtain a contradiction. Suppose that

$$K_1 + K_2 + R_3(K_1 + K_2) > K^b.$$

Then firm 1 could have invested $K_1 + R_3(K_1 + K_2)$ instead of K_1 and made profit

$$\Pi^1 + (\Pi^3 + f) \geqslant \Pi^1 + f > \Pi^1,$$

where f is firm 3's entry cost (that firm 1 need not pay to accumulate more capacity), where use is made of the fact that

$$[K_1 + R_3(K_1 + K_2)] + K_2$$

deters entry. Again, we obtain a contradiction.

Exercise 8.6

(i) The monopolist maximizes

$$(1 - q^A - c)q^A + (1 - q^B - (c - \lambda q^A))q^B$$

with respect to q^A and q^B. The first-order conditions are

$$(1 - c - 2q^A) + \lambda q^B = 0$$

and

$$1 - c + \lambda q^A - 2q^B = 0.$$

(ii) If q_1^A is not observed, it is rationally anticipated to be $\bar{q}_1^A$, say. Thus, Cournot competition occurs relative to cost $\bar{c}_1^B = c - \lambda \bar{q}_1^A$. Firm 1 cannot affect firm 2's behavior by changing q_1^A. The first-order condition is thus

$$(1 - c - 2q_1^A) + \lambda q_1^B = 0,$$

where

$$q_1^B = [1 + c - 2(c - \lambda \bar{q}_1^A)]/3 = (1 - c + 2\lambda \bar{q}_1^A)/3.$$

Simple computations, together with $\bar{q}_1^A = q_1^A$ in equilibrium, yield

$$q_1^A = \left(\frac{3 + \lambda}{6 - 2\lambda^2}\right)d.$$

If q_1^A is observed by firm 2, then firm 1 can influence firm 2's output. Thus, the first-order condition is

$$(1 - c - 2q_1^A) + \frac{d\Pi_1^B}{dc_1^B}(c_1^B, c_2^B)\frac{dc_1^B}{dq_1^A} = 0,$$

or

$$q_1^A = \left(\frac{9 + 4\lambda}{18 - 8\lambda^2}\right)d > \left(\frac{3 + \lambda}{6 - 2\lambda^2}\right)d.$$

Firm 1 gains when firm 2 observes its first-period output. By slightly increasing its output beyond $(3 + \lambda)d/(6 - 2\lambda^2)$, it incurs only a second-order loss if its rival does not change its output. But firm 2 knows that c_1^B is lower, and therefore that q_1^B will be higher. Firm 2 curtails its output, which benefits firm 1 to the first order. With a fixed cost of entry, firm 1 may want to push its output beyond $(9 + 4\lambda)d/(18 - 8\lambda^2)$ (assuming that q_1^A is observed) to deter entry (as in the Stackelberg game discussed in the text).

Of course, learning by doing is just one way of reducing future costs. Capacity accumulation (as in the text) and investment that reduces marginal cost (as in Brander and Spencer 1983) serve somewhat the same purpose but are independent of the firm's current pricing behavior.

Exercise 8.7

A decrease in firm 1's marginal cost shifts that firm's reaction curve to the left, as figure 8.22 shows. The equilibrium $x_1^* = p_1^*$ is thus reduced, which hurts firm 2. To make entry unattractive, firm 1 should reduce its marginal cost (i.e., should overinvest).

Exercise 8.8

False. A quota transforms the foreign firm into a puppy dog. If the quota is "not too small" (just below the Nash-equilibrium output), the quota commits the foreign firm to charge a price a bit above the Nash price and induces the domestic firm to raise its price. The quota imposes a direct second-order loss if the quota is close to the Nash output, and the strategic (indirect) gain for the foreign firm is a first-order one.

Exercise 8.9

Consider the (Bertrand) Nash equilibrium (p_1^*, p_2^*) in prices in the absence of government intervention. For ε small, $\Pi^1(p_1^* + \varepsilon, p_2^*)$ is equal to $\Pi^1(p_1^*, p_2^*)$ to the second order in ε (because firm 1 optimizes). Now consider a price floor equal to $\underline{p}_1 = p_1^* + \varepsilon$. See figure 8.23. Then

$$(p_1^{**}, p_2^{**}) = (p_1^* + \varepsilon, R_2(p_1^* + \varepsilon))$$

is the new Nash equilibrium. Given p_2^{**}, firm 1 would like to reduce its price; however, it cannot. Firm 1 is better off in spite of (actually, because of) the fact that its set of choices has shrunk. The price floor commits it to charge a high price. This is the "puppy dog" effect.

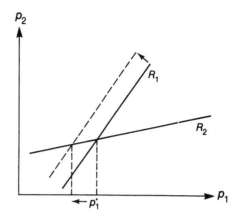

Figure 8.22

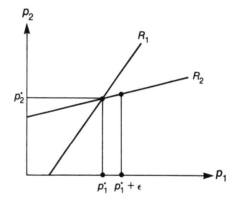

Figure 8.23

Exercise 8.10

(i) and (ii) See chapter 7.

(iii) The price of an orange is c. Hence, the residual demand for apples is

$$D_1 = (c + t - p_1)/2t.$$

Maximizing profit

$$(p_1 - c)(c + t - p_1)/2t$$

yields $p_1 = c + t/2$ and profits $\Pi^1 = t/8$.

(iv) Firm 1 gains $t/2 - t/8 = 3t/8$ by exiting the orange market. Firm 2 does not increase its profit by exiting. Thus, in the absence of exit barriers, firm 1 exits the orange market. Firm 2, therefore, enters the orange market, even if firm 1 is already in both markets (as long as the entry cost does not exceed $t/2$).

References

Arrow, K. 1962. The Economic Implications of Learning by Doing. *Review of Economic Studies* 29: 153–173.

Bailey, E., and J. Panzar. 1981. The Contestability of Airline Markets during the Transition to Deregulation. *Law and Contemporary Problems* 44: 125–145.

Bailey, E., D. Graham, and D. Kaplan. 1985. *Deregulating the Airlines*. Cambridge, Mass.: MIT Press.

Bain, J. 1956. *Barriers to New Competition*. Cambridge, Mass.: Harvard University Press.

Baldini, J. 1983. Strategic Advertising and Credible Entry Deterrence Policies. Mimeo.

Baumol, W., E. Bailey, and R. Willig. 1977. Weak Invisible Hand Theorems on the Sustainability of Prices in a Multiproduct Monopoly. *American Economic Review* 67: 350–365.

Baumol, W., J. Panzar, and R. Willig. 1982. *Contestable Markets and the Theory of Industry Structure*. New York: Harcourt Brace Jovanovich.

Baumol, W., J. Panzar, and R. Willig. 1986. On the Theory of Perfectly Contestable Markets. In *New Developments in the Analysis of Market Structure*, ed. J. Stiglitz and F. Mathewson. Cambridge, Mass.: MIT Press.

Bernheim, D. 1984. Strategic Entry Deterrence of Sequential Entry into an Industry. *Rand Journal of Economics* 15: 1–11.

Bonanno, G. 1987. Location, Choice, Product Proliferation and Entry Deterrence. *Review of Economic Studies* 54: 37–46.

Bonanno, G., and J. Vickers. 1986. Vertical Separation. Mimeo, Nuffield College, Oxford University.

Boston Consulting Group. 1972. Perspectives on Experience.

Brander, J., and T. Lewis. 1986. Oligopoly and Financial Structure: The Limited Liability Effect. *American Economic Review* 76: 956–970.

Brander, J., and B. Spencer. 1983. Strategic Commitment with R&D: The Symmetric Case. *Bell Journal of Economics* 14: 225–235.

Brander, J., and B. Spencer. 1984. Tariff Protection and Imperfect Competition. In *Monopolistic Competition and International Trade*, ed. H. Kierzkowski. Oxford University Press.

Brock, W. 1983a. Contestable Markets and the Theory of Industry Structure: A Review Article. *Journal of Political Economy* 91: 1055–1066.

Brock, W. 1983b. Pricing, Predation, and Entry Barriers in Regulated Industries. In *Breaking Up Bell*, ed. D. Evans. Amsterdam: North-Holland.

Brock, W., and D. Evans. 1983. Predation: A Critique of the Government's Case in *U.S. v. AT&T*. In *Breaking Up Bell*, ed. D. Evans. Amsterdam: North-Holland.

Brock, W., and J. Scheinkman. 1983. Free Entry and the Sustainability of Natural Monopoly: Bertrand Revisited by Cournot. In *Breaking Up Bell*, ed. D. Evans. Amsterdam: North-Holland.

Bulow, J., J. Geanakoplos, and P. Klemperer. 1985a. Multimarket Oligopoly: Strategic Substitutes and Complements. *Journal of Political Economy* 93: 488–511.

Bulow, J., J. Geanakoplos, and P. Klemperer. 1985b. Holding Idle Capacity to Deter Entry. *Economic Journal* 95: 178–182.

Caves, R., and M. Porter. 1977. From Entry Barriers to Mobility Barriers. *Quarterly Journal of Economics* 9: 241–267.

Cooper, T. 1986. Most-Favored-Customer Pricing and Tacit Collusion. *Rand Journal of Economics* 17: 377–388.

Cournot, A. 1838. *Recherches sur les Principes Mathématiques de la Théorie des Richesses*.

Cyert, R., and M. DeGroot. 1970. Multiperiod Decision Models with Alternating Choice as a Solution to the Duopoly Problem. *Quarterly Journal of Economics* 84: 410–429.

Dixit, A. 1979. A Model of Duopoly Suggesting a Theory of Entry Barriers. *Bell Journal of Economics* 10: 20–32.

Dixit, A. 1980. The Role of Investment in Entry Deterrence. *Economic Journal* 90: 95–106.

Dixit, A. 1984. International Trade Policy for Oligopolistic Industries. *Economic Journal* 94: S1–S16.

Dixit, A. 1986. Comparative Statics for Oligopoly. *International Economic Review* 27: 107–122.

Dixit, A., and G. Grossman. 1986. Targeted Export Promotion with Several Oligopolistic Industries. *Journal of International Economics* 21: 233–250.

Eaton, B. C., and R. G. Lipsey. 1979. The Theory of Market Preemption: The Persistence of Excess Capacity and Monopoly in Growing Spatial Markets. *Econometrica* 46: 149–158.

Eaton, B. C., and R. G. Lipsey. 1980. Exit Barriers are Entry Barriers: The Durability of Capital as a Barrier to Entry. *Bell Journal of Economics* 12: 721–729.

Eaton, B. C., and R. G. Lipsey. 1981. Capital, Commitment, and Entry Equilibrium. *Bell Journal of Economics* 12: 593–604.

Eaton, J., and G. Grossman. 1983. Optimal Trade and Industrial Policy under Oligopoly. Working Paper 1236, National Bureau of Economic Research.

Eichberger, J., and I. Harper. 1986. Price and Quantity Controls as Facilitating Devices. Working Paper 137, Australian National University.

Encaoua, D., P. Geroski, and A. Jacquemin. 1986. Strategic Competition and the Persistence of Dominant Firms: A Survey. In *New Developments in the Analysis of Market Structure*, ed. J. Stiglitz and F. Mathewson. Cambridge, Mass.: MIT Press.

Farrell, J., and C. Shapiro. 1986. Dynamic Competition with Switching Costs. Mimeo, Princeton University.

Farrell, J., and C. Shapiro. 1987. Dynamic Competition with Lock-in. Working Paper 8727, Department of Economics, University of California, Berkeley.

Ferschtman, C., and K. Judd. 1986. Strategic Incentive Manipulation and the Principal-Agent Problem. Mimeo, Northwestern University.

Fine, C., and L. Li. 1986. A Stochastic Theory of Exit and Stopping Time Equilibria. Working Paper 1755-86, Sloan School of Management, Massachusetts Institute of Technology.

Fisher, F. 1961. The Stability of the Cournot Oligopoly Solution: The Effects of the Speed of Adjustment and Increasing Marginal Costs. *Review of Economic Studies* 28: 125–135.

Fudenberg, D., and J. Tirole. 1983a. Learning by Doing and Market Performance. *Bell Journal of Economics* 14: 522–530.

Fudenberg, D., and J. Tirole. 1983b. Capital as a Commitment: Strategic Investment to Deter Mobility. *Journal of Economic Theory* 31: 227–256.

Fudenberg, D., and J. Tirole. 1984. The Fat Cat Effect, the Puppy Dog Ploy and the Lean and Hungry Look. *American Economic Review, Papers and Proceedings* 74: 361–368.

Fudenberg, D., and J. Tirole. 1985. Preemption and Rent Equalization in the Adoption of New Technology. *Review of Economic Studies* 52: 383–402.

Fudenberg, D., and J. Tirole. 1986. *Dynamic Models of Oligopoly*. London: Harwood.

Fudenberg, D., and J. Tirole. 1987. Understanding Rent Dissipation: On the Use of Game Theory in Industrial Organization. *American Economic Review: Papers and Proceedings* 77: 176–183.

Fudenberg, D., R. Gilbert, J. Stiglitz, and J. Tirole. 1983. Preemption, Leapfrogging, and Competition in Patent Races. *European Economic Review* 22: 3–31.

Gabszewicz, J., and J.-F. Thisse. 1986. Spatial Competition and the Location of Firms. In *Fundamentals of Pure and Applied Economics*, ed. J. Lesourne and H. Sonnenschein. London: Harwood.

Gelman, J., and S. Salop. 1983. Judo Economics: Capacity Limitation and Coupon Competition. *Bell Journal of Economics* 14: 315–325.

Ghemawat, P., and B. Nalebuff. 1985. Exit. *Rand Journal of Economics* 16: 184–194.

Ghemawat, P., and B. Nalebuff. 1987. The Devolution of Declining Industries. Discussion Paper 120, Woodrow Wilson School, Princeton University.

Gilbert, R. 1986. Preemptive Competition. In *New Developments in the Analysis of Market Structure*, ed. F. Mathewson and J. Stiglitz. Cambridge, Mass.: MIT Press.

Gilbert, R. 1987. Mobility Barriers and the Value of Incumbency. In *Handbook of Industrial Organization*, ed. R. Schmalensee and R. Willig (Amsterdam: North-Holland, forthcoming).

Gilbert, R., and R. Harris. 1984. Competition with Lumpy Investment. *Rand Journal of Economics* 15: 197–212.

Gilbert, R., and D. Newberry. 1982. Preemptive Patenting and the Persistence of Monopoly. *American Economic Review* 72: 514–526.

Gilbert, R., and X. Vives. 1986. Entry Deterrence and the Free Rider Problem. *Review of Economic Studies* 53: 71–83.

Grossman, S. 1981. Nash Equilibrium and the Industrial Organization of Markets with Large Fixed Costs. *Econometrica* 49: 1149–1172.

Hahn, F. 1962. The Stability of the Cournot Oligopoly Solution Concept. *Review of Economic Studies* 29: 329–331.

Hanig, M. 1985. A Differential Game Model of Duopoly with Reversible Investment. Mimeo, Massachusetts Institute of Technology.

Hay, G. 1976. Sequential Entry and Entry-Deterring Strategies. *Oxford Economic Papers* 28: 240–257.

Hay, G. 1982. Oligopoly, Shared Monopoly, and Antitrust Law. *Cornell Law Review* 67: 439–481.

Hendricks, K., and C. Wilson. 1985a. The War of Attrition in Discrete Time. Research Paper 280, State University of New York, Stony Brook.

Hendricks, K., and C. Wilson. 1985b. Discrete vs. Continuous Time in Games of Timing. Research Paper 281, State University of New York, Stony Brook.

Huang, C.-F., and L. Li. 1986. Continuous Time Stopping Games. Working Paper 1796-86, Sloan School of Management, Massachusetts Institute of Technology.

Itoh, M., and K. Kiyono. 1987. Welfare-Enhancing Export Subsidies. *Journal of Political Economy* 95: 115–137.

Judd, K. 1985. Credible Spatial Preemption. *Rand Journal of Economics* 16: 153–166.

Kamien, M., and Y. Tauman. 1983. The Private Value of a Patent: A Game Theoretic Analysis. Mimeo, Kellogg School of Business, Northwestern University.

Katz, M. 1987. Game-Playing Agents: Contracts as Precommitments. Mimeo, Princeton University.

Katz, M., and C. Shapiro. 1984. Equilibrium Preemption in a Development Game with Licensing or Imitation. Mimeo, Princeton University.

Klemperer, P. 1984. Collusion via Switching Costs: How "Frequent Flyer" Programs, Trading Stamps, and Technology Choices Aid Collusion. Research Paper 786, Graduate School of Business, Stanford University.

Klemperer, P. 1985a. Intertemporal Pricing with Consumer Switching Costs. Research Paper 835, Graduate School of Business, Stanford University.

Klemperer, P. 1985b. The Welfare Effects of Entry into Markets with Consumer Switching Costs. St. Catherine's College, Oxford University.

Krattenmaker, T., and S. Salop. 1985. Antitrust Analysis of Anti-competitive Exclusion: Raising Rivals' Costs to Achieve Power over Price. Mimeo, Georgetown University Law Center.

Kreps, D., and A. M. Spence. 1984. Modelling the Role of History in Industrial Organization and Competition. In *Contemporary Issues in Modern Microeconomics*, ed. G. Feiwel. London: Macmillan.

Krishna, K. 1983. Trade Restrictions as Facilitating Practices. Discussion Paper 55, Woodrow Wilson School, Princeton University.

Krugman, P. 1984. Import Protection as Export Promotion: International Competition in the Presence of Oligopoly and Economies of Scale. In *Monopolistic Competition and International Trade*, ed. H. Kierzkowski. Oxford University Press.

Leung, H.-M. 1984. Preemptive Patenting: The Case of Co-Existing Duopolists. Mimeo.

Lieberman, M. 1984. The Learning Curve and Pricing in the Chemical Processing Industry. *Rand Journal of Economics* 15: 213–228.

Londregan, J. 1986. Entry and Exit Over the Industry Life Cycle. Mimeo, Princeton University.

McGuire, T., and R. Staelin. 1983. An Industry Equilibrium Analysis of Downstream Vertical Integration. *Marketing Science* 2: 161–192.

McLean, R., and M. Riordan. 1985. Equilibrium Industry Structure with Sequential Technology Choice. Mimeo, University of Pennsylvania.

MacLeod, B. 1985. On Adjustment Costs and the Stability of Equilibria. *Review of Economic Studies* 52: 575–591.

MacLeod, B. 1986. Entry Sunk Costs and Market Structure. Mimeo, Queen's University.

Mankiw, G., and M. Whinston. 1986. Free Entry and Social Inefficiency. *Rand Journal of Economics* 17: 48–58.

Maskin, E. 1986. Uncertainty and Entry Deterrence. Mimeo, Harvard University.

Maskin, E., and J. Tirole. 1987. A Theory of Dynamic Oligopoly, III: Cournot Competition. *European Economic Review* 31: 947–968.

Maskin, E., and J. Tirole. 1988a. A Theory of Dynamic Oligopoly, I: Overview and Quantity Competition with Large Fixed Costs. *Econometrica* 56.

Maskin, E., and J. Tirole. 1988b. A Theory of Dynamic Oligopoly, II: Price Competition, Kinked Demand Curves, and Edgeworth Cycles. *Econometrica* 56.

Mathewson, R., and R. Winter. 1985. Is Exclusive Dealing Anti-Competitive? Mimeo, University of Toronto.

Matsuyama, K. 1987. Perfect Equilibria in a Trade Liberalization Game. Mimeo, Northwestern University.

Matsuyama, K., and M. Itoh. 1985. Protection Policy in a Dynamic Oligopoly Market. Mimeo, University of Tokyo.

Matutes, C., and P. Regibeau. 1986. "Mix and Match": Product Compatibility Without Network Externalities. Mimeo, University of California, Berkeley.

Maynard Smith, J. 1974. The Theory of Games and the Evolution of Animal Conflicts. *Journal of Theoretical Biology* 47: 209–221.

Milgrom, P., and J. Roberts. 1982. Limit Pricing and Entry under Incomplete Information. *Econometrica* 50: 443–460.

Modigliani, F. 1958. New Developments on the Oligopoly Front. *Journal of Political Economy* 66: 215–232.

Mookherjee, D., and D. Ray. 1986. Dynamic Price Games with Learning-by-Doing. Discussion Paper 884, Graduate School of Business, Stanford University.

Moorthy, S. 1987. On Vertical Integration in Channels. Working Paper 7, Yale School of Organization and Management.

Nguyen, D. 1986. Capital Investment in a Duopoly as a Differential Game. Mimeo, Graduate Center, City University of New York.

Ordover, J., and R. Willig. 1981. An Economic Definition of Predation: Pricing and Product Innovation. *Yale Law Journal* 91: 8–53.

Perry, M. 1984. Sustainable Positive Profit Multiple-Price Strategies in Contestable Markets. *Journal of Economic Theory* 32: 246–265.

Prescott, E., and M. Visscher. 1977. Sequential Location among Firms with Foresight. *Bell Journal of Economics* 8: 378–393.

Prescott, E., and M. Visscher. 1980. Organization Capital. *Journal of Political Economy* 88: 446–461.

Rao, R., and D. Rutenberg. 1979. Preempting an Alert Rival: Strategic Timing of the First Plant by Analysis of Sophisticated Rivalry. *Bell Journal of Economics* 10: 412–428.

Rasmusen, E. 1987. Entry for Buyout. Mimeo, University of California, Los Angeles.

Rey, P., and J. Stiglitz. 1986. The Role of Exclusive Territories in Producers' Competition. Mimeo, Princeton University.

Reynolds, S. 1987. Capacity Investment, Preemption and Commitment in an Infinite Horizon Model. *International Economic Review* 28: 69–88.

Rothschild, R. 1976. A Note on the Effect of Sequential Entry on Choice of Location. *Journal of Industrial Economics* 24: 313–320.

Salop, S. 1979. Strategic Entry Deterrence. *American Economic Review, Papers and Proceedings* 69: 335–338.

Salop, S. 1986. Practices That (Credibly) Facilitate Oligopoly Coordination. In *New Developments in the Analysis of Market Structure*, ed. J. Stiglitz and F. Mathewson. Cambridge, Mass.: MIT Press.

Salop, S., and D. Scheffman. 1983. Raising Rivals' Costs. *American Economic Review, Papers and Proceedings* 73: 267–271.

Samuelson, P. 1972. The Consumer Does Benefit from Feasible Price Stability. *Quarterly Journal of Economics* 86: 476–493.

Schmalensee, R. 1978. Entry Deterrence in the Ready-to-Eat Breakfast Cereal Industry. *Bell Journal of Economics* 9: 305–327.

Schmalensee, R. 1981. Economies of Scale and Barriers to Entry. *Journal of Political Economy* 89: 1228–1238.

Schmalensee, R. 1983. Advertising and Entry Deterrence: An Exploratory Model. *Journal of Political Economy* 90: 636–653.

Schwartz, M. 1986. The Nature and Scope of Contestability Theory. *Oxford Economic Papers* 38 (supplement): 37–57.

Seade, J. 1980. The Stability of Cournot Revisited. *Journal of Economic Theory* 23: 15–27.

Shapiro, C. 1986. Theories of Oligopoly Behavior. In *Handbook of Industrial Organization*, ed. R. Schmalensee and R. Willig (Amsterdam: North-Holland, forthcoming).

Simon, L. 1987. Games of Timing. Part I: Simple Timing Games. Mimeo, University of California, Berkeley.

Simon, L., and M. Stichcombe. 1986. Extensive Form Games in Continuous Time: Part I: Pure Strategies. Working Paper 8607, University of California, Berkeley.

Spence, A. M. 1977. Entry, Capacity, Investment and Oligopolistic Pricing. *Bell Journal of Economics* 8: 534–544.

Spence, M. 1979. Investment Strategy and Growth in a New Market. *Bell Journal of Economics* 10: 1–19.

Spence, M. 1981. The Learning Curve and Competition. *Bell Journal of Economics* 12: 49–70.

Spence, M. 1983. Contestable Markets and the Theory of Industry Structure: A Review Article. *Journal of Economic Literature* 21: 981–990.

Spence, M. 1984. Cost Reduction, Competition, and Industry Performance. *Econometrica* 52: 101–122.

Starr, R., and Y. C. Ho. 1969. Further Properties of Nonzero-Sum Games. *Journal of Optimization Theory and Applications* 3: 207–219.

Stigler, G. 1968. *The Organization of Industry*. Homewood, Ill.: Irwin.

Stokey, N. 1986. The Dynamics of Industry-wide Learning. In *Equilibrium Analysis: Essays in Honor of Kenneth J. Arrow, Volume II*, ed. W. Heller, R. Starr, and D. Starrett. Cambridge University Press.

Sylos-Labini, P. 1962. *Oligopoly and Technical Progress*. Cambridge, Mass.: Harvard University Press.

Vives, X. 1985. Potential Entrants Deter Entry. Discussion Paper 180, Center for the Study of Organizational Innovation, University of Pennsylvania.

Vives, X. 1986. Commitment, Flexibility and Market Outcomes. *International Journal of Industrial Organization* 4: 217–229.

von Stackelberg, H. 1934. *Marktform und Gleichgewicht*. Vienna: Julius Springer.

von Weizsäcker, C. C. 1980a. A Welfare Analysis of Barriers to Entry. *Bell Journal of Economics* 11: 399–420.

von Weizsäcker, C. C. 1980b. *Barriers to Entry: A Theoretical Treatment*. Berlin: Springer-Verlag. (See also review by R. Schmalensee, *Journal of Economic Literature* 21 [1983]: 562–564.)

von Weizsäcker, C. C. 1984. The Costs of Substitution. *Econometrica* 52: 1085–1116.

Waldman, M. 1987. Non-Cooperative Entry Deterrence, Uncertainty, and the Free Rider Problem. *Review of Economic Studies* 54: 301–310.

Weitzman, M. 1983. Contestable Markets: An Uprising in the Theory of Industry Structure: Comment. *American Economic Review* 73: 486–487.

Whinston, M. 1986. Exit with Multiplant Firms. Discussion Paper 1299, HIER, Harvard University.

Whinston, M. 1987. Tying, Foreclosure, and Exclusion. Mimeo, Harvard University.

Wilson, R. 1984. Entry and Exit. Notes for "Analytical Foundations of Pricing Strategy." Mimeo, Graduate School of Business, Stanford University.

Information and Strategic Behavior: Reputation, Limit Pricing, and Predation

Oligopolists are affected by many variables they cannot observe or estimate precisely: their own cost function, the cost functions of their rivals, the state of demand or the potential of the market, and their rivals' strategic decisions. To the extent that some pieces of information are private (for instance, a firm may have a good estimate of its own cost but no good estimate of its rivals' costs), we must envision market interaction as a game with asymmetric information.

The simplest case is when oligopolists compete in a static way (i.e., they meet only once). The simplicity of this case stems from the fact that, although a firm's information is at least partly revealed by its actions, no use is made of the revealed information, as there is no future. Firms thus behave myopically, and simply maximize their static profit given their private information and their assessment of their rivals' actions on the basis of their own private information. Section 9.1 addresses the case of static price competition in which firms have private information about their own cost (a special case of which is a one-shot auction). Most of the intuition for the dynamic case can be derived from this static analysis, as we will see in section 9.2.

We saw in chapter 8 how a firm can use tangible variables (capital, experience, etc.) to protect and extend its market share. However, a firm's history also matters because it conveys information to the firm's rivals and thus affects intangible variables such as beliefs. In multi-period oligopolistic interactions, a firm's behavior reveals some of its private knowledge, which the firm's rivals can later exploit. A rational firm, realizing this, seeks to manipulate its rivals' information in order to derive benefits later on. Such manipulations can be called "investments in disinformation." The investment analogy is not accidental. We will see that chapter 8's taxonomy of rival-softening strategies applies to situations of asymmetric information. Section 9.3 considers accommodation (repeated interaction in a stable industry structure) and argues that, under some conditions, asymmetric information gives producers of substitute goods incentives to raise their prices.

Sections 9.4 through 9.6 look at the more aggressive strategies associated with entry deterrence or exit inducement (predation). Section 9.4 deals with the Milgrom-Roberts reconsideration of limit pricing. Section 9.5 analyzes predation in cases of merger, section 9.6 the reputation of a multimarket firm. Sections 9.7 and 9.9 consider two other predatory behaviors: the "long purse" story (in which the predator tries to exhaust the prey's resources) and the war of attrition.[1]

9.1 Static Competition under Asymmetric Information

9.1.1 A Simple Model of Price Competition

Intuition concerning games of asymmetric information can be gained from a simple static example. Consider a two-period rivalry. The second period is the last, so the firms then behave as in the static game with the information structure defined by their posterior beliefs at the beginning of the second period. That is, the study of the static game also yields the firms' second-period payoffs as functions of the posterior beliefs. But these beliefs are the prior (date 1) beliefs updated to reflect the information conveyed by each firm's first-period behavior. The static analysis therefore demonstrates what each firm wants its rivals to believe about its private information and suggests how first-period behavior may be used for this purpose.

Here, we will consider a differentiated duopoly price game in which, for simplicity, one of the two firms has incomplete information about its rival's cost. Suppose that the demand curves are symmetric and linear over the relevant range:

$$D_i(p_i, p_j) = a - bp_i + dp_j,$$

where $0 < d < b$. (If each firm raises its price by \$1, both should lose sales. This requires $d < b$.) Assume that the two goods are substitutes and strategic complements

$(d > 0)$,[2] and that the firms have constant-returns-to-scale technologies. Firms 2's marginal cost, c_2, is common knowledge, but firms 1's marginal cost, c_1, is known only to firm 1. Suppose that for firm 2 c_1 can a priori take two values: c_1^L (with probability x) and c_1^H (with probability $1 - x$), where $c_1^L < c_1^H$. Let

$$c_1^e \equiv xc_1^L + (1 - x)c_1^H$$

denote firm 1's expected marginal cost from the point of view of firm 2. The *ex post* profits can be written as

$$\Pi^i(p_i, p_j) = (p_i - c_i)(a - bp_i + dp_j).$$

The two firms choose their prices simultaneously, so we look for the Bertrand equilibrium.[3] Firm 2 charges $p_2 = p_2^*$. Firms 1's price naturally depends on its marginal cost. Let p_1^L and p_1^H denote the prices chosen by firm 1 if it has cost c_1^L or c_1^H.

Firm 1's profit maximization yields, for a given c_1 and price p_2^* charged by its rival,

$$a - 2bp_1 + dp_2^* + bc_1 = 0,$$

or

$$p_1 = \frac{a + dp_2^* + bc_1}{2b}. \tag{9.1}$$

p_1 is an increasing function of firm 1's cost, whatever price firm 2 is expected to charge. From the viewpoint of firm 2, which does not know c_1, firm 1's expected price is

$$p_1^e \equiv xp_1^L + (1 - x)p_1^H$$

$$= x\left(\frac{a + dp_2^* + bc_1^L}{2b}\right) + (1 - x)\left(\frac{a + dp_2^* + bc_1^H}{2b}\right)$$

$$= \frac{a + dp_2^* + bc_1^e}{2b}. \tag{9.2}$$

Firm 2 is risk-neutral, so it maximizes its expected profit,

$$\mathop{E}_{c_1}\Pi^2 = x(p_2 - c_2)(a - bp_2 + dp_1^L)$$

$$+ (1 - x)(p_2 - c_2)(a - bp_2 + dp_1^H)$$

$$= (p_2 - c_2)(a - bp_2 + dp_1^e),$$

---

1. See Roberts 1987 and Ordover and Saloner 1987 for further discussions of asymmetric information in oligopoly.

2. See the introduction to part II of this book.

3. Technically, we compute a Bayesian equilibrium (see the Game Theory User's Manual).

with respect to p_2. This yields[4]

$$p_2 = \frac{a + dp_1^e + bc_2}{2b}. \tag{9.3}$$

In Nash equilibrium, $p_2 = p_2^*$. Thus, equations 9.2 and 9.3 yield prices p_1^e and p_2^*. Equation 9.1 then yields p_1^L and p_1^H. For the following we will need only

$$p_2^* = \frac{2ab + 2b^2 c_2 + ad + bdc_1^e}{4b^2 - d^2}. \tag{9.4}$$

Figure 9.1, which depicts the equilibrium, reflects the fact that firm 1's reaction function is contingent on its cost—it shifts to the right when the cost increases. Under symmetric information the Bertrand equilibrium would be at B or C, depending on whether c_1 is low or high. Under asymmetric information, everything is "as if" firm 1 had an "average reaction curve" R_1^e. Prices p_2^* and p_1^e are given by the intersection A between firm 2's reaction curve and firm 1's average reaction curve.

The crucial property for our discussion of dynamics is that (from equation 9.4) firm 2's price is an increasing function of firm 1's expected cost and therefore an increasing function of $1 - x$. Firm 2 raises its price when it becomes more likely that firm 1's cost is high, because

a high c_1 induces a high p_1 and the goods are strategic complements (i.e., the reaction curves are upward sloping).

9.1.1.1 Information Exchange

Now suppose that firm 1 can report verifiable information about c_1 costlessly. That is, firm 1 can, if it wants, perfectly reveal its cost to firm 2. It is easy to see that firm 1 will indeed do so, despite the fact that, when it has a low cost, revelation makes it look aggressive and triggers a low price p_2. When firm 1 has cost c_1^H, revelation induces (full-information) posterior beliefs $x' = 0$. From equation 9.4 and the fact that c_1^e has become equal to c_1^H, firm 2's price is as high as it can be in equilibrium.[5] Thus, a high-cost firm has every incentive to reveal its cost to soften firm 2's pricing behavior. A low-cost firm has no such incentive; however, not releasing the cost information signals that costs are low; if they were high, the information would have been released.[6]

This simple reasoning carries an important moral for future dynamic analysis. Firm 1 has an incentive to *prove* that it has a high cost before the firms engage in price competition. In the rest of this chapter, we will assume that no such direct exchange of information is feasible (cost data are not verifiable, say); rather, firm 1 will try to *signal* that its cost is high[7] through its market behavior. As we will see, such signaling will not be costless.

Exercise 9.1** Consider the previous model, but with symmetric cost uncertainty. The demand functions are $D_i(p_i, p_j) = 1 - p_i + p_j$. The firms' marginal costs are drawn independently from a common distribution with mean c^e and variance σ^2. A firm's cost is private information. Each firm can make its cost information available to its rival (information is verifiable). However, for some reason, firms cannot reveal their information *ex post* unless they have signed an agreement *ex ante* to do so. Consider the following sequence of events: (1) The firms, before knowing the realization of their costs, decide whether

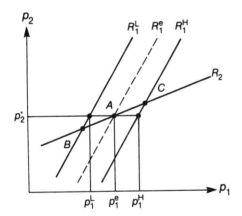

Figure 9.1

---

4. The fact that p_2 depends only on firm 1's expected price is, of course, special to the linear structure of this model.

5. That is, $(2ab + 2b^2 c_2 + ad + bdc_1^H)/(4b^2 - d^2)$.

6. The argument is formally similar to the argument that a seller with unknown quality should give a full warranty if he can do so costlessly. See example 3 in section 5 in the Game Theory User's Manual.

The argument is not limited to two potential cost levels. For instance, with three types, the high-cost type always releases cost information. Hence, the absence of release signals that the cost is low or intermediate, which induces the intermediate type to also release cost information.

7. In other instances, firm 1 will try to signal that its cost is low.

to share cost information *ex post*. (2) Firm i learns c_i ($i = 1, 2$). (3) Firms share information if they decided to do so earlier; otherwise they do not. (4) They compete in prices.

(i) Solve for the price equilibrium in the absence of information sharing. (Hint: Use the symmetry. Show that each firm's average price is $p^e = 1 + c^e$.) Show that firm i's *ex ante* profit is

$$\underset{c_1}{E} \underset{c_2}{E} \Pi^i = 1 + \sigma^2/4.$$

(ii) Solve for the price equilibrium under information sharing. Show that firm i's *ex ante* profit is now

$$\underset{c_1}{E} \underset{c_2}{E} \Pi^i = 1 + 2\sigma^2/9.$$

(iii) Conclude that the firms do not agree to share cost information. Discuss this result.[8]

9.1.1.2 Auctions

An interesting special case of price competition under asymmetric information is the case of a *first-price auction*. In its simplest form, an auction has the following features: The buyer (who stands for consumers in the price-competition model) has a unit demand. Each seller (firm) knows its private cost of supplying one unit of the good, but not its rivals'. A first-price auction chooses the lowest bidder, who receives his bid. This first-bid auction is thus equivalent to price competition with perfect substitutes (and a particular demand curve).[9]

9.1.2 Discussion

Let us now consider informally how the previous analysis relies on our assumptions on the demand functions, the nature of asymmetric information, and the type of competition. In doing so, we will focus on pre-competition incentives to reveal information.

• *Complements versus substitutes* We assumed that the goods produced by the two firms were demand substitutes ($d > 0$). Were they complements ($d < 0$), each firm would also want to pretend that its cost was high. To understand why, suppose that firm 2 believes that firm 1's cost is high. Then firm 2 believes that firm 1 will charge a high price, reducing the demand facing firm 2. Firm 2 is then led to reduce its price, which raises firm 1's demand. With demand complements, charging a low price is like supplying a public good; each firm claims that it will not supply the good in order to force its rival to do so.[10,11]

• *Information about cost versus information about demand* We assumed that the firms had private information about their costs. They can also have private information about demand. In the above example, they may not know the intercept a, for instance, but they may receive private information about it: $a_i = a + \varepsilon_i$, where ε_i is a zero-mean error around the unknown true value a. In this case it is easy to see that each firm will want to pretend that the demand is high (i.e., to announce that a_i is high). Doing so gives one's rivals an incentive to raise their prices.[12]

• *Price competition versus quantity competition* As in chapter 8, the results are usually reversed if price competition is replaced with quantity competition (i.e., "capacity" competition).[13] For instance, a firm wants to demonstrate to its rivals that it has a *low* cost. This signals high production, which forces the rivals to curtail their own production.

9.2 Dynamics: A Heuristic Approach

In the remainder of this chapter, direct disclosure of private information is ruled out. Firms try to manipulate their rivals' knowledge indirectly, by adopting a market behavior that differs from the optimal behavior under symmetric information. To focus this discussion, let us

---

8. Information sharing in oligopoly has been studied by Clarke (1983), Fried (1984), Gal-Or (1985, 1986), Li (1985), Nalebuff and Zeckhauser (1985), Novshek and Sonnenschein (1982), Ponssard (1979), Shapiro (1986), and Vives (1984).

9. For extensive surveys of the literature on auctions, see McAffee and McMillan 1987 and Milgrom 1987a. For a simple introduction to the main results in the case of two types per bidder, see Maskin and Riley 1985. For an example of resolution of equilibrium in a first-bid auction, see example 3 in section 4 of the Game Theory User's Manual.

10. In the terminology of chapter 8, goods are strategic substitutes, and firm 2's low price is equivalent to softness.

11. In the rest of this chapter, it will be assumed that the goods are substitutes and strategic complements.

12. In the case of uncertainty about the slope b, the firms would like to pretend that b is low (i.e., that demand is high). Similarly, they would like to pretend that d is high (i.e., that demand is high). See equation 9.4.

13. As long as prices are strategic complements and quantities are strategic substitutes.

suppose that firms compete in prices over two periods, and that private information pertains to own cost. If entry or exit is not an issue, a firm wants to appear unaggressive so as to induce its rivals to raise their prices. Thus, in the first period, it charges a high price to signal that it has high costs.[14] Thus, accommodation calls for the "puppy dog" strategy, in the language of chapter 8. The outcome is a more collusive one than under symmetric information. Section 9.3 informally reviews arguments along these lines.

To deter the entry or induce the exit of its rival, a firm adopts the more aggressive "top dog" strategy. Indeed, this firm wants to signal a low cost so as to induce its rival to doubt its viability in the market, so the firm charges a low price rather than a high one. This is the basis for the limit-pricing model of section 9.4. Two important variations on that model are given in sections 9.5 and 9.6. In the limit-pricing story, a low price is meant to dissuade the entry or induce the exit of a rival. When mergers are feasible, it may also help a firm to buy out a rival cheaply, because a rival who has been convinced that the market is not very profitable is prepared to sell out at a low merger price (see section 9.5). Also, predation may not be primarily geared toward inducing the exit of a current rival. It may, rather, signal to prospective entrants that entry is not profitable. For instance, a firm that has monopoly power on several geographical markets may prey on a firm that enters one of its markets not because such predation raises its profit on this market, but because it deters entry by the same or other competitors in other markets (see section 9.6).

The literature offers two kinds of intimately related models. In the *signaling* model, firm 1's price is directly observed by its rival. Sometimes, however, the price is kept secret, and what is revealed to firm 2 instead is firm 2's demand or profit (which depends on firm 1's unobserved price). Now, if firm 1 has private information

about its cost (or about the demand), the same principles apply as in the signaling framework, except that firm 1's signal is garbled by the noise in the demand function. However, in the case of price secrecy firm 1 need not have private information to try to manipulate firm 2's information. Suppose, for instance, that demand is uncertain and correlated over time. Firm 2's demand then depends on two unobserved variables: demand uncertainty and firm 1's price. Firm 2 faces a "signal-extraction problem," and is unable to fully recover the demand parameter. As we will see, a low price for firm 1 may be mistaken by firm 2 for a low state of demand, because both reduce firm 2's demand. Firm 1 then has an incentive to *jam* firm 2's inference process. Fortunately, the techniques and the intuitions for the signaling model and the signal-jamming model tend to be very similar.[15]

9.3 Accommodation and Tacit Collusion[16]

The idea that a firm may raise its price to signal high cost and soften the behavior of its rivals was developed by Ortega-Reichert. In chapter 8 of his 1967 thesis, he considered a duopoly model of two consecutive first-price auctions. (Think of auctions organized by government agencies for oil leases, medicines, or electric power equipment.) Two firms ($i = 1, 2$) draw their costs c_i of supplying one unit of the good in a common cumulative distribution $F(c_i | \lambda)$, where λ is an unknown parameter of the distribution (itself drawn from a distribution $G(\lambda)$). The costs are drawn independently between firms and between periods, so the results do not depend on serial correlation. Demand is common knowledge. The lowest-price bidder gets to supply one unit at the price he bids, and the other bidder does not sell; and this is true in each of two periods, A and B. If the first-period costs drawn, c_1^A and c_2^A, were common knowledge, the two firms could

---

14. The reason why such a strategy signals cost is that raising one's price is marginally less costly to a high-cost firm than to a low-cost firm. Mathematically,

$$\frac{\partial}{\partial c_i}\left(\frac{\partial}{\partial p_i}[(p_i - c_i)D_i(p_i, p_{-i})]\right) > 0,$$

where $D_i(\cdot)$ is the residual demand curve and p_{-i} denotes the price(s) of the rival(s). Readers who are familiar with the Spencian signaling model (see Game Theory User's Manual, supplementary section) will note that this is nothing but the usual sorting condition for signaling games.

15. Readers who are knowledgeable in dynamic games of incomplete information (see Game Theory User's Manual) may, however, note that signal-jamming models tend to have fewer equilibria. (There usually are fewer out-of-equilibrium beliefs and, therefore, less leeway in specifying firm 2's perception of the unknown parameter.) See Milgrom 1987b for some relationships between hidden-action and hidden-information models.

16. This section, though informal, will be difficult for readers who are not familiar with games of incomplete information. Section 5 of the Game Theory User's Manual should be helpful for those readers.

use them to update their beliefs about λ. However, it is assumed that firm j observes only c_j^A and its rival's first-period price, p_i^A. Thus, in the first period (A), firm i, by raising its price above what would be optimal for the period, signals that its cost c_i^A is high, and therefore that the cost distribution F is biased toward high costs.[17] Hence, firm i convinces firm j that firm i's second-period cost is also likely to be high. This information, by the now-usual reasoning, softens firm j's behavior (i.e., induces it to bid high) in period B, which benefits firm i.[18] Ortega-Reichert's model, although technically complex (like most of the models in this chapter), illustrates nicely the trade-off involved in choosing actions that reveal private information. It suggests that asymmetric information may provide firms with yet another incentive to take a nonaggressive stance in price competition in a mature industry.[19]

Mailath (1984) and Riordan (1985) have developed similar models of repeated price competition under asymmetric information.[20] In particular, Riordan shows that one can obtain something resembling conjectural variations (see chapter 5) by introducing asymmetric information. In the literature on conjectural variations, each firm believes that by raising its price by \$1 it induces its rival to raise its own price by \$$\gamma$, where γ is the coefficient of conjectural variations. As we saw in section 6.2, such beliefs are not rational in a static model: Because the rival has no time to react, the only rational conjecture is $\gamma = 0$. In a dynamic model, however, a firm may induce its rival to raise its price (in the future, not in the current period).

To see how this works, suppose that each firm's marginal cost is 0. Firm i's demand is

$$q_i = a - p_i + p_j.$$

The demand intercept a, which is unknown to both firms, is distributed along the real line (for simplicity), with mean a^e. Consider first a one-period model. Firm i maximizes

$$E(a - p_i + p_j)p_i = (a^e - p_i + p_j)p_i$$

over p_i, which yields

$$p_i = (a^e + p_j)/2.$$

By symmetry, the static Bertrand equilibrium is

$$p_1 = p_2 = a^e.$$

Now consider a two-period version of this model. The intercept a is the same in each period. Each firm observes only the realization of its demand, so its rival can secretly

---

17. Suppose that λ is a parameter of first-order stochastic dominance. Then $\lambda > \lambda'$ implies that

$F(c|\lambda) \geqslant F(c|\lambda')$

for all c. (The distribution for parameter λ puts a lot of weight on the lower tail.) Thus, a low p_i^A signals to firm j that c_i^A is low and therefore that λ is likely to be high.

18. Ortega-Reichert solves the perfect Bayesian equilibrium in closed form for a particular class of distributions—exponential for F:

$f(c|\lambda) = \lambda e^{-\lambda c}$ for c and λ positive,

gamma for G:

$g(\lambda) = \Delta^r \lambda^{r-1} e^{-\Delta \lambda} / \Gamma(r)$

for $\Delta > 0$, $r \geqslant 2$, $\lambda > 0$, where f and g denote the densities. He shows that each firm indeed develops a reputation for being a soft bidder.

What happens with more than two periods? Over time, λ is more and more precisely known, and the incentive to manipulate information decreases. The long-run behavior should thus resemble a series of identical static or myopic first-price auctions with known parameter λ. This, however, is a modeling issue. Suppose that λ, instead of being constant, is imperfectly correlated over time (this intuition is derived from Holmström 1983). For instance, it could follow a first-order autoregressive process: $\lambda_t = \rho \lambda_{t-1} + \varepsilon_t$, where $0 < \rho < 1$ and the noise ε_t is i.i.d. Then, because there constantly is new information, firms keep on charging high prices forever.

19. See chapter 6 on tacit collusion. Bikhchandani (1986) supplies an example in which repeated bidding leads the firm to build a reputation for tough rather than soft bidding. He considers repeated second-price auctions with "common values." Suppose, for instance, that two firms bid for oil leases. Each firm has private information about the amount of oil in the tract. The value is common in that one firm's information is of interest to its rival not only for the purpose of predicting the first firm's behavior but also for the purpose of assessing the value of the oil tracts. A well-known phenomenon for common values (see, e.g., Milgrom and Weber 1982) is the "winner's curse": The winning firm learns that its rival, which submitted a lower bid, did not have a high valuation of the oil tract, which is bad news. This leads firms to bid cautiously. The winner's curse *per se* does not imply that a firm manipulates information in the first period. In particular, if the valuations are distributed independently and identically and there is no serial correlation, the bidders treat the two auctions as independent. But assume now that firm 1 may or may not have an advantage over firm 2 in drilling cost, and that this is private information to firm 1. In a single auction, firm 2 bids less aggressively because of the possibility that firm 1 has a cost advantage. The winner's curse is aggravated by the fact that if firm 2 wins and firm 1 has a cost advantage, firm 1 must have had very pessimistic beliefs about the amount of oil. This implies that in a repeated auction framework, firm 1 wants to develop a reputation for having a cost advantage (i.e., for being a tough bidder). See Bikhchandari 1986 for more details. See Wilson 1985 for a brief account of this and other reputation models.

20. See also Bulow et al. 1985, Fudenberg and Tirole 1986a, and Mailath 1985a,b. Riordan's model is actually phrased in terms of quantity competition; however, as he notes, it also applies to price competition as long as one is careful about the usual reversal of results between strategic substitutes and complements.

cut price. (Technically, the model is one of signal jamming.) In our symmetric equilibrium, each firm charges price α in the first period. If the intercept is a, each firm i learns a perfectly by observing its first-period demand:

$$D_i^A = a - \alpha + \alpha = a.$$

The second-period game is one of complete information; hence, the Bertrand equilibrium in the second period has both firms charging a.[21]

Suppose that firm i deviates and charges price $p_i^A \neq \alpha$ in the first period. Firm j observes a demand of

$$D_j^A = a - \alpha + p_i^A.$$

Its perception $\tilde{a}$ of a, given by

$$a - \alpha + p_i^A = \tilde{a} - \alpha + \alpha = \tilde{a},$$

is therefore erroneous. Thus,

$$\tilde{a}(p_i^A) = a + (p_i^A - \alpha). \tag{9.5}$$

In the second period, firm j believes it is playing a game of perfect information, with intercept $\tilde{a}(p_i^A)$, so it charges $p_j^B = \tilde{a}(p_i^A)$. Using equation 9.5, we obtain the coefficient of "conjectural variations":

$$\frac{dp_j^B}{dp_i^A} = \gamma = 1.$$

A unit increase in the first-period price triggers a unit increase in the rival's second-period price.

To derive α, one proceeds as follows: Firm i, when it deviates, is not fooled about a. It therefore maximizes its second-period profit:

$$\max_{p_i^B}[a - p_i^B + \tilde{a}(p_i^A)]p_i^B.$$

Thus,

$$p_i^B = \frac{a + \tilde{a}(p_i^A)}{2}$$

$$= a + \frac{p_i^A - \alpha}{2}.$$

By the envelope theorem, the derivative of this second-period profit with respect to p_i^A is

$$p_i^B \frac{d\tilde{a}}{dp_i^A} = p_i^B.$$

The expectation of this derivative with respect to a is thus

$$a^e + \frac{p_i^A - \alpha}{2}.$$

In the first period, the expected present discounted profit of firm i is maximized. Thus, the sum of the first-period marginal profit

$$\frac{d}{dp_i^A}[(a^e - p_i^A + \alpha)p_i^A]$$

and the second-period marginal profit is 0:

$$a^e - 2p_i^A + \alpha + \delta\left(a^e + \frac{p_i^A - \alpha}{2}\right) = 0. \tag{9.6}$$

In equilibrium, $p_i^A = \alpha$, which together with equation 9.6 yields

$$\alpha = a^e(1 + \delta). \tag{9.7}$$

Each firm charges $a^e(1 + \delta)$ in the first period, rather than a^e (which would, on average, be charged under complete information about a, and which would be charged under incomplete information in a single-period model).[22]

Mailath's setup is closer than Riordan's to the Milgrom-Roberts model discussed in the next section, with observable prices and private information about cost. (The Mailath model is a signaling model.) The conclusions, however, are similar. This approach by no means justifies the static conjectural-variations approach, but it illustrates the positive effect of a firm's price on its rival's price.[23]

9.4 The Milgrom-Roberts Model of Limit Pricing

It has often been alleged that an established firm can discourage entry by charging a low price. Bain's (1949) concept of limit pricing was built around the idea that if there is a positive relationship between the pre-entry

21. The reaction curves are $p_i^B = (a + p_j^B)/2$. By symmetry, $p_i^B = p_j^B = a$.

22. Here the second-order condition is satisfied. When a has a compact support, the global second-order condition may be harder to satisfy.

23. Under quantity competition, the conclusions are naturally reversed. For instance, in the Mailath model an increase in quantity signals a low cost and therefore a high quantity tomorrow. This induces the rival to curtail output tomorrow. As Riordan notes, one then gets negative conjectural variations.

price and the speed or degree of entry, the established firm indeed has an incentive to cut its price.[24]

Although Bain's view prevailed for thirty years, many economists felt uncomfortable about applying it to antitrust analysis. To condemn a firm for making consumers pay too little seemed paradoxical. More important, it was not clear how a low price could deter entry. As Bain mentioned, a low price must convey bad news to potential entrants about their profitability in the market.

One possibility is that the price of the established firm has commitment value. That is, the entrants expect the pre-entry price to prevail after entry. However, such a theory is not very convincing. Entry into many markets is a decision that covers a period of many months or years, whereas a price can often be changed within a few days or weeks. Consequently, any loss that a potential entrant may suffer from a low pre-entry price is negligible. Prices *per se* have only a short commitment value (Friedman 1979). Now, it may be the case that a low pre-entry price is associated with a high pre-entry capacity. The capacity may have a higher commitment value than the attached price. The source of the entry deterrence is then the incumbent's capacity rather than its price (see chapter 8).

In this section we will look at industries in which capacities do not necessarily have commitment value. As we will see, the incumbent firm may nevertheless lower its price when facing the threat of entry. The paper that is crucial to the reexamination of the doctrine of limit pricing (and, more generally, in drawing our attention to the implications of asymmetric information for antitrust analysis) is Milgrom and Roberts 1982a. A simplified version of the Milgrom-Roberts two-period model is given in the following subsection.[25]

9.4.1 A Model

There are two periods and two firms. Firm 1, the incumbent, is a monopoly at date 1 and chooses a first-period price p_1. Firm 2, the entrant, then decides to enter or stay out in the second period. If it enters, there is duopolistic competition in period 2. Otherwise, firm 1 remains a monopoly.

As in the static model of section 9.1, firm 1's cost can be low (with probability x) or high (with probability $1 - x$). Let $M_1^t(p_1)$ denote the incumbent's monopoly profit when it charges p_1, where $t = L$ or H (indicating low or high cost).[26] Let p_m^L and p_m^H, respectively, denote the monopoly prices charged by the incumbent when his cost is low and when it is high. We know from chapter 1 that $p_m^L < p_m^H$. Let M_1^L and M_1^H denote the incumbent's profit when it maximizes its short-run profit, depending on its type ($M_1^t \equiv M_1^t(p_m^t)$). Assume that $M_1^t(p_1)$ is strictly concave in p_1.

Firm 1 knows its cost from the start. Firm 2 does not know firm 1's cost. For simplicity (and following Milgrom and Roberts), assume that firm 2 learns firm 1's cost immediately after entering if it decides to enter; the second-period duopoly price competition, if any, is then independent of the price charged in period 1. Let D_1^t and D_2^t denote the two firms' duopoly profits when firm 1 is of type t. (D_2^t possibly includes entry costs.) To make things interesting, assume that firm 2's entry decision is influenced by its beliefs about firm 1's cost:

$$D_2^H > 0 > D_2^L. \tag{9.8}$$

That is, under symmetric information, firm 2 would enter if and only if firm 1's cost were high. The common discount factor is δ.

Because firm 1 prefers to be a monopoly ($M_1^t > D_1^t$, for $t = L, H$), that firm clearly wants to convey the information that it has low cost. The problem is that it has no direct means of doing so, even if it indeed has a low cost. The indirect way is to signal by charging a low price, p_1^L. In our example, firm 1 may want to charge p_1^L even if it has a high cost. The loss in first-period monopoly profit may be offset by the second-period gain from remaining a monopoly. Does this mean that the potential entrant will stay out when observing p_1^L? It is not clear. A rational entrant, knowing that it is in the existing firm's self-interest to "lie" in this manner, will not necessarily infer that the incumbent has a low cost. In turn, the incumbent knows that the entrant knows about this incentive, and so on. As Milgrom and Roberts show, the correct way to analyze this dynamic game of incomplete information

---

24. For a model positing an exogenous relationship between pre-entry price and entry, see Gaskins 1971.

25. The analysis here follows section 6 of Fudenberg and Tirole 1986a.

26. Thus $M_1^t(p_1) = (p_1 - c_1^t)D_1^m(p_1)$, where $D_1^m(\cdot)$ is the monopoly demand.

is to solve for a "perfect Bayesian equilibrium" (see the Game Theory User's Manual).

There are two kinds of potential equilibria in such a model.[27] In a *separating* equilibrium, the incumbent does not pick the same first-period price when his cost is low as when it is high. The first-period price then fully reveals the cost to the entrant. In a *pooling* equilibrium, the first-period price is independent of the cost level. The entrant then learns nothing about the cost, and his posterior beliefs are identical to his prior beliefs (i.e., he still puts probability x on the cost's being low).[28]

Let us look for separating equilibria. There are two necessary conditions: that the low-cost type does not want to pick the high-cost type's equilibrium price, and vice-versa. We then complete the description of equilibrium by choosing beliefs that are off the equilibrium path (i.e., for prices that differ from the two potential equilibrium prices) and that deter the two types from deviating from their equilibrium prices. Thus, our necessary conditions are also sufficient, in the sense that the corresponding prices are equilibrium prices. In a separating equilibrium, the high-cost type's price induces entry. He thus plays p_m^H (if he did not, he could increase his first-period profit without adverse effect on entry). Thus, he gets $M_1^H + \delta D_1^H$. Let p_1^L denote the price of the low-cost type. The high-cost type, by charging this price, deters entry and obtains $M_1^H(p_1^L) + \delta M_1^H$. Thus, a necessary condition for equilibrium is

$$M_1^H - M_1^H(p_1^L) \geq \delta(M_1^H - D_1^H). \tag{9.9}$$

Similarly, the low-cost type must be maximizing his profit by choosing p_1^L. Because he could charge his monopoly price and get at worst $M_1^L + \delta D_1^L$ (at worst, p_m^L induces entry) and because in équilibrium he gets $M_1^L(p_1^L) + \delta M_1^L$, we must have

$$M_1^L - M_1^L(p_1^L) \leq \delta(M_1^L - D_1^L). \tag{9.10}$$

To make things interesting, assume that there is no separating equilibrium in which each type behaves as in a full-information context; i.e., the high-cost type would

wish to pool if p_1^L were equal to p_m^L:

$$M_1^H - M_1^H(p_m^L) < \delta(M_1^H - D_1^H). \tag{9.11}$$

To characterize the set of p_1^L satisfying equations 9.9 and 9.10, we must make more specific assumptions on the demand and cost structures. Subsection 9.4.1.1 (which ought to be skipped in a first reading) does so. For our purpose it is sufficient to note that, under reasonable conditions, equations 9.9 and 9.10 define an interval $[\tilde{\tilde{p}}_1, \tilde{p}_1]$, where $\tilde{p}_1 < p_m^L$. Thus, to separate, the low-cost type must charge a price sufficiently below his monopoly price so as to make pooling very costly to the high-cost type.

9.4.1.1   Derivation of the Interval of Separating Prices

The reason why it is more costly for the high-cost type to charge a low price is the so-called *sorting* or *single-crossing* condition (see the Game Theory User's Manual):

$$\frac{\partial[M_1^H(p_1) - M_1^L(p_1)]}{\partial p_1} > 0.$$

As we saw in section 9.2, this condition is satisfied here, because

$$\frac{\partial^2[(p_1 - c_1)D_1^m(p_1)]}{\partial p_1 \partial c_1} = -\frac{dD_1^m}{dp_1} > 0.$$

This condition ensures that the curves

$$y = M_1^L - M_1^L(p_1^L)$$

and

$$y = M_1^H - M_1^H(p_1^L)$$

cross once at most in the $\{p_1^L, y\}$ space. Next under some assumptions, the lower the incumbent's cost, the more he benefits from remaining a monopolist. Letting $D_1(p_1, p_2)$ denote the duopoly demand for firm 1 (notice that $D_1(p_1, +\infty) = D_1^m(p_1)$), letting $M_1(c_1)$ and $D_1(c_1)$ denote the monopoly and duopoly profits for cost c_1, letting p_1^d and p_2^d denote the equilibrium duopoly prices

---

27. Actually, there may exist a third kind, in which the incumbent uses a mixed strategy.

28. Bagwell (1985) analyzes whether the incumbent can signal its cost through alternative means (e.g., whether advertising can "crowd out" pricing as a

signaling instrument). He finds that wasteful advertising is not used in equilibrium: Imposing a cost of $1 for the high type to mimic the low type costs the low type less than $1 when it lowers its price, but exactly $1 when it advertises. For further elaborations (in particular, where advertising is not wasteful), see Bagwell and Ramey 1987.

(functions of c_1), and using the envelope theorem, we have

$$\frac{d[M_1(c_1) - D_1(c_1)]}{dc_1}$$

$$= \frac{d}{dc_1}\left(\max_{p_1}[(p_1 - c_1)D_1^m(p_1)]\right.$$

$$\left. - \max_{p_1}[(p_1 - c_1)D_1(p_1, p_2^d)]\right)$$

$$= -D_1^m(p_1^m) + D_1(p_1^d, p_2^d) - (p_1^d - c_1)\frac{\partial D_1}{\partial p_2}\frac{\partial p_2^d}{\partial c_1}.$$

The third term in this equality is presumably negative (because $p_1^d - c_1 > 0$, $\partial D_1/\partial p_2 > 0$, and—under mild conditions[29]—$\partial p_2^d/\partial c_1 > 0$). Thus, if the monopoly demand for firm 1 exceeds its duopoly demand, $M_1 - D_1$ decreases with c_1 and therefore

$$M_1^L - D_1^L > M_1^H - D_1^H.$$

This is the case for the unit-demand location model solved in chapter 7, where the monopoly demand was equal to the market size (i.e., was the maximum possible demand).

Using these derivations, we can obtain the interval $[\tilde{\tilde{p}}_1, \tilde{p}_1]$ from figure 9.2. $\tilde{p}_1$ is such that equation 9.9 is satisfied with equality; it is called the *least-cost* separating

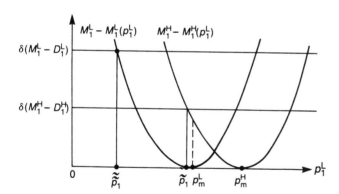

Figure 9.2

price because, of all potential separating prices, the low-cost type would prefer the one at $\tilde{p}_1$ (the closest to p_m^L).

9.4.1.2 Analysis of a Separating Equilibrium

The necessary conditions studied in subsection 9.4.1.1 are also sufficient. Let the high-cost type choose p_m^H and let the low-cost type choose p_1^L in $[\tilde{\tilde{p}}_1, \tilde{p}_1]$. When a price that differs from these two prices is observed, beliefs are arbitrary (in an unexpected event, Bayes' rule does not pin down firm 2's posterior beliefs). The easiest way to obtain equilibrium is to choose beliefs that induce entry (this way, the two types will be little tempted to deviate from their presumed equilibrium strategies), so let us specify that when p_1 does not belong to $\{p_m^H, p_1^L\}$ the posterior beliefs x' are equal to 0 (firm 2 believes that firm 1 has a high cost).[30] Now, let us check that no type wants to deviate. The high-cost type obtains his monopoly profit in the first period and thus is not willing to deviate to another price that induces entry. Nor (according to equation 9.9) does he deviate to p_1^L. And similarly for the low-cost type. Thus, we have obtained a continuum of separating equilibria.[31]

It is generally felt that only one of these separating equilibria—the least-cost one—is "reasonable." Suppose that firm 1 charges p_1 in $[\tilde{\tilde{p}}_1, \tilde{p}_1)$. Such a price is dominated for the high-cost type; that is, the high-cost type is always better off charging p_m^H rather than p_1, whatever its expectations about the effect of price on entry. At worst, p_m^H triggers entry, and at best p_1 deters entry. Even if p_1 deters entry, the high-cost type makes more profit charging p_m^H, on the basis of equation 9.9 and the concavity of the profit function:

$$M_1^H + \delta D_1^H > M_1^H(p_1) + \delta M_1^H.$$

Thus, firm 2, when observing p_1, should not believe that firm 1 has a high cost. That is, p_1 should deter entry. This implies that the low-cost firm, to signal its type and deter entry, need not charge less than $\tilde{p}_1$.

---

29. See chapter 8.

30. Whether these beliefs (which are consistent with Bayes' rule) are "reasonable" will be discussed below.

31. This continuum of separating equilibria exists for any $x < 1$. For $x = 1$, however, the low-cost firm plays its monopoly price, p_m^L. Thus, a tiny change in the information structure may make a huge difference. A very small probability that the firm has a high cost may force the low-cost firm to lower its price discontinuously in order to signal its type. Games of incomplete information (which include games of complete information) are very sensitive to the specification of the information structure.

To summarize this rather long analysis: There exists a unique "reasonable" separating equilibrium. The high-cost type charges its monopoly price and allows entry. The low-cost type charges the highest price $\tilde{p}_1$ such that the high-cost type's first-period loss of charging $\tilde{p}_1$ weakly exceeds its gain from deterring entry. Firm 1 reduces its price from p_m^L to $\tilde{p}_1$ because of the asymmetry of information. The following conclusions hold for this separating equilibrium:

Conclusion 1   Despite the fact that the incumbent manipulates his price, the entrant is not fooled. He learns the incumbent's cost perfectly. Entry occurs exactly when it would have occurred under symmetric information.

Conclusion 2   Even though the incumbent does not fool the entrant, he engages in limit pricing; the low-cost type would be mistaken for the high-cost type if it did not sacrifice short-run profits to signal its type.

Conclusion 3   Social welfare is higher than under symmetric information. The second-period welfare is not affected because entry is not affected. First-period welfare is generally increased because the low-cost type reduces its price.

Though it would be premature to conclude that limit pricing always increases welfare (see below), such a separating equilibrium shatters any illusion that low pre-entry prices obviously reduce welfare.

9.4.1.3   Pooling Equilibria

The existence of pooling equilibria hinges on whether the condition

$$xD_2^L + (1 - x)D_2^H < 0 \qquad (9.12)$$

is satisfied.

Assume that condition 9.12 is violated (with a strict inequality—for simplicity, we will not consider the equality case). Then, at the pooling price, firm 2 makes a strictly positive expected profit if it enters (as posterior beliefs are the same as prior beliefs). This means that entry is not deterred, so that the two types cannot do better

than to choose their static monopoly prices. As these prices differ, no pooling equilibrium can exist.

Assume, therefore, that condition 9.12 is satisfied, so that a pooling price p_1 deters entry. A necessary condition for a price p_1 to be a pooling-equilibrium price is that none of the types wants to play its monopoly price. If one of them were to do so, it would at worst allow entry. Therefore, p_1 must satisfy condition 9.10 and the analogous condition for the high-cost type:

$$M_1^H - M_1^H(p_1) \leqslant \delta(M_1^H - D_1^H). \qquad (9.13)$$

Again, the set of prices p_1 that satisfy both condition 9.10 and condition 9.13 depends on the cost and demand functions. Let us simply note that, from condition 9.11, there exists an interval of prices around p_m^L that satisfy these two inequalities.

Now it is easy to see that if p_1 satisfies conditions 9.10 and 9.13, p_1 can be made part of a pooling equilibrium. Suppose that whenever firm 1 plays a price differing from p_1 (an off-the-equilibrium path price), firm 2 believes that firm 1 has a high cost. Firm 2 then enters, and firm 1 might as well play its monopoly price. Thus, from conditions 9.10 and 9.13, none of the types would want to deviate from p_1.[32]

Let us consider the pooling equilibrium in which both firms charge the low-cost monopoly price p_m^L. It is easy to see that some of our conclusions for the separating equilibrium are reversed:

Conclusion 1'   The incumbent manipulates its price in a way that does not reveal cost information. There is less entry than under symmetric information (entry is always deterred, and not only with probability x).

Conclusion 2'   The low-cost type charges its monopoly price. The high-cost type engages in limit pricing to deter entry.

Conclusion 3'   The consequences of asymmetric information for welfare are ambiguous. First-period welfare is, in general, increased, because the high-cost type lowers its price. But there is less entry, which, in general, lowers second-period welfare.

---

32. We will not consider here how restrictions on beliefs can eliminate some (or, possibly, all) equilibria. (One way to eliminate equilibria is to use the Cho-Kreps criterion—see subsection 11.6.2.) For more detail in the context of the limit-pricing game, see Cho 1986.

9.4.2 Discussion

The Milgrom-Roberts model shows that limit pricing does occur, but that it is not necessarily harmful.

It turns out that the conclusions are sensitive to the data of the problem. This means that the industrial economist must have an intimate knowledge of the industry in question before drawing definite conclusions about limit pricing. First, pooling and separating equilibria differ in their positive and normative consequences. Second (as section 9.3 suggests), if the incumbent accommodates entry and if its cost is not learned by the entrant at the entry date, the incumbent charges more than the monopoly price. Thus, if the incumbent is unsure whether he will deter or accommodate entry (for instance, because he does not know the entry cost), it is not clear whether he will charge more or less than the monopoly price. Third, the previous model assumed that the incumbent's cost was unrelated to the entrant's. Consider the other polar case, in which the entrant's cost c_2 is equal to the incumbent's cost c_1 but the entrant does not know it before entering. Firm 2's duopoly profit is then a function $D_2(c_1)$. For many specifications of second-period competition, D_2 is a decreasing function of c_1. (A symmetric decline in cost tends to increase both firms' profits.) Thus, to deter entry, the incumbent must signal a *high* cost and therefore charge a price above the monopoly price in the first period (Harrington 1985).

As in chapter 8, the principles established for the deterrence of entry also apply to the inducement of exit (*predation*). Salop and Shapiro (1980), Scharfstein (1984), and Roberts (1986) have extended the Milgrom-Roberts approach to formalize post-entry predation. In their model, the established firm preys on an entrant who faces a cost of reentry in order to convey that it has bad news about the entrant's future profitability.[33] Thus, the model of limit pricing can, with small changes, be reinterpreted as one of predatory pricing.

The welfare analysis of the limit-pricing model has implications for the predation model. Suppose that two firms compete in period 1, and that at the end of period 1 firm 2 (still called the "entrant") decides whether to exit on the basis of its observation of firm 1's price. (The only difference with the limit-pricing model is that the entrant is in at date 1.) In a separating equilibrium, the entrant is not fooled, and lower prices improve the first-period welfare. We already noticed that welfare may go down if the equilibrium is a pooling one; here we have another reason to be circumspect about the benefits of limit pricing. Introduce another period (period 0), in which the entrant decides whether or not to sink an entry cost. Even if the equilibrium is separating, so that the entrant will not be fooled in period 1, the incumbent's price is lower than under symmetric information, which reduces the entrant's expected profit. Thus, in period 0, the prospective entrant is less likely to enter.[34] Predation may be *ex ante* detrimental, even though it is welfare improving when it takes place (in period 1).

More generally, the Milgrom-Roberts model and its variants offer a framework for discussing tests of predatory behavior.[35] As in the case of "barriers to entry," it is difficult to come up with a satisfactory definition of "predation." The intuitive notion refers to low prices (or high advertising levels) that are meant to induce a rival's exit so as to assure the remaining firm of higher profits in the future. As in the taxonomy of chapter 8, we can decompose the effect of a predator's action into two components. The first indicates how this action directly affects the predator's profit, if we take the rival's behavior (in particular, the exit decision) as fixed. The second reflects the influence of this action on the rival's behavior (a strategic effect). The predator, for instance, realizes that a low price may depress the rival's assessment of profitability in this market and may thus induce exit. One may define predation as the reflection of this strategic effect on the predator's behavior. These theoretical considerations, however, leave two issues open. The first is semantic: As we have seen, predation in the above sense is not necessarily socially harmful. As the word usually carries a negative connotation, this raises the issue of whether we want

---

33. A signal-jamming version of the same idea is provided in Fudenberg and Tirole 1986b. There, an established incumbent (without superior information) secretly cuts its price to mislead the recently entered firm to believe that its intrinsic profitability is low, thus trying (but not succeeding) to induce exit. As in Milgrom and Roberts' separating equilibrium, the entrant sees through

the incumbent's strategy and is not fooled. An example of signal-jamming predation is given in example 4 in section 11.5.

34. The entrant stays out for a larger range of entry costs.

35. See Ordover and Saloner 1987 for a good discussion of these tests.

to use it in cases where the strategic behavior increases welfare. The second issue is operational: As in chapter 8, it may be hard to disentangle the two components of the effect of the action on the predator's profit. A low price or a high level of advertising may simply be a competitive ("innocent") behavior intended to maximize profit (where competition is taken as given). But it may also have the strategic purpose of inducing exit. This brings us to the legal definitions of predation.

The early tests of predatory behavior (Areeda and Turner 1975; Posner 1976) were based on cost. For instance, the Areeda-Turner test, which has been embraced by U.S. courts in several antitrust cases, holds that a price below the short-run marginal cost should be unlawful and that the short-run marginal cost can be approximated by the average variable cost. There have been many discussions as to what is a good surrogate for short-run marginal cost, but the most fundamental criticism of the Areeda-Turner test is that the comparison of price and marginal cost may not be related to predatory pricing. As Joskow and Klevorick (1979, pp. 219–220) have insisted, what is important is the trade-off between the sacrifice of current profit and the gain from monopolization:

Predatory pricing behavior involves a reduction of price in the short run so as to drive competing firms out of the market or to discourage entry of new firms in an effort to gain larger profits via higher prices in the long run than would have been earned if the price reduction had not occurred.

For instance, in the Milgrom-Roberts model, predatory pricing can involve prices above or below the marginal cost. The signal conveyed to the entrant or the prey about its future profitability matters as much as the predator's current sacrifice of profits.

Although predatory behavior can be demonstrated within an abstract model, deriving empirical tests for antitrust analysis is difficult indeed. How can one measure predatory intent if the predatory price bears no systematic relation to cost?

One possibility is to look at the incumbent's intertemporal price path. For instance, suppose that the incumbent firm cuts its price when entry occurs. This might indicate predatory behavior. However, the incumbent's residual demand curve falls when a competitor enters, which may call for a lower price independent of predatory intent (Williamson 1977). Joskow and Klevorick call this labeling of a truly competitive price cut as predatory a "type-I error." Conversely, suppose that the incumbent does not lower his price when entry occurs. This does not mean that the incumbent does not engage in anticompetitive behavior. The incumbent may have been practicing limit pricing (charging a low price) before entry, and—having been unsuccessful in deterring entry —may have felt no need to cut his price further. Thus, the time-series analysis of the incumbent's price may lead to a "type-II error," in which predatory behavior goes undetected. More generally, any test will have to face these two types of errors.

One drawback of games of incomplete information[36] is the multiplicity of equilibria. In the limit-pricing game, what should firm 2 believe when it observes a price p_1 that is not an equilibrium price? Because such an event has zero probability, Bayes' rule cannot be applied. In contrast with the well-defined beliefs that characterize equilibrium strategies, any posterior beliefs are consistent with Bayesian updating.[37] Now, this engenders a large multiplicity of beliefs. Suppose that we do not want p_1 to be chosen by some type of firm on the equilibrium path. If observing p_1 is indeed an off-the-equilibrium-path event, we can choose posterior beliefs $x'(p_1)$ following p_1 as we like; so let us assume that $x'(p_1)$ is very unfavorable to the incumbent. (Here $x'(p_1) = 0$, so p_1 triggers entry.) Then, depending on p_1, it is quite possible that no type wants to choose p_1. This fulfills our earlier assumption that p_1 was off the equilibrium path. One way to reduce the multiplicity—a way that has been explored intensely in game theory in recent years—is to impose some "reasonable" restrictions on beliefs following a zero-probability event. (We used such a restriction earlier to

---

36. See Milgrom and Roberts 1987 for a fuller discussion of various limits of this approach.

37. Suppose that the low type chooses p_1 with probability α^L and that the high type does so with probability α^H. Bayes' rule determines posterior beliefs x' through the formula

$$x'[x\alpha^L + (1 - x)\alpha^H] = x\alpha^L.$$

For a positive-probability event ($\alpha^L + \alpha^H > 0$), x' is uniquely defined. For a zero-probability event ($\alpha^L = \alpha^H = 0$), any x' in [0, 1] is admissible.

single out a unique equilibrium among separating equilibria; for further "refinements," see the Game Theory User's Manual and the references therein.) Another route, taken by Matthews and Mirman (1983) and Saloner (1981), is to assume that the incumbent's first-period price[38] is observed by the entrant with some noise. For instance, the entrant could observe $\tilde{p}_1$ where $\tilde{p}_1$ follows some conditional distribution $F(\tilde{p}_1 | p_1)$. If the support of F is all of R^+, for instance, there are no longer zero-probability events, and Bayes' rule retains its power. Assuming that the incumbent's output is a strictly decreasing function of his marginal cost, Saloner shows that every type of incumbent firm engages in limit pricing (i.e., produces more than the monopoly output).

Saloner also extends this model to more than two periods. In each period, the entrant receives a noisy version of the price and decides whether to enter. Intuitively, the entrant should enter if and only if the price exceeds some history-dependent threshold. The entrant may want to wait to obtain more precise information, and therefore entry is in general delayed relative to the full-information case. However, as in the Milgrom-Roberts model, the limit-pricing behavior does not bias the delay in a clear direction, as it is anticipated by the entrant. (The delay is due to the noise and the entrant's willingness to learn.)

9.5 Predation for Merger

The purpose of this section and the next is to apply the logic of section 9.4 to predatory behavior. As we saw in that section, the limit-pricing model can be reinterpreted as a predation model. However, several economists close to the Chicago School—McGee (1958, 1980), Telser (1966), and Bork (1978)—have argued that it cannot be rational to engage in predatory pricing in order to induce exit. Their argument is that merging with the rival (if legal) is a superior way to realize monopoly power. Competition—especially predatory competition—destroys industry profit, and the rivals have incentives to avoid it. For instance, the predator could make an offer to the prey that would be preferred by both to the predatory outcome. Hence, episodes of price cutting must be attributed to other, more innocent considerations, such as a fluctuation in demand or cost or a normal reaction to a decline in the residual demand curve due to entry.

Before games of asymmetric information became standard practice, Yamey (1972) criticized the above argument on two grounds. First, the predator may face potential entry in the market in question or in other markets in which it operates. If it does not fight in the market in question but prefers to take over its rival, it may be perceived as a weakling (for instance, a high-cost firm that is afraid to engage in a price war). This may encourage other firms to enter (possibly in the other markets), because they anticipate that, rather than being preyed upon, they will make profits in those markets or else will be bought out at advantageous prices. Second, the buyout price of the prey may not be independent of the predator's pre-merger market behavior. Clearly, these two objections are linked to private information and reputation. Under complete information, predatory pricing would not affect the perceived profitability of the prey or of other potential entrants.[39]

We will take up Yamey's first argument in section 9.6. We will now examine his second argument in light of Saloner's (1987) work. But before doing so, let us see how these two arguments can be motivated with examples taken from the great merger wave of 1887–1904 (a time in which there were few impediments to horizontal mergers—see Scherer 1980, pp. 121–122).

Between 1891 and 1906, the American Tobacco Company and two affiliated corporations acquired 43 of their competitors. American Tobacco engaged in predatory pricing (sometimes of the signal-jamming variety—secretly controlled subsidiaries, known as "bogus independents," secretly cut prices, so that the rivals would attribute the decline in their profits to intensified and enduring competition or to declining demand). Burns (1986) offers evidence that predatory pricing considerably reduced American Tobacco's cost of acquiring its competitors (both those that were victims of predation and the competitors not preyed upon yet, who sold peacefully). Another famous case is that of the Standard Oil Company of New Jersey.

---

38. The authors cited actually use quantity rather than price.

39. "A bout of price warfare initiated by the aggressor, or a threat of such activity, might serve to cause the rival to revise its expectations, and hence alter its terms of sale to an acceptable level." (Yamey 1972, p. 130)

Standard Oil attained a 90 percent market share of the U.S. petroleum-refining industry in the late nineteenth century through a program of mergers *cum* predatory actions (low prices, foreclosure of supplies of crude oil and railroad transportation, and so on). (See McGee 1958 and Scherer 1980 [pp. 336–337] for views that these low prices may not have followed predatory intents.)

The rationale behind predation for mergers was recently formalized by Saloner (1987). To understand his insight, consider the following bare-bones model. Its structure is the limit-pricing model, except that after the entrant enters and before second-period price competition takes place the incumbent can make a merger offer to the entrant.[40] If the merger price is turned down, duopoly competition ensues in the second period, as was described above. If the merger is accepted, firm 1 acquires firm 2's assets and technology and remains a monopoly. For simplicity, let us assume that the entrant learns the incumbent's cost after turning down the merger offer and before waging price competition. Let us alter equation 9.8 into

$$D_2^H > D_2^L > 0. \tag{9.14}$$

That is, for any level of c_1, firm 2 would enter even if it were not bought out. Let us also assume that a monopoly makes more profit than a duopoly.[41]

The following is a separating equilibrium in this model: The high-cost type of firm charges its monopoly price, p_m^H. The low-cost type engages in limit pricing; it charges $p_1^* < p_m^L$, where p_1^* is defined by

$$M_1^H - M_1^H(p_1^*) = \delta(D_2^H - D_2^L). \tag{9.15}$$

After observing p_m^H, the entrant accepts being bought out if and only if the merger price exceeds D_2^H; after observing p_2^*, he accepts merger prices above D_2^L. The incumbent naturally offers D_2^H following p_m^H and D_2^L following p_1^*. Equation 9.15 says that the high-cost type has no incentive to masquerade as the low-cost type. By doing so, it saves $D_2^H - D_2^L$ on the merger price, but it incurs a first-period profit loss of $M_1^H - M_1^H(p_1^*)$.

Would the low-cost type not find it profitable to charge its monopoly price? As in the limit-pricing game, assume that prices above p_1^* lead to beliefs that the cost is high. By charging his monopoly price, the incumbent gains in the first period[42]

$$M_1^L - M_1^L(p_1^*) < M_1^H - M_1^H(p_1^*).$$

But he raises the merger price by $D_2^H - D_2^L$. Thus, the low-cost type does not charge its monopoly price (and, *a fortiori*, does not mimic the high-cost type), under the assumption that it wants to merge if it is perceived as having a high cost. For simplicity, we make that assumption. (For this, it suffices that the low-cost type gains more from a merger than the high-cost type. On this, see the discussion in subsection 9.4.1.1 of how the value of remaining a monopolist varies with the incumbent's cost. Saloner analyzes quantity competition in the second period, making the more satisfactory assumption that the incumbent's cost is not revealed to the entrant immediately before period-2 market competition and showing that under some conditions a merger is indeed more valuable to a low-cost type.) As in the limit-pricing model, there exist pooling equilibria.

An interesting feature of the separating equilibrium is that limit (predatory) pricing improves welfare relative to the symmetric-information case. The merger occurs in any case, and the only issue is the sell-out price. The incumbent's behavior resembles that of an aggressive army that attacks only in order to be in a superior bargaining position at the armistice talks. Fortunately, the welfare consequences may be different. Here, asymmetric information and the concomitant impulse to signal bad news to the entrant improves welfare through lower prices.[43]

In this model, firms always merge. In Saloner's variant there is a third firm, which would be ready to enter if the merger were to occur and if it believed the incumbent to

40. Saloner considers the slightly more complicated model with first-period competition between the two firms. The fact that the same effect arises with first-period competition is important because it more clearly addresses the question of eliminating an existing rival.

41. Formally, let $\bar{M}^t$ denote firm 1's monopoly profit when it owns firm 2's assets or technology for $t = L, H$. ($\bar{M}_1^t \geq M_1^t$; for perfect substitutes and if $c_2 \geq c_1^t$, $\bar{M}_1^t = M_1^t$; firm 1 then only acquires the right to prevent its rival from producing.) The assumption can be written $D_1^t + D_2^t \leq \bar{M}_1^t$.

42. Recall that $M_1^H > M_1^H(p_m^L)$, that $p_1^* < p_m^L$, and that

$$\frac{\partial}{\partial p_1}[M_1^H(p_1) - M_1^L(p_1)] > 0.$$

43. Whether mergers should be allowed is not clear cut. A merger may have the advantage of eliminating an inefficient competitor. However, it badly affects the consumer surplus by raising the market price(s) in the second period. See Saloner 1987 for a comprehensive discussion of the welfare trade-offs in this kind of model.

have a high cost. A merger between the other two firms may or may not occur.

9.6 Multimarket Reputation

In sections 9.4 and 9.5 we saw how an established firm may want to cut its price and build a reputation for toughness in order to induce its rival in its market to stay out, to exit, or to sell out at a low price. Naturally, a multimarket incumbent may adopt the same strategy in one market to improve its position in another market. By a rough analogy, the second-period market competition of sections 9.4 and 9.5 can be reinterpreted as competition in a second market. For instance, suppose that an entrant enters (at some cost) into market 1. The incumbent, who is still a monopolist in market 2, may have an incentive to prey on the market-1 entrant to signal that his costs are low. Even if such a strategy does not induce exit (and therefore loses money) in market 1, it may prevent entry by another entrant (possibly the same firm) in market 2. In order for this strategy to be viable, the incumbent's costs must be strongly positively correlated between markets. One may, for instance, think of markets as geographical units, and of the incumbent's good in each market as being the "same" and thus being produced at the same cost (except for transportation costs).[44]

Let us consider a few alleged examples of such multimarket predatory behavior. Recall first Burns' (1986) demonstration that American Tobacco succeeded in reducing acquisition costs by preying on some rivals. One remarkable finding is that the gains applied not only to the acquisition of the prey but also to that of the competitors who sold out before being preyed upon. This strategy was facilitated by the fact that many of American Tobacco's rivals sold in small territories. American Tobacco could thus attack a rival in a given marketing area without losing too much money on its overall product line (that is, it could practice discrimination to limit predatory losses).

Another example (Scherer 1980, p. 338) is that of General Foods, the producer of Maxwell House Coffee, which controlled approximately 45 percent of regular-coffee sales in the eastern United States. A rival brand, Folger's, popular in the western states, tried to expand eastward in the 1970s. General Foods counterattacked with sharp price decreases where Folger's had entered, and succeeded in stopping further entry into the northeastern states (though it did not induce exit from the already-penetrated cities).[45] In a less successful case of multimarket predatory behavior in the 1970s, the Empire Gas Corporation, which sold liquified petroleum gas in many geographical markets while most of its competitors sold in only one, tried to signal from one market to another by charging less than the wholesale price in some markets. This was meant to induce the competitors to raise their prices well above this wholesale price. Although this led to either exit or higher prices in some markets, the rivals' price increases eventually collapsed; furthermore, even where rivals had exited, other firms entered. (The barriers to entry were limited.) Empire lost money in the whole process.[46]

Multimarket predation was first formalized by Kreps and Wilson (1982) and Milgrom and Roberts (1982b).[47] Elsewhere in this book we have applied these authors' reputation model to the reputation for being a high-quality producer (section 2.6) and to the reputation for cooperative pricing behavior (section 6.5). There is clearly no point to developing an argument that is basically the same here,[48] so their model of multimarket behavior will simply be summarized.

Kreps, Milgrom, Roberts, and Wilson look at a simplified version of the previous predation game, which they then extend to several markets. In a given market, the entrant decides to enter or not. In case of entry, the incumbent has two possible courses of action: predation or acquiescence. The entrant's profit (including the entry cost) is positive if the incumbent acquiesces, and negative if he preys. One can think of preying (acquiescing) as

---

44. Posner (1979, pp. 939–940), following Yamey, argues that predation by a multimarket firm is "a plausible policy for a profit-maximizing seller to follow." He suggests that such a strategy may have been adopted by Standard Oil.

45. See Scherer 1980 (pp. 335–340) and Schmalensee 1979 for further examples.

46. See Easterbrook 1981. This example is worthy of meditation in the light of the incomplete-information approach.

47. See also Easley et al. 1985. This line of research was stimulated by Selten's (1978) chain-store paradox, according to which, under symmetric information, no predation occurs, no matter in how many markets the incumbent faces potential entry.

48. A two-market version is studied as example 1 in section 5 of the Game Theory User's Manual.

charging a low (high) price. The incumbent can be either "strong" or "weak." If he is strong, he enjoys preying and he always preys. If he is weak, preying is costly and can be worthwhile only if it raises profits in another market. Only the incumbent knows whether he is weak or strong. (Strength can be thought of as a rough approximation for having a low production cost.)

The two-market version of the game is as follows: The incumbent is in both markets. In the first stage, the market-1 entrant decides whether to enter; the incumbent then decides whether to prey (if entry has occurred). In the second stage, another entrant, who has observed the outcome in market 1, decides whether to enter market 2; if he enters, the incumbent decides whether to prey. (The *n*-market version of the game is similar.) In such a context, it may be worthwhile for a weak incumbent to prey if entry occurs in market 1. If it were not worthwhile, predation in market 1 would then reveal a strong incumbent; thus, after predation, entry would not occur in market 2. If the gain from monopolizing market 2 exceeds the predation cost in market 1, it cannot be an equilibrium for the weak incumbent not to prey in market 1. (Clearly, if entry occurs in market 2, the weak incumbent then has no incentive to prey, because there is no future—i.e., no reputation to maintain.)

In the *T*-market or *T*-stage version of the multimarket predation model, the equilibrium has the following features (if the probability of being strong is not too small): In the first markets, entry does not occur. If a firm entered by mistake, it would be preyed upon with probability 1 (i.e., by the strong and the weak types). Because the number of markets to defend shrinks over time, concerns about reputation lessen; this encourages entrants to enter, possibly stochastically (the weak entrant preys with probability less than 1). Another point of this reputation story is that, for *T* large, the probability that the incumbent is strong can be very small and still create an incentive for the weak type to prey. For a similar result, see exercise 2.9.

9.7 The "Long Purse" Story

In the theories of predatory pricing sketched in sections 9.4 through 9.6, the predator tries to convey bad news to its rivals about their profitability in its market(s). The predation does not affect the rivals' real prospects, only the *perception* of these prospects. Under rational expectations, predation may or may not succeed in driving (or keeping) rivals out of the market.

An alternative and popular theory of predatory pricing holds that cutthroat competition may affect the rivals' prospects, as the rivals cannot raise enough resources to carry on. According to this theory, a firm with substantial financial resources—the "long purse" or "deep pocket" —can prey on a weaker rival. Because the strong or big firm can sustain losses for a longer period of time, it can drive the weak or small firm out of the market.[49] If this theory is right, predatory pricing has serious consequences. First, predation is more likely to be successful than in the signaling model; therefore, it more often leads to the monopolization of the industry. Second, the remaining firm need not be the most efficient one; rather, it is the strongest financially. To monopoly pricing may be added cost inefficiency.

The "long purse" story lacked theoretical foundations, and it slowly fell from grace. Scherer writes that "perhaps because it enjoyed such frail intellectual support, the ... theory received much less emphasis in conglomerate merger cases in the 1970s" (1980, p. 560). Telser's influential 1966 article raised suspicion about the traditional "long purse" story. In that article Telser assumed that the ability of one of the firms to raise capital is limited by some upper bound. By charging a low price, that firm's rival can impose a loss until the upper bound is reached and the financially constrained firm has to quit. But, as Telser notes, predatory pricing will not even occur in equilibrium. The financially constrained firm, realizing that it will be preyed upon and lose money, has an incentive to quit as early as possible (or not to enter).[50]

---

49. "An enterprise that is big in this sense obtains from its bigness a special kind of power, based upon the fact that it can spend money in large amounts. If such a concern finds itself matching expenditures or losses, dollar for dollar, with a substantially smaller firm, the length of its purse assures it of victory.... The large company is in a position to hurt without being hurt." (Edwards 1955, pp. 334–335) See also Scherer 1980, pp. 214–215, 335–336, 560.

50. Benoit's (1983, 1984) game-theoretic treament of Telser's point shows that the absence of observed predation is due to the complete-information structure of the game. If the strong firm does not know whether its rival is financially constrained, it may pay for the latter to bluff when it indeed is financially constrained and pretend that it is not (such a strategy resembles that of the reputation model of Kreps, Milgrom, Roberts, and Wilson, studied in section 9.6).

One problem with this approach is that it is not clear why the prey faces a financial constraint. Suppose that, instead of limiting their credit, the creditors give an infinite credit line to the prey. Then there is no scope for predation. The predator acquiesces, and the "prey" makes profit each period. So it is in the interest of the creditors not to impose financial constraints. Recognizing this, Fudenberg and Tirole (1985, 1986b) argue that imperfections in the capital market are central to a reconsideration of the "long purse" story. Let us sketch how one may go about formalizing these imperfections.

Let us first consider an entrepreneur (he will later be interpreted as firm 2) who must finance a project through debt. Let K denote the size of the investment, and let E denote the entrepreneur's wealth (equity). Thus, the entrepreneur borrows an amount $D = K - E$ from a bank. The investment yields a random profit $\tilde{\Pi}$ in some interval $[\underline{\Pi}, \overline{\Pi}]$. If r denotes the rate of interest charged by the bank, the entrepreneur must reimburse $D(1 + r)$. If $\tilde{\Pi} \geqslant D(1 + r)$, he does so and retains $\tilde{\Pi} - D(1 + r) > 0$. If $\tilde{\Pi} < D(1 + r)$, his firm goes bankrupt and retains nothing. Bankruptcy costs (legal and administrative costs, or losses in the product market due to disruption) are equal to B, so the bank, which has priority in the bankruptcy process, retains $\tilde{\Pi} - B$. If F denotes the cumulative distribution of $\tilde{\Pi}$ (with density f), the firm's expected profit is

$$U(D, r) = \int_{D(1+r)}^{\overline{\Pi}} [\tilde{\Pi} - D(1 + r)] f(\tilde{\Pi}) d\tilde{\Pi}.$$

The bank's expected profit is

$$V(D, r) = (1 + r)D(1 - F(D(1 + r)))$$
$$+ \int_{\underline{\Pi}}^{D(1+r)} (\tilde{\Pi} - B) f(\tilde{\Pi}) d\tilde{\Pi}. \qquad (9.16)$$

Suppose that banks are competitive, and that the cost of

their funds is $1 + r_0$. The bank's zero-profit condition can be written as

$$V(D, r) = (1 + r_0)D. \qquad (9.17)$$

Assume that equation 9.17 defines a unique rate of interest, $r(D)$, and that $dr/dD > 0$.[51]

Will the entrepreneur invest in the project? Only if his expected profit exceeds $(1 + r_0)E$, the opportunity cost of his equity. Where W denotes the entrepreneur's net benefit from the project, this project is undertaken if

$$W = \int_{(K-E)(1+r)}^{\overline{\Pi}} [\tilde{\Pi} - (1 + r)(K - E)] f(\tilde{\Pi}) d\tilde{\Pi}$$
$$- (1 + r_0)E \geqslant 0.$$

Using equation 9.17 and letting $E\tilde{\Pi} \equiv \int_{\underline{\Pi}}^{\overline{\Pi}} \tilde{\Pi} f(\tilde{\Pi}) d\tilde{\Pi}$ denote the expectation of $\tilde{\Pi}$, we can rewrite W in a simpler manner:

$$W = [E\tilde{\Pi} - (1 + r_0)K] - [BF((1 + r)(K - E))]. \qquad (9.18)$$

where the first term is equal to the project's net value in a perfect financial world and the second term represents the expected bankruptcy cost. (The firm goes bankrupt if $\tilde{\Pi} < (1 + r)(K - E)$.)

It is now easy to see that a higher wealth or equity makes it more likely that the project is undertaken: A higher equity lowers debt $(K - E)$ as well as the rate of interest, so $dW/dE > 0$. We can interpret this result as follows: A higher equity lowers the probability of bankruptcy and therefore reduces bankruptcy costs. From the zero-profit condition, these cost savings are passed on to the entrepreneur (see equation 9.18) and make the project look more attractive.[52]

The foundations for an understanding of the optimality of a debt contract between the bank and the entrepreneur have been laid by Diamond (1984), Gale and Hellwig

---

51. The rate of interest r defined by equation 9.17 exceeds r_0 because the bank gets a return r when $\tilde{\Pi}$ is high, and less than r in case of bankruptcy.

For a given D, there may not exist a rate of interest that satisfies the zero-profit constraint. The bank may make negative profit for all r. The problem is that, by raising r, the bank raises the probability of bankruptcy and therefore raises the bankruptcy costs, so its profit may decrease. The derivative of V with respect to r is proportional to

$1 - F(D(1 + r)) - Bf(D(1 + r))$.

The derivative of

$V(D, r) - (1 + r_0)D$

with respect to D is negative if, e.g., B is "small." Thus, if the sum to be reimbursed, $D(1 + r)$, is close to the maximum profit, $\overline{\Pi}$, the profit decreases with r (assuming that f is bounded away from zero). We ignore this issue and assume in the following that $1 - F - Bf$ is positive in the relevant range and that there exists a zero-profit rate of interest (sufficient conditions for this are easy to find).

52. Alternatively, the entrepreneur may not be able to find a bank that is willing to finance the investment, if we relax our assumption that there exists a rate of interest at which the bank breaks even.

(1985), and Townsend (1979). These authors assume that the bank cannot observe the firm's profit without inspecting the firm's accounts. The cost of doing so is B. When no inspection (bankruptcy) occurs, the bank can only demand a constant amount of money: $D(1 + r)$. The optimal contract has the bank inspect, and get the residual profit, if and only if the firm is unable to meet its obligations (i.e., to reimburse $D(1 + r)$). Asymmetric information thus yields a debt contract as the optimal contract.

It is easy to see how such imperfections in the capital market provide foundations for the "long purse" story. Consider a two-period duopoly model. Firm 1 has no financial constraint. Firm 2 must finance an investment K between the two periods if it wants to remain in the market. Firm 2's equity after the first period depends on its retained earnings after first-period market competition. Now, by preying in the first period, firm 1 reduces firm 2's first-period profit and therefore reduces its second-period equity. Firm 2 must borrow more and finds continuation in this market less attractive. Predation is successful if it drives E down enough so that $W = 0$. Thus, predation is worthwhile to firm 1 if the first-period profit loss is offset by the second-period gain from becoming a monopolist.

In this version of the "long purse" story, predation can occur even in the absence of asymmetric information between the firms. Also, firm 2 may be in the market in period 1 (because it may make a profit even though it is preyed upon); it simply cannot expand (or modernize, or stay in the market) in period 2. Predation is rather associated with imperfections (asymmetric information) in the capital market.[53] And the prey exits the market either voluntarily (because the rate of interest charged by the bank is too high relative to the opportunity value of the firm's assets) or else because it cannot find financing at all (there is no rate of interest at which the bank can break even). This model addresses the effect of financial constraints on expansion, as well as the effect on exit. Exit, with or without bankruptcy,[54] is not necessarily the most common outcome of such a predation (see Scherer 1980, p. 214). As in our model, the prey can stop expanding or modernizing rather than run the risk of going bankrupt. Also, the prey can sell out its assets to the predator.[55] As Saloner (1987) notes, the "failing-firm defense" (a rarely used provision in the U.S. merger law that allows the acquisition of a company that is unlikely to survive as a viable competitor in the absence of a merger—see Scherer 1980, p. 555) may well encourage predatory behavior. (This reasoning assumes that courts have difficulty assessing predatory behavior. Otherwise, as long as predation is an offense, the prey can sue for treble damages, and this may be a better deal than it can get in a merger.)

The "long purse" story relies on the presumption that outside financing is more costly than inside financing (retained earnings). Some asymmetric information between the borrower and the lenders must underlie this cost differential. As Roberts (1987) notes, one institution that alleviates the financing problem for new firms (which are particularly likely to face financial constraints) is venture capitalism. Venture capitalists are often very involved in the day-to-day operations of a firm, which reduces the asymmetry of information between the creditors and the firm and thereby lowers the cost of financing new projects. Equity, however, has its own costs.[56] Much work remains to be done to determine the exact link between financial markets and industry structure.

---

53. Don't the bank and firm 2 have an incentive to write, before period 2, a long-term contract stating that firm 2 will always get financing (i.e., will borrow $K - E$ whatever E is)? Doing so eliminates firm 1's incentive to prey and thus raises firm 2's profit. Thus, it may pay to sign such a contract if it will be observed by firm 1 and if the bank and the firm can commit to abide by this contract. The second condition is troublesome, however. Suppose that firm 1 preys in the first period, so that financing the second-period project is no longer profitable for firm 2 (given the bank's zero-profit condition). Then firm 2 and the bank can increase their profits by renegotiating the contract and not going through with the project. Thus, the long-term contract is not credible unless it is the same as the short-term contract in the text (according to which the project will be financed only if $W(E) \geq 0$).

Bolton and Scharfstein (1987) also consider the link between long-term financial contracts and predation. Their model differs from that of Fudenberg and Tirole in two respects. First, a firm's incentive to repay a loan is linked not with the threat of bankruptcy but with that of no refinancing in subsequent periods. Second, they consider debt contracts that are either observable or unobservable by the predator, whereas Fudenberg and Tirole look only at unobservable debt contracts. Bolton and Scharfstein highlight a trade-off between incentives to perform (i.e., repay the debt) and vulnerability to predatory behavior. Creditors can only respond to the threat of predation by worsening the incentive problem (i.e., raising the probability of refinancing).

54. It would not be difficult to introduce an equilibrium probability of bankruptcy in this model.

55. Or to a financially solid rival (which also has the effect of increasing industry concentration).

56. See section 3 of Holmström and Tirole 1987 for a review of the pros and cons of debt and equity financing.

9.8 Concluding Remarks

Game theory made it possible to understand more clearly some of the earlier intuitions about the signaling properties of price and non-price competition. The theoretical foundations it provided were especially important in the case of price competition, as prices have low commitment value and therefore are, *a priori*, poor candidates for entry barriers. These foundations led many economists to reject the simplistic "Chicago view" of the world (based on perfect information) that price cuts are always natural responses to cost and demand shocks or to increased competitive pressure.

An established firm has an incentive to manipulate the information possessed by prospective entrants or established firms in each of its markets. Although there are exceptions, a sensible strategy is to charge low prices to deter entry or induce exit, and to charge high prices to promote collusion when accommodating the competition.

The welfare analysis of this manipulation of the rivals' information is ambiguous. The young game-theory approach has not yet derived operational criteria for the assessment of price behavior in specific instances. The field is now mature for such developments.

Economists may have neglected the link between financial institutions and predation. The "long purse" story relies on financial imperfections (based on the asymmetry of information in the capital market) rather than on signaling. It states that insufficient retained earnings, stemming in part from the rivals' predatory behavior, may prevent young or financially constrained firms from expanding or from renewing their equipment. Furthermore, the prospect of tough competition from the established firms may reduce entry. The welfare consequences of capital-market imperfections in oligopoly may be serious, and deserve further analysis.

9.9 Supplementary Section: Darwinian Selection in an Industry

In this section, we take up the model of the war of attrition (see chapter 8) to develop an example of "bilateral predation." We consider an industry in which there is initially a surplus number of firms, so that the departure of some is a necessary condition for the survival of the others. Predatory behavior is passive, in that each firm waits for the other firm(s) to exit first.

The war of attrition studied here, unlike that in chapter 8, has asymmetric information about payoffs. Each firm is uncertain about its rivals' profit or cost in the market. Behind the waiting strategy lies the secret hope of each firm that the war of attrition will prove very costly for its rivals. If this does not happen and a firm's rivals insist upon staying in the industry, the firm must eventually leave the industry. As we shall see, a war of attrition selects the healthiest or the most motivated firms (that is, those whose actual losses are smallest or whose future profits are highest). Beyond this Darwinian flavor,[57] the asymmetric-information war of attrition has the advantage of allowing firms to make positive expected profits.[58,59]

The idea of the war of attrition was pioneered by theoretical biologists (see, e.g., Maynard Smith 1974 and Bishop et al. 1978). Riley (1980) and Kreps and Wilson (1982) introduced an asymmetric-information version to the realm of economics. Kreps and Wilson demonstrated that although a war of attrition resembles a "war of entrenchment" and although predatory pricing behavior of the sort discussed in section 9.6 above resembles more a "war of extermination," the two behaviors are closely related in a formal sense: They both are part of the same signaling methodology.[60]

Consider a simple example of a war of attrition in an industry with increasing returns (i.e., a stripped-down version of the Fudenberg-Tirole [1986c] model). There

---

57. There also exist competitive (as opposed to strategic) models of selection in industries. The idea that the unfit are swept away is developed in Alchian 1950 and in Nelson and Winter 1982. Optimizing models of industry selection in which firms learn about their costs after entering are analyzed in Jovanovic 1982, Lippman and Rumelt 1982, and Hopenhayn 1986.

58. Recall from chapter 8 that if the war of attrition occurs at all, the firms make no expected profit: For a firm to be willing to fight, it must be the case that its rival will give up with positive probability. From this, we concluded that each firm is indifferent between staying and exiting at each instant, which means that both firms *ex ante* expect no profit. See Milgrom and Weber 1986

for a discussion of the link between complete-information and incomplete-information wars of attrition.

59. A further advantage is that under some conditions the equilibrium is unique (see below); there exist several equilibria under complete information.

60. To see the analogy, note that if a multimarket incumbent (see section 9.6) acquiesces to entry in a market and reveals that predation is costly to him, he gives up the potential benefits of future entry deterrence. Similarly, a firm that exits the market abandons the potential monopoly profit on this market.

are two firms, $i = 1, 2$. At time 0, both firms are in the industry. Before paying their fixed costs, they each earn a gross duopoly profit of $\Pi^d > 0$ per unit of time. As long as one of the firms has not left the industry, profit remains unchanged. If at moment T firm i leaves the industry, firm j earns a gross monopoly profit of $\Pi^m > \Pi^d$ per unit of time starting from this moment and continuing into the future. The two firms have fixed costs $f_1 > 0$ and $f_2 > 0$ per unit of time; the fixed costs are incurred only if the firm is in the industry. The net profit of firm i per unit of time is $\Pi^d - f_i$ in a duopoly situation, $\Pi^m - f_i$ in a monopoly situation, and 0 when the firm has left the industry.

The fixed cost of a firm may be interpreted as the operating cost that the firm must incur to be in the industry plus the opportunity cost of profits forgone in other ventures. Assume that only firm i knows f_i. Firm j, its rival, has a probability distribution $g_i(f_i)$ over f_i. Assume that g_i is defined on $[0, +\infty)$ and is continuous and strictly positive. Let $G_i(f_i)$ be the cumulative distribution $[G_i(0) = 0, G_i(+\infty) = 1]$. All the other variables (including probability distributions) are known to both firms.

Suppose that firm 1 is the first firm to leave the industry, and that it does so at moment T. Firm 2 becomes a monopolist from that moment on. (We do not allow reentry, although the equilibrium we derive remains an equilibrium even if such behavior is allowed.) The present discounted values of profit over time for the two firms are

$$V_1 = \int_0^T (\Pi^d - f_1)e^{-rt}dt$$

and

$$V_2 = \int_0^T (\Pi^d - f_2)e^{-rt}dt + \int_T^\infty (\Pi^m - f_2)e^{-rt}dt.$$

V_2 and V_1 are defined in an analogous way when firm 2 is the first one to leave and does so at moment T (where r indicates the interest rate).

From observing these profits, we can deduce the following simple results: Any firm that has fixed costs greater than the monopoly profit will never enter (or will never stay beyond date 0) because, whatever the behavior of

its rival, it will earn a negative profit in the industry. At the same time, a firm that has fixed costs smaller than the duopoly profit will enter and will always stay in the industry.

We have in mind here an industry in which the probability that the fixed costs are greater than the duopoly profit is high (i.e., $G_i(\Pi^d)$ is close to zero).[61] Thus, the industry is similar to a natural monopoly, in that each firm may be capable of surviving as a monopoly but each loses money in a duopoly. In the war of attrition that follows, the firm that is first to leave is the loser.

Each firm's strategy is simple: It amounts to a stopping time T_i at which firm i leaves the industry if firm j has not done so before. Of course, this stopping time depends on the fixed cost of the firm: $T_i(f_i)$. Therefore, let $\{T_1(f_1), T_2(f_2)\}$ be the two stopping times conditional on the fixed costs. (Since fixed costs are private information, each firm does not know the exact stopping time of its rival; rather, each has only a probability distribution over this variable derived from its probability distribution over the rival's fixed cost.)

Suppose that firm 1, with fixed cost f_1, chooses stopping time T. Then the present discounted value of its expected profit over time is equal to

$$\text{Prob}[T_2(f_2) \geqslant T] \cdot \int_0^T (\Pi^d - f_1)e^{-rt}dt$$

$$+ \int_{\{f_2|T_2(f_2) < T\}} \left(\int_0^{T_2(f_2)} (\Pi^d - f_1)e^{-rt}dt \right.$$

$$\left. + \int_{T_2(f_2)}^\infty (\Pi^m - f_1)e^{-rt}dt \right) g_2(f_2)df_2.$$

We seek the $T = T_1(f_1)$ that maximizes the above expression. (The maximization exercise for firm 2 is analogous.) Thus, we obtain a Nash equilibrium (a perfect Bayesian equilibrium, in the language of the Game Theory User's Manual). In spite of the complexity of the firms' objective functions, the solution turns out to be quite simple.

From the profit expression, it is easy to show that if $f_i > f_i'$,

$$T_i(f_i) \leqslant T_i(f_i').[62]$$

---

61. Assuming $G_i(\Pi^d) > 0$ is realistic. It also yields uniqueness of the solution. See exercise 9.2 for an example of multiplicity in the pure natural-monopoly case—i.e., the case in which $G_i(\Pi^d) = 0$.

62. To obtain this, write the two "incentive-compatibility constraints": that the firm prefers $T_i(f_i)$ to $T_i(f_i')$ when its cost is f_i and the reverse when its cost is f_i'. Adding these two constraints yields the desired result.

In other words, the higher firm i's fixed cost, the sooner that firm leaves (a Darwinian characteristic of this selection). Moreover, the function T_i can be shown to be strictly decreasing and thus differentiable almost everywhere.[63] We define

$$F_i(t) \equiv T_i^{-1}(t)$$

to be firm i's level of fixed cost such that firm i exits at date t.

We will now derive the conditions governing the functions F_i (or, in an equivalent manner, the functions T_i). To do this, we consider firm i at the moment (t) when its fixed cost is such that it decides to leave—that is, when $f_i = F_i(t)$. Now suppose that firm i decides to stay in the industry until $t + dt$ and to leave at that moment if firm j has not left. We calculate the probability that firm j leaves the industry during this time interval conditional on its not having done so before t. This last condition means that firm j's fixed cost is smaller than $F_j(t)$. Firm j will give up between t and $t + dt$ if its fixed cost falls between $F_j(t + dt)$ and $F_j(t)$, which has the conditional probability

$$\frac{g_j(F_j(t))}{G_j(F_j(t))}[-F'_j(t)dt].$$

Since firm i loses $F_i(t) - \Pi^d$ per unit of time, it must be the case that

$$F_i(t) - \Pi^d = \left(-\frac{g_j(F_j(t))}{G_j(F_j(t))}F'_j(t)\right)\left(\frac{\Pi^m - F_i(t)}{r}\right); \qquad (9.19)$$

otherwise, with fixed cost equal to $F_i(t)$, firm i could increase its expected profit by moving its departure date forward or backward.

Equation 9.19 and its analogue for firm j form a system of differential equations. To the latter are added the following "boundary conditions":

$$F_i(0) = \Pi^m \text{ and } \lim_{t \to \infty} F_i(t) = \Pi^d \text{ for all } i.$$

The first of these conditions comes from the property that a firm will enter only if it can survive as a monopoly (and if it does enter, it at least waits to see whether its rival gives up immediately[64]). The second condition is related to the fact that the instantaneous probability that a rival will leave tends toward zero as time tends toward infinity

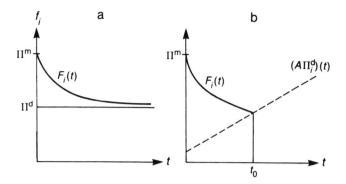

Figure 9.3
Selection in a war of attrition. (a) Stationary payoffs: infinite selection. (b) Nonstationary payoffs: possibility of finite selection.

and to the fact that a firm that is willing to fight must sustain negligible duopoly losses.

In equilibrium, selection may take a long time (in the sense that there is a positive probability that, at any moment, the industry will still be shared by the two firms and a positive probability that one of the firms will have dropped out (see figure 9.3a)). A different result can be obtained if we generalize the model by allowing the profit functions to vary over time. Fudenberg and Tirole (1986c) allow learning by doing as well as time-varying demands (i.e., a growing or declining industry). In the case of the generalized model, the selection process may stop in finite time, as a firm that is not viable as a duopoly at date 0 may become so after demand has grown or production costs have decreased. Figure 9.3b represents a finite selection process in the case of growing profits. If both firms are still in at date t_0, they will remain a duopoly forever. Thus, at t_0 firm i must be indifferent between leaving and staying in a duopoly forever when it has cost $F_i(t_0)$. This replaces the previous boundary conditions,

$$\lim_{t \to \infty} F_i(t) = \Pi^d,$$

by

$$F_i(t_0) = (A\Pi_i^d)(t_0) \text{ for } i = 1, 2,$$

where $(A\Pi_i^d)(t)$ denotes firm i's average (discounted) duopoly profit from date t on; i.e.,

$$(A\Pi_i^d)(t) \equiv \int_t^\infty \Pi_i^d(s) r \, e^{-r(s-t)} ds,$$

---

63. See Fudenberg and Tirole 1986c for a full characterization of equilibrium.

64. This has a positive probability as long as $G_j(\Pi^m) < 1$.

and $\Pi_i^d(s)$ is firm i's gross duopoly profit at date s.[65] Fudenberg and Tirole also show that the perfect Bayesian equilibrium of this game exists and is unique.

Comparative-statics results from this model are meager. However, consider the symmetric case ($G_1 \equiv G_2 = G$). It can be shown that when the cost distribution shifts toward higher costs, in the sense of a higher hazard rate $g(f)/G(f)$ for all f, selection takes longer, in that $T_i(f_i)$ increases for all $f_i \leqslant \Pi^m$.[66] (Of course, to obtain the time distribution of exit, one must also take the change in the distribution of costs into account.)

The welfare results, as in many signaling models of predation, are ambiguous. On the one hand, if the duopolists succeed in maintaining price collusion, the social value of competition is low and a social planner would like to hasten the exit process. The monopoly rent is dissipated through duplication of fixed costs during the war of attrition, rather than through low prices. In contrast, if the price under duopoly competition is close to the marginal cost, firms may exit too soon from a social point of view, as they do not internalize the gain in consumer surplus associated with competition.

There are two meanings that can be given to the Darwinian notion that competition selects the fittest firm. The first is that a given firm exits later when its cost is lower. We noted that this property always holds in wars of attrition. The second meaning compares the two firms and states that the remaining firm is more efficient than the exiting one. This property is satisfied only for symmetric profit functions and cost distributions. It is easily seen that if the two firms' costs are drawn from different distributions, competition may select the wrong firm (the one with the higher cost).

Fudenberg and Kreps (1987) ask: What is a firm's willingness to wage wars of attrition when it fights in several markets and its private information is correlated across markets? To make things concrete, suppose that firm $i = 0$ is in N geographically distinct markets. In market j, it faces firm j ($j = 1, \ldots, N$). Its fixed cost per market, f_0, is the same in all markets, and is distributed according to the distribution $G_0(f_0)$ from the viewpoint of its rivals. Firm j's fixed cost, f_j, is drawn from the distribution $G(f_j)$. The N rivals' costs are drawn independently. The markets are identical and (except for f_0) independent.

Suppose first that the behavior in one market is not observed in the other markets. Then firm 0 wages N independent and identical wars of attrition, each described as above. The exit behavior follows the differential equations 9.19.

Assume next that there is an informational leakage. Firm j observes what happens in market $j' \neq j$. The N wars of attrition are simultaneous (i.e., they start at the same time). Suppose that reentry is prohibitively costly, so that when a firm exits its rival has conquered the market forever. Fudenberg and Kreps show that the equilibrium is unchanged. That is, playing wars of attrition against N opponents is equivalent to playing against one opponent (except that payoffs are multiplied by N); information leakages do not matter. To see this, note that the differential equation for each firm j ($j = 1, \ldots, N$) is unchanged. Suppose that the incumbent, if it exits one market, exits all remaining duopoly markets simultaneously (it obviously does not exit monopolized markets, as reentry is not feasible). If $N - k$ rivals have not yet conceded at some date t, then the cost of staying per unit of time is

$$(N - k)(f_0 - \Pi^d).$$

The expected gain from staying is also multiplied by $N - k$; it is equal to

$$(N - k)\left(-\frac{g(F(t))}{G(F(t))}F'(t)\right)\left(\frac{\Pi^m - f_0}{r}\right),$$

where $F(t)$ describes the symmetric behavior of each of its rivals. Thus, the differential equation for the incumbent is unchanged, and for that reason the equilibrium is unchanged. Fudenberg and Kreps then investigate the role of the no-reentry condition and show that, under some assumptions about the nature of equilibrium when the incumbent has revealed its type, the information leakage between markets may benefit or hurt the multimarket firm.

The following exercises pertain to incomplete-information wars of attrition.

---

65. If $\Pi_i^d(s)$ is increasing, $(A\Pi_i^d)(t)$ is also increasing.

66. Equation 9.19 provides the intuition for this. The higher g/G suggests a lower slope $|F'(t)|$ for the exit function.

*Exercise 9.2**** Riley (1980) considers a war of attrition in which two animals of the same species both desire the same food source or mate. Both use up valuable time to fight for the prize. Eventually, at some date t, one of the contestants departs, and has payoff $-t$. The winner has payoff $v - t$. Animal i's valuation for the prize, v_i, is private information and is drawn from a distribution $G(\cdot)$ with density $g(\cdot)$. ($G(0) = 0$, $G(+\infty) = 1$.) Let $V_i(t)$ denote the valuation such that animal i drops out at date t.

(i) Use an intuitive argument to show that the differential equations for equilibrium are

$$V_j(t) V_i'(t) g(V_i(t)) = 1 - G(V_i(t)).$$

(ii) Suppose that $G(v) = 1 - e^{-v}$. Show that there exists a continuum of equilibria indexed by K in $[0, +\infty)$ such that $V_1(t) = K\sqrt{t}$ and $V_2(t) = (2/K)\sqrt{t}$. How does this differ from the war of attrition discussed in the present section?

*Exercise 9.3**** Kreps and Wilson (1982) consider the following war of attrition: There are two players, $i = 1, 2$. Time is continuous from 0 to 1. When one player concedes, the game ends. Each player can be either "strong" (with probability p for player 1 and q for player 2) or "weak" (with probabilities $1 - p$ and $1 - q$). A strong player enjoys fighting and therefore never concedes. A weak player 1 loses 1 per unit of time while fighting and makes $a > 0$ per unit of time when its rival has conceded; a weak player 2 loses 1 per unit of time while fighting and makes $b > 0$ per unit of time when its rival has conceded. Thus, a weak player 1 has payoff $a(1 - t) - t$ when it wins at t and payoff $-t$ when it concedes at t; similarly for player 2. There is no discounting.

(i) Show that from time 0^+ on, the posterior beliefs p_t and q_t of each player about the other must belong to the curve $q = p^{b/a}$.

(ii) Show that one of the weak types exits with positive probability at date 0 exactly (that is, a player's cumulative probability distribution of exit times exhibits an atom at $t = 0$). How are the weak types' payoffs affected by a, b, p, and q?

Answers and Hints

Exercise 9.1

(i) No information sharing: Let p_2^e denote firm 2's expected price.

$$\max[(1 - p_1 + p_2^e)(p_1 - c_1)]$$

yields

$$p_1 = (1 + p_2^e + c_1)/2.$$

Thus,

$$p_1^e = \mathop{E}_{c_1} p_1 = (1 + p_2^e + c^e)/2.$$

By symmetry, $p_1^e = p_2^e = 1 + c^e$. Firm 1's expected profit conditional on c_1 is thus

$$\mathop{E}_{c_2} \Pi^1 = (2 + c^e - c_1)^2/4.$$

Taking the expectation of this expression with respect to c_1 yields the result.

(ii) Information sharing: c_1 and c_2 are common knowledge at the date of price competition. See chapter 7.

(iii) Information sharing has two effects. First, efficiency is increased, because producers have better information about costs and demand. More efficient price or output decisions result from a finer information structure. Second, information sharing affects the nature of product-market competition, and makes it more or less "collusive." In general, the private (and social) desirability of information sharing depends on the model specification.

Most of the literature (like this exercise) considers linear demand functions. Clarke (1983) and Gal-Or (1985) show that information exchange about demand does not take place under quantity competition. Vives (1984) considers differentiated products and shows that whether information is shared depends on whether goods are complements or substitutes and on whether firms compete in price or in quantities. Shapiro (1986) considers quantity competition and allows correlation between the costs; he shows that consumer surplus falls but profit and welfare go up when information is shared.

Exercise 9.2

(i) At time t, animal 1 (say) loses dt by waiting dt longer. But it wins a price v_1 with conditional probability

$$\frac{[1 - G(V_2(t))] - [1 - G(V_2(t + dt))]}{1 - G(V_2(t))}$$

$$\simeq \frac{g(V_2(t)) V_2'(t) dt}{1 - G(V_2(t))}.$$

By definition, the loss must equal the expected benefit for $v_1 = V_1(t)$. This yields the differential equation.

(ii) For the exponential distribution,

$$g/(1 - G) = 1.$$

Hence, the differential equations become

$$V_j(t) V_i'(t) = 1.$$

The economic difference with the Fudenberg-Tirole model is that the Riley "economy" is a natural monopoly with probability $\underline{1}$. That is, it is common knowledge that both members are not viable as a duopoly (this would correspond to $G_i(\Pi^d) = 0$ for all i, in the text). This engenders a technical difference: In the text, $G_j(F_j(t))$ tends to $G_j(\Pi^d) > 0$ when t tends to infinity; here, $1 - G_j(V_j(t))$ tends to $1 - G_j(\infty) = 0$ when t tends to infinity. Looking at the differential equations, one gets an intuition as to why the natural-monopoly case loses a boundary condition at infinity, which yields the multiplicity.

Exercise 9.3

(i) Let us look for an equilibrium in which the weak types are, for all $t > 0$, indifferent between staying and exiting. Let a weak player 1 (a weak player 2) drop with conditional probability $\Pi_t dt$ ($\rho_t dt$) between t and $t + dt$. For a weak player 1 to be indifferent between staying and exiting, it must be the case that

$$1 = [(1 - q_t)\rho_t][a(1 - t)].$$

But, from Bayes' rule,

$$\dot{q}_t = q_t(1 - q_t)\rho_t.^{[67]}$$

These two equations yield

$$\dot{q}_t = q_t/a(1 - t)$$

and, by symmetry,

$$\dot{p}_t = p_t/b(1 - t).$$

Dividing, we obtain

$$\frac{\dot{q}_t}{q_t} = \frac{b}{a}\frac{\dot{p}_t}{p_t},$$

or

$$q_t = kp_t^{b/a}.$$

It is easily seen that $k = 1$. Suppose, for instance, that $k < 1$. p_t would reach 1 at date $t_0 < 1$, while $q_{t_0} = k < 1$. Player 2, convinced that player 1 is strong, drops out immediately with probability $(1 - q_{t_0}) > 0$. Thus, a weak player 1 should wait at $t_0 - \varepsilon$.

(ii) At date 0, the players are not on the curve $q = p^{b/a}$. Thus, one of them must drop out with strictly positive probability so as to reach the curve and move along this curve from then on. For more details see Kreps and Wilson 1982.

---

67. Derive this by taking the limit of Bayes' rule in discrete time:

$$q(t + dt) = \frac{q(t)}{q(t) + [1 - q(t)](1 - \rho_t dt)}.$$

References

Alchian, A. 1950. Uncertainty, Evolution and Economic Theory. *Journal of Political Economy* 58: 211–222.

Areeda, P., and D. Turner. 1975. Predatory Pricing and Related Practices under Section 2 of the Sherman Act. *Harvard Law Review* 88: 697–733.

Bagwell, K. 1985. Advertising and Limit Pricing. Discussion Paper 131, Studies in Industry Economics, Stanford University.

Bagwell, K., and G. Ramey. 1987. Advertising and Limit Pricing. Mimeo.

Bain, J. 1949. A Note on Pricing in Monopoly and Oligopoly. *American Economic Review* 39: 448–464.

Benoit, J.-P. 1983. Entry with Exit: An Extensive Form Treatment of Predation with Financial Constraints. IMSSS Technical Report 405, Stanford University.

Benoit, J.-P. 1984. Financially Constrained Entry in a Game with Incomplete Information. *Rand Journal of Economics* 15: 490–499.

Bikhchandani, S. 1986. *Market Games with Few Traders*. Ph.D. thesis, Graduate School of Business, Stanford University.

Bishop, D., C. Cannings, and J. Maynard Smith. 1978. The War of Attrition with Random Rewards. *Journal of Theoretical Biology* 74: 377–388.

Bolton, P., and D. Scharfstein. 1987. Long-Term Financial Contracts and the Theory of Predation. Mimeo, Harvard University.

Bork, R. 1978. *The Antitrust Paradox*. New York: Basic Books.

Bulow, J., J. Geanakoplos, and P. Klemperer. 1985. Multimarket Oligopoly: Strategic Substitutes and Complements. *Journal of Political Economy* 93: 488–511.

Burns, M. 1986. Predatory Pricing and the Acquisition Costs of Competitors. *Journal of Political Economy* 94: 266–296.

Cho, I.-K. 1986. Equilibrium Analysis of Entry Deterrence: Reexamination. Mimeo, Graduate School of Business, University of Chicago.

Clarke, R. 1983. Collusion and the Incentives for Information Sharing. *Bell Journal of Economics* 14: 383–394.

Diamond, D. 1984. Financial Intermediation and Delegated Monitoring. *Review of Economic Studies* 51: 393–414.

Easley, D., R. Masson, and R. Reynolds. 1985. Preying for Time. *Journal of Industrial Organization* 33: 445–460.

Easterbrook, F. 1981a. Predatory Strategies and Counterstrategies. *University of Chicago Law Review* 48: 237–263.

Edwards, C. 1955. Conglomerate Bigness as a Source of Power. In *Business Concentration and Price Policy*, NBER Conference Report (Princeton University Press).

Fried, D. 1984. Incentives for Information Production and Disclosure in a Duopolistic Environment. *Quarterly Journal of Economics* 99: 367–381.

Friedman, J. 1979. On Entry Preventing Behavior. In *Applied Game Theory*, ed. S. J. Brams et al. Vienna: Physica-Verlag.

Fudenberg, D., and D. Kreps. 1987. Reputation and Multiple Opponents I: Identical Entrants. *Review of Economic Studies* 54: 541–568.

Fudenberg, D., and J. Tirole. 1985. Predation without Reputation. Working Paper 377, Massachusetts Institute of Technology.

Fudenberg, D., and J. Tirole. 1986a. *Dynamic Models of Oligopoly*. In *Fundamentals of Pure and Applied Economics*, ed. J. Lesourne and H. Sonnenschein. London: Harwood.

Fudenberg, D., and J. Tirole. 1986b. A "Signal-Jamming" Theory of Predation. *Rand Journal of Economics* 17: 366–376.

Fudenberg, D., and J. Tirole. 1986c. A Theory of Exit in Duopoly. *Econometrica* 54: 943–960.

Fudenberg, D., and J. Tirole. 1987. Understanding Rent Dissipation: On the Use of Game Theory in Industrial Organization. *American Economic Review, Papers and Proceedings* 77: 176–183.

Gale, D., and M. Hellwig. 1985. Incentive Compatible Debt Contracts: The One-Period Problem. *Review of Economic Studies* 52: 647–664.

Gal-Or, E. 1985. Information Sharing in Oligopoly. *Econometrica* 53: 329–343.

Gal-Or, E. 1986. Information Transmission: Cournot and Bertrand Equilibria. *Review of Economic Studies* 53: 85–92.

Gal-Or, E. 1987. First Mover Disadvantages with Private Information. *Review of Economic Studies* 54: 279–292.

Gaskins, D. 1971. Dynamic Limit Pricing: Optimal Pricing under the Threat of Entry. *Journal of Economic Theory* 2: 306–322.

Harrington, J. 1985. Limit Pricing when the Potential Entrant Is Uncertain of his Cost Function. Mimeo, Johns Hopkins University.

Holmström, B., and J. Tirole. 1987. The Theory of the Firm. In *Handbook of Industrial Organization*, ed. R. Schmalensee and R. Willig (Amsterdam: North-Holland, forthcoming).

Holmström, B. 1983. Managerial Incentive Problems: A Dynamic Perspective. In *Essays in Economics and Management in Honor of Lars Wahlbeck*. Helsinki: Swedish School of Economics.

Hopenhayn, H. 1986. A Competitive Stochastic Model of Entry and Exit to an Industry. Mimeo, University of Minnesota.

Joskow, P., and A. Klevorick. 1979. A Framework for Analyzing Predatory Pricing Policy. *Yale Law Journal* 89: 213–270.

Jovanovic, B. 1982. Selection and Evolution of Industry. *Econometrica* 50: 649–670.

Kreps, D., and R. Wilson. 1982. Reputation and Imperfect Information. *Journal of Economic Theory* 27: 253–279.

Kreps, D., P. Milgrom, J. Roberts, and R. Wilson. 1982. Reputation and Imperfect Information. *Journal of Economic Theory* 27: 253–279.

Li, L. 1985. Cournot Oligopoly with Information Sharing. *Rand Journal of Economics* 16: 521–536.

Lippman, S., and R. Rumelt. 1982. Uncertain Imitability: An Analysis of Interfirm Differences in Efficiency under Competition. *Bell Journal of Economics* 13: 418–438.

McAfee, P., and J. McMillan. 1987. Auctions and Bidding. *Journal of Economic Literature* 25: 699–754.

McGee, J. 1958. Predatory Price Cutting: The Standard Oil (NJ) Case. *Journal of Law and Economics* 1: 137–169.

McGee, J. 1980. Predatory Pricing Revisited. *Journal of Law and Economics*, 23: 289–330.

Mailath, G. 1984. The Welfare Implications of Differential Information in a Dynamic Duopoly Model. Mimeo, Princeton University.

Mailath, G. 1985a. Welfare in a Simultaneous Signaling Duopoly Model. CARESS Working Paper 85-29, University of Pennsylvania.

Mailath, G. 1985b. Incentive Compatibility in Signaling Games with a Continuum of Types. Mimeo, University of Pennsylvania.

Maskin, E., and J. Riley. 1985. Auction Theory with Private Values. *American Economic Review, Papers and Proceedings* 75: 150–155.

Matthews, S., and L. Mirman. 1983. Equilibrium Limit Pricing: The Effects of Private Information and Stochastic Demand. *Econometrica* 51: 981–996.

Maynard Smith, J. 1974. The Theory of Games and the Evolution of Animal Conflicts. *Journal of Theoretical Biology* 47: 209–221.

Milgrom, P. 1987a. Auction Theory. In *Advances in Economic Theory: Invited Papers for the Fifth World Congress of the Econometric Society*, ed. T. Bewley. Cambridge University Press.

Milgrom, P. 1987b. Adverse Selection without Hidden Information. Working Paper 8742, University of California, Berkeley.

Milgrom, P., and J. Roberts. 1982a. Limit Pricing and Entry Under Incomplete Information: An Equilibrium Analysis. *Econometrica* 50: 443–460.

Milgrom, P., and J. Roberts. 1982b. Predation, Reputation and Entry Deterrence. *Journal of Economic Theory* 27: 280–312.

Milgrom, P., and J. Roberts. 1987. Informational Asymmetries, Strategic Behavior and Industrial Organization. *American Economic Review, Papers and Proceedings* 77: 184–193.

Milgrom, P., and R. Weber. 1982. A Theory of Auctions and Competitive Bidding. *Econometrica* 50: 1089–1122.

Milgrom, P., and R. Weber. 1986. Distributional Strategies for Games with Incomplete Information. *Mathematics of Operations Research* 10: 619–631.

Nalebuff, B., and R. Zeckhauser. 1985. The Ambiguous Antitrust Implications of Information Sharing. Mimeo, Princeton and Harvard Universities.

Nelson, R., and S. Winter. 1982. *An Economic Theory of Economic Change*, Cambridge, Mass.: Harvard University Press.

Novshek, W., and H. Sonnenschein. 1982. Fulfilled Expectations Cournot Duopoly with Information Acquisition and Release. *Bell Journal of Economics* 13: 214–218.

Ordover, J., and G. Saloner. 1987. Predation, Monopolization and Antitrust. In *Handbook of Industrial Organization*, ed. R. Schmalensee and R. Willig (Amsterdam: North-Holland, forthcoming).

Ordover, J., and R. Willig. 1981. An Economic Definition of Predation: Pricing and Product Innovation. *Yale Law Journal* 91: 8–53.

Ortega-Reichert, A. 1967. *Models for Competitive Bidding Under Uncertainty*, Ph.D. thesis, Stanford University.

Ponssard, J. P. 1979. The Strategic Role of Information on the Demand Function in an Oligopolistic Environment. *Management Science* 25: 243–250.

Posner, R. 1976. *Antitrust Law: An Economic Perspective*. University of Chicago Press.

Posner, R. 1979. The Chicago School of Antitrust Analysis. *University of Pennsylvania Law Review* 127: 925–948.

Riley, J. 1980. Strong Evolutionary Equilibrium and the War of Attrition. *Journal of Theoretical Biology* 82: 383–400.

Riordan, M. 1985. Imperfect Information and Dynamic Conjectural Variations. *Rand Journal of Economics* 16: 41–50.

Roberts, J. 1986. A Signaling Model of Predatory Pricing. *Oxford Economic Papers* (supplement) 38: 75–93.

Roberts, J. 1987. Battles for Market Share: Incomplete Information, Aggressive Strategic Pricing, and Competitive Dynamics. In *Advances in Economic Theory: Invited Papers for the Fifth World Congress of the Econometric Society*, ed. T. Bewley. Cambridge University Press.

Saloner, G. 1981. Dynamic Equilibrium Limit Pricing in an Uncertain Environment. Mimeo, Graduate School of Business, Stanford University.

Saloner, G. 1987. Predation, Merger and Incomplete Information. *Rand Journal of Economics* 18: 165–186.

Salop, S., and C. Shapiro. 1980. A Guide to Test Market Predation. Mimeo.

Scharfstein, D. 1984. A Policy to Prevent Rational Test-Market Predation. *Rand Journal of Economics* 2: 229–243.

Scherer, F. 1980. *Industrial Market Structure and Economic Performance*, second edition. Chicago: Rand-McNally.

Schmalensee, R. 1979. On the Use of Economic Models in Antitrust: The ReaLemon Case. *University of Pennsylvania Law Review* 127: 994–1050.

Selten, R. 1978. The Chain-Store Paradox. *Theory and Decision* 9: 127–159.

Shapiro, C. 1986. Exchange of Cost Information in Oligopoly. *Review of Economic Studies* 52: 433–446.

Telser, L. 1966. Cutthroat Competition and the Long Purse. *Journal of Law and Economics* 9: 259–277.

Townsend, R. 1979. Optimal Contracts and Competitive Markets with Costly State Verification. *Journal of Economic Theory* 21: 265–293.

Williamson, O. 1977. Predatory Pricing: A Strategic and Welfare Analysis. *Yale Law Journal* 87: 284–340.

Wilson, R. 1985. Reputations in Games and Markets. In *Game-Theoretic Models of Bargaining*, ed. A Roth. Cambridge University Press.

Vives, X. 1984. Duopoly Information Equilibrium: Cournot and Bertrand. *Journal of Economic Theory* 34: 71–94.

Yamey, B. 1972. Predatory Price Cutting: Notes and Comments. *Journal of Law and Economics* 15: 129–142.

Research and Development and the Adoption of New Technologies

This chapter has two distinct parts. The first part (sections 10.1 through 10.4) analyzes the private and social incentives to bring about technological innovations; the second is concerned with how already existing innovations are adopted in the marketplace.

Research and development (R&D) is crucial, not only in the analysis of an individual industry, but also from an economy-wide viewpoint. Solow's (1957) discovery that only a small fraction of per-capita growth (10 percent for the U.S. nonfarm sector over the period 1909–1949) was associated with an increase in the ratio of capital to labor called economists' attention to the role of technological progress in improving welfare.[1] This central role implies that careful attention should be given to the firms' incentives to innovate and to adopt new technologies.

It is customary to distinguish three stages of research: basic research aimed at deriving fundamental knowledge (pursued mainly at universities and government agencies); applied research associated with engineering; and development, which brings products and processes into commercial use. Then there is the post-research stage, during which the innovation diffuses through the industry via licensing, imitation of patented innovations, or adoption of unpatented innovations.

It is also usual to distinguish between product innovations and process innovations. Product innovations create new goods and services; process innovations reduce the cost of producing existing products. Of course, it is not always possible to draw a clear line between the two types of innovation. One firm's new product may lead to a new process for another firm. Also, a product innovation can generally be regarded as a process innovation—imagine that the new product existed prior to the innovation, and that the innovation simply reduced its production cost.

---

1. Certainly a non-negligible fraction of the residual is due to factors other than technical progress (see, e.g., Denison's [1962] high estimate of the role of an improved education of labor). But there is no denying that technical progress is a major component of the residual.

In sections 10.1 and 10.2 we will consider Schumpeter's (1943) thesis about the link between market structure and R&D. Schumpeter's basic point—that monopoly situations and R&D are intimately related—is articulated in two clearly distinct arguments: that monopolies are natural breeding grounds for R&D, and that if one wants to induce firms to undertake R&D one must accept the creation of monopolies as a necessary evil. We will ignore the first argument, which is controversial and which is not central to Schumpeter's thesis[2]; we will focus on the second argument, which accords to innovation the status of a public good, the supply of which must be encouraged by a system of patents. Any innovation created by one firm provides usable information to other firms at little or no cost. While all firms stand prepared to use such information, no one firm is willing to pay the sums of money (often huge) necessary to produce it without compensation. In practice, such compensation often comes through the granting of a patent that provides the innovating firm with a temporary monopoly and, consequently, allows it to recoup its R&D costs. (An unpatented innovation can also confer a temporary monopoly position because it involves a trade secret or because there is a lag in imitation.) The dilemma of the patent system is that, in encouraging R&D, it prevents the diffusion of innovation and consequently creates a noncompetitive situation.

The private benefits associated with an innovation protected by a patent are considered in section 10.1. Section 10.2 introduces the cost side (the R&D production process) and describes patent races. These two sections emphasize the relationship between these problems and those of product selection and investment (which were considered in chapters 2, 7, and 8). After all, innovating amounts to creating new products. Therefore, the issue of the market's incentive to engage in R&D is similar to that of competitive product diversity. On the cost side, R&D activity is an instance of investment with some specificities (the great randomness of the returns from the investment, the preemption effect of patentable innova-

tions, the public-good aspect of unpatentable ones). The welfare effects of patent protection are analyzed in section 10.3. Section 10.4 discusses alternative, more centralized methods of encouraging R&D: the prize system and the contractual mechanism. The supplementary section introduces the possibility of licensing an innovation and suggests how this can affect the value of the innovation and the race for a patent.

Inventing new products and processes is not sufficient for economic progress. The innovations must then be properly exploited and diffused through licensing, imitation, or simple adoption. (The difference between imitation and adoption is that an imitator must pay for reverse engineering—e.g., figuring out another firm's technology.) The second part of this chapter is particularly concerned with the adoption process. We assume that a new technology is available to all firms at some cost. After a brief introduction, we analyze the preemptive aspects of the adoption of new technologies. In section 10.5 we consider whether, in oligopoly, the timing of adoption is likely to involve "bunching" (almost simultaneous adoption by all firms) or "spacing of adoption" between firms. Section 10.6 reviews the recent literature on standardization and network externalities. Network externalities exist when the consumers of a given good enjoy this good all the more when it is consumed by many other consumers (as in the case of telephone networks or videocassette recorders). Such consumption externalities introduce interesting features to the adoption process.

10.1 Incentives as a Function of the Market Structure: The Value of Innovation

In his pioneering 1962 article, Arrow asked: What is the gain from innovation to a firm that is the only one to undertake R&D, given that its innovation is protected by a patent of unlimited duration?[3,4] Here we will attempt to isolate the "pure" incentive to innovate, i.e., that which is

---

2. Schumpeter remains vague about whether the first argument is associated with monopoly power or with bigness. He suggests that large firms are better qualified or more eager to undertake R&D than smaller firms because increasing returns are prevalent in R&D; because R&D activity involves a high level of risk that is difficult to eliminate with insurance (for reasons of moral hazard), and large firms are more diversified and therefore more willing to take risks; because innovation, once generated, is implemented more rapidly in a large firm because there is an appropriate production structure; and because a monopolist

does not have competitors ready to imitate his innovation or to circumvent an existing patent on this innovation.

3. The analysis here also follows Dasgupta and Stiglitz 1980. This section, as well as sections 10.2 and 10.8, draws from a survey by Guesnerie and Tirole (1985).

4. The more realistic case of a patent of limited duration or an innovation likely to eventually become obsolete or be circumvented is treated similarly.

independent of any strategic considerations of preemptive innovation. We will put off discussing the cost of innovation (which cost is usually influenced by pressure from competitors, and thus by strategic considerations) for the next section.

For an example, let us use a process innovation. To simplify, we will assume that this innovation lowers the unit production cost of a particular good from an initial high level $\bar{c}$ to a level $\underline{c} < \bar{c}$. Our thought experiment will be to ask how much the firm would be willing to pay to obtain technology $\underline{c}$ given that no one else will buy it. To construct a benchmark for evaluating the incentives offered by the market, we start by considering the firm's incentive to innovate when it is run by a social planner.

10.1.1 Social Planner

Assume that a planner's incentive to innovate is equal to the incremental net social surplus attributable to the innovation. The planner sets a price equal to marginal cost, i.e., $\bar{c}$ before innovation and $\underline{c}$ afterward. Therefore, the additional net social surplus per unit of time is equal to

$$v^s = \int_{\underline{c}}^{\bar{c}} D(c)dc.$$

If the interest rate r is constant, the discounted present value of this change (that is, the social incentive to innovate) is given by

$$V^s = \int_0^\infty e^{-rt} v^s dt = \frac{1}{r} \int_{\underline{c}}^{\bar{c}} D(c)dc.$$

10.1.2 Monopoly

Now assume that a firm is in a monopoly situation in the product market as well as with regard to R&D. Let Π^m be its profit per unit of time. From the envelope theorem, we know that

$$\frac{d\Pi^m}{dc} = \frac{d}{dc}[(p - c)D(p)]$$

$$= \frac{\partial \Pi^m}{\partial p} \frac{dp^m}{dc} + \frac{\partial \Pi^m}{\partial c}$$

$$= \frac{\partial \Pi^m}{\partial c}$$

$$= -D(p^m(c)),$$

where $p^m(c)$ is the monopoly price as a function of cost c. Therefore, the monopolist's incentive to innovate is given by

$$V^m = \frac{1}{r}[\Pi^m(\underline{c}) - \Pi^m(\bar{c})]$$

$$= \frac{1}{r} \int_{\underline{c}}^{\bar{c}} \left(-\frac{d\Pi^m}{dc}\right) dc$$

$$= \frac{1}{r} \int_{\underline{c}}^{\bar{c}} D(p^m(c))dc.$$

Since $p^m(c) > c$ for any c, we see that $V^m < V^s$. This is easy to understand, because monopoly pricing at any cost level yields underproduction as compared with the social optimum. Therefore, the monopolist's cost reductions pertain to a smaller number of units. This result is identical to that obtained in chapter 2, where it was demonstrated that, socially, a monopolist has too low an incentive to introduce a new product, because he cannot fully appropriate the social surplus (unless he can price-discriminate perfectly).

10.1.3 Competition

Finally, consider a situation that is competitive initially. A large number of firms produce a homogeneous good with a technology exhibiting marginal cost $\bar{c}$. These firms are initially involved in Bertrand price competition, so that the market price is $\bar{c}$ and all the firms are earning zero profit. The firm that obtains the new technology exhibiting cost $\underline{c}$ is awarded a patent. Let $p^m(\underline{c})$ be the monopoly price. There are two possible cases: $p^m(\underline{c}) > \bar{c}$ and $p^m(\underline{c}) \leqslant \bar{c}$. In the second case, the innovating firm sets its monopoly price and the other, less efficient firms produce nothing; then the innovation is called *drastic* or *major*. In the first case, the innovator is constrained to charge[5]

---

5. Actually, he will charge $\bar{c} - \varepsilon$ in order to corner the entire market. We assume here that the monopolist's objective function is strictly concave, so that he wants to be as close as possible to his unconstrained optimum.

$p = \bar{c}$ because there is a competitive supply from the other firms at price $p = \bar{c}$. The innovation is then called *nondrastic* or *minor*.

In the case of a nondrastic innovation, the innovator's profit per unit of time is

$$\Pi^c = (\bar{c} - \underline{c})D(\bar{c}),$$

and therefore the incentive to innovate in the competitive situation is

$$V^c = \frac{1}{r}(\bar{c} - \underline{c})D(\bar{c}).$$

Note that $\bar{c} < p^m(\underline{c}) \leqslant p^m(c)$ by assumption, and therefore $D(\bar{c}) > D(p^m(c))$ for all $c \geqslant \underline{c}$. From this, we derive

$$V^m = \frac{1}{r}\int_{\underline{c}}^{\bar{c}} D(p^m(c))\,dc < \frac{1}{r}\int_{\underline{c}}^{\bar{c}} D(\bar{c})\,dc = V^c.$$

On the other hand, $D(\bar{c}) < D(c)$ for all $c < \bar{c}$, and therefore $V^c < V^s$.

Exercise 10.1* Show that the value of a drastic process innovation for a competitive firm exceeds the value of this innovation for a monopolist but is still lower than that for a social planner.

Thus, in both cases,

$$V^m < V^c < V^s.$$

Let us summarize this analysis. Even with a patent of infinite duration, the problem of appropriating the social surplus arises (here the surplus is generated by the introduction of a new technique rather than a new product). Also, aside from any strategic considerations, the monopolist gains less from innovating than does a competitive firm, because the monopolist "replaces himself" when he innovates whereas the competitive firm becomes a monopoly. This result follows from the different initial situations; a monopolist tends to "rest on his laurels." This property, which we owe to Arrow, is called the *replacement effect*.

Exercise 10.2* V^s, V^m, and V^c provide measures of the incentive to undertake R&D and, therefore, allow us to compare the amount of research performed under various market structures. However, they are not adequate measures if we wish to consider, say, the effectiveness of subsidizing research in the monopoly and competitive

cases. Let W^m denote the increase in welfare brought about by innovation when this innovation is exploited by the monopolist (i.e., when marginal-cost pricing does not hold). Thus, W^m is equal to V^m plus the change in consumer surplus. And similarly for W^c.

(i) Show that $W^m > V^m$ and $W^c \geqslant V^c$.

(ii) Show that for a drastic innovation $W^m > W^c$. What about a nondrastic innovation? (Hint: Consider the case of a linear demand $D(p) = a - bp$, and compute how W^m and W^c change with $\underline{c}$ for $\underline{c}$ in the neighborhood of $\bar{c}$.)

Exercise 10.3* Consider an industry with n firms, linear demand $q = a - bp$, and symmetric cost $\bar{c}$. Compute the private value of a drastic innovation that reduces cost from $\bar{c}$ to $\underline{c}$, assuming Cournot competition. How does this value change with n?

Exercise 10.4** An industry is initially competitive. The price is equal to the firms' marginal cost, $\bar{c}$. Demand is linear: $q = 1 - bp$. One of the firms (and only one) has access to a cost-reducing technology. It can obtain a technology that allows production at marginal cost c by spending $\phi(c) = K(\bar{c} - c)^2/2$. K is sufficiently large that the process innovation remains nondrastic. The process innovation is made at date 0, and the patent last T units of time (after which the technology c can be used freely by all firms). The firms wage Bertrand competition, and the rate of interest is r. Following Nordhaus (1969), compute the socially optimal patent length T^*. How does T^* vary with b? With K? Interpret. (Hint: Use the envelope theorem to compute the change in the profit of the innovating firm that occurs with a change in the length of the patent.)

10.1.4 Monopoly Threatened by Entry

Consider the case of two firms in an output market. Before innovation, firm 1 is a monopolist and produces at unit cost $\bar{c}$. Firm 2, the potential "entrant," has a very high (infinite) unit cost and currently leaves the entire market to firm 1, which makes a profit of $\Pi^m(\bar{c})$.

If the monopolist is the only one who can acquire a new technology that reduces the unit cost to $\underline{c}$, we have the situation considered in subsection 10.1.2. In this case, the incentive to innovate for the monopolist is V^m.

If the potential entrant is the only one who can acquire the new technology, we have the situation of subsection 10.1.3 so long as Bertrand-type price competition prevails. Then the monopolist plays the role of a competitive fringe at price $\bar{c}$, and the value of innovation for the entrant is V^c.

Comparing these two cases suggests that innovation is more valuable for the entrant than for the monopolist, because $V^c > V^m$.

Now assume that neither firm has an acquisitional monopoly over the innovation. For example, think of a situation where a third firm, which cannot produce in this output market, generates the innovation and puts it up for bidding between the two producing firms. (A more plausible case assumes that two firms compete to discover the new technology first; see section 10.2.) Here, the concept of the value of the innovation is slightly different from that which we have considered in the three preceding subsections. Not only must an existing firm take into account the benefits connected with the innovation; it must also consider what will happen if it does not adopt the innovation and a competitor does. However, this does not affect the calculation of the value of the innovation for the potential entrant. Because it initially does not make any profits in this market, the potential entrant does not care whether or not the monopolist adopts the innovation once he has already decided not to adopt it himself. On the other hand, the monopolist who in subsection 10.1.2 expects to earn a profit $\Pi^m(\bar{c})$ per unit of time if he does not innovate finds his profit reduced by an innovating entrant. As we shall see, this new aspect of the problem invalidates the conclusion that the innovation is more valuable for the entrant than for the monopolist.

Let $\Pi^d(\bar{c}, \underline{c})$ and $\Pi^d(\underline{c}, \bar{c})$ be the profits per unit of time for the monopolist and the entrant, respectively, if the entrant alone adopts the new technology with marginal cost $\underline{c}$ and, consequently, the monopolist's marginal cost is still $\bar{c}$. For the entrant and the monopolist, the innovation values V^c and V^m can be written as follows:

$$V^c = \frac{\Pi^d(\underline{c}, \bar{c})}{r},$$

$$V^m = \frac{\Pi^m(\underline{c}) - \Pi^d(\bar{c}, \underline{c})}{r}.$$

It is reasonable to assume that in a homogeneous-good industry a monopolist does not make less profit than two noncolluding duopolists:

$$\Pi^m(\underline{c}) \geqslant \Pi^d(\bar{c}, \underline{c}) + \Pi^d(\underline{c}, \bar{c}). \qquad (10.1)$$

This property (called the *efficiency effect*[6]) must be verified for each competitive model, but it is rather intuitive; if he wishes, the monopolist can always duplicate the situation of the noncolluding duopolists. Note that in the present case the monopolist does not necessarily do strictly better. To see this point, consider the situation in which the innovation is drastic, so that $p^m(\underline{c}) < \bar{c}$. If the entrant innovates, he completely eliminates the monopolist from the market, and the potential industry profit is not dissipated by competition. In this case, $\Pi^d(\bar{c}, \underline{c}) = 0$ and $\Pi^d(\underline{c}, \bar{c}) = \Pi^m(\underline{c})$, so equation 10.1 is satisfied with equality. Equation 10.1 more generally implies that $V^m \geqslant V^c$ (with equality for a drastic innovation). We conclude that *because competition reduces profits, the monopolist's incentive to remain a monopolist is greater than the entrant's incentive to become a duopolist.* Thus, if the monopolist and the entrant were to bid for the innovation, the monopolist would bid $\Pi^d(\underline{c}, \bar{c})$, obtain the property right on it, and remain a monopolist (Gilbert and Newberry 1982).

As we shall see, this effect does not necessarily mean that in a race for a patent the monopolist will always innovate sooner than the entrant. We must also take into account the replacement effect developed above (i.e., the fact that the existing monopolist already earns monopoly profit before the innovation and, therefore, is in less of a hurry to innovate than an entrant who is "starting from scratch").

As Gilbert and Newbery (1982) note, the monopolist may want to obtain property rights on an innovation even though he will make no use of it. This occurs, for instance, if the patent relates to a production technology that is not superior to that of the monopolist. The only purpose of patenting then is to prevent the entrant from competing. A similar situation may occur when a product innovation is not sufficiently differentiated from the monopolist's product to warrant his incurring the costs of introducing the new product; the monopolist may, however, acquire the property right on the product innova-

---

6. We encountered this effect when discussing the persistence of monopoly in subsection 8.6.2.

tion in order to avoid competition. Thus, the efficiency effect may be an explanation for patent "shelving."[7]

10.2 Introduction to Patent Races

Except in subsection 10.1.4, we have considered only the pure incentive to innovate, i.e., the gain from innovating in a hypothetical situation where a firm has a monopoly over R&D activities. However, a firm does not usually have such monopoly power. Rather, R&D competition can be likened to a race for a patent. In this situation, each firm may wish to accelerate its research program at the cost of incurring additional expenses. This is reminiscent of the rent-dissipation postulate enunciated in chapter 1: Each time the market or a regulatory agency engenders a rent (here the rent is associated with the monopoly situation created by the patent), there is competition for it, and the rent tends to be partially dissipated by the additional costs incurred in an attempt to appropriate it.[8]

10.2.1 A Model

A simple model of a patent race is the "memoryless" or "Poisson" patent race associated with Dasgupta and Stiglitz (1980), Lee and Wilde (1980), Loury (1979), and Reinganum (1979, 1982).[9] The research technology is characterized by the assumption that a firm's probability of making a discovery and obtaining a patent at a point of time depends only on this firm's current R&D expenditure and not on its past R&D experience. This assumption has the merit of simplifying the analysis by abstracting from the investment aspects of R&D expenditures.

We can use this model to study the so-called persistence of monopoly. The issue, which was addressed by Gilbert and Newberry (1982) and Reinganum (1983),[10] is whether a monopolist in the product market is more likely to innovate than an entrant. In order to connect our conclusions to some previously discussed points, we shall consider the case of a monopolist producing at marginal cost $\overline{c}$ and a process innovation leading to cost $\underline{c}$. Two firms, the monopoly (firm 1) and an entrant (firm 2), are competing in R&D activities. The first firm to innovate obtains and exploits a patent.[11] For simplicity, we assume that the patent has an infinitely long life. Following the notation of subsection 10.1.4, we denote as $\Pi^m(\overline{c})$ the profit per unit of time earned by the monopolist before the innovation. The potential entrant initially earns no profit in this industry. After the innovation, the profits of the monopolist and the potential entrant are $\Pi^m(\underline{c})$ and 0 respectively if the monopolist obtains the patent, and $\Pi^d(\overline{c}, \underline{c})$ and $\Pi^d(\underline{c}, \overline{c})$ respectively if the entrant obtains the patent. As before, we assume that

$$\Pi^m(\underline{c}) \geqslant \Pi^d(\overline{c}, \underline{c}) + \Pi^d(\underline{c}, \overline{c}).$$

We assume that if firm i spends $\{x_i dt\}$ between time t and time $t + dt$, its probability of making a discovery during this interval is $h(x_i)dt$, where h is a concave, increasing function and $h'(0)$ is "very large." As was mentioned above, a firm's probability of making a discovery at time t depends only on the flow of its expenditures at this time and not on its past expenses (experience, memory). Nor does the probability of a discovery here depend on the date or on the competitor's past research program. (One could obviously think of situations in which these last

---

7. Gilbert and Newbery mention the antitrust case in which the SCM Corporation sought more than $500 million in damages alleging that the Xerox Corporation had (among other anticompetitive behaviors) maintained a "patent thicket" containing innovations that were neither used nor licensed to others. See pp. 451 and 452 of Scherer 1980 for further examples. For more on the theory of patent shelving, see Tauman and Weiss 1986.

In a number of countries, the patent law includes compulsory licensing provisions (the recipient of a patent is forced to license if it fails to utilize the innovation within a specified length of time). There may also be an annual patent renewal fee that goes up dramatically over the years. No such provisions exist in the U.S. patent law, although compulsory licensing is sometimes used as a remedy in antitrust cases. (See Pakes 1986 for a different view of patent shelving, in which the patent is an option on an uncertain return stream, firms still explore opportunities for earning returns from the use of the patent after they obtain it, and the decision whether to pay the renewal fee is derived as the solution of an optimal-stopping-time problem.)

8. We will focus on the strategic aspects of the innovation process. There is a large literature on the *decision-theoretic* approach (see Kamien and Schwartz

1982 for an extensive and clear review of this approach as well as for a good overview of the empirical literature). This literature assumes either that there is only one firm doing R&D or, more generally, that a firm's environment (including the rivals' R&D expenditures) is taken as exogenous (so that, in the multifirm case, each firm assumes that its R&D spending has no influence on its rivals' spending). Grossman and Shapiro 1986a contains a useful analysis of the optimal time path of R&D expenditures by a monopolist. (There also exists a search-theoretic literature that puts less emphasis on research expenditures and focuses on optimal search procedures and stopping time; see, e.g., Weitzman 1979 and Roberts and Weitzman 1981.)

9. See Reinganum 1984 for a review of memoryless patent races.

10. See also Gilbert and Newbery 1984, Salant 1984, and Baldwin 1987.

11. This "big bang" assumption is, of course, very debatable. Patents can be circumvented, new innovations can come along, and so on. Also, a patent may not be exploited immediately, because of uncertainty about the demand or the technology.

two elements might provide information on the probability of discovery to the firm in question, either through general technological progress or through involuntary diffusion of knowledge between firms.)

In general, R&D competition between two firms is characterized by two research-expenditure intensities specified as functions of time, $x_1(t)$ and $x_2(t)$, up to the moment when one of the two firms obtains the patent. At each date t, if neither firm has made a discovery the game starting at that moment is identical to the initial game. In other words, the absence of experience implies that the game has no memory. Consequently, the equilibrium R&D strategies x_1 and x_2 will be independent of time. This property allows us to solve the model simply.

Now we derive the present discounted value of the expected profit over time for each firm i and denote this by V_i. Since the R&D process is of the Poisson type, the probability that at time t none of the firms has made a discovery is

$$e^{-[h(x_1)+h(x_2)]t}$$

if the patent race starts at moment 0. Conditional on the absence of innovation before t, the monopolist realizes a profit of

$$[\Pi^m(\bar{c}) - x_1]dt$$

between t and $t + dt$. Moreover, with probability $h(x_1)dt$, he is first to innovate, and he earns, starting from this moment, a stream of profit over time with a discounted value of

$$\Pi^m(\underline{c})/r.$$

With probability $h(x_2)dt$ the entrant is the first to innovate, and starting from this moment the monopolist's discounted value of profits over time is

$$\Pi^d(\bar{c}, \underline{c})/r.$$

Letting r denote the interest rate, we can write V_1 as follows:

$$V_1(x_1, x_2)$$
$$= \int_0^\infty e^{-rt} e^{-[h(x_1)+h(x_2)]t}$$
$$\times \left(\Pi^m(\bar{c}) - x_1 + h(x_1)\frac{\Pi^m(\underline{c})}{r} + h(x_2)\frac{\Pi^d(\bar{c}, \underline{c})}{r} \right) dt$$

$$= \frac{\Pi^m(\bar{c}) - x_1 + h(x_1)[\Pi^m(\underline{c})/r] + h(x_2)[\Pi^d(\bar{c}, \underline{c})/r]}{r + h(x_1) + h(x_2)}.$$

In a similar manner, V_2 can be written as

$$V_2(x_1, x_2) = \int_0^\infty e^{-rt} e^{-[h(x_1)+h(x_2)]t} \left(h(x_2)\frac{\Pi^d(\underline{c}, \bar{c})}{r} - x_2 \right) dt$$
$$= \frac{h(x_2)[\Pi^d(\underline{c}, \bar{c})/r] - x_2}{r + h(x_1) + h(x_2)}.$$

A Nash equilibrium is a set of research intensities (x_1^*, x_2^*) such that x_i^* maximizes V_i given x_j^* (for any i).

Which of the two firms spends more on research (or, equivalently, which one is more likely to be the first to innovate) depends on the two effects identified in the preceding section. The efficiency effect

$$\Pi^m(\underline{c}) - \Pi^d(\bar{c}, \underline{c}) \geqslant \Pi^d(\underline{c}, \bar{c}),$$

reflected in the numerators of V_1 and V_2, suggests that the monopolist has more incentives to innovate and, therefore, spends more on R&D. The monopolist gains a net flow profit of

$$\Pi^m(\underline{c}) - \Pi^d(\bar{c}, \underline{c})$$

by preempting the entrant, while the entrant gains only $\Pi^d(\underline{c}, \bar{c})$ by being first. The replacement effect leads to the observation that the marginal productivity of R&D expenditure for the monopolist decreases with his initial profit:

$$\frac{\partial}{\partial[\Pi^m(\bar{c})]} \frac{\partial V_1}{\partial x_1} < 0.$$

This follows from the observation that, by increasing x_1, the monopolist moves the discovery date forward (on average) and therefore hastens his own replacement. In contrast, the entrant does not forgo a flow profit when discovering.

Either of the two effects may dominate. To see this, consider two extreme situations:

• First, consider the case of a drastic innovation. Since the entrant becomes a *de facto* monopolist in the case of innovation, there is no dissipation of monopoly rent, i.e., no efficiency effect. Then the replacement effect must dominate, i.e., $x_1^* < x_2^*$. Reinganum (1983) derives this result from the first-order conditions associated with the Nash equilibrium:

$$\frac{\partial V_1}{\partial x_1} = \frac{\partial V_2}{\partial x_2} = 0.$$

Therefore, we conclude that in the case of a drastic innovation there is a tendency (in a probabilistic sense) toward "entry" into the output market.[12]

• In order to eliminate the replacement effect, it is sufficient to choose an R&D technology in which the amounts committed per unit of time are considerable, so that the probability of discovery per unit of time is high. In this case, innovation is achieved early, and the monopolist is much more concerned with the possibility of innovation by the entrant than with the date of his own "replacement." Therefore, we have $x_1^* > x_2^*$ (consider, for example, the family of technologies $\{\lambda h[x/\lambda]\}$, where λ tends toward infinity[13]; see Fudenberg and Tirole 1986). Consequently, for a nondrastic innovation, there is a tendency for the monopoly to persist, because the established firm has a higher probability of obtaining the patent.

*Exercise 10.5*** Consider a symmetric patent race involving n firms. The firms initially make no profit and have a private value V for the patent. The R&D technology is memoryless. A flow of expenditure x_i yields a probability of discovery $h(x_i)$ per unit of time. Assume that $h' > 0$, $h'' < 0$, $h(0) = 0$, $h'(0) = +\infty$, and $h'(+\infty) = 0$. Time is continuous, and the rate of interest is r.

(i) Suppose that each of a firm's $n - 1$ rivals spends x per unit of time on R&D, and that this firm spends y per unit of time. Show that the firm's expected intertemporal profit is

$$\frac{h(y)V - y}{h(y) + (n - 1)h(x) + r}.$$

Compute the firm's "reaction curve" $y = R(x)$, where y denotes the firm's best research intensity given that its rivals choose x. Show that the reaction curve is upward sloping. Interpret.

(ii) Solve for the symmetric Nash equilibrium. How does the equilibrium research intensity vary with n? Show that if V is also the social value of the patent, there is socially too much R&D.

10.2.2 Discussion

Two refinements of the basic patent-race model have been developed recently. First, R&D expenditures are only one dimension of the invention process. In the basic model, firms hasten the date of discovery by spending more on R&D. In practice, they also must choose between different technologies. They may choose technologies that are more or less risky (e.g., technology A may give a fairly deterministic date of discovery, whereas technology B may lead to faster discovery or turn out to be a dead end). Also, they may choose technologies that are more or less correlated with each other. Second, the basic patent-race model makes the unrealistic assumption that firms do not learn in the R&D process. This rules out strategic behavior of the kind studied for other investments in chapter 8 (e.g., first-mover advantages).

10.2.2.1 Choice of Technology

How does the race for a patent affect the choice of R&D technologies?

Let us begin with the risk dimension. Dasgupta and Maskin (1986), Judd (1985), and Klette and de Meza (1986) have taken up the issue of risk (which was pioneered by Dasgupta and Stiglitz [1980]) and have written models of patent races that, under some assumptions, yield a market choice of excessively risky R&D technologies. That is, R&D competitors pick technologies that involve more "variance"[14] than is socially optimal. This is not entirely surprising. To the extent that a patent race resembles a "winner-take-all game," what matters is to be first, not how far behind one finishes in the patent race. Because the payoff of discovery becomes zero after a given point in time (equal to the rivals' discovery date), a firm's objective function is convex in its own discovery date, and this induces firms to choose risky technologies. But a firm, by choosing a risky technology, exerts a negative externality on its rivals. It increases its own chance of preempting the rivals when the latter would have discovered early and thus received a high payoff.

---

12. Here *entry* does not mean competition, as one monopolist replaces another.

13. When λ tends to infinity, the cost of R&D becomes almost linear in research intensity: $\lambda h(x/\lambda) \simeq x h'(0)$. It can be shown that this leads to very fast

innovation. (Recall that firms did not innovate quickly because of decreasing returns in the discovery function h.)

14. A technically more correct definition of risk is that of increasing risk or mean-preserving spreads. See exercise 10.6.

Following Dasgupta and Maskin and Klette and de Meza, suppose that both firms choose a "safe" technology that yields a discovery time distributed uniformly between 1 and 2 years. (Here we abstract from R&D expenditures to focus on technology choice.) The discovery will be superseded 4 years from now, and the firms do not discount the future.[15] If t denotes the date of discovery (expressed in years) and v the private flow profit from the patent, the patent holder gets $v(4 - t)$. Suppose that there exists as an alternative a riskier technology that yields a discovery time distributed uniformly between 0 and 3 years. Now an R&D monopolist would be indifferent between the two technologies, each of which would yield an expected profit of $2.5v$ (because the expected discovery date is 1.5). However, if these two technologies are equally costly, rivals in a patent race will choose the risky one (see exercise 10.6). The negative externality is then easy to point out: When both firms choose the safe technology, each firm is almost assured of winning when its discovery date is close to 1 (i.e., when the payoff of discovery is high). But this is not the case when its rival switches to the risky technology. Of course, this switch also makes it more likely that the firm that sticks to the safe technology will win when the discovery date is close to 2, but such wins have lower payoffs.[16]

Exercise 10.6*** Two firms are engaged in a patent race. At date 0, each chooses a technology from a family of technologies indexed by a parameter ρ. $F(t, \rho)$ denotes the probability that a firm discovers before date t; the associated density is $f(t, \rho)$. The rate of interest is 0, and the invention, which yields a flow profit v, becomes obsolete at date T (so the payoff is $v(T - t)$). For simplicity, assume that $F(T, \rho) = 1$ for all ρ. The cost of the technology ρ is $C(\rho)$, and ρ is a parameter of increasing risk (see Rothschild and Stiglitz 1970). Recall that an increasing ρ preserves the mean,

$$\frac{d}{d\rho}\left(\int_0^T tf(t, \rho)dt\right) = \frac{d}{d\rho}\left(\int_0^T F(t, \rho)dt\right) = 0,$$

and that

$$\frac{d}{d\rho}\left(\int_0^\tau F(t, \rho)dt\right) \geqslant 0$$

for all τ in $[0, T]$.

(i) Starting from arbitrary technology choices $\{\rho_1, \rho_2\}$, show that an increase in ρ_2 hurts firm 1 as long as

$$f(t, \rho) - (T - t)f_t(t, \rho) \geqslant 0$$

(as is the case for the uniform distribution). (Hint: Integrate by parts.)

(ii) Conclude that, starting from a symmetric equilibrium, both firms will be better off if they symmetrically reduce ρ slightly. More generally, show that the cooperative symmetric choice of ρ is lower than the competitive one (which, if v coincides with the social value of invention—say, because of perfect price discrimination—shows that there is socially an excessive risk in patent races). (Hint: Write the two cooperative and competitive necessary conditions and add them up; then use the answer to question i.)

Now let us consider the issue of *correlation*. If firms choose similar projects, duplication of success (i.e., almost simultaneous discoveries) can be expected to occur more often than if they chose radically different R&D technologies. There has recently been a lot of research on the issue of whether competing firms have an incentive to choose similar technologies. Bhattacharya and Mookherjee (1986) and Dasgupta and Maskin (1986) have analyzed the correlation bias when the innovation is patented, and Glazer (1986) has performed a similar analysis for a nonpatented but proprietary process innovation by a product-market duopoly. Dasgupta and Maskin have shown that, under some assumptions, the equilibrium involves socially too much correlation. The intuition for this is that, when a firm moves away from its rival in the space of research projects, the first firm increases the probability that when it is unsuccessful its rival will be successful—which is socially desirable. Hence,

---

15. Under discounting, even an R&D monopolist would enjoy mean-preserving spreads in the discovery date, because the objective function, which is proportional to $\exp(-rt)$, is convex in the date of discovery t.

16. This discussion assumes that firms maximize profits. Managers, however, may have different attitudes toward risk, because their objective function generally diverges from profit maximization (see "The Theory of the Firm"). Indeed, it is often asserted that managers are too cautious in their investment choices—see Holmström 1983, Holmström and Ricart i Costa 1986, and Lambert 1986.

there may be too much similarity in the choice of project characteristics.[17]

10.2.2.2 Experience in Patent Races

One way of formalizing experience or learning effects in patent races is to assume that a firm's probability of discovery per unit of time depends not on current R&D expenses but on experience accumulated to date. For instance, the probability of firm i's discovering between date t and date $t + dt$ is

$$h_i(\omega_i(t))dt,$$

where $d\omega_i(t)/dt = x_i(t)$ and h_i is an increasing function. The cost of accumulating $x_i(t)dt$ units of experience is

$$C_i(x_i(t))dt,$$

where C_i is an increasing, convex function. Thus, at each moment of the patent race, the game can be summarized by the vector of experiences for all firms.[18]

Experience is an instance of capital, and it is therefore not surprising that themes encountered in chapter 8 (such as natural monopoly and first-mover advantages) appear here. Let us start with a useful but not necessarily appealing result, that of "ε-preemption." Consider a patent race between two firms in which both firms make negative expected profits if neither of them drops out of the race, but each firm is viable as an R&D monopoly. This is a natural-monopoly situation, and one would expect one of the firms to drop out.[19] It seems plausible that the firm that drops out is the one with less experience (the follower), if the firms have access to the same R&D technology and have the same value for the patent. One might further conjecture that this firm might as well drop out at the beginning of the race. It does not seem reasonable to accumulate experience and then to drop out when the probability of discovery is higher. Fudenberg et al. (1983), using a model in which $x_i(t)$ equals either 0 (in which case firm i exits the race) or 1 (firm i stays in) at each instant, showed that the leader indeed obtains a monopoly on R&D, even if it enters the race only a short period of time before the follower—hence the term "ε-preemption." Harris and Vickers (1985) independently obtained the same result under considerably weaker conditions; they allowed $x_i(t)$ to be completely arbitrary (i.e., they used a variable-intensity model).

Although the ε-preemption result shows that competition in R&D may be strongly restricted by first-mover advantages and experience effects, competition is often observed at the R&D stage. To explain this, we ought to relax some of the assumptions of the previous model. Fudenberg et al. (1983) show that the key to understanding competition at the R&D stage is the possibility of the follower's *leapfrogging* the leader—i.e., accumulating more experience and jumping ahead in the race. They offer two ways in which leapfrogging can occur.

The first way is via *information lags* (i.e., firms observe their rivals' R&D efforts with some delay). To understand this, let us come back to the intuition behind ε-preemption. Consider a foot race between two athletes. Assume that it is common knowledge that the two athletes are equally good, and that they prefer to reserve themselves (run at a slow pace) rather than exhaust themselves by running at a fast pace. Suppose further that the leader has eyes in the back of his head and can monitor whether the follower is catching up. Because the leader can keep his lead by speeding up if the rival does so, there is no point for the rival in even engaging in the race. The leader can thus proceed at a slow pace without fear of being leapfrogged. But the picture changes dramatically if the two athletes run on tracks separated by a wall. Suppose that the wall has holes, so that from time to time each athlete can check his relative position. Now the leader can no longer run at the slow pace; if he did, the follower could run fast, leapfrog the leader without his noticing it, and force him to drop out of the race at the next hole. Thus, lags in information (or in reaction) engender competition. The same holds for patent races. To

---

17. This analysis again ignores managerial incentives to assume profit maximization. Holmström (1982, p. 338) has shown that firms tend to choose technologies that are too similar (correlated) in order to better monitor their managers through yardstick competition (see "The Theory of the Firm"); he argues that firms provide society with a market portfolio that is not as diversified as it would be if there were no managerial-incentive problem.

18. One can, of course, think of more complex technologies, such as ones in which the probability of discovery is contingent on the environment and on time or is not monotonic (no discovery after a certain amount of research might be bad news).

19. In a memoryless race with a constant patent value and a constant research technology, the set of firms at the date of discovery is the same as the one at the beginning of the race; no firm ever drops out.

formalize this, Fudenberg et al. consider a discrete-time, variable-intensity patent race. (Discrete time is a very crude representation of information lags: A firm's R&D intensity is not observed by the rival until the following period.) They assume that each firm can accumulate 0, 1, or 2 units of experience per period, at respective costs of 0, c_1, and $c_2 > 2c_1$. Thus, absent impatience, an R&D monopoly prefers to accumulate one unit of experience per period. In the equilibrium of the patent race between the two firms, competition is very vigorous when the firms are tied (have the same experience). Each firm accumulates two units.[20] When the leader is one unit of experience ahead, the leader randomizes between 1 and 2 and the follower randomizes between 0 and 2; thus, there is competition (with some probability). When the leader's lead is at least 2, the follower drops out of the race and the leader proceeds at the monopoly pace (1).

The second possibility for leapfrogging offered by Fudenberg et al. involves a *multistage patent race*, which allows for jumps in the experience variable (instead of continuous variation, as above). They offer a two-stage, fixed-intensity ($x_i(t) = 0$ or 1) patent race. A firm must first make an intermediate discovery (the first stage) before trying to obtain the patent (the second stage); alternatively, one could think of the two stages as research and development. In such a race, the first-stage follower can leapfrog the leader by making the intermediate discovery first. Again, the possibility of leapfrogging is shown to generate competition. Grossman and Shapiro (1987), Harris and Vickers (1987), and Judd (1985) have extended this model considerably, most notably by allowing variable R&D intensities.[21] Their conclusions are similar to those of the information-lag model. Competition is most intense when firms are even. When the lagging firm draws even, both firms intensify their research effort. The leader tends to invest more in R&D than the follower.

10.3 Welfare Analysis of Patent Protection

The recent research on innovation has focused more on the positive aspects of R&D (Is there competition? Who invests more in R&D? etc.) than on the normative side of the patent system. To be certain, the welfare analysis is relatively complex, and more work is necessary before clear and applicable conclusions will be within reach. Some very incomplete notes concerning the issue of whether the market faces enough incentive to innovate will follow, the focus of which will be product innovations. (Very similar remarks could be made about process innovations.)

A good way to begin is to think of product innovation as *product selection* (with a random introduction process). We know from chapters 2 and 7 that the market may offer too little or too much diversity. The same must undoubtedly hold for product innovations. With infinitely long-lived patents, say, a firm may have too little or too much incentive to engage in R&D. The appropriability effect, according to which the private surplus from innovation is lower than the social surplus (in the absence of perfect price discrimination), leads to too little innovation (see section 10.1). In contrast, the business-stealing effect, according to which a firm that introduces a new product does not internalize the loss of profit suffered by its rivals on the product market, suggests too much innovation. Actually, another business-stealing effect (analyzed in section 10.2) arises in patent races: By increasing its R&D effort, a firm reduces the probability of its rivals' obtaining the patent, and a typical result is that firms engaged in a patent race overinvest in R&D (if we assume away the appropriability effect)[22] and thus duplicate too much of the research effort.[23]

The current theories are much too rudimentary to be realistic. They generally presume a single patented innovation, brought about by profit-maximizing firms with a single R&D technology. We have already noted some

---

20. As long as they already have sufficient experience. Otherwise, the strategies are more complex. See Fudenberg et al. 1983 and Lippman and McCardle 1987.

21. Grossman and Shapiro also allow for the possibility of sharing intermediate results through licensing, and for that of forming a joint venture at the first stage of research.

22. See Lee and Wilde 1980 and exercise 10.5 above.

23. Of course, the existence of several independent research programs is not bad *per se*, because "two chances are better than one." (Indeed, a single firm may set up several research teams. Kamien and Schwartz [1982, p. 35] mention that the Upjohn Corporation once had six research teams pursuing six different approaches to the development of a commercial process for the synthesis of cortisone.) Rather, the overinvestment is due to the fact that firms do not internalize the loss of patent revenues incurred by their preempted rivals.

extensions—e.g., the firms may choose among several R&D technologies (involving different techniques and different amounts of risk), or they may be run by managers and therefore may not quite maximize profits (because of the separation of ownership and control). It would also be desirable to introduce various degrees of effectiveness of the patent system. In practice, patents are invented around or inventions are imitated (often with a lag). To the best of our knowledge, very little has been done concerning the optimal degree of patent protection, a crucial issue in patent law. But, on the issue of imitation, economists have long recognized that the possibility of even partial imitation of discoveries may yield particularly low incentives to do R&D (Arrow 1962; Nelson 1959).[24] Spillovers are likely to reduce the payoff of the winner of a patent race and to increase the payoffs of the losers. First, if the imitation takes place within the winner's industry, spillovers increase product-market competition and reduce the innovator's payoff. Second, spillovers increase the payoff of the losers, who "free ride" on the winner's invention (independent of whether the losers compete in the winner's product market). Here we are just reciting the public-good argument. The point, however, is that the public-good problem is particularly acute (i.e., the incentives to do R&D are low) precisely when the positive externalities on other firms (the spillovers) are large.[25] Government subsidization of R&D activity is likely to be a good substitute for a failing patent system in industries with large spillovers (Spence 1984).

Now let us depart from the single-innovation paradigm. Even in the absence of spillovers, the loser of a patent race does not always lose everything; sometimes it comes up with a patent for another product (or else with more experience for the next patent race). Furthermore, monopolies created by patents are temporary, even with strict patent protection. New technologies are continuously invented to replace old ones. Schumpeter (1943) referred to this as a "process of creative destruc-

tion." It would thus be desirable to formalize successive patent races.[26]

Even if we are successful in determining whether firms engage in too little or too much R&D, the optimal way to encourage or discourage R&D remains to be determined. The theory has focused on the optimal patent length (see, e.g., Nordhaus 1969). However, R&D incentives can be altered in a variety of ways. At the input level, R&D expenditures depend on subsidies. (For instance, the 1981 U.S. Economic Recovery Tax Act added tax credits for R&D investment; similarly, the Research Development Limited Partnership Act offered fiscal advantages to joint ventures.) At the output level, the payoff for innovation depends on the length of the patent (in the United States it is 17 years), on the scope of enforcement of patent protection, and on other factors. Little attention has been paid to the optimal package of these instruments to encourage an adequate amount of R&D.

10.4 Alternative Inducements to R&D

Patents are not necessary for producing appropriability, and therefore they are not necessary to induce R&D. In general, unpatented innovations still yield gains to their inventors, at least for a short period of time. Imitators may observe an innovation with a lag, or may not have the know-how to copy it immediately. Indeed, patents play a minor role in some industries (e.g., computers). Still, many economists agree with Schumpeter that patents, and the concomitant static inefficiency associated with monopoly power, are required to give firms proper incentives to innovate, and that patents promote dynamic efficiency (although these economists offer little information about the optimal patent length and the optimal amount of protection). But there are other methods of encouraging innovation, such as the award system and the contractual mechanism.

---

24. The following informal analysis assumes away the possibility of licensing (see section 10.8 for an analysis of licensing). In practice, the patent holder may find it profitable to license his patent (rather than let other firms inefficiently imitate) and thus obtain some of the joint surplus for licensing. It should be noted, however, that the existence of spillovers raises the licensees' status-quo (no licensing) payoff and thus strengthens their bargaining positions. Hence, even if licensing occurs, the threat of imitation reduces the licensor's payoff.

25. A mitigating factor, noted by many authors, is that the loser of a patent

race can better imitate the winner's discovery if he has kept abreast of the recent developments in the field. In particular, R&D enables firms to more easily assimilate their rivals' spillovers. One must then view "absorptive capacity" and innovation as joint products (Cohen and Levinthal 1987). This argument is sometimes offered to explain the high level of R&D in the semiconductor industry.

26. For a start on this, see Dasgupta and Stiglitz 1981, Futia 1980, Nelson and Winter 1982 (chapters 12 and 13), and Reinganum 1985.

The *award* system, in its extreme form, consists in designating a well-defined project and then granting a fixed sum of money (the "prize") to the first firm that completes the project. After the prize is awarded, the innovation falls into the public domain. Like the patent system, this method has very ancient origins; however, it is used much less frequently than the patent system. An important advantage over the patent system is that it does not produce a monopoly.

The award system is difficult to implement. First, the government must be highly knowledgeable about the feasibility of various inventions and the demand for them. Information about demand is crucial for determining the size of the award, which, in turn, influences the research incentives. Generally, firms are better informed than the government on these matters, so a less centralized solution (such as the patent system) is preferable. Indeed, one advantage of the patent system is that monopoly profits are correlated with (although different from) the social value of an invention.

In practice, the prize in the award system is likely to be determined after the innovation takes place. Because the inventor's investment is sunk at that stage, the inventor is subject to the hold-up problem noted in the chapter on the theory of the firm. The administrative and judicial bodies in charge of prizes generally estimate the values of inventions very conservatively.

Another drawback of the award system in comparison with the patent system is that with the latter it is not necessary to transmit technological information (which can be tricky when the technological know-how acquired by the innovating team is difficult to transmit or even to define).

Last, the award system implies competition at the research level. As in the case of a patent system, there is no reason why this competition should yield the optimal amount of innovative activity.

Scherer (1980, p. 458) reviews the use of the award system to stimulate inventions related to military uses of atomic energy, and relates some examples of holdups created by the Atomic Energy Commission's Patent Compensation Board.[27]

A more serious rival to the patent system is a centralized solution known as the *procurement or contractual mechanism*. Although somewhat similar to the award system, the contractual mechanism differs in that the government controls access to the research market. More precisely, the government chooses a certain number of firms[28] and signs a contract with these firms. The contract usually contains more details than are specified when an award is offered. For instance, it often specifies that a certain portion of the research costs will be borne by the government.[29] Contracts of this sort may prevent excessive duplication of research costs. However, there are incentive problems linked to limited yardstick competition. The compromise sought between these two factors depends on the research technology and the ease with which the contracting firms can be controlled.[30] As with the award system, the government must know the value of the innovation. Obviously, this is facilitated when the main customer for the innovation is the agency. This explains why the procurement system is often used in connection with space and defense projects.

10.5 Strategic Adoption of New Technologies

Technological progress depends on adoption of new technologies as much as on their invention. Whereas the previous section focused on incentives and on the process of bringing about inventions, this section and the next look at the speed of diffusion of innovations.

Few innovations are adopted instantaneously.[31] Two reasons for this are that firms may expect an increase in demand, and may be hesitant to sink the adoption cost before there is enough demand, and that they may expect a decrease in the adoption cost or in the uncertainty attached to the technology.

---

27. Scherer also reviews the use of this system to stimulate general inventions in the USSR.

28. Often only one.

29. Here we assume that the customer is the government. The customer might also be a private firm needing a particular technology or some particular machine tools.

30. See Ponssard 1981 for a discussion of how French government agencies trade off these two factors.

31. For instance, the basic oxygen furnace used to produce steel was developed in Austria in 1949. In 1960 only 3.7 percent of the U.S. steel capacity (56.9 percent in 1970, 85 percent in 1980) used the process (Oster 1982). Similarly, the technology to generate electricity using steam turbines was well known at the time of its adoption.

On average, one would expect diffusion paths to be S-shaped[32] (indicating that a few firms adopt the invention early, that the adoption process accelerates as other firms learn about the invention, and that the process decelerates when most firms have already adopted). Mansfield (1968) and his followers have indeed demonstrated that the S surve does well econometrically.[33] The precise pattern of adoption in a given industry must, as we will see, be studied in more detail, because of the strategic aspects of adoption.

In this section we will look at the diffusion process of an unpatented innovation in a concentrated industry. We will assume that an innovation made at date 0 can be adopted (in a nonproprietary fashion) by any firm at any future date t for cost $C(t)$. Adoption is a once-and-for-all process: $C(t)$ is a sunk cost. We assume that $C'(t) < 0$ and $C''(t) > 0$ (the adoption cost decreases over time, but at a decreasing rate) and that $C(0)$ is "large" (no firm wants to adopt at date 0). We formalize strategic adoption by a duopoly. Each firm must choose a time (possibly infinity) of adoption. We assume that information lags are negligible, in that firms can observe (and respond to) their rival's action without a delay. As we will see, this implies that the firms may be tempted to adopt the technology early in order to delay or prevent adoption by their rivals.[34]

Consider two polar cases associated with two different forms of rent that the new technology provides. In the first case, which involves two firms and a process innovation, adopting second is never profitable. The first adopter then benefits greatly from his adoption, and one would expect a firm to adopt the innovation early in order to preempt its competitor. The outcome is diffusion with a long lag between the two firms. Indeed, in our extreme example, the first adopter adopts "early" (in a sense defined below) and its rival never adopts. Furthermore, the monopoly rent associated with the adoption is totally dissipated by the costly early adoption. In the second example, adoption of a product innovation triggers immediate imitation. One would then expect little incentive to adopt. Adoption is delayed and occurs at the same time for both firms (actually, it never occurs in our extreme example). Thus, a key to the timing of adoption in a concentrated industry is the speed with which adoption is imitated.

10.5.1 Imitation-Deterring Innovation: Preemption and Diffusion

To illustrate our first outcome, consider a homogeneous-good Bertrand duopoly in which two firms initially have constant unit cost $\bar{c}$. Neither firm makes a profit. Adopting the innovation reduces the unit cost to $\underline{c} < \bar{c}$. Let $V = (\bar{c} - \underline{c})/r$. When only one firm has adopted, this firm makes Bertrand profit $\bar{c} - \underline{c}$ per unit of time, if $\bar{c}$ does not exceed the monopoly price at cost $\underline{c}$ ("nondrastic" innovation). Imitation never occurs in this extreme model, because Bertrand competition with identical costs yields zero flow profit. Figure 10.1 depicts the payoff of the first adopter (the leader) and that of the preempted firm (the follower). The equilibrium time of adoption, t^c, is given by $V = C(t^c)$. If firm 1 plans to adopt after t^c,

Leader's and follower's payoffs

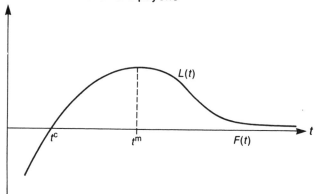

Figure 10.1
Preemption and diffusion. The leader's payoff is $L(t) = [V - C(t)]e^{-rt}$; the follower's is $F(t) = 0$.

32. This is a reference to the shape of the cumulative distribution of adoptions as a function of time.

33. Kamien and Schwartz (1982), reviewing the empirical evidence, also note that diffusion tends to be faster in nonconcentrated industries. However, see Hannan and McDowell (1984) on the adoption of automatic teller machines in various local banking markets.

34. The following is drawn from Fudenberg and Tirole 1985, 1987. Their analysis owes much to the earlier work of Scherer (1967) and Reinganum (1981a, b), who assumed that the firms choose their adoption dates irrevocably at date 0 (see Quirmbach 1986 for further results obtained by this approach). Because firms cannot revise their plans on the basis of observed adoption by their rivals, the issue of strategic preemption analyzed in this section does not arise in the analyses by Scherer and Reinganum.

firm 2 will do better to adopt just slightly earlier. Thus, any proposed equilibrium adoption time $\bar{t}$ with $\bar{t} > t^c$ is vulnerable to preemptive adoption. This intuition was informally put forward by Dasgupta and Stiglitz (1980).[35]

This zero-profit equilibrium satisfies Posner's two postulates (see chapter 1). First, the monopoly rent is totally dissipated; the adoption cost of the first adopter is equal to the subsequent monopoly profit. Second, this dissipation is completely wasteful from a social viewpoint. The consumer price, equal to $\bar{c}$, is not affected by the innovation, so the innovation does not give rise to any increase in social welfare. (The second postulate would not be satisfied if the innovation were drastic.)

If only one firm can adopt this technology (say, because it holds a patent on it), this firm will choose the date of adoption t^m so as to maximize $[V - C(t)]e^{-rt}$. The first-order condition is

$$r(V - C(t^m)) = |C'(t^m)|;$$

the interest on the delayed net profit $(V - C(t^m))$ is equal to the cost savings associated with waiting. Note in particular that $V > C(t^m)$, which implies that $t^m > t^c$. *The innovation is adopted later, when it is proprietary.*

Of course, the absence of imitation by the follower in the nonproprietary case is an artifact of our extreme model. For instance, with product differentiation, the preempted firm will end up adopting in the long run if the cost $C(t)$ falls sufficiently. A long diffusion lag between the two firms would often be a more realistic description of the adoption process.

10.5.2 Quick Imitation and Delayed Joint Adoption

Consider, as a simple example of delayed adoption, the following discrete-time model: Each duopolist initially makes profit $\Pi > 1$ per period. The current cost of adopting a new technology, C, is constant over time (this violates our previous assumptions, but in an irrelevant way), with

$$1 < C < (1 + r)/r,$$

where r is the per-period rate of interest. If only one firm (the "leader") has adopted the technology, its flow rent is $\Pi + 1$ and its rival (the "follower") has flow rent $\Pi - 1$. If both firms have adopted, their flow rent is Π again. Thus, the innovation serves merely to transfer profits from one firm to the other. The innovation can dissipate rents, but it cannot increase aggregate profit. At each date, each firm chooses whether to adopt (if it has not adopted yet) on the basis of history.

There are several perfect equilibria in this game. We will focus on the Pareto-inferior and Pareto-superior ones. Note first that reaction is always immediate: If one firm adopts at t, then the other adopts at $t + 1$, because the flow profit associated with adoption, which is equal to 1, exceeds the interest on the adoption cost, which is $Cr/(1 + r)$. The *Pareto-inferior (preemptive) equilibrium* has each firm adopt at each date (conditional on its not having adopted before), independent of whether its rival has yet adopted. In this equilibrium, each firm adopts at date 0 and has a payoff of

$$\left(\frac{1 + r}{r}\right)\Pi - C < \left(\frac{1 + r}{r}\right)\Pi.$$

Firms are made worse off by the introduction of the innovation (this could be called "super" rent dissipation). The *Pareto-superior (delayed-adoption) equilibrium* has each firm adopt only if its rival has adopted before. Thus, adoption never takes place. Each firm's payoff is

$$\left(\frac{1 + r}{r}\right)\Pi.$$

This is an equilibrium because $C > 1$. There is no super rent dissipation.[36, 37]

Although coordination mistakes are possible (each firm may suspect its rival and preempt before being preempted), one would expect both firms to coordinate on

---

35. The equilibrium turns out to require mixed strategies of a special kind, which are developed in Fudenberg and Tirole 1985.

36. If the firms never observed their rival's date of adoption, or if they were to commit themselves at date 0 to an adoption date, the unique equilibrium outcome would be the preemptive outcome described above: Given that the rival's adoption date cannot be influenced, it is a dominant strategy to adopt as

early as possible, because the extra flow profit exceeds the interest saved by delayed adoption by one period.

37. This late-joint-adoption equilibrium may depict the delayed introduction of compact cars by the U.S. automobile industry in the 1950s. White (1971) asserts that the three industry leaders recognized that if one of them introduced a small car, they would all do so; consequently, they waited until the market was large enough to accommodate all three of them, and then introduced their compacts simultaneously in 1959.

the Pareto-superior delayed-adoption equilibrium. (The argument for this equilibrium is stronger, the shorter the lag between periods. For small lags, each firm gains little by preempting and loses a large payoff if its rival decided to wait.) Because the duopoly never adopts the new technology, it automatically adopts more slowly than it would if the technology were proprietary. In the example developed here, the innovation is adopted immediately when it is proprietary. Thus, the relationship between property rights on an invention and the speed of its adoption is highly dependent on the kind of rent brought forth by the invention.

Can we build interesting models of markets that yield a payoff structure similar to the one above? The following exercise takes up chapter 7's model of product differentiation along a line and introduces a product innovation that, if adopted by a firm, raises its customers' valuation for its good by a constant. The product innovation does not increase demand (the number of customers is fixed, and they have unit demands), and the industry profit is not affected by adoption by one of the two firms as long as the innovation is "small."

*Exercise 10.7** Two firms are located at the two extremes of the city, consumers are uniformly distributed along the segment, and transportation costs are linear. The firms can introduce a product innovation that raises the quality of their good and thereby raises the consumers' valuation for the good by $\Delta \bar{s}$. The (fixed) cost of adopting the innovation is C per firm. Let t denote the transportation cost. Suppose that $\Delta \bar{s}/3 < t$ and that $C < \Delta \bar{s}(1 + r)/3r$ (where r is the discrete-time rate of interest). Compute the industry flow profit when 0, 1, or 2 firms have adopted. Conclude that when $\Delta \bar{s}$ is small, this industry profit is independent, to the second order in $\Delta \bar{s}$, of the number of firms that have adopted, and that this location model fits exactly the late-adoption paradigm considered above. Show also that the innovation, if it were proprietary, would be adopted instantaneously. (In the whole exercise, assume that the valuation $\bar{s}$ is sufficiently high that the market is covered and competitive.)

*Exercise 10.8*** Consider a duopoly. The incumbent (entrant) makes flow profit Π_0^m (respectively, 0) before adopting a process innovation. If only the entrant has adopted, firms 1 and 2 make flow profits Π_1^d and Π_2^d. If only the incumbent has adopted, it makes flow profit $\Pi_1^m > \Pi_0^m$. If both firms have adopted, each makes a

flow profit of Π^d. Suppose that $\Pi_1^d + \Pi_2^d \leqslant \Pi_1^m$ and $\Pi_1^d < \Pi^d < \Pi_2^d$. Time is continuous, and the rate of interest is r. The cost of adoption, $C(t)$, is decreasing and convex, is "high" at date 0 (no one wants to adopt initially), and eventually becomes "low" (both firms end up adopting).

(i) Interpret the assumptions about the flow profits.

(ii) Show that the entrant is a "faster second," in the sense that it reacts earlier to preemption than the incumbent.

(iii) Draw the leader and follower curves (as in figure 10.1) for the two firms.

(iv) Show that the incumbent preempts the entrant.

(v) Can you think of an alternative specification of payoffs that leads to adoption of a nonproprietary technology by the entrant first?

Katz and Shapiro (1984) look at a development game in which development leads to a property right on the innovation (contrary to the case considered here). Thus, the innovation in their model is deterministic and patented. As in the adoption game, each firm chooses an optimal date of innovation. The Katz-Shapiro model introduces two interesting possibilities: licensing and imitation. While patenting leads to obvious preemptive motives, the possibility of imitation makes the innovation more of a public good and introduces reverse incentives. Each firm then benefits when the other firm moves first. Whether the development game resembles a preemption game or a war of attrition depends on how cheap and lengthy imitation is. For instance, a reduction in the cost of imitation tends to delay development. Licensing gives rise to even more complex incentives. On the one hand, it may enhance the value of the patent (see the supplementary section) and thus favor preemption and early development; on the other hand, it may also enhance the value of being second, as the follower can, at a cost, enjoy the patent.

10.6 Network Externalities, Standardization, and Compatibility

This section examines adoption in an industry characterized by complementarity in consumption or production, and studies the influence of the existence of network externalities and compatibility decisions on the diffusion path.

Positive network externalities arise when a good is more valuable to a user the more users adopt the same good or compatible ones. The externality can be direct (a telephone user benefits from others being connected to the same network; computer software, if compatible, can be shared). It can also be indirect; because of increasing returns to scale in production, a greater number of complementary products can be supplied—and at a lower price—when the network grows (more programs are written for a popular computer; there are more video-cassettes compatible with a dominant video system; a popular automobile is serviced by more dealers). Note also that the size of the relevant network is either firm-specific (as is often the case with automobiles) or industry-wide (an extreme example is that of phonographs, because of the standardization of records).

The first issue with network externalities lies on the demand side. Because of their interdependent utility functions, users must anticipate which technology will be widely used by other users. This introduces coordination problems. Also, although they care about coordinating, different users may have conflicting preferences about which technology to coordinate on. These two considerations lead to two potential inefficiencies: excess inertia (users wait to adopt a new technology or to choose among several technologies) and excess momentum (consumers rush to an inferior technology for fear of getting stranded). These issues can be studied independent of the way the technologies are supplied. In particular, it is convenient to assume that they are supplied competitively (at marginal cost).

The second issue relates to the supply side, and the way technologies are chosen and promoted. In the presence of network externalities, standards (i.e., a choice of a particular technology to be adopted by everyone) are often mandated (or agreed upon) by the government or by private bodies such as industry committees. For instance, light bulbs, electrical sockets, and railroad tracks are usually standardized. The standards for stereo televisions in the United States were developed by an industry committee and were reinforced by the Federal Communications Commission through protection from interference by other users. One advantage of standardization is that it avoids excess inertia.[38] Another is that it reduces the users' search and coordination costs (see Carlton and Klamer 1983). Standardization may, however, be difficult. Rapidly changing technologies may impose the adoption of an inefficient approach. Also, standardization may reduce diversity.[39] A non-negligible amount of standardization is actually left to the marketplace. Technologies are then mostly sponsored by firms. A dominant firm often sets the standard. (This was the case with AT&T before its breakup. IBM has always played an important role in imposing standards in the computer industry. Home Box Office, the largest cable television service, led in defining a signal-scrambling standard.) But the adoption of a standard need not be associated with a dominant firm. The QWERTY typewriter keyboard became standard for typewriters without such an association.[40]

When technology choices are left to the marketplace, firms sponsoring incompatible technologies have an incentive to develop an "installed base" in order to obtain a competitive advantage over their rivals or to prevent the rivals from acquiring an advantage. To this purpose, they can start with low (penetration) prices and announce products before they are commercialized. Another important element in this strategy is the compatibility decision. For strategic purposes, firms can choose to keep their products incompatible, thus reducing the size of their network. Or they can achieve compatibility, either individually (through the choice of technology or by building adapters) or by reaching agreements with their competitors through committees.[41]

The implications of network externalities for industrial organization have been better understood in recent years

---

38. The adoption of AM stereo radio broadcasting in the U.S. seems to have been hampered by the lack of standards and the concomitant hesitancy of stations and listeners to sink money into technological losers.

39. Besen and Johnson (1986) argue, on these grounds, that the FCC's decision not to standardize teletext and videotext was wise.

40. Many observers believe that the Dvorak keyboard is superior to this standard, even when retraining costs are taken into account. However, it would be foolish for a firm to build this alternative keyboard and for secretaries to switch to it individually. See David 1985 for the history of the typewriter industry.

41. In general, the firms have the choice between individual adoption and agreement. They may, in particular, use the threat of "going on their own" to improve their bargaining position. An interesting contrast arises between noncooperative adoption (which, because of conflicting preferences on the choice of technology, resembles a preemption game) and cooperative adoption (which resembles more a war of attrition, with each firm waiting for its rivals to concede). Farrell and Saloner (1987) elaborate on these two themes.

because of the work of Farrell, Katz, Saloner, and Shapiro. Farrell and Saloner have concentrated on the demand side; Katz and Shapiro have focused on the supply side. Their work will be reviewed in the next two subsections. More complete reviews of the theoretical literature can be found in Besen and Johnson 1986 and in Besen and Saloner 1987.[42] (These two papers also contain interesting analyses of the development of compatibility standards—in the broadcasting and telecommunication-services industries, respectively.)

The new literature on network externalities is deeply rooted in traditional microeconomic and industrial-organization theories. On the demand side, the externalities give rise to a multiplicity of equilibria, to inefficiencies, and to a need for coordination even when the technologies are supplied competitively (these are familiar themes in the literature on public finance and, more recently, in the macroeconomics literature). On the supply side, the choice of technologies relates to the problem of product diversity. On both sides, decisions by firms and users to adopt certain technologies give rise to games of timing, the two polar cases of which are wars of attrition and preemption games.

10.6.1 The Demand Side: Users' Coordination of Expectations

Let us begin with a simple illustration of the coordination problem. Consider two users ($i = 1, 2$). They can either stick to an old technology or adopt a new one. The two technologies are incompatible, so that the size of a network is firm-specific. Let $u(q)$ denote a user's utility when he sticks to the old technology and the size of the network for the old technology is q (where $q = 1$ or 2). Similarly, $v(q)$ is a user's utility when he adopts the new technology and when that technology has network size q. (The functions u and v are net of switching or adoption costs.) Positive network externalities mean that $u(2) > u(1)$ and $v(2) > v(1)$. Assume, further, that $u(2) > v(1)$ and $v(2) > u(1)$. That is, both users prefer to coordinate their decision, whatever this decision is. (If these condi-

tions did not hold, the users would always prefer one technology to the other and the coordination problem would not arise.)

Suppose that the two users choose *simultaneously* whether to switch to the new technology. It is easy to see that there are two pure-strategy equilibria[43]: Both users stick with the old technology, or both users adopt the new one. Using a terminology due to Farrell and Saloner, we can illustrate the possibilities of excess inertia and excess momentum. *Excess inertia* arises when $v(2) > u(2)$ but the two users stick to the old technology. Coordinating on the new technology would be Pareto superior, but each user is afraid of moving alone. *Excess momentum* arises when $u(2) > v(2)$ but the two users switch to the new technology for fear of getting stranded with the old one.

Naturally, the inefficiency associated with excess momentum or inertia is an artifact of the simultaneity of the model. For instance, to avoid excess inertia, one user could (in real time) adopt the new technology and entice the other user to follow suit. Indeed, Farrell and Saloner (1985) argue in a more general framework that excess inertia is not really an issue with such congruent preferences. Similarly, excess momentum is not really an issue if a user can react very quickly to the other user's decision to switch. A user sticking to the old technology will not get stranded for very long if other users switch.[44] Thus, excess inertia and excess momentum may not be problematic except in two circumstances: when the information or reaction lags are long[45] and when the users may have conflicting preferences as to the choice of standard (but may still enjoy network externalities).

Farrell and Saloner (1985) consider a model involving potentially conflicting technological preferences. Suppose that in the previous model, a user's taste for the technologies is indexed by and varies continuously with a parameter θ in the interval $[0, 1]$—say, $u_\theta(q)$ and $v_\theta(q)$. We will interpret θ as a parameter of preference for the new technology, in the sense that $v_\theta(2) - u_\theta(1)$ increases with θ; that is, the user's willingness to join the other

---

42. Other relevant papers include Adams and Brock 1982, Arthur 1985, Dybvig and Spatt 1983, and Rohlfs 1974.

43. There also exists a mixed-strategy one, which gives a lower expected utility to both users than the two pure-strategy ones.

44. In particular, with immediate response to the other user's switch it is a weakly dominant strategy not to initiate the switching process.

45. In this circumstance, coordination is particularly important; still, one would expect that firms with congruent preferences (such as those discussed above) could communicate or could agree on a standard through a committee.

user and adopt the new technology increases with θ. Suppose further that $v_1(1) > u_1(2)$ and $v_0(2) < u_0(1)$. That is, a user with θ close to 1 prefers the new technology, independent of the other user's behavior. (Switching is a dominant strategy for such a user.) Similarly, a user with θ close to 0 always prefers the old technology. The coordination problem arises only for intermediate values of θ.

The information structure is as follows: Each user knows his own θ, but not the other user's. The parameters θ are a priori (independently) drawn from the uniform distribution on $[0, 1]$. The timing of the game has two periods, 1 and 2. (Considering more than two periods would not affect the outcome.) In each period, firms decide simultaneously whether to switch to the new technology if they have not yet done so. Switching is irreversible, and payoffs accrue at the end of date 2 (so the payoff at date 1 is taken as negligible).

Each user can pick one of three strategies: (1) never to switch, regardless of the other user's behavior in the first period; (2) to switch at date 2 if the other user has switched at date 1 (i.e., to jump on the bandwagon); and (3) to switch at date 1 (possibly initiating the bandwagon). As is easily seen, the fourth possible strategy (switching at date 2 even if the other user has not switched) is dominated; the user would then be better off switching at date 1, which would increase the probability that the other user would also switch.

Intuitively, each user ought to follow strategy 1 if it has a low θ, strategy 2 if it has an intermediate θ, and strategy 3 if it has a high θ. Indeed, an equilibrium behavior must take this form (this is just an "incentive-compatibility" condition). Figure 10.2 depicts a symmetric equilibrium (a perfect Bayesian equilibrium, in the terminology of the User's Manual). The values of the parameters θ^* and θ^{**} such that the user is indifferent between strategies 1 and 2 and between strategies 2 and 3 are given by the following equations:

$$u_{\theta^*}(1) = v_{\theta^*}(2), \tag{10.2}$$

$$v_{\theta^{**}}(2)(1 - \theta^*) + v_{\theta^{**}}(1)\theta^* = v_{\theta^{**}}(2)(1 - \theta^{**}) + u_{\theta^{**}}(2)\theta^{**}. \tag{10.3}$$

To see this, first consider the behavior of a user with parameter θ^*. Neither strategy 1 nor strategy 2 prescribes switching at date 1. The choice between the two strategies hinges on whether the user jumps on the band-

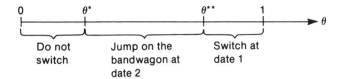

Figure 10.2
A bandwagon situation in network externalities.

wagon in period 2 if the other user has switched at date 1. (Because the user has not switched at date 1, the other user will not switch at date 2 if he has not done so at date 1.) Equation 10.2 simply expresses the indifference between sticking with the old technology and following suit.

The derivation of equation 10.3 is slightly more complex. It expresses the indifference between strategies 2 and 3. If a user switches at date 1, the other user switches at date 1 or follows suit at date 2 if and only if his parameter exceeds θ^*, which has probability $1 - \theta^*$. The first user then gets $v_{\theta^{**}}(2)$. With probability θ^*, however, switching elicits no response and the user gets $v_{\theta^{**}}(1)$. If the user adopts strategy 2 instead, he switches only if the other user has done so in the first period, which has probability $1 - \theta^{**}$. He then gets $v_{\theta^{**}}(2)$; otherwise, he gets $u_{\theta^{**}}(2)$. Equation 10.3 and the fact that $\theta^{**} > \theta^*$ imply that $u_{\theta^{**}}(2) > v_{\theta^{**}}(1)$—i.e., the user with parameter θ^{**} prefers not to switch alone. Equation 10.3 also implies that $v_{\theta^{**}}(2) > u_{\theta^{**}}(2)$.

It is easily seen that this equilibrium exhibits excess inertia. For instance, if both users have parameters θ_1 and θ_2 just below θ^{**}, they would like to coordinate on the new technology (as $v_{\theta^{**}}(2) > u_{\theta^{**}}(2)$), but in equilibrium they do not. Each user is happy to jump on the bandwagon, but neither one is sufficiently eager to set it rolling himself, as he might be adopting the new technology alone. This behavior is reminiscent of the asymmetric-information war of attrition discussed in section 9.9. Switching first is like supplying a public good, as each user would like to make sure that the other user will also switch. (Similarly, exiting a natural-monopoly industry is a "public good" from the point of view of the concerned firms, which do not want to move first.)

There are several ways to fight excess inertia. First, as Farrell and Saloner (1985) show, communication between the users alleviates the problem of (symmetric) excess inertia. Second, the users may be able to sign contracts (or reach agreements in committees[46]) that enable them to coordinate.[47] Third, as Postrell (who extends the Farrell-Saloner model to n users) shows, government subsidies to switching users also alleviates the problem of excess inertia problem: "Pump-priming" gets the bandwagon rolling (see Postrell 1986).

The earlier anology with a public good is useful but incomplete. The switching users exert a *negative* externality on those users who prefer the old technology. Farrell and Saloner (1986b) elaborate on this by considering a continuous-time model in which users arrive to the market over time. At date 0, only the old technology is around; at some later date T, the new technology becomes available and the new users have a choice between the two technologies. Like the above coordination game, such a model exhibits multiple equilibria due to network externalities. The new users may buy the old technology, so that the diffusion of the new technology never gets started. This may give rise to excess inertia; or the new users may all adopt the new technology, exerting a negative externality on the old users (the "installed base").[48] In such a situation, the welfare analysis of measures favoring the adoption of new technologies is ambiguous without a more precise knowledge of the preferences and of the way in which consumers coordinate.

Farrell and Saloner also show that it matters a great deal whether the new technology is anticipated or "preannounced." Preannouncement (i.e., announcement before introduction) may induce the consumers who arrive just before the introduction to delay their purchase. Furthermore, contracts for future delivery of the new technology at a penetration price may allow the sponsor (if any) of the new technology to build an installed base that increases the likelihood of its adoption by new users after its introduction. The welfare aspects of preannouncements and futures contracts are likewise ambiguous.

10.6.2 The Supply Side: Sponsorship and Strategic Behavior

The study of users' expectations is a building block for the study of product rivalry. Katz and Shapiro (1985a, 1986a,b) have studied penetration pricing and compatibility choices by sponsoring firms. The first of these papers focuses on the compatibility issue in a static model. Consider a duopoly offering two incompatible products. Except for their incompatibility, the two products are identical (perfect substitutes). Consumers have unit demands. One unit of product i, sponsored by firm i, yields the consumers a surplus equal to $v(q_i)$ plus a consumer-specific constant, where q_i is the size of firm i's network (the number of consumers who buy from firm i). The function $v(\cdot)$ is increasing. A generalized price $\tilde{p}_i$ for consumers can thus be defined as $p_i - v(q_i^e)$, where p_i is the price charged by firm i and q_i^e is the consumers' expectation of the size of firm i's network. Because the two products are perfect substitutes, the consumers choose the one with the lowest generalized price: $\tilde{p} = \min(\tilde{p}_1, \tilde{p}_2)$. The number of consumers buying at $\tilde{p}$ is $q = 1 - \tilde{p}$. (Consumers, who have unit demands, value good i at $\bar{s} + v(q_i^e)$, where $\bar{s}$ is distributed uniformly among them. We also assume that each consumer is negligible in the sense that he does not affect the size of the network he belongs to.)

Firms compete in a Cournot fashion (see chapter 5). They choose outputs (or capacities) q_1 and q_2 simultaneously. The market then clears at a generalized price of

$$\tilde{p} = 1 - (q_1 + q_2).$$

The firms thus charge[49]

$$p_i = v(q_i^e) + 1 - q_1 - q_2.$$

Under the assumption of a constant and symmetric marginal cost of production c, firm i's profit is

$$\Pi^i(q_i, q_j) = q_i(1 + v(q_i^e) - c - q_1 - q_2).$$

---

46. Voluntary standard committees are very important in practice. Very little theoretical work has been done on the topic; Farrell and Saloner (1987) have made a start.

47. The asymmetry of information between the users limits the efficiency of such contracts.

48. Adoption of the new technology may be inefficient, even if old and new users *ex ante* all prefer the new technology. The point is that old users want to

consume before the new technology appears, so that *after* sinking their cost they prefer the old technology.

49. Because the consumers do not observe the output choice, firms cannot influence the consumers' beliefs about the size of their network. (It is also assumed that the consumers do not update these beliefs when they observe prices that differ from the one they expect in equilibrium.) Katz and Shapiro also consider the case in which the quantities are observed by the consumers before they purchase.

Thus, the valuation for the network $v(q_i^e)$ is equivalent to a reduction in marginal cost or to an increase in the demand function.

Katz and Shapiro look for a Nash equilibrium in outputs, and then require expectations to be rational ($q_i^e = q_i$). They find a unique equilibrium under some assumptions on the $v(\cdot)$ function. They then analyze the same game assuming that the products are compatible. The consumers' valuation for the network is then $v(q_1^e + q_2^e)$. Again, a Nash equilibrium in quantities is derived. Total output is higher in the compatible case.

It is then possible to study the firms' incentive to make their products compatible. In the model, compatibility can be achieved either in a cooperative way (through agreement between the two firms, with or without side transfers) or unilaterally (through the construction of an adapter). It is found that a smaller firm has more incentive to become compatible than a larger one (of course, "smallness" or "bigness" is endogenous to the problem). But the incentive to make one's product compatible with the rival's may be socially too low or too high (as in the literature on product diversity, firms internalize neither the increase in consumer surplus nor their rivals' loss of profits).

To study penetration pricing, Katz and Shapiro (1986a, b)[50] consider a two-period model. They find that a weak firm prefers compatibility, whereas a strong firm may or may not prefer compatibility. (Incompatibility improves a strong firm's market position, but also intensifies price competition in the first period; see the papers cited for Katz and Shapiro's exact definitions of "weak" and "strong.") They also uncover an interesting "paradox": Suppose that the first product is cheaper to produce in the first period and that the second is cheaper to produce in the second period. (Think of the second product as involving a newer technology, so that there is learning.) One might expect the market to be biased in favor of the first technology, so that a firm would build an installed base in the first period and use this installed base to corner the second-period market. It turns out, however, that, with foresight on the part of the consumers, market adoption is biased toward the technology that is cheaper in the second period. This technology enables a firm to penetrate the market in the first period by pricing low; its low second-period cost commits it to a relatively low second-period price, and thus to a second-period increase in the network size. In contrast, the first technology cannot promise an extension of its installed base if its owner cannot commit in advance to a low second-period price.

10.7 Concluding Remarks

Although the main effects governing R&D (appropriability versus business stealing, spillovers versus patent protection, the efficiency effect versus the replacement effect) are relatively well understood, economists have devoted little attention to the optimal size and mix of public policies with regard to R&D (patent length and protection, R&D subsidies, and so on). A similar remark can be made concerning the adoption and diffusion of new technologies.

In addition to the desirable development of operational welfare criteria, two other R&D-related matters are wide open for further exploration. First, one can (as was mentioned above) depart from the single-innovation paradigm and envision the evolution of an *industry*, with successive and competing patents on differentiated products and/or superior technologies to produce a given good. An interesting product of research along this line may be a study of the socially optimal degree of protection of product and process innovations. Second, formal agreements between firms (e.g., licensing or joint research ventures) play a non-negligible role in the conception and diffusion of new technologies. The supplementary section contains a discussion of the link between such agreements and R&D activity. More work on the topic is warranted, if only to better develop the antitrust approach to these practices.

---

50. In these papers it is assumed that firms compete in prices. This gives rise to a multiplicity of equilibria of the sort analyzed in subsection 10.6.1. It is assumed that consumers (who have the same preferences between the two products) coordinate on the equilibrium that is best for them. (The same multiplicity of expectational equilibria can, of course, arise in Cournot competition.

However, capacity constraints restrict the flexibility of the consumers' conjectures as to the size of the networks; as Katz and Shapiro show, strong assumptions on the $v(\cdot)$ function then yield a unique equilibrium, which they cannot do under Bertrand competition.)

10.8 Supplementary Section: Patent Licensing and Research Joint Ventures

In sections 10.1 through 10.3 we assumed that the innovating firm secured the exclusive enjoyment of the patent. In this supplementary section, we consider briefly the possibility of technology transfer to other firms under licensing. We will, naturally, encounter some of the themes developed in the chapter on vertical control, together with a few new ones. We will also consider another form of contract that affects the distribution of discoveries and the incentive for R&D: research joint ventures.

10.8.1 The Incentive to License

We can distinguish two types of licensing. First, an independent inventor (or a firm specializing in R&D) may be unable to exploit a patent and therefore may license the technology to a "downstream" firm. Second, even if the inventor has production capability, he may still license a rival. The incentive to license is clear in the first case: The patent would have no value in the absence of licensing. It is less clear in the second case (or in the case in which an independent inventor licenses more than one downstream firm). The previous chapters emphasized how product competition may destroy industry profits (the so-called efficiency effect). Consider, for instance, a duopoly. A firm that licenses a process innovation to its rival may, by reducing the rival's cost, trigger tough competition and lower the industry's profits. On the other hand, licensing can occur only if it raises the two firms' (and, therefore, the industry's) profits. This suggests that there are limits to licensing—and indeed, Firestone (1971) notes that most of the patents held by corporations are used exclusively by those corporations,[51] and that most patents held by independent inventors are licensed to a single firm.

Still, licensing is a non-negligible phenomenon (furthermore, a case might be made that too little licensing takes place from a social point of view). We distinguish three motivations to license (for a corporation) or to license to more than one firm (for an independent inventor):[52]

• *Product-market incentives* Product-market competition may create incentives for the managers, who would otherwise take advantage of their monopoly position. The Rey-Tirole model reviewed in chapter 4 shows that the manufacturer of an intermediate product trades off the destruction of monopoly power and increased incentives when deciding whether to create downstream competition. An independent inventor faces the same trade-off when deciding whether to license to several manufacturers, and so does a patent-holding manufacturer when deciding whether to license to a rival (as long as this manufacturer faces managerial incentive problems due to the separation of ownership and control). Another instance of improved incentives associated with competition is formalized in the incomplete-contract models of Farrell and Gallini (1986) and Shepard (1986), who show that cross-licensing may guarantee *ex post* the quality of the licensor's product and increase the incentives for the product's users to invest in relationship-specific capital (see the chapter on the theory of the firm). We will not consider these motivations to license further.

• *Soft product-market competition* The argument that industry profit is destroyed by competition relies on strong Bertrand competition. Recall, however, from chapters 5 and 6 that product-market competition may be softened by three factors: product differentiation, capacity constraints, and intertemporal price collusion. In such cases, the industry cost savings associated with the high-cost producer's using the low-cost technology may well dominate the loss in industry profits. This is particularly clear in the case of product differentiation. In the extreme case, a firm's market position is not affected by a license to another firm that serves a nonoverlapping geographical market or produces an otherwise unrelated product. And it can appropriate some of the cost savings realized by the licensee. Licensing is then a purely vertical arrangement. The case of capacity constraints is considered below.

---

51. Of course, another reason why a firm is reluctant to license a rival is that the concomitant transfer of knowledge might allow the rival to invent around the patent, or even to develop a superior technology.

52. We will ignore here contracts that, under the pretext of licensing, serve to facilitate horizontal collusion; most patent laws are obviously concerned with such a possibility. See Scherer 1980 (pp. 173, 452) and Vaughan 1956.

• *Strategic licensing*   The first two motivations dealt with *"ex post"* licensing. Licensing can also take place *"ex ante"* (before further research takes place) to lower one's rival's incentive to invent around the initial innovation. Whereas the motivation for licensing in the last-mentioned case is to save on production costs, here the motivation is to save on R&D expenditures that are wasteful from the industry's point of view.

10.8.2   *Ex Post* Licensing and the Value of a Patent

This subsection (which is based on Kamien and Tauman 1983 and especially on Katz and Shapiro 1985b, 1986c) considers the incentive of a patent holder to license a process innovation, given that no future innovation will occur.

The first issue is the type of contract that can be signed between the licensor and the licensee. The licensor allows the licensee to use an intermediate technology to produce a final output. Kamien and Tauman (1983) consider two-part tariffs: $A + Rq$ (the licensee pays a fixed fee A for access to the technology and then a variable fee or royalty R per unit of final output produced using the intermediate technology). Gallini (1984) and Katz and Shapiro (in most of their 1985b paper) allow only fixed fees; Gallini and Winter (1985) allow only royalties. There may in practice exist information or legal reasons why contracts are restricted to simple forms such as a fixed fee or a royalty. For instance, Katz and Shapiro argue that, in some circumstances, the licensee's output (or how much of this output is produced under the licensing agreement) may not be observable by the licensor, so that it is impossible to base transfers on output. In this case the fixed-fee contract is a good approximation of reality. The evidence shows a wide variety of licensing agreements in various industries. Calvert (1964) and Taylor and Silberston (1973) observe that about 50 percent of licensing contracts specify royalties only, 10 percent a fixed fee only, and the remaining 40 percent a two-part tariff or a more complicated arrangement.

To make things concrete, consider an n-firm homogeneous-good industry in which the initial technology (available to all firms) allows production at cost $\bar{c}$. As before, an innovation is called drastic if it brings the production cost to a level $\underline{c}$ such that the corresponding monopoly price is below $\bar{c}$. We will consider the case of drastic innovation and that of nondrastic innovation.

10.8.2.1   Drastic Innovation

We start with the case of a firm "specializing in R&D." This firm generates the process innovation, but it does not have at its disposal the production structure necessary to implement it. Therefore, it transfers the innovation to a manufacturer. We assume that the manufacturer is in a monopoly situation in the output market ($n = 1$). (The purpose of beginning with the monopoly case is to separate the effects of an optimal transfer contract from the effects of competition in the output market.) Recall that the producing firm's initial unit cost is $\bar{c}$ and that the (process) innovation lowers this cost to $\underline{c} < \bar{c}$, and assume that the firm specializing in R&D may use a two-part pricing schedule (i.e., collect $A + Rq$ per unit of time). Then the true marginal cost for the producing firm is $c = (\underline{c} + R)$. Let $\Pi^m(c)$ be the profit that the producing firm can obtain (prior to paying the fixed fee) in the market when its marginal cost is c.

Exercise 10.9, which is based on the principle of residual claimancy (see chapter 4), shows that the optimal licensing contract for the licensor is

$$\{A = \Pi^m(\underline{c}) - \Pi^m(\bar{c}), R = 0\}.$$

That is, the optimal contract does not include royalties and requires a fixed fee equal to the difference in profit between using the new and the old contract. The intuition is that the absence of royalties prevents distortion of the final output, because the marginal cost facing the manufacturer is equal to the marginal cost of the vertically integrated structure. The licensor then extracts the licensee's surplus from signing the agreement through the fixed fee.

*Exercise 10.9**   Show that the optimal licensing contract includes $R = 0$.

Of course, since the monopoly is in a monopsony situation against the firm specializing in R&D, there is little chance that such a contract will be signed. (There is a bilateral monopoly situation in the "innovations market.") However, the haggling between the two firms should be over the fixed premium A (between 0 and $\Pi^m(\underline{c}) - \Pi^m(\bar{c})$), and not over R. The absence of royalties still prevents distortion at the production level and, therefore, generates the maximum total profit to be divided.

Having solved for the optimal licensing agreement, we obtain the value of the patent for the R&D firm: A (per unit of time). If the licensor can appropriate the whole surplus, $\Pi^m(\underline{c}) - \Pi^m(\overline{c})$, its incentive to innovate is the same as the one it would have if it were to merge with the manufacturer.

More realistically, the manufacturer is likely to capture some of the surplus, and the specialized firm then has less incentive to innovate than the vertically integrated structure. In the language of Williamson, part of the specialized firm's investment is expropriated, in that it is not the residual claimant for the full increase in profits. If feasible, a contract signed before R&D takes place restores the specialized firm's correct incentive to invest in cost reduction.

For a monopoly manufacturer, the argument has not made use of the assumption of a drastic innovation. Now consider the case of the specialized firm generating an innovation of cost $\underline{c}$ when the productive sector is composed of n manufacturers ($n > 1$) each using the old technology at cost $\overline{c}$. Should the firm transfer the patent to one or to many of the producing firms? What profit can it realize from its innovation? Clearly, an upper bound on achievable profit is the monopoly profit $\Pi^m(\underline{c})$ in the product market. Suppose that the specialized firm auctions off its innovation, and that this auction fixes the royalty price at zero ($R = 0$). Each producing firm is willing to pay up to $\Pi^m(\underline{c})$, since its pre-auction profit (if any) will disappear in any case. Hence, the specialized firm may obtain $\Pi^m(\underline{c})$ by selling its innovation to the highest bidder (in a first- or second-bid auction, for example). Therefore, in the case of a drastic innovation, it is optimal for the specialized firm to transfer its patent exclusively. To transfer it to many producing firms would only introduce *ex post* competition in the product market; therefore it would encourage the dissipation of rent and reduce the potential profit associated with the patent transfer. Similarly, if the patent is held by one of the manufacturers, the invention will not be licensed. Hence, *a drastic innovation is exploited by a single firm.*

10.8.2.2 Nondrastic Innovation

When the innovation is not drastic, and with Cournot competition, a nonlicensed manufacturer continues to produce a positive amount at marginal cost $\overline{c}$ (unless it incurs a substantial fixed cost). This gives rise to a productive inefficiency, and possibly to an incentive to extend the license to this inefficient manufacturer. Of course, to know if licensing really occurs, we must check that the decrease in industry revenue associated with more intense product competition (if any) does not offset the cost savings. To do so, we must make assumptions about the mode of product-market competition. Following the literature, let us assume that the manufacturers choose quantities (so the process innovation might be thought of as one that reduces the cost of installing capacities—see chapter 5). Also, for simplicity, let us consider a duopoly ($n = 2$). The patent holder is one of the two firms.

Suppose first that the licensing agreement can include a royalty (with or without a fixed fee). Gallini and Winter (1985), Kamien and Tauman (1983), and Katz and Shapiro (1985b) show that licensing always occurs. Suppose that the patent holder offers access to the technology $\underline{c}$ at royalty rate $R = \overline{c} - \underline{c}$ (no fixed fee). Because the marginal cost for the licensee has not changed ($\underline{c} + R = \overline{c}$), the product-market competition is unaffected, and industry profits are increased by ($\overline{c} - \underline{c}$) times the licensee's output (and are appropriated by the licensor). Thus, there exists a licensing contract that Pareto dominates the no-licensing situation.[53,54]

Now let us follow Katz and Shapiro and assume that only a fixed fee can be specified. With a franchise fee, franchising occurs if and only if it raises industry profit. It is easily seen that licensing does not always occur. For instance, we know from subsection 10.8.2.1 that in the drastic-innovation case licensing would reduce industry profit; this must also be the case for almost-drastic innovations. In contrast, Katz and Shapiro show that licensing does occur if the firms have very similar costs after the innovation.

---

53. The above reasoning does not apply to price competition. Under price competition, the licensor does not take the licensee's output as given, and therefore the royalties affect his marginal incentives. More specifically, an increase in the licensor's price raises the demand for the licensee's product and therefore the royalties. The presence of royalties thus softens the licensor's price behavior, and *a priori* should increase industry profits (independent of the cost savings), which makes licensing even more desirable.

54. Gallini and Winter, studying the pure royalty case (no fixed fee), show that under reasonable conditions the above royalty rate, $R = \overline{c} - \underline{c}$, is indeed the optimal contract for the licensor.

*Exercise 10.10*** Suppose that in a symmetric Cournot duopoly a small and symmetric reduction in cost increases firm (and industry) profits. (A sufficient condition for this is that the Cournot equilibrium be stable and the industry marginal revenue be downward sloping.) Assume further that, starting at symmetric cost $\bar{c}$, one of the firms innovates at $\underline{c} = \bar{c} - \varepsilon$, where ε is small. Show that licensing increases industry profits (and that licensing therefore occurs) under the fixed-fee system. (Hint: Use the symmetry of the problem.)

What about the social desirability of licensing (given that the innovation is exploited noncompetitively)? Katz and Shapiro (1985b) note that, very generally, privately desirable licensing is also socially desirable. For this it suffices that the industry output grow when one of the firms' cost decreases—a reasonable condition. Consumer surplus is then increased, and, by assumption, industry profit increases; thus, the sum of the two (i.e., welfare) increases. The converse does not hold; socially desirable licensing may not occur.[55]

Katz and Shapiro (1985b, 1986c) also look at the effect of licensing on the initial R&D effort. Clearly, licensing increases both the reward for acquiring the innovation and the reward for losing the patent race. The exact incentive to undertake R&D depends on how much of the common surplus the licensor can appropriate in the licensing agreement (which, in turn, depends on the licensor's bargaining power).

10.8.3 *Ex Ante* Licensing

Gallini (1984) and Gallini and Winter (1985) make the interesting point that licensing may not only reduce production costs but may also eliminate inefficient R&D expenditures. A licensee has less of an incentive to invent around the licensor's patent because its marginal cost has decreased, which makes innovation less desirable. A simple example illustrates their point. Suppose that firm 1,

the incumbent, is initially a monopoly and produces at cost $\underline{c}$. Suppose further that firm 2, the entrant, can, by spending K on R&D, acquire a different technology, which also gives access to marginal cost $\underline{c}$. That is, firm 2 can invent around firm 1's patent. Let Π^d denote each firm's duopoly profit. If $\Pi^d > K$, firm 2 is willing to undertake R&D. However, the two firms have an incentive to enter a licensing agreement to save the R&D cost K.

Gallini and Winter consider a duopoly model due to Reinganum (1983b) and introduce the possibility of licensing *ex ante* and *ex post*. The timing is as follows. First the firms (starting with asymmetric costs) may enter an *ex ante* licensing agreement. They then decide whether or not to undertake R&D (a zero-one decision). Undertaking R&D costs K and gives rise to a patentable process innovation at a cost drawn from some distribution. Then, in a second stage, the firms can enter an *ex post* licensing agreement (given their new costs) and finally compete on the product market. Gallini and Winter show that the overall effect of licensing is to encourage research when the initial costs are relatively symmetric, but to eliminate research when costs are far apart.

10.8.4 Research Joint Ventures

"Research joint ventures" (RJVs) are arrangements in which some firms agree to share the expenditures and the benefits associated with a given research project. Although conceptually very distinct, RJVs and licensing agreements have at least two features in common. First, they are contractual practices that considerably affect the level of R&D, and the diffusion of innovation, in the industry. Second, although initially they pertain to the input (innovation) market, they may also involve ancillary restraints on the output market.

Very little work has been done on the subject of RJVs, which is surprising in view of their potential importance

---

55. Katz and Shapiro also note that licensing is not always socially desirable. To see this, suppose that firm 1 faces cost c_1. Firm 2's cost is above $p^m(c_1)$. Suppose further that licensing brings firm 2's cost down to c_2, just under $p^m(c_1)$. Thus, firm 2 is intrinsically more inefficient than firm 1. The derivative of welfare with respect to c_2, evaluated at $c_2 = p^m(c_1)$, is

$$\frac{\partial}{\partial c_2}\left(\int_0^{q_1+q_2} P(Q)dQ - c_1q_1 - c_2q_2\right) = \frac{\partial q_1}{\partial c_2}[p^m(c_1) - c_1],$$

using the fact that $q_2 = 0$ at $c_2 = p^m(c_1)$. Now, $p^m(c_1) > c_1$. Thus, under the reasonable assumption that $\partial q_1/\partial c_2 > 0$ in Cournot equilibrium, welfare increases with c_2, meaning that licensing is not desirable. The idea is that, in this case, licensing introduces an inefficiency in the industry's production structure.

in the antitrust area (particularly for high-technology industries). However, Grossman and Shapiro (1986b) and Ordover and Willig (1985) have made progress on this subject. Let us take note of some of the issues they have raised.

Conducting R&D efficiently is both an industry goal and a social goal. Beyond exploiting complementarities of the members' R&D assets, RJVs allow the coordination of research activities between the members. For instance, they can prevent the wasteful duplication of a given research strategy. (See subsection 10.2.2.1 for a discussion of externalities between firms in the choice of research strategies.) Thus, a given R&D expenditure is likely to be better exploited through coordination between two or more firms.

However, an RJV also affects the global R&D expenditure (the incentive to do R&D). Depending on the industry, it may increase or decrease R&D activity. Two reasons have been given as to why RJVs may speed up innovation. The first is that when patent protection is not completely effective and innovations create spillovers, firms that conduct R&D individually do not internalize the positive externality on their rivals associated with an innovation. They thus tend to underinvest in R&D from an industry point of view. An RJV corrects at least the externality between its members, and thus increases R&D spending of the members. Second, it may be the case that the fixed cost of doing R&D is so high that certain firms cannot undertake it by themselves. An RJV may give such firms a means to exploit increasing returns to scale and do R&D. But it has also been noted by Grossman and Shapiro and by Ordover and Willig that in a concentrated industry an RJV may help rivals to avoid competing in the R&D market. This is especially true when the innovation redistributes rather than increases industry profit.[56] Whereas RJVs between noncompeting firms or between a few firms in a nonconcentrated industry seem socially desirable, they may well slow down research in concentrated industries.

RJVs may include ancillary restraints that prevent the firms involved from competing on the output market.

That is, the contract may facilitate horizontal collusion. For instance, a royalty per unit of output to be paid to the venture raises the firms' marginal cost, thus lowering output and raising price. An even less subtle restraint specifies the division of the product market for any patent that may emerge from the joint research. Such ancillary restraints are likely to be socially undesirable. (However, one can think of cases in which they are not. For instance, a process innovation that yields marginal cost c to two firms will create no profit if the firms compete in a Bertrand fashion. Ancillary restraints that smooth product-market competition are then necessary in order for an RJV of these firms to undertake R&D.)

To obtain a more complete view of the private and social desirability of RJVs, one ought to look at further effects (for instance, the exclusionary effect of an RJV between a subset of firms in an industry), incorporate the possibility that the market may generate too much or too little R&D in the absence of RJVs (as we have seen in this chapter), and look at the alternative public instruments that regulate R&D activity. The topic is certainly worth the effort.

---

56. To see this, go back to the delayed-joint-adoption argument of subsection 10.5.2. For instance, exercise 10.7 gives an example of a product innovation that increases the innovator's profit by an amount equal to the decrease in its rival's profit. That is, consumers benefit from the innovation, not the industry.

Instead of assuming that the innovation is nonproprietary, one can change this model slightly and assume that the innovation is covered by a patent and that the two firms are engaged in a patent race in the absence of RJV. Clearly, if the firms formed an RJV, they would not do any R&D.

Answers and Hints

Exercise 10.1

For a drastic innovation,

$$V^c = \frac{1}{r} D(p^m(\underline{c}))[p^m(\underline{c}) - \underline{c}],$$

$$V^m = \frac{1}{r} \{ D(p^m(\underline{c}))[p^m(\underline{c}) - \underline{c}]$$

$$- D(p^m(\overline{c}))[p^m(\overline{c}) - \overline{c}] \} < V^c,$$

and

$$V^s = \frac{1}{r} \int_{\underline{c}}^{\overline{c}} D(c)\,dc.$$

Figure 10.3 shows why $V^s > V^c$.

Exercise 10.2

(i) When the unit cost decreases, the monopoly lowers its price. So consumer surplus increases. Hence, $W^m > V^m$. Similarly, under competition, the consumer price goes down unless the innovation is nondrastic, in which case the consumer surplus is unchanged and $W^c = V^c$. (The innovation is then entirely devoted to cost savings.)

(ii) For a drastic innovation, the *ex post* welfare (when the cost is $\underline{c}$) is the same under monopoly and competition. But *ex ante*, the welfare is higher under competition than under monopoly. Hence, the change in welfare is higher under monopoly: $W^m > W^c$.

Let $W^m(c)$ denote welfare under monopoly and cost c. So $W^m \equiv W^m(\underline{c}) - W^m(\overline{c})$. And similarly for W^c. For a nondrastic innovation,

$$\frac{dW^m}{d\underline{c}} = - D(p^m(\underline{c}))\left(1 + \frac{dp^m}{d\underline{c}}\right)$$

and

$$\frac{dW^c}{d\underline{c}} = - D(\overline{c}),$$

with

$$p^m(\underline{c}) > \overline{c}.$$

For a linear demand,

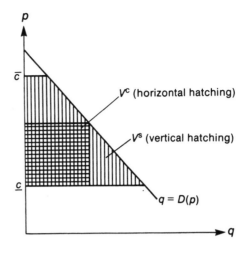

Figure 10.3

$$p^m(\underline{c}) = \frac{a + b\underline{c}}{2b};$$

thus,

$$\frac{dW^m}{d\underline{c}} = - \tfrac{3}{4}(a - b\underline{c})$$

and

$$\frac{dW^c}{d\underline{c}} = - (a - b\overline{c}).$$

Now, for *very* minor innovations, $\underline{c} \simeq \overline{c}$; hence, $W^m < W^c$.

When the innovation becomes major (drastic),

$$\frac{a + b\underline{c}}{2b} = \overline{c}$$

and

$$\frac{dW^m}{d\underline{c}} = - \tfrac{3}{2}(a - b\overline{c}).$$

This implies that $W^m > W^c$, which confirms our previous result that this inequality indeed holds for a drastic innovation. More generally, it is easy to show that $W^m < W^c$ for small innovations and $W^m > W^c$ for bigger, nondrastic ones.

Exercise 10.3

The value is equal to

$$\frac{(a - b\underline{c})^2}{4b} - \frac{(a - b\overline{c})^2}{b(n + 1)^2}.$$

Exercise 10.4

Let $\Delta \equiv \bar{c} - c$, $D \equiv 1 - b\bar{c}$, and $\zeta \equiv 1 - e^{-rT}$. If a cost reduction Δ costs $K\Delta^2/2$, the firm maximizes

$$V(\zeta) = \max_{\Delta} \left(\frac{\zeta}{r} \Delta D - \frac{K\Delta^2}{2} \right),$$

which yields

$$\Delta(\zeta) = \frac{\zeta}{rK} D.$$

The longer the patent (i.e., the higher ζ), the higher the cost reduction. Welfare is equal to

$$W(\zeta) = V(\zeta) + \left(\frac{1-\zeta}{r} \right) \left(D\Delta(\zeta) + \frac{b}{2}\Delta(\zeta)^2 \right).$$

But, from the envelope theorem, $\partial V/\partial \zeta = \Delta D/r$. Thus,

$$\frac{dW}{d\zeta} = \frac{\zeta D^2}{r^2 K} + \left(\frac{1-\zeta}{r} \right) \left(\frac{D^2}{rK} + \frac{b\zeta D^2}{r^2 K^2} \right)$$
$$- \frac{1}{r} \left(\frac{\zeta D^2}{rK} + \frac{b}{2} \frac{\zeta^2 D^2}{r^2 K^2} \right)$$
$$= 0,$$

which yields

$$\tfrac{3}{2} b\zeta^2 + (rK - b)\zeta - rK = 0.$$

The positive solution lies between 0 and 1, so the optimal patent length is finite. Differentiating this equation and using the second-order condition shows that $d\zeta/db < 0$; thus, a lower elasticity of demand calls for a longer patent. Draw a diagram, and compare the firm's profit and the consumer surplus for various values of the elasticity of demand.

Exercise 10.5[57]

(i) The probability that none of the firms has discovered by time t is

$$\exp\{-[h(y) + (n-1)h(x)]t\}.$$

Let firm 1 choose intensity y, and let firms $2, 3, \ldots, n$ choose intensity x. Firm 1's expected profit is

$$\int_0^\infty [h(y)V - y]e^{-[h(y)+(n-1)h(x)]t} e^{-rt} dt$$
$$= \frac{h(y)V - y}{h(y) + (n-1)h(x) + r}.$$

Letting $H(x) \equiv (n-1)h(x)$ and differentiating with respect to y, we obtain the first-order condition

$$[H(x) + r][h'(y)V - 1] - h(y) + h'(y)y = 0. \qquad (10.4)$$

(The objective function is strictly concave.) The first-order condition 10.4 yields $dR/dH > 0$. Thus, when the number of rivals increases or when these rivals raise their research intensity, firm 1 speeds up its research.

(ii) The symmetric Nash equilibrium is given by $x = R(x)$ or

$$[(n-1)h(x) + r][h'(x)V - 1] - h(x) + h'(x)x = 0. \qquad (10.5)$$

Assume that the left-hand side of equation 10.5 decreases with x. (This requires a "stability condition," according to which the reaction curve is not too steep—see p. 432 of Lee and Wilde 1980 for more detail.) The left-hand side of equation 10.5 is positive at $x = 0$ (because $h'(0) = +\infty$) and negative at $x = +\infty$ (because $h'(\infty) = 0$ and $h'' < 0$). Hence, there exists a unique equilibrium intensity $x^*(n)$. Differentiating equation 10.5 yields

$$[-]dx^* + \{h(x^*)[h'(x^*)V - 1]\}dn = 0,$$

where $[-]$ indicates a negative expression (the negativity follows from the s.o.c.). But from the concavity of h and the fact that $h(0) = 0$,

$$h(x) > x h'(x).$$

Thus, equation 10.5 implies that

$$h'(x^*)V - 1 > 0.$$

We thus get

$$\frac{dx^*}{dn} > 0.$$

The socially optimal expenditure per firm and unit of time is lower than x^*. Note the basic externality: When

---

57. The following analysis is drawn from Lee and Wilde 1980.

a firm lowers expenditures slightly from x^*, it incurs a second-order loss and it increases its rivals' profits to the first order.

Exercise 10.6 [58]

(i) Firm 1's expected profit is

$$\Pi^1(\rho_1, \rho_2)$$
$$= \int_0^T v(T-t)f(t, \rho_1)[1 - F(t, \rho_2)]dt - C(\rho_1).$$

Its derivative with respect to ρ_2 is equal to

$$\frac{\partial \Pi^1}{\partial \rho_2} = -\int_0^T v(T-t)f(t, \rho_1)F_\rho(t, \rho_2)dt$$

$$= -\left[v(T-t)f(t, \rho_1)\left(\int_0^t F_\rho(s, \rho_2)ds\right)\right]_0^T$$

$$+ \int_0^T v(-f + (T-t)f_t)\left(\int_0^t F_\rho(s, \rho_2)ds\right)dt$$

$$= -\int_0^T v(f - (T-t)f_t)\left(\int_0^t F_\rho(s, \rho_2)ds\right)dt,$$

after we integrate by parts. However, $\int_0^t F_\rho \geqslant 0$ for all t, so we obtain the desired result.

(ii) At a Nash equilibrium $\{\rho^*, \rho^*\}$,

$$\frac{\partial \Pi^1}{\partial \rho_1} = 0.$$

Thus,

$$\frac{d}{d\rho^*}[\Pi^1(\rho^*, \rho^*)] = \frac{\partial \Pi^1}{\partial \rho_2}(\rho^*, \rho^*) < 0$$

from (i). More generally, let $\{\rho^*, \rho^*\}$ denote a symmetric Nash equilibrium in technology choices, and let $\{\tilde{\rho}, \tilde{\rho}\}$ denote the symmetric joint profit-maximizing choices. We know that

$$\Pi^1(\rho^*, \rho^*) - \Pi^1(\tilde{\rho}, \rho^*) \geqslant 0$$

(by definition of a Nash equilibrium), and that

$$\Pi^1(\tilde{\rho}, \tilde{\rho}) - \Pi^1(\rho^*, \rho^*) \geqslant 0$$

(from joint profit maximization). Adding these two inequalities yields

$$\Pi^1(\tilde{\rho}, \tilde{\rho}) - \Pi^1(\tilde{\rho}, \rho^*) \geqslant 0,$$

which implies from (i) that $\tilde{\rho} \leqslant \rho^*$.

Exercise 10.7

Suppose that only firm 1 has adopted. The cutoff location x is given by

$$(\overline{s} + \Delta\overline{s}) - p_1 - tx = \overline{s} - p_2 - t(1-x).$$

The demand functions are then

$$D_1(p_1, p_2) = \frac{t + \Delta\overline{s} + p_2 - p_1}{2t}$$

and

$$D_2(p_1, p_2) = \frac{t - \Delta\overline{s} + p_1 - p_2}{2t}.$$

In Nash equilibrium,

$$p_1 = c + t + \Delta\overline{s}/3,$$

$$p_2 = c + t - \Delta\overline{s}/3,$$

$$\Pi^1 = \frac{(t + \Delta\overline{s}/3)^2}{2t},$$

and

$$\Pi^2 = \frac{(t - \Delta\overline{s}/3)^2}{2t}.$$

Thus, $\Pi^1 + \Pi^2 = t + (\Delta\overline{s})^2/3t \simeq t$ for $\Delta\overline{s}$ small. The condition $\Delta\overline{s}/3 < t$ ensures that firm 2 remains active. The equilibrium when either no firm or both firms have adopted is the same as in chapter 7.

The follower has an incentive to follow suit: It increases its profit by

$$\frac{1 + r}{r}\left(\frac{t}{2} - \frac{(t - \Delta\overline{s}/3)^2}{2t}\right) - C \simeq \frac{1 + r}{r}\frac{\Delta\overline{s}}{3} - C$$

for $\Delta\overline{s}$ small. On the assumption made in the exercise, this increase is positive.

---

58. This exercise follows Klette and de Meza 1986 and Dasgupta and Maskin 1986.

With much more substantial quality improvements, the leader drives its rival out of the market by adopting the innovation. The payoff for adopting first is thus very important, and the equilibrium is one of early preemption.

Exercise 10.8[59]

(i) $\Pi_1^d + \Pi_2^d \leqslant \Pi_1^m$ is the efficiency effect. $\Pi_1^d < \Pi^d < \Pi_2^d$ suggests that the new technology is superior to the incumbent's initial technology.

(ii) The optimal date for following is given by (for firm 1)

$$r\,C(T_1^F) + |C'(T_1^F)| = \Pi^d - \Pi_1^d$$

and (for firm 2)

$$r\,C(T_2^F) + |C'(T_2^F)| = \Pi^d.$$

Thus, $T_1^F > T_2^F$, owing to the fact that the incumbent already makes a profit before adopting.

(iv) The incumbent preempts at date T_2 such that $L_2(T_2) = F_2(T_2)$.

(v) Suppose that the old technology enables the entrant to produce at cost $\overline{c}$, and that the "new" technology also allows production at cost $\overline{c}$. Clearly, only the entrant will ever adopt this new technology (recall, it is non-proprietary; otherwise the incumbent might shelve the associated patent).

Exercise 10.9

For $R = 0$, the sum of the two profits (that of the specialized firm and that of the manufacturer) is equal to $\Pi^m(\underline{c})$. Thus, the vertically integrated profit is obtained. The fixed fee is then used to share this profit.

Exercise 10.10

By assumption,

$$\frac{d}{dc}[\Pi^1(c, c) + \Pi^2(c, c)] < 0.$$

But, because of the symmetry,

$$\frac{\partial}{\partial c_2}[\Pi^1(c, c_2) + \Pi^2(c, c_2)]\bigg|_{c_2 = c}$$

$$= \frac{1}{2}\frac{d}{dc}[\Pi^1(c, c) + \Pi^2(c, c)] < 0.$$

Thus, industry profit is increased when one firm's cost is decreased for almost equal costs.

---

59. This is only a sketch. For more details, see Fudenberg and Tirole 1986, pp. 36–41.

References

Adams, W., and J. Brock. 1982. Integrated Monopoly and Market Power: System Selling, Compatibility Standards, and Market Control. *Quarterly Review of Economics and Business* 22: 29–42.

Arrow, K. 1962. Economic Welfare and the Allocation of Resources for Inventions. In *The Rate and Direction of Inventive Activity*, ed. R. Nelson. Princeton University Press.

Arthur, W. 1985. Competing Technologies and Lock-In by Historical Small Events: The Dynamics of Allocation Under Increasing Returns. Discussion Paper 43, Center for Economic Policy Research, Stanford University.

Baldwin, C. 1987. Preemption vs. Flexibility in New Product Introductions. Mimeo, Harvard Business School.

Besen, S. M., and L. L. Johnson. 1986. Compatibility Standards, Competition, and Innovation in the Broadcasting Industry. Report R-3453-NSF, Rand Corporation.

Besen, S. M., and G. Saloner. 1987. Compatibility Standards and the Market for Telecommunications Services. Working Paper E-87-15, Hoover Institution.

Bhattacharya, S., and D. Mookherjee. 1986. Portfolio Choice in Research and Development. *Rand Journal of Economics* 17: 594–605.

Calvert, R. 1964. *The Encyclopedia of Patent Practice and Invention Management*. New York: Reinhold.

Carlton, D., and J. Klamer. 1983. The Need for Coordination Among Firms, with Special Reference to Network Industries. *University of Chicago Law Review* 50: 446–465.

Cohen, W., and D. Levinthal. 1987. Innovation and Learning: The Two Faces of R&D: Implications for the Analysis of R&D Investment. Mimeo, Carnegie-Mellon University.

Dasgupta, P., and E. Maskin. 1986. The Simple Economics of Research Portfolios. Economic Theory Discussion Paper 105, Cambridge University.

Dasgupta, P., and J. Stiglitz. 1980. Uncertainty, Industrial Structure, and the Speed of R&D. *Bell Journal of Economics* 11: 1–28.

Dasgupta, P., and J. Stiglitz. 1981. Entry, Innovation, Exit: Towards a Dynamic Theory of Oligopolistic Industrial Structure. *European Economic Review* 15: 137–58.

David, P. 1985. CLIO and the Economics of QWERTY. *American Economic Review: Papers and Proceedings* 75: 332–337.

Denison, E. F. 1962. *Discourse on Method*. New York: Liberal Arts Press.

Dybvig, P., and C. Spatt. 1983. Adoption Externalities as Public Goods. *Journal of Public Economics* 20: 231–247.

Farrell, J., and N. Gallini. 1986. Second-Sourcing as a Commitment: Monopoly Incentives to Attract Competition. Working Paper 8618, University of California, Berkeley.

Farrell, J., and G. Saloner. 1985. Standardization, Compatibility, and Innovation. *Rand Journal of Economics* 16: 70–83.

Farrell, J., and G. Saloner. 1986a. Standardization and Variety. *Economics Letters* 20: 71–74.

Farrell, J., and G. Saloner. 1986b. Installed Base and Compatibility: Innovation, Product Preannouncements, and Predation. *American Economic Review* 76: 940–955.

Farrell, J., and G. Saloner. 1987. Coordination Through Committees and Markets. Mimeo, University of California, Berkeley.

Firestone, O. 1971. *Economic Implications of Patents*. University of Ottawa Press.

Fudenberg, D., and J. Tirole. 1985. Preemption and Rent Equalization in the Adoption of New Technology. *Review of Economic Studies* 52: 383–401.

Fudenberg, D., and J. Tirole. 1986. *Dynamic Models of Oligopoly*. Volume 3 of *Fundamentals of Pure and Applied Economics*, ed. J. Lesourne and H. Sonnenschein. London: Harwood.

Fudenberg, D., and J. Tirole. 1987. Understanding Rent Dissipation: On the Use of Game Theory in Industrial Organization. *American Economic Review: Papers and Proceedings* 77: 176–183.

Fudenberg, D., R. Gilbert, J. Stiglitz, and J. Tirole. 1983. Preemption, Leapfrogging, and Competition in Patent Races. *European Economic Review* 22: 3–31.

Futia, C. 1980. Schumpeterian Competition. *Quarterly Journal of Economics* 94: 675–696.

Gallini, N. 1984. Deterrence through Market Sharing: A Strategic Incentive for Licensing. *American Economic Review* 74: 931–941.

Gallini, N., and R. Winter. 1985. Licensing in the Theory of Innovation. *Rand Journal of Economics* 16: 237–252.

Gilbert, R., and D. Newbery. 1982. Preemptive Patenting and the Persistence of Monopoly. *American Economic Review* 72: 514–526.

Gilbert, R., and D. Newbery, 1984. Preemptive Patenting and the Persistence of Monopoly: Comment. *American Economic Review* 74: 238–242.

Glazer, J. 1986. The Choice of Research Techniques with Uncertain Success Probabilities in Rivalrous Situations. Mimeo, Bell Communications Research.

Grossman, G., and C. Shapiro. 1986a. Optimal Dynamic R&D Programs. *Rand Journal of Economics* 17: 581–593.

Grossman, G., and C. Shapiro. 1986b. Research Joint Ventures: An Antitrust Analysis. *Journal of Law, Economics, and Organization* 2: 315–337.

Grossman, G., and C. Shapiro. 1987. Dynamic R&D Competition. *Economic Journal* 97: 372–387.

Guesnerie, R., and J. Tirole. 1985. L'Economie de la Recherche-Developpement: Introduction à Certains Travaux Théoriques. *Revue Economique* 36: 843–870.

Hannan, T., and J. McDowell. 1984. The Determinants of Technology Adoption: The Case of the Banking Firm. *Rand Journal of Economics* 15: 328–335.

Harris, C., and J. Vickers. 1985. Perfect Equilibrium in a Model of a Race. *Review of Economic Studies* 52: 193–209.

Harris, C., and J. Vickers. 1987. Racing with Uncertainty. *Review of Economic Studies* 54: 1–22.

Holmström, B. 1982. Moral Hazard in Teams. *Bell Journal of Economics* 13: 324–340.

Holmström, B. 1983. Managerial Incentive Problems—A Dynamic Perspective. In *Essays in Economics and Management in Honor of Lars Wahlbeck.* Helsinki: Swedish School of Economics.

Holmström, B., and J. Ricart i Costa. 1986. Managerial Incentives and Capital Management. *Quarterly Journal of Economics* 101: 835–860.

Judd, K. 1985. Closed-Loop Equilibrium in a Multi-Stage Innovation Race. Discussion Paper 647, Kellogg Graduate School of Management, Northwestern University.

Kamien, M., and N. Schwartz. 1982. *Market Structure and Innovation.* Cambridge University Press.

Kamien, M., and Y. Tauman. 1983. The Private Value of a Patent: A Game Theoretic Analysis. Discussion Paper 576, Northwestern University.

Katz, M., and C. Shapiro. 1984. Perfect Equilibrium in a Development Game with Licensing or Imitation. Discussion Paper 85, Woodrow Wilson School, Princeton University.

Katz, M., and C. Shapiro. 1985a. Network Externalities, Competition, and Compatibility. *American Economic Review* 75: 424–440.

Katz, M., and C. Shapiro. 1985b. On the Licensing of Innovations. *Rand Journal of Economics* 16: 504–520.

Katz, M., and C. Shapiro. 1986a. Technology Adoption in the Presence of Network Externalities. *Journal of Political Economy* 94: 822–841.

Katz, M., and C. Shapiro. 1986b. Product Compatibility Choice in a Market with Technological Progress. *Oxford Economic Papers* 38: 146–165.

Katz, M., and C. Shapiro. 1986c. How to License Intangible Property. *Quarterly Journal of Economics* 101: 567–590.

Klette, T., and D. de Meza. 1986. Is the Market Biased against R&D? *Rand Journal of Economics* 17: 133–139.

Lambert, R. 1986. Executive Effort and the Selection of Risky Projects. *Rand Journal of Economics* 17: 77–88.

Lee, T., and L. Wilde. 1980. Market Structure and Innovation: A Reformulation. *Quarterly Journal of Economics* 194: 429–436.

Lippman, S., and K. McCardle. 1987. Dropout Behavior in R&D Races with Learning. *Rand Journal of Economics* 18: 287–295.

Loury, G. C. 1979. Market Structure and Innovation. *Quarterly Journal of Economics* 93: 395–410.

Mansfield, E. 1968. *Industrial Research and Technological Innovation—An Econometric Analysis.* New York: Norton.

Mansfield, E., M. Schwartz, and S. Wanger. 1981. Imitation Costs and Patents: An Empirical Study. *Economic Journal* 91: 907–918.

Nelson, R. 1959. The Simple Economics of Basic Research. *Journal of Political Economy* 67: 297–306.

Nelson, R., and S. Winter. 1982. *An Evolutionary Theory of Economic Change.* Cambridge, Mass.: Harvard University Press.

Nordhaus, W. 1969. *Invention, Growth, and Welfare.* Cambridge, Mass.: MIT Press.

Ordover, J., and R. Willig. 1981. An Economic Definition of Predation: Pricing and Product Innovation. *Yale Law Journal* 91: 8–53.

Ordover, J., and R. Willig. 1985. Antitrust for High-Technology Industries: Assessing Research Joint Ventures and Mergers. *Journal of Law and Economics* 28: 311–333.

Oster, S. 1982. The Diffusion of Innovation among Steel Firms: The Basic Oxygen Furnace. *Bell Journal of Economics* 13: 45–56.

Pakes, A. 1986. Patents as Options: Some Estimates of the Value of Holding European Patent Stocks. *Econometrica* 54: 755–784.

Ponssard, J.-P. 1981. Marchés Publics et Innovation: Concurrence ou Régulation? *Revue Economique* 32: 163–179.

Postrel, S. 1986. Bandwagons and the Coordination of Standardized Behavior. Mimeo, Massachusetts Institute of Technology.

Quirmbach, H. 1986. The Diffusion of New Technology and the Market for an Innovation. *Rand Journal of Economics* 17: 33–47.

Reinganum, J. 1979. Dynamic Games with R&D Rivalry. Ph.D. dissertation, Northwestern University.

Reinganum, J. 1981a. On the Diffusion of a New Technology: A Game-Theoretic Approach. *Review of Economic Studies* 48: 395–405.

Reinganum, J. 1981b. Market Structure and the Diffusion of New Technology. *Bell Journal of Economics* 12: 618–624.

Reinganum, J. 1982. A Dynamic Game of R&D: Patent Protection and Competitive Behavior. *Econometrica* 50: 671–688.

Reinganum, J. 1983a. Uncertain Innovation and the Persistence of Monopoly. *American Economic Review* 73: 741–748.

Reinganum, J. 1983b. Technology Adoption under Imperfect Information. *Bell Journal of Economics* 14: 57–69.

Reinganum, J. 1984. Practical Implications of Game Theoretic Models of R&D. *American Economic Review, Papers and Proceedings* 74: 61–66.

Reinganum, J. 1985. Innovation and Industry Evolution. *Quarterly Journal of Economics* 100: 81–100.

Roberts, K., and M. Weitzman. 1981. Funding Criteria for Research, Development, and Exploration Projects. *Econometrica* 49: 1261–1288.

Rohlfs, J. 1974. A Theory of Interdependent Demand for a Communication Service. *Bell Journal of Economics* 5: 16–37.

Rothschild, M., and J. Stiglitz. 1970. Increasing Risk I: A Definition. *Journal of Economic Theory* 2: 225–243.

Salant, S. 1984. Preemptive Patenting and the Persistence of Monopoly: Comment. *American Economic Review* 74: 247–250.

Scherer, F. 1967. Research and Development Resource Allocation under Rivalry. *Quarterly Journal of Economics* 131: 359–394.

Scherer, F. 1980. *Industrial Market Structure and Economic Performance*, second edition. Chicago: Rand-McNally.

Schumpeter, J. 1943. *Capitalism, Socialism and Democracy*. London: Unwin University Books.

Shepard, A. 1986. Licensing to Enhance Demand for New Technologies. Mimeo, Yale University.

Solow, R. 1957. Technical Change and the Aggregate Production Function. *Review of Economics and Statistics* 39: 312–320.

Spence, M. 1984. Cost Reduction, Competition and Industry Performance. *Econometrica* 52: 101–122.

Tauman, Y., and Y. Weiss. 1986. Shelving and Licensing of Innovations. Mimeo, Tel-Aviv University.

Taylor, C., and Z. Silberston. 1973. *Economic Impact of Patents*. Cambridge University Press.

Vaughan, F. 1956. *The United States Patent System*. Norman: University of Oklahoma Press.

Weitzman, M. 1979. Optimal Search for the Best Alternative. *Econometrica* 47: 641–654.

White, L. 1971. *The Automobile Industry Since 1945*. Cambridge, Mass.: Harvard University Press.

Noncooperative Game Theory: A User's Manual

Noncooperative game theory has become an important tool for analyzing strategic interaction between players and has found many applications in the field of industrial organization. This chapter is intended to introduce the aspects of the theory that have proved most useful in industrial organization and to familiarize the reader with their applications. It will help the reader to develop a kit of game-theory tools that he or she will be able to call upon when studying industrial organization. The kit will be composed of four basic tools, starting with the concept of Nash equilibrium for static games of complete information and continuing with its natural extensions to dynamic games of complete information, to static games of incomplete information, and to dynamic games of incomplete information.

The analysis is intentionally informal, and it is not meant to be a complete overview. It borrows freely from Fudenberg and Tirole 1986c (and also, in the portion devoted to dynamic games of incomplete information, from Tirole 1983). Serious students of game theory are strongly advised to study the more formal literature.[1]

11.1 Games and Strategies

There are two ways of formalizing a game. One is to describe the *extensive form*, which specifies the order of play, the information and choices available to a player whenever it is his turn to play, the payoffs for all players (contingent on all players' choices), and (possibly) a probability distribution for moves by "nature."[2] The "tree" of the game (an ordering of "nodes") depicts this extensive form. The tree represented in figure 11.1 describes the following two-player game: At "time $t = 1$," only player one makes a decision. He faces two choices, referred to as

---

1. For more formal treatments see Friedman 1986, Luce and Raiffa 1957, Moulin 1982, Kohlberg and Mertens 1986, Kreps and Wilson 1982, and Myerson 1984. Moulin's book contains an impressive selection of exercises.

2. See Kreps and Wilson 1982 or Luce and Raiffa 1957 for more formal definitions.

"Left" (L) and "Right" (R). At "time $t = 2$," and observing player 1's initial decision, player 2 makes a decision. He chooses between "left" (ℓ) and "right" (r). Since each player plays during only one period, it is unnecessary to index the actions and strategies per period. For convenience, both players' utilities (or payoffs) appear at the bottom of the tree. (They may represent the sum of payoffs received along the tree.) For example, if $(a_1, a_2) = (L, \ell)$, where a_i denotes agent i's action, player 1 receives utility equal to 2 and player 2 receives zero utility.

In this game, player 2 observes player 1's action before picking his own action. The case in which he would not (where both actions are chosen "simultaneously") is depicted in figure 11.2. In that figure, the oval connecting player 2's nodes, which indicates that he has the same information whether player 1 has moved (or is moving, or will move) Left or Right,[3] is called player 2's *information set*. (In game 1, each node is a separate information set.) In the sequential game (game 1), player 2 could have had different choices of actions in the two nodes; in the simultaneous game (game 2), he necessarily has the same actions available, as otherwise he would be able to distinguish the two nodes. In the jargon of this chapter, game 2 is a *static game* and game 1 a *dynamic game*; this is because in the latter, but not in the former, a player (player 2) has the possibility of observing and reacting to the other player's actions. At a formal level, these two types of games need not be separated; however, this distinction makes the progressive introduction of extensions of the Nash concept more convenient.

We assume that the entire structure of the tree is "common knowledge": All players know it, know that their opponents know it, and so on.[4] Any exogenous uncertainties (i.e., moves of nature) must be incorporated into the tree.[5]

In our discussion of games 1 and 2, we talked about the players moving left or right. These are called *pure strategies*. A pure strategy is the choice by a player of a given action with certainty. In contrast, a player (say, player 1) might randomize between left and right, i.e., play left with

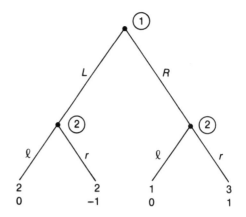

Figure 11.1
Game 1.

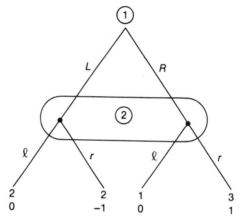

Figure 11.2
Game 2.

probability x and right with probability $1 - x$, with x in [0, 1]. Such a strategy is called a *mixed strategy*.[6] A pure strategy is a special case of a mixed strategy (with $x = 0$ or 1 in the previous example).

The *normal-form* representation of an extensive-form game is a summarized description of the extensive form. The normal form is a collection of the pure strategies available to each player at each of his information sets in the extensive form. In games 1 and 2, player 1 has two pure strategies: $a_1^1 = L$ and $a_1^2 = R$. In game 1, player

---

3. We could represent this game equally well by the extensive form in which player 2 moves first but player 1's information set includes two nodes.

4. On the notion of common knowledge, see Aumann 1974, 1976 and Milgrom 1981a.

5. See sections 11.4 and 11.5.

6. More accurately, in an extensive-form game, a behavioral strategy for player i specifies for each of his information sets a probability distribution over the actions that are feasible in that set. The term *mixed strategy* is often reserved for the normal form (see below). Kuhn (1953) has shown that the two concepts are equivalent as long as each player recalls at any point in the tree what he knew previously (i.e., at earlier nodes). So we will identify both concepts.

2 has four pure strategies: $a_2^1 = \{\ell, \ell\}$, $a_2^2 = \{r, r\}$, $a_2^3 = \{\ell, r\}$, and $a_2^4 = \{r, \ell\}$, where, for instance, $a_2^3 = \{\ell, r\}$ means that player 2 reacts to a_1^1 by playing left and to a_1^2 by playing right. In game 2, player 2 has only two pure strategies, which correspond to the strategies a_2^1 and a_2^2 of game 1. The normal form also maps pure strategies into payoffs for each player. For instance, in game 1, player 1's payoff for pure strategies $\{a_1^1, a_2^3\}$ is $\Pi^1(a_1^1, a_2^3) = 2$, because player 1 plays Left and player 2 reacts by also playing Left. The normal forms are often depicted by matrices, as in figure 11.3.

More generally, one can define a normal-form game as a set of feasible pure strategies or actions A_i and payoff functions

$$\Pi^i(a_1, \ldots, a_i, \ldots, a_n)$$

for each player i.

As in the extensive form, one can enlarge the strategy space and allow mixed strategies. A mixed strategy for player i is a probability distribution over A_i. (The strategy space is thus $\bar{A}_i$, the set of probability distributions over A_i). The payoffs for mixed strategies are simply the expected values of the corresponding pure-strategy payoffs.

Exercise 11.1* Consider the extensive-form game depicted in figure 11.4.

(i) What are player 2's information sets? What are player 1's?

(ii) Write this game in normal form.

11.2 Nash Equilibrium

In this section we will be using exclusively the normal-form representation. To make an optimal decision, a player must generally foresee how his opponents will behave. The first and indisputable basis for such a conjecture is that one's opponents should not play dominated strategies. If an action always gives a lower payoff to a player than another action, whatever the other players do, we may assume that the player will not pick that action. Consider, for instance, the normal form of game 1. Playing a_2^1, a_2^2, or a_2^4 is (weakly) dominated by playing a_2^3 for player 2. Thus, player 2 plays a_2^3 if he is "rational," and player 1 should expect a payoff of 2 or 3 if he plays Left (a_1^1) or Right (a_1^2). So he plays Right, and we have obtained a well-defined outcome for this game: $\{a_1^2, a_2^3\}$. Note that

Game 1

Player 2 \ Player 1	$a_2^1 = (\ell, \ell)$	$a_2^2 = (r, r)$	$a_2^3 = (\ell, r)$	$a_2^4 = (r, \ell)$
$a_1^1 = L$	2,0	2,−1	2,0	2,−1
$a_1^2 = R$	1,0	3,1	3,1	1,0

Game 2

Player 2 \ Player 1	$a_2^1 = \ell$	$a_2^2 = r$
$a_1^1 = L$	2,0	2,−1
$a_1^2 = R$	1,0	3,1

Figure 11.3
Normal form.

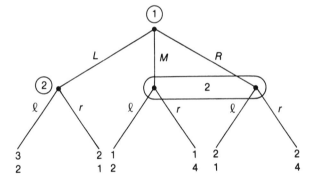

Figure 11.4
Game 3.

playing Left is not *a priori* dominated for player 1. However, it becomes so after player 2's dominated strategies have been eliminated. More generally, one can proceed by *successive elimination of dominated strategies* on the normal form. At each stage, the elimination of dominated strategies for some players at the previous stage uncovers dominated strategies for other players. The process stops when no more dominated strategies can be found.

The elimination of the dominated strategies also gives a unique answer in the famous "prisoner's dilemma" game, depicted in figure 11.5. The story behind this game is that two people are arrested for a crime. The police lack sufficient evidence to convict either suspect and, consequently, need them to give testimony against each other. The police put each suspect in a different cell, and are able to prevent the two suspects from communicating with each other. The police tell each suspect that if he testifies against (finks on) the other, he will be released—provided the other suspect does not fink on him—and will receive a reward for testifying. If neither suspect finks, both will be released on account of insufficient evidence, and no rewards will be paid. If one finks, the other will go to prison; if both fink, both will go to prison, but they will still collect the rewards for testifying. In this game, both players simultaneously choose between two actions. If both players cooperate (*C*) (do not testify), they get 2 each. If they both play noncooperatively (*F*, for *fink*), they obtain −2. If one finks and the other cooperates, the latter is rewarded (gets 3) and the former is severely punished (gets −3).[7]

Clearly *F* is a dominant strategy for both players. So {*F*, *F*} is the only plausible outcome. This outcome is very bad for both players; by cooperating, each would be able to obtain 2 instead of −2. However, self-interest leads to a Pareto-inefficient outcome. (The reader who thinks that this outcome is not reasonable—in particular, that the players should be able to sustain cooperation—should question the description of the game, i.e., the way a real-life situation is depicted, but not the way the outcome is selected.)

*Exercise 11.2**   A seller has one indivisible unit of an object for sale. The *n* bidders have valuations $0 \leqslant v_1$

Player 2 / Player 1	F	C
F	−2,−2	3,−3
C	−3,3	2,2

Figure 11.5
The prisoner's dilemma.

$\leqslant v_2 \leqslant \cdots \leqslant v_n$ for the object, and these valuations are common knowledge. Bidders submit bids b_i simultaneously. The highest bidder wins the object and pays the second bid; i.e., if *i* wins, he has utility

$$\Pi^i = v_i - \max_{j \neq i} b_j.$$

The others do not pay anything.

(i) Show that bidding one's valuation ($b_i = v_i$) is a dominant strategy for bidder *i*.

(ii) Conclude that bidder *n* wins and has a surplus of $v_n - v_{n-1}$.

(iii) Would these results be affected if each trader knew his own valuation but not those of the other bidders?

*Exercise 11.3**   There are *n* consumers, with utility functions

$$\Pi^i \equiv t_i + g_i(a, \theta_i),$$

where t_i is consumer *i*'s income, *a* is a public decision (for instance, the quantity of a public good), $g_i(a, \theta_i)$ is consumer *i*'s valuation for decision *a*, and θ_i is a utility parameter. The functions g_i are common knowledge. The monetary cost of decision *a* is $C(a)$.

(i) Show that for a planner who knows all the parameters $\{\theta_i\}_{i=1}^n$, the socially optimal decision, $a^*(\theta_1, \ldots, \theta_n)$, maximizes

$$\sum_i g_i(a, \theta_i) - C(a)$$

(the Samuelson rule).

---

7. In an example of an I.O. game, *C* would stand for "charging a high price" and *F* for "charging a low price."

(ii) Suppose that θ_i is known only to consumer i. The planner tries to design a mechanism that induces the consumers to announce their valuations truthfully and implement the socially optimal decision. Consider the following game: Consumers are asked to announce their valuations simultaneously. $\tilde{\theta}_i$ is consumer i's announcement (it may differ from the truth). The planner then implements the decision $a^*(\tilde{\theta}_1, \ldots, \tilde{\theta}_n)$ (i.e., the decision that is optimal if all consumers tell the truth), and gives transfers:

$$t_i(\tilde{\theta}_1, \ldots, \tilde{\theta}_n) = K_i + \sum_{j \neq i} g_j(a^*(\tilde{\theta}_1, \ldots, \tilde{\theta}_n), \tilde{\theta}_j)$$
$$- C(a^*(\tilde{\theta}_1, \ldots, \tilde{\theta}_n)),$$

where K_i is a constant. Show that telling the truth ($\tilde{\theta}_i = \theta_i$) is a dominant strategy for consumer i. Conclude that the planner can implement the first-best (full-information) allocation.

Unfortunately, in many games the elimination of dominated strategies does not go very far toward selecting a unique "reasonable" outcome (or a limited set of them). An example is given by the simultaneous game 2. None of the four strategies is dominated, and this method leaves us with an indeterminate outcome. Similarly, in Bertrand or Cournot games of simultaneous choices of prices or quantities (chapter 5), the optimal action for one firm depends on that of the other firm, which means that one already has a lot of undominated strategies.

Two other famous two-player simultaneous-choice examples are depicted in figure 11.6. In "matching pennies," players choose heads or tails. If the choices match, player 1 receives 1 from player 2; and vice versa when they don't match. In "battle of the sexes," each player chooses between going to a movie or to a play. The two players always prefer going somewhere together to going anywhere alone, but player 1 prefers the movie and player 2 the play.

In such cases, the notion of *Nash equilibrium* yields a weaker concept of "reasonable outcome."

Definition A set of strategies $\{a_i^*\}_{i=1}^n$ is a pure-strategy Nash equilibrium if and only if, for all a_i in A_i,

$$\Pi^i(a_i^*, a_{-i}^*) \geqslant \Pi^i(a_i, a_{-i}^*),$$

where $a_{-i}^* \equiv (a_1^*, \ldots, a_{i-1}^*, a_{i+1}^*, \ldots, a_n^*)$. In other words, a Nash equilibrium is a set of actions such that no player,

Matching pennies

Player 1 \ Player 2	H	T
H	1,−1	−1,1
T	−1,1	1,−1

Battle of the sexes

Player 1 \ Player 2	M	P
M	3,2	1,1
P	1,1	2,3

Figure 11.6

taking his opponents' actions as given, wishes to change his own action. This definition is, of course, straightforwardly extended to allow mixed strategies by letting $\tilde{A}_i$ (the set of probability distributions over A_i) be player i's strategy set and letting Π^i denote the expectation over the mixed strategies.

Matching pennies illustrates the possibility of the inexistence of a pure-strategy equilibrium. If player 1 plays H, player 2 plays T, which induces player 1 to want to play T, and so forth. But there exists a mixed-strategy equilibrium: Each player plays H and T with equal probabilities. For this to be an equilibrium, it must be the case that both pure strategies yield the same payoff to each player. Playing H yields to player 1

$$\tfrac{1}{2}(1) + \tfrac{1}{2}(-1) = 0,$$

whereas playing T yields him

$$\tfrac{1}{2}(-1) + \tfrac{1}{2}(1) = 0.$$

Pure-strategy equilibria need not exist in general games, but mixed-strategy equilibria always do (see the supplementary section).

The battle of the sexes illustrates the possibility of multiple equilibria. $\{M, M\}$ and $\{P, P\}$ are the two pure-strategy equilibria. There also exists a mixed-strategy equilibrium, in which player 1 plays M with probability $\tfrac{2}{3}$ (and P with probability $\tfrac{1}{3}$) and player 2 plays P with probability $\tfrac{2}{3}$ (and M with probability $\tfrac{1}{3}$). In such cases, it is not clear which prediction should be made. No equilibrium is superior to the others for both players. On the other hand, some elements of history (not included in the description of the game) may suggest a "focal" equilibrium (for instance, that the two players have previously alternated, and last week they went to a movie, so that the "natural" thing to do this week is to go to a play).[8] This type of selection among Nash equilibria involves much personal judgment (as opposed to the use of a systematic method).

Often, A_i is a continuous space ($\mathbb{R}$, say) and Π^i has nice differentiability properties. One can then obtain a pure-strategy equilibrium, if any, by differentiating each player's payoff function with respect to his own action. The first-order condition is thus

$$\Pi_i^i(a_i^*, a_{-i}^*) = 0,$$

where $\Pi_i^i \equiv \partial \Pi^i / \partial a_i$ denotes the partial derivative with respect to own action. (The local second-order condition is $\Pi_{ii}^i \leqslant 0$.) The first-order conditions give a system of n equations with n unknowns, which, if solutions exist and the second-order condition for each player holds, yield the pure-strategy Nash equilibrium (or equilibria). For instance, suppose that two firms (producing differentiated goods) compete through prices, so $a_i = p_i$. The demand for the good produced by firm i is

$$q_i = D_i(p_i, p_j) = 1 - bp_i + dp_j,$$

with $0 \leqslant d \leqslant b$. If firm i has unit cost c, then

$$\Pi^i = (p_i - c)(1 - bp_i + dp_j).$$

Note that Π^i is concave in p_i. The first-order conditions are, for $i = 1, 2$,

$$1 + dp_j + bc - 2bp_i = 0.$$

The pure-strategy Nash equilibrium is unique and symmetric:

$$p_1^* = p_2^* = \frac{1 + bc}{2b - d}.$$

Now let us return to games 1 and 2. The simultaneous-move game (game 2) has two pure-strategy equilibria: $\{a_1^1, a_2^1\}$ and $\{a_1^2, a_2^2\}$. The sequential-move game (game 1) admits these two Nash equilibria plus a third: $\{a_1^2, a_2^3\}$, which yields the same actions (and, therefore, the same payoffs) as the second. For the simultaneous game, both Nash equilibria look reasonable.[9] This is not the case for the sequential-move game, for which we argued that

there exists a unique reasonable solution (after elimination of dominated strategies). The issue, as we will see, is that the concept of Nash equilibrium is appropriate only when all decisions are made simultaneously (once and for all); it is generally too weak when sequential decisions are involved.

*Exercise 11.4** Find the pure strategy Nash equilibria for the game defined in exercise 11.1.

*Exercise 11.5*** Consumers are located uniformly along a linear city of length 1. Each consumer wants to buy one unit of a good from one of the existing firms. The transportation cost for the consumer is proportional to the distance to the firm he buys from. The law prohibits any form of competition through price or service (other than location), so consumers go to the nearest firm. A firm's utility is equal to the number of its customers. Firms located at the same location get the same number of customers.

(i) There are two firms, and they choose their locations simultaneously. Show that there exists a unique pure-strategy Nash equilibrium, and that both firms locate in the middle of the segment.

(ii) Show that with three firms there exists no pure-strategy Nash equilibrium.

*Exercise 11.6*** There are n consumers. Each consumer i spends an amount of money p_i on a public good. The choices are simultaneous. Consumer i has utility

$$U_i(p_1, \ldots, p_n) = g\left(\sum_{i=1}^{n} p_i\right) - p_i,$$

where $g(0) = 0$, $g'(0) > 1$, $g' > 0$, $g'' < 0$, and $\lim_{x \to \infty} g'(x) < 1$. Compute the Nash equilibrium. Discuss the multiplicity. Show that there is too little public expenditure.

11.3 Perfect Equilibrium

In a Nash equilibrium the players take their opponents' strategies as given and therefore do not consider the pos-

---

8. Schelling's (1960) examples of focal equilibria may be more convincing.

9. Except that the payoffs (3, 1) for the second exceed those (2, 0) for the first.

It might be argued that the two players should coordinate on the second, but one can change the example slightly so that this does not occur.

sibility of influencing them. In games in which a player chooses some actions after observing some of his opponents' actions (what we call *dynamic* games), this conjecture is naive and leads to some absurd Nash equilibria, as we saw in the previous section. This section introduces a refinement of Nash equilibrium for dynamic games that mitigates the deficiencies of Nash equilibrium.

Consider again the sequential game 1 (figure 11.1) and the Nash equilibrium $\{a_1^1, a_2^1\}$. Player 1 does not play R because player 2 threatens to play ℓ in this case. But suppose that player 1 plays R. Then player 2, faced with a *fait accompli*, benefits from playing r, since he then obtains 1 instead of 0. Therefore, player 2's threat is not credible. Player 1, who should anticipate this, plays R, which gives him a payoff of 3—greater than what he obtains by playing L. Thus, the proposed Nash equilibrium is based on a noncredible threat, i.e., a threat that would not be carried out if the player were put in the position to do so.

The basic idea of perfect equilibrium is to select Nash equilibria that do not involve noncredible threats, by (roughly) requiring that the players' behavior be optimal even in situations that are not reached on the equilibrium path. For instance, player 2's decision to play ℓ when player 1 has played R is not optimal; the reason why $\{a_1^1, a_2^1\}$ is a Nash equilibrium nevertheless is that this suboptimal decision does not cost player 2 anything, because player 1 is supposed to play L (in the jargon of game theory, player 1's playing R is a zero-probability event). In contrast, a perfect equilibrium requires that player 2 play optimally whether player 1 plays Right or Left. This amounts to eliminating dominated strategies for player 2, which is why perfection gives the same answer as the iterated elimination of dominated strategies for this game. (See below for a class of games in which the two methods give the same answer.)

To obtain the perfect equilibrium, we work "backwards": By knowing player 2's optimal reaction to each of player 1's potential actions, we can "fold back the tree," as in figure 11.7. Player 1's (respectively, player 2's) *valuations* are 2 and 3 (respectively, 0 and 1) when player 1 has played left and right. (The valuations represent the payoffs that the players obtain when they reach a certain location in the game tree.) The game then boils down to a single-decision-maker problem in which player 1 chooses R. The process of backward induction in the tree is called *Kuhn's algorithm* (Kuhn 1953).

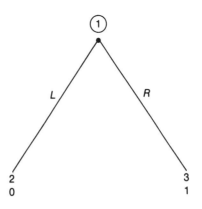

Figure 11.7

For more general games, let us define a (proper) *subgame* as a subset of the initial game tree that (1) begins with an information set that contains only one node, (2) is closed under succession (if a node is in the subgame, so are all of its successors), and (3) is such that all the information sets of the subgame are information sets of the initial game.

In particular, a game itself is one of its subgames. For instance, game 1 has three subgames: itself and the two subgames starting after player 1 has moved. In contrast, game 2 is its only subgame, because of requirement 1. A (subgame) *perfect equilibrium* (Selten 1965) is a set of strategies for each player such that in any subgame the strategies (truncated to this subgame) form a Nash equilibrium. Thus, *perfection requires that strategies be in equilibrium whatever the location (understand subgame) in the game tree, and not only along the equilibrium path.* A perfect equilibrium is necessarily a Nash equilibrium (take the big subgame constituted by the game itself). In game 1 the two second-period subgames are single-decision-maker problems. Nash equilibrium in these subgames simply means that the decision maker (player 2) chooses his best action.

There are two types of commonly used games for which perfection is powerful: games of perfect information and games of "almost perfect" information.

11.3.1 Games of Perfect Information

Roughly, in these games the player whose turn it is to play knows (has perfect information about) all the actions that have been chosen before this play. There is no element of simultaneity at all. Formally, all information sets have only one node. Game 1 is an example of such a game; the Stackelberg game of chapter 8 and the short-run-commitment price game of chapter 6 are others. The interesting thing about these games is that the iterated elimination of weakly dominated strategies on the normal form yields perfect equilibria (at least for finite games). To see this, start from the terminal period or the terminal nodes (there are two such nodes in game 1). (First-stage) elimination of dominated strategies for the player playing last yields his optimal behavior at each terminal node. When the last-period behavior is folded back into valuations, the next-to-last period becomes the last one, and again the (second-stage) elimination of dominated strategies yields optimal behavior, and so forth. Thus, the iterated elimination of dominated strategies satisfies backward induction in the tree (Kuhn 1953). (The two concepts are almost equivalent. For an example in which they differ, replace the payoff 3 in game 1 by payoff 2. $\{R, r\}$ is a perfect equilibrium, but is ruled out by the elimination of weakly dominated strategies. The reader will check that the iterated elimination of strongly dominated strategies on the "agent normal form" yields exactly the set of perfect equilibria. See subsection 11.6.1 for the definition of agent normal form; see Moulin 1982 for results on the elimination of weakly dominated strategies.)

Example 1 Let us consider an algebraic example with the two-period structure of game 1. For this, consider the same price game as in section 11.2, except that firm 2 observes firm 1's price before choosing its own. The backward-induction logic requires that firm 1 foresee that firm 2 will react optimally to *any* choice of p_1. That is, firm 1 should solve the second-period optimization problem for firm 2 before tackling his own, first-period one. Knowing p_1, firm 2 maximizes

$$(p_2 - c)(1 - bp_2 + dp_1);$$

thus,

$$p_2 = R_2(p_1) = (1 + dp_1 + bc)/2b,$$

where R_2 denotes firm 2's (optimal) reaction. So firm 1 maximizes

$$(p_1 - c)[1 - bp_1 + d R_2(p_1)].$$

Note that it takes into account the effect of p_1 on p_2. The solution is then

$$p_1^* = \frac{(2b + d)(1 + bc) - d^2 c}{4b^2 - 2d^2}$$

and

$$p_2^* = R_2(p_1^*).$$

(The prices are higher in the sequential game than in the simultaneous game. See the explanation in terms of strategic complements in chapter 8.)

Example 2 Consider Rubinstein's (1982) bargaining game in which two players, who must share a pie of size 1, make sequential, alternating offers. At date 1, player 1 makes offer x_1 in $[0, 1]$; player 2 accepts or refuses x_1. If he accepts, he obtains $1 - x_1$, leaving x_1 for player 1. If he refuses, he makes offer x_2 in $[0, 1]$ at date 2. If this offer is accepted, he gets $1 - x_2$ in period 2 and player 1 gets x_2; if player 1 refuses this offer, he gets to make an offer x_3 in the third period, and so on. The players alternate making offers until one of them accepts his opponent's offer. The payoffs are $\delta^t x_t$ for player 1 and $\delta^t(1 - x_t)$ for player 2 if they agree at date t on a share x_t for player 1. The discount factor δ belongs to $(0, 1)$. Impatience will be the driving force that leads to agreement in this model. This is a game of perfect information. Each player, when making or responding to an offer, knows all actions taken before his move. Suppose that there are T periods. To solve for the perfect equilibrium, look at the last period first. Clearly, the player who makes the offer at T demands the whole pie because the other player will not be able to make a further offer. So, $x_T = 0$ if T is even and $x_T = 1$ if T is odd. At $T - 1$, the player who makes the offer gives the other player a share of the pie such that the latter is indifferent between getting this share at $T - 1$ and getting the whole pie at T. And so forth.

Exercise 11.7** Solve the previous bargaining game for $T = 2, 3, \ldots$. Show that x_1 tends to $1/(1 + \delta)$ when T goes to infinity.

Rather than solve the finite-horizon case (see exercise 11.7), we focus on the infinite-horizon case, to show how direct backward induction can be replaced by the use of valuation functions. Let us assume that the horizon is infinite. Conditional on the game's not being terminated (no offer has been accepted), the game "looks the same" at all odd periods; and similarly for even periods. Let us thus look for "stationary strategies": When player 1 makes an offer, he always offers x_1. When player 2 makes an offer, he always offers x_2. These offers and any that are more favorable for the responding player are always accepted; any that are less favorable for the responding player are rejected.

Let V_i denote player i's valuation when it is his turn to make an offer; that is, V_i is the payoff that i expects when making an (optimal) offer. And let W_i denote player i's valuation when it is the other player's turn to make an offer. Note that because strategies are stationary, these valuations do not depend on time. Note also that from the definition of x_1 and x_2

$$V_1 = x_1, \; W_2 = 1 - x_1; \; V_2 = 1 - x_2, \; W_1 = x_2$$

and that

$$V_1 + W_2 = V_2 + W_1 = 1.$$

Now, when player 1 makes the offer, he offers player 2 a share that makes the latter just indifferent between accepting now and waiting one more period (offering more would be pointless). Thus,

$$1 - x_1 = \delta(1 - x_2)$$

or

$$W_2 = \delta V_2.$$

And similarly when player 2 makes the offer:

$$x_2 = \delta x_1$$

or

$$W_1 = \delta V_1.$$

Because the game is symmetric, $V_1 = V_2 = V$ and $W_1 = W_2 = W$. Thus, $W = \delta V$ and $V + W = 1$ lead to $V = 1/(1 + \delta)$ and $W = \delta/(1 + \delta)$. So the player who makes the offer gets $1/(1 + \delta)$, and the other gets the rest of the pie: $\delta/(1 + \delta)$. The equilibrium strategies are these: The offering player offers a share $\delta/(1 + \delta)$ to the responding player; the latter accepts any share at least equal to $\delta/(1 + \delta)$ and rejects any lower share.

Note that this equilibrium is the limit of the finite-horizon equilibrium when T goes to infinity (see exercise 11.7). Rubinstein showed that this is also the unique equilibrium of the infinite-horizon game.[10]

Exercise 11.8*** Show that the infinite-horizon equilibrium is unique. Hint: Introduce the following valuations. $\overline{V}_i$ (respectively, $\underline{V}_i$) is the highest (respectively, the lowest) possible payoff for player i in the set of perfect equilibria when it is his turn to make the offer. Define $\overline{W}_i$ and $\underline{W}_i$ similarly. What are the relationships between these numbers? Conclude that $\overline{V}_i = \underline{V}_i = 1/(1 + \delta)$ and $\overline{W}_i = \underline{W}_i = \delta/(1 + \delta)$.

Exercise 11.9* Consider the following simple-minded inspection game: A firm may pick an anticompetitive action (i.e., may prey) or not. Preying yields it an (extra) monetary payoff of $g > 0$. Antitrust authorities can inspect or not. The cost of inspection is $c > 0$. If the firm has preyed and inspection occurs, the firm pays a penalty $p > g$; the antitrust authorities' payoff is then $s - c > 0$. If the firm has not preyed and inspection occurs, or if no inspection occurs, no penalty is paid and the authorities' payoff is $-c$ or 0, respectively.

(i) Suppose that the antitrust authority observes whether predation occurred before choosing whether to inspect. Draw the game tree. What is the perfect equilibrium?

(ii) Assume that whether predation has occurred is not observed before the inspection decision. Draw the game tree. Argue that there exists no pure-strategy equilibrium. Compute the mixed-strategy one. How does a change in the penalty affect this equilibrium?

11.3.2 Games of "Almost Perfect" Information

Suppose that the game can be decomposed into a number of periods $t = 1, 2, \ldots, T$ (where T is finite or infinite), and that at each date t the players simultaneously choose actions knowing all the actions chosen by everybody at dates 1 through $t - 1$. Because such a game introduces simultaneity only within a period, we call such extensive forms *games of "almost perfect" information*. The simplest example of such a game is the "repeated game" in which a simple one-period simultaneous-move game (such as those depicted in figures 11.2, 11.5, and 11.6) is repeated T times and, at date t, players know all the moves before t. In a repeated game there is no physical link between the periods.[11] In contrast, the sequential quantity-price game

---

10. In general, infinite-horizon games may have other equilibria than the limits of the equilibria of the finite-horizon game when the horizon tends to infinity. See chapter 6 and subsection 11.3.2 for examples. See Fudenberg and Levine 1983 for an investigation of the link between the two.

11. The one-period simultaneous-move game is called the *constituent game.* Each period starts a proper subgame for each history of past moves.

of chapter 5 and the entry, accommodation, and exit games of chapters 7 through 9 involve physical links through all kinds of investments. For instance, when firms learn by doing, price competition at t does not look the same as that at $t-1$ because the cost structure have changed. A brief introduction to repeated games should suffice here. (For more on repeated games, see chapter 6.)

Example: Repeated games   Let us return to the "prisoner's dilemma" game described in section 11.2, and let us assume that the players play this same game repeatedly (and learn past moves along the way). Assume that each player's payoff is equal to the present discounted value of his per-period payoffs over the time horizon (with some discount factor δ in $(0, 1)$). Suppose first that there are a finite number of periods T. To solve for a perfect equilibrium, work backwards from the end of the horizon. At date T, the strategies must specify a Nash equilibrium for any history. Since payoffs at date T are separable and not affected by history, the strategies must specify a Nash equilibrium of the one-period game. So, from section 11.2, for any history, $a_1^*(T) = a_2^*(T) = F$. Both players fink. Consider period $T-1$. Strategies must form a two-period Nash equilibrium for any history. However, the last two periods are physically independent of history, and the period-T outcome is independent of what happens at $T-1$. Hence, the strategies at $T-1$ must also form a one-period Nash equilibrium. Hence, both players fink at date $T-1$. By backwards induction, they fink at all periods. This is part of a more general result: If the one-period-game equilibrium is unique, the T-period-game equilibrium is simply a repetition of this equilibrium T times.[12] This property does not hold when $T = +\infty$ (there is a "discontinuity at infinity"). Both players finking at each period, whatever the history, is still a perfect equilibrium: Given that the future outcomes are not affected by what is played now (they will fink anyway), both players should maximize their instantaneous payoffs

by finking. But there exist other equilibria. Consider, for instance, the following symmetric strategies: At any date t a player cooperates if and only if both players have always cooperated between periods 1 and $t-1$. At date 1, both cooperate. This forms a perfect equilibrium if $\delta > \frac{1}{5}$: In a subgame starting at date t in which one player has finked in the past, both fink forever. We already know that such strategies are perfect (and, therefore, Nash). In a subgame in which no one has yet finked, the strategies also form a Nash equilibrium; they yield

$$2(1 + \delta + \delta^2 + \cdots) = 2/(1 - \delta)$$

from t on. If a player deviated and finked at date t, he would get

$$3 - 2(\delta + \delta^2 + \cdots) = 3 - \frac{2\delta}{1 - \delta}$$

because from time $t+1$ on both strategies will specify "fink forever." Thus, for a player to cooperate we need

$$\frac{2}{1 - \delta} > \frac{3 - 5\delta}{1 - \delta}$$

(the long-run gain from sustaining cooperation exceeds the short-run gain from deviating), which amounts to $\delta > \frac{1}{5}$.

There are many other equilibria for the infinite horizon. The so-called folk theorem gives an exact characterization of the set of perfect equilibria of general repeated games with infinite horizon when the discount factor is very near 1.[13]

11.4   Bayesian Equilibrium

11.4.1   Games with Imperfect or Incomplete Information

Game theorists make a distinction between imperfect information and incomplete information. Roughly speaking,

---

12. The combinations of one-period equilibria are only some of many equilibria if the one-period game has multiple equilibria. See Benoit and Krishna 1985 for a general result; see Frayssé and Moreaux 1985 for a simple application to the repeated Cournot game.

13. The folk theorem asserts that any feasible payoff above the "individually rational payoffs"—the individually rational payoff for player i is the minimum payoff that other players could force i to get in the one-period game:

$$\min_{a_{-i}} \max_{a_i} \Pi^i(a_i, a_{-i})$$

—can be sustained on average as a perfect-equilibrium payoff of the infinitely repeated game for $\delta = 1$ (Aumann and Shapley 1976; Rubinstein 1979) or, under a weak condition, for δ close to 1 (Fudenberg and Maskin 1986). For instance, in the prisoner's dilemma game the individually rational payoffs turn out to coincide with the equilibrium payoffs $(-2, -2)$ of the one-period game. The set of equilibrium payoffs in the infinitely repeated game is thus the set of convex combinations of the four payoff couples of figure 11.4. For discount factors of less than 1, see Abreu 1984. The supplementary section of chapter 6 contains a more complete discussion of the folk theorem.

a player has imperfect information when he does not know what the other players have done beforehand.[14] On the other hand, a player has incomplete information when he does not know his rivals' precise characteristics (preferences, strategy spaces). For example, consider research and development (R&D) competition among firms. The dynamic game played by firms seeking a patent is one with incomplete information if the firms do not know their rivals' unit research costs (or the quality of their engineers), but it is one with imperfect information if, at a given point in time, they do not know how much their rivals have spent so far on R&D. Actually, this distinction is somewhat semantic—a game with incomplete information may be transformed into one with imperfect information by first introducing a new player, "nature," who chooses the characteristic or the type of each player, and then assuming that the players, other than the particular one in question, are not informed of the choice of the player's type (see Harsanyi 1967–68).[15] The equilibrium concept described in section 11.5 encompasses games of incomplete and imperfect information.

The characteristic (or *type*) t_i of a player i embodies everything that is relevant to this player's decision making.[16] In practice, it is often posited that t_i is some parameter of player i's objective function (cost or demand parameter, for instance) known to player i. One further assumes that it is common knowledge that types are *a priori* drawn from some known distribution

$$p(t_1, \ldots, t_i, \ldots, t_n).$$

Player i thus has conditional probability

$$p_i(t_{-i} | t_i)$$

on his opponents' types

$$t_{-i} \equiv (t_1, \ldots, t_{i-1}, t_{i+1}, \ldots, t_n)$$

given his own type t_i.

11.4.2 Static Games of Incomplete Information

In this subsection we will be concerned only with games in which players move simultaneously, so no player has the opportunity to react to another's move. Hence, we can abstract for the moment from the issue of perfection discussed in section 11.3. And, importantly, we need not worry about the inferences made by players about their opponents' types, because all the actions are taken before any actions are observed. Hence, inferences are consequenceless. Dynamic games of incomplete (or imperfect) information will be considered in section 11.5. (Note that in a dynamic game the question of inferences can become important.)

We assume that player i picks some action a_i in A_i (as before, A_i can be extended to include mixed strategies) and has an *ex post* payoff of

$$\Pi^i(a_1, \ldots, a_n, t_1, \ldots, t_n).$$

Player i's decision naturally depends on his information t_i: Let $a_i(t_i)$ denote this action. Harsanyi's Bayesian equilibrium is the natural generalization of Nash equilibrium to games of incomplete information. It assumes that each player i correctly anticipates what actions all players $j \neq i$ choose. Because these actions depend on types, he correctly computes the functions $\{a_j(t_j)\}_{j \neq i}$.

Definition A *Bayesian equilibrium* is a set of type-contingent strategies $\{a_i^*(t_i)\}_{i=1}^n$ such that each player maximizes his expected utility contingent on his type and taking the other players' type-contingent strategies as given: $a_i = a_i^*(t_i)$ maximizes

$$\sum_{t_{-i}} p_i(t_{-i} | t_i) \Pi^i(a_1^*(t_1), \ldots, a_i, \ldots, a_n^*(t_n), t_1, \ldots, t_i, \ldots, t_n).$$

In other words, player i anticipates that player j will play $a_j^*(t_j)$ if the latter has type t_j; however, not knowing t_j, the former must compute his payoff in expectations. One could as well think of a player i as having several incarna-

---

14. In particular, one can describe a simultaneous game as a game of imperfect information by assuming that one player chooses before the other and that the latter does not know the action chosen by the former. (See, e.g., game 2.)

15. Suppose that each player's characteristics are known by this player, but that from the point of view of the $n - 1$ other players the characteristics are drawn from some known probability distribution. One can introduce a $(n + 1)$st player, whose strategy consists of choosing characteristics for each of the n

original players at the start of the game. Each player observes only his own characteristics and thus has imperfect information about nature's choice of his opponents' characteristics. (To endow nature with an objective function, one can assume that it is indifferent among all choices of characteristics and that it randomizes according to the initial probability distribution.)

16. See Harsanyi 1967–68, Mertens and Zamir 1983, and Brandenburger and Deckel 1985.

---

tions, such as a player i with type t_i and another, different player i with type t_i'. Which incarnation plays against the other players is drawn according to the prior distribution. Thus, a Bayesian equilibrium can be seen as a Nash equilibrium with $\sum_i |T_i|$ players, where $|T_i|$ is the number of potential types for player i.

Example 1 Let us start with a straightforward example. In the two-player, simultaneous-move game depicted in figure 11.8, player 1 has only one type (player 2 has complete information about player 1). Player 2 has two possible types: t_2 and t_2'. While player 2 knows his type, player 1 puts equal probabilities on the two types. Each player has two possible actions (up or down for player 1, left or right for player 2). Each cell represents the payoffs of players 1 and 2. For instance, the upper leftmost cell says that if player 1 plays U and player 2 has type t_2 and plays L, they get 3 and 1, respectively. Note that player 1's payoff depends only on the chosen actions, and not on who player 2 is. Solving for a Bayesian equilibrium here is straightforward. Each type of player 2 has a dominant strategy. Regardless of what player 1 does, t_2 chooses L and t_2' chooses R (that is, $a_2^*(t_2) = L$ and $a_2^*(t_2') = R$). Now everything is as if player 1 faced an opponent who played L and R with equal probability, because t_2 and t_2' are equally likely. Thus, by playing U (respectively, D), player 1 gets $\frac{1}{2}(3 + 2)$ (respectively, $\frac{1}{2}(0 + 4)$). Hence, $a_1^* = U$.

	Type t_2		Type t_2'	
Player 2 Player 1	L	R	L	R
U	3,1	2,0	3,0	2,1
D	0,1	4,0	0,0	4,1

Figure 11.8
Game 4.

Example 2 Consider a duopoly with Cournot (quantity) competition. Let firm i's profit be quadratic: $\Pi^i = q_i(t_i - q_i - q_j)$, where t_i is the difference between the intercept of the linear demand curve and firm i's constant unit cost ($i = 1, 2$) and q_i is the quantity chosen by firm i ($a_i \equiv q_i$). It is common knowledge that, for firm 1, $t_1 = 1$ (firm 2 has complete information about firm 1). Firm 2, however, has private information about its unit cost. Firm 1 knows only that $t_2 = \frac{3}{4}$ or $\frac{5}{4}$ with equal probabilities. Thus, firm 2 has two potential types, which we will call the "low-cost type" ($t_2 = \frac{5}{4}$) and the "high-cost type" ($t_2 = \frac{3}{4}$). The two firms choose their outputs simultaneously. Let us look for a pure-strategy equilibrium. Firm 1 plays q_1, firm 2 plays q_2^L (if $t_2 = \frac{5}{4}$) or q_2^H (if $t_2 = \frac{3}{4}$). Let us start with firm 2:

$$q_2(t_2) \in \arg\max_{q_2}[q_2(t_2 - q_2 - q_1)]$$
$$\Rightarrow q_2(t_2) = (t_2 - q_1)/2,$$

where "arg max" denotes the set of values that maximize the objective function. Let us now consider firm 1, which does not know which type it faces.

$$q_1 \in \arg\max_{q_1}[\tfrac{1}{2}q_1(1 - q_1 - q_2^H) + \tfrac{1}{2}q_1(1 - q_1 - q_2^L)]$$
$$\Rightarrow q_1 = (1 - Eq_2)/2,$$

where $E(\cdot)$ denotes an expectation over firm 2's types. However,

$$Eq_2 = \tfrac{1}{2}q_2^H + \tfrac{1}{2}q_2^L = (Et_2 - q_1)/2 = (1 - q_1)/2.$$

One thus obtains $\{q_1 = \frac{1}{3}, q_2^L = \frac{11}{24}, q_2^H = \frac{5}{24}\}$ as a (provably unique) Bayesian equilibrium. This simple example illustrates how one can compute the Bayesian equilibrium as a Nash equilibrium of a three-player game.[17]

Example 3 Assume that two players bid simultaneously for an indivisible object ($a_i \equiv b_i$). The highest bidder gets the object and pays his bid. (Thus, if $b_i > b_j$, i gets the object and pays b_i to the seller. If $b_i = b_j$, the object is sold at the common bid randomly—the specification of the auction in this case does not matter, because identical bids will have probability 0.) A player's type t_i is his valuation for the object, so player i gets $t_i - b_i$ if he wins

---

17. See Saloner 1987 for more on this game. See section 11.6 for the sequential (i.e., Stackelberg) version of the game.

and 0 if he loses. Types t_i are drawn independently from the uniform distribution on $[0, 1]$. Let us look for a Bayesian equilibrium in which a player's bid is a strictly increasing and differentiable function of his valuation for the good. And, because the game is symmetric, let us derive symmetric-equilibrium strategies: $b = b^*(t)$. Player i's payoff when he is of type t and bids b is

$$\Pi^i = (t - b)\operatorname{Prob}\{b_j < b\},$$

where Prob stands for "probability that." Because strategies are strictly increasing,

$$\operatorname{Prob}\{b_j < b\} = \operatorname{Prob}\{b_j \leqslant b\}.$$

But, from player j's strategy,

$$\begin{aligned} \operatorname{Prob}\{b_j < b\} &= \operatorname{Prob}\{b^*(t_j) < b\} \\ &= \operatorname{Prob}\{t_j < b^{*-1}(b) \equiv \Phi(b)\} \\ &= \Phi(b), \end{aligned}$$

where $\Phi(b)$ denotes the inverse function of b^* (in words, $\Phi(b)$ is player j's valuation when he bids b), and use is made of the uniform distribution of types (if θ is distributed uniformly on $[0, 1]$ and $k \in [0, 1]$, then $\operatorname{Prob}\{\theta \leqslant k\} = k$). Thus, player i maximizes

$$\Pi^i = (t - b)\Phi(b),$$

which yields the first-order condition

$$-\Phi(b) + (t - b)\Phi'(b) = 0.$$

Now, in order for $b^*(\cdot)$ to also be player i's optimal strategy, it must be the case that the latter is of type $t = \Phi(b)$ when bidding b. Hence,

$$\Phi(b) = [\Phi(b) - b]\Phi'(b).$$

This differential equation has the obvious solution $\Phi(b) = 2b$. Thus, a Bayesian equilibrium of the game has each player bidding half of his valuation: $b^*(t) = t/2$.[18] Similar techniques are used to solve "wars of attrition"; see section 9.9.

Exercise 11.10[**] Consider an n-bidder first-bid auction. Each bidder's valuation is drawn independently from the cumulative distribution: $F(t) = t^\alpha$ on $[0, 1]$. Show that, in equilibrium, the bid function is linear in the bidder's valuation. What happens when n tends to infinity?

Exercise 11.11[**] Suppose that each bidder's estimate of the value of an object affects the other bidders' own valuations for the object. The extreme case of this situation is the common-value auction in which the *ex post* value of the object (e.g., an oil lease) is the same for all bidders and each bidder has a private and imperfect estimate of the common value. Winning then conveys bad news to the winner, who learns that the other bidders attached a low value to the good. This winner's curse must be anticipated by a rational bidder. Consider a first-bid auction for a good with common value $\theta = x_1 + x_2$. The parameters x_1 and x_2 are independently drawn from the uniform distribution on $[0, 1]$. There are two bidders, $i = 1, 2$. Bidder i knows x_i but not x_j.

(i) Argue informally that bidder i's payoff, if he wins, is necessarily smaller than $x_i + \frac{1}{2} - b_i$ (where b_i is the winning bid).

(ii) Look for a symmetric equilibrium. Let $x = \Phi(b)$ denote the inverse bid function. Argue that, for a given x_i, b_i ($= \Phi^{-1}(x_i)$) maximizes

$$\{x_i + E[x_j | x_j \leqslant \Phi(b_i)] - b_i\}\Phi(b_i).$$

(iii) Compute the equilibrium bid function. (Hint: It is linear.)

Example 4 Simultaneous-move games of *complete* information often admit mixed-strategy equilibria. Some researchers are unhappy with this notion because, they argue, "real-world decision makers do not flip coins." However, as Harsanyi (1973) has shown, mixed-strategy equilibria of complete-information games can often be vindicated as the limits of pure-strategy equilibria of slightly perturbed games of incomplete information. Indeed, we have already noticed that in a Bayesian game, once the players' type-contingent strategies have been computed, each player behaves as if he were facing mixed strategies by his opponents. (Nature creates uncertainty through the choice of types rather than the choice of the side of the coin.) To illustrate the mechanics of this con-

---

18. The second-order condition for each bidder is satisfied. For more on auctions, see Myerson 1979 and Milgrom and Weber 1982. On characterization and uniqueness in the first-bid auction, see Maskin and Riley 1983.

Player 1 \ Player 2	I	N
I	−1,−1	1,0
N	0,1	0,0

Figure 11.9
A game of "grab the dollar."

struction, let us consider the one-period version of the "grab the dollar" game represented in figure 11.9. Each player has two possible actions: investment and no investment. In the complete-information version of the game, a firm gains 1 (i.e., wins) if it is the only one to make the investment, loses 1 if both firms invest, and breaks even if it does not invest. (We can view this game as an extremely crude representation of a natural monopoly market.) The only symmetric equilibrium involves mixed strategies: Each firm invests with probability $\frac{1}{2}$. This clearly is an equilibrium: Each firm makes 0 if it does not invest and makes $\frac{1}{2}(1) + \frac{1}{2}(-1) = 0$ if it does invest. Now consider the same game with the following incomplete information: Each firm has the same payoff structure, except that when it wins it gets $(1 + t)$, where t is uniformly distributed on $[-\varepsilon, +\varepsilon]$. Each firm knows its type t, but not that of the other firm. Now, it is easily seen that the symmetric *pure* strategies, "$a(t < 0)$ = do not invest, $a(t \geqslant 0)$ = invest," form a Bayesian equilibrium. From the point of view of each firm, the other firm invests with probability $\frac{1}{2}$. Thus, the firm should invest if and only if $\frac{1}{2}(1 + t) + \frac{1}{2}(-1) \geqslant 0$, i.e., $t \geqslant 0$. Because for a given type a player has a unique best action, there is no problem with the player resisting the prescription to randomize with a given probability ($\frac{1}{2}$ before). When ε converges to zero, the pure-strategy Bayesian equilibrium converges to the mixed-strategy Nash equilibrium of the complete-information game.

Because games of complete information are an idealization (in practice, everyone has at least a slight amount of

incomplete information about the other players' objectives), Harsanyi's argument shows that it is hard to make a strong case against mixed-strategy equilibria on the ground that they require a randomizing device.[19]

11.5 Perfect Bayesian Equilibrium

We now study dynamic games of incomplete (or imperfect) information. The tricky feature in these games is that a player who reacts to another player's move can extract information from that move. It is natural to suppose that the inference process takes the form of Bayesian updating from the latter player's supposed equilibrium strategy and his observed action. The equilibrium notion is a combination of the (subgame) perfect-equilibrium concept for dynamic games and the Bayesian-equilibrium concept for games of incomplete information. This section introduces the simplest such notion: perfect Bayesian equilibrium (PBE)[20] and gives four simple applications of the concept.

To motivate the notion of equilibrium, we begin with the simple game of imperfect information depicted in figure 11.10. This game has three players and takes place over three "periods." In period 1, player 1 can choose from among three actions: "Left" (L_1), "Middle" (M_1), and "Right" (R_1). If player 1 chooses one of the latter two, player 2 gets to choose between "Left" (L_2) and "Right" (R_2), although he is not informed of player 1's exact choice (he knows only that player 1 did not choose L_1). The imperfect information of player 2 is represented by an information set $\{M_1, R_1\}$, characterized by an oval around the two corresponding nodes (n_2 and n_3). Given his state of information, player 2 is faced with the same choices at nodes n_2 and n_3. Finally, for move $\{M_1, R_2\}$ or $\{R_1, L_2\}$ player 3 must choose between "Left" (L_3) and "Right" (R_3) in the third period without knowing which of the nodes (n_4 or n_5) the game has attained. The values of the objective functions are written at the bottom of the tree. For example, for moves (M_1, L_2, R_3) player 1 receives 3, player 2 receives 2, and player 3 receives 0.

The following parable should prove helpful in understanding the equilibrium concept. Suppose that an econo-

---

19. See Milgrom and Weber 1986 for sufficient conditions on the objective functions and information structure so that the limit of Bayesian equilibrium strategies when the uncertainty becomes "negligible" forms a Nash equilibrium of the complete-information limit game.

20. The refinement of this notion is discussed in section 11.6.

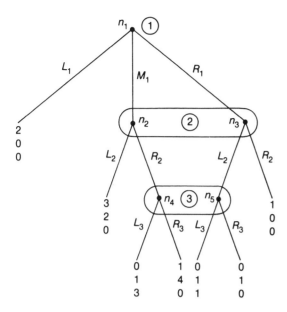

Figure 11.10
Game 5.

mist has to solve game 5 and, not knowing what to do, he turns to two people who have very specific talents.

The first consultant is a game theorist. He is well versed in the method of solving perfect equilibria of dynamic games, as described in section 11.3. On the other hand, he is sufficiently familiar with decision theory to understand the concept of expected utility (payoff). However, he is not aware of Bayes' law for calculating posterior probability distributions. Glancing at the problem described in figure 11.10, he first tries to solve player 3's decision problem. Unfortunately, he realizes that he can formulate this problem as a classical decision problem only so long as player 3 attributes some subjective probability (say, μ_3) to the game being at node n_4 (so the conditional probability of n_5 is $1 - \mu_3$). Similarly, player 2's decision problem depends on the probability (μ_2) that he attributes to the game being at node n_2. Then the game theorist behaves in a scientific manner. Admitting his ignorance of the probabilities attached to each informational set (here, $\mu = (\mu_2, \mu_3)$), he makes the following remark: "If I am given subjective probabilities μ, the game is identical to a perfect-information game, which I can

solve." In fact, given μ_3, player 3 chooses the action that maximizes his expected payoff. Player 2 knows the optimal strategy of player 3, and he also maximizes his expected utility given the subjective probability μ_2. Finally, given the other players' optimal strategies, player 1 chooses according to his own self-interest. Therefore, the game theorist reports to the economist the correspondence between the subjective probabilities μ and the optimal strategies obtained by backward induction:

$$a^*(\mu) = \{a_1^*(\mu), a_2^*(\mu), a_3^*(\mu)\},$$

where a_i^* can be a mixed strategy.

The second consultant is a Bayesian statistician. Calculating posterior probability distributions is second nature to him; however, he is familiar with neither game theory nor decision theory. Possessing a scientific mind, he makes the following remark: "If I am given the set of strategies $a = \{a_1, a_2, a_3\}$, I can calculate the probabilities the players should attribute to the various nodes." For example, if player 1 plays each of his actions with probability $\frac{1}{3}$, player 2 must assign a probability of $\mu_2 = \frac{1}{2}$ to node n_2 if the game attains his informational set. Moreover, if $a_2 = R_2$, player 3 assigns probability $\mu_3 = 1$ to node n_4. What happens if player 1 plays $a_1 = L_1$ (with probability 1)? Then player 2 can attribute any probability μ_2 to node n_2, since every probability is compatible with Bayes' law (because the event "the game attains player 2's informational set" has zero probability).[21] The statistician reports for each set of strategies the set of beliefs that are compatible with these strategies in a Bayesian sense: $\mu^{\text{Bay}}(a)$.

The conclusion to this parable is easy to guess. The economist calls in his two consultants. The statistician proposes that the strategies he uses to calculate the probability be the strategies actually chosen by the players, which the game theorist should give him. In turn, the game theorist suggests that the players' subjective probabilities be based on a study of the other players' behaviors, and calls on the statistician to provide him with these probabilities. Then both agree that the notion of equilibrium should make explicit these two types of compatibility. Consequently, they define a *perfect Bayesian equilibrium* as a set of strategies a that satisfy

---

21. However, we can, following Kreps and Wilson 1982, require that μ_3 be consistent with μ_2. For example, if $\mu_2 = \frac{1}{2}$ and player 2 plays L_2 with probability $\frac{2}{3}$, then $\mu_3 = \frac{1}{3}$ (see below).

$$a \in a^*(\mu^{\text{Bay}}(a)), \qquad (11.1)$$

and they associate with these strategies a system of beliefs that sustain the equilibrium by satisfying

$$\mu \in \mu^{\text{Bay}}(a^*(\mu)). \qquad (11.2)$$

Thus, the optimal strategies (and the associated beliefs) satisfy a fixed-point condition:

(P) Strategies are optimal given beliefs.
(B) Beliefs are obtained from strategies and observed actions using Bayes' rule.

The concept of perfect Bayesian equilibrium was introduced into the formal game-theory literature by Selten (1975) as "perfect equilibrium" and by Kreps and Wilson (1982) as "sequential equilibrium."[22] Although Selten pioneered this concept, Kreps and Wilson must be credited for putting more emphasis on beliefs,[23] making the concept more applicable, and paving the way for refinements based on restrictions on beliefs for zero-probability events (see section 11.6 for an example).

Remark We have been very informal about what Bayesian updating means. At the very least, the information sets that are reached with positive probability on the equilibrium path should be assigned beliefs consistent with Bayes' rule. This yields a very weak definition of PBE, which coincides with sequential equilibrium only in some simple games (e.g., the signaling game of section 11.6). In more complex games, further restrictions on the consistency of beliefs off the equilibrium path must be added to produce a stronger and more reasonable version of PBE. The consistency requirement of Kreps and Wilson (see subsection 11.6.1) is one such restriction.

How do we calculate the perfect Bayesian equilibrium (or equilibria) of a game? The characterization of a PBE as a fixed point of a correspondence suggests a method of calculation. However, calculating a fixed point is extremely tedious. Quite often, intuition allows us to solve the problem directly if the definition is well understood. There exists no general method; however, a few systematic tricks are of use in solving these games. The game

depicted in figure 11.10 is actually trivial. Player 3 has a dominant strategy that consists of playing L_3; therefore, regardless of μ_3, $a_3 = L_3$. Hence, we can convert the game to the two-period, two-player game depicted in figure 11.11. (Since player 3 does not play in this game, we omit the values of his objective function.)

We observe that player 2 now has a dominant strategy: L_2. Therefore, player 1's optimal action is M_1. Consequently, the unique PBE is given by $a = (M_1, L_2, L_3)$, and it has associated to it a set of beliefs ($\mu_2 = 1, \mu_3 \in [0, 1]$).

This game is indeed trivial. Because of the existence of dominating strategies, the game theorist finds the equilibrium path without the help of the statistician.

We now solve four simple but nontrivial games that are relevant to industrial organization. In these games (in contrast with the previous game) there is interaction between backward induction and forward Bayesian inference. The first two are games of incomplete information in which an informed party may reveal information when choosing between two actions. In the third game, a player's private information can be revealed through a complex (two-dimensional) action. There, simple economic reasoning indicates what the economic path must be. The fourth game gives an example of a game of imperfect information.

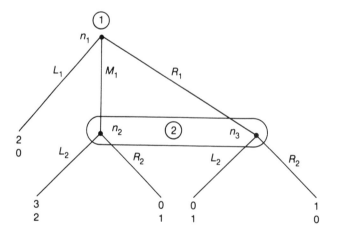

Figure 11.11
Game 6.

22. Kreps and Wilson have shown that perfect and sequential equilibria coincide for almost all games.

23. Selten defined his concept of "trembling hand" perfect equilibrium on the normal form. Beliefs, although easy to compute, are implicit rather than explicit.

11.5.1 A Two-Period Reputation Game

The following is a much simplified version of the Kreps-Wilson-Milgrom-Roberts reputation story. There are two firms ($i = 1, 2$). In period 1, both firms are in the market. Only firm 1 (the "incumbent") takes action a_1. The action space has two elements: "prey" and "accommodate." The profit of firm 2 (the "entrant") is D_2 if firm 1 accommodates and P_2 if firm 1 preys such that $D_2 > 0 > P_2$. Firm 1 has one of two potential types t_1: "sane" and "crazy." When sane, firm 1 makes D_1 when it accommodates and P_1 when it preys, where $D_1 > P_1$. Thus, a sane firm prefers to accommodate rather than to prey. However, it would most prefer to be a monopoly, in which case it would make M_1 per period, where $M_1 > D_1$. When crazy, firm 1 enjoys predation and thus preys (its utility function is such that preying is always worthwhile). Let p_1 (respectively, $1 - p_1$) denote the prior probability that firm 1 is sane (respectively, crazy).

In period 2, only firm 2 chooses an action a_2. This action can take one of two values: "stay" and "exit." If it stays, it obtains payoff D_2 if firm 1 is actually sane and payoff P_2 if firm 1 is crazy. The idea is that, unless it is crazy, firm 1 will not pursue any predatory strategy in the second period because there is no point building or keeping a reputation at the end. (This assumption can be derived more formally from the description of the second-period competition.) The sane firm 1 gets D_1 if firm 2 stays and $M_1 > D_1$ if firm 2 exits. We let δ denote the discount factor between the two periods.

We presumed that the crazy type always preys. The interesting thing to study is, then, the sane type's behavior. From a static point of view, a sane firm 1 would want to accommodate in the first period. However, by preying it might convince firm 2 that it is of the crazy type, thus inducing exit (as $P_2 < 0$) and increasing its second-period profit.

Let us begin with a taxonomy of potential perfect Bayesian equilibria.

A *separating* equilibrium is an equilibrium in which firm 1's two types choose two different actions in the first period. Here, this means that the sane type chooses to accommodate. In a separating equilibrium, firm 2 has complete information in the second period: If μ denotes the entrant's second-period (posterior) beliefs about the incumbent's type, then

$$\mu(t = \text{sane}|\text{accommodate}) = 1$$

and

$$\mu(t = \text{crazy}|\text{prey}) = 1.$$

A *pooling* equilibrium is an equilibrium in which firm 1's two types choose the same action in the first period. Here, this means that the sane type preys. In a pooling equilibrium, firm 2 does not update its beliefs when observing the equilibrium action:

$$\mu(t = \text{sane}|\text{prey}) = p_1.$$

There can also exist *hybrid* or *semi-separating* equilibria. For instance, in the reputation game, the sane type may randomize between preying and accommodating (i.e., between pooling and separating). One then has

$$\mu(t = \text{sane}|\text{prey}) \in (0, p_1)$$

and

$$\mu(t = \text{sane}|\text{accommodate}) = 1.$$

Let us first look for conditions of existence of a separating equilibrium. In such an equilibrium, a sane firm 1 accommodates and thus reveals its type and obtains $D_1(1 + \delta)$. (Firm 2 stays, because it expects $D_2 > 0$ in the second period.) If firm 1 decided to prey, it would convince firm 2 that it is crazy and would obtain $P_1 + \delta M_1$. Thus, a necessary condition for the existence of a separating equilibrium is

$$\delta(M_1 - D_1) \leqslant (D_1 - P_1). \tag{11.3}$$

Conversely, suppose that condition 11.3 is satisfied. Consider the following strategies and beliefs: The sane incumbent accommodates, and the entrant (correctly) anticipates that the incumbent is sane when observing accommodation; the crazy incumbent preys, and the entrant (correctly) anticipates that the incumbent is crazy when observing predation. Clearly, these strategies and beliefs form a separating PBE.

Let us now look at the possibility of a pooling equilibrium. Both types prey; so, as we saw, $\mu = p_1$ when predation is observed. Now, the sane type, who loses $D_1 - P_1$ in the first period, must induce exit (at least with sufficient probability). Therefore, it must be the case that

$$p_1 D_2 + (1 - p_1)P_2 \leqslant 0. \tag{11.4}$$

Conversely, assume that condition 11.4 holds, and consider the following strategies and beliefs: Both types prey, and the entrant has posterior beliefs $\mu = p_1$ when predation is observed and $\mu = 1$ when accommodation is observed. The sane type's equilibrium profit is $P_1 + \delta M_1$; it would become $D_1(1 + \delta)$ under accommodation. Thus, if condition 11.3 is violated, the proposed strategies and beliefs form a pooling PBE. (If condition 11.4 is satisfied with equality, there exists not one but a continuum of such equilibria.) If conditions 11.3 and 11.4 are violated, the unique equilibrium is a hybrid PBE (with the entrant randomizing when observing predation).

The following exercise extends this analysis to n periods.

Exercise 11.12***

(i) Selten (1978) offers the following paradox. A chain store (the incumbent) is located in n geographically separated markets. It faces n potential entrants, one in each market. The potential entrants must make their entry decisions sequentially. At date i ($i = 1, \dots, n$), entrant i, who has observed what happened in the $i - 1$ preceding markets, decides whether to enter (I, for *in*) or not enter (O, for *out*). If it enters, the incumbent chooses whether to prey (P) or acquiesce (A); the payoffs in market i are as shown in figure 11.12 (the first payoff refers to the incumbent, the second to entrant i). The entry and predation decisions in market i are observed before entrant $i + 1$ decides whether to enter. The incumbent's payoff is the sum of its n payoffs. Show that with one potential entrant ($n = 1$), the unique perfect equilibrium has the entrant enter and the incumbent acquiesce. Then demonstrate Selten's chain-store paradox: No matter how large n is, all the entrants enter and the incumbent never preys.

(ii) Now, suppose with Kreps, Milgrom, Roberts, and Wilson, that the entrants do not know the incumbent's

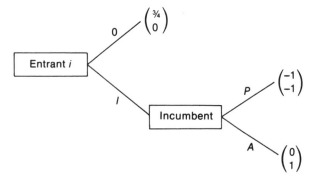

Figure 11.12

objective function perfectly. With probability $1 - x$, the payoffs are as above; with probability x, the incumbent gets $\frac{1}{2}$ (say) instead of -1 when preying (the payoffs are otherwise unchanged). Solve the one-entrant case. Then, by backward induction, derive the equilibrium for entrant i for posterior beliefs x_i at the beginning of date i. How big should $x_1 = x$ be to keep entrant 1 out?

11.5.2 Sequential Bargaining with Incomplete Information

Bargaining usually involves asymmetric information. For instance, the seller (respectively, the buyer) may have incomplete information about the buyer's willingness to pay (respectively, the seller's reservation price). To the extent that bargaining proceeds through a series of offers, refusals, counteroffers, and so on, it is natural to model it as a dynamic game of incomplete information. A simple instance of such a formalization is given here. (A straightforward reinterpretation of such a game was used in formalizing intertemporal price discrimination by a monopolist in chapter 1.)

Consider the following simple bargaining problem: A buyer and a seller negotiate over one unit of a product (or a contract). The seller makes an initial offer of p_1, which the buyer either accepts or refuses. If the offer is refused, the seller makes a second offer, p_2. If the second offer is also refused, each party goes his own way and the seller keeps his product. The value of the product is s for the seller and b for the buyer. (*Value* must be interpreted in a broad sense that includes the possibility of outside exchanges with other parties.) Assume that the discount factor is δ_s for the seller and δ_b for the buyer and that both parties are risk-neutral. Therefore, the utilities of the seller and the buyer are $[p_1, b - p_1]$ if p_1 is accepted, $[\delta_s p_2, \delta_b(b - p_2)]$ if p_2 is accepted, and $[\delta_s s, 0]$ if p_2 is refused. Incomplete information is restricted to the following aspect: The seller does not know whether the value of the product is $\overline{b}$ or $\underline{b}$ ($\underline{b} < \overline{b}$) for the buyer. The seller puts equal probabilities on these two values, whereas the buyer knows b. Both parties know everything else. We assume that there is always some potential gain from exchange: $s < \underline{b} < \overline{b}$. Moreover, we assume that $\underline{b} > (\overline{b} + s)/2$. This condition implies that if the seller were authorized to make only one offer, he would choose to sell surely (by charging $\underline{b}$) rather than run the risk of losing the sale (by trying to sell at price $\overline{b}$). We now define the strategies and the beliefs.

First, the seller makes an offer p_1. The buyer accepts ($d_1 = 1$) or refuses ($d_1 = 0$), depending on p_1 and on his willingness to pay. Thus, the buyer's strategy can be denoted as $d_1(p_1, b)$. If the buyer refuses p_1, the seller deduces from this a posterior probability that the buyer's willingness to pay is equal to $\bar{b}$, which we denote as $\mu(\bar{b}|p_1)$. Obviously, $\mu(\underline{b}|p_1) = 1 - \mu(\bar{b}|p_1)$. The seller then makes a subsequent offer, $p_2(p_1)$. Finally, the buyer accepts p_2 ($d_2 = 1$) or refuses p_2 ($d_2 = 0$), according to the decision rule $d_2(p_1, p_2, b)$. (In equilibrium, p_1 will not be an argument of d_2.)

(1) The first step consists of writing the "self-selection constraints" that must be satisfied by an equilibrium path. By self-selection constraints we mean (in a general enough way) the constraints expressing the fact that in equilibrium a player of a given type does not strictly prefer to adopt a strategy other than his own (such as that of the same player when he is of a different type). Here, the buyer can be of two types, $\underline{b}$ and $\bar{b}$. We refer to "the buyer of type $\underline{b}$" (respectively, "type $\bar{b}$") to designate the buyer who attaches a value $\underline{b}$ (respectively, $\bar{b}$) to the product. During the second period, self-selection constraints are trivial; the buyer of type b buys if and only if $p_2 \leqslant b$. Analogously, the buyer of type b will accept an offer p_1 during the first period if and only if

$$b - p_1 \geqslant \delta_b\{\max[b - p_2(p_1), 0]\}. \tag{11.5}$$

Equation 11.5 represents the following: If the buyer accepts offer p_1, his utility is $b - p_1$; and if he refuses, the seller charges $p_2(p_1)$.

Writing equation 11.5 for $\underline{b}$ and $\bar{b}$ shows that if the buyer of type $\underline{b}$ accepts p_1, then, _a fortiori_, the buyer of type $\bar{b}$ accepts p_1 (simply because he attaches more value to the product than the buyer of type $\underline{b}$ and is, therefore, more eager to buy).

(2) The second step is to look at the consequences of the self-selection constraints on the seller's posterior probability distribution over b. Clearly, we may assume that p_1 was refused (otherwise, bargaining is completed, and the distribution no longer matters). Since an offer accepted by the type-$\underline{b}$ buyer is automatically accepted by the type-$\bar{b}$ buyer, the probability of facing the latter type when the offer is refused is, at most, $\frac{1}{2}$.

(3) The third step is to return to the strategy space by examining the effects of this distribution on the strategy of the seller in the second period. When the seller can make only one offer, and his distribution over b is uniform he behaves cautiously by assumption (that is, he charges $\underline{b}$). _A fortiori_, when his subjective probability of facing buyer $\bar{b}$ is less than $\frac{1}{2}$ he must also behave cautiously; therefore, regardless of p_1, we have $p_2(p_1) = \underline{b}$. Now the final two steps of the characterization of the equilibrium are obvious.

(4) Forecasting that the seller will charge $\underline{b}$ if he refuses the first offer, the buyer of type $\underline{b}$ accepts it if and only if $p_1 \leqslant \underline{b}$. Buyer $\bar{b}$ accepts p_1 if and only if $\bar{b} - p_1 \geqslant \delta_b(\bar{b} - \underline{b})$, or simply

$$p_1 \leqslant \tilde{b} = \delta_b \underline{b} + (1 - \delta_b)\bar{b}.$$

(5) Finally, the seller chooses p_1 in order to maximize his expected profit. He chooses between $\underline{b}$ and $\tilde{b}$ depending on whether $\underline{b}$ is greater or less than

$$(\tilde{b} + \delta_s \underline{b})/2. \tag{11.6}$$

If he proposes $\underline{b}$, this offer is accepted by both types of buyer. On the other hand, if he proposes $\tilde{b}$, he benefits from buyer $\bar{b}$'s impatience, knowing full well that he will be able to enter into an exchange in the second period if the buyer turns out to be of type $\underline{b}$. Because during our characterization we defined the players' strategies and beliefs for each history of the game, we conclude that the game has a unique perfect Bayesian equilibrium.

A more general analysis of this model, including the case in which the buyer also has incomplete information about the value of the product to the seller, can be found in Fudenberg and Tirole 1983.

11.5.3 Warranty as a Signal of Quality

A buyer is willing to buy one unit of a product of uncertain quality (for example, a used car). More precisely, the product has a probability Π of working properly and a probability $1 - \Pi$ of being defective. The seller knows Π; so Π is his "type." The buyer knows that Π belongs to an interval $[\underline{\Pi}, \bar{\Pi}]$, and he has a prior probability distribution defined over this interval. The buyer receives utility $\bar{u}$ if he does not purchase from this seller (for example, $\bar{u}$ is the utility he receives if he does not consume the product; alternatively, $\bar{u}$ is the buyer's reservation utility which is related to his willingness to pay for searching among other sellers). Let I_1 be the gross monetary value of a working product, and I_2 the gross monetary value of a nonworking product ($I_1 > I_2$). The seller offers a contract (p, g), where p is the price of the product and g is the indemnity payment if the product does not work. The consumer's utility is $u(I_1 - p)$ in the first case; it is $u(I_2 - p + g)$ in the second, where the utility function of the buyer who consumes the product is assumed to be strictly concave. The seller, whom we assume to be risk-neutral, has an expected profit of $p - (1 - \Pi)g$ if the buyer accepts the contract (p, g). The buyer and the seller meet only once, which rules out product-reputation concerns. What contract will the seller propose? Economic intuition, based on the theory of insurance, conjures up the following points:

(1) In the case of complete information (i.e., the buyer knows Π), all the Pareto optima have the property that the buyer is completely insured. In other words, the warranty always specifies $g_0 = I_1 - I_2$.

(2) In the case of incomplete information, if the seller proposes the indemnity payment g_0, the buyer's utility when he consumes the product does not depend on his subjective probability distribution over Π. Therefore, he accepts any price that does not exceed p_0, where p_0 is defined by

$$u(I_1 - p_0) = u(I_2 - p_0 + g_0) = \bar{u}.$$

(To simplify the analysis, we assume that $p_0 - (1 - \underline{\Pi})g_0 > 0$.) When the seller proposes $c_0 = (p_0, g_0)$, the buyer obtains zero surplus for any Π.

(3) The contract c_0 is Pareto optimal for any Π.[24] On the other hand, the seller would offer some other contract $c = (p, g)$ only if he expected to make more profit than with c_0. Since any other contract is suboptimal, the buyer will derive a negative surplus from such an exchange, and therefore he should not make the purchase. In other words, a rational buyer should be suspicious if the seller does not offer a complete warranty.

In a two-period game, we formalize our intuition that the seller proposes the contract c_0 in equilibrium. First, the seller proposes a contract, $c = (p, g)$, which depends only on his own information, i.e., $c(\Pi)$. Then, the buyer chooses to buy ($d(c) = 1$) or not to buy ($d(c) = 0$). His behavior depends on his beliefs about Π and, more precisely, on the expected Π, given the buyer's prior probability distribution over Π and the information in the

contract proposed by the seller, $c = (p, g)$. Let $\mu(c)$ be this posterior expectation. In perfect Bayesian equilibrium, $c(\Pi)$ maximizes the seller's expected profit with his objective probability specified by Π and with $d(\cdot)$ taken as given. $\mu(c)$ is consistent with the function $c(\cdot)$ in the Bayesian sense, and $d(c)$ maximizes the buyer's expected utility given $\mu(c)$.

Assume that the seller, who has probability Π, proposes a contract $c = (p, g)$ that differs from $c_0 = (p_0, g_0)$. Since $d(c_0) = 1$, the seller's expected profit for c must satisfy

$$p - (1 - \Pi)g \geq p_0 - (1 - \Pi)g_0. \tag{11.7}$$

This inequality must be satisfied for all the values of Π for which the seller chooses c. Since $\mu(c)$ is (from Bayes' law) a weighted average of these values, we have

$$p - [1 - \mu(c)]g \geq p_0 - [1 - \mu(c)]g_0. \tag{11.8}$$

On the other hand, the buyer's surplus is non-negative (otherwise, he would not make the purchase, and the contract could not be optimal for the buyer). Therefore,

$$\mu(c)u(I_1 - p) + [1 - \mu(c)]u(I_2 - p + g) \geq \bar{u}$$

$$= u(I_1 - p_0). \tag{11.9}$$

Using Jensen's inequality (if $f(x)$ is strictly concave, then $f(Ex) > Ef(x)$, where the expectation operator refers to x), we get

$$\mu(c)(I_1 - p) + [1 - \mu(c)](I_2 - p + g) > I_1 - p_0. \tag{11.10}$$

It is easy to see that 11.8 and 11.10 are contradictory (using $g_0 = I_1 - I_2$).

Once we have observed that for any Π the equilibrium offer should be c_0, which is accepted by the buyer, it is elementary to construct a PBE that generates this equilibrium path. Any contract c different from c_0 must have zero probability in equilibrium. Therefore, we can choose the beliefs freely (while $\mu(c_0)$ is necessarily the expectation of Π for the prior distribution, given pooling and Bayes' rule). It suffices to assume that the buyer believes that such a contract is proposed by the "worst" seller (the seller with the lowest probability $\underline{\Pi}$). Therefore, if the

---

24. The buyer obtains full insurance under c_0 and, therefore, does not care about the true value of Π.

seller proposes contract $c = (p, g)$, the buyer accepts it if and only if

$$\underline{\Pi}u(I_1 - p) + (1 - \underline{\Pi})u(I_2 - p + g) \geqslant \bar{u}.$$

However, it is clear from this inequality that the seller's expected profit is less than if he had proposed c_0.[25]

11.5.4 Signal Jamming

Each of the preceding three examples involved a player with private information who attempted to manipulate another party's beliefs about this information. This fourth example shows how beliefs can be manipulated under imperfect (but not incomplete) information. In this example, a player garbles the payoff-relevant information received by another player by choosing an unobservable action.

The simplest such model involves two firms, two actions, two types, two profit levels, and two periods. Firms 1 and 2 compete in period 1. Firm 1 has two possible actions: S (*soft*; accommodate) and T (*tough*; prey). Firm 2's action is not described here (one can think of it as always accommodating). Firm 1 has perfect information about its own payoff. From a single-period point of view, it prefers playing S. Playing T costs $c > 0$. This is common knowledge. Firm 2 has two potential profit levels: H and L, with $H > 0 > L$. The *a priori* distribution puts weight α on H and weight $1 - \alpha$ on L if firm 1 plays S. (Thus, there are two "types," H and L; the terminology is abused here, because we will assume that firm 2 does not know its type.) However, if firm 1 plays T, firm 2 makes profit L regardless of its type. Firm 2 does not observe whether firm 1 plays S or T in the first period and does not know its type. Instead, it must infer this type from the observation of its profit and what it expects firm 1 to have played. Except for firm 1's action, the two firms have the same information. In period 2, firm 2 decides whether to stay. Profits are the same in the two periods (as long as both firms are in and firm 1 takes the same action). Firm 1, which we assume is always profitable, stays and chooses action S (since this is the last period, firm 1 plays its single-period dominant strategy). The discounted second-

period gain of becoming a monopoly for firm 1 is $g > c$. (For simplicity we will assume that g and c do not depend on firm 2's type, although this is not essential.) Firm 2 earns zero profit in the second period if it leaves.[26]

To solve for equilibrium, let us consider the two potential actions for firm 1 in period 1. Suppose it plays S in equilibrium. Firm 2's first-period profit is identical to, and therefore perfectly informative about, its second-period profit. Thus, it stays if and only if it makes profit H in the first period. Now, S must be the equilibrium action: Playing T does not increase firm 1's profit. By playing T in the first period, firm 1 loses c, but gains g whenever it changes firm 2's decision to stay. This occurs when firm 2 is of type H. Playing T gives firm 2 a profit L, and that firm—thinking firm 1 has played S—leaves. Thus, a necessary condition for S to be an equilibrium action is

$$c \geqslant \alpha g. \tag{11.11}$$

Conversely, if condition 11.11 is satisfied, firm 1's playing S and firm 2's use of the exit rule "exit if and only if first-period profit is equal to L" form a perfect Bayesian equilibrium.

Second, suppose that T is the equilibrium action. Then profit is L whatever firm 2's type: The first period profit is uninformative. So the posterior beliefs when observing L are the same as prior beliefs. Firm 2 stays when observing L if and only if

$$\alpha H + (1 - \alpha)L \geqslant 0. \tag{11.12}$$

If condition 11.12 is satisfied, T cannot be an equilibrium action. Firm 1 could save c without any change in second-period profit. If 11.12 is not satisfied, then playing T is an equilibrium action as long as the cost of doing so (c) is lower than the gain, αg (if firm 1 deviates and plays S, firm 2 exits if and only if it is of the low-profit type). So T is an equilibrium action if and only if both 11.11 and 11.12 are violated.

When condition 11.11 is violated and 11.12 is satisfied, we already know that no pure-strategy equilibrium exists. Hence, if an equilibrium exists (we actually know it does—see section 11.6), it must involve firm 1's mixing

---

25. The concept discussed above originated in the discussion that followed the publication of Spence's 1977 article on consumers' perceptions of product quality. Our discussion has followed Grossman 1980. See also Milgrom 1981b.

26. This signal-jamming game is a simplification of that in Fudenberg and Tirole 1986a. Other signal-jamming games can be found in Holmström 1983, in Riordan 1985, and in Gibbons 1985.

between S and T. Suppose that firm 1 plays T with probability y (and S with probability $1 - y$), and that firm 2, when observing profit L, exits with probability z (and stays with probability $1 - z$). For firm 1 to randomize, it must be indifferent between the two actions; hence,

$$c = \alpha z g. \tag{11.13}$$

(Playing T modifies firm 2's decision only when it is of type H, and this decision is changed only with probability z.) Because condition 11.11 is violated, condition 11.13 defines a unique z in $(0, 1)$. Next, for firm 2 to be indifferent about exiting or staying when observing L, it must be the case that

$$\eta H + (1 - \eta)L = 0,$$

where η denotes the posterior probability that firm 2 is of type H. From Bayes' rule,

$$\eta = \frac{\alpha y}{\alpha y + (1 - \alpha)}.$$

[When the true type is H (respectively, L), the probability of ending up with profit L is equal to the probability y of predation (respectively, 1).] Thus, we need

$$\alpha y H + (1 - \alpha)L = 0. \tag{11.14}$$

Because condition 11.12 is satisfied, condition 11.14 defines a unique y in $(0, 1]$. We thus conclude that there exists a unique equilibrium in this game.

These four games were selected for their simplicity. In particular, each of them has a unique equilibrium. Often, however, dynamic games of incomplete or imperfect information are plagued by a multiplicity of equilibria. This is due in particular to the fact that Bayes' law has no bite when the observed move has a probability of zero.[27] The leeway in specifying conjectures in such events may give rise to a great number of equilibria. The supplementary section provides examples of multiple equilibria and shows how one may select from among these using refinements of perfect Bayesian equilibrium.

11.6 Supplementary Section

11.6.1 Existence of Equilibrium

The basic existence result concerns the existence of a Nash equilibrium. The existence of Bayesian, perfect, and perfect Bayesian equilibria is proved through simple reinterpretations of this result. Consider a normal-form game with a finite number of players ($i = 1, \ldots, n$). Let A_i denote the set of player i's feasible actions, $a = (a_1, \ldots, a_i, \ldots, a_n)$ the vector of actions (where a_i belongs to A_i), and $\Pi^i(a)$ player i's payoff. The following theorem is a special case of one contained in Debreu 1952. (Debreu also allows a player's set of feasible actions to depend on the other players' actions.)

THEOREM   If, for all i, A_i is a compact and convex subset of a Euclidean space, and Π^i is continuous in a and quasi-concave in a_i, there exists a Nash equilibrium, i.e., a vector a^* such that, for all i and a_i in A_i,

$$\Pi^i(a^*) \geqslant \Pi^i(a_i, a^*_{-i}).$$

This theorem (which can be proved by a fixed-point method) has a straightforward application to games with a finite number of actions. It shows that for such games an equilibrium always exists in mixed strategies (it need not exist in pure strategies; see, e.g., the game of matching pennies): Let $\bar{A}_i$ denote the set of probability distributions over the finite set A_i of pure strategies. So we enlarge the action set to allow mixed strategies: $a_i \in \bar{A}_i$. $\bar{A}_i$ is homeomorphic to a simplex, and hence is compact and convex. Π^i becomes an expectation over pure-strategy outcomes; it is therefore linear (hence, quasi-concave) in a_i and polynomial (hence, continuous) in a. So, there always exists a mixed-strategy equilibrium (Nash 1950).

The above theorem (or variants thereof) also provides conditions for the existence of an equilibrium in games with a continuum of actions. However, some games in industrial organization (e.g., auctions, Cournot competition, location games) have discontinuous and/or nonquasi-concave payoff functions. See Dasgupta and Maskin

---

27. In the predation game, the crazy type always preys, so "preying" is a positive-probability event (Bayes' rule applies); and "accommodating" always signals the sane type. Thus, the leeway does not exist. Similarly, in the bargaining game, "refusing" is a positive-probability event in the interesting region for price offers (prices above $\underline{b}$, which are rejected by type $\underline{b}$). The warranty game is special in that the Pareto-optimal action (which is the equilibrium action under complete information) is the same for all types. In the signal-jamming game, the incumbent's move is not directly observed.

1986 for sufficient conditions for a pure-strategy equilibrium (with quasi-concave payoff functions) and a mixed-strategy equilibrium (in the absence of quasi-concavity) to exist.

The theorem can also be used to prove the existence of equilibrium for versions of the Nash concept for incomplete information or dynamics. Let us assume that each player has only a finite number of feasible pure strategies. Similarly, under incomplete information, each player i has only a finite number of potential types $|T_i|$ (i.e., nature has only a finite number of pure strategies).

11.6.1.1 Existence of a Bayesian Equilibrium

It suffices to transform the game between the n players into a game between $\sum_{i=1}^{n} |T_i|$ players. That is, each player has $|T_i|$ incarnations that play in their own interest. (Player i, when of type t_i, does not care about the payoff he would have were he of type t_i'.) This is still a game with a finite number of players and a finite number of pure strategies. Hence, it admits a mixed-strategy equilibrium. The equilibrium strategies in the transformed game are clearly equilibrium strategies of the original game.

11.6.1.2 Existence of a Perfect Equilibrium

For games of perfect information, Kuhn's algorithm of backward induction yields a constructive proof of the existence of a perfect equilibrium. More generally, the existence of a perfect equilibrium results from the general proof for perfect Bayesian equilibrium (although for games of almost perfect information there exist simpler proofs).

11.6.1.3 Existence of a Perfect Bayesian Equilibrium

A "trembling hand" perfect equilibrium (Selten 1975) is a slightly more refined concept than Kreps and Wilson's (1982) sequential equilibrium, which itself is a bit more refined than perfect Bayesian equilibrium; thus, it yields existence of a PBE and sequential equilibrium as by-products.

Consider the normal form of a game. For a given set of actions A_i for player i, we can define the set of totally mixed strategies for that player:

$$\tilde{A}_i^0 = \left\{ \sigma_1 \in R^{|A_i|} \,\middle|\, \sum_{a_i \in A_i} \sigma_i(a_i) = 1, \, \sigma_i(a_i) > 0 \text{ for all } a_i \right\}.$$

That is, $\sigma_i(a_i)$, the probability that player i plays a_i, is required to be strictly positive.

Fix ε, and let $\{\varepsilon(a_i)\}_{a_i \in A_i}$ denote a set of numbers such that $0 < \varepsilon(a_i) < \varepsilon$ for all a_i. Now, consider the following maximization problem for player i:

$$\max_{\sigma_i} \Pi^i(\sigma_i, \sigma_{-i}) \text{ subject to } \sigma_i(a_i) \geqslant \varepsilon(a_i) \text{ for all } a_i, \quad (11.15)$$

where $\sigma_{-i} \equiv (\sigma_1, \ldots, \sigma_{i-1}, \sigma_{i+1}, \ldots, \sigma_n)$ denotes the mixed strategies played by the other players. In other words, player i is constrained to play each of his possible strategies with at least a small probability.

An "ε-perfect equilibrium" is a set of (totally mixed) strategies $\{\sigma_i\}_{i=1}^{n}$ such that, for some $\{\varepsilon(a_i)\}_{a_i \in A_i}$ with $0 < \varepsilon(a_i) < \varepsilon$, σ_i solves 11.15 for each player i. In other words, an ε-perfect equilibrium is a Nash equilibrium of a constrained game. For given $\{\varepsilon(a_i)\}$, such a Nash equilibrium exists from Debreu's theorem. (The only difference with the proof of existence of a mixed-strategy equilibrium is that mixed strategies must belong to subsets of the simplices; however, this is irrelevant, because the subsets are compact and convex.)

A "trembling hand" perfect equilibrium is any limit of ε-perfect equilibria as ε tends to zero. Because the strategy spaces are compact, such a limit exists (there always exists a converging subsequence). Because the profit functions Π^i are continuous, any limit is a Nash equilibrium (from condition 11.15).

Remark 1 When a player plays at various information sets, this equilibrium concept ends up being not quite refined enough. Selten introduces a second refinement, which operates like the first but on the so-called *agents' normal form*. (The agents' normal form consists in considering each information set as a distinct player, with the objective function the player of whom it is an incarnation. This defines a normal form with a larger number of players, to which the preceding techniques can be applied. The difference with the previous approach is basically that a player's trembles at different information sets must be independent, so there are fewer "trembling hand" perfect equilibria. The concept of a "trembling hand" perfect equilibrium actually refers to this second refinement). For a discussion, see Fudenberg and Tirole 1986c.

Remark 2 The main point is that a "trembling hand" perfect equilibrium is not only a Nash equilibrium; it is also a PBE. This is where Selten's trick of introducing trembles pays. The perturbed game, with the required minimum trembles $\varepsilon(a_i)$, has no zero-probability action. Hence, in an extensive form (with the normal form defined by the above game) there is no zero-probability event. Bayes' rule bites everywhere, and Nash equilibria automatically satisfy the perfection requirement. (To visualize this, go back to game 1. If player 1 is forced to play R with probability at least $\varepsilon(R) > 0$, player 2 necessarily puts as much weight as he can on r following R. Hence, ℓ will not be a limit of optimal reactions to R, even when $\varepsilon(R)$ tends to 0. On the normal form of game 1, Selten's construction yields only the unique perfect equilibrium.) Thus, noncredible threats are not part of a Nash equilibrium of a perturbed game, nor are they part of a "trembling hand" perfect equilibrium in the limit.

Remark 3 Whereas Selten works on the normal form, Kreps and Wilson (1982) use the extensive form and put more emphasis on beliefs at information sets. They consider PBEs satisfying a consistency requirement. That is, the set of strategies and beliefs in a PBE must be the limit of a sequence of sets of strategies and beliefs such that the strategies are totally mixed and the beliefs are consistent with strategies and Bayes' rule. Along this converging sequence, the strategies need not be optimal given the beliefs, even in Selten's constrained sense. Only in the limit must they be optimal. It is easy to see that in the signaling game studied in subsection 11.6.2.1 this consistency criterion has no bite. However, in more general games it (among other things) imposes consistency between beliefs of different players or of the same player at different information sets, even in zero-probability events. Kreps and Wilson have shown that for "almost all games," sequential equilibria and "trembling hand" perfect equilibria coincide.

11.6.2 Refinements

An issue that was carefully eluded in the text is the common and high multiplicity of equilibria in dynamic games with incomplete or imperfect information. To understand why this issue often arises, consider a game in which player 1 has private information and plays first and player 2, who cares about player 1's information, reacts to player 1's action. (Such a game will be called a *signaling game* below.) Suppose that we want to rule out some action a_1 as an equilibrium action for player 1. To this purpose, let us assume that a_1 is indeed not optimal for player 1 (that is, a_1 has "probability 0 in equilibrium"—i.e., is an "off-the-equilibrium-path" or an "out-of-equilibrium" event). In this event, Bayes' rule has no bite and any beliefs about player 1's type after a deviation to a_1 are admissible. In many games there exist types for player 1 that, if they were common knowledge, would induce player 2 to take some action that would hurt player 1 considerably. For instance, if player 2 thinks that player 1 has a high marginal cost or that demand is high, he will enter the market or accumulate a large capacity. Now, if we specify that after observing a_1 player 2 believes that player 1 is of such a type, so that player 2 indeed takes an action detrimental to player 1, then player 1 does not want to choose a_1 after all. The leeway in specifying off-the-equilibrium-path beliefs usually creates some leeway in the choices of equilibrium actions; by ruling out some potential equilibrium actions, one transforms other actions into equilibrium actions. Hence, it is not surprising that one often ends up with a continuum of perfect Bayesian equilibria.

But multiplicity, as usual, raises doubts about the very nature of equilibrium. How do players coordinate on a particular equilibrium? Do they choose a "focal" one? Do they learn? If they do, what is the learning process? Many of the recent developments in game theory concern the refinement of the notion of equilibrium by placing restrictions on off-the-equilibrium-path events, where Bayes' rule does not place restrictions. We are now endowed with nearly a dozen refinements of perfect Bayesian equilibrium. Although the field is changing rapidly and these notes will soon be outdated, let us consider two such refinements which have been used often and are easy to apply.[28]

Subsection 11.6.2.1 (which follows Fudenberg and Tirole 1986c) describes the simplest game in which the issues of updating and perfection arise: the signaling game. Because of the complexity of dynamic games with incomplete information, industrial-organization economists have

---

28. For more complete discussions of refinements, see Fudenberg and Tirole 1986c, Cho and Kreps 1987, and the references in these two papers.

derived many (perhaps too many) applications of this basic game. We consider how to apply the two refinements to this game. Subsection 11.6.2.2 solves examples.

11.6.2.1 The Signaling Game

The following game is called a signaling game because a variant of it was used by Spence (1974) to study job-market signaling. There are two players. Player 1 is the leader (also called the sender, because he sends a signal); player 2 is the follower (or receiver). Player 1 has private information about his own type t_1 in T_1, and chooses action a_1 in A_1 (the set of probability distributions over A_1 is $\tilde{A}_1$). Player 2, whose type is common knowledge for simplicity, observes a_1 and chooses a_2 in A_2. Payoffs are equal to $\Pi^i(a_1, a_2, t_1)$, where $i = 1, 2$. Before the game begins, player 2 has prior beliefs $p_1(t_1)$ about player 1's type.

Player 2, who observes player 1's move before choosing his own action, should update his beliefs about t_1 and base his choice of a_2 on the posterior distribution $\tilde{p}_1(t_1 | a_1)$. How is this posterior distribution formed? As in a Bayesian equilibrium, player 1's action ought to depend on his type; let $a_1^*(t_1)$ in $\tilde{A}_1$ denote this strategy (as before, this notation allows a mixed strategy). Thus, by figuring out $a_1^*(\cdot)$ and observing a_1, player 2 can use Bayes' rule to update $p_1(\cdot)$ into $\tilde{p}_1(\cdot | a_1)$. In a world of rational expectations, player 1 should anticipate that his action will also affect player 2's through the posterior beliefs.

Definition A *perfect Bayesian equilibrium* (PBE) of the signaling game is a set of strategies $a_1^*(t_1)$ and $a_2^*(a_1)$ and posterior beliefs $\tilde{p}_1(t_1 | a_1)$ such that

(P_1) $\quad a_2^*(a_1) \in \arg\max_{a_2} \sum_{t_1} \tilde{p}_1(t_1 | a_1) \Pi^2(a_1, a_2, t_1)$

and

(P_2) $\quad a_1^*(t_1) \in \arg\max_{a_1} \Pi^1(a_1, a_2^*(a_1), t_1)$.

(B) $\tilde{p}_1(t_1 | a_1)$ is derived from the prior $p_1(\cdot)$, a_1, and $a_1^*(\cdot)$ using Bayes' rule (when applicable).

(P_1) and (P_2) are the perfectness conditions. (P_1) states that player 2 reacts optimally to player 1's action given his posterior beliefs about t_1. (P_2) demonstrates the optimal Stackelberg behavior by player 1; note that he takes into account the effect of a_1 on player 2's action. (B) corresponds to the application of Bayes' rule. The quantifier "when applicable" stems from the fact that if a_1 is

not part of player 1's optimal strategy for some type, observing a_1 is a zero-probability event and Bayes' rule does not pin down posterior beliefs. *Any* posterior beliefs $\tilde{p}_1(\cdot | a_1)$ are then admissible.

Both of the refinements below put restrictions on "reasonable" beliefs $\tilde{p}_1(\cdot | a_1)$ following an out-of-equilibrium action a_1.

Elimination of Weakly Dominated Strategies

Let a_1 and a_1' denote two actions in A_1.

Definition 1 $\quad a_1$ is weakly dominated by a_1' for type t_1 in T_1 if, for all a_2 and a_2' in A_2,

$$\Pi^1(a_1, a_2, t_1) \leqslant \Pi^1(a_1', a_2', t_1) \tag{11.16}$$

(with at least one strict inequality for some (a_2, a_2')). a_1 is weakly dominated for type t_1 if it is weakly dominated by some action a_1' for type t_1.

Now suppose that a_1 is not an equilibrium action (i.e., is never played in equilibrium by any type). Although Bayes' rule allows any posterior beliefs $\tilde{p}_1(\cdot | a_1)$, player 2 should not put any weight on types for whom a_1 is (weakly) dominated. Thus, we define, for the given action a_1,

$$J = \{t_1 \in T_1 | a_1 \text{ is weakly dominated for type } t_1\}.$$

A "reasonable" restriction on beliefs following a_1 is that $\tilde{p}_1(\cdot | a_1)$ have support $T_1 - J$, i.e.,

$$\sum_{t_1 \in J} \tilde{p}_1(t_1 | a_1) = 0.$$

(We assume that T_1 is countable and use the summation sign, but this is irrelevant to the argument.) Because we restrict beliefs, we reduce the number of potential off-the-equilibrium-path payoffs, and therefore we make it harder for an equilibrium to be sustained.

We can further refine the equilibrium notion by enlarging the set of weakly dominated strategies. Definition 1 requires that a_1 be dominated by a_1' for any reactions a_2 and a_2'. But not all reactions are plausible. After all, player 2, whatever his posterior beliefs, will adopt an optimal reaction. So, let us introduce the set of best reactions (responses) to some action a_1 for arbitrary posterior beliefs $\tilde{p}_1$:

$$\mathrm{BR}(\tilde{p}_1, a_1) \equiv \arg\max_{a_2 \in A_2} \left(\sum_{t_1 \in T_1} \tilde{p}_1(t_1) \Pi^2(a_1, a_2, t_1) \right).$$

Further, let

$$\mathrm{BR}(I, a_1) \equiv \bigcup_{\{\tilde{p}_1 : \tilde{p}_1(I) = 1\}} \mathrm{BR}(\tilde{p}_1, a_1)$$

denote the set of player 2's best responses when his posterior beliefs put all the weight in a subset I of types. In particular, $\mathrm{BR}(T_1, a_1)$ is the whole set of potential best reactions to a_1.

A stronger restriction on out-of-equilibrium beliefs begins by replacing "for all a_2 and a_2' in A_2" in definition 1 with "for all a_2 in $\mathrm{BR}(T_1, a_1)$ and a_2' in $\mathrm{BR}(T_1, a_1')$." This increases the number of weakly dominated strategies and tightens the allowable support of posterior beliefs. (Requiring that a_2 and a_2' be best responses is in the spirit of the iterated elimination of dominated strategies discussed in the text.)

Elimination of Equilibrium Weakly Dominated Strategies

Often there are too few types for which a_1 is weakly dominated for the support of posterior beliefs to be pinned down sufficiently. The "intuitive criterion" of Kreps (1984) and Cho and Kreps (1987) offers to increase the number of dominated strategies by looking at strategies dominated by the proposed equilibrium outcome.[29] Consider a proposed equilibrium with payoff $\Pi^{1*}(t_1)$ for type t_1. Suppose that player 1 deviates from his equilibrium strategy and plays the out-of-equilibrium action a_1.

Definition 2 a_1 is equilibrium weakly dominated for type t_1 in T_1 if, for all a_2 in $\mathrm{BR}(T_1, a_1)$,

$$\Pi^1(a_1, a_2, t_1) \leqslant \Pi^{1*}(t_1) \tag{11.16'}$$

with at least one strict inequality for some a_2 in $\mathrm{BR}(T_1, a_1)$.

We can again consider the set J of type t_1 such that a_1 is equilibrium weakly dominated, and require that player 2 put weight only on types t_1 in $T_1 - J$. The idea is that if everybody really believes that the proposed equilibrium is the one being played (a basic tenet of the equilibrium notion), player 2 knows that types in J have no incentive to play a_1—whatever the associated posterior beliefs, they do not do better than if they follow their equilibrium strategy. A weakly dominated strategy is automatically an equilibrium weakly dominated strategy.

Thus, it seems natural to restrict beliefs to $T_1 - J$ (see, however, footnote 32). Some problems may arise, however. For instance, $T_1 - J$ may be empty. Hence, the intuitive criterion needs to restrict beliefs to $T_1 - J$ only when some other condition is satisfied. For instance, Cho and Kreps (1987) suggest restricting beliefs to $T_1 - J$ when the following condition is met: For all a_2 in $\mathrm{BR}(T_1 - J, a_1)$, there exists t_1 (in $T_1 - J$) such that

$$\Pi^1(a_1, a_2, t_1) > \Pi^{1*}(t_1). \tag{11.17}$$

Condition 11.17 states that, no matter what posterior beliefs are formed that do not put weight on J, there exists some type t_1 who would like to deviate.

The intuitive criterion thus requires a perfect Bayesian equilibrium to exhibit no off-the-equilibrium-path action a_1 and no subset J of types such that a_1 is weakly dominated for all types in J and condition 11.17 is satisfied. (For finite games, a perfect Bayesian equilibrium that does not satisfy the intuitive criterion is not a part of a stable component in the sense of Kohlberg and Mertens [1986].[30] Thus, from the Kohlberg-Mertens existence result, an equilibrium satisfying the intuitive criterion exists.)

11.6.2.2   Examples

Example 1

Consider the following game (Spence 1974): Player 1 (a worker) chooses an education level e and then demands a wage w from player 2 (a firm). Thus,

$$A_1 = \{(e, w)\} \subset R^2.$$

---

29. See Banks and Sobel 1987 and Cho and Sobel 1987 for a similar approach, and McLennan 1985 for a different approach. Cho and Kreps 1987 contains a very helpful discussion of the link between the various refinements and of their connection with the "stability criterion" of Kohlberg and Mertens (1986). Our version of the intuitive criterion follows Cho and Kreps.

See Cho 1986 for an analysis of ideas related to the elimination of equilibrium-dominated strategies in more general games. See Farrell 1985, Grossman and Perry 1986, and Okuno and Postlewaite 1986 for substantially different refinements.

30. See Kreps 1984 and Cho and Kreps 1987. Cho and Sobel (1987) identify simple conditions (including the single-crossing property and the property that senders of all types have the same ordering concerning the receiver's response to a given message) such that the signaling game has a unique stable equilibrium (this equilibrium is then the one selected by the elimination of equilibrium-dominated strategies).

Player 2 then accepts or refuses to employ the worker at wage w, so

$$A_2 = \{\text{yes}, \text{no}\}.$$

The passivity of the firm in this game is meant to represent the bidding by several firms for the worker.

A worker can be of two types, indexed by their productivity (expressed in dollars) within any firm: $L < H$ (so $t_1 = L$ or H), where $L > 0$. The worker knows his type, and the firm has prior beliefs $p_1(L) = \alpha$ and $p_1(H) = 1 - \alpha$. Let

$$M \equiv \alpha L + (1 - \alpha)H$$

be the mean or average productivity computed from the prior beliefs. The posterior beliefs are denoted

$$\tilde{p}_1(L|a_1) = \eta(a_1)$$

and

$$\tilde{p}_1(H|a_1) = 1 - \eta(a_1).$$

The worker invests $e \geqslant 0$ in education. For simplicity, we assume that the worker's level of education has no influence on his productivity. The cost of education to the worker, however, depends on the worker's type. A more productive worker learns at a lower cost (this condition is often called the single crossing, sorting, or Spence-Mirrlees condition). For instance, let us assume that the cost of education is e/t_1. The payoff for player 1 with type t_1 receiving wage w is

$$\Pi^1 = w - e/t_1.$$

The indifference curves for the two types are represented in figure 11.13. Type L's indifference curve is steeper than type H's because a given increase in education is more costly to type L and, therefore, requires a higher wage raise to keep this type at the same utility level.

The firm accepts the offer only if $w \leqslant E(t_1|a_1)$. Any $w \leqslant L$ is always accepted for any level of education (in particular, 0), and any $w > H$ is always refused.

First we will consider the perfect Bayesian equilibria of this game. We will look at the two potential types of pure-strategy equilibria (separating and pooling), and we

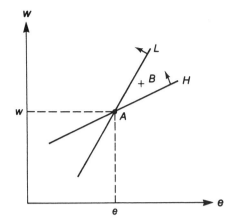

Figure 11.13

will examine whether or not these equilibria satisfy the two criteria discussed above.

Separating equilibrium   The two types of workers choose two different levels of education. Type t_1 receives wage t_1.[31] The low-productivity type, L, necessarily chooses $e(L) = 0$. (If he invested $e > 0$, his utility, equal to $L - e/L$, would be lower than that obtained for no education, which is at least L.) The high-productivity type chooses education $e > 0$. Let us define the levels of education $0 < s < r$ by

$$L = H - s/L$$

and

$$L = H - r/H.$$

In words, the low-productivity type is indifferent between not investing in education and being recognized (getting wage L) and investing s in education and being taken for a high-productivity type (able to demand wage H). And the high-productivity type would not want to invest more than r to be recognized (while he could get a wage at least equal to L by not investing). Clearly, a separating PBE has education level e in the interval $[s, r]$, because it must satisfy the incentive-compatibility constraints $L \geqslant H - e/L$ and $H - e/H \geqslant L$. Conversely, any e in $[s, r]$ is part of a PBE. It suffices to specify that for out-of-equilibrium education levels e' not in $\{0, e\}$, the

---

31. One could also think of equilibria in which $E(t_1|a_1) > w(a_1)$; however, such equilibria actually do not satisfy the refinement criteria.

firm puts all the weight on the low-productivity type $\eta(e') = 1$. Thus, the worker with education e' cannot demand more than L, and, as is easily verified, type L chooses education 0 and type H chooses education e. So we have a *continuum of separating equilibria*.

However, only one separating equilibrium survives once we eliminate weakly dominated strategies when forming out-of-equilibrium beliefs. For this purpose, notice that any e strictly greater than s is dominated by education level 0 for type L. (By investing 0, the low-productivity worker gets at least L; by investing e, he gets at most $H - e/L < L$.) In particular, any e in $(s, r]$ should lead to $\eta(e) = 0$ (so that $w = H$ can be demanded). Thus, to be recognized, type H need not invest more than s, and we are left with a unique separating equilibrium, in which the high-productivity type invests at the "least-cost separating equilibrium level" s. (This equilibrium also satisfies the intuitive criterion.)

Pooling equilibria There also are a lot of pooling PBEs. Suppose that both types choose education level e. The corresponding wage that can be demanded is M. To enforce such an equilibrium, one is best off choosing out-of-equilibrium beliefs $\eta(e') = 1$ for $e' \neq e$ (so that the wage is equal to L following e'). This, as before, gives the least incentive to deviate from e. Now, with such beliefs, the most profitable deviation is to choose $e' = 0$. So for e to be a pooling equilibrium we need $M - e/L \geq L$ and $M - e/H \geq L$. Hence, any education level e satisfying $M - e/L \geq L$ defines a pooling equilibrium. Thus, we have a continuum of pooling equilibria with education levels in an interval $[0, v]$, where $0 < v < s$.

The simple elimination of weakly dominated strategies does not reduce the set of pooling equilibria. In contrast, the intuitive criterion eliminates them all. To see this, look at figure 11.13. Suppose both types pool at point

$A = \{e, w\}$. Suppose that player 1 deviates and chooses

$B = \{e + \delta e, w + \delta w\}$.

Point B involves more education, and a wage raise that more than offsets the increase in education for the high-productivity type but not for the low-productivity one. Choosing B is thus equilibrium-dominated for type L (but not for type H). So, after point B, the firm should form beliefs $\eta = 0$ and expect profit $H - (w + \delta w)$. But $w \leq M < H$, so for δw small the firm should accept offer B. And, therefore, type H should pick B rather than A.[32] Hence, the pooling equilibrium at A does not satisfy the intuitive criterion. (Actually, the intuitive criterion does not always eliminate all pooling equilibria. A counterexample is another signaling game, the limit-pricing game—see Fudenberg and Tirole 1986c. Other examples can be built in more complicated games, such as bargaining games.)

Hence, in this game the intuitive criterion selects a unique pure-strategy equilibrium.[33] The intuitive criterion also disposes of the mixed-strategy (or hybrid or semiseparating) equilibria.[34,35]

We shall now develop an industrial-organization example with a very similar structure. The treatment closely follows that of the job-market signaling example.

Example 2

Consider the Cournot game with asymmetric information used to illustrate the notion of Bayesian equilibrium in the text, but played in a sequential rather than simultaneous manner (Gal-Or 1987). There are two firms ($i = 1, 2$). Firm or player 1 chooses output $a_1 = q_1$. Firm or player 2 chooses output $a_2 = q_2$ after observing q_1. Payoffs are

$$\Pi^i = [t_1 - (q_1 + q_2)]q_i,$$

---

32. However, if the firm is convinced by the high-productivity type's speech that a low-productivity type would never deviate to point B, it should also have some doubts as to whether A is really a pooling allocation. In other words, if it is common knowledge that a speech attempting to convince the firm that point B is chosen by type H is successful, point A necessarily signals that the worker is of type L, as he would have deviated to B if he had been of type H. Hence, the firm turns down offer A, and even type L is better off offering B than A. Hence, it is not clear that it can be common knowledge that a deviation to B signals the high-productivity type. (This argument was offered by Joseph Stiglitz.) See Cho and Kreps 1987 for a discussion of this point.

33. For an alternative method of selecting this equilibrium, see Riley 1979.

34. The equilibrium chosen by the intuitive criterion or the stability criterion is discontinuous in the firm's beliefs about the worker. When $\alpha = 0$ (that is, when it is common knowledge that the worker is of type H), the worker does not invest in education and obtains wage H. When α is strictly positive, the type-H worker still gets wage H but must invest $e = s$ in education (where s is constant in, and therefore does not converge to 0 with, α). This discontinuity is a general property of the Spencian signaling model. For more on this issue, see Fudenberg et al. 1986.

35. To see this, begin by duplicating the reasoning used above for pooling equilibria.

where t_1 can be thought of as the intercept of the linear demand curve (minus a common unit cost, say). If t_1 is common knowledge (the full-information case), we know that firm 2 has reaction function

$$q_2 = R_2(q_1) = (t_1 - q_1)/2$$

and firm 1 maximizes

$$[t_1 - q_1 - R_2(q_1)]q_1.$$

This leads to $q_1 = t_1/2$ and $q_2 = t_1/4$. Profits are $\Pi^1 = (t_1)^2/8$ and $\Pi^2 = (t_1)^2/16$.

Now assume that firm 1 (the incumbent) has superior information about demand. Before choosing q_1, it learns t_1. This parameter or type can take the value L or H, with $0 < L < H$. Firm 2 has prior probabilities $p_1(L) = \alpha$ and $p_1(H) = 1 - \alpha$. Before choosing q_2, it observes only q_1 and updates its beliefs:

$$\tilde{p}_1(L|q_1) = \eta(q_1),$$

$$\tilde{p}_1(H|q_1) = 1 - \eta(q_1).$$

Clearly, firm 2 reacts optimally given its posterior beliefs, so it maximizes

$$q_2(\{\eta(q_1)L + [1 - \eta(q_1)]H\} - q_1 - q_2).$$

The optimal reaction,

$$q_2 = R_2(q_1) = \{\eta(q_1)L + [1 - \eta(q_1)]H - q_1\}/2,$$

grows with firm 2's beliefs that demand is high. Hence, firm 1 has an incentive to convince firm 2 that demand is low.

Let us first derive the "monotonicity property" from the incentive-compatibility conditions. Roughly, firm 1 chooses a higher quantity when demand is high.[36] Let q_1 and q_1' denote optimal actions for types L and H, respectively. (We allow the possibility that several such actions

exist.) Optimality requires that

$$q_1(L - q_1 - R_2(q_1)) \geqslant q_1'(L - q_1' - R_2(q_1'))$$

and

$$q_1'(H - q_1' - R_2(q_1')) \geqslant q_1(H - q_1 - R_2(q_1)).$$

Adding these two inequalities yields

$$(q_1' - q_1)(H - L) \geqslant 0,$$

which yields the desired monotonicity.

We now look for (pure strategy) separating and pooling equilibria. We will impose a number of conditions. These conditions are met for, e.g., $H = 4$, $L = 3$, and $\alpha = 0.8$ (these numerical values simplify computations).

Separating equilibria In a separating equilibrium, the firm's type is revealed by its output. Type H, therefore, plays its full-information quantity $H/2$.[37] The incentive-compatibility constraints require that type t_1 not want to choose the quantity chosen by type t_1'. Clearly, type L does not want to choose $H/2$. First, $H/2$ is not profit maximizing for type L under full information about L; second, playing $H/2$ conveys the information that demand is high, and leads to a greater output for firm 2 than under full information. The relevant incentive constraint is thus that the high-demand type not want to play the low-demand type's quantity q_1; that is,

$$\frac{H^2}{8} \geqslant q_1\left(H - q_1 - \frac{L - q_1}{2}\right). \tag{11.18}$$

To make things more interesting, let us assume that condition 11.18 is violated at type L's full-information output ($q_1 = L/2$):

$$\frac{H^2}{8} < \frac{L}{2}\left(H - \frac{3L}{4}\right). \tag{11.19}$$

---

36. This condition, which can be derived in a much larger class of games (including the previous job-market signaling game), stems from the Spence-Mirrlees condition, which can be written here as

$$\frac{\partial}{\partial t_1}\left(\frac{\partial \Pi^1}{\partial q_1}\right) > 0.$$

37. If type H were to play q_1 in equilibrium, its profit would be

$$q_1\left(H - q_1 - \frac{H - q_1}{2}\right)$$

$$\leqslant \frac{H}{2}\left(H - \frac{H}{2} - \frac{H - H/2}{2}\right)$$

$$\leqslant \frac{H}{2}\left(H - \frac{H}{2} - \frac{t_1^e(H/2) - H/2}{2}\right),$$

where the first inequality comes from the full-information maximization and the second from the fact that the expectation of t_1 conditional on firm 1's playing $H/2$ cannot exceed H.

It is easily checked that 11.19 is satisfied if L is sufficiently close to H. (The intuition is that at $L \simeq H$ the change in output by type H to claim he is type L has only a direct second-order effect on his profit but yields a first-order decrease in firm 2's output and, therefore, an indirect first-order increase in firm 1's profit.) Inequality 11.19, the monotonicity of output with respect to type, and the concavity of the right-hand side of 11.18 imply that the separating output q_1 must not exceed $s < L/2$, where s is the smallest root of 11.18. (For instance, for $H = 4$ and $L = 3$, $s = 1$.) On the other hand, q_1 cannot be too small (otherwise, type L would not want to choose q_1 even though it conveys the information that demand is low), so a necessary condition is

$$q_1 \left(L - q_1 - \frac{L - q_1}{2} \right) \geq \max_x \left[x \left(L - x - \frac{H - x}{2} \right) \right],$$

(11.20)

where the right-hand side is computed on the most pessimistic assumption that output x conveys the information that demand is high. It is easy to see that 11.20 and our previous analysis imply that q_1 must belong to some interval $[r, s]$, where r is the smallest root of 11.20. (For $H = 4$ and $L = 3$, r belongs to $(0, 1)$.)

Conversely, any q_1 in $[r, s]$ is type L's output of a separating PBE. To obtain this result, it suffices to specify that for out-of-equilibrium quantities q_1' not in $\{q_1, H/2\}$, firm 2 believes that demand is high. From 11.20, type L prefers playing q_1. From the definition of $H/2$, type H prefers playing $H/2$. Thus, there is a continuum of separating PBE.

As in example 1, the elimination of weakly dominated strategies leaves us with a unique separating equilibrium: the least-cost separating one at s. This results from the fact that playing $q_1 < s$ is dominated by playing $H/2$ for type H (from the definition of s). So, for $q_1 < s$, firm 2 should believe that demand is low. In turn, type L need not choose an output lower than s to signal that demand is low.

Pooling equilibria   Let q denote a pooling quantity. (Both types play q in equilibrium.) Firm 2's posterior belief about the intercept following output q_1 is unchanged:

$$M = \alpha L + (1 - \alpha) H.$$

Thus, type t_1's profit is

$$q_1 \left(t_1 - q_1 - \frac{M - q_1}{2} \right) = q_1 \left(t_1 - \frac{M}{2} - \frac{q_1}{2} \right).$$

The best way to sustain q_1 as a pooling output of a PBE is to assume that firm 2 believes that demand is high when it observes $q_1' \neq q_1$. So q_1 will indeed be a pooling equilibrium output if and only if

$$q_1 \left(L - \frac{M}{2} - \frac{q_1}{2} \right) \geq \max_x \left[x \left(L - x - \frac{H - x}{2} \right) \right]$$

(11.21)

and

$$q_1 \left(H - \frac{M}{2} - \frac{q_1}{2} \right) \geq \max_x \left[x \left(H - x - \frac{H - x}{2} \right) \right]$$

$$= H^2/8.$$

(11.22)

As is easily checked, 11.22 defines an interval of allowable q_1 that includes $H/2$. Inequality 11.21 also defines an interval located to the right of r. Indeed, given our numerical values ($H = 4$, $L = 3$, $\alpha = 0.8$), this interval also contains $H/2$. Thus, the set of pooling outputs is an interval containing $H/2$.

To eliminate this continuum of pooling equilibria, we can use the intuitive criterion. Let q_1 be a pooling equilibrium output. Define $q_1' < q_1$ by the smallest root of

$$q_1' \left(H - q_1' - \frac{L - q_1'}{2} \right) = q_1 \left(H - q_1 - \frac{M - q_1}{2} \right).$$

(11.23)

Now playing $q_1' - \varepsilon$ (for ε positive and small) is equilibrium dominated for type H, but not for type L. So firm 2's posterior beliefs should put all the weight on type L following output $q_1' - \varepsilon$. But, from 11.23, type L prefers playing $q_1' - \varepsilon$ to playing q_1. Thus, q_1 is not a pooling output anymore.

*Exercise 11.13**   Consider the Stackelberg game, except that t_1 is continuously distributed on the interval $[L, H]$ instead of having only two atoms at L and H. Look for a separating equilibrium. Type t_1 chooses output $q_1 = Q_1(t_1)$, where Q_1 is strictly increasing and differentiable; the inverse function of Q_1 is T. Thus, $T(q_1)$ is the type that chooses output q_1.

(i) Show that T satisfies the differential equation

$$q_1 T'(q_1) = T(q_1) - 2q_1.$$

(ii) What is the boundary condition? Check that the solution is

$$T(q_1) = \left[2 + 2 \ln \left(\frac{H/2}{q_1} \right) \right] q_1.$$

(iii) Argue that $T(s) > L$, where s is the least-cost separating output in the discrete case.

Exercise 11.14**[38] We saw in chapter 4 that, in the absence of uncertainty, a monopoly manufacturer makes a monopoly retailer (or wholesaler) the residual claimant for his sales. That is, the manufacturer charges an intermediate price equal to his marginal cost and captures the retailer's profit through a lump-sum transfer (the franchise fee). This exercise shows that when the manufacturer has private information about the demand for his product, he may want to charge more than the marginal cost (and reduce the franchise fee) for signaling purposes. A monopoly manufacturer with marginal cost c charges a two-part tariff to a monopoly retailer: $T(q) = A + p_w q$, where q is the quantity bought and resold by the retailer, p_w is the intermediate price, and A is the franchise fee. The final demand for the product is $q = t_1 - p$, where p is the consumer price chosen by the retailer. For simplicity, the cost of retailing is zero. Player 1 (the manufacturer) moves first and offers a contract $a_1 = \{A, p_w\}$. Player 2 (the retailer) accepts or refuses the contract and, if he accepts it, chooses a consumer price. So $a_2 = \{$yes or no, $p\}$. He accepts the contract if and only if his expected profit is non-negative.

(i) Rederive the result that under full information about t_1 the equilibrium contract is $p_w = c$ and $A = (t_1 - c)^2/4$.

(ii) Suppose that only the manufacturer knows t_1. This parameter (type) can take value L or H ($0 < L < H$). The retailer learns t_1 after signing the contract but before choosing p. Reanalyze examples 1 and 2 to show that type L charges an intermediate price equal to c and type H charges an intermediate price strictly exceeding c. (Show that the intermediate price is a nondecreasing function of t_1. Look for separating and pooling equilibria. Use the elimination of dominated strategies and the intuitive criterion.)

---

38. This exercise stems from discussions with Eric Maskin.

Answers and Hints

Exercise 11.1

(i) There are three information sets.
(ii) This is straightforward.

Exercise 11.2

(i) Let $b = \max_{j \neq i} b_j$. Varying b_i in $(b, +\infty)$ has no effect on bidder i's welfare; he gets the object and pays b in any case. Similarly, varying b_i in $[0, b)$ has no effect on his welfare. Suppose that $v_i > b$. Then bidding $b_i < b$ rather than v_i reduces bidder i's welfare by $(v_i - b) - 0 > 0$. If $v_i < b$, bidding $b_i > b$ reduces his welfare by $0 - (v_i - b) > 0$. If $v_i = b$, bidder i is indifferent between getting the object (at price b) and not getting it. He may as well bid $b_i = v_i$.

(ii) Straightforward.

(iii) The reasoning in answer i was independent of the level of b, so bidding $b_i = v_i$ is optimal for any b. Therefore, bidding the true value is always optimal (and a dominant strategy) in a second-bid auction.

Exercise 11.3

(i) Social welfare is equal to

$$\sum_i \Pi^i = \sum_i t_i + \sum_i g_i(a, \theta_i)$$

$$= -C(a) + \sum_i g_i(a, \theta_i) + \text{constant},$$

from the government's budget constraint.

(ii) With these transfers, and for any announcements

$$(\tilde{\theta}_1, \dots, \tilde{\theta}_{i-1}, \tilde{\theta}_{i+1}, \dots, \tilde{\theta}_n) \equiv \tilde{\theta}_{-i}$$

by the other consumers, consumer i's payoff function is

$$t_i(\tilde{\theta}_i, \tilde{\theta}_{-i}) + g_i(a^*(\tilde{\theta}_i, \tilde{\theta}_{-i}), \theta_i)$$

$$= K_i + \sum_{j \neq i} g_j(a^*(\tilde{\theta}_i, \tilde{\theta}_{-i}), \tilde{\theta}_j) + g_i(a^*(\tilde{\theta}_i, \tilde{\theta}_{-i}), \theta_i)$$

$$- C(a^*(\tilde{\theta}_i, \tilde{\theta}_{-i})).$$

But from the definition of a^* we have for all a,

$$\sum_{j \neq i} g_j(a^\star(\theta_i, \tilde{\theta}_{-i}), \tilde{\theta}_j) + g_i(a^\star(\theta_i, \tilde{\theta}_{-i}), \theta_i) - C(a^\star(\theta_i, \tilde{\theta}_{-i}))$$

$$\geqslant \sum_{j \neq i} g_j(a, \tilde{\theta}_j) + g_i(a, \theta_i) - C(a).$$

That is, $a^\star(\theta_i, \tilde{\theta}_{-i})$ is optimal for the profile of preferences $(\theta_i, \tilde{\theta}_{-i})$. This inequality holds, in particular, for any $a = a^\star(\tilde{\theta}_i, \tilde{\theta}_{-i})$ that consumer i can induce by lying and announcing $\tilde{\theta}_i$ instead of θ_i. Hence, announcing θ_i is optimal whatever the other consumers' announcements.

The planner can thus implement the first-best allocation as long as monetary transfers are socially costless. This mechanism is due to Clarke (1971) and Groves (1973).

In general, the government's budget,

$$\sum_i t_i - C(a),$$

is not balanced. Actually, Green and Laffont (1977) have shown that, in general, there exists no dominant strategy mechanism that implements the first-best allocation and balances the budget. First-best allocation and a balanced budget can be obtained if one is willing to accept a weaker concept of equilibrium: the Bayesian equilibrium concept developed in section 11.4 (see Arrow 1979 and d'Aspremont and Gerard-Varet 1979).

Exercise 11.4

The pure-strategy Nash equilibria are

$$\{a_1^\star = L, a_2^\star(L) = \ell, a_2^\star(M, R) = \ell \text{ or } r\}$$

and

$$\{a_1^\star = R, a_2^\star(L) = r, a_2^\star(M, R) = r\}.$$

Exercise 11.5

(i) If locations differ, moving toward one's rival increases one's market share (which is equivalent to profit, in the absence of price competition). Thus, the locations must be identical. If the common location is not the middle of the segment, moving slightly toward the center increases one's market share.

(ii) Suppose first that the three firms are not located at the same point. A firm located alone at the left or the right would gain market share by moving slightly toward

its rivals. Thus, firms must be located identically and get one-third of the market each. However, by moving slightly either to the right or to the left of this common location, a firm can get approximately half of the market, or more. So no pure-strategy equilibrium exists. On the existence of a mixed-strategy equilibrium, see Dasgupta and Maskin 1986.

Exercise 11.6

Let $P_{-i} \equiv \sum_{j \neq i} p_j$. Consumer i maximizes

$$g(P_{-i} + p_i) - p_i,$$

which yields

$$g'(P_{-i} + p_i) = 1.$$

This first-order condition is sufficient, and defines a unique optimum as the objective function is strictly concave and $g'(0) > 1$, $g'(+\infty) < 1$. The total contribution ($P \equiv P_{-i} + p_i$) is thus given by

$$g'(P) = 1.$$

There is clearly too little public expenditure (due to the free-rider problem). The optimal public expenditure, P^*, maximizes $\{ng(P) - P\}$, so that $g'(P^*) = 1/n$, implying $P^* > P$. Although the total expenditure P is determinate, the individual ones are not. Any $\{p_1, \ldots, p_n\}$ such that $p_1 + \cdots + p_n = P$ is an equilibrium.

A multiplicity of equilibria similar to the one in this exercise arises when the size of the public good is fixed (for example, a project is implemented only if $P \geqslant \overline{P}$). However, multiplicity does not arise in all models of private provision of a public good.[39]

Exercise 11.7

Let $T = 2$. Player 2 makes the last offer, so he offers $x_2 = 0$, which is the lowest share accepted by player 1. Player 2 thus gets 1. He will accept giving x_1 to player 1 in period 1 only if $1 - x_1 \geqslant \delta(1)$. Thus, player 1 offers $x_1 = 1 - \delta$.

Let $T = 3$. We know that if player 2 makes the offer in period 2, he gets $1 - \delta$, because there are exactly two periods left. So player 1 in period 1 must give him at least

---

39. As an exercise, consider "convex contribution costs"—$C_i(p_i)$, with $C_i' > 0$, $C_i'' > 0$, $C_i'(0) \leqslant 1$, and $C_i'(+\infty) \geqslant 1$—and show how P can be computed as a

fixed point. What happens if the consumers have different g_i's instead of different C_i's?

$1 - x_1 \geqslant \delta(1 - \delta)$.

Hence, $x_1 = 1 - \delta + \delta^2$.

Let $T = 4$. From the three-period game, we know that if player 2 rejects the offer at date 1 he gets $1 - \delta + \delta^2$. Thus,

$$1 - x_1 = \delta(1 - \delta + \delta^2) \Rightarrow x_1 = 1 - \delta + \delta^2 - \delta^3.$$

By induction on the number of periods, we get in the limit

$$x_1 = 1 - \delta + \delta^2 - \delta^3 + \cdots$$

$$= \frac{1 - \delta}{1 - \delta^2}$$

$$= \frac{1}{1 + \delta}.$$

Exercise 11.8

The following beautifully simple version of Rubinstein's proof of uniqueness is from Shaked and Sutton 1984. Suppose player 1 makes the offer at some date. Because player 2 gets at most $\overline{V}_2$ in the next period (perfectness requires that equilibrium is also sustained from the next period on), the offer x_1 such that $1 - x_1 = \delta \overline{V}_2$ is accepted. Hence,

$$\underline{V}_1 \geqslant x_1 = 1 - \delta \overline{V}_2. \tag{11.24}$$

Similarly, the most player 1 can get now is $\overline{V}_1 \leqslant 1 - \underline{W}_2$; but $\underline{W}_2 \geqslant \delta \underline{V}_2$ because player 2 can always reject and wait for his turn. Hence,

$$\overline{V}_1 \leqslant 1 - \delta \underline{V}_2. \tag{11.25}$$

Similar equations hold when player 2 makes the offer:

$$\underline{V}_2 \geqslant 1 - \delta \overline{V}_1, \tag{11.26}$$

$$\overline{V}_2 \leqslant 1 - \delta \underline{V}_1. \tag{11.27}$$

Now 11.24 and 11.27 give

$$\underline{V}_1 \geqslant 1 - \delta + \delta^2 \underline{V}_1 \Rightarrow \underline{V}_1 \geqslant 1/(1 + \delta), \tag{11.28}$$

and 11.25 and 11.26 give

$$\overline{V}_1 \leqslant 1 - \delta + \delta^2 \overline{V}_1 \Rightarrow \overline{V}_1 \leqslant 1/(1 + \delta). \tag{11.29}$$

Because $\underline{V}_1 \leqslant \overline{V}_1$ by definition,

$$\underline{V}_1 = \overline{V}_1 = V_1 = 1/(1 + \delta).$$

Similarly,

$$\underline{W}_1 = \overline{W}_1 = W_1 = \delta/(1 + \delta).$$

The same equations hold for player 2. Since valuations are unique, it is easy to see that the equilibrium strategies are also unique, and that they are those described in the text.

Exercise 11.9

(i) The game tree has three nodes, which are also information sets. Use Kuhn's algorithm of backward induction: The authority inspects if and only if it observes predation. Hence, the firm does not prey in equilibrium.

(ii) The game tree is the same as in question i, except that the two nodes following the firm's decision form a single information set. If the firm preys in equilibrium, the authority inspects and thus the firm ought not to prey. If it does not prey in equilibrium, no inspection occurs, so preying would be profitable. Thus, there exists no pure-strategy equilibrium. Suppose that the firm preys with probability x and the authority inspects with probability y. Because the two parties must be indifferent between their two pure strategies, x and y are given by

$$x(s - c) - (1 - x)c = 0 \Leftrightarrow xs = c$$

and

$$-y(p - g) + (1 - y)g = 0 \Leftrightarrow yp = g.$$

Exercise 11.10

A bidder with valuation t maximizes

$$(t - b)F^{n-1}(\Phi(b)).$$

The first-order condition is thus, after simplification,

$$(t - b)\Phi'(b) = \frac{F(\Phi(b))}{(n - 1)f(\Phi(b))}.$$

This condition must be satisfied at $t = \Phi(b)$, which yields a first-degree differential equation in $\Phi(b)$.

For $F(x) = x^\alpha$, one obtains $\Phi(b) = kb$, where

$$k = 1 + \frac{1}{\alpha(n - 1)}.$$

The bid tends to the true valuation (i.e., k tends to 1) when the number of bidders tends to infinity.

Exercise 11.11

(i) and (ii) The winner's *ex post* payoff is

$$x_i + E(x_j | x_j \leqslant \Phi(b_i)).$$

Because $\Phi(\cdot)$ is a nondecreasing function,[40]

$$E(x_j | x_j \leqslant \Phi(b_i)) \leqslant E(x_j) = \tfrac{1}{2}.$$

This is a much more general result; see Milgrom 1981b.

(iii) Suppose that $\Phi(b) = kb$. Writing the first-order condition and imposing $\Phi(b_i) = x_i$, one obtains $k = 2 - 1/k$, or $k = 1$. Each bidder bids his private information.

Exercise 11.12

(i) Solve by backward induction. If the single entrant enters, the firm is better off acquiescing. Hence, the entrant does enter. With multiple entrants, in the last period the incumbent acquiesces to entry; hence, the last entrant enters. Because the outcome in the last period is independent of what happened before, the incumbent acquiesces to enter at date $n-1$; so entrant $(n-1)$ enters. And so on.

(ii) *Single entrant:* Clearly, the entrant stays out if $x > \tfrac{1}{2}$ and enters if $x < \tfrac{1}{2}$. It is indifferent between entering and not entering if $x = \tfrac{1}{2}$. *Multiple entrants:* Consider date $n-1$, and suppose the entrant enters. Suppose further that the "soft" incumbent (with payoff -1 in the case of predation) acquiesces with probability 1. Then predation signals a "tough" incumbent who enjoys preying and always preys. Entrant n stays out, whereas it would enter if it observed acquiescence at $n-1$. By preying, the soft incumbent gets $-1 + \tfrac{3}{4} = -\tfrac{1}{4}$ instead of $0 + 0 = 0$. So the soft incumbent does not prey; and again the entrant enters if $x_{n-1} < \tfrac{1}{2}$ and stays out if $x_{n-1} > \tfrac{1}{2}$ (and is indifferent for $x_{n-1} = \tfrac{1}{2}$). The picture changes at date $n-2$. Suppose that the soft incumbent acquiesces with probability 1. Then it makes $0 + 0 + 0 = 0$. By preying, it deters future entry (because $x_{n-1} = 1$ then) and makes $-1 + \tfrac{3}{4} + \tfrac{3}{4} > 0$. Can the soft incumbent prey with probability 1? Then after predation at date $n-2$ one has $x_{n-1} = x_{n-2}$. Recall that the entrant stays out at $n-1$ if

$x_{n-1} > \tfrac{1}{2}$. So if $x_{n-2} > \tfrac{1}{2}$, the incumbent preys with probability 1. If $x_{n-2} < \tfrac{1}{2}$, the soft incumbent must randomize between preying and acquiescing, so that $x_{n-1} = \tfrac{1}{2}$: Let y_{n-2} denote the probability of predation by the soft incumbent. From Bayes' rule,

$$\frac{1}{2} = \frac{(1 - x_{n-2})y_{n-2}}{(1 - x_{n-2})y_{n-2} + x_{n-2}}.$$

The entrant at date $n-2$ is willing to enter if

$$(-1)[x_{n-2} + (1 - x_{n-2})y_{n-2}] + (1)[(1 - x_{n-2})(1 - y_{n-2})]$$
$$\geqslant 0.$$

Using the previous Bayesian updating rule, this inequality can be written as

$$x_{n-2} \leqslant \tfrac{1}{4}.$$

(For $x_{n-2} = \tfrac{1}{4}$, the entrant randomizes.) More generally, entrant 1 stays out if $x > 1/2^{n-1}$ and enters if $x < 1/2^{n-1}$.

Exercise 11.13

(i) Firm 2 reacts to q_1 by

$$q_2 = \frac{T(q_1) - q_1}{2}$$

since q_1 reveals that firm 1's type is $T(q_1)$. Hence, type t_1 maximizes

$$q_1 \left(t_1 - q_1 - \frac{T(q_1) - q_1}{2} \right).$$

The first-order condition with respect to q_1 must be satisfied at type $t_1 = T(q_1)$ for firm 2 to have rational expectations. This yields the differential equation. It is easily checked (using the first-order condition as an identity) that the second-order condition is satisfied.

(ii) Type H might as well choose its full-information output, $H/2$; so $T(H/2) = H$.

(iii) For instance, for $H = 4$ and $L = 3$, $s = 1$ and $T(1) = 2 + 2 \ln 2 > L$. With lots of types, there are more incentive constraints than with only two types: Type H

---

40. To prove this formally, take two values x_j and x_j' and write the "incentive-compatibility equations": The optimal bid for x_j yields at least as much payoff as the optimal bid for x_j' when the information is x_j; and conversely. This is the

method of proof that we used in chapter 1 to show that a monopoly price is a nondecreasing function of marginal cost.

must not play type $(H - \varepsilon)$'s output, the latter type must not play type $(H - 2\varepsilon)$'s output, and so on. Type L needs an even lower output to separate from type H, for example.

Exercise 11.14

(i) The retailer maximizes

$$(p - p_w)(t_1 - p) - A,$$

so the highest franchise that can be demanded is

$$A(p_w) = (t_1 - p_w)^2/4$$

and the retail price is

$$p(p_w) = (t_1 + p_w)/2.$$

The manufacturer then maximizes

$$A(p_w) + (p_w - c)(t_1 - p_w)/2.$$

(ii) To obtain the monotonicity, write the two incentive-compatibility constraints. In equilibrium, the low-demand type is revealed, so efficiency requires that $p_w = c$. But the high-demand type "proves" that demand is high by choosing $p_w > c$. This is because a positive margin is more important when demand is high than when demand is low. So the low-demand type is less tempted to forgo the reduction in the franchise fee required to claim that demand is high in exchange for a positive margin.

To eliminate the pooling equilibria using the intuitive criterion, start from a pooling contract $\{p_w, A\}$ and consider a new contract with a slightly higher intermediate price and a slightly lower franchise fee, which type H (but not type L) prefers to the pooling contract.

References

Abreu, D. 1984. Infinitely Repeated Games with Discounting: A General Theory. Mimeo, Harvard University.

Arrow, K. 1979. The Property Rights Doctrine and Demand Revelation under Incomplete Information. In *Economics and Human Welfare.* New York: Academic.

Aumann, R. 1974. Subjectivity and Correlation in Randomized Strategies. *Journal of Mathematical Economics* 1: 67–96.

Aumann, R. 1976. Agreeing to Disagree. *Annals of Statistics* 4: 1236–1239.

Aumann, R., and L. Shapley. 1976. Long Term Competition: A Game Theoretic Analysis. Mimeo.

Banks, J., and J. Sobel. 1987. Equilibrium Selection in Signaling Games. *Econometrica* 55: 647–662.

Benoit, J.-P., and V. Krishna. 1985. Finitely Repeated Games. *Econometrica* 53: 890–904.

Brandenburger, A., and E. Dekel. 1985. Hierarchies of Beliefs and Common Knowledge. Mimeo.

Cho, I.-K. 1986. A Refinement of Sequential Equilibrium. Mimeo, Princeton University.

Cho, I.-K., and D. Kreps. 1987. Signaling Games and Stable Equilibria. *Quarterly Journal of Economics* 102: 179–221.

Cho, I.-K., and J. Sobel. 1987. Strategic Stability and Uniqueness in Signaling Games. Mimeo, University of Chicago.

Clarke, E. 1971. Multipart Pricing of Public Goods. *Public Choice* 2: 19–33.

Dasgupta, P., and E. Maskin. 1986a. The Existence of Equilibrium in Discontinuous Economic Games, I: Theory. *Review of Economic Studies* 53: 1–26.

Dasgupta, P., and E. Maskin. 1986b. The Existence of Equilibrium in Discontinuous Economic Games, II: Applications. *Review of Economic Studies* 53: 27–42.

d'Aspremont, C., and L. A. Gerard-Varet. 1979. Incentives and Incomplete Information. *Journal of Public Economics* 11: 25–45.

Debreu, G. 1952. A Social Equilibrium Existence Theorem. *Proceedings of the National Academy of Sciences* 38: 886–893.

Farrell, J. 1985. Credible Neologisms in Games of Communication. Mimeo, Massachusetts Institute of Technology.

Fraysse, J., and M. Moreaux. 1985. Collusive Equilibria in Oligopolies with Finite Lives. *European Economic Review* 24: 45–55.

Friedman, J. 1986. *Game Theory with Applications to Economics.* Oxford University Press.

Fudenberg, D., and D. Levine. 1983. Subgame-Perfect Equilibria of Finite and Infinite Horizon Games. *Journal of Economic Theory* 31: 251–268.

Fudenberg, D., and E. Maskin. 1986. Folk Theorems for Repeated Games with Discounting or with Incomplete Information. *Econometrica* 54: 533–554.

Fudenberg, D., and J. Tirole. 1983. Sequential Bargaining with Incomplete Information. *Review of Economic Studies* 50: 221–247.

Fudenberg, D., and J. Tirole. 1986a. A Signal-Jamming Theory of Predation. *Rand Journal of Economics* 17: 366–376.

Fudenberg, D., and J. Tirole. 1986b. A Theory of Exit in Duopoly. *Econometrica* 54: 943–960.

Fudenberg, D., and J. Tirole. 1986c. Noncooperative Game Theory for Industrial Organization: An Introduction and Overview. In *Handbook of Industrial Organization*, ed. R. Schmalensee and R. Willig (Amsterdam: North-Holland, forthcoming).

Fudenberg, D., D. Kreps, and D. Levine. 1986. On the Robustness of Equilibrium Refinements. *Journal of Economic Theory*, forthcoming.

Gal-Or, E. 1987. First Mover Disadvantages with Private Information. *Review of Economic Studies* 54: 279–292.

Gibbons, R. 1985. Incentives in Internal Labor Markets. Mimeo, Massachusetts Institute of Technology.

Green, J., and J.-J. Laffont. 1977. Characterization of Satisfactory Mechanisms for the Revelation of Preferences for Public Goods. *Econometrica* 45: 427–438.

Grossman, S. 1980. The Role of Warranties and Private Disclosure about Product Quality. *Journal of Law and Economics* 24: 461–483.

Grossman, S., and M. Perry. 1986. Perfect Sequential Equilibrium. *Journal of Economic Theory* 39: 97–119.

Groves, T. 1973. Incentives in Teams. *Econometrica* 14: 617–631.

Harsanyi, J. 1967–68. Games with Incomplete Information Played by Bayesian Players. *Management Science* 14: 159–182, 320–334, 486–502.

Harsanyi, J. 1973. Games with Randomly Disturbed Payoffs: A New Rationale for Mixed Strategy Equilibrium Points. *International Journal of Game Theory* 2: 1–23.

Holmström, B. 1983. Managerial Incentive Problems: A Dynamic Perspective. Mimeo.

Hotelling, H. 1929. The Stability of Competition. *Economic Journal* 39: 41–57.

Kohlberg, E., and J.-F. Mertens. 1986. On the Strategic Stability of Equilibria. *Econometrica* 54: 1003–1038.

Kreps, D. 1984. Signalling Games and Stable Equilibrium. Mimeo.

Kreps, D., and R. Wilson. 1982. Sequential Equilibrium. *Econometrica* 50: 863–894.

Kuhn, H. 1953. Extensive Games and the Problem of Information. *Annals of Mathematics Studies*, No. 28. Princeton University Press.

Luce, R., and H. Raiffa. 1957. *Games and Decisions.* New York: Wiley.

McLennan, A. 1985. Justifiable Beliefs in Sequential Equilibrium. *Econometrica* 53: 889–904.

Maskin, E., and J. Riley. 1983. Uniqueness of Equilibrium in Open and Sealed Bid Auctions. Mimeo, University of California, Los Angeles.

Mertens, J.-F., and S. Zamir. 1985. Formulation of Bayesian Analysis for Games with Incomplete Information. *International Journal of Game Theory* 14: 1–29.

Milgrom, P. 1981a. An Axiomatic Characterization of Common Knowledge. *Econometrica* 49: 219–222.

Milgrom, P. 1981b. Good News and Bad News: Representation Theorems and Applications. *Bell Journal of Economics* 12: 380–391.

Milgrom, P., and R. Weber. 1982. A Theory of Auctions and Competitive Bidding. *Econometrica* 50: 1089–1122.

Milgrom, P., and R. Weber. 1986. Distributional Strategies for Games with Incomplete Information. *Mathematics of Operations Research* 10: 619–631.

Moulin, H. 1982. *Game Theory for the Social Sciences.* New York University Press.

Myerson, R. 1979. Optimal Auction Design. *Mathematics of Operations Research* 6: 58–73.

Myerson, R. 1983. Bayesian Equilibrium and Incentive Compatibility: An Introduction. Northwestern MEDS Discussion Paper 548.

Myerson, R. 1984. An Introduction to Game Theory. Discussion Paper 623, Kellogg School of Business, Northwestern University.

Nash, J.-F. 1950. Equilibrium Points in *N*-person Games. *Proceedings of the National Academy of Sciences* 36: 48–49.

Okuno-Fujiwara, M., and A. Postlewaite. 1986. Forward Induction and Equilibrium Refinement. Mimeo, University of Pennsylvania.

Riley, J. 1979. Informational Equilibrium. *Econometrica* 47: 331–360.

Riordan, M. 1985. Imperfect Information and Dynamic Conjectural Variations. *Rand Journal of Economics* 16: 41–50.

Rubinstein, A. 1979. Equilibrium in Supergames with the Overtaking Criterion. *Journal of Economic Theory* 21: 1–9.

Rubinstein, A. 1982. Perfect Equilibrium in a Bargaining Model. *Econometrica* 50: 97–110.

Saloner, G. 1987. Predation, Merger and Incomplete Information. *Rand Journal of Economics* 18: 165–186.

Schelling, T. 1960. *The Strategy of Conflict.* Cambridge, Mass.: Harvard University Press.

Selten, R. 1965. Spieltheoretische Behandlung eines Oligopolmodells mit Nachfrageträgheit. *Zeitschrift für die gesamte Staatswissenschaft* 12: 301–324.

Selten, R. 1975. Reexamination of the Perfectness Concept for Equilibrium Points in Extensive Games. *International Journal of Game Theory* 4: 25–55.

Selten, R. 1978. The Chain-Store Paradox. *Theory and Decision* 9: 127–159.

Shaked, A., and J. Sutton. 1984. Involuntary Unemployment as a Perfect Equilibrium in a Bargaining Model. *Econometrica* 52: 1351–1364.

Spence, M. 1974. *Market Signaling.* Cambridge, Mass.: Harvard University Press.

Tirole, J. 1983. Jeux Dynamiques: Un Guide de l'Utilisateur. *Revue d'Economie Politique* 4: 551–575.

Vickrey, W. 1961. Counterspeculation, Auctions and Competitive Sealed Tenders. *Journal of Finance* 16: 8–37.

Review Exercises

Some of the following exercises merely review or apply ideas introduced in the text; others use techniques developed there to analyze new and interesting questions.

The bracketed numbers refer to the most relevant chapters; however, the reader should feel free to use ideas developed in other chapters or not developed at all in the present book. (The chapter on the theory of the firm is referred to as [0], and an exercise that appeals to many of the chapters does not refer to any particular one.)

Some of these exercises are taken from MIT problem sets and examinations prepared by J. Harris, P. Joskow, G. Saloner, R. Schmalensee, and the author.

Exercise 1 [0]**

(i) Define "relationship-specific investment" or "transaction-specific investment" (terms used by Williamson, Klein, Crawford and Alchian, and others).

(ii) In a simple two-period model, show that if an input supplier who must make relationship-specific investments *ex ante* cannot contract on the price at which transactions will take place *ex post*, the result will be underinvestment in relationship-specific capital.

(iii) How might the above result change if both the buyer and the seller were required to make relationship-specific investments *ex ante*?

(iv) Several alternative explanations for why a firm might find it advantageous to integrate forward or backward, or to rely on complex contractual arrangements to mediate exchange between levels of the production process, have been proposed. Discuss one or more alternatives to the "relationship-specific investment" rationale for vertical integration. What type of empirical evidence would you look for, and how would you use it to distinguish between competing explanations of vertical integration?

Exercise 2 [0, 4]*

A monopoly manufacturer of an intermediate good sells a quantity q to a monopoly retailer. The retailer faces demand $q = 1 - p$, where p is the final price. The retail cost is 0, and the manufacturer's cost is $C(q) = q^2/2$.

(i) What is the aggregate profit under vertical integration?

(ii) What are the profits Π^m and Π^r under the optimal linear tariff, $T(q) = p_w q$, for the manufacturer?

(iii) What are these profits under a two-part tariff?

Suppose now that *before* the manufacturer chooses the tariff, the retailer can choose to invest to increase demand. At cost ε (where ε is small and positive), the demand is increased from $q = 1 - p$ to $q = 2 - p$. (At cost 0, the demand remains $q = 1 - p$.) The investment choice is observed by the manufacturer, who *then* chooses a tariff (so the manufacturer cannot commit before the retailer's investment).

(iv) What is the level of investment under a linear tariff?

(v) What is the level of investment under a two-part tariff? Does the manufacturer make more profit than under a linear tariff? Explain.

Exercise 3 [1]**

Consider a monopolist facing a linear demand curve $q = a - bp$ and producing at marginal cost c.

(i) Show that the elasticity of demand (defined as a positive number) is an increasing function of b.

(ii) Compute the welfare loss due to monopoly pricing. How does the relative welfare loss (dead-weight loss over welfare under marginal cost pricing) vary with b?

Exercise 4 [1]**

A monopolist has constant marginal cost c and faces a twice-differentiable demand of $q = D(p, d)$, where d is a demand parameter ($\partial D/\partial d > 0$). Let $p^m(d)$ denote the (a?) monopoly price for parameter d.

(i) Show that a sufficient condition for p^m to be a nondecreasing function of d is that $\partial^2 D/\partial p \partial d \geqslant 0$. First prove this by assuming that the monopolist's profit is concave in price. Then prove it more generally. (The second-order condition may not be satisfied, so the monopoly price may not be unique for a given demand parameter. Show that any monopoly price for d' does not exceed any monopoly price for d when $d' < d$. Use the reasoning that was used in chapter 1 to prove that the monopoly price increases with marginal cost.)

(ii) Discuss the sufficient condition. Give a simple demand curve for which it is not satisfied and for which the monopoly price does not depend on d.

Exercise 5 [1]*

Consider a monopolist facing demand $q = 1 - p$ in each of two periods. Its marginal cost is equal to c in the first period and $c - \lambda q_1$ in the second period (where λ is positive and "small"). Compute the optimal pricing strategy for the monopolist. Compute the Lerner index in each period and comment. Does output increase or decrease over time?

Exercise 6 [1, 2, 3]**

In his paper "Demand Uncertainty and Sales" (mimeo, Graduate School of Business, University of Chicago), Peter Pashigian lists a number of different types of sales and some explanations for these sales. Consider pre-season sales (e.g., August sales of winter clothes), white sales, within-season random sales, and clearance sales.

Think of potential explanations (including ones not offered in the text) for these sales (uncertainty, information acquisition about consumers' tastes, peak-load pricing, various forms of price discrimination, etc.), and give a critical assessment of these explanations.

Exercise 7 [2, 3, 7]*

(i) A private railway company considers building a railroad between cities A and B. No such service commonly exists; there may be alternative ways of moving passengers and freight (e.g. cars, trucks, and barges), but these are assumed to be competitive if they exist. Using chapter 2, compare the private company's incentive to build the railroad with the social planner's.

(ii) Would you amend your conclusion if there existed an alternative and differentiated transportation mode run monopolistically by the railways company (see chapter 2 or 3) or another company (see chapter 7)?

Exercise 8 [2, 5]**

In *The Economics of Regulation* (Wiley, 1971), Alfred Kahn argues that a "prominent imperfection that may make unrestricted competition particularly injurious to consumers is their own limited ability to judge the quality of products and hence to keep it at acceptable levels even when they have a wide range of competitive suppliers to choose from." "Consumer protection," he notes, "can be equally necessary when price competition is very intense. The decline in price to average variable costs can lead to a skimping on safety, reliability and frequency of service that consumers may have difficulty in detecting promptly...." (volume 2, p. 176) This exercise builds an example in which price competition lowers incentives to maintain a reputation (and may lower welfare).

There are two periods ($t = 1, 2$) and a single good. Consumers are all identical and have unit demands. The valuation for the good is $v + s_t$, where s_t is the quality of the good: high ($s_t = 1$) or low ($s_t = 0$). The extra cost for a firm to supply the high quality is c'. The production cost of the good is c. The quality cannot be ascertained at the date of purchase, and no warranty is feasible. However, all parties observe the date-t quality at the end of date t.

A firm can be of two types: With probability $1 - x$, the extra cost of supplying quality is $c' > 0$. With probability x, the low quality is not cheaper to produce (or else, the firm is "honest"). A firm knows its type, but the consumer (or the firm's rival, if any) does not. Assume that $\delta x > c'$ (where δ is the discount factor).

(i) Consider a monopoly situation. Show that the following is an equilibrium path: The firm, whatever its type, charges $p_1 = v + 1$ and produces the high quality in the first period. It charges $p_2 = v + x$ in period 2, and it produces the high quality in that period only if this is cheaper. Show that the expected welfare is equal to

$$(v - c)(1 + \delta) + x(1 + \delta) + (1 - x)(1 - c').$$

(ii) Consider a duopoly situation. Show that, for any price charged by the firms in the first period, it cannot be the case that both firms supply the high quality with probability 1 in that period. (Hint: What would Bertrand competition imply in period 2?)

Look for a symmetric equilibrium. Show that, if $\frac{1}{2}c' > \delta(1 - x)$, each firm produces the low quality in the first period if it is cheaper to do so. Compute the welfare, and show that if the above two conditions are satisfied, and if $x\delta < 1 - c'$, welfare is lower in duopoly than in monopoly.

Exercise 9 [2, 5, 7]*

There are two goods. The demand for good 1 is

$$q_1 = a - bp_1 + dp_2,$$

and that for good 2 is

$$q_2 = a - bp_2 + dp_1,$$

where a and b are strictly positive and $|d| < b$. The production cost of each good is 0.

(i) Are the goods differentiated?

(ii) Suppose that the two goods are produced by the same firm (a monopoly). Compute the optimal prices. Compare the Lerner index and the inverse of the elasticity of demand for each good. Comment.

(iii) Are the goods strategic complements, or substitutes?

(iv) The firms choose prices simultaneously, taking their rival's price as given. Compute the Nash-equilibrium prices, and compare them with the results in question ii.

Exercise 10 [3]*

Assume that a monopoly supplier of a good makes sales to customers located in different regions of the country. The demand functions for the good in each region are

$$q_1 = 1 - p_1$$

and

$$q_2 = \tfrac{1}{2} - p_2.$$

Assume in what follows that production and transport costs are zero.

(i) Assuming that the monopolist must charge a uniform (linear) price to the two regions, calculate the profit-maximizing uniform price.

(ii) Assume that the monopolist can engage in third-degree price discrimination. Calculate the profit-maximizing price for each region.

(iii) Does third-degree price discrimination increase or decrease welfare, as measured by the sum of consumers' plus producers' surplus, in this case? Is this a general result when one compares uniform monopoly prices with third-degree price discrimination?

(iv) Assume that the monopolist is selling an intermediate product, and that the demand functions above are the derived demands for the intermediate product of two competitive downstream industries. If third-degree price discrimination is not possible, show that the monopolist can achieve the same result by integrating forward into one of the downstream markets. Which one will he integrate into, and why?

Exercise 11 [3]*

There are two goods: the "basic good," produced by a monopolist at no cost, and the "complementary good" (services), produced and sold by a competitive industry at cost c per unit. Each consumer can consume (a) nothing, or (b) one unit of the basic good, or (c) one unit of the basic good and one unit of the complementary good. The consumer then has net surplus (a) 0, or (b) $v - p$, or (c) $w - p - c$, where $w > v > 0$ and p is the price of the basic good.

There are two types of consumers: type-1 ("low demand") consumers, who have valuations v_1 and w_1 for the basic good and the bundle, and type-2 ("high-demand") consumers, who have valuations $v_2 \geqslant v_1$ and w_2. Let $(1 - \alpha)$ and α denote the respective proportions of consumers. Assume that

$$w_2 - v_2 > c > w_1 - v_1$$

and

$$\alpha(w_2 - c) < v_1.$$

In answering the following, indicate when you recognize an instance of first-, second-, or third-degree discrimination. (Up to question v, the monopolist cannot tie the complementary good.)

(i) What are the socially efficient consumptions of the basic and complementary goods by the two types?

(ii) Suppose that the monopolist knows which consumers are of type 1 and which are of type 2. What prices will he charge?

(iii) Suppose that the monopolist cannot tell the customers apart. Show that the monopoly price still leads to the socially efficient allocation.

(iv) Suppose that the monopolist gets a "signal." Students are all of type 1. Conditional on a consumer's not being a student, the probability that he is of type 2 is $\beta > \alpha$. Assuming that $\beta(w_2 - c) > v_1$, compute the optimal prices to students and nonstudents. Show that discrimination leads to an inefficient outcome.

(v) Return to question iii (no signal), but assume that the monopolist can tie the complementary good. Show that he sells the basic good alone at price v_1 and the bundle at price $v_1 + (w_2 - v_2)$, and that his profit increases as a result of the tie-in.

For more on these issues, see J. Ordover, A. Sykes, and R. Willig, "Nonprice Anticompetitive Behavior by Dominant Firms toward the Producers of Complementary Products," in *Antitrust and Regulation*, edited by F. Fisher (MIT Press, 1985).

Exercise 12 [3]*

Consider a monopoly supplier of aluminum. Aluminum is used as an input in the production of numerous final goods. For purposes of this exercise, assume that there are only two final goods that use aluminum. Each of the goods has a different demand for aluminum.

(i) If explicit price discrimination is not possible, show that the monopoly input supplier will have an incentive to integrate into the production of at least one of the final goods.

(ii) Show that if the monopolist integrates into one final-goods market, it will integrate into the market with the most elastic demand.

(iii) Why will final-goods competitors in the integrated market by "squeezed" out of business?

Exercise 13 [3]*

Disneyland used to offer a variety of admission fees. For a given fee, the purchaser was entitled to a certain number of rides once in the park. (For example, there might have been an "economy" package that cost $10.00 and included tickets for five rides and an "adventure" package that cost $15.00 and included tickets for ten rides.)

(i) Using diagrams and/or equations, explain why Disneyland's management might have found this scheme profitable. Why didn't they simply charge a fee per ride?

(ii) There are numerous products for which there is a fixed charge to use the service and then a charge per usage. Examples are Polaroid cameras and film and electrofax copying machines and paper. How does the optimal pricing for these products differ from that of

Disneyland, and in what respects is it similar? Explain the reasons for the similarities and the differences.

Exercise 14 [3]*

(i) A "monopolist" faces a single consumer, with demand function $q = a - p$. His marginal cost is 0. The monopolist faces a competitive fringe at price $p_0 < a$ (that is, a perfect substitute is available at price p_0). What is the optimal pricing scheme under a linear tariff? Under two-part pricing?

(ii) Suppose now that there are two types of consumers, with demands $q = a_1 - p$ (in proportion x) and $q = a_2 - p$ (in proportion $1 - x$), where $p_0 < a_1 < a_2$. Consider linear pricing and third-degree price discrimination. Would uniform (linear) pricing increase welfare? (Think of the case in which $a_2/2 > p_0 > a_1/2$.) How does the result compare with the Robinson-Schmalensee one on uniform versus discriminatory pricing under linear demands?

(iii) Consider the two types of consumers of question ii, but look at *second*-degree price discrimination. Compare the monopoly price under linear pricing and the marginal price under a two-part tariff.

Exercise 15 [3, 4]*

Review the various motives for tie-ins. Explain how you might distinguish between them empirically.

Exercise 16 [3, 4]**

The Chicken Delight company (CD) owned the rights to a particular recipe for making fried chicken and the associated trademark. CD manufactured nothing itself, but licensed franchisees to make and sell fried chicken in local retail outlets using the CD recipe and trademark. It did not charge a franchise fee; however, it required each franchisee to purchase a specified number of cookers and fryers and to purchase a variety of supplies (including cups and napkins) from CD. CD purchased these pieces of equipment and supplies from third parties. There was nothing unique to CD about the equipment and supplies.

(i) Define the term *tie-in sale*.

(ii) Why might a company like CD enter into the arrangement described above with its franchisees?

(iii) How would you expect the prices CD charged its franchisees for the equipment and supplies it sold to them to compare to the prices the franchisees would have paid had they not been required to purchase from CD?

(iv) Why might CD have used a tie-in arrangement rather than a franchise fee?

(v) Why might CD have used a tie-in arrangement rather than taking a share of each franchisee's profits?

(iv) Why might CD have required the franchisee to purchase several types of inputs from it rather than just a single input such as the frying equipment or the mix for the chicken coating?

If this example excites you, see *Siegal* v. *Chicken Delight* 448, F.2d 43 (9th Circuit 1971) for more details. Chicken Delight was enjoined from engaging in these practices and subsequently went out of business.

Exercise 17 [3, 7]*

Consider the model of differentiation on a line with unit-demand consumers located uniformly along a segment of length 1 and facing transportation cost t per unit of distance, and with two firms located at the two extremeties of the segment and having marginal cost c. The firms compete in a Bertrand fashion.

(i) Show that under uniform pricing the consumers' generalized cost varies between $c + t$ and $c + 3t/2$ (if consumer surplus is sufficiently high).

(ii) Suppose that the duopolists can price-discriminate depending on the location of the consumer (i.e., can each choose one delivery price per location). What type of price discrimination is this? Show that in Bertrand equilibrium the consumers' generalized cost varies between $c + t/2$ and $c + t$. How does this compare with the results obtained in the case of a monopoly in chapter 3?

Exercise 18 [3, 7]**

Tim Bresnahan, in his paper "Competition and Collusion in the American Automobile Industry" (*Journal of Econometrics* 35 [1981]: 457−482), estimates a noncooperative model of vertical product differentiation for the automobile industry. A car's quality is taken to be one-dimensional and is measured by a "hedonic function" of its characteristics (length, weight, horsepower, etc). Bresnahan finds that larger vehicles have larger price-cost margins and that larger vehicles are farther apart in the product-quality space. Can you think of models (or varia-

tions thereof) that would explain either or both of these findings?

Exercise 19 [4, 7, 8]**

(This exercise follows Rey and Stiglitz's 1986 mimeographed paper "The Role of Exclusive Territories in Producers' Competition" [Princeton University].) Two manufacturers $(i = 1, 2)$ produce imperfect substitutes. The demand for good i is $q_i = D_i(p_i, p_j)$, and demands are symmetric: $D_1(\cdot, \cdot) = D_2(\cdot, \cdot)$. Let

$$\varepsilon(p_1, p_2) \equiv -\frac{\partial D_1}{\partial p_1} \bigg/ \frac{D_1}{p_1}$$

denote the own-price elasticity of demand, and let

$$\tilde{\varepsilon}(p_1, p_2) \equiv \frac{\partial D_1}{\partial p_2} \bigg/ \frac{D_1}{p_2}$$

denote the cross-price elasticity. Let $\varepsilon(p) \equiv \varepsilon(p, p)$. The unit manufacturing cost is c.

(i) Suppose first that the manufacturers distribute the good themselves (at no cost). Show that in Nash equilibrium the two firms charge price p such that

$$(p - c)/p = 1/\varepsilon(p).$$

(ii) Suppose now that each manufacturer i distributes his good through two retailers. Each of these two retailers carries only brand i and pays $A_i + p_{w_i} q_i$ to manufacturer i (where p_{w_i} is the wholesale price). The retailers of a given brand are undifferentiated and face no distribution cost. All four retailers choose prices simultaneously in the second stage of the game. In the first stage, producers choose retail contracts simultaneously. Argue that A_i must be equal to zero, and that the outcome is the same as in question i.

(iii) Suppose now that each manufacturer uses a single (exclusive) retailer. (Equivalently, each could give exclusive territories to its two retailers.) Retailer i thus maximizes

$$(p_i - p_{w_i})D_i(p_i, p_j) - A_i$$

over p_i. Let $p_i^*(p_{w_i}, p_{w_j})$ denote the Nash-equilibrium retail prices (obtained by solving the competition between retailers for given wholesale prices). Let

$$m(p_{w_1}, p_{w_2}) \equiv \frac{\partial p_1^*}{\partial p_{w_1}} \bigg/ \frac{p_1^*}{p_{w_1}}$$

and

$$\tilde{m}(p_{w_1}, p_{w_2}) \equiv \frac{\partial p_1^*}{\partial p_{w_2}} \Big/ \frac{p_1^*}{p_{w_2}}$$

denote the own- and cross-elasticities of retail-price responses. Assume that m and $\tilde{m}$ are positive. Comment on this assumption. Argue that

$$A_i = [p_i^*(p_{w_i}, p_{w_j}) - p_{w_i}] D_i(p_i^*(p_{w_i}, p_{w_j}), p_j^*(p_{w_i}, p_{w_j})).$$

Show that the first-period equilibrium in contracts between the manufacturers implies a symmetric retail price satisfying

$$\frac{p - c}{p} = \frac{1}{\varepsilon - \tilde{\varepsilon}\tilde{m}/m}.$$

What does this suggest concerning the private desirability of retail competition in this model? What strategy in the taxonomy of chapter 8 does the choice of monopoly retailing resemble?

Exercise 20 [5]*

Consider a duopoly with concave inverse demand function $P(q_1 + q_2)$ and convex costs $C(q_1)$. Consider the standard static Cournot game. Prove that firm i's best-response function $R_i(q_j)$ is monotonic in q_j and that the slope of $R_i(q_j)$ is between -1 and 0.

Exercise 21 [5]*

Discuss various rationing rules, their relevance, and why the choice of the rule may matter when one is formalizing oligopoly pricing.

Exercise 22 [5]*

(i) Compute the Cournot equilibrium with n firms when the firms face the inverse demand function $p = P(Q) = Q^{-1/\varepsilon}$ (with $\varepsilon > 1$) and have identical constant marginal cost c.

(ii) Show that each firm's profit goes down when c goes up.

(iii) Take $n = 2$. Show that q_2 is a strategic complement for q_1 if $0 \leqslant q_2 \leqslant (1/\varepsilon)q_1$.

Exercise 23 [5, 6]*

Consider an industry that produces a homogeneous good. Any firm can produce as much as it wants at a constant marginal cost of c per unit. Assume that all firms have price as the strategic variable.

(i) If the firms choose prices simultaneously and non-cooperatively and the market lasts for only one period, what price will prevail? Why?

(ii) Suppose that the firms meet repeatedly. Can the firms "tacitly collude"? (Describe various theories of repeated interaction and the stylized facts they are meant to explain.)

Exercise 24 [5, 7]**

In chapter 7 we saw that a free-entry equilibrium in general may involve too much or too little entry in an industry. This exercise follows von Weizsäcker 1980 and Mankiw and Whinston 1986 (see chapter 7 for references) to study the level of entry in the special case of a homogeneous-good industry. We start with a Cournot example, and then sketch Mankiw and Whinston's more general approach.

Suppose that firms face an entry cost f, and that entry is free. The industry inverse demand function is $p = P(Q)$, where Q denotes aggregate output. A firm that enters has cost function $C(q)$, where q is individual output ($C(0) = 0$, $C'(q) \geqslant 0$, $C''(q) \geqslant 0$). In a symmetric equilibrium in which n firms enter, the output per firm is $q(n)$ (so that aggregate output is $Q(n) = n q(n)$).

Compare the free-entry equilibrium not with the first-best optimum (which, because of product homogeneity, would have a single firm, pricing at marginal cost if $C'' = 0$), but with the socially optimal number of firms subject to the constraint that the social planner is unable to control the behavior of a firm once it is in the market. Let n^c and n^* denote the number of firms in the free-entry equilibrium and the constrained welfare optimum. In questions i and ii, assume that these are real numbers (i.e., ignore the integer constraint).

(i) Assume that $P(Q) = a - bQ$ and $C(q) = cq$. Show that if entering firms compete in a Cournot fashion, then

$$q(n) = \frac{1}{n+1} \frac{a-c}{b}$$

and

$$(n^c + 1)^2 = (n^* + 1)^3 = \frac{(a-c)^2}{bf}.$$

In the free-entry equilibrium, is there socially too little entry, or too much?

(ii) Following Mankiw and Whinston, make the following more general assumptions concerning post-entry market behavior:

A1: $Q(n)$ increases with n.

A2: $q(n)$ decreases with n (business-stealing effect).

A3: $P(Q(n)) - C'(q(n)) > 0$ (market power).

Show that the profit per firm decreases with the number of entering firms (n^c is such that this profit is equal to zero). Next, show that the social welfare,

$$\int_0^{Q(n)} P(x)dx - n\,C(q(n)) - nf,$$

is decreasing at $n = n^c$. Then show that $n^c > n^*$.

(iii) Reintroducing the integer constraint, Mankiw and Whinston show that $n^c \geqslant n^* - 1$. Can you think of an homogeneous-good industry in which $n^c < n^*$? (Hint: Recall chapter 2.)

Exercise 25 [5]***

Go through the Kreps-Scheinkman proof that, under efficient rationing, the outcome of the two-stage capacity-and-then-price game is the Cournot outcome for the following demand function:

$$D(p) = \begin{cases} 1 & \text{for } p \leqslant 1 \\ 0 & \text{for } p > 1 \end{cases}.$$

Compute the reduced-form profit functions and the equilibrium (pure or mixed) strategies.

Exercise 26 [5, 7, 8]*

A great deal of empirical work in industrial organization has focused on the estimation of relationships such as

(Profit rate)_i
$\quad = a + b \cdot \text{(Concentration ratio)}_i$
$\quad\quad + c \cdot \text{(Minimum efficient scale)}_i$
$\quad\quad + d \cdot \text{(Advertising/sales ratio)}_i$
$\quad\quad + e \cdot \text{(Capital/output ratio)}_i$,

where each variable is measured at the industry (i) level and where observations for n industries are used to estimate the relationship.

(i) Define the concentration-ratio and minimum-efficient-scale variables.

(ii) Why are economists interested in estimating relationships such as this?

(iii) Is industry concentration a good proxy for the degree of competition in an industry?

(iv) What are the other right-hand-side variables supposed to pick up in this relationship?

(v) Can you interpret such a relationship as causal?

Exercise 27 [7, 8]**

Michael Whinston, in "Tying, Foreclosure, and Exclusion" (mimeo, Harvard University, 1987), argues that bundling may deter entry in a market.

(i) Consider the following model: There are two completely unrelated markets and two firms. Market A is monopolized by firm 1. Consumers have unit demands. A fraction x (respectively $1 - x$) of consumers has valuation $\overline{v}$ (respectively $\underline{v}$) for good A with $\overline{v} > \underline{v} > c_A$ (where c_A is firm 1's unit cost of production for good A). Assume that the firm cannot perfectly price-discriminate and that $x(\overline{v} - c_A) < \underline{v} - c_A$. Market B is served by firm 1 and firm 2. It is a differentiated market on the line. Transportation costs are linear (t per unit of distance). The density of consumers is uniform and equal to 1 along the segment of length 1. Firms 1 and 2 are located at the two extremes of the city. Their marginal cost for good B is c_B. Consumers have unit demands in market B as well, and the demands in the two markets are independent. (A consumer's probability of having valuation $\overline{v}$ for good A is independent of his location in market B.) Let p_A be firm 1's price in market A, and let p_1 and p_2 be firm 1's and firm 2's prices in the differentiated market. Suppose that firm 1 sells the two goods separately. What is p_A? Compute the reaction curves $p_i = R_i(p_j)$ in market B. What is the Nash equilibrium in market B?

(ii) Consider the following timing: Firm 1 can "bundle" its two goods or not; firm 2 enters (at its extremity of the city) and pays an entry cost F or stays out; the firms choose their prices simultaneously. Bundling is a technological decision that forces firm 1 to sell the two goods together (it then charges a single price $\overline{p}$). If firm 1 does not bundle, it sells the two goods separately, and the equilibrium is as before. (For simplicity, we will not consider mixed bundling.) Suppose that firm 1 bundles and firm 2 enters. Show that there exist two cutoff locations on the line. Show that firm 1's demand is

$$[p_2 - (\bar{p} - v^e) + t]/2t,$$

where $v^e \equiv x\bar{v} + (1 - x)\underline{v}$. Show that firm 1's new reaction curve satisfies

$$\tilde{R}_1(p_2) < R_1(p_2) + \underline{v}.$$

Informally determine whether bundling is good for entry deterrence and for entry accommodation.

Exercise 28 [8]*

Consider an industry consisting of three firms. Each firm has the same cost structure, given by

$$C(q_i) = 5 + 2q_i$$

for firm i. Industry demand is given by the inverse demand function

$$P(Q) = 18 - Q,$$

where $Q = q_1 + q_2 + q_3$. The production timing is as follows: Firm 1 produces its output first. Knowing firm 1's output, firm 2 produces its output. Knowing both firm 1's and firm 2's output, firm 3 then produces its output. Each firm knows that this is the timing of production; thus, firm 1 (for example) knows when it makes its production choice that it will be followed by firms 2 and 3. The industry demand and cost functions are known to each firm.

What will the equilibrium values of q_1, q_2, and q_3 be? What standard duopoly model is this an extension of?

Exercise 29 [8]**

(i) Describe the use of various strategic effects to deter entry or accommodate a rival in two-period settings. (Think of puppy dogs and other cute animals.)

(ii) Answer the following (in words) and explain:

• A foreign firm that competes in prices with a domestic firm in the domestic market suffers from facing a quota. True or false?

• Two firms are in the market in period 1. Firm 2 does not know firm 1's marginal cost. Firms compete in prices. Is cutting price a good strategy for firm 1 if it wants to drive firm 2 out of the market? If it wants to accommodate firm 2?

• "Advertising is like capital. An incumbent should over-invest to deter entry." True or false?

• "The principle of differentiation (say, in spatial competition) is an instance of a puppy dog effect." True or false?

Exercise 30 [8]**

There are two firms, with demand functions $D_i = 1 - 2p_i + p_j$. Firm 2's (the entrant's) marginal cost is 0. Firms 1's (the incumbent's) marginal cost is initially $\frac{1}{2}$. By investing $I = 0.205$, the incumbent can buy the new technology and reduce its marginal cost to 0.

(i) Consider the timing: The incumbent chooses whether to invest; then the entrant observes the incumbent's investment decision; then the firms compete in prices. Show that in perfect equilibrium the incumbent does not invest.

(ii) Show that if the investment decision is not observed by the entrant, the incumbent's investing is an equilibrium. Comment.

(iii) Explain why the conclusion in question i may be affected if the entrant faces a fixed entry cost. Does it matter whether the potential entrant makes its entry decision before or after the incumbent's investment decision? (Just give the argument; do not compute anything.)

Exercise 31 [7, 8]**

In a single-period framework, offering a most-favored-nation clause is equivalent to charging a uniform price (as long as customers have perfect information about trading prices). Consider the following model: There are two markets and three firms. Each market is one of differentiation on the line, with two producers located at each extremity. The transportation cost is t per unit of distance (that is, we assume linear transportation costs). Consumers are uniformly distributed along the segment, and the numbers of consumers in each market are equal (and are normalized to 1). The only difference between the markets is their length. Market i has length l_i, with $l_1 \geqslant l_2$ (so the products are, in a sense, more differentiated in market 1). Firm 0 (the "chain store" or "national firm") serves both markets. The other extremities of each market are occupied by firm 1 (market 1) and firm 2 (market 2) ("local or regional firms"). The production cost in each market for existing firms is c.

(i) Suppose that firm 0 charges different prices in the two markets (i.e., it price-discriminates). Solve for the

Nash equilibria in prices. Show that market 1 is more profitable than market 2.

(ii) Suppose from now on that firm 0 can commit to a most-favored-nation clause (that is, it uses uniform pricing across markets). Show that nothing is changed if $l_1 = l_2$. So assume that $l_1 > l_2$. Show that uniform pricing lowers prices in market 1 and raises prices in market 2. Show that firm 0 loses from imposing the price-protection policy. Derive the intuition. (Hint: how does the uniform price change when $l_1 + l_2$ is kept constant and $l_1 - l_2$ increases?) Show that a social planner's preventing firm 0 from price-discriminating would lower welfare. (Hint: Welfare can be identified with transportation costs in this simple model.) Why isn't the Robinson-Schmalensee result concerning the desirability of uniform pricing with linear demand curves (see chapter 3) applicable? (After all, the *residual* demand curves for firm 0 are linear.) The model used in this exercise is considered by Patrick DeGraba in "The Effects of Price Restrictions on Competition between National and Local Firms" (*Rand Journal of Economics*, 18 [1987]: 333–347). DeGraba assumes quadratic transportation costs.

An interesting aspect of DeGraba's model is that the locations of the local firms are not exogenously fixed. These firms can choose to locate near or far from the national firm in their respective product spaces. With endogenous location choices, uniform pricing changes the nature of competition even when $l_1 = l_2$. The reason for this is that a local firm's moving closer to the center of the segment (and thus closer to the national rival) triggers a smaller price cut by the national firm under uniform pricing, as the latter has no reason to cut its price in its other market. And indeed the local firms do not choose maximal differentiation under uniform pricing, whereas they do under discriminatory pricing (see the result of d'Aspremont et al., discussed in chapter 7). For his specification, DeGraba finds that transportation costs are lower and welfare higher under uniform pricing.

Exercise 32 [8]*

Consider a new industry. Firm 1 can choose one of two technologies. Technology A requires a fixed cost f_A and can produce goods at a cost of c_A per unit. The costs with technology B are f_B and c_B. After firm 1 has chosen its technology, firm 2 can consider entering. It has only one technology choice, with costs f_2 and c_2.

(i) Why might the magnitude of f_2 determine which technology firm 1 chooses?

(ii) Might firm 1 adopt a different technology if it were not facing entry? Why or why not?

(iii) Relate this model to the ideas of Spence and Dixit discussed in chapter 8.

Exercise 33 [8, 9]**

When a near-monopolist sets its price so low that a small rival goes out of business, the smaller firm is likely to charge the larger one with predatory pricing.

(i) Is the conduct described above always welfare-reducing? If not, indicate when welfare might be enhanced. (No formal analysis is necessary.)

(ii) Areeda and Turner (*Harvard Law Review* 38 [1975]: 697–733) argued that the larger firm's price should be held to be predatory if and only if it is below that firm's short-run marginal cost, and they further contended that average variable cost could be used as a proxy for short-run marginal cost. Evaluate both components of this argument.

(iii) Should established firms be found guilty of a predatory response to entry if and only if they increase their own output when entry occurs?

(iv) Describe what standards you think the courts should use to evaluate charges of predatory pricing. Should evidence of intent be considered? Market structure? Costs? Comment on the welfare properties and the administrative feasibility of your proposal.

Exercise 34 [8, 10]**

Can you find a rationale for a law specifying the compulsory licensing of patents in cases of nonuse or insufficient use without "legitimate excuse" within n years from the date of the grant of the patent? Discuss potential problems of enforcing such a law.

Exercise 35 [9]**

Two firms compete in prices. Firm i's demand is

$$q_i = a - bp_i + dp_j,$$

where $b > 0$ and $-b \leqslant d \leqslant b$. Each firm's unit cost can be low (c_L) or high (c_H) with equal probabilities. Each firm knows its unit cost but not its rival's.

(i) Solve for the price equilibrium in a one-period framework.

(ii) Suppose that firms compete in price in each of two periods. Does the previous one-period equilibrium yield the first-period equilibrium prices? If not, explain what happens (if you are courageous, solve for the dynamic equilibrium). Does the sign of d make a qualitative difference?

Exercise 36 [9]*

Review the various theories linking predation and asymmetric information, and compare them.

Exercise 37 [9]**

(i) Consider the model of product differentiation on a line. The line has length 1. The consumers are uniformly distributed along it; they face transportation cost t per unit of distance and have unit demand, with valuation v for the good. Suppose that $3t/2 \geqslant v \geqslant t$. Firm 1 is located at the left end of the segment. Firm 2 may or may not be located at the right end of the segment. (Firms have at most one product each.) Production costs are 0. Show that if firm 2 does not enter, firm 1's monopoly profit is $v^2/4t$. Show that if firm 2 enters, each firm's duopoly profit is $\frac{1}{2}(v - t/2)$ and the duopoly price is $v - t/2$.

(ii) Consider the Milgrom-Roberts model for the setup outlined in question i. At date 1, firm 1 is a monopolist. Firm 2 observes firm 1's first-period price and decides whether to enter. Firm 1 has private information not about the production cost (which is 0), but about the common demand parameter v, which can take as a value $\underline{v}$ or $\overline{v}$, where $3t/2 \geqslant \overline{v} \geqslant \underline{v} \geqslant t$. Suppose for simplicity that firm 2 learns v before second-period product-market competition if it decides to enter. Suppose that the entry cost lies between $\frac{1}{2}(\underline{v} - t/2)$ and $\frac{1}{2}(\overline{v} - t/2)$. The discount factor is δ. Look for a separating equilibrium. What is the price charged by firm 1 when $v = \overline{v}$? Write the condition(s) to be satisfied by the price p_1 charged by firm 1 when $v = \underline{v}$ (how does p_1 compare with $\underline{v}/2$?). Show that for $\delta = 1$ and $\overline{v} = 3t/2$, the least-cost separating price is $p_1 = t/2 < \underline{v}/2$.

Exercise 38 [9, 11]**

Consider the following game between an incumbent firm and an entrant: First the entrant decides whether to enter (E) or not (N). Then if the entrant enters, the incumbent decides whether to prey (P) or acquiesce (A). The incumbent and the entrant get 4 and 0 if N, 1 and -1 if E and P, and 2 and 1 if E and A.

(i) Compute the perfect equilibrium of this game.

(ii) Suppose that the game is repeated twice (the discount factor is $\delta = 1$, say). What is the equilibrium?

(iii) Suppose that the game is repeated twice. With probability α, the incumbent has payoff as described above. With probability $1 - \alpha$, he has payoff 3 when E and P (that is, he enjoys preying) and otherwise he has the same payoff as before. Only the incumbent knows his payoff. Does the incumbent with payoffs as before play the same strategy as in question ii? Does the entrant learn the incumbent's "type" in period 1?

(iv) Solve the game described in question iii (consider two cases depending on whether α exceeds $\frac{1}{2}$ or not).

Exercise 39 [11]***

One interesting issue in a situation of repeated interaction between two asymmetrically informed parties is whether these parties increase or decrease the "stakes" of their relationship over time. Consider two examples. In the first, a lender makes a loan to a borrower, who can reimburse or default. The lender has incomplete information about the borrower's honesty. It is shown that the size of the loan (the stake) increases over time, conditional on the previous loans having been reimbursed. The second example is the predation model of chapters 9 and 11. The entrant can enter two markets held by the incumbent sequentially, one big and one small. He does not know whether the incumbent enjoys preying. In equilibrium, he enters the big market first (decreasing stakes). Meditate on the difference between these examples. The first example was inspired by J. Sobel's paper "A Theory of Credibility" (*Review of Economic Studies* 52 [1985]: 557–574); the second was suggested by Drew Fudenberg.

Increasing Stakes

In a given period, a lender can give $C(A)$ to a borrower (with $C(0) = 0$, $C'(0) = 0$, $C'(A) > 0$ for $A > 0$, $C''(A) > 0$). This investment yields A. The borrower can default (keep A) or reimburse (give A to the lender). The lender has incomplete information about the borrower's honesty. An honest borrower (probability x_1) always reimburses. A "dishonest" borrower (probability $1 - x_1$)

maximizes his expected payoff. Let A^* and A^{**} be defined by $C'(A^*) = 1$ and $C'(A^{**}) = x_1$.

(i) Interpret A^* and A^{**}.

(ii) Suppose that there are two periods (1 and 2). The lender makes loan $A_1 \geqslant 0$ and then $A_2 \geqslant 0$. Whether the borrower has defaulted in the first period is observed before the lender makes the second-period loan. The discount factor is $\delta < 1$. Show that, in equilibrium, $A_2 = A_1/\delta$ if the first loan was reimbursed and $A_2 = 0$ otherwise. (Hint: Show that for $A_1 \leqslant \delta A^{**}$, A_1 is always reimbursed and that for $A_1 \geqslant \delta A^*$ it is not reimbursed by the dishonest type. What happens for $\delta A^{**} < A_1 < \delta A^*$?)

Decreasing Stakes

Consider the chain-store paradox (exercise 11.12). There are two periods and two markets. With prior probability $1 - x_1$, the incumbent is "sane," and the payoff structure is as in figure 11.12 in the "small market"; in the "big market," all the payoffs in figure 11.12 are multiplied by 2. With prior probability x_1, the incumbent always preys (and the entrant's payoff is the payoff or twice the payoff indicated in figure 11.12). The discount factor is $\delta = 1$, and $x_1 < \frac{1}{2}$. The entrant can enter only one market per period and can choose which market to enter first.

(iii) Show that the entrant enters the big market in the first period, and (possibly) the small market in the second period.

Exercise 40***

Think of a private rationale for, and potential social consequences of, the following practices relating to patents and licensing:

(i) "package licensing" (licensing of all patents owned in a particular field and refusal to grant licenses for less than the entire group of patents)

(ii) "grant-back licensing" (requiring the licensee to assign or grant back to his licensor an innovation or improvement discovered in using the patent)

(iii) "patent pool and cross-licensing" (in which two or more members of an industry make their patents mutually available).

Exercise 41**

True, false, or uncertain?

(i) "A durable-good monopolist prefers leasing to selling."

(ii) "Price discrimination may destabilize a cartel (understand: tacit collusion)."

(iii) "Entry promotes competition and increases social welfare."

(iv) "The dominant firm always preempts other firms in the choice of investments, in product positioning, or in the adoption of new technologies."

(v) "Price adjustments in oligopoly are more sluggish for an upward shock in demand than for a downward shock."

Exercise 42*

Discuss the following assertion: "In a monopoly situation, the monopoly profit is part of the dead-weight loss." (Think of various situations where it is true, false, or in between.)

Exercise 43**

Schmalensee, in his chapter on inter-industry studies of structure and performance in the forthcoming *Handbook of Industrial Organization*, offers a useful synthesis of cross-sectional evidence. Go through his list of stylized facts, and think of various theories that are consistent with each of them. Here are a few examples to work through:

(i) The price-cost margin and the accounting rates of return are weakly correlated (stylized fact 3.1).

(ii) In cross-section comparisons involving markets in the same industry, seller concentration is positively related to the level of price (stylized fact 4.1).

(iii) Legal restrictions on local advertising in the United States are associated with higher retail prices (stylized fact 4.2).

(iv) Seller concentration is positively related to estimates of the minimum market share of an efficient plant, and to capital intensity (stylized facts 5.2 and 5.3).

Index

Milgrom-Roberts model, 306, 367–374
Mobility, barriers to, 316
Money-back guarantee, 85
Monopolization, 194–196, 377
Monopoly
  bilateral, 21–25, 411
  and future competition, 79–87
  natural, 19–21, 311–312, 338, 341, 398, 407
  persistence of, 348, 350–352, 394
  threatened by entry, 392
Monopoly power, 280, 338
  and intermediate price controls, 17
  and price discrimination, 17, 73
Monopoly pricing, 50, 66–75, 145–146, 219, 334
  formula for, 23
Monopsony, 65, 411
Monotone-likelihood-ratio property, 265
Moral hazard, 35, 51, 54, 106, 116, 171
  adverse selection and, 44
  bilateral, 178
  downstream, 177–178
  quality and, 107–108, 111–112
Most efficient scale, 19, 288, 352
Most-favored-customer clause, 85, 241, 330–332
Multidivisional-form (M-form) firm, 47–48
Multimarket behavior, 376–377
Multimarket contact, 243, 251
Multiproduct monopoly and pricing, 69–70, 105, 137

Nash bargaining solution, 25, 30
Nash equilibrium, 206, 207, 214, 258, 268–270, 281, 283, 296–297, 323–324, 363, 381, 395, 444–445
  in game theory, 206, 425–428
  mixed-strategy, 427, 435–436, 444–445
  perfect, 206, 245, 257, 269, 403, 428–432, 438, 445
  pure-strategy, 427
Nash point, 208
Nelson effect, 120
Neoclassical methodology, 48–50
Network externalities, 196, 404–409
Nonintegration, 31

Observability, 38, 44, 52
Obsolescence, planned, 86–87
Oligopoly, 205, 221, 257, 314, 334, 361, 380
  informative advertising in, 292–294
  multimarket, 332–333
  as noncooperative game, 206
  price competition and, 209
  and pricing, 212–218
Opportunism, 25, 27
Opportunity cost, 312
Optimal-control theory, 345
Optimal insurance, theory of, 35, 52
Ordinary-demand function, 10

Organizational culture, 49
Outside pressure, 44
Overinvestment, 323, 325

Parametrized distribution formulation of uncertainty, 53
Pareto optimality, 6–7, 36, 109, 113, 120, 156, 412, 442
  allocation and, 250
  price discrimination and, 139, 151
Participation constraint, 39–40
Patent races, 394–399
Patents, 323, 390, 394, 399–401, 411–413
Poison pills, 43
Poisson process, 312
Predation, 372–373
  advertising and, 373
  bilateral, 380
  limit pricing and, 372
  in "long purse" story, 377–379
  mergers and, 374–376
  monopolization and, 377
  multimarket, 376
  and price reduction, 373
Preemption, 346–351
  diffusion, and, 402–403
  ε-, 398
Price competition, 262–264, 279–281, 296, 330
  asymmetric information and, 366
  capacity constraint and, 214–216
  compatibility and, 233, 336
  dynamic, 243–245, 364–365
  model of, 233, 362–364
  oligopoly theory and, 209
Price-cost margin, 156–157. *See also* Lerner index
Price discrimination, 133–135
  arbitrage and, 134–135, 140
  multimarket, 137–142
  perfect, 135–137, 144–145
  second-degree, 142–152
  third-degree, 137–142
  tie-in sales and, 146–148
  vertical control and, 141
  and welfare, 137–140, 142, 149
Price games, 228–234, 327
Price-protection plan, 85, 330
Price rigidities, 253–256
  kinked demand curve and, 265–268
Price squeeze, 193–194
Price-taking behavior, 7
Price wars, 240, 241, 248, 265
  recession and, 252
Pricing
  average-cost, 19, 284
  basing-point, 241
  linear, 170–173
  nonlinear, 153–162